VIRGINIA

A Guide to the Old Dominion

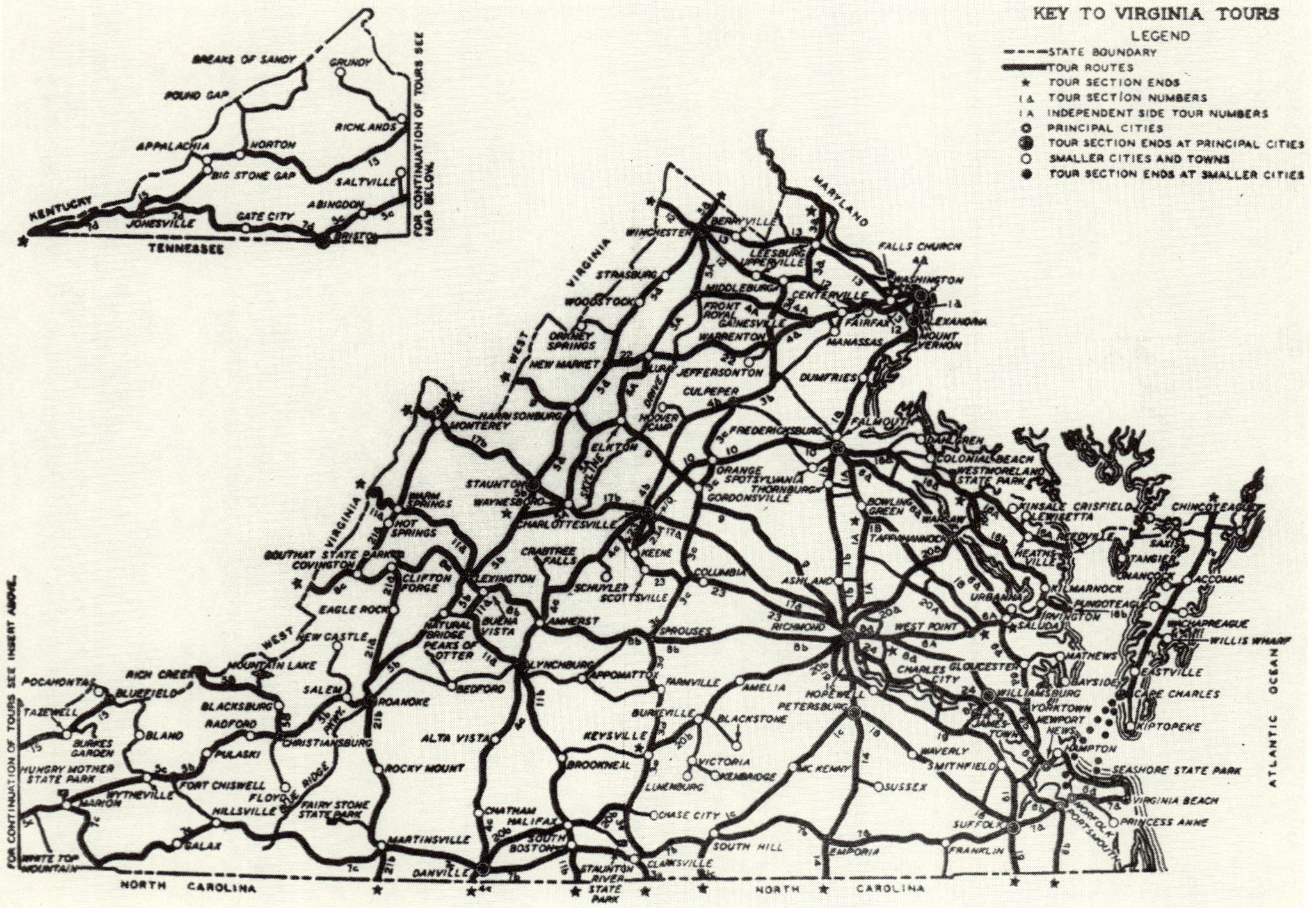
KEY TO VIRGINIA TOURS
LEGEND
STATE BOUNDARY
TOUR ROUTES
TOUR SECTION ENDS
TOUR SECTION NUMBERS
INDEPENDENT SIDE TOUR NUMBERS
PRINCIPAL CITIES
TOUR SECTION ENDS AT PRINCIPAL CITIES
SMALLER CITIES AND TOWNS
TOUR SECTION ENDS AT SMALLER CITIES
FOR CONTINUATION OF TOURS SEE MAP BELOW.
FOR CONTINUATION OF TOURS SEE INSERT ABOVE.
BREAKS OF SANDY
GRUNDY
POUND GAP
RICHLANDS
APPALACHIA
NORTON
BIG STONE GAP
SALTVILLE
KENTUCKY
ABINGDON
JONESVILLE
GATE CITY
BRISTOL
TENNESSEE
MARYLAND
WEST VIRGINIA
WINCHESTER
BERRYVILLE
LEESBURG
UPPERVILLE
FALLS CHURCH
WASHINGTON
STRASBURG
MIDDLEBURG
CENTERVILLE
WOODSTOCK
FRONT ROYAL
GAINESVILLE
FAIRFAX
ALEXANDRIA
MOUNT VERNON
MANASSAS
ORKNEY SPRINGS
WARRENTON
NEW MARKET
LURAY
JEFFERSONTON
DUMFRIES
CULPEPER
HOOVER CAMP
HARRISONBURG
MONTEREY
FREDERICKSBURG
FALMOUTH
DAHLGREN
COLONIAL BEACH
ELKTON
SKYLINE DRIVE
ORANGE
SPOTSYLVANIA
THORNBURG
WESTMORELAND STATE PARK
STAUNTON
WAYNESBORO
GORDONSVILLE
WARM SPRINGS
HOT SPRINGS
CHARLOTTESVILLE
BOWLING GREEN
TAPPAHANNOCK
WARSAW
KINSALE
CRISFIELD
LEWISETTA
REEDVILLE
CHINCOTEAGUE
SAXIS
HEATHSVILLE
TANGIER
ONANCOCK
ACCOMAC
GOUTHAT STATE PARK
COVINGTON
CRABTREE FALLS
KEENE
COLUMBIA
CLIFTON FORGE
LEXINGTON
SCHUYLER
SCOTTSVILLE
ASHLAND
KILMARNOCK
URBANNA
IRVINGTON
PUNGOTEAGUE
SALUDA
EAGLE ROCK
NATURAL BRIDGE
BUENA VISTA
AMHERST
SPROUSES
RICHMOND
WEST POINT
WACHAPREAGUE
WILLIS WHARF
NEW CASTLE
PEAKS OF OTTER
LYNCHBURG
APPOMATTOX
MATHEWS
GLOUCESTER
CHARLES CITY
EASTVILLE
RICH CREEK
MOUNTAIN LAKE
POCAHONTAS
BLUEFIELD
SALEM
BEDFORD
FARMVILLE
AMELIA
HOPEWELL
WILLIAMSBURG
BAYSIDE
CAPE CHARLES
TAZEWELL
BLACKSBURG
ROANOKE
PETERSBURG
YORKTOWN
JAMESTOWN
NEWPORT NEWS
BLAND
RADFORD
BURKEVILLE
BLACKSTONE
KIPTOPEKE
BURKES GARDEN
CHRISTIANSBURG
PULASKI
ALTA VISTA
KEYSVILLE
WAVERLY
HAMPTON
HUNGRY MOTHER STATE PARK
FORT CHISWELL
ROCKY MOUNT
VICTORIA
KENBRIDGE
MC KENNY
SMITHFIELD
SEASHORE STATE PARK
ATLANTIC OCEAN
WYTHEVILLE
FLOYD
BLUE RIDGE PKWY.
BROOKNEAL
LUNENBURG
SUSSEX
MARION
HILLSVILLE
FAIRY STONE STATE PARK
CHATHAM
HALIFAX
CHASE CITY
NORFOLK
VIRGINIA BEACH
SUFFOLK
PORTSMOUTH
PRINCESS ANNE
GALAX
MARTINSVILLE
SOUTH BOSTON
SOUTH HILL
EMPORIA
FRANKLIN
WHITE TOP MOUNTAIN
DANVILLE
STAUNTON RIVER STATE PARK
CLARKSVILLE
NORTH CAROLINA

VIRGINIA

A Guide to the Old Dominion

Compiled by Workers of the Writers' Program
of the Work Projects Administration
in the State of Virginia

Virginia State Library and Archives

in cooperation with the Virginia Center for the Book

Richmond • 1992

Library of Congress Cataloging-in-Publication Data

Virginia : a guide to the Old Dominion / compiled by workers of the Writers' Program of the Work Projects Administration in the State of Virginia.
p. cm.
Originally published: New York : Oxford University Press, 1940, in series: American guide series.
Includes bibliographical references and index.
ISBN 0-88490-173-4 : $35.00
1. Virginia. 2. Virginia—Guidebooks.
I. Virginia Writers' Project.
F226.V894 1992
917.5504'43—dc20 92-28334

Virginia State Library and Archives, Richmond, Virginia.

Standard Book Number: 0-88490-173-4
Printed in the United States of America.

First published in May 1940 in the American Guide Series by Oxford University Press.

This book is printed on acid-free paper meeting the requirements of the American National Standard for Permanence of Paper for Printed Library Materials.

FOREWORD

The Enduring Spirit of Virginia

BY GARRETT EPPS

Of all rhetorical modes, Virginians are most comfortable with the elegiac. Almost from the earliest days of English settlement in Virginia, its people have been complaining that the great days are gone, that outside forces have overwhelmed the old way of life, and that the things that made the Old Dominion unique have now fled, never to return. These laments for a vanished past have taken on new intensity in the half century since this book was published. Indeed, many thoughtful people now believe that regionalism is a spent force in American life and that the geographical peculiarities that inspired the WPA state guides survive only as faded memories.

Certainly the pace of change has been merciless, and the forces of centralization strong. Television, computers, telecommunications, air travel, the interstate highway system, corporate integration, and mass migration have remade every institution—from family, to farm and workplace, to local, state, and federal government. In the 1990s, Americans are entering a new period of transformation, with changes occurring on a global scale and at a computerized pace. Decisions made in Tokyo and Riyadh increasingly determine the texture of life in American cities, towns, and farms. All this has given added force to the sense of separation disappearing, to the idea that the South, as a distinct region in American life, is "a Civilization gone with the wind."

In this context we would do well to recall the words of French historian Fernand Braudel, who charted the course of history in the Mediterranean through many centuries. Braudel concluded from his study that civilizations are like sand dunes, blown and shifted by winds that may replace each individual grain of sand, yet, after storm and change, are found standing in much the same place. "We shall not allow ourselves to repeat the often-voiced opinion that 'civilizations are mortal,'" Braudel wrote. "Mortal perhaps are their ephemeral blooms, the intricate and short-lived creations of an age, their economic triumphs and their social trials, in the short term. But their foundations remain. They are not indestructible, but they are many times more solid that one might imagine. They have withstood a thousand supposed deaths, their massive bulk unmoved by the monotonous pounding of the centuries."[1]

Throughout its history, I would argue, Virginia has been the center of a highly distinctive civilization—a place where European settlers and their descendants faced unprecedented problems and forged original, often flawed, and almost always influential solutions. Virginia, I think, remains a distinctive civilization to this day.

This is not to deny that we would search in vain for the sleepy, segregated, rural dominion described in the pages of *Virginia: A Guide to the Old Dominion.* The years since 1940 have transformed the nation in fundamental ways, and they have had more impact on the South than on the nation as a whole. If the South has changed more than the rest of the country, Virginia has changed more than most of the South. Statistics cannot tell the story, but they may indicate its magnitude. When *Virginia* was published, the state had a population of 2.7 million, nearly two-thirds of whom lived in rural areas. Its per capita personal income ranked thirtieth among the forty-eight states. Today, Virginia's people number 6.2 million. Slightly more than two-thirds live in cities, and their per capita income ranks twelfth in the nation. Fifty years ago, Virginia was proud but poor and backward, living on the psychic capital of a historic past and isolated intellectually, economically, and socially from the life of the nation. Today, instead of lagging behind the nation, Virginia is cutting further into the future than any of its neighbors.

The economic changes, sweeping though they are, are only a

small part of the transformation that Virginia has experienced in the last fifty years. When *Virginia* was written, the state was a part of the segregated South; a reader will find the chilling traces of segregation in its listings, which primly note how many hotels, picture houses, swimming pools, and tennis courts in each town are open to "Negroes." The segregated system is nearly forgotten today, or remembered at most as a period of aberrant bigotry. But segregation, as it existed in the South from the turn of the twentieth century until the 1960s, was in fact unique in American history: a comprehensive racial, social, and legal system that oppressed all those it governed, black and white. It bears comparison with South African apartheid, and it was the closest thing Americans have ever created to an authentic native totalitarianism.

For the more than half a century of its life, segregation stunted every aspect of southern life. It was an inner wound that rendered social progress impossible and made the southern states pariahs in the American family. That system was dismantled through the courage and creativity of southern black people and the integrity of federal law, and its destruction was the final step that liberated the energies of southern whites and blacks. Before the civil rights movement, Virginia, like other southern states, was caught in inner stalemate and hopelessness. After the movement's success, the region and the state became a place where anything seemed possible. Virginia's new-found prosperity and optimism flow from that liberating peaceful revolution.

Perhaps the best way to gauge the transformation of Virginia since then would be to repeat the "symbolic approach" Douglas Southall Freeman recommended in his introduction to the first edition of *Virginia*—"a southward journey from the bridge that joins the Lincoln Memorial with Arlington." That river crossing, Freeman wrote in 1940, carried the traveler into a land where "life itself has a different tempo . . . more leisured without being essentially indolent." Today, the Memorial Bridge hurtles passengers into the bustling futurescape of northern Virginia, a populous, affluent network of cities and suburbs where mass transit, computers, and the automobile are combining to create the prototype for an entirely new type of community. There is a different tempo—but it is faster not slower, and newer not older, than that of the central city north of the Potomac.

The rest of Virginia's landscape today is a similar panorama of confidence and change. The old eastern cities, which not long ago were sad, sleepy, and dependent on an agricultural economy, are now rich, busy, and diversified. They are centers for finance, transport, manufacturing, and services. Much of the farm economy has been remade by technology, the global market, and the growth of corporate agriculture.

What, then, has become of the Old Dominion we will read about in *Virginia*? In the midst of the new landscape, I would suggest, the continuity is striking. The glossy new surface of Virginia covers a familiar skeleton.

What makes Virginia what it is? The first answer is water. The Chesapeake Bay and the rich system of rivers that feeds it—the Potomac, the York, the Rappahannock, the James, and their countless tributaries—made Virginia a natural site for colonization and exploration and fostered the growth of a plantation economy. The lapping of those waters is the unceasing, rhythmic refrain to all of Virginia history. They were the waterways that brought European settlers in the seventeenth century and learning to the cosmopolitan planters of the eighteenth century. They carried tobacco and cotton to the metropolitan markets of Europe; they created the battle lines of the Civil War; and their rise and fall even today infuse the tempo of the state's economic and social life. And the water gives to much of eastern Virginia—the rural areas of the Northern Neck and the Eastern Shore—a sensual, timeless sweetness that is found in few other places on earth.

Land is the second foundation of Virginia's civilization—the dense, wet, fertile Virginia soil that proved so fatally well adapted to the growth of tobacco. As much as any other influence, tobacco has made Virginia what it is today. It was tobacco, with its promise of overnight wealth, that drew settlers to Virginia in the seventeenth and eighteenth centuries. It was tobacco, with its peculiar need for intense hand cultivation, that led Virginia planters, desperate for cheap labor, to create the American system of slavery. It was tobacco, with the relentless demands it placed on the soil that grew it, that caused the agricultural collapse that nearly ruined the state in the early nineteenth century. It was tobacco that helped create the post–Civil War sharecropping system, and it is tobacco in the twentieth century that forms a troubling pillar of the state's economy. The current legal and political struggles over tobacco's future, though they may be fought in boardrooms, legislative chambers, and courtrooms, are simply one more expression of the central tension of Virginia history—a manifestation of the same historical forces that pushed the state into the frontlines of the American Revolution, the Civil War, and the struggle over civil rights. A third constant in Virginia's history is the role of public life. The House of Burgesses that met in 1619 was the beginning of representative government in the English colonies. Since then, Virginia society has placed a high—some would say inordinate—value on politics and government. As a result, Virginia has traditionally been a kind of political laboratory for the rest of the nation. The popular uprising of 1676, known to history as Bacon's Rebellion, was an early indication of the social tensions that would power the Revolution a century later; and Bacon's Rebellion, with its confused cries by those left out of the colonial aristocracy for representation, liberty, and greater freedom to exploit racial minorities (in this case the Indians), also foreshadowed with almost eerie precision the tangled history and eventual failure of most American populist movements.

The plantation society of the eighteenth century was the source of many basics of American liberal thought. Thomas Jefferson wrote the Declaration of Independence; James Madison forged the radical notion of church-state separation and took the lead in writing the Constitution; George Washington led the new republic in war and peace. By 1832, when the hope and generosity of the revolutionary era were a distant memory, Virginia responded to Nat Turner's slave revolt by designing, and nearly adopting, a peaceful legal end to slavery. When that movement failed, Virginia thinkers like George Fitzhugh and Thomas Dew led the South in forging the grim proslavery argument, the rigid southern ideology of racism and states' rights that later inspired the secession movement. During the civil rights era, Virginia politicians and editors again took the lead in resistance; it was in Virginia that the arguments were first heard that southern states had the right to "nullify" the Supreme Court's school-desegregation rulings by interposing state authority between the citizen and the national government. These arguments were advanced, in the main, peacefully in Virginia; but farther south and west, they were potent weapons in the hands of less-scrupulous demagogues, and they played a major role in making the late 1950s and early 1960s a time of regional convulsion.

Virginia's political institutions today exist just across the river from the nation's capital. That proximity may be the most important single legacy left by the generation that founded the Republic. Being close to Washington has created northern Virginia, whose growth now forms the foundation of Virginia's wealth and dynamism. Being close to Washington, with its legions of ambitious activists and lawyers, has created a constant pressure on Virginia's legal and political system that has sparked a revival of the state's public creativity.

In fact, Virginia today is again a political laboratory for the South and for the nation. In the early 1980s, Virginia politicians and preachers such as Richard Viguerie, Jerry Falwell, and Pat Robertson pioneered in direct-mail fund-raising, single-issue politics, and the use of satellite and cable-TV technology to build national constituencies through the potent mixing of religion and politics. And there are signs as well of a more hopeful creativity: In 1989, Virginia became the first state to elect a black man, L. Douglas Wilder, as its governor. In the midst of a grim decade of race-baiting at the highest national levels, the success of Wilder's campaign may foreshadow a time when racial diversity will be a positive force in American politics and when the old code words and covert appeals to racism will have lost their sting—a time, perhaps not too far off, when Virginia can lead the nation forward again.

The Virginia that greets travelers today—in all its wealth, self-assurance, and "un-Southern" bustle—is a direct outgrowth of those earlier Virginias. No state in the Union can repay a patient and enterprising tourist with as rich a lesson in the bright and dark sides of American history as Virginia can. Indeed, it is not too much to say that Virginia is worth any amount of time and travel that can be devoted to it, from a three-day holiday to a lifetime of research.

The tours recommended in this guidebook—to Jamestown and Williamsburg, where English settlers first lived in the New World; to Yorktown, where Washington's troops turned the old order upside down; to Monticello, where Jefferson dreamed of liberty in a stately mansion built by slaves; to Richmond, where Jefferson

Davis and Robert E. Lee tried vainly to build a nation around the "peculiar institution"; to the Booker T. Washington birthplace in Franklin County, where visitors have a rare chance to see slavery through the eyes of slaves; to the grim battlefields near Fredericksburg, where one-quarter of those killed in the Civil War died; to Danville, where public officials in the 1960s tried to crush the civil rights movement using laws written for use against slave revolts; to the tidewater, where nuclear submarines sail over the graves of the *Monitor* and the *Virginia*; and to the mountains and valleys of southwestern Virginia, with their dusty coalfields, breathtaking bluegrass pastures, and rugged farmlands—all outline a rich, passionate history that is a beacon of hope, and a warning, to all those who care about this country.

A trip through Virginia—with our eyes open to all the magnificence and pain preserved in its buildings and landscape—reminds us of historian C. Vann Woodward's words: "The South has had its full share of illusions, fantasies, and pretensions, and it has continued to cling to some of them with an astonishing tenacity that defies explanation. But the illusion that 'history is something unpleasant that happens to other people' is certainly not one of them—not in the face of accumulated evidence and memory to the contrary."[2]

Virginia's history teaches us that our decisions matter. The ways one generation chooses to govern its economic, social, and environmental life can leave a lasting legacy, for good or ill. And it teaches further that a people can survive the shocks of history—riches and poverty, victory and defeat, glory and shame—without losing the things that make them, and their way of life, unique.

Notes

[1] Fernand Braudel, *The Mediterranean and the Mediterranean World in the Age of Philip II* (New York: Harper and Row, 1973), 2:775–776.

[2] C. Vann Woodward, "The Irony of Southern History," in *The Burden of Southern History* (Baton Rouge: Louisiana State University Press, 1960; reprint, New York: Mentor Press, 1969), 136.

NOTE TO READER

Virginia: A Guide to the Old Dominion was first published in 1940 by Oxford University Press as a volume in the American Guide Series launched several years earlier by the New Deal's Federal Writers' Project. A team of publicly funded researchers and writers, working under the expert direction of Virginia Writers' Program supervisor Eudora Ramsay Richardson, spent three years digging in the collections of the Virginia State Library and visiting hundreds of communities across the state gathering material for the book. *Virginia: A Guide to the Old Dominion* quickly went into a second printing in 1941, and several subsequent printings followed after the end of World War II.

Although perspectives on the past have changed significantly in the years since the guide first appeared, it remains in great demand more than a half century later for the wealth of historical information it contains as well as for the insights it provides into life in mid-twentieth-century Virginia. The modern interstate highway system has superseded many of the routes recommended by the guide, yet the time-tested scenic byways still beckon adventurous and curious travelers. *Virginia: A Guide to the Old Dominion* offers both the avid voyager and the armchair tourist a nostalgic sojourn through a Virginia that in many ways no longer exists—yet, a Virginia whose enduring tradition and character continue to shape and inspire the future.

This reprint edition of the Virginia guide is essentially a photographic reproduction of the book as it appeared in its fourth printing in 1947, with the following minor exceptions. Ten pages of preliminary material, paginated with parenthetical roman numerals, have been added at the beginning of the book. The entire text of the 1947 printing, with its original title page and numbering, follows the new front matter. Eighty-seven of the original 101 photographs have been located in the files of the

Picture Collection of the Virginia State Library and Archives and are reproduced here. Twelve of the fourteen missing illustrations have been photographed from the original volume. Virtually identical period photographs in the State Library's collection have been substituted in the remaining two cases—that of "Lower Brandon (18th Century), Prince George County" and of the "Aircraft Carrier on the Ways, Newport News." The illustration captions have been reset for this edition as they appeared in the original. The artwork printed on the front endpaper of the original guide, a "Key to Virginia Tours," has been reproduced here as the frontispiece. The foldout map of Virginia and Richmond, tucked in a special sleeve attached to the inside back cover of the original guide, has not been included in this reprint edition.

Many individuals contributed to the production of this volume. Jon Kukla, former director of the State Library's historical publishing program, conceived the project and commissioned the new foreword. Garrett Epps graciously agreed to contribute the foreword and has patiently awaited its appearance in print. Susan Bracy Sheppard, Sarah Shields Driggs, and Stacy Gibbons Moore, with the assistance of Carolyn S. Parsons and Petie Bogen-Garrett, did an outstanding job of identifying the original photographic images. Pierre Courtois and Mark Fagerburg expertly copied the aging photographs to ensure their preservation and reproduction quality. Emily J. Salmon copyedited and proofread the new material and ably guided the book through production. Special thanks go to Beverly J. Bagan and the members of the board of the Virginia Center for the Book for their enthusiastic support of and financial assistance to this project.

Sandra Gioia Treadway, *Director*
Division of Publications and Cultural Affairs

VIRGINIA

A Guide to the Old Dominion

VIRGINIA

A GUIDE TO THE OLD DOMINION

Compiled by workers of the Writers' Program
of the Work Projects Administration
in the State of Virginia

AMERICAN GUIDE SERIES

ILLUSTRATED

Sponsored by James H. Price, Governor of Virginia

OXFORD UNIVERSITY PRESS · NEW YORK

FIRST PUBLISHED IN MAY 1940
Second printing October 1941
Third printing, with corrections, 1946
Fourth printing, 1947

VIRGINIA CONSERVATION COMMISSION
State-wide Sponsor of the Virginia Writers' Project

FEDERAL WORKS AGENCY
JOHN M. CARMODY, *Administrator*

WORK PROJECTS ADMINISTRATION
F.C.HARRINGTON, *Commissioner*
FLORENCE KERR, *Assistant Commissioner*
WILLIAM A. SMITH, *State Administrator*

PRINTED IN U.S.A. BY THE OXFORD UNIVERSITY PRESS

COMMONWEALTH OF VIRGINIA

GOVERNOR'S OFFICE

RICHMOND

JAMES H. PRICE
GOVERNOR

IT gives me pleasure to commend this Guidebook, and express the hope that Virginia's future contributions to the welfare of all the nation may equal its past record and present-day progress.

Virginia welcomes the traveler throughout the year. The oldest state is favored by rugged physical beauty from seashore to mountains, a pleasant climate, excellent transportation facilities, diversified manufacturing and agricultural pursuits, and a rich tradition of accomplishment. Our people, largely of Anglo-Saxon blood, are friendly.

We welcome the visitor because he brings a freshness of view and helps us to appreciate our common heritage. We believe that to see Virginia, to know Virginia, is to like our people.

James H. Price

Governor

Preface

AS *The Virginia Guide* is about to be transformed into a book through the alchemy of printer's ink, the staff of the Virginia Writers' Project finds an alloy in its pleasure. We are thinking not so much of what has gone into the book as of all that was necessarily omitted. Compressing the story of Virginia within the covers of one volume was a painful task—particularly for the State supervisor, whose duty it became to delete more words than she allowed to remain. As first written, the *Guide* was perhaps four times its present length and then, according to the judgment of some of our staff, not long enough to do justice to our country's oldest commonwealth. Through amputations gradually and torturously performed, the book was reduced to meet the publishers' practical demands. We hope we have said much in few words. To those Virginians, however, who are saddened by our omissions, we promise to make the reserved material available in other books. The deleted passages are not dead; they merely sleep in files carefully guarded by Pauline Davis.

The Virginia Guide is the result of many people's efforts. A collaboration it certainly is; a mosaic we hope it will appear, with its component parts so fitted together as to present an accurate picture of our State's yesterday and today. This book was begun in April 1937 and finished three years later. Parts of the essay section were contributed by generous specialists; the city and highway sections, however, are wholly the products of workers on the Virginia Writers' Project. Men and women in the field gathered data that were sent to the office in Richmond and carefully checked and amplified by a dozen or more workers in the State Library. After the material had been assembled and the points of interest listed with their approximate locations, workers traveled along the highways and byways and visited every city, town, and hamlet, checking mileages, taking notes on the contemporary scene, and gathering stories unavailable in histories or musty records. All the writing was done in the Richmond office, and in its final form represents the craftsmanship of five writers, with the state supervisor as co-ordinator.

No manuscript that went into the making of the book—no highway tour, no essay, no city description—is in its entirety the work of one person, for within the office we developed experts who through emphasis upon their special fields became as useful to the co-ordinator as they were sometimes annoying. John Sherwood Widdicombe, a graduate of the University of Virginia and of Oxford and a student of architecture, wrote the descriptions of all our important houses; H.Ragland Eubank, a graduate of the College of William and Mary, made us toe the mark of historical accuracy; and Frank A. Browning contributed all that the *Guide* has to say about battlefields, wars, and rumors of wars and much more that can be exhumed from the files for a military history of Virginia. Fortunately, Fillmore Norfleet, having a law degree and a doctor's degree in French, having taught languages, having worked upon biographies, and failing—though a native Virginian—to take his State too seriously, frequently brought his cynical pedagogism to the aid of the harassed supervisor. Likewise, Ann Heaton—still more Irish than Virginian—refrained from specialization and injected color of sorts into the tours she touched with her Hibernian hand. The essay on the Negro and Negro sections of several other essays are the work of Roscoe E. Lewis, of Hampton Institute and the staff of the Virginia Writers' Project.

Altogether we have become authorities on Virginia history—not infallible perhaps, yet capable of blasting many an error and tradition oft-repeated by our forerunners. Whatever of untruth our specialists have allowed to remain in the telling of Virginia's story, we hope to correct in subsequent editions of *The Virginia Guide*, for in a book filled with the minutiae of history we have surely been guilty of minor errors here and there.

The essays in their final form are largely the work of the editorial staff. Those contributed by experts in their several fields were of necessity cut and adapted to the requirements of the book. For *Agriculture and Farm Life* we are indebted to Wilson Gee, Director of the Institute for Research in Social Sciences at the University of Virginia; for *Industry, Commerce, and Labor* to George Talmage Starnes, associate Professor of Commerce and Business Administration at the University of Virginia; for *The Theater* to Helen Clarke, Business Manager, Richmond Theatre Guild; for *Natural Setting* to Arthur Bevan, State Geologist, C.O.Handley, Leader Virginia Co-operative Wildlife Research Unit in the United States Department of Agriculture, and R.J.Holden, Professor of Geology; for *Architecture* to H.I.Brock of *The New York Times*; for material on social life and racial elements incorporated in *History* to Thomas P. Abernethy, associate Professor of History at the University of Virginia, and Richard Lee Morton, Professor of History at the College of William and Mary; and for source material used in *Transportation* to John B. Mordecai, Traffic Manager for the Richmond, Fredericksburg & Potomac Railroad. We are grateful also to Fiske Kimball and Eugene Bradbury, who checked many architectural descriptions.

Members of the advisory committee appointed by our sponsor, Governor James H. Price, gallantly read and constructively criticized the manuscript of the book, which was parceled out to them in sections. So we extend our gratitude and the Governor's to Wilmer Hall, State Librarian; H.J.Eckenrode, Director of the Division of History and Archaeology for the Virginia Conservation Commission; Sidney B. Hall, Virginia Superintendent of Public Instruction; Blake Tyler Newton, division Superintendent of Schools, Westmoreland and Richmond Counties and Member State Board of Education; E.G.Swem, Librarian of the College of William and Mary and author of *Swem's Index*; and F.B.Kegley, historian of Southwest Virginia. This heroic committee read carbon copies on onion skin paper and sent to us no complaint.

Virginians must have wanted a book that tells the story of Virginia, where dramatic episodes of history were enacted, for people all over the State were quick to respond to our requests for co-operation. State departments opened to us their doors and their files. Though we must have annoyed the Highway Department no end, daily using their graphs and getting up-to-date information on new routing and surfacing of roads, the officials continued agreeably helpful. Draftsmen from the department prepared two maps used in the *Guide*. The State Library, that happy hunting ground of historians and genealogists, never lost patience with our painstaking research workers. The Conservation Commission gave us facts and pictures and always a hearty welcome. The National Park Service drew base maps for us and gave us much battlefield information. The State Chamber of Commerce and chambers in Virginia cities were unstinting in their co-operation; local historians everywhere answered our queries and checked our manuscripts; houses were opened to us, and we were given pictures or allowed to take them. We are sorry that it is not possible to make our gratitude more specific.

Withal, we have tried to write without bias of a Virginia that worked for democracy through Colonial years, whose statesmen led the fight for freedom from British autocracy and for the establishment of a republic, of a Virginia that lost its leadership in 1825 and in subsequent years has striven to regain a place among the commonwealths, of a Virginia that passed through its commemorative era and seems about to launch upon new accomplishment. We welcome the traveler to our shrines, and we shall always share with him our spoonbread, Smithfield ham, Brunswick stew, peanuts, and tobacco if he will but listen to the tales we like to tell of our worthy ancestors. In our book we have striven to record the exploits not only of those 'not born to die,' but also of those 'to fortune and to fame unknown,' who but for us would not have escaped undeserved oblivion.

EUDORA RAMSAY RICHARDSON
State Supervisor

Preface to the Second Printing

We have taken advantage of this new printing of *The Virginia Guide* to include appendices of 1940 population figures, recent changes in highway routes and numbers, a list of radio stations with the latest frequency allocations, and an enlarged index, which has discarded the topical plan used in the first printing. Minor errors that, in a book dealing with many minutiae, were inevitably discovered by our staff and by specialists in various fields of Virginia history, have been carefully assembled for the second edition, which we hope will be published in the not too distant future.

E.R.R.

Contents

Part III. Tours

Part IV. Appendices

Illustrations

HEAD AND TAIL PIECES BY EDWARD A. DARBY

Maps

General Information

Railroads: The Richmond, Fredericksburg, and Potomac R.R. from Washington to Richmond, handles trains of the Atlantic Coast Line and the Seaboard Air Line, both lines continuing southward to the Gulf States; the Southern Ry. crosses the State diagonally from Washington to the North Carolina line near Danville and has in addition lines from Richmond to Danville, from Danville to Norfolk, and in the Southwest; the Chesapeake and Ohio Ry., the Norfolk and Western Ry., and the Virginian Ry. cross the State from the Hampton Roads area to the western boundary; the Seaboard enters Norfolk from North Carolina; the Pennsylvania R.R. traverses the Eastern Shore from Maryland to Cape Charles and enters Norfolk by ferry; the Baltimore & Ohio R.R. and the Southern Ry. traverse the Shenandoah Valley; and numerous small lines operate in the vicinity of Norfolk, of Northern Virginia, and in the Southwest.

Highways: Paved Federal and State highways form a network over the State; county roads, taken over by the State secondary road system except in three counties, form networks within the larger pattern. The State has 9,432 miles of primary road, of which 82 per cent are hard-surfaced. There are 36,356 miles of secondary road, of which more than half have been paved or improved.

Bus Lines: Interstate lines cover the main north-south and east-west highways; intrastate lines cover many of the sectional areas.

Air Lines: Eastern Air Line stops at Richmond: New York—Richmond, four trips; New York—Miami (Pan American); New York—Atlanta (Piedmont Flyer); New York—San Antonio (Southwestern); and New York to Tampa. Pennsylvania Central Airlines, Norfolk—Washington, connects for north and west. American Airlines, Albany, N.Y.—Fort Worth, Texas, stops at Lynchburg, Roanoke, and Bristol.

Waterways: Merchants and Miners Line, Norfolk to Philadelphia and to Boston; Old Dominion Line, Norfolk to New York and to Miami; Baltimore Steam Packet Company (Old Bay Line) and Chesapeake Line, Norfolk to Baltimore; Chesapeake Line, West Point to Baltimore. Ferries run regularly from Norfolk, Little Creek, and Old Point Comfort to Cape Charles.

Traffic Regulations: Operation of private out-of-state cars is limited to six months unless reciprocal agreements permit of longer operation. Maximum speed: on highways, 55 m.p.h.; residential districts, 25 m.p.h.; business districts and when passing schools, 15 m.p.h.; passing stationary school buses, 5 m.p.h. Norfolk and Richmond (latter on trial) have parking meters and both cities enforce ordinances against jaywalking.

Accommodations: All the cities and many towns have good modern hotels; there are many tourist homes, generally near communities. Tourist camps are at frequent intervals, some with trailer grounds; inquiry as to quality is advisable. Campsites are in the National forests and in the Shenandoah National Park. Cabins are available in State parks (reservations made at Virginia Conservation Commission, Richmond). On the Skyline Drive are many cabins, lodges, and several campsites.

Climate: Virginia climate is generally mild and equable, with short periods of severe temperature in winter and in summer. The annual average temperature is about 57° F.

Recreational Areas: National forests and National and State parks for various amusements; waters along Atlantic Coast and Chesapeake Bay for saltwater bathing and fishing; Skyline Drive and Blue Ridge Parkway and the mountains for scenic pleasures. Inquire of local communities for diversified recreations.

National Parks: Arlington National Cemetery, across the Potomac River from Washington; Colonial National Historical Park, on the peninsula between the York and James Rivers; Fredericksburg and Spotsylvania National Military Park, around Fredericksburg; George Washington Birthplace National Monument, 37.5 m. E. of Fredericksburg off State 3; Petersburg National Military Park, around Petersburg; Richmond National Battlefield Park, near Richmond; Shenandoah National Park, extends 70 m. along the west of the Blue Ridge, traversed by Skyline Drive.

National Forests: George Washington National Forest, in three parts, headquarters at Harrisonburg; Jefferson National Forest, headquarters at Roanoke.

State Parks: Douthat, entrance 3 m. E. of Clifton Forge, off US 60; Fairystone, 20 m. NW. of Martinsville, off State 57; Hungry Mother, 3 m. W. of Marion, off US 11; Seashore, 3 m. W. of Cape Henry, off US 60; Staunton River, SE. corner Halifax County, off US 360; Westmoreland, 40 m. E. of Fredericksburg, off State 3.

Federal Recreational Areas: Chopawamsic Recreational Demonstration Area, 2 m. W. of Triangle, off US 1 (30 m. S. of Washington); Swift Creek Recreation Park, 13 m. SW. of Richmond, off State 10; Blue Ridge Parkway, under construction, will extend from North Carolina line to Shenandoah National Park; Bull Run, 4 m. W. of Manassas.

Cautions: Fires: In the National forests and parks fires should be built only at designated campgrounds. *Poisonous Snakes*: Rattlesnakes in the western mountains; copperhead moccasins are widely distributed; and cottonmouth moccasins are restricted to the Dismal Swamp area.

Information Bureaus: The Virginia State Chamber of Commerce and the Virginia Conservation Commission issue literature descriptive of the State and its attractions; local chambers of commerce furnish information generally restricted to their vicinities; hotels, railroad stations, automobile clubs, and gas companies supply general information as to travel; and stations in the National forests and National parks are equipped to give guidance in their particular areas.

Admission to Private Houses: Where conditions of admission to private houses and estates have been established those conditions are given. Houses that strangers may enter only by invitation of the owner are marked *private*. Most of those that are named without mention of conditions of admission or without the warning *private* are the homes of Virginians who are happy to receive the courteous visitor, even though he is wholly a stranger within their gates—provided that he appears at seasonable hours, preferably in mid-afternoon, and does not stay too long. Grounds should not be used for picnicking.

Calendar of Events

('nfd' means *no fixed date*; as many dates are subject to slight changes, items are listed in approximate sequence.)

JANUARY		
19	Stratford Hall	Robert E. Lee Birthday Celebration
MARCH		
midmonth	Warrenton	Warrenton Hunt Point-to-Point Races
last half	Gloucester and Mathews Counties	Gloucester-Mathews Narcissus Tour
nfd	Norfolk	Annual Camellia Show
nfd	Middleburg	Middleburg Hunt Point-to-Point Races
APRIL		
nfd	Richmond	Deep Run Hunt Race Meet
nfd	Foxville	Fauquier Field Trials Association—Spring Trials
13	Charlottesville	Founders Day Celebration (Jefferson's Birthday) at University of Virginia
nfd	Alexandria	Annual Narcissus Show of the Garden Club of Virginia
midmonth	Norfolk	Annual Spring Flower Show
midmonth	Middleburg	The Middleburg Races—flat and steeplechase
midmonth	Alexandria	Alexandria Association Old Home Interiors Tour
nfd	Middleburg	Middleburg Spring Meet
nfd	Hot Springs	Spring Tennis Tournament

26	Cape Henry	Cape Henry Pilgrimage, commemorating the first landing on April 26, 1607
nfd	Lynchburg	Lynchburg Junior Horse Show
last week	State-wide	Garden Week in Virginia; many private homes open
last Tuesday	Norfolk	Annual AKC Dog Show, sponsored by Hampton Roads Kennel Club, Inc.
last Wed. and Thurs.	Richmond	Virginia Kennel Club Show
last Sat.	Alexandria	Old Dominion Kennel Club Show
last week or first of May	Winchester	Shenandoah Apple Blossom Festival

MAY

1st week	Stratford Hall	Spring Celebration, sponsored by the Robert E. Lee Memorial Foundation
nfd	Warrenton	Stuyvesant School Horse Show
nfd	Warrenton	Virginia Gold Cup Race
nfd	Virginia Beach	Cavalier Horse Show
nfd	Warrenton	Warrenton Country School Horse Show
nfd	Norfolk	Tidewater Horse Show
13	Jamestown	Jamestown Day; commemorating the founding of the first English colony
2nd Sun.	Fredericksburg	Mary Washington Mother's Day Celebration
midmonth	Virginia Beach	Rose Show, sponsored by Princess Anne Garden Club
23	Richmond	Powhatan Hill Festival, celebrating the arrival of the English to the site of Richmond
nfd	Hampton	Hampton Horse Show

nfd	Richmond	Deep Run Hunt Club Horse Show
last weekend	Richmond	National Championship Motorcycle Races and Hill Climb
nfd	Bristol	Virginia Dogwood Festival
nfd	Warrenton	Gymkhana
nfd	Blacksburg	V.P.I. Horseshow
nfd	Fort Myer	Military Horse Show
nfd	Norfolk	Maury Regatta
30	State-wide	Memorial Day
May to Nov.	Middleburg	Polo Matches every Thursday and Sunday
June		
1st week	Place varies	State Woman's Golf Tournament
nfd	Culpeper	Culpeper Horse Show
9	Petersburg	'The Ninth of June,' celebrating the origin of Memorial Day
nfd	Tasley	Potato Blossom Festival
nfd	Bassett	Bassett Horse Show
nfd	Upperville	Upperville Colt and Horse Show
nfd	Virginia Beach	Virginia Amateur Golf Tournament
nfd	Warrenton	Warrenton Pony Show
July		
1–2	Richmond	National Outboard Regatta Trials
nfd	Norton	Rhododendron Festival
4	West Point	Outboard Motor Regatta
4	Stratford Hall	Celebration in honor of two signers of the Declaration of Independence born at Stratford Hall, Francis Lightfoot and Richard Henry Lee

week of 4th	Hampton	Yacht Club Regatta, including Virginia Gold Cup, Inboard Motor Races, Sailboat Regatta
1st half	Charlottesville	Institute of Public Affairs
nfd	Hot Springs	Mixed Golf Tournament
nfd	Hot Springs	Midsummer Tennis Tournament
last Thurs.	Chincoteague Island	Pony Penning Day
nfd	Hot Springs	Skeet Tournament
nfd	Front Royal	Horse Show at U.S. Army Remount Station

AUGUST

2nd Thurs. and Fri.	Hot Springs	Bath County Horse Show
2nd Fri. and Sat.	White Top Mtn.	White Top Folk Music Festival
3rd Thurs. Fri. and Sat.	Berryville	Clarke County Horse Show
nfd	Keswick	Keswick Hunt Club Horse Show
nfd	Irvington	Rappahannock River Yacht Club Regatta
27–30	Hot Springs	Golf Tournament
nfd	Manassas	Annual Dairy Fair

SEPTEMBER

1st Sat. to Mon.	Warrenton	Warrenton Horse Show
nfd	Norfolk	Regatta Norfolk-Portsmouth Yacht Racing Association
nfd	South Boston	National Tobacco Festival and Pageant
nfd	Upperville	Upperville Horse Show
nfd	Fairfax	Fairfax Horse and Pony Show
nfd	Orange	Orange Horseman's Show
last week	Richmond	Virginia State Fair

OCTOBER		
nfd	Charlottesville	Farmington Hunt Club Horse Show
12	Stratford Hall	Anniversary of the death of General Robert E. Lee
19	Yorktown	Yorktown Day—Anniversary of Cornwallis's Surrender
nfd	Norfolk	Navy Day Observance at Naval Operating Base
nfd	Fredericksburg	Dog Mart
October to March	State-wide	Fox hunting at more than a dozen nationally recognized hunts, chiefly in northern Virginia

PART I
Virginia's Background

The Spirit of Virginia

BY DOUGLAS SOUTHALL FREEMAN

THE best symbolic approach to Virginia is a southward journey from the bridge that joins the Lincoln Memorial with Arlington. When the traveler turns his back on Washington and sees before him the portico of General Lee's mansion, the wheels of the motorcar may turn as rapidly as before, but life itself has a different tempo. It is neither the nervous *accelerando* of the East nor the common time of the Deep South. Life is more leisured without being essentially indolent. Human relations are somewhat more intimate. Tempered by the reserve of a certain personal dignity, friendliness prevails. Everywhere the dark laughter of the Negro is to be heard. Old houses outnumber modern, but the exclamation points of new factory stacks punctuate a landscape familiar to three centuries of white residents. From north to south, along the coastal plain, the scenery and the people change scarcely at all.

It is among these people, or some of them, that traditional Virginia life is to be observed. In the cultured circles of the larger eastern cities of the Commonwealth, there is a curious commingling of yesterday and today. New York is the objective of the natives' most frequent journeying, and to Europe they go often; but they always will stop chattering about a new play on Broadway to listen to a Negro story, and the elders seldom talk fifteen minutes without some reference to the War between the States. There is a deliberate cult of the past along with typically American business activity. All eastern Virginians are Shintoists under the skin. Genealogy makes history personal to them in terms of family. Kinship to the eighth degree usually is recognized. There are classes within castes. Alumni of the various colleges have different affiliations. A pleasant society it is, one that does not adventure rashly into new acquaintanceship but welcomes with a certain stateliness of manner those who come with letters from friends. If conversation rarely is brilliant, it is friendly and humorous and delightsome to the alien except when it passes to genealogical abstrusities.

The rural life of Tidewater is more clearly divided in economic status. A few families have contrived for 200 years to hold to baronial estates, though sometimes by making themselves the slaves of their houses and their gardens. More often, Virginians who have grown rich in the North, or Virginia women who have married men of fortune, come back in a desire to re-establish the old plantation life. Some of them succeed in making the river estates more beautiful than in the eighteenth century, but the difference between the fine appearance of these properties and the dilapidation of smaller holdings near by is the difference between income spent on the farm and money derived from farming. There probably is not a single great plantation in eastern Virginia that can be called self-sustaining otherwise than by sentimental, rather than actuarial bookkeeping.

If the traveler who comes from the North to Richmond or to Norfolk will turn westward, he will find after 150 miles of travel that the scenery and the people change with every hour's driving. Orange County and the border of Albemarle seem the home of Richmonders who have craved a sight of the mountains; the Warrenton and Middleburg districts are suburbs of Washington or are the hunting grounds of New Yorkers. Around Charlottesville is a society *sui generis*, with an English flavor somewhat less pronounced today than it was a generation ago.

Once the Blue Ridge is passed and the exquisite Shenandoah Valley is reached, the motorist is among people who take religion and farming more seriously. Many of these Valley folk came into Virginia from Pennsylvania, and adhere to creeds that were Quaker in origin. Other residents of the Valley, particularly between Staunton and Lexington, are of stout Scotch-Irish stock and have the unflagging belief of their race in education and in hard work. To the southwestward, one may go into counties where cattle raising overtops agriculture. The Negro population of those counties never was large. Politics, for that reason, have not been swayed by race questions. Northward from Staunton, down the Valley, one comes to the great apple-growing country. There the admixture of stock is most interesting: the descendants of Scotch-Irish and the Pennsylvania Germans live side by side with families that went to the Valley from the Alexandria district and northern Tidewater before the American Revolution.

Along the crest and among the coves of the Blue Ridge, and in the Alleghenies that guard the Valley on its westward side, live the mountaineers proper. That some of them ever wrest a living from their steep and narrow fields even a student familiar with squalor would find it difficult to believe; but they hold tenaciously to their small farms and they send surplus sons to the mines or to the nearby new industries, the establishment of which is perhaps the most thrilling chapter in the recent economic history of Virginia.

Among 2,500,000 people of habitat so diversified, what common inheritance is there to justify the assertion that there is a distinctive spirit of Virginia? The answer is a definition, perhaps the only definition, of that spirit. By hundreds of thousands, Virginians have gone into other States, but those who have remained in the Old Dominion are of the same stock and have no deep admixture of recent foreign blood. In Richmond, for example, the percentage of foreign born was only two and three-tenths in 1930 as against thirteen in 1860. No large cities serve as electromagnets for a melting pot. The presence of the Negro has kept out the foreigner who in other States competes with the native manual laborer to get his start in America.

The experience of an immense, common tragedy has strengthened the homogeneity of the population. In Virginia, strangers often are amazed to find how near seems the War between the States. The reason is that the conflict reached every family, brought all of them together in defense, left most of them impoverished, and then produced during reconstruction a type of government that made political unity a racial necessity. Prior to 1860, Virginia was divided not unevenly between Whigs and Democrats. After the war, disfranchisement and the carpetbaggers' venal misguidance of the freedmen made men Democrats because they were white and had been Confederates.

Virginia's emergence from reconstruction and her progress in recovery placed her for a generation and a half under the direction of men who had confident faith that nothing which could happen to them was as bad as that which they had survived. Courage, patience, and cheer, as exemplified by the Confederate veterans, left so deep a mark that even in the blackest days of the great depression of 1929–36, there was far less of anxious concern in Virginia than in most American States.

Likewise to the war and to the reconstruction are to be traced the respect for leadership that is one of the characteristics of the spirit of Virginia. The Virginians of the '60s were unrelenting individualists, reared on their own land, but they learned from Lee and from Jackson how discipline could offset odds. Thanks to the wise planning of Alexander H. H. Stuart and others, these men saw their State readmitted to the Union within less than six years after Appomattox. It was a lesson they did not soon forget. Even poor leadership long was better than the lack of any.

Folkways and religion have contributed in the same manner to the persistence of a distinctive Virginia spirit. Although the movement from farm to town has torn thousands of Virginia families from the soil, there has been a continuity of life among people of similar tradition and of Protestant faith. If courtesy and neighborliness are more general than in many parts of the Union, it is because courtesy is due old friends. In their migrations, Virginians have carried with them the *Lares et Penates* of ancestral altars. Had the altars not been old, the household gods would not have been so cherished.

Much of the spirit represented by these political and historical influences should persist and doubtless will. That is the hope of those who share a common pride in Virginia at the same time that they refuse to shut their eyes to the shadows of a pleasant picture. There is, in Virginia, too high a birth rate among those least able, economically or intellectually, to rear stalwart children. The backwardness described in the essay on education in this informative volume is not overpainted in its indigoes and black. Negroes gradually have been forced from the skilled trades, despite all that has been done for their training at Hampton and at such smaller schools as St.Paul's at Lawrenceville. The choice of the Negro now lies between the extremes of overcrowded profession and underpaid common labor or domestic service. No middle class is being developed.

Many rural communities are depressed. Virginia farmers by tens of thousands still seek pathetically to eke a living from eroded or starved land. Much of the industrial development of the State requires only the semiskilled worker whose wage is adequate if he is unmarried but is insufficient for the support of a family.

The course of the sun will lighten some of these dark colors. Industrially, Virginia will continue to progress. Those manufactories that are not maintained by great corporations simply to prepare materials for finish or fabrication in the North gradually will be forced by competition to improve the quality of their product and, in so doing, to demand skilled labor at higher wages than ever will be paid semiskilled operatives. This is reasonably certain. Virginia's opportunity lies in the preliminary vocational training of workers who can advance along with industry. In agriculture, which will remain the largest vocation in Virginia for at least another generation, progress depends on leadership and on adequate governmental support. For the advance of Virginia, Blacksburg is the key position. Industrialists from the North often say that the honesty and the economy of government in Virginia are among the considerations that bring them to Virginia; but honesty is a virtue that ought to be inherent, and economy is a mockery and a misnomer when it is attained by neglect of public health or at the expense of children's education.

If industry prospers and yields a larger tax-revenue, Virginia can hope to improve steadily her educational system in all its parts from the rural Negro school, which remains a deep disgrace, to the institutions of higher learning. Virginia seems aware of this: the average of citizenship will never be better or worse than the standards of the primary and secondary schools, but leadership increasingly will depend on the colleges, the universities, and the professional institutions. It will be a mistake to diffuse the limited funds Virginia can devote to higher education, and equally will it be a mistake to undertake too wide postgraduate and professional study at an early date. Prudently, and as fast as she may, Virginia must offer this training within her borders. She has suffered much already from the loss of those superior young men and women who go North for advanced instruction, and never return. Virginia's heaviest loss is through the export of brains. In the attainment of her larger industrial future, Virginia will perceive, also, that short-sighted persistence in the underpayment of Negro workers has driven away and will continue to deprive her of thousands of willing hands and strong bodies.

Politically, the ominous conditions in Virginia are the gradual atrophy of local self-government, the failure of well-educated, unselfish men and women to participate actively in the public service, and the abstention of tens of thousands from the exercise of the franchise. It is difficult to say which of these three is potentially the most serious. Local boards of supervisors and city councils long were training schools for public service. Membership, if unsolicited, was regarded as a duty. It no longer is so. Among Virginians of means and education, the balance between activity and complacency too often is tipped on the wrong side. The civic conscience is stronger than the political. Recruits for community service never are lacking, but for men who unselfishly will assume public office, the drums are beaten in vain. Politics no longer are the avocation of the gentleman as in 1765–89. That avocation must be revived. Virginia's future never will be secure until there is larger participation by intelligent voters in elections and in public office.

Perhaps it is indicative of the changing spirit of Virginia, that this introduction to *The Virginia Guide* should include as much of confession as of eulogium, and more concerning present needs than past glories. This should not be taken to mean that Virginia is losing either her pride or her faith. Rather should these paragraphs be read as evidence that Virginia is looking forward in a consciousness of her responsibility to justify her past. Her sons and her daughters are not content to say, 'We have Abraham for a Father.'

Natural Setting

ALTHOUGH three centuries of political change have gradually reduced the vast range of Virginia's original domain, the topography of the State is still unusually varied. As chartered in 1609, the Old Dominion extended from the Atlantic to the Pacific, and from the approximate latitude of Columbia, South Carolina, to a parallel above the southern boundary of the present State of Pennsylvania. Until 1784 it stretched far northwest of the Ohio River and west of the Mississippi. Kentucky was part of Virginia until 1792; West Virginia became a separate State in 1863. But, notwithstanding this contraction, Virginia retains its characteristic trend 'across the grain' of the continent and also a diversity of geographic, topographic, and geologic features somewhat different from that of other Atlantic seaboard States.

The outline of the State is roughly the shape of a triangle. Its base is the almost straight southern boundary, which divides Virginia from North Carolina and Tennessee. With slight variation, this line follows parallel 36° 22′ from the Atlantic shore to Cumberland Gap, at 83° 41′ west longitude. The little village of Cumberland Gap on the Virginia-Tennessee border is about 25 miles farther west than the meridian of Detroit, Michigan. On the western side of the triangle the jagged and tortuous ridge lines of some of the Appalachian ranges demark Virginia from Kentucky and West Virginia as far northeast as latitude 39° 28′. The eastern boundary of the mainland is defined by the Potomac River, Chesapeake Bay, and the Atlantic Ocean. Below the mouth of the Potomac the line crosses Chesapeake Bay to cut off from Maryland a long outer peninsula known as the Eastern Shore.

The total area of Virginia is 42,627 square miles, of which 2,365 square miles are water surface. Along the southern boundary from the Atlantic to Cumberland Gap the maximum length of the State is about 432 miles. Its maximum width north and south is 200 miles. By highway, Cumberland Gap is about 510 miles from Washington, D.C. The extreme airline distance diagonally across the State from the northeast corner of Accomac County on the Eastern Shore peninsula to Cumberland Gap is about 470 miles.

Virginia is divided physiographically into five distinct provinces—the

Coastal Plain, the Piedmont Province, the Blue Ridge Province, the Valley and Ridge Province, and the Appalachian Plateau.

Coastal Plain: 'Tidewater' is the name generally given to the broad belt of undulating and river-gashed plain that borders the eastern seaboard of Virginia from the Potomac to the North Carolina line. This province decreases in width from 120 miles near Bowling Green, 35 miles north of Richmond, to 80 miles near Norfolk in the south, and is traversed by great estuaries, which drain into Chesapeake Bay. The interstream ridges are narrow and relatively flat. In general the plain descends gently from an altitude of 300 feet at its western edge near Washington to sea level, at a rate of less than three feet to the mile. Tidal channels of four rivers sever the northern and central part of the plain into three long peninsulas, whose eastern extremities—with the peninsula of the Eastern Shore—border the lower Chesapeake Bay and form a magnificent system of natural harbors. This pattern of bays, deep tidal rivers, and long intervening necks of arable land has had a profound influence upon the social and commercial life of Tidewater Virginia.

Piedmont Province: There is no sharp line of division between the Coastal Plain and the Piedmont Province, which broadens southward from a width of 40 miles at the north to about 185 miles at the North Carolina line. Imperceptibly rising toward the foothills of the Blue Ridge, the province ranges in altitude from about 300 feet at the east to from 500 to 1,000 feet at the base of the mountains, reaching its greatest height in the southwestern part. The surface has been so channeled by streams that, with a few notable exceptions, flat areas are few. Hills or ridges dot the general surface near the western border. Some of these are outlying spur ridges and foothills of the Blue Ridge; others are isolated ridges and low mountains. They rise to altitudes as great as 2,200 feet.

Blue Ridge Province: The Blue Ridge rises rather abruptly above the western part of the Piedmont. In the northern half of the State it is a distinct ridge, bordered here and there on each side by subordinate ridges and with numerous deep coves in each slope. Some of the peaks have altitudes of more than 4,000 feet. In its southern part the Blue Ridge Province is a high, broad, somewhat rugged plateau—a region of rolling uplands, deep ravines, and high peaks. The highest mountains in Virginia, Mount Rogers (5,719 feet) and Whitetop (5,520 feet), are in the extreme southwestern part. At the North Carolina line the Blue Ridge Plateau is about 60 miles wide, with a general elevation of about 1,500 feet above the Piedmont upland.

Most of Virginia west of the Blue Ridge Province lies in the Appalachian

Valley, commonly called the Valley of Virginia. The width of the province in the north, between the Blue Ridge and the West Virginia line, is about 35 miles; along the Tennessee line it is about 100 miles. Altitudes vary from approximately 300 feet above sea level at Harper's Ferry, on the Potomac, to 4,500 feet at the highest points of numerous ridges. In length, the Valley of Virginia extends 360 miles from the Potomac River southwestward to Tennessee. It is in reality a series of elongate valleys separated by transverse ridges, plateaus, or narrow gaps. The largest and best known of its principal units, Shenandoah Valley at the north, is about 150 miles long and from 10 to 20 miles wide. It contains a number of natural wonders. Above its center this valley is divided into two parts by Massanutten Mountain, a long high ridge. Other units in the Valley of Virginia, from north to south, are Fincastle Valley, Roanoke (Salem) Valley, Dublin Valley, Abingdon Valley, and Powell Valley. Dublin and Abingdon valleys, in the southwestern part, are from 2,100 to 2,400 feet above sea level.

Appalachian Plateau: Designated by some geographers as the Southwestern Plateau, the Appalachian Plateau in Virginia embraces parts of the Cumberland and Kanawha plateaus, which extend a relatively short distance into Virginia from Kentucky. The general elevation is between 2,700 and 3,000 feet, but the plateau is channeled by streams into a maze of deep narrow ravines and winding ridges. Cumberland Mountain, overlooking Powell Valley, marks the eastern boundary. Other mountains lie along the boundary farther northeast. In place of the elongate conformations of the Valley and Ridge Province, there is a multitude of irregular hills and peaks. The rock formations, in a few places, dip sufficiently to create more or less definite northeast-southwest ridges, but in general the only elevations that have a directional trend are inter-stream ridges.

CLIMATE

Virginia's climate is on the whole mild and equable, with refreshing seasonal changes that vary somewhat in different areas.

Southeastern Tidewater, within a 50-mile radius of Norfolk, has a particularly even climate. Thermometer readings in winter are rarely lower than 15° above zero, and the average temperature of the coldest winter month is about 40° above. This lower Chesapeake region has an average of about 258 days of sunshine a year and an average growing season of 200 days. Summer temperatures are only a little warmer than in the Piedmont-Tidewater zone to the north and west.

In the remainder of the Tidewater and in the Piedmont, average summer and winter temperatures are slightly lower than in the Norfolk region. The coldest winter temperatures in Piedmont are from 5° to 15° above zero; the summer maximum of from 105° to 107° is infrequently reached.

In the Appalachian zone, which includes the mountain and valley regions to the west and the upper reaches of Piedmont near the Blue Ridge, zero weather is frequent in winter. The average temperature for December, January, and February ranges around freezing point. Summer temperatures in the Shenandoah Valley average a little above 75° with an occasional 'high' of 90°; but the nights are cool because of mountain breezes that dispel the quickly radiated heat of the lower levels.

Rainfall in Virginia averages from 40 to 45 inches a year, and is well distributed. There is ample precipitation from May to September, when rain is needed for growing crops. June, July, and August are the months of greatest rainfall, and November is the driest month.

Snowfalls are moderate over most of the State and melt quickly, except in the mountain section and the northern part of the Shenandoah Valley, where the annual snowfall is from 25 to 30 inches a year. In the southeastern Tidewater the fall is commonly less than 10 inches; in the Piedmont it is 18 inches or more.

Midwinter days (from sunrise to sunset) in the latitude of Richmond are about half an hour longer than in the latitude of Boston and Detroit; midsummer days are about half an hour shorter. Clear days are most frequent in the fall and spring and average 12 a month throughout the year. Cloudy days average 9 a month, and partly cloudy 10 a month.

In the eastern section, fogs are frequent during the cooler season. They are likely to occur in the early morning and to disperse in a few hours. Heavy summer fogs occur in the mountain and valley regions about three times a month.

Virginia in general escapes both the rigorous cold of States farther to the north and the debilitating summer heat of more southerly regions. The climate fosters a well-balanced variety of agricultural products and has attracted to the State many industries to which conditions of temperature and humidity are important.

GEOLOGY

The mystery obscuring the pre-Cambrian eras—dim ages of the early geologic past that were longer, possibly, than all subsequent time—is not clarified by their rock remains in Virginia. If life existed during the vast era of creation known as the Archeozoic, it was of a nature too primal and transitory to leave traces. In looking for clues among the next younger Algonkian rocks, too, the geologist is baffled by a profound metamorphism that reduces theory to conjecture. Rocks in the Piedmont and the Blue Ridge prove that the surface-formed materials of the pre-Cambrian eras included both sedimentary strata and lava flows.

The story becomes more legible in the fossil-bearing strata of the Paleozoic era, deposited long before the present Appalachian Mountains were formed. During most of the era the portion of Virginia west of the Blue Ridge, as well as a part of the Piedmont, was submerged in great inland seas that advanced in the Cambrian period over the Mississippi Valley. Erosion of the Piedmont uplands supplied sediment that was spread over the beds of the seas to the west. Enormous volumes of lime silt accumulated in these seas, giving rise later to the limestone valleys, such as the Shenandoah. Great coal swamps existed during the later Paleozoic era. Later a series of great lateral thrusts from the southeast uplifted the sea beds of sediment to mountainous heights, folding and faulting the strata and expelling the sea from the interior of Virginia.

Here, at the close of Paleozoic time, occurred one of the greatest revolutions in the earth's history. The shrinkage of the earth had produced accumulated stresses that crumpled the weaker sediments in the sea trough, pushed up the old Appalachian mountain system, and drove the interior seas from the continent, never to return over such a vast area. The Appalachian Mountains as they are now known, however, were not produced until the Mesozoic and Cenozoic eras.

In the Triassic period, first of the Mesozoic era, erosion of the recently elevated mountains furnished a large amount of débris to be carried down the eastern slopes and deposited in the deltas and on flood plains of rivers flowing toward the Atlantic and in numerous down-warped basins. Triassic muds and sands (Newark series) of Virginia were laid down in various basins of the central Piedmont. The drainage of the Cretaceous period deposited sands, muds, and some limy materials in lakes, swamps, and estuaries over much of the Coastal Plain.

The Cenozoic era, during which forms of modern life first appeared on the earth, embraces the Eocene, Miocene, and Pliocene epochs of the Tertiary or mammal age. Most geologists include in this era the 'age of man,' the Quaternary, or ice age; by others this period is designated as the first in the Psychozoic era. Invading the land from the east, the Atlantic laid the Tertiary deposits of sediment at least as far westward as the present fall line and over the whole of what is now the Coastal Plain. Later in the

Cenozoic era, rivers spread sand and gravel widely over the Tertiary sediments.

The recent chapters of the geologic story of western Virginia are written in topography rather than in sedimentary deposits. Yielding to erosion, the mountainous surface of the region diminished in Mesozoic time to a nearly flat surface, slightly above sea level. A vertical uplift in the late Cretaceous period raised this plain to a height of from 1,000 to 2,000 feet above the sea, and another vertical uplift of approximately the same force toward the close of the Tertiary age further increased the altitude without folding the strata. Erosion by the rejuvenated streams carved valleys in the softer limestone and shales and left the resistant beds standing high as great elongate mountain ridges.

The geologic divisions of Virginia today coincide with the physiographic divisions. Each of the provinces is distinguished by characteristic groups of rocks—sedimentary, igneous, and metamorphic—and its boundaries are delimited chiefly by the character and structure of its rocks.

The geologic structure of the Coastal Plain is simple. Beds of sedimentary rock dip gently seaward and are exposed in wide belts of successively older rocks from the coast to the fall line. Clays, sandstones, greensands, diatomaceous earth, and shell marl (Cretaceous and Tertiary) range from loose to well-indurated materials. The province contains true rocks in the geologic sense, although few of the formations are well consolidated. Superficial mantels of sand and gravel (Quaternary) occur along the main streams and the coast. Dismal Swamp, southwest of Norfolk, is underlain by peat.

By deep borings (2,251 feet) it has been proved that the basement rocks of the Coastal Plain are crystalline, like those of the Piedmont Province. Artesian supplies of water are easily obtained in many parts of the province.

The Piedmont is predominately an area of very old (pre-Cambrian) crystalline rocks, both igneous and metamorphic. It abounds in granites, gneisses, schists, and greenstones. Slate (early Paleozoic), soapstone, and marble occur in many places. Metamorphic rocks have been so changed from their earlier condition that the character of many of the original rocks is indeterminate. The major types of rock masses extend northeast and southwest in long and relatively narrow belts. Broad elongate lowlands of general southwest trend are underlain by much younger (Triassic) red sandstone and shale. The most extensive belt of these formations occurs in the northwestern part of the Piedmont Province and in the Richmond Basin southwest of Richmond. The latter contains important bodies of coal and some natural coke.

While simple in its broad outlines, the structural arrangement of crystalline rocks in the Piedmont Province is complex in detail. The prevailing dip of foliation in the metamorphic rocks is toward the southeast. In places the schists and gneisses are much contorted. Granites and other igneous rocks have been intruded more or less along the trend (strike) of the foliation or grain of the older rocks. The grain of the province is northeast and southwest, with the different rocks in a somewhat belted type of arrangement. Numerous faults occur in parts of the province.

Rocks in the Blue Ridge Province are chiefly crystalline, such as granite, gneiss, and greenstone. Schists and altered rhyolite occur in the southwestern plateau portion. The northwest flank is covered by sandstone and quartzite (early Paleozoic) that dip under the Valley of Virginia.

The geologic structure, especially in the plateau part of the Blue Ridge, is somewhat similar to that of the Piedmont region, except that more of the rocks are in massive crystalline bodies, like granite and greenstone. The ridge part of the province in the north is a huge uphold of granite and greenstone that has been thrust northwestward for miles along a great fault.

The Valley and Ridge Province is underlain by sedimentary rocks (Paleozoic). The Valley of Virginia is dominantly a limestone (Paleozoic) region, although broad belts of shale are common. Adjoining ridges and those within the valley are capped with hard sandstone. Anthracitic coal occurs in the middle part, particularly in the vicinity of New River and Roanoke. In the Valley and Ridge sections to the west, beds of hard sandstone support the ridges along their crests. There are outcroppings of limestone and shale along their slopes, and most of the intermontane valleys are on shale or sandstone. Some valleys are dominantly limestone. Formations in the Appalachian Valley have a total thickness of about eight miles.

Laterally the sedimentary strata of the Appalachian Valley have been squeezed into a series of great anticlines (upfolds) and synclines (downfolds), the folds generally being overturned toward the northwest and trending southwest parallel to the ridges and valleys. Many of them have been broken into great fractures or faults, so that large blocks or long thick horizontal slices of the earth's crust have been shoved miles to the northwest. These faults cause a marked repetition in the outcrop of various limestones and other formations and add to the valley's complexity of structure and diversity of topography.

In the order of their formation, the bedrocks of Virginia represent most of the periods in the four more recent eras of geologic time. The oldest, or pre-Cambrian rocks of igneous and metamorphic origin, are found at the surface only in the Piedmont region and in the Blue Ridge. An analysis of radioactive mineral from the Blue Ridge indicated that some of the rocks are eight hundred million years old. Paleozoic rocks are west of the Blue Ridge, except for small areas of older Paleozoic in the Piedmont. The upper Cambrian and part of the subsequent Ordovician limestone are sometimes designated collectively as 'valley limestone.' The Mesozoic rocks in Virginia crop out only in the Piedmont and along the western edge of the Coastal Plain. The Cenozoic is represented by Tertiary marine deposits and Quaternary sand and gravel. Most of the Coastal Plain is covered by unconsolidated Tertiary sands, clays, gravels, and marls, chiefly of Miocene age. To the Quaternary age belong upland sands and gravels scattered over the higher lands, as do lower terrace sands and gravels of the Chesapeake Bay region and the estuaries.

Fossil remains of marine invertebrates, such as corals, snails, clams, and crustacea, occur in many of the Paleozoic shales and limestones of the Valley and Ridge Province. Some of the limestones contain colonies of fossil seaweed. Of the Mesozoic era, when reptiles dominated land and sea, Virginia's fossil records are meager. Dinosaur footprints have been preserved in Triassic sandstones of Loudoun County. Scant records, too, exist of the vertebrates of the Cenozoic age, which saw the rise and dominance of mammals—although the sediments of the Coastal Plain have yielded teeth and vertebræ of whales, and there are fragmental remains of elephants in western Virginia. Some beds abound in invertebrate shells, the cliffs near Yorktown having yielded more than 100 species.

Fossil plants in Virginia are confined mainly to coal beds (the remains of swamp vegetation) and to the shales associated with such beds. They include types of ferns, rushes, and conifers that have, in the main, become extinct. One of the formations in the Coastal Plain contains a peculiar and industrially valuable earth, diatomite, composed of millions of tiny plants called diatoms.

NATURAL RESOURCES

The diversified geography and topography of Virginia account for natural resources that are both varied and abundant. Many types of soils are present; water resources range from rushing mountain streams and underground reservoirs to deep navigable outlets to the sea; mineral deposits are numerous; plant and animal life thrives in great variety.

Soils: The soils of the Coastal Plain are of three general types. The most fertile is the black stiff loam of tidal lowgrounds. Though boggy in wet weather and impregnably hard in dry weather, this soil requires little fertilization. The light sandy loams just west of the lowgrounds are easily cultivated and yield readily to fertilization for the growing of truck crops. The still higher clay and sand loams of the Coastal Plain, even though impoverished, react favorably to crop rotation and produce a wide variety of staple and special crops.

The Virginia Piedmont lands are generally fertile. The limestone and a part of the clay lands produce bluegrass, grains, and fruits. Virginia's tobacco belt lies in the central and southern portions of the Piedmont.

Limestone soils predominate in the valley areas west of the Blue Ridge. Toward the north in the Shenandoah Valley is the apple country of the State. Here also, along with grain, hay, and vegetables, are raised fine beef cattle, and poultry production is a profitable enterprise. In the southwestern section, the raising of livestock is of chief agricultural importance.

Soil conservation in Virginia has been largely concerned with the rehabilitation of lands impoverished by tobacco culture. Tidewater soils, exhausted in the Colonial period by intensive tobacco cultivation, were saved from utter ruin by the introduction of crop rotation and the use of marl as a neutralizing agent.

The present soil conservation problem centers in the Piedmont, where soils were depleted by the production of bright tobacco. Used in cigarette manufacture the world over, bright tobacco afforded an annual harvest of gold until the serious decline of prices in the late 1920's. The land on which tobacco had been grown, moreover, was unfit for subsistence crops. In limiting the tobacco crop to raise prices, some of the land was retired, hills were terraced, dikes were built in water courses, and legume crops were planted on acres once devoted to tobacco.

Erosion does comparatively little damage to the soils of the flat Coastal Plain or in the mountain region where outcropping strata and the quick-growing bluegrass hold the precious top soil; but many clay hills of the Piedmont have been washed of their former fertility.

Water: Virginia has a tidal shore line of 1,280 miles and contains all or part of eight river systems. About 2,365 square miles of its area are covered with water.

The Potomac River—including the north and south forks of its tributary, the Shenandoah—has a drainage area of 5,960 square miles, and its tidal section is 117 miles long. The Rappahannock River system, of which the Rapidan is chief tributary, lies entirely in Virginia, with its headwaters in the Blue Ridge and a course stretching 105 miles to the fall line. All the James River system, descending from high Allegheny ridges to Hampton

Roads, is in Virginia, except a few headwater creeks that extend into West Virginia. While the Chowan River itself lies in the Tidewater region of North Carolina, its three main tributaries, the Meherrin, the Nottoway, and the Blackwater, are Virginia streams. The Roanoke River, with the Dan as its principal tributary, also flows into North Carolina but has a course of 240 miles in Virginia, from the Valley of Virginia to the southeastern Piedmont. The New River (paradoxically one of the oldest rivers in North America) rises in western North Carolina and flows north and west to cut through the Valley Ridges across the Blue Ridge Plateau and the Valley of Virginia into West Virginia. The Holston, Clinch, and Powell Rivers, draining the southern part of the Valley of Virginia southwestward, are the State's principal tributaries of the Tennessee River system.

Uniform rainfall gives the numerous streams of Virginia a fairly even flow, and all the nontidal waters are suitable for ordinary industrial use. The steep gradient from headwaters in the mountains makes Virginia's larger streams a potential source of hydroelectric development with an estimated capacity of 459,000 horsepower.

Mineral Resources: Coal, the State's most important commercial mineral resource, occurs in three principal areas. The largest of these, the southwest Virginia field, on the eastern side of the Allegheny Plateau, covers 1,550 square miles and contains some 30 billion tons of bituminous coal. Next in importance is the Valley Field, in the Valley of Virginia, which covers 100 square miles and contains more than a billion tons of semianthracite coal. The third field, the Richmond Basin in the eastern Piedmont, covers 150 square miles and contains more than a billion tons of bituminous coal. This latter field was the first to be mined in the United States (1750) but has been worked little since the opening of mines in the mountains (1880). Natural gas in commercial quantities is found in the southwestern part of the Valley of Virginia.

Next in importance is a wide variety of nonmetallic minerals used in building and manufacturing. Principally, these are limestone, dolomite, shale, and sandstone in the Valley and Ridge regions; granite on the eastern Blue Ridge slope, in the central Piedmont, and along the fall line; calcareous marl in the Tidewater; and brick clays widely distributed throughout the State.

Other nonmetallic minerals, not so general in their distribution, are salt and gypsum in southwest Virginia; glass sand in the Valley region; barite in southwest Virginia and the Piedmont; kaolin and black marble in the Shenandoah Valley; greenstone, slate, soapstone, and talc in the central

Piedmont; feldspar, mica, and cyanide in the southern Piedmont; ocher in southwest Virginia and the Tidewater regions; and diatomite in the Tidewater.

Iron occurs in greater quantities in Virginia than does any other metal, lower grades of ore being widespread in the Valley Ridges, the central Blue Ridge, and the western edge of the central and southern Piedmont. Manganese ores are common in the Valley Ridges and western Piedmont. Gold, the first to be mined in the United States, occurs in a middle belt through the northeastern Piedmont and at one place in the Blue Ridge Plateau. Lead and zinc occur in southwest Virginia; pyrite and pyrrhotite in the southern Blue Ridge Plateau and central Piedmont; and titanium in the Piedmont. Copper occurs in the southern Piedmont; arsenic, asbestos, and graphite in the southern and central Piedmont; nickel and cobalt in the southern Bluc Ridge; and tin in the central Blue Ridge; but none of these appears in commercial quantities.

FLORA AND FAUNA

On the Coastal Plain in Virginia are vast stretches of pine woods, interspersed with hardwood trees and splashed in early spring by flowering redbud and dogwood. Broomsedge covers many an impoverished field, and near the tidal rivers and inlets are acres of waving marsh grass. Hardwood and pine areas extend throughout the Piedmont, broken by hillsides where broomsedge and weeds provide scant coverings. In the mountains are great slopes and ridges of hardwood and small tracts of pine, spruce, and hemlock. At the higher levels, rhododendron and mountain laurel abound; and bluegrass carpets the uncultivated fields of the valleys.

Though the original timber has long since been cut and the subsequent growth periodically exploited, more than 65 per cent of Virginia's area still consists of woodland. Among the varieties of trees found in the State are twelve kinds of oak, five of pine, four of hickory, three each of cedar, maple, birch, and elm, and two each of walnut, locust, gum, and poplar. In the Coastal Plain, pines are of first commercial importance, but other trees having general distribution are oak, red cedar, gum, poplar, beech, hickory, persimmon, ash, walnut, locust, dogwood, and redbud, with cypress and southern white cedar in isolated areas. The Piedmont forests contain oak, poplar, beech, gum, walnut, dogwood, redbud, persimmon, locust, and (less generally) red cedar and pine. The mountain forests are also principally of hardwood, containing oak, poplar, maple, beech, basswood, hickory, locust, walnut, red cedar, ash, dogwood, redbud, and cucumber magnolia. Pine, hemlock, and red spruce, though important, are less common in the mountains.

An adequate system of forest fire control has been developed. Individuals, corporations, and the State collectively maintain lookout towers and employ fire fighters. Two National forests, a National park, and six State parks hold a vast area of the State's woodland in reserve.

The principal native grasses of Virginia are marsh, crab, wire, and blue grass. Marsh grass, limited to the salt flats of the Coastal Plain, serves as a natural protection against erosion caused by encroachment of the sea and provides valuable grazing. Crab grass on the arable lands of the coast is cut for hay. The wire grass indigenous to all sections and bluegrass in the mountains provide grazing and help to prevent erosion.

Many wild flowers are indigenous to Virginia. On mountain and cliff are trailing arbutus, rhododendron, many kinds of azaleas, and mountain laurel. Peculiar to the Alleghenies are the Canby's mountain lover, an evergreen; St.John's wort, with its large pale-yellow blossom; the mountain spurge, its purple blooms hidden under low leaves; mountain mint or Virginia thyme with its lavender-tipped white flowers; and trailing wolfsbane. Among the more notable flowers characteristic of the lowland woods and fields are the abundant blue lobelia, which originated in Virginia; prolific and dainty quaker-ladies or bluets; sturdy erect blue lupine with blossoms similar to those of the wisteria vine, which is also abundant throughout the State; the poison-rooted May apple; the rare spring beauty; false rue anemone; morning glory; chicory, the root of which is often blended with coffee; lowland laurel; and delicate yellow dogtooth, Confederate, and wood violets.

Though Virginia's animal life is still varied and plentiful, civilization has levied a costly toll upon many species of earlier fauna. Some mountainous regions in the western part of the State are still primitive enough to shelter a small herd of elk, a few black bears, and an occasional wildcat; and the Dismal Swamp is still the habitat of bears and wildcats. But the bison that once fed on Virginia bluegrass are gone; beavers, wolves, and panthers are extinct. The otter and the mink have dwindled to an alarming degree and survive mainly along isolated water courses. Deer, because of conservation measures and their own shy habits, are increasing; and the prolific muskrat is safe despite much trapping. The fox, raccoon, opossum, squirrel, mole, rat, and mouse have adapted themselves to civilization; and so, in a more limited way, have the skunk and the ground hog. Public opinion and restricted fox hunting protect the red and gray fox. Protective laws have saved the raccoon from extinction, and the unobtrusive opossum has managed to survive in spite of the epicures who would garnish him with sweet potatoes. By canny foraging on farm gardens, the rabbit still maintains a comfortable livelihood.

Game birds flourish under a protective conservation program. The bob-white is widely distributed throughout the State; the wary wild turkey still inhabits the woods; the ruffed grouse is found in hilly areas; mourning doves and woodcock, though reduced in number, exist in nearly every section of the State; and sora appear annually in the coastal marshes.

Although only a few game waterfowl nest in Virginia, others migrating to the South either spend the winter or find an intermediate resting place here. Gray and black mallards, as well as wood or summer ducks, nest in the State or pass through on their semiannual journeys; canvasbacks, shovelers, goldeneyes, redheads, scaups or bluebills, and many of the lesser diving ducks winter in Virginia waters; the mallard, black duck, and pintail are plentiful in marshes and shallow waters; Canada geese and brant remain all winter on coastal feeding grounds. Of nongame waterfowl, bitterns, herons, several varieties of gulls, and numerous shore birds haunt the tidal waters and marshes.

Bald and golden eagles are now restricted to a few coastal and mountain areas. Virginia has more than a dozen species of hawks, ranging from the large marsh hawk to the diminutive sparrow hawk; and eight species of owls, from the great horned to the small screech owl. Hawks and owls are commonly killed without discrimination in Virginia, though only five of the hawk species and one of the owl are considered more destructive than beneficial. The turkey buzzard and the black buzzard, despite their attacks on small farm animals and their reputation as spreaders of disease, are tolerated as scavengers.

Great numbers of song birds make Virginia their home. The belligerent English sparrow dominates bird life near human habitations, and his many cousins are common over the countryside. The mockingbird sings both night and day; but his cousin, the catbird, is a temperamental artist who varies his monotonous grating cry only on special occasions. Robins and bluebirds are ever present in the fields and woods. Other birds common in Virginia are the crow, bluejay, cowbird, meadow or field lark, oriole, purple martin, cliff and barn swallows, house and marsh wrens, nuthatch, titmouse, several species of woodpecker and tanager, chuck-will's-widow, whippoorwill, nighthawk or bullbat, chimney swift, hummingbird, kingbird or bee martin, starling, wood thrush, and the glorious cardinal or redbird.

Virginia's poisonous snakes are the pit viper or rattlesnake, the copperhead, the cottonmouth moccasin, and the water moccasin. The rattlesnake, found in the western mountains and in some isolated eastern regions, is a dark brown or yellowish color with contrasting darker spots. The bronze and yellow-banded copperhead has a rather wide distribution and is the State's most treacherous serpent. The cottonmouth moccasin, short, thick, and vicious-looking, is restricted to the Dismal Swamp.

Of the nonpoisonous group, the black snake is the most common, but blue and black racers are particularly prevalent. These constrictors are valuable as enemies of small rodents. The black chicken snake, the mountain or pilot black snake, and the corn snake, all larger than the racer, are found in the mountains. The king snake, another of the constrictor group, feeds on other snakes as well as on rodents. Other harmless serpents are two species of garter snake, the milk snake or cowsucker, green snake, water snake, ringneck snake, spreading adder or puff snake, and pine snake—largest of all Virginia snakes.

In the category of turtles, the diamondback terrapin, green sea turtle, and snapping turtle are prized as food. More common are several kinds of mud turtles and the dry-land box turtle. Among the frogs are the spring peeper, green frog, tree frog, toad-frog, and bullfrog. Several kinds of lizards and salamanders inhabit the state.

Inland waters contain bass of three kinds—the rock bass or redeye, the smallmouthed black bass in the clear highland streams, and the largemouthed black bass in the sluggish rivers and ponds of the flat country. Throughout the entire State are bream, silver and yellow perch, pike, carp, and common catfish. Only in the New River, however, is found the giant Mississippi catfish. Speckled and rainbow trout are restricted to certain mountain streams, as are the few pickerel in the State.

The salt-water fish, besides being of great commercial importance, include several varieties caught for sport. Most common in tidal waters are the croaker, hogfish, spot, white perch, gray and spotted trout, striped bass or rockfish, alewife, menhaden, flounder, bluefish, shad, catfish, eels, angelfish, dogfish, and shark. Sturgeon and sheepshead, once common, are now scarce. The shellfish of importance are oysters, clams, scallops, blue crabs, and shrimps. All the salt-water bottoms contain oyster beds. Clams are restricted to the lower regions of Chesapeake Bay, and scallops to the seacoast inlets. Blue crabs and shrimps are found in tidal waters.

Indians

AT THE dawn of the seventeenth century, three distinct groups of Indian tribes, representing three different linguistic stocks, occupied the territory that is now Virginia. Along the coast and up the tidal rivers to their falls were the many palisaded settlements of the Algonquian group, the Powhatan confederacy, enemy of the Siouan stock composed of the Monacan and Manahoac federations that spread from the banks of the upper James and the headwaters of the Potomac and Rappahannock Rivers to the Allegheny Mountains. The bellicose and scattered Iroquoian stock was represented by the Conestoga (Susquehanna) tribe of nearly 600 warriors living in fortified towns near the headwaters of the Chesapeake Bay; the Rickohockan, or Rechahecrian (who are identified with the Cherokee by most ethnologists, as the Yuchi by John Reed Swanton), occupying the mountain valleys of the southwest; and the Nottoway in the southeast.

During their first years in Virginia the colonists of the London Company found along the rivers and coast some 200 villages under the leadership of Wahunsonacock, known to the colonists as Powhatan. This chief of an Algonquian confederation, which consisted of about 2,400 warriors, had inherited the territories of the Powhatan, Arrowhatock, Appamatuck, Pamunkee, Youghtanund, and Mattapament, to which, by later conquest, he had added other tribes, bringing the number under his dominion up to 30. Of the 36 'King's howses' or tribal capitals, Werowocomoco, on the left bank of the York River, was Powhatan's favorite, and the one in which, as a prisoner in 1608, Captain John Smith first saw the powerful chieftain.

> Arriving at *Weramocomoco* [Werowocomoco] their Emperour proudly lying uppon a Bedstead a foote high, upon tenne or twelve Mattes, richly hung with manie Chaynes of great Pearles about his necke, and covered with a great Covering of *Rahaughcums*. At [his] heade sat a woman, at his feete another; on each side sitting uppon a Matte uppon the ground, were raunged his chiefe men on each side the fire, tenne in a ranke, and behinde them as many yong women, each [with] a great Chaine of white Beades over their shoulders, their heades painted in redde: and [Powhatan] with such a grave Maiesticall countenance, as drave me into admiration to see such state in a naked Salvage.

Displacement of the Indians began almost simultaneously with the finishing of the first stockade at Jamestown. Before the colony was two years old, the principal Indian settlements had been seized, Powhatan had withdrawn to a remote town on the Chickahominy River, and the Indians were so intent on revenge that no Englishman was safe outside the fort. Temporary suspension of hostilities, however, was established by the marriage of John Rolfe and Powhatan's daughter, Pocahontas, in 1614, after which the colonists 'had friendly trade and commerce, as well with *Powhatan* himselfe, as all his subjects.'

In the treaty of peace that followed, the Indians acknowledged the British as their masters. But the chief of the Pamunkey tribe, Opechancanough, who succeeded Powhatan in reality though not nominally, was determined to annihilate the white invaders. In 1622 his carefully planned attack resulted in the massacre of some 350 settlers. The colonists who escaped, forewarned by a converted Indian boy, retaliated at once, and during the autumn of 1622 and the following winter killed so many Indians and destroyed so many of their settlements that for more than 20 years there was a truce. But in 1644, Opechancanough, now old and feeble, decided upon a last effort. In the uprising that began on April 18 with a sudden massacre along the whole border, the Indians were routed and Opechancanough was captured and brought to Jamestown, where he was murdered by an outraged colonist. In October 1646 his successor made a treaty of submission by which the Indians agreed to abandon everything below the falls of the James and Pamunkey Rivers and to restrict themselves on the north to the territory between the York and the Rappahannock.

The Jamestown settlers' contact with the Indians of Siouan stock was limited. A week after landing, on May 21, 1607, Christopher Newport with a party of 23 pushed up the James to the falls, where they were told by Pawatah (Powhatan) that it was a 'Daye and a halfe Iorney to Monanacah . . . his Enmye,' who 'came Downe at the fall of the leafe and invaded his Countrye.' In the autumn of 1608 Captain Christopher Newport, 'with 120 chosen men,' went up 'fortie myles' past the falls and discovered on the south bank of the James two Monacan towns. The first, Mowhemenchouch (Mowhemcho), was an open settlement, through which John Lederer passed in 1670, calling it Mahock, which Francis Louis Michel, a visitor in 1702, called Maningkinton, and which a Huguenot colony took possession of in 1699. It later became Monacan Town. The second village, 14 miles distant, was Massinacack. In August 1608 Captain Smith with 12 men and the Indian guide Mosco, 'a lusty Salvage of *Wighcocomoco*,' ascended the Rappahannock, had an encounter with Manahoac Indians (of whom some 12 tribes wandered over the Rapidan-Rappahannock area of the Piedmont section), and from an Indian named Amoroleck received the information about the Siouan tribes that is contained in his *Description of Virginia* (1612):

> Upon the head of the river of *Toppahanock* [Rappahannock] is a people called *Mannahoacks.* To these are contributers the *Tauxanias,* the *Shackaconias,* the *Ontponeas,* the *Tegninatoes,* the *Whonkenteaes,* the *Stegarakes,* the *Hassinnungaes,* and divers others; all confederats with the *Monacans,* though many different in language, and be very barbarous, living for most part of wild beasts and fruits.

The Monacan confederacy, dwelling 'upon the head of the Powhatans' along the James above the falls, consisted, according to Smith's enumeration, of the Monacan proper, 'the *Mowhemenchughes,* the *Massinnacacks,* the *Monahassanughs,* the *Monasickapanoughs,*' together with other tribes not named. The 'chiefe habitation' of this confederacy of five tribes, whose generic name of Monacan applied also to the territory they occupied, was Rasauweak (Rassawek), at the confluence of the James and Rivanna Rivers. The allied Monacan and Manahoac confederacies were constantly at war with the Powhatan and the Iroquois (the Massawomek of John Smith and the Massawomees of Jefferson), 'their most mortall enemies.'

Banded into a league late in the sixteenth century, the powerful Iroquois began thereafter their gradual descent upon these weaker tribes of the south, annihilating some and causing others to flee, eventually to merge for protection—thus completely shattering the tribal pattern existing in 1607. About 1656, 'the Mahocks and Nahyssans,' according to Lederer, but more probably the Shackoconian tribe of the Manahoac confederacy, seeking a new dwelling place, 'sett downe near the falls of James river, to the number of six or seaven hundred.' In an attempt to dispel them, the English, who were joined by the Pamunkey under Totopotomoi, precipitated what was perhaps the bloodiest Indian battle ever fought on the soil of Virginia, the last great fight between Siouan and Algonquian tribes. The Powhatan, who had suffered even more at the hands of the English than at those of the Iroquois, became by 1665 mere dependents of the colony, submissive to the stringent laws enacted that year, which compelled them to accept chiefs appointed by the governor. After the Treaty of Albany in 1684, the Powhatan confederacy all but vanished.

The exploratory trip made in 1670 by John Lederer, a German who received a 'commission of discovery' from Governor Berkeley, lifted the veil that had so long covered the activity of these Siouan tribes. Drastic changes, caused by the hostile wedge formed by the Iroquois in the north and by the English in the east, had taken place among the confederations in a little more than half a century. Leaving the falls of the James, Lederer went southwest 'toward the Monakins,' then 'from Mahock' (Mohemcho), the tribe's town, 'into the province of Carolina,' finding in 'these parts . . . formerly possessed by the Tacci, alias Dogi,' the tribe of Nahyssan (the Monahassanugh of John Smith) still living at their village on the James. This tribe, called Hanohaskie by Thomas Batts (1671), became in later narratives the Tutelo (Totero or Todirish-roone), a generic Iroquoian name applicable to all Siouan tribes in Virginia and Carolina. A subtribe of the Tutelo was the Saponi (the Monasickapanough of John Smith), who had moved from the Rivanna to a tributary of the upper Roanoke, where their town of Sapon was visited first by Lederer and then by Batts. Other tribes of Siouan stock were the Nuntaneuck (the Tauxanias of Smith); the Akenatzy (Occaneechi), who lived on an island in the Roanoke River; the Managog (Manahoac), who had but lately roamed the upper Piedmont region; and the Monakin or Monacan, who occupied the village of Mohemcho. All these tribes were of Siouan stock.

Between 1671 and 1701 the Saponi and Tutelo tribes withdrew from their position at the base of the mountains, directly in the path of the Iroquois, and settled on two islands in the Roanoke River near the one inhabited by their kinsmen the Occaneechi, an important tribe whose island was the great trading center 'for all the Indians for at least 500 miles.' The Occaneechi's wealth, however, was their undoing. In 1676, the Susquehanna (Conestoga), driven from their Chesapeake Bay home by the Iroquois and the English, fled to the Occaneechi, whom they tried to dispossess. In the battle that ensued, the Susquehanna were driven from the island. In May of the same year, Nathaniel Bacon,Jr., with 200 Virginians, arrived there in pursuit of the Susquehanna, joined the Occaneechi, and put the Susquehanna to flight. The latter settled near the Nottoway tribe, their Iroquois kinsmen, and became the Meherrin. Afterwards the whites turned on the Occaneechi, whereupon this tribe abandoned its island home, fled into Carolina, and eventually combined with the Saponi, Tutelo, and other tribes of Siouan stock in a body numbering about 750 persons. In 1705, according to Robert Beverley, the Indian population within the explored portions of Virginia numbered fewer than 500 able-bodied men, of whom 350 were remnants of tribes once belonging to the Powhatan confederacy.

Through the persuasion of Governor Spotswood, who hoped to protect them from the Iroquois and at the same time to make them a barrier between the Virginia settlements and the hostile southern tribes, the Saponi, Tutelo, 'Stukarocks,' and federated tribes moved in a consolidated group from Carolina to the vicinity of Fort Christanna, shortly after the opening of the Tuscarora War (1711–12). Here Spotswood, to secure the fidelity of the smaller tribes, began a school to which were admitted as pupils—

and hostages—the children of chiefs. But this seed of civilization fell on sterile ground. The Saponi, or, as they were then commonly called, the Christanna Indians, were still at war. Quarrels persisted between them and the neighboring Nottoway and Meherrin; while the more distant Iroquois, who cherished toward these people 'so inveterate an enmity' that it could be 'extinguished' only by their 'total Extirpation,' continued their attacks.

Finally, Governor Spotswood, hoping to put an end to the warfare between the Iroquois and the southern tribes, in 1722 promoted the Albany (N.Y.) Conference, at which a peace treaty was signed by the Five Nations of the Iroquois and their allies, the Tuscarora, Shawnee, and others on the one hand, and by Virginia and its tributary Indians on the other. Thus the long war ended and peace finally came in Virginia to 'the Nottoways, Meherrins, Nansemonds, Pamunkeys, Chichominys, and the Christanna Indians'—called 'Todirich-roones' by the Iroquois, and comprising 'the *Saponies*, *Ochineechees*, *Stenkenocks* [Stegarakes], *Meipontskys*, [Ontponeas] & *Toteroes*,' all of whom were grouped at 'Sapponey Indian town,' which was 'about a musket-shot from the fort.' Dissatisfied with the proximity of white settlements and at peace with the Iroquois, the restless Saponi, Tutelo, and such allied tribes as the Occaneechi and the Stegarake (only survivor of the Manahoac confederacy) abandoned the settlement near Fort Christanna about 1740, went first to Pennsylvania and then to New York, where they placed themselves under the protection of their traditional enemy, becoming in 1753 a part of the Six Nations.

During the first half of the eighteenth century the Shenandoah Valley—last frontier of Virginia—was the hunting ground of such nonresident Indian tribes as the Delaware, Catawba, and Shawnee, among whom there was continual warfare. After the completion of a chain of forts along the border for the protection of white settlers, the Indians suddenly withdrew from the valley in 1754, but returned in 1756 at the beginning of the French and Indian War. Depredations continued until the end of the war in 1763, after which the valley was left in peace. The Cherokee, as the white settlements pressed upon them in their mountain fastness, moved gradually westward.

In 1768, Governor Francis Fauquier, answering a question propounded by the Lords of Trade and Plantation, revealed the state to which the aborigines of Virginia had been reduced. 'The number of Indians residing in the known parts of this Colony,' he wrote, 'is very small, there being only some remains of the Eastern Shore and Pamunkey Indians, who are so far civilized as to wear European dress, and in part follow the customs of the common Planters. Besides these there are some of the Nottoways, Meherrins, Tuscaroras and Saponeys; who tho' they live in peace in the midst of us, lead in great measure the Life of wild Indians. The number of all these decrease very fast owing to their great fondness for Rum.'

These remnants were the amalgamation of some of the numerous tribes that had roamed the forests of Virginia. The Nottoway, strong during the first settlement period and greatly outnumbering the Powhatan in the provincial census of 1669, were by 1820 reduced to 27 persons, of whom only three spoke the tribal language. The Meherrin, the other Virginia tribe of Iroquoian stock, equaled in number the Pamunkey—originally the strongest tribe of the Powhatan confederacy—in 1699, after which they rapidly vanished. The Nansemond tribe of the Powhatan confederacy, composed of some 300 warriors in 1622, had dwindled to 45 men by 1669. In 1744 they joined the Nottoway. Today, in Virginia, there are several groups and scattered families of Indian descent, comprising 779 persons. The State recognizes three tribes: the Pamunkey, the Mattaponi, and the Chickahominy.

Description of the sedentary Powhatan Indians in their 'pallizadoed townes' formed much of the substance of early writings on Virginia. 'Their habitations or townes' were 'for the most part by the rivers, or not far distant from fresh springs, commonly upon a rise of a hill.' Many settlements, particularly those on the Bay, were protected by encircling palisades, as depicted in the water-color drawings of Secotan and Pomeioc (in Carolina) made in 1585 by 'Maister Jhon White, an Englisch paynter.' Where there was less danger of attack, the habitations of the Algonquian spread out unprotected on the river shore. Werowocomoco, Powhatan's favorite village, and Kecoughtan (at or near the present site of Hampton) were typical. '*Kegquouhtan* . . . conteineth eighteene houses,' wrote Smith in *Newes from Virginia*, 'pleasantly seated upon three acres of ground, uppon a plaine, halfe invironed with a great Bay of the great River . . . the Towne adioyning to the maine by a necke of Land of sixtie yardes.' 'Placed under the covert of trees,' the houses—all alike, 'scattered without forme of a street,' and 'warm as stoves, albeit very smoakey'—were like 'garden arbours.' A framework of poles was set in two parallel rows inclosing the floor space. Opposite poles were bent over and lashed to one another in pairs to form a series of arches of equal height, and these arches were joined by horizontal poles placed at intervals and securely tied together 'with roots, bark, or the green wood of the white oak run into thongs.' Each of the flat ends had a door hung with mats. Outside stood a wooden mortar and pestle for grinding corn. The smoke from the fire kindled on the ground inside escaped through a small vent in the roof. The coverings were generally of bark or mats of rushes, occasionally of boughs. The ordinary dwelling, which housed from 6 to 20 people, contained but one room, on each side of which were platforms or bedsteads about a foot high and covered with 'fyne white mattes' and skins. In 'square plotts of cleered grownd' near these bark-covered houses, the women raised tobacco and such vegetables as corn, beans, an herb called 'melden,' squash, 'pumpons and a fruit like unto a musk millino.' Maize was so important that platforms were erected in the fields, where watchers were stationed to protect the crop from birds, and the shelled corn filled storage baskets that took 'upp the best part of some of their houses.' Among the roots used for food were groundnuts (*Apios tuberosa*) and tuckahoe (*Peltandra Virginica* and *Orontium aquaticum*). In March and April the Powhatan lived on their 'weeres,' feeding on 'fish, turkies and squirrells,' the fish being caught in fish dams or shot with 'long arrows tyed in a line'; in May they 'set their corne'; and in the 'tyme of their huntings' they gathered 'into companyes' with their families and went 'toward the mountaines,' where there was 'plenty of game.'

The empire ruled over by Powhatan was reduced to subdivisions, each with a governmental hierarchy consisting of the *cockarouse* or sachem, the *werowance* or war leader, the tribal council, and the priests. Nor did the scheme vary under Opechancanough. 'This revolted Indian King with his squaw,' wrote Thomas Martin in 1622, 'commaundeth 32 Kingdomes under him. Everye Kingdome contayneigne ye quantitie of one of ye shires here in England. Everye such Kingdome hath one speciall Towne seated upon one of ye three greate Rivers . . .' Dwellings and gardens were owned privately, but all other property was held in common.

Typical of the Iroquoian type of town was the village of the Nottoway, which William Byrd visited in 1728. A strong palisade, about 10 feet high, surrounded a quadrangle dotted with long communal 'cabins . . . arched at the top, and covered with bark.' Inside there was no furniture except 'hurdles' for repose. The fortification served as a place of refuge for members of the tribe living in outlying districts. The towns of the Siouan tribes were similar. Within the inclosure of those that were palisaded stood the prominent round 'town house' surrounded by the 'arbour-like' dwellings of the people. The Cherokee towns spread out along the banks of mountain streams or in a valley. Close by the dwellings of logs chinked with clay stood a conical earth-covered lodge known as the 'winter hot house.' On an artificial mound in the center of the village was the large oblong 'council house,' center of all tribal ceremonies.

The male Indian costume consisted of garments of skins or woven fiber, and moccasins; the women wore skirts of fringed deerskin or woven silk-grass fiber (silk weed or Indian hemp, *Asclepias pulchra*), which reached from the waist to the middle of the thigh. Members of both sexes wore in winter mantles made of skins and feathers. Feathered headgear, necklaces of clam shells, beads, or pearls, copper pendants, wampum head rings, and body tattooing completed the garish personal decoration. The Siouan Indians of 'Sapponey Town,' visited by Byrd in 1728, had probably varied little since early days in their traditional war dress. With 'feathers in their hair and run through their ears, their faces painted with blue and vermilion, their hair cut in many forms,' they were 'really . . . very terrible.' Both men and women greased their bodies and heads with bear's oil or walnut oil mixed with paint, either of which yielded an 'ugly smell.' The 'Sweating-houses,' little huts built with wattles, were also tribal survivals. Heated by red-hot pebbles, they were used by sick Indians to sweat out maladies, 'a remedy . . . for all distempers.'

The handicrafts were exclusively woman's province—the making of wooden dishes and trays, 'earthern pottes,' and the thread spun from 'barks of trees, deare sinews, or a kind of grasse they call *Pemmenaw*,' which was used variously as 'lines for angles,' 'nets for fishing,' sewing the deerskin mantles, and the making of baskets and 'aprons . . . women wear about their middles, for decency's sake.'

In their monotheistic religion, according to Lederer, the Indians worshiped *Okee*, called also *Mannith*, the 'creator of all things.' 'To him alone the high priest or *Periku*' offered sacrifices. 'The government of mankind' was assigned to 'lesser deities, as *Quiacosough* and *Tagkanysough*—that is, good and evil spirits.' Smith, however, says 'their chief God' was 'the Devil, him they call Okee.'

Burial customs varied among the different tribes. Within most of the temples were the image of *Okee* and the sepulchers of kings. The Algonquian buried ordinary members of the tribe in pits; while the bodies of the chiefs were disemboweled, dried, stuffed with sand, wrapped in skins and mats, and then laid in the temple. Henry Spelman, who lived among tribes along the Potomac prior to 1610, described a burial resembling the type used by Indians of the Plains. The body, wrapped in mats, was laid on a scaffold about three or four yards high. Ossuaries were common among the southern Algonquian and the Siouan tribes of the Piedmont. The bones of the dead, in a reburial ceremony, were deposited in great pits until a huge mound was formed.

Today, along the shores of Chesapeake Bay and the banks of many of its

The Old Dominion

CAPTAIN JOHN SMITH'S MAP

Photograph by courtesy of the Virginia Conservation Commission

ST. JOHN'S CHURCH (1741), RICHMOND

hotograph by courtesy of the Virginia State Chamber of Commerce

SCENE OF BRITISH SURRENDER—MOORE HOUSE (c. 1750), NEAR YORKTOWN

THE CAPITOL (1701–05, RECONSTRUCTED 1929), WILLIAMSBURG

hotograph by courtesy of the Virginia Conservation Commission

Photograph by courtesy of the Virginia State Chamber of Commerc

MONTPELIER (1760, 1793, 1907), HOME OF PRESIDENT MADISON, NEAR ORANGE

ASHLAWN (1796–98), HOME OF PRESIDENT MONROE, NEAR CHARLOTTESVILLE

Photograph by courtesy of the Virginia Conservation Commissio

Photograph by courtesy of the Virginia Conservation Commission

MOUNT VERNON (1743–87), HOME OF PRESIDENT WASHINGTON, NEAR ALEXANDRIA

MONTICELLO (1770–75, 1798–1809), HOME OF PRESIDENT JEFFERSON, NEAR CHARLOTTESVILLE

Photograph by courtesy of the Virginia Conservation Commission

Photograph by courtesy of the Virginia Conservation Commission

HOUDON'S STATUE OF GEORGE WASHINGTON (1785–96), THE MARBLE ORIGINAL—STATE CAPITOL, RICHMOND

ıotograph by courtesy of the New York Historical Society

PORTRAIT OF THOMAS JEFFERSON BY REMBRANDT PEALE

Photograph by Homier-Clark Studi

STATUE OF ROBERT E. LEE BY H. M. SCHRADY AND LEO LENTELLI, CHARLOTTESVILLE

tributaries are heaps of oyster shells, containing bits of pottery and stone implements, which mark the position of many ancient Algonquian settlements, some having flourished long after 1607. Westward, along the valley of the James from the falls to the mountains, in the section once dominated by the Siouan tribes, are traces of their village and campsites on the banks of streams, where fragments of pottery and stone implements are scattered over the surface. The same district contains soapstone quarries and occasionally a macabre ossuary. In the Rappahannock-Rapidan area most of the mortars, long cylindrical pestles, hammers, discoidal stones, and pipes have been garnered; but occasionally axes, projectile points, and bits of pottery are brought to the surface by freshets or turned up by the plow.

History

WHEN on May 14, 1607 the *Sarah Constant, Goodspeed*, and *Discovery* landed at Jamestown the colonists sent by the Virginia Company of London, years of futile effort to achieve British colonization in America were terminated in the establishment of a permanent settlement in the New World. All North America not Spanish or French was then called Virginia, in honor of the Virgin Queen. In 1578 Sir Humphrey Gilbert had obtained authority from Elizabeth to colonize lands on the Western Hemisphere not already claimed by any Christian prince or people, but he had failed to plant an enduring settlement. Groups of adventurers sent out by Sir Walter Raleigh either returned disheartened to England or mysteriously disappeared.

In 1606, however, King James granted a joint charter to two companies—one, with headquarters in London, authorized to settle southern Virginia; and the other, with headquarters in Plymouth, authorized to settle northern Virginia; but neither to plant within 100 miles of the other. The expeditions sent out by the Plymouth Company met with failure, but the London Company established the settlement at Jamestown. The years between 1607 and 1624, encompassing the overlordship of the Virginia Company of London, assured the permanence of the first English colony in America.

On April 26, 1607 (O.S.) the colonists landed on a point of land they called Cape Henry, opposite another point they named Cape Charles, honoring two sons of their king. An indication of future trouble came toward evening when a band of Indians arrived 'creeping upon all foure from the Hills, like Beares, with their Bowes in their mouthes.' The adventurers ascended the river and landed at a place they named 'James Towne' to honor the king himself.

Leadership aboard the three little boats left much to be desired; the men had quarreled grievously among themselves; malaria lurked in the marshy lands; and supplies were insufficient. John Smith, the most able man in the company and the one fitted for almost any emergency by a life of incredible adventure, was in chains when the little band reached Virginia. Fortunately, however, the opening of the sealed orders of the king

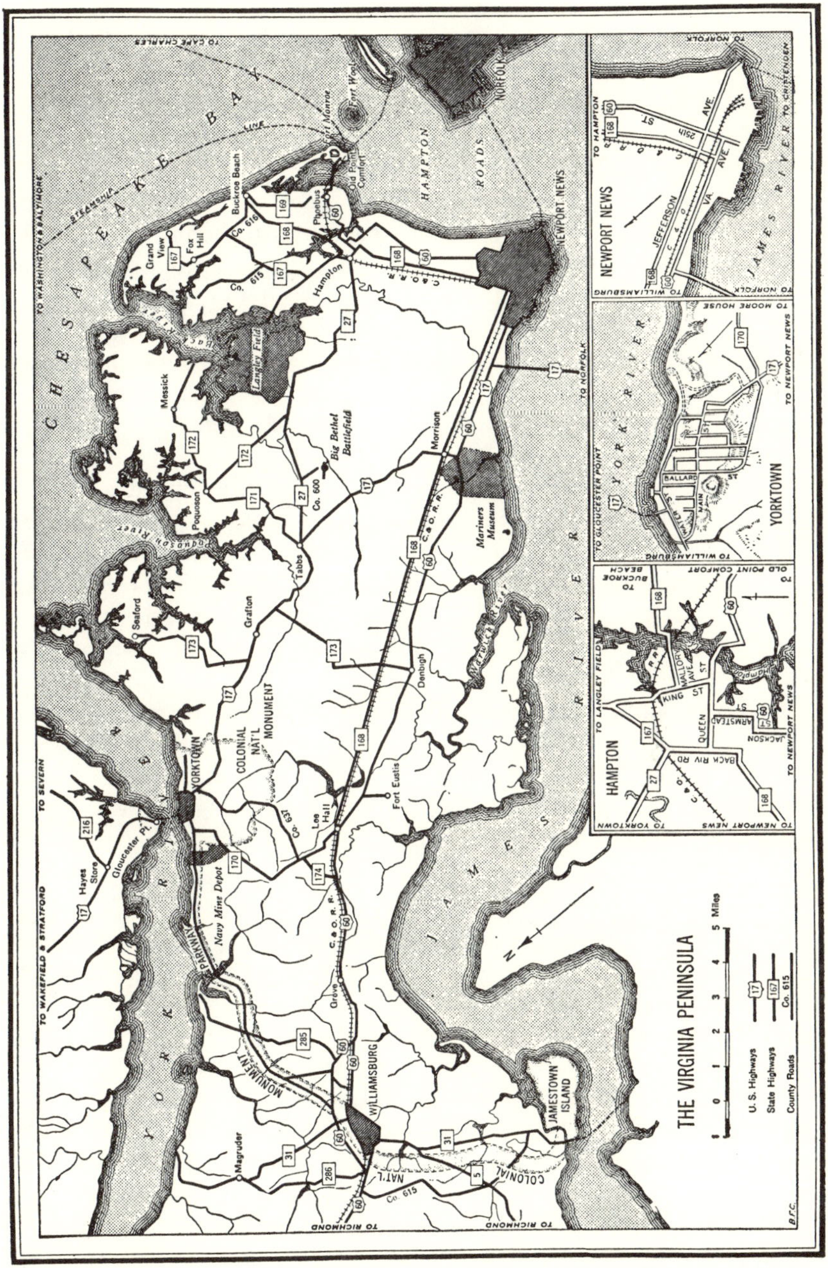
THE VIRGINIA PENINSULA
U.S. Highways
State Highways
County Roads
Co. 615
0 1 2 3 4 5 Miles
CHESAPEAKE BAY
YORK RIVER
JAMES RIVER
HAMPTON ROADS
STEAMSHIP LINE
TO WASHINGTON & BALTIMORE
TO CAPE CHARLES
TO WAKEFIELD & STRATFORD
TO SEVERN
TO RICHMOND
TO NORFOLK
Fort Monroe
Fort Wool
Old Point Comfort
NORFOLK
NEWPORT NEWS
Phoebus
Hampton
Buckroe Beach
Grand View
Fox Hill
Messick
Langley Field
Back River
Poquoson
Poquoson River
Seaford
Grafton
Tabbs
Big Bethel Battlefield
Morrison
Mariners Museum
Denbigh
Warwick River
Fort Eustis
Lee Hall
COLONIAL NAT'L MONUMENT
YORKTOWN
Gloucester Pt.
Hayes Store
Navy Mine Depot
PARKWAY
Grove
WILLIAMSBURG
MONUMENT
Magruder
JAMESTOWN ISLAND
COLONIAL NAT'L
C. & O. R.R.
Co. 616
Co. 615
Co. 600
Co. 637
HAMPTON
TO LANGLEY FIELD
TO BUCKROE BEACH
TO OLD POINT COMFORT
TO NEWPORT NEWS
TO YORKTOWN
KING ST
QUEEN
MALLORY AVE
BACK RIV RD
ARMSTEAD
JACKSON
YORKTOWN
TO GLOUCESTER POINT
TO WILLIAMSBURG
TO MOORE HOUSE
BALLARD
MAIN
NEWPORT NEWS
TO HAMPTON
TO WILLIAMSBURG
TO CRITTENDEN
JEFFERSON
VA. AVE.
25th ST
B.F.C.

named him a member of the council along with Edward Maria Wingfield, Christopher Newport, Bartholomew Gosnold, John Ratcliffe, John Martin, and George Kendall. The incompetent Wingfield was made president of the council. Smith demanded trial for the charges that had been preferred against him, was released, and by force of personality became the acknowledged leader. On June 22, Newport sailed for England, leaving in Virginia 100 men, more than half of whom were 'gentlemen,' unfit for the tasks involved in making a wilderness habitable. Bickering was the order of the day. In September Wingfield was deposed; and Ratcliffe, who subsequently proved himself unequal to the responsibility, was elected president of the council. Whether or not credence can be given to the story of Pocahontas's saving John Smith's life, there is no doubt that Smith became the hero of Jamestown, exploring the new land, wheedling supplies from the Indians, and effectively using the strong arm in emergencies.

The London Company, with stockholders looking toward gains that might be derived from the finding of a passage to the South Sea and from the discovery of precious metals in the New World, was guilty of inadequate stewardship. The 'First Supply,' brought by Newport on January 2, 1607 (January 12, 1608, N.S.), contained insufficient provisions and 70 new colonists. Likewise Newport's 'Second Supply,' arriving in September of the same year, bringing again some 70 settlers, added little to the welfare of the colony. Then it was that John Smith, having been chosen president of the council, composed the letter known as 'Smith's Rude Answer,' in which he replied to the London Company's demand that the colonists send commodities sufficient to pay the cost of the voyage, a lump of gold, assurance that they had found the South Sea, and one member of the lost Roanoke Colony. He wrote:

> When you send againe I entreat you rather send but thirty Carpenters, husbandmen, gardiners, fishermen, blacksmiths, masons and diggers up of trees, roots, well provided; than a thousand of such as we have: for except wee be able both to lodge them and feed them, the most will consume with want of necessaries before they can be made good for anything.

Chiefly because of Smith's leadership, most of the 200 settlers survived the winter and in the spring set about planting and building cheerfully enough. In August seven of the nine ships that had left England with Sir Thomas Gates landed their colonists at Jamestown. In October John Smith, having been severely injured, returned to England for medical treatment, and the settlers faced the long and terrible winter of 1609–10 without competent leadership. Supplies were soon exhausted; no one was capable of intimidating or cajoling the Indians; the water was unfit for drinking; 'sicknesse' took its ghastly toll. In May when Gates, whose ship had been wrecked on the Bermudas, reached Jamestown as first governor, he found only a few wretched survivors. Five hundred strong at the beginning of winter, the colonists—numbering but 65 pitiable creatures—started back to England on June 7, 1610. They had reached Mulberry Island, 14 miles distant, when Lord De la Warre arrived with supplies and new settlers. All turned back, weary but determined to carry on.

The kindly De la Warre, returning to England in the spring of 1611, left as deputy governor George Percy, succeeded soon by Sir Thomas Dale, whose absolutism the colonists found difficult to endure. Meanwhile, by two clever strokes, John Rolfe became the savior of Virginia: in 1612 he introduced the cultivation of tobacco, ending the futile search for gold; and in 1614 he married Pocahontas, effecting a convenient alliance with the Powhatan confederacy. George Yeardley, who became deputy governor in 1616, set up the first windmill in America, imported a herd of blooded cattle, turned his attention to the fertilization of the soil, and encouraged the cultivation of tobacco. But Sir Samuel Argall, appointed in May 1617, virtually reduced the colonists to the status of slaves until his flagrant misconduct caused his removal.

By April 1619 the colony under Sir George Yeardley, now governor, had apparently achieved a degree of stability that augured well for continued prosperity. Plantations had been established eastward and westward on both sides of the James River. A few women had crossed the Atlantic to convert the wilderness into a home, and plans were afoot for the sending of 150 maids, who arrived by 1621 to become wives of the settlers. From a Dutch man-of-war were obtained in 1619 the first Negroes landed in Virginia—20, who were received as indentured servants and not as slaves for life.

VIRGINIA ACHIEVES REPRESENTATIVE GOVERNMENT

But the most far-reaching event of 1619 was the meeting of the house of burgesses, the first democratically elected legislative body to convene in the New World. Each of the 11 duly constituted plantations sent two members to represent it in this epoch making body. The early deliberations of the burgesses centered about education. In 1618 the City of Henricus had been selected as suitable site for a proposed university. The East India School, which was to be established at Charles City Point, was planned to prepare students for the college; money had been subscribed for both institutions; and the revenues from an iron foundry at Falling Creek were to be used for the support of the university.

Representative government in Virginia, however, had come through an evolutionary process. The charter of 1606—giving to the Plymouth and London Companies authority to colonize Virginia between 34° and 45° north—provided for a superior council in England appointed by the king, and a local governing council appointed by the superior council, the local council to elect its own president. The charter gave to the colonists small hope of gain, for the property—held in common stock—belonged to the London Company. The second charter, however, obtained on May 23, 1609, and drafted by Sir Edwin Sandys, leader of the Liberal party in Parliament, gave the London Company direct administration of the colony and power to prescribe the form of government to be established, but was less democratic than the first in that the governor was to be appointed by the council in London and not by the council in Virginia. The territory, redefined, had a frontage 200 miles south and 200 miles north of Point Comfort, and extended 'up into the land, throughout from sea to sea, west and northwest.'

Almost at once the government of the colonists became the talking point of liberals in Parliament, who wanted to increase the rights enjoyed by British subjects in the face of Stuart absolutism. It was under the more liberal charter of 1612, also drafted by Sandys, that the colonists were able to achieve representative government. More important, however, were the reaffirmation of those privileges the second charter had granted and the clear statement that all laws governing Virginia were to be made by the London Company. The execution of the order was delayed, however, by Argall, who arrived as deputy governor in May 1617; connived with Sir Robert Rich in England to plunder the 'common stock'; and continued martial law in the colony. As Lord De la Warre, sent by the London Company with authority to arrest Argall, died on his way across the ocean, it was not until the arrival of Yeardley, on April 19, 1619, that the new government was put into effect, incorporating the principles of 'the Great charter of privileges, orders, and laws' drawn up in 1618 by Sir Edwin Sandys and Sir Thomas Smyth. Settlers were given their own tracts of land; martial law and common holding came to an end; lands to be tilled by servants during indentureship were laid out for the support of officials, in order to relieve the people of taxation 'as much as may be'; four 'corporacouns' were constituted, each with a proposed capital city; and through the creation of the house of burgesses the colonists shared in making the laws.

Soon after affairs had begun to run smoothly in the colony, Virginia narrowly escaped an invasion of the Pilgrim Fathers, whose expedition—financed mainly by members of the London Company—was authorized to settle south of the Hudson River in southern Virginia. Thrown off their course, the Pilgrims set foot on a rock off the coast of northern Virginia. So did chance take a hand in determining the course of history.

A 'deadly stroake' was dealt the southern colony in 1622 when the Indians attempted by wholesale butchery to rid the country of white invaders. From the marriage of John Rolfe and Pocahontas in 1614 till the death of Powhatan in 1618 a state of comparative peace had emboldened the colonists to spread their plantations along both banks of the James River and to neglect their stockades. But the implacable Opechancanough, who had succeeded Powhatan as chief of the Indian confederacy, was scheming with diabolical cleverness. On March 22, 1622, at precisely the same hour the Indians struck along a 140-mile front. Three hundred and forty-seven colonists were killed instantly and 18 died later, reducing the settlement by more than a third. Jamestown suffered less, however, than the outlying plantations, for Chanco, a converted Indian, working at the plantation of Richard Pace across the river, informed his master of the plot. Though the surviving settlers did not desert Virginia and though others arrived almost at once, it was many years before the colony recovered from the disaster. Plans were abandoned for the East India School and the university, which were to be established to Christianize and educate the Indians.

The days of the Virginia Company of London, moreover, were numbered. The widening breach between the liberals and the king had been reflected in James's denunciation of Sir Edwyn Sandys. In answer to the king's command in 1620, 'Choose the devil if you will, but not Sir Edwin Sandys' as company treasurer, Sandys stepped aside in favor of his friend, the Earl of Southampton, whom the king found equally unacceptable. It was Sandys, however, who drew up the liberal instrument known as the Virginia Constitution of 1621. In 1622 the king granted the London Company a monopoly of the sale of tobacco in England. The condition that 40,000 pounds of Spanish tobacco be also imported was not satisfactory to Spain, whose favor James sought as he looked toward an alliance between his son and the Infanta. Through the scheming of the wily Count of Gondomar, Spanish ambassador, an investigation was ordered of the London Company both in England and Virginia. When the commission returned from the colony in June 1624 with an unfavorable report, only partially true, the King's Bench revoked the charter of the London

Company and Virginia became a royal colony, extending from modern Pennsylvania to Florida and indefinitely westward.

Anglo-Saxon love of personal liberty continued to express itself in the Virginia colony. All the revolutionary pronouncements that emanated from Virginia between 1763 and 1776 had their antecedents in the period that immediately followed the dissolution of the London Company. Just before the revocation of the company's charter the general assembly had resolved, forecasting the words of Parliament's petition to Charles five years later and in amazing prophecy of the doctrine condemning taxation without representation, that 'the governor shall not lay any taxes or impositions upon the colony, their lands or commodities, other than by authority of the General Assembly . . .'

The king's failure to provide for a house of burgesses in the governmental plans he instituted after the demise of the London Company had little effect upon the progress of the democratic principle. After James had commissioned a council to take charge of affairs in Virginia, had appointed the governor, and, forthwith, had died, Virginians sent Yeardley across the ocean to urge the king to 'avoid the oppression of governors in colonial affairs' and to continue the general assemblies. Until royal recognition of the house of burgesses came in 1628, governors Francis Wyatt, George Yeardley, and Francis West were wise enough to allow the burgesses to assist the council unofficially in the passing of 'proclamations, ordinances, and orders.' The principle of taxation by representation was reiterated in resolutions passed in 1631, in 1632, in 1642, in 1652, and many other times before a Virginian gave the Declaration of Independence to the world.

The behavior of liberty-loving Virginians must have sorely tried the royal Stuarts, whose edicts brought forth either argument or disobedience. During the investigation of the London Company, the clerk of the council had lost his ears for giving the king's commissioners certain official papers. Virginians dared to ask that the charter of the London Company be renewed. Other evidences of insubordination followed. There was, for instance, Virginia's protest against Lord Baltimore's proprietary—carved from Virginia territory by royal grant in 1632. For some strange reason there had been no trouble when Sir Robert Heath had received patent in 1629 to that part of southern Virginia styled 'Carolana.' Chief among the agitators against Lord Baltimore was William Claiborne, who, anticipating the grant, had established on the Isle of Kent within the Maryland territory a trading post and colony. The conflict, however, was not between Virginia and Lord Baltimore, but was a contest that Claiborne carried on with the aid of his settlers.

Interposed in the general confusion was the not inconsiderable matter of 'thrusting' a royal governor out of Virginia. Sir John Harvey was appointed in 1628. His arrival having been delayed, the council continued Captain Francis West as acting governor, and the assembly convened. It refused to agree to the king's demand regarding English monopoly of Virginia tobacco, and sent West abroad as the first of a long line of agents who presented the colony's cause to the king. Dr. John Pott was then named acting governor. When Harvey finally reached Virginia, in 1630, he discredited Pott, usurped the powers of the general assembly, and refused to forward to the king the general assembly's 'denial' of the tobacco monopoly. Finally, when the governor dissolved the assembly, the house of burgesses defiantly continued its sessions. In peaceful revolution the governor was 'thrust out,' and the council in 1635 named John West his successor. Though Harvey took his appeal to the king, who ruled that the deposed governor must return to Virginia as governor if just for a day, Virginia's first popular revolution was successful. In 1639 the king appointed Sir Francis Wyatt governor.

In the meantime new governmental machinery had been installed. In 1634 the four 'corporacouns' that had been created in 1619 gave place to eight shires, later designated as counties. All free male citizens had the right to vote for members of the house of burgesses and for county officers.

Then came Sir William Berkeley, who supplanted Wyatt in 1641 and continued in office until 1652. Though the staunchest of royalists, Sir William endeared himself to Virginians at once by exercising justice and good sense. After the massacre of 1644, led by the aged Opechancanough, had wiped out about 300 colonists, Berkeley dealt with the Indians courageously and promptly. The civil war in England was reflected, however, in Berkeley's intolerance toward dissenters. When three pastors from the Massachusetts Bay colony accepted Captain Richard Bennett's invitation to settle in Virginia, they were ordered to return 'with all convenience.' The oppressive act against nonconformists passed in 1647 caused many Puritans in Virginia to migrate to more tolerant Maryland.

Berkeley's intense loyalty to the Crown furnishes the key to his character. He went to England to offer aid to Charles I; after the execution of his sovereign, he refused to recognize Cromwell; and he extended to Charles II an invitation to make his home in Virginia. When Virginia was at last 'reduced' to Parliament, the loyal servant of the king retired to Green Spring near Jamestown.

Under the Commonwealth Virginia enjoyed almost complete political freedom. Fortunately, the Navigation Act, first passed in 1651 limiting colonial trade to England and her possessions, was not strictly enforced. That Virginians had learned to govern themselves was attested by the averting of a civil war that was threatened by the inhabitants of the eastern shore. These isolated settlers, in a protest drawn up on March 30, 1652, embodying a complaint that dated back to 1647, based their refusal to pay taxes on the grounds that, since they had received no summons for election of burgesses, they considered themselves 'disjointed and sequestered from the rest of Virginia.' Moreover, without authority from the general assembly, they had made their own reprisals against the Dutch among them, who they claimed had been selling arms to the Indians. No blood was shed in the settlement of the difficulty, and the eastern shore, then Northampton County, remained within Virginia.

The Restoration ushered in one of Virginia's darkest eras. The chaotic situation in England and the death of Governor Mathews in 1660 caused Virginia to turn again to their old leader. Accordingly, the house of burgesses elected Sir William Berkeley governor, and soon thereafter Charles II reappointed him.

Though it was quite another Berkeley who resumed office, he worked at first in the interest of the colonists. The Navigation Act of 1660, more thoroughly enforced than Cromwell's, imposed real hardship upon Virginia planters by requiring all trade with Virginia to pass through English ports with payment of high duties. Governor Berkeley traveled to England in 1661 to make personal protest against the obnoxious regulation that was reducing the price of Virginia tobacco, and in 1664 he endeavored to obtain the co-operation of Carolina and Maryland in concerted restriction of tobacco planting. The governor also had a hand in the general assembly's inauguration of a works program, by means of which factories were established both to provide employment and to furnish the colonists with needed commodities.

His philosophy, however, was that of the benevolent despot, who would brook no opposition to his authority. Satisfied with the representatives whose election he had influenced in 1661, when reaction against the Commonwealth had increased his popularity, he issued no other writ for an election until forced to do so by the rebellion that ended his career. Accordingly, control of the colony fell into the hands of an oligarchy that controlled Virginia for 15 years. Restriction of the franchise to 'freeholders and housekeepers' who were 'answerable . . . for levies' further strengthened the throttle hold of Berkeley's political machine. Charles II's grant of the Northern Neck—the area lying between the Potomac and the

Rappahannock from the Chesapeake back to the headwaters of both rivers —to four royal favorites in 1669 was deeply resented by Virginians.

VIRGINIA'S FIRST REBELLION

In 1674 a young man came out of England with courage to defy autocratic rule. His name was Nathaniel Bacon; his family was old and distinguished; he had been educated at Oxford, and he had traveled extensively. Upon taking up lands in Virginia, he was almost at once made a member of the council. Though the fundamental cause of unrest in Virginia was economic and brought about by dire distress of the small farmers, liberty-loving Anglo-Saxons were holding responsible for their plight the arrogant rule of the governor, who they believed had deprived them of the freeman's right to petition for redress. The immediate occasion of what is known as Bacon's rebellion was an Indian uprising, which Berkeley failed to handle with dispatch.

Following depredations of the Susquehannock in northern Virginia in 1675, which Berkeley had sent troops to punish, and the unfortunate killing of Indians who came bearing a flag of truce, the Susquehannock had sought revenge upon the whites and had enlisted other tribes as allies. Although the governor authorized an expedition to be led by Sir Henry Chicheley, suddenly disbanding the militia, he remained inactive while atrocities continued. When Virginians petitioned for commanders to lead them in defense of their 'lives and estates,' the governor not only refused but forbade further requests 'under great penalty.' Then it was that Nathaniel Bacon assumed leadership and sent messengers to the governor asking that he be given a commission. When Berkeley lost no time in refusing and in declaring Bacon a rebel, the affair took on the nature of an insurrection. An autocratic governor had arrogantly offended a man who became over night the spokesman of the aroused masses.

While fighters flocked to Bacon's ranks, the governor issued a writ for the election of a new house of burgesses. Having already dealt summarily with the Indians, Bacon was elected a burgess. Though Berkeley had dubbed him 'the greatest rebel that ever was in Virginia,' he was pardoned and again took his seat as a member of the council. The rebellion was not at an end, however. Soon Bacon, hearing that Berkeley plotted against him, left Jamestown, again without a commission to proceed against the Indians. Thenceforth the rebels concentrated their attack upon Berkeley's government. With his motley followers, Bacon appeared again at Jamestown and forced the governor to sign the commission so long sought. Under

Bacon's influence the burgesses liberalized the laws of the colony. The unhappy governor left Jamestown, finally going to the eastern shore, and Nathaniel Bacon was for a time the virtual head of government. From Middle Plantation, now Williamsburg, he issued a proclamation calling upon Virginians to 'consult with him for the present settlement of His Majesty's distressed colony.' The people came and 'none or very few' failed to sign an oath that pledged them to aid in the Indian war, to oppose the governor, and to resist any effort that England might make to suppress Bacon until the king could be acquainted with the 'grievances' of the colony.

The young leader then made his fatal mistake. He seized the British guardship, put two of his lieutenants in command, and sent it across the bay to capture Berkeley without first removing the British captain. Upon arrival at the eastern shore, the captain delivered the ship to the governor, and Bacon's men were held captive. When Berkeley returned to Jamestown, Bacon followed and stormed the capital. Berkeley fled to the guardship, and Bacon set fire to Jamestown. From Berkeley's home, Green Spring, 100 years before another Virginian phrased the Declaration of Independence Bacon issued a proclamation declaring that, should Berkeley be upheld by England, Virginians must defend their liberties or abandon the colony. The young leader then set out upon a grand tour of Virginia. In Gloucester County he was stricken with a fever and died before his leadership could be challenged by the king.

Virginia's second rebellion against autocracy ended with the terrible vengeance of an old man who believed that the divine right he represented had been defied. In demented fury Berkeley hanged without trial more than 20 men and confiscated the property of many others. Charles II snorted in disgust upon hearing the news: 'That old fool has hanged more men in that naked country than I have done here for the murder of my father.' Recalled to England, Sir William Berkeley died within a year. In Virginia, however, a fire had been rekindled, which succeeding decades of conservatism were powerless to extinguish.

Although self-government in Virginia was immediately threatened, the uprising served as a warning to other governors and prepared Virginia to accept joyfully the expulsion of James II. In particular the experience created among the poorer planters a sense of solidarity. Bacon's Rebellion was the first organized and violent resistance on a large scale to British authority in America.

Out of the confusion following Berkeley's departure emerged a succession of even more incompetent governors who, as royal agents through the decade preceding the 'Glorious Revolution,' despoiled the colony and sought to destroy popular government in Virginia. Against even the determination of James II, however, the burgesses successfully defended their two most precious prerogatives: control over general taxation and initiation of legislation.

After the trying first years, life in Virginia had soon taken on—except for the effects of Negro slavery and eighteenth-century affluence—the character it retained in Tidewater even after the newer colonists of Piedmont and the Valley altered radically the total picture. In the seventeenth century Virginia society had been divided into three main classes: a small group, privileged and secure, if not wealthy; the vastly preponderant yeomen, who were to become a true middle class after slavery had been thoroughly introduced; and the indentured servants. Static among the nonfree laborers was the Negro minority. Members of the miniature aristocracy owned large, but rarely enormous, tracts of land, stretching back from the wooded banks of the great rivers or on navigable tributary creeks, and lived in comfortable houses. No one had very many slaves or the more usual indentured servants. A few leaders managed a little better, usually by doing something besides raising tobacco. Planter William Fitzhugh practiced law and engaged in trade; William Byrd I traded and speculated in frontier land. These big planters monopolized the seats in the governor's council and, with him, ran the colony. M.Durand—a Huguenot forerunner of the French to come later—observed in 1687: 'There are no lords, but each is a sovereign on his own plantation. The gentlemen called Cavaliers are greatly esteemed and respected, and are very courteous and honorable. They hold most of the offices in the country.'

Mention of books from the earliest days and the existence later of fair-sized libraries indicate a respectable level of education among the few. Many small collections of books were recorded during this period. In 1667 a Mr.Mathew Hubard died in possession of more than 30 volumes, including John Smith's *Historie of Virginia* and the poetry of John Donne; and an inventory of Colonel Ralph Wormeley's library in 1701 listed above 500 titles. The office-holding planters of substance had their children taught at home and frequently sent eldest sons to schools in England. In 1681 there had been an abortive attempt to establish a printing press in the colony.

Without luxury and reduced to bare necessities for the majority, life in seventeenth-century Virginia was not, however, without merriment. There was time for a good deal of drinking, it seems, and a good deal of convivial visiting. And everybody smoked. A decade after Bacon's Rebellion,

M.Durand could say in a pamphlet designed to attract his persecuted coreligionists: 'The land is so rich and so fertile that when a man has fifty acres of ground, two men-servants, a maid and some cattle, neither he nor his wife do anything but visit among their neighbors . . . When a man squanders his property he squanders his wife's also, and this is fair, for the women are foremost in drinking and smoking.'

In 1682 another rebellion was launched by Virginians. Bumper crops and the failure of the government to authorize a year's cessation brought the price of tobacco in London down to the point of crisis. Taking cessation into their own hands, desperate planters rode through the night tearing up tens of thousands of young plants. It took several months and the execution of six 'plant-cutters' to discourage the practice. Robert Beverley, formerly a loyalist, suspected of instigating the riots, was imprisoned. This unofficial crop control was only a temporary and slight tonic. Lord Culpeper, a proprietor of the Northern Neck and then governor, wrote the Privy Council in 1683, the year following the Tobacco Riots: 'I soe encouraged the planting of tobacco that if the season continue to be favorable . . . there will bee a greater cropp by far than ever grew since its first seating. And I am confident that Customs next year from thence will be £50,000 more than ever heretofore in any one year.' Though admitting that 'the great Cropp then in hand would most certainly bring that place [Virginia] into the utmost exigencies again,' he promised to put down any disturbances that might result! The effect on the Exchequer of the consequent decline in price of tobacco was offset by raising the rate of customs, already over 300 per cent. Taxes in Virginia were also raised.

In 1689, however, Virginia made a fresh start. Amid rumors of a projected Indian-Catholic massacre and threats of another revolt, the happy news arrived of the expulsion of James II and the peaceful accession of William and Mary. Later that year the passage in England of the Bill of Rights cleared the way for Anglo-American progress. In 1693 education was given a real impetus in Virginia by the founding of the College of William and Mary, the second college in America. Finally, the beginning of the new era was marked symbolically by the removal in 1699 of the capital from Jamestown to Williamsburg. By 1700, when the population had reached about 70,000, the most important new trends were under way: quantity production of tobacco on a vast scale; the consequent growth of slavery as the foundation of the colony's economy with the parallel suppression of Virginia's sturdy yeomanry; the immigration of new racial elements; and westward expansion.

The essential history of Virginia from 1690 to 1776 is a record of the economic and territorial expansion of a maturing colony. Henceforward tobacco dominated Colonial Virginia. A comparatively prosperous decade following the Revolution in England was terminated by the War of the Spanish Succession (Queen Anne's War), which virtually closed most of the ports of Europe to British trade and thus deprived Virginia of a world market. Cut into by export duties in Virginia and the tax on tobacco entering England—600 per cent by 1705—profits almost vanished. It became clear that America's real enemy, responsible for adverse legislation, was the middle class in England, made up of businessmen who were determined to force empire trade through English channels at all costs.

Negro slavery was the inevitable answer to Virginia's economic impasse. After 1690, and especially after 1710, the proportion of Negro immigration rose sharply. Negro slaves increased from about 5 per cent of the population in 1670 to 9 per cent in 1700, 25 per cent in 1715, when they numbered about 23,000 against a total population of about 95,000, and to about 40 per cent by the middle of the century. Having prospered briefly after 1689, the hardy, independent 'peasantry' never recovered from the blow inflicted by the Spanish War. Many migrated to other colonies, particularly Pennsylvania, but most of them either sank to become the new class of 'poor whites' or rose to become petty, slaveholding planters.

The colony did not come into its 'great days' easily. Overproduction soon resulted from the importation of too many slaves, and a semiprohibitive duty was imposed in 1710. Many attempts to limit or prohibit the slave trade were obstructed by the British government, which acquired a monopoly of the valuable traffic in slaves in 1713 by the Treaty of Utrecht. Tobacco depressions gave a slight encouragement to the development of manufactures—in spite of opposition in England—and to the export of naval stores and other raw materials. Governor Spotswood established the first successful smelting furnace in 1715, and other furnaces were set up a few years later in the Valley of Virginia. Except for coarse 'Virginia cloth' and farm implements, however, manufacturing made small headway in Colonial Virginia, without skilled artisans or an invigorating climate. During this period pirates also interfered with trade, but Governor Spotswood did much to discourage piracy when he destroyed Blackbeard and his crew in 1718.

Regulation of the tobacco trade became a necessity. From about one and a third million pounds in 1640, exportation had risen to more than 18,000,000 pounds by 1688, to considerably more by 1699, and—after the war slump—had climbed back to about 20,000,000 pounds in 1731. A new inspection law, enacted in 1730 through the efforts of Sir John Randolph sent to London by the general assembly to present the case of Virginia planters, brought about an era of prosperity by providing for the issuance of notes in receipt for crops stored in public warehouses. In 1755, when there were about 175,000 whites and 120,000 Negroes in the colony, more than 42,000,000 pounds of tobacco were exported.

Geographic, racial, religious, and social changes marked the first half of the eighteenth century. Steadily new plantations were developed as the frontier was pushed westward. Governor Spotswood and a cavalcade mixing business with pleasure paid the first formal visit to the Valley in 1716. As early as 1650–51, however, Abraham Wood and Edward Bland, seeking a new fur-trading field distant from the encroachments of Maryland, had made into the southwest a journey of exploration, which was followed sporadically by other pilgrimages. In 1728 William Byrd II headed a commission that surveyed the Virginia-North Carolina line from the ocean about 240 miles westward. By this time pioneers from Tidewater had begun to take up Piedmont land. Large grants, made in 1749 to the Loyal Company and the Ohio Company, threw much of the western territory into the hands of speculators and stimulated exploration. That year Christopher Gist reached the falls of the Ohio, the site of the present Louisville.

During the period 1699–1755 several racial strains, other than the African, were added to the English stock of Virginia. From the beginning, small groups of foreigners had come to the colony; eight 'Dutch-men' and Poles, sent over in 1608 to make 'soap-ashes' and glass; a few Frenchmen in 1620 to help found a silk industry; and from time to time a sprinkling of Swedish, Polish, German, and other artisans. Elias Legardo, Joseph Moise, and Rebecca Isaacke, who arrived from England in 1624, were the first Jews to reach Virginia. The last of many convicts—felons or rebellious victims of oppression, who were shipped out frequently over a period of about 60 years against the protest of Virginians—were 52 Scottish prisoners in 1678, probably Covenanters. Throughout the seventeenth century small groups of intransigent Irish had been sent over as political prisoners. In 1699, however, members of the first large influx of foreigners began to come: French Huguenot refugees fleeing from persecution following the Revocation of the Edict of Nantes in 1685. The small groups of Germans, who came in 1714 and 1717 to settle at Germanna, the site of Governor Spotswood's iron furnaces, later joined their compatriots in the Valley. Scottish immigrants constituted another valuable ingredient in Virginia's new 'melting-pot.' Having previously ventured across the Atlantic in search of religious freedom, these Presbyterians came freely after the Toleration Act was passed in 1689 and on equal terms with the English after 1707, when the Union of Scotland with England was accomplished.

By far the largest and most far-reaching infusion into Virginia's racial stock, however, was the invasion of the tramontane Valley by Germans, Scotch-Irish, English Quakers, and a scattering of Welsh Baptists, who had settled in Penn's tolerant colony. About 1730, just when outpost settlement advancing from Tidewater had reached the mountains on the east, these people—industrious merchants, yeomen, and peasants—began a migration into the Valley that continued in full spate beyond the middle of the century. These nonconformists brought a dissent that was to destroy the Anglican establishment and a tough philosophy that was later to override Tidewater and take the lead in revolt against British oppression.

HEYDAY OF COLONIAL LIFE

By the middle of the eighteenth century Colonial Virginia had achieved its heyday. Affluence had polished the manners and enriched the life of old Tidewater and newer Piedmont gentry, while a 'hardy race had settled in the Valley; and beyond the mountains hunters and pioneers were pushing toward the Ohio.' Estates had expanded along with tobacco production and slavery until several nabobs held vast domains. Upon these rose the great Georgian Colonial houses of eastern Virginia, most of which were built between 1730 and 1760. Libraries grew in number and size. William Byrd II, with nearly 4,000 volumes, owned the largest, perhaps, in America at the time. As early as 1724 the Reverend Hugh Jones was recording: '. . . good Families . . . live in the same neat manner, dress after the same Modes, and behave themselves exactly as the Gentry in London; most Families of any Note having a Coach, Chariot, Berlin, or Chaise.'

Virginians preferred the country. The well-known mansion of brick or stone, with its various outbuildings, was the center of an almost self-sufficient community. Poor farmers lived in small houses of frame or brick, far more numerous than the 'great' houses. Stories were long told of remote planters haunting the nearest roadside to watch for the weekly stage, hoping to find a traveler who could be persuaded to stop over for a day or a week or a month. Early in the century Governor Spotswood had 'showed small Concern in reporting that upon an official Occasion he had entertained four Hundred Guests at Supper.' Colonel James Gordon of Lancaster County noted one day in his diary: 'No company, which is surprising.'

During this mid-eighteenth-century period, life in the Valley was vastly different from that in the Tidewater. The Germans, who peopled the lower region, and the Scotch-Irish, whose province became the upper Valley, brought traditions of hard work from their native lands. They built small stone houses that were strongholds against the Indians, still inhabiting this frontier country. Just behind the vanguard of these industrious folk sprang up mills, furnaces, forges, and even small factories. The rich land was turned rapidly into profitable farms. Nonconformist churches soon flourished here, and education was not far behind.

Defense of Virginia's western frontier in the 1750's provided a seminary for the Revolution. The French and Indian War, begun in 1754, schooled Americans to fight British regulars and thrice baptized in leadership their future commander in chief. Land was behind it all. The Anglo-Americans were pushing farther and farther westward into the 'Great Woods'; while the French, having long intended to make the Alleghenies—if not eventually the ocean—their eastern boundary, were setting up outposts in territory already granted to the new land companies. By 1753 the French had begun stirring up unfriendly Indian tribes and pushing eastward to implement their claim to the Allegheny westward. On the basis of the royal charters of 1606, 1609, and 1612, Virginia laid claim—later established—to the West and Northwest as far as British territory extended. Twice Governor Dinwiddie had sent George Washington out to protect the interests of Virginia and the land companies—the first time to deliver a formal protest and soon afterwards to join Colonel Joshua Fry's small force. Washington fell into command when Colonel Fry was killed accidentally. A fort, originally planned by the British at the site of the present Pittsburgh, had been built by the French and named Duquesne. The French, advancing from their stronghold, forced Washington to evacuate Fort Necessity, which he had built at the present Farmington, Pennsylvania. Because the British Government was eager to prevent backdoor encroachments of the French, General Edward Braddock and British troops were sent to Virginia in 1755 to lead an offensive. With two complete regiments of regulars, several companies from Virginia and two other colonies, and with Washington on his staff, Braddock reached a spot near Fort Duquesne in July. The general led his redcoats forward in formation to engage the French and Indians. Surrounded by an enemy hidden behind trees, his men were cut to pieces as they fled, and General Braddock was mortally wounded in the rout.

Washington, left once more in command, was soon recommissioned as a colonel and made commander in chief of Virginia forces. Troops were collected and drilled and forts were built along the immediate frontier. Though attempts were made to take Fort Duquesne, it was not occupied until late in 1758 and then only after the French, deserted by their Indian allies and hotly engaged farther north by the British, had blown it up. Washington and his Virginians were first to enter the smoking ruins. This war, which ended in America the following year on the Plains of Abraham and was formally closed by the Treaty of Paris in 1763, marked Virginia's coming of age. The defeat of the British leadership and British regulars in 1755 had vindicated 'bush-fighting' and given Americans a new self-confidence. Events during these war years had revealed also the need and the value of intercolonial co-operation.

The West had become a permanent scene of action. No sooner was the Treaty of Paris signed than George III issued his restrictive proclamation of 1763, prohibiting trade with the Indians or grants of land beyond the Alleghenies. This challenge trod on too many Virginia toes to be taken seriously, but settlement was further opposed by a renewal of border warfare with the Indians. Other troubles were in store for Virginia. In 1769–70 the Walpole Company was formed by associates in England and France, as well as in America, who began negotiations for a tract on a scale that would have dwarfed its predecessors. When it became generally known that 20,000,000 acres within Virginia's domain were involved, and that the king contemplated a new colony to be known as Vandalia, opposition flared. Even reactionary Governor Dunmore, who arrived in 1771, took Virginia's part in protests that ran on into 1773–74 and forestalled the enterprise.

A long series of frontier 'outrages' became general war again in 1774. Governor Dunmore led a detachment of Virginia troops into the West and ordered Major Andrew Lewis forward with another. While the governor was negotiating peace with the Indians at a point some distance away, the Battle of Point Pleasant took place on October 10 at the junction of the Ohio and Great Kanawha Rivers, and the Indians were driven back across the river. The whole campaign may have been intended to divert public attention from the political crisis then at hand. Nevertheless, pacification followed speedily in the West, and it was possible to form the County of Kentucky in 1776, before troubles—incident to the Revolution—broke out again on the frontier.

VIRGINIA DEFIES THE KING

No sooner had the curtain fallen on the prologue, with the Treaty of Paris in 1763, than it rose on the first act of the pre-Revolutionary drama. Young Patrick Henry shouted the first frank challenge at the king. Failure of the tobacco crop had obliged the Virginia assembly in 1758 to pass the Two Penny Act, providing that for 12 months obligations should be paid in currency at the rate of two pence per pound of tobacco, the price of which had then risen to six pence per pound. The clergy complained to the Board of Trade and Plantations and, after the king vetoed the act, brought suit for their usual quantity of tobacco and for damages. When Patrick Henry appeared for the defense in the Parsons' Cause in Hanover County in 1763, he spoke so eloquently, declaring that 'by this conduct the King, from being the father of his people, had degenerated into a tyrant and forfeited all his right to his subjects obedience,' that the crowd broke into a tumult. The jury's award of only one penny damages to the plaintiff amounted to denying the right of the king's action. Already the old order was on the way out.

Although Anglo-American economic rivalry was the basic cause, expenses resulting from the war and consequent taxes became the occasion for the quarrels with the British Government, which believed itself justified in taxing America to help pay its own debt. The colonies held an opposite opinion. The Sugar Bill in 1764 was the first of many attempts to tax the colonies without their consent. The Virginia assembly was the first legislative body to take an official step in facing the Stamp Act issue. Burgesses and council protested against both the Sugar Bill and a proposed stamp tax as violations of constitutional rights, asserting that no subjects of Great Britain could justly be made subservient to laws passed without their consent.

The Stamp Act, passed in March 1765, evoked an immediate response from Virginia. Patrick Henry on May 29 stirred the Virginia general assembly to pass the Virginia Resolves on the following day, setting forth Colonial rights according to constitutional principles, and carried mainly by the representatives of a united interior, voting against those from eastern Virginia. 'Caesar had his Brutus,' cried the young orator, 'Charles I his Cromwell, and George III—may profit by their example. If this be treason, make the most of it.' Governor Fauquier was obliged to dissolve the assembly, but the die had been cast. Governor Hutchinson of Massachusetts declared, 'Nothing extravagant appeared in the papers till an account was received of the Virginia Resolves.' Nine years later Edmund Burke in his speech on Colonial taxation gave Virginia credit for arousing the general resistance to the Stamp Tax.

In the decade that began in 1764 Virginia continued to lead constitutional opposition to the new British policy. On February 8, 1766, the Act was flatly outlawed by the Northampton County court, which declared that 'the said act did not bind, affect, or concern the inhabitants of this colony, inasmuch as they conceive the same to be unconstitutional, and that the said several officers may proceed to the execution of their respective offices, without incurring any penalties by means thereof.' On February 27 the outstanding planters of northeastern Virginia, led by Richard Henry Lee, met at Leedstown in the Northern Neck—115 strong—and leveled against the Stamp Act resolutions that embodied the principles later written into the Declaration of Independence. Another association in Norfolk, the 'Sons of Liberty,' met on March 31 and made similar protests. The most important single instrument, however, to form American opinion during this period was probably *An Enquiry into the Rights of the British Colonies*, a pamphlet in which Richard Bland presented in March 1766 the first printed argument that Virginia, like the other colonies, was 'no part of the Kingdom of England,' but united with the British Empire solely through its allegiance to the Crown—a doctrine the American people afterwards accepted as the ground upon which they resisted Parliament. This was a remarkable statement of the political theory actually underlying the Empire but not recognized by statute until 165 years later.

Virginians were delighted at the repeal of the Stamp Act on March 18, 1766. After more than a year of surface tranquility, the Revenue Act was signed by the king on June 29, 1767. This external tax on glass, paper, white lead, painters' colors, and tea gave rise to memorials from burgesses and council and to protests from county after county.

In the autumn of 1768 Lord Botetourt arrived as Virginia's new governor. Leadership was slipping into the hands of a new element from Piedmont and farther west. When news reached Williamsburg early in 1769 of the order to transport the Boston rioters to London for trial, Virginians were incensed. The assembly, meeting in May, drafted resolutions condemning the attempt to transport Americans across the sea for trial, claiming the right of the colonies to concerted action and appeal, reiterating the exclusive right of the colony's assembly to levy taxes. Sympathetic Governor Botetourt was obliged to dissolve the disloyal burgesses, who withdrew to the Raleigh Tavern, where they signed a strict agreement not to import any slaves, wines, or British manufactures. The Non-Importation Agreement was soon adopted in all the colonies. The British Government was forced to give up the idea of transporting the patriots of Massachusetts for trial and by April 12, 1770, had rescinded all except the tax on tea and the principle involved. Beloved Governor Botetourt having died, haughty Lord Dunmore reached Virginia late in 1771. A royal order forbidding assent to any restriction of the slave trade led the Virginia assembly in February 1772 to send the king a petition, in which the trade was castigated as a 'great inhumanity' and one endangering 'the very existence of your Majesty's American dominions.'

Early in 1773 Virginia took a step that was to organize revolution. Renewal of the threat to transport Americans for trial in England emphasized the need for greater co-operation among the colonies. Led by Richard Henry Lee, a group of legislators, including Thomas Jefferson, Patrick Henry, and George Mason, proposed—and the legislature created—a standing committee of correspondence, representing the lower house, to inform the other colonies through similar committees, which they recommended be set up, of Virginia's reaction to the latest moves of the British ministry, to receive theirs in return, and to keep in touch with Virginia's London agent. Unlike the local and unofficial committees of correspondence, originated by Samuel Adams a year earlier to consolidate anti-British sentiment in the faction-torn townships of Massachusetts, this Virginia committee was an official, centralized body modeled on the permanent standing committee originated in 1759 to correspond on similar business with an agent in London. This committee, active until 1772, left four of its members to the new committee. The effort to transport Americans for trial was abandoned, and before the year was out Parliament repealed the duty on tea—not without retaining, however, the three-penny custom collectable in American ports. Associations against tea drinking were revived. Virginia had its 'tea-party' near Yorktown, similar to the one that took place in the Boston harbor.

From the moment in May 1774 that news reached the colonies of the Boston Port Bill, closing that harbor in punishment of the tea dumpers, events moved swiftly to successive climaxes. The Virginia assembly resolved to set aside June 1, when the bill was to take effect, as a day of fasting and prayer. Governor Dunmore dissolved the legislature, and members gathered the next day at the Raleigh Tavern, declared common cause with Massachusetts, recommended that a general congress be held annually, that no East India Company commodity be imported, and advocated a general commercial boycott of Great Britain. Revolution was in the air when Virginia's first convention met in Williamsburg on August 1, pledged supplies to Boston, suspended transatlantic debts and commerce, and elected delegates to a continental congress.

Peyton Randolph of Virginia was made president of the First Continental Congress held in Philadelphia in September. Here Washington, without pretensions of eloquence, shone as a man of 'solid judgment and information.' At the Second Virginia Convention, opening on March 20, 1775, Patrick Henry again was the central figure of high drama. Giving his impassioned plea for 'embodying, arming and disciplining' Virginia militia, he closed with the fiery words:

> Gentlemen may cry 'Peace! Peace!' but there is no peace. The war is actually begun! . . . Is life so dear or peace so sweet as to be purchased at the price of chains and slavery? Forbid it, Almighty God! I know not what course others may take, but, as for me, give me liberty, or give me death!

Patrick Henry's resolution was adopted and steps were taken for establishing manufactories to make both arms and other commodities that had formerly been imported from England.

On April 20 Governor Dunmore provoked the first armed resistance in Virginia by ordering the gunpowder stored in the public magazine in Williamsburg to be removed to a warship. Although the governor filled his palace with marines and threatened to 'proclaim liberty to the slaves and reduce Williamsburg to ashes' if he or his affairs suffered any injury, he was forced by the approach of Patrick Henry at the head of troops from Hanover and other counties to pay £ 320 for the powder. As soon as the little army had dispersed, his lordship declared Henry an outlaw—matching Governor Berkeley's treatment of Bacon just a century earlier. The burgesses, called by Lord Dunmore to consider Lord North's proposals, met once more on June 1. They rejected the 'Olive Branch' and, to defray the expense of the late Indian war, proposed a tax of £ 5 per head on imported slaves. To protect the slave trade the king's representative exercised his veto power for the last time in Virginia. When the burgesses were ready for his assent to bills passed, the governor refused to leave the *Fowey*, the ship to which he had fled on the night of June 8, and the burgesses adjourned on June 20, never to meet formally again. On June 15 the Continental Congress had elected George Washington commander in chief of American forces. The Third Virginia Convention, meeting in July, quickly provided for a committee of safety, for the raising of regular regiments, and for dividing the colony into 16 military districts. Lord Dunmore retired to Norfolk, where—lacking troops—he remained inactive for several months among a nest of Tories.

Meanwhile the Fourth Virginia Convention passed scathing resolutions condemning Lord Dunmore and announcing that the people of Virginia were ready to protect themselves 'against every species of despotism.' In November the ex-governor had declared the colony to be in revolt and had proclaimed all slaves in Virginia free. On December 9 his defending forces were routed at Great Bridge by 'shirt men,' militia acting under the Committee of Safety. Having taken to his ships, he bombarded Norfolk on New Year's Day. It was not until the following July, however, that he was finally driven from the Chesapeake. Washington, having invested Boston in November, drove out the British under General Howe by March 1776. Virginia had sent up supplies as well as Daniel Morgan with his frontier marksmen, who could pick off captains at 'double the distance of common musket shot.' Morgan had soon gone on to distinguish himself before Quebec, carrying Virginia's offensive far afield.

Virginians remained ideologically in the forefront of opposition. Radicals were at the helm when the Fifth Virginia Convention opened in Williamsburg on May 6, 1776. Declaring on May 15 the colony a free and independent State, the Convention instructed Virginia delegates in Congress to propose separation from Great Britain. In obedience to the mandate from his State Richard Henry Lee rose in Congress on June 7 and proposed independence, contraction of foreign alliances, and establishment of a plan of confederation. Three days later, a committee was appointed to draft a declaration of independence. On June 12 the Virginia Convention, serving as a legislative body, adopted George Mason's Bill of Rights and on June 29 approved a constitution. The bill of rights and the constitution were to serve as patterns for other States and for the Nation itself. Lee's resolutions were adopted on July 2, 1776 and, when Jefferson's Declaration of Independence was approved by Congress on July 4, the United States of America was born.

For the next three years, while the war was being waged north and south and Virginia was contributing her full share of men and treasure and defending the western frontier, her legislators were laying the foundations of a new society. The progressives, led by crusading Thomas Jefferson, went far toward destroying the old regime. The new government, which endured without change for 54 years, consisted of a house of delegates, with the sole power to originate legislation; a senate, in place of the former council; a council of eight, limited to an executive function; and a chief magistrate. Both council and governor were chosen, the governor yearly, by the two houses voting together. When the legislature met in October 1776, several courts were set up immediately, and Jefferson, Pendleton, and Wythe were given the task of revising the whole body of Virginia law in conformance with the new constitution. By a legislative act of 1778 Virginia became the first State in the world to make a person engaged in the slave traffic guilty of a criminal offense. An amendment, however, that proposed freedom for all children born to slaves after the enactment of the bill was defeated. The laws of entail and primogeniture, legal basis of a social hierarchy, were abolished by bills that Jefferson presented now and that were passed a few years later.

Besides sending aid to the theaters of conflict north and south, Virginia began waging singlehanded a war in the West, where the British occupied a chain of forts from Detroit to Kaskaskia. On the strength of the battle of Saratoga, in which Daniel Morgan and his riflemen were important factors, Virginia sent into the Northwest George Rogers Clark in command of four companies. On July 4, 1778, General Clark surprised the fort at Kaskaskia and shortly afterward entered Vincennes without opposition from the friendly French residents. Later, during Clark's absence, Vincennes was retaken by British Governor Hamilton. On February 24, 1779, Clark returned, surprised the small garrison, and sent Hamilton to Williamsburg as a prisoner. Forts built to the mouth of the Ohio enabled Clark to hold the territory until the end of the war.

In May 1779 actual conflict was carried into the heart of Virginia, when Sir George Collier sailed into Hampton Roads with 2,000 troops. Using Portsmouth as their base, they raided surrounding country, destroyed the navy yard at Gosport (Portsmouth) and large quantities of stores. When reinforcement from Sir Henry Clinton in New York failed to arrive, the attempted blockade of Virginia was abandoned, and the colony's trade with the West Indies, now an American lifeline, continued.

Following a summer of American reverses on several fronts, rumor spread in 1780 that dismemberment of the Continental union and devastation of Virginia were planned. In October, General Alexander Leslie, having entered the Chesapeake with 3,000 troops, made Portsmouth his base. Upon news of the British defeat at King's Mountain, however, Leslie went south to join Cornwallis. At the end of December, Benedict Arnold with about 1,000 troops appeared in the Bay, advanced by water and land to Richmond, where he burned stores, and then established his base at Portsmouth. General William Phillips, joining forces with Arnold, undertook raids on a larger scale. At Petersburg, Phillips died a week before Cornwallis's arrival there on May 20, 1781. After General Nathanael Greene's move into the Deep South had left Virginia uncovered, General La Fayette, commanding part of the Continental army, came to Virginia, advancing southward as far as Petersburg. Nearly 7,000 strong and well armed, the British began their pursuit of La Fayette, who retreated toward Fredericksburg, was joined by General Anthony Wayne, and then continued southwestward. Cornwallis dispatched Colonel John G. Simcoe with 500 men to Point of Fork to destroy an arsenal and stores that General von Steuben was unable to defend, and Colonel Banastre Tarleton with 250 men to Charlottesville to capture Thomas Jefferson and the Virginia legislature. Reunited without these prizes at Elk Hill, the British moved eastward toward Williamsburg, followed by La Fayette, whose troops numbered about 5,000 after General von Steuben had joined him. On July 4 Cornwallis left Williamsburg, paused near Jamestown, where a part of his forces fought the inconsequential Battle of Greenspring, crossed the James, and proceeded to Portsmouth and thence to Yorktown, which he entrenched as a naval base.

With the arrival of 3,000 French regulars from the fleet under Admiral de Grasse, the initiative slipped irretrievably into the hands of the patriots, who strung themselves out across the peninsula. Washington and General Rochambeau arrived on September 15, and seven days later the Continental army reached Jamestown by water from the North. While the French fleet prevented the arrival of British re-enforcements, the combined American and French forces began on September 28 to converge on Yorktown. The siege ended on October 19, with General Cornwallis's surrender.

VIRGINIANS IN THE MAKING OF THE CONSTITUTION

In the movement toward stronger union that resulted in the adoption of the Constitution, Virginia again played the leading part. Under the Articles of Confederation the Government was without power to regulate trade, raise revenue, or make foreign treaties—all pressing needs. James Madison, justly called the father of the Constitution, introduced into the Virginia general assembly in 1785 the resolution inviting commissioners from Maryland to meet with commissioners from Virginia to discuss common problems of trade and navigation. The conference, which opened in March at Alexandria and was continued at Mount Vernon, resulted in a plan for the two States' joint regulation of commerce and was the first step toward permanent union of the thirteen commonwealths. On January 21, 1786, the general assembly of Virginia adopted resolutions inviting all other States to meet for the purpose of considering the trade of the United States. Five States sent commissioners to the Annapolis Convention of September 11–14, 1786. Though navigation and commerce were still the points at issue, Washington and Madison were seeing the meeting of representatives of the several States as another step toward a stronger union. At Annapolis the Virginians were reinforced by Alexander Hamilton of New York. The convention adopted Hamilton's address that pledged the delegates to endeavor 'to procure the concurrence of the other states in the appointment of commissioners, to meet at Philadelphia, on the second Monday in May next to take into consideration the situation of the United States.'

George Washington was elected president of the convention that opened in Philadelphia on May 14, 1787. Governor Edmund Randolph of Virginia presented the 'Virginia Plan,' which incorporated James Madison's ideas and furnished the basis of deliberations. Madison spoke more frequently than any other delegate, kept copious notes that have enlightened historians, and wrote 20 of the 85 Federalist papers, which created a public opinion favorable to the adoption of the Constitution. The seven Virginia delegates—George Washington, George Wythe, George Mason, James Madison, Edmund Randolph, John Blair, and James McClurg—fought for the inclusion of a bill of rights, for the immediate cessation of the slave traffic, and for a progressive program of abolition. Because a bill of rights was omitted, because the Deep South and New England traders forced a compromise that continued the slave traffic until 1808 and failed to provide for the ultimate abolition of slavery, and because a mere majority of Congress was permitted to determine tariff policies, George Mason and Edmund Randolph refused to sign the instrument. James McClurg and George Wythe were absent. George Washington, James Madison, and John Blair signed, believing that the faults could be corrected immediately by amendments.

Virginia was the tenth State to ratify the Constitution. Meeting on June 2, 1788, the rank and file of delegates to the State convention split on sectional lines, Tidewater and the northwest favoring ratification, while Piedmont and the slaveless southwest, refusing to sanction the compromise between commercial North and plantation South over slavery and the tariff, fought for a second convention and revision. Among the leaders, Mason and Henry, encouraged by Richard Henry Lee writing from Chantilly, directed the opposition; Madison, Wythe, Pendleton, Henry Lee, and even Randolph, backed up by Washington's letters from Mount Vernon, conducted a successful defense. The attempt by the Northeastern States, acting through John Jay in 1786, to surrender navigation on the Mississippi to Spain had aroused such suspicion of New England's intentions that it took all of visionary Madison's persuasive talents to win ratification at last on June 26 by a small margin, and then only with the assurance that the first Congress would submit to the States amendments constituting a bill of rights, and with the clear proviso that the people of Virginia could cancel ratification setting up the Union 'whenever the powers granted unto it should be perverted to their injury or oppression.' The convention suggested 40 amendments, which were the bases of the 10 that became the Bill of Rights in the Constitution—the first nine introduced by James Madison and the tenth by Richard Henry Lee.

Meanwhile Virginia had been undergoing important geographical changes. Byrd's line between Virginia and North Carolina was extended west in 1779, although the exact location was disputed for another century; and the north-south boundary between Virginia and Pennsylvania, agreed upon that same year, was run in 1784–85. Within a year of the peace treaty, which recognized Virginia's claims, the Old Dominion surrendered the entire Northwest Territory—the vast section between the Ohio River and the Canadian border west from Pennsylvania to the Mississippi, and including the Great Lakes area—to the United States. In 1792 Kentucky became a State, thus fixing the limits Virginia preserved until 1861. Meanwhile, an interior change of territorial status had taken place—the disappearance of the great proprietary of the Northern Neck. Taken up first in 1673 by Thomas, Lord Culpeper, who acquired five-sixths of the territory from the original grantees, the proprietary had passed in 1689 by marriage into the family of the fifth Lord Fairfax and was abolished by the general assembly in 1786.

George Washington, who took office as first President under the new Government on April 30, 1789, exerted a calming influence upon a decade of growing pains and political turmoil. Back from Paris in December 1789, Thomas Jefferson was appalled at the antidemocratic spirit he found in the highest places. Three months later Washington chose him Secretary of State. In opposition to Secretary of the Treasury Alexander Hamilton, he began to marshal the growing ranks of antifederal extremists who were to overthrow the conservatives in 1800. In the meantime the conservatives were ascendent. Led by Hamilton, they forced through the Assumption Bill in 1790, which Virginia and the other Southern States, with the exception of South Carolina, opposed on the ground that their debts were almost paid and the Government's assuming the debts of the Northern States inflicted an unfair hardship upon the South. As a sop to the agrarian opposition, they threw in the Southern choice of a site on the Potomac for the National capital, for which Virginia had already ceded territory. The next year Jefferson fought Hamilton's creation of the Bank of the United States. When war broke out between England and France in 1793 and John Jay negotiated a thoroughly Federalist treaty with England, attitudes split squarely; the banking and commercial imperialists, led by Hamilton, sympathized with England; the agrarian progressives, led by Jefferson, remained true to the cause of revolution and to America's old ally. In 1796 President Washington, having served two terms, retired to Mount Vernon, expressing regret that the 'increasing weight of years' admonished him 'to decline being considered among the number of those out of whom a choice is to be made,' but over Adams's administration he watched benevolently. In 1798 the Federalists enacted the infamous Alien and Sedition Laws, which made it possible to deport persons of less than 14 years' residence and to throw into jail others who should express un-American sentiments—in other words, ideas openly and severely in opposition to administration policies.

THE VIRGINIA DYNASTY

The accomplishments of Thomas Jefferson's administration, antithetical to that of Adams, were the clear articulation of democratic philosophy, the acquisition of a vast territory, and the futile enunciation of the principle that peace was more to be desired than the profits of commerce.

This man who had sprung from privileged aristocracy had from his youth espoused the cause of the masses. Upon assuming office, he discarded the monarchical rituals that had characterized the first two administrations and at once abolished from public entertainments all precedents as to rank and distinction. Opposed to the aristocratic doctrines of Alexander Hamilton and distressed because of Washington's conservatism, he had left the cabinet in 1794. As vice president during Adams's administration he had fought the Alien and Sedition Laws and had drafted the Kentucky Resolutions that eloquently protested the silencing, as he said, 'by force and not by reason the complaints and criticisms, just or unjust, of our citizens against the conduct of our agents.' The first of the alien laws, raising the number of years for naturalization from 5 to 14, was repealed in April 1802; the third, permitting the President to order 'dangerous' aliens out of the country, died at the end of the two-year period to which it was originally limited; and the sedition law, classifying as a crime criticism of the Government and of Federal officials, expired in March 1801. The establishment of a citizen's right to expatriation was a further expression of Jeffersonian democracy.

In acquiring the Louisiana Territory, Thomas Jefferson exceeded his constitutional authority to the great advantage of the United States. Robert R. Livingston, whom Jefferson had appointed minister to France, had expressed naive faith in existing treaties and apparently did not share Jefferson's belief that French occupation of Louisiana would be 'very ominous to us.' An ocean, moreover, separated Jefferson from Livingston, and letters were in danger of interception. So the President sent to France as an envoy extraordinary and minister plenipotentiary another Virginian—his trusted friend, James Monroe—without written authorization to purchase the whole territory. Livingston, somewhat piqued, tried to consummate the purchase while Monroe was on the ocean, but failed. So, to the vision of Thomas Jefferson and the immediate diplomacy of James Monroe belongs the credit for striking the bargain by which the United States almost doubled its area for the sum of $15,000,000. Though the Constitution gave the Federal Government no authority to buy and hold territory, Jefferson decided to postpone asking Congress to pass an amendment lest Napoleon change his mind. Jefferson sent two Virginians, Meriwether Lewis and William Clark, to explore the vast western territory. The expedition started from the mouth of the Missouri in the spring of 1804, and the explorers returned to the vicinity of St.Louis in the fall of 1806, having reached the mouth of the Columbia River.

Napoleon's Berlin and Milan Decrees and the British orders in Council—three decrees that restricted American trade and led to the impressment of American soldiers and the search and seizure of American ships—brought about the Embargo Act of 1807, which Jefferson considered preferable to war. Off the Virginia capes the American *Chesapeake* had been fired upon by the British *Leopard*, with consequent fatalities and the impressment of American sailors. When the money changers cried for war, Thomas Jefferson substituted economic sanctions. America's experiment was doomed to failure, however, for the New England traders and owners of vessels were so vociferous in protest that Congress in 1809 repealed the Embargo Act and, hoping to stimulate home manufactures, passed in its stead the Non-Intercourse Act.

Jefferson's mantle fell in 1809 upon the shoulders of another Virginian, James Madison. The peace policies of Jefferson collapsed during Madison's administration, chiefly because the popular demand for war made inroads upon the thinking of cabinet members and lawmakers. In June 1812 Congress declared a state of war to exist between the United States and Great Britain. Again the Virginia coast became a British target. In February 1813 Admiral George Cockburn, commanding British vessels, entered the Chesapeake, made headquarters at Lynnhaven Bay, landed a force of 1,800 men, and plundered coastal plantations. In April the British *St.Domingo* captured the *U.S.S.Dolphin* in the Rappahannock River. In June, though Cockburn had been reinforced by Admiral Borlasse Warren, the enemy fleet was repulsed in its effort to take Norfolk and Portsmouth. A few days later, however, Cockburn successfully pillaged the little town

Architecture I

Photograph by W. Lincoln Highton

JACOBEAN GABLE-END, BACON'S CASTLE (c. 1655), SURRY COUNTY

Photograph by courtesy of the Virginia State Chamber of Commer

WILTON (1762), MIDDLESEX COUNTY

ADAM THOROUGHGOOD HOUSE (c. 1634), PRINCESS ANNE COUNTY

Photograph by courtesy of the Virginia Conservation Commissi

Photograph by courtesy of the Virginia State Chamber of Commerce

WESTOVER (1730–35), CHARLES CITY COUNTY

LOWER BRANDON (18th CENTURY), PRINCE GEORGE COUNTY

Photograph by courtesy of the Virginia Conservation Commission

Photograph by W. Lincoln Highton

BREMO (1815–19), FLUVANNA COUNTY

CARTER'S GROVE (1751), NEAR WILLIAMSBURG

Photograph by W. Lincoln Highton

Photograph by W. Lincoln Highton

GUNSTON HALL (1755–58), FAIRFAX COUNTY

ANNEFIELD (1790), NEAR BERRYVILLE

Photograph by W. Lincoln Highton

Photograph by courtesy of the Virginia Conservation Commission

'GREAT ROOM,' KENMORE (1752–77), FREDERICKSBURG

otograph by W. Lincoln Highton

ROLFE HOUSE (c. 1651) INTERIOR, NEAR SURRY

VICTORIAN PARLOR, VALENTINE MUSEUM (WICKHAM HOUSE, 1812), RICHMOND

otograph by courtesy of the Virginia Conservation Commission

Photograph by W. Lincoln Highto

ENTRANCE HALL, CARTER'S GROVE (1751), NEAR WILLIAMSBURG

of Hampton, but soon thereafter turned his attention to the Carolinas. Despite Cockburn's return to the Chesapeake Bay in August 1814, Virginia suffered during the rest of the war little more than the shock of seeing Washington burned and President Madison and his plumply pretty wife Dolly seek refuge on its soil. The ratification of the Treaty of Ghent in February 1815, establishing the principle of the freedom of the seas, brought peace to the last year of Madison's second term, and sounded the death knell of the Federalist party, which had been expiring for some time with painful gasps. In addition, it paved the way for the 'era of good feeling' coincident with the two terms of James Monroe, the last of the Virginia dynasty.

As President of the United States, Monroe prevented the fortification of the Canadian border, acquired the Floridas, was party to the Missouri Compromise, and enunciated the great doctrine that has continued to dominate the foreign policy of the United States. Madison had wanted war vessels removed from the Great Lakes. Monroe all but achieved the goal. He sent to the British ministry 'a precise project for limiting the force'; in January 1817 Lord Castlereagh accepted the proposal; the actual reduction became effective the following year. The powers agreed to the maintenance of but one vessel on Ontario, two on the upper lakes, and one on Champlain. Thus the unfortified border made possible permanent peace between Canada and the United States and proved that disarmament promotes good will and security.

In annexing all Florida Monroe merely completed the task he had set out to accomplish when he went to France as Jefferson's special representative in 1803 and again in 1804. When Napoleon had sold the Louisiana Territory, he had said clearly that West Florida was included. Both Monroe and Livingston thought that the entire area had been purchased—only to be rudely awakened soon after the bargain was sealed. Later an uprising of the Seminoles, which was speedily, though unauthoritatively, quelled by General Andrew Jackson, expedited the settlement of the Florida question. On February 22, 1819, Secretary John Adams arranged the treaty that effected the purchase from Spain of all East and West Florida.

The Missouri Compromise, framed by Virginia-born Henry Clay, was passed in March 1820. Jefferson had consistently opposed slavery; Madison had spoken of it as a 'dreadful calamity.' Monroe took steps toward the repatriation of the blacks to Africa. In Liberia, where the town of Monrovia still bears his name, several colonization projects were undertaken with his encouragement.

On December 2, 1823, Monroe sent to Congress his annual message that embodied the principles later known as the Monroe Doctrine. The Holy Alliance, created to suppress liberalism, was about to interfere with the new republics in South America. Jefferson, who had stood consistently against entangling alliances, corresponded with Monroe immediately before the message was written. Thus the doctrine protesting future European colonization in America and the extension on this hemisphere of such systems as those the Holy Alliance promoted was the contribution of both Thomas Jefferson and James Monroe.

The treaty with Russia signed on January 11, 1825, establishing the northwest boundary of the United States, was one of the last significant accomplishments of Monroe's administration.

Meanwhile sectionalism in Virginia had reared its head in a contest between a cismontane and a tramontane people. Unbalanced political representation between the two parts of Virginia led to threats of State dismemberment. In 1816, the year of James Monroe's presidential election, a compromise was reached by which the west 'obtained a representation in the Senate based upon white numbers in exchange for a law equalizing land values for purpose of assessment.' Slavery agitation subsided, internal improvements began, and a crop of young politicians matured. The rising spirit of nationalism was typified by the American System, which had crept into Virginia with the demand for better means of communication between the eastern and western sections.

Partly because of this system Virginia moved into an epoch of solidification and construction. The general assembly authorized in 1816 the President and Directors of Public Works. The whole State united in 1819 against the establishment of Federal banks. But with agriculture, the case was different. Between 1817 and 1830 the eastern part of the State experienced a great industrial decline and loss of population. Tobacco planters gave up their impoverished farms to briars and broomsedge and moved to the western frontiers or into the new Southern cotton states. Fairfax County by 1833 had become a ruin; Norfolk, said Henry Ruffner in 1847, had lost half its commerce in 25 years. In much of the Piedmont and Tidewater, plantations were so run down that they could support only their owners; land values fell from $206,000,000 to $90,000,000 from 1817 to 1830; the total increase in the white population was only 91,213 in the decade following 1820. Similarly, the decrease of Virginia's exported goods fell from $8,212,860 in 1817 to $3,340,185 in 1828. The eastern part of the State was left with only the resource of surplus Negroes.

During the years following 1818 Virginia was enveloped in one of America's periodic depressions. The planters of Tidewater and Piedmont discarded tobacco for cotton and tried to rejuvenate wornout land. They attributed their failure to the American System's doctrine that a high protective tariff was essential for making the nation self-supporting. Western Virginia, however, was developing rapidly. Wheat, sheep, and iron were coming to the front as economic products. But the inefficiency of the State in supplying this section with adequate means of communication brought dissatisfaction. Unable to fit slavery into their industrial scheme, the mountaineers turned against the American System just at the time that the depleted land of the east was being brought back to fertility and the sale of slaves had become an important economic factor.

Sectionalism was nowhere so apparent as in education. Only on the promise that free schools should later be established did the western part of Virginia consent to an annual appropriation of $15,000 for a proposed university. When the University of Virginia was founded in 1819, the site chosen was close to the mountains.

The Missouri Compromise had thrown the balance of political power to the North. The slavery question was dimmed, however, by agitation that centered about the tariff. The 'Tariff of Abominations,' enacted in 1828, caused the South to unite solidly against the North and brought about talk of secession.

SECTIONAL STRIFE AND SLAVE BREEDING

Although Andrew Jackson, elected in 1828, was against the American System, he did nothing at first toward lowering the high tariff. After South Carolina's Nullification Act, Governor John Floyd announced that any attempt to cross Virginia's territory would be met with armed resistance. Talk of secession was temporarily suspended by the passage of Clay's compromise tariff, providing for a gradual reduction of rates until 1841, and after 1842 for no duties above 20 per cent.

At the Whig Convention of 1839, presided over by James Barbour of Virginia, were nominated the party's first successful candidates, William Henry Harrison and John Tyler, both Virginians. Tyler, who followed Harrison's short tenure of office (March 4 to April 4, 1841), pursued the policies of the Virginia dynasty and fought the attempted revival of the American System. During Tyler's administration the Treaty of Washington was signed (1842), fixing the Canadian boundary as far west as the Rocky Mountains, and Texas was annexed. Though Governor William Smith called out three regiments for participation in the Mexican War

(1846–48) and only one was accepted, the war's two heroes were Virginians—Zachary Taylor and Winfield Scott.

The question of slavery now dominated the scene. With the exhaustion of Tidewater soil and the rise of King Cotton, eastern Virginians were driven into a nefarious traffic—that of supplying the new South's demand for more slaves. As the interstate slave trade increased, Virginia was dubbed the 'breeder of slaves.' In the western part of the State, abolitionists came to the front. In Virginia the slave industrial system was in a death grapple with the free industrial system. Nat Turner's slave insurrection of 1831 crystallized sentiment for and against abolition. Citizens flocked to one of three standards: removal of free Negroes from the Tidewater and Piedmont sections; deportation of the entire Negro population; and a plan for gradual emancipation. In the legislature of 1832 an act that provided for colonization of free Negroes and another that would have brought about emancipation were lost by narrow margins. Later the 'Atherton Gag,' preventing discussion of slavery, was passed by the National House.

The Wilmot Proviso intensified hatred and misunderstanding. Virginia declared itself against the proposed exclusion of slavery from all territory to be acquired from Mexico. A crisis was averted, however, by Clay's Compromise of 1850. During 1852, the year *Uncle Tom's Cabin* was published, the Virginia branch of the American Colonization Society sent 243 Negroes to Liberia. The slavery question was revived in 1854 by the Kansas-Nebraska Bill, allowing local option as to slavery in new Territories; and in 1857 by the Dred Scott Decision. On the night of October 16, 1859, John Brown's band seized the United States arsenal at Harpers Ferry. At night 100 marines under Colonel Robert E. Lee arrived, surrounded the arsenal, and captured the raiders. In a swift trial, John Brown was convicted of murder and treason and hanged.

But Virginia remained union minded and declined South Carolina's proposal for a Southern convention. By 1860, however, the State needed only the shot fired at Fort Sumter by Edmund Ruffin, a Virginian, to crystallize anti-union sympathies. When Lincoln issued a call for troops on April 15, 1861, Governor John Letcher refused to supply Virginia's quota. On the 17th the State Convention voted to secede from the Union. On April 23 Governor Letcher placed Robert E. Lee in command of Virginia troops. On the 25th Virginia joined the Confederate States. On May 21, 1861, Richmond was made the capital of the Confederacy.

The Virginia that seceded from the Union retained the forms, if not the substance, established during the half century that ended with the inauguration of John Quincy Adams. The caste system placed its entire weight on slavery. Just above the slave was the free Negro, fettered with legal restrictions, despised by 'poor whites,' that great mass of miserable people strewn about the Tidewater and Piedmont. In contrast were the poor 'mountain whites,' primitive, rugged, proud. Above these was the yeoman farmer class, independent, self-respecting, deeply religious. The planter class, at the top, had its own strata—'the rabble of small planters,' possessing few slaves; the middle-class planters; and lastly a handful of upper-class planters. In 1860 out of a white population of 1,047,299 only 52,128 persons owned slaves; half of these held from one to four, and only 114 individuals owned as many as 100 slaves.

In mid-century Virginia shared with the rest of the States in the spate of immigration that followed the collapse of liberal movements in Europe when the revolutions of 1848 failed. Among the newcomers, who settled chiefly in Richmond, were many Jews. Although they had filtered into the colony from the beginning and there were 26 heads of families in Richmond who organized in 1789 Virginia's first Jewish congregation, Jews had not been attracted to agrarian Virginia. By the end of the eighteenth century they were coming in steady, if thin, streams, which swelled abruptly in 1848.

Except for the few towns, Virginia's Tidewater and Piedmont landscape was a patchwork of farms wedged between plantations. In the 'big house' the table was weighted with food and wines, and entertaining was on a grand scale. As many as 20 people often dined at Bolling Hall and remained the night, subjected only to a little 'doubling up.' Henry Barnard, who visited Shirley in 1833, left a minute description. At eight o'clock the family had breakfast—a cup of coffee or tea drunk 'fashionably,' cold ham 'of the real Virginia flavor,' and a variety of hot breads. About one o'clock the invited guests arrived, the gentlemen consumed 'grog,' and at three o'clock dinner was served. After champagne, the upper cloth was removed for the elaborate desserts. 'When you have eaten this, off goes the second table cloth, and then upon a bare mahogany table is set the figs, raisins, and almonds and . . . 2 or 3 bottles of wine.' The planter, as a rule oft-married and sire of many children, bought his whiskey by the barrel, fraternized at the tavern, went to barbecues, hunted, and took his daily tour of the plantation.

The slaves, grouped together in the 'quarter,' had plenty of fuel and a daily ration of a quart of corn meal and half a pound of salt pork for each adult, supplemented by vegetables in season. Coarse winter clothing, shoes, and blankets were issued in October; and medical attention was provided. They had their dances, baptizings, 'preaching,' house-raisings, and hunted rabbit, 'coon, and 'possum. The plantation was a factory, a school, a parish, a matrimonial bureau, a nursery, and a divorce court.

After 1835, the growing of wheat began to predominate south of the James, particularly in Tidewater; and farm land increased enormously in value, rising from $216,401,543 in 1850 to $371,761,661 in 1860. Industry's output in Virginia rose from $29,602,507 in 1850 to $50,602,507 in 1860.

BATTLE GROUND OF THE 'SIXTIES

Virginia was the central battle ground of the war. Hoping for a quick subjugation, Federal armies occupied Alexandria and western Virginia (admitted as a separate State on June 20, 1863), reinforced the garrison at Fort Monroe, and threatened to enter the Valley near Harpers Ferry. Outmaneuvered north of Winchester and decisively defeated at Manassas on July 21, 1861, the North began molding a finer military organization; while the South, except for unsuccessful efforts to recover western Virginia, awaited the next Federal move.

Declaration of martial law around Richmond, the Hampton Roads posts, and other threatened zones, early in March 1862—followed by the battle between the *Monitor* and the *Merrimac* on March 9, the evacuation of Norfolk on May 9, and preparations for the evacuation of Richmond the following week—was the result of Federal activities in the fall of 1861 and the winter following. Union forces took the forts at Cape Hatteras in August and those at Roanoke Island in February, thereby opening the back door to Norfolk. The coast of South Carolina below Charleston was occupied in November. Fort Henry on the Tennessee River and Fort Donelson on the Cumberland were captured in February, leading to the loss of Kentucky, half of Tennessee, and of Nashville, for the duration of the war. The *Trent Affair*—purely naval—in November and December almost culminated in war between the United States and Great Britain and momentarily raised Confederate hopes. The capture of New Orleans in April closed the mouth of the Mississippi. The battle of Shiloh on April 6 and 7 resulted in the loss of General Albert Sidney Johnston. The loss of Island No.10 on April 8 opened the upper stretches of the Mississippi to the Union fleet and resulted in the subsequent evacuation of Corinth and Fort Pillow and in the Battle of Memphis and the consequent destruction of the Confederate river fleet.

Military movements on a large scale began in Virginia in March 1862. General Joseph E. Johnston withdrew from the vicinity of Washington to the Rappahannock. McClellan transferred his army to the vicinity of Fort Monroe and in May began an advance on Richmond, retarded by Johnston, now on the Peninsula; and Jackson's Valley campaign kept Washington on tenterhooks. The Federal fleet steamed up the James River to aid in taking Richmond, but on May 14, was effectively stopped at Drewry's Bluff—a fortification never taken.

After the indecisive battle of Seven Pines on May 31–June 1, 1862, Lee was placed in command of the Army of Northern Virginia. He defeated McClellan and relieved Richmond and began to withdraw to strike at Pope in northern Virginia. In August a decisive victory at Manassas over Pope—now commanding most of McClellan's army as well as his own—produced a near panic in Washington and necessitated the hurried restoration of McClellan to command. Lee's invasion of Maryland, coincident with Confederate advances in Kentucky, culminated in the indecisive battle of Sharpsburg, or Antietam, on September 17 and gave Lincoln his opportunity to claim a Northern victory and to announce on September 22 his purpose to proclaim emancipation. McClellan followed Lee back to Virginia, but his inertia again proved his undoing. He was supplanted by Burnside on November 7, 1862. Burnside was effectively disposed of at Fredericksburg on December 13, 1862, and Hooker, who succeeded him, ended an energetic campaign ingloriously at Chancellorsville in May 1863, though there the South sustained the irreparable loss of Stonewall Jackson.

When Lee's army invaded Pennsylvania in June 1863, panic reigned throughout the North. With Gettysburg, July 1–4, came defeat and the Confederacy's loss of all hope that European powers might intervene. Lee returned slowly to Virginia, followed by Meade who temporized throughout the fall and winter, unwilling to tilt lances again with an always dangerous foe.

The last phase of the war began in March 1864. Then Grant, who had had numerous successes in the west—including Vicksburg in July 1863, and Chattanooga in November—was placed in command of all Union armies. Under his plan Sherman began the march across the near South to cut off supplies from Virginia, Sigel moved down the Valley of Virginia for the same purpose, Butler advanced from Fort Monroe toward Richmond, and Grant remained with Meade to oppose Lee. Butler's and Sigel's movements came to naught. After Grant and Meade crossed the Rapidan on May 4, 1864, the battles of the Wilderness, Spotsylvania, North Anna River, Totopotomoy Creek, Cold Harbor, and the assault on Petersburg followed in rapid succession, all indecisive. General Early, whom Lee sent from Cold Harbor to the Valley, advanced to Washington and Baltimore in July, but returned to the Valley when additional troops arrived to protect the Federal capital. When Sheridan, placed in command in the Valley in August, defeated Early at Winchester and at Fisher's Hill in September and at Cedar Creek in October, the Valley was lost to the South. Grant reached Petersburg in June, having suffered more than 60,000 casualties on the way, and attempted encirclement of the city and the cutting of rail communications. Heavy blows, failing to break Lee's lines, pushed the Federal lines gradually westward. The Crater fiasco, six months' work on the Dutch Gap Canal undertaken to permit entrance of the fleet, several efforts to break through east of Richmond, attempts to destroy the Virginia Central Railroad and the James River Canal, and repeated drives against the roads south and west of Petersburg were all unsuccessful. Federal failures in Virginia, from the beginning of the war until the final breaking of Lee's lines, repeatedly depressed Northern spirits. Sheridan's victories in the Valley and Sherman's march through Georgia, however, were of sufficient brilliance to re-elect Lincoln. Though heavy operations ceased, the winter proved hard for the ill-equipped and ill-fed Southern army. On February 3, 1865, a conference in Hampton Roads between Lincoln and Seward and Confederate commissioners effected nothing.

With the coming of spring, Sheridan returned from the Valley, Grant became active along his entire line, and on the morning of April 2, 1865, Lee's lines broke southwest of the city. During the following night Richmond and Petersburg were evacuated; and Lee moved westward in an attempt to join Johnston in North Carolina. Grant sent one corps into Richmond, left another near Petersburg, and with the remainder—four corps and Sheridan's cavalry—began a running fight with Lee that terminated at Appomattox on April 9, 1865. With the surrender of Lee, the struggle ceased in Virginia, and the Confederacy collapsed.

At last it was over—the strange, intangible thing for which men had fought and women had sacrificed and suffered. The privileged minority knew perhaps that they had been protecting the wealth ancestors had accumulated at the price of black men's liberty; the small planters had blindly followed an example they had seldom questioned; and from the ranks of the poor whites men and boys had enlisted, or later had been drafted. They had fought a good fight. Now it was over, and few were sorry. Soldiers would return to the hearth and the plow. The favored minority had lost much; the masses could continue to dig a living out of the soil that had not failed their forefathers.

VIRGINIA ACCEPTS RECONSTRUCTION

But a different South—a different Virginia—lay about them. Great houses had been burned; churches and courthouses were heaps of ashes; rare books, valued records had been destroyed. People were filled with awe and bewilderment—planters who had once been rich, poor whites, Negroes. Adversity had leveled the great and the small. And the conquerors had come down to take possession of Virginia. The war was over, but days of Reconstruction were at hand.

The State was without civil government; farms were ruined, and farmers had no implements, stock, seeds, or money; factories were reduced to ruins; merchandise was depleted and credit was gone; railways were in a state of dilapidation, and the canal was scarcely serviceable; Negro labor had uncertain status and white labor was scarce; West Virginia, now a new State, had assumed no part of the *ante-bellum* debt, now $48,567,040—an increase of $16,628,896 since 1860; and Virginia had $27,709,319 in unproductive stocks. The total loss, exclusive of slaves, amounted to $104,205,720.53.

The Federal army assumed command of the State and remained in virtual control until 1870. On May 9, 1865, President Johnson recognized the 'Restored Government' of Virginia—the Government had consented to a division of the State—and on May 26 Governor F.H.Pierpont moved from Alexandria to Richmond. On June 15 the Bureau of Refugees, Freedmen, and Abandoned Lands set up offices in the State. On June 27 all Virginia, except Fairfax County, became the Military Department of Virginia under command of General Alfred H. Terry.

Governor Pierpont was conservative. Through his action in securing sanction for a revision of the Alexandria Constitution of 1864 to enfranchise disqualified Confederates, he incurred the animosity of the radicals, who wished to gain control through the Negro vote. When his term expired on April 4, 1868, his successor was appointed by military order.

In the spring of 1865 there were about 500,000 Negroes in the State and about 700,000 whites. Most cities had their Negro population doubled almost overnight; around rural Bureaus squalid villages arose; and the mortality rate among Negroes increased appallingly. Independent courts were instituted in which all complaints, generally against whites, were heard. Authorized to function for one year after the declaration of peace, the Freedmen's Bureau was extended to January 1, 1869, though its educational and financial activities continued until June 20, 1872. Negroes did not gain suffrage until late in 1869 and radicals never controlled the State.

The failure of legislators in Virginia and other Southern States to ratify the Fourteenth Amendment gave a radical Congress excuse for severity. By the Reconstruction Act, passed on March 2, 1867, and supplemented on March 23, Virginia became Military District No.1, commanded by General John M. Schofield.

The constitutional convention, for which the act had provided, convened in Richmond on December 3, 1867. Two-thirds of its 105 members were radicals, 25 of these Negroes. Judge John C. Underwood, who had gained notoriety by impaneling a mixed jury and presiding at the attempted trial of Jefferson Davis in May 1867, was elected president. Two clauses of the constitution drafted by the convention effected the undoing of the radical element: one provided for the disfranchisement of a large number of military officers and governmental officials; the other prohibited from holding public office any person who had voluntarily aided the South during the war. General Schofield, addressing the convention on April 17, 1868—the day the instrument was approved by that body—and failing to prevent the insertion of these clauses, refused to authorize the expenditure of funds necessary for ratification.

President Grant having recommended to Congress that the people be allowed to vote on the objectionable clauses separately, the election, held on July 6, 1869, resulted in the adoption of the constitution without the two disfranchising clauses. Gilbert C. Walker of New York, a conservative Republican, was elected governor; and the legislators were two-thirds conservative—of 181 Senators and delegates 55 were radicals of which 24 were Negroes; three Negroes were conservative. The legislature convened on October 5 and on October 8 ratified the Fourteenth and Fifteenth Amendments. Virginia had complied with the terms of the Reconstruction Act. On January 26, 1870, the Old Dominion ceased to be Military District No.1.

FROM COMMEMORATION TO ACHIEVEMENT

Then the State began its slow climb to recovery. The slave system had produced unhealthy economic conditions, false standards, and gross inequalities; and the war had brought about destitution. On March 2, 1870, a start was made toward the goal set by Thomas Jefferson almost 100 years before; a department of public education was established with Dr. William H. Ruffner as superintendent. Though impoverishment caused progress to be slow, by the turn of the century the State had laid the foundations for a system of secondary education, had somewhat strengthened its colleges for men, and had provided two normal schools, one for women and another for Negroes. Within the three decades railroads relaid their trackage, built new lines to connect remote areas with centers of population, and established great terminals. Steamships, increasing in numbers, carried commercial tonnage on inland waterways and north and south from coastal ports. Factories began to add an industrial economy to the almost wholly agrarian economy that had formerly characterized Virginia.

The attempt to fund the State's *ante-bellum* debt gave rise to a powerful political party that stirred racial hatreds, ran the gamut of political passions, dragged Virginia through State and National courts, and died with the downfall of its principal figure, General William Mahone. An act of the assembly in 1871 provided for funding the State debt of more than $45,000,000 and tentatively assigned one-third to West Virginia. Mahone, first postwar railroad magnate, entered the political field in 1873. Under the Democratic banner he virtually nominated the successful candidate for governor and, during the next four years, built up a small following on the debt question. Failing, however, to secure the gubernatorial nomination in 1877, he organized the Readjuster party and built up in two years a powerful machine composed chiefly of Negroes and disgruntled Democrats. In 1879, having elected a legislature that sent him to the United States Senate, he began to institute throughout the State a spoils system strong enough to survive the downfall of its creator. Later Mahone allied himself openly with the Republican party, elected a Readjuster governor in 1881, and dispensed Federal patronage in Virginia. The dispute that had to do with the State debt became more violent and involved; fights and riots occurred; some laws were defeated, and others that were passed were vetoed or fought in the courts; and corruption prevailed. In 1883, however, control was wrested from Mahone's machine. The financial difficulties were adjusted in 1891–92 to the satisfaction of the State's creditors. It was not until 1915, however, that the Supreme Court of the United States rendered the opinion that West Virginia must assume its proportion of those obligations incurred when it was a part of Virginia.

But the constitution of 1868 continued to be a thorn in the flesh of white Virginians. It did not discourage Negroes from voting, and it had made possible as late as 1888 the election from the Fourth Congressional District of a Negro to the National House of Representatives. The delegates to the constitutional convention that assembled on June 12, 1901, wrote into the new instrument the 'understanding clause,' which was to be effective until 1904 and then to be superseded by an intelligence test which required voters to interpret the constitution. The payment of three years' poll tax six months before general elections was also made a prerequisite to voting—an imposition that has decreased the size of both the white and the Negro electorate. The constitution was not ratified by the voters but 'proclaimed' by the convention and 'approved' by the legislature.

In the constitution of 1902 special provision was made for Virginia cities in line with the old precedent, reminiscent of England, by which they were politically independent of counties. Despite various inducements to found towns, Colonial Virginians had preferred to live on plantations. Each of the four 'corporacouns' constituted in 1619 was to have a capital city; in 1662 an act provided for the building of five towns; acts passed in 1680 and 1691 sought to establish towns. Though a few towns came into existence, the majority of Virginians continued to live on plantations. The political independence of the Virginia city had its origin in the act of 1705, which authorized 16 towns and provided that a community might become a 'free borough' when it had accumulated as many as 30 families, and after the acquisition of 60 families that its constitution should 'be held perfect' and that it might then send a representative to the general assembly. Yet during the Colonial period only three municipalities had their own burgesses: Jamestown, the first capital; Williamsburg, the second; and Norfolk, the only free borough. Richmond, when rechartered with city status in 1842, became under the commonwealth the first independent municipality. Now there are in Virginia 24 cities that administer their own affairs and bear to counties only geographic relationships.

The constitution written largely to its liking, Virginia saw the end of its commemorative era that had been characterized by mourning, monuments to the illustrious dead, and nostalgia for the days that were no more, and launched upon twentieth-century accomplishments. The State was not crushed by the panic of 1907; the depression of 1921 had no serious State-wide consequences; and the cataclysm of the early 1930's was far less devastating than in most other States. The explanation is to be found in Virginia's small bonded indebtedness and the diversification of the industries that were established during the first third of the century. Between 1899 and 1929 the value of products manufactured in Virginia rose from $108,644,150 to $745,910,075, and the number of industrial workers was almost doubled. The foundation, accordingly, was laid for a solid prosperity that made progress possible in many fields. Virginia began in 1922 to lift itself literally out of the mud with the reorganization of a highway department under a competent commissioner, and has achieved a system of roads comparable to any other in the country. The more than 8,000 miles of hard-surfaced roads in the State have been brought about without a bond issue and by means of a gasoline tax imposed in 1926. And no 'nuisance' taxes have been imposed in Virginia. The $4,000,000 annual revenue from the sale of alcoholic beverages in State-owned stores has been in a measure an antidote for depression.

Woodrow Wilson, another Virginia-born President, was inaugurated in 1913. His administration was marked not only by high idealism and emphasis upon human welfare but also by a sound fiscal and economic policy. The Owen-Glass Federal Reserve Bank Act, credited with preventing the old type of money panic, was the handiwork of Virginians. Robert L. Owen of Oklahoma, chairman of the Senate Committee on Currency and Banking, was born in Virginia; and Carter Glass, then representative from Virginia, was serving as chairman of the House Committee on Currency and Banking.

The old wounds of the unreconstructed rebels within the State, salved by the Spanish American War, were completely healed during the World War. A Democratic President, born in the Old Dominion, was at the helm; the Nation and Virginia held common cause in what the people believed to be an honest effort to safeguard those principles of self-government for which the oldest one of the United States had stood since the settlers at Jamestown demanded representative government. War brought prosperity to Virginia: factories; munitions plants; Camp Lee, where 50,000 soldiers were trained; Camp Humphreys for engineers; Camp Stuart for embarkation; and Langley Field for aviators. With the signing of the Armistice, cities that had come into existence or doubled their size almost overnight found a way to recover from the postwar slump through the establishment of new industries.

Virginia's principal progress during the twentieth century, however, has been made in relation to human welfare, particularly owing to the emphasis laid upon it by Governor Westmoreland Davis (1918–22). Though the State still lags far behind in education, the May Campaign of 1905, which had the essential characteristics of a religious revival, immediately resulted in better rural schools and more emphasis everywhere upon secondary education. Consolidated high schools, a start toward vocational education in cities and counties, a better State university that since 1920 has admitted women to its graduate and professional departments, the second oldest institution of learning in America converted into a coeducational State college, an agricultural and polytechnic institute that is sending its tentacles into many fields, a military institute that possesses traditions close to the hearts of Virginians, new buildings made possible to a large extent through Federal aid, and public insistence upon increased appropriations bear testimony to the progress made in the first four decades of the twentieth century. In 1916 foundations were laid for a modern public health program, which has steadily grown in the years that have followed. The State Board of Public Welfare, modestly established in 1908 as the Board of Charities and Corrections, received its new name in 1922. Its functions, consistently broadened, now include the administration of the eleemosynary and penal work of the State. The prisons, the four reform schools, the asylums for the insane, the sanitaria for tubercular patients, aid to dependent children, old age assistance, and much else come under its jurisdiction.

During the gubernatorial administration of Harry Flood Byrd the government of Virginia underwent complete reorganization. A commission on the simplification of State government had been appointed by Governor E. Lee Trinkle in 1924 and had recommended changes that became the basis of the new plan. The reorganization act of 1927 provides that only three State officers be elected by the people—the governor, lieutenant governor, and the attorney general. State government functions under 12 major departments: Taxation, Finance, Highways, Education, Corporations, Labor and Industry, Agriculture and Immigration, Conservation and Development, Health, Public Welfare, Law, and Workmen's Compensation. The heads of all these, with the exception of the department of law, are appointed by the governor. The governor may inspect all records and, when the legislature is not in session, may suspend any State executive officer except the lieutenant governor.

The constitution has been several times amended but not rewritten. The legislature is bicameral and meets biennially. The house has a maximum membership of 100, elected for a two-year term; the senate, a maximum membership of 40 elected for a four-year term. Justice is administered by a supreme court of appeals, circuit courts, city courts, trial justices, and justices of the peace. The general assembly elects the seven supreme court judges for twelve-year terms and all circuit and city judges for eight-year terms. Citizens of the United States who have lived in the State one year, the county or city six months, and the election precinct 30 days are entitled to vote. Though many city and county officers are still paid out of fees collected, a board fixes the maximum compensation each officer may receive, thus removing one objectionable feature from the system. Governor James H. Price, inaugurated in January 1938 and now in the midstream of his administration (1939), is emphasizing efficiency in government and human welfare.

Between the industrial North and the still agrarian South, between political left and right wings, between extremes of poverty and wealth, between the advocates of States' rights and the proponents of centralized government, Virginia even now stands on middle ground. Its democratic forms are sound; and, more than ever before, Virginia is aware of the necessity to raise educational standards and to ameliorate the condition of its vast submarginal population. Virginia still cherishes the heritage passed down from liberty-loving first settlers, who defied British kings; from Nathaniel Bacon and Patrick Henry, who roused the people against autocracy; from Thomas Jefferson, who enunciated the principles of democracy; from Robert E. Lee, who could turn defeat into spiritual victory. The weary travelers who disembarked at Jamestown established not only the first permanent English settlement in America, but a democratic ideal that may wane but will never die.

The Negro

VIRGINIA was the Negro's first home in the British Colonies of North America. Anthony, one of the Negroes in the shipload that arrived in 1619, married Isabella, and the son born to them in 1624, of whom there is record, was the first native Negro of Virginia. The infant was taken from his home in Kecoughtan to Jamestown in 1625, and there christened William in honor of Captain William Tucker.

Another Anthony, who probably came in 1622, and his wife Mary were bound servants in 1625; but by 1651 Anthony Johnson had secured his freedom and accumulated enough funds to import five servants, on whose headrights he acquired 250 acres on the eastern shore. First free Negro and first Negro landowner of Virginia, Anthony Johnson perhaps has the added distinction of being the first person in the colony, white or black, to hold as a lifetime servant a Negro who had committed no crime. Johnson petitioned the court of Northampton County in 1653 for the return of one John Casor, a runaway Negro whom he claimed for life. Although Casor protested that he had already been held 'seven years longer than he should or ought,' he was returned to his master for life. As far as is known, this was the first judicial sanction in the English colonies of life servitude where crime was not involved.

A court decree of 1661 that runaway Negroes were 'incapable of making satisfaction to their masters by the addition of time' to their terms of service gave legal recognition to a system already in general application. As an increasing supply of Africans became available, Virginians learned to do without white indentured servants. In 1672 the Royal African Company, with the Duke of York at its head, gained exclusive rights to the African slave trade; and in 1698 the trade was thrown open to the public. Slavers traveled the 'middle passage' to Virginia, their holds packed with African captives.

For the great majority of Negroes in Colonial Virginia, the 'sun-up to sun-down' routine in the tobacco fields was a lifelong ordeal from which there was no escape. Far more fortunate than these field hands were the slaves who worked in and around the 'big house.' Here the Negro played an important role. Many owners provided special uniforms for their house servants, and planters vied with one another in presenting before their guests the best appareled and most courtly butlers. In the kitchen the Negro cook was supreme, and the slave nurse or 'Mammy' helped to rear the children of the 'big house.'

Many mansions owed much of their beauty and durability to slave artisans, and Negroes were sometimes encouraged to develop their other talents or unusual gifts. An advertisement in the Virginia *Gazette* in 1760 offers for sale 'a young healthy Negro fellow who has been used to wait on a gentleman and plays extremely well on the French horn,' and another solicits the return of a runaway slave who 'can play the violin and took his fiddle with him.' Sy Gilliat, slave to Lord Botetourt in Williamsburg, was a fiddler at official State balls. Also skilled as a violinist was Robert Scott, free Negro of Charlottesville, who with his wife and three sons—all accomplished musicians—entertained La Fayette when the Marquis visited Monticello in 1825. Thomas Fuller, 'African calculator' of Alexandria, won fame for himself and bets for his master by his ability to answer 'all questions of time, distance and space.' Thomas Jefferson's servant, Henry Martin, became in later years bell ringer at the University of Virginia.

About 300 Negroes were in the colony in 1650, about 6,000 in 1700, and about 30,000 in 1730. By 1776 there were 270,262 slaves and 297,352 free persons (several thousands of whom were Negroes). From the beginning many Virginians opposed the traffic in human beings; while others, like Patrick Henry, were 'drawn along by ye general Inconvenience' of living without slaves. Thomas Jefferson voiced the sentiments of both groups when he inserted into the first draft of the Declaration of Independence a severe indictment of the English king for having 'waged cruel war against human nature itself, violating its most sacred right of life and liberty in the person of a distant people who never offended him, captivating and carrying them into slavery in another hemisphere.' This clause was struck out, wrote Jefferson afterwards, 'in complaisance to South Carolina and Georgia, who . . . still wished to continue [the trade]. Our Northern brethren also, I believe, felt a little tender under these censures.'

Ignoring northern and southern interests, the Virginia legislature during the Revolution barred all slave importations into the State after 1778. This action antedated by 30 years a similar ban imposed by the National Government. In 1782, Jefferson prevailed upon the legislature to legalize the manumission of slaves. Although a wave of freedom grants swept the State, the provision that the master must continue to support the slaves he freed was a serious deterrent to emancipation. Virginia delegates to the

National Constitutional Convention of 1787 fought valiantly for the immediate prohibition of the slave traffic and the gradual abolition of slavery. But the slave traders of New England and the cotton planters of the Deep South forced a compromise that continued the traffic until 1808 and failed to provide constitutional relief for the slaves.

Several mass uprisings, both before and after the Revolution, revealed the extent to which doctrines of the rights of man had penetrated 'slave row.' In September 1800 two frightened slaves reported to a white storekeeper of Richmond that Gabriel Prosser, a free Negro of the city, was plotting to capture Richmond and kill all who resisted, 'except the French inhabitants.' When a slave named Scott 'astounded his master by accidently pulling 10 dollars from a ragged pocket,' the conviction grew that a conspiracy was afoot. Prosser was captured in a vessel about to sail for Norfolk and later was hanged without having implicated a single confederate.

Other slave deliverers were to come, foremost among whom was Nat Turner. The Negro son of a mother who attempted to kill her baby rather than have him grow up a slave, and of a father who 'never accepted' slavery, Turner with a small band of followers cut a wide swath of death across Southampton County in August 1831. Two months later, Governor John Floyd recommended to the State legislature that all laws be revised to 'preserve in due subordination, the slave population.' While hundreds of petitioners urged that the 'black menace' be dispelled, Thomas Jefferson Randolph, grandson of Thomas Jefferson, offered the proposal that all slave children born after a certain year be purchased by the State and hired out until sufficient funds were accumulated to remove them from the United States. By a vote of 65 to 58, however, the legislature declared it 'inexpedient' to attempt to abolish slavery at that time, and laws were passed that forbade reading and writing among slaves and that banned all Negroes, slaves or free, from preaching or holding religious meetings unattended by a licensed white minister.

Of the 517,105 Negroes in Virginia in 1830 less than 10 per cent were free. Although the charge was made in the slavery debates of 1831–32 that free Negroes 'incited slaves to rebel,' the records reveal that many of the free Negro class in Virginia were industrious and law-abiding members of the community. Most slaveholders encouraged the American Colonization Society in its efforts to transport free Negroes to Liberia on the west coast of Africa, and about 3,000 of Virginia's 50,000 free Negroes were thus colonized. In Petersburg, according to Dr.Luther P. Jackson, in 1830 there were 503 free Negro heads of families who owned property of considerable value, including numerous slaves. Free Negroes would purchase their slave relatives for the nominal sum of five shillings each—an amount that was written into the deed of manumission but was seldom paid. By holding these relatives ostensibly as slaves, free Negroes evaded the legislative act of 1806, banishing from the State within 12 months all Negroes thereafter emancipated.

After 1808, when Negroes could no longer be legally imported from Africa, Virginia became a breeding place for slaves needed in the cotton country. Exhausted tobacco lands and curtailed foreign markets had made slaves a liability in Virginia. But Eli Whitney's revolutionary cotton gin and the acquisition through the Louisiana Purchase of a vast area suitable for cotton cultivation had created a demand for slave labor in the Deep South and Southwest. 'Dealing in slaves has become a big business,' noted the editor of *Niles' Register*; while Thomas Jefferson Randolph asked the legislature in 1832, 'How can an honorable mind, a patriot and a lover of his country, bear to see this ancient dominion . . . converted into one grand menagerie, where men are to be reared for market like oxen for the shambles?'

In the decade from 1830 to 1840, when slave trading was at its height, Virginia's Negro population dropped from 517,105 to 498,829, although Frederic Bancroft assumes that the natural increase of slaves during the decade must have been about 24 per cent. Bancroft places the yearly exportation at 11,793, a figure that checks closely with Thomas Marshall's estimate in 1830 of an exportation from Virginia of 10,800 Negroes.

'Nigger-traders' roamed the countryside and added slaves to their coffles at every stopping place. 'Dammit, how niggers has riz!' a planter is said to have exclaimed at a Richmond slave auction, when one Negro was 'knocked down' for $2,000. Robert Lumpkin's slave jail in Richmond was better known to the Negroes of the city as the 'Devil's Half-Acre.'

While thousands of Virginia slaves were on their way to the Deep South, hundreds of others were setting their course by the north star. The Fugitive Slave Law, enacted in 1850, was first invoked in the case of a fugitive from Norfolk, named Shadrach, who was arrested in Boston. While prominent lawyers of that city prepared a defense, 'a crowd of sympathizing colored persons, at broad noon day . . . surrounded the prisoner . . . fled with him pell-mell . . . and placed him beyond reach of his pursuers.' Boston was draped in mourning by protesting citizens when Anthony Burns, fugitive from Alexandria, was carried back to Virginia in chains. In Richmond, crowds visited Lumpkin's slave jail to see the 'nigger who wanted to be free.' Sold by his owner for $900, Burns was later redeemed by a Virginia-born abolitionist for $1,300 and allowed to return North. In 1856, James A. Smith, a shoe dealer of Richmond, fastened Henry Brown in a box two feet eight inches deep, two feet wide, and three feet long, containing 'a large gimlet, a bladder of water and a few biscuits.' Supposedly filled with shoes, the box was labeled 'This Side Up With Care.' When the lid was pried off in Philadelphia and Brown stepped out, contemporary newspapers made much of the case, and the fugitive became famous as 'Box Brown.' His benefactor, caught preparing two other Negroes for similar shipment, was imprisoned.

In 1860, when war clouds were fast gathering, there were 548,907 slaves, 53,042 free Negroes, and 1,047,299 whites in Virginia. Although Virginia slaves knew the great hope offered by 'Marse Lincum's boys,' during the war many continued to work faithfully at home, and to guard the women and children of the plantation. At the front, Negro servants tended masters, eased the latter's last moments, brought sorrowful news back home, and served in the Confederate army—cooking, digging redoubts, building fortifications, and caring for horses.

When United States troops first invaded Virginia soil at Alexandria, Negroes of the city cheered and prayed as soldiers released 'an old man, chained to the middle of the floor by the leg' in Kephart's slave jail, and turned the building into a prison for captive Confederates. When General Benjamin F. Butler moved into Fortress Monroe and declared homeless Negroes contraband of war, thousands of refugees flocked to 'de freedom fort' at Old Point Comfort. On an expedition along the North Carolina coast, one gun carriage of the *U.S.S.Minnesota* was manned by contraband volunteers, and General Butler reported that 'no gun in the fleet was more steadily served than theirs, and no men more composed than they when danger was supposed to be imminent.'

Negro soldiers participated in two major battles in Virginia. During the Battle of the Crater on July 30, 1864, after three white divisions of the Federal forces had failed to advance through the breach in the Confederate lines, a Negro division was sent in. A gallant charge, in which more than 1,000 Negroes were killed, wounded, or captured, resulted in failure when Federal support was not forthcoming. On September 29 of the same year, 3,000 of General Butler's Negro infantry marched up the slope toward Fort Harrison at New Market Heights into a withering fire from the Confederates. When the first line of defense was reached, the column broke ranks and captured the fort, thus breaking Lee's line around Richmond for the only time before the Confederacy's final collapse.

On a Sunday morning in April 1865, after a solemn-faced orderly had interrupted Jefferson Davis's worship at St.Paul's Church in Richmond, the news spread like wildfire that the city had to be evacuated. Negro soldiers marched in the next morning and, singing 'John Brown's Body,' paraded through rows of flaming buildings. To the resounding cheers of Richmond's Negroes, they halted without command at Lumpkin's slave jail to pay a moment's tribute to the throng that packed the windows, while the joyous strains of 'Slavery Chain Done Broke at Last' rang through the bars.

After Lee's surrender, the Freedmen's Bureau began systematic efforts to provide food, clothing, and homes for about 100,000 Negro refugees. Efforts also were made to educate the ex-slaves. Stories are told of prayers and 'schoolin's' under 'Emancipation Oak,' a towering tree that still stands on the pike between Hampton and Old Point Comfort. In 1866 General Samuel Chapman Armstrong, director of the eastern district of the Freedmen's Bureau, envisaged Hampton as 'the strategic spot for a permanent and great educational work' and suggested to the American Missionary Association that a school for freedmen be established there as the Hampton Normal and Industrial Institute. This later became the scene of Booker T. Washington's early labors. Close by the spot where Mary L. Peake, a free Negro woman, had taught the first contrabands, a plot of land was purchased and in April 1868 classes were begun. When the Reverend Richard Colver of Boston sought in Richmond a building in which to start a school for Negroes, Mary Jane Lumpkin donated the use of the slave jail that had made her husband famous.

The earning of a living was the chief concern of freedmen. Rumors of re-enslavement caused Negroes to distrust white bosses. In Virginia, moreover, the scale of wages was for a decade lower than in any other Southern State except South Carolina. In 1869, when the Virginia Freedmen's Bureau reported 'an excessive supply of laborers with a small demand,' a State commission was set up to encourage foreign white labor to migrate to Virginia.

While the masses struggled for a livelihood, their leaders were fighting for the rights of citizenship that the Federal Government was promising. At the State convention called in 1867 to draft a new constitution, 25 of the 103 delegates were Negroes. The election of 1869, by the largest vote in the State's history, placed 21 Negroes in the house of delegates and 6 in the State senate. Dr.Thomas Bayne, who had escaped from slavery in 1858 and returned to Norfolk as a dentist in 1865, was the leader of the Negro group. He was 'one of the shrewdest politicians of his day, whose ready tongue enabled him easily to turn aside the ridicule that met any

Negro representative who rose to speak.' The Norton brothers—Daniel, a physician of Yorktown, and Robert, a merchant of Williamsburg, both educated in New England—were outstanding members of the legislature. James Bland, reputedly the son of old Pompey Bland, gaming-house proprietor of Farmville, displayed in the senate 'every characteristic and mannerism of the gentlemen who in pre-war days had patronized his father's establishment.'

Negro legislators had their greatest success in the session of 1880–82, when their support helped to repeal the poll tax and establish a Negro insane asylum at Petersburg. But perhaps the most important achievement was the passage of a bill establishing a college for Negroes. Sponsored by A.W.Harris, Negro representative from Petersburg, the act authorized the expenditure of $100,000 for the erection of Virginia Normal and Collegiate Institute and provided $20,000 annually for its support.

The climax of the Virginia Negro's brief political career was reached in 1888 with the election of John M. Langston to Congress, from the Fourth District. Although his opponent was seated, Langston contested the election and was finally declared victor when only a few months of the term remained. On September 23, 1890, he took the oath of office as Virginia's only Negro representative in Congress. In the final decade of the century, fraud and intimidation were rife at elections, and violence was not unusual. John R. Holmes, a Negro candidate for State senator in 1892, was shot to death by a white man in Charlotte County. This act, described as 'a very extreme example of intimidation,' solved the dilemma for the district, since no other Negro candidate presented himself.

With the turn of the century came the virtual elimination of the Negro from Virginia politics. Delegates to the State constitutional convention of 1901 adopted a poll tax and 'understanding' requirement for prospective voters, and wildly cheered Carter Glass when he declared: 'This plan will eliminate the darkey as a political factor in this state in less than five years . . . The article of suffrage . . . does not necessarily deprive a single white man of the ballot, but will inevitably cut from the existing electorate four-fifths of the Negro voters.' The *Lynchburg News* found in 1905 that of the 147,000 Negro voters qualified under the former constitution, only 21,000 were registered and of these less than half had 'paid their poll taxes and qualified.' But, in the words of the *Richmond Planet*, the Negro had 'long since abandoned the field of politics for the field of finance and industrial endeavor.'

Fraternal insurance offered the most lucrative field for the Negro entrepreneur, and in 1890 some 200 companies were operating in this field in Virginia. As deposits multiplied, few of the companies resisted the temptation to enter fields of higher finance, particularly banking. Richmond in 1902 had three Negro banks—W.W.Browne's Savings Bank of the True Reformers, John Mitchell's Mechanics Savings Bank, and Maggie Walker's St.Luke's Penny Savings Bank. Of 25 Negro banks organized in the State but three have survived: the Consolidated Bank and Trust Company (formerly the St.Luke's Penny Savings Bank) of Richmond, the Crown Savings Bank of Newport News, and the Savings Bank of Danville.

Richmond at the beginning of the century was the religious, as well as the economic and political, center of Negro Virginia. James H. Holmes, whose First African Baptist Church had 5,000 members, held the world's record in baptisms—847 converts in a single hour. John Jasper preached the Sixth Mount Zion Baptist Church out of debt with his famous sermon, 'De Sun Do Move.' Throughout the State the church has been the Negro's most successful institution. According to the 1926 Federal religious census, 378,742 Negroes in Virginia were members of religious bodies in that year. Of the 2,261 Negro churches, 1,900 were in rural areas, and 70 per cent of all the church members were in rural sections. The rural church is the common meeting ground for the Negro community, where young and old gather to chat, to pray, and to be inspired by 'that old time religion.'

Although all orthodox sects exist in Virginia, with Baptists and Methodists predominating, numerous 'messiahs' have large followings. The waters of Virginia rivers have 'washed the sins' from many Negroes, whose strong belief is that baptism 'takes' best in open water. At Newport News, Elder Lightfoot Michaux established the Church of God, with mass baptism in the James River as an important part of its ritual. 'Daddy' Grace, dynamic Portuguese 'Bishop,' also has a 'mission' by the James and conducts spectacular baptizings.

The charge that Virginia Negroes put church building ahead of home building is dubious. Whereas only 23.9 per cent of all Negro homes in the United States were owned by their occupants in 1930, in Virginia 43.6 per cent of the Negro homes were owned by those who lived in them. Yet in the low-rent districts of every city thousands of Negro tenants live in rickety tenements and squalid shacks. Near Newport News, Aberdeen Gardens, a housing project sponsored by Hampton Institute and the Farm Security Administration, is a notable example of the attempts to provide for Negroes better homes in more healthful surroundings.

Notwithstanding extensive migration to the cities, farming is still the principal economic activity of the Negro in Virginia. In 1935 the State had a Negro farm population of slightly more than 269,000, and 43,211 of its farms were being operated by 27,662 Negro owners, 37 managers, and 15,512 tenants. While the number of Negro tenant farmers increased by only 364 from 1930 to 1935, the number of owner-operators increased by 3,214 in the same period.

Although various Federal, State, and private agencies have labored to improve conditions in the rural sections, a low standard of living still prevails. A recent study reveals that 50 per cent of all rural families in Virginia and 60 per cent of the Negro rural families in the State have gross incomes of $600 or less, and 25 per cent of the Negro rural families have gross incomes of $259 or less. Such marginal and submarginal populations, according to William E. Garnett of the Virginia Polytechnic Institute, represent a 'human erosion' far more costly than the 'soil erosion which occasions extensive programs.' It is among such groups that health standards are lowest and mortality rates highest. In 1930 the death rate for Negroes in Virginia was 17.8 per thousand as compared with only 10.4 per thousand for whites, while the infant mortality amounted to 11.5 deaths per thousand births for Negroes, and 5.9 deaths per thousand births for whites.

In Virginia, as throughout the South, the relatively heavy concentration of Negroes in the larger cities gives rise to many acute problems. From 15.4 per cent of the total Negro population in 1870, the proportion of Negroes in Virginia cities had increased to 32.8 per cent in 1930. Richmond with 52,988 Negroes and Norfolk with 43,942 have the largest Negro populations.

Life is especially hazardous for Negro youth in the cities. With public parks, playgrounds, and athletic fields 'traditionally prohibited,' Negro children haunt city alleys and dumps. Richmond, Lynchburg, and Norfolk have taken the lead in providing community centers or recreation fields for Negro boys and girls. Since 1910, when Negro reformatories were authorized by the State legislature, the Industrial School for Colored Girls under Janie Porter Barrett and the Hanover Manual Labor School for Colored Boys under S.B.Layton have achieved remarkable results in rehabilitating delinquents.

While the rate of illiteracy among Virginia Negroes has dropped in the decade from 1920 to 1930, it is still far higher than the figure for the State's white citizenry. In 1920, 23.5 per cent of the Negro population and 5.9 per cent of the white population 10 years of age or over were unable to read and write. By 1930 illiteracy had dropped to 19.2 per cent for Negroes and to 4.8 per cent for whites. Of the 162,588 illiterates in Virginia in 1930, more than 50 per cent were Negroes, nearly two-thirds of whom lived in rural sections.

In Virginia, as in the entire South, the children of unskilled workers do not go far in school, and uneducated Negroes find only unskilled occupations. Virginia municipalities universally exclude from public positions all Negroes except teachers. In Richmond, the largest center of Negro population in the State, all street cleaners, garbage collectors, and elevator operators in municipal buildings are white. The State's industry has been traditionally open shop, although in recent years labor union affiliation is growing among both Negro and white workers. Negro school teachers, laundry employees, railway freight workers, truck drivers, motion picture operators, and station and service employees are partially organized in various trade unions. The Hampton Roads port area has 5,000 dock workers who are enrolled in the International Longshoremen's Association, an American Federation of Labor affiliate, with George W. Millner, a Negro of Norfolk, as its international vice-president. The State Federation of Labor, however, preserves segregated unions. Since 1935 thousands of Negro tobacco, fertilizer, peanut, and candy workers have joined unions affiliated with the Congress of Industrial Organizations.

While rural Negroes are migrating to the cities, lack of jobs has in recent years prompted wholesale migration to Northern industrial centers. Whereas the State's total population increased from 2,309,187 in 1920 to 2,421,851 in 1930, the Negro population declined from 690,017 (29.9 per cent of the total) to 650,165 (26.8 per cent of the total). In the 10-year period, 259,317 Negroes left Virginia, while only 72,644 Negroes born elsewhere moved into the State. The ratio of loss of Negro population is greater than that of any other South Atlantic State. Estimates indicate that the decline of Negro population in Virginia will be revealed as even greater when the census figures for 1940 are made available.

Migration has taken Virginia-born Negroes to positions of prominence and responsibility in other States. The presidents of 21 Negro academies and colleges, the editors of five leading Negro newspapers, many prominent Negro lawyers, ministers, and scholars were born or reared in Virginia. Robert R. Moton, Carter G. Woodson, Charles Sidney Gilpin, Leslie Pinckney Hill, William R. Valentine, Charles S. Johnson, Anne Spencer, Eugene Kinckle Jones, Salem Tutt Whitney, and Bill (Bojangles) Robinson are a few Virginia Negroes whose names are widely known. Within the State, achievement is occasionally recognized. William M.

Cooper of Hampton Institute and Lutrelle F. Palmer of the Huntington High School in Newport News were named, in 1938 and 1939 respectively, as distinguished Virginians on the 'honor roll' of the Richmond *Times-Dispatch*; and William H. Moses, Jr., of Hampton Institute, submitted the successful design in a contest for a plan of Virginia's exhibit at the New York World's Fair of 1939.

The lure of the crowd is strong among Virginia Negroes; every city and town has a 'street' that serves as the social and business center of Negro life. Here Negroes from every walk of life congregate to purchase from Negro merchants, to ply their trades, to discuss the latest developments in Negro America, or simply to see who else is abroad. Here race pride is triumphant; drug stores, cafes, barber shops, pool rooms, grocery stores, theaters, beauty parlors, and garages are operated by and for Negroes. To the uninitiated, the crowd is a group of idlers wasting time in meaningless banter. That banter, however, is the Negro's escape from a day of labor in the white man's world. No matter how carefree the outward appearance of Negroes may be, behind their happy dispositions is the imprint of poverty, disease, and suffering—birthmarks of a people living precariously, but of a people wholly Virginian.

Transportation

THE evolution of Virginia's economic and social life is revealed in the story of transportation. The earliest settlers, having built their homes beside bays, rivers, creeks, or inlets, traveled by water. The first roads followed Indian trails and temporarily slaked the thirst of commerce. Then iron highways suddenly shot through productive sections and dominated the scene until the advent of the macadamized road.

During the sixteenth century several navigators cruised along the Atlantic coast and presumably saw the Virginia shore: Verrazzano (1524), Gómez (1525), and Thevet (1556); and Menéndez (1570), who ascended the Potomac River almost to its navigable head. Bartholomew Gosnold, who skirted the Virginia shore in 1602, came again in 1607 bringing some of the first settlers to Jamestown. In the next year came the exploration and mapping of Virginia rivers and the Chesapeake Bay by Captain John Smith; and, as the colonists pushed their shallops and pinnaces up the navigable waterways to barter with the natives for corn, the history of transportation in Virginia began.

In John Rolfe's tobacco garden, planted in 1612, were sown the seeds of Virginia's economic future. By 1620 40,000 pounds of tobacco were shipped to England. As civilization began its slow sweep up the James, York, Rappahannock, and Potomac toward the fall line, vessels from Glasgow, Bristol, and London became as familiar sights as the native craft. Traffic increased, despite such obstacles as the Navigation Act (1660), a tornado that demolished many tobacco barns about 1666, the wanton destruction of boats in rivers by invading Dutch fleets (1667 and 1673), and Bacon's Rebellion (1676). At the dawn of the eighteenth century the population, spread from Tidewater to mountains, numbered between 60,000 and 70,000 persons, including some 6,000 Negroes. On the tobacco leaf had been built a prosperous agricultural community that used water as its medium of transportation. The river barons reached the full tide of success early in the eighteenth century, and the marshes in front of their palatial homes were spanned with wharves that welcomed ships of commerce ready to exchange the luxuries of Europe for a cargo of golden leaf.

For the first century and a half of Virginia's history land transportation in the Tidewater section existed more in theory than in fact. Horses, brought over first in 1610 and intermittently thereafter, multiplied, furnishing the only means by which land trips of any consequence could be undertaken. Yet a few roads developed early. By 1624 Jamestown Island had not only a cartway but two roads—one, subsequently called the 'Old Greate Road,' leading from Back Street of 'New Towne' to the blockhouse at the head of the island, and another that passed along the river side. Communication with other settlements—all on the James River or Accomac shore—was by boat or sloop. In 1633, the year the act was passed for 'Seatinge of the Middle Plantation' (Williamsburg) and two years after the first settlement was established on the York River, the general assembly ordered highways to be laid out 'according as they might seem convenient.' Settlements had begun to spring up in the interior, reached first on horseback over Indian trails and then, later, by carts. As the population increased—by 1652 it was approximately 20,000—and new counties were formed, the parish churches, courthouses, ferries, and ordinaries (taverns) became the focal points for roads that led from crude interplantation lanes.

In 1658 surveyors of roads were appointed, and in 1662 vestries were given the power to 'order out laborers in proportion to the tithables.' These men worked under surveyors ordered to keep the roads 40 feet wide. Nathaniel Bacon in 1676 doubtless used the Iron Bound Road leading from Jamestown to Williamsburg (starting point of an old Indian trail that traversed the peninsula to the Pamunkey River), and Governor Spotswood had a road built to haul crude iron from his furnaces at Germanna to his wharf below Fredericksburg. By 1772 'most families of any note in Williamsburg had a coach, chariot, Berlin or chaise,' according to Hugh Jones, 'and every ordinary person' kept a horse. In 1738 regulations by Alexander Spotswood establishing definite postal routes fostered permanency.

An English traveler in 1746 found that the roads from Yorktown to Williamsburg and Hampton were 'infinitely superior' to most roads in England. Still, most travelers in Tidewater from 1776 to 1782 discovered that the roads were 'not being kept in repair.' As soon as one was in bad order, another was made in a different direction. During wet seasons the roads were 'hopeless seas of mud with archipelagoes of stumps.' Private coaches—Sir William Berkeley possessed one in 1677—soon grew in number and were manufactured in Richmond by 1786, the year in which slow stagecoaches were already lumbering southward from Portsmouth and

Alexandria to Petersburg, and from Richmond to Hampton. These vehicles, covered with mud from top to wheel, rattled along, sometimes overturning, frequently sinking into bogs, and always uncomfortable.

From an Indian trail along the Potomac emerged the Potomac path, along which developed Dumfries, Colchester, and Alexandria. Branching from this road at Cameron Run on Hunting Creek was a road, known as 'the new Church road' in 1742, that extended by Falls Church to Vestal's (now William's) Gap, and then to Winchester. The Ox Road ran southeastward from inland Occoquan. In 1752 Lewis Elzey and others were ordered to open a road 'from Alexandria to Rocky Runn Chappell.' Called the Newgate Road, it became, after 1755, Braddock's Road. The Halifax Road led from Petersburg south; and the Carolina Road was developed, after many changes, from the Shenandoah Hunting Path (extending in the seventeenth century from Conoy Island in the Potomac to Occaneeche Island in the Roanoke), from the Monocacy Trail, and the Iroquois Trail. Starting at Bull Run Mountains, it ran through Louisa County to Norman's Ford on the Rappahannock and then into Prince William and Caroline Counties. Known as the Rogues' Road throughout the last part of the eighteenth century, it finally became little more than a path.

Tobacco was responsible for the development of many of the early roads. The leaves were packed in huge hogsheads fitted with a shaft at each end that allowed the unwieldy container to be rolled along the ground behind an ox or a horse. Recognition of these paths was made by the general assembly in 1712 and 1720. Soon 'rolling roads' leading to 'public warehouses' at markets generally located in Tidewater ports, such as Leedstown and Falmouth, became as much a part of the landscape as the increasing network of ferries. But, withal, water remained the preferred carrier, and boats transported the tobacco from the warehouses at the fall line to the down-river settlements. By the middle of the eighteenth century, when there were some 330 ships and 3,000 sailors in the tobacco trade between Virginia and England, transportation was quickened by pack-horse travel. Moving in single file along the narrow trails called 'tote-roads,' 'pack-roads,' or 'horse-ways,' the horses carried traffic between the older towns and the frontier posts that had suddenly become more numerous. The numerous small agriculturists in the Tidewater area, stifled by the large-scale production of tobacco that low-priced Negro labor had made possible, had begun an exodus to fresher fields. Many went to the vague mountain section that had already unveiled its charms to such explorers as Major (later Major General) Abraham Wood, between 1650 and 1671, and Governor Spotswood in 1716. Up river and over Indian trails flowed the mass of yeomen. As the pioneers trekked westward, extending the transportation system from water across the land, the heads of navigation at the fall line of the principal rivers became cargo transfer points, thus creating Petersburg, Richmond, Fredericksburg, and Alexandria.

In the mountainous sections, trails gradually became roads. In 1760, William Byrd III, leading an expedition against the Cherokee, cut a path through southwestern Virginia. The 'tote-paths,' following usually a well-defined system of primitive traces, widened into crude wagon roads to accommodate the gaily caparisoned and swaying Conestoga freight wagons that had appeared. By 1782 carriages could cross the Blue Ridge by Rock Fish Gap. The war path of the Delaware and Catawba Indians that ran the length of the Shenandoah Valley was known at the beginning of the nineteenth century, when organized migration began, as the Indian Road, a name subsequently discarded for the Wagon Road, then for the Valley Road, and after 1840 for the Valley Turnpike. Along the foothills of the Alleghenies ran Back Road, to the east of which, at an early date, was the Ox Road (later called the Middle Road) that stretched from Harrisonburg to Woodstock. The Wilderness Road, over which so many pioneers trekked to Kentucky, began some miles northeast of Fort Chiswell, crossed the New River at Ingles' Ferry, and continued beyond Abingdon to Block House. Vehicles began to pass over its length only after the legislature made it a wagon road in 1795. On the east side of the Blue Ridge ran a parallel road that led down the Piedmont, a section traversed by such roads from the Tidewater as the Three Chopt (or Three Notched) Road and the River Road, both beginning at the falls of the James and extending by different routes into Albemarle County, terminus likewise of the Mountain Road that began just north of Richmond. From these trunk lines diverged lateral routes, ever pushing into virgin territory and increasing in importance as the land travel changed from north-south to east-west—especially after 1773 when Virginians changed the course of empire westward through Cumberland Gap.

Ferries and bridges were necessarily an early part of Virginia transportation. From Jamestown a ferry crossed the James River at an early date. In 1702, antedating by about 20 years many ferries on the James, York, and Rappahannock Rivers, a ferry line was established between Portsmouth and Norfolk; it exists today as the Portsmouth and Norfolk County Ferry Company. In 1748, 1760, 1764, and almost every year thereafter until the Revolution, the general assembly passed acts authorizing new 'publick ferries' to transport pedestrians, hogsheads of tobacco, livestock, coaches, chariots, wagons, and carts. In the mountainous sections were such early ferries as Castleman's (1764), Snicker's (1766), and Buchanan's (1811). When traffic became heavy, bridges were built. William Byrd crossed bridges in southern Virginia in 1728. In 1752 the general assembly passed an act permitting the Appomattox to be spanned for the first time, and in 1785 Mayo's bridge cast its shadow over the route that Patrick Coutts's ferry had long used between Manchester and Richmond. During the turnpike era—the first decades of the nineteenth century—many covered bridges were built, particularly in the mountains.

In the first half of the nineteenth century Virginia's attempts to encourage water transportation resulted in the construction of canals. During the preceding century, George Washington, recognizing the necessity for commercial routes across the Appalachian range to connect the waters of eastern Virginia with the Ohio River, had urged public developments of both waterways and highways. After the general assembly had passed acts in 1772 for opening the falls of both the James and the 'Potomack' Rivers, the Revolution intervened. The projects, therefore, lapsed and were not carried out until 1784, when two canal companies—the James River and the Potomac—were incorporated.

The James River Company, promoted by such men as George Washington, Edmund Randolph, and John Marshall, opened in 1790 the first commercial canal in the United States, stretching from Richmond to Westham and paralleling the James for seven miles. The Potomac Company's plan of linking by a canal Alexandria and Georgetown to Cumberland at the base of the Alleghenies began to materialize in 1802, when the first section was completed past the falls of the Potomac. Soon the aqueduct, constructed under the supervision of Claude Crozet, spanned the Potomac from Georgetown to the Virginia side. When the canal was finished, some $12,000,000 had been spent by Maryland and Virginia.

After appointing commissioners in 1810 to 'view certain rivers within the Commonwealth' with the idea of developing more water transportation, the general assembly, in 1816, created the Board of Public Works to supervise such transportation enterprises and turned over to this unit a 'Fund for Internal Improvement,' from which the State subscribed to the stock of eight water transportation companies. The Dismal Swamp Canal, though chartered by Virginia and North Carolina in 1787, was not completed until 1828. This canal, which connects Chesapeake Bay with Albemarle Sound, fell into disuse for some time but was reopened from Deep Creek to South Mills, North Carolina, in 1899, and in 1929 was acquired by the Federal Government, which also owns the Albemarle and Chesapeake Canal connecting Elizabeth River with North Landing River.

Production and commerce having increased with the opening of the canal, the James River Company was by 1808 an exceedingly profitable enterprise. But by 1820 the lean years had come and the canal was taken over by the State. In 1835, the canal property and rights were acquired by the James River and Kanawha Canal Company, chartered in 1832 to carry out the original plans and construct the canal to the Ohio waters. By 1840 this company had extended the narrow waterway to Lynchburg; and regular lines of packet or passenger boats, pulled by horses six to eight miles an hour, plied the 156 miles to Richmond.

In 1851 the canal was continued to Buchanan, the limit of its extension. Here the James River and Kanawha Turnpike across the Appalachian range provided access to the Kanawha and Ohio Rivers. Paralleling the James and constructed at a cost of more than $8,000,000, the canal was one of Virginia's most important early public works and the greatest freight and passenger carrier in the State. It was mutilated, however, during the War between the States; almost swept away by the flood of 1877; considered financially worthless in 1879; and, having been sold in 1880 to the Richmond and Allegheny Railroad, was acquired along with that road in 1888 by its competitor, the Chesapeake and Ohio Railway.

As the heavy traffic caused dirt roads to become all but impassable, especially in winter, the necessity for adequate thoroughfares became evident. The result was the turnpike, created by chartered companies that charged a toll for using it. From 1802 to 1818 eight turnpike companies were incorporated to establish roads out of Richmond: Manchester Turnpike (1802) to Falling Creek; Richmond Turnpike (1804) running by the Deep Run Coal Pits to the Three Notched Road at Short Pump; Richmond and Columbia Turnpike to Goochland Courthouse; Brook Turnpike (1812) to Williamson's Tavern (now Solomon's Store); Westham Turnpike (1816) from Richmond to Leonard's Tavern near Westham; Manchester and Petersburg Turnpike (1816) laid out by Claude Crozet; Mechanicsville Turnpike (1817); and the Richmond and Osborne's Turnpike (1818), running to a ferry that crossed the James to Osborne's Wharf. By 1828 the State, from its 'Fund for Internal Improvement,' had subscribed to stock in 12 turnpike companies. In mid-century many miles of hard-surfaced roads were completed, particularly in the mountainous section. One of the most ambitious of these enterprises, a corollary to the James River Canal, was the turnpike constructed in 1830 from Rockfish Gap to Scottsville. The peak of this attempt to hurry traffic over land was reached in 1850 when the road down the Shenandoah Valley was macadamized from Winchester to Staunton. During this same decade appeared many of the planked roads, such as the Jerusalem, Orange, and Boydton.

With the advent of canals and turnpikes came transformation on the water, peacefully content up to the War of 1812 with its sloops and swift sailing packets. Only twice had the supremacy of the sailing vessel been questioned. In 1784 Virginia granted James Rumsey the right to construct and navigate boats 'upon his model' for a period of 10 years in the waters of the State. The year that Rumsey operated successfully his ingenious device on the Potomac (1787), John Fitch obtained the privilege of operating steamboats on Virginia waters for 14 years. These sporadic attempts soon gave way to commercial steamboats on Chesapeake Bay and its tributaries. In 1813 were launched the *Washington* and the *Richmond*, the first running from Washington to Marlboro and the second from Washington to Richmond. The *Eagle* began its round trips between Baltimore and Richmond in 1815, and the *Powhatan* its regular trips between Richmond and Norfolk in 1816. The run between Baltimore and Norfolk was appreciably reduced in time by the *Virginia*, built in 1817, and the *Norfolk*, put in service in 1819, the year the *Washington* extended its run to Norfolk. During the two decades preceding the War between the States, the *Union* ran between Washington and Norfolk; the *Osceola* plied weekly from Baltimore to Norfolk; the *Columbia*, largest boat on the river, ran regularly after 1837 for many years on the Washington-Norfolk-Baltimore route; and the *William Selden* linked Baltimore to Fredericksburg. Between Aquia Creek and Washington ran such early vessels as the *Chesapeake*, *Augusta*, and *Washington*. The boats of the Baltimore Steam Packet Company (the Old Bay Line) organized in 1840, running between Norfolk and Baltimore, competed with the iron ship *Philadelphia*, which ran between Norfolk and Seaford, Delaware. In 1852 the Merchants and Miners Transportation Company was organized. In 1859, the *Mount Vernon*, of 700 tons, opened a regular service between New York and Washington. When war came, several of the substantial Potomac ships were impressed by the Federal Government. Between 1869 and 1873 the Plant Line operated the *Lady of the Lake* and the *Jane Mosely* between Washington and Norfolk. In 1874 the boats of the Chesapeake Steamship Company connected Baltimore with West Point, Virginia, and between 1871 and 1891 the Potomac Steamboat Company operated the *George Leary* and the *Excelsior* between Washington and Norfolk. A continuation of this company is the Norfolk and Washington Steamboat Company, chartered in 1890. The boats of this line, the Old Bay Line, the Chesapeake Steamship Company, and the Merchants and Miners Transportation Company still plow the Bay, its tidal rivers and numerous estuaries served now, as formerly, by an adequate system of freight boats, foremost among which are those of the Buxton Lines, Inc., and the Eastern Steamship Lines, the York River Line, and the Philadelphia and Norfolk Steamship Company.

Virginia's policy of subscribing to the capital stock of companies engaged in public transportation had its most beneficial effect between 1828 and 1861 when the railway came to deliver traffic from the semiparalysis of coach and canal. Because of the great need to connect hinterland with Tidewater, these swift land carriers were built rapidly, lacing through the productive areas and stimulating commerce. The confirmation by the assembly, on March 8, 1827, of the charter granted by Maryland to the Baltimore and Ohio Railroad Company was Virginia's first official railroad record, but that road did not begin operating in Virginia until after 1839. In 1831, when there were little more than 100 miles of railroad completed in the United States, the horse-drawn Chesterfield Railroad, chartered three years earlier, was opened to haul coal from mines in Chesterfield County to Richmond. The charter of this pioneer company, which was operated throughout its existence by horsepower, antedated by only two years the charter of the Petersburg Railroad Company, the first steam railroad to operate in the State. Its terminus, Weldon, North Carolina, became also the terminus of the Portsmouth and Roanoke Railroad, chartered in 1832, completed in 1837, and now the oldest unit in the Seaboard Air Line Railway Company. In 1832 a charter was granted also to the Winchester and Potomac Railroad Company, which completed its tracks through the fertile Shenandoah Valley to the Potomac River at Harpers Ferry in 1836. In 1848 it was purchased by the Baltimore and Ohio Railroad. The Richmond, Fredericksburg and Potomac Railroad Company, chartered in 1834, developed its route by a series of progressions and did not reach Washington until after the War between the States. In 1837 the tracks were extended to Fredericksburg, where passengers took a coach to Marlboro Point on Potomac Creek and thence traveled to Washington by steamboat. In 1872 the line was extended to join the Alexandria and Washington Railroad and thus form an all-rail route from Richmond to Washington. Among other carriers of this early epoch were the Richmond and Petersburg Railroad Company and the Louisa Railroad Company, both chartered in 1836. The tracks of the Louisa Railroad (oldest unit in the present Chesapeake and Ohio Railway system) opened the following year to Frederick Hall. The company announced in unabashed manner an 'Unrivalled Line to Charlottesville,

Staunton and the Virginia Springs,' although the railroad stopped short of Charlottesville by 44 miles and passengers were conveyed the rest of the way by coach. The South Side Railroad Company, chartered in 1846, was completed in 1854 between Petersburg and Lynchburg. Fostered by the State, the Blue Ridge Railroad Company was chartered in 1849. Under the direction of Claude Crozet the tracks, passing through several long tunnels, were completed in 1858 from Blair Park to Waynesboro. The mountainous and isolated southwest was opened up in 1856 by the Virginia and Tennessee Railroad, a company chartered in 1849; while, in the opposite side of the State, the Norfolk and Petersburg Railroad by 1858 was hurrying traffic to the sea.

In 1861 Virginia's investments in 'Public Works' ceased. The State had purchased a total of $48,000,000 worth of stock in turnpike, toll bridge, canal, and water and rail transportation. During the war the railroads, operating 1,290 miles of track, were the most sought-after prize of the contending armies. The important Baltimore and Ohio lines, comprising two-thirds of Virginia's mileage and controlled by Union sympathizers, became a Federal bulwark. The military requirements of the Confederacy fell heavily on the remaining roads, particularly on the Petersburg and Weldon, the Richmond and Danville, and the Virginia Central—so important as arteries of supply for Lee's army that about them centered Federal offensive and Confederate defensive movements.

Following the war numerous railroads began to consolidate into the great 'through lines' that gird the State today. In 1885 the 32 railroads in Virginia had an aggregate length of 2,430 miles. Mileage increased steadily until 1915, and then dropped when 10 short systems disappeared. The present group of railroads, owning some 7,242 miles of track, includes 18 separate companies ranging from the Nelson and Albemarle Railroad with 18 miles of track to those with an elaborate system. The Norfolk and Western Railway is a vast system that started with the merger in 1870 of three railroads extending from Norfolk to Bristol. The Baltimore and Ohio Railroad consists in Virginia of the former Valley Railroad, chartered in 1866, and the Winchester and Potomac Railroad. The Seaboard Air Line Railway had its beginning in 1900 with the purchase of the Virginia and Carolina Railroad. The Southern Railway, incorporated in 1894, took over the lines of the Richmond and Danville Railroad, and in 1899 those of the Atlantic and Danville Railway. The Atlantic Coast Line Railroad is a continuation of the Richmond and Petersburg Railroad, chartered in 1836. The Chesapeake and Ohio Railroad has developed since 1869 from the Virginia Central Railroad and the unfinished Covington and Ohio

Railroad. The Virginian Railway is a continuation of the Tidewater Railway, chartered in 1904. The Norfolk Southern Railroad developed from the Elizabeth City and Norfolk Railroad, incorporated in 1875. The tracks of the hardy Richmond, Fredericksburg and Potomac Railroad are used by trains of the Seaboard Air Line Railway and the Atlantic Coast Line Railroad.

At the beginning of the twentieth century Virginia's roads were poor. In 1919, however, the State highway commission took over road construction, and now an excellent primary system of 9,250 miles includes 24 United States highways, which form the principal interstate traffic arteries, and a secondary system of 37,000 miles, which reaches even the remotest parts of the State. With the improvement of the State highways since 1923 transportation by public motor vehicles has developed rapidly. The early short lines have been extended and consolidated into great corporations. While they were started to furnish transportation in sections where other facilities were lacking, the great preponderance of motor common carrier operations now closely parallel the railroads and have become their most formidable competitors. Since 1923 the State corporation commission has issued 384 certificates to freight common carriers and 1,112 certificates to common carriers of passengers, chief among which are the Greyhound System, Peninsula Transit Corporation, Norfolk Southern Bus Corporation, and Virginia Stage Lines, Inc.

The ports surrounding Hampton Roads, termini for eight railroads, handle a vast tonnage of export, import, coastwise, and intercoastal freight passing through the Virginia Capes not only on foreign ships but also on the five regular steamship lines that use the numerous docks and coal piers. Deep water terminal docks on the James near Richmond are in the process of construction. Steam ferries link the cities of Hampton Roads and extend the service to Cape Charles; other ferries connect the Potomac, James, and Rappahannock Rivers, making 13 in the State. Across the mouth of the James River the Newport News-James River Bridge, finished in 1928 at a cost of $5,500,000, is the 'world's longest all-over-water bridge'; and over the Rappahannock River is the long Downing Bridge, finished in 1927, that has opened up the isolated Northern Neck section.

Commercial aviation, the last phase of the transportation scene, has developed slowly in Virginia since the Eastern Air Transport, Inc. established in 1928 a pioneer mail line from New York to Atlanta via Richmond. Its passenger service was begun August 18, 1930. By 1936 the planes of two companies, flying 3,640 air miles daily over Virginia, served four cities in the State in addition to the Washington Airport, on the Virginia bank of the Potomac. Today, by private, municipal, and Federal funds, 36 airports have been licensed, emergency landing fields provided, and air mileage has been lighted.

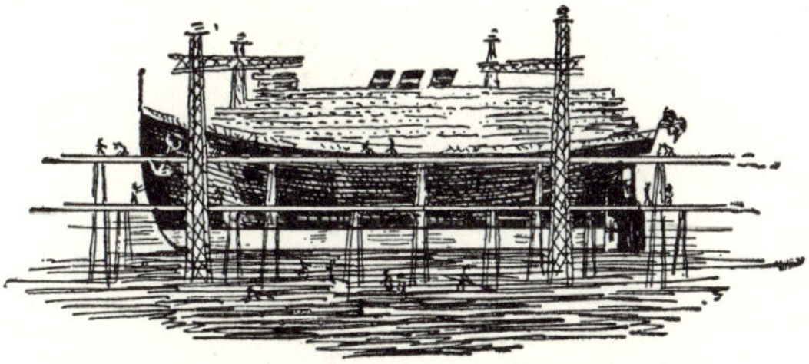

Agriculture

THE predominant interests and character of Virginia have been agricultural ever since its establishment. In 1930, of a total population of 2,421,851, 67.6 per cent was rural and 39.3 per cent actually resided on farms. There were in that year 170,610 farms in Virginia, comprising 64.9 per cent of the total land area of the State. The total value of all property on these farms was $992,824,691, and the gross income from crops and livestock combined amounted to $154,380,000. The prosperity and welfare of Virginia are mainly based upon the soundness of its agricultural development.

The idea of founding an agricultural civilization in the New World did not bulk large in the minds of the members of the London Company, which sponsored the settlement of Virginia. The primary interest of these promoters was to discover immediately in the virgin areas great supplies of pitch, tar, soap ashes, resin, flax, cordage, iron, copper, glass, and timber for shipbuilding and other purposes. For many years prior to the permanent settlement at Jamestown, the mother country had been forced, through its own diminishing supply, to import these commodities from such uncertain sources as Germany, Poland, Russia, and Sweden. Although the first efforts of the early colonists were devoted to finding and delivering the needed commodities, it soon became manifest to leaders like Captain John Smith that the labor supply in the struggling colony was inadequate for such a task. In order to survive, the adventurers had to concentrate their energies upon securing food and upon building houses and forts. Thus, whether they came into the New World by way of Jamestown, Virginia, or Plymouth, Massachusetts, or Charles Town, South Carolina, farming was their occupation.

To a much larger degree than is commonly recognized, the colonists were beneficiaries of the Indians. Of more lasting value than the actual supplies they obtained were the agricultural plants and practices they adopted from the natives. Experiments enabled them eventually to acclimate many European plants, but at the outset they depended upon such native crops as Indian corn, potatoes, and tobacco, the yields of which on virgin soil were quick and certain.

With the arrival of more colonists from the Old World, the farm clearings increased in extent, and the red man was driven farther and farther westward. No epic in all history is more colorful than this subduing of a great wilderness to the purposes of civilized man. European livestock was introduced, principally the English breeds, and in the course of a few years the new settlers became independent as far as the necessities of life were concerned.

Two economic characteristics stand out prominently in colonial agriculture—its extensive character, with a thin application of labor and capital on a large area of land, and its self-sufficiency. While not completely isolated from commercial relations with Europe, the colonists generally produced for home consumption rather than for sale. Self-sufficiency was a most important feature of the early American farm. By and large, only luxuries were bought and the only buyers were the well-to-do. Necessary clothing was produced at home. The flax, the wool, and later the cotton were carded, spun, and woven by slaves or members of the farmer's family, and from home-grown products. Leather came from cattle on the place and was fashioned by a shoemaker on each plantation. Homemade implements usually sufficed for tilling the fields and for carpentry. The farm provided a bountiful food supply. Practically the only articles of diet it did not yield were salt, molasses, rum, tea, and coffee. Salt was a necessity, and rum a customary and popular beverage; both were important in the internal trade of the times. Tea and coffee were little used by farmers in the pre-Revolutionary days, though shortly after the Revolution their use was widely extended.

The typical Virginia farmer of colonial days did not own a large mansion and numerous slaves. Admiral Chadwick in *Causes of the Civil War* estimates that of the 52,128 Virginia slaveholders in 1860 one-third held but one or two slaves, half held one to four, and only 114 persons owned as many as 100 each. T.J.Wertenbaker's study of rent rolls in a number of Tidewater counties indicates clearly that most of the colonial farmers were yeomen and that many of these rose from the estate of indentured servants. Such findings have a disturbing effect upon widely current tradition, but they in no wise obscure the stability and worth of the early farming classes. Nothing can detract from the luster of the civilization achieved by the old Virginia planter. Thomas Nelson Page, in his collection of essays entitled *The Old South*, wrote:

> It has been assumed by the outside world that our people lived a life of idleness and ease, a kind of hammock-swing, 'sherbet-sipping' existence, fanned by slaves, and in their pride, served on bended knees . . . Any master who had a successfully con-

> ducted plantation was sure to have given it his personal supervision with an unremitting attention which would not have failed to secure success in any other calling. If this was true of the master, it was much more so of the mistress.

The early manor was based on the self-sufficient principle that characterized all the farms of Virginia. Negroes were taught trades as blacksmiths, carpenters, masons, millers, shoemakers, weavers, and spinners. But when the wolf of material want had been driven from the door, the colonists looked for some agricultural product that could be exchanged for the luxuries of the Old World, and they found it in tobacco. John Rolfe, husband of Pocahontas, is reputed to have been the first to experiment with the cultivation of tobacco. The plant grown by the Indians was of inferior quality and could not compete with the West Indian product. By 1614, however, it is said that Rolfe had succeeded in growing a tobacco leaf as 'strong, sweet and pleasant as any under the sun.'

In England the demand for tobacco was increasing. The London Company, disappointed in its hope of obtaining iron, naval stores, and the like from the colony, encouraged the growth of tobacco. A first shipment was made in 1619—singularly enough, the year in which a Dutch privateer brought the first cargo of slaves to this country. From the outset tobacco was the leading article of export from the New World. During the Colonial period it constituted between one-fourth and one-half of the total export of North America. In 1775 the tobacco sent abroad was valued at about $4,000,000. Although this exchange crop brought much wealth and luxury to Virginia planters, the methods of agriculture that it involved rapidly impoverished the soil, and after the middle of the eighteenth century many farmers in the Tidewater region began to look toward the virgin lands of the Middle West.

As late as 1830 virtually all farm work other than plowing and harrowing was being done by hand; but by 1866, except in the more backward portions of the country, most of this work was being performed by horse-driven machinery. Thomas Jefferson contributed to the perfection of the moldboard of the plow, and by 1834 Cyrus McCormick of Rockbridge County, Virginia, had developed his reaping machine. Canals, steamboats, and railroads, supplemented later by automobiles and trucks, revolutionized transportation and brought commercial markets closer to the farmer. While Virginia farmers still cling to a greater extent than farmers in most other States to a self-sufficing type of economy, their agriculture is now chiefly commercial, varied in its total output, but with specialization of crops or livestock in each region.

Cotton is commonly regarded as the plant that most widely absorbs the energies of Southern farm folks. The term 'cotton economy' has become almost synonymous with the one-crop system of the South and its numerous attendant evils of high tenancy ratios, low living standards, and impoverished soils. 'Tobacco economy' closely parallels that of cotton. But though extensive areas in Virginia today are devoted to the raising of tobacco and limited areas are planted to cotton, the physical factors of climate, topography, and soils have operated to insure here such a diversity of agricultural interests as prevails in few other States. As a result, the farmers of Virginia have not all suffered in the same manner or degree as those elsewhere during the recent years of agricultural depression.

Virginia is divided into five major agricultural divisions that are not identical with the natural divisions of the State. The soils of the Tidewater region are mainly alluvial in nature, and this area yields the corn, wheat, alfalfa, clover, and grasses of general farming. Proximity to the Atlantic Ocean, with its modifying effect upon temperatures and assurance of adequate rainfall, and the presence of light sandy loams make this section suited to the efficient and economic production of truck crops on a large scale. The eastern shore counties of Accomac and Northampton are among the largest potato-producing counties in the United States. Because of its favorable geographical situation, Virginia is able to place its vegetables in Northern markets after the peak season is over in the Carolinas and before New Jersey and Long Island produce has matured. The Tidewater division is the principal peanut-growing region of the State, and Virginia ranks high among the leading States in the production of this commodity. Some cotton is grown in a few Tidewater counties.

Middle Virginia is one of the best general farming sections of the State. Its varied soils permit of a wide diversification in crops. Corn, tobacco, wheat, hay, and oats are the principal products; but truck crops, legumes, and fruits also thrive here. A large part of the tobacco produced in the Old Dominion is grown in the southern portion of middle Virginia. This division of the State is well adapted to livestock because of a grazing season from nine to ten months long; dairying flourishes, particularly in the northern part, which is accessible to Washington and other eastern markets.

In Piedmont Virginia the soils are generally underlain with red clay, and, with proper rotation of crops and appropriate fertilizers, can be brought to a high state of productivity. There is much general farming in this region, and both soil and climate make the Virginia Piedmont one of the best fruit-growing sections in the world. Here the Albemarle pippin has its home, and winesaps and other standard varieties of apples are extensively grown, along with peaches, pears, plums, and grapes.

The Valley of Virginia is made up of fertile limestone soils, among the best to be found anywhere. Wheat is grown extensively in this area. So characteristic is this crop that during the War between the States the Shenandoah Valley was known as the Granary of the Confederacy. Bluegrass flourishes here and provides pasturage for livestock. Here, also, conditions are ideal for apple growing, and many parts of the valley are becoming vast apple orchards, producing fruit of exceptionally fine quality.

The altitude of Appalachia or southwest Virginia varies from 1,000 to 3,000 feet or more; the region is traversed by ranges of the Alleghenies. Much of the soil of this section, enriched by limestone, produces bluegrass for grazing, and cattle constitutes a leading resource of the region. General farming and truck gardening are also important in this area. Cabbages and late potatoes figure prominently among the products. Burley tobacco is extensively grown in a few southwestern counties.

The estimated gross income from farm production in Virginia in 1935 (the latest year for which complete estimates are available) was $162,008,000. Of this total $84,080,000 was derived from crops of various sorts, and $77,928,000 from livestock and livestock products. The principal crops in terms of 'farm value' (obtained by multiplying quantities produced by average selling prices) were: corn, $29,787,000; tobacco, $18,765,000; hay, $12,667,000; apples, $11,686,000; wheat, $7,196,000; Irish or white potatoes, $5,443,000; peanuts, $4,939,000. The products of farm gardens were valued at $9,100,000, and the products of forests on farm land at $6,661,000. Truck crops had a farm value of $5,550,000. Cotton and cottonseed yielded only $1,950,000—less than the sweet potato yield of $2,466,000 and the miscellaneous grain yield of $2,041,000. In the category of livestock and livestock products, the principal items were: milk, $28,295,000; hogs, $13,748,000; eggs, $13,494,000; and poultry, $9,073,000. In the production of tobacco Virginia ranked next to North Carolina and Kentucky, and in apples next to Washington and New York.

In 1920 the farm population of Virginia comprised 1,064,417 persons, or 46.1 per cent of the total population. But by 1930, as a result of the marked urban trend all over the United States, the number had dropped to 950,757, or 39.3 per cent of the total population in that year. The economic depression of recent years has operated to check this downward tendency, and in 1935 the farm population was 1,053,469—a gain of 102,712 for the five-year period.

In 1935, 17,645,000 acres, or 68.5 per cent of Virginia's total land area, consisted of land in farms. Of such farm land, about 8,000,000 acres were available for crops and about 3,900,000 acres were under cultivation. The total number of farms was 197,632, representing a combined value for land and buildings of $593,855,000, an average per farm of approximately $3,000. While the average value of land and buildings per acre was $51.16 in 1930, under the influence of the depression this figure had declined to $33.66 by 1935.

During the 75 years from 1850 to 1925 the average acreage per farm in Virginia decreased from 340 to 88.8. By 1930 the average had risen a little, to 98.1; but a declining tendency was again manifest in the 1935 figure of 89.3. Of the 197,632 farms in 1935, 140,618 or considerably more than two-thirds contained fewer than 100 acres each, and 52,585 contained fewer than 20 acres each. Those containing 500 acres or more numbered only 3,306, and only 691 contained 1,000 acres or more.

Of those who in 1935 were operating Virginia's 197,632 farms, 58,386 or 29.5 per cent were tenants on the land they cultivated, and of such tenant farmers 42,874 or 73.4 per cent were white and 15,512 or 26.6 per cent were Negroes. The ratio of tenants to owners in 1935 was virtually the same as in 1880, when the first census of farm tenancy was taken. Among all the Southern States, only Florida, West Virginia, and Maryland have a lower tenancy ratio, and all others except Florida show a substantial increase in tenancy since 1880.

The lowest percentage of tenancy recorded in the State since 1880 was in 1925, when tenant farmers were cultivating 25.2 per cent of all farms and 19.7 per cent of all land in farms. In 1930 the corresponding percentages were 28.1 and 22.9; while by 1935 they had increased to 29.5 and 25. The increase since 1930 has been chiefly among white tenants and in the mountain areas. Of the Tidewater counties, where tenancy ratios are highest, several have recorded decreases. Nevertheless, in some counties of Virginia half or more of all the farms were being operated by tenants in 1935.

The relative economic status of owner and tenant farmers is indicated to some degree by the facts that, in 1930, 21.6 per cent of the owners but only 7.2 per cent of the tenants had telephones; 9.3 per cent of the owners but only 2.7 per cent of the tenants had electric lights; and 10.8 per cent of the owners but only 3.4 per cent of the tenants had water piped into their dwellings.

While the total farm mortgage debt in Virginia increased from $24,000,000 in 1910 to $75,128,000 in 1935, the latter sum represented only about 12.7 per cent of the total value of farm land and buildings in the State—

$593,855,000. Of Virginia's 197,632 farms in 1935, 43,451 or 22 per cent of the total were mortgaged. Virginia's percentage of mortgaged farms was the lowest of any State in the Union in 1935, with the exception of West Virginia with 16.5 per cent and New Mexico with 19.9 per cent. In that year also Virginia had next to the lowest farm real estate tax per $100 of true value among all the 48 states, the rate being 70¢ as against a National average of $1.14.

In common with many other States, particularly those in the South, Virginia confronts a serious problem in the matter of soil conservation. Historians have shown that soil exhaustion was an important factor a century or more ago in the extensive migration from the rural areas of Virginia to other States in the West and farther south. The wasteful practices of a frontier civilization, especially in the extensive and continuous growing of tobacco, led to impoverishment of the soil over wide areas, so that one of the major agricultural problems of the State is that of rehabilitating worn-out lands. While the gravity of the problem has long been recognized and measures have been advocated for its amelioration within the State, particular focus has been brought to bear on the matter in recent years by the Soil Conservation Service of the Federal Government. A Nation-wide erosion survey was made in the fall of 1934, and the situation was found to be so serious that in 1937 more than 400,000 acres of farm lands were included in the co-operative projects of Virginia farmers with the Soil Conservation Service. The principal areas concerned are near Danville, Lynchburg, and Charlottesville, and demonstrations are being made here of an eleven-point erosion control program designed to check wasteful processes that lead to soil devastation and to restore the fertility of depleted soil, not only in the demonstration areas but throughout the State.

A notable force in the agricultural development of the State has been the Virginia Polytechnic Institute at Blacksburg. Through its farm and home demonstration work and its agricultural experiment stations, it has strongly influenced sound agricultural practices in Virginia. The State Department of Agriculture and Immigration has also functioned for many years as a regulatory and informational agency, with great benefit to Virginia agriculture. In co-operation with the United States Department of Agriculture, it maintains a crop reporting service, which collects and distributes statistical material of indispensable value to farmers of the State. Three National farm organizations, the Grange, the Farm Bureau, and the Farmers' Union, operate helpfully in Virginia; and in addition, there are several organizations devoted to various specialized interests, such as horticulture and dairying.

During more than 300 years of agriculture in Virginia, significant changes have occurred. The outstanding single trend has been away from a self-sufficing type of agriculture to that of a more commercial kind. The introduction of heavy machinery into farming, together with improved transportation, give a comparative advantage to western farmers in wheat, corn, and hogs; and the rapid increase of population in eastern metropolitan areas is stimulating in Virginia, as elsewhere in the East, the production of such bulky and perishable agricultural products as milk, vegetables, and fruits. With less than half of its available crop land actually used for crops in 1934, the State's fullest agricultural development still lies far in the future.

Industry, Commerce, and Labor

INDUSTRY in Virginia had its beginning in 1608 with the establishment of a glass factory at Jamestown. The next year settlers were producing not only glass ornaments for the Indian trade but also nets and seines, pitch, tar, and soap ashes. By 1609 artisans were turning out timber products of various sorts, and in 1611 the colonists began the manufacture of bricks. Though John Rolfe's introduction of tobacco culture in 1612 retarded industrial development, the London Company sent to Virginia in 1619 workmen skilled in many crafts and 'out of Sussex about forty; all framed to Iron-workes.' At Falling Creek that year a foundry was established that achieved 'a very great forwardness' before all its workers were killed in 1622 by the Indians.

Shipbuilding, off to a creditable start soon thereafter, was interrupted by several Navigation Acts passed by a jealous England. Salt, manufactured on the eastern shore as early as 1620, was being exported to Massachusetts by 1633. Silk worm culture and the making of textiles had an early beginning; and basic necessities were soon produced in all settlements. English statutes in restraint of trade, however, and the evolution of plantation rather than community economy combined to curb industrial progress in Virginia. The small farmer instituted a subsistence program in the production of clothes, food, and implements; and the large planter exchanged his tobacco for imported luxuries.

Nevertheless, in the later years of the seventeenth century Virginians had established several flour and grist mills that served areas beyond their immediate neighborhoods. In 1692, under the encouragement of Governor Andros, weaving and fulling mills began operation.

Virginia's first industrial community sprang up around Governor Alexander Spotswood's foundry, established at Germanna in 1715. Soon other iron works were flourishing in the Tidewater and the land beyond the mountains. During the Revolution arms and ammunition were manufactured in Virginia, and in 1817 the Bellona Arsenal, which had been founded near Richmond in 1810, began to supply ordnance for the Federal Government.

For 50 years after the Revolution, however, the industrial graph of

Virginia shows no upward trend. During this period many Virginians entertained strong prejudices against factories or corporations of any kind. They preferred the plantation and the freedom of farm life to the factory and its 'accompanying evils.' Freeholder and freeman were synonymous to the liberty-loving Virginian, and it was thought that diversion of people to manufactures would undermine her civil institutions. Factory employees were thought to lack the economic independence, the moral fiber, and the physical aggressiveness required to defend political liberty.

Between 1820 and 1840 the attitude in Virginia toward factories became more friendly. In 1827 the legislature was asked to encourage cotton manufacture and to ascertain whether Negro labor could be employed in that industry. One year later the *Petersburg Virginian* published an essay favoring the establishment of a cotton factory in Petersburg. In 1836 two cotton mills, with 400 spindles, 170 looms, a machine shop, and a sizing house, were erected at Appomattox. In encouraging the development of cotton manufacturing in Virginia during that early period, the advocates of factories emphasized the advantages of a cheap labor supply. Figures exist showing that a man's wage was $2.75 per week in Virginia, while it was $7 in Massachusetts; that a woman's wage was $1.58 per week in Virginia, while it was $2.60 in New Hampshire. By 1839 there were three cotton mills in the State, with numbers of spindles ranging from 5,000 to 25,000, and five having 5,000 spindles or fewer.

During the War between the States several new factories were built hastily to meet the needs of the Confederacy. By 1863 there were 66 tanneries, 16 spinning mills, 14 flour mills, 5 iron works, 9 coal mines, 9 salt works, and 1 paper mill operating in Virginia. Many of these factories were destroyed before the close of the war.

After the war, Virginia, like the rest of the South, had to pass through a period of economic reconstruction. Conditions had improved greatly, however, by 1880, when the volume of industry in Virginia was greater than ever before. Richmond had resumed its position as an important flour-milling center. Iron smelting, cotton manufacture, tanning and leather-making, tobacco processing, and other forms of manufacture were making real progress. During this period the State was already being affected by millowners' fruitful migration southward in search of cheap labor.

Industrial development in Virginia has been pronounced since 1900. Although the State is still classified as agricultural, a large proportion of its people is supported by industrial wages. In 1937 its manufacturing industries employed 132,643 wage earners, as compared with 66,233 in 1899.

During the same period the total annual wages paid to industrial workers increased from $20,273,889 to $112,773,796; the annual value of manufactured products increased from $108,644,150 to $908,222,316. The primary horsepower installed in Virginia manufactures increased from 136,696 in 1899 to 646,251 in 1929.

A rich supply of raw materials, adequate fuel and water-power resources, a mild climate, a plentiful supply of labor, and good transportation facilities have helped to attract new industries. At present industries are more diversified in Virginia than in any other Southern State. No single type is predominant, and this variety promotes stability in employment and wages. The recent tendency to decentralize manufactories has also helped Virginia, since several outstanding Northern industries have established branches in the State.

Most of the factories in Virginia produce consumer goods, including food products, shoes, clothing, hosiery, rayon, silk goods, cotton goods, and tobacco products. In 1929 approximately 56 per cent of Virginia's industrial workers were employed in the production of consumer goods, as compared with 47 per cent for the country as a whole. According to the Virginia Department of Labor and Industry, the increase in employment in the State since 1932 has resulted chiefly from the development of consumer-goods industries, which employed 65 per cent of Virginia's industrial workers in 1937. Almost two-thirds of the wage earners added to industrial pay rolls since 1932 have been employed in consumer-goods industries. The predominance of light over heavy industries in Virginia is due largely to the character of natural resources that include neither iron ore nor types of coal suitable for smelting and to the character of the available labor, offering a larger supply of semiskilled and unskilled workers than of skilled.

On the basis of the value of the product, the most important industry in Virginia is tobacco, including the manufacture of cigarettes, cigars, pipe and plug tobacco, and snuff, with cigarettes and cigars well in the lead. In the production of cigarettes Virginia is second only to North Carolina, having produced about 53,000,000,000 in the year ending July 1937—more than one-fourth of the National output. This manufacture is concentrated in Richmond, although there are a few factories elsewhere. In 1937 this industry, with a product in Virginia valued at $279,329,749, employed nearly 5,000 workers earning an aggregate wage of $5,092,146. Of the total output of Virginia industry in 1937, valued at $908,222,316, the tobacco industry as a whole accounted for $303,381,676 or 33.4 per cent. The value added by manufacture was $72,019,292 or 21.4 per cent of the value added to the product of all Virginia industry. Nearly 9,000 workers were engaged in the tobacco industry and were paid $8,743,377 in wages in 1937. These figures contrast sharply with those for 1909, when 7,882 workers were paid $2,162,000 by the tobacco industry in Virginia, and the product was valued at $25,385,000. The growth of Virginia, and Richmond in particular, as a center of tobacco manufacture has been due in large part to the proximity of an ample supply of semiskilled labor to the source of the raw material—the tobacco fields. Policies of the State government, especially favorable to local industry in regard to taxation, have been an important factor.

The textile industry made considerable progress during the first quarter of the present century. While Virginia has most of the advantages for textile manufacture enjoyed by other Southern States, the industry has not developed here too rapidly or as much out of proportion to other industries as in some other areas. The number of workers employed by this industry rose from 9 per cent of all industrial wage earners in Virginia in 1909 to 22 per cent in 1935. In 1937 there were more than 130 textile mills in Virginia. These included 10 cotton mills, 29 knitting mills, 17 woolen mills, 17 silk mills, 3 jute mills, and 3 dyeing and finishing plants. Employment in men's clothing factories increased 286 per cent from 1909 to 1929, and 54 per cent more by 1935; silk and rayon manufacture, exclusive of rayon yarn, increased 175 per cent and 69 per cent during the same periods; and knit goods 82 per cent and 29 per cent.

The manufacture of furniture has made rapid progress in Virginia in the past 30 years. Among the Southern States the Old Dominion is now second only to North Carolina in furniture production. Employment in this industry increased 759 per cent between 1909, when it accounted for only 1 per cent of the State total, and 1937, when it accounted for nearly 7 per cent. The United States Census of Manufactures for 1937 listed 49 furniture plants in Virginia, employing 8,504 workers, paying annually wages of $6,601,638, and turning out products valued at $30,016,087.

Though not new in Virginia, the chemical industry has recently taken on new vitality. The manufacture of fertilizers has long been considerable in Virginia. In recent years, however, it has increased in importance because of a greater demand. In 1937, the 49 plants listed by the United States census employed 2,460 wage earners, paid annually wages amounting to $1,474,587, and manufactured products valued at $20,495,097. Chemical factories in Virginia produce, in addition to fertilizers, soda ash, caustic soda, bicarbonate of soda, cellulose, rayon, fixed nitrogen, and a number of heavy chemicals. The plant of the Solvay Process Company of

Hopewell, successor to the Atmospheric Nitrogen Corporation, is said to be the largest nitrogen plant in the world.

In a brief period the manufacture of rayon yarn has become an important factor in the State's industrial development. Virginia mills producing rayon and allied products employed 10,637 workers in 1937, paid annual wages of $12,999,444, and produced goods with a total annual value of $55,897,047. Among the factors that have brought about the rapid expansion of the rayon industry in Virginia have been a water supply with a low dissolved iron content and a none too high priced labor supply. The fact that one large company, when its employees struck for better working conditions, closed its plant permanently and moved its machinery to South America indicates the importance placed upon docile labor.

The development of transportation facilities in Virginia has been responsible for the growth here of industries producing and repairing transportation equipment. In 1937 railroad repair shops in Virginia gave employment to more than 9,000 workers and paid total wages of more than $13,500,000. Shipbuilding, another important Virginia industry, employed in 1937 about 11,000 workers, paid an annual wage bill of about $20,000,000, and turned out products valued at almost $41,000,000. This industry—both in private hands and in the Norfolk Navy Yard—is concentrated in the Hampton Roads area, having been attracted here largely by the commerce and deepwater facility of this great port.

Virginia has also a large number of other industries of importance. Food products of various kinds, including both fish and vegetable canneries; paper and printing; leather and its products; and machinery, contribute to the State's income. In addition, much capital is invested in the mineral industries, chief among which are the mining and processing of coal, clay, limestone, and sand and gravel. Most of the titanium produced in North America comes from Virginia; and the State is the largest producer of soapstone. Cement manufacture is also important. The annual valuation of the raw materials mined and quarried ranges in normal years from $35,000,000 to $50,000,000. Between 300 and 400 different mines and quarries are in operation from year to year.

Virginia has maintained a happy balance between industry and agriculture. Because its industries are diversified, stability of employment is fostered, and workers are given some freedom in selecting a trade. Diversification, moreover, has its advantages in times of general business depression, since during such periods all industries are not affected alike.

Virginia has been more fortunate than most other Southern States, however, in that several of the industries that have located within its boundaries have been in the high-wage class. Many lowest-wage industries have passed over Virginia because more favorable conditions for their operations could be found farther southward. Nevertheless, a considerable number of low-wage industries have come to the State. This situation is fostered and encouraged by the offer by many localities of free factory sites, tax exemptions for a number of years, free rent, and other subsidies. Many of the firms accepting these offers are marginal firms, which seek to prolong their existence by low production costs. Most of them employ a large proportion of women workers and seek to take advantage of the low labor standards that can be found in Virginia. Such concerns have been found to be an economic and social liability to the State. It is now generally recognized that permanent industrial progress in Virginia can be secured only through the encouragement of industries that can offer continuous employment and that can afford to pay such wages as will enable workers to enjoy a decent standard of living.

COMMERCE

Since early Colonial times commerce has played an important part in the economic development of Virginia. For a long time after the first settlers reached Virginia, the tidal waterways and rivers afforded the most satisfactory means of transportation in the eastern part of the colony. English ships, loaded with manufactures of various kinds, visited the wharves of the many plantations along the rivers to exchange their wares for Virginia's chief product, tobacco.

These waters are still used by bay and river vessels, but their traffic is small in comparison with the rail traffic in the State. Virginia's real commercial development has been to a large degree the result of the railroad, which made possible connection of Tidewater ports with the regions west of the mountains.

Much of Virginia's foreign and domestic trade passes through the ports of Hampton Roads. Eight trunk-line railroads have their terminals in this area, and deliver to the docks products of the South, the Middle West, and the North. As a shipping center and railroad terminal the Hampton Roads area has grown to be the third-largest commercial center along the Atlantic seaboard, and its facilities have played a significant part in making Virginia an industrial center.

Most of the exports of the Hampton Roads ports are products from Virginia and the States near by. The value of exports through the customs district of Virginia in 1935, as reported by the United States Department of Commerce, was $122,580,000. Leaf tobacco and cigarettes accounted for $102,601,000 of the total. Seventy per cent of all the leaf tobacco exported from the United States in 1935 passed through Hampton Roads. Most of the leaf tobacco sent through the Hampton Roads ports is the bright flue-cured leaf of Virginia and North Carolina. In addition to tobacco exports, the records show that cotton piece goods, cotton linters, lumber, coal, tanning extracts, iron and steel scrap, steel sheets, and chemicals are important items in the export trade of Hampton Roads, both in value and in volume.

Virginia's exports greatly exceed its imports. Imports into the customs district of Virginia in 1935 were valued at $29,188,000, or less than one-fourth the value of exports. The most important products imported into the State were molasses, cotton and burlap, cigarette tobacco, bananas, ores, inedible oils, and crude gypsum.

The coastwise trade of the Hampton Roads area in 1935 totaled 16,600,000 tons, made up of 14,900,000 outbound and 1,700,000 inbound. Coal accounted for 14,000,000 tons of the outgoing cargo. Other commodities in the coastwise movement of products into and out of Virginia ports were cotton piece goods, petroleum products, leaf and manufactured tobacco, peanuts, lumber, and vegetables.

Virginia's water-borne commerce constitutes only a small part of her total trade. In 1935 there were 2,123 wholesale establishments in the State, with a total net sales return of $502,951,000. At the same time there were 26,757 retail stores, with net sales of $471,329,000. The annual sales per store amounted to $22,759, and the sales per capita were $246.42.

LABOR

Notwithstanding the existence of several large cities, Virginia's labor supply resides preponderantly in small towns and rural districts. The population of the State in 1930 was 2,421,851. Of this number 785,537—or 32.4 per cent—lived in urban centers, and 1,636,314—or 67.6 per cent—lived in rural sections. Although between 1920 and 1930 the number of towns and cities with populations of 2,500 or more increased from 38 to 45, the percentage of people living in urban communities increased by only 3.2 per cent. Thus, while the industrial development of the State is steadily drawing people from farms to urban centers, Virginia is still predominantly rural; and there are still thousands of people in rural districts who constitute a potential labor supply for new factories. Many of the industries recently established in Virginia are drawing upon this labor reserve.

A large rayon company chose a site with the expectation of drawing most of its personnel from a city near by. At the end of the first year, however, it was found that only 11 per cent of its workers lived in that city, while 89 per cent came from the rural area within a radius of 25 miles from the plant.

According to the census of 1930, only 23,820 people—less than 1 per cent of Virginia's population—were foreign born. Industrial expansion in Virginia began just as the great era of immigration into America was coming to an end, and the bulk of it has taken place since the World War, when immigration practically ceased. The rural reserve of native labor has further discouraged immigration into the State.

In 1930 nearly one-fourth, or 650,165, of the total population of the State was Negro. In 1935 there were 37,568 Negro workers employed in manufacturing plants in Virginia. There is no evidence, however, that Negro workers have come into competition with white workers except in the unskilled trades. For instance, in the tobacco industry, Negro labor is employed almost entirely in rehandling tobacco. In this branch of the tobacco industry 4,130 Negro females and 2,892 Negro males were employed in 1935, while only 182 white males and no white females were similarly occupied. On the other hand, in the manufacture of cigarettes 2,655 white females and 1,439 white males were employed, as compared with 809 Negro females and 965 Negro males. A large number of Negro male and female workers were employed in the manufacture of food and kindred products, and almost 6,000 Negro males were employed in the wood products industries.

Most of the consumer-goods industries give employment to a large number of women workers. These and other light industries with modern machines have attracted women tenders into many industries formerly closed to them. The Virginia State Planning Board found that from 1909 to 1929 the total number of persons employed by Virginia industries increased 13.4 per cent, but that the gains in the number of women employed accounted for 90 per cent of the total. Employment of males during the same period did not keep pace with the growth of population, while female employment increased more than five times as fast as did the number of people in the State. The lower wage scale prevailing for women has contributed to this increase. The annual report of the Virginia Department of Labor and Industry in 1935 showed 43,365 female workers employed by industries in Virginia. Of these, 12,256 were Negroes. Ninety-five per cent of nearly 50,000 female industrial workers in Virginia in 1937 were engaged in the production of consumer goods, particularly in the manufacture of tobacco, food products, and textiles.

Studies made by the Bureau of Labor Statistics of the United States Department of Labor show that, while the wages paid by employers in Virginia are higher on the whole than those paid in other Southern States, they are only about two-thirds as high as those paid in the North. In 1930 the average full-time weekly wage of employees in the cotton goods industry in Virginia was $15.43, for a work week of 54.7 hours, as compared with $20.92 for an average work week of 51 hours in six Northern States. In 1932 Virginia workers in the hosiery industry received an average full-time weekly wage of $14.04 for 54.6 hours, as compared with $22.94 in Massachusetts for 48.2 hours, $23.52 in New Jersey for 47.7 hours, and $24.92 in New York for 48.1 hours. In the manufacture of underwear Virginia workers received $12.43 for an average work week of 49.7 hours, as compared with $19.39 in Massachusetts for 48 hours, and $18.89 in Pennsylvania for 52.9 hours. In the furniture industry the difference in wages was even greater. In 1931 workers in furniture plants in Virginia received an averate full-time wage of $12.98 for a work week of 55 hours; in Illinois similar workers were paid $24.45 for 51 hours, in Massachusetts $28 for 48.4 hours, and in New York $24.01 for 51.4 hours.

No authoritative study has been made of the relative efficiency of workers in the North and those in Virginia and other Southern States. It is certainly true, however, that Virginia workers generally reflect the influence of a predominantly rural rather than urban environment. Not only do they come from folk, especially in the mountain sections, that have been inclined to be satisfied with standards lower than obtain in more mature industrial areas, but also they have yet to develop fully the traditions of craftsmanship and skill characteristic of an older and more instinctively urban, industrial society.

Slow to organize in Virginia and still far behind the National average, labor unions, nevertheless, have helped to protect Virginia workers, to offset the disadvantage of a labor supply in excess of the demand, and to lessen exploitation of rather docile unskilled and semiskilled industrial employees. Although the present labor movement had its real beginning in Virginia in the period 1885–90, the first local union in the State was organized four years before the War between the States. Early in the *antebellum* period there had been loose associations of workmen, embryonic trade unions, and even unsuccessful strikes at intervals, as when the white puddlers and rollers at the Tredegar rolling mill in Richmond struck on a Sunday in May almost 100 years ago. The first organization was a local of the Typographical Union, chartered in Petersburg in 1857. This local, with a membership of 16 in 1858, was disbanded two years later, but two other local unions, in Richmond and Alexandria, were chartered in 1865, as the union idea slowly gathered force in Virginia.

In 1886, when the Knights of Labor held their National convention in Richmond, there were 20 local unions in the State, with a membership estimated at more than 1,367. The Knights of Labor, having just experienced a phenomenal growth, had swelled from 100,000 members to 700,000 throughout the country during the previous year and was then the largest labor organization on American soil. In Virginia whites and Negroes had entirely separate local and district assemblies. When a group of non-Southern delegates to the convention made an issue of racial segregation, a storm of reaction was aroused in Richmond and the South generally. This controversy became the most widely advertised aspect of the convention and, by hurting the Knights of Labor, which then symbolized the labor movement, acted as a severe setback for labor organization in Virginia.

Unionization went forward, however, and at the turn of the century the need for better organization led to the establishment of the Virginia Federation of Labor as well as of central labor unions in most Virginia cities. Most active during the war years, the latter have dwindled since then. By 1914, when there were 102,820 industrial workers in Virginia, there were 244 active local unions with a membership estimated at 14,367. The peak of unionization was reached in 1920, when there were 46,796 workers in 446 locals—about 40 per cent of the industrial wage earners in Virginia. Seven years later the figures had dropped to 334 locals and 21,413 members—about 19 per cent of all those employed in Virginia industry—but had risen again by 1930 to 370 locals and 29,543 members. Organized strikes occurred with irregular frequency and only partial success. In 1918 there were 37, while in 1922, the year of the great railroad strike, there were only five. The three strikes of 1930 included the unsuccessful strike of the workers in the textile mills of Danville. The failure of this union effort, the most outstanding in the history of the labor movement in Virginia, retarded further organization of textile workers in the South generally.

The labor union scene was altered sharply in 1937, when the American Federation of Labor, with which the great majority of locals were affiliated, was split by the emergence of the Congress of (then Committee for) Industrial Organization. The A.F. of L., having had a membership that year of about 30,000 or about 24 per cent of all industrial workers in the State, lost nearly 15,000 upon the withdrawal of the mine workers, who formed the backbone of the C.I.O. Added to the secessionists were about

5,000 workers, especially in the tobacco and textile industries, newly organized by C.I.O. forces. By May 1938 the C.I.O. had reached a membership in Virginia of nearly 29,000.

The effect of the activities of this new and more militant labor organization, along industrial rather than craft lines, was to stimulate unionization of labor throughout Virginia. The C.I.O. welcomed into its membership women and Negroes, who have been organized as never before, although they still—women particularly—form an extreme minority in Virginia's labor movement as a whole. Most unions now admit Negroes on an equal footing with whites, but there are few mixed locals. Particularly, a wave of strikes—18 in all—in 1938 dramatized the labor situation and led to a substantial growth of both labor groups. In May 1939 the C.I.O. could report a membership above 31,000, and the A.F. of L. one above 35,000.

Today, unionization in Virginia lags behind the National average but is about equal to the Southern norm. Considering the primarily agricultural economy of the State and the opposition with which attempts at organization have been met, the size of the movement is truly remarkable.

One of the most important problems connected with the industrial growth in Virginia has been the protection of the health, welfare, and life of workers in manufacturing establishments. The experience of older industrialized States has shown that adequately to protect such workers it is desirable that social legislation keep pace with industrial progress. More has been done for the protection of workers in Virginia than in many other Southern States.

Almost from the beginning of her industrial growth, Virginia has had a law for the protection of children against hazards of the factory system. A law enacted in 1889 for the protection of women and children in industry provided that no child under 12 years of age should be employed in manufacturing industries and prohibited night work for children under 14 in manufacturing, mechanical, and mining operations. The law also limited the hours of work to 10 in 24. This early law has been amended from time to time, and at present Virginia's child labor law provides that no child under 14 years of age may work in a factory, and none less than 16 may work without a school certificate showing physical fitness and evidence of age. Children under 16 are not permitted to work more than 6 days or more than 44 hours weekly or more than 8 hours a day. Night work for children is prohibited.

One phase of Virginia's labor problem relates to the protection of women in industry. Virginia's hours law for women was not changed to any important extent in 37 years. In 1938, however, the legislature amended the law and reduced the maximum daily hours of women from 10 to 9 and added a weekly limit of 48 with a number of exemptions. The Federal Wages and Hours Law, applicable to both men and women in those industries defined as interstate, has focused thought upon the need of a State law giving protection to men as well as to women. A few other laws that have been enacted for the regulation of working conditions and for the protection of the health of women workers are below the average standard of similar laws in more highly industrialized States.

Virginia has a good workmen's compensation law. Under its provisions the responsibility of employers is definitely fixed and compensation is provided for workers injured in the course of industrial employment. The law applies to all concerns within the State employing 11 or more workers. Such employers must insure the payment of compensation in a company approved by the State Corporation Commission, or must insure themselves in such manner as to satisfy the Industrial Commission of their ability to fulfil such obligations.

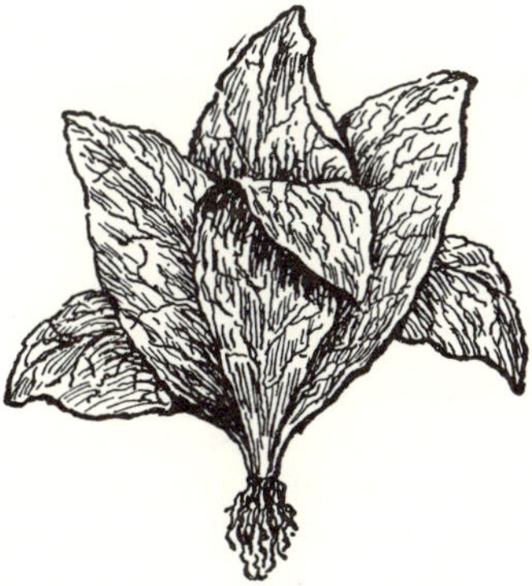

Education

VIRGINIA was the first English colony in America to lay plans for establishing a university, the first to found a free school, and the first to propose a system of public education. Yet today, in every comparative rating of the public schools of the United States, Virginia is near the bottom.

A carefully compiled table of statistics, published in the *Virginia Journal of Education* in February 1938, discloses the high rank that Virginia takes in its ability to pay for a public school system and the low place it occupies at present in actual expenditures. Virginia ranks seventh in Federal taxes in millions and fourteenth in total taxes collected; but it drops to forty-second in the percentage of income spent on education, to forty-first in the value of school property per pupil enrolled, and to forty-third with respect to teachers' salaries; in literacy the State is forty-second; in power to hold pupils between the ages of 14 and 17 years, Virginia drops to the forty-second place.

Dr.Sidney B. Hall, superintendent of public instruction, in his report for 1936–37, states that Virginia still falls below the minimum of five books to a pupil. The Virginia State Library is doing heroic missionary work in the field of extension libraries. On a parsimonious allowance, it sends traveling units to rural schools and clubs to furnish an indispensable instrument of twentieth-century education.

On the other hand, Virginia's revised curriculum, developed under the direction of Dr.Hall, has attracted wide attention. It has been called, however, an excellent machine without the motive power of adequate appropriation. Conditions in the rural schools of the State, where this curriculum should be functioning most efficiently, have been characterized by authorities in the *Virginia Journal of Education* as 'deplorable.' In an address delivered on April 12, 1939, before the State Chamber of Commerce, the superintendent of public instruction again called attention to the State's failure to support her public schools: 'Virginia is adding 11 millions this year [1937–38] to the value of school property, without making adequate financial provision for its operation and use.' In regard to teachers' salaries, he said that, 'because of the decrease in the purchasing value of the dollar, teachers are paid less today on the basis of the work done than they have been for more than a generation.'

RISE OF THE PUBLIC SCHOOL SYSTEM

Free education in Virginia had its beginnings soon after the founding of the colony. In addition to the Syms Free School, founded in 1634, and the Eaton Free School, established a few years later, there were seven other very early institutions generally known as parish schools. In 1646 the Virginia assembly passed its first apprenticeship law (confirmed in 1672, 1705, and 1748), which prescribed that poor orphans, neglected children of indigent parents, and all apprentices should be taught the elements of an education, given religious instruction, and trained in a good calling or trade. There is even some evidence of attempts in the seventeenth century to establish trade schools in the Virginia workhouses. The schools for 'all the children within the bounds' or for poor orphans and apprentices were supported by private philanthropy. Unfortunately, association of free primary education with the poor orphan produced what has been called an 'orphan fixation,' which for more than 200 years proved an obstacle to the development and general acceptance of a public school system and even after 1869 prevented a wholehearted support of free education for all classes.

The idea that education is a State function evolved slowly in Virginia, as elsewhere. Its first great American champion, Thomas Jefferson, was 100 years in advance of his time. Within a few days after his election in 1779 as governor of Virginia, he submitted to the assembly his plan for education: 'A Bill for the More General Diffusion of Knowledge.' Its aim was to safeguard democracy by educating the people. Jefferson hoped to end the old horizontal system of schools for the rich and schools for the poor, and sought to remove the blight of pauperism from free education.

The plan proposed three years of free elementary education for all children regardless of class or condition, free secondary education for those who had the ability to profit by it, and free college and university education for those with still greater endowments. The weakness of the plan came from its author's fear of centralization. He proposed to finance the schools mainly by a direct tax locally imposed. The bill, which would have given primary education to boys and girls alike, did not go through at the time, but some of its provisions were enacted into law in 1796.

In 1818 Jefferson led another assault on the indifference to popular education. The assembly of 1810, prompted by Governor John Tyler,Sr., had passed a law establishing the Literary Fund, a form of school support intended to take the place of a local tax. This law, still functioning in Virginia, provides that all fines, escheats, and confiscations accruing to the State shall be used for the founding of a university, for the education of poor children, and for the encouragement of learning. Jefferson's amended education bill of 1818 was intended to establish a pyramidal system of education, a system of primary and secondary schools and district colleges, with the university the capstone of the structure. As only the primary schools and the university were founded, the result was a feeble substructure, a vigorous top, and nothing between by which free-school children could climb upward. Such as it was, however, the system functioned until about 1860. Amendments and re-enactments did not change its inherent weakness, which lay in the permissive nature of the provisions. The bill left the matter of setting up primary schools in a locality to the men of substance, who naturally did not hasten to tax themselves to educate the children of their poor neighbors. Before 1860 not more than half a dozen counties had established district free schools.

A growing sentiment in favor of extending educational opportunity was reflected in the educational conventions of 1841, 1845, 1856, and 1857. In the western counties a rising middle class was founding schools and colleges and demanding a State-supported system of free schools. The descendants of Scotch and Scotch-Irish settlers were the most powerful factors in this movement. Official recognition of free education actually came in 1851. Then through revision of the constitution it was provided that one-half of the capitation tax might be applied to free primary schools.

Even before the educational revivals of the 1840's and 1850's, Virginia had experimented with two other forms of free popular education, both originating in England. The first, the secular Sunday school, was welcomed here with enthusiasm, reached its crest of favor in the 1830's, and then rapidly waned in popularity. As initiated by Robert Raikes, the plan provided instruction for the poor in reading, writing, and religion, using the Bible and the catechism as the basis of teaching. The classes, in which all ages and all social strata were mingled, were held on Sunday, sometimes continuing all day. The aristocratic lion in some sections fed with the proletariat lamb. Jefferson's democratic ideal seemed on the eve of realization. The teachers were volunteers, and the cost was so low that prophets hailed this innovation as a solution of the problem of popular education. It proved a false dawn. The glow faded, but the democratic leveling had helped to inoculate the public with the idea of free schools disassociated from charity.

Almost at the same time the Lancasterian plan for popular education invaded Virginia. This monitorial system, invented by Joseph Lancaster, employed older pupils to teach the younger under the supervision of an adult teacher. The schools were supported by private contributions and municipal appropriations. Norfolk had a Lancastrian Academy in 1815, and the Lancastrian, or Lancasterian, School at Richmond, founded in 1816, functioned successfully until the establishment of the public school system in 1869.

In spite of all obstacles, the State was moving toward a genuine system of public education under the stimulus of the educational conventions and the efforts of such advocates as Dr.Henry Ruffner, Governor James McDowell and Governor Henry Alexander Wise, when the conflict over slavery and states' rights drew into its vortex the best energies of a generation. After the war, Virginia faced a new social order and founded her system of State-supported public schools for both white and Negro children. According to the mandate of the Federal Government, a constitutional convention was summoned to meet in Richmond on December 3, 1867, to frame a new State constitution. Firmness and patience helped the minority of native sons to shape the educational provisions in accordance with the spirit of Virginia.

These provisions required that public schools for both races should be set up and functioning by 1876. The general assembly met in March 1870 and elected Dr.William Henry Ruffner the first State superintendent of public instruction, requiring him to frame within 30 days a plan for a uniform system of public schools. In July 1870 this plan became a law. Illiteracy among both races had gained noticeably during the war. With this burden and financially impoverished, Virginia started on a new course.

By 1871 the public schools, had an enrollment of 150,000, but shipwreck threatened just ahead. In the lean years of 1877–79 the public school system found itself almost without funds. The Literary Fund had been diverted to other channels. Though Dr.Ruffner and other stalwart friends of education saved the system from complete disaster, the next two decades show a downward curve on the educational graph—the result of an alliance between school administration and politics. But the new State constitution of 1902 in large measure divorced the schools from political influence. The power of the State board was increased, appropriations were cut off from schools not under exclusive control of the State, and it was provided that the superintendent of public instruction should be an experienced educator elected by the people for a term of four years.

A series of educational conferences promoted by Robert C. Ogden of New York was held at various centers in the South in the opening years of the twentieth century. In Virginia they resulted in the May campaign of 1905. State officials were bombarded with appeals for improvement of the public school system. Better school laws were enacted, high schools and normal schools were established, and facilities for industrial and agricultural education were set up. In 1884 the State had founded a normal school for women at Farmville, and between 1908 and 1912 three more such schools were opened at Harrisonburg, Fredericksburg, and East Radford. These schools have since evolved into teachers' colleges.

In 1937–38 Virginia's expenditures for educational purposes amounted to $29,140,234.86, a sum which, according to careful estimates, was $10,000,000 less than the amount needed. In 1937–38 the expenditure per pupil in average daily public school attendance was $45.56, as against a National average of $74.30. The largest sum spent for a single specialized purpose in 1937–38 was $907,777 for vocational education; but, according to the superintendent of public instruction, this sum fell far short of what was needed. In 1937–38 the State employed 17,249 teachers, white and Negro, whose average annual salary (exclusive of supervisors and supervising principals) was $792. The average annual salary, including all types of instruction, was $886. Of the 735,198 children of school age in the State, 583,556 were enrolled in the public schools, with an average daily attendance of only 493,266.

Virginia's revised curriculum proves, however, that those who planned it were intent on changing the gears of the educational machine to meet the demands for twentieth-century efficiency. It proves also that Virginia's low educational rating is not the fault of her educators but of those who dispense the public funds.

THE ACADEMY MOVEMENT

Before the widespread establishment of private schools, wealthy planters engaged tutors and invited the children of neighboring plantations to share the instruction and the expense; girls attended with their brothers or were taught by governesses. The enrollment lists of Eton, Cambridge, and Oxford show that many sons of wealthy Virginia families went overseas for their education. Frequently small planters or successful merchants set up community schools known as Old Field schools, sometimes patronized for convenience by the upper class. Here the instruction varied

Architecture II

otograph by courtesy of the Virginia Conservation Commission

THE ROTUNDA (1822–26), UNIVERSITY OF VIRGINIA, CHARLOTTESVILLE

Photograph by courtesy of the Virginia Conservation Commissi

STATE CAPITOL (1785–92, 1904–05), RICHMOND

otograph by courtesy of the Virginia Conservation Commission

ARLINGTON (1802–20), NEAR ALEXANDRIA

WHITE HOUSE OF THE CONFEDERACY (1818, 1844), RICHMOND

otograph by courtesy of the Virginia Conservation Commission

Photograph by courtesy of the Virginia Conservation Commissic

BRUTON PARISH CHURCH (1710–15), WILLIAMSBURG

otograph by courtesy of the Virginia State Chamber of Commerce

GOVERNOR'S PALACE (1705–20, RECONSTRUCTED 1930), WILLIAMSBURG

WREN BUILDING (1695–99, RESTORED 1928), COLLEGE OF WILLIAM AND MARY, WILLIAMSBURG

otograph by courtesy of the Virginia Conservation Commission

Photograph by courtesy of the Virginia Conservation Commissi

STRATFORD HALL (1729), WESTMORELAND COUNTY

POHICK CHURCH (1774), FAIRFAX COUNTY

Photograph by W. Lincoln High

hotograph by W. Lincoln Highton

HANOVER COURTHOUSE (1733), HANOVER COUNTY

ST. LUKE'S CHURCH (17th CENTURY, RESTORED 1887), NEAR SMITHFIELD

hotograph by courtesy of the Virginia Conservation Commission

Photograph by W. Lincoln Hight

RUINS OF BARBOURSVILLE (c. 1820), ORANGE COUNTY

from the rudiments of knowledge to mathematics and the classics, under an educated master.

The academy movement, which started in mid-eighteenth century, carried Virginia to pre-eminence through the number and quality of secondary schools and the high cost of board and tuition. From 1776 to 1870, when the academy gave way to the public high school, 218 such institutions were chartered: 127 for boys, 71 for girls, and 20 that were coeducational. The academy responded quickly to the conditions of a changing economic life. It included in its curricula practical subjects needed in a new country—navigation, surveying, engineering, sciences, and modern languages. In *Scientific Interests in the Old South*, Dr. T. C. Johnson reveals through minute documentation the extent to which the sciences were taught in these academies, seminaries, or institutes, as they were variously known. Often the scientific instruction was strengthened by lectures from a professor at a neighboring college. When the academy movement waned, some of these institutions survived to form the nuclei of future colleges and universities.

An educational chart of Virginia, designed to display the scope and quality of the instruction given in girls' schools between 1790 and 1860, would show surprising variations. While the catalogue of one Virginia seminary was promising to 'temper the severities of arithmetic to the delicacy of the female mind,' another was publishing in its prospectus the stern requirement that the young ladies were 'expected to study philosophy from the original text of the master and use no easy compendiums'; and at Llangollen in Spotsylvania, the Lewis School for both sexes, in separate classes, was putting the 'delicate female mind' through the same severe intellectual discipline as was given the boys. This was in 1815, and the advertisement of other schools for girls, then and later, list Latin and Greek, with emphasis on Euclid 'to strengthen the mind,' and a surprising array of the sciences. Between 1835 and 1838, according to Dr. Johnson, nearly all the 100 advertisements of girls' schools in Virginia listed some natural sciences in the course of study. But few of these schools omitted the teaching of shellwork, beadwork, and the making of wax flowers, or neglected the 'captivating accomplishments' of music, French, and dancing. Intelligent Virginians—Thomas Ritchie, editor of the *Richmond Enquirer*, among them—grew more and more critical of the trivial and superficial education given to girls and argued for 'more masculine breadth and substance.' In response to this demand and as part of a Nation-wide educational awakening, schools were founded to provide girls in Virginia with the same educational opportunities as were offered young men.

COLLEGES AND UNIVERSITIES

Higher education has always been Virginia's favorite child, while the free or public school has been left like Ishmael to sojourn in the desert. Before the Jamestown settlement was ten years old, ambitious schemes were afoot both in Virginia and in England to found a college or university at Henricopolis in the corporation of Henrico, with an endowment of $45,000 and a domain of 10,000 acres. The Massacre of 1622, however, discouraged all efforts toward higher education, and not until 1693 was the College of William and Mary founded by royal charter at Williamsburg.

Now Virginia has 24 senior colleges and universities, 10 of which are controlled by the State. The University of Virginia was founded at Charlottesville by Thomas Jefferson in 1819. The College of William and Mary passed into State control in 1906. Virginia's two military colleges, the Virginia Military Institute at Lexington (founded 1839) and the Virginia Polytechnic Institute at Blacksburg (founded 1872), combine military and technical training with courses in the liberal arts. The four teachers' colleges, to which men are admitted only in the summer sessions, now confer the degree of bachelor of arts. Since William and Mary passed into State control, Hampden-Sydney College (opened January 1, 1776 as Prince Edward Academy) has become the senior private institution for higher education in Virginia. Hampden-Sydney was the progenitor of Union Theological Seminary, now in Richmond, and of the Medical College of Virginia, organized in 1838 as Hampden-Sydney medical department. This medical college, also in Richmond and now a State-controlled coeducational institution, is the largest medical center south of Baltimore. Scotch-Irish zeal for education is responsible for the beginnings of Washington and Lee University, chartered in 1782 as Liberty Hall Academy. During the third decade of the nineteenth century several other colleges were established—the University of Richmond, Randolph-Macon College at Ashland, and Emory and Henry College at Emory. In addition to the senior colleges and universities, Virginia has 12 institutions of junior college standing. Of these, nine are for women and three are coeducational, including the Eastern Mennonite School at Harrisonburg, the only one of this sect in the State.

State-controlled higher education in Virginia has been predominantly for men. Until 1918 no State-supported college admitted women. In that year the Virginia Polytechnic Institute and the College of William and Mary became coeducational. In 1920 the University of Virginia opened to women its graduate and professional schools. Women are still virtually excluded from the winter sessions of the university's school of liberal arts, though they may receive the degree of bachelor of arts by attending courses in the summer.

While Virginia has no college for women that ranks with the so-called 'Big Seven,' she can offer a list of several distinctive institutions, the oldest dating from the educational revival of the 1840's, and all except Randolph-Macon Woman's College and Sweet Briar College developing from a female seminary or institute. Hollins College near Roanoke, founded in 1842 as a coeducational institute, stands foremost among the pioneers. The Mary Baldwin Seminary in Staunton was opened, also in 1842, as the Augusta Female Seminary. Patterned after those in the men's colleges, the early courses at these two schools were exacting. Westhampton College, opened in 1915 as co-ordinate college for women at the University of Richmond, had as its first students 'co-eds,' who for several years had been tolerated on a masculine campus.

Randolph-Macon Woman's College at Lynchburg, founded by Methodists in 1893, has the distinction of being the first fully accredited woman's college in Virginia. Sweet Briar College, one of the youngest of Virginia's colleges for women, was opened near Amherst in 1906 as a strictly liberal-arts institution.

NEGRO EDUCATION

The apprenticeship act of 1646 required masters to instruct and catechize their Negroes, as well as their white apprentices and indentured servants. In the eighteenth century occasional efforts were made in Virginia to give the Negro an elementary education and to train him in some craft or industry. At Bremo, the old Cocke homestead on the upper James, is still preserved the eighteenth-century slave schoolroom. Before 1764 the editor of the *Virginia Gazette* had established a school for Negroes in Williamsburg, as an entry against his estate, 'To paid Ann wages for teaching the Negro school,' furnishes evidence. In December 1827 *The Richmond Whig* advertised a school for 'free Negro boys' taught by a Joseph Sheppard, who sought to 'elevate them from mental thralldom and degradation.' When the foreign slave trade was abolished in 1808, Virginia became, in the words of President Dew of the College of William and Mary, 'a Negro-raising state for other states.' Her slaves were in demand because of their excellent training. House-servants were often taught to read and write, to increase their economic value. But steadily mounting unrest among the slaves, the increase of abolitionist propaganda, and fear of another Nat Turner insurrection produced a reaction against educating the Negro. Stringent laws were passed in 1849 penalizing Negro instruction or 'assemblages.'

At the close of the War between the States, Virginia was too impoverished to educate even her white children. It was then that the Freedmen's Bureau and the Peabody Fund, both Northern philanthropies, gave money and moral support for Negro education. They were aided in their efforts by the almost 60,000 free Virginia Negroes, many of them literate and property owners. In 1868 the Hampton Normal and Agricultural Institute was established by the American Missionary Association of New York, which had conducted schools for Negroes on Hampton River since 1861.

Not until 40 years after the establishment of Virginia's public school system was the vocational training of the old apprenticeship system restored to both whites and Negroes. Virginia Randolph, a Negro teacher in a rural school of Henrico County, started a movement in 1906 for the return of vocational and industrial training. Her plan so transformed the rural Negro schools of the county that it was successfully adopted elsewhere in Virginia and North Carolina. She was the first supervisor to be aided by the Jeanes Fund.

Negro education in the South has been vitally assisted by four funds established by Northern philanthropists. The Slater Fund, the earliest, provided $1,000,000 for Negro rural schools and the training of Negro teachers. It was founded in 1882 by a Connecticut merchant, J.P.Slater. The Jeanes Fund, endowed in 1905 by a Philadelphia Quaker, Miss Anna Jeanes, finances supervisors for the rural schools. The Phelps-Stokes Fund, founded by Miss Caroline Phelps-Stokes in 1909, aids the public rural schools of both races. The Rosenwald Fund for rural Negro education, with a munificent endowment of $22,000,000, was founded in 1912 by Julius Rosenwald of Chicago. In 1930, near the old Syms School in Elizabeth City County, the Rosenwald Fund erected the five thousandth of the school buildings it has distributed throughout the rural South. The Slater Fund and the Jeanes Fund were merged in 1937 as the Southern Education Foundation, Incorporated.

In 1928, Dr.Michael Vincent O'Shea of the University of Wisconsin made an exhaustive report on public education in Virginia to the Virginia commission of education. He found the Negro rural schools seriously handicapped by short terms, poor physical equipment, inefficient teachers, low salaries, and lack of effective supervision. Dr.Sidney B. Hall, Virginia's present superintendent of public instruction, lists as needs of the Negro schools more and better buildings, increased and improved transportation facilities, better teachers, higher salaries, and consolidation.

In addition to Hampton Institute, Virginia has three other Negro colleges. One of these, Virginia State College at Petersburg, is supported by State funds. Another, Virginia Union University, had its lowly origin in a building known as Lumpkin's jail, or slave pen, in Richmond. Virginia Theological Seminary and College was founded in 1888; its alumni serve many of the churches of the State.

Other Negro institutions in the State, however, give some college courses. In the heart of the 'black belt' in Brunswick County, the Reverend James S. Russell, an Episcopal minister, started in 1888 the St.Paul Normal and Industrial School, now a coeducational junior college and teacher-training institution. The northern branch of the Presbyterian Church controls the Ingleside-Fee Memorial Institute at Burkeville, which gives an accredited high school course and two years of college work; and the Roman Catholic Church maintains the St.Emma Industrial Institute for Negroes at Rock Castle on the James River. The Bishop Payne Divinity School at Petersburg trains Negroes for the ministry.

The editor of the Richmond *Times-Dispatch* on May 19, 1937, commended the award of the Roosevelt Memorial Association to Dr.James Hardy Dillard, in recognition of half a century of wise and devoted work on behalf of the Negro, and said: 'School superintendents find it easier now in the South to give Negro pupils new schools than they did 20 or 30 years ago . . . Some of these superintendents are growing bold enough to discuss the disparity between the salaries of the white and the colored public teachers.' But for all advances that have been made in recent years, many inequalities with respect to Negro and white education still exist in the public school system of Virginia.

In 1937–38 there were 27 counties without public schools for Negroes and 26 counties and two cities without Negro high schools. The total number of accredited, qualified, and certified Negro high schools in the State is 63. In 1937–38 the expenditure for each Negro pupil in average daily attendance was $26.08 in city schools and $12.19 in rural schools, as against corresponding expenditures of $47.62 and $24.01 for the white pupil. In 1937–38 the average annual salary paid Negro elementary teachers was $518, while white elementary teachers received $773. The average salary paid Negro high school teachers was $848, while white high school teachers received $1190.

THE FUTURE PROGRAM

Although the Virginia legislature at its 1938 session adopted only a part of the program advanced by educators for lifting standards in the schools of the State, public opinion has been so aroused that necessary appropriations cannot be indefinitely withheld. The following three-point unified program was adopted in January 1938 by the Virginia Educational Association: a minimum school term of nine months with a minimum average salary for teachers of not less than $720 per school year; an actuarially sound retirement law for teachers; textbooks furnished pupils in the public schools at the expense of the State. Although this program has not yet been achieved, public attention has been focused on the need, and additional appropriations constitute a step in the right direction.

The comptroller's report for 1938 lists Federal aid for education in Virginia to the amount of $1,244,267, distributed among the funds for rehabilitation, for vocational education, for home economics courses given in 71 per cent of the accredited high schools, and in the College of William and Mary, the Medical College of Virginia, the Virginia Polytechnic Institute, and the Virginia State College for Negroes.

In 1938 the general assembly of Virginia made appropriations to help the local school boards develop already existing programs for adult education. These local programs are to be set up in community centers, unifying all phases of the education of adults.

Delinquents, formally committed by the courts, are placed in private homes or sent to four industrial schools maintained by the State. A State institution cares for white epileptics and feeble-minded persons, and one for Negroes is now being built (1939). The State supports white and Negro institutions for the deaf and blind. The Virginia Commission for the Blind maintains workshops in three cities and gives effective aid in conserving sight. In 1936 the general assembly established an annual appropriation of $950,000 for the support of these institutions.

Besides these State institutions, there are a number of schools and homes for normal and subnormal youth supported by private philanthropy—Masonic and sectarian.

Thomas Jefferson wrote in 1795: 'I do most anxiously wish to see the highest degrees of education given to the highest degrees of genius, and to all degrees of it, so much as may enable them to read and understand what is going on in the world, and to keep their part of it going on right; for nothing can keep it right but their own vigilant and distrustful superintendence.' And in 1820 he noted hopefully: 'Surely Governor Clinton's display of the gigantic efforts of New York towards the education of their citizens will stimulate the pride as well as the patriotism of our Legislature, to look to the reputation and safety of their country, to rescue it from the degradation of becoming the Barbary of the Union.'

Today in the education field, courageous and versatile leaders are pushing toward the goal set by Thomas Jefferson. With the fourth decade of the twentieth century at the threshold, there is already good hope that in the early 1940's Virginia will recapture her traditional prestige in education and link her present with her past.

Newspapers

BUT I thank God, there are no free schools nor printing and I hope we shall not have, these hundred years, for learning has brought disobedience, and heresy, and sects into the world, and printing has divulged them, and libels against the best government. God keep us from both.' Thus wrote Governor William Berkeley, reporting to the Commissioners of Plantations in 1671. Within little more than a decade thereafter, William Nuthead sponsored by John Buckner, set up in Gloucester County a press (the second to be established in America) and in 1682 printed two sheets of the Acts of the Virginia Assembly. Though Berkeley had been recalled to England, a spirit of intolerance toward 'liberty of presses' persisted. Buckner was summoned for this printing of the Laws, and Charles II ordered in 1683 that no person use any press in the colony. Massachusetts had set up a printing press in 1639, but it was 1704 before any newspaper was regularly published in the colonies and 1763 before a daily paper appeared regularly.

More liberal views prevailed in Virginia in 1730, for in that year William Parks of Annapolis, Maryland, was appointed public printer by Governor Gooch and set up a press in Williamsburg. This was the first permanent printing press in Virginia. Three years later, Parks printed a collection of all the acts of assembly then in force, one of the typographical monuments of Colonial America. In 1736 he founded the *Virginia Gazette* with a subsidy from the governor and the house of burgesses. A tablet commemorating this pioneer printer was presented to Williamsburg by the Virginia Press Association in 1930.

Three newspapers, or gazettes as they were commonly called, were published in Williamsburg before and during the Revolutionary period. The original *Virginia Gazette* was edited successively by William Hunter and Joseph Royle and then by Alexander Purdie, with John Dixon as associate. On December 29, 1774, Purdie dissolved the partnership with Dixon and launched a paper of his own; while Dixon, with William Hunter, Jr., as co-editor, continued to edit the *Virginia Gazette*. Being a Tory, Hunter later found it wise to disappear, and Thomas Nicolson became Dixon's partner. After Alexander Purdie's death in April 1779, the gazette that he had founded some four years previously was published until December 9, 1780, by John Clarkson and Augustine Davis.

In the troubled years preceding the Revolution, the first gazette was too subservient to the British Crown to be acceptable to the liberals. So in 1766, encouraged by Thomas Jefferson, William Rind came down from Maryland and founded a paper, first called *Rind's Virginia Gazette* but later dropping the name of its editor. Rind died on April 19, 1773, and Clementina Rind, his widow, published the paper until her own death on September 25, 1774. Immediately thereafter John Pinkney became the publisher 'for the benefit of Clementina Rind's Estate' and continued the paper until February 3, 1776.

Thus it will be seen that the *Virginia Gazette* revived in 1930 has a rather complicated ancestry. Similarly in other cities, rival gazettes had their day and ceased to be. The controversies before, during, and following the Revolution caused this multiplication of newspapers. Each shade of opinion strove to find expression in an organ of its own. A free press was born of this rivalry, and monopoly of news and ownership was ended. Before the eighteenth-century gazette was generally abandoned, Richmond had supported nine, Winchester three, and Norfolk two—including one issue by the British navy during the Revolution.

Thomas Jefferson, however, was in part responsible for this liberation. *Rind's Virginia Gazette,* virtually Jefferson's official organ, published Benjamin Franklin's views on the repeal of the Stamp Act in 1766. Fourteen years later, during the high tide of the Revolution, the general assembly declared that 'a good printing press is indispensable for the right information of the people and for the public service,' a concise definition of the true mission of journalism. Governor Jefferson then invited John Dunlap and James Hayes, skilled printers of Baltimore, to settle in Virginia. Setting up their press in Charlottesville, they made that town the fourth center of printing in Virginia, following Williamsburg, Richmond, and Norfolk. By 1781 Dunlap and Hayes had moved to Richmond, leaving Charlottesville without a paper until 1820, when the *Central Gazette* was established.

Other communities responded to the stirring spirit of the Revolutionary era. In 1774 the *Norfolk Intelligencer* was founded in what was then Virginia's most populous town; the *Alexandria Gazette* began publication in 1784; later came the *Petersburg Gazette,* which changed its title in 1800 to *The Intelligencer*; and the *Virginia Herald* was founded at Fredericksburg in 1787 by Timothy Green. The *Herald* began as either a weekly or a semi-weekly, and continued for nearly 100 years. The *Alexandria Gazette,* the oldest daily in the United States published continuously, was owned and edited by various members of the Snowden family from 1800 to 1900.

Lynchburg and Staunton had newspapers by 1793, and Leesburg followed in 1798 with the *True American.* The farthest outpost captured by the press in the eighteenth century was Fincastle in Botetourt County, where the *Herald of Virginia* appeared in 1800. The Shenandoah Valley was distinguished by a German weekly newspaper issued in 1807 as *Der Virginische Volkberichter und Neumarketer Wochenschrift.*

The Scotch, Scotch-Irish, and German pioneers of southwest Virginia, with their keen interest in education, were not long in founding newspapers, although isolated by mountain barriers and served by poor roads. The first newspaper published west of the mountains was the *Holston Intelligencer and Abingdon Advertiser*, which appeared in 1806. The *Abingdon Virginian* flourished from 1839 to 1917, bearing at its masthead this notice: 'Established as the People's Friend. Devoted to farm, education, good habits, news, politics, morals, religion, and amusement in the home.'

In format and content these early journals had little in common with the modern newspaper. The front page was usually cloaked in lucrative advertisements and in stodgy philosophy expressed in either verse or prose. The *Virginia Gazette* on April 24, 1751, tediously applauds in labored verse 'Infidelity, or Atheism Disproved, by a Gentleman of Virginia.' Then follow a quotation from Horace, unwisely in the original, and a pompous essay on the importance of acquiring wisdom in youth. Mind in the mid-eighteenth century was definitely superior to matter—on the front page. Nor had radical innovations arrived even as late as 1816. On September 20 of that year, page 1 of the *Richmond Compiler*, the city's first daily paper, is heavy-laden with advertisements; page 2 has a meager slice of foreign news more than two months old, engulfed by accounts of domestic events; while page 3 naïvely chronicles a bee-swarming on one of Richmond's streets—a Virgilian episode somewhat dwarfed by notices of slave sales and rewards for runaways.

For more than 100 years newspaper headlines were models of restraint. Five days after one of Richmond's greatest disasters, the burning on December 26, 1811, of the theater on Academy Square, the *Richmond Enquirer* headed an account of the tragedy with the one word 'Narrative' in type scarcely larger than the text. And in its issue of January 30, 1830, the same paper assigned to an obscure paragraph, without fanfare or headlines, news of an 'atrocious attempt to rob the Early Union Stage Line between Richmond and Baltimore.' Nor did the death of George IV in 1830 create a ripple in the journalistic calm; the insignificant paragraph devoted to the king's undramatic demise had all the earmarks of *lèse-majesté*.

Yet as far as human nature is concerned, the old papers prove the truth of the French proverb, *Plus ça change, plus c'est la même chose*. A poem entitled 'The Lady's Complaint,' published in the *Virginia Gazette* of October 15–22, 1736, might have been written by a plaintive feminist of 200 years later:

Custom, alas! doth partial prove
Nor give us equal measure.
A pain it is for us to love,
But it is to men a pleasure.

They plainly can their thoughts disclose,
Whilst ours must burn within,
We have got tongues and eyes in vain,
And truth from us is sin.

Men to new joys and conquests fly,
And yet no hazard run.
Poor we are left if we deny,
And if we yield undone.

Then equal laws let custom find,
And neither sex oppress.
More freedom give to womankind,
Or give to mankind less.

A twentieth-century chamber of commerce might have sponsored this appeal to industrialists in the *Richmond Compiler* of May 16, 1816: 'Capitalist! We invite you to settle among us. Here is a field for the employment of your capital. Richmond is destined to be great.'

Changes in methods of transportation are duly reflected in these early papers. The *Richmond Compiler* for August 5, 1816, proudly announces a new stage line, leaving 'Columbian Hotel on Main Street at 8 a.m.' and arriving at 'French's Tavern in Petersburg at 2 p.m.,' some 20 miles incredibly accomplished in five hours! But 14 years later the development of steam travel on land and water inspired the following prophetic lines, published in the *Richmond Enquirer* of January 2, 1830:

Tell John to set the kettle on,
  I mean to take a drive;
I only want to go to Rome,
  And shall be back by five.

Tell cook to dress those hummingbirds
  I shot in Mexico;
They've now been killed at least two days,
  They'll be *un peu trop haut*.

As travel by rail gained popularity, a bard (although no prophet), writing in elegiac mood for the *Richmond Dispatch* of February 19, 1852, lamented the passing of the turnpike:

> For the Steam-King rules the travelled world
> And the old Pike's left to die.
>
> . . .
>
> For the dust lies still upon the road
> And the bright-eyed children play
> Where once the clattering hoof and wheel
> Rattled along the way.
>
> . . .
>
> We have circled the earth with an iron rail
> And the Steam-King rules us now.

The spirit of liberalism, lusty at the turn of the century, had begun to assume a bilious complexion by the 1820's. Stimulated by the ever-mounting temperature of political and economic controversy, many new journals entered the field in the years between 1824 and 1861. The industrial and commercial North was arrayed against the agrarian South in a clash over the tariff, and the admission of new States into the Union brought the question of Negro slavery to the front. The Virginia press both reflected and directed the sectional controversy in a community that represented the widest range of opinion and feeling. The Whig press, supported mainly by the conservative planters and merchants of Tidewater Virginia, advocated greater control by the National Government and a greater centralization of power. The Democratic party, faithful to Jefferson's principles, championed states' rights. The dominant organ of Jeffersonian Democracy was the *Richmond Enquirer*, founded by Thomas Ritchie in 1804; that of the Whigs was the *Richmond Whig*, founded in 1827 by John Hampden Pleasants. The Piedmont section, Jefferson's own, remained loyal to his brand of democracy, but the Whigs controlled the *Lynchburg Virginian* and the *Leesburg Washingtonian*. The Scotch and Irish in the Shenandoah Valley, keener about internal improvements than about political theories and having few slaves or none, were chiefly represented by the *Lexington Gazette* and the *Staunton Spectator*.

Vital statistics of Virginia newspapers reflected the accelerated tempo of the day—both birthrate and deathrate mounted. Editors were propounding the question, 'Can the Union be peacefully dissolved?' Papers ceased to be impartial dispensers of news and became guides to public opinion. Intensified partisan passions caused one noted duel. John Hampden Pleasants, founder and editor of the *Richmond Whig*, challenged Thomas Ritchie, Jr., editor of the *Enquirer* during his father's absence in Washington, and fell on the field of honor. John Moncure Daniel, extreme secessionist and dynamic editor, started the *Richmond Examiner*—a paper patterned to compete with the *Richmond Dispatch*, which made its appearance in 1850 as a nonpartisan journal. The *Virginia Sentinel* of Alexandria, founded to combat the growing power of the Federal Government, exerted a profound influence on the trend of public opinion. John Brown's Raid in 1859 caused such a fusing of these disparate elements that when the war broke out in 1861 the South had virtually a united press east of the Alleghenies. The newspapers discriminated between 'the Cause' and the Confederate Government, criticizing the first at times but upholding the second throughout the conflict.

From the days of the first newspaper in Williamsburg to the War between the States, the methods of news-gathering hobbled through a slow evolution. The masthead of the *Virginia Gazette* carried the boast, 'Containing the freshest Advices, Foreign and Domestick.' But in its issue of March 21, 1744 the 'freshest Advices,' dealing with the seizure of the Austrian Silesian provinces by Frederick the Great, were more than two months old and had doubtless been brought by the 'good Ship, *Virginia*' reported 'safe in York river 10 weeks after leaving Bristol, England.' By May 9 news of chaotic Europe had given way to matters of more local interest, among these being Bishop Berkeley's treatise on the virtues of Tar Water—a medicine before the onslaught of which such dreaded diseases as scourge, smallpox, consumption, and asthma fled in truly miraculous fashion.

In pretelegraph days, news was commonly carried by pony express, a laborious method partially improved upon by the *American Beacon* of Norfolk, which sent relays of riders through Washington to New York and then had the dispatches collected en route brought down to Hampton Roads by boat. Along with the Mexican War came the telegraph and a new journalistic era. Richmond had a telegraphic service by 1847; but it was expensive. As an economy measure the city's newspapers copied press dispatches from New York and relayed them to other Virginia cities by pony express. In 1861 the newspapers of Richmond combined to secure a joint telegraphic news service, and the Associated Press of the Confederacy was organized.

Mortality among Virginia newspapers was high during the war. By January 1863 nine-tenths of the papers had perished, leaving but 13 survivors. Of the 16 pro-Southern papers founded during the conflict, only three were alive in 1865. The Federal forces started 20 newspapers during their occupation of various sections in the South, but all ceased publication upon Lee's surrender. The press, along with all else in the State, felt the pinch of privation. Because of the scarcity of newsprint, some publications used wallpaper and wrapping paper for their issues. The tone of the following notice that appeared in Abingdon during the war demonstrates the acuteness of the need: 'We call upon everybody who has rags, rich or poor, young or old, learned or unlearned, to send them to us and get 4 cents a pound or more if demanded. We are obliged to have them or stop printing. So send them along for humanity's sake and help us keep the machine in motion.'

Since the appearance in 1865 of the first Negro newspaper in Virginia, more than 40 papers, most of them weeklies, have been launched and edited by Negroes. *The True Southerner*, the pioneer of this field, was founded in Hampton by a white man, Colonel D.B.White. In 1866 the paper, with Joseph T. Wilson as editor, was moved to Norfolk, where a political contest with Mayor Lamb ended its career. Thereupon Wilson started the short-lived *American Sentinel* in Petersburg. In 1888 he founded *The Industrial Day* in Richmond, a monthly concerned mainly with the interests of labor. Another Negro paper devoted to the same subject was started at about the same time in Lynchburg by a prominent young journalist, I.Garland Penn, author of *The Afro-American Press*. *The Leader*, a Republican Negro weekly, was begun in Washington in 1888; two years later the founder and editor, Magnus L. Robinson, moved the paper to Alexandria, where it underwent various mutations of title that ended in its present designation.

The foremost Negro newspapers of today in Virginia are the *Richmond Planet*, the *Newport News Star*, and the *Norfolk Journal and Guide*. The first named, a Republican weekly, was founded in 1883 by E.A.Randolph; but it was a later editor, John Mitchell, who gave it National distinction as a champion of Negro rights. As founded by M.N.Lewis in 1901, the *News Star* succeeded the *Evening Recorder*, which began publication in 1897 as the *Recorder*—the first Negro daily in Virginia; since Lewis's death in 1926, Thomas Newsome has edited the *News Star*. The *Journal and Guide*, an independent weekly, was founded in 1901 by P.B.Young,Sr.

In the decade following the close of the War between the States, Virginia's newspapers increased in number from 40 to 80, and 180 were being issued by 1896. A marked recession followed, owing to various causes. Not only Virginia, but the entire country, felt its impact. The major factor in this recession was the increased cost of operating a newspaper plant. Competing newspapers found it necessary to merge in order to meet the complex demands of modern journalism. Swifter means of transportation enabled the metropolitan newspapers to serve the rural areas, thus tending to eliminate the rural press. Combined circulation greatly increased, while the number of individual papers declined. Today no competition exists between the dailies in any Virginia city. In each, both morning and evening papers are owned and controlled by one company.

The merger trend had important effects for several Richmond newspapers. The *State*, founded in 1876 by John H. Chamberlayne, united in 1896 with the *Star*, established in 1893. In January 1903 a double wedding reduced the number of Richmond's leading papers from four to two, when James A. Cowardin's *Dispatch*, dating from 1850, united with Joseph Bryan's *Times*, established in 1886, to form a morning daily, the *Times-Dispatch*, and the *News* and the *Evening Leader* combined to form an afternoon daily. The *News* was founded in 1899, the *Leader* in 1888. In Norfolk a series of consolidations brought about the *Virginian-Pilot* and the *Ledger-Dispatch*, which in 1933 came under the ownership of Norfolk Newspapers Incorporated but continued publication without change of names.

The excellence of Virginia newspapers has been recognized in awards made by both State and National agencies. The Richmond *Times-Dispatch* received the highest honor in 1933 from the Virginia Press Association for front-page make-up and advertising display, and in 1936 this paper stood near the top among contestants for the National N.W.Ayer Award. The *Lynchburg News*, founded in 1866 by R.E.Withers, won top honors for typographical excellence among American papers with a circulation of 10,000 or less in 1938, when it was selected among 935 contestants to receive the Ayer Award. The *Roanoke World News*, an afternoon daily, captured three first awards from the Virginia Press Association in 1937 for excellence of general make-up. In 1929 Louis Isaac Jaffe, editor of the Norfolk *Virginian Pilot*, received the Pulitzer award for the best editorial of the year.

Governor William Berkeley's prayer has not been answered. The State now (1939) supports 32 daily newspapers, 6 semiweeklies, and 120 weeklies. Learning has brought about many things feared by the autocratic old governor, 'and printing has divulged them.'

Folklore and Music

PIONEERS and restless settlers moving from the more populated settlements of New England and Pennsylvania drifted down the Valley of Virginia into western North Carolina. Later, they migrated back into the Cumberlands, into pockets of the Blue Ridge and a vast hinterland between Virginia and West Virginia. This was a region of deep hollows, swift streams, verdant forests, and hard living—the haunt of game and legends, overhung with blue mists and smoke from stillhouses and cabins perched precariously on mountain slopes.

A proud people, not vain or impeccably attired as were the lowland planters, the mountain folk retained all the mannerisms of isolated and nonconformist sects, whose beliefs were largely formed by a wilderness environment and strict adherence to Biblical laws. Although the kinship between lowlander and mountain whites was close, mountain folkways remained earthy and rough; their speech and manners hardened; the minuet became a jig; and sentimental arias were replaced by original story-ballads dealing with a regional legend, a feud, or an individual feat. Divided by geographical and cultural barriers, the people developed customs, games, songs, and patterns of speech, art, and work that indicated the culture of a particular time and place.

The industrial revolution, bringing with it a challenge to old methods of manufacture and agriculture, spread its influence into outlying villages and towns, until the structure of rural life showed the effects of an expanding civilization. In the hills, this change marked the end of pioneering. It marked the end, to a large extent, of the independence and isolation that were so much a part of the hill people. 'Furriners' came and went in increasing numbers, leaving behind them their own restlessness, a desire—usually confined to the younger generation—to escape a rather monotonous and impoverished life and join kinsmen or friends outside. Machinery planted the food and machinery prepared the food for use. Patches of sorghum and tobacco disappeared; the spinning wheel and flax gave way to 'sto' boughten' goods; snuff came in cans, and a plug or twist of factory-made tobacco supplied the stains on the filling-station stove; squirrel-path roads were straddled by Model T's; magazines of the confession type replaced almanacs; and stragglers from the mills brought visions of Judgment Day to God-fearing hill men and women. But new ways did not entirely destroy the old—as the mountaineer went to the city, he carried deep-rooted convictions and beliefs, a code of morals and a way of living that defied both the machine and Old Scratch.

Midwives and yarb doctors took up their abode in the shacks of factory towns. Doorways were hung with open-end horseshoes to ward off bad luck. Men and women entered mill and factory gates with the left hind foot of a graveyard rabbit in their pocket or hung asafetida about their necks as protection against sickness. It was bad luck to have to return to the house when something was forgotten or to go in one door and out another. Many a lovesick youth sat on the porch and recited:

Starlight, starbright,
First star I've seen tonight,
Wish I may—wish I might,
Dream of my true love tonight.

Children repeated the verses their parents and grandparents sang. Lord Darnell, one of the oldest ballads in the State, tells of a young farmer lad who met his death when led astray by Lord Darnell's wife:

She placed her eyes on little Matthew Groves,
And these words to him did say:
'You must go home with me this night;
This live-long night to stay.'

'I can't go home with you this night,
I cannot for my life,
For by the ring on your finger
You are Lord Darnell's wife.'

Ring games, of both local and Old Country origin, are built around rhymes. 'Lady Fair,' a choosing game, is gay and fast moving:

In this ring is a lady fair,
Dark brown eyes and curly hair,
Rosy cheeks and dimpled chin,
Take someone and choose them in. (*Choose a boy*)

Now you've married and married for life,
La, la, la, what a pretty little wife.
Pretty little wife and husband too,
Kiss him twice if once won't do.

'Cumberland Gap,' a banjo piece and ditty song of the days of the War between the States, passed out of the hills and into nearly every State:

I've got a gal
In Cumberland Gap.
She's got a baby
That calls me pap.

Another version derided the haughty mien of local damsels, asserting that:

Cumberland gals,
   Are getting so gran'
Won't go to meeting
   With an hones' man.

A more serious story-ballad, composed about 1864, tells of 'The Gladeville Skirmish,' beginning:

The Yankees from Sandy
Upon us did run,
They captured our boys
And broke up our guns.

Primitive religious sects (Pentecostal), with a membership drawn largely from lower-income groups, frequently compose their own songs, as stark as the economic life of the congregation. One song creates a realistic and gruesome picture of Death:

Oh, Death, please let me see,
   If Christ has turned his back on me.
When you were called and asked to bow,
   You would not heed, 'You're too late now.'

I'll fix your feet so you can't walk;
   I'll lock your jaws so you can't talk,
I'll close your eyes so you can't see,
   This very hour come and go with me.

As civilization closed in and changes took place in the speech, dress, and behavior of hill folk, the old ballads found their counterparts in more modern songs, such as 'The Lick Branch Explosion,' 'Wreck of Old 97,' variations of 'Birmingham Jail,' and the Tin Pan Alley 'feudin'-piece,' 'The Martins and McCoys.' Facing a losing fight, the hills still protected their own. Scientific predictions for crops and weather fell upon deaf ears. When katydids chirped, it was only 40 days until frost; if a cat turned its back to the fire, there would be bad weather; if hornets built their nest high, it signified a mild winter; if drops of water or ice hung to the timber on St. Valentine's Day, it was a sure sign that there would be plenty of fruit; and even kids in a new brick school 'over yonder to town' knew the verse:

Evening red and morning gray
Sets the traveler on his way.
Evening gray and morning red
Brings down rain upon his head.

In time of sickness some store-bought patent medicine might be resorted to, but with money scarce and stores distant, cures were most commonly taken from the fields and woods. Pipsissewa, of fragrant blossom and evergreen leaf, was used for dropsy; snakeroot for headache; sarsaparilla and sassafras teas were used as spring tonics; smoke-dried Jimson leaves, for asthma; cabbage or poke weed leaves, as a poultice for boils and sores. A mixture of mullein leaves, ratsbane, wild-cherry bark and molasses made a cough syrup; a liberal dose of whiskey or brandy was a cure for snake bite; peppermint tea was an aid for indigestion. A posthumous child is believed to be able to cure digestive disorders of children by blowing down their throats, and the seventh child of a seventh child is said to possess extraordinary healing powers.

The salt marshes, bays, and riverland of Tidewater Virginia supported a social life entirely different from that of the rugged wilderness farther westward. Large plantations, the method of appointment to office, and the use of indentured or slave labor developed a landed aristocracy retaining the domestic, social, and religious customs of Britain. Except in the gentle art of political oratory and the craft activities of the skilled artisans and tradesmen employed by the estates, their social pattern was not conducive to an indigenous artistic expression. As freed servants became landholders and, after Bacon's Rebellion, factors in government, the folkways and beliefs of peasants and prisoners captured in the Scotch and Irish wars were partly absorbed into middle-class society. The general use of Negro slaves about the middle of the eighteenth century created an impoverished class of poor whites and was responsible for the migration or escape of thousands of white indentured servants to join the Scotch-Irish and Germans in mountain pockets of the back country. As a consequence, such folklore as remained was confined to isolated groups along the coast and on islands a few miles off the mainland.

Masters of large estates held constant open house, where hard drinking was the order of the day, with persimmon beer, apple cider, cherry bounce, brandies, corn whiskey, wines, and juleps made of rum, water, and sugar. Gambling was common, and young people indulged in such games as 'cross and pile,' 'putt,' 'buttons, to get pawns for redemption,' 'grind the bottle,' 'fox in the warner,' and 'break the Pope's neck.' Negroes and whites attended the races, cock fights, and boxing matches, and talented servants supplied music for the dances. Life was not entirely devoted to entertaining, however, for there was work to be done, and the forces of nature were rough in a region swept by winds and tide and storm.

In an area swept by winds and tides and constantly threatened, not only by the forces of nature, but also by pirates who infested the coast, it is not strange that people gave credence to stories of haunts, dints, and witches. Lynnhaven Bay was a hiding place of Blackbeard, the Pirate. When conditions are right, his gun is still heard on certain nights. Blackbeard's skull, tradition says, was made into a cup and still remains in Tidewater. Taylor's Bridge was guarded for some years by a headless man, who exacted a toll of fourpence-half-penny of all who passed, and dealt harshly with those who refused to pay. The method of determining murder by the 'ordeal of touch,' practiced in Tidewater during the seventeenth century, was based on an old English and Scotch superstition that a murderer brought into the presence of his victim would cause the victim's wounds to bleed anew. Harder to get rid of is the bogy of Craddock's Creek, who leaves peculiar foot-marks and eludes capture with a weird cry of 'Yahoo! Yahoo!'

Pecatone, an estate between the Yeocomico River and Machodoc Creek, dates from 1650 and is responsible for the legend of a mistress who was a petty tyrant among her overseers and Negroes. In her last days she, her coach, and her coachman 'were borne aloft in a terrible hurricane and lost to sight.' From that time until destruction in 1888, the home was haunted by lights, groans, and shrieks at night.

In Princess Anne County, during the early days, Grace Sherwood was accused of being a witch and of having blighted Jane Gisburne's crop of cotton. According to Elizabeth Barnes, she assumed the appearance of a black cat, visited the Barnes's home, jumped over the accuser's bed, drove and whipped her, and left by a keyhole or crack in the door. Hailed into court as a witch, Grace Sherwood was found guilty and condemned to a ducking from what has since been known as Witch Duck Point. The Cape Henry area supplies several Grace Sherwood legends, and in Gloucester County two witches are said to have practiced their dark profession.

Portobago on the Rappahannock was the home of Sir Thomas Lunsford, a professional soldier who fled to Virginia from the British Roundheads. Known as the 'childeater,' he was ridiculed in verse by Royalist Cleveland:

> The Post that came from Banbury,
> Riding on a red rocket,
> Did tidings tell how Lunsford fell,
> A child's hand in his pocket.

At the eastern point of Gloucester County live a people, known as Guineamen, whose backgrounds are lost to history. These fisherfolk and truckers speak with a Middle English accent, but there is nothing in dress or mannerism to indicate their origin. The women wear sunbonnets and put shoes on only when they attend the Church of God, a Holy Roller sect. The men are usually clad in blue denim and either go barefooted or use hip boots to reach boats anchored in the shallows. Typical of their attitude and manner of living is the story about a Guineaman who shipped a load of potatoes to Baltimore. The merchantman sold them, subtracted the freight charges and his commission, and sent the farmer a bill for 50¢. The Guineaman remarked: 'Oi don't mind feeding dem poor hungry people in Baltimore, but Oi'll be damned if Oi'll pay em to eat my victuals.'

Customs retaining the flavor of *ante-bellum* days have survived among the Negroes in rural areas and small towns and even in the Negro districts of cities. Group participation in plantation labor meant social participation in play-party games, dances, molasses boilings, tobacco strippings, and corn huskings. A pseudo-spiritual of slavery days evidently refers to secret religious meetings in a secluded spot. The title, 'Lie Low, Lizzie, Lie Low,' implies, as much as the song, a message between the lines:

Lie low, Lizzie, lie low,
Cause dey ain't gwine be no meeting here tonight.
Meat selling nine pence a pound,
And coan five dollars a barrel.
So lie low, Lizzie, lie low.
Cause dey ain't gwine be no meeting here tonight.

Ain't gwine be no meeting here tonight.
Don' you know, don' you know?
Creek's all muddy, and de pond all dry.
Warn't fo' de tadpole, de fish all die.
So lie low, Lizzie, lie low.
Cause dey ain't gwine be no meeting here tonight.

Another Gloucester Point song was probably used in a festive dance when the beer was ripe and includes the following verse:

Juba boys, Juba, Juba up, Juba down,
Juba round Simmon town.
Juba dis, en Juba dat,
Juba round de simmon vat.

A cakewalk song from the same region reflects an even more abandoned spirit of gayety:

When er fellah come a knocking
De holler, 'Oh shoo.'
Hop high ladies,
Oh, Miss Loo.
Oh, swing dat yaller gal,
Do boys, do.
Hop light yallers,
Oh, Miss Loo.

Stories of the Uncle Remus type were a source of entertainment, especially brief 'hoodle-tales,' such as 'Why the Frog Lives in the Water,' 'In the Bee-tree,' 'The Ugliest Animal,' and 'Buzzard Makes Terrapin His Riding Horse.' Slightly humorous, the tales frequently contained a moral and were directed at both animals and human beings.

More universal are the work-gang or track-lining songs found wherever a railroad lays its track. Like sea chanteys and the ribaldries of urban laborers, many of the gang songs are too rough for the printed page, but two innocuous rhymes are:

Little red rooster ain't got no comb,
Just like a rounder ain't got no home.
Hey boys! Get right again.

Jack de rabbit,
Jack de bear.
Shake it back, boys,
Just a hair!

The natural musical talents of the Negro were noticed by Thomas Jefferson in his *Notes on Virginia*: 'In music they are more generally gifted than the whites with accurate ears for tune and time, and they have been found capable of imagining a small catch.' But general recognition of the artistic value of Negro songs and music and interest in their preservation are comparatively modern, and no successful attempt to collect them was made before 1830. William Francis Allen, Charles Pickard Ware, and Lucy McKim Garrison published their collection of *Slave Songs of the United States* in 1867. *Cabin and Plantation Songs as Sung by the Hampton Students* was compiled in 1874 by Thomas P. Fenner, and *Religious Folk-Songs of the Negroes as Sung on the Plantation* was arranged from this work by the musical director of Hampton Institute in 1909. In 1918 Hampton Institute published *Negro Folk Songs* collected and edited by Natalie Curtis Burlin. Songs of the Negroes of some of the counties of Mississippi, Georgia, North Carolina, and Tennessee were gathered by Howard W. Odum and Guy B. Johnson of the University of North Carolina and compiled in their book *The Negro and His Songs*, published in 1925. Since many Negroes in these States spring from slaves originally bought in Virginia, their songs partly represent the Old Dominion. Dorothy Scarborough of Columbia University made a collection of songs from several Southern States, including Virginia, for her book, *On the Trail of the Negro Folk-Songs*, also published in 1925. Negro workers on the Federal Writers' Project have recorded many Negro songs, hymns, and spirituals that otherwise would have died with the last of the ex-slaves.

Negro singing, first made known to the general public by singers from Fisk University in Tennessee, was then popularized by singers from

Hampton Institute, and later by those from other Virginia Negro schools. Thomas P. Fenner came from Providence, Rhode Island, to Hampton Institute in 1872 to establish a department of music. The Hampton singers at first numbered 17, and the first concert to raise money for Virginia Hall was given in Lincoln Hall, Washington,D.C., February 15, 1873. Hampton now has a regular choir that tours America. Each year the Virginia State College Choral Society from Petersburg gives a concert in honor of the governor of Virginia.

Negro spirituals are strangely haunting. Those current among the Virginia Negroes today differ little from those sung several decades ago. 'Swing Low, Sweet Chariot' was noted in Fisk Jubilee Songs, 1871. The Hampton version is a variant. This theme, or one similar to it, occurs in the first movement of Dvorak's *New World Symphony*, and the same theme also occurs in John Powell's 'Negro Rhapsody.' 'My Lord Delivered Daniel' was noted in *Slave Songs of the United States*, *Jubilee Songs* (1872), and *Hampton Plantation Songs*. 'The Old Ship of Zion,' a spiritual widely current in Virginia, has many variants. 'Go Down Moses,' a song of slavery, is an interpretation of Hebrew history. 'Deep River' is a spiritual highly prized in Virginia. 'Steal Away to Jesus' was first sung as a notice to the other slaves on the plantation that a secret religious meeting would be held that night.

The spiritual or religious songs of the 'fasola' singers are an important aspect of Southern folk music. Singing schools utilizing the rural shape-note method were established in the Shenandoah Valley by Yankee singing masters and spread south, southeast, and west along with the shape-note hymn books of Ananias Davisson and James P. Carrell of Harrisonburg. The former's *The Kentucky Harmony*, was published about 1817, and *The Supplement to the Kentucky Harmony* appeared in 1821. The latter's *Songs of Zion* and *The Virginia Harmony* appeared in 1820 and 1831, respectively.

In the eighteenth century Joseph Funk and his father settled in Singer's Glen, near Harrisonburg. Here, more than a century ago, Joseph Funk began to teach vocal music and to publish song books. His *Choral Music*, a collection of German songs, was published in 1816; and he continued in this work until just before the War between the States. The shop fell into disrepair, but was set up later by Funk's grandson, Aldine Kieffer, who founded *Musical Millions*, a monthly publication devoted to rural music and singing schools. Kieffer's 'Twilight Is Falling,' set to music by B.C.Unseld, is popular throughout the rural South.

John Powell has made numerous settings for ballads, folk-songs, hymns, and dances. *Twelve Folk Hymns*, from the old shape-note hymnbooks and oral tradition which Mr.Powell edited, and for which he, Annabel Morris Buchanan, and Hilton Rufty wrote musical settings, was published in 1934. A collection of such folk-music was included in Mrs.Buchanan's publication, *Folk Hymns of America*. Mr.Rufty has done the musical settings for the *American Anthology of Old World Ballads*, compiled and edited by Dr.Reed Smith of the University of South Carolina and published in 1937.

Although individual collectors and composers have rendered valuable assistance in the appreciation, use, and preservation of old ballads, songs, and stories, unless there is active community interest in the folkways and music of various regions and peoples, the work of academicians is no insurance against the ultimate disappearance of certain examples of American speech, anecdote, rhyme, and handicraft. Arthur Kyle Davis,Jr., editor of *The Traditional Ballads of Virginia*, has completed the work begun by the late Professor C.Alphonso Smith, former archivist of the Virginia Folklore Society. The White Top Festival, first held in 1931 on the summit of White Top Mountain in southwest Virginia, has developed out of increased interest on the part of musicians and laymen alike in the contributions of folk artists in the hinterland. This festival is the meeting place each August for folklorists and music makers of the South and neighboring States. Equally important is the annual summer get-together held at Galax, where the atmosphere is less academic and participants are free of the inhibitions common to most public performances of this nature.

As hard-surface roads reach inward to the hollows and settlements, bringing or following radios, gas stations, movies, and dine-and-dance halls, the old customs undergo a gradual change. Some compromise with urban ways of living is necessary when the last frontier may be only a few hundred yards from an express highway, sandwiched between a billboard and a mountain. On fence lines, telephone poles, and barn sides, from mining towns in southwestern Virginia to farm lanes in the Shenandoah Valley, posters proclaim the union of hinterland and city and advertise the virtues of 'EFFIE, the Hillbilly Striptease Dancer.' This type of artist, born of crossroad and urban music hall, appears at local theaters with a noisy hoedown band that probably had its origin in the woods of Manhattan and borrowed its folk-songs from Tin Pan Alley. But it is by such blending that a people will find themselves and create a native art and culture—a culture that ranges from symphonic compositions of the city to Negro spirituals of the lowlands and from story-ballads of the hills to trade rhymes of heavy industries. It is Virginia and America.

Art

FOR one brief moment in the late sixteenth century, European art flared faintly on the shores of the Virginia colony. Among the stalwarts of Raleigh's 'Second Colonie' that clutched for a foothold on the new continent in 1585 was John White (Johannes Wyth), later to become Virginia's second governor (1587–90) and the grandfather of Virginia Dare. The water-color drawings made in 1585–86 by this 'English paynter . . . sent into the countryc by the queenes Maiestye, onlye to draw the description of the place' and 'to describe the shapes of the Inhabitants their Apparell, manners of Livinge, and fashions . . .' were 'cutt in copper' and issued by Theodore de Bry in 1590 to illustrate John Hariot's *Narrative*. From the 18 drawings still in existence it is evident that White attempted to produce a full pictorial account of the life of the aborigines.

Handicrafts were the only native art of seventeenth-century Virginia. Hardly a year after the founding of Jamestown, Sir Christopher Newport brought to the colony a number of Dutch and Polish glassmakers. The industry continued to the 'Starving Time,' when it languished and finally became extinct. In 1621 Captain William Norton and four skilled Italians, in a second attempt at glassmaking, produced chiefly beads for Indian trade until the enterprise was wiped out by the massacre of 1622. During the next decades such crafts as cobbling, tanning, weaving, and pottery making were carried on.

The 'Artickles of Agreemt' between Dennis Whit and Morgan Jones in 1667 probably contain the earliest reference to Virginia pottery: 'a condicon or agreemt for to be copartners for ye term of five years in making and selling of Earthen warre . . .' With the growth of population toward the turn of the century—from some 40,000 in 1670 to about 70,000 in 1700—handicrafts increased.

The fine arts developed more slowly. Though art was appreciated from the beginning, as indicated by the early importation of British paintings and *objets d'art*, a number of factors hindered local creation. Prosperous Virginians remained, as a rule, intensely loyal to the British Crown, regarding the mother country as their real home; even the gentlemen who flocked to Virginia after the fall of Charles I in 1649 endeavored to transmit the English tradition to their children and frequently sent their sons 'home' to be educated. Nor was social life on the widely scattered plantations—with an occasional trip to fashionable Williamsburg—of the kind to stimulate native artistic activity.

During the eighteenth century, however, visiting artists were attracted to the colony. Charles Bridges, who arrived in Williamsburg in May 1734 is the first known professional painter in Tidewater Virginia. Having done portraits of the Byrd children 'and several others in the neighborhood,' the artist in 1735 received from William Byrd II a letter of introduction to Governor Spotswood that resulted in several important commissions. Bridges flourished in the colony until about 1750 and, like most of his contemporaries, did various types of decoration in addition to portrait painting. In 1740, 1,600 pounds of tobacco were sold by Caroline County to pay Bridges 'for drawing the King's Arms for the use of the County Court.' In 1743 Alexander Gordon (1692–1754) came from England to Virginia, where he combined painting with the professions of musician and teacher of languages.

The Swedish painter Gustavus Hesselius (1682–1755), one of America's most noted art pioneers, had settled in Delaware and traveled through coastal Virginia, painting portraits rich in character and individuality. His son John (1728–78) also did portraits for prominent Virginia families. Between the years 1758 and 1767 an Englishman, John Wollaston,Jr., executed in Virginia many portraits in a style suggestive of Kneller, though he gave his sitters rather puffy hands and eyes with so peculiar a slant toward the nose that critics dubbed him 'The Almond Eyed Artist.' Henry Warren, another 'limner,' is known only by an advertisement in the *Virginia Gazette* in 1768 that announced his establishment in Williamsburg and his readiness to paint 'night pieces' and 'family pieces.'

The many portraits painted in Virginia between 1764 and 1775 by the Huguenot, John Durand, another of the group that traveled from town to town earning a precarious livelihood, are hard and dry, though of pleasing color and, as Robert Sully reflected, 'with less vulgarity of style than artists of his *calibre* generally possess.' Henry Benbridge (1744–1812), a Philadelphian with European training, settled in South Carolina upon his return from London in 1770 and radiated over the Southern field, executing many portraits, family groups, and an occasional deft miniature. In 1799 youthful Thomas Sully discovered Benbridge hard at work in Norfolk. In order to acquire a knowledge of oil painting, Sully sat for his portrait and profited by Benbridge's 'useful and kind instruction.'

To this group of eighteenth-century portraitists belong also Robert Edge Pine (1730–88), an Englishman who painted Washington at Mount Vernon in 1785, and William Williams (1759–1823), a New York portraitist who toured the South working in oil, pastel, and miniature. In 1793, the Masonic Lodge in Alexandria, having received President Washington into the order, commissioned Williams, then living in Philadelphia, to 'paint him as he is,' and the result was a somewhat inartistic pastel portrait (now in Alexandria) that is, perhaps, a good likeness. Williams also executed a portrait of 'Light Horse Harry' Lee. Of 'Manley, Taylor, Frazier, and Caine,' mentioned by William Dunlap as painters who worked in Virginia during this time, nothing is known except that Frazier's works kindled in Charles Willson Peale the ambition to paint.

During the early Republican period, roughly from 1783 to 1820, Colonial portraiture gave way before the influence of the classicist Benjamin West (1738–1820), whose school in London was attended by many post-Revolutionary American artists. Foremost among West's pupils was versatile Charles Willson Peale (1741–1827), who had worked as a saddler and at many other trades. On a trip to Norfolk to buy leather, he was so much impressed by the paintings of 'a certain Frazier' that on his return to Maryland he took up the study of art with John Hesselius at Annapolis. In 1766 he entered West's studio. While living in London, he obtained through his friends in Maryland the commission to paint the full length portrait of *Lord Chatham* that Edmond Jennings sent to Virginia as a gift to the 'Gentlemen of Westmoreland County.' Returning to America in 1769, Peale executed many portraits, group compositions, miniatures, and silhouettes of Virginians and in 1772 painted at Mount Vernon his most notable portrait—that of George Washington in the costume of a colonel in the Virginia militia.

Gilbert Stuart (1755–1828), foremost painter of the young republic and renowned for his many portraits of Washington, established himself at the new National capital from 1803 to 1805; among his sitters were John Randolph of Roanoke, James and Dolly Madison, and Colonel John Tayloe and his wife, of Mount Airy and the Octagon House.

Among the later group of West's pupils who worked in Virginia were William Dunlap (1766–1839) and Thomas Sully (1783–1872). Dunlap, author of the *History of the Rise and Progress of the Arts of Design in the United States*, painted many portraits in Virginia during the winters of 1819–21. At 16 Sully, who was born in England but brought up in Charleston,S.C., joined his brother Lawrence, who was painting miniatures in Norfolk. Later, he obtained instruction from Fraser, the miniaturist, and from Benbridge and West. His numerous portraits of Virginians, particularly residents of Petersburg and Richmond, were done during the period stretching from 1804 to about 1855 and are representative of his fluent, easy style.

The surge of classicism that produced so many historical and allegorical canvases during the early Republican period received in Virginia a powerful stimulus through Thomas Jefferson's architectural designs and his enthusiasm for the study of the arts. The 'intellectual collaboration' (to quote Bernard Faÿ) between France and America that marked this epoch was further exemplified by the founding in Richmond in 1786 of the Academy of Sciences and Fine Arts of the United States of America, the first institution of its kind in the new country, by the visionary Chevalier Quesnay de Beaurepaire. With funds subscribed in Virginia and elsewhere, Beaurepaire erected a building near Capitol Square. The project, however, came to naught—the building was burned, and the Chevalier himself was swept into the vortex of the French Revolution. In 1785 the French sculptor Jean-Antoine Houdon (1741–1828), commissioned by the legislature to execute a statue of Washington, arrived at Mount Vernon; he made a life mask and painstaking measurements of Washington. At the end of the year he returned to France and began work on the magnificent marble statue—probably the most celebrated in the United States—which was placed in the rotunda of the State capitol in 1796.

Between 1808 and 1811, Felix Sharples, son of the English pastel painter James Sharples, executed pastels in Norfolk, Suffolk, and many of the Tidewater counties. As security for money borrowed, he left in the State a large collection of pastels by himself and other members of his family, which formed the nucleus of the Sharples Collection in Independence Hall. The French émigré, Julien Févret de Saint-Mémin (1770–1852), came to Richmond during the Aaron Burr trial in 1807, when the town was crowded with important personages. He remained not quite a year, producing—with the aid of a machine called a physionotrace—profile drawings in crayon and white chalk; Saint-Mémin's delicate miniature engravings were made by reducing these drawings on copper plates with a pantograph. John Wesley Jarvis (1780–1839), Anglo-American portrait and miniature painter, made seasonal trips to the cities and estates south of Baltimore during the early decades of the nineteenth century.

Local artists of Richmond at this time were Philip A. Peticolas (1760–1843), copyist and painter of miniatures, and James Warrell, an Englishman, who in 1812 was offering his services to the citizens 'as a Portrait Painter in Oil.' Among Warrell's canvases was the *Sena Soma*, or the

Sword Swallower, now at the Valentine Museum. In 1814 he designed *Peter Francisco's Gallant Action . . . in Amelia County, Virginia*, later engraved by D.Edwin. In 1816 Warrell, with Richard Lorton, a Petersburg artist, aided in establishing in Richmond a museum of art and natural science known as the Virginia Museum. Music and displays of fireworks were used to entice the public to the museum, where paintings were exhibited among a miscellaneous collection of *objets d'art*. Here were shown a group of Gilbert Stuart's portraits and John Vanderlyn's *Ariadne*, the first study of a nude unveiled publicly in Richmond.

Between the War of 1812 and the middle of the century the English tradition in portraiture survived in the work of English-born William J. Hubard (1807–62), Edward F. Peticolas, and Robert M. Sully (1803–55), nephew of Thomas Sully. In 1829, Chester Harding (1792–1866) exhibited in Richmond his 'portraits of many distinguished men,' to which he added those of several Richmonders.

With the expansion of commerce and the growth of National sentiment, American landscapes and scenes from everyday life found their way into local painting. Foremost among the genre painters was George Caleb Bingham (1811–79), who was born in Augusta County but worked mainly in Missouri. Bingham's paintings constitute a record of the domestic and political life of the frontier. His later work shows the influence of the anecdotal school of Düsseldorf in Germany, to which American painters had begun to turn for instruction.

The name Hudson River School has been applied to a loosely defined indigenous movement in landscape painting. In this tradition worked William Louis Sontag (1822–1900), a Pennsylvanian, whose *Morning in the Alleghanies* is representative of his many landscapes of western Virginia. Views of Mount Vernon, a popular subject, were painted by William Henry Bartlett (1809–94).

The paintings inspired by the War between the States are linked artistically with the impulse to record local scenes and events. John A. Elder (1833–95), who had studied at Düsseldorf under Emmanuel Leutze, settled in Richmond, where he painted battle scenes and portraits of *Robert E. Lee* and *Stonewall Jackson*. Conrad Wise Chapman (1842–1910), born in Washington,D.C. and brought up in Rome, came to the South during the war, entered the army, and, while attached to General Beauregard's forces at Charleston, S.C., was detailed to make paintings of the city's fortifications. He produced 31 canvases (now at the Confederate Museum, Richmond), of which *Sunset Gun, Fort Sumter* is the most beautiful. E.L.Henry (1841–1919), James Hope (1818–92), Sandford R. Gifford (1823–80), and David Blythe (1815–65) depicted military operations in the region of the Potomac.

The Hudson River School broadened under the influence of the French Barbizon group with its subjective poetic interpretations of landscape. Robert Loftin Newman (1827–1912), born at Louisa, exemplifies this later phase of nineteenth-century American painting. After studying in Paris under Couture, and absorbing the Barbizon style, he returned to America to paint landscapes distinguished for their color harmonies. Benjamin West Clinedinst (1859–1931) was born near Woodstock and after a period of study in Paris executed many portraits and genre paintings. Elliott Daingerfield (1859–1932), born at Harpers Ferry, came early under the Barbizon influence and achieved wide recognition as a landscapist and figure painter. Prince Pierre Troubetzkoy, society painter, was a resident of Albemarle County and died in Charlottesville in 1936.

A number of native Virginia painters have done most of their work outside the State. Carle John Blenner (b.1864) whose work is primarily in portraiture, was born in Richmond, studied in Germany and France, and now lives in New York. F.Graham Cootes (b.1879), New York painter and illustrator, was born in Staunton. A native of Petersburg, Jerome Myers (b.1867) is among the leaders of modern realism in American painting; he works in a variety of media, specializing in New York street scenes. Hugh Henry Breckenridge (b.1870), whose paintings are to be seen in many prominent institutions throughout the country, was born in Leesburg and trained in Paris. He has been an instructor at the Pennsylvania Academy of Fine Arts since 1894.

On the other hand, several artists from other sections have incorporated themselves into Virginia life. Gari Melchers (1860–1932), outstanding Detroit-born artist, settled at Falmouth after working in Düsseldorf, Paris, and Holland, where he did many admirable studies of Dutch peasants. While on a visit to America to execute murals, he was attracted by the color and local types of the Virginia mountains and made his home in the State until his death, taking part in the establishment of the Virginia Museum of Fine Arts and in other art activities. Born in New York, W.Sergeant Kendall (b.1869), a pupil of Thomas Eakins, has contributed outstanding landscapes of the Virginia scene.

The development of sculpture in Virginia began in the nineteenth century, chiefly under the domination of the Italian School. One of Virginia's first sculptors was Alexander Galt (1827–63), a native of Norfolk who studied in Florence; he died before he reached artistic maturity, and many of his best works were burned during the evacuation of Richmond in 1865.

Edward V. Valentine (1838–1930), of Richmond, who studied in France, Italy, and Germany, returned to his native city in 1865 and became a leading artistic influence there. His works in the State include statues of *Jefferson Davis* and *Thomas Jefferson*, a recumbent marble statue of Lee, and the figure studies, *Andromache and Astyanax* and *The Blind Girl.* Among the few examples of his work that Sir Moses Ezekiel (1844–1917), who studied in Germany, sent to his native State from his studio in the Baths of Diocletian were two statues of *Jefferson*, a bust of *General Edward W. Nichols*, and the *Confederate Memorial* at Arlington. After service in the War between the States and study in Paris, William Ludwell Sheppard (1833–1912), best known for his genre painting and studies of the soldiers of the Army of Northern Virginia, executed many notable statues and a bronze haut-relief, *The Color Bearer*. Master of a variety of media, Paris-trained Augustus Lukeman (1872–1935), a native of Richmond, settled in New York, where he executed bas-reliefs, monuments, and portrait busts, including the *Jefferson Davis* in the Federal capitol. William Couper, who was born in Norfolk in 1853, returned from the studios of Munich and Florence and established himself in New York in 1897 as a portraitist and sculptor of busts in the modern Italian manner; he is represented in Virginia by a heroic bronze statue of *Dr.Hunter Holmes McGuire* and a statue of *Captain John Smith.*

Sculptors from outside the State have contributed important monuments memorializing Virginia personalities and events. In Richmond, grouped around Houdon's busts of *Washington* and *Lafayette* in the capitol rotunda, are seven statues of Virginia-born presidents, by Charles Keck, Charles Beach, Harriet Frishmuth, Attilio Piccirilli, and F.William Sievers, a native of Indiana but long a resident of Richmond. Other sculptors with representative works in Richmond are John Frazee (1790–1852), pioneer American-born sculptor, Thomas Crawford (*c.*1813–57), and Randolph Rogers, all of New York; Joel Hart (1810–77), of Kentucky; and Frederick Volck. In Charlottesville is statuary by Robert I. Aitken, Charles Keck, Karl Bitter, and Gutzon Borglum, while Williamsburg preserves Richard Hayward's eighteenth-century memorial statue of *Norborne Berkeley.*

Among the beginnings of graphic art in Virginia were Saint-Mémin's profile engravings and his etched view of Richmond's water front—a scene also depicted in line and mezzotint by Peter Maverick (1780–1831). To this early period belong, too, Joseph Wood (1798–1852), aquatintist, and the French engraver Blouet, both of whom did views of the State penitentiary in Richmond. Thomas Sully was not above occasional commercial lithography, and John Gadsby Chapman executed some 1,400 drawings, resembling steel engravings, that served as illustrations; Benjamin West Clinedinst in the 1890's and William Ludwell Sheppard also made contributions in this field. Among etchers associated with Virginia were William Louis Sontag, Elliott Daingerfield, and James D. Smillie. The drawings and book illustrations of Dugald Stewart Walker (1884–1937), a native of Richmond who received instruction in Virginia and New York, are lavish in detail, and distinguished by an oriental richness of design. Jerome Myers captures realistically the types of New York's east side in his admirable lithographs.

The problems of readjustment that followed the War between the States impeded public activity in the arts until 1892 when the Valentine Museum was founded in Richmond to house collections in art, archeology, and anthropology. Native art was fostered by the Art Club of Richmond, organized in 1895; and in later years, by the Virginia League of Fine Arts and Handicrafts, formed in 1917 by two Richmond artists, Adele Clark and Nora Houston; and by the Academy of Sciences and Fine Arts of the United States, revived in 1930, which encourages creative work through lectures, classes, and frequent exhibitions. In Richmond, Confederate relics are housed in the Confederate Museum; a representative group of eighteenth-century portraits in the home of the Virginia Historical Society; and a large collection of contemporary paintings, statuary, and *objets d'art* in the Virginia Museum of Fine Arts, founded in 1934. The Norfolk Museum and the Bayly Museum of Fine Arts at the University of Virginia are important contributors to local art appreciation; while the specialized Mariners' Museum near Newport News contains interesting carved figureheads and a great variety of exhibits relating to maritime life. The Conservation Commission of Virginia established in 1937 the Virginia Art Index, directed by Julia Sully, for the purpose of recording all historic portraits in the State.

Today, many native artists are producing portraits, landscapes, and studies of local types and of characteristic Virginia scenes; realistic genre painting seems to be the dominant influence among the younger artists. The Negro wood-carver, Leslie Bolling (b.1898), has produced admirable statuettes of racial types. Among those active in the graphic arts are Lois Wilcox, engraver and lithographer, and the wood engravers Charles W. Smith (b.1893) and Julius J. Lankes (b.1884). An attempt has also been made in recent years to revive the handicrafts. In the mountains, mission groups started in 1923 to teach weaving, rug making, needlecraft, bookbinding, cabinet making, wood carving, and allied crafts; and this work has been taken up by various schools and guilds, and by the Handicraft Projects of the Works Progress Administration. Among the flourishing potteries now in the State is the interesting James Towne Collony Pottery, which duplicates old pieces discovered during the Williamsburg and Jamestown excavations.

Interest in art seems to be growing throughout the State. Art festivals are held in many Virginia centers, and a series of exchange exhibitions has been conducted—followed in 1938 by the first All-Virginia Exhibition of paintings sent to New York City, and the inauguration of a Biennial Exhibition of Contemporary Painting by the Virginia Museum of Fine Arts. Federal Art Galleries located at Big Stone Gap, Lynchburg, Fairfax, and Richmond are contributing to the artistic education of Virginians through classes, exhibitions, and lectures. In 1938 the Negro Art Center was established in Richmond, offering, under a Negro instructor, classes in painting, wood carving, modeling, and other branches of the arts and crafts. Art departments in various colleges and flourishing summer art schools are promoting art appreciation and training Virginia's artists of tomorrow.

Literature

VIRGINIA is producing at last a literature both indigenous to its soil and imbued with a realism that may be said to capture the major portion of the truth about its people and its civilization. This contemporary flowering has saved the State from cults of extremists that had their day before the clatter of Virginia typewriters was heard throughout the land.

Late in the nineteenth century Virginians seriously took up writing as a profession. In the early Colonial period the struggle for existence precluded authorship as a conscious art and brought forth a pragmatic literature that described the new country for a curious English people, chronicled the daily life of the colonists, catalogued laws, and finally evolved into formal history. In the late Colonial days emphasis was placed on statesmanship and forensics to the exclusion of imaginative writing. Following the establishment of the republic, to which the Virginia intelligentsia gave its best thought, the sectional strife of the Fiery Epoch produced statesmen and orators rather than creative writers. When slavery flourished, wealth was confined to a few large planters, on the whole uninterested in professions; and the masses of tenants and small landowners were too busy digging a living out of the soil to cultivate the arts.

The War between the States left Virginians in dire poverty. 'Literature on a large scale,' says Dr. Alphonso Smith, 'implies authorship as a profession, and authorship as a profession has never flowered among a poor people . . . Literary productiveness, in other words, is vitally related to industrial productiveness, both being correlative manifestations of the creative spirit.'

The birth year of the new industrialism in the South, 1875, was also the birth year of a new Southern literature. It was then that Lanier attained National fame. Immediately thereafter other writers—Virginians among them—loomed upon the horizon, where before only the lonely figures of Poe, Timrod, Hayne, Simms, and Father Ryan had been silhouetted. The Reconstruction literature of Virginia, however, which endured well into the twentieth century, was characterized by a nostalgia for the past and a romantic idealism that evaded facts. However, many voices are at last being lifted against those artificial traditions that were memorialized by Virginians who wrote during the four decades after the War between the States.

The chroniclers of pioneer experiences wrote with spicy frankness. George Percy, who was governor of Virginia from 1609 to 1610, and Ralph Hamor, secretary of the colony, who arrived in 1609, took chronological lead with their 'true discourses,' 'true relations,' and 'observations' concerning Virginia and Virginians. Captain John Smith spun yarns that are still merry reading whether they deal with New England, the Summer Isles, or the story of Virginia. Two writers of this early period wandered along the pleasant bypaths of poetry and metrical translation. Richard Rich invites passing notice as the first of Virginia's versifiers. In 1610 he wrote *A Ballad of Virginia*, describing his voyage from England and his experiences in the new colony. A much more notable poet was the Oxford-bred George Sandys, who was treasurer of the colony for seven years and completed at Jamestown his metrical translation of Ovid's *Metamorphoses* (1626).

Then for 50 years there were neither chroniclers nor romancers. The drama of Bacon's Rebellion, however, inspired the anonymous *Burwell Papers*, which recounted the abortive effort of the people to overthrow entrenched autocracy, and eulogized the young rebel leaders. The chronicles of William Byrd II, appearing after 1741, when Virginia was about to settle down to an era of tobacco prosperity, are written in amusing and expansive vein. 'A Journey to the Land of Eden' (in *Westover Manuscripts*), which describes the pilgrimage of commissioners sent to fix the State's southern boundary, not only makes the early eighteenth century live again but still causes Virginians to chuckle over the strange ways of North Carolinians. Byrd's account of the Dismal Swamp area, of the beginnings of the iron industry, and of manners and morals in general has become increasingly valuable with the passing years. Hugh Jones, a clergyman and lawyer, rounded out the social and economic picture with the publication in 1724 of *The Present State of Virginia*, though his book is rather more for study than for entertainment. But perhaps the most delightful bits of writing that have emerged from the Colonial period are the diaries of Philip Vickers Fithian, tutor at Nomini Hall, who dealt with the goings on of belles and beaux, family dinners and neighborhood parties, work and games, foods and clothes, flirtations and stolen kisses.

The writing of formal history was initiated by Robert Beverley, whose *History of the Present State of Virginia* was published in London in 1705 and subsequently translated into French. Soon thereafter William Stith, using the notes he inherited from Sir John Randolph, compiled *The History of Virginia from the First Settlement to the Dissolution of the London Company*, which was published in 1747. As authoritative source for students of the early Colonial era, Stith's history is second only to the far different and more comprehensive work of W.W.Hening, which accurately records the statutes of Virginia from 1619 to 1792.

The era preceding and immediately following the Revolution is marked by a literature forceful, lucid, and as definitely creative as fiction, drama, or poetry. The Virginia prose of that period not only brought forth a Nation but stands today among the permanent models of expository writing. In a *Letter to the Clergy on the Two-Penny Act* (1760), Richard Bland enunciated the principles actuating those colonists who had wearied of supporting the privileged few; and his pamphlet entitled *An Inquiry into the Rights of the British Colonies* (1766), declaring Virginia no part of the Kingdom of England and united with the Mother Country only by the Crown, was amazingly prophetic of a philosophy much later to be translated into statute. *The Leedstown Resolutions*, which were written by Richard Henry Lee and adopted by 115 patriots in 1766 and which set forth the doctrine later incorporated into the Declaration of Independence; the speeches of Patrick Henry and of George Washington; James Madison's notes and contributions to the *Federalist Papers*; many speeches and pamphlets by other authors; and everything penned by Thomas Jefferson rank in clarity, force, and purity of English among the literary monuments of America.

In Revolutionary Virginia the leading contributors to *belles lettres*—as distinct from political treatises—were lawyers, physicians, and clergymen. The same breadth of culture that had emanated from the pulpit oratory of Samuel Davies characterized the preaching of the blind James Waddell. The political satires of St.George Tucker are less noteworthy than two of his lyrical compositions, 'Resignation' and 'Days of My Youth,' which, despite defects of style, have found places in most American anthologies. Dr.James McClurg, the delegate from Virginia to the Federal Constitutional Convention of 1787, who out-Hamiltoned Hamilton in his advocacy of monarchical forms for America, found escape from medicine and forensics in a pleasing bit of society verse, 'The Belles of Williamsburg,' a tribute to the pretty girls of the Colonial capital; and much fugitive verse, some of no mean quality, appeared in issues of the *Virginia Gazette*. Literature sustained a loss in 1808 when John Daly Burk, a gallant young Irishman, was killed in a duel ten years after his coming to Virginia. His tragedies, *Bunker-Hill* (1797) and *Bethlem Gabor* (1807), contain interesting local allusions, and his *History of Virginia* (1804–16) is of lasting value.

Deliberate biography of National heroes—an art unknown in England until Izaak Walton published his *Life of Donne* in 1640, and practiced little for many years thereafter—was introduced into American letters by a Virginian who chose a Virginian as his subject. Mason Locke Weems, better known as 'Parson' Weems, published in 1800 his highly imaginative *Life of Washington*, which put the cherry tree and dollar-throwing myths into permanent circulation and a set fashion in anecdotal writing that has endured even to this day. The quixotic parson followed his first success with biographies of Francis Marion, Benjamin Franklin, and William Penn—all so entertaining as to make their historical inaccuracies somewhat pardonable. The five volume study of Washington published between 1804 and 1807 by John Marshall, Chief Justice of the United States Supreme Court and author of epoch-making decisions, is a scholarly work vastly different from Weems's fairy tale. But William Wirt, highly successful in his *Letters of a British Spy* (1803) and in a series of essays published as *The Old Bachelor* (1810–13), made a dismal contribution to biography in his *Sketches of the Life and Character of Patrick Henry* (1817).

Though other Virginians wrote during the first half of the nineteenth century, only one deserves more than passing comment. Anne Royall, who spent 15 years of her childhood as a captive of the Indians, first recounted her experiences among the red men and then wrote readable travel books. *Letters to a Young Relative* by John Randolph, the poems of William Munford, *Swallow Barn* (1832), a novel of the Tidewater, and *Memoirs of the Life of William Wirt* (1849) by John Pendleton Kennedy of Maryland are not altogether forgotten. Yet no writer foreshadowed Virginia's greatest literary genius, Edgar Allan Poe.

'I am a Virginian,' Poe declared on one occasion to a friend. 'At least I call myself one.' Born in Boston, he was adopted less than three years later by the Allans of Richmond and educated in Richmond, in England, at the University of Virginia, and briefly at West Point. Though his earliest poems were published in the North and though he set out upon his career as man of letters in Baltimore, Poe achieved recognition through the *Southern Literary Messenger*, which published his first short stories and of which he became editor in 1835.

As poet, essayist, and creator of the modern short story, Poe holds in American literature a pre-eminence accentuated by the passing years. Discerning a new esthetic, he was among the first to catch in both prose and poetry the dark spirit of individuality that fascinated Baudelaire, through whose translations Poe became one of the chief progenitors of the Symbolist Movement and took his place as a real force in the development of

Western literature. There is a close relationship between Poe's genius and the atmosphere of Virginia, with its 'mists and mellow fruitfulness,' its classical background, and its drowsing mansions.

One of Poe's contemporaries who escaped oblivion through a recent reprinting of his remarkably prophetic book, *The Partisan Leader*, secretly published in Washington in 1836 and subsequently suppressed, was Judge N.Beverley Tucker, author also of a novel, *George Balcombe* (1836). Philip Pendleton Cooke, a contributor to the *Southern Literary Messenger* from Martinsburg (now in West Virginia), wrote at 17 'The Song of the Sioux Lover,' but his best-known poem is the memorial lyric, 'Florence Vane,' which has been translated into several languages. John Reuben Thompson, who succeeded Poe as editor of the *Messenger*, later composed stirring war lyrics that have found places in anthologies. George Bagby, whose editorship of the *Messenger*—assumed in 1860—was interrupted by his service in the Confederate army and ended by the death of the magazine in 1864, was a popular essayist and humorist.

From the death of Poe to the War between the States, though Virginia produced no other genius of the first rank, the years were not barren of all literary production. Into this period falls the work of Bishop William Meade, whose *Old Churches, Ministers and Families of Virginia*, published in 1857, is the authoritative source of early parish history in Virginia. General Winfield Scott wrote clearly of infantry tactics and army regulations; and Sarah Barclay Johnson illustrated *The City of the Great King* by her father, James Turner Barclay—published in 1857—and the next year brought out her own book, *The Hadji of Syria*. Disguised as a Mohammedan woman, she entered the tomb of David and sketched the first picture of it ever made public.

The literature produced in Virginia immediately after the War between the States was diverted into channels of thought deepened by the conflict. John Esten Cooke was the outstanding historical novelist and biographer of the period. After serving on Stonewall Jackson's staff, he wrote biographies of both Jackson and Lee. His three best-known novels, still greatly loved throughout the South, are *The Virginia Comedians* (1854), *Surry of Eagle's Nest* (1866), and *Mohun* (1869), which has recently been republished.

The spirit that characterized Virginia at the close of the war is revealed in such books as *Women: or Chronicles of the Late War* (1871) by Mary Tucker Magill; *The End of an Era* (1902) and *The Lion's Skin* (1905) by John Sergeant Wise; *The Birth of the Nation* (1907) by Sarah Agnes Pryor; the excellent dialect stories of La Salle Corbell Pickett, whose husband

General George Edward Pickett was made famous by his gallant charge at Gettysburg; *Diary of a Southern Refugee during the War* (1867) by Judith Brockenbrough McGuire; and *A Girl of Virginia* (1902) by Lucy Meecham Thruston. Mrs.S.A.Weiss, however, who began writing prose as a war prisoner at Fort McHenry, sought escape through such books as *The Crime of Abigail Tempest* and *The Last Days of Poe,* and through the writing of poetry. Her books had a wide circulation in England and were translated into both French and German.

In the poetry of the immediate postwar period, John Reuben Thompson was perhaps the most studied artist; but Father Abram Joseph Ryan, laureate of the South, was the most beloved poet. Under the pen name Moina, he wrote ringing war lyrics that were recited by all literate Southerners. The moods induced by the war are vividly expressed also in the devotional verse of Margaret Junkin Preston, the clarion battle songs of James Barron Hope, and the sharply pointed lines of Father John Banister Tabb. A place among the poets should be given also to Christopher P. Cranch, who published in 1875 what is probably the best American translation of Virgil's *Aeneid.*

But the war's aftermath distorted the creative spirit in curious ways. Writers, glorifying the days that were no more, sought to crystallize in memory a past that had never existed as they portrayed it. Possessing no iconoclasm and much conservatism, Southern literature was for 30 years an inaccurate picture of the times it professed to reproduce, but it was pleasingly written and provided a narcotic that the South welcomed. The singing optimism of Thomas Nelson Page offered an escape from depressing realities. Page's first published work appeared in *Scribner's Monthly* in 1877, but his recognition as a writer dates from the publication of *Marse Chan* ten years later. His novels, following in quick succession, are still among the sentimental classics of the South. In another kind of reaction Thomas Dixon of North Carolina, who lived for a time in Virginia, wrote novels of Southern life—*The Leopard's Spots* (1902) and *The Clansman* (1905)—as special pleas for hatred. Later *The Trail of the Lonesome Pine* (1908) and other fiction of John Fox,Jr., beatified the mountain whites with unlikely virtues and started the spurious lore of the 'hill billy,' which is now being amplified by radio.

Neither Virginia nor the South can be held wholly accountable for this trend. When Frances Hodgson Burnett wrote *Little Lord Fauntleroy* (1886), inspired, it is said, by the little son of a friend with whom she was staying in Norfolk, the book was devoured by sentimental readers throughout the English-speaking world. Two continents shed tears during this era over 'Sweet Alice, Ben Bolt,' which Thomas Dunn English wrote while visiting a friend in Tazewell County, Virginia. The immense success in Victorian England of Du Maurier's *Trilby* (1894) absolves Virginia from full responsibility for the sentimentalism of an era that cherished Thomas Nelson Page's *Two Little Confederates* (1888) and the self-effacing Southern mammy of fiction.

Marion Harland responded to the same influence. Born Virginia Hawes, in Amelia County, she married Edward Payson Terhune, a Presbyterian minister, and is the mother of Albert Payson Terhune and Virginia Terhune Van de Water. Her novels were immensely successful, though she won wider renown as the author of a cookbook and as a writer on domestic economy.

The twentieth century was well on its way when the new Southern literature came into being. In the forefront of the novelists it has produced stand three Virginians: Mary Johnston, Ellen Glasgow, and James Branch Cabell; and Virginia may claim also Willa Cather, who was born in Winchester.

Mary Johnston wrote through one era and into another. Beginning as a romanticist, she evolved into realism and finally into mysticism. Even in her earliest historical novels, however, where she was at her romantic best, Miss Johnston's genius for truthful detail is apparent. From the landing of the women in 1620 through the stirring 1860's, her story of Virginia is written with keen feeling for dramatic values and historic verity. Though she made no effort to debunk, she has not surrounded her heroes with traditional glamour. Her Stonewall Jackson in *The Long Roll* (1911), the mad general threatened with the mutiny of his soldiers, was disturbing to the hero-worshipers who demanded that greatness and perfection be considered synonymous. Yet students have been unable to prove that the portrayal was not in accord with the records. In *Hagar* (1913) Miss Johnston brought her chronicle up to the present day and then set out with the mystics to discover the fourth dimension, writing such books as *Michael Forth* and *The Exile*. Sympathetically and yet unsparingly, she treated of a way of life that had to give place to modernity. While arguing in behalf of social reform, she gave with remarkable fairness the case of both plaintiff and defendant, and truthfully presented Virginia caught in transition.

The novelist who presents the most nearly complete picture of the South is undoubtedly Ellen Glasgow. In order that her literary achievement may be correctly evaluated, Miss Glasgow's work must be viewed in its entirety. Among the 20 books she has written in 41 years, there are no failures. At the beginning of her career, the local color novel had not yet run its course in America. It had, according to Carl Van Doren, invented few memorable plots, devised no new styles, added few notable characters to fiction, but had contented itself with the creation of types and puppets. Sentimentality was its dominant characteristic. Therefore, when she began writing of the Virginia she knew so well, Miss Glasgow must have consciously resisted the sentimentalism of her contemporaries. Her strongly ironical vein probably saved her. Sometimes laughing at Virginia, loving it but knowing it, she has given to the world a realism touched with whatever there is of romance that rings true. With the pen of a realist, this novelist of changing manners has dared to fight sentimentality and has defied a public she knew to be demanding what she has called 'an evasive idealism, a sham optimism, and a sugary philosophy.'

Miss Glasgow is the most significant novelist writing of the South today, because her canvas is the broadest. In depicting the reconstructed South, she deals not only with the aristocracy that gave her birth, but with the common people whom she has learned to understand so well. The best known of her books are perhaps *Barren Ground* (1925), *The Romantic Comedians* (1926), and *They Stooped to Folly* (1929).

James Branch Cabell belongs also to the literature of protest against Philistia. Having fled to Poictesme, Cabell sends his iconoclastic shafts against spiritual conservatism and by means of a new romance pierces the old with the cool steel of his inimitable irony. The South furnished the background for his emergence into a realm of his own making. Lichfield—or Richmond—offers too narrow an horizon for the sort of genius that is Cabell's. In Poictesme there is freedom for the mind that would wander unfettered by the limitations actuality imposes. Here Cabell, the imaginative genius, is able to reveal truth higher than that to be found in realism. Here it is that Manuel, the Redeemer, can study 'the secret of preserving that dissatisfaction which is divine where all else falls away with age into the acquiescence of beasts'; and here Jurgen, the pawnbroker, can wage his halfhearted, though ineffectual, fight to escape the rule of Koschei, the deathless.

With the perspective Poictesme provides, Cabell ridicules the sentimentality, the orthodoxy, and the unreality of the Philistia in which his predecessors—and, alas, many of his contemporaries—dwell in inane but scarcely blissful ignorance. Since his mixture of symbolism and factual writing sometimes baffles the constituency rightfully his, it is no wonder that the literal-minded ones are left either perplexed or aghast. Yet in the literature of disillusionment James Branch Cabell holds high rank. In 1929 at the age of 50 he completed the 20 books he chose to call his 'biography,' dropped James from his name, and as Branch Cabell started upon a new literary career.

Among Virginia-born novelists, however, Willa Cather is perhaps best assured of lasting favor. Though she does not use Virginia scenes, her matured and careful art reflects the State in its sense of background and its leisured grace of style. Something similar may be said of the Far-Eastern novels of Pearl Buck, who is a Virginian by descent and a graduate of Randolph-Macon Woman's College. For many years the stories, essays, and novels of Margaret Prescott Montague, who spends her winters in Richmond, have delighted literary esthetes. *Closed Doors; Studies of Deaf and Blind Children,* published in 1915; and the articles that were appearing at that time in the *Atlantic Monthly* assured Miss Montague of an important place in literature. Henry Sydnor Harrison presented in *Queed* (1911), *V.V.'s Eyes* (1913), and *Angela's Business* (1915) a truthful picture of life in the South, though his method was somewhat reminiscent of the Victorians. His Angela, seated behind the steering wheel of her little Fordette, constantly about her business of pursuing men, was drawn with a scathing irony of which Southern men had formerly not been guilty. Amélie Rives, in private life the Princess Troubetzkoy, published her first book in 1888 and has subsequently written drama, fiction, and poetry of high literary quality.

Other Virginia novelists of the twentieth century whose work has brought far-flung recognition are Kate Langley Bosher, author of *Mary Cary* (1910) and other best sellers; Sally Nelson Robins, whose books were founded upon experiences shared by many of her neighbors in Virginia; Helena Lefroy Caperton, whose versatile pen has recreated the Richmond of other days and sketched humorously the present-day Richmond she knows so well; Emma Speed Sampson, whose 'Miss Minerva' books are quoted by old and young; Roy Flannagan, whose realistic typewriter is hammering out tales of a South that romanticists have striven to hide; and Clifford Dowdy, whose war story *Bugles Blow No More* achieved immediate popularity.

Blair Niles, author of *Black Haiti* (1926) and *Condemned to Devil's Island* (1928), is a Virginian. Sherwood Anderson bought two newspapers in Marion, Virginia, lived there awhile, and still gives Marion as his permanent address. Frances Parkinson Keyes, novelist and associate editor of *Good Housekeeping,* was born in Charlottesville. Agnes Rothery (Mrs. Harry Rogers Pratt) has achieved recognition in America and abroad as the author of travel books. Her *New Roads in Old Virginia* appeared in 1929 and has been followed by authoritative books on foreign countries.

Virginius Dabney, editor of the Richmond *Times-Dispatch*, has written with detached eloquence of *Liberalism in the South* (1932).

In biography and history Virginians have done the scholarly work that was to be expected from their tradition. Especially distinguished are the names of Alexander Brown, author of *The Genesis of the United States* (1890) and *The First Republic in America* (1898); Philip A. Bruce, author of *Economic History of Virginia in the Seventeenth Century* (1895), *Social Life of Virginia in the Seventeenth Century* (1907), and *Institutional History of Virginia in the Seventeenth Century* (1910); Lyon Gardiner Tyler, former president of the College of William and Mary, who wrote *The Cradle of the Republic* (1900) and many other historical books, and founded the *William and Mary Quarterly*; William G. Stanard, editor of the *Virginia Magazine of History and Biography*, and Mary Newton Stanard, who wrote *The Story of Virginia's First Century* (1928) and furnished the first accurate account of Bacon's Rebellion and its real significance; E.G.Swem, editor of the *William and Mary Quarterly* and compiler of *Swem's Index*; William Henry Squires, author of many historical works dealing with Virginia; Thomas Jefferson Wertenbaker, who stands at the forefront of contemporary American historians; William E. Dodd, former ambassador to Germany, historian, and author of biographies of Jefferson Davis, Woodrow Wilson, and Nathaniel Macon; James Southall Wilson, editor of *The Virginia Quarterly Review* (1925–30) and of several authoritative works on Edgar Allan Poe; Carter G. Woodson and Luther P. Jackson, Negro historians and scholars; Eudora Ramsay Richardson, author of *Little Aleck; A Life of Alexander H. Stephens* (1932), *The Influence of Men—Incurable* (1936), *The Woman Speaker* (1936), and short stories and essays; Hamilton James Eckenrode, author of biographies of Jefferson Davis, Nathan Bedford Forrest, Rutherford B. Hayes, and James Longstreet, and of a novel, *Bottom Rail on Top* (1935), conceived in the modern vein of candor; and William Cabell Bruce, whose biography of Benjamin Franklin won the Pulitzer award in 1918.

Foremost among Virginia biographers is Douglas Southall Freeman, whose monumental *R.E.Lee* won the Pulitzer award in 1935. Dr.Freeman's great book is more than a biography; it is a military history of the War between the States.

The turn of the century brought popular recognition to the Virginia poets James Lindsay Gordon, W.Gordon McCabe, Charles W. Coleman, B.B.Valentine, and Henry Aylett Sampson. In modern verse Edwin Quarles, Carlton Drewry, Virginia Moore, Aline Kilmer, Virginia McCormick, Josephine Johnson, Emma Gray Trigg, Francis Mason, Anne

Spencer, Nancy Byrd Turner, Leigh Hanes, John Richard Moreland, Julia Johnson Davis, Marion Sartorious Ott, Marjory Howell, Mary Willis Shelburne, Virginia Stait, Elkanah East Taylor, and Florence Dickinson Stearnes have done interesting work. Lawrence Lee, Virginia Tunstall, Caroline Giltinan, and Henry E. Baker are adopted Virginians. George Dillon, winner in 1932 of the Pulitzer Prize for poetry, claims Richmond as his home, though he is now editor of *Poetry*, published in Chicago. Some of the best current verse in Virginia appears in *The Lyric*, *Lyric Virginia Today*, an anthology edited by the gifted lyricist, Mary Sinton Leitch, and in the *Virginia Quarterly Review*. The *Lyric* was founded in 1920 by the distinguished poet, John Richard Moreland. During his editorship and that of his successor, Virginia McCormick, the magazine was published in Norfolk. Now, however, it emanates from Roanoke, the home of Leigh Hanes, the present editor. John Moreland is the author of many books of verse and appears in many important anthologies. Leigh Hanes, whose collected work is published in two volumes, is best known for his 'Song of the New Hercules.'

The *Reviewer*, a little monthly magazine, appeared in Richmond in 1921 and during the four years of its existence promised to rival the prestige of the *Southern Literary Messenger*. Its founder and editor, Emily Clark, has written in *Innocence Abroad* (1931) a vivid account of the writers connected with the publication. The *Reviewer* published the first work of Julia Peterkin, Frances Newman, and Gerald Johnson; the first prose of DuBose Heyward; and some of Paul Green's earliest writings. James Branch Cabell edited the monthly for three issues, and its brief but brilliant course was an eloquent reply to H.L.Mencken's designation of the South as the 'Sahara of the Bozart.' The *Southern Literary Messenger* was reborn in 1939 under the editorship of F. Meredith Dietz.

In time not too far distant Virginia may unite the channels that have hitherto separated the literary trends of North and South. The birthplace of the Nation is as probable a place of origin as any other for a National literature that will combine romance, the social graces, and a coherent culture with dramatic vitality and spiritual vision.

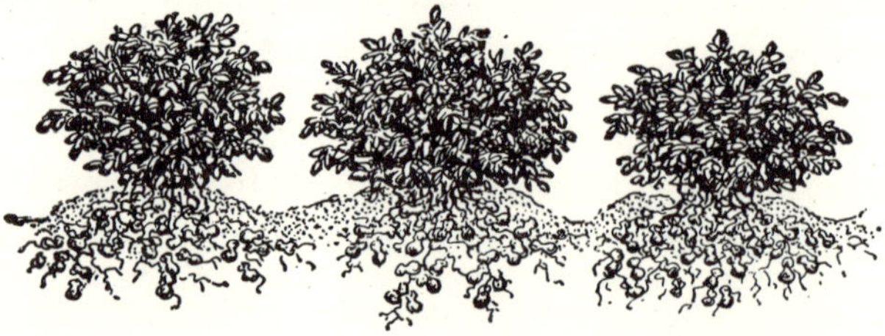

The Theater

VIRGINIA has always cherished the drama. The pleasure-loving Cavaliers were not sympathetic with the dour denials of enjoyment that prevailed in some of the other colonies. Fragmentary records of Virginia's first century reveal the not infrequent appearance of amateur plays and strolling players. Just what the plays were and where they were produced are unknown, except for a court record of Accomac County, dated 1655, which sets forth a charge made by a pious gentleman against several persons for presenting a play entitled *Ye Bear and Ye Cub*. The court adjudged the play harmless, and charged the complainant with costs.

In 1716 the first playhouse in America was erected at Williamsburg. Built by William Levingston, who entered into contract with Charles and Mary Stagg, dancing teachers, the theater was designated for the acting of 'Comedies, Drolls, and other kind of stage plays . . . as shall be thought fitt to be acted there.' Though Levingston's theater was used for both amateur and professional performances, it was frequently in financial difficulties. Governor Spotswood, in a letter written June 24, 1718, tells of having been slighted by eight committeemen who failed to accept his invitation to a celebration of the king's birthday or to 'go to the play that was acted on the occasion.' Other references are found to presentations, by students of the College of William and Mary, of *Cato*, *The Busybody*, *The Beaux' Stratagem*, and *The Recruiting Officer* by 'the company.'

In 1745 the theater was presented to the city for use as a town hall. But in the fall of 1751 another playhouse was built, 'by way of subscription,' just back of the capitol. This was opened on the night of October 21, with a performance of *Richard III* by Thomas Kean, Walter Murray, and Charles Somerset Woodham of New York. After a few performances the company moved on to Petersburg but returned to Williamsburg in the following spring. In May it played at Hobbs' Hole (Tappahannock), and at Fredericksburg during the June fair.

The playhouse in Williamsburg housed the first well-rounded and well-trained dramatic company to arrive in the New World from England. In June 1752, the Hallams—Lewis, senior, his wife, and two children—with a supporting company disembarked from the *Charming Sally* at Yorktown and made their way to Williamsburg. 'A select company of Commedians,' they were styled by the *Virginia Gazette*. 'The Scenes, Cloaths, and Decorations are entirely new, extremely rich and finished in the highest taste . . . so that Ladies and Gentlemen may depend on being entertained in as polite a manner as at the Theatre in London.'

The barnlike playhouse was altered 'at great expense . . . into a regular Theatre fitt for the reception of Ladies and Gentlemen and the execution of their own performance.' In September the Hallam company opened with the first performance in America of *The Merchant of Venice*, and remained in Williamsburg for 11 months. Reference to later performances occurs in a letter mentioning that *Othello* and a pantomime were played on October 9, with 'the Emperor of the Cherokee Nation, his Empress and their Son, the Prince, attended by several of his warriors, the Great Men and their Ladies, present at the play.'

On February 6, 1768, a group of players known as the Virginia Company of Comedians appeared in Norfolk. In Williamsburg on April 4 of the same year this group presented a tragedy called *Douglas*, and later continued its season with a repertory that included *The Drummer*, *The Beggar's Opera*, *Miss in Her Teens*, *The Harlequin Skeleton*, *Venice Preserved*, and *The Constant Couple*.

In the winter of 1770 the 'American Company,' as the Hallams and their group were then called, played a short season in Williamsburg. In 1771 another company presented *King Lear*. In 1772 the American Company was back in Williamsburg, appearing before large and brilliant audiences.

The theaters of this early day were crude and flimsy structures built entirely of wood, with benches in 'the pit' for common folk and boxes for the gentry. They were heated in winter by a stove in the foyer, around which the half-frozen audience would gather between the acts. Posters in the lobbies 'respectfully requested' the audience 'not to spit on the stove,' and notices on the house bills or programs suggested that 'Ladies and Gentlemen bring their own foot warmers.'

Candles were used for illumination. In the midst of a performance it was not uncommon for a stagehand to snuff a smoking candle in the footlights. Performances usually began at six o'clock, and for hours before the rise of the curtain Negro servants solemnly held seats for their masters and mistresses. The evening's entertainment generally consisted of a prologue, a complete drama, a farcical afterpiece, and often singing or dancing.

A system of benefit performances, prevalent in this period and lasting for many years thereafter, provided the actor with a substantial part of his income. According to this custom, actors 'who were of good talents, industrious habits and of fair character . . . were allowed the privilege, toward the close of the season, of a benefit night.' The cards of actors and the playbills solicited 'the patronage of the Ladies and Gentlemen' of the community; and if the actor was well esteemed, his receipts were usually substantial.

For a decade or two before the Revolution, the theater at Williamsburg was the scene of some of the gayest and most brilliant gatherings in the colony. When the Virginia general assembly was in session, the town overflowed with visitors, the inns were filled to capacity, and every house in town entertained guests. Theaters elsewhere in the colony also did a thriving business. Washington from his youth was fond of the theater. His ledger contains many entries for 'play tickets,' and often his diary records that he 'went to the play.' But the Provincial Congress, meeting on October 24, 1774, issued a warning against extravagance and dissipation, naming among other things 'gaming, cock-fighting, exhibition of shows, plays and other expensive diversions and entertainments.' Theaters were closed; many actors departed for the English West Indies; and the first period of Virginia's theatrical history ended.

After the Revolution, however, interest in the theater revived. In 1779 the capital of Virginia was moved to Richmond. Though many plays had been staged in the old Market House there, the first theater in the new capital was opened in a building erected on Shockoe Hill in 1786. The *Virginia Gazette and Advertiser* announces a performance of *The Recruiting Officer* 'at the new theatre on Shockoe Hill on Saturday Evening next, November 17th, 1787,' with *Lethe, or Aesop in the Shades* as the afterpiece. Among subsequent announcements are those of 'the tragedy of *Romeo and Juliet* to which will be added a farce called *The Citizen*, to be presented November 30th, 1787'; and a benefit for Mr.Bissett on December 7,1787, presenting *The Beggar's Opera* 'to which will be added (particular desire) Macklin's celebrated farce of *Love à la Mode* . . . the whole to conclude with the comic song of *Four and Twenty Fiddlers All in a Row* by Mr.Bissett.' Edgar Allan Poe's mother appeared many times on the stage of the Shockoe Hill Theater, closing her professional career there in 1811, in December of which year she died.

The burning of this theater, in 1811, was one of the most tragic episodes in Richmond's history. Before a holiday audience on the night of December 26, a benefit was being held for two players, Alexander Placide and his daughter. The curtain had been rung down on the feature, *The Father, or*

Family Feuds. During the afterpiece, *Raymond and Agnes, or The Bleeding Nun*, a lamp drawn up into the scenery started a blaze, which soon became a seething inferno. The governor of the State and 72 others lost their lives. After this tragedy, people hesitated to congregate in large buildings, and theaters all over the country were affected.

It was seven years before Richmond ventured to build another playhouse. The list of subscribers who in 1818 made possible the new building at Seventh and Broad Streets included many well-known Richmonders, among them Chief Justice John Marshall, for whom the theater was named. It was a much longer time, however, before the theater came into fullest use. According to the *Southern Literary Messenger* of February 1835, 'the commodious theatre which succeeded the old one . . . which is placed in a far more eligible situation and is of much safer construction, is only occasionally patronized when the appearance of some attractive star or celebrated performer is advertised.' Among the most famous of these celebrated performers was Junius Brutus Booth, who on July 13, 1821, made his first appearance in America on the stage of the Marshall Theater in *Richard III*.

Richmond's 'golden age of the theater' began toward the middle of the nineteenth century. Great plays were then given, with great actors who remained throughout the season. The names of William Charles Macready, Edwin Forrest, the Booths, and James W. Wallack appeared in the playbills; and William Rufus Blake, Joseph Jefferson, and John Wilkes Booth served at various times as stage managers at the Marshall.

A collection of old playbills of this theater, covering the years from 1848 through 1852, is owned by the Poe Shrine at Richmond. It is mounted in yellow ledgers, with marginal notations and records of receipts in code written by the managers. Beside a handbill advertising *Romeo and Juliet* on January 14, 1850, is written: 'Clear night but very wet walking. Mr. Wise's speech at the capitol on the slavery question and the people fools enough to listen to a dishonest politician.' On April 1 of the same year is this terse statement. 'Mr. Booth was *Drunk* and *Did Not Appear*.'

The great Jenny Lind sang in Richmond at the Marshall Theater in 1850. Another outstanding local event was the appearance in 1854 of Ole Bull, immortal Norwegian violinist, in the old Exchange Hall and in the African Church. Adelina Patti sang to delighted audiences from the rostrum of the same church.

By the middle 1850's Richmond had become one of the four or five most important dramatic centers in the United States, and for years every notable actor of the American stage played in this city more or less regularly. Richmond's verdict in matters dramatic became authoritative, and there were times when plays were tried out in Richmond before presentation in New York.

The Marshall Theater burned during the night of January 2, 1862. Almost before the bricks were cold, Mrs.Elizabeth McGill, its owner, began the building of a new theater on the same site; and in 1863 this new playhouse, the Richmond, was opened with *As You Like It*, presenting Ida Vernon and D'Orsay Ogden in the leading roles. Though the War between the States was now at its height, the theater in Virginia suffered less than it had during the Revolution. As Mrs.McGill (later Mrs.Powell) wrote, 'Everyone seemed to need relaxation and the house was full every night. President Davis used to come often with his cabinet.' Sally Partington, a favorite among the soldiers, played opposite most of the celebrated male actors of the day. Strangely enough, the soldiers seemed to prefer tragedy to comedy, and during the war many of America's great tragedians were seen in Virginia's capital.

A memorable performance of the postwar years in Richmond was that of Edwin Booth and Lawrence Barrett, who in 1888 appeared together in *Othello*. Among other actors who thrilled and charmed Richmond audiences in the early postwar decades were Charlotte Cushman, the elder Salvini, John McCullough, Francis S. Chanfrau, Laura Keene, Adelaide Histori, Fanny Janauscheck, Sarah Bernhardt, Helena Modjeska, Fanny Davenport, Adelaide Neilson, Mary Anderson, George L. Fox, Edward A. Sothern, Richard Mansfield, and Robert B. Mantell.

Other theaters were erected in Virginia during these years—among them the Theatre of Varieties in Richmond, introducing vaudeville. The most prominent of Richmond's later playhouses, the Academy of Music, was opened in 1886 with a presentation of Gilbert and Sullivan's *Mikado*. Here, in the last decade of the century, came Signor Salvini in *Othello*, Henry Irving and Ellen Terry in *The Merchant of Venice*, Frederick Warde in *King Lear*, and Creston Clarke in his role of Edgar Allan Poe. In memorable performances of *Rip Van Winkle* and *The Rivals* at the Academy in 1902, Joseph Jefferson bade farewell to a city that he had loved throughout his professional career.

Among outstanding Virginians in the theater toward the end of the nineteenth century were Wilton Lackaye (1862–1932), born in Loudoun County, a character actor, and George Fawcett (1861–1939), a native of Fairfax County, also a character actor, first on the stage, then the screen. A pioneer in motion pictures is Francis Xavier Bushman born in Norfolk in 1884, who had the lead in 402 early films. Jack Holt (b.1881), a native of Winchester, began his screen career in 1913. Acting both on the stage and screen are James Harlee Bell, born in Suffolk, in 1894, and Margaret Sullavan (b.1911), a native of Norfolk. The career of Randolph Scott, born in Orange County in 1903, has been wholly in motion pictures. The outstanding success of the Negro actor, Charles Sidney Gilpin (1878–1930), born in Richmond, was the role of Brutus Jones in Eugene O'Neill's *Emperor Jones*. Equally at home on stage or screen is the Negro tap dancer, Bill (Bojangles) Robinson, who was born in Richmond in 1878. The role of Amos in radio's ceaseless skit *Amos 'n Andy* belongs exclusively to Freeman Gosden, a native of Richmond.

In Virginia, as elsewhere, developments and trends that were radically to alter the theater's destiny began to gather headway late in the nineteenth century and to gain greatly intensified momentum early in the twentieth. Some of these were a reflection of changes in the general pattern of American economic and social life; others had their origin within the theater itself. Abuses of the star system; the rise of the great theatrical syndicates; the increasing domination of Broadway and the decline of 'the road'; the competition at first of vaudeville and then of motion pictures—these were some of the factors that accounted for the rapid recession of the theater's golden age and (outside a few of the largest metropolitan centers) reduced the legitimate stage from opulence to poverty.

Hunger for the legitimate drama brought about a renaissance of stock companies during the early part of the present century. For several years the Academy was the home of a stock company known as the Giffen Players, some of whose members (including Richard Bennett, Margaret Illington, Lucille LaVerne, and Ralph Morgan) later became nationally prominent on stage or screen. The little theater movement, which started later, had its genesis in small groups of idealists eager to experiment with new methods and new media.

Little theaters have been organized and are actively functioning in most of Virginia's larger communities, including Richmond, Lynchburg, Staunton, Danville, Norfolk, and Petersburg. The Lynchburg Little Theatre has a building of its own. The Richmond Theatre Guild is not only the largest nonprofessional theater organization in the State, but also one of the largest in the country. Spiritual successor to many earlier acting societies and dramatic clubs in Richmond, the Guild is a direct descendant of the Little Theatre League, organized in 1918.

Within the past few years, colleges and universities have placed greatly increased emphasis upon dramatic instruction and presentations. The dramatic departments and the players of the College of William and Mary, the University of Richmond, and the University of Virginia are outstanding in this field.

Both little theater and college groups are ambitious in their undertakings. Their repertoires range from miracle and morality plays, through the works of Elizabethan and Restoration dramatists and the foreign playwrights of all eras, down to recent Broadway successes. In their workshops they are producing plays, training actors, designing scenery, and developing an enthusiasm for the drama that is not likely to be extinguished. The next chapter in the history of the Virginia theater, it seems safe to predict, will be written chiefly by the little theaters and the dramatic departments of colleges and universities.

Architecture

ARCHITECTURE in Virginia started with 'two faire rows' of houses built between 1611 and 1615 at Jamestown and three 'streets' at the city of Henrico, for the first settlers built merely shacks or huts.

According to Ralph Hamer, secretary of the colony at the time, the Jamestown houses were 'all of framed Timber, two stories and an upper Garrett, or Corne loft, high.' More particular description there is none; but mention is made of 'three large and substantial Store Howses joyned togeather,' of the defenses, 'newly and strongly impaled,' and of 'some very pleasant and beautiful howses . . . without the towns.'

We have a hint of the outward aspect of Virginia's two most considerable communities when the colony was less than ten years old and learn, incidentally, that already the Virginians were building 'pleasantly and beautifully' in the open country. So they have preferred to do ever since.

Sir Thomas Dale and Sir Thomas Gates seem to have been responsible for this construction. Gates brought with him from England not only smiths and carpenters but also bricklayers and brickmakers. Though the brick church at Jamestown, of which only the ruined tower now survives, was not begun until 1639, it is possible that a brick church was built at Henrico—as some reports have it—before the Indian massacre of 1622. If so, nothing is left of it. The Indian onslaught completely wiped out the settlement below the falls of the James and narrowly missed extinguishing the colony.

The log cabin was unknown in Virginia, as in England, at this date, and for many years afterwards. The roofed pen of logs was a contrivance of Scandinavian origin and did not establish itself on this continent until the Swedes brought it over to Delaware. Once it was introduced, diffusion of the type was inevitable, peculiarly adapted as it was to rough-and-ready shelter in a rude country of forests.

In any case, the earliest Virginia construction for lodging purposes that can be dignified with the name is the frame house of the rows at Jamestown. The most familiar aspect of Virginia villages, even today, is such rows of frame houses. No Virginia frame house of the first half of the seventeenth century has survived, and very few are left that can be authenticated as belonging to the latter half. But the fashion of building these houses, adapted from contemporary English models, persisted all through the eighteenth and well into the nineteenth century.

The prototype essentially was the English timber cottage, with wooden weatherboarding applied to the frame over all, although in the old country the common practice was to let plaster or other filling serve as outer covering. Since the older surviving frame houses in Virginia are filled in with plaster or brick nogging and the weatherboard is an added protection (as the name itself implies), it is reasonable to suppose that the first Virginia builders, having an abundance of wood, which was very scarce in England, used this method in the beginning, and that the frame house, covered only with boards, was a later development.

The typical form of the Virginia frame house, examples of which are still scattered over the Tidewater and Piedmont sections, is a house one room deep and two rooms wide, or two rooms and a passage wide. This house has a gable roof of steep pitch, which nowadays usually has dormers to light the upper half-story. But in the primitive form, the dormers were probably lacking. The roof may still (perhaps under a modern sheathing of tin) be covered with shingles, which presently usurped the place of the thatch commonly used in England.

If the house has two rooms, separated by a 'passage'—passage is the correct word and 'hall' a pretentious intrusion, involving the misuse of a word correct in its proper place—we find, as a rule, massive chimneys at each end with the chimney stacks standing free of the building above the half-story fireplace. As the family increased, another unit of the same pattern was often set L-fashion at the back with another outside chimney. Or the original unit was extended lengthwise beyond the chimney at one end or both, often with roofs of lower pitch on the additions, omitting the dormers, which by that time had become standard.

Much less often there are two stories under the steep roof, in which case lower dormered wings may extend from both ends. That, however, came later. It suggests the influence of the Georgian principle of symmetrical arrangement—a main block with flanking pavilions—which reached the colony early in the eighteenth century. This is characteristically expressed in the brick houses of that century, such as Westover (1730).

Not essentially different in design from the typical frame house and still Gothic is the simplest type of seventeenth-century brick house. This is illustrated in a number of houses still, or until recently, extant. The Thoroughgood House in Princess Anne County and Winona in Northampton

County, both probably built before 1650, follow the one-room deep plan with steep gabled roof and dormers (added later to the Thoroughgood House). More elaborate were Bacon's Castle or Allen's Brick House in Surry County and Fairfield, the Burwell seat in Gloucester County, the latter fortunately photographed before its destruction in 1900. Each presents an unmistakable Tudor aspect, with clustered chimney stacks; and the first has curved and stepped gables on the main section and a closed porch on one long side and a stair tower on the other.

Nothing is left today but the foundations of the colony's manor house, Green Spring, where Sir William Berkeley maintained a gaol—still standing—for political offenders and common malefactors alike. Before it was pulled down after the Revolution sketches of the house were made by William Ludwell Lee of the Stratford family. It is known, therefore, that Green Spring likewise revealed Tudor or Gothic elements, including a steeply pitched roof with dormers.

Both Green Spring and Bacon's Castle were certainly built before Bacon's Rebellion of 1676, for the hot-headed young Nathaniel Bacon, leader of the rebels, used the governor's country house as his headquarters for his siege of Jamestown, and Allen's Brick House sheltered some of his followers.

It is broadly true, as Fiske Kimball pointed out many years ago, that American Colonial architecture was chiefly dependent upon the architectural development in England. Our seventeenth-century expression in wood was primarily an adaptation to local materials and conditions, and it produced an unmistakable American type, both in Virginia and in New England. Variations in the type up and down the Atlantic Coast, creating a recognizable Virginia architecture and an equally recognizable New England architecture, were owing largely to differences in climatic conditions and habits of living.

The style of building that was brought over by the first settlers, both in Virginia and in New England, was already old-fashioned in the old country. The changes made in it over here, while the type held, did not reflect changes going on across the water. They were made in America to suit conditions in various regions, while the general way of building persisted in the heads of workmen transplanted from England along with the original model. Not until the eighteenth century was well into its second quarter were the English architects' books (rising in flood tide at home) brought to America where the new English fashion in architecture captured the imagination of the colonists.

These folios spread abroad the elegant Renaissance mode that began with Inigo Jones, before Charles I walked out of Jones's own White Hall to the scaffold. This mode received magnificent illustration in churches and public buildings at the hands of Christopher Wren, right on from the second Charles's time to that of the dull Hanoverian Georges. Curiously, however, it does not seem to have been in general use for gentlemen's private houses, even in England, until the reign of William and Mary, or thereabouts.

Most of Virginia's extant English Renaissance, or so-called Georgian, houses were built after 1720, and it is difficult not to assume that the way they were built was much affected by the public buildings in Williamsburg, which rose up under William and Mary, Anne, and the first George.

Middle Plantation (now Williamsburg) had taken the place of Jamestown as the capital of the colony only in 1699. It had been appointed as the site for the College of William and Mary in 1693. From a wayside village, boasting a church and a few houses, Middle Plantation, between the James and the York Rivers, had to be made over into a seat of government and of learning. The latest fashions in polite urban buildings were available for an entire setup. This elegant new mode was used and thus was handsomely advertised throughout His Britannic Majesty's Old Dominion.

Every person of condition in the colony attended upon the general court or the house of burgesses and saw what Governor Alexander Spotswood and his associates had wrought. Not until the Williamsburg public buildings were restored in the image of the originals was it possible for this generation to measure their influence in their own time and on the generation that saw them built. Without the restoration that influence might have gone almost unsuspected. With the restoration the evidence is in plain view. The Wren Building at the College of William and Mary and the reconstructed Governor's Palace and the capitol exhibit the special characteristics of English Renaissance architecture that became the hall mark of Virginia's Georgian style.

Westover, its builder a member of the council while Spotswood was governor, is obviously like the Governor's Palace, the construction of which had been begun in 1705 and completed under Spotswood's supervision. Colonel William Byrd's seat, to be sure, is larger—it is a country house, not a town lodging. It may well be that Byrd, an accomplished and traveled person, used as his principal guide in designing his mansion another architect's book and gathered hints, besides, from fashionable houses he had seen and admired in England. But the essential pattern is the same.

Built about the same time as Westover, Christ Church in Lancaster County, near Robert Carter's vanished seat Corotoman, employs all the characteristic Williamsburg elements. So does Colonel Thomas Lee's Stratford Hall (1727–30) in Westmoreland County, though a pair of quadruple chimneys, linked with arches into the semblance of towers, furnishes the dominant accent of the Lee house.

Ampthill, in Chesterfield County, was the seat of Archibald Cary, whose father and grandfather were both directly and practically concerned in the construction of the Williamsburg public buildings. It seems to have started life (completed in 1732) as a long house, a single room deep on each side of a passage after the seventeenth-century fashion. But as it stands, transplanted to the other side of the James, it has grown into the newer foursquare style, two rooms deep, with the passage sweeping through from back to front in the manner already noted as a Virginia specialty—one not borrowed from common practice in England, but climatically acquired.

Carter's Grove, in James City County, built in 1751 by Carter Burwell, resembled, before its roof was lifted a few years ago, Ampthill rather than Westover. It gave less effect of height than either Westover or any Williamsburg model a few miles away—including Brafferton Hall (1723) and the President's House (1732) at the college.

But the characteristic elements are there, and the basic pattern holds both for main house and dependencies, which in all these cases were lower flanking buildings, originally unconnected with the main mass but later usually joined on by what the Marylanders call 'hyphens.' The interior of the first floor was usually paneled to the ceiling with pine, painted white. Stratford, however, which has a true 'hall,' uses the paneling there only. Often, as at Carter's Grove and at Brandon, a Harrison seat on the James, the paneling is elaborated with pilasters in the classic order.

Rosewell, in Gloucester County, through the building of which two generations of Pages beggared themselves, is now a fire-gutted shell. It outdid the Governor's Palace, not only in ground extent and the number of stories, but in count of cupolas, for it had two. But it followed the palace fashion, in the manner of the brickwork—Flemish bond and random-glazed headers (neither used at Ampthill) with rubbed brick for trim —and in the orderly arrangment of dependencies.

At Rosewell, as in Christ Church and at Westover, stone and brick are combined in the decoration but used sparingly. Houses built wholly of stone are unusual, since the Tidewater lacked that material, and are of later date. Outstanding examples are Mount Airy in Richmond County, built by Colonel John Tayloe in 1758, and Prestwould in Mecklenburg, built by Sir William Skipwith about the same time.

As the typical Virginia plantation house of the eighteenth century sat in the midst of broad acres of plowed field, pasture, and woodland, remote from neighbors, so the typical Virginia church of that century was the crossroads church, set by itself in a field or a wood, at a point convenient to a group of plantations that covered a great stretch of country. The difference was that the 'big' house was revealed among gardens, lawns, and groves, and framed in outlying buildings—set in order to right and left, or flanking a curved forecourt, as at Mount Vernon, or defining a court at the back, as at Shirley on the James. But the sunlight, which dappled the mellow red brick walls and the gray shingled roof with the shadows of the trees in the churchyard, fell only on the church and the tombstones, parading their coats of arms and the names and titles of dead parishioners. There was not even a rectory in sight. The rector of the parish was provided with a glebe—a lesser plantation—and with indentured servants and slaves.

The Brick Church in Isle of Wight County (named St.Luke's after the Revolution), probably the oldest extant church building in the original thirteen colonies, comprises a rude square tower at the west end and a nave with Gothic buttresses and brick-mullioned windows, including a great window lighting the chancel at the east end. It has suffered damage and restoration, but these features seem to have belonged to the original structure. The tower at Jamestown—all that is left of the fifth church, begun in 1639—is likewise of brick and unmistakably Gothic.

St.Peter's, New Kent County, the main part of which was built in 1701–03, is a quadrangular, high-gabled block, with a square tower (1740) and crude corner finials, set on a Norman arched porch. Bruton Parish Church in Williamsburg, called the 'Court' Church, was the first Virginia church to be built under the influence of the new fashions. It was erected in 1710–15 under Governor Spotswood's supervision. The handsome square tower, however, was not set in front of the original cruciform structure until a generation later.

Christ Church, Alexandria, where Washington had a pew and where the Mount Vernon coach, all green and gold with four horses, used to set down the general and his lady of a Sunday morning, was begun in 1767 and completed in 1772. It has a tower topped by Wrenish pepperpots that was added as late as 1818. St.John's, Richmond, where Patrick Henry cried out for liberty or death, is one of the few surviving wooden churches of the regular Anglican establishment. It goes back to 1741, or not long after Colonel Byrd founded the city at the falls of the James. St.John's tall wooden tower, also crowned with Wrenish pepperpots, did not exist when Patrick Henry poured out his burning eloquence upon the Virginia Convention in 1775. The characteristic Virginia church was the crossroads church—as it continues to be even today, to a very considerable extent.

Virginia's Colonial churches, of which about 50 survive, fall into six general groups: (1) those with small naves and huge towers (1630–1700); (2) middle-colonial type with rectangular plan and steeply pitched gabled roof (1690–1740); (3) T-shaped buildings with three sharp end-gables (1700–60); (4) regular cruciform type with gabled roof (1710–50); (5) Greek-cruciform type with all four transepts equal (1730–70); and (6) late-colonial Wren quadrangular type with hipped roof (1760–76).

Requirements of the interior chiefly determined the shape of the building, the main object being to have the communicants close to the pulpit. This problem was solved finally with the creation of the late, nearly square Wren block, when the pulpit was placed at the center against a side wall.

Among churches of each group are minor variations. Two buildings of the first period, St.Luke's and Jamestown, differ from their fellows by reason of their Gothic buttresses. The earliest of the second period, represented by Merchant's Hope in Prince George County, had a swag roof. Characteristics of this the largest group, of which Old Church in King and Queen County is also a representative, are compass windows and the door in the south wall near the east end. Churches of all groups except the first have galleries, and the groups after the second generally have pedimented doors of rubbed and carved brick. In a few instances the pediments are of stone. The oldest T-church, Yeocomico (1706) in Westmoreland County, has irregularly spaced windows and, as originally, a swag roof. Among later representatives are Vauter's in Essex County, St.John's in King William, and Blandford in Petersburg. The regular cruciforms, except Bruton Parish Church, had no tower during the Colonial period, whether in rural or urban areas. St.John's in Hampton and Mattapony in King and Queen County belong to this group. Greek-cruciform buildings, with a door in north, west, and south ends and all-round cornice, divide themselves into two subtypes—(a) those with gabled roof and single tier of windows, such as North Farnham in Richmond County and Abingdon in Gloucester, and (b) those with hipped roof and two tiers of windows, represented by Aquia Church in Stafford County and St.Paul's in King George. Aquia Church (1757), with quoining of stone, differs from others of its type because of the tower above its front transept. Here again is an instance of a tower in a strictly rural section. The late Wren blocks with hipped roofs fall into two subgroups—(a) with single tier of tall compass windows, represented by Lamb's Creek in King George County and Payne's Church (now destroyed) in Fairfax, and (b) with two tiers, square-headed below and round-arched above, as shown in Pohick in Fairfax County. This type, except in the case of Christ Church in Alexandria, has a door at the center of the south wall, with the main entrance at the west end. Every Colonial church stands due east and west.

Even before the surrender of Cornwallis at Yorktown ended for practical purposes the War for Independence, Thomas Jefferson had started to make over the architecture of Virginia. He did not like what is known as 'Georgian' architecture. He was bored by it, as was Sir Christopher Wren in his time by the Gothic. When the master of Monticello followed Patrick Henry as governor, he drew a plan (which was never executed) for remodeling the Governor's Palace in Williamsburg in the semblance of a classic temple with a portico. The new capitol in Richmond he modeled after the Roman temple at Nîmes known as the *Maison Carrée.* And the style of architecture called Early Republican, distinguished to the common eye by tall columns and pedimented porticos, though it derives through the sixteenth-century Italian Palladio from its original Greco-Roman sources, is principally, as an American expression, the child of Jefferson's ardent fancy.

The architects, professional and amateur, native and foreign, whom he proselyted and with whom he collaborated, included Stephen Hallet ('The first approved professional among us'), Benjamin Latrobe, Charles Bulfinch, William Thornton—all of whom worked on the Capitol in Washington—and Robert Mills, who had two years under the master's own eye as student and draftsman at Monticello. All these spread the new gospel over the country in the form of buildings in classic style. In Virginia, it was Jefferson who built all the houses with stately porticos that crown the river bluffs and the hilltops from the Chesapeake to the Blue Ridge Mountains and beyond. Even if somebody else drew the plans, still Jefferson was the real builder. Monticello, the University of Virginia, Bremo, and his home of refuge, Poplar Forest—these, to be sure, are directly the works of the master's hand and attest authentically his title as Virginia's architect paramount. But all those other houses in Virginia that were built new with porticos and pediments or had their Georgian fronts 'lifted' by means of porticos and pediments—from Jefferson's time almost up to the War between the States—also stand as witnesses to clinch the title.

A house of dignity in the Old Dominion was Jeffersonian or nothing. The change came about the more easily because the deep Tidewater—where the statelier family seats of eighteenth-century vintage clustered, and where they still linger as patches of orange-brickcolor among their trees and overgrown gardens—was left aside by the movement of population westward to the hills. That movement Jefferson himself had led. He had pegged it down by shifting the seat of government from Williamsburg to Richmond and by building the University of Virginia—the crowning achievement of his old age.

Much more might be written about Jeffersonian architecture in its rural setting; for example, of the Greek Revival stage that owed its primary local impulse to that capitol of his on its acropolis above the James—notwithstanding that the model temple itself is classed as Roman. This was the phase that produced Berry Hill (*see Tour 11b*), with the Parthenon for inspiration, and encouraged the practice of covering clean red brick with stucco in imitation of stone.

Much might be written also about Virginia architecture as it developed in the cities, when cities began to grow to a size that gave them urban character. In all the older towns are distinctly urban and urbane types of red brick houses with Georgian fronts and cornices, with a lurking seventeenth-century suggestion in the steeply-pitched roofs and gables. Especially there are the houses that Robert Mills built, in which the red brick is usually covered with stucco.

Monumental Church, standing with its dome in Broad Street, Richmond, solemnly commemorates the great theater fire of 1811 that cost the lives of the governor of the commonwealth and 70-odd besides. That church is the monument, as well, of Robert Mills, who is best known as the architect of the great colonnade of the Treasury in Washington and of the Washington monuments in Washington and Baltimore.

Best of all Mills's works in Virginia are the stuccoed houses of the 1820's and 1830's that faced upon the streets of Richmond with plain fronts, except for modest Doric or Ionic framed doorways or small entrance porches in the same styles. Very sober town houses they looked. But, at the back, where the land sloped toward the river and the walled garden dropped its terraces, was the tall columned portico, with hanging balconies clinging to the backs of the columns to leave clean the upward sweep of the shafts to the roof. Thus, as one walked through the hall (no longer a mere passage) from the front door to the back door, the city house of formal dignity turned into a country house with a large gracious air and a sense of comfortable seclusion.

The house of John Wickham, who defended Aaron Burr, survives as the Valentine Museum in Richmond and is little changed. It serves as a reminder of how proficient Mills was in this manner, though he was content, in this instance, to use a one-story portico across the side-bayed garden front, which today looks out on the same walled garden. The White House of the Confederacy, so called, or the Jefferson Davis Mansion, not far away also survives. This house, which Mills built for Dr. John Brockenbrough, retains both the sedate and urban front on the street and the lofty portico at the back. But an attic story has been piled on top, and the garden is so crammed that much of the original effect is lost.

It is not too much to say that the architecture of Virginia, as a distinctive thing, perished with Virginia's own great builder and at that builder's own hands. For Jefferson made his Palladian architecture not Virginian only, but National. Houses in this manner, generally speaking, sprang up all over the country, bigger, if not better, than the Virginia houses. This was true, especially in the new States west of the Alleghenies, whither men from the seaboard States moved with their families and gear and set up on a grand scale on large tracts of land, received often as public grants in recognition of services in the Revolution.

Building in Virginia has tended since the middle of the nineteenth century or earlier to follow the current American fashion in building and to match very closely in any given period the run of the mill in the rest of the country.

Virginia felt as early as the 1820's the first wave of the Gothic Revival from England—exemplified in General John Hartwell Cocke's lodge, Recess, close to and almost contemporaneous with his classic seat, Bremo in Fluvanna County, mainly planned by Jefferson himself. Virginia caught the subsequent fever engendered by Sir Walter Scott's romances, suffered the irruption of mock medieval designs, dressed up in jigsaw scrollwork and jimcrackery, which we identify as the Victorian Gothic. It fell a victim to the jerry-building plague that swept in from the railroad shack towns of the fast-moving West. It did not escape the rage for the Second French Empire baroque, which in the late 1860's and 1870's possessed the land in the vulgarized and brutalized version now called the General Grant Style. It succumbed to the fad of patchwork quilt polychromy trailing after the introduction by Richardson of the Romanesque style into American architecture. Sham fronts faced with a checkerwork of roughhewn green and brown stones insulted with their presence the proudest of the dim-shaded streets in the larger towns. Poverty, which the War between the States left in its wake, saved the smaller towns and villages from a like desecration, and enabled them to escape that architectural plague only to be devastated later by the universal bungalow blight.

Even when people were not seduced by the new idols and tried to build in the old tradition, the quality was almost certain to be lost. For the fine art of brickwork had fallen into neglect, and the sturdy craft of carpentry was being crowded out by millwork. Proportions perished; design was forgotten. Flattened tin roofs reduced to vulgar insignificance the once gracious, if small and simple, Virginia home, set back from the high road in the grove of trees in the country or tucked in its white-fenced yard along the village street.

Better times brought better buildings. They brought also the eclectic taste, the hodgepodge of styles that the American Beaux Arts architects, fresh from Paris, dumped upon their defenseless stay-at-home fellow citizens. Virginia built like the rest of the country, and the fashionable new suburbs of her cities became, as everywhere else, samplers of the past styles of every country but our own.

The range was from Richardsonian Romanesque derivatives, with massive rough walls, heavy arches, and round excrescences like stone tents, through the regular Italian palace and French chateau effects to Elizabethan manors, some of which were copied, others imported like Virginia House in Richmond, formerly Sulgrave Manor.

Tobacco built the houses of the eighteenth-century Virginia nabobs. Tobacco likewise built most of these new mansions in assorted exotic styles, and some of them were—and are—very handsome, even if they have nothing to do with Virginia architecture as such. 'A refreshing, if entirely alien, note arrived in Richmond in the 1890's with the Jefferson Hotel, a vision of old Seville conjured up by Carrère and Hastings, just back from setting up Spanish scenery for the Florida winter-resort stage. With terrace, arches, fountain court, and towers, and a dress of cream-colored brick and terracotta, it looks across Franklin Street at the classic portico of Peter Mayo's big square gray house and is not one whit abashed.

Another building fashion swept the whole Nation, indirectly starting the movement that within the last two decades has restored Virginia's own architecture to favor with Virginians and awakened pride in the local tradition. This pride, in turn has created the current very active revival of building consciously, and even determinedly, in the old manner. The return tidal wave of the classic that swept the country after the Chicago World's Fair of 1893 had, with its dramatic Roman-holiday scenery, fired the imagination of an American people peculiarly susceptible at the moment to expressions of magnificence and illusions of grandeur. Virginia went in enthusiastically for the architectural stuff of which the White City beside Lake Michigan was made. A new crop of porticos and pediments grew up.

Meantime, however, Stanford White had come down to the University of Virginia to restore Jefferson's Rotunda, which had been wrecked by fire in 1895. From this building, an adaptation of the Pantheon in Rome, the inspiration came to White and his partner, Charles F. McKim (who had already started an American Colonial revival, based on a study of old houses in New England), to create after the same Pantheon model the libraries of Columbia and New York Universities.

Thus the dazzling light of the new White City, or *fin de siècle* fashion, caused the rediscovery of the forgotten man, Thomas Jefferson, the Architect—for 50 years among his own people completely lost in the magnitude of the political fame of Jefferson, Father of Democracy. Those red brick buildings with their white columns framing the Lawn at Jefferson's university, those old porticoed houses scattered about the countryside and entangled in local traditions as tenacious as the ivy that mantled their walls—these buildings were, it appeared, not merely venerable relics of an old time and an extinct fashion. In them was embodied a Virginia achievement as distinguished as any other of her contributions to the sound beginnings of the American union of States. Very soon the new porticoed and pedimented houses began to look more like the native old houses and less like the latest imported models advertised in Chicago. The red brick of a country based on one of the reddest of red clay beds in the world gained favor over the alien pale stone of the new classic fashion.

It was rather blind groping at first, so completely had knowledge of the older architectural traditions faded out in a half century sliced off from its past by the sword of a destructive war. Actually the distinction had been lost between the true Colonial—the so-called American Georgian or adapted English Renaissance of the eighteenth century—and the Palladian-Jeffersonian, which Fiske Kimball named Early Republican.

Indeed, the Virginians, like the rest of the country a generation ago, habitually called the revived Jeffersonian style Colonial when they did not call it Southern.

Since the outstanding monuments of the Jeffersonian vintage were still in active use—as the capitol and university buildings—and since many of the upcountry plantation mansions, including Monticello itself, have escaped serious damage, the volunteer salvage corps concentrated their attention on the neglected Tidewater—and thus rediscovered the true Colonial, almost by accident. In this field, the process of pious restoration by private hands and through patriotic organizations—in which the women have taken the lead—has set going surveys and investigations by architects and antiquarians, the sum of which has created for the first time a body of dependable knowledge covering Virginia's building methods and styles as far back as the last quarter of the seventeenth century.

The return of Virginia to its own version of the architecture that came from England has been encouraged—as it has been made possible on a solid basis of authenticity—by the recreation of the Colonial capital at Williamsburg, financed by John D. Rockefeller,Jr. and carried out with extraordinary care and completeness. As we have seen, the originals launched the fashion in which the finest and most distinctive Virginia houses and churches were built—at least, before Mr.Jefferson came along. So that it is only reasonable that the restoration should have potent effect on today's revival of that style.

The vertical fashion of skyscrapers, which America invented and developed as its principal contribution to the most compendious of the arts, has not missed the larger Virginia cities. But it expresses itself here, as everywhere, in standard skyscraper patterns. The rival horizontal fashion, which exploits shining metal and glass, the professedly international style, has made little headway in Virginia.

The Valley of the Shenandoah—the river called Euphrates by Colonel Spotswood's Knights of the Golden Horseshoe—was settled by two main streams of migration. One went over the mountain from the Piedmont and the Tidewater and took with it its accustomed manner of living and building—the Virginia manner of the period of migration. The other stream—much the more important numerically and made up largely of Ulstermen (usually called Scotch-Irish in Virginia) and of Germans—came down into the Valley from the North, chiefly through Pennsylvania. They brought with them the architecture that is distinguished as the Pennsylvania-Dutch type, with its solid foursquare houses of stone—the natural building material of a mountainous country.

The two types (west and east) are essentially the same in stylistic derivation, according to date. Either they show characteristics of the Medieval or Gothic—like the steep-roofed, narrow-gabled house of Virginia's architectural beginnings—or they follow Renaissance block patterns and are adapted to the local material of which they are built, the use to which they are put, and the climatic and other conditions of living that they serve.

An example is Augusta Church, built between 1740 and 1750, a solid foursquare structure with walls laid in stones of odd shapes after a manner characteristic of Pennsylvania stone houses and churches of the first half of the eighteenth century. Topping it is a steep roof, having the gables clipped off diagonally half-way—the so-called jerkin-head roof, although, as a matter of fact, the same style of roof is used in the deep Tidewater in houses built before 1750.

The original Valley counties, Augusta and Frederick, were not created until 1738 and not organized until some years later. Augusta Church is therefore not merely a characteristic piece of Valley of Virginia architecture but probably the oldest surviving example of the type of architecture that may be said to be peculiarly the Valley's own.

In general, the architecture that is Virginia's own, in right of happy adaptation to her countryside and the manners, custom, and genius of her people, is of two types.

First is the Colonial, derived directly from English models: Early Colonial, built on the still lingering Medieval pattern of the seventeenth-century common usage in the homeland; and Late Colonial following the Renaissance mode as interpreted by English architects of that century and made the new fashion of building for persons of distinction through most of the century succeeding.

Second is the Jeffersonian, which was artfully taken from Palladio's bag of tricks but which received a stamp that makes it both distinctive and distinguished. Houses in Virginia have still an unmistakable Virginia character, no matter how obvious the derivation. They carry the conviction of belonging to the country as surely as the clay and wood of which they are composed and the field and forest in which they are framed.

PART II

Cities

Alexandria

Railroad Station: Union Station, W. end of King St., for Richmond, Fredericksburg & Potomac R.R., Chesapeake & Ohio Ry., Seaboard Air Line Ry., and Southern Ry.
Bus Station: 109 N.Washington St., for Greyhound Lines.
Airport: Washington Airport, 4 m. N. on US 1, for Eastern Air Lines, American Airlines, and Pennsylvania-Central Airlines; taxi $1.25.
Taxis: Fare 20¢ within city limits, $1.50 to Washington.
Local Busses: SE. corner Pitt and Cameron Sts. for busses to Washington, fare 15¢, 8 tokens for $1; to Mount Vernon, fare 25¢; to Episcopal Theological Seminary, fare 10¢.
Pier: Norfolk and Washington Steamboat Co., E. end of Prince St., for boat to Old Point Comfort and Norfolk, 7 p.m. daily except when river is frozen.
Traffic Regulations: No U-turns in business district, one hour parking limit on King St.

Accommodations: 4 hotels; tourist homes, trailer camp.

Information Service: Chamber of Commerce, 201 S.Washington St.

Radio Station: WJSV (1460 kc.).
Motion Picture Houses: 5, including 1 for Negroes.
Swimming: Alexandria Municipal Pool, NE. corner Cameron and Harvard Sts., fee 20¢, children 10¢, suits 25¢, open 9 a.m.–10 p.m. weekdays, 2–6 Sun., from May 30 to Labor Day.
Boating: Rowboats for rent at E. end of Prince and Duke Sts., fee 50¢ for 1st hour, 35¢ each additional hour.

Annual Events: Tour of historic houses and gardens, sponsored by St.Paul's Church and the Alexandria Association, one Sat. in May and one Sat. in June, $1 for full day and afternoon tea.

ALEXANDRIA (52 alt., 24,149 pop.), hugging the western bank of the Potomac River, stretches south from the sinuous Four Mile Run to the marshes of Hunting Creek. West of the sweeping curve made through the city by the tracks of the Richmond, Fredericksburg and Potomac Railroad, scattered suburbs cover a succession of ridges. Caught in the wedge made by vast Potomac Yards, where seven railroads meet to exchange freight, and the industrial section along the river front, lies old Alexandria, a ragged pentagon neatly laid out in squares, and divided almost equally by King Street. This crowded business thoroughfare, flanked by ill-assorted faces of commercial buildings, extends westward from the water's edge toward the George Washington Masonic Memorial Temple.

Within view of the glistening white belfry of Christ Church and the spire of City Hall are scores of Georgian Colonial and early Federal houses of mellow red brick, gray stucco, or white weatherboarding. Here and there are long narrow houses resembling halves of gabled houses, called locally 'flounder' houses. With sloping shed-roofs and their tallest side walls windowless, they are said to owe their unusual architectural style to owners' attempts to evade taxation by reporting construction unfinished. Flounder houses are common in the older sections of Philadelphia, and inasmuch as many early residents of Alexandria were Pennsylvania Quakers it is thought that this type of house may have originated there. The façades of most houses in Alexandria are even with the sidewalk, the doorways with shining brass knockers often painted in bright colors to match the shutters. Front or side yards are few; most old residences have narrow terraces or courtyards in back that enclose boxwood, mimosa, and an arbor of dangling wistaria within old brick walls.

Among the streets running east to the river, Prince Street in its final block is probably the most interesting. Its cobbled bed slopes down between Lombardy poplars and two rows of odd small houses with doors and shutters painted bright green, red, blue, or yellow. Along the river front, where the prevailing odor is of fish and fertilizer, are wooden wharves and vacant shabby warehouses that recall the days when Alexandria was an important port. Boat clubs occupy two old buildings on the river bank, where speedboats, launches, and sailboats tie up beside weather-beaten craft of local fishermen. In a few small eating places there is still a semblance of the old barroom and tavern atmosphere.

Alexandria's diurnal noises give way at night to a silence broken by puffing trains, the occasional whistling of steamers, and the drone of airplanes flying low for a landing or taking off at Washington Airport. On Saturday night the shops of King Street glitter and swarm with people, for Alexandria is still a country town; while down Washington Street passes a queue of automobiles. On Sunday a lethargy descends on Alexandria. In the principal Negro quarter, a section of nondescript row houses just north of King Street and west of Washington Street, groups sit chatting in doorways, on stoops, or in rocking chairs on the sidewalks, as they watch children at play and couples *en promenade* displaying their Sunday best. Negroes live in every section of Alexandria and the professional group and government workers have substantial residences.

Old Alexandrians and newcomers constitute two distinct groups. The 'Foreign Legion,' as recently acquired citizens are called, discovered Alexandria just after the World War, restored old houses, moved in, and since 1932 has gained many recruits from Washington's officialdom. Streets were lengthened to accommodate new houses, fashioned after eighteenth-century models. People who once could recite the genealogy of every neighbor worth knowing find their refurbished city a bit perplexing, grateful as they are for the prosperity the 'Foreign Legion' has brought.

Although Captain John Smith ascended the Potomac to the falls in 1608, the west shore of the river was the last of Virginia's Tidewater fringe to be settled. In 1669 Governor Berkeley granted Robert Howsing 'six thousand acres of land situate . . . upon the freshes of Potomac River on the west side.' Captain John Alexander, who surveyed this tract, including the site of Alexandria, bought the Howsing grant the year following, and sporadic settlement began.

The section suffered in 1675 because of the Susquehannock War, when the Indians crossed the Potomac to attack new settlers. Colonel John Washington with a Virginia force joined Major John Truman's Maryland troops in a campaign against the Indians on Piscataway Creek (Maryland). During a truce, Maryland soldiers killed the Indian conferees. The Susquehannock, bent on revenge, advanced southward and aroused other Indians, thus bringing about conditions that led to Bacon's Rebellion. The century had ended before the Indians were driven out and permanent settlements established.

Plantations flourished after 1713, when Queen Anne's War ended and tobacco trade expanded. Indian trails then became 'rolling roads,' along which hogsheads of tobacco were drawn or 'rolled' by oxen or horses to public warehouses. The first warehouse in this vicinity was authorized in 1730 on the south side of Hunting Creek 'upon Broadwater's land.' The site was found unsuitable, and establishment of a warehouse 'upon Simon Pearson's land upon the upper side of Great Hunting Creek' was confirmed in 1732 by the general assembly. In 1740 a public ferry was established 'from Hunting Creek warehouse, on land of Hugh West . . . to Frazier's point in Maryland,' and from 'the plantation of John Hareford in Doeg's Neck . . . to Prince George County in Maryland.' A tavern was erected here, on the main thoroughfare between New England and the South, and the community was called Belhaven. By 1742, when fees of tobacco inspectors were fixed, Hunting Creek Warehouse and that 'on the land of the Honourable Thomas Lee, Esquire, at the Falls of Patowmack,' were important shipping points.

In that year Fairfax County was cut from Prince William, and in 1748 the general assembly authorized the establishment of a town for Fairfax County 'at Hunting Creek warehouse,' to be named Alexandria for the family that had once owned the site. The following year the county surveyor, John West,Jr., assisted by young George Washington, laid off the town in streets and 84 half-acre lots. Among the purchasers were Lawrence Washington of Mount Vernon and his brother Augustine. Soon a busy port and an important stage stop, Alexandria grew quickly to commercial prominence. In 1752 it was made the county seat.

The export of wheat became in time even more important to Alexandria than that of tobacco. Grain growing increased as settlement pushed westward, making the colony self-sufficient in flour and meeting the demands of an expanding market in England and the West Indies. By 1776 caravans of 'flour waggons' were coming from as far as Winchester and returning laden with merchandise from England. In 1781 Alexandria was first on Virginia's flour inspection list.

Taverns such as the City Tavern, the Bunch of Grapes, and the Indian Queen opened for the accommodation of travelers and for the entertainment of the 'gentry'—Washingtons, Fairfaxes, Masons, and other plantation owners with fine mansions in or near town. Scottish merchant-shippers, like the partners Carlyle and Dalton, built handsome town houses, and George Washington had a house in town. Parties and balls were frequent, while the populace sought amusement in fairs, political rallies, and other gatherings held in Market Square. Washington, who raced his own horses, was a steward of the Alexandria Jockey Club.

Washington's first command—troops recruited in Alexandria—was drilled in Market Square before proceeding against the French in 1754. Alexandria was the mobilization point for Maryland troops and for one New York company in preparation for the second campaign in 1755. Here they joined Virginia troops and British regiments under the command of General Edward Braddock. Before starting, the general held a conference in Alexandria with the governors of five colonies. Washington set out as an aide to Braddock but assumed command after Braddock's death.

In July 1774 Washington presided in the courthouse here at a meeting to elect delegates to the first Virginia convention and to protest against the Boston Port Bill. 'If Boston is forced to submit, we will not,' the citizens declared. The Fairfax Resolves, drawn by George Mason, stated Virginia's position on taxation, Parliament, and the Crown, suggested a common platform, and affirmed that 'every little jarring interest and dispute which hath ever happened between these Colonies should be buried in eternal oblivion.'

When the town was incorporated in 1779, Alexandria acquired a seal picturing 'a ship in full sail with a balance equally poised above the ship.' Some of the streets were paved by Hessian prisoners, labor procured through Dr. William Brown, one of the first surgeons general of the Revolutionary army and compiler during the war of the first American *Pharmacopoeia for the Use of Army Hospitals*. A lodge of Masons was organized in 1783. The next year a daily newspaper was established, now the oldest in America, and in 1785 an academy was founded to which Washington contributed annual gifts. He also endowed a short-lived charity school, the first free school in northern Virginia.

In that same year representatives from Virginia and Maryland met in Alexandria to discuss boundaries and commercial relations between the two States. This meeting, continued at Mount Vernon, led to the Annapolis Convention of 1786 and to the Constitutional Convention at Philadelphia in 1787.

In 1789 Virginia gave Alexandria away. Along with a generous slice of Fairfax County, the city later became part of the District of Columbia, laid out in 1791, and the stone marking the southern corner, still in place at Jones Point, was planted with a Masonic ceremony. The presiding official was Dr. Elisha Cullen Dick, who executed two oil paintings of Washington and was consulting physician during Washington's last illness.

Alexandria's exile had its highlights. The Bank of Alexandria, first in the present area of Virginia, was organized in 1792. Two years later the Library Company of Alexandria was founded; many sea captains subscribed, and carried its books on long voyages. A brick building (1767–73) had been erected to replace the wooden parish church, and the Presbyterian Meeting House, completed in 1790, was followed in 1795 by St. Mary's, the first permanent Roman Catholic church in Virginia. When the British sacked the city of Washington in 1814 and jeopardized Alexandria, town officials surrendered to the invaders, who burned a ship at anchor and loaded their vessels liberally with supplies. Alexandria's most serious fire occurred in 1824. An event of quite another sort took place in 1836: the tweaking of President Jackson's nose by Lieutenant Robert Randolph, U.S.N., aboard the steamboat *Sydney*. Randolph, whom Jackson had dismissed for defaulting with Government funds, was knocked down, then hustled ashore and placed under arrest; he was not punished for the assault.

In 1846 homesick Virginians asked Congress to give them back to the Old Dominion. Their petition was granted. In 1847 the general assembly created Alexandria County with Alexandria its seat. In 1898 Clarendon became the county seat, and in 1920 the name of the county was changed to Arlington.

But good fortune was mixed with alloy. The Baltimore & Ohio Railroad reached Winchester and the Cumberland coal fields, and in the 1840's it diverted trade to Baltimore. Though Alexandria achieved city status in 1852, it was soon outstripped by Baltimore and its new fleets of clipper ships.

The War between the States brought about another period of exile. After sending four companies, including a battalion of artillery, to Harpers Ferry in 1859 to suppress John Brown's raid, Alexandria at the beginning of the war was severed from the rest of Virginia. In April 1861, when Robert E. Lee assumed command of Virginia's armed forces, he was followed by many Alexandrians. The next month Federal troops took possession of the city. In August 1863, two months after West Virginia had been admitted to the Union, Governor Francis Pierpont proclaimed Alexandria capital of the 'reorganized government' of Virginia, and it remained so to the end of the war.

Safe behind Federal lines Alexandria escaped the havoc that obliterated evidences of the past in other Virginia cities, but it continued to fall behind newer commercial centers. The city passed through several decades of sluggish economic development before its recent rejuvenation. Today, however, it has the second largest freight classification yards in America and numerous industries: two large fertilizer plants; a plant for the construction and repair of refrigerator cars; chemical works; an automobile assembling plant; iron works; foundries; a shirt factory; a brick kiln; and a pottery. Its industrial pay roll of some $6,000,000 is distributed annually among approximately 3,600 employees.

POINTS OF INTEREST

1. The CITY HALL AND MARKET HOUSE (*open daily*), Cameron St. between Royal and Fairfax Sts., a red brick building with corner pavilions and a lofty spire upon a clock tower, is a highly stylized version of late eighteenth-century architecture. The massive central motif on the Cameron Street façade, crowned with a mansard roof, aggravates the eclectic style of the building. Erected in 1817 and burned in 1871, it was rebuilt and enlarged in 1873.

A courthouse for Fairfax County was erected on Market Square in 1754. A school, apparently the first in Alexandria, occupied the ground floor. In 1782 a larger brick structure over a massive arcade was built on the northwest corner of the square. This was incorporated in the building erected in 1817. Until 1789 the seat of Fairfax County was on this site. For 11 years after the area comprising Alexandria was ceded to the Federal Government, county business continued to be conducted here. From 1847 to 1898 the courthouse of Alexandria County remained in the city.

In the courthouse is a SET OF STANDARD WEIGHTS AND MEASURES stamped 'The County of Fairfax 1744,' said to be the only complete set in the United States of early standards authorized by England.

The ALEXANDRIA-WASHINGTON LODGE OF MASONS is in the central part of the Cameron Street side of the building. Chartered in 1783 under the Grand Lodge of Pennsylvania, it transferred to the Grand Lodge of Virginia in 1788, when Alexandria Lodge No.22 was chartered and George Washington was named its first Worshipful Master. In 1805 'Washington' was added to 'Alexandria,' the only instance in the history of Masonry of a lodge altering its name without a new charter.

The MASONIC MUSEUM (*open 9–5 weekdays; adm. 10¢*) contains two portraits of Washington, an oil by C.P.Polk and a pastel done by William Williams in 1794; the high leather-covered library chair Washington presented and used as Master; his personal Masonic relics; and his bedchamber clock with its hands, stopped by Dr.Dick, still pointing to ten minutes past ten, the moment of Washington's death. Among other portraits are one of La Fayette at 27 by Charles Willson Peale, and one of Thomas, sixth Lord Fairfax, painted in London by Sir Joshua Reynolds.

2. GADSBY'S TAVERN (*open 9–5 weekdays, 2–5 Sun.; adm. 25¢*), 132 Royal St., is a two-story brick structure with a taller brick addition next

---

KEY TO ALEXANDRIA MAP

1.City Hall and Market House 2.Gadsby's Tavern 3.Carlyle House 4.Ramsay House 5.Alexandria Gazette Building 6.Stabler-Leadbeater's Drug Store 7.Old Presbyterian Meeting House 8.Craik House 9.Coryell House 10.La Fayette House 11.Old Lyceum Hall 12.Lord Fairfax House 13.Robert E. Lee House 14.Hallowell School 15.Philip Fendall House 16.Lloyd House 17.Christ Church 18.Friendship Fire Engine House 19.George Washington Masonic National Memorial Temple

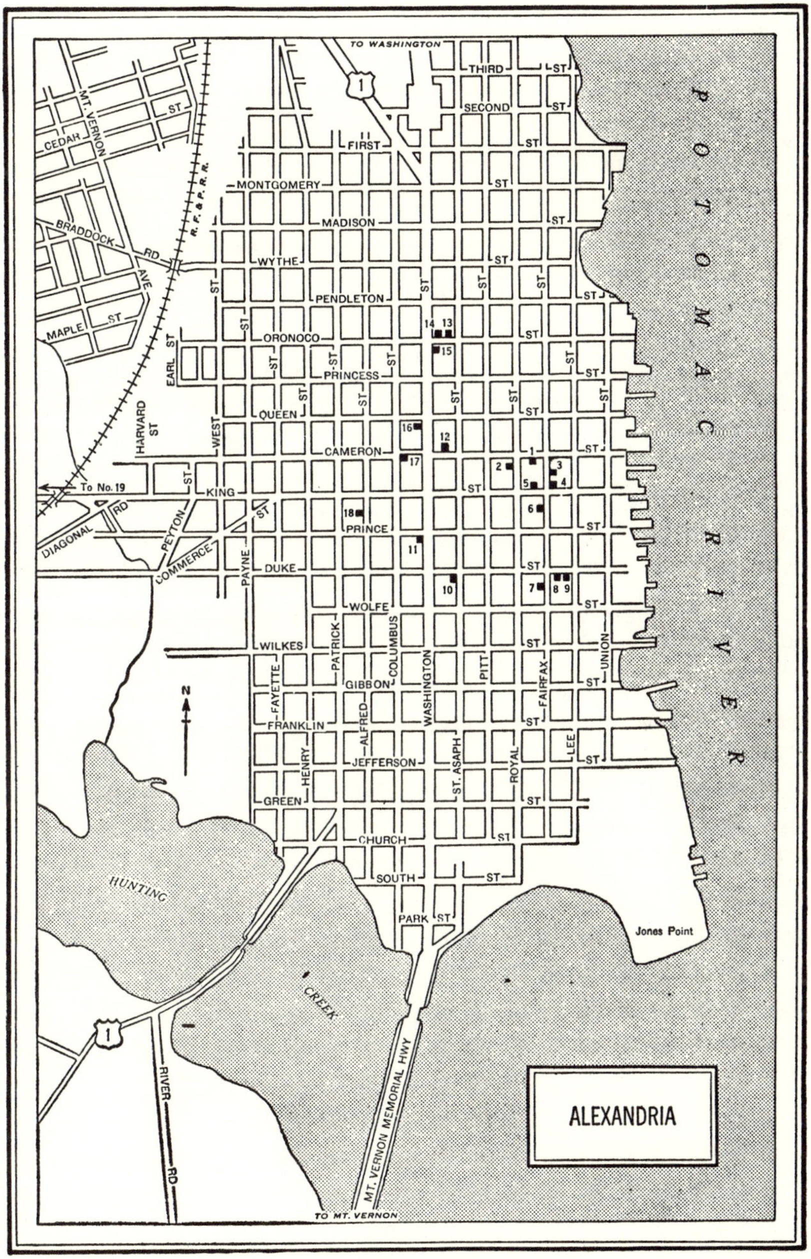
TO WASHINGTON
THIRD
SECOND
FIRST
MONTGOMERY
MADISON
WYTHE
PENDLETON
ORONOCO
PRINCESS
QUEEN
CAMERON
KING
PRINCE
DUKE
WOLFE
WILKES
GIBBON
FRANKLIN
JEFFERSON
GREEN
CHURCH
SOUTH
PARK ST
MT. VERNON
CEDAR
BRADDOCK RD
AVE
MAPLE
EARL ST
HARVARD ST
WEST
R. F. & P. R. R.
To No. 19
DIAGONAL RD
PEYTON
COMMERCE
PAYNE
FAYETTE
PATRICK
HENRY
ALFRED
COLUMBUS
WASHINGTON
ST. ASAPH
PITT
ROYAL
FAIRFAX
LEE
UNION
POTOMAC RIVER
HUNTING CREEK
Jones Point
RIVER RD
MT. VERNON MEMORIAL HWY
TO MT. VERNON
ALEXANDRIA

door. The older building is topped by a gabled roof above a modillioned cornice with fretwork along the lowest molding. The roof is pierced by three dormers, large keystones accentuating the flat arches above the window openings. Fluted pilasters flank the central entrance and support a broken pediment that rises through a stringcourse above a round-arched transom with a tall keystone. The portal, the winged flat arches, and large key-blocks of stone over the windows are typical of late eighteenth-century Georgian Colonial design. In the restored courtyard stands an eighteenth-century coach, as if waiting for the hostler's slothful boy to bring out the horses. From this structure, built in 1752 and long known as the City Tavern, Washington recruited for his first command in 1754, and he used it several times as headquarters during the French and Indian War.

John Wise, who bought the City Tavern in 1792 and built the addition, was succeeded as host two years later by John Gadsby, an Englishman. An inventory in 1802 showed ten buildings, including stables, kitchens, and laundry, grouped about a courtyard. John Davis, an English traveler, said 'that Gadsby keeps the best house of entertainment in America.' Washington attended two celebrations of his birthday here, one in 1789 and his last in 1799. When he reviewed Alexandria troops from these tavern steps in November 1799, he ended his military career where he had begun it 45 years before. The townspeople gave General La Fayette a brilliant reception here in 1824.

Both buildings of the tavern are restored. Although the splendid paneling of the ballroom in the corner structure has been acquired by the Metropolitan Museum of Art, both interiors are still notable for the quality and extent of their carved woodwork. The basement kitchen contains a collection of Colonial utensils.

3. The CARLYLE HOUSE (*open 9–5 weekdays; adm. 15¢*), 123 N. Fairfax St. (entrance through Wagar Building), is a large, two-story stuccoed brick building in Georgian Colonial style. The hip roof is pierced by dormers and a chimney at each end of the ridge. Along the garden side spreads a wide terrace. On the west front a long flight of stone steps leads to the double door with an elliptical fanlight and stone arch, on the keystone of which is carved *Humilitate*, motto of the Carlyle family. Porches and other modifications have not improved a once handsome exterior, but the interior is still distinguished by fine paneled woodwork. From the transverse hall, the stairway ascends gracefully in one continuous curve. Decorative features of the outstanding Blue Room include pediments broken into sweeping scrolls over both doors, an elegant fireplace with pale blue marble facing, a shallow mantel supported by pilasters, a low dado with Greek key molding, and a deep cornice with modillions and rosettes. A museum since 1914, the house contains an extensive collection of early American furniture.

The house was built in 1752 by John Carlyle, a Scottish merchant, who came to America in 1740. In April 1755 Carlyle, then commissary of the Virginia forces, offered his house to General Braddock, Commodore Keppell, and the governors of five colonies, who met in the Blue Room to plan a concerted campaign against the French and Indians. Colonel George Washington was present and received his commission as an aide on the general's staff.

4. The RAMSAY HOUSE (*open daily*), NE. corner King and Fairfax Sts., a two-and-a-half-story building of brick covered partly with clapboard and partly with flush boarding, is the oldest house in Alexandria. It has three pedimented dormer windows on the front, and the roof slopes away in a broad half-gable toward the rear. This rather odd structure was built in 1749–51 by William Ramsay, a Scottish merchant who was one of the founders of Alexandria and its first postmaster.

5. The ALEXANDRIA GAZETTE BUILDING, 317 King St., a modern stone structure, houses the oldest daily newspaper in the United States. First issued on February 5, 1784, by George Richard & Company as the *Virginia Journal and Alexandria Advertiser*, it has undergone changes of name and ownership, but the *Gazette* of today is a continuation of the original paper. The office file lacks only a few of the earliest issues and those of 1861, when the *Gazette* was suppressed by Federal authorities for its strong secessionist sentiment, and its building was burned by Federal soldiers. Publication was continued surreptitiously during the war in a little sheet called *Local News*.

6. STABLER-LEADBEATER'S DRUG STORE (*open* 10–4:30; *adm. free*), 107 S.Fairfax St., one of the oldest drug stores in America, operated until 1933 on the ground floor of this three-story brick building. It was restored by the Landmarks Society of Alexandria, sponsored by the American Pharmaceutical Association, and opened to the public in 1939. Flint glass bottles, mortars with pestles, old thermometers, scales, weights, and measures are part of the shop's authentic equipment.

Founded in 1792 by Edward Stabler, a Quaker from Petersburg, the store was patronized by Drs. Craik, Dick, and Brown. The account books and prescription files show drugs sold to Henry Clay, John Calhoun, Daniel Webster, and the Washington, Lee, Custis, and Fairfax families. A note in Martha Washington's hand is preserved: 'Mrs.Washington desires Mr.Stabler to send by bearer a quart bottle of his best Castor Oil and a bill for it, Mt.Vernon, 1802.' In 1852 John Leadbetter of Philadelphia, who had married the granddaughter of the founder, took over the store. Robert E. Lee was making a purchase here when Lieutenant J.E.B.Stuart delivered orders to him to suppress John Brown's Raid in 1859.

7. The OLD PRESBYTERIAN MEETING HOUSE (*open* 9:30–5 *daily, Apr. to Oct.; adm.* 10¢), 321 S.Fairfax St., is a large, rather austere, red brick hall with a broad gabled roof and two tiers of regularly spaced windows. A tall square tower at the west end is crowned by a latticed balustrade and a handsome square wood cupola with pilasters. The white-painted interior, with box pews, open gallery, and a semidomed recess in the end wall behind the centered pulpit, has a severity more common to New England than to the South.

The first Meeting House, attended by Scottish colonists and their descendants, was begun in 1774 but finished only after an act of 1790 allowed the trustees 'to raise by one or more lotteries' money enough for 'completing the building.' Struck by lightning in 1835 and burned, it was succeeded the following year by the present building erected on the same lot. In 1886 the meeting house was abandoned as a place of worship.

The white marble table tomb of an Unknown Soldier of the Revolution stands in the treeless yard among the graves of many Revolutionists of Scottish ancestry, including Dr. Craik, Major John Carlyle, and Colonel Dennis Ramsay.

8. The CRAIK HOUSE (*private*), 210 Duke St., is a dilapidated three-and-a-half-story red brick building with brick stringcourses marking the floor levels and a large dentil cornice along the façade. The gabled roof is pierced by two round-arched dormer windows.

The house, built about 1790, was the home and office of Dr. James Craik (1730–1814), a Scottish surgeon, who accompanied Washington on his campaigns in the French and Indian War and was with him in every battle from Great Meadows to Yorktown. He was appointed assistant director-general of hospitals in the Continental Army in 1779. Dr. Craik, in attendance at Mount Vernon when Washington died, is mentioned in his will as 'My old and intimate friend, Dr. Craik.'

9. The CORYELL HOUSE (*private*), 208 Duke St., of 'flounder' type, built in 1790, is an unpainted frame building leaning against the Craik House. George Coryell, who lived here, and his father Cornelius Coryell of New Jersey ferried Washington across the Delaware River on Christmas Eve 1776.

10. The LA FAYETTE HOUSE (*private*), SW. corner Duke and St. Asaph Sts., is a large red brick house with white stone arches above each window and a balustrade along the front parapet of the gable roof. A wide, round-arched entrance portal, with delicately traced fan- and sidelights, is the most notable exterior feature. Attractive interior woodwork is well preserved. The house is one of the best examples of Federal or post-Colonial architecture in the city. Built by Thomas Lawrason in 1795, it was lent by his widow in 1825 to La Fayette, who stayed here during his last visit to America.

11. The OLD LYCEUM HALL (*private*), SW. corner Washington and Prince Sts., erected in 1839, is a two-story stuccoed brick building painted yellow and lined to simulate stone blocks. A tall Doric portico, with four fluted columns and a continuous triglyphed entablature, gives this Greek Revival building an air of serenity.

In 1834 gentlemen of the town, led by Benjamin Hallowell, the Quaker schoolmaster, formed a society devoted to literature, science, and history. Hallowell, elected president, delivered the first lecture, on vegetable physiology. This building was erected five years later. During the War between the States it was used as a hospital. Today (1939) the Little Theater presents occasional productions here.

12. The LORD FAIRFAX HOUSE (*private*), 607 Cameron St., is a three-story town house with a long two-story ell at the rear. Two white stringcourses cut across the tall red brick façade. Above a recessed vestibule, within which delicately carved pilasters and small columns flank the

portal, a stuccoed surface arch rises from the first stringcourse and embraces the central windows of the two upper stories. The interior retains much of its fine original woodwork. In the hall a graceful stairway with mahogany banisters winds above an oval well. The house was built in 1816, and bought in 1830 by Thomas, Lord Fairfax, ninth Baron of Cameron.

13. The ROBERT E. LEE HOUSE (*private*), 607 Oronoco St., is a two-and-one-half-story building of pink brick with white trim. A dormer window pierces the long gabled roof on each side of a small eave pediment, the latter rising above a slightly projecting central pavilion. The Georgian Colonial doorway and windows, with keystoned flat arches of white stone, are widely spaced. The interior is notable for original mantels and a graceful staircase. An acre of garden at the rear remains almost as it was a century ago.

The house was owned in 1795 by John Potts and purchased in 1799 by William Fitzhugh. In 1818 when Robert E. Lee was 11 years old, his mother, Ann Hill Carter Lee, moved here from another house in Alexandria where the family had lived since 1811. Here General La Fayette paid his respects to Mrs.Lee in 1824, and met her son, who had been assistant marshal of the welcoming parade.

14. The HALLOWELL SCHOOL (*private*), 609 Oronoco St., shares a common chimney with the Lee House next door. Built about 1793, this house accommodated the school opened in 1825 by Benjamin Hallowell (1799–1877), a Pennsylvania Quaker, and was attended by sons of prominent families in the community and by students from Canada and Latin America. Robert E. Lee was prepared here for entrance to the United States Military Academy.

15. The PHILIP FENDALL HOUSE (*private*), 429 N.Washington St., is a frame-covered brick structure in early Federal style with a Victorian front porch. It rises two stories to an attic with latticed windows under plain eaves, and has a long gabled wing at the rear.

Built shortly after the Revolution, it was the home of Philip R. Fendall, attorney, whose first wife was Elizabeth Steptoe, widow of Philip Ludwell Lee, and whose second wife was Mary Lee, sister of 'Light Horse Harry' Lee. The house came into possession of Richard Bland Lee, brother of 'Light Horse Harry,' in 1792 and for the next half-century the house was a home of the Lee family. On December 15, 1799, friends assembled here to make arrangements for Washington's funeral.

16. The LLOYD HOUSE (*private*), 220 N.Washington St., perhaps the finest example of formal domestic architecture in Alexandria, is a large, square, red brick house of post-Colonial design. The broad gabled roof has three dormer windows with slender pilasters supporting a diminutive gable pediment. The modest but beautifully designed doorway is framed by Corinthian pilasters and a broken pediment over the round-arched fanlight. Two tiers of windows with flat-arched lintels complete a dignified façade. Fine brickwork is matched by the interior woodwork in modified Adam style. The house was built in 1793 by John Hooe and acquired by the Lloyd family in 1832.

17. CHRIST CHURCH (*open 9–5 weekdays; adm. 10¢; services Sun.*), SE. corner Cameron and Columbia Sts., is a late Georgian Colonial building of dark red brick laid in Flemish bond. Centered on the west façade is a square tower supporting an octagonal belfry in three stages, and a domed cupola. White stone quoining emphasizes the corners of the main structure, and white keystones accent the flat-arched brick lintels of the first tier of windows and the arched brick headings of those above. The broad hip roof rises above a continuous denticulated cornice to a short ridge. The east wall is pierced in the center by a fine Palladian window with four square pilasters and a broken pediment. A balcony extends around three sides of the chaste white interior beneath an aquamarine ceiling. The canopied pulpit, originally against the north wall, is centered before the Palladian window.

Preceded by a frame building and known until early in the nineteenth century as Alexandria or Lower Church, the present structure was built in 1767–73. The tower and cupola and probably the balcony were added in 1818, the year in which the small graceful wrought-brass and crystal chandelier was brought from England, where it was purchased for $140 at George Washington's expense. Two of the white box pews are marked by silver plates: the one owned by Washington, a vestryman of the parish for three months in 1765; the other of Robert E. Lee.

18. FRIENDSHIP FIRE ENGINE HOUSE (*open occasionally, adm. 10¢*), 107 S.Alfred St., is a small red brick building with classical trim painted white, castiron acanthus leaves topping stone pilasters and iron ornaments upon the projecting lintels of two tall windows. The figures 1774 (the year the fire company was formally organized) fill the low pediment above the wide door and are inscribed again on the square wooden base of the tall octagonal cupola.

The building was erected perhaps as early as 1775 and housed the local fire company of which Washington was a member and honorary captain shortly before his death. Among exhibited memorabilia of early fire fighting is a copy of the fire engine, now preserved in Baltimore, Maryland, that Washington brought from Philadelphia in 1774 and presented to the Friendship Fire Company.

19. The GEORGE WASHINGTON MASONIC NATIONAL MEMORIAL TEMPLE (*open 9–5 daily*), on Shooter's Hill, King St. and Russell Rd., a gray stone monument in neo-Classic style, occupies the site first proposed for the National capitol. On a massive square base structure, from the center of which juts a Doric portico, a vast tower rises through three colossal stages to a stepped pyramid reaching more than 400 feet above the summit of the terraced hill.

The idea of a monument to George Washington, the Mason, originated with Charles H. Callahan of Alexandria. The movement got under way at a meeting of the Alexandria-Washington Lodge in 1910, and the cornerstone was laid on November 1, 1923. Designed by Harvey Wiley Corbett of New York and costing $5,000,000 contributed by 3,000,000 Masons, the temple will eventually house the portraits and relics in possession of the Alexandria-Washington Lodge of Masons.

POINTS OF INTEREST IN ENVIRONS

Mount Eagle (Lord Fairfax Country Club), 1.5 *m.*; Woodlawn, 8.8 *m.*; Mount Vernon, 9.4 *m.*; Fort Belvoir, 9 *m.* (*see Tour 1a*). Arlington National Cemetery, Arlington, Fort Myer, 7.5 *m.* (*see Tour 12*). Episcopal High School, 3 *m.*; Protestant Episcopal Theological Seminary, 3.2 *m.* (*see Tour 13*). Falls Church, 8.8 *m.* (*see Tours 4a and 13*).

Charlottesville

Railroad Stations: Union Station, Main and 7th Sts. for Southern Ry. and Chesapeake and Ohio Ry.; Water St. at Monticello Rd. for Chesapeake and Ohio Ry.
Bus Stations: Water and 5th Sts. and at University Book Store, The Corner, Main St. and University Ave. for Virginia Stage Lines, and Scottsville Bus Line.
Taxis: Fare 25¢ within city limits.
Local Busses: Fare 5¢.
Traffic Regulations: Numbered cross streets are one-way thoroughfares, alternately N. and S.

Accommodations: 3 hotels; tourist homes in city and university; country inns near by.

Information Service: Chamber of Commerce, Monticello Hotel, Courthouse Square; Monticello Hotel Office.

Motion Picture Houses: Four.
Golf: McIntire Municipal Park, Rugby Ave. between Park St. and Rugby Rd., 9 holes, greens fee 25¢ per hour, 50¢ per day; Farmington Country Club, 3 m. W. on US 250, 18 holes, adm. by arrangement, greens fee $1.50; University of Virginia Golf Club, 7 holes, greens fee 25¢.
Swimming: Fry's Springs, W. end of Fry's Springs Rd., fee 25¢, children 15¢; Farmington Country Club, 3 m. W. on US 250, adm. by arrangement, fee 25¢; Seminole Club, 7 m. W. on US 29 (L), fee 25¢; Blue Ridge Pool, 7 m. W. of university on County 678 (R) off US 250, fee 25¢, children 15¢.
Tennis: McIntire Municipal Park, Rugby Ave. between Park St. and Rugby Rd., 13 courts, free; university courts, adm. free by arrangement; Washington Park, NE. corner Preston Ave. and 10th St. for Negroes, 3 courts, free.

Annual Events: Founder's Day (Jefferson's birthday) Apr. 13 (State holiday); Jefferson Day, July 4; Institute of Public Affairs, two weeks early in July; horse shows at intervals; fox and drag hunting with packs near by, early Sept. to late Mar.

CHARLOTTESVILLE (480 alt., 15,245 pop.), Thomas Jefferson's city and home of the University of Virginia, is situated among the red clay foothills of the Blue Ridge Mountains near the Rivanna River. As the seat of Albemarle County, it has been an important crossroads since late Colonial times. Its Main Street follows Three Chopt Road, one of the first trails from Tidewater to the West. Roads approaching the city roll and wind between wooded hills and fertile pastures, orchards and tilled land. In spring the hillsides are bright with apple trees in bloom, for the county surrounding Charlottesville rivals the Shenandoah Valley in fruit growing and is the home of the luscious Albemarle pippin, Queen Victoria's favorite apple. The best view of the city is from the crest of Pantops, the last and steepest hill on the new road coming from the east. Thickly planted with trees, Charlottesville in its natural bowl appears as an immense many-pavilioned garden.

'Downtown,' the compact business district around the east end of

Main Street, is filled with unhurried shoppers, local housewives doing the day's marketing between gossiping pauses in street or store, and country folk 'in for the day.' On court days and on Saturdays, 'downtown' is crowded until late evening, for the city is market and convivial gathering place for much of the county. Here, close by a hodgepodge of brick store fronts, are a few old buildings that were in the center of eighteenth-century Charlottesville. At the western end of Main Street, which has reached out to the once-distant university, hatless students predominate.

In spite of several small factories, Charlottesville is primarily a university and residential city. Most of its streets, lined with small, attractive houses and thickly shaded by trees, remain undisturbed by the bustle of commerce. The number of fine statues in squares and parks is remarkable for a city of this size. Along the railroad tracks, however, and at the edges of the city are slum sections, where most of the Negroes and folk from the surrounding mountains live. The majority of Charlottesville Negroes are employed as domestic servants.

In 1735, following the first patents for land hereabout in 1727, Abraham Lewis received 800 acres that embraced the present grounds of the university, and Nicholas Meriwether, 1,020 acres including land on which the eastern part of Charlottesville stands. Two years later William Taylor patented 1,200 acres between the Meriwether and Lewis grants, owned later by Richard Randolph. Meanwhile, Peter Jefferson acquired the estates of Shadwell and Monticello. Few patentees, however, settled upon their estates. Thomas Jefferson said that his father 'was the third or fourth settler, about the year 1737, of the part of the county in which I live.' In 1761 the county purchased a 1,000-acre tract from Richard Randolph, built a new courthouse, and laid out 50 acres in streets and lots adjacent to the courthouse square. In 1762, when it was 'represented' that 'a town for the reception of traders . . . would be of great advantage to the inhabitants' of the county, the general assembly 'established a town,' which was named for Queen Charlotte, wife of George III. The county sold the town lots, and taverns and stores sprang up around the courthouse. Other acres of public grounds were sold as 'outlots,' for agricultural use by town residents. Until well into the nineteenth century the Rivanna River was Charlottesville's chief avenue for commercial traffic.

The tumult of war has never seriously disturbed Charlottesville, although the Revolution touched it immediately on two occasions. The establishment of 'The Barracks' near by for the 'Convention Troops,' about 4,000 prisoners taken when Burgoyne surrendered at Saratoga in 1777, aroused no bitter feeling. These troops—English officers and soldiers and a large number of Hessian mercenaries—arrived in January 1779 and remained until October 1780, but many of the Germans escaped into the mountains, where their names survive among mountain folk today. Colonel Banastre Tarleton's raid in 1781 was a more serious business. Cornwallis hoped to capture the most important Revolutionary leaders and send them to England. Ex-governor Jefferson, Acting Governor Fleming, and members of the general assembly, warned in the nick of time by Jack Jouett, hastily fled to Staunton. Tarleton and his men destroyed military stores, clothing, and tobacco, raided the county courthouse, and destroyed all the order books. Court records, dating from 1748, escaped destruction.

In its youth Charlottesville and the county of which it was social and commercial center produced several men, besides Thomas Jefferson, whose lives contributed richly to the Nation. In order to be near Jefferson, James Monroe came to Charlottesville in 1789 and later moved to Ashlawn (*see Tour 23A*) close by Monticello. James Madison was a frequent visitor here. Two men whose expeditions identify Charlottesville with the opening of the great West were George Rogers Clark, born at Buena Vista, two miles east, and Meriwether Lewis, born near Ivy, about seven miles west.

Though situated on one of the main east-west roads, Charlottesville remained a small social center until after the first quarter of the nineteenth century. Thomas Jefferson said in 1822: 'In our village . . . there is a good degree of religion, with a small spice of fanaticism. We have four sects, but without either church or meeting house. The courthouse is the common temple, one Sunday in the month to each. Here Episcopalian and Presbyterian, Methodist and Baptist meet together, . . . listen with attention and devotion to each others preachers, and all mix in society in perfect harmony.' Construction of the first church in the town was begun in 1824. When the university was opened a year later Charlottesville contained 'a courthouse, a half finished church, and three or four taverns, which constitute the whole of its public buildings,' and its inhabitants numbered about 600.

The War between the States only brushed Charlottesville. Most of the university buildings were turned into hospitals, and temporary structures were erected, in which university doctors looked after the wounded. During the last year of the war Union forces under Sheridan occupied the town, but did little damage.

After the Virginia Central Railroad, now the Chesapeake and Ohio, reached Charlottesville in 1848, putting an end to river traffic, industries were established on a modest scale. One of these, the Charlottesville Woolen Mills, reorganized in 1868, still survives. In 1801 Charlottesville was chartered as a town. In 1888 it was chartered as a city, its population then being 4,200. Charlottesville now has several factories, employing about 2,000 workers, with a $1,500,000 annual pay roll. The large woolen mill produces 'cadet gray,' the material used for uniforms by the United States Military Academy at West Point and other military institutions. Smaller textile mills produce underwear and artificial silk goods.

The university and the lively influence of the 'Sage of Monticello,' who is still called 'Mr. Jefferson,' have made Charlottesville and the surrounding section a cultural center. With its hospitality and peaceful beauty the community has attracted visitors who never leave—people who enjoy contemplation or working, not too hard, or simply good living.

POINTS OF INTEREST

1. ALBEMARLE COUNTY COURTHOUSE (*open 9–5 Mon.–Fri., 9–1 Sat.*), NW. corner Jefferson and Park Sts., is a large red brick building

with a tall white portico in Ionic style. Half of the structure was built in 1803, the front part was erected in 1860, and the portico was added in the early '70s. The archives contain some of Jefferson's correspondence. The north wing was used at first as a church, 'the common temple' to which Jefferson referred. Madison, Monroe, and Jefferson worshiped here. Old red brick buildings, in which judges and lawyers of Charlottesville still have offices, once crowded more completely around the square and the streets leading out from it on the south side.

Albemarle County was cut from Goochland in 1744 and embraced a wide area on both sides of the James River. Its first seat, established near Scottsville to the south, served until 1761, when the present site was chosen. The legislature met in the first courthouse in 1781. Pillory, stocks, and a whipping post stood in the square when it was enclosed in 1792.

2. The SITE OF THE OLD SWAN TAVERN (*private*), NE. corner Jefferson and Park Sts., is now occupied by the Red Land Club in a small red brick structure. The tavern was built about 1773 by John Jouett, father of Jack, whose warning saved Thomas Jefferson and the assembly. Jack Jouett moved to Kentucky in 1782. His father died in 1805.

3. JACKSON MONUMENT, NE. corner Jefferson and E.4th Sts., is an exceptionally vigorous figure of Stonewall Jackson on Little Sorrel, bending forward in his saddle, his strong chin thrust forward. The work of Charles Keck, it was unveiled in 1921.

4. The McINTIRE PUBLIC LIBRARY (*open 9–6 Mon.–Fri.; 9–5 Sat., 7–9 p.m. Mon. and Fri.*), SE. corner Jefferson and E.2nd Sts., is a small, well-proportioned pink brick building with a semicircular portico in free classical style. Designed by Walter Dabney Blair and built in 1920, it was given to the city by Paul Goodloe McIntire. The library contains about 8,000 volumes.

5. LEE MONUMENT, Jefferson St. between 1st and E.2nd Sts., begun by H.M.Schrady and finished after his death by Leo Lentelli, was dedicated in 1924. This figure on Traveller convincingly portrays Lee's calm serenity and patient wisdom.

6. The OLD ARMORY OF THE MONTICELLO GUARDS (*open daylight hours*), Market St. between E.5th and E.7th Sts., is a large brick hall built in 1895. The Monticello Guard is successor to the Albemarle County Militia, organized in 1745 with Peter Jefferson as lieutenant colonel, and has taken part in many battles. In 1824, when La Fayette visited Monticello, the organization was rechristened the La Fayette Guard. On ceremonial occasions the guard turns out in its Colonial uniform with cocked hats, knee breeches, and leggings. The old armory has been superseded by a new building two blocks eastward.

7. THE FARM (*private*), E. end of Jefferson St., erected in 1825, is a square brick house with a flat-roofed, one-story portico. Close by is a small stucco-covered house with large end chimneys, built before the Revolution on the Nicholas Meriwether estate. The older house was the home of Meriwether's heir and grandson, Colonel Nicholas Lewis.

Tarleton, dashing up from the ford where the woolen mill now stands, greeted Mrs.Lewis with, 'Madam, you dwell in a little paradise.' He established headquarters here for the single night he spent in Charlottesville, sleeping wrapped in his cloak on the parlor floor.

8. The LEWIS AND CLARK MEMORIAL, Ridge and Main Sts., unveiled in 1919, is a group in bronze by Charles Keck. The two explorers are gazing into the distance, while behind them crouches Sacajawea, the Indian woman who guided them in the Northwest. Pending negotiation of the Louisiana Purchase (1803), Jefferson sent his secretary, Meriwether Lewis, and the latter's close friend, William Clark, to explore the vast new territory beyond the Mississippi.

9. The GEORGE ROGERS CLARK MEMORIAL, Main St. and Fry's Springs Rd., is a bronze group by Robert Aitken, unveiled in 1921, commemorating the conquest of the Northwest Territory. George Rogers Clark, astride his horse, is shown among scouts and Indians.

The UNIVERSITY OF VIRGINIA, W. end of Main St., founded by Thomas Jefferson in 1819, occupies a large, roughly triangular tract of rising ground between the convergence of Fry's Springs and Ivy Roads. Most of its fine buildings are designed in a classical style peculiarly American. In spite of quantities of ancient trees shading the grounds, every white portico of nearly 100 red brick structures is framed at some angle by a vista. In the center on the highest ground are Jefferson's buildings set in four parallel lines separated by lawns and gardens. A rotunda joining the northern end of the terraced central rectangle serves as focal point. Jefferson's 'quadrangle' was closed by the erection of Stanford White's group at the south end of the Lawn in 1898.

In 1814 Jefferson, then retired from public life at Monticello and able to give most of his time to educational interests, was elected a trustee of the Albemarle Academy, a school for boys incorporated in 1803. As early as 1779 he had sponsored a bill to establish a university. Under the pressure of his friend, Joseph Carrington Cabell, the general assembly authorized in 1816 the establishment of Central College at a point just west of Charlottesville. The cornerstone of the first building, now Pavilion VII on West Lawn, was laid on October 6, 1817. In 1818 Jefferson's bill to provide a university, though much mutilated, passed the general assembly, and a commission was named to select the site. Under Jefferson's influence, the commission recommended Central College as the place for the university and the legislature in 1819 confirmed the decision. The official corporate name of the university, chosen then, remains 'The Rector and Visitors of the University of Virginia.' Jefferson, rector of the board of visitors until his death, was the builder, administrator, and dominating power of the institution. When the first session opened in March 1825 there were 40 students and 7 faculty members. Before Jefferson's death on July 4, 1826, the number of students had increased to more than 140, the two lawns and two ranges were complete, and the rotunda was nearly finished.

Jefferson introduced several innovations. For the first time in America higher education was independent of a church. 'The institution will be based on the illimitable freedom of the human mind. For here we are not afraid to follow the truth wherever it may lead or to tolerate any error so long as reason is left free to combat it.' He replaced the customarily prescribed curriculum with the elective system, giving the widest choice of subjects or 'schools' taught in any American university at that time. The university was one of the first to include music and the liberal arts among its curricula. The conventional grouping of students into classes was disregarded. Discipline was reduced to a minimum, though before his death Jefferson found it necessary to modify this principle. Instead of a president, there was a rotating chairman of the faculty, and final authority was vested in a board of seven visitors.

Jefferson expected students from all social strata to take their places on equal terms and to obtain a degree of cultivated intelligence in harmony with the architectural environment. In accordance with his prohibitions, the university has never conferred an honorary degree. He counseled: 'Enlighten the people generally and tyranny and oppressions of body and mind will vanish like spirits at the dawn of day.'

Aided by the honor system, introduced in 1842, university students outgrew their early taste for violence and insubordination. The honor committee, composed of the presidents of the five principal schools, still administers the code; any student proved guilty of violating his pledged word or of knowing and failing to report such violation is dismissed. This system frees the student body from strict surveillance and keeps individual liberty from degenerating into license. Its operation extends to student relations with residents of Charlottesville.

The university became almost at once the most important in the South and grew steadily until the War between the States, during which it was kept open for a few students. It suffered the crushing effects of Reconstruction, but by 1904 renewed growth led the board of visitors to discard Jefferson's executive pattern and choose, as first president, Edwin Anderson Alderman, who was succeeded after his death in 1931 by John Lloyd Newcomb. The plant has been enlarged since 1904 by nearly two dozen principal buildings. Women were admitted to the winter session in 1920, as a result of efforts led by Mary Cooke Branch Munford (1865–1938), who in 1926 was appointed a member of the board of visitors. With an enrollment (1938–39) of 2,920, including less than 200 women, the university is

---

KEY FOR CHARLOTTESVILLE MAP

1.Albemarle County Courthouse 2.Old Swan Tavern 3.Jackson Monument 4.McIntire Public Library 5.Lee Monument 6.Old Armory of the Monticello Guards 7.The Farm 8.Lewis and Clark Memorial 9.George Rogers Clark Memorial

KEY FOR UNIVERSITY OF VIRGINIA MAP

10.Entrance Gate 11.Medical School and University Hospital 12.Brooks Museum 13.East Range 14.Serpentine Walls 15.The Lawn 16.Rotunda 17.Statue of Jefferson 18.Statue of George Washington 19.Cabell Hall, Rouss Physical Laboratory, and Mechanical Laboratory 20.Statue of Homer 21.University Commons 22.West Range 23.Alderman Memorial Library 24.McConnell Statue 25.University Chapel 26.President's House 27.Fayerweather Hall 28.Bayly Art Museum 29.Madison Hall 30.Monroe House 31.Clark Memorial Hall 32.Dawson's Row 33.McCormick Observatory

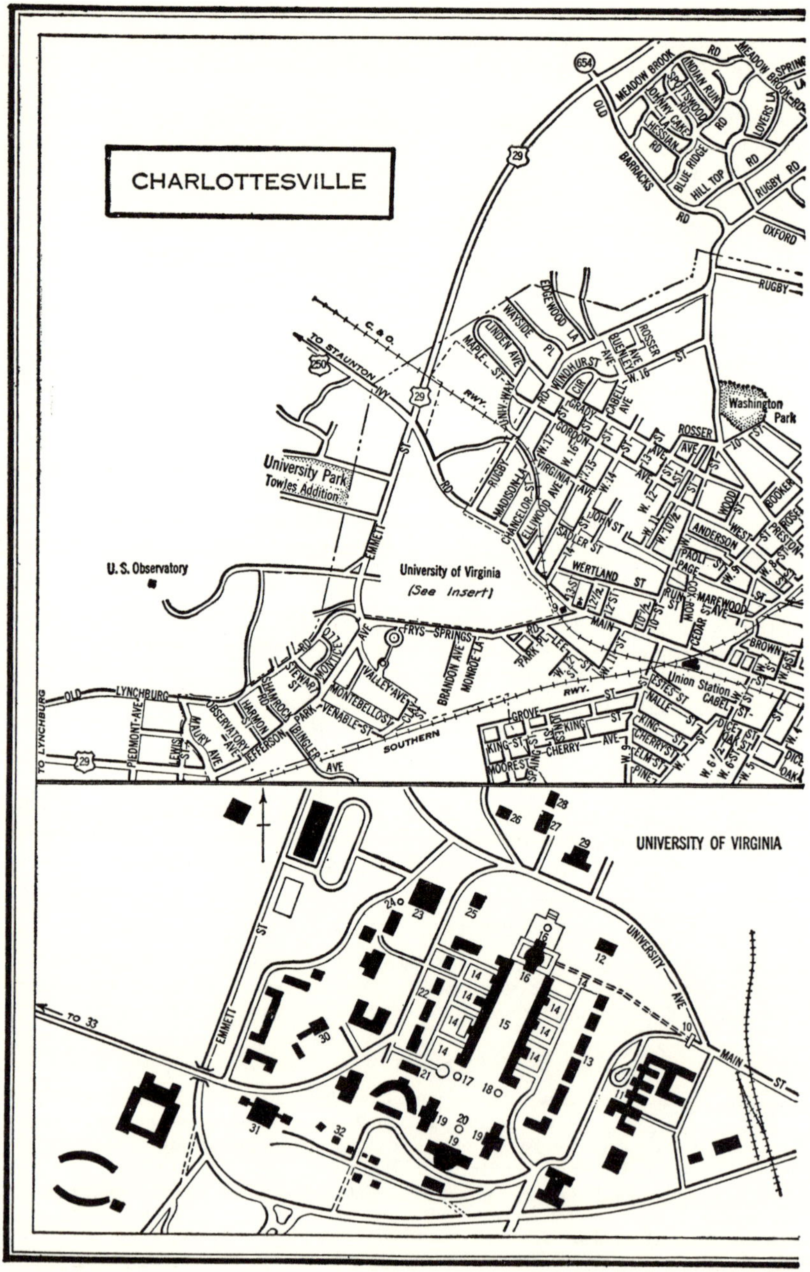
CHARLOTTESVILLE
University Park
Towles Addition
U. S. Observatory
University of Virginia
(See Insert)
Washington Park
Union Station
UNIVERSITY OF VIRGINIA

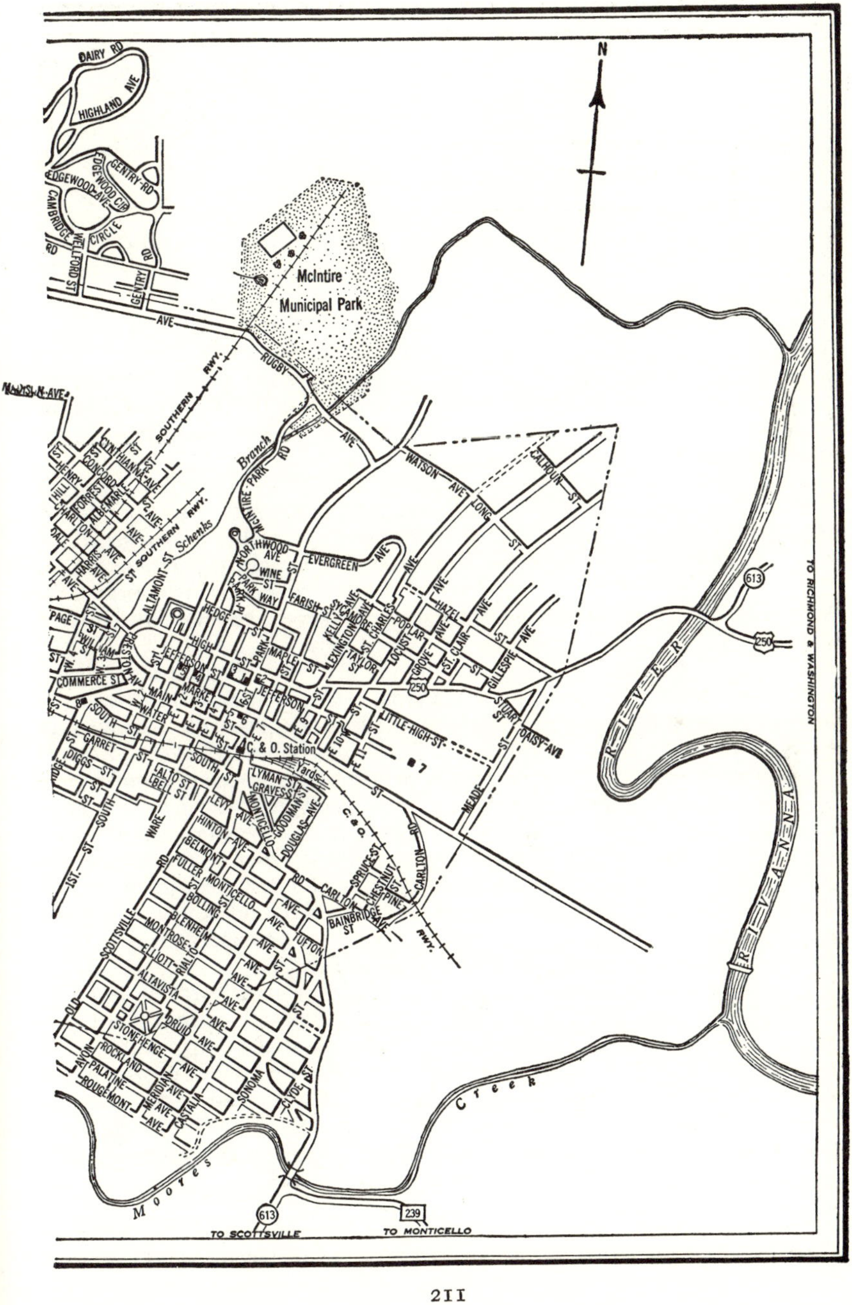
N
DAIRY RD
HIGHLAND AVE
EDGEWOOD
EDGEWOOD CIR
GENTRY RD
CAMBRIDGE
CIRCLE
WELLFORD ST
GENTRY
AVE
McIntire
Municipal Park
RUGBY
AVE
SOUTHERN RWY.
SOUTHERN RWY.
Schenks
Branch
MCINTIRE PARK RD
WATSON AVE
CALHOUN ST
LONG ST
NORTHWOOD AVE
EVERGREEN AVE
WINE ST
PARK WAY
FARISH ST
KELLY AVE
LANDRE
HAZEL
POPLAR
ST. CHARLES
LOCUST
LEXINGTON
TAYLOR
GROVE
ST. CLAIR AVE
GILLESPIE AVE
HENRY
CONCORD
CYNTHIANNA AVE
FORREST
ALBEMARLE
CHARLTON
HARRIS
ALTAMONT ST
HEDGE
HIGH
PAGE
WILLIAM
COMMERCE ST
PRESTON AVE
JEFFERSON
MARKET
MAIN
WATER
PARK
MAPLE
JEFFERSON
SOUTH
GARRET
DIGGS ST
C. & O. Station
Yards
LITTLE HIGH ST
STUART
DAISY AVE
MEADE
ALTO ST
BEL ST
LYMAN ST
GRAVES ST
LEVY AVE
MONTICELLO
GOODMAN ST
DOUGLAS AVE
HINTON AVE
BELMONT
FULLER
MONTICELLO
C. & O.
CARLTON RD
SPRUCE ST
CHESTNUT
PINE
CARLTON
BAINBRIDGE ST
RWY.
BOLLING
BLENHEIM
MONTROSE
SCOTTSVILLE
ELLIOTT
RIALTO
ALTAVISTA
TUFTON
STONEHENGE
DRUID
ROCKLAND
PALATINE
ROUGEMONT
AVON
MERIDIAN
CASTALIA
SONOMA
CLYDE ST
WARE
1ST ST
RIVANNA RIVER
Moores Creek
613
250
239
TO RICHMOND & WASHINGTON
TO SCOTTSVILLE
TO MONTICELLO

coeducational in only the graduate and professional schools. The summer session is wholly coeducational.

UNIVERSITY TOUR

(Points of interest are numbered to correspond with the city and university map. Buildings are open during school hours unless otherwise indicated.)

10. The brick ENTRANCE GATE, Main St. and University Ave., unpretentious but dignified, was designed by Henry Bacon, architect of the Lincoln Memorial in Washington, and was given to the university by Mrs.Charles Senff of New York.

11. The MEDICAL SCHOOL and UNIVERSITY HOSPITAL are housed in a group of large modern brick buildings, construction of which was begun in 1900. The department of medicine has a long and distinguished list of alumni, including Henry Rose Carter, father of modern quarantine; Walter Reed, investigator of yellow fever; and John Anderson, who discovered the cause of typhus fever.

12. BROOKS MUSEUM (*open* 8:30–5 *Mon.–Fri.*, 8:30–1 *Sat.*), built in 1877–78, is the one architectural tragedy on the university grounds. To excuse its yellow-trimmed, red brick presence, a tradition has grown up that it was put here by mistake. Besides mineralogical and geological collections and part of the university's zoological collection, it contains the School of Geology and the State Geological Survey, the first in America, founded in 1836.

13. EAST RANGE (*private*) is a line of students' single rooms in five low red brick structures facing east across a tree-shaded terrace from behind an arcade. Backing on a series of gardens that separate it from East Lawn, it parallels West Range, which lies similarly beyond West Lawn. In one garden is MERTON PINNACLE, a weather-beaten piece of stone carved in Gothic style. Erected in 1451 on Merton College, Oxford, it was removed during restoration and presented to the university in 1928.

14. SERPENTINE WALLS of native red brick surround nearly all the gardens between lawns and ranges. Averaging about six feet in height, the walls are one brick thick, to economize on material, and built on a serpentine plan to give them added strength. They were designed and built by Jefferson, following a practice he had seen in France.

15. THE LAWN, heart of the university, is a large terraced and tree-bordered rectangle. Five two-story, templelike pavilions in a variety of classical styles, most of them with porticoes, are spaced down each of the two long sides and linked by one-story blocks behind Tuscan colonnades. Although these buildings were erected between 1817 and 1826, when the Greek Revival was well under way, Jefferson remained faithful to Palladio and designed them in Academic Roman style. With walls of red brick, trim and columns painted white, they were intended to illustrate the classical orders.

Jefferson envisioned students and their preceptors living together in 'academic villages' with a familylike unity productive of intellectual co-operation. Originally ten unmarried professors, as specified, lived in the upper stories of the pavilions and held their classes in the rooms below. Students lived in the rows of rooms between. Most of the rooms are still occupied by students in their final years; but now professors, with families, live in only six of the pavilions.

16. The ROTUNDA, which, with its encircling balustraded terrace, closes the north end of the Lawn, is an adaptation on one-half the diameter of the Pantheon in Rome. Begun as the library in 1822, it was not completed until 1826, after Jefferson's death. A shallow portico six columns wide on its north face balances the immense portico, six columns wide and three deep, facing the Lawn. Fine Corinthian capitals replace and duplicate those of Carrara marble commissioned in Italy by Jefferson and destroyed by fire in 1895. A few of the least damaged original capitals have been placed in the gardens between lawns and ranges. Broad flights of steps lead down from the porticoes. On the north a second flight drops to a paved and buttressed lower terrace. A huge annex, added in 1851–53, covered this space and obscured the Rotunda until the fire providentially destroyed it. The terraces were arranged in 1898 when the rotunda was restored by Stanford White. The LIBERTY BELL STATUE OF THOMAS JEFFERSON by Sir Moses Ezekiel, a replica of the monument in Louisville, Kentucky, a bronze figure placed upon a pedestal in the shape of the Liberty Bell, has stood in the center since 1907. Inside, where the main library was housed until 1938, stands a life-size white marble figure of Jefferson by Alexander Galt of Norfolk, set up in 1868.

17. At the south end of West Lawn is a small formal garden with a fine seated STATUE OF JEFFERSON in its center. Unveiled in 1915, it is a copy of the figure made by Karl Bitter to commemorate the Louisiana Purchase.

18. Facing it and terminating East Lawn is a similar garden around a bronze STATUE OF GEORGE WASHINGTON, cast from Jean Antoine Houdon's study in the capitol at Richmond.

19. The south end of the rectangle, an open field in Jefferson's day, is occupied by three buildings erected in 1898 and designed by Stanford White, who once exclaimed that the Lawn 'embodies everything that matters most to me: Perfect harmony, perfect symmetry.' CABELL HALL, named for Joseph Carrington Cabell, who, next to Jefferson, did most to create the university, faces the rotunda and is flanked by the ROUSS PHYSICAL LABORATORY on the east and the MECHANICAL LABORATORY on the west. The shallow portico has six Ionic columns and a pediment filled with symbolic figures by G.J.Zolnay. The semicircular rear of the structure contains the university auditorium. The large painting that forms the background for the platform is a reproduction of Raphael's *The School of Athens*, copied by George W. Breck in 1900. The auditorium is used for concerts, by the University Players, and for sessions of the Institute of Public Affairs, which, since 1927, has brought to the university for two weeks early in July men and women qualified to speak on national and international affairs.

20. In the center of this group a bronze STATUE OF HOMER by

Sir Moses Ezekiel rests on a stone pedestal. A boy with a lyre is seated against the poet's knee.

21. The UNIVERSITY COMMONS, a dining hall for students and faculty members, is a rectangular brick building with a shallow Tuscan portico. It was designed by McKim, Mead, and White, and completed in 1908.

22. Occupying a hall in the middle section of WEST RANGE ('Rowdy Row') is the JEFFERSON SOCIETY ROOM, a literary and debating society formed in 1825. Jefferson refused honorary membership because of his connection with the university as rector, but Madison, Monroe, and La Fayette accepted. Poe was a member and read a paper to the society in 1826. Here hangs a portrait of Jefferson by John Trumbull. The WILSON ROOM (*open summer, on application winter*), No.31, was occupied by Woodrow Wilson in 1879–80 and is marked by a tablet. POE'S ROOM (*open on application*), No.13, is maintained by the Raven Society, founded in 1904. POE ALLEY, the drive nearest Poe's room southward, is marked at the east end by a vague, circular design in the pavement. The head of Pallas, whereon the raven perched, half obscures the ominous bird in bluish stone.

23. The ALDERMAN MEMORIAL LIBRARY (*open* 8:30 *a.m.*–10:30 *p.m. weekdays*, 2–10:30 *Sun.*), on the crest of a steep declivity, is a wide brick building with engaged Tuscan columns along its tall one-storied southern façade. The library has nearly 300,000 books and more than 500,000 manuscripts. The most important collections are the Virginiana, especially rich in manuscripts, the James collection on the Negro, the Tunstall collection of Southern poetry, the Lomb optics collection, the Hertz classical collection, and the John Bassett Moore collection on international law. The material available here on Jefferson, Poe, and the Lees is of National importance.

24. The McCONNELL STATUE by Gutzon Borglum is a memorial unveiled in 1919 to James R. McConnell, member of the Lafayette Escadrille and the first student of the university killed in the World War. The bronze figure of a youth, wearing an aviator's helmet, and with pinions on his outstretched arms, is poised on a globe as if for flight.

25. The UNIVERSITY CHAPEL (*open by arrangement*) was finished in 1890 and was a gift of alumni and the Ladies' Chapel Society. The ivy-clad little Neo-Gothic building with its gargoyles seems out of place among the more grandiose structures in classical style. It is now used only for weddings and funerals of students and instructors.

26. The PRESIDENT'S HOUSE (*private*), on Carr's Hill, occupying the highest site in the university grounds, is a large brick house with a tall classic portico of Greek Doric style. Apparently the last building designed by Stanford White, it was completed in 1908 after the architect's death.

27. FAYERWEATHER HALL is a long rectangular brick structure with a particularly fine Corinthian portico at the south end, designed by Carpenter and Peebles and erected in 1893. The eight columns are the only ones at the university so true to their Roman prototypes as to have fluted shafts. Formerly the gymnasium, the building is occupied by the School of Art and Architecture, which was established in 1918–19 by Paul

Goodloe McIntire with its chair first occupied by Sydney Fiske Kimball. A basement entrance leads to the FINE ARTS LIBRARY (*open* 9–6, 7:30–9:30 *Mon.–Fri.;* 9–1 *Sat.; summer* 9–4 *Mon.–Fri.*).

28. The BAYLY ART MUSEUM (*open* 12–4:30 *Tues.–Sat.;* 1:30–4:30 *Sun.; June* 15–*Sept.* 15, 10–12, 4–6 *daily except holidays*), completed in 1935 as a memorial to Thomas H. Bayly, was designed by Edmund S. Campbell in the Palladian style. The museum contains a Thomas Sully portrait of Jefferson once owned by Madison, a fine portrait of Washington by Rembrandt Peale, and numerous busts and other portraits, including a portrait of Chief Justice John Marshall by John B. Martin, George Julian Zolnay's bust of Poe, cast in 1899, and a portrait by E.H.Foster of Professor William H. McGuffey, widely known for his school readers.

29. MADISON HALL, designed by Parish and Schroeder of New York, was completed in 1907. The center section has a Roman-Ionic portico on the front and small Roman-Doric porticoes terminating two side wings. The building is the home of the Student Union, organized in 1932, to which all students belong. It was the gift of Miss Grace Dodge of New York in 1905 to commemorate the fiftieth anniversary of the founding at the university of the first college Y.M.C.A. in the world, an event celebrated two years later. Most of the porticoed buildings behind it, stretching down Madison Lane and Rugby Road, are FRATERNITY HOUSES, some of them very good architecturally.

30. MONROE HOUSE (*private*), on the crest of Monroe Hill, is a brick residence painted white. James Monroe purchased this property and built or remodeled the house when he first came to Albemarle County in 1790 and lived here until he moved to Ashlawn. He had law offices in one of the arcaded outbuildings. The house is now a part of the university.

31. CLARK MEMORIAL HALL, the law building, erected in 1932, is a large brick structure with a curious pyramidal roof over the central portion, supported by six Corinthian columns set between anta walls. The building was given by W.Andrew Clark. In the main hall are murals by Allyn Cox, illustrating the origins of Mosaic and Roman law.

32. Stretching down the hill beside Clark Hall is DAWSON'S ROW, erected in 1859, the only student quarters built between Jefferson's day and 1929, when the eight NEW DORMITORIES, facing west toward the mountains from behind Monroe Hill, were completed.

33. The McCORMICK OBSERVATORY (*open by arrangement*), about 1 *m.* W. of Clark Hall on a hilltop, was given to the university by Leander J. McCormick. Its original 26-inch refracting telescope, the larger of two now in use, was the largest in the world when the observatory was opened in 1884. This observatory replaced one established by Jefferson—among the first in America—and housed in a building on this site in 1828.

POINTS OF INTEREST IN ENVIRONS

Bentivar, 7.1 *m.* (*see Tour 4b*). Buena Vista, 2.7 *m.* (*see Tour* 10). Shadwell, 4.4 *m.*; Edgehill, 5.4 *m.* (*see Tour 17a*). Farmington, 4.1 *m.*; Ivy (Locust Hill), 7.4 *m.* (*see Tour 17b*). Michie Tavern, 2 *m.*; Monticello, 2.5 *m.*; Ash Lawn, 4.9 *m.* (*see Tour 23A*).

Fredericksburg

Railroad Station: Lafayette Blvd. between Caroline and Princess Anne Sts. for Richmond, Fredericksburg and Potomac R.R.
Bus Station: Princess Anne and Wolfe Sts. for Greyhound Bus Line, Great Eastern Line, and Virginia Stage Lines.
Taxis: Fare 25¢ within city, 10¢ each additional passenger.

Accommodations: 7 hotels, including 2 for Negroes; tourist homes.

Information Service: Chamber of Commerce, City Hall, Princess Anne St. between William and George Sts.

Motion Picture Houses: 3.
Golf: Mannsfield Hall, 3.9 m. S. on US 17–State 2, 9 holes, greens fee 75¢, weekends and holidays $1.
Swimming: Mannsfield Hall, 3.9 m. S. on US 17–State 2, 25¢.
Tennis: Mannsfield Hall, 3.9 m. S. on US 17–State 2, free.

Annual Events: Local horse shows, Apr. and Oct.; Dog Mart, Oct.

FREDERICKSBURG (50 alt., 6,819 pop.), where George Washington attended school for four months and his mother spent her last years, where Monroe practiced law, John Paul Jones had his only home, and the armies of the 1860's fought their bloodiest battles, is at the head of navigation on the Rappahannock River.

The city's eastern boundary is the river, crossed by a railroad bridge and by Free Bridge, which passes over a tiny island. Northward is the old town of Falmouth, and southward and westward residential areas rise toward pleasant fields on rolling land. Old Fredericksburg is a rectangular plot from the river to the higher level of Princess Anne Street. Straight streets, under arching trees, crisscross at right angles. Commerce follows William Street from the center of the city to Caroline Street, where grocery stores, meat markets, hardware stores, motion picture houses, and restaurants are in full possession. Negroes and factory workers live in small old houses huddled together beside the river and in several outlying areas.

Houses, cemeteries, and monuments tell of two centuries of distinguished people and stirring events. Tourist conscious now, the city presents an almost universal gleam of fresh paint, applied to white clapboards, green shutters, and to the trim of red brick Colonial buildings.

Fredericksburg has long been the urban center of a fertile agricultural region. Its people still trade with country folk who market and buy here. The city's industrial plants, with an annual pay roll of $2,500,000, manufacture flour, clothing, textiles, shoes, crates, and boxes. But Fredericksburg is primarily an old residential community that cherishes the profitable aura of its past.

The dog mart, held in the city park each October, perpetuates an old custom. It is preceded by a bench show, street parade, and hornblowing contest, and is followed by a ball. The story goes that first settlers brought fine hunting dogs with them, of which the Indians were so covetous that a day was set each year when settlers traded dogs for furs and other articles. The barter was begun in 1698 and continued until interrupted by the Revolutionary War. In 1927 it was revived.

Fredericksburg's authenticated record begins in 1608 with a visit by Captain John Smith. In 1671 John Buckner, Robert Bryan, and Thomas Royston patented here a tract called later the Lease-land. In 1722 there was a public ferry across the river 'from Mrs.Fitzhugh's plantation . . . to the wharf on the leased land of Thomas Buckner and John Royston.' About 1723 William Levingston moved here and built 'a dwelling and kitchen.' In 1727 the general assembly directed that 50 acres of the Lease-land be laid out, and established a town for Spotsylvania County by the name of Fredericksburg—for Frederick, Prince of Wales and father of George III. Colonel William Byrd II, visiting the sparsely settled town five years later, was impressed by the stone prison, 'strong enough to hold Jack Shepherd,' and by the versatility of 'Mrs.Levistone,' who was a 'Doctress and Coffee Woman,' and 'qualify'd to exercise 2 other callings.' He noted that 'the Court-house and the Church are going to be built here, and then both Religion and Justice will help to enlarge the Place.'

The town grew as a port. Ships lay 'close to the Wharf, within 30 Yards of the Public Warehouses, which are built in the figure of a Cross.' Wagons jolted in from the countryside with wheat and tobacco for export. Rows of buildings, many of brick, began to rise on Sophia and Caroline Streets, and mansions were built on the 'hill.' In 1734 a new ferry was authorized 'on Rappahannock river, from the warehouse landing, at the town of Fredericksburg . . . to the land of William Thornton.' A French traveler wrote in 1765: 'Back settlements send down to Fredericksburg great quantities of butter, cheese, flax, hemp, flower and some tobacco.' Soon wheat and flour led the exports.

During the Revolution the town furnished leaders for the Continental army and arms from its 'gunnery.' In an old order book, dated September 18, 1783, is an entry 'to Mary Driskell, a nurse in the Continental Hospital at Fredericksburg, from January 9, '79, to May '82, by which appears to be due the amount certified, £266 : 19.'

In 1781 Fredericksburg was incorporated as a town. After the Revolution it prospered steadily. In 1807, however, during the obsequies of William Stanard, an overturned candle started a fire that reduced half the town to ashes. But Fredericksburg recovered. As center for a large number of slave-holding landed proprietors, some of whom lived in town, it entered a period of luxury, when racecourses, wine cellars, and balls reached their apogee. Great canvas-covered wagons, some as high as 12 feet, lumbered in from 'up country' with loads of grain, tobacco, and other produce, drawn by four to eight horses with bells jangling on their collars. They returned laden with groceries, wines, housefurnishings, and other imported supplies. Two hundred of these huge conveyances were often in Fredericksburg at one time, 'bringing business for the many vessels, some of them large three-masted schooners, which came from all parts of the globe to anchor at the wharves.' In 1822 Fredericksburg was made a central point for the distribution of mail to five States, and the mails became so heavy that surreys were used instead of postriders. During this era of prosperity even funerals were occasions for entertaining, refreshments being served in dark wrappings and wine drunk from glasses festooned with long black ribbons. In 1840 there were 73 stores, 4 semiweekly newspapers, 3,974 inhabitants, and exports amounted to about $4,000,000 yearly.

Fredericksburg's distinguished men were not all of the Revolutionary period. Matthew Fontaine Maury, the great marine cartographer, spent part of his life here. Another native was Maury's brother-in-law, William Lewis Herndon, who worked with him for a time at the National Observatory and, in 1851, was apparently the first to explore the Amazon to its headwaters.

The War between the States struck Fredericksburg down. Situated halfway between Washington and Richmond and on main roads and a rail route, it was a major objective of both armies. It changed hands seven times during the conflict and achieved, with its immediate neighborhood, the unhappy distinction of being one of the bloodiest battlegrounds of history.

In 1879 the general assembly created 'the city of Fredericksburg . . . one body politic, in fact and in name.' By the beginning of the twentieth century the scars of battle and Reconstruction were fairly smoothed out, and since then improvements have changed a sleepy community into a modern little city. In 1912 Fredericksburg exchanged its councilmanic form of government for the city manager plan.

POINTS OF INTEREST

(Buildings to which the public is admitted are usually open unofficially earlier and later than hours stated. Guide service at $1 per hour can be arranged at the chamber of commerce.)

1. CITY HALL (*open 9–5 weekdays*), Princess Anne St. between William and George Sts., is a gray-painted two-story brick building, with one-story wings. Narrow steps lead to three entrance stoops. Built in 1813, it houses city offices and the chamber of commerce. Council records preserved here date from 1782. In 1824 La Fayette was given a public reception in the assembly room. The hall housed soldiers of General Whittle's Confederate brigade in 1862, and later was used as Union barracks and hospital.

2. ST.GEORGE'S CHURCH (*open daily*), NE. corner Princess Anne and George Sts., is a gray brick edifice of Victorian design, with tower and spire centered on the front. Built in 1849, it is the third on this site. The first was erected in 1732 by Colonel Henry Willis, 'top man of the place.' The first rector of St.George's Parish to officiate in this building was the Reverend Patrick Henry, uncle of the orator; Charles Washington and James Monroe were vestrymen; the bell was given in 1751 by Colonel John Spotswood, son of the Colonial governor.

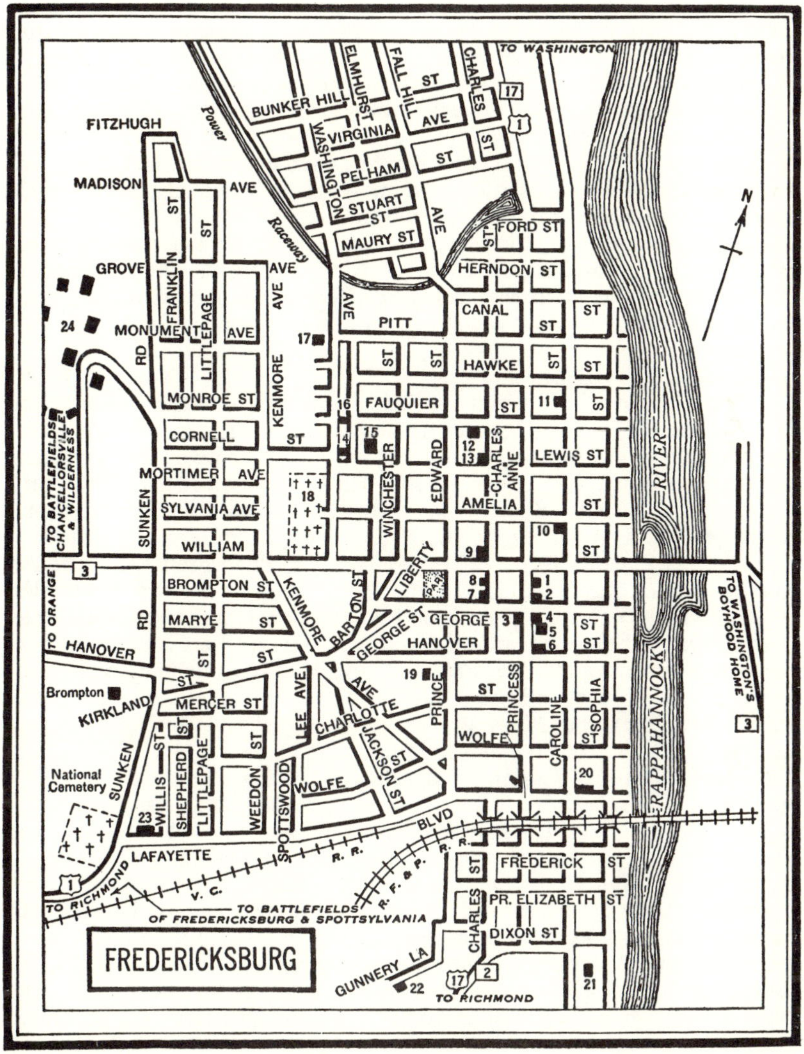

1.City Hall 2.St.George's Church 3.Presbyterian Church 4.Wallace Library 5.Courthouse 6.Masonic Lodge 7.Masonic Cemetery 8.James Monroe Law Office 9.Slave Block 10.Hugh Mercer's Apothecary Shop 11.Rising Sun Tavern 12.Horse Chestnut Tree 13.Mary Washington's House 14.George Rogers Clark Memorial 15.Kenmore 16.Mercer Monument 17.Mary Washington Monument 18.Confederate Cemetery 19.Federal Hill House 20.John Paul Jones House 21.Sentry Box 22.Gunnery Springs 23.National Park Service Headquarters and Museum 24.Mary Washington College

Among the graves in the churchyard are those of William Paul and of John Dandridge, Washington's father-in-law. Colonel Fielding Lewis and two of his children are buried beneath the steps of the church.

3. The PRESBYTERIAN CHURCH (*open daily*), SW. corner Princess Anne and George Sts., built in 1833, is a red brick building with a recessed portico having two Tuscan columns between anta walls, a plain pediment, and a square white cupola. Clara Barton, founder of the American Red Cross, attended the wounded here when the church was used as a Federal hospital. Two cannon balls have been built into the left column of the portico, where balls struck during the bombardment of Fredericksburg.

Presbyterianism was established in Fredericksburg in 1806 by Dr.Samuel B. Wilson. Annoyed at the Rising Sun Tavern by men 'drinking, cursing, and gambling,' he believed the town needed regeneration and started his church.

4. The WALLACE LIBRARY (*open* 3–6 *weekdays*), SE. corner Princess Anne and George Sts., a small tan brick building containing more than 6,000 volumes, was opened in 1911.

5. The COURTHOUSE (*open* 9–5 *Mon.–Fri.*, 9–1 *Sat.*), Princess Anne St. between George and Hanover Sts., built in 1852, is a two-story buttressed gray stucco structure in Victorian Gothic style. The bell, in a central domed tower, was made in the Paul Revere Foundry at Boston.

This site has been the court green since 1732, when Fredericksburg became the seat of Spotsylvania County. Before and during the Revolution it was the rendezvous of patriots and soldiers. Among the debtors confined to the green on their honor was 'Light Horse Harry' Lee. During the battle of Fredericksburg in 1862, Federal General D.N.Couch had headquarters in the courthouse, and the tower was his signal station. Records in the vault include the will of Mary Washington, Augustine Washington's commission (1742) as a trustee of Fredericksburg, and the official bill of expenses for the entertainment of La Fayette in 1825.

6. The MASONIC LODGE (*open* 8:30–5 *weekdays*, 1:30–5 *Sun.; adm.* 25¢, *large groups* 15¢), NE. corner Princess Anne and Hanover Sts., is a plain two-story building of brick painted gray, with twin end chimneys, erected in 1815. Having functioned under a dispensation after 1752, when George Washington 'entered apprentice,' Lodge No.4 was chartered in 1758 by the Provincial Grand Lodge of Massachusetts under the Grand Lodge of Scotland and accepted a charter from the newly organized Grand Lodge of Virginia in 1778. The Scottish charter is still displayed. An interior doorway and two canopies from the old building on Caroline Street are preserved here, as well as the Bible on which Washington was sworn, the minute book with a record of three degrees conferred on Washington, and a Gilbert Stuart portrait of Washington.

7. MASONIC CEMETERY, NW. corner Charles and George Sts., a half acre of turf dotted with mossy tombstones and enclosed by a stone wall, is one of the oldest Masonic burial grounds in America. The land was bought in 1784 by Fredericksburg Lodge No.4. Here is an impressive array of chiseled names, virtue-claiming epitaphs, and coats of arms. Basil Gordon (1768–1817), one of the first millionaires in North America, Robert

Lewis, private secretary to his uncle, George Washington, and twice mayor of Fredericksburg, and officers of three wars are buried here.

Covered with wild vines in a far corner is the grave of Lewis Littlepage, born in Hanover County in 1762 but a resident of Fredericksburg during his early years. As a boy of 18, after writing poetry at the College of William and Mary, he went to Madrid as protégé of John Jay, American minister to Spain, with whom he later quarreled. He joined the Duc de Crillon, distinguished himself in the storming of Gibraltar, and met La Fayette. He visited Poland, was knighted by King Stanislaus, made minister in the Polish cabinet, and sent to conclude a treaty with Catherine of Russia. The Empress 'borrowed' him and sent him against the Turks in the Black Sea, where his fellow townsman, John Paul Jones, was an admiral in the Russian fleet. He served against Russia during the Polish revolution of 1791 and joined Kosciusko in storming Prague in 1794. After an unfortunate love affair with a princess of North Poland and the capture of King Stanislaus by the Russians, Littlepage retired to Fredericksburg, where he died in 1802.

8. The JAMES MONROE LAW OFFICE (*open 9–6 daily; adm. 25¢, large groups 15¢*), Charles St. between George and William Sts., is a long, story-and-a-half red brick building with small, green-shuttered windows, two simple doorways, three chimneys, and three dormers along the low gabled roof. The whitewashed rear wall faces a little old-fashioned garden. Built in 1758, the building is little altered since the days of Monroe, who practiced law here from 1786 to 1790. The house contains original Monroe furniture of the Louis XVI period, purchased when he was minister to France in 1794, and later used in the White House when Monroe entered it as President in 1817, following its burning by the British in 1814. The Monroe Room in the White House is furnished with reproductions of these original Monroe pieces, copied by craftsmen under the direction of Mrs.Herbert Hoover.

In the building are the desk on which Monroe wrote his message to Congress in 1823 enunciating the principles of American foreign policy known as the Monroe Doctrine; his Revolutionary gun, dueling pistols, and sword; a portrait of him by Rembrandt Peale, a portrait by John Trumbull (painted on a wooden panel), a miniature by Semé, a bronze bust of La Fayette presented by him to Monroe; letters from La Fayette, Adams, Madison, Jefferson, and others; the dispatch box Monroe carried while negotiating the Louisiana Purchase; the court dress he wore at the court of Napoleon; and many other belongings. The collection also includes Mrs.Monroe's court dresses, jewelry, wedding slippers, dressing table, and other possessions.

9. The SLAVE BLOCK, NW. corner Charles and William Sts., is a circular block of sandstone three feet high, but taller before the street level was raised. One side is hewn to form a step to the top, from which, in *ante-bellum* days when the Planters Hotel stood behind it, ladies mounted their horses and slaves were auctioned.

10. HUGH MERCER'S APOTHECARY SHOP (*open 9–6 weekdays; adm. 25¢*), SW. corner Amelia and Caroline Sts., is assumed to have been in this small story-and-a-half clapboarded structure. The southern portion

of the building, older than the shop, was built in the mid-eighteenth century. Washington kept a desk here for transacting business when in Fredericksburg.

Dr.Hugh Mercer, a Scottish Jacobite, met disaster at Culloden as an army surgeon with Bonnie Prince Charlie, emigrated to America, fought in the French and Indian War, became a close friend of Washington, and on his advice settled in Fredericksburg. Here he practiced medicine and conducted his apothecary shop. He entered the Revolution as a colonel of militia but was a brigadier general when he was killed at the Battle of Princeton.

During restoration, the removal of lath and plaster revealed the shelves, drawers, and pigeonholes of an old shop, some of the drawer fronts bearing labels apparently in Dr.Mercer's handwriting. The interior is completely furnished with a large collection of apothecary bottles and implements, some found on the place, others belonging to Mercer's descendants. A little garden is maintained as it used to be, with lavender, thyme, and other herbs.

11. The RISING SUN TAVERN (*open* 9–5 *weekdays, adm.* 25¢), Caroline St. between Fauquier and Hawke Sts., a one-and-a-half-story frame building covered with broad hand-beveled clapboards, is approached by a small stone porch, recently restored. Its gabled roof is pierced by three tiny dormers and built-in end chimneys. The banquet room includes a paneled corner fireplace and a handsome built-in cupboard.

The building was erected before the middle of the eighteenth century by John Gordon. Situated on the main north-south highway, it was a stage stop and post office. In the hands of 'Mine Host' Weedon it was a social and political center, where the fiery patriot served sedition as well as wine. Weedon, born in Westmoreland in 1734, was the son of George Weedon and a descendant of a Westmoreland pioneer but often identified as a German named von der Wieden. Here George Mason, George Wythe, Edmund Pendleton, Thomas Jefferson, and Thomas Ludwell Lee met on January 13, 1777, and outlined the bill that Jefferson later phrased and Madison presented to the Virginia assembly in 1785, when it passed as the Statute of Virginia for Religious Liberty. A Peace Ball, attended by Washington and his mother, his officers, La Fayette, Rochambeau, de Grasse, and others, in celebration of victory at Yorktown, was supposedly held in 1781 in the assembly room, long since burned.

12. The HORSE-CHESTNUT TREE, Fauquier St. between Charles and Edward Sts., a large old tree standing close to the walk, is the only survivor of 13 planted by George Washington to symbolize the 13 original States.

13. MARY WASHINGTON'S HOUSE (*open* 9–12, 1–6 *weekdays;* 1–6 *Sun. only in summer; adm.* 25¢), NW. corner Lewis and Charles Sts., is the simple white frame structure in which Washington's mother lived from 1772 to 1789. The middle section, built by Washington in 1772, rises two stories from a simple doorway to a plain gable roof. The south wing, part of the original house, has a gabled garret with dormers above the main floor; the north wing, added after Mary Washington's death, has a steep gam-

brel roof with shallow 'Dutch' dormers. The interior is restored and furnished as it might have been when Mary Washington occupied it.

Beyond wide porches at the rear is the old-fashioned garden with the original sundial and part of the box-bordered brick walk along which Mrs. Washington went each day to her daughter's home near by. The boxwood she planted still flourish. Here also is the old stone kitchen with the equipment Colonial cooks used—along with 'conjur' perhaps—to prepare the food that helped to create Virginia's reputation for hospitality. Preceding the Revolution Washington persuaded his mother to move from Ferry Farm on the river to the comparative safety of a town house.

Mary Washington, it seems, never visited her son at Mount Vernon. In making clear his wish that she remain away from his house, which resembled a 'well resorted tavern,' Washington wrote, 'This would, were you to be an inhabitant of it, oblige you to do one of 3 things: 1st to be always dressing to appear in company; 2d, to come . . . in a dishabille, or 3d to be as a prisoner in your bedchamber. The first you'ld not like, . . . the second I should not like, . . . And the 3d, . . . would not be pleasing to either of us.' So the old lady stayed in Fredericksburg. Her complaint that she had 'never lived so poore' caused a movement in the general assembly for granting her a pension. Washington besought a friend to stop the proceedings, but Mary Washington continued to talk of her poverty and to borrow from neighbors. George Washington, to end the gossip, ceased to rent his mother's 'quarter' a few miles below Ferry Farm, explaining, 'What I shall then give, I shall have credit for,' and avoid being 'viewed as unjust and undutiful son.' Washington frequently visited his mother at Fredericksburg, and on March 11, 1789, he came to say goodby before starting for New York and his inauguration as first President. Mary Washington died the following August.

14. The GEORGE ROGERS CLARK MEMORIAL, Lewis St. and Washington Ave., is a small granite block in a circular grass plot, erected in 1929 'in grateful acknowledgment of the valor and the strategic victory' that acquired the Northwest Territory for Virginia. Clark spent part of his childhood about 15 miles south of Fredericksburg.

15. KENMORE (*open 9–6 daily, adm.* 50¢), Washington Ave. between Lewis and Fauquier Sts., was the home of George Washington's sister, Betty Washington Lewis. Set among tall trees in a walled yard, the two-story red brick house with its low water table of molded brick stands between a pair of detached wings. The gabled roof is pierced by two square built-in end chimneys. The simply framed entrance doors are surmounted by rectangular transoms. Over the rear door a modest portico with four Tuscan columns faces the garden, which has been restored with the box-bordered walk that led to Mary Washington's house.

The fine mahogany stairway in the entrance hall is adorned with a carved lotus motif, and the tall clock standing here belonged to Mary Washington. The reassembled gun over the door at the left is the only firearm extant known to have come from the Fielding Lewis Gunnery, where it was made in 1781. Through this door is the dining room with ceiling, mantel, and cornice elaborately ornamented in putty stucco. Portraits by John Wollaston of Colonel Fielding Lewis and of his wife, Betty Washington, hang in this room. The end of the hall opens into the parlor or 'great room.' The rich plaster ornament of the ceiling, from which a fine Waterford crystal chandelier is suspended, includes four horns of plenty. Above the handsome carved mantel, which is supported on classic consoles, is a panel framed with Georgian 'dog-ear' trim and embellished with a delicate plaster bas-relief representing Aesop's fable of the fox and crow. The subject of this decoration is said to have been suggested by Washington, and the work seems authentically to have been that of Hessian prisoners. The ceilings were executed by a man whom Washington called 'that Frenchman.' The house is filled with furniture and relics, many of which belonged to the Washington or Lewis family; some are gifts or loans from the Metropolitan Museum.

The four panels of the ceiling in the library represent the four seasons with palm, grape, acorn, and mistletoe. The over-mantel panel frames a decorative basket of flowers and festoon in plaster relief. The bedrooms upstairs are furnished chiefly with heirlooms.

On a plantation of 861 acres purchased from Richard Wyat Royston, Fielding Lewis began to build in 1752 for his second bride, 19-year-old Betty Washington, the only sister of George to reach maturity; but the house was not complete in detail until after 1777. Before that, the home of the Fieldings had become a center of political and social life. Washington frequently recorded visits here.

Fielding Lewis was an earnest patriot. He wrote resolutions, endorsed by a large gathering in Fredericksburg, commending Patrick Henry's resistance to Governor Dunmore. He fitted out soldiers at his own expense. As chief commissioner for the manufacturing of small arms in Fredericksburg, he used his own money when public funds ran out. When he died in 1781, he left a debt of £7,000 and a mortgage on the house later known as Kenmore.

Mrs.Lewis continued to live here until she sold the house in 1796. Early in the nineteenth century it was bought by the Gordon family, who changed its name to Kenmore. It served as a hospital and military headquarters during the War between the States, when it was considerably damaged, and later it housed a boys' academy.

In 1922 a band of women formed the Kenmore Association to save the house from being pulled down, and raised the money for its purchase and restoration. Woodwork, ceilings, nearly all hardware, and floors are original. The dependencies were completely reconstructed upon excavated foundations. In the kitchen a Negro 'mammy' serves tea and gingerbread to visitors.

16. The MERCER MONUMENT, center of Washington Ave. at Fauquier St., is a bronze figure of General Hugh Mercer by Edward V. Valentine, erected by Congress in 1906.

17. The MARY WASHINGTON MONUMENT, Washington Ave. and Pitt St., a 50-foot granite obelisk near the grave of Mary Washington, was erected by the women of the National Mary Washington Monument As-

sociation and dedicated in 1894 with President Grover Cleveland as the speaker. A monument was begun here in 1833, but it stood incomplete until battered to ruins during the War between the States.

18. The CONFEDERATE CEMETERY (*open 9–5 daily*), entrance Washington Ave. and Amelia St., a large rectangular tract with scattered trees and mossy tombstones behind a four-foot brick wall, was established in 1865 by the Fredericksburg Ladies' Memorial Association. On May 10 of that year the association held a Memorial Day service here, possibly the first in the South. Here are buried 1,470 Confederate soldiers and officers—1,140 of them unidentified—who fell on battlefields near by.

19. FEDERAL HILL HOUSE (*open by arrangement*), behind church on SW. corner of Hanover and Prince Edward Sts., is a plain two-and-a-half-story residence, its thick brick walls covered with white clapboards. The interior is handsomely ornamented. A paneled transverse hall contains a fine staircase and leads through an elegantly arched doorway to a drawing-room that runs the full length of the house.

The builder and the date of construction are unknown. After the Revolution Robert Brooke, governor of Virginia (1794–96) and a founder of the Federal party, bought the house and renamed it Federal Hill. During the war, it was used as a Federal hospital.

20. The JOHN PAUL JONES HOUSE (*private*), NE. corner Lafayette Blvd. and Caroline St., a small half-brick, half-frame structure, is the only house in America the naval hero could call home. It was owned by his older brother, William Paul, who conducted a tailoring business here after migrating from Scotland in 1758.

John Paul (1747–92) was born in Scotland. He first visited Virginia as a lad of 12, apprenticed to a shipmaster. During the next nine years he was acting midshipman, third and first mate on slavers, shipmaster, and finally master of his own boat. When his crew mutinied, he killed the ringleader and fled to his brother in Fredericksburg. In 1775, after seven years of obscurity, he appeared in Philadelphia, calling himself John Paul Jones and bearing a commission as senior lieutenant in the Continental navy. Then began his incredible career as a naval officer. He successfully attacked New Providence in the Bahamas and for a time convoyed supply ships into New York harbor; in a seven-week free-lance cruise between Bermuda and Nova Scotia he captured six brigantines, one sloop, and one ship and destroyed six schooners, one ship, and one brigantine; he cut his way through ice to save Americans on Isle Royale, burned a warehouse on the Acadian coast, took four transports, and on his way home captured another transport and a sixteen-gun privateer. Sailing to France with dispatches, he picked up two prizes and forced a British sloop to strike her colors. With the clumsily remodeled *Bonhomme Richard*, obtained for him by Benjamin Franklin, he entered upon a series of successful engagements and, in one of the great sea fights of history, caused the *Serapis* to ask for quarter. He often paid officers and sailors out of his own pocket and was not reimbursed until after the war. In 1787 Congress awarded him a gold medal. The next year, on Thomas Jefferson's advice, he accepted Empress Catherine's invitation to reorganize the Russian Navy. Though made an admiral and sent to the

Black Sea against the Turks, he was never given the superior command and lost Catherine's good will through the intrigue of rivals.

After the Revolution Jefferson spoke of him as a man of 'disinterested spirit' and the 'principal hope of our future efforts on the ocean . . .' He died in Paris at the age of 45 and was buried there in St.Louis Cemetery for Protestants. In 1813 his body was removed to the Naval Academy Chapel at Annapolis.

21. The SENTRY BOX (*private*), Caroline St. near E. end Dixon St., is a long frame house with gray weatherboarding, end chimneys, and a slender-columned front porch. It is somewhat remodeled, but the central portion remains much as it was. Overlooking the river, it was used during the War of 1812 and the War between the States as a lookout for enemy ships. In the garden to the left are the remains of an underground passage. The house was built in 1783–85 by the Revolutionary general George Weedon and later owned by General Hugh Mercer's son, Hugh Tennent Weedon Mercer.

22. GUNNERY SPRINGS, off Gunnery Lane, an extension of Ferdinand St., flow in a meadowy field below a steep hill. A concrete and brick covering over the springs was erected by the Daughters of the American Revolution in commemoration of early women patriots. The Virginia Convention of 1775 ordered the establishment here of a manufactory of small arms and ammunition, of which Charles Dick and Colonel Fielding Lewis were active commissioners. 'A hundred stands of arms a month' was the estimated output, besides repair to damaged guns. In 1781 Dick wrote Governor Jefferson that 'the Gentlemen of this town and even the Ladys have very spiritedly attended at the Gunnery and assisted to make up already above 20,000 Cartridges with Bullets . . . as also above 100 Good Guns from this Factory.'

23. NATIONAL PARK SERVICE HEADQUARTERS AND MUSEUM (*open* 9–5 *daily*), NE. corner Lafayette Blvd. and Sunken Road, a two-story red brick structure in late Georgian Colonial style, exhibits military relics, a diorama of shell-torn Fredericksburg, and a model in relief of the battlefield. Slide lectures are given to explain battles in the neighboring area.

24. MARY WASHINGTON COLLEGE, entrance off Sunken Road at Monroe St., a group of 14 buildings on an 80-acre campus, overlooks the city from above the wooded slope of Marye's Heights. Established in 1908 as the State Normal and Industrial School for Women in Fredericksburg, it became the Fredericksburg State Teachers College in 1924 and was renamed Mary Washington College in 1938. Bachelor degrees have been conferred since 1935. The 1937–38 enrollment in the college was 1,428, in the training school 1,097, and the faculty numbered 48.

POINTS OF INTEREST IN ENVIRONS

Brompton, 1.3 *m.*; Fredericksburg Battlefield Park, 1.7 *m.* (*see Tour* 1*b*). Chancellorsville Battlefield, 10 *m.*; Spotsylvania Courthouse Battlefield, 11.1 *m.*; Wilderness Battlefield, 14.4 *m.* (*see Tour* 10). Chatham, 0.5 *m.*; Ferry Farm, 1.6 *m.* (*see Tour* 16*a*).

Hampton

Railroad Station: Washington St. and Depot Ave. for Chesapeake and Ohio Ry.
Bus Station: King and Queen Sts. for Greyhound and Peninsula Transit Lines.
Taxis: Fare 25¢ within city limits.
Streetcars: Local and interurban, fare 5¢ within city and 5¢ for each zone outside.
Traffic Regulations: 15-minute and 1-hour parking limits in business district; 3 public parking lots.

Accommodations: 2 hotels; inns and tourist homes.

Information Service: Tidewater Auto. Ass'n., Langley Hotel, 111 Queen St.

Motion Picture Houses: 2.
Golf: Chamberlin Golf and Country Club, 1 m. E. on US 60, 18 holes, greens fee $1.
Swimming: Chamberlin Golf and Country Club, 1 m. E. on US 60, by arrangement. Sea bathing at Buckroe Beach, 4 m. E. on State 169 off US 60.
Tennis: Chamberlin Golf and Country Club, 1 m. E. on US 60, 1 court, fee 75¢; for other courts, inquire at information service.

Annual Events: Hampton Horse Show, May; Hampton Yacht Club Regatta, including Gold Cup event, 1st week in July.

HAMPTON (3 alt., 6,382 pop.), where settlers came in 1610 and scene of the first free school in the colonies, is the oldest English community in America.

The little city on Hampton Roads is cut by jagged arms of Hampton Creek. Its early bow-and-arrow street pattern is still explained by old-timers: Queen Street, shooting through the center of the city, is the arrow; Hope and Court Streets curve to form the bow; taut between them stretches King Street—the string. From this tiny area streets extend in a fairly symmetrical pattern to Bright, Sunset, and Hampton creeks and northward into the narrow peninsula. Along the water fronts mounds of oyster shells and odors of fish and marshland are reminders that the sea is close by.

Large packing plants are centered on Hampton Creek in the northeastern section of the city. On the shore line farther north are several imposing homes of fishing magnates and southward are the cottages of tongers and small fisherfolk. The rest of the city is given over to late Victorian houses and bungalows. Of the 200 boats that operate in surrounding creeks, at least two-thirds are used for fishing and about 40 of these are trawlers that fish off the capes. In 1938 100,000 barrels of crabs, 50,000 gallons of oysters, and 30,000 bushels of unshucked oysters were shipped from Hampton.

Everywhere in Hampton are soldiers, enlisted men, and officers from the Coast Artillery post at Fort Monroe and from Langley Field. Crowds, far out of proportion to the size of the city, move in leisurely fashion, and army cars pass continually along Queen Street. From May through September holiday throngs go through Hampton to and from Buckroe Beach.

Among the Negro population, 44 per cent of the whole, are many educated men and women. The Peoples Building and Loan Association of Hampton has more shareholders and a larger cash revenue than any similar Negro association. Along the waterfront, however, and in several other slum districts live many illiterate and economically distressed Negro families.

Originally Hampton was called Kecoughtan (pronounced Kick-o-tan). Sir Christopher Newport's band of adventurers paused here in 1607 to exchange greetings with the Kecoughtan Indians, named the point to the eastward Point Comfort, then continued to Jamestown. Fort Algernourne was built at Point Comfort in 1609. After the Kecoughtans ceased to be friendly, Sir Thomas Gates drove them away and in 1610 built two stockades on Hampton's rivulet, which Lord Delaware had named Southampton (Hampton) River for the Earl of Southampton, leading spirit of the London Company. The stockades were named Fort Henry and Fort Charles for the sons of James I, and in 1613 each had 15 soldiers. In the vicinity of the stockades were a few planters, and Hamor, secretary of the colony, said there were 'goodly seats and much corn about them, abounding with the commodities of fish, fowle, Deere, and fruits, whereby the men liued there with halfe that maintenaunce out of the Store which in other places is allowed.'

When in 1619 the colony was divided into four 'incorporations' with a proposed chief city for each division, a wide territory on both sides of the James was named Elizabeth City. When the 'incorporations' were divided into counties in 1634, the territory embracing Kecoughtan became Elizabeth City County. In 1620 the land between the creek and Chesapeake Bay was appropriated for public uses, and the portion on the bay called Buck Roe was assigned to the growing of grapes and mulberry trees.

Hampton's first business man, William Claiborne, arrived in 1630 with authorization from the governor's council 'to make discoveries in the Chesapeake Bay and to trade with the Indians.' He established a profitable post on Kent Island, then thought to be a part of Virginia, and set up a storehouse and a trading base on his 150-acre grant at Kecoughtan. Here he lived during the tumultuous years after 1634 when Lord Baltimore's colonists, with a map that showed Kent Island within their domain, found him and his underlings most mutinous subjects. When the system of inspecting and storing tobacco was inaugurated in 1633, one of the first seven warehouses was established at 'Southampton river in Elizabeth City.' The town of Hampton was formally established and named in 1680.

The community knew too well the pirates that infested the Virginia coast in the late seventeenth century. Hampton citizens continually protested the drunkenness and inefficiency of Captain Aldred, who commanded the *Essex-Prize*, a pirate-chaser that always lay up for repairs when its services were needed. When the man-of-war *Shoreham* replaced the *Essex-Prize* in 1700, Peter Heyman, collector of customs for the James River, was among the Virginians killed in a ten-hour battle that resulted in defeat of the pirates. Governor Nicholson, who had risked his life aboard the *Shoreham* to watch the engagement, reported that 'Peter Heyman had behaved himself very well in the fight.' Heyman was appointed postmaster in 1692 for all the plantations in Virginia and Maryland, and endeavored to set up an efficient Colonial postal system. In 1718 Captain Henry Maynard, a citizen of Hampton, killed Edward Teach, alias Blackbeard, the most notorious of all the Colonial brigands of the sea, and helped bring piracy to an end.

More than 1,100 Acadians came to Hampton in 1755, and while their ships lay at anchor in Hampton Roads, Governor Dinwiddie and the council engaged in lengthy conferences and much letter writing. The poor exiles were greatly feared, for, said the governor, Virginia had been 'much harassed by that perfidous nation in our back country.' 'It was unkind of the Governor of Nova Scotia,' he continued, 'to send such a number of people here without the least previous notice.' Nevertheless, the Acadians were allowed to land and were cared for until the following spring when Virginia appropriated money for their deportation.

Among the prominent citizens or natives of Hampton were George Wythe (*see Williamsburg*); James Barron, commodore of the American Navy during the Revolution; Commodore Samuel Barron, commander of a United States squadron in the Tripolitan War; another Commodore James Barron (*see Norfolk*); and Commodore Lewis Warrington, commander of an American squadron during the War of 1812.

This seaport town also has a military history. Though the British several times skirted Hampton during the Revolution, and though Hampton furnished its share of soldiers, no fighting took place in the immediate vicinity. During the War of 1812, however, the British, exasperated by their failure to take Portsmouth, attacked Hampton in June 1813. Momentarily repulsed by Virginia militia under Major Stapleton Crutchfield, the British rallied and entered Hampton as the Virginians retreated westward. Hampton was incorporated as a town in 1849, though it was authorized by the 'Act of Cohabitation' in 1680. In August 1861 Hampton suffered its greatest loss when the town was burned by its own inhabitants to prevent occupation by the Federals; only five houses remained standing.

At the end of the war ragged soldiers came home to rebuild the city. Hampton Institute became an important center of Negro education. In 1882 a rail line was completed from Richmond to the mouth of the James. Another fire in 1884 wiped out 33 of the newly built residences and stores on Queen Street. Fishermen and oystermen began to bring in their wares for shipping; sea-food plants were started on a small scale and flourished. The establishment of important industries in the Norfolk area helped to bring about Hampton's revival, and in 1908 it was chartered as a city. Langley Field near by, opened in 1917 as a training field, became an important army air base. Hampton carries on today in a manner that is neither aggressive nor wholly complacent. It remains a little city not straining to be large.

POINTS OF INTEREST

ELIZABETH CITY COUNTY COURTHOUSE (*open* 9–5 *Mon.–Fri.*, 9–1 *Sat.*), NW. corner King and Court Sts., is a plain red brick building with a low white wooden dome and a portico with four modified Doric columns. The main block was erected in 1876. The first courthouse on this site was erected in 1715 when the county seat was moved to 'Hampton town.' In 1781 the general assembly granted justices permission to hold court elsewhere 'while the court house in Hampton is occupied by troops of our allies as a hospital.'

ST.JOHN'S CHURCH (*open daily*), NW. corner Court and Queen Sts., is a church of Elizabeth City Parish, which was first called Kecoughtan and established in 1610. Compact and cruciform, its sturdy walls belong to the original structure built in 1728. This replaced the second church erected in 1667 on Pembroke Farm. St.John's was ill-attended in the reaction following the Revolution, and was ransacked during the War of 1812. The vigorous challenge in 1825 of Mrs.Jane Barron Hope, daughter of Commodore James Barron—'If I were a man I would have those walls built up'—brought about restoration of the church in 1827–28, when it was named St.John's. Though partly burned in 1861, the 'old walls honestly built' by Colonial workmen stood firm. The church was restored again in 1869.

A Breeches Bible dated 1599 and a vestry book dated 1751 are preserved here, in addition to a plain silver chalice and paten, hall-marked 1619, sent by Mary Robinson from England. In the churchyard lie many of the city's founders.

BRADDOCK MONUMENT, E. end of Victoria Ave., is a large fat cannon mounted on a stuccoed pedestal, overlooking Hampton Creek. It was erected in 1916 to mark the spot at which General Braddock and his British troops landed in February 1755, preparatory to the tragic expedition against Fort Duquesne.

LITTLE ENGLAND, S. of E. and Victoria Ave., is the flat area lying behind Capps' Point along Sunset Creek. Now occupied by car barns and a power station, it was originally an estate of 500 acres patented by William Capps. The Battle of Hampton was fought here in 1813, following the repulse of the British in their attempt to take Portsmouth.

BLACKBEARD'S POINT, SE. from E. end Victoria Ave., is a triangle occupied by sea food industries. Here in 1718 Captain Henry Maynard set on a pole the head of 'Blackbeard,' brought back when he returned with nine prisoners from the battle that practically ended organized piracy. The prisoners, tried at Williamsburg, were later hanged.

SYMS–EATON ACADEMY, E. end Cary St., in a brick building erected in 1902, is an amalgamation of two of the earliest schools in America. Syms is the oldest free school and the first endowed educational institution in the United States. In 1634 Benjamin Syms left 200 acres and 8 cows to provide a free school for children of the parish. In 1659 Thomas Eaton, a 'cururgeon,' left 500 acres including buildings, livestock, and two Negro slaves for a school to serve Elizabeth City County. The schools were so popular that in 1759 an act was necessary to provide for the attendance of only poor children at Eaton School. In 1805 the schools were merged by act of the general assembly, and called Hampton Academy. In 1852 the academy became part of the public school system. Its building was burned in 1861 and rebuilt after the war.

SITE OF THE FIRST ELIZABETH CITY PARISH CHURCH, Tyler St. near College Place, is in an ancient graveyard identified by an iron fence and marker. Cobblestone foundations have been uncovered, and it is known that a frame church stood here in 1624.

HAMPTON INSTITUTE (*open* 9–4:30 *daily, guide service*), E. end of Queen St., one of the foremost Negro educational centers in the world, covers 74 acres on the east bank of Hampton Creek. Its 139 buildings, nearly all of red brick, are scattered over immaculate grounds shaded by fine old trees. Hampton Institute grew out of temporary measures taken when former slaves came to Fort Monroe to satisfy their desire for 'book larnin.' Gathered under the trees, one of which is still called 'Emancipation Oak,' illiterate Negroes of all ages shouted out the letters of the alphabet. At the suggestion of General Samuel Chapman Armstrong, then chief of the Freedmen's Bureau, the American Missionary Association in 1867 purchased the farm where Hampton Hospital had been maintained by the Federal Government during the war. The school opened in the old hospital barracks in April 1868, with Armstrong as principal, two assisting teachers, and 15 pupils. It was chartered as the Hampton Normal and Industrial Institute in 1870. One-third of the $285,000 accruing to the State, after Virginia accepted the provisions of the Morrill Land-Grant Act of Congress that year, was allotted to the institution. Depending largely, however, on contributions from friends of Negro education, especially in the North, it grew rapidly. In 1878, 17 young Indian prisoners of war were sent here from Florida by the Federal Government to be educated. Indians were enrolled until 1923. In the winter session of 1936–37 there were about 200 instructors and 1,024 students. Between 600 and 700 teachers attend the summer school each year. Hampton, now a private corporation, confers the degrees of bachelor of arts, bachelor of science and, in the summer school, a master of science degree in education. The school publishes the *Southern Workman*, a monthly magazine on general education.

Under General Armstrong's program, the boys were put to 'planting and digging potatoes, while the girls were taught to make and mend clothes, and were instructed in the rudiments of plain English Education.' The students are still trained in hand, as well as mind, and taught primarily how to make a living. There are two main divisions: the trade school teaching everything from bricklaying to tailoring; and the collegiate schools, teaching agriculture, business, education, home economics, library science, and nursing.

The ADMINISTRATION BUILDING, facing the central plaza in the middle of the campus, houses the offices of the president and other school executives. The MUSEUM (*open 9–5 weekdays*) on its upper floor contains exhibits collected by friends and students of Hampton in Africa, Hawaii, and the Philippines. The African exhibits include musical instruments and fetishes from the upper Congo. The Indian collection, contributed mainly by ex-students, includes a variety of rare items from various American Indian tribes.

OGDEN HALL, E. of the Administration Building, is the main assembly hall, with a stage for the presentation of debates and plays; it seats 2,000. Students gather here each Sunday evening at 7:30 to sing spirituals. This service is open to the public.

The COLLIS P. HUNTINGTON MEMORIAL LIBRARY (*open 9–5 weekdays, 3–7:30 Sun.*) seats 300 in its main reference room and has special seminar rooms. Among its 55,000 volumes is a special collection of books and pamphlets dealing with the Negro and slavery.

VIRGINIA HALL, facing Ogden Hall, was 'sung up' by Hampton singers shortly after the institute was founded. In 1870 General Armstrong led a group of Hampton singers on a tour of New England and Canada. This and successive tours netted most of the total cost of $98,000. The building contains dining rooms and the girls' dormitory.

DUPONT HALL houses the departments of biology, chemistry, physics, and mathematics, and an auditorium used for seminars and the showing of educational motion pictures.

The SLATER MEMORIAL TRADE SCHOOL includes the 13 trade departments where 200 students work at their respective trades, paying their way by construction and repair work. In 1932 the BEMIS LABORATORIES were erected entirely by student builders as an addition to the trade school. Many buildings on the campus were designed in the Bemis Laboratories and constructed under the direction of students.

The GEORGE P. PHENIX ELEMENTARY HIGH SCHOOL, just S. of campus gate, was erected in 1931. Six hundred pupils from the community attend the school, which serves as a laboratory for education students.

The ARMSTRONG MEMORIAL CHURCH, of Italian Romanesque architecture, is a gift of Frederick Marquand. Most of the construction work was done by trade school students.

WHIPPLE FARM, 80 acres adjoining the campus to the east, and SHELLBANKS FARM, 800 acres on Back River adjoining Langley Field, provide agricultural training. Among Hampton's distinguished graduates are Booker T. Washington, Dr. Robert Moton, and Mrs. Janie Porter Barrett, head of the Virginia Industrial School.

POINTS OF INTEREST IN ENVIRONS

Old Point Comfort and Fort Monroe, 3.3 *m.*; Langley Field, 3 *m.*; Buckroe Beach 4 *m.* (*see Tour 8a*).

Hampton Roads Port

Commercial Airport: Norfolk; Municipal Airport, 7 m. E. off Cape Henry Blvd. (US 40), for Pennsylvania Central Airlines.
Government Airports: Naval Air Station, Norfolk, Hampton Blvd. and 99th St.; Army Air Station, Langley Field, 3 m. N. of Hampton on State 27.
Piers: Norfolk: Front St. (continuation of W. York St.) for Norfolk and Washington Steamboat Co.; W. end Brooke Ave. for Rappahannock River and Mobjack Bay Lines; W. end W. Main St. for Baltimore Steam Packet Co. and Merchants and Miners Transportation Co.; W. end Water St. for Buxton Lines to Richmond; S. end Jackson St. for Chesapeake Steamship Co.; W. end Boissevain Ave. for Eastern Steamship Lines (Old Dominion). Portsmouth: E. end High St. for tug to Norfolk connecting with boat to Baltimore, 6 p.m. daily, no fare.
Ferries: Norfolk: S. end Commercial Place, to Portsmouth, fare 5¢, automobile and driver, 25¢; Pine Beach, W. end 99th St., to Newport News, fare 20¢, automobile and driver, $1 and $1.25; W. end Ocean View Ave., to Old Point Comfort and Fort Monroe, fare 20¢, automobile and driver, 75¢ and $1; Little Creek, Shore Drive, to Cape Charles, fare 50¢, automobile $2.50 and $3; W. end Brooke Ave. to Old Point Comfort, fare 25¢, automobile $1 and $1.25, to Cape Charles, fare 70¢, automobile $2.50 and $3, and to Newport News, fare 35¢. Portsmouth: E. end High St. to Norfolk, fare 5¢, automobile, 25¢, passengers additional to driver, 5¢ each, to Berkley, fare same as to Norfolk; Seaboard Air Line Wharf, E. end High St. for boat to Newport News, fare 30¢, no automobiles. Newport News: 23rd St. and River Rd., to Norfolk, fare 30¢; E. end Jefferson Ave. to Norfolk (Pine Beach), fare 20¢, 2-passenger car and driver, $1, 4-passenger car and driver, $1.25, round trip $1.50, extra passenger, 20¢.
Canals: Albemarle and Chesapeake Canal; Dismal Swamp Canal; both are sections of Atlantic Coastal Waterways, no tolls.
Toll Bridges: Norfolk-Portsmouth Bridge, US 460, car and driver, 25¢, pedestrians, 5¢; James River Bridge, US 17, car, $1.25.

Government Establishments: Immigration Offices, Norfolk, Post Office Bldg., Granby and Charlotte Sts.; Newport News, Post Office, West Ave. and 25th St.
Naval Operating Base, Norfolk, Hampton Blvd. and 99th St.
Naval Hospital, Portsmouth, N. end Green St.
Norfolk Navy Yard, Portsmouth, S. end First and Fourth Sts.
Customhouses, Norfolk, Main and Granby Sts.; Newport News, Post Office Bldg., West Ave., and 25th St.
Coast Guard Headquarters, Norfolk, Post Office Bldg., Granby and Charlotte Sts.
Quarantine Stations, Old Point Comfort and Craney Island.
Fort Monroe, Old Point Comfort.
State Rifle Range, Virginia Beach.

HAMPTON ROADS is the channel through which the waters of the converging James, Nansemond, and Elizabeth Rivers flow into Chesapeake Bay. This four-mile roadstead, 40 feet deep and navigable throughout the year, is bounded on the north by the shore line from Newport News to Old Point Comfort, on the east by the Rip Raps and Willoughby Spit, on the south by Willoughby Bay and Sewall Point, and on the west by a line from Newport News to Sewall Point. Because of its central location on the

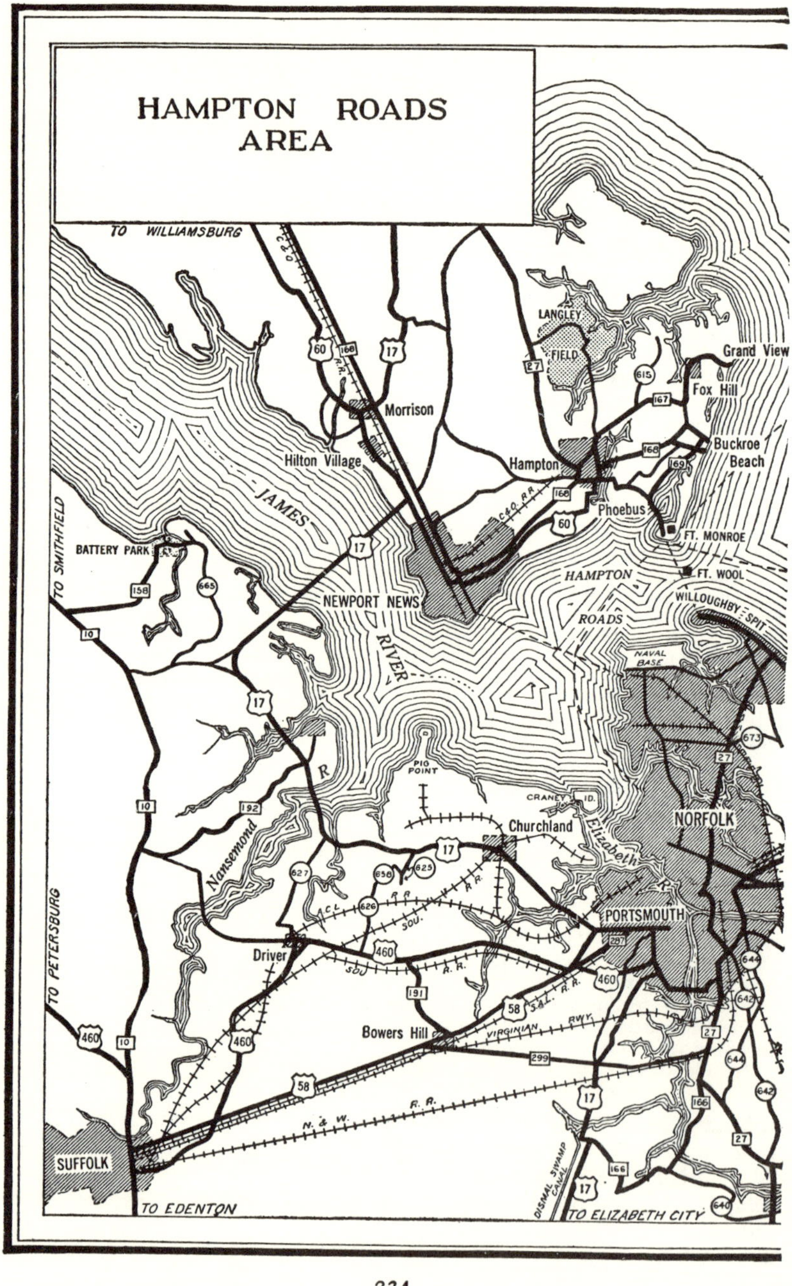
HAMPTON ROADS AREA
TO WILLIAMSBURG
LANGLEY FIELD
Grand View
Fox Hill
Morrison
Buckroe Beach
Hilton Village
Hampton
Phoebus
JAMES
FT. MONROE
TO SMITHFIELD
BATTERY PARK
HAMPTON
FT. WOOL
NEWPORT NEWS
ROADS
WILLOUGHBY SPIT
RIVER
NAVAL BASE
PIG POINT
CRANEY ID.
NORFOLK
Churchland
Nansemond
Elizabeth R.
PORTSMOUTH
TO PETERSBURG
Driver
Bowers Hill
VIRGINIAN RWY.
N. & W. R. R.
SUFFOLK
DISMAL SWAMP CANAL
TO EDENTON
TO ELIZABETH CITY

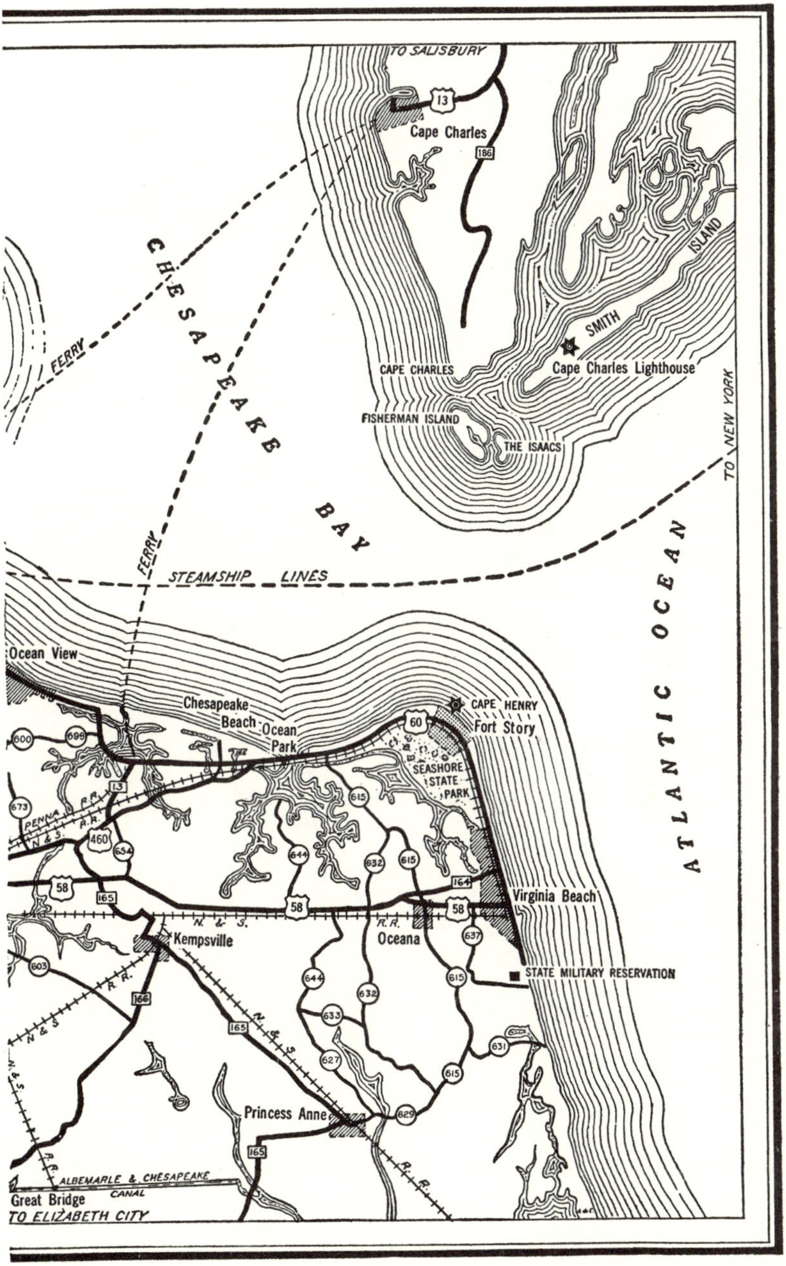
TO SALISBURY
13
Cape Charles
186
CHESAPEAKE
BAY
FERRY
FERRY
STEAMSHIP LINES
SMITH
ISLAND
Cape Charles Lighthouse
CAPE CHARLES
FISHERMAN ISLAND
THE ISAACS
TO NEW YORK
ATLANTIC OCEAN
Ocean View
Chesapeake
Beach
Ocean
Park
60
CAPE HENRY
Fort Story
SEASHORE
STATE
PARK
600
699
673
13
PENNA. R.R.
N. & S. R.R.
460
654
644
615
632
615
58
165
58
164
58
Virginia Beach
N. & S.
R.R.
Kempsville
Oceana
637
STATE MILITARY RESERVATION
603
R.R.
166
N & S
644
632
615
633
165
N. & S.
627
615
631
Princess Anne
629
165
R.R.
ALBEMARLE & CHESAPEAKE
CANAL
Great Bridge
TO ELIZABETH CITY

Atlantic seaboard and its many railroad facilities, Hampton Roads is one of the most important harbors in the country and the east-coast rendezvous of the United States navy. There is a combined water frontage of about 50 miles, of which some 22 miles have been improved or developed.

Spacious Hampton Roads seems never crowded. The pattern of boats on its ample surface changes as constantly as the color of the water, the spots of oily bilge, the seaweed, and the circling gulls. Freighters parade in and out the Capes, followed by a black plume of smoke. Some set their course to or from the upper Chesapeake Bay, but most steam straight in or out from the open sea. Trim steam ferries shuttle back and forth, and tugs tow barges filled with freight cars, lumber, or brick. Scattered about are tramp steamers, anchored and swinging in the tide or nosing toward the black skeletons of coal piers. Warships and cruisers, gray and lean against the horizon, thread their way toward dry docks. Sporadically, government boats tow large red targets into the glittering distance and hurriedly move away as Fort guns boom in target practice. Occasionally, the Virginia pilot boat that lies in wait for incoming vessels off the Capes weighs anchor and comes in for supplies and fuel. Trawlers and oyster boats chug toward hidden fishing banks, while elegant yachts and cabin cruisers glide toward less trammeled waters. Along the shore bob dories, bateaux, and rowboats, filled with fishermen. At dusk the white-painted Bay and coastwise passenger steamers sidle up to Old Point's dock, then steam away into the gathering darkness. The lights of Buckroe Beach, the Fort, and Newport News blink at those of Ocean View, the Naval Base, and feeble farmhouse lights to the west. Precise and intermittent gleams from lighthouses cut arcs across the water, and channels are marked by swaying light buoys and doleful bell buoys. Bridges arch across river mouths, their concrete length festooned with yellow lights broken at the draw by green and red.

Newport News, at the mouth of the James, and Norfolk and Portsmouth, along the Elizabeth River and its several branches, with their harbors, anchorage, customs, and other facilities, constitute the Port of Hampton Roads. Federal services and regulations of port activity consist of quarantine, under the Public Health and Customs services, Treasury Department; Immigration Service, under the Department of Labor; and the improvement of rivers, harbors, and other waterways under direction of the Secretary of War and the Chief of Engineers of the United States Army. Local jurisdiction over the port is vested in the State Port Authority of Virginia, created in 1926, which is charged with development of the port and promotion of its commercial and maritime interests. It regulates such services as fire protection, pilotage, dockage, towage, and handling of cargoes.

The total tonnage of water-borne commerce handled through the port in 1938 was 24,083,019, of which 826,739 tons were imports and 1,992,564 were exports. Wood pulp and ore were the largest items of import; coal and scrap iron the largest items of export, the latter reflecting the current trend toward international rearmament. Petroleum products, sugar, gypsum, and paper manufactures were other important items of import.

Exports include grain, tobacco and tobacco products, lumber and logs, cotton and textiles.

The Norfolk Navy Yard, on the Portsmouth side, and the United States Naval Operating Base in Norfolk consume a great volume of coal and have created many industries deriving power from the same source. These government properties themselves, worth about $50,000,000, add to the port's commercial stature. Within Norfolk are the United States Public Health Service Hospital, a branch of the United States Hydrographic Office, the Navy's principal fuel reserve depot, a naval air station, a submarine base, and the St.Helena Reservation, now used as a naval air base.

From 1607, when Sir Christopher Newport brought his band of pioneers to effect the first permanent English settlement in America, throughout the Colonial period, Hampton Roads was a point of entry to the seat of government in Virginia. Ships bringing other settlers and supplies sailed through its broad waters into the James. Later it was the hunting place of pirates and hostile British ships, and, during the War between the States, the scene of important naval conflicts.

On June 22, 1807, occurred a naval engagement rising from the presence of four alleged British deserters on the American vessel, *Chesapeake*. The British frigate *Leopard* pursued the *Chesapeake* through the Capes, then fired a broadside into the American vessel, which surrendered without firing a shot. The *Chesapeake* was boarded and the deserters were taken. Commodore James Barron (1769–1851), commander of the *Chesapeake*, was afterwards court-martialed 'for neglecting in the probability of an engagement, to clear his ship for battle,' and deprived of rank and pay for five years. On his return to duty, he was refused an active command through the influence of Commodore Stephen Decatur,Jr. This resulted in a duel between Barron and Decatur in 1820, and Decatur was killed. Barron was later commandant of the Gosport Navy Yard in Portsmouth.

On the afternoon of March 8, 1862, occurred the battle that changed naval warfare. The *Virginia*, formerly the *Merrimac*, a wooden ship which had been sunk, raised by the Confederates, and converted into an ironclad, attacked the Federal fleet, which was armed with 204 guns and aided by land batteries. By six o'clock the *Virginia* had sunk the *Cumberland*, burned the *Congress*, driven the *Minnesota* ashore, and compelled the *St. Lawrence* and the *Roanoke* to seek shelter under the guns of Fort Monroe. On March 9 the *Virginia* encountered the *Monitor*, an ironclad more heavily armored and more efficient by reason of her light draught and revolving gun turret. For four hours the two ironclads battered each other, until at last a shell from the *Virginia* exploded on the eyeslit of the *Monitor's* pilot house, blinding her commander, Captain John L. Worden. 'Tactically,' said R.S.Henry in *The Story of the Confederacy*, 'it was a drawn fight, in its results a victory for the Monitor.'

FORT WOOL, mid-channel on the ferry course, is on a man-made island, constructed of rocks sunk on a shoal called Rip Raps from the rippling of the water. Begun after 1830 and called Fort Calhoun, the fortification was not complete when war broke out in 1861. Hurriedly mounted guns, however, aided in silencing Confederate batteries on Sewall Point and Willoughby Spit on May 9, 1862, when Union forces crossed these waters to take Norfolk. The fort was renamed for General John E. Wool, Union commander of the department of Virginia. During the World War defense nets were spread from its foundations to trap submarines.

Norfolk

Railroad Stations: Union Depot, Lake Ave. and Main St., for Norfolk and Western Ry., Norfolk Southern R.R., and Virginian Ry.; ferries, foot of Brooke Ave., to Chesapeake and Ohio Ry. and Pennsylvania R.R.; ferry, W. end of York St., to Atlantic Coast Line R.R.; ferry, foot of Jackson St., S. of W.Main St., to Southern Ry.; ferry, foot of Commercial Pl., to foot of High St. (Portsmouth), for Seaboard Air Line Ry., Virginian Ry.
Bus Stations: Union Bus Terminal, NE. corner Monticello Ave. and Tazewell St., for Greyhound Lines, Norfolk Southern Bus Corp., Carolina Coach Co., Peninsula Transit Corp., and Virginia Coach Lines.
Taxis: Fare 25¢ first half mile, 10¢ each additional half mile, $2 per hour for 5 passengers or less.
Streetcars and Busses: Fare 10¢, 3 tokens 25¢; weekly pass $1.
Traffic Regulations: Limited free parking on many downtown streets; parking meters on some streets, 5¢ for one hour; a few one-way streets east and west.

Accommodations: 14 hotels; tourist homes.

Information Service: Chamber of Commerce, 107 W.Main St.; Tidewater A.A.A., Monticello Hotel, City Hall Ave. and Granby St.

Radio Station: WTAR (780 kc.).
Theaters and Motion Picture Houses: Colonial Theater, Tazewell St., occasional road shows; Little Theater, W.York and Duke Sts., local productions; 17 motion picture houses, including 3 for Negroes.
Golf: Ocean View Municipal Golf Course, N. end Granby St., 18 holes, greens fee 60¢, weekends and holidays 75¢; Norfolk Golf Club, Sewall Point Rd. W. of Granby St., 18 holes, open by arrangement, greens fee $1, weekends and holidays $1.50; Army Base Golf Course, E. side Hampton Blvd. opposite U.S. Supply Base, 9 holes, greens fee 25¢; Municipal Golf Course, Memorial Park, between Corprew and Highland Aves., 9 holes, greens fee 25¢.
Baseball: High Rock Park, Church and Rugby Sts.
Football: High Rock Park, and Foreman Field, Hampton Blvd. and Bolling Ave.
Swimming: Navy Y.M.C.A., NE. corner Brooke Ave. and Boush St., adm. 25¢; Foreman Field gymnasium, Hampton Blvd. and Bolling Ave., open 9–4, adm. 25¢; surf bathing, Willoughby Beach, Ocean View, Chesapeake Beach, Virginia Beach, and Ocean Breeze Beach (Negro), adm. 10¢, children 5¢, and Norfolk Municipal Bathing Beach (Negro), free, on Shore Drive.
Tennis: Lafayette Park, Granby St. and La Vallette Ave., 11 courts, open sunrise to sunset, free; Fergus Reid Tennis Club, Orapack St. between Colley and Westover Aves., open by arrangement 9–6 daily, 50¢ for 3 sets.
Riding: Restmere Riding Academy, Sewall Point Rd. W. of Granby St., $1.50 per hour; Pinewell Saddle Club, Ocean View, $1 per hour; Norfolk Saddle Club, Sewall Point Rd. 0.4 m. W. of Granby St., open by arrangement.

Annual Events: Negro Emancipation Day Parade, Jan. 1; Cape Henry Pilgrimage, Apr. 26; Hampton Roads Kennel Club Show, Apr.; Norfolk Fair, early Sept.; Navy Day, Norfolk Navy Yard and U.S. Naval Operating Base keep 'open house,' Oct. 27.

NORFOLK (7 alt., 129,710 pop.) is a fusion of land and sea, of boats and brick houses, of civilians and sailors. Pressed between a ragged western shore line and a zigzag eastern boundary, it stretches north from the eastern branch of the Elizabeth River to a curving sand beach on Chesapeake Bay. Into its flat surface, partly wrested from the river, reach the salty multiple fingers of three estuaries: Mason's Creek, its mouth well guarded by the Naval Base; wide Lafayette River (Tanner's Creek), lined with the mansions of the commercial and professional aristocracy; and the eastern branch of the Elizabeth River, its muddy shore a jumble of boats, wharves, warehouses, and industries extracting life from the sea. On the western shore, constantly washed by the swift tides of the Elizabeth River and Hampton Roads, numerous docks, railroad piers, grain elevators, and other developments make a dense fringe of geometric design.

Linked with Portsmouth by ferries and a bridge, old Norfolk, a maze of rectangles that form narrow, somber streets, hides behind its bulwark of river-front buildings except for occasional tall structures that look out over dark funnels and graceful masts. Plowing through the oily surface of the harbor are powerful little tugs with barges in tow, gleaming white coastal and Bay passenger steamers, rusty-hull coastal freighters, tramp steamers, battleships, trawlers and oyster boats, and less frequently transatlantic steamships. In narrow, tree-lined streets are old brick houses, some in large yards kept green and damp by sheltering boxwood, magnolia, and crape myrtle, and others shoulder to shoulder, flush with sidewalks. Between drab low buildings in tawdry neighborhoods cobbled alleys twist like arteries too cramped for the life that pulses through them. The dense traffic of commercial Granby Street, a narrow canyon of business establishments, motion picture houses, restaurants, and hotels, is duplicated in Church and Bank Streets, both teeming with people and filled with shops, and the streets surrounding the large brick Municipal Market and the Municipal Armory, circled by an open-air flower market. Some six blocks along Brewer and Market Streets are daily lined with trucks and stalls, where produce is sold by white and Negro farmers and hucksters, among them thick-bearded Mennonites dressed in traditional costume. From the Confederate Monument to the sharp rise of Berkeley Bridge, East Main Street, its elegant old brick houses of the Colonial elite now in decay, unrolls its wares in curio shops, wienie bars, tattoo clinics, shooting galleries, beer gardens, and cheap rooming houses. Nightly this quarter is patrolled by paired M.P.'s, whose brassards and billies come most into play when Saturday shore leave spills recruits from the naval base, sailors from ships, and a goodly number of marines into downtown Norfolk. Most of the enlisted men, however, find their distractions in the motion picture houses, beer bars, the large Navy Y.M.C.A., and numerous dance halls that give them an equal chance with civilian swains for reducing Norfolk's list of eligible spinsters.

Beginning with tree-shaded Ghent which is pierced by the Hague, a horseshoe-shaped yacht harbor, Norfolk's numerous white suburbs stretch northward and spread east and west where inlets and marshes allow. Without perceptible lines of demarcation, swank sections merge into those of people on limited budgets. In the sandy and pine-covered region near the Bay are many houses with a perpetual holiday air, for in the distance are the green-and-white-striped roof tops of Ocean View's tousled casino and numerous seasonal concessions. Here within city limits proletarian Norfolk swims, picnics, dances, and plays during the sultry summer, the scene always enlivened by white-jacketed gobs from the naval base and the faraway procession of ships to and from the Capes.

A good portion of Norfolk's 40,000 Negroes live along dingy Charlotte and East Freemason Streets and in scattered suburban settlements, Huntersville, Lindenwood, Broad Creek Boulevard, and in thrifty Titustown, which supplies the city with many domestics. In contrast, extending north from Brambleton Avenue to Princess Anne Road are slums where Negroes live in dreary lines of shell-like hovels that pass for dwellings, fronting on unpaved and often muddy streets.

The stable population of Norfolk consists of a few millionaires, families in moderate affluence whose daughters make their debut at the Christmas german, and the rank and file at work in Norfolk's 275 industries. A museum of fine arts, the Hermitage Foundation that fosters public art exhibitions, lectures, and publications, a symphony orchestra some 20 years old, and a generous sprinkling of poets supply Norfolk's local culture, while a country club tops the list of numerous places of diversion suitable to every purse and taste. Under the stimulus of civic pride Norfolk is being beautified (1939) by the planting of thousands of azaleas. In future springs the public parks and incoming roads will be banked with blossoms.

As a maritime town, Norfolk was thwarted by a curious series of reverses until development of railroads made it the outlet of an immense back country, including the Virginia and West Virginia coal fields. Today factories produce fertilizers, agricultural implements, lumber, cotton and silk goods, roasted peanuts, and other materials with an annual value of about $100,000,000. The Norfolk area supplies eastern markets with oysters, fish, and crabs. The city is a distributing center for sea food, fresh and frozen, to several Southern States. During the winter months it handles large shipments of fish from sources as far distant as the Great Lakes and Alaska. Large quantities of inedible fish from local fisheries are used for fertilizer.

But in the eyes of nearly a million yearly visitors, the main lure of Norfolk is the access it offers to an all-year playground. Twenty-five miles of beach near by attract surf bathers from May till November. Myriads of waterfowl find haven in the Back Bay section, a favorite resort of hunters. Most of the coastal inlets abound in snipe, sora, wild ducks, and geese. The weird natural wonderland of the Dismal Swamp, a few miles south, is a haunt of fur-bearing game, including black bear. Several lakes near Norfolk invite fresh-water fishermen, and there is good sea fishing off Ocean View. The vicinity of Cape Henry and Seashore State Park offer hiking and riding among sunny dunes.

Norfolk's site on the Elizabeth River embraces a grant made to Captain Thomas Willoughby in 1636. Development began here in 1680, when, in the 'Act of Cohabitation' providing for a town for each county, the general assembly directed that, 'in Lower Norfolk county . . . on the Easterne Branch on Elizabeth river at the entrance of the branch,' 50 acres be 'measured about, layd out and appointed for a towne.' Though Charles II in 1681 suspended the Act of 1680, 'the ffeoffees' proceeded with the purchase of the site, 'on Nicholas Wise his land,' effecting the transaction in 1682 for 'tenn thousand pounds of tobacco and caske.' When in 1691 the statute of 1680 was re-enacted to provide for 'ports of entry,' the town was described as 'the land appointed . . . and accordingly laid out and paid for and severall dwelling houses and ware houses already built.' In 1705 the house of burgesses named it Norfolk for Norfolk County, England.

Trade with the mother country and the West Indies made this the largest municipality in Colonial Virginia. The first wharves were built of pine logs fastened together by cross beams and extending from the shore to the channel. Here 'twenty brigs and smaller vessels rode constantly.' Norfolk ships carried tobacco, meat, flour, and lumber to the West Indies and returned with cargoes of sugar and molasses. Trade with the Carolinas, however, was hindered by pirates until Governor Alexander Spotswood took determined measures against the sea robbers (*see Hampton*).

In 1736 'the town of Norfolk' was 'erected into a borough, by the name of The borough of Norfolk . . . a body corporate, consisting of a maior, recorder, eight aldermen, and sixteen common council men . . . with power to elect and send one burgess to sit in the house of burgesses.' Of 16 towns authorized in 1705 to acquire borough status—a unit politically separate from the county—Norfolk was the only one that became a borough.

Samuel Boush was the first mayor, and Sir John Randolph served as recorder. Male citizens took turns at patrolling the streets to restrain the exuberance of transient sailors. Early streets were improved and new ones were formed by filling in creeks and marshes.

The town had to reclaim ground from tidal sloughs as the population grew. Church Street led across the neck of a peninsula to the mainland. Main (then Front) Street, bordering the waterfront, was crowded with warehouses, residences, shops, sailors' boarding houses, and ordinaries. Most of the early citizens quenched their thirst at taverns, the only source of drinking water being a public spring near the corner of Main and Church Streets. Water for other uses came from the river and, in case of fire, was passed along from hand to hand by bucket brigades.

Norfolk by 1740 had a population of about 1,000, composed of English and Scottish residents and some Irish. The merchants were mainly anti-Jacobite Scots. Importing most of their luxuries from Great Britain and conducting a lucrative trade with the mother country, the well-to-do merchants leaned toward Tory conservatism. In recognition of their loyalty, Governor Robert Dinwiddie in 1753 presented the corporation with a mace.

Though Norfolk protested boldly against the Stamp Act and later contributed its share of minutemen, it became early in the Revolution a rallying point for Tories. Lord Dunmore, the royal governor, chose Norfolk and Portsmouth as bases for his ships. Landing at Norfolk, he dismantled the printing office of John Holt and seized two printers publishing revolutionary literature. He was finally forced to retire (*see Portsmouth*).

The Virginia regiments under Colonel William Woodford occupied Norfolk, and Dunmore attempted to drive them out by bombarding the borough, January 1, 1776. When firing ceased, the riflemen continued to plunder and burn buildings without the interference of officers. Finally Colonel Woodford forbade the burning of houses under severe penalty, but two-thirds of Norfolk was in ashes. In February the rest of the town was burned, by order of the Colonial government, to rid it of Tories and to deprive Dunmore of shelter. Only the borough church (St.Paul's) was spared. After assisting 'poor people' in finding shelter elsewhere, troops abandoned the area.

After peace was signed in 1783, the Tories returned to Norfolk and began restoring the borough's former commercial prestige. In 1794 Norfolk was overrun with several thousand French refugees from the Negro insurrection in Santo Domingo. It had then, said Moreau de St.Méry, a population of 3,000, a brick theater, a hospital, an academy, two gazettes, and a Catholic chapel where 'a zealous Irishman with a red face has come to preach to the wretched French refugees.' The women 'are pretty in Norfolk,' noted Moreau de St.Méry, 'but their complexion is sallow and . . . the length of their feet is also somewhat disagreeable.'

Norfolk soon became the port for water-borne trade from the inland country. The town suffered from a disastrous fire in 1799. During the Napoleonic wars Norfolk's commerce increased only to be lost to the French, Spanish, and British privateers. The anger of Norfolk shipowners reached a peak in 1807, when the *Chesapeake* was fired upon by the British frigate *Leopard.*

During the War of 1812 men of Norfolk, Portsmouth, and other towns, with a reinforcement of marines from the frigate *Constellation*, joined to form defenses. On June 22, 1813, Fort Norfolk and Fort Nelson repulsed a British attack on Portsmouth by land and afterwards, aided by batteries on Craney Island, routed an assault by barges.

Peace in 1815 promised to restore Norfolk's prosperity, though New York was a strong trade rival. In 1822 the first steam ferry made a trial trip between Norfolk and Portsmouth. In 1845 the general assembly made Norfolk a city. With a population of 14,000 in 1854, it began to regain some of its earlier prestige. In 1855, however, it met with a setback in an epidemic of yellow fever, which destroyed about a tenth of the population. The hero of the scourge was a Negro gravedigger, who buried the dead until he, too, was struck down by the plague. He is remembered as 'Yellow Fever Jack,' and a monument in a cemetery here testifies to his faithfulness.

Margaret Douglas, a white woman from North Carolina, started Virginia's first Negro free school in Norfolk in 1853. When the enrollment increased to 25 she was sentenced to 30 days in jail on the charge that several pupils were slaves.

Hardly had the city recovered from the epidemic when the War between the States brought on a new series of disasters. After the secession of Virginia, the Federal command evacuated and burned the navy yard in Portsmouth. But when Roanoke Island, south of Norfolk, was occupied in

February 1862, the situation of Norfolk became precarious; and, though the *Virginia* (*Merrimac*) gained temporary victories in March, Norfolk fell to Union forces under General John Ellis Wool, May 10, 1862. The city was never again in Confederate hands.

With the coming of peace Norfolk had little trade and no apparent future, but a hope came to fulfilment through the development of railroads. The Norfolk and Petersburg Railroad, laid in 1858, was merged in 1870 with the Southside and the Virginia & Tennessee as the Atlantic, Mississippi and Ohio Railroad. This system, reorganized in 1881 as the Norfolk and Western Railroad Company, brought the first carload of coal into Norfolk in 1882 and began the traffic that made Norfolk a commanding coal port.

Meanwhile, the Norfolk and Southern (now Norfolk Southern) Railroad Company, chartered in 1875 as the Elizabeth City and Norfolk Railroad Company, laid tracks between Norfolk and Elizabeth City, North Carolina. When the road was extended to Albemarle Sound, Norfolk became a port through which fruit, vegetables, and other perishable products of the South pass quickly to Northern markets. The Virginian Railway (organized as the Tidewater Railway in 1904), which brings coal from West Virginia, and the Belt Line, connecting all railroads with terminals at Norfolk and Portsmouth, are more recent developments in transportation.

Norfolk has extended its boundaries several times. In 1906 it annexed Berkley, a town on the east side of the river's southern branch.

The Jamestown Tercentennial Celebration (Jamestown Exposition) was held in 1907, on a 340-acre site at Sewall Point. A Congressional Act of 1905 provided for a celebration of 'the birth of the American Nation, the first permanent Settlement of English-speaking people on the Western Hemisphere, by the holding of an international naval, marine, and military celebration in the vicinity of Jamestown.' Virginia erected many buildings; many States built duplicates of early homes to create a 'Colonial City'; and the Federal Government contributed buildings and a pier. The exposition was formally opened by President Theodore Roosevelt. Today the grounds are occupied by the Naval Training Station.

Norfolk boomed during the World War. For two years training stations and munitions factories hummed with activity; camouflaged ships sailed in and out; soldiers and sailors and their followers overflowed the city; officers came to Norfolk for diversion. With the coming of peace in 1918 the munitions plants were closed, but since then the city has steadily pulled itself out of postwar depression and acquired more territory. In 1919 it adopted the city-manager plan of government. Industrially, Norfolk is now one of the foremost cities of the New South. For the traveler—and Norfolk is a traveler's town—there are few places that rival its varied attractions.

POINTS OF INTEREST

1. The CONFEDERATE MONUMENT, Main St. and Commercial Place, is a towering pedestal of white Vermont granite surmounted by the

bronze figure of a soldier. The pedestal was erected in 1889 on the center lot of the original town of Norfolk. In 1907, when more funds were collected, the monument was completed by the addition of the statue designed by William Couper, Norfolk sculptor.

2. ST.PAUL'S CHURCH (Episcopal) (*open* 8:30–5 *daily, except* 8:30–1 *Thurs. and Sun.*), NW. corner N.Church St. and E.City Hall Ave., standing in a placid, brick-walled graveyard strewn with ancient tombstones, of which the oldest bears the date 1673, incorporates much of the walls of the only building that survived the bombardment by Dunmore's ships and the subsequent burning of Norfolk in 1776. A cannon ball is embedded in the south wall. Beneath a thick mantle of ivy the building shows good proportions. Small 'rose' windows, late Georgian Colonial vestibules, and a short, semidetached tower built in 1901 are recent alterations. The transepts and the roof were reconstructed about 1892.

The first church on this site was erected in 1639–41, but the present building dates from 1739. Long known as Borough Church, it still serves Elizabeth River Parish, constituted about 1634.

On the second floor of the adjacent brick Parish House is ST.PAUL'S MUSEUM (*open* 8:30–5 *weekdays except* 8:30–1 *Thurs.;* 8:30–12 *Sun.; adm. free*). Here are displayed documents and pictures relative to the history of old Virginia churches and portraits of ecclesiastical and secular leaders.

3. The NORFOLK COURTHOUSE, SE. corner E.City Hall Ave. and N.Bank St., built between 1847 and 1850, has a portico with six Tuscan columns. The front of the two-story building is of faced granite, the rest is stuccoed. A colonnaded dome rising 110 feet above the street looks down on magnificent shade trees that cover a neat lawn. When first erected, this building was the city hall. The CLERK'S OFFICE, back of the courthouse, was built, apparently, at the same time as the main structure.

4. The MYERS HOUSE (*open* 9–6 *daily, adm.* 25¢), SW. corner E. Freemason and N.Bank Sts., built in 1789–91, has one of the finest Adam style interiors in America. The walls are thickly covered with ivy. A fine cornice continues across the gable ends, which are pierced by fanlights. The well-proportioned windows in two tiers have heavy flat arches of stone with raised keys. Twin entrances, opening on each side of the outer corner and approached by short, double flights of white marble steps between iron railings, have mahogany doors protected by arched pedimented hoods supported on slender fluted columns.

KEY TO NORFOLK MAP

1.The Confederate Monument 2.St.Paul's Church 3.The Norfolk Courthouse 4.The Myers House 5.The Masonic Temple 6.Old Norfolk Academy 7.The First Baptist Church 8.Norfolk's Mace 9.The United States Customhouse 10.The Sams House 11.The Greene House 12.The Chinese Baptist Church 13.The Whittle House 14.The Selden House 15.The Norfolk Public Library 16.The Milhado House 17.Fort Norfolk 18.The Museum of Arts and Sciences 19.Christ-St.Luke's Church 20.The Female Orphan Society 21.Tazewell Manor 22.The Norfolk Division of the College of William and Mary and Branch of V.P.I. 23.The United States Marine Hospital 24.The United States Naval Operating Base.

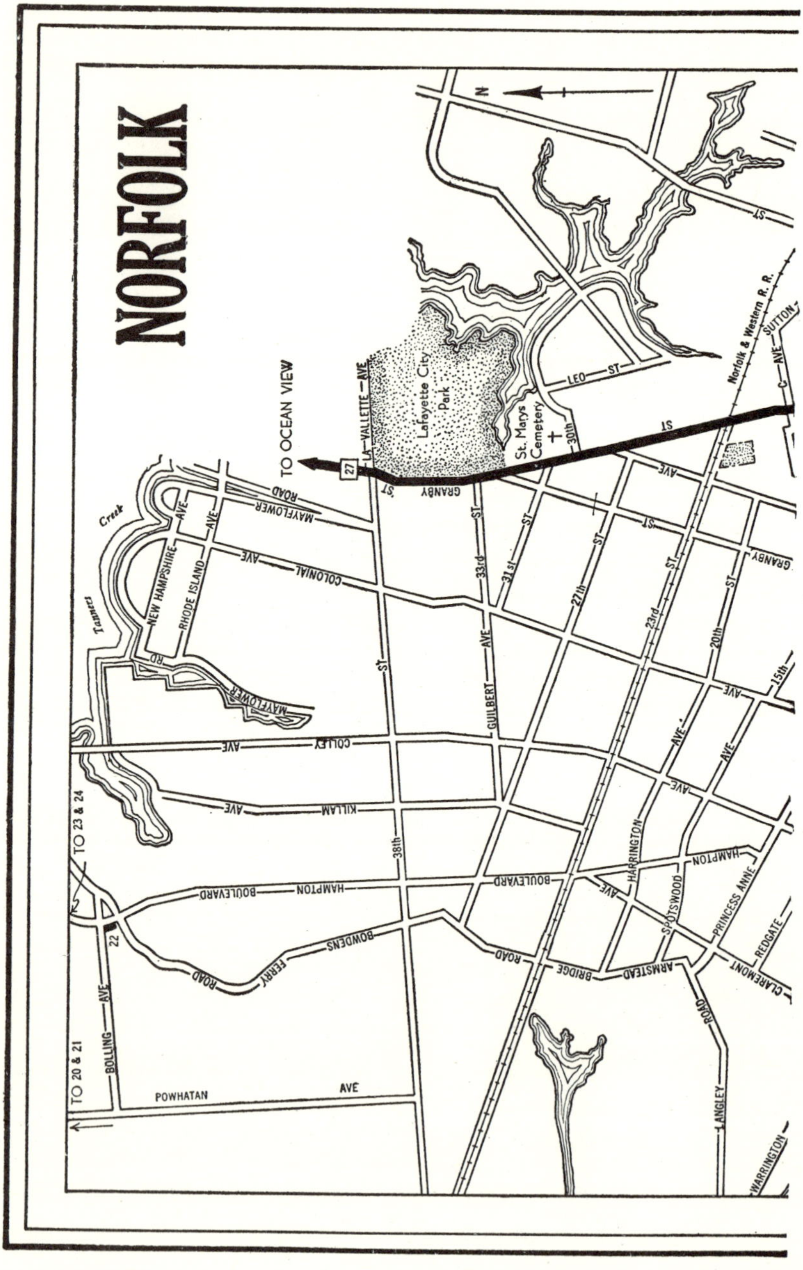
NORFOLK
TO OCEAN VIEW
Lafayette City Park
St. Marys Cemetery
Norfolk & Western R. R.
LA VALLETTE AVE
GRANBY ST
LEO ST
SUTTON
C AVE
30th
33rd ST
31st ST
27th ST
23rd ST
20th ST
15th
MAYFLOWER ROAD
NEW HAMPSHIRE AVE
RHODE ISLAND AVE
COLONIAL AVE
Tanners Creek
MAYFLOWER RD
GUILBERT AVE
38th ST
COLLEY AVE
KILLAM AVE
HAMPTON BOULEVARD
HARRINGTON AVE
SPOTSWOOD AVE
PRINCESS ANNE
REDGATE
CLAREMONT
ARMSTEAD BRIDGE ROAD
BOWDENS FERRY ROAD
ROAD
LANGLEY
WARRINGTON
BOLLING AVE
POWHATAN AVE
TO 23 & 24
TO 20 & 21
22
27
N

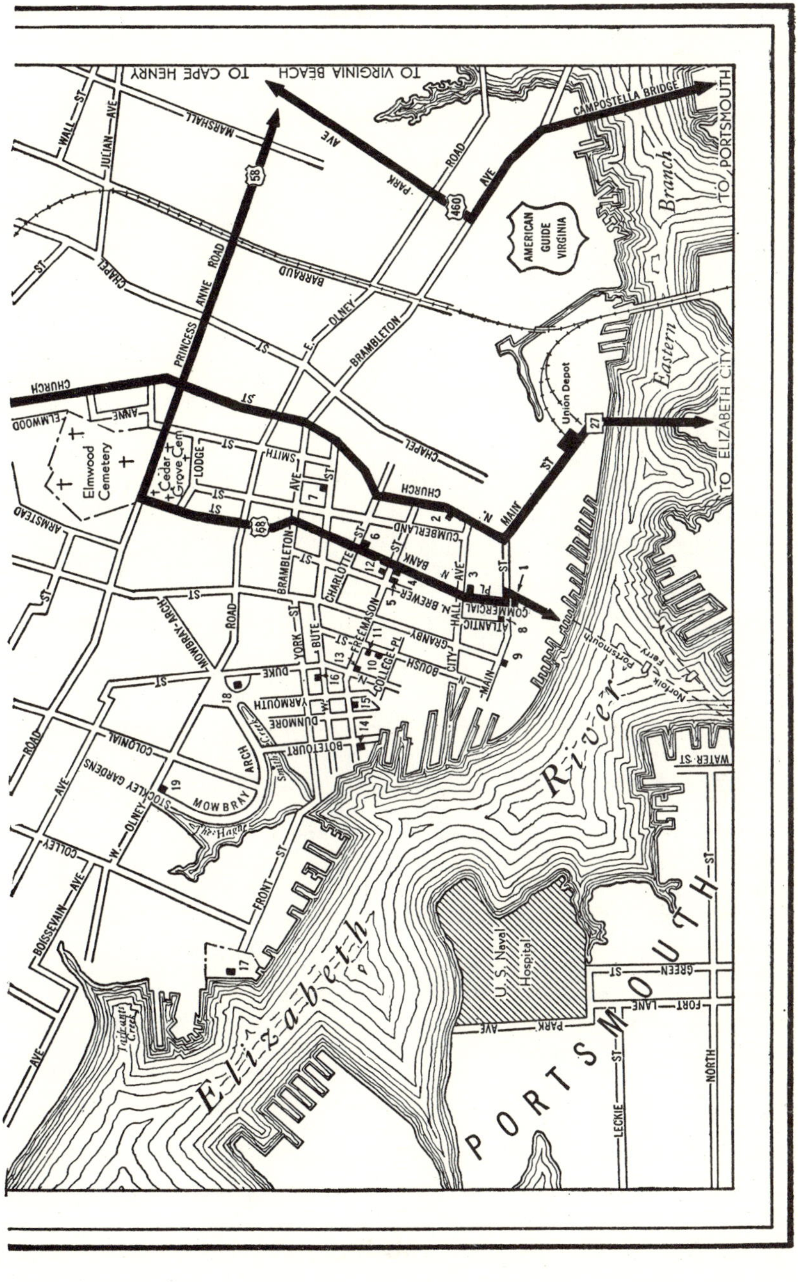
TO CAPE HENRY
TO VIRGINIA BEACH
TO PORTSMOUTH
CAMPOSTELLA BRIDGE
TO ELIZABETH CITY
AMERICAN GUIDE VIRGINIA
Eastern Branch
Union Depot
Elizabeth River
PORTSMOUTH
U.S. Naval Hospital
Elmwood Cemetery
Cedar Grove Cem.
Norfolk Portsmouth Ferry
The Hague
58
460
27
168
WALL ST
JULIAN AVE
MARSHALL AVE
PARK AVE
ROAD
CHAPEL ST
BARRAUD
PRINCESS ANNE ROAD
E. OLNEY
BRAMBLETON AVE
CHURCH ST
ELMWOOD
ANNE
SMITH
LODGE ST
N. MAIN ST
CUMBERLAND
CHARLOTTE ST
BANK ST
N. BREWER
COMMERCIAL PL
ATLANTIC
GRANBY
BOUSH
CITY HALL AVE
FREEMASON
COLLEGE PL
YORK ST
BUTE
DUKE
YARMOUTH
DUNMORE
BOTETOURT
MOWBRAY ARCH
COLONIAL
STOCKLEY GARDENS
W. OLNEY ROAD
COLLEY AVE
BOISSEVAIN AVE
FRONT ST
ARMSTEAD
WATER ST
GREEN ST
FORT LANE
PARK AVE
LECKIE ST
NORTH ST

The ceiling of the spacious hall along one side is ornamented with beautiful plaster work in low relief above a delicate cornice and deep frieze. With variations of design the ceilings are similar in all the principal rooms, and paneled dadoes lead around to mantlepieces of the finest Adamesque delicacy. The dining room and the rooms above it were added about 1800.

Built by Moses Myers, merchant and consul of Dutch-Jewish ancestry who moved here from New York, the house was occupied continuously by members of his family until 1931, when it was opened as a museum. Besides a large quantity of furniture of good American and English design, there are portraits of Moses Myers and of his wife, Eliza Judd of Canada, by Gilbert Stuart, a Thomas Sully portrait of their eldest son, John, and others.

5. The MASONIC TEMPLE, SE. corner E.Freemason and N.Brewer Sts., is a brick building appropriately erected, in 1875, on the street that was designated Freemason on the 'Boush Plan,' a map of Norfolk made in 1762. First chartered in 1741, the lodge subsequently surrendered its charter, and a new one was granted in 1786.

6. OLD NORFOLK ACADEMY, N.Bank St., between Grigsby Pl. and E.Charlotte St., is an austere brick building in Greek Revival style modeled on the plan of the Temple of Theseus and painted gray. The façade has a double portico supported by six Doric columns. Built about 1840, the building housed the Norfolk Academy until it was acquired by the city in 1916. It accommodates the juvenile and domestic relations court.

7. The FIRST BAPTIST CHURCH (Negro), 418 E.Bute St., is a brownstone building, the fourth on this site, completed in 1904 by the oldest Baptist organization in the city. Organized in 1800 by the Reverend James Mitchell, an Englishman, the congregation first met in a hall, then in the 'Borough Church' (St.Paul's). In 1816 all the white members except the minister's family withdrew and organized a new church.

8. NORFOLK'S MACE rests within a specially designed plate glass case in the vault of the National Bank of Commerce Building (*open* 9–4 *weekdays*, 9–12 *Sat.*); NE. corner N.Atlantic and E.Main Sts. Of pure silver, the mace weighs six-and-a-half pounds and is 41 inches long. The staff, composed of six sections, is embellished with leaves and scrolls. Under the openwork of the crown surmounting the head are the arms of Great Britain, the letters C.R., and the initials of Fuller White, London silversmith who fashioned the mace. Around the paneled periphery are the emblems of England, Scotland, France, and Ireland.

At the base is the inscription: 'The gift of the Honble Robert Dinwiddie Es^{qr} Lieu^{t} Governour of Virginia to the Corporation of Norfolk 1753.'

Despite the date, the mace was not presented until 1754, when it was 'thankfully received.' Carried for safe keeping to Kemp's Landing when Norfolk was burned in 1776, it was subsequently returned, making only two appearances, in 1836 and 1857, until May 1862, when Mayor W.W.Lamb (1835–1909), liberal editor of the *Daily Southern Argus*, alarmed at the Confederate evacuation, buried the 'beautiful and bright though ancient

Agriculture

'hotograph by W. Lincoln Highton

DAFFODILS FOR THE MARKET, GLOUCESTER COUNTY

Photograph by courtesy of the Virginia Department of Agriculture

COTTON, GREENSVILLE COUNTY

EASTERN SHORE POTATO FIELD

Photograph by courtesy of the Virginia State Chamber of Commerce

otograph by W. Lincoln Highton

SPINACH FIELD IN EARLY SPRING, NEAR SMITHFIELD

TOBACCO, CHARLOTTE COUNTY

otograph by courtesy of the Virginia Department of Agriculture

Photograph by United States Forest Servic

APPLE ORCHARDS, NEAR SALEM

HARVEST FIELD IN THE BLUE RIDGE

Photograph by courtesy of the Farm Security Administratic

otograph by courtesy of the Virginia Conservation Commission

APPLE 'RUNNER,' WINCHESTER

Photograph by W. Lincoln Highton

PLOWING IN THE PIEDMONT

WALNUT GROVE, WHERE THE McCORMICK REAPER WAS INVENTED (1831)

Photograph by W. Lincoln Highton

Photograph by W. Lincoln Highton

SPRING PLANTING, NEAR WOODSTOCK

VALLEY FARM, NEAR ROANOKE

Photograph by W. Lincoln Highton

Photograph by W. Lincoln Highton

SKY MEADOW, NEAR SALTVILLE

DAIRY HERD, ROCKINGHAM COUNTY

Photograph by courtesy of the Virginia Department of Agriculture

silver mace' under the hearthstone of his house. It was discovered in 1894 among a litter of old records in a room at the police station.

9. The UNITED STATES CUSTOMHOUSE, Main and Granby Sts., is a large stone building, completed in 1857. The Corinthian capitals of the portico and the columns of the interior are of cast iron. Some of the original floors, of black and white marble in checkerboard pattern, have been replaced.

The first customhouse, built in 1819 at Church and Water Streets, was converted into a Federal prison during the War between the States, after which it was burned.

10. The SAMS HOUSE (*private*), 311 N.Boush St., is a yellow painted brick structure, rising two stories above an English basement. It has a high, classical porch and a double iron-railed flight of steps. The name of the builder, Robert Boush, a great-grandson of Norfolk's first mayor, who purchased the land in 1715, is cut in one of the bricks; two other bricks bear the date 1800. Descendants of the Boush family owned and occupied the house until 1847, when it was purchased by Conway Whittle. Here Conway Whittle Sams wrote the *Conquest of Virginia.*

11. The GREENE HOUSE (*private*), 317 N.Boush St., set back from the street in a neat greensward, is a square frame building in early Federal style. Twin flights of steps ascend behind iron railings to a stoop. This house was probably built by John Pryor, who bought the land in 1786. In 1796 it became the property of Eli Vickery, and in 1883, of the Greene family.

12. The CHINESE BAPTIST CHURCH, 206 E.Freemason St., a brick building erected in 1879 by the First Christian Disciples, has a Chinese minister and a Sunday school attended by some 70 Chinese children. Church work among the Chinese, begun in 1901 by an interdenominational group, was turned over in 1918 to the Baptist Union of Norfolk and Portsmouth, which in 1930 sponsored the organization of this church.

13. The WHITTLE HOUSE (*private*), SE. corner N.Duke and W. Freemason Sts., a dignified brick building in Georgian Colonial style, has a Palladian window and a pedimented entrance approached by a flight of wide and well-worn sandstone steps. The house was built about 1791 by an English architect, who made it his home until 1795. In 1803 it was purchased by Richard Taylor. Colonel Walter H. Taylor, who served throughout the War between the States on the staff of General Robert E. Lee, was born in this house.

14. The SELDEN HOUSE (*private*), SW. corner W.Freemason and Botetourt Sts., a post-Colonial frame building with broad chimneys, was built in 1807 as a country house for Dr.William B. Selden (1773–1849), originally of Hampton, who settled in Norfolk after a medical education in Philadelphia and Edinburgh, and became a leading physician.

When Norfolk was occupied by Federal troops from 1862–65, General Egbert L. Vielé, military governor of the city, occupied the Selden house. Egbert L. Vielé,Jr., born here in 1864, settled in France at an early age and under the name of Francis Vielé-Griffin became an outstanding poet and *vers librist.* Robert E. Lee, during his last visit to Norfolk in 1870, was a guest in this house, then occupied by Dr.Selden's son, Dr.William Selden (1808–87), formerly a surgeon in the Confederate army.

15. The NORFOLK PUBLIC LIBRARY (*open 9–9 weekdays*), 345 W. Freemason St., the gift of Andrew Carnegie, is a large stone building in French Renaissance style built on land donated by the daughters of Dr. William Selden: Julia, Charlotte, Caroline, and Mary. In the fireproof William Henry Sargeant Memorial Room there is a valuable collection of Virginiana. The library, which has about 94,000 volumes, maintains seven branches, including one for Negroes.

16. The MILHADO HOUSE (*private*), 250 W.Bute St., a tall brick building, has a dormer-windowed attic and two front entrances, one in the English basement and the other, more formal, through a portico to the floor above. In the rear stands the old kitchen. Erected 'in the fields,' probably by John Smith, the first occupant, the house was bought in 1768 by Dr.Alexander Gordon. While serving as surgeon in the British army during the Revolution, Colonel Gordon was captured and imprisoned at Norfolk. Exchanged for an American officer in 1775, he returned to England, where he died. Aaron Milhado II (1808–51), Colonel Gordon's grandson, and a subsequent owner of the house, was one of Norfolk's leading citizens.

17. FORT NORFOLK (*open by permission from District Engineer's Office, War Department, Post Office Building*), W. end of Front St., with gunless ramparts and a smooth lawn that sweeps to a sea wall, long ago outlived its usefulness as a fortress and is now district headquarters of the United States Engineers and a storage place for ammunition.

Built in 1794 by the State of Virginia, the fort was sold the following year to the Federal Government. From its key position, it aided American troops in opposing the British at the Battle of Craney Island, June 22, 1813. Abandoned by the garrison upon Virginia's secession, it was held by the Confederates until Norfolk was evacuated in 1862.

18. The MUSEUM OF ARTS AND SCIENCES (*open 12–5:30 Tues.–Sat.; 2:30–5:30 Sun.; free*), SE. corner Yarmouth St. and Mowbray Arch, a limestone building of Italian Renaissance design, was opened in 1933. American Indian artifacts and pottery, Mexican idols, Chinese ceramics, stoneware and early porcelain are on display as permanent and loan collections. An extensive library specializes in genealogical works. The museum conducts special exhibitions of contemporary art, publishes the quarterly *Tidewater Arts Review*, and presents frequent lectures on art, music, literature, and the drama.

19. CHRIST–ST.LUKE'S CHURCH (Episcopal) (*open 8–5 Mon.–Fri., 8–2:30 Sat. and 6–1:30 Sun.*), SE. corner W.Olney Rd. and Stockley Gardens, is a gray granite building with limestone trim designed in a modified Tudor Gothic style. A high tower above the entrance is finished with elaborate finials. Foremost among the decorations are a bas-relief carved in Caen stone after Leonardo da Vinci's *Last Supper*, and stained glass windows by Meyer of Munich.

The building was erected in 1909. The congregation has been formed by the merger of three churches: Christ Church, founded in 1798 on its separation from the Borough Church (St.Paul's); St.Luke's Church, organized in 1871; and St.Andrew's Church, formed about 1912.

20. The FEMALE ORPHAN SOCIETY, 5505 Powhatan Ave., cares for Norfolk girls from two-and-one-half to twelve years of age who are orphans or from broken homes. Organized in 1804 by Bishop Francis Asbury and a group of women, the society opened its first home in 1817.

21. TAZEWELL MANOR (*private*), 6225 Powhatan Ave., Edgewater, is a two-story frame house, its hip roof slate-covered and pierced at each corner by a brick chimney. A small portico has four Tuscan columns. The wings are later additions. Built in 1784 on Tazewell St., the house was moved to its present location in 1902. The front lawn, edging the Elizabeth River, overlooks Hampton Roads and the distant mouths of the James and Nansemond rivers. Tazewell Manor was built by John Boush, great-grandson of Norfolk's first mayor, and was subsequently purchased by Governor Littleton Waller Tazewell.

22. The NORFOLK DIVISION OF THE COLLEGE OF WILLIAM AND MARY and a branch of the VIRGINIA POLYTECHNIC INSTITUTE, SW. corner Hampton Blvd. and Bolling Ave., providing college courses for local students, are housed in a former public school building acquired in 1930 and a large brick structure built in 1936. On the grounds is FOREMAN FIELD, containing a concrete stadium with a seating capacity of 18,000, erected in 1936.

23. The UNITED STATES MARINE HOSPITAL, E.Hampton Blvd. facing Lafayette River, is a large structure of concrete, stone, and brick, built in 1922 and greatly enlarged in 1933. With a capacity for 400 patients, it admits persons certified for hospital and out-patient treatment by the U.S. Public Health Service.

24. The UNITED STATES NAVAL OPERATING BASE (*open 8 a.m. to sunset daily*), Hampton Blvd. and 99th St., occupies the 850-acre site of the Jamestown Exposition on Hampton Roads. Established in 1917, it is one of the most modern naval bases in the world. Scattered about are 453 buildings valued, with equipment, at $30,000,000. Major units are the Navy Supply Depot, 12 warehouses that handle supplies for the entire fleet; the Marine Corps Depot of Supplies, supply base and assembling point for marines assigned to foreign duty; Marine Barracks; the Training Station, consisting of a drill department for recruits, Service Schools Department for the technical training of enlisted men, and a preparatory school for enlisted candidates for the Naval Academy; and the Naval Air Station, a repair base for fleet aircraft.

POINTS OF INTEREST IN ENVIRONS

Adam Thoroughgood House, 8 *m.*; Seashore State Park, 14 *m.*; Cape Henry, 17 *m.*; Fort Story, 17.5 *m.*; Virginia Beach, 18 *m.* (*see Tour* 8*a*). Norfolk Navy Yard, 1 *m.* (*see Portsmouth*).

Portsmouth

Railroad Stations: Broad St. between Hartford and Woodrow Sts., Port Norfolk, for Atlantic Coast Line R.R. and Southern Ry.; E. end of High St., adjacent to Portsmouth-Norfolk ferries, for Seaboard Air Line Ry. and Chesapeake and Ohio ferry, leaving 8:45 a.m. daily for Newport News, for Virginian Ry., Norfolk & Western Ry., Chesapeake and Ohio Ry., Pennsylvania R.R. and Norfolk Southern R.R.
Bus Stations: Greyhound Bus Terminal, 119 High St., for Atlantic Greyhound, Penn. Greyhound, Richmond Greyhound, Norfolk Southern, Virginia Coach, Carolina Coach, and Peninsula Transit Lines.
Taxis : Fare 25¢ for 1st m., 10¢ for each additional half m.; no charge for extra passengers.
Local Bus: Fare 7¢; 116 High St., for busses to Deep Creek, fare 25¢, round trip 40¢, and to Bowers Hill, fare 20¢, round trip 30¢.
Traffic Regulations: No U-turns under traffic lights, parking limits in business district from 10 minutes to 2 hours day and night in most congested district.

Accommodations: 4 hotels; numerous tourist homes, especially on highways leading out of the city.

Information Service: Chamber of Commerce, 215½ High St.; Tidewater Auto Ass'n, Monroe Hotel, NE. corner Court and High Sts.

Motion Picture Houses: 4, including 1 for Negroes.
Baseball: Sewanee Field, Washington St. between Lincoln and Henry Sts., for games of Portsmouth 'Truckers,' Piedmont League.
Golf: Portsmouth Country Club, Glensheallah, 0.5 m. NW. of city limits, off W. end High St., 9 holes, open by arrangement, greens fee 25¢ for 9, 40¢ for 18 holes weekdays, 50¢ for 18 holes Sun.; Portsmouth Municipal Golf Course, Portsmouth City Park, 1.5 m. W. of city limits at end of King St., 9 holes, greens fee 25¢, 40¢ for 18 holes, Sat. and Sun. 30¢, 50¢ for 18 holes.
Swimming: Y.M.C.A., 527 High St.; Portsmouth Country Club, 0.5 m. NW. of city limits off W. end High St., adm. by arrangement, fee 25¢; surf bathing at Ocean View, 10 m. NE. of city limits via Granby St., Norfolk, and Virginia Beach, 20 m. E. of city limits on US 58.
Tennis: Portsmouth City Park, W. end King St., 4 courts, no fee; Portsmouth Country Club, 0.5 m. NW. of city limits off W. end High St., open by arrangement.

Annual Events: Pilgrimage to Cape Henry, Apr. 26; tour to Dismal Swamp and Lake Drummond, round trip fare $1.25, Oct.; Navy Day, Oct. 27 (inspection of shops and ships in dry docks).

In PORTSMOUTH (12 alt., 45,704 pop.) the sea dominates. The odors of brine and creosote fill the air, and the hollow sound of boat whistles floats eerily from the water. Commercial fisheries lie at the end of cobbled alleys and near docks and freight piers. Blue-jacketed sailors hurry to some long-anticipated rendezvous or idle in groups. Less conspicuous are the old families of Portsmouth, who cherish their traditions and customs, and find diversions at the country club and cotillion.

The city occupies a waterlocked point of flat land penetrated by numerous arms of the oily Elizabeth River and its southern and western branches. Its geometric blocks, bisected by many railroad tracks, spread from a rich truck-farming section on the southwest to the circling water's edge, lined on the east with piers that look across the river to the jagged Norfolk skyline. The two cities are connected by a tollbridge and profitable ferries—commercial shuttles that are crowded with weekend pleasure vehicles.

Along Portsmouth's tree-lined streets, walled in by close-set rows of comparatively modern residences, are occasional survivals of eighteenth-century buildings, many overlooking narrow gardens planted with boxwood, magnolia, and other shrubbery of the South. From dingy Crawford Street, divided by railroad tracks and edged with raucous beer bars intermingled with commercial houses, streets run at right angles to cut their way through the old town, the center of which is occupied by the extensive Seaboard Air Line Railway shops. The commercial life of Portsmouth flourishes along wide and lengthy High Street, which begins opposite the ferry landing, runs between shops and restaurants, lighted at night in a blaze of neon, then past churches and the courthouse, traverses a Negro section, and finally leads into an area of homes. Residential Court Street, a wide north-south artery, begins at the water's edge, runs through midtown, and ends in a cluster of all-night food-and-beer bars at the guarded entrance of the Navy Yard. During working hours Navy Yard employees hurry along the shaded length of these two thoroughfares, while at night shipbound sailors and marines trudge its darkened sidewalks. Westward stretch the suburbs, densely populated, shaded, flat, and frozen or cooled, according to the season, by winds sweeping across the wide mouth of the Western Branch. Living in numerous sections is Portsmouth's Negro population (41 per cent of the whole), which supplies the city with sea-food workers, fishermen, marine yard employees, and domestics. Along parts of County and High Streets, and for several blocks on streets extending toward Scott's Creek, life teems in ramshackle houses that rise flush from the sidewalk. The homes of the business and professional class meet much higher standards. Despite too-evident poverty, the Negroes support a theater, and many 'cook shops' and general stores.

Portsmouth's industrial life is carried on in the 40 freight piers that edge the water front, in buildings on the ragged peninsula just beyond the Navy Yard, and in various factories and mills scattered about the city. Cottonseed oil, fertilizer, paint, hosiery, chemicals, foundry products, and lumber constitute the major part of the city's industrial output. The aggregate annual pay roll exceeds $12,000,000.

The palisaded village of the Chesapeake Indians had long disappeared when Captain William Carver, mariner, acquired a plantation in 1664 along the brackish southern banks of the Elizabeth River. Later, despite the high offices he held, Captain Carver, 'deciding to risk his old bones against the Indian rogues,' participated in Bacon's Rebellion (1676), even attempting to capture Governor Berkeley. For this treasonable escapade, he was afterwards hanged. His confiscated land was granted in 1716 to

Colonel William Crawford, who in 1750 'laid out a parcel of land . . . into one hundred and twenty-two lots, commodious streets, places for a court house, market, and public landings for a town . . . and made sale . . . to divers persons . . . desirous to settle and build thereon speedily.' Naming the place Portsmouth, he presented it to Norfolk County. In 1752 the general assembly 'enacted . . . that the said . . . parcel of land be . . . established a town . . . and retain the name of Portsmouth.'

Among the traders, merchants, and shipbuilders, chiefly Scots, who flocked to the new town, was Andrew Sprowle. Acquiring land immediately to the south, he started the village of Gosport—named after the town opposite Portsmouth, England—by building a marine yard and tenements for workers. The British Government, recognizing the value of this enterprise, soon took over the yard as a repair station and appointed Andrew Sprowle navy agent.

When royal government ended in Virginia in 1775, Governor Dunmore fled to Sprowle's home in Gosport, where he lived 'riotously upon his friend.' For several months, he rallied Tories and Negroes about him and plundered the countryside, until his defeat at Great Bridge. Immediately afterwards he joined the British fleet, accompanied by Sprowle.

Following the burning of Norfolk in 1776, Dunmore and his Tories took possession of Portsmouth and remained until the eccentric General Charles Lee arrived with his forces, and Dunmore sailed away with his whole following. Finding the town a hotbed of Tories, General Lee, 'to quell this Toryism,' had the houses 'of the most notorious Traitors' demolished. Sprowle's property and the abandoned marine yard were seized. Later, Fort Nelson, named for General Thomas Nelson, was erected on Windmill Point.

One May morning of 1779, a great gray British fleet, carrying 2,000 men and commanded by Sir George Collier, anchored in Elizabeth River. General Edward Mathew of the fleet burned Fort Nelson and the marine yard, and the British departed. Portsmouth was the landing place and base for three other invading British expeditions under Leslie, Arnold, and Phillips.

The Revolution had repercussions in Portsmouth. Filled with refugees from burned Norfolk, the town, tolerant at first, soon flamed with indignation. About 1784 'those execrable miscreants called Tories' were told 'to leave this town immediately' or 'measures' would be taken. Thus banished, the 'Tories' went back to ruined Norfolk.

In 1784 Andrew Sprowle's confiscated property, Gosport, was divided into lots and made a part of Portsmouth. A decade later, the navy yard, which the State had retained, was lent to the Federal Government, Captain Richard Dale was placed in command, and the keel of a frigate was laid. The *Chesapeake*, the first ship built by the Federal Government, was completed in 1799. In 1801 the Government purchased the Gosport Navy Yard (now Norfolk Navy Yard) for $12,000. In 1798 a visitor remarked that 'one might walk from Portsmouth to Norfolk on the decks of vessels at anchor.'

In an attempt to take Portsmouth and the navy yard during the War of 1812, the British landed 2,600 men at Port Norfolk (now a part of Portsmouth), but the guns of Fort Nelson and Fort Norfolk stopped the invasion. A fresh onslaught was made on sandy Craney Island, lined with redoubts. Approaching in barges, the British were met with a bombardment that sank several vessels and caused an immediate retreat.

After extending its town limits in 1811, Portsmouth witnessed the opening of the Dismal Swamp Canal in 1812, a 'boat containing 10,000 shingles' being the first to pass over the mingled waters of Chesapeake Bay and Albemarle Sound. In 1821, when the first horseboat ferry was built, the town was swept by a fire of incendiary origin, but it was soon rebuilt. The land on which Fort Nelson lay was augmented by a 61-acre tract in 1826, the old fort was demolished, and on its site a naval hospital was begun. The town's first railroad was chartered in 1834, and public schools were established in 1846.

During this period Portsmouth attended its jockey, cricket, and quoit clubs; frequented racecourses; watched the launching of the *Lady of the Lake* (1830), which 'moved by its own steam'; and welcomed such visitors as Andrew Jackson (1833) and Henry Clay (1844).

Yellow fever, brought by a ship just returned from the tropics, decimated the inhabitants of Portsmouth in 1855. Of the 4,000 people who remained in the town during the epidemic, 1,089 died. In 1858 Portsmouth was chartered as a city.

When Virginia seceded from the Union, the Gosport Navy Yard was evacuated and burned, after which Virginia troops occupied the area. In May 1862 the Confederates burned the navy yard and evacuated the area. Then Federal forces moved in, established martial law in Portsmouth, and again took possession of the navy yard.

Another phase of Portsmouth's commercial era began in 1837 with the completion of the Portsmouth and Roanoke Railroad. Subsequently this line was incorporated in the Virginia and Carolina Railroad, which in 1900 became the Seaboard Air Line Railway, with its coastal terminus at Portsmouth. Branches of two other railroads, the Atlantic Coast Line and the Southern, bring inland produce to the city. Since taking over the lines of the Atlantic and Danville Railway in 1894, the Southern has built an elaborate system of freight piers on the Western Branch.

At the beginning of the twentieth century, Portsmouth started extending its wharves along the water front, and, as necessity demanded, demolished its old houses to make way for modern business establishments.

POINTS OF INTEREST

The NORFOLK COUNTY COURTHOUSE (*open* 9–5 *Mon.–Fri.*, 9–1 *Sat.*), NW. corner Court and High Sts., is a brick building with broad stone steps leading to a shallow, four-columned portico. The first courthouse for Norfolk County, erected 1691–93, stood on land later part of Norfolk City, was burned by Dunmore in 1776, and was rebuilt between 1784 and 1788. In 1801–03 a courthouse was built in Portsmouth on this, the third site. The present building, erected in 1844–46, was later remodeled. New Norfolk County was formed in 1636 from Elizabeth City

County and the next year divided into Upper Norfolk and Lower Norfolk. The present Norfolk County was cut from Lower Norfolk in 1691.

TRINITY CHURCH (*open* 9:30–5 *daily*), SW. corner Court and High Sts., is a brick building, stuccoed tan, with green classical trim. One of the original churches of Portsmouth Parish formed from Elizabeth River Parish in 1761, it was erected in 1762, partly rebuilt in 1829, and later remodeled. The bell, which cracked while pealing the news of Cornwallis's surrender, was recast. The church is on one of the four corner lots that Colonel William Crawford gave for public buildings in 1750.

Because its greensward was the first public burying ground in Portsmouth, Trinity stands among the tombs of the city fathers. The oldest stone, dated 1763, memorializes Alexander Scott, editor of a Norfolk newspaper, who lived in Gosport; others identify Commodore James Barron (1768–1851), commander of the *Chesapeake*; Colonel Bernard Magnein, aide to La Fayette; and the Reverend John Braidfoot, second rector of Portsmouth Parish (1774–85) and a chaplain in the Continental army.

UNITED STATES NAVAL HOSPITAL (*open* 6 *a.m.*–9 *p.m. daily; adm. by arrangement*), N. end Green St., occupies a beautiful peninsula in the Elizabeth River. The main unit, a three-story brick and stone structure on a high basement, is stuccoed in white and gray. Long stone steps lead up to the ten Doric columns of the portico. Among the 51 other buildings to the west is the Pharmacist's Mates School, in which an average of 325 men are trained annually. A swimming pool, athletic field, and tennis courts provide diversion for the 572 enlisted men and civilian employees. The institution serves navy and marine corps, their dependents, and the Virginia and North Carolina war veterans.

The naval hospital was begun in 1827 under the direction of John Haviland, Philadelphia architect, and was opened in 1830. During the yellow fever epidemic of 1855 nearly 600 patients were cared for here. Its capacity was taxed during the War between the States and the Spanish-American War. In 1902 the Hospital Corps Training School was instituted. Between 1907 and 1909 the main building was demolished, except for the portico, and a new one erected.

On the grounds are two monuments. One, designed by John Haviland, is a memorial to Major John Saunders, commander of Fort Nelson in 1805; the other, of rough granite surmounted by a cannon, marks the site of Fort Nelson.

In the BURYING GROUND, NW. corner of the grounds, are tombstones bearing inscriptions in many languages. Here lie the bodies of yellow fever victims, of many members of the Confederate and the Union navies, of those who drowned when the ship *Huron* was wrecked in 1877, and of many Spanish-American and World War veterans. The STONE CAIRN, surmounted by a pillar and an urn, is in memory of 300 men lost when the *Cumberland* and *Congress* were sunk by the Confederate ironclad *Virginia* (*Merrimac*) in 1862.

The RICHARD DALE MONUMENT, intersection of Washington and North Sts., is composed of three massive slabs of granite with a bronze tablet. It was erected in 1917 to honor the Revolutionary naval hero,

Richard Dale (1756–1826), who served first in the Virginia Navy, transferred his allegiance to the British, and then returned to fight for the American cause. Captured by the British, he escaped to France and became lieutenant on the *Bonhomme Richard.* In 1794 Dale was put in command of the Gosport Navy Yard. Jefferson, in 1801, raised his rank to commodore and sent him in command of a squadron to blockade the Tripolitan ports. The following year Dale resigned from the service and settled in Philadelphia.

The WATTS HOUSE (*private*), NW. corner Dinwiddie and North Sts., a frame building with a gabled roof, has three porches with fluted columns and a fanlight over the main entrance. The interior woodwork remains intact from heart pine floors to hand-carved mantels and graceful curving stairway. Colonel Dempsey Watts built the house in 1799. It passed to his son, Captain Samuel Watts, who entertained Chief Black Hawk here in 1820, and Henry Clay in 1844.

The PORTER HOUSE (*private*), 23 Court St., a tall stuccoed brick structure, has a hipped roof with elaborate cornice and a classically framed portal. Built just before the War between the States, it was acquired by John L. Porter, designer of the ironclad *Virginia,* and was his home until the Confederate evacuation of Portsmouth.

The BALL HOUSE (*private*), 213 Middle St., set back from the street, is a frame building with paired chimneys at each end of a steeply curbed green-shingled roof, and five dormers are set closely along the lower roof surface. It was built about 1784 by John Nivison at the corner of Crawford and Glasgow Streets. After the building had served as barracks during the War of 1812, subsequent owners entertained La Fayette in 1824 and Andrew Jackson in 1833. It was moved to the present site in 1869.

The BUTT HOUSE (*private*), 327 Crawford St., is a two-and-a-half story brick building with leaded-glass windows. It was built about 1826 by Dr.Robert Bruce Butt and used during the War between the States as commissary headquarters for the Federal army.

The CASSELL–McRAE HOUSE (*private*), 108 London St., two-and-a-half stories of brick, painted gray, has a steep gabled roof and twin chimneys. The house has stone lintels over the windows, a graceful fanlight over the entrance door, large outside locks, paneled doors, and deep wainscoting on the interior. About 1825, when the house was being constructed, Captain John W. McRae, the builder, is thought to have left on a long voyage and to have been lost at sea.

The CRAWFORD HOUSE (*open day and night*), SW. corner Crawford and Queen Sts., is a tall brick building with four dormer windows in the gabled roof. Aaron Milhado I, a Spaniard who had just migrated to America, built the house in 1779 as a residence. For many years it served as the Centennial House, an exclusive hotel frequented by naval officers and their families. About 1835 its name was changed to Crawford House in honor of Portsmouth's founder. Remodeled and painted cerise, it was used for several years as a warehouse and store, but since 1938 has housed the Helping Hand Mission.

The IRONMONGER HOUSE, NE. corner Crawford and High Sts., a

large brick building built in 1822 by John Thompson, has been gaily painted and metamorphosed into shops. Here, in 1853, was born Frank M. Ironmonger, youngest soldier of the Confederacy. Enlisting when not quite eleven years old, he acted for a time as courier then participated in important battles. Captured within the Federal lines in 1865 and sentenced to be shot as a spy, he escaped and served until the end of the war.

The BILISOLY HOUSE (*private*), 801 Court St., a white frame building, has one gable end facing the street, and the other is broken by paired chimneys. In the yard stands a two-story kitchen, formerly detached, but now joined to the main unit by an addition. The house was built sometime after 1797, the date that Captain Andrew W. Kidd purchased the property. It passed to the Bilisoly family, French refugees who came to Portsmouth in 1799.

The NORFOLK NAVY YARD (*open* 8:30–4:30 *daily; adm. free, pass issued at gate*), entrances S. end First and Fourth Sts., is one of the two largest navy yards in the United States. Scattered over 453 acres are 212 low brick buildings, including the marine barracks, housing machine and training school shops; and plants manufacturing from government formulae and specifications such widely divergent articles as paint, gases, metal furniture, and turbine blades. Along the water front are 6 dry docks varying in length from 324 to 1,011 feet, 30 berths totaling 9,000 feet, for ships of every class, immense steel framework building ways, a reservation for ships condemned to be sold, and a base station for the lighthouse service. In addition to the ever-changing enlisted personnel, some 5,000 civilians are steadily employed.

TROPHY PARK, reached through First St. gate, is a tree-shaded reservation established to preserve Confederate and other American weapons of war and equipment of historic value from old ships.

After its acquisition by the Federal Government in 1801, the Gosport Navy Yard, as it was known until the War between the States, remained under the somewhat inadequate direction of navy agents until 1810; then Commodore Samuel Barron was appointed the first commandant, a position to which his brother, Commodore James Barron, later succeeded. The year after the launching of the *Delaware* (1820), the first battleship built in a government-owned navy yard, a school for midshipmen was established here aboard the frigate *Guerrière*. A dry dock was opened in 1833 in the presence of President Andrew Jackson and his cabinet. Here in 1861–62, the *Merrimac* was converted into the ironclad *Virginia*. During the World War a fourth dry dock was added, one of the largest in the world.

POINTS OF INTEREST IN ENVIRONS

Dismal Swamp and Lake Drummond, 20.6 *m.* (*see Tour 6b*); Virginia Beach, 20 *m.* (*see Tour 8a*).

Newport News

Railroad Station: 23rd St. and River Rd. for Chesapeake and Ohio Ry.
Bus Stations: NW. corner 28th St. and Washington Ave. for Greyhound and Peninsula Transit Lines; SE. corner 28th St. and Washington Ave. for Great Eastern Lines.
Taxis: Fare 10¢ and upward, according to distance.
Streetcars and Busses: Local and interurban; fare 5¢ within city limits, 5¢ for each zone outside city.
Traffic Regulations: No all-night parking in main part of city, 1 hr. parking 8–6 on Washington Ave.

Accommodations: 3 hotels; tourist homes.

Information Service: Tidewater Auto Ass'n, Warwick Hotel, 25th St. between Washington and West Aves.

Radio Station: WGH (1310 kc.).
Motion Picture Houses: 3, including 1 for Negroes.
Golf: James River Country Club, 5.3 m. W. of city limits on US 60, 18 holes, open by arrangement, greens fee $2; Old Dominion Golf Club, 16th and Chestnut Sts., 18 holes, greens fee 40¢ for 18 holes, 25¢ for 9 holes.
Swimming: James River Country Club, open 10 a.m. to 10 p.m. daily, guest fee 40¢.
Tennis: James River Country Club, 5.3 m. W. of city limits on US 60, no fee for guests; Huntington Park, 1 m. W. of city limits on US 60, 4 courts, no fee; Woodrow Wilson School Grounds, Maple Ave. and Kecoughtan St., 1 court, no fee; Newport News Baseball Park, 28th and Wicham Sts., 1 court, no fee.
Ice Skating: Old Dominion Skating Rink, near Old Dominion Golf Club, 16th and Chestnut Sts., open 8–11 p.m. in winter, adm. 40¢.
Boating: Boats for hire at piers, S.end of Warwick Ave.

Annual Events: Newport News Regatta, usually in late summer.

NEWPORT NEWS (25 alt., 34,417 pop.), at the mouth of the James River and at the head of Hampton Roads, is the Tidewater terminus of the Chesapeake and Ohio Railway and the home of one of the largest shipyards in the world. The area of the city is roughly triangular, with its base stretching across the marshy lowlands of Virginia's most historic peninsula and its sides the James River and Hampton Roads.

Overlooking the waters, new and comfortable homes present a sharp contrast to clustered slums. The better residential district, beginning at the northernmost limits, is contiguous to the shipyard. Southward, parks stretch to meet the great railway terminal, which dips into the city behind more than a mile of river front. At the apex of the triangle is the terminus of the Chesapeake Ferry Company and close by are the municipal pier and a harbor for small boats. On the Hampton Roads shore line is a confusion of industrial plants and warehouses. A residential section at the eastern edge of the city has been named Kecoughtan for its remote ancestor.

Men in uniform frequent the streets of Newport News—sailors and naval officers from Norfolk or from cruisers anchored in the bay; army officers and enlisted men from Langley Field and Fort Monroe. Newport News has a festive air when the shipyard launches a new vessel or when a man-of-war casts anchor in Hampton Roads and sends ashore its pleasure-seeking crew.

Negroes make up 39 per cent of the population of Newport News. Most of the men have stable and comparatively well-paid employment in industry, particularly in the shipyard, where many hold skilled jobs, and the Negro business and professional group is increasing.

Newport News, though on the site of a very old settlement, became a city in recent years. It lies within the original Kecoughtan area, which extended from the Chesapeake Bay westward to Skiffe's Creek and northward to Back River. In 1607 the first English settlers entering the James River named the apex of the triangle Point Hope. In 1611 Robert Salford, with his wife and son, came to the creek now in the eastern part of the city. The name of the stream, Salford Creek, was changed through usage to Salter's. Other land within the limits of present Newport News was patented in 1621 by the Newce brothers, Thomas and Sir William, who came from Ireland. Sir William Newce had offered to transport 1,000 persons to Virginia, but brought 'only a few weak and unserviceable people, ragged and not above a fortnight's provisions, some bound for three years, and most upon wages.' For his failure William Capps impatiently dubbed him 'Sir William Naughtworth.' But there was some reason for Sir William's failure to bring the thousand persons—he died in 1621.

Daniel Gookin, an Englishman who had moved to Port Newce in County Cork, Ireland, followed the Newces to this area, bringing with him 'fifty men of his owne, and thirty Passengers, exceedingly well furnished with all sorts of Prouision.' It was he who probably named the community—some say for his home in Ireland; others, to honor Newce and Captain Christopher Newport; and still others, for the good news that Newport brought the starving colonists—the most likely origin since old inhabitants still call the city Newport's News. That the name was current in 1626 is attested by the minutes of the general court, which record a transfer to Daniel Gookin of land 'situate above Newport's News at a place called Marie's Mount.'

Though tracing its ancestry to Kecoughtan and sharing in Colonial and American vicissitudes, Newport News was merely an area of farm lands and a fishing village until the coming of the railroad and the subsequent establishment of the great shipyard. In 1852 an act of the general assembly 'to legalize a wharf at Newports News,' gave the Warwick County Court 'the same powers in regard to said wharf as are possessed by the county court of James City in regard to the Grove Wharf on the lands of Thomas Wynne.' In 1873 Major Robert H. Temple surveyed a railway line from Richmond to the mouth of the James River. Seven years later Collis P. Huntington, the industrialist, found Major Temple's wooden markers intact and undertook to build the road along that route. The railroad was completed in 1882, and a town was plotted without formal authorization by the general assembly. Four years later the Chesapeake Dry Dock and Construction Company, now the Newport News Shipbuilding and Dry Dock Company, was begun and boom years followed. In 1900 the population was 19,635; and in 1920, 35,596.

Humanity's flotsam and jetsam landed upon an area that came to be known significantly as Hell's Half Acre, a district between 18th and 23rd Streets now occupied by a railway yard. When Newport News was incorporated as a city in 1896, Hell's Half Acre lay outside its limits. Shacks were hurriedly built to house its motley population, estimated during the World War at about 2,000 persons almost equally divided between Negroes and whites, whose barrooms and brothels catered to water-front workers and visiting seamen. It is said that the area then averaged a murder a week. At the end of the war, however, Newport News annexed Hell's Half Acre and the adjacent Negro district known as Poverty Row, and instituted a program of law enforcement. Between 1925 and 1927 all the land of both sections was bought by the Chesapeake and Ohio Railway, and the disreputable shacks were razed.

Now, in addition to the giant shipyard and the sea terminus of a great railway, the city's industries include the manufacture of soft drinks, ice and ice cream, mattresses and pillows, metal fixtures, automobile parts, caskets, hotel and hospital supplies, and building accessories.

POINTS OF INTEREST

The COURTHOUSE (*open* 9–5 *Mon.–Fri.*, 9–1 *Sat.*), NW. corner Huntington Ave. and 25th St., is a red brick structure, built in 1891–93 and used for only three years as the courthouse of Warwick County. In 1896, the year of its incorporation as a city, Newport News held its courts in this building. The courthouse, later bought by the city, is now used by the corporation court of Newport News and the circuit courts of Warwick and Elizabeth City Counties.

The PUBLIC LIBRARY (*open* 9–5, 7–9 *weekdays*), SW. corner West Ave. and 30th Sts., is of modified Federal architecture with pink brick and white pilasters. It was designed by Charles Robinson and built in 1928 under the direction of the Newport News Library, Inc., organized in 1908 through the efforts of local clubwomen. The library contains nearly 24,000 volumes.

The PLANT OF THE NEWPORT NEWS SHIPBUILDING AND DRY DOCK COMPANY (*open by arrangement*), Washington Ave. between 35th and 49th Sts., stretching nearly a mile along the James and covering 125 acres, has been an important factor in the development of Newport News. The vast plant of red brick shops is dominated by the numerous giant trellises of two steel cradles and three dry docks—one capable of accommodating the largest ships afloat. The clean and orderly appearance of the whole yard displays the high standards of the founder, Collis Potter Huntington, whose statement, 'We shall build good ships here at a profit if we can, at a loss if we must, but always good ships,' is inscribed in bronze on a giant rock within the entrance. Organized in 1886, it is one of the largest private shipbuilding yards in the world. It occupies a perfect situation with respect to tides, deep water, and proximity to the sea. The first dry dock was completed in 1889. Normally employing about 7,000 men, it enlarged its working force to 14,000 during the World War. More than 350 vessels have been constructed here for the Merchant Marine and United States Navy. After the World War the equipment was modified to produce locomotives and other heavy machinery, particularly hydraulic turbines. Some of these turbines, among the largest in the world, were built for Boulder Dam, Muscle Shoals, and for Dnepropetrovsk, the huge power development project of the Soviet Republics on the Dnieper River. Safety regulations, medical and surgical services, noncontributory pensions, and workers' insurance have functioned since about 1916, and recreational activities are sponsored by the plant. A system of employee representation has been in operation since 1927. In 1919 an apprentice school was established, providing a four-year course in craft training with wages. Increased naval appropriations of 1938–39 resulted in immediate acceleration of work at the shipyard, where the largest passenger vessel ever built in America is under construction (1939).

The CHESAPEAKE AND OHIO RAILWAY TERMINAL, bounded by 23rd St., the river, Newport News Ave., and Warwick Ave., spreads over more than 300 acres and is the largest single terminus in the world. Ten piers, including four covered merchandise piers, two coal piers, and a passenger pier, extend into the river along a mile and a half of frontage. Two piers have facilities for emptying an entire gondola carload of coal into a ship in one rapid operation. There are extensive warehouses, especially for tobacco, of which the volume moving through Hampton Roads is unrivaled. This section was chosen in 1880 by Collis P. Huntington as the deep-water terminal for his railroad. Coal dumpings rose from 575,000 tons in 1882 to 51,488,060 in 1935. More than 62,000,000 tons of other commodities were moved in 1935 as against 1,150,000 tons in 1882.

The SOLOMON LIGHTFOOT MICHAUX TEMPLE, SW. corner Jefferson Ave. and 19th St., a blue-painted brick building, is the headquarters of Elder Michaux, Negro evangelist, who once sold fish on the streets of Newport News. By sharp business acumen, particularly in becoming chief local purveyor of fish to the United States Navy during the World War, he accumulated a fortune, which he expends liberally in charity to black and white unfortunates. He has large congregations in New York, Philadelphia, and Washington, besides local followers, who meet most often on the shore at the foot of Jefferson Avenue in an open-air tabernacle seating 5,000.

The SITE OF CEELEY'S, 225 Chesapeake Ave., is occupied by a residence. First the home of Thomas Ceeley, it was later the plantation seat of the Cary family. Thomas Ceeley, the younger, a burgess from Warwick Plantation in 1629 and from Warwick County in 1639, sold the property to William Wilson, from whom it passed with his daughter's hand to Miles Cary and to Miles's son, Wilson Miles Cary. George Washington is supposed to have courted one of Wilson Miles Cary's daughters until he was discouraged by her father. Considering young George too poor a match,

Mr.Cary is reported to have told him rather haughtily that she had a coach of her own to drive.

The VIRGINIA STATE SCHOOL FOR COLORED DEAF AND BLIND CHILDREN, NW. end of Pear (Sampson) Ave., occupies a group of seven brick buildings on spacious grounds, including on its 140 acres a farm, workshops, and an infirmary. It was founded in 1906 through the efforts of William C. Ritter, himself deaf, who was superintendent until 1937. Opened in 1908 with 25 children, the school had an enrollment of 100 in 1937 with 9 instructors. The ratio of blind to deaf is about 40–60. Training is provided in farming, arts, crafts and trades, and in the 'three R's.' There is also a creditable school orchestra.

The NEWPORT NEWS HOMESTEADS, around the intersection of Aberdeen and Newmarket Rds., is a model community built by the Farm Security Administration to provide low-cost housing for Negro industrial workers. Seventy-nine double houses are scattered over a 436-acre tract of rich trucking land well drained and planted with trees. The 158 semidetached units, on half-acre lots providing garden space, are constructed of red brick, and are connected by double garages. They range in size from three to five rooms and are uniform in design except for minor variations. They rent from $11.50 to $18 per month, and, after their first year of occupancy, are offered to renters for sale upon payments spread over 40 years. A large brick community house, including an auditorium and school rooms, provides a center for recreation and education. A guidance and supervisory program includes instruction in vegetable gardening and in living under modern conditions. Except for architectural design, the project has been carried out entirely by Negroes.

POINTS OF INTEREST IN ENVIRONS

Mariner's Museum, 5.3 *m.*; James River Country Club and Golf Museum, 7.1 *m.*; Old Point Comfort and Fort Monroe, 9.8 *m.*; Buckroe Beach, 10.5 *m.* (*see Tour* 8*a*).

Lynchburg

Railroad Stations: Southern Station, Kemper St. off Park Ave., for Southern Ry.; Union Station, foot of 9th St., for Chesapeake and Ohio Ry. and Norfolk & Western Ry.
Bus Stations: 5th and Church Sts. for Atlantic Greyhound Bus Line; 212 8th St. for Virginia Stage Line.
Taxis: Fare 25¢ within city limits, 10¢ each additional passenger.
Streetcars and Local Busses: Fare 7¢, 4 tokens for 25¢.
Traffic Regulations: No U-turns in business district, one-hour parking limit 7 a.m.–7 p.m., no parking 2–7 a.m.

Accommodations: 6 hotels, including 2 for Negroes; tourist places.

Information Service: Chamber of Commerce, 203–10 Lynch Bldg., 9th and Main Sts.; A.A.A., Virginia Hotel, 8th and Church Sts.

Theater and Motion Picture Houses: Little Theater, 420 Rivermont Ave.; 5 motion picture houses, including 1 for Negroes.
Golf: Oakwood Country Club, Rivermont Ave.–Boonsboro Rd. at Peakland Pl., 18 holes, greens fee 75¢, Sat., Sun., and holidays, $1; Boonsboro Country Club, 4.2 m. NW. on US 501, 18 holes, greens fee $1.
Swimming: Miller Park and Riverside Park, daily fee 10¢; Guggenheimer Playground, 1900 block of Grace St., fee 10¢; Oakwood Country Club, Rivermont Ave.–Boonsboro Rd. at Peakland Pl., fee 55¢.
Tennis: Oakwood Country Club, Rivermont Ave.–Boonsboro Rd. at Peakland Pl., fee 55¢; Guggenheimer Playground, 1900 block of Grace St.; Miller Park, Park Ave. between Memorial and Fort Aves.

Annual Events: Tri-County Fair, Sept.

LYNCHBURG (800 alt., 40,661 pop.), the largest market for dark tobacco in the South and one of the largest in the country, winds its hilly way along the banks of the James River and extends into the foothills of the Blue Ridge on the northwest.

Through its steep streets pass the tracks of the Southern Railway and the Norfolk and Western Railway. The Chesapeake and Ohio Railway, however, clings to the edge of the river, where vestiges of the Kanawha Canal still form part of the city's boundaries. Above the bluffs along the river a wide residential section follows meandering streets and roads. Separated from it by an unpopulated, hilly region, another series of neat, small houses rambles southwestward beyond 'downtown's' industrial belt. Slum sections turn up unexpectedly around the corner from tree-lined avenues. Bridges for trains and automobiles cross into the countryside to the northeast, and in the river are two slender islands. The principal Negro district follows Blackwater Creek up from the river.

Lynchburg industry employs about 8,000 workers, who are paid annually more than $8,000,000. Tobacco gave the city birth, brought it up, and still contributes to its support. Nearly 8,000,000 pounds of tobacco are marketed here annually. Lynchburg shoe factories, fourth in National importance, have an annual pay roll of $3,000,000. Other industries include the world's largest tannin extract plant, foundries, an overall factory, and lumber, paper, flour, cotton, silk, and hosiery mills.

Seventeen-year-old John Lynch established a ferry here in 1757, supplanting a difficult ford, and dwellings were built on the navigable river near his ferry house. John Lynch was the son of Charles Lynch, an Irishman who served his indentureship in Louisa County, where in 1733 he married Sarah Clark, ardent Quakeress and daughter of his master. Somewhat later he patented land near the present Lynchburg and lived at a house named Chestnut Hill.

Tobacco was early the economic stimulus of this largely Quaker community. Before 1786, when the general assembly authorized a town on his land, John Lynch had built the first tobacco warehouse north of the river on the bluff above his ferry. Tobacco in hogsheads was 'rolled' in from the surrounding fields and let down by ropes from the warehouse to bateaux on the river below, and this point became a trade center for dark tobacco—a coarse-leaf variety used as chewing and pipe tobacco and for the making of cigars. The first warehouse on the south bank was built in 1791, and four more warehouses were added between 1800 and 1805. The village was incorporated as a town in the latter year.

Strict attention to quality at that time made the town the world center for dark leaf tobacco. Stemming was begun here in 1804 by Charles Johnson, and tobacco inspectorship was established in 1806. The partners Hare and Labby (L'Abbé) were the first to use licorice in the treatment of tobacco.

Before the days of canal and railroads, fleets of bateaux bore tobacco down to Richmond. Three husky slaves manned each bateau. From planked gunwales the two strongest propelled it with long iron-shod poles, and the third used a large oar as rudder. They were furnished with 60 pounds of meat and two bushels of meal for the trip and helped themselves to potatoes, corn, and tobacco from the down cargoes and to salt, sugar, molasses, and whisky from return cargoes. Poling demanded a high degree of strength, courage, and skill, and the Negroes took great pride in their job.

In 1829, when the population of the town was 4,630, a visitor recorded that 500 bateaux left the wharves of Lynchburg and described the place as a bustling business center with an incredible number of stores and 15 tobacco factories.

A curious figure of this period was Colonel Augustine Leftwich, born in Bedford, England, in 1794, who came here at 18 and made a fortune in tobacco. In summer he would stroll to his factory like an Indian nabob, dressed in spotless white linen with a slave behind him holding aloft a great green umbrella.

The James River and Kanawha Canal reached Lynchburg from Richmond in 1840. In 1852, when the population was more than 8,000, Lynchburg received its city charter, and that year the first train steamed in.

During the War between the States the city was an important Confederate supply base, with hospitals and an arsenal.

By 1870, when the community began to rise out of postwar depression, railroads were almost the exclusive carriers of industrial products. Former industries were continued; new ones were founded, including the manufacture of shoes, started in 1870. John W. Carroll the same year started the manufacture of 'Lone Jack' and 'Brown Dick,' widely known smoking and chewing tobaccos. A great gambler down on his luck, Carroll drew a 'lone jack,' which, with the three others he held, won a pot of more than $5,000 and the chance to recoup his fortunes. In 1882 James A. Bonsack revolutionized the tobacco industry by inventing a cigarette making machine. In 1886 more than 30,000,000 pounds of tobacco were marketed from Lynchburg. Soon thereafter other industries were established. At the close of the century the city had survived a depression that followed the boom and had increased its population to 19,709.

In 1883 Theodore Presser founded *The Étude*, a publication for music teachers and pianists; Randolph-Macon Woman's College was opened in 1893; the Art Club was organized in 1896 and revived in 1925, and the Civic Art League was established in 1932 by Bernard Gutmann; in 1912 Mrs.John H. Lewis organized the Equal Suffrage League; and the Little Theater came into being in 1920.

Lynchburg is the home of Carter Glass, United States senator, former Secretary of the Treasury, and author of the Federal Reserve Act.

POINTS OF INTEREST

1. The CITY COURTHOUSE (*open 9–5 Mon.–Fri., 9–1 Sat.*), 9th and Court Sts., is a white stuccoed brick building of Greek Revival architecture. The dome that rises from the center of the gabled roof suggests the Roman tradition, but the four-columned portico is Greek. Completed in 1855, the courthouse was designed by W.S.Ellison, Philadelphia architect, and succeeds a frame building erected in 1812. The site was donated to the city by John Lynch,Sr., with the stipulation that it revert to his heirs if used for any other purpose.

2. MONUMENT TERRACE, continuation of 9th St. between Church and Court Sts., designed by Aubrey Chesterman of Lynchburg and dedicated in 1928, is a granite and limestone stairway with 13 landings, ascending a steep, 70-foot hill between terraced lawns. At the top is a bronze STATUE OF A CONFEDERATE INFANTRYMAN with bayonet fixed, designed by James O. Scott of Lynchburg and erected in 1898. The flight of steps, with Italianate balustrades, gives access to small buildings that cling to the hillside. At the bottom is a bronze STATUE OF A DOUGHBOY, designed by Charles W. Keck of New York and erected in memory of the 47 Lynchburg soldiers killed in the World War.

3. LYNCHBURG BOULDER, E. end of 9th St., a rounded, smoke-grimed, quartz boulder about five feet high, on a small grass plot among intersecting railroad tracks, marks the spot where John Lynch built his ferry house in 1757.

4. TOBACCO WAREHOUSES (*open by arrangement*), Commerce St. between 10th and 13th Sts., are cavernous brick and frame buildings where tobacco has been marketed since 1791. In a new building at Commerce and 10th Streets are incorporated part of the walls of Springhill, the first warehouse in present Lynchburg. The three largest warehouses in Lynchburg are now MARTINS, SE. corner 10th and W.Commerce Sts., built in 1806; FARMERS, SE. corner 13th and W.Commerce Sts.; and BOOKERS, SW. corner 13th and W.Commerce Sts. During the season about 2,500,000 pounds of tobacco are handled in each of these, but the biggest year was 1886, when 37,208,100 pounds were sold.

5. The OLDEST HOUSE IN LYNCHBURG (*private*), SW. corner Madison and 10th Sts., a red brick cottage, is said to have been built soon after John Lynch established his ferry (1757). Before it became a dwelling, it was used as a school.

6. The TERRELL-LANGHORNE HOUSE (*private*), SW. corner Jackson and 5th Sts., is a small red brick building erected about 1800 and now in disrepair. It was occupied first apparently by Dr.Edward Terrell, who returned to his farm at Rock Castle in 1803. His son, Dr.Christopher Terrell; grandson, Dr.John Terrell; and great-grandson, Dr.Alexander Terrell, practiced medicine in Lynchburg. 'Staunton' John Lynch, nephew of the city's founder, lived in this house. Mrs.John H. Lewis, a veteran fighter for social reform, aunt of Lady Astor and Mrs.Charles Dana Gibson, started housekeeping here.

7. The bronze STATUE OF JOHN WARWICK DANIEL, in the triangle bounded by 9th and Floyd Sts. and Park Ave., designed by Sir Moses Ezekiel and erected in 1913, represents Major Daniel (1842–1910) seated and holding a crutch. Affectionately dubbed 'the Lame Lion of Lynchburg,' he served in the Confederate army, and a wound at the Battle of the Wilderness made him a cripple. He was one of Virginia's foremost orators and was elected to the United States Senate for four consecutive terms.

8. The SITE OF OLD LYNCHBURG COLLEGE, Wise St. between 10th and 11th Sts., is occupied by two of the original Victorian Gothic gray stuccoed buildings, now residences, in which the first Methodist Protestant College in the South and the first college in Lynchburg once functioned. Founded by the faculty of Madison College, Uniontown, Pennsylvania, in 1855, it was moved to this site the next year. In February 1861 the college ceased to exist. The buildings were used as a Confederate hospital, and after the war as Federal barracks.

KEY FOR LYNCHBURG MAP

1.City Courthouse 2.Monument Terrace 3.Lynchburg Boulder 4.Tobacco Warehouses 5.Oldest House in Lynchburg 6.Terrell-Langhorne House 7.Statue of John Warwick Daniel 8.Site of Old Lynchburg College 9.Virginia Theological Seminary and College 10.Spring Hill Cemetery 11.Fort Early 12.Lynchburg College 13.Lynchburg Female Orphan Asylum 14.Point of Honor 15.Little Theater 16.Jones Memorial Library 17.Claytor-Miller House 18.Hull of the Packet Boat *Marshall* 19.Randolph-Macon Woman's College 20.Lynchburg Federal Art Gallery 21.Virginia Episcopal School

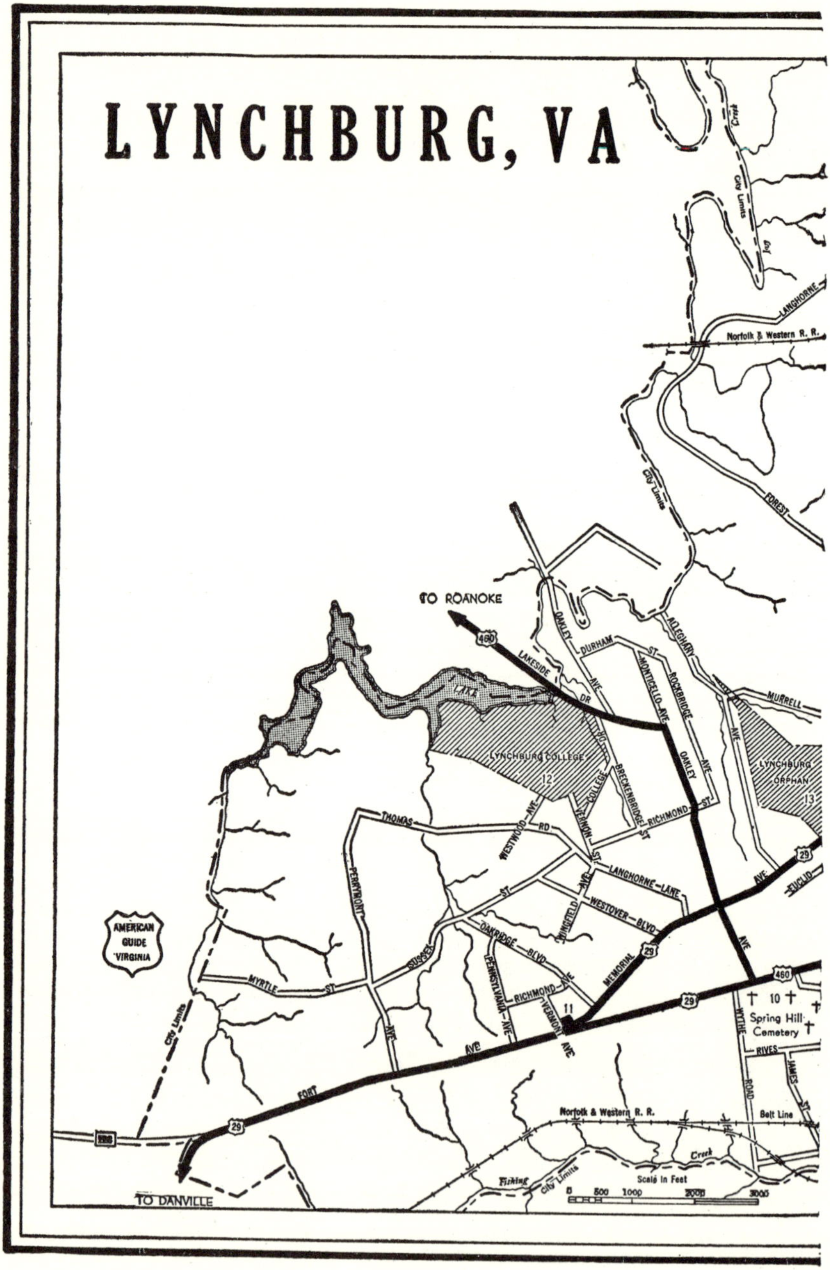
LYNCHBURG, VA
City Limits
Creek
LANGHORNE
Norfolk & Western R. R.
FOREST
TO ROANOKE
460
LAKESIDE
DR
OAKLEY
AVE
DURHAM
ST
MONTICELLO
ROCKBRIDGE
ALLEGHANY
MURRELL
LAKE
LYNCHBURG COLLEGE
12
LYNCHBURG
ORPHAN
13
BRECKENRIDGE
RICHMOND
THOMAS
RD
WESTWOOD
VERNON
COLLEGE
PERRYMONT
LANGHORNE LANE
WESTOVER BLVD
SPRINGFIELD
29
EUCLID
MEMORIAL
OAKRIDGE BLVD
SUSSEX
PENNSYLVANIA AVE
VERMONT AVE
MYRTLE ST
11
10
Spring Hill Cemetery
WYTHE
ROAD
RIVES
JAMES
AMERICAN GUIDE VIRGINIA
FORT
Belt Line
Fishing
Scale in Feet
0 500 1000 2000 3000
TO DANVILLE

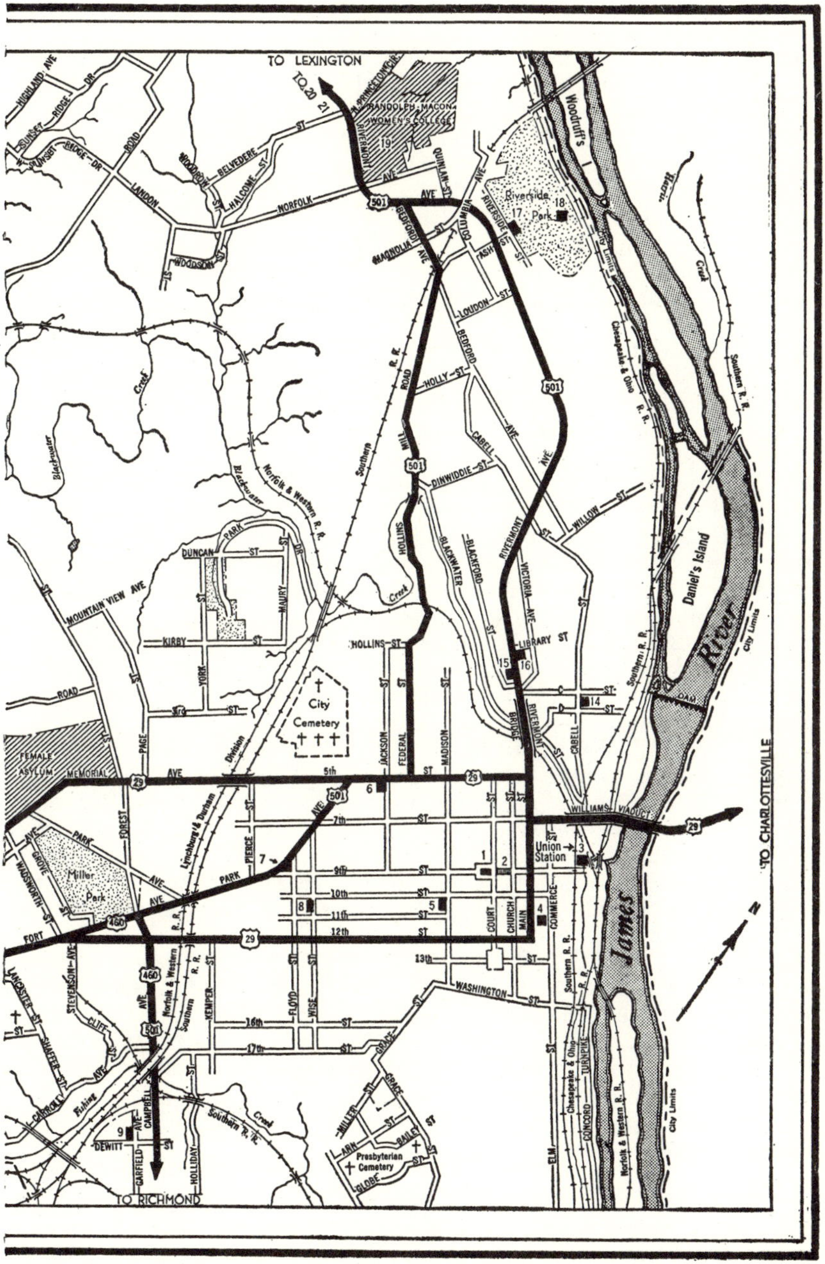
TO LEXINGTON
TO 20
21
RANDOLPH-MACON WOMEN'S COLLEGE
19
Riverside Park
17
18
Woodruff's
TO RICHMOND
TO CHARLOTTESVILLE
City Cemetery
Miller Park
FEMALE ASYLUM
Union Station
Daniel's Island
River
James
DAM
City Limits
Presbyterian Cemetery
WILLIAMS VIADUCT
MEMORIAL AVE
FORT AVE
PARK AVE
MOUNTAIN VIEW AVE
RIVERMONT AVE
BEDFORD AVE
MILL ROAD
Southern R.R.
Norfolk & Western R.R.
Chesapeake & Ohio R.R.
Linchburg & Durham R.R.
Blackwater Creek
5th ST
7th ST
9th ST
10th ST
11th ST
12th ST
13th
16th ST
17th ST
WASHINGTON ST
COMMERCE
MAIN
CHURCH
COURT
LIBRARY ST
HOLLINS ST
DINWIDDIE ST
HOLLY ST
LOUDON ST
NORFOLK AVE
CAMPBELL AVE
DEWITT ST
HOLLIDAY
ELM
CONCORD TURNPIKE
1
2
3
4
5
6
7
8
9
14
15
16

9. The VIRGINIA THEOLOGICAL SEMINARY AND COLLEGE (Negro), N.W. corner Garfield Ave. and Dewitt St., a Baptist institution occupying several gaunt brick buildings, was incorporated in 1888 'to prepare Christian preachers, teachers, and workers for work among the Negroes.' The college is coeducational and confers bachelor degrees in arts and sciences; the seminary confers the degree of bachelor of divinity. Of the 500 graduates, 150 are preachers and 25 are foreign missionaries. Enrollment in 1937–38 was 120.

10. SPRING HILL CEMETERY (*open daily*), Fort Ave. between Lancaster St. and Wythe Rd., is a 45-acre landscaped tract shaded by trees and surrounded by a high brick wall. The land was bought in 1853 by Bishop John Early and other citizens. When neighbors objected to the proximity of a graveyard, John Crouse, who sold the land, pleaded that he had not known the difference between a cemetery and a seminary. An injunction suit having failed, the first grave was dug in 1855; pall bearers and other mourners carried firearms.

Here are buried three Confederate generals—James Dearing (1840–65), Jubal A. Early (1816–95), and Thomas Taylor Munford (1831–1918)—Bishop Early (1786–1871), Senator John W. Daniel, and a child of General J.E.B.Stuart.

11. FORT EARLY (*open*), NE. corner Fort and Vermont Aves., entered through a semicircular stone archway, is a restored square earthwork built during the Lynchburg campaign. Confederate forces, commanded by General Jubal A. Early, repulsed General Hunter's attack here in June 1864. A CLUBHOUSE (*open by arrangement*), erected in 1922, is sheltered by the grass-covered breastworks. The EARLY MONUMENT, opposite the fort on a grassy triangle, is a tall granite obelisk erected in 1920. General Early lived in Lynchburg from 1869 until his death.

12. LYNCHBURG COLLEGE, NW. end of Vernon St., a coeducational institution controlled by the Christian Church, occupies a group of three modern brick buildings and the renovated WESTOVER BUILDING. The latter, a large, many-turreted frame structure, was the Westover Hotel when purchased in 1903. Virginia Christian College was chartered and classes began in the remodeled hotel in the same year. In 1919 it was rechartered as Lynchburg College. In 1937–38 it had a faculty of 30 and a student body of 250.

13. LYNCHBURG FEMALE ORPHAN ASYLUM (*open by arrangement*), 2400 block of Memorial Ave., known as Miller Orphans' Home, a four-story turreted building designed by General John Elliott in Victorian Gothic style and set in a 100-acre park, was opened in 1875. The institution cares for 65 white orphans under 18 years old and operates a day nursery for 20 children between the ages of two and eight. The grave of Samuel Miller, philanthropist who endowed the orphanage, is marked by a granite shaft.

14. POINT OF HONOR (*open 9–4 daily*), 112 Cabell St., is a plaster-covered brick mansion built in 1806 by Dr.George Cabell. The early Federal atmosphere of the interior is preserved in the lofty ceilings, the finely carved woodwork, the gracious sweeping stairway, and an elaborate

chandelier. This mansion, named according to local tradition by young William Lewis Cabell after the satisfactory culmination of a duel, was the birthplace of Mary Virginia Ellett Cabell (1839–1930), an organizer of the Daughters of the American Revolution. Lent to the city, Point of Honor is now a playground and manual training and recreational center for children.

15. LITTLE THEATER (*open by arrangement*), 420–22 Rivermont Ave., is the first theater erected and owned by a little theater league in Virginia. Built of gray concrete and brick, its auditorium seats 300. Two interior murals by the Lynchburg artist, Scaisbrook Abbott, depict tragedy from an early American melodrama and comedy from a scene in *Twelfth Night*. The Little Theater League was organized in 1921, and the present building was opened in 1930 with a production of Arnold Bennett's *Milestones*.

16. JONES MEMORIAL LIBRARY (*open 9–9 weekdays*), SE. corner Rivermont Ave. and Library St., above a series of lawn and stone terraces, is a cream-colored brick structure with classic gray stone trim and an entrance loggia adorned with six Ionic columns between anta walls. It was presented to the city by Mrs.George M. Jones and opened in 1908. The library contains nearly 55,000 volumes and has three branches, including one for Negroes.

17. The CLAYTOR–MILLER HOUSE (*not open*), in Riverside Park at Ash St. entrance, built about 1792–93 by John Miller, is a two-story white frame building with a steep gabled roof. About 1819 it was the home of Owen and Jane Hughes Owens, originators of the first circulating library in Lynchburg, who used part of their house as a school. Thomas Jefferson, while stopping here, is said to have demonstrated to one of the Owens children that the tomato was not a poisonous ornament but a luscious food. Sam Claytor owned the house about 1825. When it was about to be razed to make way for a new building, the Lynchburg Historical Society moved it from 8th and Church Streets to its present site.

18. The HULL OF THE PACKET BOAT *MARSHALL*, Riverside Park at Look Out Point, is all that remains of the canal boat on which the body of 'Stonewall' Jackson was carried to Lexington for burial.

19. RANDOLPH–MACON WOMAN'S COLLEGE, Rivermont Ave. between Norfolk Ave. and N.Princeton Circle, the first accredited college for women in Virginia, is housed in 16 red brick buildings, several in Neo-Gothic, the rest in Georgian Colonial styles. Surrounded by nearly 80 acres of lawns and groves, the buildings overlook the James River and command a distant view of the Blue Ridge Mountains. Scattered throughout the buildings are excellent examples of modern art, including paintings by George Bellows, William Chase, Gari Melchers, Childe Hassam, Jules Guerin, and John Carroll. Randolph-Macon Woman's College was opened in 1893, with Dr.William Waugh Smith as first president. A chapter of the Phi Beta Kappa Society, the first in an independent college for women in the South, was established here in 1917. The college confers the degree of bachelor of arts. In 1937–38 it had a faculty of 72 and an enrollment of 630. The LIBRARY (*open daily*), erected in 1929, contains about 45,000

volumes and a room in which a few valuable old books and manuscripts are displayed. Among outstanding alumnae of the college is Pearl Buck (Mrs.Richard J. Walsh), who as Pearl Sydenstricker was graduated in 1914.

20. The LYNCHBURG FEDERAL ART GALLERY (*open* 10–5 *Mon.–Fri.*, 3–5 *Sun.*), 1331 Oak Lane, Peakland, sponsored by the Lynchburg Art Alliance, was established in 1936. Classes in painting, modeling, and crafts are held for adults and children, besides extension classes for Negroes and whites.

21. The VIRGINIA EPISCOPAL SCHOOL, Williams Rd. and Virginia Episcopal School Rd., opened in 1916, is a boys' preparatory school housed in four large red brick buildings on 140 acres of grounds. The LANGHORNE MEMORIAL CHAPEL (*open*), a red brick building, was given by Chiswell Dabney Langhorne and his daughter, Lady Astor. In 1937–38 the school had a faculty of 11 and a student body of 117.

POINTS OF INTEREST IN ENVIRONS

Sandusky, 4.1 *m.*; Quaker Memorial Presbyterian Church, 4.2 *m.*; Sweetbriar College, 12.1 *m.* (*see Tour 4c*). Poplar Forest, 8 *m.* (*see Tour 11a*). Appomattox Courthouse, 23.6 *m.* (*see Tours 11b and 3d*).

Petersburg

Railroad Stations: 501 2nd St. for Atlantic Coast Line R.R. and Norfolk and Western Ry.; Dunlop and Appomattox Sts. for Seaboard Air Line Ry.
Bus Stations: 115 W.Washington St. for Greyhound Bus Line; 13 Sycamore St. for Carolina Coach Line; Wythe St. near Sycamore St. for Richmond-Petersburg Bus Line.
Taxis: Fare 25¢ within city limits, 35¢ across town, $1 per hour.
Local Busses: Fare 7¢.
Traffic Regulations: No U-turns in business district; 30-minute parking limits.

Accommodations: 7 hotels; tourist homes.

Information Service: Chamber of Commerce, 209 N.Sycamore St.; A.A.A., Hotel Petersburg, 16 W.Tabb St.

Motion Picture Houses: 8, including 3 for Negroes.
Golf: Country Club of Petersburg, Johnson Rd. at Lee Park, 9 holes, adm. by arrangement, greens fee $1; Municipal Golf Course, Lee Park, S.Boulevard and Johnson Rd., under construction (1939).
Swimming: Lee Park, S.Boulevard and Johnson Rd., open 9–7:30 weekdays, 1–7:30 Sun., May 15 to Sept. 15, fee, adults 10¢ a.m., 15¢ p.m., children 5¢ a.m., 10¢ p.m., suits 25¢ and 35¢.
Tennis: Lee Park, S.Boulevard and Johnson Rd., 9 courts, free; Country Club of Petersburg, Johnson Rd. at Lee Park, 4 courts, adm. by arrangement.

Annual Events: 'The Ninth of June,' Memorial Day observance; Southside Virginia Fair, 2nd week in Oct.; Virginia Amateur Field Trials, Camp Lee, Nov.

PETERSBURG (100 alt., 28,564 pop.) stretches southward under a mass of trees from the island-studded Appomattox River, spanned by two lofty vehicular bridges, to an undulating countryside where the fields are planted with tobacco and peanuts. Despite industrial encroachments the city retains a certain charm.

Along the short narrow streets of the downtown commercial section, survivals of the more remote past hold their own with false fronts of the late nineteenth century and with modern buildings. Within sight of a tangle of tracks surrounding the union depot is Petersburg's water front, a bottled-up arm of the Appomattox formed by a peninsula containing the old town of Pocahontas. Both sides of this estuary are lined with factories and wharves, and in the stream weather-beaten barges, generally loaded with lumber, pick their way among anchored pleasure craft.

Lengthy Sycamore Street mounts southward and crosses busy railroad tracks into a residential section. Past the deep landscaped ravine cut by Lieutenant Run the widened thoroughfare swerves through the fashionable suburb of Walnut Hills, wedged between former battlefields and Lee Memorial Park, Petersburg's summer playground. Just back of the river-front buildings lies a slum district, composed of white and Negro families, that finds counterparts in the sections bordering sinuous Halifax Street, midtown. At intervals, the brick hulks of enormous tobacco plants cling to the Atlantic Coast Line tracks that pass through the heart of the city. On industrial East Bank Street, peanut processing plants mingle with tobacco warehouses, while trunk and bag factories give a commercial air to the West End, pressed on the south by a park, the fair grounds, and Alms House Farm.

The city has its share of ancestor worshipers, counterbalanced by citizens looking toward personal and group achievement. The art of gracious living survives in clubs and homes, and old inhabitants retain Virginia idioms that have all but disappeared in many other parts of the State. People are still 'right much' interested in family trees, refer to kitchens as 'cook rooms,' and call relatives 'kinfolks.'

Although the Negroes of Petersburg, 44 per cent of the population, have developed an educated group, with a social and cultural life that centers about two educational institutions, the majority still live in crowded sections and gain their livelihood by menial and domestic work.

The beginning of Petersburg dates from 1645, when the general assembly directed that Fort Henry be built at the falls of the Appomattox River. The next year the assembly provided that the fort be given to Abraham Wood for three years, on condition that he keep ten men there for its protection. He established a trading post and cultivated friendly relations with Indians, who furnished guides and hunters. Thus reinforced, between 1650 and 1671 Wood undertook two journeys of exploration westward.

Peter Jones, who married Wood's daughter, succeeded his father-in-law as manager and proprietor of the trading post, which became known as Peter's Point. The settlement figured prominently in Bacon's Rebellion (1676), when unfriendly Indians were driven from the village.

William Byrd II in 1733 envisaged two cities, 'one . . . to be called Richmond, and the other at the Point of the Appamattuck River, to be nam'd Petersburgh.' The strategic position at the head of navigation indicated to him the future growth of Petersburg. As it is today, the city represents the amalgamation of Petersburg, laid out in 1748; Blandford, established the same year; Pocahontas, constituted a town in 1752; and Ravenscroft, a settlement that meanwhile had grown up on a triangle enclosed today by Halifax, Sycamore, and Shore Streets. These four were united and incorporated in 1784, and 'stiled the town of Petersburg.'

During the Revolutionary War the city was too important to be overlooked by the adversary. In 1781 General Benedict Arnold and General William Phillips, commanding 2,500 British troops, destroyed stores in Petersburg and pillaged the community despite the valiant efforts of General von Steuben and General Muhlenburg. British forces, augmented on May 20, 1781, by the army of Cornwallis, started from Petersburg four days later on the journey that ended at Yorktown.

For years before the Revolution and until the War between the States, a race track, a theater, many comfortable and merry taverns, and hospitable homes made Petersburg a popular stopping-place for travelers and a jolly center for long visits. When George Washington paused here on his southern tour (1791), he found, according to his diary, that Petersburg, containing 'near 3,000 souls,' received 'at the Inspections nearly a third of the Tobacco exported from the whole State besides a considerable quantity of wheat and flour.' He wrote also of telling a lie: 'Having suffered very much by the dust yesterday, and finding that parties of Horse, and a number of other Gentlemen were intending to attend me part of the way to day, I caused their enquiries respecting the time of my setting out, to be answered that, I should endeavor to do it before eight o'clock; but did it a little after five.' The mayor of Petersburg is said to have bestowed upon Washington during this visit the title 'father of his country.'

Across from the town of Petersburg, according to Thomas Anburey's *Travels in the Interior Parts of America* (1776–81), was 'a kind of suburb, independent of Petersburg, called Pocahunta . . . the principal trade of Petersburg arises from the exporting of tobacco, deposited in warehouses and magazines . . . up to which sloops, schooners, and small vessels continually sail.'

During the War of 1812 the territory furnished a company under Richard McRae, which distinguished itself at Fort Meigs. These soldiers, jauntily wearing cockades, gave President Madison occasion to call Petersburg the 'Cockade City,' a name that has held through the years. In Petersburg, John Daly Burk, Irish refugee, began his history of Virginia; Aaron Burr and his daughter, Theodosia, lived here in 1805; Winfield Scott started his brief law career; and the returning La Fayette was lavishly entertained here. Joseph Jenkins Roberts (1809–76), who migrated to Liberia in 1829, was born in Petersburg. The American Colonization Society appointed him in 1842 the first Negro governor of Liberia; when the country was proclaimed a republic in 1847, Roberts was elected the first president.

After 1812 Petersburg overshadowed Richmond in many respects. Theatrical companies, booked for Petersburg, went to Richmond incidentally. Disastrous fires occurred in 1815 and 1826. The first general conference of the Methodist Episcopal Church, South, meeting in Petersburg in 1846, made history through the organization of Southern Methodism. Four years later Petersburg achieved the status of city. The *Southern Star*, the first steamboat to reach Petersburg, was appropriately welcomed in 1858.

The War between the States ravaged the little city on the Appomattox. Though at first no battles were fought near by, Petersburg sent 17 companies to the front. In 1864 the city became the 'last ditch of the Confederacy.' Railroad lines through Petersburg constituted an artery of supply for Richmond and made the city a Federal objective. The long and terrible siege of Petersburg marked the downfall of the Confederacy. Here the South made its last stand against superior Federal forces. The fall of Petersburg led directly to the surrender at Appomattox.

The city made a new start after 1865. By 1880 there were 70 more industries than existed here 20 years earlier. Census tabulations of ensuing years showed steady gains. In 1888 a Negro, John Mercer Langston, born in Surry County in 1848, was elected to Congress from the Fourth Virginia

Congressional District. He had studied law in Ohio, had been minister to Haiti and president of the Virginia Normal and Collegiate Institute. Although his election was contested, and although he was not seated until two months before the expiration of his term, Langston holds the distinction of being the only Virginia Negro Congressman.

Modern Petersburg takes pride in its industries. Here some 4,000 wage earners are paid annually about $4,000,000. With a plug and twist tobacco factory, preparing annually 6,000,000 pounds for export; a large cigarette factory, making more than 4,000,000,000 cigarettes annually; two stemmeries and rehandling plants; and three auction warehouses employing 2,100 people, chiefly Negroes, whose annual wages are $1,200,000, Petersburg has earned an important position in the manufacture of tobacco. It boasts, in addition, a luggage factory that employs 1,500 people. Among other industries are pen and pencil plants, a silk mill, a pants and overall factory, a mill that makes napkins and tablecloths, three peanut factories, and plants that produce optical lenses, flour, woodwork, and furniture.

POINTS OF INTEREST

1. GOLDEN BALL TAVERN (*open*), SE. corner Grove Ave. and N.Market St., is an unpainted frame building with brick ends and dormers along its gabled roof. Now a lunch room, this tavern was built about 1750. From the time of its erection until 1825, its sign of a large golden ball was famous in Virginia. The tavern was host to Washington in 1791 and was popular with settlers and trappers. During the British occupation of Petersburg in 1781 the scarlet-coated officers had quarters here.

2. The OLD MARKET PLACE (*open daily*), bounded by Grove Ave., Rock St., River St., and Cockade Alley, is an octagonal red brick building with twin chimney pots at each angle and a roof extending over the sidewalks. It was erected in 1879 to supersede a simple frame building. The site for a public market was donated in 1805 by Robert Bolling. In its early days it was the only place where meats and vegetables could be sold. The building is now leased by operators of a grocery store and meat market.

3. The COURTHOUSE (*open* 8:30–5 *weekdays*, 8:30–1 *Sat.*), E. end of Courthouse Ave., facing N.Sycamore St., erected in 1835, is a brick building in Greek Revival style with a gray stucco finish. The wide portico has four fluted stone columns in free classical design. An ornate cupola with a clock is surmounted by a figure of Justice.

4. WEST HILL (*private*), E.Tabb St. between Monroe and Adams Sts., is a long frame house on a very high stuccoed-brick basement. Tall narrow dormers line the gabled roof, and within there is a fine Chippendale staircase. The house was built shortly after the Revolution by Robert Bolling and was the home of the family until the larger mansion, Center Hill, was erected. West Hill later housed the stewards of the Bolling estate.

5. CENTER HILL (*open by arrangement*), on a court off N. side Franklin St. between Jefferson and Adams Sts., is a two-story brick mansion of 30 rooms approached by a circular drive. The house has a low hip roof and wide columned verandas facing north and south. Built about 1825 and re-

modeled in 1850, Center Hill, which succeeded Bollingbrook Hill as the residence of the Bolling family, was noted during three-quarters of a century for entertainment on a grand scale. Following Lee's evacuation of Petersburg, Center Hill became the headquarters of the Federal Major General George L. Hartsuff. Lincoln made the quip while visiting here, 'General Grant seems to have attended sufficiently to the matter of rent.' The house has been acquired by the Government to be used as a museum and headquarters of the National Park Service.

6. EAST HILL is on a knoll between N. Jefferson St. and the Atlantic Coast Line tracks. This is the SITE OF BOLLINGBROOK, Colonial house of the Bollings. Erected by Major Robert Bolling about 1725, it was originally two separate buildings; the larger burned in 1855 and the smaller was razed in 1915. Twice headquarters of the British in 1781, it was bombarded by La Fayette. While Phillips and Arnold had headquarters here, Phillips died. From his deathbed he remarked querulously that the Americans would not even let him die in peace.

7. BLANDFORD CEMETERY (*open 9–5 daily*), E. side Crater Road at city limits, stretches placidly beneath large, ancient trees. The oldest stone, marking the grave of Richard Fairbrough, reads 1702. Veterans of six wars are buried here, including 30,000 Confederates killed in the Siege of Petersburg. Among the epitaphs are those of William Skipwith, Baronet and Cavalier, who fled Cromwell's wrath; of Herbert, plain squire and stout Roundhead; of the British commander, General Phillips; of John Daly Burk, Irish refugee and historian, who was killed in a duel; of the Corsican, Antommatti, who shot himself in the church, for unrequited love. A shaft commemorates Captain Richard McRae and his Petersburg Volunteers, who 'consecrated their valor at the Battle of Fort Meigs' in 1813.

The claim is made for Blandford, as for several other Virginia cemeteries, that here was the scene of the first Memorial Day ceremony. The story goes that Mrs. John A. Logan, wife of the commander of the Grand Army of the Republic, visited the cemetery in 1866 and spied Miss Nora Fontaine Davidson, a schoolteacher, and her pupils putting flowers and tiny Confederate flags on the soldiers' graves. Shortly afterward General Logan issued a proclamation for the observance of Memorial Day.

BLANDFORD CHURCH (*open 9–5 daily; key at office*), W. edge of cemetery, is a gabled T-shaped brick building, standing peacefully among trees draped, like itself, with ivy. The walls bear scars of bullets fired in 1864–65. The Colonial building—'the Brick Church of Bristol Parish'—is now a Confederate memorial chapel. Here among marble tablets erected to honor

---

KEY FOR PETERSBURG MAP

1. Golden Ball Tavern 2. Old Market Place 3. Courthouse 4. West Hill 5. Center Hill 6. East Hill 7. Blandford Cemetery 8. Central Park 9. The Lawn 10. Southern College 11. William R. McKenney Free Library 12. Wallace-Seward House 13. Municipal Market 14. Trapezium Place 15. Stirling Castle 16. Beasley House 17. Bishop Payne Divinity School 18. Battersea 19. Pride's Tavern 20. Mountain View 21. Virginia State College for Negroes

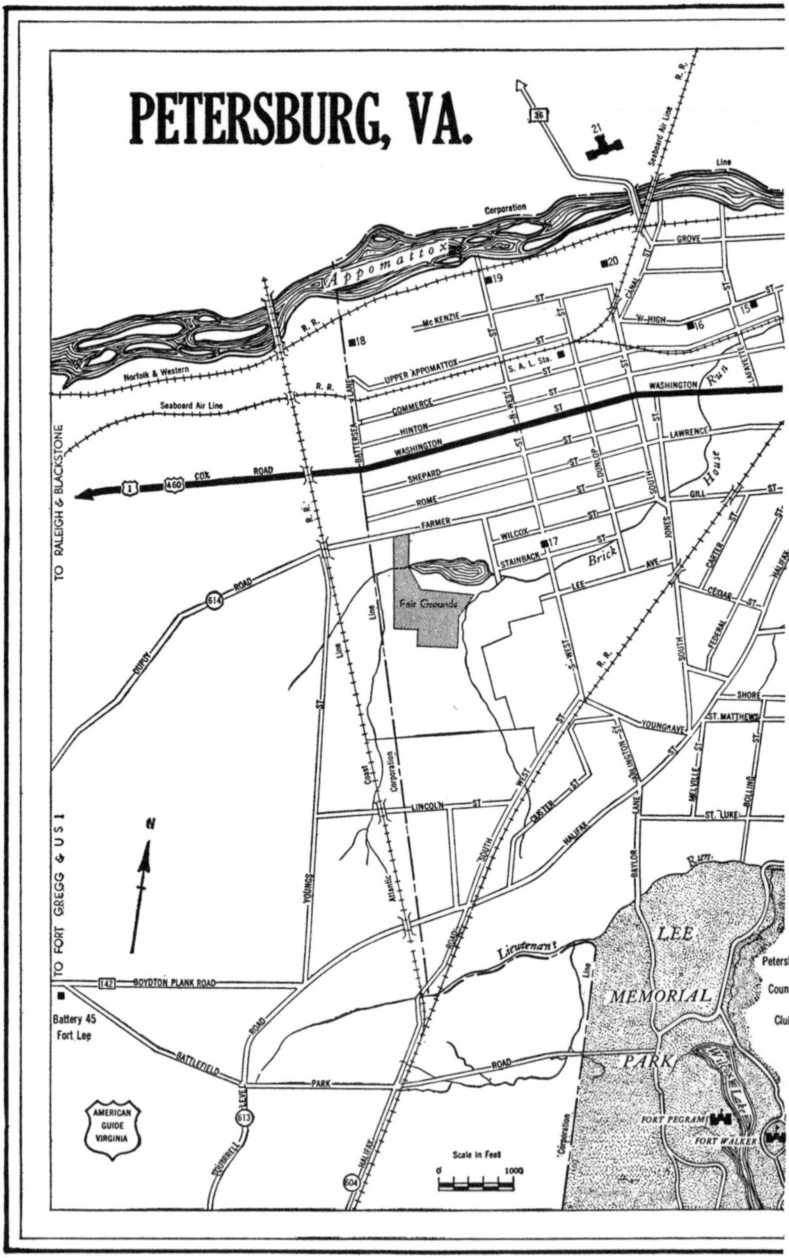
PETERSBURG, VA.
Appomattox
Corporation
Norfolk & Western
Seaboard Air Line
R. R.
TO RALEIGH & BLACKSTONE
TO FORT GREGG & U S 1
COX ROAD
WASHINGTON
LAWRENCE
GROVE
CANAL
HIGH
McKENZIE
UPPER APPOMATTOX
S. A. L. Sta.
COMMERCE
HINTON
SHEPARD
ROME
FARMER
WILCOX
STAINBACK
BATTERSEA LANE
N. WEST
DUNLOP
SOUTH
JONES
LAFAYETTE
GILL
Brick House Run
LEE
AVE
CARTER
CEDAR
HALIFAX
FEDERAL
SHORE
ST. MATTHEWS
YOUNG AVE
ARLINGTON
MELVILLE
BOLLING
ST. LUKE
Fair Grounds
DUPUY ROAD
Coast Line
Atlantic
Corporation Line
YOUNGS
LINCOLN ST
CUSTER
SOUTH WEST
BAYLOR LANE
Lieutenant Run
BOYDTON PLANK ROAD
Battery 45
Fort Lee
BATTLEFIELD
PARK
ROAD
LEE MEMORIAL PARK
Petersburg Country Club
FORT PEGRAM
FORT WALKER
Willcox Lake
AMERICAN GUIDE VIRGINIA
Scale in Feet
0
1000
SQUIRRELL LEVEL
N
1
460
614
142
613
604
36
15
16
17
18
19
20
21

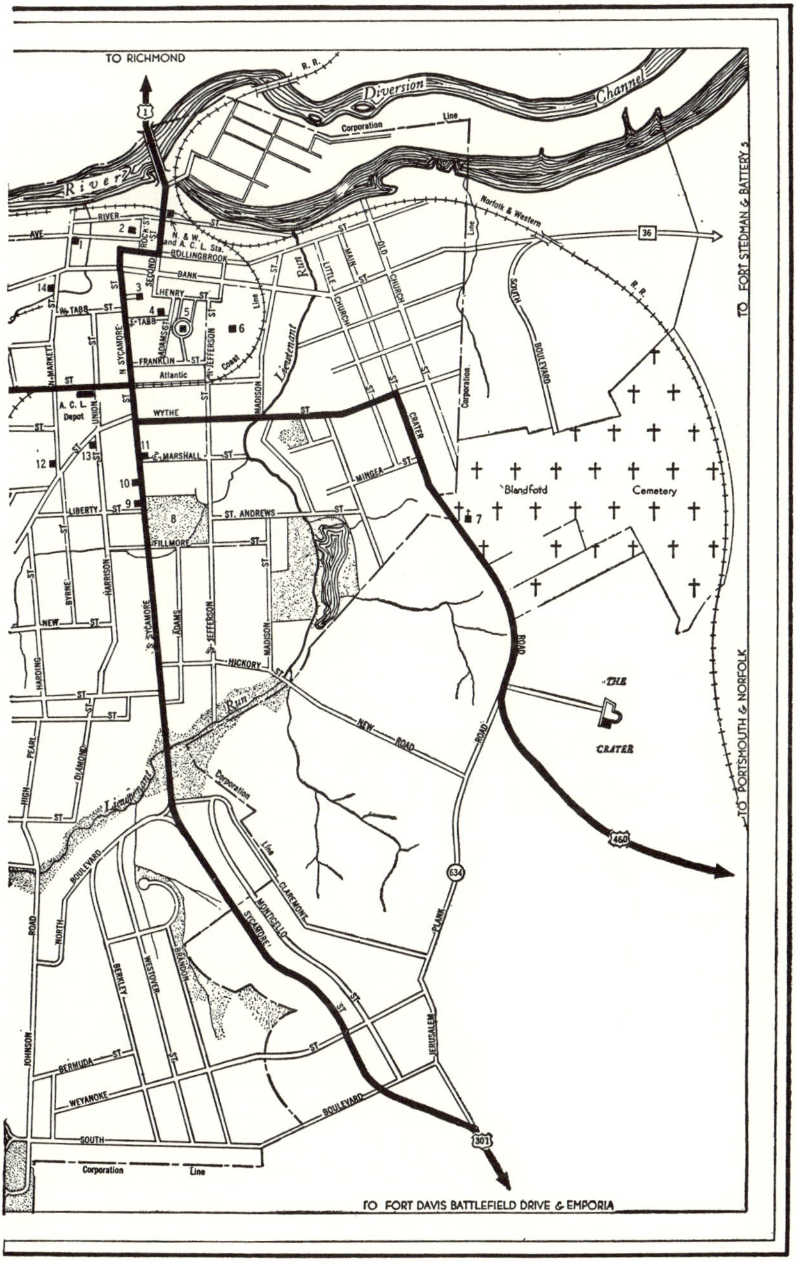
TO RICHMOND
R. R.
Diversion
Channel
Corporation
Line
River
Norfolk & Western
TO FORT STEDMAN & BATTERY 5
RIVER
ST
AVE
N. & W. and A. C. L. Sta.
BOLLINGBROOK
BANK
HENRY
ROCK ST
SECOND
W. TABB
E. TABB
ADAMS ST
N. JEFFERSON
FRANKLIN
Coast Line
Atlantic
N. MARKET
N. SYCAMORE
UNION
A. C. L. Depot
WYTHE
MADISON
Lieutenant
Run
LITTLE CHURCH
MAIN
OLD CHURCH
CRATER
SOUTH BOULEVARD
Corporation
MARSHALL
MINGEA
LIBERTY
ST. ANDREWS
FILLMORE
Blandford
Cemetery
BYRNE
HARRISON
NEW
S. SYCAMORE
ADAMS
S. JEFFERSON
HICKORY
HARDING
PEARL
HIGH
DIAMOND
NEW ROAD
ROAD
THE CRATER
TO PORTSMOUTH & NORFOLK
Corporation Line
CLAREMONT
MONTICELLO
SYCAMORE
NORTH BOULEVARD
BERKLEY
WESTOVER
BRANDON
PLANK
JERUSALEM
JOHNSON
ROAD
BERMUDA
WEYANOKE
SOUTH
BOULEVARD
Corporation Line
TO FORT DAVIS BATTLEFIELD DRIVE & EMPORIA

Revolutionary patriots and between memorial windows, one given by each Southern State, are inscriptions in bronze to commemorate incidents and personages of the 1860's. On a tablet is inscribed an elegy, written in 1841 and attributed to Tyrone Power I.

The church was first a rectangular structure, erected in 1735–37 on Wells' Hill. The long transept on the north side was begun in 1752 and completed in 1764. In 1757 a wall was built around the churchyard. When Petersburg was incorporated, the boundary was run so as to embrace the 'Church on Wellses Hill.' After St.Paul's Church was built in 1802–06, Blandford was abandoned. The Petersburg Ladies Memorial Association in 1901 restored it as the memorial chapel.

8. CENTRAL PARK, NE. corner S.Sycamore and E.Fillmore Sts., now shaded by lofty trees, was formerly a smooth green known as Poplar Lawn. Scene of demonstrations and open forum for distinguished orators, the site has served as race track, drill and mobilization ground, and was a hospital area during the siege of 1864–65. Here, mounted upon a stone base, is the POCAHONTAS BASIN, a roughly oblong piece of gray stone, hollowed out. In it, according to local legend, bathed the Indian princess.

9. The LAWN (*private*), 244 S.Sycamore St., a tall red brick house with ivy blanketing its walls and massive chimneys obscuring its gable ends, extends back among magnolias and boxwood bushes. It was erected about 1825 by George Bolling.

10. SOUTHERN COLLEGE (*open by arrangement*), 220 S.Sycamore St., occupying several gray buildings of brick and frame construction, was granted a charter in 1863, a year after its founding by William Thomas Davis, and was first called Southern Female College. The land it occupies was part of the settlement of Ravenscroft.

11. The WILLIAM R. McKENNEY FREE LIBRARY (*open 9–9 Mon., Wed., Fri.; 9–6 Tues., Thurs., Sat.*), NE. corner S.Sycamore and E.Marshall Sts., formerly a residence, is a two-story building of stuccoed brick. The mid-nineteenth-century house was built by John Dodson, then mayor of Petersburg, and was later the home of General William Mahone. The library contains about 30,000 volumes; Virginiana, including Nimo's Notes; and a small museum.

12. The WALLACE-SEWARD HOUSE (*private*), 204 S.Market St., a red brick house with a high front porch supported by iron columns, was built in 1855 by Thomas Wallace and described at the time as 'a costly, well designed, and handsome residence.' For a few hours following the evacuation of Petersburg the abandoned building was occupied as headquarters by General Grant. On the porch Grant discussed with President Lincoln, just arrived from City Point, the terms of the expected surrender of General Lee.

13. The MUNICIPAL MARKET, on the triangle formed by Halifax and Harrison Sts. and South Ave., is a large brick building erected in the third quarter of the nineteenth century. In stalls within the building are sold all manner of meats, fruits, and vegetables, shipped from afar or brought by farmers from neighboring counties. On the sidewalks are vendors' stands, tempting purchasers with bright flowers and fresh vegetables.

14. TRAPEZIUM PLACE (*open by arrangement*), 244 N.Market St., is a three-story red brick house with no right-angled corners and no parallel walls. This architectural curiosity was erected in 1815 by an eccentric Irishman, Charles O'Hara. He followed, it seems, the plans of a West Indian servant, who claimed that the peculiar construction of the house would ward off evil spirits. For years the place was known as 'Rat Castle,' because of the pet rats O'Hara kept. He is believed to have served in the British army, and his habit of appearing on the Queen's birthday, dressed in a uniform, earned him the title of 'General.'

15. STIRLING CASTLE (*private*), 320 W.High St., a two-story white frame house on a red brick foundation, has a square portico with fluted Ionic columns. Neat servants' quarters stand in the rear. The house was built in 1735 by Peter Jones III on a site eight miles from present Petersburg. After Jones's death the 'wooden castle' was rebuilt in the newly established town.

16. The BEASLEY HOUSE (*open by arrangement*), 558 W.High St., is a two-story frame building, mildly mid-Victorian. From November 1–28, 1864, General Lee had headquarters here. A small weatherboard building in the yard was used as Lee's office.

17. The BISHOP PAYNE DIVINITY SCHOOL (*open by arrangement*), S.West St. between Wilcox and Stainback Sts., occupies two brick and two frame buildings. Organized in 1884, it has (1939) four full-time professors and 13 students. It is the only seminary in the United States for Negro clergymen of the Protestant Episcopal Church and has trained two-thirds of the Negro ministers of that denomination.

18. BATTERSEA (*private*), N. end of Battersea Lane, in spite of shabbiness, can still be described in the words of the visiting Marquis de Chastellux (1781): 'The house is decorated in the Italian rather than the British or American style, having three porticoes at the three principal entrances, each of them supported by four columns.' The house consists of a hip-roofed main part extended by passage-linked wings. The interior woodwork, including a Chippendale stairway, is exceptionally fine. Prior to the Revolution Battersea was built by Colonel John Banister, first mayor of Petersburg. Because of his active participation in the patriotic movement, Banister seems to have been 'a particular object of spite to the British,' who visited his home in 1781, destroyed his furniture, and mutilated the house.

19. PRIDE'S TAVERN (*closed for restoration*, 1939), N.West St. near Norfolk & Western R.R. tracks, is a group of red brick buildings dating from the Revolutionary period. Long offering travelers the comfort for which Petersburg 'ordinaries' were renowned, it was a meeting place for wealth and fashion, especially while Pride's Race Track operated near by.

20. MOUNTAIN VIEW (*private*), McKenzie St. opposite N. end South St., a red brick residence, stands on what is believed to be the site of Fort Henry. It is claimed that fragments of the fort are incorporated in the house and that the low stone building at one end of the lot was the home of Captain John Flood, first commander of the fort. Mountain View was owned in 1830 by Dr.Donald McKenzie, president of the early Peters-

burg Railway Company. During the War between the States General Henry A. Wise had headquarters here; later the Federal commander, Lloyd Collins, occupied the house.

21. VIRGINIA STATE COLLEGE FOR NEGROES, N. end of Campbell's Bridge, covers 300 elevated acres above the Appomattox River. On the campus of 37 acres are 31 brick buildings; the rest of the land is an experimental farm. Established in 1882 as the Virginia Normal and Collegiate Institute, it was created largely through the activities of public-spirited Negroes, particularly A.W.Harris, of Petersburg, who introduced the bill to establish the institution. Inadequate State support long retarded its progress. In 1902 the name was changed to Virginia Normal and Industrial Institute, and in 1920 the institute was made the Negro land-grant college of Virginia. The college has steadily increased its enrollment and the standard of its 23 courses of instruction, which include liberal arts, agriculture, manual crafts, and a department of education. In 1930 the name of the institution was changed by the legislature. Enrollment in 1937–38 was 1,005, of which 576 were women.

POINTS OF INTEREST IN ENVIRONS

Turnbull House, 3 *m.* (*see Tour* 1c). Federal Tunnels and Museum, 2.5 *m.*; Fort Davis, 3.1 *m.* (*see Tour* 14). The Crater, 2.6 *m.*; Petersburg National Military Park, 3.3 *m.* (*see Tour* 18).

Richmond

Railroad Stations: Main Street Station, 15th and Main Sts., for Chesapeake and Ohio Ry. and Seaboard Air Line Ry.; Broad Street Station, Broad St. between Davis Ave. and Robinson St. for Atlantic Coast Line R.R., Norfolk & Western Ry., and Richmond, Fredericksburg & Potomac R.R.; Hull Street Station, 2nd and Hull Sts., for Southern Ry.
Bus Stations: Union Bus Depot, 412 E.Broad St., for Atlantic Greyhound, James River Bus Line, Richmond Greyhound, and Peninsula Transit Corp. Line; Richmond Bus Center, 9th and Broad Sts., for Carolina Coach Co., Richmond-Ashland Bus, and Virginia Stage Lines.
Airport: Richard Evelyn Byrd Flying Field, 4.3 m. E. of city limits on side road (L) off Charles City Rd. (R) off US 60, for Eastern Air Lines; taxi $1.50.
Taxis: Fare 35¢ within city limits.
Pier: S. end 32nd St., Fulton, East Richmond, for Buxton Lines to Norfolk (and James River landings); excursions down river in warm season on *Robert E. Lee*.
Streetcars and Local Busses: Fare 7¢ on streetcars, 7¢ and 8¢ on busses.
Traffic Regulations: No U-turns in congested district, speed limit 25 m.p.h., in business district 15 m.p.h.

Accommodations: 16 hotels, including 2 for Negroes; tourist homes.

Information Service: Chamber of Commerce, State Planters Bank Bldg., 9th and Main Sts.; *Richmond News Leader*, 110 N.4th St.; State Chamber of Commerce, 111 N.5th St.; Auto Club of Virginia, 111 N.5th St.

Radio Stations: WRTD (1500 kc.), WMBG (1350 kc.), WRVA (1110 kc.), WRNL (880 kc.).
Theaters and Motion Picture Houses: Lyric Theater, 9th and Broad Sts.; The Mosque (auditorium), Main and Laurel Sts.; City Auditorium, Cary and Linden Sts.; 26 motion picture houses, including 6 for Negroes.
Baseball: Tate Field, Mayo Island, S. end of 14th St., Richmond 'Colts' of Piedmont League.
Golf: Laurel Golf Club, 5.2 m. W. of city limits on US 33, 18 holes, greens fees 35¢ for 9, 75¢ for 18 holes Mon.–Fri., 65¢ and $1 Sat., Sun., and holidays; Glenwood Golf Club, 0.5 m. NE. of city limits on Creighton Rd. (L), off State 33, 18 holes, greens fees 50¢ for 9, 75¢ for 18 holes Mon.–Fri., 65¢ and $1 Sat., Sun., and holidays; Chesterfield Golf Club, 4.8 m. SW. of city limits off County 681 (R), off County 679 (L), off State 147 (L), 9 holes, greens fees 50¢ Mon.–Fri., 75¢ Sat., Sun., and holidays.
Swimming: Shields Lake, Byrd Park, S. end of Boulevard at Idlewood Ave., open summer months, free; Negro pool, Sledd and High Sts. and Old Chamberlayne Ave., open summer months, free.
Tennis: Powhatan Hill, Williamsburg Rd. and Northampton Ave., 3 courts; Hotchkiss Field, 700 Brookland Park Blvd., 6 courts; William Byrd Park, Boulevard and Idlewood Ave., 12 courts; Carter Jones Park, 28th and Bainbridge Sts., 6 courts; Luck's Field, Rogers and T Sts., 4 courts; Oakwood, 31st and Kuhn Sts., 4 courts for Negroes; all open daylight hours, free.
Skeet: Richmond Skeet Club, 3.8 m. W. of city limits off US 250 (L).

Annual Events: Deep Run Hunt Race Meet, Curles Neck Farm, early Apr.; Garden Club Week, Apr. or May; Virginia Kennel Club Show, Apr. or May; National Motorcycle Races and Hill Climb, May; Deep Run Horse Show, Broad Street Rd., May; Virginia State Fair, Boulevard and Hermitage Rd., late Sept. or Oct.

RICHMOND (115 alt., 182,929 pop.), capital of Virginia, at the head of navigation on the James, has spread from its seven hills to include a vast territory along the rocky course of the river and across rolling country to the north and south. The westward trend of population left old Richmond forlorn and deserted, and caused a new city to be built and old houses to be razed in order that the uses of business might be served. So today the former capital of the Confederacy has the appearance of a modern city with a residential section reaching toward fashionable suburbs and slum areas, with retail streets and factory districts progressive and far from distinctive. Parks and playgrounds provide the city with a decorative fringe.

From Church Hill, the heart of old Richmond, six long streets extend to the west end of the city, where they open fanwise to include many shorter streets. Handsome residences and apartment houses extend from Monroe Park to the city limits and southward on the Boulevard. Across the river South Richmond, formerly Manchester but now a part of the city and connected with the north side by four highway and four railroad bridges, retains its business districts and separate community life. Suburban areas extend westward along both sides of the river and northward across rolling terrain.

The largest Negro district spreads in a southeasterly direction from Union University through a section known as Jackson Ward, although it is no longer a political subdivision. This is largely a district of squalid houses, but along Marshall and Clay Streets, once outside of the ward but now a part of it, are many fine old residences occupied by well-to-do Negro families.

The principal retail district is concentrated on Broad, Grace, and Franklin Streets between 1st and 9th Streets. The financial district is on Main Street between 7th and 12th Streets; and, for many blocks east of 10th Street, Cary Street is given over to commission merchants and manufacturers of tobacco.

In the river near by, Belle Isle—the site of a Confederate prison and now occupied by an iron mill—Mayo's Island, and numerous smaller islands and jutting boulders block navigation beyond the intermediate turning basin near Nicholson Street. A combined Federal and city outlay of $5,690,000 has provided three cut-off canals and a river channel 25 feet deep and 300 feet wide. Richmond is a United States Customs Port of Entry, and handles annually some 2,000,000 tons with a valuation in excess of $90,000,000.

The beauty of an earlier day survives on Capitol Square in a few buildings that have escaped the wreckers' tools—and in the memory of old Richmonders. Despite the inroads of progress, the city has inexplicably retained its atmosphere. Although outwardly its traditional exclusiveness no longer exists, Richmond still has its inner circle. But there is a paradox in the liberal attitude of old Richmonders. Social discriminations have not precluded social justice. From old circles have come leaders who are intent upon bringing about better civic conditions, and who work with people of all races, creeds, and previous conditions.

Richmond's Negro population, constituting nearly one-third of the whole, is made up chiefly of laborers and domestics, though a fairly stable business and professional class is developing with the aid of rapidly improving educational facilities. Negro men and women prominent in business and the professions have found sincere co-operation among 'the best white people.' Negroes operate a hospital, two successful insurance companies, a bank, a Y.M.C.A., and a Y.W.C.A.

The city's social season, from late fall to Ash Wednesday, retains its old ritual, with the Monday germans as highlights. Tea in darkened drawing rooms, dinners served by tradition-trained butlers, frosted mint juleps in ancient goblets, and Smithfield ham and beaten biscuits are part of the ceremonial that has continued with no deviation. It is still proper in old Richmond to refer to a guest as So-and-So's granddaughter or the descendant of a founding father. The very broad *a* and the added *y* are indispensable to good breeding. Guests come by street and motor *cyar* to have tea in the *gyarden* at *hälf päst* five, and no *tomātoes* are served in Richmond.

The city pursues culture through groups that promote the arts by cultivating creative and appreciative faculties and through clubs that dwell upon Richmond's contribution to history. On Capitol Square and in hotels close by the political pot is continually boiling. Yet citizens of Richmond take only mild interest in government affairs and pay small attention to legislators who congregate biennially for sessions of the general assembly.

The industries of Richmond are diversified. Annual sales of manufacturers reach $250,000,000, and the capital investment in 300 manufacturing enterprises is $97,690,000. More than 2,600 retail stores and 413 wholesale houses bring the annual pay roll to $61,000,000. The city has one of the largest fertilizer plants and one of the largest cigar factories in the world, several book manufacturing and paper plants, and a flour mill with a capacity of 600,000 barrels a year. As the seat of the Fifth Federal Reserve Bank, Richmond is the financial center of five States and the District of Columbia. Tobacco, however, is the staple product. Downtown Richmond is fragrant with the odor of the cured leaves being converted into cigars, cigarettes, and smoking and chewing tobacco. The city has its own water and gas companies and a municipally-owned plant generates electricity for lighting streets and public buildings.

A week after the English landed at Jamestown in 1607, Captain Christopher Newport set out to explore the James River. On the '27th daye of May,' coming upon some falls, the party set up a cross on a small island near the foot of the present 9th Street. Two years later, sent by John Smith, Captain Francis West purchased a site at the falls from the Indians and erected a fort that he called Fort West. After trouble with the Indians the settlement was abandoned. In 1610 Lord Delaware led an expedition to the falls, vainly sought minerals, and returned to Jamestown. In 1637 Thomas Stegg established a trading post at the head of navigation on the James and was later granted lands about the falls. His son, Thomas Stegg II, who had acquired property on both sides of the river, in 1670 left his holdings to William Byrd I, a nephew, then only 18.

After the massacre of 1644 the settlers established Fort Charles at the head of navigation and offered freedom from taxation to anyone who would establish a home near by. Young Nathaniel Bacon had taken up land near the falls. In this neighborhood the Susquehannock incited other Indians to the depredations that precipitated Bacon's Rebellion in 1676. The settlement at Fort Charles, encouraged by 'certain privileges' granted William Byrd I for inducing able-bodied men to live there as a defense against the Indians, became a trading post for furs, tobacco, and other commodities and was known as Byrd's Warehouse or Shocco.

In 1733 William Byrd II 'laid the foundation of two Citys': Petersburg and Richmond. Colonel Byrd combined truth with prophecy when he wrote: '. . . these two places being the uppermost Landing of James and Appamattux Rivers, are naturally intended for Marts, where the Traffick of the Outer Inhabitants must Center.' Four years later Major William Mayo plotted on what is now Church Hill 32 squares for Richmond 'with Streets 65 Feet wide,' and named the place after Richmond on the Thames. In 1742, when the population was 250, the general assembly enacted that the 'piece or parcel of land . . . at the falls of the James River . . . be . . . constituted . . . a town.' Ten years later, the assembly appointed nine trustees 'to lay off and regulate the streets and to settle the bounds of the lots in the said town.' In 1769 William Byrd III 'laid out another parcel of his lands, on the north side of the James river . . . at a place called Shoccoes.' That year, moreover, a town later called Manchester was established at Rocky Ridge on the south side of the river.

During the next two decades Richmond grew slowly, with vicissitudes that included the destructive 'great freshet' of 1771. In 1775 three epoch-making conventions met in the town. The First Virginia Convention, held in Williamsburg in August 1774, had elected delegates to the First Continental Congress and adopted a system of nonintercourse with Great Britain. The Second Convention opened on March 20, 1775, at St.John's Church in Richmond. Patrick Henry made his impassioned plea for liberty or death and put through his resolution for 'embodying, arming, and disciplining' the militia. The Third Convention, meeting in Richmond in July, appointed the Committee of Safety, proposed the enlisting of recruits, and inaugurated a plan for financing the war; and the Fourth Convention was organized in Richmond but adjourned to Williamsburg.

In 1779 Richmond was made the capital of Virginia. The following year, when Governor Jefferson moved into a rented house and the assembly convened in temporary quarters, there were but 684 people living in Richmond. The town played an important part in the last days of the Revolution, suffered pillaging by Benedict Arnold in January 1781, was rescued from the British under Arnold and Phillips the following April by the arrival of La Fayette, and in June was on Cornwallis's line of march eastward.

With peace came a new era of growth. The *Virginia Gazette* was moved from Williamsburg to Richmond, and three other newspapers were established in the new capital. In 1782 Richmond was incorporated as a town, though it was called a city in deference to its status as capital. William Foushee was elected mayor. The general assembly held sessions that led to a convention of other States for the framing of a Federal Constitution, which—amid verbal fireworks—Virginia ratified in 1788. Thomas Jefferson's beautiful building went up on Capitol Square. By 1790 the population had increased to 3,761, and by 1800 had reached 5,730.

In 1802 Benjamin Henfry, a Scotsman, demonstrated lighting by gas before citizens in Haymarket Garden, present terminus of the Atlantic Coast Line Railway, and heard his 'tea kettel apparatus' ridiculed; Richmond missed the opportunity of being the first American city to install street lighting. In 1803 came Tom Moore, Irish poet, 'whose songs were sung to every guitar and harpsichord in Richmond.' In 1807 Aaron Burr was tried for high treason behind the portico of the Jeffersonian capitol. In 1811 a theater fire took the lives of 73 people. That year the Allans of Richmond adopted Edgar Allan Poe, an orphaned baby. His youth here and his later connection with the *Southern Literary Messenger* are justification for Poe's declaring, 'I am a Virginian. At least, I call myself one.'

Like most cities Richmond grew with the development of transportation. Though it was not until 1840 that freight was shipped by canal between Richmond and Lynchburg, a canal was proposed by the Reverend Robert Rose in 1750. The general assembly passed an act in 1764 'for extending navigation of the James River from Westham (seven miles) downward through the Falls.' In 1784 the James River Navigation Company was chartered, and the following year George Washington was elected its president. In 1790 the canal was opened from Richmond to Westham, and in 1836 the Richmond, Fredericksburg and Potomac Railroad carried its first passengers out of Richmond, at the terrifying speed of 10 miles an hour. When the James River and Kanawha Canal was completed in 1840, Richmond was linked with the Piedmont country.

The city became as gay and fashionable as Williamsburg had been in its heyday. Hostesses vied with each other in elaborate entertaining. In 1842, the year that Richmond became a city in reality as well as in name, Charles Dickens at a dinner given in the Exchange Hotel was toasted as 'the artful dodger' because he had 'dodged Philadelphia and Baltimore,' but not Richmond. Theaters presented stars of the European and American stage—the Booths, Joe Jefferson, Jenny Lind.

But the 'Fiery Epoch' had begun. Sectional misunderstanding had thwarted a movement within the State for the emancipation of slaves. The capital city was caught up in the excitement of war. On the night of April 19, 1861, Richmond blazed with fireworks and 'ten thousand hurrahing men and boys carried torches' to celebrate Virginia's secession. On May 29, the Confederate capital was moved from Montgomery, Alabama, to Richmond.

For a time the city was headily gay. Officers, resplendent in new uniforms, strolled beside hoop-skirted beauties, whose very curls danced with patriotism. Sewing circles culminated in 'danceable teas,' and pretty heads were forever planning balls, parties, and theatricals. But there was bickering, too. Richmond ladies were critical of the wives of new officialdom. 'This Cabinet of ours,' wrote Mary Boykin Chestnut on July 27, 'are in such bitter quarrels among themselves—everybody abusing everybody.'

As the war years deepened Richmond was the center of political wrangling and the objective of an invading army. Privation stifled gaiety and feuds. Wounded soldiers were brought to hurriedly equipped hospitals. In May 1862, McClellan came within sight of Richmond. Defeated in the Seven Days' Campaign, he changed his base from the York to the James, where he remained until recalled in midsummer.

Foremost among the war heroines was Sally Tompkins, who as head of a hospital was commissioned captain in the Confederate army. Elizabeth Van Lew heroically toiled for the Union and emancipation, sending daily communications to Federal officers and helping blue-clad soldiers to escape from crowded Libby Prison, a ship chandlery and tobacco warehouse built by William Libby in 1845 at Twentieth and Cary Streets. On February 9, 1864, she aided Colonel Thomas E. Rose and 108 Federals in a daring break from the prison. On April 3, 1865, Richmond was evacuated and burned by its own people.

After the war Richmond began the slow task of rebuilding. Elizabeth Van Lew became postmaster—the only woman ever to hold so important a government post in the city; the canal was reopened; railroads were repaired; a system of public education was established; and the emancipated Negro began to find his place in the economic scheme. In 1887 horse-drawn streetcars, which had been running since 1861, were supplanted by electric cars.

A romantic literature, characterized by nostalgia for bygone days, gave place in time to the writing of history and realism. Mary Johnston became America's foremost historical novelist; Ellen Glasgow held the mirror before the people she knew—too close for their happiness; and James Branch Cabell created a medieval realm in which he ridiculed the Philistia about him. Edward V. Valentine, Sir Moses Ezekiel, Dugald Stewart Walker, and others achieved National recognition in the world of art. John Powell took front rank among musicians. Schools and colleges increased in number and size and strengthened their curricula. Richmond became a hospital center for Virginia and other Southern States. In 1910 Manchester across the river was annexed as a unit of greater Richmond. Women, under such leaders as Lila Meade Valentine and Mary Cooke Branch Munford, began to participate in public affairs. Negroes set out to learn the use of new tools that freedom and education had given them. Commerce and the arts built a new Richmond, which while celebrating its bicentennial in 1937, refreshed its memory by means of a historical pageant.

POINTS OF INTEREST

1. CAPITOL SQUARE, bounded by Bank, N.9th, Capitol, and Governor Sts., is shaded by large trees, patterned by worn brick walks, and inhabited by tame squirrels. Half its 12 acres slope steeply. The act by which the capital was moved from Williamsburg set apart 'six whole squares' for public buildings, provided for the erection of a 'house' for use

of the general assembly, and for temporary buildings elsewhere. The grounds were laid out in 1816 by Maximilian Godefroy.

The WASHINGTON MONUMENT, NW. corner of the Square, is probably Richmond's finest sculptural group. A bronze equestrian statue of George Washington stands on an elaborate stone base flanked by nine-foot bronze figures of George Mason, Patrick Henry, General Andrew Lewis, John Marshall, Thomas Nelson, and Thomas Jefferson. Around the base are female figures seated on trophies of victory.

Public subscriptions for a monument were first raised in 1817 by a committee under John Marshall. The 60-foot monument, unveiled in 1858, was completed with the figure of Marshall in 1867. Thomas Crawford executed all the figures except those of Nelson and Lewis, which were done by Randolph Rogers after Crawford's death. The base and pedestal were designed by Robert Mills.

The STATE CAPITOL (*open* 8–5 *Mon.–Fri.*, 8–4 *Sat.*) raises a proud Ionic portico above the trees on the steep hill. Robert Mills, one of America's first professional architects, wrote: 'I remember the impression it made on my mind when first I came in view of it coming from the South. It gave me an idea of the effect of those Greek temples which are the admiration of the world.' The lofty portico and the rectangular mass of the main block are tied together by an unbroken cornice and pilaster treatment, which continues the effect of columns around the sides and back. Short passages lead to side wings—modified miniatures of the older building.

Thomas Jefferson sent from France a plaster model he had prepared in collaboration with the French architect, Charles Louis Clarisseau, as a modified design of the Maison Carrée, late Roman temple at Nîmes. The capitol antedated by more than 20 years the Madeleine in Paris, first example in Europe of similar quasi-literal temple architecture. The cornerstone was laid in 1785 but the capitol was not completed in time to house the ratification convention in June, 1788, although the general assembly met in the unfinished building in October. The original portion was finished in 1792 under the supervision of Samuel Dobie and the brick was covered with stucco in 1798. The wings and the long flight of steps were built in 1904–05.

Here, where one of the world's oldest representative legislatures still meets, events of National importance have taken place: in 1807 the dramatic trial of Aaron Burr on charges of treason; in 1861 the secession convention, which met here for part of 54 days of bitter debate; sessions of the Congress of the Confederate States of America, 1861–65; and a notable tragedy, the 'Capitol Disaster' in 1870, when the floor of the old Hall of the House of Delegates collapsed, killing 63 persons and injuring 60.

Beneath the dome of the rotunda stands the noted marble FIGURE OF GEORGE WASHINGTON, by Jean Antoine Houdon. Washington is portrayed in military uniform, a plowshare and small implements of war about his feet, his left arm resting on a fasces. One day while Houdon was following Washington about Mount Vernon to catch a characteristic pose, he watched him bargaining for a yoke of oxen. When Washington, his arm on a fence post, explosively protested about the price, Houdon went at once to mold his figure. Niches in the encircling wall are occupied by busts of the seven other Virginia-born Presidents of the United States and Houdon's bust of La Fayette. A marble plaque in memory of Lila Meade Valentine (1865–1921), Virginia's leader in the fight for enfranchisement of women, is in the House of Delegates.

Along the north side of Capitol Square are three bronze figures: The STATUE OF GOVERNOR WILLIAM SMITH, a work of W.L.Sheppard, unveiled in 1906; the STATUE OF GENERAL THOMAS J. JACKSON, by J.H.Foley,R.A., presented in 1875 by Beresford Hope as a gift of English admirers of 'Stonewall'; the STATUE OF DR.HUNTER HOLMES MCGUIRE, a work of William Couper, unveiled in 1904. Dr.McGuire (1835–1900), born in Winchester, was an eminent physician.

The GOVERNOR'S MANSION (*private*), NE. corner of the Square, a two-story brick house painted white, is designed in simplified early Federal style, with a single-story Doric portico and four chimneys rising from the ridge corners of the deck roof. Built in 1813, it was the second governor's house on this site. When Richmond became the capital, the State made no provision for the executive's residence, and Governor Jefferson was forced to rent one. Nineteen years later, however, the State erected on this site a four-room makeshift, which was dubbed 'The Palace' and made to serve until pleas—especially those of Governor Tyler—convinced the legislature that a more appropriate one should be built. Virginia's governors, from James Barbour to James H. Price, have occupied this mansion. In more expansive times it was customary during legislative sessions to keep a huge bowl always full of toddy. Here the Prince of Wales (later Edward VII), Marshal Foch, Winston Churchill, several Presidents of the United States, and other notables have been entertained.

The VIRGINIA STATE LIBRARY (*open 9–5 Mon–Fri., 9–12:30 Sat.*), E. side of the Square, is cramped in an undistinguished pale yellow brick building with gray stone trim, but is soon to be moved to a new building being erected (1939) near by. A library bill presented by Jefferson in 1779, the first attempt to obtain a public library for Virginia, was unsuccessful. An act of the Virginia Assembly in 1823 provided the meager proceeds from the sale of Hening's *Statutes at Large* for a library to be used by the court of appeals, general court, and general assembly. In 1828 'the room in the southeast corner of the Capitol' was chosen for a library. The present building was completed in 1892 and enlarged in 1908 and in 1920.The library contains more than 250,000 volumes, files of old newspapers, historical maps and charts, and more than 1,000,000 manuscripts. Here also are a bronze bust of Commodore Matthew Fontaine Maury by Edward Valentine, a very early map of Virginia (1590), and several early portraits and copies. Source material of inestimable value is made available to research workers by a staff that guards the irreplaceable books and documents. Wilmer Hall is the librarian, and Coralie H. Johnston has been in charge of the reading room since 1916.

The OLD BELL TOWER (*open by arrangement with park keeper*), near SW. corner of the Square, is a mellowed red brick building. The little thickset square tower was built in 1824, replacing one of wood. Calls to the colors have pealed from both towers.

2. ST.PAUL'S EPISCOPAL CHURCH (*open* 10–4 *Mon.–Fri.*, 10–12 *Sat.; Sun. services*), SW. corner N.9th and E.Grace Sts., of brick stuccoed dark gray, was designed in classical style by Thomas Stewart of Philadelphia and dedicated in 1845. A wide Corinthian portico is surmounted by a towering cupola. St.Paul's is known as the 'Church of the Confederacy,' associated as it is with Jefferson Davis and Robert E. Lee, who worshiped there during the War between the States. Jefferson Davis was confirmed in this church and was attending services there when he received news on April 2, 1865, of the proposed evacuation of Petersburg and Richmond. The Lee Memorial Window is noteworthy. A mosaic reproduction of Leonardo da Vinci's *Last Supper* above the altar is illuminated upon request.

3. The JOHN MARSHALL HOUSE (*open* 9–5 *Mon.–Fri.*, 9–2 *Sat.; adm.* 25¢), NW. corner N.9th and E.Marshall Sts., is a square brick building of post-Colonial simplicity, designed and built soon after 1789 by Chief Justice John Marshall, who lived here until his death in 1835. The gable, above one of two little formal porches that flank the outer corner, is pedimented. The interior, including high mantels, simple paneling, and cornices with plaster relief, is characterized by classical serenity.

John Marshall (1755–1835), born near Germantown (*see Tour 4a*), was related through his mother, Mary Randolph, to Thomas Jefferson and the Lees. After taking an active part in the Revolution, he went to the College of William and Mary in 1780 to study briefly under George Wythe. In 1782 Marshall was elected to the Virginia Legislature and moved to Richmond, where he married Mary Ambler in 1783 and hung out his shingle. He exerted great influence in the ratification convention of 1788, championed Washington's administration and Hamilton's financial measures, and became the Federalist leader in Virginia. He was elected to Congress in 1799, served as President Adams's Secretary of State, and in 1801 became Chief Justice of the Supreme Court. Bitter antagonist of his cousin, Thomas Jefferson, he made precedent-setting conservative decisions for 34 years. By his decision in the case of *Marbury* v. *Madison* he established the Supreme Court's power of judicial review of National legislation. Marshall presided in 1807 at the trial of Aaron Burr.

4. The VALENTINE MUSEUM (*open* 10–5 weekdays), SW. corner E.Clay and N.11th Sts., a two-story house of brick stuccoed gray, conceals a terraced garden dotted with trees and shrubbery. It was designed by Robert Mills for John Wickham, chief attorney for Aaron Burr, and built in 1812. A sweeping stairway and a parlor, proudly retaining every detail of furnishing in lushest Victorian style, stand out among the rooms.

Mann S. Valentine purchased the house and left it to the city in 1892; it was restored and opened to the public in 1930. In the garden at the rear is the original carriage house, used for 30 years as a studio by Edward Virginius Valentine, and acquired by the city in 1937. The museum houses the Mann S. Valentine collection of oriental casts and some of Edward V.

Valentine's best work, including the plaster cast of his recumbent statue of Robert E. Lee, furniture of the eighteenth and nineteenth centuries, rare books, cultural history material from Europe, the Orient, Africa, Polynesia, and North America, and a series of miniature groups depicting Richmond's history.

5. The CONFEDERATE MUSEUM or WHITE HOUSE OF THE CONFEDERACY (*open 9–5 Mon.–Fri., 9–2 Sat.; adm. 25¢*), SE. corner N.12th and E.Clay Streets, is an angular white stuccoed-brick house with a shallow, flat-roofed portico in Roman-Doric style. A small cupola stands rather incongruously in the center of the roof. Built in 1818, this is one of the few buildings designed by Robert Mills in the city, but its original lines were altered in 1844 by a third-story addition.

Known as the Brockenbrough Mansion, it was bought and furnished by the Confederacy as a 'worthy White House' for the Davis family. Here was born Winnie Davis, 'Daughter of the Confederacy,' and here died little Joseph Davis after falling from a porch. The house was occupied for five years after the war by the Federal Government, and served as Central School for 20 years, and finally, in 1893, was saved from ruin by the Confederate Memorial Literary Society, which made it a treasure house of 'things Confederate.' Here, among other exhibits, are Robert E. Lee's sword, the original Great Seal and provisional constitution of the Confederacy, Jackson's sword and cap, and the military equipment of General Joseph E. Johnston and General J.E.B.Stuart.

6. MEDICAL COLLEGE OF VIRGINIA, scattered about the corner of E. Marshall and N.12th Sts., is a group of 13 major buildings. The Egyptian Building, first permanent building of the institution, erected in 1854 from the design of Thomas S. Stewart of Philadelphia, is (1939) being restored.

The Medical College was founded in 1838 as a department of Hampden-Sydney College but was granted a separate charter in 1854. After John Brown's raid of 1859, Dr.Hunter Holmes McGuire persuaded some 300 Southern medical students in Pennsylvania universities to transfer *en masse* to Southern medical schools. Of these, 140 enrolled in the medical college here. Dr.McGuire founded the rival University College of Medicine in 1893, but after years of bitter competition, amalgamation of the two colleges was effected in 1913. Women were admitted in 1918.

The institution, one of the largest medical plants in the South, consists of 11 units: the Memorial, Dooley, St.Phillip's, and Crippled Children's Hospitals; McGuire and Cabaniss Halls; the Egyptian Building; the Library; the dormitory and educational unit for St.Phillip's Hospital School for Nursing; the clinic and laboratory building; and the staff dormitory. New units are in process of construction (1939). Enrollment in 1937–38 was about 700, and the faculty numbered 223.

7. MONUMENTAL CHURCH (*open 9–1, 2–5 weekdays; Sun. for services*), E.Broad St. between N.12th and College Sts., is a stuccoed brick building of Classical Revival architecture. The body of the building, an octagonal domed auditorium, is extended on four faces, and the entrance portico is of brown sandstone with columns between anta walls. It was

completed in 1814 from the design of Robert Mills; no similar example of his work survives. Here is preserved a baptismal basin, dated 1733, from the last church at Jamestown.

On this site stood the Richmond Theater, where Edgar Allan Poe's mother acted. Governor George William Smith and many other prominent citizens were burned to death December 26, 1811, during a performance of *The Bleeding Nun.* A stalwart slave, Gilbert Hunt, saved the lives of about 20 women and children by catching them in his arms as they were dropped from flaming windows. Laws in Virginia and elsewhere to prohibit the opening inward of theater doors resulted from this tragedy.

8. CRAIG HOUSE (*open* 10–12, 2–6 *daily*), NW. corner N.19th and E.Grace Sts., a two-story white frame building built by Adam Craig late in the eighteenth century, is set back in a picket-fenced corner garden. This is the birthplace of Jane Craig, Poe's 'Helen.' A Negro art school is conducted here and in the restored brick kitchen in the yard.

9. MONTE MARIA ROMAN CATHOLIC CONVENT, E.Grace St. between N.22nd and N.23rd Sts., occupies a group of brick buildings, including an old galleried house built by William Taylor in 1859. The Sisters of the Visitation of Baltimore established themselves here in 1866, altered the interior, and erected a small church.

10. ST.JOHN'S CHURCH (*open* 8:45–5:30 *daily, Sun. for services*), E.Broad St. between N.24th and N.25th Sts., is a simple white frame building with a three-tiered square tower over the front entrance. The central part was built in 1741 on ground given by William Byrd together with 'wood for burning bricks into the bargain.' The church has been enlarged several times. The Second Virginia Convention met in St.John's on March 20, 1775, and heard Patrick Henry rhetorically ask for liberty or death. Among the graves in the churchyard are those of George Wythe (*see Williamsburg*), the first professor of law in the United States; Elizabeth Arnold Poe, mother of the poet; and Dr.James McClurg, one of Virginia's delegates to the Constitutional Convention in 1787.

McClurg (1746–1823) was born near Hampton and was graduated from the College of William and Mary and from the University of Edinburgh. During the Revolution he served as physician-general and director of hospitals for Virginia and in 1779 was appointed professor of anatomy and medicine at the College of William and Mary. When that chair was discontinued in 1783, he moved to Richmond. Dr.McClurg was the only Virginian at Philadelphia to advocate monarchial forms of government for the United States.

11. CHIMBORAZO PARK, E.Broad St. between 32nd and 35th Sts., a landscaped promontory overlooking the wharves and many of Richmond's largest manufacturing plants, was whimsically named for a mountain in the Andes. In 1862 Dr.James B. McCaw established here a hospital of 150 buildings and 100 tents—then the largest military hospital in the world. Seventy-six thousand patients were cared for, with a mortality of less than 10 per cent. The park site was purchased by the city in 1874. The stone that once marked Powhatan's grave stands here on the bluff above the site of the old chief's village.

12. The HENRICO COUNTY COURTHOUSE (*open* 9–5 *Mon.–Fri.*, 9–1 *Sat.*), SW. corner S.22nd and E.Main Sts., a red brick building erected in 1896, occupies a half-acre lot deeded for county use to William Randolph in 1750, about the time the first courthouse was built here. Henrico, formed in 1634, was one of the eight original counties, and was named for Henry, Prince of Wales. It first embraced a wide area extending westward on both sides of the river.

13. EDGAR ALLAN POE SHRINE (*open* 9:30–5:30 *daily; adm.* 25¢), 1916 E.Main St., is a little gray stone cottage with dormers along its gabled roof. Inscribed on the front wall are the letters 'J.R.,' believed to be the initials of 'Jacobus Rex,' James II, King of England. This is apparently the oldest house in Richmond, erected about 1686. Beyond a sheltered garden at the rear is an ivy-covered loggia, built with material salvaged from the Southern Literary Messenger Building, which stood on a corner near by. On exhibition here are many of Poe's manuscripts and other objects associated with his life in Richmond.

14. MASONIC HALL (*open by arrangement* 9–4:30 *Mon.–Fri.*, 9–1 *Sat.*), 1805 E.Franklin St., a white frame building, was erected in 1785, largely through the efforts of Chief Justice John Marshall. It has been occupied by the Masonic order longer than any other building in America. La Fayette was feted here in 1824.

15. The VIRGINIA HISTORICAL SOCIETY HEADQUARTERS (*open* 9–4:30 *Mon.–Fri.*, 9–1 *Sat.*), 707 E.Franklin St., is a three-story brick building with a high Doric porch. It dates from 1845 and is typical of prosperous mid-nineteenth-century Richmond dwellings. From 1862 until June 1865 it was the residence of General Lee's family. After Appomattox the defeated hero rode to this house amid the cheers of Union soldiers occupying the city. In its front room he declared, on hearing of Lincoln's assassination, 'This is the hardest blow the South has yet received.'

The Virginia Historical Society has occupied the building since 1892. Organized in 1831 with John Marshall as president, the society has preserved many valuable books, manuscripts, and a large collection of portraits, which are on exhibition in a fireproof addition. These include a portrait of La Fayette by Charles Willson Peale, Thomas Sully's *Pocahontas*, and a death mask of Lee.

16. ELLEN GLASGOW'S HOUSE (*private*), 1 W.Main St., is an imposing square gray stuccoed building with deck-roof, built by David Branch about 1839. At the rear is an enclosed formal garden. Ellen Glasgow (1874–   ) is the author of 20 novels that deal with aspects of the Virginia scene (*see Literature*).

17. The CASKIE HOUSE (*private*), NW. corner E.Main and N.5th Sts., is a two-story octagonal red brick building, the only one of this type in Richmond. It was built about 1815 and was once the home of William Wirt (1772–1834), author and member of counsel in the prosecution of Aaron Burr.

18. SHOCKOE HILL CEMETERY (*open* 8–5 *daily*), N. end of 3rd St., a twelve-and-a-half-acre tract sheltered by ancient elms and magnolias and enclosed by a buttressed red brick wall, was used chiefly be-

tween 1825 and 1875. Here are buried Peter Francisco, 'Hercules of the American Revolution'; Chief Justice John Marshall and his wife, Mary Ambler; Elizabeth Van Lew, whose grave is marked with a Roxbury 'pudding-stone' from Boston's Capitol Hill; Claude Benoit Crozet, French engineer, who built the Afton tunnel; and Jane Craig Stanard, inspiration of Poe's 'To Helen.'

19. The SIXTH MT.ZION BAPTIST CHURCH (*open* 9–12, 1–5 *daily*), NE. corner Duval and St.John's Sts., is a red brick structure. Here John Jasper, a Negro preacher, acquired a National reputation by his sermon, 'The Sun Do Move and the Earth Am Squaar,' delivered for the first time March 28, 1879. His theme was Joshua's saving of the Gibbonites. Jasper would say, 'Dey had an orful fight, . . . but yer might know dat Ginr'l Joshwer wuz not up dar ter git whip't . . . As a fac', Joshwer wuz so drunk wid de bat'l . . . dat he tell de sun ter stan' still tel he cud finish his job. What did de sun do? Did he glar down . . . an' say, "What you talkin' 'bout my stoppin' for, Joshwer; I ain't navur startid yit . . . ?" Naw, he ain't say dat. But wat de Bible say? It say dat it wuz at de voice uv Joshwer dat it stopped. I don' say it stopt; 'tain't fer Jasper ter say dat, but de Bible, de Book uv Gord, say so, But, I say dis; nuthin' kin stop untel it hez fust startid . . . It stopt fur bizniz, an' went on when it got through . . . an I derfies ennybody to say dat my p'int ain't made.' Jasper was once offered £400 to go to London, but he refused to forsake his church. A bust of Jasper by Edward V. Valentine is in the church.

20. The ACADEMY OF SCIENCES AND FINE ARTS OF THE UNITED STATES OF AMERICA (*open* 10–4:30 *weekdays, July and Aug.* 10–12 *Sat., adm.* 10¢), 102 E.Franklin St., occupies a pleasant red brick house in what is known as Linden Row. In 1786 the Chevalier Alexandre Marie Quesnay de Beaurepaire, an enthusiastic young French officer, after ten years of effort founded an academy with this title. A building was erected in Richmond, and the academy was affiliated with the Royal Academy of Sciences and the Paris Royal Academy of Sculpture and Painting. Beaurepaire was recalled to France by the Revolution, and with him went active interest in the academy.

A second institution was established in 1817, with the sponsorship of the Virginia legislature. A building for a Museum of Art and Natural Science was erected on what is now Capitol Square. After 1822, however, interest died, and the collection was publicly auctioned. The Virginia League of Fine Arts was formed in 1918, and the present Academy was chartered in 1930. It led the movement to establish the Virginia Museum of Fine Arts and now sponsors the Federal Art Project in Virginia. Art classes for children and adults are conducted, art exhibitions are held, and a Children's Federal Art Gallery is maintained.

21. The RICHMOND CITY LIBRARY (*open* 9–9 *weekdays*), SE. corner E.Franklin and N.1st Sts., moved in 1930 into this gray sandstone building of simple contemporary design by Baskerville and Lambert, which has been described as 'an outstanding example of austere beauty combined with practical realization of function.'

The first public library in Richmond, besides the State Library, was opened in 1924 at 901 W.Franklin Street. The present building, containing about 125,000 volumes, was the gift of Mrs.Sallie M. Dooley, as a memorial to her husband, James H. Dooley.

22. The TREDEGAR IRONWORKS, S. end of 6th St., between the Canal and James River, a jumble of blackened brick buildings spread disconsolately over a 25-acre lot and interspersed with heaps of rusty scrap iron, is the oldest plant of its kind south of the Potomac. Business has been carried on here since 1836, the plant having contributed munitions and supplies to the Confederacy and to the United States in all foreign wars since its establishment. Here were rolled the plates that armored the *Merrimac-Virginia* (*see Hampton Roads Port*), terror of the Union Navy. The plant is named after Tredegar, England, notable for its ironworks.

23. HOLLYWOOD CEMETERY (*open summer* 7–6:30, *winter* 7–5 *daily*), entrance SW. corner Cherry and Albemarle Sts., a 115-acre tract rising to a bluff overlooking the James, is cut by ravines and thickly set with fine trees. The cemetery was dedicated in 1849 and named for its magnificent holly trees. Among those buried here are John Randolph of Roanoke, Commodore Matthew Fontaine Maury, President Jefferson Davis, Presidents Monroe and Tyler, many Virginia governors, and Confederate officers.

24. The CATHEDRAL OF THE SACRED HEART (*open* 7–6 *daily*), in a triangular plot formed by Laurel St., Park and Floyd Aves., is a limestone structure of Italian Renaissance design, with dome and portico, and an ambulatory at one side. The cathedral was built in 1906 with funds donated by Mr. and Mrs.Thomas Fortune Ryan.

25. VIRGINIA UNION UNIVERSITY (Negro), 1500 N.Lombardy St., occupies 15 buildings on a tree-shaded 55-acre campus, 8 of them constructed of gray, roughhewn Virginia granite in a modified Romanesque style. This university represents the fusion of four institutions and had a twin beginning in 1865 when the American Baptist Home Mission Society founded in Richmond a theological school for freedmen under Dr.J.C.Binney and the Wayland Seminary in Washington.

The Richmond school, which opened in 1867 under Dr.Nathaniel Colver in Lumpkin's Slave Jail, united in 1899 with the Wayland Seminary, which in 1869 had absorbed the National Theological School, founded in Washington in 1865. By act of the Virginia Legislature in 1900 the name was changed to Virginia Union University. In 1932 Hartshorn Memorial College, a Negro woman's college near by, founded in 1883, was co-ordinated with Union University.

The university has two divisions, the Theological Seminary and the College of Arts and Sciences, besides an extension in Norfolk. Enrollment in the college exceeds 550 students, of whom slightly more than half are women; there is a faculty of 30. The library contains about 28,000 books and pamphlets, including the McClay Collection of books by or about Negroes. The bachelor degrees of arts, science, theology, and divinity are conferred. Nearly 2,000 graduates include such Negro leaders as Eugene

Kinckle Jones, T.Arnold Hill, Charles S. Johnson, Dr.Joshua B. Simpson, and Dr.Bessie B. Tharps.

26. UNION THEOLOGICAL SEMINARY (Presbyterian), Chamberlayne Ave. between Melrose and Westwood Aves., occupying 11 brick buildings around an open lawn, was founded in 1812 at Hampden-Sydney and was moved to Richmond in 1898. The enrollment in 1937–38 was 163.

The GENERAL ASSEMBLY'S TRAINING SCHOOL FOR LAY WORKERS, 3400 Brook Road, quartered in two large buildings of pink brick with light stone trim in early Federal style, erected in 1922, was established in 1914 by the Presbyterian general assembly. Bachelor and master degrees in religious education have been conferred since 1933. The enrollment in 1937–38 was 91.

MONUMENT AVENUE, a continuation of W.Franklin St., the most fashionable residential street in the city, is a tree-shaded thoroughfare with a central parkway of grass and shrubs, dotted with statues of distinguished Virginians.

27. The J.E.B.STUART MONUMENT, at Lombardy St., a dramatic equestrian bronze of the great cavalry leader, was executed by Fred Moynihan and erected in 1907.

28. The LEE MONUMENT, at Allen Ave., a bronze figure of the general upon his horse, Traveller, stands on an ornate stone pedestal. The monument was unveiled by Lee's West Point classmate and friend, General Joseph E. Johnston, in 1890. Because the sculptor, Jean Antoine Mercié, thought 'the brow of Lee too noble to be hidden under a hat,' this was the first equestrian statue with bared head erected in the United States.

29. The bronze JEFFERSON DAVIS MONUMENT, at Davis Ave., portrays the Confederate President in an oratorical pose, backed by an open, semicircular colonnade and a classical column supporting an allegorical female figure. This work of Edward V. Valentine was unveiled in 1907.

30. The STONEWALL JACKSON MONUMENT, at Boulevard, designed by F.William Sievers and dedicated in 1919, is a bronze figure of the general astride his horse, Little Sorrel.

31. The COMMODORE MATTHEW FONTAINE MAURY MONUMENT, at Belmont Ave., is a bronze figure of Maury, in a chair below a massive bronze globe.

32. The JAMES BRANCH CABELL HOUSE (*private*), 3201 Monument Ave., home of the author, is a brown stone building. James Branch Cabell (1879–) has written 30 books, including satirical fiction and essays. Since 1929 he has been writing under the name of Branch Cabell (*see Literature*).

33. The CONFEDERATE MEMORIAL INSTITUTE or BATTLE ABBEY (*open* 10–5 *weekdays*, 2:30–5:30 *Sun.; adm.* 25¢), N.Boulevard between Kensington and Stuart Aves., set in landscaped grounds of six acres, is an oblong, windowless building of white marble with a tall Ionic portico, completed in 1913. Charles 'Broadway' Rouss of New York, a Confederate veteran, donated $100,000 in 1896 toward such a building.

The State of Virginia appropriated $50,000, and various contributions made up a total to equal the initial donation. The institute houses a large collection of portraits of Southern heroes and is distinguished also by the mural series of the French artist, Charles Hoffbauer, depicting Confederate battle scenes. Hoffbauer made preliminary sketches in 1914 before his enlistment in the French army, destroyed them upon his return, and enriched by personal knowledge of war painted the present murals.

34. The CONFEDERATE SOLDIERS' HOME (*open 9–5 daily*), N.Boulevard between Stuart and Grove Aves., a group of six frame buildings, comprises a chapel, hall, museum, two cottages, and a combination hospital and mess hall. It was founded in 1884 for disabled Confederate veterans. In 1936, because its original 300 inmates had dwindled to 17, eight buildings were razed. Now (1939) only seven old soldiers remain. Little Sorrel, 'Stonewall' Jackson's horse, has been mounted and placed in the museum. A cannon used in Fort Sumter's defense stands lonely guard over a lawn shaded by oaks and sycamores.

35. HOME FOR CONFEDERATE WOMEN (*private*), 301 N.Sheppard St., is a white stone building of modified French Renaissance style. The central section, with an Ionic portico, is connected by solaria to its wings. Chartered in 1896 to care for needy daughters, widows, mothers, or sisters of Confederate soldiers, the home has been twice moved. The present building, first occupied in 1932, has accommodations for 75.

36. The VIRGINIA MUSEUM OF FINE ARTS (*open* 9:30–5 *Tues.–Sat., adm.* 25¢; 2–5:30 *Sun., adm. free*), NW. corner N.Boulevard and Grove Ave., is a pink brick building of modified Federal architecture. It is the first unit of a building that will be much larger. Built in 1934 after a $100,000 gift by Judge John Barton Payne and another of $100,000 from 11 sponsors, the museum has a notable permanent collection, the nucleus of which is the John Barton Payne collection presented to the Commonwealth of Virginia in 1919, containing a Del Sarto, a Rubens, a Murillo, a Canaletto, a Reynolds, and others. Judge Payne also bequeathed $50,000 for the purchase of paintings by American artists. On indefinite loan is the Henry P. Strause collection of clocks, gold, and silverplate. The museum sponsors lectures, special exhibitions, research, and restoration work.

37. WILLIAM BYRD PARK, entrance S. end of Boulevard, is a 300-acre recreation area with roads through peaceful groves and around three artificial lakes, in one of which a fountain is colorfully lighted at night. The park dates from 1874, when the city council bought 60 acres for a reservoir. It has bathing, tennis, and other athletic facilities. In the southwest corner is Virginia's memorial to World War dead, the CARILLON, a 240-foot tower of pink brick, designed in Georgian Colonial style. Erected in 1932, it contains 66 bells, cast in England, that are seldom played. On the ground floor is a MUSEUM OF WORLD WAR RELICS (*open* 10–12, 2–4 *weekdays,* 3–5 *Sun; adm. free*).

A bronze STATUE OF CHRISTOPHER COLUMBUS, by Feruccio Legnaioli, is in the northwest section of the park.

38. REVEILLE (*private*), Cary Street Rd. between Lafayette St. and Woodlawn Ave., is a tall, white-painted brick house of simple eighteenth-

century design, rambling back into a large garden with box-bordered flower beds. When built, it was a plantation house far outside the city. Tradition attributes its title to the Revolutionary period, but the name is not found in deed books earlier than 1852.

39. VIRGINIA HOUSE (*private*), S. side Sulgrave Rd. in Windsor Farms, is a large gabled Tudor manor house of brownstone surrounded by English gardens. Alexander Weddell, ambassador to Spain, brought materials for the house from Warwick Priory, Warwick, England, and reconstructed the house on this site in 1925. Eventually the Virginia Historical Society will be housed here.

40. AGECROFT HALL (*private*), S. side Sulgrave Rd. in Windsor Farms, a Tudor mansion of plaster and half-timber construction, was built about 1490 and later enlarged, in Lancashire, England, and reconstructed on its present site in 1926–28.

41. AMPTHILL (*private*), S. end Ampthill Rd. off Cary Street Rd., is the stolid red brick house built by one of the Henry Carys—father or son (*see Williamsburg*). The hip-roof central section is flanked by gable-roofed wings. Exterior detail is severe, but the full interior paneling is handsomely designed. Before being moved in 1929–30 the main house and its formerly detached buildings stood beside Falling Creek, on the south bank of the James. Built many years before 1732—if its then obsolete bonding be taken as evidence—the house appears to have been enlarged subsequently. The interior woodwork and the outhouses probably date from about 1750–60, during the ownership of Archibald Cary, chairman of the committee that directed the Virginia members of the Continental Congress in 1776 to move for independence.

42. WILTON (*open 9–5 weekdays*, 9–12, 3–6 *Sun.; adm.* 25¢), S. end Wilton Rd. off Cary Street Rd., built by William Randolph III about 1750 on the north bank of the James six miles below Richmond, is a well-proportioned brick mansion. A broad hip roof raises its plain surfaces between tall end chimneys. The entrance doors, framed by Ionic pilasters, and a crowning cornice are the chief exterior ornaments. The interior is fully paneled and has been refurnished in the style of the period. Beneath the cornice of a bedroom is inscribed: 'Sampson Darrell put up this Cornish in the year of our Lord 1753.' The house was moved to this site in 1935 and restored.

43. The UNIVERSITY OF RICHMOND, College Rd. W. of Three Chopt Rd., is housed in 16 buildings scattered in groups over nearly 300 acres of rolling ground. The T.C.Williams School of Law, founded 1870, and the Evening School of Business Administration, founded 1924, branches of the University, are in downtown Richmond.

The light red brick buildings of Richmond College, to the northeast, are designed in various styles of architecture ranging from modern to Collegiate Gothic. A nine-acre artificial lake separates this campus from that of WESTHAMPTON COLLEGE, where red brick buildings of Collegiate Gothic style were designed by Ralph Adams Cram. On a steep slope above the lake, screened by great oaks is the LUTHER H. JENKINS OUTDOOR THEATER.

Apparently the first organized movement by the Baptists for education in the new commonwealth began in 1788, when a committee of 10 was organized to 'forward the business respecting the seminary of learning,' but, after 21 years, the project was given up because of lack of funds. The attempt was renewed in 1830 with the formation of an 'Educational Society,' and in 1832 the Virginia Baptist Seminary was founded, with Robert Ryland as principal and sole teacher and with fourteen theological students. In 1840 the institution was chartered as Richmond College. Almost destroyed and closed by the war, it was reopened in 1866. Coeducation was begun in 1898, with the matriculation of four young women.

Westhampton, a separate women's college, was founded in 1914 to come within the University of Richmond, which was created by charter several years later. At the same time the Baptist Women's College of Richmond, an independent school, turned its property over to the new organization. The modern plant has been constructed since 1914.

The university libraries house about 67,000 volumes. Bachelor and master degrees in arts and science and LL.B. degrees are conferred. The total enrollment (1939), including the schools of law and business administration, a summer school, and the graduate department, is about 1,500.

POINTS OF INTEREST IN ENVIRONS

Du Pont de Nemours Manufacturing Plant, 6.7 *m.* (*see Tour 1c*). Seven Pines Battlefield, 8.5 *m.* (*see Tour 8a*). Mechanicsville and the National Battlefield Park Route, 6.5 *m.* (*see Tour 20a*). Fort Harrison, Park Headquarters and Museum, 8.9 *m.* (*see Tour 24*).

Roanoke

Railroad Stations: Shenandoah Ave. and Randolph St. for Norfolk and Western Ry.; Jefferson and Walnut Sts. for Virginian Ry.
Bus Stations: 16 W.Church Ave. for Greyhound Lines; 608 S.Jefferson St. for Pan-American Lines.
Taxis: Fare 25¢ within city limits.
Streetcars: Fare 7¢, 4 tokens 35¢, weekly pass $1.

Accommodations: 13 hotels; tourist homes.

Information Service: Chamber of Commerce, 13 W.Church Ave.

Radio Station: WDBJ (930 kc.).
Theaters and Motion Picture Houses: Roanoke Theater, 15 W.Campbell Ave.; Academy of Music, S. side of W.Salem Ave. near Park (5th) St., concerts and road shows; 7 motion picture houses, including 1 for Negroes.
Golf: Monterey Golf Club, 1.2 m. N. on County 605 (R) off State 115, 18 holes; Blue Hills Golf Club, 1.5 m. N. on County 605 (R) off State 115, 18 holes; greens fees for both $1 Sat., Sun., and holidays, 75¢ other days.
Swimming: Lakeside, 2.5 m. W. of city limits on State 24, open 9–8; Roberts Pool, 0.8 m. W. on US 11, open 7 a.m.–8 p.m.; adm. at both 25¢, children 15¢; Blue Hills Golf Club pool, open 6:30 a.m.–7:30 p.m., adm. 25¢.
Tennis: Courts in 10 of 12 parks in city (2 courts for Negroes), free.

Annual Events: Roanoke County Fair, Sept.

ROANOKE (950 alt., 69,206 pop.) lies in a bowl formed by the Blue Ridge and Allegheny Mountains and ranks third in population among Virginia cities, though in 1880 it was only the small town of Big Lick. Within the southern corporate limits rises Mill Mountain, detached from surrounding ranges. Its summit commands a view of twisting streams, ridges, valleys, and distant peaks. From the mountain's base extend streets, cut by railroad tracks, creeks, the winding course of the Roanoke River, and by parks generously scattered throughout the city.

It is perfectly evident that the population is not preponderantly Virginian, for people seem always in a hurry. Industrial executives, factory workers, merchants, and professional people make up the majority of those seen on the streets.

The era of architectural ugliness in which Roanoke was born and the city's precocious growth have complicated the task of the planning commission created in 1928. Shops and factories are near the center of the city as well as toward the outskirts, and better sections are close to those not so good. There are unsightly areas of houses quickly built and poorly kept, and junk heaps near historic places. The retail district, with Jefferson Street as its axis, is crowded between railroad tracks and Tazewell Avenue. Houses in the older residential section are late Victorian, but suburban developments give evidence of an architectural renaissance.

The Negro population, 18 per cent of the whole, finds work principally in factories and railroad shops and yards. Negroes are skilled in manipulating the immense car wheels, a task that requires a delicate sense of balance. Though several Negro residential districts reflect a wage scale higher for Negroes than that prevailing in most other Virginia cities, many districts show the need for slum clearance.

The opening of the Blue Ridge Parkway from a point 25 miles south of Roanoke to the Pinnacles of the Dan and the completion of the Skyline Drive to Rockfish Gap near Waynesboro bring thousands of visitors through Roanoke annually. Plans for the ultimate development of the two scenic highways involve the parkway's circling Roanoke and joining the drive north of the city.

One hundred and sixty-one industries and 11 utility companies thrive in Roanoke, annually paying 17,711 people salaries that total $23,893,840.32. Though the railroad shops and the enormous cellulose factories are the mainsprings of industrial prosperity, and though the city owes its origin wholly to the establishment here of a railroad terminal and shops, the surrounding country with its fertility and wealth of natural resources has contributed to the miraculous growth of Roanoke.

The country around Roanoke was once a favorite hunting ground of the Indians, attracted by the abundance of game drawn to the salt deposits, or 'licks,' within the limits of the present city. In 1654 Abraham Wood passed this way, and in 1671 his son Thomas came through, having set out from the Indian town of Appomattox 'in order to discover the South Sea,' he wrote in his diary.

When Augusta County was formed in 1738, the valley of the Roanoke lay within its boundaries. Settlements were made here as early as 1740. In 1749 Dr.Thomas Walker of Albemarle organized the Loyal Land Company and on a trip to explore the country found squatters in the valley. At the 'Great Lick they bought corn for their horses from Michael Campbell' and farther on 'lodged at James Robinson's.'

The French and Indian War almost wrecked these frontier settlements, yet a few stalwart people continued to hold their homes, and others came to set up homesteads. About the turn of the century Old Lick, already a stage on the Great Road down the valley, became an important crossroads when it was reached by the turnpike running west from Lynchburg.

In 1834 the community made its first effort to become a town. Streets were laid out and lots were sold, but only the little town of Gainsborough materialized. Salem, and not Big Lick, was made the seat of Roanoke County when it was created in 1838.

In 1852 the Virginia and Tennessee Railroad built a depot at Big Lick and a few shops and stores followed immediately. In 1858 Isham M. Ferguson established a tobacco factory in the village, and 10 years later a canning factory was put in operation. Big Lick was chartered as a town in 1874; John Trout was elected mayor; the council met regularly in Rorer's

Hall; and the town even erected a calaboose 12 feet square. Four years later *The Big Lick News* printed its first edition.

In 1881 it was noised abroad that two railroads, the Shenandoah Valley and the Norfolk and Western, were seeking a junction point. John C. Moomaw suggested that the council offer inducements that would bring the terminal to Big Lick and started on a 50-mile ride to Lexington, where he was to confer the next day with railroad officials. He had arranged that a messenger convey to him at Buchanan in the morning details of the town's offer. The council promised a terminal and $10,000. Charles W. Thomas rode to Buchanan and delivered the papers to Mr. Moomaw, who hurried on to Lexington. The junction was awarded to Big Lick.

In 1882 the town changed its name to Roanoke (Ind., shell money) and extended its limits. In 1881 there had been less than 700 inhabitants; in 1883 there were 5,000, and Roanoke received its city charter the next year. In 1906 the Virginian Railway came, bringing its shops and its great coal traffic. Mark Twain was a passenger on the first Virginian coach that entered the city. In succeeding years many industries have been attracted to Roanoke.

POINTS OF INTEREST

ELMWOOD PARK, Jefferson St. between Bullitt and Elm Aves., is a seven-and-a-half-acre landscaped municipal park and children's playground. A large cream-painted brick house with Dutch-style stepped gable ends, built by Jonathan Tosh in 1820, stands on the crest of the steep, wooded knoll in the center. The house is occupied by the PUBLIC LIBRARY (*open 10–9 weekdays, 3–6 Sun. and holidays*), founded by local women in 1920 and opened in 1921. The city donated the park grounds and provided financial support. The library maintains four branches, one for Negroes, and has more than 58,000 volumes, including a collection of illuminated manuscripts and local Virginiana.

LONE OAK (*private*), SW. corner Franklin Rd. and King George (16th) Ave., on a hill facing Mill Mountain and overlooking the Roanoke River, is a red-painted brick house of modern appearance. Its central block, with walls two feet thick, was built by the Tosh family, incorporating an earlier log house. It was known originally as 'Rock of Ages' from the rock ledge on which it stands, and was probably the first brick house in this part of the valley. The house is surrounded by five acres of lawn and gardens restored to their Colonial character—all that is left of the Tosh land.

MILL MOUNTAIN (2,183 alt.), S. edge of city limits, rises more than 1,000 feet above the city. For some distance up the tree-covered side facing Roanoke, new and old houses cling like Swiss chalets on the mountain's almost vertical flank. In 1910 an incline trolley line was built to the summit, which affords a magnificent view of mountains and valley and of the city itself. The popularity of precipitous LAUREL ROAD (*toll 50¢ for car and 2 persons, 10¢ each additional person*), off Ivy St. S. from Walnut St., caused the cable car to be abandoned in 1930, and its track was removed in 1934. From the foot of the mountain issues CRYSTAL SPRING, E. side of S. Jefferson St. and Wellington Ave. between Hamilton Terrace and McClanahan St. It has a flow of 5,000,000 gallons daily and provides water for the city.

The AMERICAN VISCOSE CORPORATION PLANT (*open by arrangement*), S. end of E.9th St., one of the largest artificial silk factories in the world, occupies a neatly kept plant on a 120-acre tract where a Saponi Indian village once stood. Opened in 1917, it has expanded swiftly. With a production capacity in 1937 of 30,000,000 pounds, the company employs nearly 5,000 workers. The plant was originally owned by British capital.

The viscose process was developed from the inventions of three Englishmen, Cross, Bevan, and Topham. It is the latest and now most generally used of four methods of rayon manufacture. Spruce wood pulp, before reaching the plant, is ground and pressed into creamy-white, blotterlike sheets about two feet square and an eighth of an inch thick. It is piled in 250-pound batches, which are identified by number through every step in the process in order to balance exactly the quantity of chemicals with which they are to be treated. The batches are mercerized by steeping in a caustic soda solution, drained, shredded into a damp, cottony mass of 'crumbs,' aged for several hours in temperature-controlled rooms, and treated with carbon bisulphide to form orange-colored cellulose xanthate. Dissolved in another caustic solution, the material becomes a brown, sticky, viscous liquid. Pipes carry this modified cellulose from filters to hundreds of tanks in the cellars, where it is stored at an even temperature, and then fed under pressure to the spinning machinery. Each unit consists of a 'spinnerette,' a nozzle perforated by invisibly fine orifices, through which the brown fluid oozes into a precipitating medium—a dilute sulphuric acid bath, flowing in troughs. The coarse thread that forms immediately is stretched and slightly twisted as it is wound into a small cylinder in a 'bucket' revolving 6,000 to 10,000 times a minute. Solidification of the fluid is instantaneous, and swiftly moving thread is made, within a few inches of the 'spinnerette,' out of 50 to 150 separate filaments, depending on the number of perforations. Washing and drying the 'cakes' taken from the 'buckets' removes most of the acid solution and strengthens the thread, which is then unwound into skeins and treated with sodium sulphide to desulphurize and refine the greenish-yellow yarn. Bleaching gives it a silken lustre. Again washed and dried, the yarn is sorted, inspected, loosely wound on spools, then rewound tightly on cones. During the winding processes several vast halls are filled with the deafening hum of thousands of whirling spools and cones. Six or seven days elapse between the shredding of impure cellulose and the last act in the transformation of spruce logs into thread.

The CARR HOUSE (*private*), Dale Ave. (Vinton Rd.) between 22nd and 23rd Sts., a sturdy, two-story building with brick end chimneys, was built entirely of hand-hewn logs about 1800 by Colonel George W. Carr. It was first the home of the Akers family and then the plantation home of Colonel Carr, who served in the Mexican War. Near the house stand FOUR SLAVE CABINS, snug two-story houses in excellent repair, also of hand-hewn logs with plaster chinking. Three are occupied by white tenants, but in the fourth lives Aunt Winnie Divers, believed to be (1939) about 107 years old.

The NORFOLK AND WESTERN SHOPS (*open*), Norfolk St. E. of Randolph St., including several vast brick buildings and numerous smaller sheds, all blackened by smoke, spread over a 145-acre tract in the center of the city. Beneath the lofty roof of one immense building, the mottled gray and red shell of a new locomotive may hang in the easy clutches of a giant overhead crane, while deafening blows contribute to its completion. At another end of this shop, a powerful locomotive, new or reconstructed, may straddle a pit, as workmen paint its gleaming flanks. Machines are everywhere—snarling lathes, saws that eat into steel as though it were butter, casting molds, and welding tools that send off showers of sparks. Shouts rise above the clanging din in the ENGINE-ERECTING SHOP to make way for a gigantic new engine part suspended from a traveling crane overhead. In the PAINT SHOP rows of wheelless new coaches or freight cars receive protective coats of orange paint. Among the buildings are a blacksmith shop, machine shop, boiler shop, foundry, planing mill, car-erecting shop, lumber yards, storehouses, lumber kiln, and a 22-stall engine house.

These main repair shops of the Norfolk and Western Railway have a production capacity of 4 locomotives per month and 20 freight cars per day. With the rest of the railroad's local facilities, they constitute Roanoke's chief industry, employing about 6,000 workers at an annual pay roll of $9,350,000. The shops, acquired by the railroad in 1883, were started two years earlier as the Roanoke Machine Works and have been enlarged several times.

HOME OF BIG LICK GARDEN CLUB (Negro), SE. corner Lynchburg Ave. and E.4th St., a small two-story frame structure built about 1837, was long thought to be the first Roanoke postoffice. During the days of the stagecoach, however, mail was exchanged and delivered at hostelries. The first authorized postoffice was in the little depot of the Virginia and Tennessee Railroad and was moved about 1868 to the Neal House near by. The Big Lick Garden Club was organized in 1930 and has 40 members. There are four other Negro garden clubs in Roanoke—the Ideal, Sunset, Magic City, and Homemakers.

The RALEIGH TAVERN (*private*), Lynchburg Ave. between E.2nd and E.4th Sts., is a long, unpainted frame building with a two-story gallery porch and a pair of brick end chimneys. Built about the beginning of the nineteenth century and long known as Pate's Tavern, it was for several decades a popular stopping place for travelers on the north-south stages or on the road from Lynchburg west to Seven Mile Ford. Passengers could alight on the tavern's broad steps, which still hug the dirt road. During the War between the States local women nursed wounded soldiers here. In a little frame house opposite lives (1939) Aunt Martha, a former slave, more than 95 years old.

The MUNICIPAL MARKET, bounded by Campbell Ave., Salem, Nelson, and Wall Sts., is housed in a commodious three-story brick building. The market was established in 1885 in quarters that have been subsequently enlarged. On a vast expanse of first-floor space are vendors' stalls, displaying products from neighboring farms and distant places. On the second floor a matron keeps children happy while mothers make purchases or sell their wares. The third floor is given over to offices of market executives and to a large auditorium where dances and public meetings are held. On the sidewalks around the building country folk set up stands, gay from early spring till late fall with many-colored flowers, fruits, and vegetables. A paved parking square is continually crowded with automobiles and hucksters' trucks.

BELMONT (*private*), in Monterey Golf Course on Tinker Creek, just across bridge (R) off State 115, long known as 'Monterey,' is a wide one-story log house painted white, with several rooms and wide stone-flagged porch. The 530-acre tract called Bell Mount upon which the house was built was conveyed by Israel Christian to William Fleming, who had married Christian's daughter in 1763. Dr.Fleming, member of the Continental Congress in 1779–80 and the only man from west of the Blue Ridge ever to sit in that body, landed at Norfolk in 1755. This Jedburgh-born Scot and graduate of Edinburgh, having quit His Majesty's Navy in which he was a surgeon for several years, began almost at once to play a militant part in his adopted country. He joined Major Andrew Lewis as a lieutenant and surgeon on the 'Sandy Creek Voyage,' the unsuccessful expedition sent out by Governor Dinwiddie in 1756 to join the friendly Cherokee against the Shawnee and the French along the Ohio; he became an ensign in the First Virginia Regiment, commanded by Washington, and was made a captain in 1760; later he practiced medicine at Staunton; and moved to his new home here in 1768. He commanded the Botetourt regiment at Point Pleasant in 1774. Though shot twice in the arm and once through the chest, he assumed command when all the other leaders had fallen, and his shouted commands forced part of his lung through the bullet hole in his chest. In 1781 he was a member of Governor Jefferson's council. After the expiration of Jefferson's term on June 1, Colonel Fleming acted as governor for nearly two weeks before a successor could be appointed. Fleming fled before Tarleton with the legislature to Staunton. While he was 'holding his court' in Staunton, the nervous legislature indulged in a second run for its life on a false rumor that Tarleton had crossed the Blue Ridge—a flight so precipitate that Patrick Henry is said to have left Staunton wearing only one boot. Colonel Fleming died at Belmont in 1795 and lies buried somewhere near the house.

POINTS OF INTEREST IN ENVIRONS

Veterans' Facility Hospital, 6.9 *m.*; Hollins College, 7.7 *m.*; (*see Tour 5b*).

Staunton

Railroad Stations: Middlebrook Ave. and S.Augusta St. for Chesapeake and Ohio Ry.; Greenville and Waynesboro Aves. for Baltimore & Ohio R.R.
Bus Station: NW. corner Johnson and New Sts. for Atlantic Greyhound, Virginia Stage Lines, and Pan American Lines.
Taxis: Fare 25¢ for 2 passengers, within city limits.
Traffic Regulations: Halfhour parking one side of street only in business district.

Accommodations: 4 hotels; tourist homes.

Information Service: Staunton-Augusta Chamber of Commerce, 112 W.Frederick St.; Shenandoah Valley, Inc., Stonewall Jackson Hotel, Market and Johnson Sts.

Motion Picture Houses: 3.
Golf: Gypsy Hill Park, Churchville and Thornrose Aves., 9 holes, greens fee 25¢; Stonewall Jackson Tavern, 2.3 m. N. on US 11, 18 holes, greens fee $1.25.
Swimming: Gypsy Hill Park, Churchville and Thornrose Aves., free.
Tennis: Gypsy Hill Park, Churchville and Thornrose Aves., 3 courts, open daily, fee 10¢ per hr., children 5¢.

Annual Events: Staunton Motorcycle Hill Climb, July 4; Staunton Fair, 6 days in late summer; Gold Star Mothers' Pilgrimage to birthplace of Woodrow Wilson, autumn.

STAUNTON (pronounced Stăn'ton, 1,385 alt., 11,990 pop.), in the Shenandoah Valley, originated the city-manager form of government and is the birthplace of Woodrow Wilson.

The city is set among mountains. Round about are fertile fields, grazing lands, and acres of orchards, in spring snowy with blossoms that distil their fragrance through the countryside and in fall heavy with fruit and pungent with the cidery odor of ripe apples.

Streets in Staunton drop and wind perilously, following trails once used by Indians, stagecoaches, and bell-decked wagon caravans. Old homes of mellowed brick and of clapboard, not too recently painted, stand close to sidewalks and hide gardens tucked behind them. Children's children have lived in these houses, content to remodel but unwilling to destroy.

At the center of the city is the crowded business district. Narrow streets that are laid here at right angles curve and broaden slightly as they climb toward residential sections. Within the circle roughly defining the city limits are a lake around which a race track has been laid; a cemetery, spacious and landscaped; the grounds of the Western State Hospital and of the Virginia School for the Deaf and Blind; the small neat campuses of two colleges; a park; and a line of railroad tracks running through unsightly slums.

From September till June youth rules Staunton. Boys from two preparatory schools—confident that brass buttons and uniforms are irresistible—and pretty girls who are wise enough to study fashion magazines as well as classical subjects find time to be admired. Undergraduates from men's colleges near by flock to Staunton for delightful—though vigilantly chaperoned—hours with the girls of Mary Baldwin and Stuart Hall.

Negroes, not so numerous here as they are in many other Virginia cities, are a stable element in the population. Sue M. Brown, author, organizer, and leader in racial and interracial work, was born in Staunton.

Local industrial plants manufacture furniture, men's garments, woolens, hosiery, flour, and dairy products. An ingenious woman dresses period dolls so originally as to have won National notice. Staunton is the market for one of the richest agricultural counties in America. The principal farm products—hay, corn, wheat, fruit, milk, butter, and poultry—have an annual value of more than $7,000,000.

In 1736 William Beverley was granted a large tract of land embracing the present city of Staunton, 'in consideration for inducing a large number of settlers to the community.' In 1738, when Augusta County was formed, extending from the Blue Ridge Mountains to the Mississippi River and south from the Great Lakes to North Carolina, no provision was made for a county seat. Beverley gave a small stone building at Mill Place, earliest name of the settlement, for use as the county courthouse. In 1761 the general assembly authorized the town of Staunton. Some say the name honored Lady Gooch, wife of Governor William Gooch and a member of the Staunton family, others that the town was named for Staunton, England.

The town was advantageously situated at the crossing of the Valley Pike and the Midland Trail. Travelers westward bound and those journeying southward or northward stopped in Staunton. Here they refreshed themselves at taverns, rested their horses, and replenished their supplies. Through Staunton were shipped luxuries that East sent West, and along the streets of the frontier city great droves of hogs passed on their way to eastern markets. In 1796 Isaac Weld, an Irish traveler, wrote, 'As I passed along the road in the great valley and the village called Staunton, I met with great numbers of people from Kentucky and the new state of Tennessee, going towards Philadelphia and Baltimore and with many others going in a contrary direction, "to explore," as they call it, that is to search for lands conveniently situated for new settlements in the western country. This town called Staunton carries on a considerable trade with the back country and contains nearly two hundred dwellings, mostly built of stone, together with a church. Nowhere, I believe, is there such a superfluity of . . . military personages as in the town of Staunton.' In 1797 the Duc de la Rochefoucauld-Liancourt, a French philosopher, visited Staunton on his way to Monticello, and commented in his diary upon the town: 'There are eight Inns, fifteen to eighteen stores and about 800 inhabitants . . . The inhabitants, like the generality of Virginians, were fond of gambling and betting.'

Throughout vast Augusta County Indians gave no end of trouble, for the unreasonable savages resented the white man's theft of their land. Among the Indian fighters was 'Mad Ann' Bailey, intermittently a resident of Staunton. She came to America from England as an indentured servant, married Richard Trotter, and brought forth a son. After her husband was killed by the Indians, Ann set out to avenge his death. She 'halways carried a hax and a hauger and could chop as well as hany man.' Dressed in men's clothes, equipped with rifle, tomahawk, and knife, she became a spy, messenger, and scout, killed more than one person's share of Indians, saved stockades, and lived to the creditable age of 83.

Staunton was once the capital of Virginia, though the distinction was unpremeditated and short-lived. In 1781, when the British Colonel Tarleton approached Charlottesville, the general assembly fled to Staunton and continued its sessions in Old Trinity Church.

After the Revolution Dr.Alexander Humphreys, pioneer surgeon and teacher of medical science, who died in 1802, lived in Staunton. Ephraim McDowell, pioneer in the science of ovariotomy, William Wardlaw, Samuel Brown, and other distinguished physicians were pupils of Dr.Humphreys. In 1788, after the disappearance of a visiting Englishman, Dr.Humphreys was suspected of murder when a bag that bore his name and contained the bones of a man was found in a cave. He sued his accuser and received a verdict of 'slander.' Later Dr.McDowell positively identified the hair as that of a Negro whose corpse Dr.Humphreys probably had used for dissection.

The town was chartered in 1801. The Central Railroad completed its tracks as far west as Staunton in 1854. During the War between the States no battles were fought in the immediate vicinity of Staunton, but both armies used the city as a base for supplies. Staunton became a city in 1871.

It is one of the few cities that have made original contributions to government. In conceiving the city-manager plan, adopted in 1908, it set a pattern that has been followed by about 500 other cities. This wholly American form, based upon methods used in business corporations, has been adopted in several foreign countries. In Staunton a unicameral council of five members, elected by the voters, appoints a city manager, who administers municipal affairs.

Staunton has been visited by many notables, including Washington, Jefferson, Jackson, and Lee. President Coolidge, while spending his summers in Virginia, worshiped in Staunton at the First Presbyterian Church. Since 1936 the Gold Star Mothers of America have held annual conventions here.

POINTS OF INTEREST

CITY HALL, 100 block E.Beverley St., originally a small rectangular frame structure erected in 1871 and known as Grangers Hall, was entirely remodeled in 1931 and built of red brick. On the second floor is the HEADQUARTERS OF THE STONEWALL BRIGADE BAND (*open 9–5 weekdays*), organized in 1845 as the Mountain Saxe Horn Band. At the beginning of the War between the States the band was mustered in as the Fifth Virginia Regimental Band, and General Jackson raised its rank to the Stonewall Brigade Band. General Grant at Appomattox allowed members to take home their instruments. When Grant, making his first trip south as President, passed through Staunton, the band serenaded him at the station—the first welcome he received by a southern organization, he said. At his funeral in New York the band was given the post of honor, and in 1897 it played at the dedication of Grant's Tomb on Riverside Drive. During the summer months the band plays regularly in Gypsy Hill Park. The original instruments, preserved here, are the only complete set known to have been manufactured by Antoine Saxe in Brussels. A bugle in the band's collection was used in the Revolution, the War of 1812, the Mexican War, and the War between the States, and sounded the call to colors for the Spanish-American War and the World War.

MARY BALDWIN COLLEGE, Frederick St. between New and Market Sts., a large group of yellow buildings, brightened by white colonnades and sitting on a terraced hillside, is the second oldest Presbyterian college for women in the United States and the oldest of uninterrupted history in the South. Established in 1842 by the Reverend Rufus W. Bailey as the Augusta Female Seminary, it was kept open during the War between the States and Reconstruction by Miss Mary Julia Baldwin, principal for 34 years. By act of the general assembly in 1895–96 the seminary was named for Miss Baldwin. In 1923 it became a college and now confers the degree of bachelor of arts. The enrollment is more than 300. President Wilson was baptized in Waddell Chapel, in which his father preached before it became part of the college.

WOODROW WILSON'S BIRTHPLACE (*open* 8:30–5 *Mon.–Fri.*, 8:30–12 *Sat.; adm.* 25¢), 24 N.Coalter St., is a square house of gray-painted brick. A flat-roofed portico, somewhat altered and now at the rear, was originally the main entrance. Its two-story columns face the garden, landscaped to conform with the old pattern. The house was built in 1846 as the manse of the First Presbyterian Church. Woodrow Wilson was born here December 28, 1856, while his father, the Reverend Joseph R. Wilson, was pastor of the church. The building was purchased by Mary Baldwin College in 1931, and sold in 1938 to the Commonwealth of Virginia. As a part of the annual convention of Gold Star Mothers a pilgrimage is made to this house.

KALORAMA (*private*), 19 S.Market St., a large frame house, incorporates the foundations, four rooms, and a hall of Beverley Manor House, built about 1737. Carter Beverley, a grandson of William Beverley, rented the house from Daniel Sheffey, who bought it in 1805. After Mr.Sheffey's death in 1831, Mrs.Sheffey and her two daughters opened a school for 'young ladies' here.

AUGUSTA COUNTY COURTHOUSE (*open* 9–5 *Mon.–Fri.*, 9–1 *Sat.*), NE. corner Johnson and Augusta Sts., a classic structure in cream brick with large stone columns, is the fifth courthouse on this site. The limestone corner marker planted at the end of the first day's surveying of the Beverley grant in 1736 is in the courtroom. In the same room hang portraits of early justices and judges, including one of Chief Justice Marshall—the work of Robert Sully.

STUART HOUSE (*private*), 120 Church St., is a large, red brick building with plain white portico and fine interior woodwork, perhaps designed by Thomas Jefferson. The house was built in 1791 by Archibald Stuart, member of the Virginia Convention of 1788 and a close friend of Jefferson. Except for a wing added in 1845, the house has not been altered. When the British approached Williamsburg in 1780, Judge Stuart's son, Alexander H. H. Stuart, was a student of the College of William and Mary and an officer of the newly founded Phi Beta Kappa Society. Fleeing from the city, he carried with him the seal of the society, which was later found in this house in a secret drawer.

OLD TRINITY CHURCH (*open 9–6 weekdays, Sun. services*), Beverley St. between Church and Lewis Sts., built in 1855 and third on this site, is of Gothic Rivival style in dull red brick, with a 30-foot tower half covered with ivy. The interior, except for the brick-lined chancel, has fine walnut woodwork, and some of the stained glass is excellent. The first church of Trinity Parish, organized in Augusta County in 1747, was erected in 1760–63 on land acquired from William Beverley for £6. The vestry ordered the work done 'in a fashionable and workmanlike manner.' The Virginia assembly met in this building in 1781, after crossing the mountains to escape the British. A bronze tablet near the gate bears the names of assemblymen who took refuge in the church.

SMITH THOMPSON HOUSE (*open by arrangement*), 701 W.Beverley St., half log and half brick beneath white clapboarding, was built in 1790 by Smith Thompson. All the nails, latches, and locks are hand-wrought. The fireplaces have wide flagstone hearths and high mantels. Thompson, a barber, was a Revolutionary soldier. He boasted of having shaved Washington and displayed the razor he used.

STUART HALL, 325–29 W.Frederick St., a preparatory school for girls, occupies a group of eight cream-painted brick buildings on a small campus. The older buildings have white porticoes with tall square columns. It was founded in 1843 as a small day school in 'Old Main'—a fine example of the Greek Revival—now used as a dormitory and for classrooms.

Known first as the Virginia Female Institute, the college was renamed in 1907 to commemorate Mrs. J.E.B. Stuart, widow of Virginia's cavalry leader, who became principal in 1880. Robert E. Lee and Bishop William Meade served on its board. It is owned and operated by the three Episcopal dioceses of Virginia, and had an enrollment in 1938 of about 120 girls.

STAUNTON MILITARY ACADEMY, Prospect St. between Market and N.Coalter Sts., occupies a group of white-trimmed gray stone buildings on a hilltop overlooking the city. It is a private military school founded by Captain William K. Kable in 1859 as the Charles Town Male Academy at Charles Town, now West Virginia. It was moved to Staunton in 1884 and is a unit of the Reserve Officers' Training Corps.

VIRGINIA SCHOOL FOR THE DEAF AND BLIND (*open by arrangement*), E.Beverley St. at New Hope Rd., is a group of brick and stone buildings on one of Staunton's hills at the edge of 98 farm acres. Construction of the three-story brick central portion of the administrative building, with six fine Doric columns, was begun in 1843. This structure is flanked by two newer buildings, which follow its Greek Revival style. The school was established in 1838. State-supported, it is a coeducational institution with an enrollment of 350 students who receive general education and vocational training.

WESTERN STATE HOSPITAL (*open by arrangement*), Greenville Ave. S. of Waynesboro Ave., with a capacity of 2,438 (including the De Jarnette semiprivate sanatorium, 1.5 m. E. on US 250), is the largest of three State asylums for white insane. The group of more than a dozen brick buildings is in the corner of 966 acres of farm land, from which the institution derives most of its food. There is a golf course for patients. The hospital was established in 1825 as the Western Lunatic Asylum.

By 1866 nearly 2,000 patients had been treated. According to a newspaper report in that year, 'of patients treated during the last ten years, 23 became deranged because of "the war"—from disappointed love 7; from intemperance and dissolate [*sic*] habits, 30; from religious excitement, 1; from the use of tobacco, 5; jealousy, 4; idleness, 5.' Since 1935 the plant has been improved with Federal funds, and overcrowding eliminated through enlargement.

POINTS OF INTEREST IN ENVIRONS

Bellefont (home and grave of John Lewis), 2.2 *m.*; Augusta Church, Augusta Military Academy, 8.6 *m.* (*see Tour 5a*).

Williamsburg

Railroad Station: N. end of Boundary St. for Chesapeake and Ohio Ry.
Bus Station: College Shop, Duke of Gloucester and Boundary Sts., for Greyhound and Peninsula Transit Corp. Lines.
Taxis: Fare 25¢ within city.
Traffic Regulations: Halfhour parking limit on Duke of Gloucester St.; large public parking lots adjoining business area; speed limit on Duke of Gloucester St. and around college, 15 m.p.h., elsewhere 25 m.p.h.

Accommodations: 2 large, 10 small inns, numerous guest houses; seasonal rates.

Information Service: Information Bureau of the Restoration, Craft House, S.England St. beside Williamsburg Inn; Chamber of Commerce, New Shop Buildings, W. end Duke of Gloucester St.; booth on Richmond Rd. during tourist season.

Motion Picture Houses: One.
Golf: Yorktown Golf Course, 13 m. SE. on Colonial National Parkway, 18 holes, greens fee $1.
Swimming: Yorktown Beach, 13 m. SE. on Colonial National Parkway, suit 25¢, bath house 25¢.

Annual Events: Garden Week, late Apr. or May; Alumni Day at College of William and Mary, early June; General Assembly of Virginia meets in Colonial Capitol once during each biennial legislative session.

WILLIAMSBURG (78 to 84 alt., 3,778 pop.), capital of Virginia from 1699 to 1780 and now the showplace among Colonial restorations, is spread upon a ridge in the peninsula between the James and York Rivers. Queen's Creek and College Creek (called in early days Archer's Hope) partly encircle the city. Round about, fields roll toward the water or stretch inland to meet pine woods. On the outskirts are new houses of brick or wood. East-west Duke of Gloucester Street, wide, straight, and tree-shaded, bisects the little city from the college to the capitol.

Eighteenth-century Williamsburg, lately a straggling, dusty ghost, is today a lively reincarnation of the busy and important Colonial capital. Bordering deep sidewalks, with benches at the curbs, are shops behind façades of eighteenth-century design and signs in flowing script. Set close to the street, most of the dwellings have green shutters and gambrel or gabled roofs pierced by a line of dormer windows. Those of frame are small, with vast single-buttressed brick chimneys; a few, built of brick, are large and formally designed, while many have rambling additions. But whether of pink brick or white clapboard they appear old in pattern only. In the interiors, paneling and wainscoting are freshly painted or of polished natural woods, and walls are tinted 'Williamsburg blue' or covered with fresh paper. Gardens, where old-fashioned flowers bloom from early spring till late fall, have great boxwood trees or hedges of dwarf box planted in intricate patterns.

The past constitutes Williamsburg's livelihood, its present, and its future. The colonists' homes and taverns, where all classes of Virginians lived and assembled, and the palace and its gardens, where royal governors surrounded themselves with such splendor as would make their 'barbarous exile' more endurable, illustrate like a picture book the long fight waged by liberty-loving people against privileged aristocracy. Today boys and girls in college clothes and tourists hurrying from house to house contrast ludicrously with Negro guides and attendants in eighteenth-century costumes. Williamsburg—without patina—is the only Colonial city that appears today much as it did before the Revolution. Old and new buildings, in about equal proportion, glisten with pristine freshness; and now, as always, handicrafts represent the only local industries.

The 'Act for the Seatinge of the Middle Plantation,' passed in 1633, encouraged settlement in the area where Dr. John Pott was living. Middle Plantation stood just within the six-mile palisade built across the peninsula to protect settlers from a repetition of the Massacre of 1622. The 'pallisades . . . bounded in by two large Creekes' gave 'all the lower part of Virginia . . . a range for their cattle, near fortie miles in length and in most places twelve miles broade.' Middle Plantation suffered in the Massacre of 1644, and two years later a new palisade was ordered to replace the neglected original. On August 3, 1676, at the house of Otho Thorpe occurred the taking of the 'Oath of Middle Plantation,' an important event in Bacon's Rebellion. Here William Drummond and other principals in that abortive assertion of independence were hanged by Governor Berkeley. Jamestown having been destroyed by Bacon, Middle Plantation became for a short time the seat of restored royal Government. Though citizens of York signed a petition urging the temporary capital as most fit to become permanent, Jamestown was rebuilt.

The choice of Middle Plantation by the assembly in 1693 as the site of 'a free schoole & college' to be known as William and Mary and the burning of the State House in Jamestown caused Middle Plantation, still only a loose concentration of plantation dwellings, to be designated in 1699 as the new capital, renamed Williamsburg in honor of William III. Immediate provision was made for construction of a capitol and for platting the new city according to the survey of Theodoric Bland.

The new capital rapidly attained the size and appearance it presents today. Alexander Spotswood, who arrived in Virginia as lieutenant governor in 1710, had several ravines filled and the streets leveled, and assisted in erecting college buildings, a church, and a magazine for the storage of arms. He was patron of one of the earliest theaters in America, built in 1716 by William Levingston, who brought musicians and actors from England to perform 'comedies, drolls, and other kinds of stage plays.' The theater was conducted by Charles Stagg and his wife Mary, America's first 'leading lady.' The first successful printing press in Virginia was set up at Williamsburg in 1730 by William Parks, who founded the colony's first newspaper six years later and Virginia's first paper mill about 1744.

Incorporated in 1722, Williamsburg became the political and educational center of Virginia and the scene of the most 'fashionable' social life in Colonial America. During legislative sessions substantial planters emerged from rural isolation to occupy 'town houses,' comfortable rooms at inn or tavern, or to lodge with friends. Sycophants and adventurers swelled the throng. English visitors testified that balls, races, fairs, and other entertainment composed a 'season' not greatly inferior to London's in amusement and elegance.

The tranquillity of this scene was broken in 1765 when Patrick Henry, undeterred by cries of 'Treason!' incited the burgesses to pass resolutions against the Stamp Act. Here in 1773 were developed the intercolonial activities of a committee of correspondence that grew out of the standing committee originated in 1759 to communicate with the colony's London agents. The house of burgesses, meeting in Williamsburg in 1774, called the First Continental Congress. The First Virginia Convention, indirectly resulting from closure of the port of Boston, met at Williamsburg in the summer of 1774 to elect delegates to a general Colonial congress. Fear of Lord Dunmore and of a British man-of-war near by in the York River caused the next three conventions to meet in Richmond. The fifth and most noted Virginia Convention met in Williamsburg on May 6, 1776, and began the open move toward American freedom by declaring Virginia an independent commonwealth and by instructing the Virginia delegates to the Second Continental Congress to propose American independence.

Williamsburg began to decline when the capital was moved to Richmond in 1780 to escape the invading British. In 1781, before and during the Siege of Yorktown, Williamsburg was headquarters first of the British and then of the Continental and French forces. From the capitulation of Cornwallis in October until the following summer the French army was quartered near by. Though these closing events of the war temporarily animated Williamsburg, the population dwindled from more than 2,000 in 1779 to about 1,200 in 1795, and in 1804 the former capital was described as very 'decayed.' Between 1770 and 1790 the Reverend Mr.Moses, who seems to have been the first Negro preacher in Virginia, had organized the Williamsburg Baptist Church, undaunted by opposition that was at times physical. The church, its membership recruited almost entirely from the city's Negroes, survived under the Reverend Gowan Pamphlet and other Moses protégés.

Except for brief revivals brought about by two wars, Williamsburg dozed for a century and a half as shopping center for the surrounding country. Many residents owned small farms near by and managed to live with a minimum of enterprise. The Battle of Williamsburg took place on May 5, 1862, when a Union corps engaged Confederates retreating from Yorktown toward Richmond. The city suffered at the hands of the Union troops, and reached the nadir of its fortunes when the College of William and Mary was closed in 1881. After 1889, when the college reopened, a slow recovery began and continued until the little community was aroused suddenly in 1917 by the location on its outskirts of a munitions factory with nearly 15,000 workers. Hastily constructed cheap buildings disfigured the Colonial city.

In its newborn ugliness Williamsburg dozed again. In 1926 John D. Rockefeller, Jr., came to Williamsburg at the invitation of Dr. W.A.R. Goodwin, who had been responsible for the restoration of Bruton Paris Church, of which he was rector, and of the Wythe House. Mr. Rockefeller was enthusiastic over Dr. Goodwin's plan for restoring the city to its eighteenth-century appearance. On Mr. Rockefeller's authorization most of the property in the Colonial area was acquired by Colonial Williamsburg, Inc., and within a decade most of the research and restoration was completed. Research covered Colonial documents and records in libraries, museums, and family archives in America, England, and France. Buildings totaling 459 were torn down, 91 of the Colonial period rebuilt, 67 restored, and a new shopping center in Colonial style was provided. Six new houses were built in the Negro section in 1929. Negroes, 23 per cent of the local population, whose ancestors raised the Colonial structures, are chiefly employed as domestics or as costumed attendants at Colonial buildings.

Nearly 200,000 tourists come annually to Williamsburg and the little city has a rapidly widening influence throughout America. The eighteenth century as mirrored in Williamsburg inspires styles of dress, furniture, interior decorations, and domestic architecture.

POINTS OF INTEREST

(*Numbers identify each point of interest on the accompanying map and on the pictorial map supplied free by the Restoration. Points of interest treated here are given the numbers used in Williamsburg Restoration literature. At the Information Office in the Craft House* (73) *where maps are obtainable, combination tickets are sold for* $1.50 *each,* 75¢ *for children under* 16, *providing admission to all exhibition buildings of Colonial Williamsburg, Inc.: The Capitol, Public Gaol, Raleigh Tavern, Ludwell-Paradise House, and Governor's Palace.*)

The COLLEGE OF WILLIAM AND MARY, the second oldest college in America, was the first to establish an honor system, an elective system of studies, schools of law and modern languages, and second to establish a school of medicine—all in 1779. The Phi Beta Kappa Society was founded here December 5, 1776.

The three original buildings of the college are set in the fenced and elm-shaded triangle formed by the convergence of Jamestown Road and Richmond Road. Grouped behind them in adequate harmony are the many new buildings constructed since 1919.

'Their Majesties Royal College of William and Mary, in Virginia,' established by charter from King William and Queen Mary in 1693, revived the 'University of Henrico,' which had been chartered in 1618 but given up after the Massacre of 1622. The college opened in temporary buildings in 1694. It was given a seat in the house of burgesses and was supported by taxation of a penny per pound on tobacco exported from Maryland and Virginia, quitrents in Virginia, 20,000 acres (for which the college still pays two copies of Latin verse yearly as rent to the governor), £3,000 pledged by London merchants, and £300 donated by several pirates who had been pardoned through intercession by Commissary James Blair. In 1694 it received from the College of Heralds the only coat of arms ever granted an American college. Three Presidents of the United States, Thomas Jefferson, James Monroe, and John Tyler, were educated here; three signers, besides the author, of the Declaration of Independence, Benjamin Harrison, Thomas Nelson, Jr., and George Wythe; and many other distinguished Revolutionary patriots, including Richard Bland, Peyton Randolph, John Blair, and Edmund Randolph. George Washington became chancellor in 1788. The first recorded college club, the Flat Hat, was organized here in 1750; and in 1770 the first collegiate prizes in America were awarded, when Lord Botetourt presented gold medals. In 1784 the first course in political economy in America was established, and in 1803 the first school of history.

After the beginning of the nineteenth century the college was gradually eclipsed by the University of Virginia. It was suspended from 1861 to 1865, closed in 1881, and reopened in 1889. In 1906 the property was deeded to the State. Women, now more than half the student body, were admitted in 1918. The next year a program of rapid expansion gave new life to the old college. Enrollment in 1937–38 was 1,299.

1. The WREN BUILDING (*open 9–5 daily*) is the oldest academic building in America and the only structure in America designed by Wren. Though 'first modelled by Sir Christopher Wren,' it was 'adapted to the Nature of the Country by the Gentlemen there,' and has the simple solidity typical of American building in the early eighteenth century, when nice spacing and proportion of windows were the chief external ornament. The sandy pink brick of the long rectangular mass is set in courses of Flemish and English bond. A steep hip roof above two full stories is pierced by 12 dormers and surmounted by a plain cupola between two huge chimneys near the ends.

The foundation was laid in 1695, and the building was so far advanced by 1699 that the general assembly could meet in the great hall while the capitol was being built. In 1781 the structure was used as the main hospital for the French army. Although it was burned in 1705, 1859, 1862, and rebuilt each time, the original walls were still standing when restoration was undertaken in 1928. An illustrative copperplate in the Bodleian Library and a plan drawing by Jefferson have made it possible to retain the old walls and to approximate the appearance of the building in 1705. A portrait of Robert Boyle in black gown, painted about 1689 by Friedrich Kerseboom, and a faded one of James Blair, first president, by Charles Bridges, hang among others in the wide, paneled Blue Room, where officers of the college have always met.

In the south wing is the Chapel, built by 'overseer' Henry Cary, Jr., in 1729–32. Its high-paneled interior is richly restored in late Jacobean style. Among those buried beneath its floor are Governor Botetourt, Sir John Randolph, Peyton Randolph, John Randolph 'the Tory,' and Bishop James Madison, cousin of the fourth President of the United States and president of the college from 1777 to 1812.

1A. The COLLEGE LIBRARY (*open* 8:30–1, 2–6, 7–*midnight daily*), formerly housed in the Wren Building occupies a plain pink brick building in Georgian Colonial style. This was erected in part in 1908 with funds from Andrew Carnegie and other friends of the college and subsequently enlarged twice. The library contains 125,000 volumes, including a large collection of rare books and about 250,000 manuscripts, largely Virginiana.

Among more than 200 paintings in the library are portraits of John Page (1627–92) by Sir Peter Lely; of several Lewis family members by John Wollaston; of Fielding Lewis Taylor by William J. Hubard; and a St.Mémin engraving of St.George Tucker. There is a mezzotint said to have been done from an original painting of General George Washington by 'Alexander Campbell of Williamsburg,' got up hastily in London to satisfy curiosity about the American rebel leader and published in 1775. The 'Frenchman's Map,' dated 1782, has been useful in restoration work by showing the location of every house then standing.

2. The BRAFFERTON BUILDING (*open school hours*), with two stories of pink brick and a half-story beneath the tall hip roof, was built in 1723, possibly under the direction of Henry Cary,Jr., to house the first permanent Indian school in the colonies. Five semicircular steps approach

---

KEY FOR WILLIAMSBURG MAP

NOTE: *Names in capital letters are described in text.*

1.WREN BUILDING 1A.COLLEGE LIBRARY 2.BRAFFERTON BUILDING 3.STATUE OF LORD BOTETOURT 4.PRESIDENT'S HOUSE 5.New Shop Buildings 6.New Fire House 7.Taliaferro-Cole House 8.Pulaski Club 9.The Rectory 10.Maupin Shop 11.James Galt House 12.John Custis Tenement 13.Travis House 13A.Repiton House 14.Colonial Prison 15.PUBLIC MAGAZINE 16.Market Square Tavern 17.Lightfoot House 18.Captain Orr's Dwelling 19.BLAND–WETHERBURN HOUSE 19A.Tarpley's Store 20.Charltons Inn 21.Purdie's Dwelling 22.Kerr House 23.COLONIAL CAPITOL 24.Public Records Office 25.Colonial House 26.Colonial House 27.RALEIGH TAVERN 28.The Sign of the Golden Ball 29.Davidson Shop 30.Teterel Shop 31.Virginia Gazette Printing Office Site 31A.Pitt-Dixon House 32.DR.BLAIR'S APOTHECARY SHOP 33.LUDWELL–PARADISE HOUSE 33A.Blair's Brick House 34.OLD COURTHOUSE 35.Norton House 36.James Geddy House 37.BRUTON PAR-ISH CHURCH 38.Armistead House 39.JOHN BLAIR HOUSE 39A.Parish House 40–41–42.New Shop Buildings 43.Timson House 43A.MATTHEW WHALEY SCHOOL 44.Minor House 44A.Deane House 45.WYTHE HOUSE 45A.Deane Shop and Forge 46.Carter-Saunders House 47.GOVERNOR'S PALACE 48.Brush House 50.Levingston House 51.ST.GEORGE TUCKER HOUSE 52.Archibald Blair House 53.SIR JOHN and PEYTON RANDOLPH HOUSE 54.Colonial House 55.Colonial House 56.PUBLIC GAOL 57.COKE–GARRETT HOUSE 58.Dr. Robert Waller House 59.Site of the Second Williamsburg Theater 60.Benjamin Waller House 61.BASSETT HALL 63.Asycough Shop 64.SEMPLE HOUSE 65.Colonial House 66.Chiswell-Bucktrout House 67.Wig-Maker's House 68.Ewing House 69.Moody House 70.Colonial Dwelling 71.Powell-Hallam House 72.Williamsburg Inn 73.Craft House 74.Orrell House 75.The Quarter 76.Masonic Lodge 77.Bracken House 78.Allen-Byrd House 79.Site of First Courthouse 80.TAZE-WELL HALL 80A.Williamsburg Lodge 81.CUSTIS KITCHEN 81A.EASTERN STATE HOSPITAL 82.Griffin House

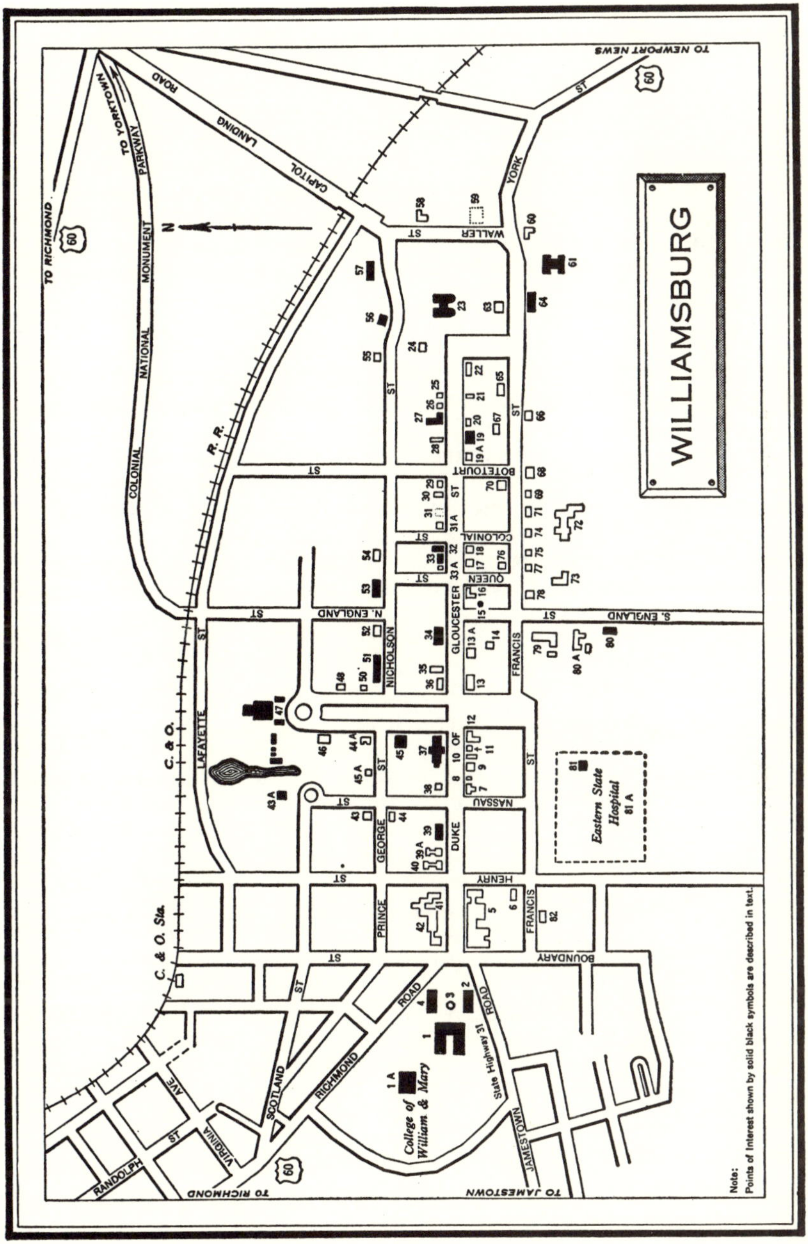
WILLIAMSBURG
TO RICHMOND
TO YORKTOWN
TO NEWPORT NEWS
TO JAMESTOWN
COLONIAL NATIONAL MONUMENT PARKWAY
CAPITOL LANDING ROAD
R. R.
C. & O.
C. & O. Sta.
LAFAYETTE ST
N. ENGLAND ST
S. ENGLAND ST
NICHOLSON ST
GLOUCESTER ST
DUKE OF GLOUCESTER ST
FRANCIS ST
BOTETOURT ST
COLONIAL ST
QUEEN ST
WALLER ST
YORK ST
NASSAU ST
HENRY ST
GEORGE ST
PRINCE GEORGE ST
BOUNDARY ST
SCOTLAND ST
RICHMOND ROAD
JAMESTOWN ROAD
State Highway 31
RANDOLPH ST
VIRGINIA AVE
College of William & Mary
Eastern State Hospital
Note:
Points of Interest shown by solid black symbols are described in text.

the plain central door beneath a small pediment. By 1712 20 Indians were assembled in the school established on the income from part of a £4,000 fund left for 'pious and charitable' uses by Robert Boyle, English scientist and seventh son of the Earl of Cork. Governor Spotswood's Indian School was moved here from Fort Christanna about 1722. The building was named after the English manor in which the fund was invested. Never very successful, the school was closed when the Revolution began, and the income was diverted to the West Indies for Negro education. Although of the three original buildings it is the only one that was never burned, it had been stripped of interior woodwork long before it was fully restored in 1932. The alumni office and information bureau are in the rebuilt KITCHEN close by.

3. The STATUE OF LORD BOTETOURT, in front of the Wren Building, is a life-size white marble figure of Virginia's royal governor. Hatless but bewigged and protected by flowing baronial robes and a fur muff, the noble lord holds an easy stance upon a baroque pedestal. Commissioned by the general assembly, Richard Hayward of London executed the figure in 1773. It stood originally in the piazza of the capitol and was moved here in 1801. The Right Honorable Norborne Berkeley, Baron de Botetourt (pronounced Botytot in Virginia) came to Virginia in 1768 and died in 1770, mourned as 'best of governors and best of men.' The statue was cleaned twice a year by order of the assembly, even during the Revolution, and escaped all but slight damage when once overturned by hoodlums.

4. The PRESIDENT'S HOUSE (*private*), built in 1732 under the direction of Henry Cary,Jr., is similar to the Brafferton Building but somewhat larger. Its central door is approached by a flight of square stone steps. James Blair, first president, lived here for ten years before his death in 1743. He was largely responsible for the establishment of the college, having suggested it to the assembly, which sent him to England in 1691 to interest Their Majesties in the proposal. He brought back the charter, royal and private endowments, and Wren's design for the main building. The 20 presidents of the college have lived here. This building was the headquarters of Cornwallis for ten days prior to the Battle of Green Spring and of the French surgeon general during the Siege of Yorktown. It was then accidentally burned but was repaired at the expense of Louis XVI. In 1931 it was restored. Among portraits of Colonial Virginians that hang within are several of the Page family by John Wollaston.

15. The PUBLIC MAGAZINE (*open* 10–5 *daily; adm.* 25¢, *children* 10¢), lately called 'Powder Horn,' stands in the southern part of Market Square. The octagonal building, with brick walls two feet thick, has a peaked roof and an encircling wall ten feet high. It was built in 1715–16 under the 'overseership' of John Tyler and the supervision of Governor Spotswood to store 'all Arms, Gun-Powder, and Ammunition, now in the Colony, belonging to the King.' The protecting wall, recently restored, was built in 1755 during the alarms of the French and Indian War, and was pulled down in 1855. Early on the morning of April 20, 1775, Governor Dunmore removed powder stored here, precipitating the outbreak

of revolution in Virginia. Patrick Henry, leading Hanover County troops, compelled payment of twice the powder's equivalent in sterling.

19. The BLAND–WETHERBURN HOUSE, an unrestored frame building, is still used as an inn. Almost certainly the birthplace in 1710 of Richard Bland, 'Great Virginia Patriot' and statesman, this house, genuinely ancient-looking in spite of a Victorian porch, was sold by Bland's father about 1716 and became a tavern. In 1738 Henry Wetherburn, formerly of the Raleigh, bought this tavern and, until his death in 1760, ran it along with three others acquired by marriage to their keepers' widows. Thus one of the earliest 'hotel chains' was established. Wetherburn enlarged the building and named the rooms, but his 'Arrack punch' glorified the establishment. For a single 'biggest bowl' of it Peter Jefferson acquired 400 acres of land in Albemarle (then Goochland) County from William Randolph of Tuckahoe.

23. The COLONIAL CAPITOL (*open 10–6 daily summer, 10–5 winter; adm. 75¢*), a pink brick building within a brick-walled yard, is a reconstruction of the first capitol and is built on the original foundations of the 'best and most commodious pile' in Colonial America. It is H-shaped, composed of two parallel units with two-story semicircular bays at the southern ends and a connecting gallery over an arcaded piazza. The gallery roof is surmounted by a slender white cupola bearing the arms of Queen Anne, in whose reign the building was erected, and a clock and the Union Jack high above. The legislative chambers are accurately refurnished according to ample records. The house of burgesses and the office of the clerk of the house are on the first floor of the east wing. Occupying similar positions in the west wing are the general court and the office of the secretary of state. The original speaker's chair in the house of burgesses, with its graceful cabriole legs and high paneled and pedimented back, is centered against the wainscoted wall of a circular platform at the end of the room and is effectively silhouetted against a large bull's-eye window.

Here Bob Cooley, Negro custodian of the capitol during the Revolutionary period, would dust off a chair for each entering statesman 'with the solemn aspect of the dignitary who sat in it.' In the office of the clerk of the house hangs a full-length portrait of Washington by Charles Willson Peale, a replica of one in Philadelphia. On the second floor are council and committee rooms. The Council Chamber in the south bay of the west wing is a stately oval room above the general court, decorated in Palladian style with 14 Jacobean chairs around the green baize-covered table; here hangs a good portrait of Queen Anne after the school of Kneller. The gallery over the lower central arcade was used as a conference room where councilors and burgesses met together. Among other portraits in the capitol are those of Queen Mary by Sir Godfrey Kneller; of William III by Sir Peter Lely; and of Queen Elizabeth, full length, by Marc Gheerardts.

The original building, erected under the 'overseer-ship' of Henry Cary between 1701 and 1705, was burned in 1747 and rebuilt in 1751–53. The second building, which had a western portico admired by Jefferson, was burned in 1832. Restoration began in 1929.

The general assembly met here from 1704 until 1779, having used the Wren Building of the college during the five previous years. Many important events of the Revolutionary period took place here. On December 24, 1779, the assembly met here for the last time before its removal to Richmond.

On the eastern side of the capitol is the SITE OF THE OLD EXCHANGE, an open space that served as official trading center of the colony.

24. Near by on the west is the PUBLIC RECORD OFFICE, a brick building under reconstruction (1939). It was erected about 1751 for the 'preservation of the Public Records and papers of the colony' after the capitol had burned. Once popularly known as the 'Secretary's office,' it is the only building still standing that was used by the Colonial government for administrative purposes.

27. RALEIGH TAVERN (*open 10–6 daily summer, 10–5 winter; adm. 50¢*), an L-shaped white weatherboard building with 18 dormer windows, has been completely reconstructed on its original foundation. A bust of Sir Walter Raleigh is above the door. The interior is faithfully furnished in late eighteenth-century style. The rear wing is a modern kitchen. Built sometime before 1742, the tavern was once owned by John Blair; its first known keeper was Henry Wetherburn.

In 1769 the Raleigh began its career as a center of sedition when the burgesses, dissolved because of resolutions against the British Revenue Act, convened in the Apollo Room as the 'late representatives of the people' and adopted the Non-Importation Agreement. *Hilaritas sapientiae et bonae vitae proles* (jollity is the offspring of wisdom and good living) is the motto over the mantel. This room was the frequent rendezvous of Jefferson, Henry, and other Revolutionary patriots. They met here in 1773 to develop intercolonial committees of correspondence. Dissolved by Dunmore, the burgesses met again in the Apollo Room in May 1774. The tavern was an institution. Auctions as well as balls were held under the Raleigh's aegis. La Fayette was entertained at a banquet here in 1824, and the building was still used as a tavern until it burned in 1859. Portraits of La Fayette by Samuel Lovett Waldo and of Henry St.George Tucker by W.J.Hubard hang here.

32. DR.BLAIR'S APOTHECARY SHOP (*open 9–5 weekdays*) is one of the earliest drug stores in America. This small brick building, once called the 'Unicorn's Horn,' was erected early in the eighteenth century by Archibald Blair. Its swag roof, gabled with a 'kick out,' is not unusual in Tidewater Virginia. Prentis & Company, occupants at the time of the Revolution, were consignees of the shipment of tea that a 'Yorktown Tea Party' threw into the river from a British ship in 1774.

33. The LUDWELL–PARADISE HOUSE (*open 10–6 daily summer, 10–5 winter; adm. 25¢*) is a rectangular brick building erected about 1717 by Philip Ludwell II, stepson and heir of Sir William Berkeley's widow. The architecture of this typical early Georgian Colonial house is notable for the pleasing arrangement of the 18-pane windows and the basket-weave effect of its Flemish bond brick, accented with glazed headers. The compact low hip-roof building has a fine denticulated cornice. A lean-to at

the back provides additional space. The white frame kitchen, the cover of the well, and the brick stables at the end of the long narrow garden have all been reconstructed from their foundations. The Ludwells, who probably used this town house during the legislative season, were wealthy planters. Eccentric Lucy Ludwell Paradise, daughter of Philip Ludwell and widow of John Paradise, a scholarly Londoner who was a friend of Dr. Johnson, returned in 1805 to live here until she was confined in the asylum. She horrified London society by pouring hot tea on a gentleman who displeased her, and it is said that in this house she received visitors in her coach, which was rolled back and forth in the hall. Well preserved, the house needed slight repair by the Restoration.

34. The OLD COURTHOUSE (*open* 9–9 *daily*), on Courthouse Green, is a well-proportioned T-shaped one-story brick building with a cupola. The entrance is protected by a cantilevered, gabled hood. It was erected in 1770 to serve as hustings court of the city and courthouse for James City County, in which only half of Williamsburg originally lay. The building now houses the WILLIAMSBURG RESTORATION ARCHEOLOGICAL EXHIBIT, a collection of objects recovered during excavation of building sites, a series of photographs showing progressive stages of restoration, and the eighteenth-century Bodleian copperplate of Williamsburg's public buildings.

37. BRUTON PARISH CHURCH (*open* 9–12, 1–5 *daily*), apparently the oldest Episcopal church of uninterrupted use in America, is a mellow red brick building of early Virginia Colonial design. Tall white-shuttered windows, well proportioned and nicely spaced, run along the sides and east end. Above the cornice of the square tower at the west end rises a two-tiered octagonal steeple. Within is the spacious box pew of the Colonial governor, sheltered by an elegant canopy and bearing the royal insignia.

Bruton Parish was created in 1674 through the union of two earlier parishes. A new church on land donated by Colonel John Page, ordered built in 1679 and completed in 1683, was inadequate for the fashionable crowds after Williamsburg became the capital. Governor Spotswood drew the plans and supervised construction of the present structure, which was built in 1710–15. The tower was not constructed, it seems, until 1769. The interior was altered in 1838–40 but restored in 1905–07 under supervision of the rector, Dr. Goodwin. Beneath the aisles and in the yard are buried many distinguished Virginians, including Governor Edward Nott, Lieutenant Governor Francis Fauquier, Judge John Blair, and three secretaries of state. The church preserves a seventeenth-century marble font from Jamestown, Bibles, and three communion services. A silver flagon, dated 1756, chalice dated 1764, and alms basin are supposed to have been given to Bruton Parish by Governor Fauquier between 1759 and 1768. The silver service presented by Lady Rebecca (Staunton) Gooch to the college is kept here. The cup has the hallmark of London's Peter Maraden, and the plate is dated 1737. The third service preserved here is the chalice, paten, and basin given by Acting-Governor Francis Moryson in 1661–62, 'For the use of James City Parish Church.'

39. The JOHN BLAIR HOUSE (*private*), a snug story-and-a-half frame house with a chimney set in the middle of the roof and five dormers unevenly spaced, was built about 1747 by John Blair,Sr., enlarged later to accommodate two families, and recently restored. John Blair,Sr., twice acting-governor, was a merchant and father of John Blair,Jr., ardent supporter of the cause of independence and a signer of the Non-Importation Agreement in 1769. He served as a judge and chief justice of the general court and as judge of the Virginia high court of chancery. He was grand master of the first Grand Lodge of Masons in Virginia, organized in 1778. Chancellor Blair was one of the Virginia delegates to the Constitutional Convention in 1787 and a signer of the Constitution. Washington appointed him in 1789 a justice of the United States Supreme Court, from which he resigned in 1796. John Marshall probably lived in this house while studying law with George Wythe.

43A. The MATTHEW WHALEY SCHOOL (*open school hours*), N. end Nassau St., only public school for white children in Williamsburg, is a large, well-equipped brick building of simple design, completed in 1931. Its name revives that of the school founded in 1706 for the poor of Bruton Parish by Mary Whaley and provided with £50 by her will in 1742, to 'eternalize the name of Matty's School by Matty's name forever.' Matty died in 1705, aged nine. The original 'Matty's Free School' occupied three frame buildings just outside town and continued 'the teaching of the neediest children of the Parish of Bruton in the art of reading, writing, and arithmetic' probably until the Revolution, but without benefit of the legacy. Payment was refused by Mrs.Whaley's executor, and the suit dragged on for more than 120 years. In 1866 the College of William and Mary, as new trustees, received $8,470 and the following year opened the 'Grammar and Matty School' in Brafferton Hall.

45. The WYTHE HOUSE (*open* 9–1, 2–5 *weekdays*, 2–5 *Sun.; adm.* 25¢), a rectangular brick mansion, has two built-in chimneys and a hip roof. The simplicity and disposition of the windows is unusually satisfying. Richard Taliaferro, 'one of our most skillful architects,' built the house in 1755 and left it in 1775 to his son-in-law, George Wythe. Admitted to the bar at 20, Wythe was the first professor of law in America, the teacher of Thomas Jefferson, John Marshall, James Monroe, and Henry Clay; the first Virginia signer of the Declaration of Independence; chairman of the committee that designed the seal of Virginia; delegate to the Constitutional Convention, although absent when the Constitution was signed; and chancellor of Virginia from 1778 to 1801. In his opinion on the case of *Commonwealth* v. *Caton*, 1782, Wythe established himself as one of the first formulators of the American theory of judicial review: 'If the whole legislature . . . should attempt to overleap the bounds . . . I, in administering the public justice of the country, will meet the united powers at my seat in this tribunal; and pointing to the Constitution, will say to them, Here is the limit of your authority; and hither shall you go but no further.' He died in 1806 from poison administered by a nephew—an impatient heir—and is buried in St.John's Churchyard, Richmond.

The house was Washington's headquarters before the Siege of Yorktown and Rochambeau's afterward. Restored under the supervision of the Reverend Dr. William Goodwin, it was deeded in 1931 to Bruton Parish and used as a parish house until 1937. Here hangs the only known portrait of George Wythe, copied from a lost original.

47. The GOVERNOR'S PALACE (*open* 10–6 *daily summer*, 10–5 *winter; adm.* $1) is an authentic reconstruction of the brick house erected as a residence for royal governors soon after Williamsburg became the capital. A wide green flanked by a double driveway leads to the palace and its dependencies. At the end of the green the driveway turns in a loop before a fine iron-grilled gate. This stately entrance, topped with an elaborately scrolled heading and flanked by the British lion and unicorn, leads into a formally landscaped forecourt enclosed by the palace building, two dormered flankers, and a curving brick wall at the front.

The palace rises two full stories to a denticulated cornice beneath a steep and many-dormered hip roof, surmounted by a balustraded platform and a tall lantern cupola rising in two octagonal stages between multiple chimneys. The design of the five-bay façade is in keeping with the earliest phase of the Georgian style—narrow many-paned sash windows with wide architraves set almost flush with the brick openings, a simple square-transomed doorway beneath a centered wrought-iron balcony, and a brick string course between the first and second stories. The plan of the main block was originally square, but in 1751 it was extended by the addition of a 'ball-room' wing at the rear. In the gable end of this wing the royal arms of the first Georges, wood-carved and gaily painted, overlook the palace gardens.

About a reconstructed KITCHEN and SCULLERY, close to the west side, cluster small brick outbuildings—smokehouse, laundry, dairy; and there are still others on the east side. The huge formal gardens, roughly square in total plan, embrace a CANAL and FISH POND along the western edge. There are ten separate gardens including box, fruit, and kitchen gardens, a maze, and a bowling green—all completely restored, their rectangular forms thickly set in eighteenth-century fashion with trim hedges and walks in intricate geometrical patterns.

The interior is notable for its fine woodwork. The wide entrance hall, most of the passages, and several smaller rooms are fully paneled. In other rooms the wall surfaces and some of the woodwork have been painted in the original soft shades of gray-green, yellow, and blue. The walls of the library, directly above the entrance hall, are covered with antique Spanish tooled leather. Furnishings and interior decoration, chiefly in mid-eighteenth-century style, have been restored in lavish detail. As mentioned by Lord Botetourt, coronation portraits of George III and Queen Charlotte, by the court painter Allan Ramsay, hang against the pale blue walls of the large and stately ballroom, flanking the door to the music room. Among other portraits in the palace are those of the Honorable Mary Howard, by Sir Peter Lely; of Charles II and Catherine of Braganza, after the school of Lely; and of Charles I and Queen Henrietta Maria, by Van Dyck.

The construction of this haven for 'exiled' royal lieutenants was begun in 1705 under Henry Cary. The bulk of the work was accomplished under the direction of Governor Spotswood, and the building was completed by 1720. The palace was the hub of Virginia social life—convivial symbol of royal prestige and fount of royal authority until 1775. Governor Fauquier held intellectual bachelor dinners with Dr.William Small, George Wythe, and Thomas Jefferson. Here Sy Gilliat, slave violinist to Governor Botetourt, played for entertainments. Possessed of 50 suits, Gilliat usually wore a 'powdered brown wig, with side curls and a long cue,' and 'His manners were as courtly as his dress.' The building burned in 1781, while in use as a hospital for American soldiers wounded at Yorktown. Two smaller structures facing the forecourt were torn down in 1863.

The entire establishment and extensive gardens have been reconstructed since 1930 upon their excavated foundations according to a plan drawn by Jefferson; an illustration of the buildings as they appeared between 1732 and 1747, which was found on a copperplate in the Bodleian Library at Oxford; and almost 300 pages of source material. Minute inventories taken by three governors and many contemporary descriptions have made possible accurate restoration and refurnishing.

51. The ST.GEORGE TUCKER HOUSE (*private*), though large and built in the Early Republican period, has the simplicity of an earlier day. From the central portion the white clapboard structure rambles pleasantly beneath dormered gable roofs at descending levels. The restored kitchen, with its massive chimney at the western end, is again in use. St.George Tucker, a native of Bermuda, bought the property from Edmund Randolph in 1788 and enlarged the house to its present size. Tucker, successor to George Wythe as professor of law at the College of William and Mary, wrote the *Annotated Edition of Blackstone's Commentaries* (1804), first American text on law.

53. SIR JOHN AND PEYTON RANDOLPH HOUSE (*adm. by arrangement*) is a long rectangular frame dwelling erected about 1715. Built as two dwellings, the house was bought in 1724 by Sir John Randolph, whose 'person,' according to *The Virginia Gazette*, was 'of the finest turn imaginable.' Sir John was an enlightened economist whose services as Virginia's representative in London ushered in the colony's greatest period of prosperity. His mission in 1729 resulted in a loosening of restrictions on colonial trade, and led, through passage of Virginia's tobacco inspection law in 1730, to the vast expansion of tobacco trade during the next half century. On his trip in 1732 to present 'The Case of the Planters of Tobacco in Virginia' he played an important part in the controversy over Sir Robert Walpole's tobacco excise bill. His grasp of the theory and advantages of excise taxation so impressed Walpole that he was knighted—the only native Virginian ever so honored—by George II, then under Walpole's thumb. He was the first to report legal cases in Virginia and collected papers used later by William Stith, his nephew, as sources for the first comprehensive Virginia history.

Sir John's son, Peyton Randolph, who inherited the home, was chairman of the first three Virginia conventions and first president of the First Continental Congress. His service in the cause of revolution ended by his death in 1775. The generals, Rochambeau and La Fayette, had headquarters here before the Siege of Yorktown. Mrs.Mary Monroe Peachy, owner of the house in 1824, entertained La Fayette. 'When he left the tavern nearly all the company followed him to his quarters at Mrs.Peachy's where a number of ladies assembled to see him.'

56. The PUBLIC GAOL (*open* 10–6 *daily summer*, 10–5 *winter; adm.* 50¢), an irregular red brick building, restored to its appearance in 1773 for exhibition only, was Virginia's first 'penitentiary.' Its thick walls, partly original, with small barred windows—unglassed during the eighteenth century—extend around a narrow exercise yard. The cells, behind stout nail-studded doors, were formerly crowded with prisoners who suffered sometimes fatally from winter cold. Early in the eighteenth century the gaol was called a 'strong, sweet prison for criminals'—far too 'sweet' in 1718 for nine of Blackbeard's pirates, whose term ended on what was afterwards known as Gallows' Road. In front of the building stand reproductions of the original pillory and stocks. Built simultaneously with the capitol and enlarged several times, the public gaol, where important political prisoners were held during the Revolution, served the colony as general prison until 1779, when it became the city jail.

57. The COKE-GARRETT HOUSE (*private*) is a rambling white frame building 90 feet long in landscaped grounds including a large wheel-shaped rose garden. The severe porch on the center section is supported by five square, fluted columns. The oldest part, the west wing, built before 1750, has a fine Chinese Chippendale staircase. John Coke, a goldsmith, owned the house from about 1750 until his death in 1767, when it was inherited by his son Robey. Shortly after the Revolution it passed to the Garrett family.

61. BASSETT HALL (*private*), approached by an avenue of fine old elms, is a white frame building in Georgian Colonial style; its attractive outbuildings, partly original, stand in an extensive garden. Built before 1753, Bassett Hall was owned until 1800 by Colonel Philip Johnson, a burgess, who sometimes let it as a tavern. He sold it to Burwell Bassett, a nephew of Martha Washington. It is said that here the Irish poet, Thomas Moore, wrote 'To the Firefly,' after seeing lightning bugs for the first time. Thought until recently to have been owned by President John Tyler, the house actually belonged to Abel P. Upshur, a member of his cabinet. Damaged by fire in 1930, the restored hall is now the Williamsburg home of John D. Rockefeller,Jr.

64. The SEMPLE HOUSE (*private*), fully restored, a dignified white frame building in early Federal style, shows the restraining influence of the Adam mode. The two-story central portion with an unusually high ceiling presents its gable to the street and opens on probably the finest porch in Williamsburg—small, gabled, and supported by two slender Doric columns. The home of two judges of the general court—James Semple, professor of law at the College of William and Mary, and John B. Christian—and perhaps of a third, Hugh Nelson, it was long identified as the home of Peyton Randolph until his will, discovered in 1911, was later consulted, locating his house on Nicholson Street.

80. TAZEWELL HALL (*private*), a large, unrestored, unpainted frame house with a shallow double porch, was built about 1760 across the end of England Street by John Randolph, last royal attorney general for the Virginia colony, and shifted to its present site about 1918. A staunch loyalist, Tory John Randolph's sympathies were quite unlike those of his brother, Peyton, and of his son, Edmund, who became the first Attorney General of the United States and then Secretary of State. At the beginning of the Revolution John moved to England, where he died impoverished and longing for Virginia. This lavish establishment was the main dwelling on a 1,500-acre plantation. Tory John took pride in the extensive gardens and wrote a *Treatise on Gardening*. The house was bought by Justice John Tazewell in 1778.

81. The small brick structure in the exercise yard of the Eastern State Hospital was the KITCHEN OF THE OLD CUSTIS HOUSE, built about 1714. Daniel Parke Custis, Martha Washington's first husband, lived here for many years.

81A. EASTERN STATE HOSPITAL (*adm. by arrangement*), S. side Francis St., occupying a group of stone and brick buildings on 800-acre grounds, is the oldest public asylum for the insane in America. Originally called the Lunatic Hospital and known as 'Mad House' or 'Bedlam,' it was chartered in 1768 and opened in 1773. James Galt, whose family managed the asylum through four generations, was the first superintendent. This hospital, the first to relinquish the idea that a lunatic asylum is a place of horror, is the first of its kind to care for Negro insane. Free Negroes were taken in from the beginning, and slaves after 1846, but Negroes have had separate quarters since 1850. The original buildings burned long ago. The institution (1939) cares for more than 1,600 patients.

POINTS OF INTEREST IN ENVIRONS

Yorktown, 13 *m.* (*see Tour 6b*). Carter's Grove, 6.3 *m.* (*see Tour 8a*). Jamestown, 6.7 *m.* (*see Tour 8A*). Green Spring, 6.5 *m.* (*see Tour 24*).

Winchester

Railroad Stations: Piccadilly and Kent Sts. for Baltimore & Ohio R.R. and Winchester and Wardensville R.R.; Boscawen St. near Amherst St. for Pennsylvania R.R.
Bus Station: Braddock St. between Amherst and Boscawen Sts. for Greyhound, Brenner Motor, Blue Ridge Lines, Potomac Motor Lines, and Virginia Stage Lines.
Taxis: Fare 25¢ for 2 passengers, within city.

Accommodations: 4 hotels; tourist homes and inns.

Information Service: Chamber of Commerce, Cameron St. and Rouss Ave.

Motion Picture Houses: 2.
Golf: Winchester Golf Club, 1.5 m. E. on Cork St. extended, 9 holes, greens fee $1.50 per day, caddie 50¢ for 18 holes.
Swimming: Rouss Spring Park, SE. edge of city on Millwood Rd., children only, free; Winchester Golf Club, 1.5 m. E. on Cork St. extended, adm. by arrangement.
Tennis: Rouss Spring Park, SE. edge of city on Millwood Rd., free in morning, 15¢ per hour in afternoon; Winchester Golf Club, 1.5 m. E. on Cork St. extended, adm. by arrangement.

Annual Events: Apple Blossom Festival, spring, when blossoms appear in near-by orchards; Blue Ridge Hunt Club Horse and Colt Show, Carter Hall, June.

WINCHESTER (725 alt., 10,855 pop.), near the northern entrance to the Shenandoah Valley, is the seat of Frederick County and the oldest Virginia city west of the Blue Ridge. In the eighteenth and early nineteenth centuries stagecoaches and wagons lumbered through its muddy streets, carrying adventurers westward and southward. Here crossed two old trails, which are today arterial highways serving the uses of commerce and vacationists.

In spring, when the rolling countryside is beautiful and fragrant, Winchester's Apple Blossom Festival attracts thousands of people, who come to behold the beauty of the 700,000 apple trees that bloom each year in Frederick County. Then the little city abandons itself to two days of festivity. Queen Shenandoah is crowned on the steps of Handley School. Surrounded by ladies-in-waiting, Her Majesty views a pageant enacted by 1,000 children. In the late afternoon there is an aerial show at Admiral Byrd Airport, southeast of town. The first evening is crowded with a reception for the queen and her court; a parade of Virginia fire companies, cadet corps from military schools, and World War veterans, marching to the music of many bands; street dances in roped-off areas; and a ball at the apple palace. On the second day school children re-enact their pageant; the queen is entertained; a parade with elaborate floats again enlists bands and soldiers; and at a late hour the queen's ball begins, bringing the festival to a close.

Town Run and the tracks of the Baltimore & Ohio Railroad traverse Winchester. The comparatively level older portion of the city rises toward flat-topped hills: on the north Fort Hill, on the east Church Hill, on the south Potato Hill, on the west Academy Hill, Powell's Ridge, and Apple Pie Ridge, an undulating checkerboard of apple orchards.

Though many first settlers in Winchester were English, its neat compactness is attributable to Germans from the Northern colonies. Houses, built flush with the street, have tiny gardens tucked behind them and stoops that steal space from sidewalks. On the outskirts of the city, however, newer homes have indulged themselves in the luxury of surrounding lawns. In 1732 Joist Hite crossed the Potomac at Pack Horse Ford, near present Shepherdstown, West Virginia, bringing 16 families from Pennsylvania to settle at Opequon, five miles south of Winchester. From Isaac and John Van Meter, Hite purchased lands that were a part of the Northern Neck proprietary of Thomas, Lord Fairfax.

Though Frederick County was sliced in 1738 from Orange County, the story of Winchester, first Fredericktown, did not begin until 1744, when James Wood laid out a courthouse square and 26 lots. Frederick County held its first court in a log house Wood built at the present Glen Burnie. If Lord Fairfax had had his way, Stephens City would have been made the county seat. James Wood, however, outwitted him by serving one of the justices enough toddy, and the deciding vote was cast for Frederick. In 1752 the town was laid out and named for Winchester, England.

Already settlers knew the lad, George Washington, who had been surveying Lord Fairfax's vast holdings since 1748. Washington was 16 years old—redheaded, freckle-faced, and very eager—when he set out in March 1748 for Winchester and his first job, and his eyes were busy as he 'went through most beautiful groves of Sugar Trees and spent ye best part of ye Day in admiring ye Trees and richness of ye Land.'

After General Braddock's defeat in 1755, Lieutenant Colonel Washington, placed in command of frontier forces, 'rid post to this place . . . and found everything in the greatest hurry and Confusion, by the back Inhabitants flocking in, and those of the town removing out. . . No Orders are obey'd, but what a Party of Soldiers, or my own drawn Sword, Enforces.' He set about to quiet a frightened people and to build Fort Loudoun for their protection.

Men of Winchester played a conspicuous part in the Revolutionary War. Their leader was Daniel Morgan, who moved there from New Jersey in 1753. After the Battle of Bunker Hill he organized a company of northern Virginia riflemen. Commissioned captain of militia under General Benedict Arnold, he pressed with his company into Canada, was held prisoner in Quebec, fought in both battles of Saratoga, and as hero of the Battle of Cowpens is given credit for the defeat of General Tarleton. Morgan spent the last ten years of his life in Winchester.

Between the Revolution and the 1860's Winchester grew and prospered. In 1779 the general assembly authorized its incorporation as a town.

Early in the nineteenth century stage lines operated between Winchester and Harpers Ferry, continuing even after the Winchester and Potomac Railroad was completed in 1836.

From the beginning till the end of the War between the States Winchester was a center of military activities. Crops and cattle, mills and factories made the valley an important requisitioning area for the Confederacy, and Winchester was a vantage point coveted by both armies. When General Thomas J. Jackson was given command of the Department of the Shenandoah in October 1861, he cleared Winchester of invading Federal troops; in March 1862 Union forces under General Banks forced him to evacuate the town; but on May 25 he moved in again. Until the summer of 1864 Winchester changed hands many times, and more than 100 military engagements took place in the surrounding area.

Fighting at an end, Frederick County looked again to fields and orchards, and its principal town to marketing. Winchester was chartered as a city in 1874 and adopted the city manager form of government in 1918. It owes its recent prosperity to near-by orchards. Though the Virginia apple was not important commercially until after the War between the States, its fame had spread long before. After the establishment of the Virginia Agricultural and Mechanical College—now the Virginia Polytechnic Institute—serious attention was given to apple culture. The Institute's department of horticulture was founded in 1888. Today almost 400 fruit farms in Frederick County produce more than 650,000 barrels of apples annually. Winesaps, Pippins, Staymans, the Delicious, Black Twigs, and all their manifold kin enter the packing houses; but York Imperials—crisp, pungent, and juicy—make up 60 per cent of the apples that pass in and out of Winchester. In enormous warehouses, situated at the approaches to the city and capable of handling nearly 1,000,000 barrels, apples are sorted, packed, and shipped. One of the storehouses, with a 500,000-barrel capacity, is the largest in the world. In other plants apple by-products are manufactured. Winchester also has a brick plant and factories producing woolen and knitted wear, gloves, flour, and other commodities. The annual pay roll is $3,000,000.

Even in winter, when the trees are bare and only the cidery pungence from the packing houses and the big apple in front of the Elks Club bear testimony to its principal industry, Winchester, on main-traveled highways, is still a goal for travelers.

POINTS OF INTEREST

The tree-shaded PUBLIC SQUARE, bounded by Loudoun, Boscawen, Cameron Sts., and Rouss Ave., was donated in 1744 by James Wood. Eleven buildings, as well as stocks, a whipping post, and a pillory were once in the square. The FREDERICK COUNTY COURTHOUSE (*open* 9–5 *Mon.–Fri.*, 9–1 *Sat.*), Loudoun St. between Boscawen St. and Rouss Ave., a large white-painted brick building with a tall Doric portico, was completed in 1840 and succeeded two earlier log structures. A stone jail, built about 1764, occupied the east side of the square until a brick market house took its place in 1821. The CITY HALL, Cameron St. between Boscawen St. and Rouss Ave., was erected in 1900, partly with funds contributed by Charles 'Broadway' Rouss. Born in Maryland, Rouss was sent to school in Winchester at the age of 10. At 15 he started his career in a local general store and at 18 opened his own store with a capital of $500. Later he made a fortune as a merchant on Broadway, New York City. His gifts to Winchester amounted to more than $200,000.

OLD TAYLOR HOTEL, 225 N.Loudoun (Main) St., a large brick building, its ground floor occupied by a chain store, retains many-columned verandas on its second and third stories. As the Coffee House, McGuire's Tavern, the General Washington, and as Taylor's Hotel, it was a center of business and social life for 150 years. During the War between the States the building was occupied by Confederate and Union officers. 'Stonewall' Jackson had temporary headquarters here, and General Banks used it at one time as a hospital. Burned in 1845 and rebuilt three years later, it was maintained by various owners until closed in 1905. Among its guests were Washington, John Marshall, Henry Clay, and Daniel Webster.

MOUNT HEBRON CEMETERY, E. end of Boscawen St., was established in 1844 as a cemetery and adjoined the original Lutheran burial ground. At the left of the entrance stand the RUINS OF THE OLD LUTHERAN CHURCH—one thick stone wall, jagged and ivy-grown, with two arched window openings. German Lutherans, organized before 1753 and given this site by Lord Fairfax in that year, began their church in 1764. It was used as a barracks during the Revolutionary War, and was burned in 1864. The grave of Daniel Morgan is southeast of the ruins. Near by lie five of the six men constituting Morgan's 'Dutch Mess,' his bodyguard throughout the Revolution.

In STONEWALL CEMETERY, bounded by Greenwalt Ave., Cork St., East and Woodstock Lanes, is the CONFEDERATE MONUMENT TO UNKNOWN DEAD, a tall shaft commemorating 829 unknown soldiers killed in or near Winchester. More than 3,000 identified soldiers are also buried in this cemetery.

In the NATIONAL CEMETERY, opposite Stonewall Cemetery across Woodstock Lane, five acres purchased by the Federal Government in 1866, lie 2,110 known and 2,381 unknown Union soldiers killed in the Winchester area.

The FIRST PRESBYTERIAN CHURCH, 304 E.Piccadilly St., a barnlike gray structure of rubble fieldstone, built about 1790, was the first church of the Winchester Presbytery. The building was sold in 1834 to a white Baptist congregation and later to a Negro Baptist congregation. Union troops used it as a stable during the War between the States. In 1925 it was converted into a Negro school but is now used as an armory.

The SITE OF FORT LOUDOUN, Loudoun St. between Clark and Peyton Sts., is a half acre over which Winchester's main street now passes. Part of the SOUTHWEST BASTION, NW. corner Peyton and Loudoun Sts., still stands above the surrounding level—all that is left of the redoubt built by Colonel George Washington in 1756–57. The fort, named for the

Earl of Loudoun, commander in chief of Colonial forces, was garrisoned with 450 men and defended by 24 guns. It was never attacked and its guns were never fired, but it served its purpose: the French at Fort Duquesne reported it impregnable.

STONEWALL JACKSON'S HEADQUARTERS, 415 N.Braddock St., obscured by surrounding trees and houses, is a brick house designed in Gothic Revival style. General Jackson had headquarters here in 1861.

The HANDLEY LIBRARY (*open* 10–9 *daily in winter*, 10–7 *in summer*), NW. corner Braddock and Piccadilly Sts., a richly ornamented Italian Renaissance villa, was opened in 1913. It contains about 30,000 volumes and has a lecture hall seating 300. The library and Winchester's magnificent public school were gifts from Judge John Handley.

SHERIDAN'S HEADQUARTERS, SW. corner Braddock and Piccadilly Sts., owned by the Elks Lodge, is a large brick house painted white, with a two-story Corinthian portico. The building served as headquarters for General N.P.Banks in 1862, for General R.H.Milroy during the next year, and for General Philip Sheridan in the autumn and winter of 1864–65. In the front yard stands a painted red APPLE about five feet high, made of concrete and plaster and set here in 1932 after its use in a pageant.

DANIEL MORGAN'S HOUSE (*private*), 226 W.Amherst St., a many-windowed stuccoed dwelling almost hidden by trees, was built by George Flowerdew Norton and later enlarged. General Daniel Morgan lived here two years before his death in 1802.

CHRIST CHURCH, NE. corner Washington and Boscawen Sts., a rectangular brick building in simple Neo-Gothic style, was built in 1828–29 to replace the log church on the 'Public Lotts.' The tomb of Thomas, sixth Lord Fairfax of Cameron, is in the basement of the church. The body of Lord Fairfax was first buried in the old church and later moved here, but its exact location was forgotten. In 1926 Robert T. Barton,Jr., a Winchester lawyer, employed the Negro sexton to search for the bones. After unprofitable days of digging he ordered the work discontinued. The Negro, however, returned the following morning, declaring that the spot had been revealed to him in a dream. 'If I find dem bones, Boss,' he argued, 'you pay me. If I don't find 'em, you don't.' Digging continued, the bones were discovered, and Lord Fairfax (1693–1781), proprietor of the Northern Neck, was reburied beneath the floor of the church.

GLEN BURNIE, W.Amherst St. near city limits, is a rambling red brick house in the midst of trees surrounded by a wide low meadow, which is encircled by a stone wall and crossed by a meandering stream. The house was built by Robert Wood in 1794 to replace a log house built before 1743 by his father, Colonel James Wood. General James Wood, governor of Virginia (1796–99), and brother of Robert, was born here.

SHENANDOAH VALLEY MILITARY ACADEMY, Amherst St., occupying several buildings on 22 acres of tree-shaded grounds, is one of the oldest in America. It was founded in 1764 as the Winchester Academy, and sessions have been held continuously, except during the War between the States, at least since 1785. The average enrollment is 100.

WASHINGTON'S OFFICE (*now open*), NE. corner Cork and Braddock Sts., a one-story gabled-roof building, is in two sections. The newer part is built of rough stone, the older of hewn logs covered with clapboards. The small windows have solid outside blinds. In the log section two doors with old facings swing on large H- and L-hinges. George Washington used the older part as an office while surveying for Lord Fairfax. Behind the building is a small cannon from Alexandria and a stone monument commemorating Braddock's line of march.

The SITE OF WASHINGTON'S QUARTERS, 204 S.Loudoun St., is occupied by a stone house built in 1792. In a log building here Washington had his quarters in 1755 while he built Fort Loudoun.

RED LION TAVERN (*adm. by arrangement*), SE. corner Cork and Loudoun Sts., is a pleasantly proportioned two-story house built of limestone. Now a residence, it was a thriving tavern about the time of the Revolution. George Washington stopped here several times. Peter Lauck of Daniel Morgan's 'Dutch Mess' was proprietor in 1783.

POINTS OF INTEREST IN ENVIRONS

Home of Isaac Parkins, 0.8 *m.*; Site of the First Battle of Winchester, 2.2 *m.*; Star Fort, 2.3 *m.*; Kenilworth, 5.8 *m.* (*see Tour 5a*).

PART III

Tours

Tour 1

(Washington,D.C.)—Alexandria—Fredericksburg—Ashland—Richmond —Petersburg—Dinwiddie—South Hill—(Henderson,N.C.). US 1. District of Columbia Line to North Carolina Line, 199.5 *m.*

Concrete roadbed throughout, three- or four-lane Washington to Petersburg.
Richmond, Fredericksburg & Potomac R.R., over the tracks of which pass trains of Seaboard Air Line Ry. and Atlantic Coast Line R.R., parallels route between Washington and Richmond; Seaboard Air Line Ry. and Atlantic Coast Line R.R., over the tracks of which pass the trains of Norfolk & Western Ry., between Richmond and Petersburg; Seaboard Air Line Ry. between Petersburg and North Carolina Line.
All types of accommodations.

Following, more or less, the route of the Indian Trail that became the Potomac Path and then the King's Highway, US 1 passes through the northeastern Piedmont and then skirts the western rim of the forest-covered Coastal Plain, crossing the Rappahannock, James, and Appomattox Rivers at their fall line. Agricultural pursuits predominate in this slightly rolling country. South of Petersburg the highway, veering west, penetrates 'Southside' Virginia, a region of clay soil with thin forests and tobacco farms. Except in the well-populated environs of the few cities, US 1 gives the impression of mere distance in what Gertrude Stein has called 'all the miles of uninhabited Virginia.'

Section a. DISTRICT OF COLUMBIA to FREDERICKSBURG; 49.8 *m.*

Beginning at the south bank of the Potomac and paralleling the river, US 1 has along its upper end myriads of commercial signs and tourist cabins, tawdry blots that vanish as the road plunges through the region of small farms and restored manor houses on river bluffs, and of towns that once flourished through trade in world markets.

US 1 crosses the District of Columbia Line at the south end of the Fourteenth Street Bridge, 0 *m.*, at a point 2 miles from the zero milestone in the District.

Right here to the Mount Vernon Memorial Highway, an alternate route, built by the Federal Government in 1932, that passes landscaped lagoons of the Potomac and the ROACHES RUN SANCTUARY for waterfowl and rejoins US 1 at Alexandria, 4 *m.*

HOOVER AIRPORT (R) 0.2 *m.*, is the commercial landing-field for Washington.

ALEXANDRIA, 4.6 *m.* (52 alt., 24,149 pop.) (*see Alexandria*).

In Alexandria is a junction with State 7 (*see Tour* 13).

Left from US 1 in Alexandria 8.9 *m.* on another section of the Mount Vernon Memorial Highway to MOUNT VERNON (*open winter* 9–4 *weekdays,* 1–4 *Sun.*; *summer* 9–5 *weekdays,* 1–5 *Sun.; adm.* 25¢, *children* 15¢). At the end of a long vista is the white frame mansion flanked by numerous outbuildings, also frame, arranged symmetrically on the estate laid out by George Washington.

The rectangular mass of the two-story Georgian Colonial house, joined to the nearest outbuildings by curving arcades, has a modillioned cornice and a hip roof with a low central pediment and widely spaced dormers. A graceful cupola pierces the roof midway between the two chimneys at the ridge ends. The house, its sides covered with pine slabs beveled to simulate stone blocks, faces east from behind the tall columns of its familiar piazza. The tree-bordered lawn, encompassed by a ha-ha wall, slopes steeply to the Potomac.

Furnished copiously with Washington's belongings, the handsome interior expresses, no less eloquently than the stately exterior, the character of the first President. Every room possesses relics of interest. In the central hall, where the Colonial color has been restored, hangs the key to the Bastille, a gift from La Fayette. The dining room has a plaster ceiling, cornice, and overmantel plaque designed in Adam style. In this room hangs Wollaston's portrait of Lawrence Washington, the builder of the house. Across the south end of the house is the general's study, where copies of most of the books he possessed have been restored to the shelves. Here he wrote innumerable letters and made notes in his voluminous diary. At the north end of the house is the spacious banquet hall, a story-and-a-half high, with coved and plaster-decorated ceiling and a Palladian window. The Italian marble mantel opposite was the gift of a London admirer, who also presented the two vases standing upon it. Portraits of Washington by Charles Willson Peale and Gilbert Stuart hang here. In the music room stands again the £1,000 harpsichord Washington imported for his little step-granddaughter, Nelly Custis. Upon it lies the flute that Washington never learned to play. The bedrooms on the second floor are completely furnished.

The numerous outbuildings are those that were essential to the self-sufficient plantation of the eighteenth century: smoke house, dairy, wash house, greenhouse, coach house, spinning house, barn, and others. An information booth occupies part of the restored kitchen, in the south wing; and farther away, to the northwest, a reproduction of the slave quarters contains a museum in which a large number of relics are displayed, notably the bust of Washington that Houdon made and used as a model for his marble statue in Richmond. The 5,000 acres of the original grant stretch along the Potomac between Dogue Creek and Little Hunting Creek. John Washington—great-grandfather of George—and Nicholas Spencer applied for a patent to the land in April 1669. Half the property—the part called Hunting Creek—descended to Lawrence, the son of John Washington, and then to Lawrence's daughter Mildred, who sold it in 1726 to her brother Augustine, father of George Washington. In 1735 Augustine Washington built a house here and moved from Wakefield, bringing with him his three-year-old son, George. In 1738, however, Augustine Washington moved again, this time to Ferry Farm (*see Tour* 16*a*).

Lawrence, the half-brother of George Washington, inherited Hunting Creek in 1743 and that year built a house for his bride, Anne Fairfax, the daughter of Colonel William Fairfax, probably on the foundations of his father's house, which had burned a few years before. He called the place Mount Vernon for his old commander, Admiral Edward Vernon of the British navy. Richard Blackburn was the architect. At the age of 16 George Washington came here to live with Lawrence. In 1752 Lawrence died. He left the estate to his daughter Sarah, subject to the dower rights of her mother, stipulating that if Sarah died without heirs Mount Vernon should descend to his half-brother George. On Sarah's death and her mother's remarriage a few months later, George Washington assumed possession of the estate. In 1754 he purchased his sister-in-law's right to the property and later the 2,500 acres that had once belonged to Nicholas Spencer. Subsequently he bought adjacent land.

To Mount Vernon in 1759 George Washington brought his bride. He had great plans for becoming the leading agriculturist in America and operated the estate as five separate farms. He tried out crop rotation, kept elaborate notes, and conferred with friends who were similarly experimenting. In 1773 he added the third story to the house, with the six bedrooms beneath the eaves and drew plans for the north and south additions. Called to lead the army of his rebellious country, he left the management of the estate and the execution of his building plans to his distant cousin, Lund Washington. He was at home again just in time to supervise the decoration of the ceiling in the great banquet hall. In 1783 George Washington returned to Mount Vernon to devote himself, as he told both diary and friends, to agriculture and domesticity. His field yielded harvests vastly satisfying; he was awarded 'a premium for raising the largest jackass' by the Agriculture Society of South Carolina.

In 1787 he was called to preside at the Constitutional Convention in Philadelphia. In 1789 he became the first President of the United States. Washington returned to Mount Vernon in 1797 for two quiet years. With him and his wife lived his step-grandchildren, Nelly and George Washington Parke Custis, whom he had adopted. On December 14, 1799, George Washington died; Martha Washington died three years later.

In 1853 Ann Pamela Cunningham of South Carolina set out to organize a society that would purchase and restore Washington's estate, then in the hands of descendants of his brother. The Mount Vernon Ladies' Association of the Union was formed in 1856, and in 1860, after having raised $200,000 for the purchase, it acquired the mansion and part of the land.

On the hillside near the house is the little ivy-covered mausoleum in which Martha and George Washington are buried in two simple sarcophagi in the outer vault.

Right from Mount Vernon on State 235 to WASHINGTON'S GRIST MILL (R), 11.8 *m.*, a tall, gable-roofed structure of rubble stone that is a reproduction on old foundations. It is equipped as a pre-Revolutionary mill. The white clapboard MILLER'S COTTAGE is also a restoration. In 1760 George Washington said that the mill, built by Augustine Washington, was 'decayed and out of order.' He then repaired it, did some rebuilding in 1770, and in 1795 reconstructed the millrace. Near the two mill ponds, vanished long ago, stood also the miller's house, the distillery, the blacksmith's shop, and the cooper's shop. George Washington asserted that his flour was 'equal in quality to any made in this country.' It was used at Mount Vernon, by the neighboring gentry, and was shipped to distant markets aboard Washington's 'schooners.' On one of his fre-

---

KEY FOR ALBEMARLE COUNTY MAP

1.University of Virginia 2.Blue Ridge Sanatorium 3.Michie Tavern 4.Monticello 5.Tufton 6.Ashlawn 7.Morven 8.Ellerslie 9.Blenheim 10.Redlands 11.Ruins of Viewmont 12.Plain Dealing 13.Christ Church 14.Glendower 15.Chester 16.Tallwood 17.Enniscorthy 18.Estouteville 19.Edgemont 20.Bally-Les-Braden 21.Farmington 22.Site of Locust Hill 23.Seven Oaks 24.Emmanuel Church 25.The Barracks 26.Carrsbrook 27.Bentivar 28.Site of Indian Village 'Monasukapanough' and Site of Mound examined by Jefferson 29.Franklin 30.Buena Vista 31.Shadwell 32.Edgehill 33.Grace Church 34.Castle Hill 35.Boyd's Tavern

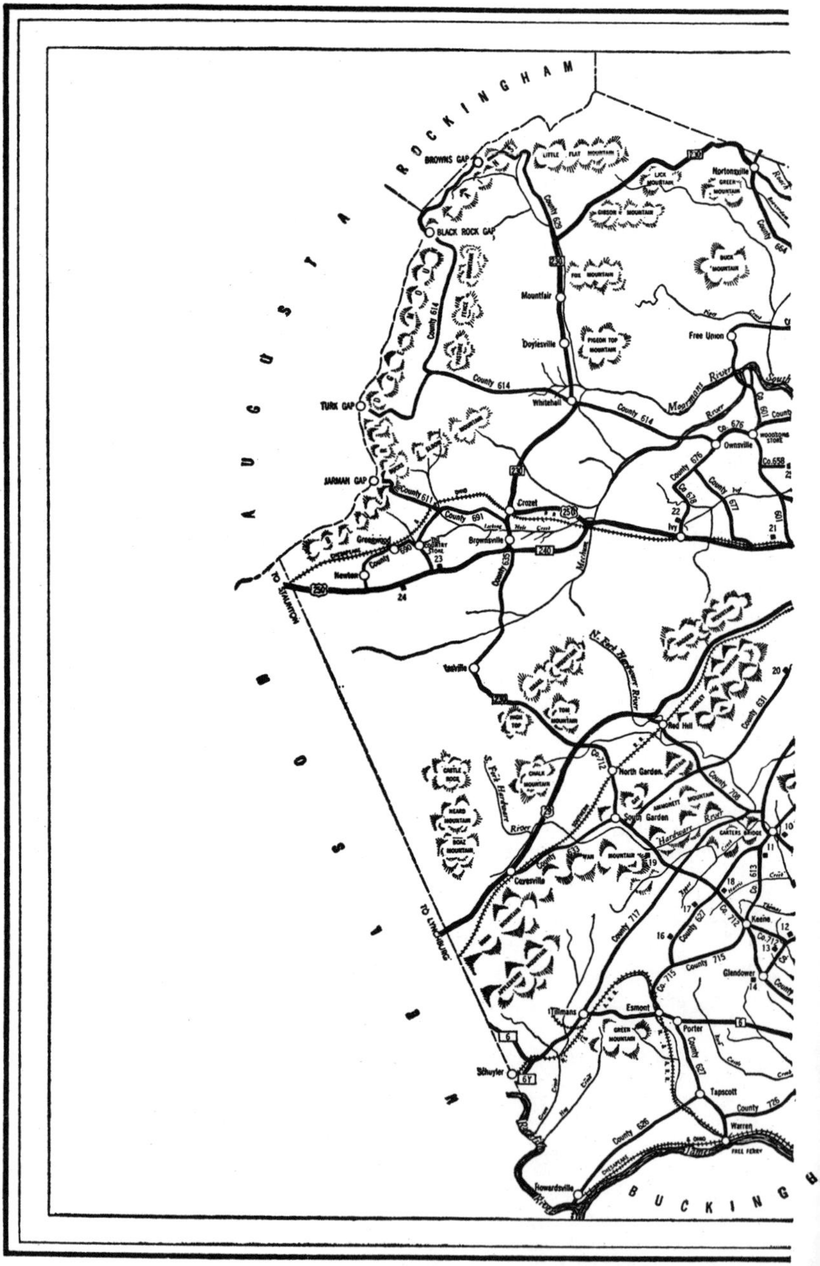
ROCKINGHAM
AUGUSTA
NELSON
BUCKINGH
BROWNS GAP
BLACK ROCK GAP
TURK GAP
JARMAN GAP
LITTLE FLAT MOUNTAIN
LICK MOUNTAIN
GIBSON MOUNTAIN
GREEN MOUNTAIN
BUCK MOUNTAIN
FOX MOUNTAIN
PIGEON TOP MOUNTAIN
Nortonsville
Mountfair
Doylesville
Free Union
Whitehall
Moormans River
Owensville
WOODSONG STORE
Crozet
Ivy
Greenwood
Brownsville
Newtown
Yancey Mills
Batesville
N. Fork Hardware River
S. Fork Hardware River
Red Hill
North Garden
South Garden
CASTLE ROCK
HEARD MOUNTAIN
CHALK MOUNTAIN
GAY MOUNTAIN
ARMORETT MOUNTAIN
Hardware River
CARTERS BRIDGE
Covesville
TO STAUNTON
TO LYNCHBURG
Keene
Glendower
Tillmans
Esmont
Porter
GREEN MOUNTAIN
Schuyler
Tapscott
Warren
FREE FERRY
Howardsville
James River
County 614
County 611
County 691
County 635
County 676
County 677
County 631
County 717
County 627
County 715
County 712
County 726
County 626
County 664
County 629
Co. 601
Co. 658
Co. 712
Co. 613
Co. 715
250
240
29
6
67

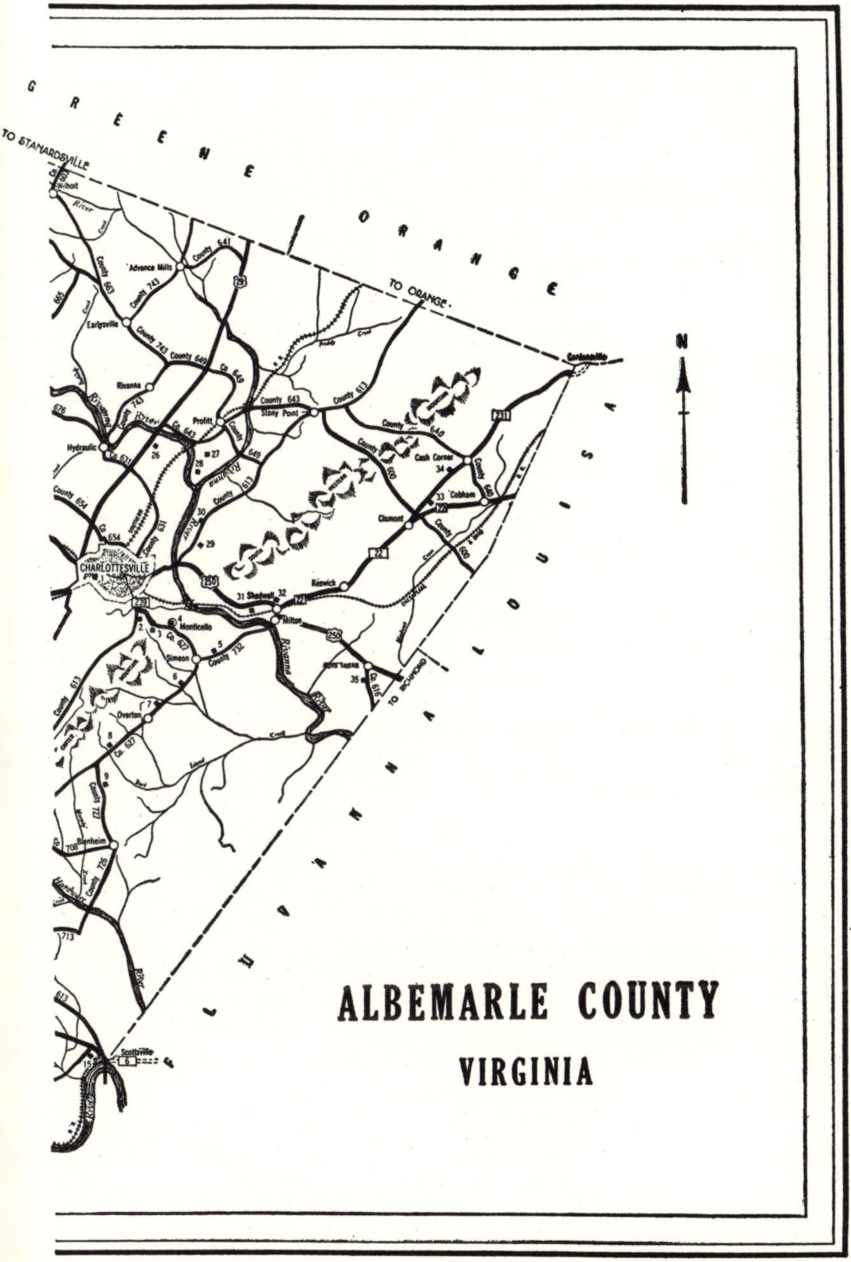

ALBEMARLE COUNTY

VIRGINIA

quent inspection tours to the mill, Washington caught the cold that resulted in his last illness.

At 12.1 *m.* is a junction with US 1 (*see below*).

HUNTING CREEK, 5.7 *m.*, is a marshy resting place for ducks in autumn and winter. In the vicinity in 1676 a 'fort or place of defence on Potomac river' was built as a protection against the Susquehannock Indians, whose depredations led to Bacon's Rebellion (*see History*).

At 5.8 *m.* is a junction with a private road.

Right on this winding road to MOUNT EAGLE, 0.3 *m.* The drive ends in a circle before a white winged structure with a Georgian pediment. The house, now the Lord Fairfax Country Club, was built late in the eighteenth century and was the home of the Reverend Bryan Fairfax (1735–1802), who became the eighth Lord Fairfax. A mild Tory, friend of Washington, and rector of the Fairfax Parish from 1789 to 1792, the Reverend Mr.Fairfax remained nonpartisan during the Revolution. When in 1800 Bryan inherited the title of Lord Fairfax and the right to a seat in the House of Lords, he chose to remain in Virginia.

Embedded in the long reaches of wooded parkway (R), 6.5 *m.*, is a remnant of the line of forts—O'RORKE, WEED, FARNSWORTH, and LYON—that formed part of the southern defenses of Washington during the War between the States.

At 10.2 *m.* is a junction with State 235 (*see above*).

The entrance (R) to WOODLAWN (*open during April Garden Week*) is at 13.4 *m.* The square, rose-red brick house designed in Georgian Colonial style with Classic Revival innovations, on the crest of shaded Gray Heights, was designed by Dr.William Thornton in 1805. The central unit with brick walls laid in Flemish bond rises two stories—with flat arches of stone over the windows—to a gable roof with hipped ends. A central pediment pierces the roof like a dormer. The house is extended by two low balancing wings connected with the main structure by low galleries. A high brick wall joins the wings with outbuildings. The house has two central halls connected by an elliptical stairway that rises in a long simple sweep, and has been lately embellished with fine eighteenth-century woodwork salvaged from the Barton House in Fredericksburg.

The 2,000-acre estate, once part of Mount Vernon, was willed by Washington to his nephew, Lawrence Lewis, who became the husband of Eleanor (Nelly) Custis, granddaughter of Martha Washington, 'about candle light' on Washington's last birthday, February 22, 1799. Woodlawn, 'grandeur in decay,' was bought in 1902 by the dramatist Paul Kester (*see Tour 16a*) and his brother Vaughan, who immediately restored it.

The brick columned entrance to FORT BELVOIR (L) is at 13.6 *m.* (*visitor's pass obtained at gate*). This military reservation of the United States Corps of Engineers was formerly Fort Humphreys. The neat parade ground, surrounded by staff headquarters, officers' quarters, and enlisted men's barracks, occupies a wide peninsula, part of the Belvoir estate, which once belonged to the Fairfax family. On the east side are a U.S. FISH HATCHERY and EXPERIMENT STATION.

Commerce and Industry

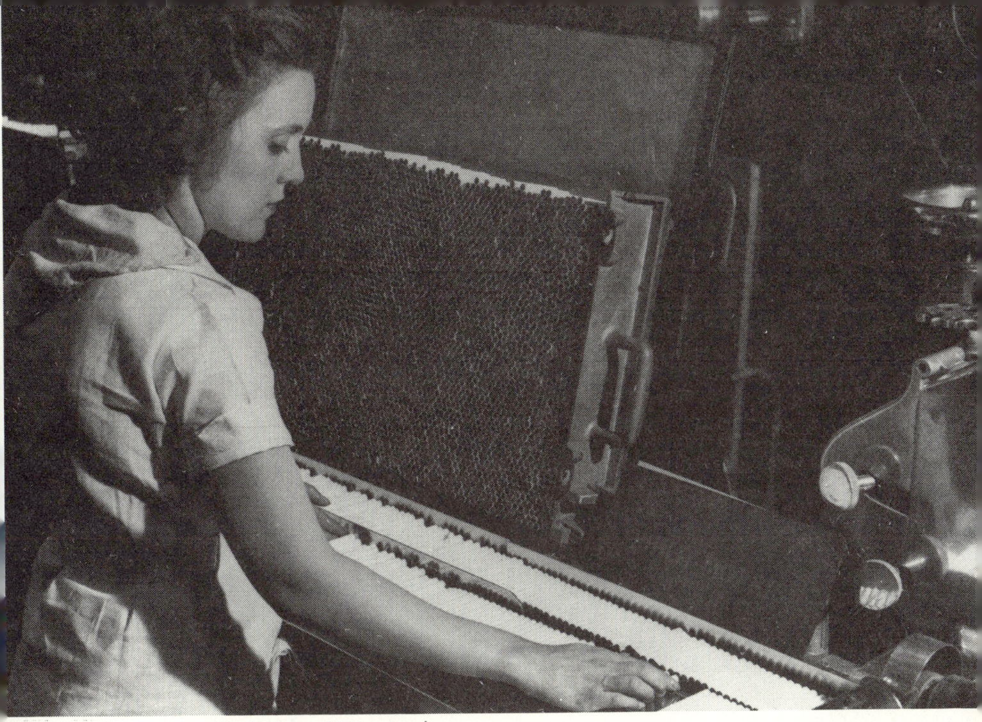

Photograph by courtesy of the *Richmond News Leader*

CIGARETTE GIRL, TOBACCO ROW, RICHMOND

HOSIERY WORKER IN A STAUNTON MILL

Photograph by courtesy of the *Richmond News Leader*

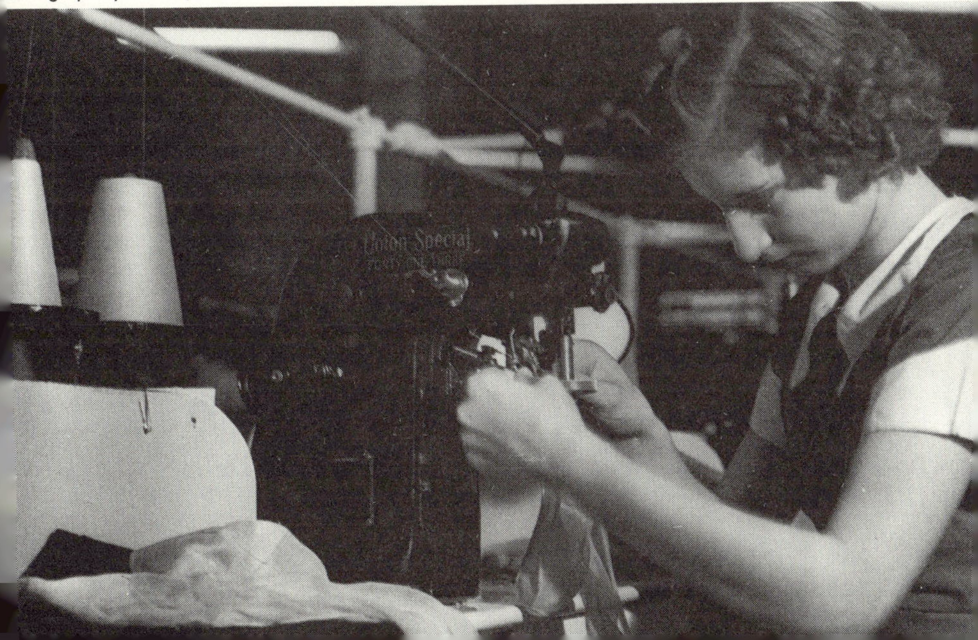

Photograph by W. Lincoln Highton

LIME WORKS, EAGLE ROCK

IN THE POCAHONTAS COAL FIELD

Photograph by W. Lincoln Highton

otograph by W. Lincoln Highton

COVINGTON

TEXTILE MILLS ALONG THE DAN, DANVILLE

otograph by W. Lincoln Highton

Photograph by courtesy of the Norfolk Advertising Boa

OYSTERING, OFF NORFOLK

Photograph by courtesy of the *Richmond News Leader*

ROASTING PEANUTS, SUFFOLK

COAL CUTTER, SOUTHWESTERN VIRGINIA

Photograph by Robert McNeill

Photograph by courtesy of the *Richmond News Leade*

PULP AND PAPER MILL, WEST POINT

LOADING LUMBER FOR BALTIMORE, NORTHERN NECK

Photograph by W. Lincoln Highto

ograph by W. Lincoln Highton

PUMPING SALT FROM UNDERGROUND, SALTVILLE

Photograph by courtesy of the Newport News Shipy

AIRCRAFT CARRIER ON THE WAYS, NEWPORT NEWS

NORFOLK TIDEWATER TERMINAL

Photograph by courtesy of the Norfolk Advertising Bo

On the grounds are the RUINS OF THE BELVOIR MANSION, gutted by fire in 1783, and completely demolished by the British in 1814. Belvoir was set aside in 1741 for Colonel William Fairfax by his cousin, the proprietor of the Northern Neck, Lord Thomas Fairfax (*see Tour 5A*). Colonel Fairfax (1691–1757) settled first in the Bahamas, then at Salem, Massachusetts. In 1734 he came to Virginia as agent for his cousin and in 1741 built the brick house 'of nine rooms and suitable outhouses.' George William Fairfax (1724–87), who inherited Belvoir, became Washington's intimate friend and associate in many enterprises, and Washington, during early manhood, was a frequent visitor here—especially when Mary Cary, sister of Mrs.George William Fairfax, was also a guest.

POHICK CHURCH (L), 16.4 *m.*, is surrounded by old trees and a quiet graveyard. The rectangular building, partly a restoration, has walls laid in Flemish bond and two tiers of windows framed with brick—flat-arched below, round-arched above. The high hip roof rises above a denticulated cornice with an unusually wide overhang. Local sandstone was used for the heavy quoining and the enframement of the three portals, two on the main façade and one on the south. Each portal has Ionic pilasters, full entablature, and a severe pediment.

In 1765 the northern part of Truro Parish became Fairfax Parish, leaving Truro with only one church—Pohick, a frame building, not on the present site. After building Payne's Church in 1768, the vestry, of which Washington was a member, planned to replace the frame church by one of brick, but had a hard time deciding upon a site. It was not till September 21, 1769, that the 'spott' was chosen. The church was completed in 1774. During the War between the States one wall, the interior, and the furniture, except the marble font, were destroyed. The church was renovated in 1874, and again in 1906.

At 18.2 *m.* is a junction with County 600.

Left here to GUNSTON HALL, 3.7 *m.* (*open during April Garden Week*), the home of George Mason (1725–92), author of the Virginia Bill of Rights, model for the first ten amendments that make up the Bill of Rights in the Federal Constitution. The simple story-and-a-half Georgian Colonial house, with stone quoining and walls of brick, has a gabled roof with dormers and four built-in chimneys. Both front and rear porches are noteworthy, the former closely following the lines of the Temple of Tyche at Eumenia, the latter eight-sided with pointed arches—a rare example of American Colonial Gothic. A delicate cornice upholds 'kicked-out' eaves. The broad central hall, which has plastered walls, a paneled dado, and deep cornice, contains a stairway with very low risers and very broad treads. The music room has Chinese Chippendale trim and the drawing room an elaborate mantel and overmantel flanked by semicircular niches, which are framed by pilasters and topped with broken pediments. Nearly all the doorways and windows have full entablature and pilasters. The house was restored in 1920.

The George Mason who built Gunston Hall (1755–58) was fourth of that name in Virginia. The architect was William Buckland, a skilled draftsman of Oxford whom Mason's brother had brought under indenture from England in 1754. The master of Gunston Hall was the author of the Fairfax Resolutions in 1774 and the following year became a member of the Virginia Committee of Safety. In 1776 he drafted the Virginia Constitution and the Bill of Rights. In 1787, as delegate to the Constitutional Convention in Philadelphia, he refused to sign the instrument because it failed to abolish slavery, because it contained no bill of rights, and because he objected to the large and too indefinite powers it gave to Congress. Although one of the real mentors of the Revolution, he returned to Gunston Hall after each public activity, fervently hoping —it is said—never again to be called from his home.

At 19.9 *m.* is a junction with County 611.

Left here to COLCHESTER, 0.9 *m.*, laid out in 1753 and once prosperous but now merely two old buildings, a few modern houses, and a dock on Occoquan Creek.

THE ARMS OF FAIRFAX, a former ordinary, is a small story-and-a-half clapboard structure on a high foundation. The large dining room with wide, fluted cupboards, once assuaged the hearty appetites of many self-confessed gourmands. In his *Travels of Four Years and a Half in the United States of America* (1798–1801), John Davis, English tutor of Nathaniel Ellicott's children at Occoquan, wrote of 'Mr. Gordon's tavern:' 'Every luxury that money can purchase is to be obtained at the first summons . . . The richest viands cover the table . . . and ice cools the Madeira that has been thrice across the ocean . . . Apartments are numerous and at the same time spacious . . . carpets of delicate texture cover the floors; and glasses are suspended from the walls in which a *Goliah* might survey himself.'

At 21.1 *m.* on US 1 is a junction with State 9.

Right here to OCCOQUAN (Ind., hooked inlet), 2.1 *m.*, directly across the river from the DISTRICT OF COLUMBIA WORKHOUSE and close to the DISTRICT REFORMATORY.

In 1801, John Davis, sailor with an ebullient flair for poetry and prose, arrived to tutor the children of Nathaniel Ellicott, a local landowner. 'Occoquan,' he wrote, 'consists of a house built on a rock, three others on the river side, and a half a dozen log-huts scattered at some distance.' But he found the settlement 'romantic beyond conception.' Three years after his departure, the town, long planned, came into being. By 1830 Occoquan was well-known to travelers for its roasted canvasback ducks, which the local inn served even for breakfast and sold, uncooked, for 'a shilling sterling apiece.' The village was in a flourishing condition until silt filled Occoquan Creek, and vessels could no longer reach the mills.

The ruins of the MERCHANT'S GRIST MILL, built in 1759 and destroyed in 1924, are close to the bridge. The high stone walls (L) are the remnants of one of the first COTTON MILLS in Virginia. Built in 1828 by Nathaniel Janney, the four stories hummed with 1,000 spindles until they were silenced by fire during the War between the States. South of these ruins, stands ROCKLEDGE, now called The Den, a two-story rock house with dormers, built in 1759 by John Ballendine, on designs by William Buckland. Under the gabled roof runs a fine denticulated cornice. With window panes that time has made iridescent and a crane swinging in the huge kitchen fireplace, Rockledge preserves the solid qualities of its builder, one of the earliest captains of industry in the agricultural south.

Legended gateposts mark the entrance (L), 24.3 *m.*, to RIPPON LODGE, a story-and-a-half frame house, now much modernized. Three dormers, piercing a gabled roof, project just above the balustraded roof of a recessed porch with six small Doric columns. The hall and dining room are paneled. In the upper hall an aperture in the north wall formerly led to a secret stairway that connected with a tunnel extending from the basement to a ravine. The brick office is still standing as is also the guardhouse with iron-grilled windows, in which Thomas Blackburn quartered troops during the Revolution.

Rippon Lodge was built about 1725 by Colonel Richard Blackburn of Ripon, England, an architect who later designed both the original Mount Vernon and the first Falls Church. Two daughters of the house of Blackburn became mistresses of Mount Vernon: Julia Anne, daughter of Colonel Thomas Blackburn, married Bushrod Washington; and Jane Charlotte, her niece, became the bride of John Augustine Washington.

At 25.4 *m.* is a junction with County 610.

1. Right here to a junction with County 638, 0.1 *m.*; R. again 0.3 *m.* to a footbridge that crosses once navigable NEABSCO CREEK (Ind., at the point of rock) on which in 1697 'four houses for stores and garrisons' were built for use in fighting Indians. On the shore of the creek, covered by briars, are the ruins of the NEABSCO IRON FOUNDRY, which John Tayloe (1687–1747) operated in 1734 after he had abandoned Bristol Iron Works (*see Tour 16a*).

At 4.9 *m.* from US 1 on County 610 is a junction with a narrow lane; L. here to the entrance gate (L) of BEL AIR 5.2 *m.*, a small gabled brick house. Bel Air, on a hilltop, has fine paneling in its large first-floor rooms, a wide-treaded stairway, and high basement kitchen. The view from the house is exceptional; on clear days Washington landmarks are visible.

Bel Air was built about 1740 by Major Charles Ewell. Marianne Ewell, his daughter, was married here to Dr. James Craik, surgeon general of the Continental armies; and in 1795, Fanny Ewell, granddaughter of the builder, married Mason Locke Weems (1759–1825). Weems, a Marylander, was ordained a clergyman by the Archbishop of Canterbury in 1784 and returned to take charge of a Maryland parish. He was not particularly happy in the church and had such difficulty making a living that he exchanged preaching for book peddling. Marriage anchored him only temporarily. After the death of his father-in-law, Colonel Jesse Ewell, in 1806, Parson Weems, who had become both author and bookseller, moved his family to Bel Air (on which he held a mortgage), where he visited them briefly at intervals as he journeyed up and down the Atlantic seaboard. His many moral tracts and his biographies of William Penn and General Francis Marion were eclipsed by that egregious mixture of fact and fiction: *A History of the Life and Death, Virtues and Exploits of General George Washington, With Curious Anecdotes Equally Honorable to Himself and Exemplary to His Young Countrymen.* The chronicler of the 'cherry tree' and 'Spanish dollar' episodes lies in the Ewell graveyard behind the house.

2. Left from US 1 on County 610, 0.3 *m.*; R. here on a sharply ascending path to the SITE OF LEESYLVANIA, 1 *m.*, birthplace of Henry 'Lighthorse Harry' Lee (1756–1818), Princeton graduate (1773), Revolutionary officer, governor of Virginia, and father of Robert E. Lee.

DUMFRIES, 29 *m.* (325 pop.), clings to a curve in the highway overlooking the creek that once gave it life. After the bars to Virginia's profitable tobacco trade were lifted by the Navigation Law of 1707, Scottish merchants immediately concentrated their activities around Quantico Creek. As early as 1713 a 'factory' and an 'agent's house' had been built and by 1749 the town had been established. In 1762 Dumfries became the seat of Prince William County. Filled at the apogee of its commercial activity with 2,000 people concerned only with exporting tobacco, Dumfries reckoned without the vagaries of nature and more insidious mankind. Silt began to clog Quantico Creek and boats, in search of flour as well as tobacco, sailed by its entry to Alexandria's more approachable wharfs. Improvident Dumfries gradually forwent its tea drinking, balls, and drama, and dwindled to comparative nothingness.

Two-storied brick STAGECOACH INN (R), a pre-Revolutionary hostelry known first as William's Ordinary, then as Love's Tavern, has stone quoins on the front corners and around the doorway.

The brick, limestone-trimmed HENDERSON HOUSE corner of Duke and Fairfax Sts., was built about 1785 by Colonel Alexander Henderson. The old house has preserved its dignified air despite additions. Alexander Henderson organized what was probably the first chain of stores in America with shops in Alexandria, Colchester, Occoquan, and Dumfries. One of his six sons, Archibald Henderson, was the first commander of the U.S. Marine Corps, from 1820 to 1859.

At TRIANGLE, 30.5 *m.*, a cluster of neon-decorated buildings, is the landscaped entrance (L) to the MARINE CORPS BASE (*visitor's pass at post gate*), eastern training center of the U.S. Marine Corps. The little town of QUANTICO stretches out from the railroad station, neon-festooned restaurants, little hotels, and other structures. The large government reservation fringing the curving Potomac is dotted with regimental and disciplinary barracks, three storehouses, commissary, bakery, a rifle range, Brown Flying Field, and numerous other buildings and equipment sufficient to accommodate some 400 officers and 3,000 enlisted men. The Marine Corps School is attended, sometime during their career, by all Marine officers.

The site of Quantico (Ind., by the long stream) was a 'naval base,' established to serve the vessels of the 'Potomac Navy' during the Revolution. When the United States entered the World War in 1917, Quantico was selected as a training camp and maneuver field for the Marine Corps, and in 1918 became a permanent post.

Right from Triangle on County 626 to CHOPAWAMSIC RECREATIONAL DEMONSTRATION AREA, 2 *m.*, about 14,500 acres of submarginal land being developed by the National Park Service. At present (1940) there are four camps with recreational facilities and cabins with accommodations for 435 persons, besides picnic areas.

CHOPAWAMSIC CREEK (Ind., by the separation of the outlet), 32.7 *m.*, was long a difficult problem for the early road builders and one of the causes for the near-disappearance of the road for a time. Testy John Randolph of Roanoke likened the Chopawamsic Swamp to the Serbonian bog that swallowed the unwary forever. The advent of the automobile stimulated engineers to efforts that eventually brought the road back to utility.

The large bronze CRUCIFIX 36.3 *m.*, designed by George J. Lober, is a memorial to the first English Catholic settlers in Virginia—Giles, Margaret, and Mary Brent who, around 1650, built homes on Aquia Creek. George Brent, their nephew, was one of four men who on February 10, 1686, obtained from James II a Proclamation granting 'free exercise of their religion' on 30,000 acres 'for the encouragement of inhabitants to settle' in this area, known as the Brenton Tract. Giles, Margaret, and Mary Brent had arrived in Maryland in 1638 and for many years were prominently identified with affairs there. In 1650 Giles Brent first patented land in Virginia. His other patents and those of his sisters followed in quick succession.

Mistress Margaret Brent, who is called in Maryland records 'Margaret Brent, Gentlemen,' was one of the most remarkable women in Colonial history. She appears frequently in the records of her two States, negotiating transactions of her own and acting as attorney for her brother, her sister, and neighbors who needed her help. She was the first woman in America to ask for 'voyce & vote allso.' Because Leonard Calvert, governor of Maryland, made her his sole executrix in an oral will that tersely instructed her 'to take all and pay all,' and because the Maryland Council made her administratrix of Lord Baltimore's revenues, she argued before the assembly in 1648 that she should be given full rights of citizenship. When the request was denied, she declared that she would protest all action taken by the assembly if she were not present and granted 'as aforesaide voyce & vote allso.' Her brother's difficulties with Lord Baltimore, arising from Giles Brent's claims to land he considered due him because of his marriage to the daughter of the Piscataway chief, and Margaret Brent's indignation that Lord Baltimore should resent her having paid hired soldiers out of his revenues, were responsible for the Brents' moving to Virginia and for the speedy colonization of much of that territory then known as Northumberland County.

On Aquia Creek (Ind., bush nut), the northern frontier of Virginia for ten years after the Indian War of 1676, was established the first English speaking Catholic colony in Virginia. Close by the bank of the creek rose the Catholic town of Aquia near which, in mid-eighteenth century, was built a small log chapel. This community was frequently visited by John Carroll, who in 1789 became the first Catholic bishop of the United States.

Left from the Crucifix on County 637 to a junction with a private road, 0.2 *m.*; R. here to the AQUIA (or BRENT) ROMAN CATHOLIC CEMETERY (R), 0.5 *m.*, salvaged from a tumble of briars and enclosed by a brick wall since its discovery in 1924. Within this graveyard lie five generations of Brents. Decipherable still are tombstones to 'Flora, 1681'; to George Brent's second wife, Mary (died in 1683), daughter of Lady Baltimore by her first husband, Henry Sewell, Secretary of Maryland; and to Pettyjohn Doyle 'who ended his life July 18, 1725, 50 years upward.'

By the cemetery wall is a bronze tablet dedicated to the memory of Jesuits who in the 1580's established a mission in the vicinity and shortly afterward were killed by the Indians, one of whose sons they had enslaved. Reprisals by the Spanish from St. Augustine aroused among the natives hostility that had not been forgotten when the Jamestown colonists arrived.

AQUIA CHURCH (L), 37.4 *m.*, erected in 1757 and still serving Overwharton Parish, is remarkably large and fine for its day. The outer angles of the walls, of large-sized brick, are heavily quoined with stone. The same gray stone frames the large center doorway and one in each end of the transept. The hip roof, above two tiers of windows and a generous cornice, has a stocky, square cupola with its base embedded in the western hip directly above the main entrance.

The interior has square, high-backed box pews with doors, a walnut altar rail, a gallery supported on graceful columns, and a triple-decked pulpit. White marble is set in the stone floor at the intersection of the aisles. The silver communion service, inscribed: 'The gift of the Rev. Mr.Alexander Scott,A.M., late minister of this Parish Anno 1739,' and dating from that year, was buried during three wars—1776, 1812, and 1861.

Overwharton Parish, formed before 1680, once covered the greater part of the original Stafford County. The Reverend John Moncure, who served as rector from 1738 to 1764, is buried beneath a stone bearing the inscription: 'In memory of the Race of the House of Moncure.' The present structure replaced a church built in 1751 and destroyed by fire three years later. This had succeeded an earlier church at another site. Tablets commemorate the vestry that built the church, the rector, and 'Mourning Richards, undertaker, and William Copein, mason.' By 1837 Aquia Church was in a dilapidated condition; it was restored about 40 years later.

STAFFORD, 40.3 *m.* (75 pop.), seat of Stafford County since 1715, clusters around the COURTHOUSE, a brick building erected in 1922. Most of the early county records disappeared during the War between the States; a few of the documents, discovered in the New York Public Library, have been returned.

Called a mother of counties, Stafford, formed from Westmoreland in 1664, was gradually reduced as the population spread westward. It was the scene of 'Parson Waugh's Tumult,' an abortive religious insurrection started in 1688 by John Waugh, who believed the story of an Indian, later discredited, and inflamed the people through sermons that told of a Catholic plot against Protestants.

Left here on County 212 to County 608, 3 *m.*; L. here to County 621, 6.3 *m.*, and R. to MARLBOROUGH POINT, 9.1 *m.*, near the site of the town of Marlborough, one of those authorized in 1680, and an early seat of Stafford County. It flourished briefly, on tobacco and herrings, then quickly disappeared.

In this region, near the mouth of Potomac Creek, was the Indian village Patawomeke, where in 1613 Pocahontas, while visiting the Potomac Indians, was kidnapped by the English. Through the trickery of Iapazaws, 'an old friend of Captaine Smiths,' the Indians 'betraied the poore innocent Pocahontas aboard' the vessel of Captain Samuel Argall for the price of a 'Kettle and other toies.' Conveyed to Jamestown, the princess was held as hostage for the 'swords, peeces, tooles, &c. hee [Powhatan] trecherously had stolne.' It was during this period of captivity that the 'Namparell of Virginia' met and married John Rolfe. An Indian village here is being explored; many artifacts and skeletons have been found.

At 48 *m.* on US 1 is a junction with County 652.

Right here to ELLERSLIE (R), 0.7 *m.* a two-and-a-half story, square brick house built in 1748 by Dr. Michael Wallace who, at 15, had been indentured to Dr. Gustavus Brown, of Charles City County, Md., to learn 'physical surgery and pharmacy.' Towards the end of his six years' apprenticeship, in 1747, he eloped—a classic ladder-and-second-story episode—with 'one of the nine Miss Browns who had twenty-seven husbands between them.' Settling in Falmouth the following year, he acquired land and built this stately house. Dr. Wallace's practice soon extended into Culpeper, Fauquier, and Loudoun Counties.

FALMOUTH, 48.2 *m.* (500 pop.), perched above the falls of the Rappahannock, carries on its life amid the decayed charm of its former lively self. Destined as a port for the tobacco and flour trade, Falmouth was laid out as a town in 1727 on land that lay just above the beach on which Captain John Smith and his 'Souldiers,' guided by the Indian Mosco, had landed, fought the Indians, set up a cross, and sought gold in 1608. Market for all the fertile country extending to the Blue Ridge, the town dotted with storehouses grew rapidly. From London in 1773 came urbane trappings—a fire engine and 40 leather buckets. In its streets drivers of wagon trains met sailors from foreign ships. On the banks of the Rappahannock (R) an iron foundry, operated as early as 1732 by Augustine Washington, ran full tilt during the Revolution under the management of James Hunter in order to furnish the American army and navy with such articles as pots, pans, camp kettles, anchors, and bayonets. To protect the foundry the governor of Virginia ordered General George Weeden to establish a camp —Camp Hunter—on the hill adjacent. In 1786, Timothy Green published the town's first newspaper, *The Falmouth Advertiser*; and in 1813 progress took another turn—a bridge replaced the ferry. As industry thrived, Scotch Basil Gordon (1768–1817) carried on a business that made him one of America's first millionaires.

Before and after the Battle of Fredericksburg (*see Tour 1b*) Falmouth was the headquarters of the Federal Army and of T.C.S.Lowe, 'Chief of Aeronauts,' U.S.A. Hovering over the town, he successfully conveyed one of the first air messages of the war. 'Balloon in the air, April 29, 1863,' started the communiqué.

George Washington, so it is said, received his early education here, between the ages of seven and eleven, attending the school kept by 'Master Hobby,' nickname of William Grove, who was brought from England by Augustine Washington, sponsor of his early undertakings. Here were born James Alexander Seddon (1815–80), Confederate Secretary of War, and Dr.Kate Waller Barrett (1858–1925), staunch advocate of social reform.

Beyond the road descending to the site of HUNTER'S IRON WORKS is the stone-pillared entrance (L) to BELMONT, a two-story frame building, painted white, erected in 1761, enlarged in 1843, and again in 1916, by a studio wing, when purchased by Gari Melchers (1860–1932), portrait and landscape painter. Trained at Düsseldorf, Melchers achieved a reputation in Europe for his pictures of Dutch peasant life. In Virginia, his favorite subjects were mountaineer types such as those in *The Pot Boils*.

Right from Falmouth on State 17 traversing the lower Piedmont and bordered by small plots devoted to farming and dairying. Its undulating upper end passes into a region of whitewashed fences, stud farms, and impressive estates.

John Lederer, a 'German Chirurgeon,' on August 20, 1670, set out from the Falls of Rappahannock, accompanied by 'Col. Catlet of Virginia, nine English horse, and five Indians on foot.' He proceeded up the north bank of the river toward the 'top of the Apalataean Mountains,' his goal, but on the way the Englishmen found fault with their leader and returned to Williamsburg and discredited his discoveries.

Along the highway near BEREA, 4.2 *m.*, the Army of the Potomac moved westward on January 20–21, 1863, toward the fords of the Rappahannock, in an attempt to approach Lee's army from the rear. As the troops advanced a storm arose and converted the road into such a quagmire that the 'Mud March' was abandoned.

At 8.3 *m.* is a boundary of the former gold mining district of Stafford County. The ore was discovered by German miners (*see Tour 3b*), who believed it held silver. Their story was discredited and the region remained unworked until much later.

RICHLANDS, 9.6 *m.* (25 pop.), has grown up on the vast Richland estate, part of four large grants made in 1703 to Robert 'King' Carter (*see Tour 16b*), who in the following year built a tobacco warehouse here. On this land the master of Corotoman started inland colonization and established three 'quarters.' On his death in 1732, Stanstead Quarters came under the management of his son, Charles Carter.

GROVE BAPTIST CHURCH (L), 14.2 *m.*, is a gray stone building erected in 1811. William L. Royall, Jr., a 19-year old Confederate scout, was captured by a Federal cavalry detachment and placed in this church for safe keeping. Shortly afterward he was led to the Presbyterian Church, directly across the road, tried by a 'drumhead court-martial' for being a bushwhacker, and acquitted. The verdict had not been easily reached, for orders had arrived to hang the first bushwhacker caught. Fortunately, Lieutenant Colonel Timothy O'Bryan, in command, had frequently been a guest at Mount Ephraim, the Royall home, and had promised Mrs. Royall that her son would go unharmed if he were ever caught.

At 15 *m.* is a junction with County 651.

Left on this road 0.8 *m.* to the LIBERTY GOLD MINE (L), worked extensively before the War between the States; it was finally abandoned in 1937. A shaft, hoist, and several beehive rock crushers—spherical globes of reinforced concrete some 10 feet in diameter—are visible from the highway.

In MORRISVILLE, 18.6 *m.* (50 pop.), still a crossroads, once stood Richard Coventon's Ordinary.

Where the crossroads settlement of LOIS, 21.4 *m.*, now stands, the Virginia assembly made a gesture in 1798 toward establishing a town to be called Fayetteville, but the enterprise failed.

At 26.4 *m.* on State 17 is a junction with State 295 (*see Tour 4a*).

In OPAL, 29.9 *m.*, on State 17 is a junction with US 15 (*see Tour 3b*).

FREDERICKSBURG, 49.8 *m.* (50 alt., 6,819 pop.) (*see Fredericksburg*).

In Fredericksburg are junctions with State 3 (*see Tour 16a and Tour 10*), US 17 (*see Tour 6a*), and State 2 (*see Tour 1A*).

Section b. FREDERICKSBURG to RICHMOND, 56 m.

This section of the highway passes from the rolling country of hazy distances into the flat sand-clay outer fringes of the Coastal Plain, covered with small farms dwarfed by vast reaches of forest.

In FREDERICKSBURG, 0 *m.*, US 1 swings R. on Lafayette Blvd. to a junction with the Sunken Road at 1.1 *m.* Straight ahead is the entrance to the National Military Cemetery on the slope of Marye's Heights, where are buried 15,206 victims of the War between the States—only 3,000 of them identified. At the junction is (R) the NATIONAL PARK SERVICE HEADQUARTERS AND MUSEUM (*see Fredericksburg*) of the Fredericksburg-Spotsylvania National Battlefield.

The Battle of Fredericksburg took place in December 1862 during the fourth major drive by the Northern army for the capture of Richmond. A hundred and twenty thousand strong, the Army of the Potomac, commanded by General Ambrose E. Burnside, marched south from Warrenton and, blocked by General R.E.Lee's army on the hills below Fredericksburg, camped from November 17 to November 20 on Stafford Heights across the Rappahannock. On December 11 Burnside bombarded Fredericksburg (already evacuated) and then, under fire, laid five pontoon bridges and within two days took most of his force across the river. On December 13 he ordered two attacks: the first at Hamilton's Crossing (*see below*), around which General T.J.Jackson had massed his corps, began about 10 o'clock. Under a blanket of thick fog General W.B.Franklin drew up his men in battle formation on the plains below the hill. As the fog lifted, the Confederates saw waving flags and the gleam of 48,000 bayonets. The first charge, led by General G.G.Meade, was repulsed, but a second charge, in which Meade was supported by another division, broke through General Jackson's line. Despite fierce fighting, the Federals were driven back and the Confederate line was restored. No more fighting took place there.

The second and more costly venture was General E.V.Sumner's attack on Marye's Heights. The Sunken Road at the base of the hill is protected by a stone retaining wall. From behind this parapet the Confederate troops successfully repulsed seven major attacks. As one division left its wounded and dead, retreating in disorder under fire from the heights, another moved forward in the icy wind to take its place. Two days later the Union army recrossed the Rappahannock, having lost a total of 12,653 men as against 5,377 Confederates.

Right from US 1 on the Sunken Road to BROMPTON (L), 0.2 *m.*, a two-story brick house with one-story wings, built about 1837 by John Lawrence Marye. The high gabled roof of the main unit extends forward to form a portico—its pediment pierced by a lunette—supported by four slender Ionic columns. An elliptical fanlight over the door and the delicate detail of the portico cornice, repeated under the eaves of the wings, are noteworthy. Inside, a hall extends across the front. The drawing rooms, in the wings, have mantels of Italian marble imported for the White House but discarded because of slight defects. Brompton's peaceful existence on its hillside came to an abrupt end in December 1862, when Confederate officers used the porch as a vantage point to observe the progress of Federal troops below.

At 1.7 *m.* on US 1 is a junction with a park road.

Left here through a part of the Fredericksburg-Spotsylvania National Battlefield Park to HAMILTON'S CROSSING, 5.4 *m.*, scene of action during the Battle of Fredericksburg. The park road winds along a ridge through landscaped grounds, passing a Contact Station (*information*) and restored trenches and gun pits.

Left from Hamilton's Crossing on County 634 to a junction with US 17 (*see Tour 6a*), 6.2 *m.*

At 4.4 *m.* on US 1 is a junction with State 51.

Right on this road to SPOTSYLVANIA 6.7 *m.* (*see Tour* 10).

At 4.7 *m.* on US 1 is a junction with County 636.

Left here to the SITE OF LEE'S HEADQUARTERS (L), 1 *m.*, occupied after the Fredericksburg campaign.

MASSAPONAX CHURCH (R), 8.7 *m.*, a rectangular brick structure, built in 1859 and owned by a Baptist congregation, witnessed at least one battle during the War between the States—a long battle of words inscribed by soldiers on the rear wall of the gallery. 'How many traitors have you killed and where are you now?' wrote one Yankee. 'I don't know,' was the scribbled answer, followed by, 'In the hospital, I hope,' signed Rebel. 'John G. Hamilton, from Richmond. Homeward bound,' stands out among lines of vitriolic verse, scathing denunciations of leaders on both sides, crudely drawn cartoons—all tied together with faintly penciled signatures.

THORNBURG, 13 *m.*, a crossroads, was called formerly Mud Tavern.

Left here on County 606 to NORTH GARDEN (L), 1.8 *m.*, and STONEWALL JACKSON SHRINE (L), 5.6 *m.* (*see* Tour 1*A*).

At 16.1 *m.* on US 1 is a junction with State 208.

Left on this road is the entrance to BRAYNEFIELD (L), 5.9 *m.* (*See Tour 1A*).

Every few miles along US 1 in this area are markers calling attention to various episodes and the movements of troops through this section.

LADYSMITH, 21.2 *m.*, a collection of garages and restaurants.

1. Left from Ladysmith on County 639 to WRIGHT'S CHAPEL (L), 3.8 *m.*, a frame building. In 1774 William Wright, a communicant of the Established Church, strayed into a Methodist camp meeting and became so enthusiastic over the new doctrine that he invited the minister to hold meetings in his own house. Quarterly and protracted Methodist meetings, begun then in the home, continued for the rest of Wright's life and during his son's lifetime. The first Wright did not himself profess Methodism until the day of his death. The son, on his death in 1835, donated this land for a chapel that was replaced about 1890.

2. Right from Ladysmith on State 229 to COUNTY LINE CHURCH (R), 4.4. *m.*, a brick building covered with brown stucco lined to simulate stone. This church, built in 1841 on the opposite side of the road, was rebuilt on the present site in 1894. The first building owned by the congregation, on still another site, was so named because of its proximity to the line between Caroline and Spotsylvania Counties. The Baptist congregation was organized in 1784 when some members of Waller's Church withdrew and elected William Edmund Waller (1746–1830), brother of John Waller (*see below*), as their pastor.

At 5.1 *m.* is a junction with State 51; R. here 7.2 *m.* to WALLER'S CHURCH (R), a comparatively new brick building belonging to a Baptist congregation that was constituted December 2, 1769. The planting of Baptist churches in this section was effected through the preaching of Samuel Harris and James Read. When Waller's Church, called at first Lower Spotsylvania Church, was organized, John Waller (1741–1802) became the first pastor. Until his baptism in 1867 this pioneer Baptist had a reputation for recklessness and profanity and was known as 'Swearing Jack Waller' and 'the Devil's Adjutant.'

Back of a white clapboard house (R) in GOLANSVILLE, 24 *m.*, is a QUAKER BURYING GROUND, a little fenced-in plot covered with ivy and periwinkle beneath maple and paulownia trees; there are no markers.

At MT.CARMEL, 27.5 *m.*, in a triangle is CARMEL CHURCH (R), a red brick building with a gabled roof extending forward to form a high pediment. It was built in 1874—the third church on this site—and repaired in 1923. The Baptist congregation was constituted in 1773—another church 'planted by S.Harris and J.Reed' (Read). Called at first Polecat Church, it was later named Burruss' Church for the first pastor. In 1809 this church had 162 white and 342 Negro members and rose to the point of ordaining Negro deacons.

At one time the congregation organized a temperance society, which carried on militant activities from an adjacent building. The frame structure was moved eventually to a village near by, where it became a saloon.

1. Right from Mt.Carmel on County 658 to a deserted MORMON CHAPEL (R), 3.6 *m.*, a small frame building that was probably built sometime after the War between the States. The establishment of this sect here was bitterly resented, particularly by Major John Page, who explained the reason for his feelings: 'I can't afford to let two of my neighbors be confirmed in the theory of Mormonism, who have lived in the practice of it all their lives!'

2. Left from Mt.Carmel on State 207 to the cedar-lined entrance (L) of ELLERSLIE, 2.2 *m.*, a two-story frame house on a high basement, with outside end chimneys and one wing. It was built before 1800 by James Gatewood. The delicate tracery of a cut-leaf mulberry brushes the unpainted clapboard. Frame outbuildings, former kitchen and slave quarters, still stand.

Across the North Anna River, 30.5 *m.*, the armies of Lee and Grant faced each other from May 23 to May 26, 1864. Grant, frustrated in several attempts to secure vantage ground south of the river, moved eastward and crossed at Hanovertown.

ELLINGTON (R), 30.9 *m.*, is a square brick house behind square columns of a two-story portico. Built by the Thomas H. Fox, whose initials 'T F' are cut high above the entry door, Ellington was used before and after the War between the States as a boys' academy called Fox School. Under spreading tree branches is the two-story brick building that held the classrooms. In 1864 General R.E.Lee, whose army was encamped by the North Anna River, stopped here for a glass of buttermilk. He was about to drink when a shot fired by a Federal battery passed close by him and imbedded itself in the door frame. He slaked his thirst, then rode quickly away. The buttermilk was blamed for a subsequent illness lasting several days.

At 32.5 *m.* is a junction with County 688.

Left here to DOSWELL, 0.2 *m.*, a crossroads named for the Doswell family, which acquired Bullfield and converted it into a stud farm from which came the progenitors of *Epinard* and other thoroughbreds. In *ante-bellum* days Negro jockeys of the area achieved considerable reputation.

At 35.4 *m.* on US 1 is a junction with State 51.

Right here to the former HANOVER ACADEMY (R), 2.8 *m.*, on a wide lawn shaded by oaks. The school was established in 1849 by Lewis Minor Coleman, later professor of Latin at the University of Virginia. Only two of the old buildings remain: a remodeled two-story, clapboard structure with dormers, two outside chimneys, and spacious porch; and a story-and-a-half clapboard-covered log building.

FORK CHURCH (R), 4.4 *m.*, built in 1735, is a church of St.Martin's Parish. Conventionally rectangular, the structure has brick walls laid in Flemish bond above a heavy watertable. Two small and somewhat ungainly porticos that shelter the doors must have been later additions.

Inside, across the west end, is the usual gallery. Renovations made at intervals have removed all other distinctive old features.

Behind the church is a long, narrow brick-walled enclosure containing a single row of gravestones. Near by are tombstones of the Nelson and Page families.

Fork Church was so called because of its proximity to the confluence of the North and South Anna Rivers.

Left from Fork Church 2.5 *m.* on County 685 to SCOTCHTOWN (R), a severe-looking rectangular house suggesting the pictures of Noah's Ark. Broken trees and tattered box are all that remain of once beautiful grounds and gardens. Standing on a high brick foundation, this unusually large frame house, 100 feet long and 50 wide, has a high gabled roof, pierced by four chimneys, that would give a barren appearance if the ends of the ridge were not hipped. The unpainted clapboard walls, now silvery with age, are topped with carefully spaced corbels that strike a surprising note of elegance. Stone steps lead to small porches.

Colonel Charles Chiswell, a Scot who was accustomed to hop into his coach and rattle down Negro Foot road to Williamsburg when the 'Season' opened, built Scotchtown about 1732. That year William Byrd stopped here to ask information and advice, and recorded: 'I arrived about two o'clock, and saved my dinner. I was very handsomely entertained, finding everything very clean, and very good . . . I retired to a very clean lodging in another house, and took my bark, but was forced to take it in water, by reason a light fingered damsel had ransacked my baggage, and drunk up my brandy. This unhappy girl, it seems, is a baronet's daughter, but her complexion, being red-haired, inclined her so much to lewdness that her father sent her, under the care of the virtuous Mr. Cheep, to seek her fortune on this side of the globe . . . Mr. Chiswell made me reparation . . . by filling my bottle again with brandy.

In 1771 Scotchtown was acquired by Patrick Henry for £600. His first wife, Sarah Shelton Henry, died in 1776, and the following year Henry, then living in the Governor's Palace in Williamsburg, sold Scotchtown—not without a profit—to Colonel Wilson Miles Cary, one of the wealthy lower peninsula planters fearful of British invasion.

John Payne, the Quaker, became the next owner. Dorothea, one of his many children, who later married James Madison, preserved in her *Memoirs* a vivid impression of Scotchtown. In 1783 John Payne gave up the struggle with the poor soil and the battle with his conscience over the ownership of slaves and moved to Philadelphia.

Scotchtown has more legends than the average old house: the usual story is told of Tarleton's having ridden up the steps and through the halls; there are hints of an Indian raid, of a duel—responsible for the 'bloodstain' on the hall floor—and of a woman chained by her husband in the 'dungeon'—a fearful name for what was doubtless the sweet-potato pit.

At 9.6 *m.* on State 51 is a junction with County 601; R. here 0.5 *m.* to OFFLEY (L), once the home of Thomas Nelson (*see Tour 6b*). Nothing remains of the house but one gaunt chimney in the midst of three wide-spreading oaks.

On State 51 at 10 *m.* is the junction with County 601; L. here 3.2 *m.* to the entrance of OAKLAND (R). The L-shaped frame house was built in 1899 on the charred foundations of a house erected not long after the Revolution. The oak-shaded circular drive touches the porch steps on the low dormer-windowed wing. In the living room are many portraits: *Nell Gwynn* by Sir Peter Lely; *Addison* by Sir Godfrey Kneller; *Dr. Johnson*, *Dickens*, and *Thomas Nelson, Jr.* by Chapman; the *Artist Opie*, and others.

At Oakland was born Thomas Nelson Page (1853–1922), who, after graduating from Washington College and from the University of Virginia, practiced law in Richmond until 1893.

In 1884 the *Century Magazine* published 'Marse Chan,' Page's first story. Later he wrote numerous novels, essays, short stories, and verse. Some are in Negro dialect, and almost all show the author's pride in the class from which he sprang and his nostalgia for the *ante-bellum* days he depicted with more charm than realism. Oakland is the locale of his story *Two Little Confederates*. Among his best known works are: *In Ole Virginia*, *Red Rock*, *The Burial of the Guns*, and *Robert E. Lee, Man and Soldier*. He was ambassador to Italy from 1913 to 1918. At Oakland lived his brother, Rosewell Page (1858–1939), historian and biographer.

ASHLAND, 39.8 *m.* (1,297 pop.), is a sprawling little town with its central street cluttered by noisy and very profitable railroad tracks. Victorian residences sit back on shaded lawns, aloof from the bright façades of the business block. A leisurely town of commuters, merchants, railroad employees, and professors, Ashland has an air of its own created by the students of Randolph-Macon College, who swarm the streets, overflow the drug stores, and rattle about in 'jalopies.' Unacademic industry throbs in one lone building—a shirt factory.

In 1848, Edwin Robinson, president of the Richmond, Fredericksburg & Potomac Railroad, bought 155 acres of wilderness—'slashes'—and around a well of mineral water created a health resort, Slash Cottage. Richmond came to dance in the ballroom; trains waited to let hungry passengers dine here. Churches sprang up. By 1855 the village discarded its earlier name and adopted Ashland, the name of Henry Clay's estate in Kentucky. Selected as a mustering place for Confederate troops when the War between the States began, it was later occupied alternately by both Northern and Southern troops.

In Ashland lived the Sheltons, whose daughter, it is said, was the inspiration for Poe's *Lenore.*

In 1866, the unsold part of the land passed into the possession of the railroad company, which, to foster growth, induced the Methodist Church —by means of a land donation—to move Randolph-Macon College here.

RANDOLPH-MACON COLLEGE was the first college founded in the United States by the Methodist Episcopal Church. The rambling, brick buildings are hidden by tall trees. The campus, of about 35 acres, is particularly delightful in spring when thousands of daffodils cover the lawns. The school, founded at Boydton in 1830, was moved here in 1868. Rapid growth followed. In 1890 the Randolph-Macon system was organized (*see Tour 5A and Lynchburg*); its three institutions are affiliated with the Baltimore and Virginia Conferences of the Methodist Episcopal Church, and are controlled by one self-perpetuating board of trustees.

Left from Ashland on State 54 to a junction with County 662, 1.5 *m.*; L. here 1.3 *m.* to the entrance (R) to HICKORY HILL (*open during April Garden Week*), tall structure of irregular shape. It was built in 1734 and, after a fire, rebuilt in 1875 after designs of the day. In extensive gardens the outstanding feature is an ancient box walk, 307 feet long and arched 30 feet above the broad path. Hickory Hill has long been owned by the Wickham family. During the War between the States, it was the home of William F. Wickham, the father of General William C. Wickham of the Confederate army. One of General Robert E. Lee's sons, General W.H.F. (Rooney) Lee, while recovering here from a wound in 1863, was seized by a Federal cavalry detachment and taken to Fortress Monroe.

HANOVER, 6.6 *m.* (*see Tour 1A*) on State 54 is at a junction with State 2 (*see Tour 1A*).

At 46.4 *m.* on US 1 is a junction with a paved road.

Left here 0.5 *m.* to a junction with another paved road, the old Telegraph Road between Fredericksburg and Richmond; R. to the STUART MONUMENT (R), 0.6 *m.*, a tall granite obelisk 'erected by some of his comrades to commemorate his virtues.' Upon this field, on May 11, 1864, General J.E.B.Stuart, having interposed his cavalry between that of General Philip Sheridan and the city of Richmond, was wounded during the second of two attacks by the Federal troops. Shot by a dismounted cavalryman, he was taken to Richmond, where he died on the following day.

SAINT JOSEPH'S VILLA (R), 48.6 *m.*, a Catholic orphanage for girls, was erected in 1930–31 with part of the income derived from a $3,000, 000 trust left in 1922 by Major James H. Dooley for the establishment of three eleemosynary institutions. On a beautiful landscaped tract are 14 buildings of buff-colored brick trimmed with terra cotta and roofed with green Spanish tile. The domed Romanesque church and a statue of Joseph with Jesus rise in the center of the plaza formed by a curving drive fringed by the octagonal administration building and by the school building and auditorium. In 1834 three Sisters of Charity opened an orphanage and school in Richmond, called St.Joseph's; the institution here is its successor.

The remains of EARTHWORKS at 50 *m.* were part of Richmond's outer fortifications during the War between the States. At this point General Philip Sheridan's cavalry, pushing toward Richmond, broke through on May 11, 1864, after the fight at Yellow Tavern, but turned eastward before reaching the city.

At 50.9 *m.* is a junction with State 2 (*see Tour 1A*).

RICHMOND, 56 *m.* (15 to 206 alt., 182,929 pop.) (*see Richmond*).

In Richmond are junctions with US 33 (*see Tour 9*), US 250 (*see Tour 17*), State 6 (*see Tour 23*), State 10 (*see Tour 19*), State 5 (*see Tour 24*), US 60 (*see Tour 8*), and US 360 (*see Tour 20*).

Section c. RICHMOND to NORTH CAROLINA LINE; 93.7 *m. US* 1.

South of Richmond US 1 is lined with tourist cabins, garages, and lunchrooms swathed in neon signs that at night convert the road as far as Petersburg into a glittering midway. Below the Appomattox River, the highway passes through southside Virginia, an undulating sand-clay country covered with tobacco farms and extensive pine and oak forests. It suggests Gertrude Stein's comment on Virginia: 'There were no houses, no people to see, there were hills and woods and red earth out of which they were made and there were no houses and no people to see.'

South on 9th Street from the State capitol in RICHMOND, 0 *m.*, to rejoin US 1 (L), 2 *m.*

At 5.3 *m.* is a junction with County 1209.

Left here on a cinder road to a fork, 0.4 *m.*; R. here 1 *m.* to the RICHMOND-DEEP-WATER TERMINAL, erected in 1938–39 at an approximate cost of $1,750,000.

Near by is the SITE OF WARWICK, which was flourishing in 1748. In April 1781 the British came up the James and bombarded the village, burning Colonel Archibald Cary's flouring mill—a serious blow to the Commonwealth since the mill supplied much flour for the Revolutionary forces.

The landscaped and brick-pillared entrance (L) to the DU PONT DE NEMOURS MANUFACTURING PLANT is at 6.7 *m.* In the brick buildings covering 26 acres, rayon, cellophane, and synthetic fiber are manufactured through the viscose process. This site was selected in 1927 because of the supply of labor and the proximity to water with a low iron content.

On this tract stood Ampthill, which was moved to Richmond in 1929. Archibald Cary (1721–86), dubbed by a recent biographer the 'Wheelhorse of the Revolution,' in 1749 inherited Ampthill, built by his father, Henry Cary, Jr., and carried on and enlarged already established manufacturing interests: an iron foundry, the flouring mill at Warwick, and a ropery at Richmond. Called 'the Old Bruiser' and, at times, 'Old Irons,' Archibald Cary was known for his peremptory manner. Once, so it goes, Washington was a guest at Ampthill. When he rose to take his leave, Colonel Cary objected, not once but several times. Finally Washington made a definite move to depart. Insistent Archibald Cary banged his fist on the table with a 'By God! You shall stay.' And Washington stayed.

The unused arched stone bridge, spanning Falling Creek, 7.5 *m.*, was on the Manchester-Petersburg Turnpike laid out in 1826 by Colonel Benoît Claude Crozet (*see Tour 17b*).

At 8.5 *m.* is a junction with County 609.

Left here to DREWRY'S BLUFF, 0.8 *m.*, rising high above the James River. Fortifications built here in 1862 on the land of Captain A.H.Drewry enabled the Confederate forces on May 15, 1862, to drive back the Union fleet, which was attempting to reach Richmond. Among the five Union boats was the ironclad *Monitor*, which had engaged the *Merrimac* (*Virginia*) in Hampton Roads two months earlier.

FORT DARLING, 200 yards R., was equipped for the most part with naval guns and commanded a wide bend in the river to the south. The fort and its connecting land defenses have been partly restored.

On May 14–16, 1864, some 40,000 of General B.F.Butler's men were held back in the vicinity of the bluff by hastily gathered detachments of Confederate troops and county home guards until the arrival of General P.G.T.Beauregard. Defeated, Butler withdrew to Bermuda Hundred (*see Tour* 19) where, as General Grant expressed it, he was 'bottled up.' Earthworks, thrown up by the Federals on the 14th and relinquished two days later, are still visible.

On July 23, 1863, a Confederate naval school was established here on the *Patrick Henry*, with Lieutenant William Harwar Parker as commandant. The 126 midshipmen engaged in many skirmishes, and fought more than they studied.

Beginning at 9 *m.* and extending a mile along US 1 is a double row of sodium vapor highway lamps installed in February 1936 by the Virginia Electric & Power Co. The object of the experiment is to determine the degree to which accidents may be decreased by highway lighting.

HALF-WAY HOUSE (L), 11.3 *m.*, was so named because of its position between Richmond and Petersburg. This rectangular frame building was first an academy, then a stage house, and is again an inn. The long double porch at the rear was added in 1918; new, too, are the log cabin in the yard and the shed that covers a well used for many generations by travelers.

At 12.6 *m.* is a junction with County 616.

Left here to a junction with County 615, 0.2 *m.*; L. 2.5 *m.* to OSBORNE'S WHARF. Dredging operations here, begun in October 1936, are part of the James River development project. A channel has been cut of sufficient depth and width to permit passage of ocean-going vessels. A modern steam dredge continued work begun in 1611 by Sir Thomas Dale, who, according to a method he had learned while campaigning in Holland, cut across a neck of land a ditch known as Dale's Dutch Gap.

The land in this vicinity was settled in 1625 by Captain Thomas Osborne. Public tobacco warehouses erected in 1748 at this bend of the river made the place an important shipping terminus for a number of years. On April 27, 1781, Benedict Arnold with his troops burned 25 vessels anchored here; and the following month, La Fayette's troops camped on the sloping banks.

At 1.5 *m.* on County 616 is a bridge crossing the old channel of the James to FARRAR'S ISLAND; on the island is a fork, 1.9 *m.*; L. here 1.5 *m.* to another fork; then L. 0.6 *m.* on a road that skirts the north side of the island to the site of HENRICOPOLIS, or the City of Henricus, third settlement in the colony, founded in 1611 by Sir Thomas Dale, high marshal of Virginia, and named for his patron, Prince Henry, eldest son of James I. Lulled into security by the Indians' apparent friendliness, the settlers of Jamestown felt safe in moving up the river. Dale, with 350 men (chiefly German laborers), came to what is now called Dutch Gap, began to clear the wilderness, and built the town of which Ralph Hamor, secretary of the colony, wrote: 'There is in this town three streets, of well framed houses, a handsome church, and the foundation of a more stately one laid of brick, in length an hundred foote, and fifty foote wide, beside store houses, watch houses, and such like; there are also, as ornaments belonging to this town, upon the verge of this river, five faire block-houses, or commanders, wherein live the honnestes sort of people, as in farmes in England, and there keep continuall centinell for the townes security . . .'

In 1618 Governor Yeardley was instructed to choose a suitable site at the City of Henricus for 'the college and university of Virginia,' already imposed in the town's charter. Accordingly, 10,000 acres were set aside, £1,500 were collected in England, and George Thorpe was appointed superintendent. To provide additional revenue, tenants were established on the land, and, in 1619, an iron foundry was built. But in March 1622 came Opechancanough's carefully planned massacre. Henricopolis was wiped out.

At 13.6 *m.* is a junction with State 10 (*see Tour* 19).

COLONIAL HEIGHTS, 21 *m.* (2,331 pop.), is a speed-conscious town with service stations and stores compact along the highway and suburban residences spreading east and west.

VIOLET BANK, at the end of Arlington Place, is a one-story clapboard house with hipped gambrel roof, outside chimneys—stuccoed white—and a high basement. Breaking the long line of the façade is a graceful portico, which extends from a recess created by two bays. The slender fluted columns of the portico support a roof surmounted by a solid balustrade. In this gray building, overlooking a shrub-enclosed lawn shaded by the far reaching branches of a gigantic cucumber tree, General R.E.Lee had his headquarters from June to September 1864.

The first building on this site was erected in 1770 by Thomas Shore, a shipping merchant. Luxuriously appointed with English furniture and numerous *objets d'art*, this earlier Violet Bank, named for the thousands of violets that grew under the oaks once shading the adjacent hill, was chosen by La Fayette as headquarters in 1781. The first mansion burned in 1810.

OAK HILL, Carroll Avenue, also called Archer's, Hector's, or Dunn's Hill, consists of two one-story clapboard structures connected by a deep inside porch that extends an uncovered section toward the street.

From the lawn of this house in May 1781 General La Fayette, with cannon behind a boxwood hedge that still fringes the hill, shelled Petersburg, then occupied by the British.

PETERSBURG, 22.3 *m.* (14 to 85 alt., 28,564 pop.) (*see Petersburg*).

The CENTRAL STATE HOSPITAL (L), 25.2 *m.*, is devoted exclusively to the treatment of insane, epileptic, and feeble-minded Negroes. The 30 buildings, chiefly of brick, are on an estate of 1,814 acres, half of which is a farm worked by the patients. The capacity of the hospital is 3,465, and the number of inmates, 3,506 (1938). The institution was established in 1870 as Freedmen's Hospital at Howard's Grove near Richmond. In 1885 it was moved to its present site.

The frame TURNBULL HOUSE (R), 25.3 *m.*, was General Lee's headquarters from November 1864 to April 1865. From the house Lee saw his soldiers retreating when his lines were broken under a concerted Federal attack in the early light of April 2.

At 26.8 *m.* is a junction with State 142.

Left here to the SITE OF FORT GREGG, 0.9 *m.*, an artillery position held by 300 Confederates, April 2, 1865, until Lee could form a new line—from Fort Lee towards the Appomattox—and prepare to evacuate Richmond and Petersburg.

In a field a short distance north at 27 *m.*, General A.P.Hill, while trying to reach his corps, was killed by two Federal stragglers. General Hill, prominent in most of the major engagements of the Army of Northern Virginia, was one of Lee's most reliable officers.

In the stagecoach era, this section of US 1 was the Boydton Plank Road, over which traveled the fashionable world on its summer visits to the mineral water resorts in the hills. The coachman's horn once echoed through the countryside, giving advance notice to passengers and to landlords, who knew by the number of blasts how many guests would soon be seated at the long tables of the inn.

Around Burgess Mill, on HATCHER'S RUN, 31.3 *m.*, a battle was fought on October 27, 1864. The Second Corps of Grant's army, moving toward the Southside Railroad in an attempt to cut Lee's communications and supported by two corps, attacked Confederate works on Hatcher's Run to the east and here encountered earthworks that stopped its advance. Unexpected resistance caused Grant to order a withdrawal.

BECK'S BEACH (R) is a popular resort with boats, bath houses, and a dance pavilion.

At 31.6 *m.* is a junction with County 613, the White Oak Road.

Right along this dirt road behind entrenchments, rested Lee's right wing in the early spring of 1865. General G.K.Warren, attacking Lee's works on March 31, was driven back, but returned with reinforcements, forcing the Confederates to retreat.

At FIVE FORKS, 6.4 *m.*, Sheridan and Warren attacked Lee's extreme right on the afternoon of April 1, 1865, and overwhelmingly defeated infantry and cavalry under Generals George E. Pickett and Fitzhugh Lee. On the following morning a general Federal assault broke Lee's line south of Petersburg, causing the evacuation of that city and Richmond; the surrender at Appomattox took place one week later.

DINWIDDIE, 38.2 *m.* (250 pop.), seat of Dinwiddie County, tapers from widely spaced residences strung along the highway to braces of stores, banks, and churches, which cluster around the court green. Dominating the sloping square is the rectangular brick COURTHOUSE, painted white. The four-columned portico that shields an iron balcony over the entry door, pilasters between the windows of the sides, and a right one-story wing somewhat relieve the building's severity of line. Dwarfed by this solid-looking structure is the tall granite CONFEDERATE MONUMENT, its aloof soldier at rest.

Dinwiddie County, named in honor of Robert Dinwiddie, governor of Virginia (1751–58), was formed from Prince George County in 1752. Many valuable early records were destroyed during the 1860's.

Dinwiddie's history reaches back to May 1607, when Jamestown colonists came to the falls of the Appomattox River—an exploration that Captain John Smith duplicated the following year. Fort Henry, built here in 1646, became a trading post, and finally a town (*see Petersburg*). General P.H.Sheridan's large cavalry force, leading a westward movement to encircle Petersburg, occupied this village on the evening of March 29, 1865. Two days later the forces of General Fitzhugh Lee and General George E. Pickett drove back Sheridan's entire corps and camped near the courthouse for the night. Learning that Sheridan had been reinforced, the Confederates began to withdraw to Five Forks.

Diagonally across from the court green is the two-story, clapboard building that was WINFIELD SCOTT'S LAW OFFICE. Born in Dinwiddie County July 13, 1786, Scott graduated from the College of William and Mary (1805) and then entered the law office of David Robinson in Petersburg with whom he rode the circuit, which included Dinwiddie Court. His military career began in 1808. Commissioned captain of light artillery, he participated in the War of 1812 and the Mexican War, and rose to the highest rank in the U. S. Army. He retired in 1861 and died in 1866.

At 42.7 *m.* is a junction with County 646.

Left here to a junction with County 655, 5.2 *m.*; L. here 0.5 *m.* to SAPONEY CHURCH, of Bath Parish. The small frame rectangular structure, low-pitched with a gabled roof extending forward, was built in 1880 of material from the church of 1726.

In this region lived the Saponey, 'the honestest, as well as the bravest Indians we have ever been acquainted with,' according to William Byrd II, who camped in this section on his return from surveying the Virginia-North Carolina boundary (1728). 'All the grandees of the Sapponi nation did us the honor to repair hither . . .' he wrote. With them came 'four young ladies of the first quality.' The deliberate lure of these 'copper colored beauties' and their surprising 'air of cleanliness' were wasted on the swampy air. 'We resisted their charms,' soliloquized Mr.Byrd, 'notwithstanding the long fast we had kept from the sex, and the bear diet we had been so long engaged in. Nor can I say the price they set upon their charms was at all exhorbitant. A princess for a pair of red stockings cannot, surely, be thought buying repentance much too dear.'

WARFIELD, 57.5 *m.*, a hamlet, is the SITE OF EBENEZER ACADEMY (L), the first Methodist school established in Virginia, founded by Bishop Francis Asbury (1745–1816) in 1793. It passed out of the hands of the church but remained a noted school for many years.

The SITE OF OLD BRUNSWICK COUNTY COURTHOUSE (L) is at 64 *m.* When the county was formed in 1720, it was directed that a courthouse, prison, pillory, and church be built here, though the courthouse was not erected until 1732. After Lunenburg County had been cut from Brunswick in 1746, the county seat was moved eastward.

SOUTH HILL, 78.7 *m.* (439 alt., 1,405 pop.), a comparatively new town with a spacious look, is the third largest bright-leaf tobacco market in the State. Auctions are held almost daily during the selling season, from October 1 to March 1, in four large warehouses, each with its own name and something of an individual atmosphere. There are also several large drying and rehandling plants, a large stemmery, and other facilities for handling tobacco.

Early in the winter mornings scores of springless wagons and automobile trucks, piled high with the golden leaves, come in from the rural district. Throughout the day buyers, growers, auctioneers, and others thread their way through the lanes of tobacco 'in the loose' on the warehouse floors. The leaves, heaped in large flat baskets, are arranged in rows, the size of the piles varying. The lingo used by the auctioneers is understood only by the buyers, who represent the leading tobacco manufacturers. Although nearly all business done here during the tobacco-selling season is on a credit basis, the growers pay cash for their purchases after they have disposed of their crops. With the opening of the season, the town takes on new life, business booms, and an air of prosperity prevails.

South Hill is also one of the leading cotton markets in Virginia. A large lumberyard lies on the outskirts of the town.

In South Hill is a junction with US 58 (*see Tour 7b*), with which US 1 coincides to 84.8 *m.*

On the Roanoke River, 89.5 *m.*, one of the first waterways used for transportation to the western part of the State, a well-organized fleet of flatboats operated as early as 1825.

Returning from a trip to 'settle the bound' between Virginia and North Carolina, William Byrd II and the other Virginia commissioners crossed here in November 1728.

At 93.7 *m.* the highway crosses the NORTH CAROLINA LINE, 23 miles north of Henderson, N.C. (*see North Carolina Guide*).

Tour 1A

Fredericksburg—Bowling Green—Hanover—Richmond; 53.8 *m.* State 2.

Asphalt-paved roadbed; heavy trucks barred.

State 2, an alternate to US 1 (*see Tour 1b*) between Fredericksburg and Richmond, is almost curveless. It follows roughly a Colonial trail over gently rolling terrain covered for the most part with pine forests.

State 2 branches southeast from US 1 (*see Tour 1b*), 0 *m.*, in FREDERICKSBURG at the intersection with Lafayette Blvd. and coincides with US 17 to a junction at 5.8 *m.* (*see Tour 6a*).

At 8.4 *m.* is a junction with County 612.

Left on this road to ROUND OAK CHURCH (L), 0.2 *m.*, a large T-shaped brick building. The Baptist congregation (white) to which it belongs was constituted in 1840 as the result of the Reverend Lawrence Battaile's zeal for religious work among Negroes. When he expressed a desire to go to Africa, his father suggested that he do missionary work at home and built a frame chapel on his estate for the purpose. Soon there was a large congregation of both white and Negro members. After the War between the States, the Negroes formed a separate congregation. The main part of the present building was erected in 1852, and the transepts were added in 1915.

GRACE CHURCH (L), a plain brick structure just south of the junction with County 612, was built in 1833 and is one of two churches that supplanted—on different sites—a Colonial church of St.Mary's Parish. Many of the communicants became members of the congregation at Round Oak.

At 11 *m.* is a junction with County 606.

Right here to a junction with County 609, 2.3 *m.*; L. here 1.2 *m.* to MILL HILL (L), birthplace of John Taylor (1754–1824). Now abandoned, the house seems a part of the exhausted soil. Orphaned at ten, Taylor was adopted by his cousin and maternal uncle, Edmund Pendleton, who sent him to Robertson's Academy (*see Tour 1B*) and in 1770 to the College of William and Mary. After his graduation Taylor studied law under Pendleton's tutelage and then launched into his career as soldier, statesman, politician, and agriculturist (*see Tour 6a*).

At 3 *m.* on County 606 is a junction with a lane bordered by Lombardy poplars; R. here 0.2 *m.* to the STONEWALL JACKSON SHRINE (*free*), a small one-story white clapboard building, in which General Thomas J. Jackson on May 10, 1863, 'crossed over the river' to 'rest under the shade of the trees.' Accidentally shot by his own men, Jackson was taken first to Wilderness Tavern and then brought to Guinea Station near by—away from the war zone. This house, then the office of Fairfield, home of the Chandler family, is now maintained by the National Park Service. In the rear room are mementos and the bed in which Jackson died.

On County 606 at 6.8 *m.* is NORTH GARDEN (R), a frame house, two-storied, with additions through which rise outside chimneys. Dominating the crest of a gently sloping hill, the house stands among an elaborate array of modern buildings. It was built not long after the Revolution by Captain Harry Thornton, who was devoted to racing and cockfighting—the wide hall of North Garden was frequently covered with blood and feathers. Captain Thornton became financially involved and spent many an anxious moment, hopping—when the sheriff arrived—across the dividing line between Caroline and Spotsylvania Counties, which conveniently ran through his yard. One day sheriffs of both counties came simultaneously. In an offhand manner the captain mounted a horse and rode off. At a safe distance he wheeled about, raised his hat, and said, 'Gentlemen, I have the honor to wish you a very good day.' Soon after this escapade he moved to the less annoying confines of Kentucky.

At 8.6 *m.* is a junction with US 1 (*see Tour 1b*).

VILLBORO (R), 13 *m.*, a two-and-a-half story frame building with gable roof and a right wing, clings tenaciously to its treeless hill at the crossroads. This surviving part of a much larger building has felt no painter's brush, apparently, since it was profitable Todd's Ordinary—one of five Colonial taverns between Fredericksburg and Hanover. Liquor prices were fixed by a patriarchal court: 'Rum, the gallon, eight shillings; Virginia brandy, six shillings; Punch or Flipp, the quart, with white Sugar, one and three pence, with brown Sugar, one shilling; . . . a hot Dyet, one shilling; . . . a Lodging with clean Sheets, six pence; Oats, the gallon, six pence; Pasturage, the day, six pence per Head.'

Right from Villboro on State 208 to County 639, 3.4 *m.*; L. here 0.9 *m.* to BLENHEIM (L), a sturdy, two-story house of brick laid in Flemish bond. A graceful front portico, topped with a balustrade, is echoed on the left side and at the rear. Blenheim has lost none of its dignified charm despite lack of proprietary care. Here was born in 1846 James Hoge Tyler, Governor of Virginia from 1898 to 1902.

On State 208 at 10 *m.* is a junction with US 1 (*see Tour 1b*).

BOWLING GREEN, 19.6 *m.* (463 pop.), is the seat of Caroline County. New churches, service stations, and spacious-porched Victorian houses have not dissipated the atmosphere preserved by the buildings near the court green. One vestige of the 1890's lingers in fading letters—Bullard's Opera House. The little town wakes on court day when farmers assuage their often-thwarted gregarious instinct. From the old monthly court has grown the Social Court, a pleasant event that flowers the second Monday in every month. On these occasions anything can be bought on the streets from puppies to plantations.

Hemmed on two sides by rows of one-room lawyers' offices, the verdant green is dominated by the centrally placed square brick COURTHOUSE (1803–09), with a belfry and an arcaded loggia. The small brick jail, looking none too secure, is to the rear (R), and opposite is the brick Clerk's Office. On the green are a pump; a tall granite shaft topped with a moustachioed Confederate soldier, menacingly erect; and a marker announcing that La Fayette, on his way from Maryland to Richmond, camped here the night of April 27, 1781. Within the courthouse benign and rather modern portraits of Washington, Edmund Pendleton, John Taylor, and General William Woodford look out through the arches of the portico.

In 1727 Essex, King William, and King and Queen Counties contributed territory that became Caroline County and by its name honored the wife of George II. In 1742 another section of King and Queen County was given to Caroline. The courthouse, at the first county seat, about two miles north of the present one, was not without regal air, for Charles Bridges, an English artist, was paid 1,600 pounds of tobacco in 1740 to decorate the façade with the king's arms. In the clerk's office at the old seat Edmund Pendleton served as apprentice and studied law. Later, Pendleton tutored in law two of his nephews who became men of note—John Penn (1741–88), who moved to North Carolina in 1774 and two years later was among the signers of the Declaration of Independence, and John Taylor.

The town grew up about a tavern at a junction of two roads on the Bowling Green estate of John Hoomes, who in 1794 donated four acres here for a new county seat and a building for a courthouse 'until one could be built of the same size and material as the former one.' When, however, one Kenner petitioned for two additional acres for public use, Hoomes appealed to the general assembly, requesting that the seat of justice be re-established at its former site. Kenner's petition prevailed, more taverns were built, the clerk's office was moved here, and the present courthouse was erected.

In 1868, during Reconstruction, Alice Scott Chandler (1839–1904) founded The Home School, later renamed Bowling Green Female Seminary. In 1901 the school was removed to Buena Vista.

A bronze marker, at the junction with County 626, within the town, commemorates the 'heroism' of Baptist ministers imprisoned in the jail at the old seat in 1771 for 'teaching and preaching the gospel without having episcopal ordination or a license from the General Court.' Brought to trial, the Reverend Bartholomew Chewning, James Goodrich, and Edward Herndon were remanded to gaol, there to remain till they gave 'security, each in the sum of twenty pounds & two securities each in the sum of two pounds for their good behaviour twelve months and a daye.' Similar charges were preferred against other ministers, and the same punishment was meted out. Patrick Henry, on one occasion, hurried from his home in Hanover County to the old courthouse to defend the ministers.

OLD MANSION (R), 20 *m.*, was center of the original Bowling Green estate. Its weatherboarded bulk rises a story-and-a-half between ends of brick in Flemish bond. The steep hipped gambrel roof has dormers above a wide porch—a later addition. Old Mansion still overlooks a terraced garden and a circular drive lined with huge box bushes, gnarled and twisted. Although built by Major John Hoomes on land patented by him in 1670, Old Mansion is associated principally with Colonel John Waller Hoomes, a sportsman and importer of thoroughbred horses. His sons died one by one, under strange circumstances. Seated one day in the long dining room at a table set for 13, Hoomes distinctly heard horses' hoofs galloping around the track outside the house. No horses were visible. The following day Hoomes's eldest son became ill and died. With but slight variation, the same event preceded the death of his other sons.

But even then the Old Mansion was not done with drama. The Woodfords, later tenants, came under its spell. The story is that the husband, having transferred his affections from an invalid wife to a buxom housekeeper, to cut the Gordian knot swathed himself in a sheet, placed a jack-o-lantern over his head, appeared before Mrs.Woodford's window, and frightened the poor woman into the arms of death. When rumor of the escapade got abroad, Woodford left the community—accompanied.

At 22.5 *m.* is a junction with State 14 (*see Tour 1B*).

The SITE OF NEWMARKET (R), 23 *m.*, is an open field. The owner of this outstanding Colonial mansion, John Baylor III (1705–72), was a colonel of militia and a burgess, better known as an importer and breeder of thoroughbred horses. *Fearnaught*, imported in 1764, cost him 1,000 guineas and brought forth a footnote by Patrick Nisbett Edgar in his pioneer studbook: 'Until the day of *Fearnaught* no other than quarter races were run in Virginia. Speed had been the only quality sought for.'

Colonel Baylor, contrary to custom, sent his daughters, as well as his sons, to England to be educated. Colonel George Baylor (1752–84), born here, as chief of Washington's staff carried the news of the Battle of Trenton to Congress, which presented him 'a horse, properly caparisoned for service.' Major Walker Baylor commanded the 'Washington Life Guards' at Germantown. One of his sons, Robert E.B.Baylor, was a member of the convention that framed the constitution for the State of Texas and in 1845 one of the founders of Baylor University, which was named for him. James Bowen Baylor passed his boyhood here. A representative of the U.S. Coast and Geodetic Survey, he determined the elements of the earth's magnetism from Canada to Mexico and was instrumental in determining several state boundary lines.

At 39.1 *m.* is a junction with County 614.

Left here to HORN QUARTER (L), 4.1 *m.*, an *ante-bellum* plantation. The brick house dominates three terraces rising from a sluggish little stream that mirrors fringing box bushes. Above a high basement, its two stories are topped with a steep hip roof that terminates in a balustraded deck. The wide cornice rests on an elaborate frieze of circle and anchor design, no less ornamental than the carved wood panels set between the upper and lower windows. The front portico has columns in pairs at each side with pilasters behind them. On the lawn are two rectangular, one-story brick structures—one formerly the office, the other the kitchen.

The place was originally one of three adjacent plantations owned by the same family. Here was the 'quarter' where the horn was blown to summon the slaves from the fields. The present house was built during the first of the nineteenth century by George Taylor, who equipped an entire regiment of the Confederate army and donated to the 'Cause' all surplus crops grown on the estate during the war.

At 39.4 *m.* on State 2 is a junction with State 54 (*see Tour 1b*).

HANOVER, 39.7 *m.* (125 pop.), seat of Hanover County, spreads along intersecting roads, away from the main thoroughfare.

The COURTHOUSE (L), dominating the large, brick-walled green, is a charming one-story T-shaped structure with an arcaded piazza across the front, a tall hip roof covering the bar of the T, a fine cornice with heavy dentils, and walls whose glazed headers still emphasize the Flemish bonding. The courthouse was built about 1733.

In the courtroom among portraits of notable Hanover residents are those of Henry Clay, Patrick Henry, Thomas Nelson Page, and the Reverend Samuel Davies (*see below*).

On the shaded green is (R) the small new stone jail. Box-lined walks lead past the courthouse to the CONFEDERATE MONUMENT, a granite shaft pleasingly simple, beyond which is the old one-story brick Clerk's Office. About 1920 a duplicate of the original office was erected with a passage connecting it with the first.

In 1720 by enactment of the general assembly that part of New Kent County 'which lyeth in the Parish of St.Paul' was given the name of Hanover County—in honor of the Elector of Hanover. It was in this county, through the preaching of the Reverend Samuel Davies, founder of the College of New Jersey (now Princeton University), that Presbyterianism in Virginia secured a strong footing. The Reverend Mr.Davies,who later rebuked George II for interrupting him in the midst of a discourse in England, came to the county in 1747. Patrick Henry accepted Davies's sermons as models of oratory and acquired from him ideas of religious liberty.

In the courthouse here Patrick Henry pled the Parsons' Cause on December 1, 1763, the case that won him first fame. From the beginning of the colony ministers' salaries had been paid in tobacco, fixed in 1696 at 16,000 pounds annually and, after 1748, 'laid in nett tobacco.' In 1758, a year when the price of tobacco was high, the general assembly re-enacted the law of 1755, providing that all tobacco debts be paid in currency at the rate of two pence per pound. The clergy, demanding the usual quantity of tobacco, appealed to the king, who sided with them. Then various clergymen sued for the remainder of salaries due them for 1758. Chief of these cases was instituted here by the Reverend James Maury. When the suit was tried in November 1763, the court found in Maury's favor. Moreover, a special jury was summoned to determine whether the plaintiff had sustained any damages. Apparently, the clergy had won. Accordingly, John Lewis, counsel for the defense, retired from the scene. It was then that the defendants employed Patrick Henry to represent them in the damage suit.

Patrick Henry's father, John Henry, one of the justices, presided at the trial. An uncle, the Reverend Patrick Henry, heeding his nephew's warning that unpleasant remarks about the cloth would be made, retired from the court green. Patrick Henry delivered an impassioned speech, defending the Act of 1758. The king, he said, had forfeited all rights to his subjects' obedience. As for the clergy, they had changed from shepherds to wolves 'so rapacious' that they would not hesitate to take away 'the last blanket from the lying-in woman.' At that the righteous gentlemen bristled and left the courtroom. The case ended. The jury retired and spent five minutes in awarding the Reverend Mr.Maury one penny damage—a verdict that also smacked the throne.

HANOVER TAVERN (R) spreads its long, frame, L-shaped bulk between gabled roof and a high basement of brick. A long veranda fills in the angle of the L. The tavern, erected about 1723, has grown with the years. Here Patrick Henry was living when he appeared in the Parsons' Cause. His father-in-law, John Shelton, had acquired the tavern in 1760, and Henry had moved here that year—to be near the courthouse. Lord Cornwallis in 1781, while pursuing La Fayette westward, stopped here awhile. The Marquis de Chastellux collected the story during his own visit after the Revolution: 'Mr. Tillman, our land-lord at Hanover Court House . . . though he lamented his misfortune in having lodged and boarded Lord Cornwallis and his retinue without his Lordship's having made the least recompense, could not help laughing at the fright which the unexpected arrival of Tarleton spread among a considerable number of gentlemen who had come to hear the news, and were assembled in the Court House.'

At 40.9 *m.* is a junction with County 605.

Left here to a private road, 0.4 *m.*; L. here 0.5 *m.* to the VIRGINIA MANUAL LABOR SCHOOL for delinquent Negro boys. Its many buildings are spread along a winding drive bordered with clipped privet. Founded in 1897 by Dr.John H. Smythe (Negro) to carry out the ideas of the Negro Reformatory Association of Virginia, the institution in 1920 was taken over by the State. Outside the classrooms and trade school, the overalled boys work in shops, on the farm, and in the gardens.

At 42.5 *m.* on State 2 are junctions with County 643 (L) and County 657 (R).

1. Left on County 643 to the VIRGINIA INDUSTRIAL SCHOOL (L), 1.2 *m.*, a State institution for delinquent Negro girls. Lining the circular drive are five large buildings. The average annual enrollment is 100. The girls are kept busy in classrooms and developing their aptitudes for home economics, gardening, and poultry raising. There are physical training classes and recreational facilities. The school was founded in 1915 by the Virginia State Federation of Colored Women's Clubs, which purchased here a 148-acre farm with a small building and grist mill. From its beginning the institution has had as superintendent Janie Porter Barrett (Negro), whose interest in delinquent children was responsible for its founding.

2. Right from State 2 on County 657 to a junction with County 656, 2.9 *m.*; R. here 0.2 *m.* to SLASH CHURCH (L), a frame building erected in 1729. Like its contemporaries, Slash Church has a steep gabled roof and denticulated cornice. Used now by a congregation of the Christian denomination, it was formerly a church of St.Paul's Parish, of which the Reverend Patrick Henry was rector when his nephew flouted British rule in 1763.

County 656 continues northward and becomes County 654; at 1. *m.* is a junction with a private road; R. here 0.2 *m.* and L. 0.5 *m.* to the SITE OF CLAY SPRING, now occupied by a cottage. Near by is a MONUMENT constructed of millstones, commemorating Henry Clay, who was born here April 12, 1777. He attended the log school and carried grain to the mill of 'The Slashes,' studied law under George Wythe, and was admitted to the bar at the age of 20. He moved to Kentucky in early manhood. Called 'the Mill Boy of the Slashes' and 'the Great Pacificator,' Henry Clay was thrice

Speaker of the House of Representatives, four times senator, Secretary of State under John Quincy Adams, thrice candidate for president, defender of the American tariff system, and author of the Missouri Compromise and of the Omnibus Bill of 1850. He freed his own slaves and advocated the plan of purchasing all slave children and setting them free. But acceptance by his followers of his political philosophy only served to postpone what Clay himself saw was inevitable—a clash between the North and South.

HANOVER WAYSIDE PARK (L), 44.7 *m.*, is a wooded area (*picnic facilities: campsites and trailer-sites; free*) bordered by a large artificial lake (*no boating or swimming*).

At 47.7 *m.* is a junction with County 640.

Left on this road to a junction with County 606, 0.6 *m.*; L. here 0.8 *m.* to a private road; L. 1.1 *m.* to TOTOMOI, long home of the Tinsley family. Two other structures had already occupied the site before the present rectangular house—with clapboarding and gabled roof—was built in 1792. Additions since then include small wings, a lean-to, and a two-deck porch, partially engulfed in folds of blue-green box. Half hidden by additions, tall twin chimneys form a solid wall extending to the second floor before separating. This well-preserved house rambles under the protecting branches of huge catalpa trees that cast shadows over a line of tall box. Back of the dwelling extends a broad formal garden in which box-edged flower beds radiate from the axis of a summer house and are welded together by a surrounding hedge of lilacs.

County 606 continues eastward, crossing TOTOPOTOMOY CREEK, 2.1 *m.* The stream was named for Totopotomoi, chief of the Pamunkeys and faithful ally of the English. Totopotomoi was killed in battle near here in 1656 while assisting the colonists in resisting the Ricahecreans (*see Tour 6A*). Grant's army, attempting to get between Lee and Richmond, in 1864 tried to cross this creek. Finding Confederate resistance too stubborn, Grant moved southward to Cold Harbor.

RURAL PLAINS (R), 2.3 *m.*, a brick residence erected in the late seventeenth century stands on a shaded lawn. The story-and-a-half house has four front and five rear dormers in a hip-on-gambrel roof above a denticulated cornice. The windows, now widened, once had iron bars across them. Massive doors of maple have large English locks with small brass knobs.

Patrick Henry in his nineteenth year was married here in 1754 to Sarah Shelton, granddaughter of William Parks, editor of *The Virginia Gazette.* After his own house on a neighboring farm, Pine Slash, had been destroyed by fire in 1757, Henry lived here temporarily with his father-in-law.

At 6.6 *m.* is a junction with County 700; R. here 0.4 *m.* to the SITE OF THE STUDLEY HOUSE (L), marked by foundations and old trees. Patrick Henry was born here on May 29, 1736, the son of John Henry and Sarah Winston Syme Henry. His mother's first husband was John Syme, and her son, John Syme, was heir to Studley. Soon after Patrick Henry and his brother William were born, the family moved to Colonel Henry's home, Mount Brilliant, where Patrick Henry spent most of his childhood. Later Studley was acquired by Judge Peter Lyons, and here Henry's opponent in the 'Parsons' Cause' passed his last years.

In *A Progress to the Mines* Colonel William Byrd tells of a visit to Studley in 1732, when Patrick Henry's mother was yet the widow of John Syme: 'This Lady, at first Suspecting I was some Lover, put on a Gravity that becomes a Weed; but so soon as she learnt who I was, brighten'd up into an unusual cheerfulness and Serenity. She was a portly, handsome Dame . . . and seem'd not to pine too much for the Death of her Husband . . . The courteous Widow invited me to rest myself . . . and go to Church with Her but I excused myself, by telling her she woul'd certainly spoil my Devotion. Then she civilly entreated me to make her House my Home whenever I visited my Plantations.'

County 606 again crosses TOTOPOTOMOY CREEK at 8.7 *m.* Here, on June 13, 1862, General J.E.B.Stuart encountered Federal cavalry while on his memorable ride around the Federal army. Stuart, with 1,200 cavalry, had left Richmond June 12 to learn the position of the Federals, disrupt their supply base and lines of communication, and procure provisions for the Confederate army. He returned to Richmond June 15, having passed around McClellan's entire army. Federal cavalry, after attempting to stop him here, fell back for a further resistance a short distance southwestward.

LINNEY'S CORNER, 9.8 *m.*, is the scene of the clash between Stuart's men and Federal cavalry June 13.

At 10.1 *m.* is a junction with US 360 (*see Tour 20a*).

At 53.8 *m.* on State 2 is the southern junction with US 1 (*see Tour 1b*).

RICHMOND, 58.9 *m.* (15 to 206 alt., 182,929 pop.) (*see Richmond*).

Tour 1B

Junction with State 2—Sparta—St.Stephen's Church—King and Queen—Centerville; 58.1 *m.* State 14.

Asphalt-paved except for a few miles east of Sparta.

State 14 parallels the north bank of the Mattaponi River and southeast of St.Stephen's Church traverses a narrow peninsula called 'the Shoe String.' The region produces corn, wheat, tobacco, and vegetables. Along the way are patches of pine and oak forests richly sprinkled with dogwood, laurel, and holly.

State 14 branches southeast from a junction with State 2 (*see Tour 1A*), 0 *m.*, at a point 2.9 miles south of Bowling Green.

MULBERRY PLACE (R), 0.3 *m.*, has a late eighteenth-century house with a steep hip roof and four wide chimneys. Across the back are double galleries. This estate, named for a mulberry grove that once spread over more than 100 acres, was established by John George Woolfolk (1750–1819). His son Jourdan added to the fortune by operating the stage-coach line run in connection with the railroad between Petersburg and Occoquan. In 1836 the railroad company advertised that 'the Stage Travelling, which is conducted by Messrs.J.Woolfolk & Co. . . . in the handsomest manner, being now only 67 miles, is becoming rapidly reduced by the extension of this Rail Road.'

At 6 *m.* is a junction with County 640.

Right here to WHITE PLAINS (L), 0.2 *m.*, a weatherboarded house, painted white. The gabled roof, pierced by dormers, has an air as distinctive as that of the delicate Georgian portico. One of the outside chimneys has been partly engulfed by a one-story wing.

The estate, once a part of Edmundsbury (*see below*), was given by Edmund Pendleton to his nephew, another Edmund Pendleton, who probably built this house. White Plains has been the home of three Baptist ministers; Andrew Broaddus I (1770–1848),

Andrew Broaddus II (*c.*1815–1900), and Andrew Broaddus III, who for more than 100 years were successively pastors of Salem Church. The first Andrew was the son of John Broaddus, commissary in the Continental army and an opinionated fellow, who so bitterly opposed dissenters that he published several pamphlets ridiculing them.

On County 640 at 1.8 *m.* is a junction with County 643; L. here 0.5 *m.* to the SITE OF EDMUNDSBURY (R), once the home of Edmund Pendleton (1721–1803), who, before he was 14 years of age, had been bound by the court of Caroline County 'unto Benjamin Robinson, clerk of this court, to serve him the full end and term of six years and six months as an apprentice.' He purchased and read law books and was licensed to practice law before the expiration of his apprenticeship. Pendleton finally settled here, where he acquired a large estate. In 1774 he was a member of the First Continental Congress, in 1775–76 chairman of the Committee of Safety, president of the Virginia Conventions of 1775 and 1776, and later head of the State's judiciary department.

At the outbreak of the Revolution, Pendleton was a leader of the 'cavalier' party. His wish was, he said, 'a redress of grievances and not a revolution of Government.' Although he opposed Patrick Henry's proposal to arm the militia, when the measure carried, he helped to put it into effect. He believed in a liberal suffrage and equality of man before the law and denied that government should be controlled by the wellborn or wealthy. In 1799 he published a document supporting the principles of Jefferson's party.

In SPARTA, 6.8 *m.* (40 pop.), among hills, several roads converge.

SALEM BAPTIST CHURCH (R) is a massive rectangle of brick, painted white, with a gabled roof extending forward over a heavy pediment supported by tall Doric columns. The congregation was organized in 1802 as the result of the Great Revival that spread over Virginia in 1788.

NEWTOWN, 16.7 *m.* (50 pop.), is a hamlet of scattered old and new buildings.

1. Left from Newtown on County 625 to a junction with an unimproved private road, 1.5 *m.*; L. here 0.7 *m.* to THE GLEBE OF DRYSDALE PARISH. The square, story-and-a-half brick house, built about 1763, was the home of rectors until the glebes were confiscated in 1802.

2. Right from Newtown on County 625 to a junction with County 628, 2.6 *m.*; L. 0.8 *m.* to the SITE OF ROBERTSON'S ACADEMY (R) in a grove of oaks. About 1755 Donald Robertson, a Scot, established here a classical school for boys. James Madison attended Robertson's Academy while staying in this vicinity with his grandparents. Among other pupils were George Rogers Clark and John Taylor of Caroline.

At 25 *m.* on State 14 is the junction with a private road.

Left on this road to SMITHFIELD, 0.6 *m.*, among locust trees, bridal wreath, japonica, and forsythia. The two-story frame house, built in 1783 by William Hill, has a hip roof and massive end chimneys. The original beaded, heart poplar weatherboarding, fastened to oak studding by handmade nails, is intact. The interior is distinguished by much hand-carved detail and doors with brass hinged rings instead of knobs.

At 25.5 *m.* on State 14 is a junction with County 628.

Right here to GREEN MOUNT (L), 0.9 *m.* The long frame house, with a two-story central unit and one-story wings, has been made still longer by an addition placed between the main building and one of the wings. Dr. Benjamin Fleet built Green Mount about 1840. After his death his widow, Maria Louisa Wacker Fleet, an early advocate of higher education for women, conducted a girls' school here.

ST. STEPHEN'S CHURCH, 26.6 *m.* (*see Tour 20a*), is at a junction with US 360 (*see Tour 20a*).

At 28.1 *m.* on State 14 is a junction with a private road.

Right here to FARMINGTON, 0.8 *m.*, an L-shaped frame house, on a hill overlooking broad fields. Robert Ryland, born here in 1805, became the principal of the Virginia Baptist Seminary, first president of Richmond College, a teacher in the National Theological Seminary (Negro), a founder of the Baptist Female Institute, and president of the Shelbyville (Ky.) Female College. From 1841 to 1865, while president of Richmond College, he was pastor of the First African Church.

BRUINGTON CHURCH (R), 31.4 *m.*, in a quiet grove, is a large rectangular red brick building with white trim. In the gable above the front entrances is a graceful fanlight. The building belongs to a Baptist congregation brought together in 1780 through the preaching of John Waller, James Greenwood, and William Stovall. This building, the third, was erected in 1851.

Within the iron-fenced cemetery is the grave of the Reverend Dr. Robert Baylor Semple (1769–1831), first pastor of Bruington and historian of the Baptist denomination. The College of William and Mary, though formerly a unit of the Established Church and adversely affected by disestablishment, conferred upon this pioneer Baptist the degree of doctor of divinity, as did Brown University.

At 32.8 *m.* is a junction with County 629.

Right here to County 634, 1.8 *m.*; L. here 2.4 *m.* to HILLSBORO (R), a story-and-a-half house on a wide lawn, near the Mattaponi River. It has a brick basement, brick gable ends with double chimneys, frame front and rear, and narrow windows. The interior is elaborately paneled in walnut and has a black walnut stairway of unusual design. Hillsboro was built about 1730 by Colonel Humphrey Hill (1706–75). During the Revolution it was raided by British soldiers, and during the War between the States, by Union troops. A hole in the ceiling of the hall was made by a Federal soldier who, foraging for meat in the attic, fell through the plastering.

At 2.7 *m.* on County 629 is a junction with a dirt road; L. here 0.4 *m.* to the SITE OF RYE FIELD (L), birthplace of Dr. Thomas Walker (1715–94), physician, soldier, explorer, and land agent (*see Tour 17a*).

Colonel Thomas Walker settled here about 1700, acquiring an estate that bordered for 10 miles on the Mattaponi River.

WALKERTON, 3 *m.* (90 pop.), on County 629, was once a thriving shipping point on the Mattaponi River. Now tomato packing is its chief activity. It was created a town in 1709. In 1748 the burgesses passed an act 'to prevent the building of wooden chimneys in Walker Town and also to prevent the inhabitants thereof from raising and keeping Hogs.' This act the king vetoed in 1751, and the general assembly, in an 'humble Address to His Majesty,' explained that 'what chiefly induced your Assembly to pass this Act was the prevention of the public warehouses for the reception of Tobacco in this town from the danger of fire.'

Before the War between the States, four or five two-masted vessels would be docked here at the same time; but after the building of the railroad between Richmond and West Point in 1860, the village lost its importance.

County 629 continues southward crossing the river; at 3.6 *m.* is ENFIELD (L), a story-and-a-half frame house above a curve in the Mattaponi. The oldest part of the house was built by a member of the Waller family on land granted during the reign of Charles II. Near the house is a gnarled paper mulberry tree with bent limbs that have taken root and sent new shoots in many directions.

At 5.4 *m.* on County 629 is a junction with State 30 (*see Tour 20A*).

STEVENSVILLE, 37.3 *m.* (50 pop.), is an old crossroads community. Here was Bunker Hill, the ancestral home of the Bagby family and birthplace of John Garland Pollard (1871–1937), governor of Virginia from 1930 to 1934. Pollard was editor of the *Virginia Code, Annotated* and held among other posts those of attorney general of Virginia and dean of the Marshall-Wythe School of Government and Citizenship of the College of William and Mary.

At 37.7 *m.* is a junction with County 631.

Right here 1.5 *m.* to DAHLGREN'S CORNER, where young Colonel Ulric Dahlgren, Federal cavalry officer, was mortally wounded in a night skirmish with a home guard unit on March 2, 1864. In February 1864 Colonel Dahlgren and General H.J. Kilpatrick attempted to enter Richmond to release Federal prisoners. Frustrated and separated from most of his command, Dahlgren, with 165 officers and men, made his way to this vicinity, pillaging and destroying property. A lock of Colonel Dahlgren's hair, his watch, ring, and memoranda book were preserved by Juliet Jeffries Pollard—grandmother of Governor Pollard—and, after the war, were sent to his father, Admiral John A. Dahlgren in Philadelphia.

LOCUST COTTAGE (R), 38.3 *m.*, in a grove of trees, is a small frame house that has replaced a building that housed Locust Cottage Seminary for girls, founded in 1838 by Mira Ann Southgate and her husband, James S. Southgate. Locust Cottage ceased to be a school in 1852.

BEL AIR (R), 39.2 *m.*, now with two full stories, was originally one-and-a-half stories high, with a gambrel roof and dormers, outside end chimneys, and end lean-to's. This frame house was built about the beginning of the eighteenth century by the Lumpkin family. Major Thomas Jeffries acquired it about 1800 and gave it to his daughter Juliet, who married John Pollard, grandfather of Governor John Garland Pollard.

In a wide churchyard (R), 40.3 *m.*, shaded by old trees is MATTAPONY CHURCH, built about 1755. The walls of the cruciform structure are laid in Flemish bond. This was a church of St.Stephen's Parish, constituted in 1691. Abandoned after the disestablishment, it was acquired in 1824 by the Baptists, who continue to use it. In 1922 it was gutted by fire.

At 43.4 *m.* is a junction with County 631.

Right on this road to a private road, 1.0 *m.*; R. here to the SITE OF NEWINGTON, 1.8 *m.*, birthplace of Carter Braxton (1736–97), a signer of the Declaration of Independence. The house was destroyed by fire after the War between the States, and only out-buildings remain.

George Braxton (1677–1748) acquired Newington about 1710. His only son, George Braxton who married Mary Carter, was the father of Carter Braxton.

KING AND QUEEN, 44.5 *m.*, seat of King and Queen County, is no smaller and no larger than it was when a visitor from Detroit saw it in 1897 and said: 'We found the village to consist of the following buildings—courthouse, clerk's office, . . . a diminutive jail, in which one lone prisoner languished, a general country store, and a farmhouse of moderate size, dignified as "the Hotel." '

The COURTHOUSE, a small one-story brick building, cruciform and set upon a neat greensward, was erected after the War between the States, to replace a building destroyed during the war. Among the numerous portraits of native sons are those of Alexander Fleet, author of Virginia's poor debtors' law; John Robinson, speaker of the house of burgesses; Thomas R. Dew, president of the College of William and Mary; Dr.Robert B. Semple, Baptist minister and historian; Carter Braxton, signer of the Declaration of Independence; the Reverend Andrew Broaddus, Baptist minister; William Boulware, diplomat; and Thomas Ruffin, Chief Justice of the Supreme Court of North Carolina.

King and Queen County, named for William and Mary, was formed in 1691 from New Kent County; its first seat was south of the Mattaponi River. When in 1701 that part of the territory became King William County, a new seat was established here. The community that sprang up after a courthouse had been built was wiped out entirely in March 1864 when Kilpatrick and his cavalry burned its buildings.

At 52.5 *m.* is a junction with County 611.

Right here to a private road, 1.5 *m.*; R. here 0.3 *m.* to the SITE OF PLEASANT HILL, built about 1740 by Colonel Augustine Moore when his daughter Lucy became the second wife of John Robinson (1704–66). 'Of cultivated mind and polished manners,' Robinson was born at Hewick (*see Tour 6a*). In 1738 he became speaker of the house of burgesses and treasurer of the colony and held both offices until his death. He was presiding when George Washington appeared as a member of the house of burgesses at the end of the French and Indian War. When resolutions commending his military services were passed, Washington rose to thank his colleagues but fumbled for words. 'Sit down, Mr.Washington,' said Speaker Robinson. 'Your modesty surpasses your valor, and that is beyond any language at my command.'

OLD CHURCH (R), 53.1 *m.*, in a quiet triangle was erected about 1720 and is typical of the middle-Colonial rectangular church—low-pitched, with a gabled roof, compass windows, a main door in the west end, and a side door in the south wall. The 'Upper Church' of Stratton Major Parish, it replaced an earlier frame church. As finally constituted, Stratton Major Parish had two churches—Upper and Lower. When New Church (*see below*) was completed in 1768 for communicants of the entire parish, Old Church was closed, and its windows and doors were boarded up. After the Revolution it served as a school but after 1800 was again used as a church by both Methodists and Baptists. Twice it was damaged by fire and twice restored. When contention arose between Baptists and Methodists for possession of this building, the court ordered it sold; and the buyer in turn sold it to the Methodists. Though New Church disappeared, Upper Church is still a sound building.

At 54.8 *m.* is a junction with a private road.

Right here to a private road, 0.3 *m.*; R. again to the SITE OF LANEVILLE, 0.7 *m.* Foundations, measuring 285 feet from end to end, are the remains of a house built about 1750 by Richard Corbin.

There is a story that Corbin and his wife maintained only formal relations. Living at one end of his lengthy house, he assigned apartments to her at the other end. But he would call on her formally once a year. Then he would enter his 'coach and four' in full regalia and be driven the length of the house. Richard Corbin procured for George Washington his first commission as an officer of the Virginia militia.

To Laneville his son-in-law, Carter Braxton, sent in 1775 the request that Corbin, receiver-general of the king's revenues, pay for the powder that Governor Dunmore had taken from the Powder Horn in Williamsburg. Corbin remained loyal to the king during the Revolution but lived here quietly and did nothing to thwart the Revolutionists.

In a woods at 57 *m.* is the SITE OF THE NEW CHURCH (L), completed in 1768 and destroyed in 1825. Since Stratton Major Parish already had two good brick churches, the decision to build a new church appears to have been based on a desire to surpass the elaborate new Poplar Spring Church (*see Tour 6a*) of neighboring Petsworth Parish. On February 27, 1760, it was directed that a church 'be Built on some part of the old field belonging to the Honble: Richd: Corbin Esqr: called Goliahs, 80 feet long and 50 feet wide in the Clear, the Foundations to be began 5 Bricks thick & so continue to the Surface of the Earth, from thence 4½ Bricks thick to the water Table which is to be 4 foot above the top of the Earth, thence 4 Bricks thick to 27 foot Pitch from the Surface of the Earth.' In 1664 it was agreed 'that the Honble: Richd: Corbin Esqr: send home to England for a Communion Table Cloth, a Cloth for the Desk, & 2 Surplaces for the use of the New Church.' Also, the New Church had an organ in 1769. Contrary to custom, the seats were not sold or rented to the parishioners but were assigned free according to social position. The communicants of the Lower Church were given pews on the north side and those of the Upper Church on the south side. Despite its splendor, New Church enjoyed but a brief period of glory. The Revolution and a quarrel between the vestry and the Reverend Mr.William Dunlap ended services here in 1777.

Mr.Corbin forgot to give the parish title to the land. When the church stood abandoned in the early nineteenth century, a purchaser of Goliah's Field pulled the church down and sold the bricks.

CENTERVILLE, 58.1 *m.*, is at a junction with State 33 (*see Tour 6A*).

Tour 2

(Pocomoke City, Md.)—Accomac—Onley—Exmore—Eastville—Cape Charles; US 13.
Maryland Line to Cape Charles, 62.2 *m.*

Concrete-paved throughout.
Pennsylvania R.R. parallels route.
Ferries cross Chesapeake Bay from Cape Charles to Old Point Comfort and Norfolk; for costs and schedules see below.
Small hotels on Chincoteague Island, in Accomac, Eastville, and a few other towns; tourist homes in villages; a few tourist camps.

US 13 drops down the middle of Virginia's Eastern Shore on a fairly straight course to Cape Charles near the tip of the narrowed peninsula that separates Chesapeake Bay from the ocean. The fertile land of Accomac County—the northern two-thirds of this peninsula—is abundantly wooded and rolls gently out to marshy flats along both coasts, which are interlaced by innumerable inlets and shallow bays. A chain of low islands along the east protects the mainland from the full winter force of Atlantic storms. These sheltered waters abound with fish and shellfish, which form one of the chief sources of local income. Most of Northampton County, the other third of the peninsula, is absolutely flat. Truck farms dotted with neatly-kept white frame houses stretch away to the dark green walls of pine woods, which form windbreaks against wintry gales. This landscape makes a curious impression; it is as though everything in sight had been laid out with T-square and compass. At the end of long side roads, houses, occasionally of brick and very old, stand in solitude on meadowy lawns close to the water.

The Eastern Shore can boast an unusual number of small seventeenth- and eighteenth-century houses. They are generally story-and-a-half frame structures on brick foundations with dormered gambrel roofs—often with brick end walls—or, somewhat later and more numerously, designed in a style peculiar to this region: the 'big house, little house, colonnade, and kitchen.' This type evolved to keep pace with families that grew in size and prosperity. A single unit sufficed at first. Another was built adjoining it, and finally—unless it had been constructed along with the first—the 'kitchen' at the end of a short, enclosed passage called the 'colonnade,' though quite innocent of columns. In fishing communities by the water T-shaped houses with gable roofs were more popular. Some fair-sized brick mansions date from the latter half of the eighteenth century.

All is prosperous looking in this world of vast vegetable gardens. The potato has long been the staple crop here. When its price is up, the people live well; when its price is down, sadness prevails. The principal industries are closely related to agriculture: chiefly canning of fruit and vegetables, manufacture of containers, production of fertilizer, and lumbering.

The Indians called all of the lower peninsula Accawmacke (land beyond the water). It was first settled by whites in 1614 and in the early years Crown messages were sent: 'To our faithful subjects of ye Colonie of Virginia and ye Kingdom of Accawmacke.' Accomac was one of the eight shires into which Virginia was divided in 1634.

US 13 crosses the Maryland Line, 0.0 *m.*, 6 miles south of Pocomoke City, Md. (*see Maryland Guide*). The boundary between Virginia and Maryland was not clearly established across the peninsula until 1894. This settled a controversy between these states reaching back to the early days of Lord Baltimore's Proprietary. In 1663 Colonel Edmund Scarburgh, surveyor general of Virginia, was ordered by the general assembly to run a line setting the limits of the territories. Attended by five companions and 'about fourty horsemen,' whom he took with him 'for Pomp of safety' and 'to repell that Contempt' which, he was informed, 'some Quakers and a foole in office had threatened to obtrude,' he dragooned the inhabitants into submission to Virginia. The recalcitrants were arrested 'to answer their Contempt and Rebellion'; and, where they could obtain no security, their goods were seized and 'the broad arrow set on the doore.' Nor was the opportunity to harass dissenters neglected. George

Johnson, one of those arrested, was stigmatized by Scarburgh in his report as 'ye Proteus of heresy,' notorious for 'shiffting, scismatticall pranks.' What the Virginia assembly had intended simply as a surveying expedition was converted into a war of conquest and a religious crusade. In 1668 another survey was made—called the Calvert-Scarburgh line—and became the basis for a long-drawn-out controversy between the States.

NEW CHURCH, 1.7 *m.* (50 pop.), a scattered handful of houses, recalls a church that once stood here.

Left from New Church on County 709 to HORNTOWN, 4.2 *m.*, a group of frame houses and two or three shops, long a trading place for the people of Chincoteague. Its name was derived from a habit fish peddlers had of blowing horns to advertise their wares.

SHEPHERDS' INN (*open*), SE. angle of crossroads, a log structure built before 1731 with end chimneys, has been weatherboarded.

WELBOURNE (L), built about 1811 by Drummond Welbourne, is now a roofless, crumbling shell of brick. An arcaded loggia on one side and indications of a once gracefully sloping roof hint at former beauty. Having planned beyond his means, Welbourne was unable to complete his house and is said to have committed suicide out of consequent sorrow.

Left from Horntown 0.4 *m.* on County 679 to a dirt road; R. here to CORBIN HALL, 1.5 *m.*, a brick mansion on Chincoteague Farm built in 1725 by Samuel Welbourne and remodeled in 1787 by George Corbin. Below the gabled roof is a modillioned cornice. Renovations in 1895 included a slate roof and a small vestibule projecting from the façade below a tiny Palladian window dating from 1787. A wide Victorian porch faces Chincoteague Bay. The attractive old interior trim includes pilasters rising to an arch across the hall. Beneath the house lies a drainage system constructed in the eighteenth century. North of the house are the graves of the Corbins.

At about 2.8 *m.* the tracks of the Pennsylvania Railroad are seen (R). In the 1880's the first tracks were laid down the peninsula by the New York, Philadelphia & Norfolk Railroad to meet ferries from Norfolk across the bay. The initials of the company, NYP & N, became the local name for the line—'the Nip and N.'

At 4.1 *m.* is CHINCOTEAGUE (Ind. large stream, inlet; pronounced *shin-ca-teeg*) CROSSROADS.

Left here on State 175, which traverses flat marshland cut by several inlets, over a series of causeways and bridges to CHINCOTEAGUE ISLAND (*guides and equipment for fishing*), 9.8 *m.* (2,130 pop.). Dozens of small fishing boats hug little wharves that jut out from amongst piles of oyster shells along the shore where the center of the island community is concentrated in neatly-kept white frame buildings. Houses and commercial structures along the water front are set upon brick piers. The principal street continues north and south as a shore road; several side roads lead off through pine groves and low meadowland across the long, narrow island.

Oysters, clams, and fish provide a source of income for a majority of the islanders, though poultry raising and catering to amateur fishermen have begun to bring in more cash. The local importance of commercial fishing is evident in the long lines of nets hung out to dry, boats being built or repaired in little home yards, figures of speech used by everyone, and the blue overalls, pea jackets, and hip boots of the men at work. Fishing goes on the year round, clams, oysters, and crabs being the chief catches. Chincoteague oysters have always been notable. Seed or small oysters are brought here from natural beds and put down on hard sand bottoms rented from the State.

Various devices are used in this area for commercial fishing. The pound-net or weir —called locally 'ware'—is most common, but gill nets, haul nets, and even purse nets are used—though the latter, pulled behind a motor boat, are strictly illegal in Virginia waters. Public opinion, however, regards purse netting much as it did bootlegging during prohibition. Full of disaster for the hard-working fishermen are the hazards of their enterprise: ice that may tear nets and storms that damage boats as well as nets and sometimes bury oyster beds under silt and débris. The fresh seafood is sold on the local wharves to buyers for Northern markets, the prices being fixed by the wholesale marketers.

Widely known too are the Chincoteague ponies, which, like those on the neighboring Assateague Island, used to roam over the island pastures. The origin of these animals—stunted horses rather than real ponies—is obscure, but all accounts agree that they are descendants of horses that strayed or were abandoned in early Colonial times. Their present size is probably the result of a marsh grass diet over many generations. Romanticists prefer to believe that these ill-behaved Houyhnhnms descend from Arabian mounts left by pirates in the heyday of the Spanish Main, or that such horses swam ashore from a Spanish galleon, wrecked off this coast. Annual Pony Penning Day, the last Thursday in July, is an important local event, drawing a large crowd of visitors. The ponies, taller and more graceful than Shetlands, are corralled, the foals branded, and many sold at auction. Visitors buy colts the size of large dogs, which they carry off in their automobiles. The island wears a carnival air for a day, with amusement concessions; but the revels of a century ago are known no more, especially since fencing laws have thrown the business entirely into the hands of a few.

On October 25, 1662, Chincoteague Island was granted to Captain William Whitington by Wachawampe, Emperor of the Gingo Teagues, and regranted twice later. Wachawampe's will of 1656 is on file at Eastville.

ASSATEAGUE ISLAND, separated from Chincoteague by an inlet dotted with flat little islands (*reached by boat; hire 50¢*), is a long strip of land with an excellent beach stretching its wooded and meadowy area, without habitation, outside Chincoteague and far up the Maryland coast. Wild ponies roam this island freely, and one of the most interesting sights of Pony Penning Day is the spectacle of their being forced to swim across the inlet to the auction.

TEMPERANCEVILLE, 7.9 *m.* (140 pop.), another loose gathering of modern frame dwellings and shops, was early settled by Quakers and named, it is said, for a Mr. Temperance, who owned a plantation near by. Most of the Quakers moved away about 1657 to avoid stringent laws passed against them.

Right from Temperanceville on State 288, which becomes County 695 at 1.6 *m.*, to a dirt road, 5.6 *m.*; R. here 0.5 *m.* to the MAKEMIE MONUMENT (L), a stone figure of Francis Makemie (1658–1708) in clerical garments on a roughhewn granite pedestal near the site of his house. A small truncated pyramid of brick fragments from the house marks the probable site of the family graveyard.

Makemie, born in Ireland, came to this country in 1683 as a Presbyterian missionary and trader. Settling in Accomac, he acquired much property and a wife, Naomi Anderson, daughter of a wealthy merchant. He moved to the Barbadoes, stayed until 1698, then returned to Accomac. When he was arrested for preaching without a license, he pleaded his cause in such a manner that he was later granted a license to preach; his 'dwelling house in Pocomoke near the Maryland line, and at Onancock . . .' were recognized meeting places. After organizing several congregations and importing two missionaries from London, he formed at Philadelphia in 1706 the first presbytery in America.

County 695 becomes a dirt road, 8.2 *m.*, on a causeway that crosses marshy flats dotted by clumps of trees on firmer ground, to SAXIS ISLAND, 11.5 *m.* (500 pop.), a fishing settlement of widely scattered houses not far from little wharves on the bay side. Here, as in other fishing communities on the eastern shore, the mainstay is the seafood industry. Windmills pump water in summer for muskrats, which are the source of income for at least one islander.

MAPPSVILLE (105 pop.), 11.5 *m.*, is a roadside huddle on US 13.

Left from Mappsville on County 689 to County 679, 1.3 *m.*; L. here to County 689, 1.5 *m.*; R. to a dirt road, 1.8 *m.*; L. to WHARTON PLACE, 2.3 *m.*, an almost square brick house at the far end of a field above Assawoman Creek. The openings have white stone lintels, and once-decorative wooden plaques break the space between upper and lower windows. Though the general design suggests 1825 as the approximate date of construction, it is known that at the time of the Revolution a distinguished smuggler, John Wharton, lived here. Smuggling was common throughout the colonies, and respectable.

Southward the highway runs through well-cultivated farms, on which Irish and sweet potatoes and many other vegetables are grown. The decline in potato prices has encouraged diversification. The marketing season of 1936 was the occasion for picketing of the highways by farmers in this area in an effort to enforce organized selling of crops to maintain prices.

Tenant houses dot the far edges of fields along the roads. Whole tenant families work during harvest time, women and children 'graveling' potatoes, picking fruit, or gathering vegetables, while the men load and carry the produce from the fields in two-wheeled carts, called locally 'tumble carts.' The pine woods, alternating everywhere here with the fields, have a park-like trimness.

PASTORIA, 18.6 *m.* (50 pop.), is so scattered that only a few houses and a filling station are visible at the crossroads. Colonel John Donelson and his wife Rachel Stockley, who lived in this neighborhood sometime before 1766, became the parents of Andrew Jackson's wife, Rachel.

Right from Pastoria on State 176 to PARKSLEY, 2.5 *m.* (800 pop.), an inharmonious union of commercial district full of garish signs on shabby buildings and a spacious, regularly laid out residential section wearing a pleasant late-Victorian air. Factories here can and ship fruits and vegetables.

At 21.3 *m.* on US 13 is a junction with County 662.

Left here to the entrance (L) to MOUNT CUSTIS, 2.5 *m.*, three separate houses knit into a compact hodgepodge by passages. Attractive dormers are perched on its red gabled roofs. The house stands on land patented by John McKeel or Michael, a Scotchman who migrated about 1640 to Virginia and married the daughter of his friend and fellow traveler, John Custis. McKeel built the house, to which a west end was added in 1710 and an east wing in 1834.

At 21.9 *m.* on US 13 is a junction with County 652.

Left here to BOWMAN'S FOLLY (R), 2.5 *m.*, on a knoll almost surrounded by creeks. The white frame structure has brick ends and a gabled roof above a cornice with delicate corbels. A Palladian window above a simple porch and five dormers give some distinction. Two small and perhaps older buildings ramble out as a low wing at one side, and several others stand about in the picket-fenced yard.

The first house on this site was built by Edmund Bowman, who considered his migration to Virginia a folly when his only son died here of 'slow fever' in 1660. The present house was built for General John Cropper (1755–1821), who married Bowman's daughter Gertrude. General Cropper, says the inscription on his tomb here, 'was an officer in the Revolution and did continue until the end.' On February 12, 1779, while at home on leave, he was surprised by a raiding party from the British-Bermudian sloop *Thistle Tender*, which had come up Folly Creek, a deep inlet that reaches the foot of the lawn. Cropper escaped in his underclothes and went for aid, but the only companion he could find deserted when near the house. Cropper held his ground, fired his weapons in quick succession, and shouted, 'Come on, my braves.' The British fled, thinking he had brought many defenders. Cropper found his wife and daughter locked in an outhouse, the main house planted with gunpowder, and his plate, jewelry, and 30 slaves missing.

ACCOMAC, 22.5 *m.* (41 alt., 700 pop.), seat of Accomac County, is a leisured little center of affairs for two-thirds of the Virginia eastern shore, with plenty of old trees and several houses surviving from the middle of the eighteenth century. In 1786 the general assembly voted that 'ten acres of land, the property of Richard Drummond, adjoining to Accomack courthouse, shall be . . . laid out into lots of half an acre each, with convenient streets,' as 'a town by the name of Drummond.'

Henry Alexander Wise (1806–76), a native of Accomac, was governor of Virginia from 1856 to 1860. During the trial of John Brown and his associates, Governor Wise went himself to Harpers Ferry to see that the laws of Virginia were properly carried out; and, after the prisoners were condemned, he ordered troops to Charles Town to guard them. In the army of the Confederacy he served with distinction as brigadier general.

The COURTHOUSE (R), which in the late 1890's replaced a charming Colonial building, is of bright red brick, its appearance somewhat ameliorated by a row of several little old frame law offices at one side of its yard. Accomac (Ind., otherside place) was formed in 1655 from Northampton County (*see below*), though the boundary was not officially defined until 1662.

At a court trial held in Accomac in March 1679, a jury of women was summoned. The case concerned the alleged murder of an infant, born of Mary Andrews, unmarried daughter of Sarah Carter and stepdaughter of Paul Carter. By the 'ordeal of touch,' which involved digging up the body of the baby and causing it to be 'stroaked' by the accused persons, the jury of 12 women found Paul Carter guilty, for—while he was 'stroaking' the child—black and 'sotted' places on its body grew 'fresh and red.'

Anthony Johnson of Accomac County, one of the first African captives brought to Virginia, was the first free Negro, the first Negro landowner, and the first Negro slaveowner in the Colony. Freed in 1622 or 1623, Anthony Johnson by 1651 was able to pay for the importation of five persons into Virginia, on whose 'head rights' he received 250 acres of land. On the Pungoteague Creek Anthony Johnson established the first Negro community in America. In 1654 he was able to persuade the court that he was entitled to the services 'for life' of one John Casor, a Negro—a decision that marks, so far as the records reveal, the first judicial sanction of life servitude except as punishment for crime.

The DEBTOR'S PRISON (R) is a small brick building, stuccoed and vine-covered, with a gabled roof over its one story.

ST. JAMES' CHURCH, N. side of street between US 13 and Back St., is a very pleasant example of Greek Revival design. Before the yellow stuccoed end of the rectangular, brick body stand four Greek-Doric columns of a portico.

The DRUMMOND HOUSE, E. side Back St., a weathered red brick dwelling, is composed of three units: a large, two-and-a-half story section with the ridge of its gabled roof parallel to the street; a smaller, two-story section with its gable end forming part of the façade; and a low connecting passage. The house was built in 1750 by one of the many land-holding Drummonds.

Right from Accomac on State 177 to County 661, 3.1 *m.*, which turns L. to a dirt road, 4.9 *m.*; R. here to HILL FARM, 5.7 *m.*, by the water. The red brick house, built about 1685, is large for that date. It has one long, full story on a high foundation and a half-story lighted by dormers set closely on the tall gabled roof. A formal porch, a small frame extension at one end, and the sash windows topped by flat brick arches, as well as the dormers must have been added in later years. This land was patented about 1663 by a Captain Richard Hill, who seems to have come to Accomac in 1632 and whose daughter was later married to John Drummond, the immigrant.

TASLEY, 24.7 *m.* (250 pop.), is a railway shipping point. The annual Potato Blossom Festival, held here about the first of June, centers around the crowning of a young girl as queen of the pink and white blossoms.

Right from Tasley on State 178 to ONANCOCK (Ind., foggy place), 2.2 *m.* (1,240 pop.) (*boats for charter to Tangier Island;* $10.), with inlets bringing water to the foot of many streets. Away from the business district lawns are wide and houses, several of them old, are pleasantly shaded by trees. This is a storage point for oil and gasoline, which are brought in by boat and distributed in tank trucks.

Onancock was an Indian village when John Pory was a guest of Ekeeks, king of the Onancocks in 1621. At the feast the visitors were introduced to oysters and 'batata' or potatoes. After burning his mouth on hot potatoes, Master Pory said, 'I would not give a farthing for a shipload.' Onancock was established in 1680 as one of the 19 places designated by the general assembly in the Act of Cohabitation, to provide 'ports of entry.' Onancock became the county seat the year it was created, and so remained until 1786.

During the Revolution it was headquarters for the troops under General John Cropper. In these years the Eastern Shore suffered from frequent raids by British privateers. On November 30, 1782, occurred the Battle of the Barges, so called because of the crude craft used. Commodore Whaley of Maryland sallied forth with four barges to attack the marauders. He pursued the enemy vessels, caused them to strike their colors, but was killed when the powder on his barge exploded.

The KERR (pronounced, car) PLACE (R) is a large red brick house at the end of a very deep tree-shaded lawn. The two-story façade is heightened by a pediment that rises from the cornice of the gabled roof above a formal central entrance. Considerable length is added by a wing set back slightly at one end. The house was built in 1779 by John Shepard of Scotland.

TANGIER ISLAND (1,225 pop.) (*reached by mail boat from Crisfield, Md.; noon daily, fare 50¢*), in Chesapeake Bay about 12 miles from the mainland, is almost unspoiled by the machine age. Descendants of early settlers live in freshly painted frame houses surrounded by picket fences along straight, narrow streets. In the front yards are many tombstones, though burials are now in a public cemetery. People in Tangier fish, worship, live peaceably, and are intimate with rain, sun, and the sea. Their transportation needs are met by boats, pushcarts, wheelbarrows, and bicycles. Their speech retains old words, phrases, and pronunciations. Retaining a doctor, whom they pay by assessing each family, the islanders have demonstrated the efficiency of co-operative medicine.

Yet the outside world is reaching Tangier. Visitors now bring strange notions and even flasks in pockets or handbags. Time was when no islander dared be seen on the streets during church hours, but customs have changed since the death of a pastor who was known to break beer bottles and pour their contents into the sea.

When Captain John Smith explored the bay in 1608, he found Tangier inhabited by the Pocomokes. On his map of 1612 Tangier and Watt Islands bear the name 'Russels Isles,' honoring Dr. Walter Russell, the physician who accompanied Smith. In 1670 Tangier was granted to Ambrose White; and in 1686 John Crockett and his eight sons settled here. About a third of the present inhabitants bear the name of Crockett.

The hero of the island is the early minister, Joshua Thomas, whose prayers were those of a righteous man. As a fisher lad, he prayed for large catches and was heard. He prayed that the girl he loved would marry him; and then, praying for a home, he was led to Tangier. That was not so long after America became a republic. Then came the War of 1812, when the British used the island as a base for their operations in the Bay. Brother Joshua, sorely distressed, invited the enemy to come to his temple in the grove. There he prayed that their efforts would meet failure and, in a stirring sermon, declared their cause to be unrighteous and prophesied their defeat.

ONLEY, 26.1 *m.* (476 pop.), a few dwellings and stores at a bend of the road, is headquarters of the Eastern Shore Produce Exchange, a co-operative marketing agency, organized in 1899.

KELLER, 31.8 *m.* (300 pop.), is a railroad shipping point.

1. Left from Keller on State 180 to KELLER FAIRGROUNDS (L), 1 *m.*, where the Keller Agricultural Show has been held annually since the early 1880's.

WACHAPREAGUE (Ind., little city by the sea), 5.3 *m.* (675 pop.), on the site of the Indian town of the Machipungoes, is a base for sport fishing.

2. Right on State 180 to PUNGOTEAGUE (Ind., place of fine sand), 3.4 *m.* (150 pop.), seat of Accomac from 1662 to 1677. Court was held at the tavern of John Cole, who vainly attempted to keep the court day trade by offering to furnish bricks and woodwork for a courthouse. On August 27, 1665, the first theatrical performance in Virginia was given in this town. For presenting *Ye Bare and Ye Cubb,* Cornelius Wilkinson, Phillip Howard, and William Derby were ordered to appear before the court (on the complaint of a busybody named Edward Martin) 'in those habilmets that they then acted in, and give a draught of such verses, or other speeches and passages which were then acted by them.' After presenting their wares, the men were acquitted of the charge of immorality; the complainant was fined.

On May 30, 1814, the British admiral, Sir George Cockburn, landed on Pungoteague Creek with 500 marines and fought the Eastern Shore militia. Fearing capture, he retired to Tangier Island.

Right from Pungoteague 0.3 *m.* on State 178 to (L) ST.GEORGE'S CHURCH (open 10–5), a rectangular, early eighteenth-century building of brick with gabled roof. The front wall, which has been rebuilt above the simple entrance, is laid in Flemish bond—the dull glazed headers still making a strong pattern. This is only a remnant of a much larger church, which was cruciform in plan. During the War between the States this building was used by Union forces as a stable. The two transepts were so badly damaged that when the church was restored they were taken down; their bricks were used to restore the part that remains. The church preserves an early Bible and prayer book and, though now in St.George's Parish, still uses on special occasions the communion service presented to Accomac Parish by Queen Anne.

PAINTER, 34.5 *m.* (200 pop.), is a modern settlement around a railroad station.

Left from Painter on State 182 to County 605 in the little settlement of QUINBY, 3.8 *m.*; R. on County 605 to WARWICK (L), 4.7 *m.*, long and low, half brick and half frame. The steep gabled roof has five dormers on each slope. The house has been restored and extended by a porch-girt addition facing the water. Another house faces it across the yard, a slightly later frame dwelling of three units. The brick part of Warwick was built in 1672 by Arthur Upshur as his seat on 2,000 acres granted him by 'Pyony, King of the Machipungoe' for 'four good coats.' Rachel, Upshur's wife, was bitten by a rabid fox near the well and developed hydrophobia. To save her from the agonies of death from rabies—or in an effort to prevent her from injuring herself—her attendants smothered her to death between two feather beds.

At 37.5 *m.* on US 13 is a junction with State 181.

Right here to a junction with State 178 in BELLE HAVEN STATION, 0.7 *m.*; straight ahead on State 178 to County 613, 3.4 *m.*; L. here to County 612, 6 *m.*; R. here to County 611, 6.7 *m.* and L. to HEDRA COTTAGE (L), 7.2 *m.*, a 'big house'—not so big—and a little house both gray and weather-beaten. The two units are connected by a 'colonnade.' The larger house, two-storied, is older than the tiny story-and-a-half cottage and replaced Occahannock House, the home of Edmund Scarburgh II, villain of the early Eastern Shore drama.

The first Edmund Scarburgh settled on the Eastern Shore in the early days and patented much land. The story goes that his son, the second Edmund Scarburgh, was a bold and unscrupulous man. He accumulated wealth to the hurt of his friends; yet he was once a powerful person, even for a time speaker of the house of burgesses. Charged with piracy and debt, he had fled from the Eastern Shore sometime before 1653; in that year he had been disabled from holding office, and a warrant had been issued for his arrest. In March 1655 he had been pardoned by the governor and council. He played a part in Virginia history till his death during a smallpox epidemic in 1671. This Edmund had two sons. One of these, another Edmund, sided with Berkeley in Bacon's Rebellion of 1676. Charles, however, the second son, sided with Bacon and later became a trustee of the new College of William and Mary.

EXMORE, 39 *m.* (37 alt., 700 pop.), shipping point at the junction of several roads, has comfortable brick and frame houses.

Left from Exmore on State 183 to WILLIS WHARF, 1.5 *m.* (467 pop.), on flat marshes facing warehouses. Spic and span modern houses stand beside those mellowed by time and salt air. Cargoes of iced seafood are sent from the wharves to Northern ports. Fertilizer is manufactured here from fish unsuited for the market. Oyster shells from the packing plant are used for road surfacing and are converted into lime.

Southeast of Willis Wharf across Hog Island Bay is HOG ISLAND, 11 *m.* (300 pop.) (*mail boat to Willis Wharf daily, fare 50¢*), a narrow strip of land with a 9-mile beach on the Atlantic Ocean. The island is the home of fisherfolk, who, like those on Tangier Island, have retained many of the customs of their forefathers. Hog Island is one of the few places in Virginia and the country where gasoline is sold legally without a State tax. Because the beaches are used as roads, nature has eliminated the expense of road building, for which the tax is collected elsewhere.

Along the highway in NASSAWADOX, 43.4 *m.* (1,000 pop.), are unpainted frame houses and a canning factory. William Robinson, a Quaker who entered the colony about 1656 and was promptly arrested on the complaint of the Anglican churchmen, was eventually released and aided fellow-Quakers by pretending to help them leave the colony. Actually he landed the dissenters on Nassawadox Creek, where Levin Denwood provided them with a log-cabin meeting house.

BIRDSNEST, 46.3 *m.*, bears some resemblance to its name.

Right from Birdsnest on County 620 to County 618, 0.7 *m.*; R. here to County 619, 1.6 *m.*; L. here through woods of straight, longleaf pine mixed with oak and occasional holly to HUNGAR'S CHURCH (L), 3 *m.*, built in 1751. Its urbane charm is unexpected in the woods. Rectangular, of old-rose brick in Flemish bond with the headers making a faint blue design, it has blankets of ivy here and there. S and T irons give support to the old walls, and the façade is broken by twin entrances with semicircular brick arches set off by white stone keys and springers. A long window, similar in design, is set above and between them.

After the Revolution the organ was dismantled, the pipes being melted down for the manufacture of weights for fishing nets. When the building was restored in 1850, the wall at one end was re-erected some distance behind the former one, shortening the church. Vestments presented to the parish by Queen Anne are in the clerk's office at Eastville. Hungar's, formed with the first settlement here and once divided into two parishes, was in 1691 again made a single parish, because the 'small number of tithables . . . are soe burderned that they are not able to maintain a minister in each . . .'

The entrance (L) to WINONA (*open by arrangement*), is at 3.6 *m*. Standing on a high foundation in a meadow near the water, the story-and-a-half house has a modern shingled roof, pierced by pairs of reconstructed eighteenth-century dormers, and is flanked by two modern frame additions. The bricks of the walls, mellow rose except for a bright red section restored on the front, are laid in Flemish bond. Hidden by the addition at one end is the most striking feature of the house, a buttressed chimney topped by three tall clustered stacks that rise high above the roof. Winona and Bacon's Castle (*see Tour* 19) have the only chimneys of this type that have survived in Virginia. None of the old woodwork remains.

The land was patented in 1644 by Edwyn Conaway, who received it for John Severne, then under age. As he came of age in the following year, Severne repatented it. This house may have been built at about that time. The initials 'J.S.' are on bricks in the wall near the south door, and in the chimney is a brick with a date that looks very like 1645.

At 4.2 *m*. is a junction with County 622; R. here 1.4 *m*. to HUNGAR'S GLEBE, a neglected but sturdy survivor from 1745. The dark red brick walls rest on a high foundation with pronounced water table and are broken by windows with flat-arched heads of brick. The end chimneys have molded tops, and the unusual gabled swag roof has dormers irregularly spaced.

On County 619 is VAUCLUSE, 7.6 *m*., a white frame house in a grove of trees by the water. Two-storied and rectangular, the building has brick ends and a gabled roof over denticulated cornice. The twin formal porches that shelter both entrances and the irregular additions were added long after the house was built about 1784 by Littleton Upshur, father of Abel P. Upshur (1791–1844), who lived here for many years. Abel Upshur was Secretary of the Navy (1841–43) and then succeeded Daniel Webster as Secretary of State. He was killed with others on February 28, 1844, when a gun exploded on the *Princeton*.

At 52 *m*. on US 13 is a junction with a dirt road.

Right here to KENDALL GROVE, 1.2 *m*., in a forest. The main part of the large gray-white frame house is a tall gabled unit with a central pediment; there are lower, gabled extensions at the sides. Outbuildings at the rear include several tiny frame cabins. The nearest dependency, the kitchen, is reached through a 60-foot arched colonnade.

Built in 1796, this delightful house stands on the site of one erected by Colonel William Kendall, one of many men of that name prominent in Northampton County. After Bacon's Rebellion, when it was decreed that pardons be granted all rebels who would take the oath of obedience and give security for their good behavior, Colonel Kendall appeared before the court held at Berkeley's home in 1677, and took the prescribed oath.

At 52.7 *m*. on US 13 is a junction with County 630.

Right here to HUNGAR'S WHARF, 2.9 *m*., near the mouth of Mattawaman Creek. White sand beach and the water of the bay gleam through the trees at the site of what was once a private port for the numerous ships of John Kendall, trader with the West Indies. On one of his ships worked Stephen Girard (1750–1831), later a financier and philanthropist of Philadelphia. While playing cards with Kendall years later, according to tradition, he won Kendall's holdings. But when he sold the house, the new owner brought an ejection suit. Kendall's two daughters faced the sheriff with a goose gun each time he came to serve the papers. Possession was gained while the family was visiting neighbors.

EASTVILLE, 53.4 *m.* (37 alt., 387 pop.), seat of Northampton County, is a prosperous little town spread out neatly around the courthouse. Both old and new houses are set pleasantly in wide yards.

The COURTHOUSE, built in 1899, is a typically nondescript brick building with a double-galleried porch. Here are kept county records, continuous from 1632.

When the county that formerly embraced all the Virginia Eastern Shore and was first called Accawmacke (Accomac) was divided, the new upper county assumed the old name, and the lower county retained the one adopted in 1643. Eastville became the county seat in 1680, succeeding Town's Field.

Three small old structures in the square have a pleasantly antiquated charm. A former CLERK'S OFFICE, probably the courthouse built in 1731, is of ivy-covered brick, with high foundation and a steep gabled roof. Behind this office and connected with it by part of a wall that once bounded a prison yard is the DEBTORS' PRISON, a small, plain brick building. Here is kept the old whipping post.

CHRIST CHURCH (R), a small building of sandy pink brick, stands with its graveyard behind a modern brick wall. Beneath a little belfry is a crude portico. This church was built in 1826 to take the place of Magothy Church. The communion service was given to the congregation in 1741 by John Custis IV.

TAYLOR TAVERN (R), south of the courthouse, now the Eastville Inn, is a long, two-story frame building painted white, with gabled roof and wide weatherboarding. Along its whole length runs a veranda, close to the walk. Although remodeled and enlarged, the core of this building has been a public house since pre-Revolutionary times.

CESSFORD (R), on the southern edge of town, is a shallow, rose-red brick house in a large yard. Turning a gable end toward the highway, the handsome little mansion displays identical façades to north and south—with a columned porch on each. Windows in two tiers are headed by white stone lintels, and dormers are along both sides of the roof. The house, built in 1815 by Dr. John Kerr, was named for the seat of the Scottish clan of Kerr. During the War between the States it was occupied by General H.H. Lockwood. An order signed by Lincoln, instructing the soldiers to leave the house in the condition in which they found it, is on the wall.

Left from Eastville on State 185 to INGLESIDE (R), 0.6 *m.*, a large, well-kept house painted saffron. The two-and-a-half story gabled main part is extended at one side by a wing. The design of the beautiful garden is elaborate. Wallpaper in the hall, showing Egyptian scenes, was hung when the house was built about 1810.

At 54 *m.* on US 13 is a junction with County 634.

Right on County 634 to a junction with a dirt road, 1.1 *m.*

1. Right here 0.8 *m.* across level fields to ELKINGTON (*open*), a two-and-a-half story frame house in a white-fenced grove. The gabled roof is extended on the chimney side by rambling additions. In the hall is scenic French wallpaper, depicting the hunt. The library and parlor are paneled with heart pine. The house was built about 1800 by a descendant of the Savage family and named for the first wife of Captain John Savage,

Ann Elkington. Captain Savage was a burgess from Northampton in 1666–67. His father was Thomas Savage (*see White Cliff, below*).

2. Left here 1.4 *m.* to OLD CASTLE, a dilapidated frame house with brick ends, a curbed roof over its rectangular body, and an insignificant addition at one end. It was probably built about 1721 by John Stratton, who gave aid to Governor Berkeley during Bacon's Rebellion, turning over to him one of his own vessels, which was later wrecked. The house was remodeled, however, in 1794.

County 634 continues to a dirt road at 2.1 *m.*; R. here along a strip of pine woods undergrown with holly to WHITE CLIFF, 3.4 *m.* a frame house, with unsymmetrical wings, on land jutting into a body of water known as the gulf.

Nearer the water once stood the house of Thomas Savage, who came to Virginia in 1608 with Christopher Newport and was given to Powhatan—whose fancy the 13-year-old boy had taken—in exchange for Namotacke, an Indian youth. Later, because of the jealousy of Opechancanough, brother of Powhatan, Savage was sent by Powhatan, who called him Newport, to live near this site with Debedeavon, 'the Laughing King' and chief of all 'Accawmacke.' According to his statement in 1633, Debedeavon 'had given that neck of land from Wissaponson Creek to Hungar's Creek' to Governor George Yeardley and the 'south side of Wissaponson [Savage's Neck] to his son, Thomas Newport' (Thomas Savage).

When Captain John Smith visited the Eastern Shore in 1608, this king, whom Smith called 'the comliest, most proper, civill Salvage we incountered,' told him 'of a strange accident lately happende him, and it was, two children being dead, some extreame passions, or . . . phantasies, or affection moved their parents againe to revisit their dead carkases, whose benumbed bodies reflected to the eyes of the beholders such delightful countenances, as though they had regained their vitall spirits. This . . . drew many to behold them, all which . . . not long after dyed, and but few escaped.'

At 55.3 *m.* on US 13 is a junction with a dirt road.

Right here to EYREVILLE, 1.8 *m.*, a large, comfortable-looking brick house, painted red. Gabled roofs two-and-a-half stories above the basement cover the two main parts of the structure and an irregularly connecting link. The dates 1798, 1800, and 1803 on chimney bricks tend to substantiate the tale that it took 10 years to build. The estate, first called Newport, was later won and lost three times by gambling Severn Eyre (*see below*).

At 56.7 *m.* on US 13 is a junction with a dirt road.

Right here to EYRE HALL, 1.1 *m.*, a large, delightfully rambling white frame house among numerous outbuildings in a large grove of trees. The most important, and probably oldest, part of this eighteenth-century house has a gambrel roof above a single line of green-shuttered windows. Lower extensions form a square with one open side. Behind the well-kept house is a formal brick-walled garden—one of the most attractive on the Eastern Shore.

This was the center of the Eyre estate, which once extended across the peninsula, and the home of Severn Eyre, who was a burgess from 1766 to 1773.

At 58.3 *m.* on US 13 is a junction with County 639. One of the largest canneries on the peninsula stands near this crossroads.

Right here to a junction with County 640, 0.9 *m.*, and L. to a fork, 1.7 *m.*; L. here on a dirt road to another fork, 1.8 *m.*; R. here to TOWN FIELDS, 2.6 *m.*, a farm on flat lands also called Secretary's Plantation. The present house, a white frame structure with beaded weatherboarding built apparently late in the eighteenth century, may incorporate a much earlier dwelling; one brick end forms part of the wall facing the water closeby.

Accawmacke Plantation, one of the first settlements on the eastern shore, was established here in 1620 to provide commodities from the peninsula, especially salt, from the mother settlement. The governor and council directed that 'Mr. Pory, the Secretary, and his successors in that place (office) should have five hundred acres of land,' that 'twenty Tenants' should be 'planted thereupon,' and that 'the Secretary then, from henceforward, should receive no fees for himself,' because he was to have the quitrents and the purchase price from any land sold. In 1664 Accawmacke Plantation became the seat of Northampton County and in 1680 it was laid out as a town.

At 59 *m.* on US 13 is a junction with State 186.

Left here to County 645, 4.4 *m.*; R. 0.8 *m.* to County 644; R. here to the SITE OF ARLINGTON (L), 2.3 *m.*, the ancestral estate for which George Washington Parke Custis named the more celebrated Arlington (*see Tour* 12).

With the rise of the Parliamentarians in England John Custis fled to Holland and about 1640 to Virginia. His son John Custis II (1630–96), born in Rotterdam, built on this land the house in which Governor William Berkeley took refuge in July 1676 during Bacon's Rebellion and from which he launched his surprise attack upon Giles Bland and William Carver, two of Bacon's followers sent to capture him.

Near the site of the house is the CUSTIS GRAVEYARD, where are buried several members of the family, including John Custis II. The tomb of John Custis IV (1678–1749) bears this inscription:

Under this Marble Tomb lies ye Body
of the Honorable John Custis Esqr.
of the City of Williamsburg and Parish of Bruton
Formerly of Hungars Parish and the Eastern Shore of
Virginia and County of Northampton the
Place of his Nativity
Aged 71 years and Yet liv'd but Seven Years which
was the space of time He kept a Batchelers
house at Arlington on the Eastern Shore
of Virginia.

This epitaph was the last word in a long quarrel between John Custis and his wife, Frances, the daughter of Daniel Parke, governor of the Leeward Islands. Young John had been the gay blade of Virginia, and his lady the reigning belle. After their marriage these self-willed people found it impossible to get along together. They would address each other through a slave, Pompey. Then, one day, Frances accepted Colonel John's invitation to take the air in his carriage. Her husband helped her to her seat and then silently drove straight ahead into the bay. At last, when the water was above the floor board, Mrs. Custis asked: 'Where are you going, Colonel Custis?' 'To hell, madam,' he replied. 'Drive on,' she answered. 'Any place is better than Arlington.'

He turned his carriage around and drove home, with the remark, 'Madam, I believe you would as lief meet the Devil himself if I should drive to hell.' 'Quite true, Sir,' she answered. 'I know you so well I would not be afraid to go anywhere you would go.' This incident apparently cleared the air enough for an agreement settling property differences. But Colonel John ordered the last word inscribed on his tombstone.

Near the Custis tombs is the SITE OF MAGOTHY CHURCH, an early church of Hungar's Parish. The first was the Fishing Point Church, built in 1629 'neare the ffishinge poynte' at Dale's Gift (*see below*).

The Reverend Francis Bolton, a pioneer minister in this parish, was paid '10 pounds of tobacco and one bushel of corne for everye planter and trader above the age of sixteen alive at the crop.' The rectors ruled with an iron hand. In 1637 the second one, Mr.Cotton, reported one Henry Charlton to the court for not paying his tithes. Three men testified that they 'heard Henry Charlton saye if he had had Wm. Cotton without the church yeard, he would have kickt him over the Pallysadoes, calling of him Black catted (coated) raskall.' Upon the 'complaynt of Mr.Cotton against the syd Charlton,' it was ordered that the said Charlton should 'for the syd offence buyld a pare of stocks, and sett in them three severall Sabouth days in the time of Dyvine Servis, and there ask Mr.Cotton forgiveness.'

On State 186 at 11.1 *m.* from US 13 is KIPTOPEKE, a post office and railroad station among fields and evergreen woods that were formerly on the Hallet Plantation.

This is near the tip of the peninsula, the point of land named Cape Charles on April 26, 1607, when the three ships of the London Company entered the Chesapeake on their way to Jamestown. The name honored the prince who was later Charles I, younger brother of Henry, Prince of Wales, for whom the opposite cape was named.

East of the tip of the peninsula lies flat SMITH ISLAND (*no regular boat service*). In 1608 Captain John Smith left Jamestown to explore the Chesapeake Bay. He touched this island, and on the cape met two Indians who directed him to 'Accahawacke,' home of their chief. He was hospitably received and then cruised along the bay shore to the Pocomoke River.

In 1614 Governor Dale sent 20 men, under Lieutenant William Craddock, to this peninsula to make salt by boiling down the sea water and to catch fish for the colonists. They settled along Old Plantation Creek at Dale's Gift (*see below*) but established the salt works on Smith Island.

The salt makers' residence on the faraway peninsula was looked on as the equivalent of exile. But they found that in the sandy soil corn, vegetables, and fruit would grow in abundance; that fish abounded in the ocean, bay, and inlets; that wild fowl of many kinds swarmed in the marshes; that game could be had for the shooting; that the climate was delightful; and that the Indians were friendly. The exiles were soon envied by the James River settlers.

At 60 *m.* on US 13 is a junction with County 641.

Left here to County 642, 0.2 *m.*, and L. to STRATTON MANOR (R), 0.6 *m.*, approached along a short avenue of trees in four lines. The weatherboarded white frame house, with brick ends painted red, has three little dormers in the red shingled gabled roof. Outside end chimneys have wide bases. Across the front stretches a full-length veranda; additions straggle at the rear. The house, built about 1694 by Benjamin Stratton (1657–1717), was enlarged in 1764.

CAPE CHARLES, 62.2 *m.* (8 alt., 2,527 pop.) (*ferries to Little Creek, near Norfolk*, 7, 9, 11:15 *a.m.*, 1:30, 3:45, 5:45, 7:45, *and* 10 *p.m.; fare* 50¢, *automobiles* $2.50 *and* $3. *Ferries to Old Point Comfort and Norfolk*, 6:10 *a.m., berths available after* 11 *p.m. previous evening;* 12:20, *and* 4:15 *p.m. weekdays*, 12:50 *and* 4:45 *p.m. Sun.; fares* 50¢ *to Old Point Comfort and* 75¢ *to Norfolk, automobiles* $2.50 *and* $3).

The town has a seaside air with its beach along the bay. Behind a miniature 'board walk' are brick and frame residences looking more like resort cottages; a single business thoroughfare faces the railroad tracks and ferry slips along the little harbor. Houses, in generous yards, are all late Victorian or modern. Down the middle of every street runs a slender, sodded strip set with boulevard lights. Tugs with the railroad car barges they haul between the terminals here and at Norfolk are always present in the harbor, which is protected on the north by a breakwater. The shore southward to the tip of the peninsula shows an unbroken line of white sandy beach against a background of blue-green pine woods.

Although Cape Charles was reborn when the railroad arrived in 1884, it is a belated successor to the first two settlements on the Eastern Shore: Secretary's Plantation to the north and Dale's Gift to the south.

This area was occupied by Federal forces early in the War between the States, as a precaution against use of the peninsula as an attacking base by the Confederacy. When the Federal troops landed here, the residents, thinking there was to be a battle, armed themselves with whatever odd weapons they could lay hands on, only to find that no fighting was contemplated. The false alarm has been called the Battle of Three Ponds.

Though General H.H.Lockwood, who commanded the Federal forces, established friendly relations with the people, most men of the Eastern Shore who enlisted chose the Confederate side.

Tour 3

(Frederick, Md.)—Leesburg—Middleburg—Warrenton—Culpeper—Orange—Palmyra—Farmville—Clarksville—(Oxford, N.C.). US 15. Maryland Line to North Carolina Line, 239.8 *m.*

Hard-surfaced roadbed, chiefly asphalt.
Southern Ry. parallels route between Warrenton and Orange, Chesapeake & Ohio Ry. between Orange and Dillwyn, Southern Ry. between Keysville and North Carolina Line.
All types of accommodations except along the southern half of route, where only tourist homes and small hotels in the infrequent towns are available.

US 15 runs almost due south in Virginia. The upper section traverses open farming country close to the western edge of the Piedmont Plateau, within sight of the Blue Ridge foothills. Woodland predominates in the central third of its course, and in the lower third tobacco fields predominate.

Section a. POTOMAC RIVER to WARRENTON; 51 *m. US* 15

US 15 winds past the green sides of Catoctin Mountains, a low outlying range of the Blue Ridge, and traverses broad rolling country, which slopes toward the foothills and for nearly 100 miles varies little in type. Since 1900 this section has attracted wealthy Northerners interested in raising and training blooded horses. Farms have been turned into horse-training establishments; *ante-bellum* houses have been restored as seasonal homes; hunt clubs, horse shows, and racing meets that flourished before the war have been revived; and sleepy towns have taken on new and prosperous life.

US 15 crosses the Maryland Line, 0 *m.*, on the south bank of the Potomac River at a point 18 miles south of Frederick, Md. (*see Maryland Guide*).

In the Potomac is HEATER'S ISLAND, first called Conoy Island for the Piscataway Indian tribe (of the Algonkin family) that bore the Iroquois name of *Conoy* at the time of its migration from Maryland. An ally of Colonial Maryland against the hostile Senecas (Susquehannas) and Iroquois, this obscure but important tribe, reduced to the confines of a reservation in 1669, was by 1685 'miserably poor and low.' Persecuted by Iroquois and believing that Maryland intended complete annihilation, the tribe looked across the Potomac for asylum. In 1697 the Piscataways, under their new name, moved to Virginia. Two years later they established themselves on this island, building a large fort, with 18 cabins inside the enclosure and 9 without. Maryland, realizing her loss, entreated the Indians to return, but the tribe remained in its new home. About 1705 an epidemic of smallpox descended on the island, causing the Indians to leave —forever.

CHESTNUT HILL (R), 1.8 *m.*, a spacious two-and-a-half-story house of stone with gabled roof and long two-story portico, is on a shaded knoll with the green Catoctins in the background. Chestnut Hill was built about 1800 by Samuel Clapham, whose great-uncle, Josias, acquired land here in 1739. Samuel Clapham's father, Josias II, was a notable figure in local affairs—militia officer and member of the assembly (1770–88) and of the Revolutionary conventions. He built the Catoctin Iron Works and provided water power for its operation by cutting a 500-foot channel from the Potomac through the rocky end of what is still called Furnace Mountain. During the Revolution his little gun factory with '5 or 6 hands' turned out 'good musquets' for the Continental army.

At 5 *m.* is a junction with County 663.

Left on this road to County 657, 1.5 *m.*; L. here to the NOLAND HOUSE (R), 4.4 *m.*, a large building of red brick. It is believed to have been built about 1770 by Thomas Noland, whose ferry across the Potomac near here was a link in the old Carolina Road. This road, important in the history of early Colonial settlement, was first the 'plain path' between Susquehannock villages in Pennsylvania and Occaneechee Island in the Staunton, and a route of the Iroquois who avoided Tidewater settlements in their sallies southward. Many Scotch-Irish and German immigrants followed this route before crossing the Blue Ridge to settle in the great Valley. Soon pack trains and lumbering Conestoga wagons of pioneers journeyed toward the great meadows of Kentucky. Later trade flowed northward with droves of cattle, horses, hogs, and sheep bound for Northern markets. By 1842 horse- and cattle-thieving had given it the name of 'Rogues' Road,' and necessitated an act of assembly requiring drovers to carry evidence of having bought their herds.

ROCKLAND (L), 8.1 *m.*, a two-and-a-half-story house of deep red brick, with dormers and a formal porch having double columns below a deep cornice, has an unpretentious charm. The broad-arched front doorway is noteworthy for its graceful fanlights and sidelights. Rockland was built about 1822 by General George Rust (1788–1857) on a plantation that swept back northward to the Potomac River.

Imposing, white-pillared SELMA (R), 8.2 *m.*, in which are incorporated parts of an earlier house, was built about 1900. The farm was part of the 10,000-acre tract bought about 1741 by Mrs.Ann Thomson Mason, whose eldest son was George Mason of Gunston Hall (*see Tour 1a*). The first house at Selma was built by the grandson of 'Madam Mason,' General Armistead Thomson Mason (1787–1819), United States Senator. General Mason was killed by his cousin and neighbor, Colonel John Mason McCarty, in a duel that grew out of political rivalry. Mason had ignored his cousin's challenge and the affair had almost blown over, when, returning by stagecoach from Richmond, he met his old friend, General Andrew Jackson, who advised Mason not to let the challenge pass. McCarty, who had cooled, tried to avert the encounter by making ridiculous suggestions for carrying it out. However, Mason wrote that he 'was extremely anxious to terminate once and forever this quarrel.' To avoid Virginia's recently enacted anti-dueling law, the affair took place near Bladensburg, Maryland, February 6, 1819. Mason was killed and McCarty was dangerously wounded.

At 8.9 *m.* is a junction with County 655.

Left on this road to WHITE'S FORD, 1.3 *m.*, where in September 1862 Confederate troops crossed the Potomac.

Raspberry Plain (R), 9.2 *m.*, is a modern successor to the first house on 'the raspberry plain' built by one Joseph Dixon, a blacksmith, who acquired title to 322 acres from Lord Fairfax in 1731. In 1754 Dixon sold his 'houses, buildings, orchard, ways and watercourses' to Aeneas Campbell, who in 1757 became the first sheriff of Loudoun County. The new county having no buildings, Campbell is said to have built a little brick jail with stocks and pillory in his yard.

The Site of Goose Creek Chapel (R) is at 9.6 *m.* This little 'chappel of Ease' was erected about 1733 for parishioners of Truro parish living 'above Goose Creek.'

Springwood (R) 9.7 *m.*, built of brick about 1840, has had extensive frame additions, all painted white. The first house on the estate, its name derived from the Great Spring near by, was built by Francis Aubrey about 1728. Builder of the present house was Captain George Washington Ball of the Confederate army, grandson of Colonel Burgess Ball.

By a junction at 10.6 *m.* is a small granite Monument commemorating the Battle of Ball's Bluff, which took place about one mile eastward. Early in the morning of October 21, 1861, a small Union force crossed the Potomac from Maryland and drove back a similar force of Confederates. Reinforcements from fortifications by Potomac fords turned the tide. The invaders, pushed back over the steep bluff above the river, were slaughtered by volleys of gunfire poured down from the crest. A bayonet charge completed the rout. Among the wounded was a 20-year-old first lieutenant of the Twentieth Massachusetts Infantry, Oliver Wendell Holmes, afterward Associate Justice of the U.S.Supreme Court. A national cemetery, with rows of graves marked 'unknown,' is on the bluff.

LEESBURG, 12 *m.* (313 alt., 1,650 pop.), seat of Loudoun County, has developed about the courthouse square, where white-pillared buildings are shaded by elms and oaks; old houses of stone and brick, with ivy-clad walls, fanlighted doorways, and massive knockers, still sit placidly between small business places on two sides of the green. Smaller houses, close to the sidewalk, have been disguised with new store fronts; and close to the sidewalks along side streets are squat, slant-roofed, cottages with dormers. The first settlement here, log houses huddled at the intersection of the Carolina and Ridge Roads, was called Georgetown. But when 'proper streets' were laid off on lands of Captain Nicholas Minor near the new courthouse, the 1758 assembly ordered the town incorporated under the name of Leesburg, probably for Francis Lightfoot Lee and Philip Ludwell Lee, local landholders who were among the town's first trustees.

The COURTHOUSE, built in 1894, is a somewhat ornate red brick structure with white Corinthian columns supporting a pediment cupola with clock and belfry. On the courthouse lawn are the Confederate memorial, a handsome and alert soldier on a block of roughhewn granite, and a stone shaft bearing names of county soldiers who died in the World War. Loudoun County was created in 1757 from the northwestern end of Fairfax County, as settlement spread westward. Its name is probably the only Colonial honor given John Campbell, fourth Earl of Loudoun, who in 1756–57 was in command of British forces in America and titular governor of Virginia, although he never came to the colony.

The COUNTY OFFICE BUILDING, a rectangular, two-and-a-half-story structure of red brick with a full-width portico and simple cornice was built about 1844 as the Leesburg Academy, a boys' school.

Leesburg is at the junction with State 7 (*see Tour* 13).

Right from Leesburg on County 699 to County 698, 0.7 *m.*; R. here to the entrance (R) of MORVEN PARK (*private*), 1 *m.*, home of Westmoreland Davis, governor of Virginia (1918–22). Beyond lodge gates and nearly a mile of tree-lined drive, the large, two-story house extends to an unusual length and is ornamented by a Doric portico. Cattle stray over the 1,000 parklike acres of the estate.

Westmoreland Davis (1859–   ) is a lawyer, agriculturist, and publisher. His administration as governor was distinguished by a new emphasis upon general welfare and the formulation of a progressive social program in Virginia.

OATLANDS (L), 18.7 *m.*, a large mansion built in 1800–03 by George Carter, is visible through a screen of woodland. A tall white portico with Corinthian columns stands before the central and highest of the boxlike sections of the brick structure. The sides are extended in octagonal bays, and the whole composition is graceful in spite of angularity. The land was bought by Robert ('Councillor') Carter of Nomini Hall for his son George. George Carter was his own architect and he also laid out the vast terraced gardens and boxwood avenues.

OAK HILL (*private*), 21.8 *m.*, built (R) in 1820–23 by James Monroe (*see Tour 23A*), is a brick mansion painted a creamy yellow. It stands at the head of an avenue of trees. A main block with gabled roof is extended laterally by flat-roofed wings with gabled half-stories along their centers. A double, curving flight of steps with iron railings rises to the recessed entrance—beautifully severe with delicately traced fanlights and sidelights. The wings terminate in small porticoes, and a huge Roman Doric portico on a high foundation overlooks the garden and rolling country southward to the Bull Run Mountains. The simple interior is ornamented by two very handsome marble mantels sent by La Fayette from Europe.

Construction of Oak Hill was begun during Monroe's first term as President, and it was built with the assistance of James Hoban, Irish architect of the White House and a protégé of Thomas Jefferson. The building shows the influence of Jefferson, and it may even have been based on plans Jefferson is known to have made for Ash Lawn, but which were never used there. The mansion was greatly enlarged in 1923.

Monroe spent much time here, making trips to and from the Capital on horseback and carrying state papers in his saddlebags. After retiring from public life in 1825, he remained here until Mrs.Monroe's death five years later, when he went to live with his daughter in New York.

At 23.8 *m.* is a junction with US 50 (*see Tour* 12); R. here on US 50. A new 22-mile section of US 15 connects this point with Warrenton (*see below*).

ALDIE, 24.9 *m.* (175 pop.), with a church, an old grist mill, a schoolhouse, stores, and dwellings, took its name from the former home of Charles Fenton Mercer (1758–1857), member of the Virginia House of Delegates, brigadier general in the War of 1812 and member of Congress. The MERCER HOUSE stands in an oak grove above the highway at the center of the village.

The SITE OF THE HOUSE OF JOHN CHAMPE is at 26.4 *m.* Champe was the 23-year-old Revolutionary soldier, chosen in 1780 by Major General 'Light Horse Harry' Lee, at Washington's request for a volunteer to go on the hazardous mission of desertion to the British in a plan to capture Benedict Arnold and frustrate a suspected conspiracy involving Continental officers. Washington's words to Lee were, 'Whoever comes forward . . . will lay me under great obligations personally, and in behalf of the United States I will reward him amply.' Secrecy thrown about Champe's movements almost led to his undoing as he left the Continental camp on the Hudson River. His comrades, not aware of his errand, pursued him with vigorous realism, and he escaped their fire only by abandoning his horse and hiding along the river bank until rescued by British gunboats. Champe was able to join Arnold's dragoons, but Washington's plans came to nothing, for the night Arnold was to have been trapped the British were ordered to take ship for Virginia to join Cornwallis.

MIDDLEBURG, 30.2 *m.* (300 pop.), once 'the middle burg' and overnight stop on the stagecoach journey between Alexandria and Winchester, has taken on new life since the turn of the century as a center of a community where horses and hounds dominate business and social life. Old stone and brick houses, dormered cottages, and an old stone inn survive beside chain groceries, garages, filling stations, a bank, a motion picture theater, and antique shops.

Right from Middleburg on County 626 to FOXCROFT, 3.8 *m.*, a girls' preparatory school, occupying seven brick buildings.

In Middleburg is a junction with County 626; L. here on County 626.

THE PLAINS, 38.7 *m.* (565 alt., 372 pop.), has a lumber mill and stores. Here is a junction with State 55 (*see Tour 4A*) and State 17; straight ahead on State 17.

At 49.8 *m.* State 17 forks, offering Alternate State 17 (L) through Warrenton.

WARRENTON, 51 *m.* (635 alt., 1,651 pop.) (*see Tour* 22), is at the junction with US 29–211 (*see Tour 4a*), US 211 (*see Tour* 22), and US 15–29.

Section b. WARRENTON to CULPEPER; 24.9 *m.* *US* 15–29

US 15–29 runs through prosperous dairying country dotted with horse-lovers' estates. Plantations with Colonial history and battlefield sites add interest to the scene. The northern end of the route is part of the old turnpike between Falmouth and Winchester.

South of WARRENTON, 0 *m.*, is OPAL, 7 *m.*, at a junction with State 17 (*see Tour* 1*a*).

At 11 *m.* is a junction with State 295 (*see Tour* 4*a*).

REMINGTON, 13.1 *m.* (300 pop.), known during the War between the States as Rappahannock Station, is a rural center.

The PELHAM MEMORIAL (R), 16.2 *m.* is a marble shaft honoring Confederate Major John Pelham, 24-year-old chief of General J.E.B.Stuart's Horse Artillery, who was mortally wounded March 17, 1863, at Kelly's Ford, four miles southeast.

A granite marker at 17.3 *m.* commemorates the Battle of Brandy Station. On June 9, 1863, Stuart's cavalry, gathered near here for a review by the General Staff, was attacked by Union cavalry under General Alfred Pleasonton. For several hours the heaviest cavalry fighting of the war raged around this hill. About 10,000 troops were engaged on each side. Besides being the first cavalry battle, this was the first engagement that Union cavalry provoked. Having come over in dangerous force, they inflicted heavy damage and left in good order. Stuart, although forced back locally, kept his fighting forces together, held the field, and was able to screen the movement of Lee's divisions northward. The Federals lost 936, the Confederates 523.

BRANDY STATION, 18.4 *m.*, is a small trading center by a railway station.

CULPEPER, 24.9 *m.* (423 alt., 2,379 pop.), seat of Culpeper County, is the trade center of a well-to-do farming area. Rows of brick and frame buildings line a long Main Street, backing on tree-shaded residential areas.

A hill overlooking the western side of the town was the muster place in 1775 for the Culpeper Minute Men, volunteers from Culpeper, Orange, and Fauquier Counties. With a coiled rattlesnake and the legends, 'Don't tread on me' and 'Liberty or Death' on their flag, fringed deerskin trousers and hunting shirts, bucktails flying from their hats and scalping knives and tomahawks at their belts, they had a warlike appearance as they marched to Williamsburg to answer Governor Patrick Henry's call for volunteers in 1777. John Marshall, statesman and Chief Justice of the U.S.Supreme Court, was a youthful lieutenant in the Fauquier company of his father, Captain Thomas Marshall.

Confederates camped not far away in the winter of 1862–63, and officers stayed at the old Virginia Hotel. That polished army boots bound for social events might escape the quagmire, a boardwalk was built across Main Street. Wounded from the battles of Cedar Mountain, from Kelly's Ford, and from Brandy Station were brought to churches, homes, and vacant buildings here. Later, Union officers made headquarters at the Virginia Hotel, and soldiers were billeted in public buildings; General Grant and his staff stayed at the hotel during April 1864.

The COURTHOUSE, built about 1870, is a brick structure painted a vivid red, with ornate white portico and cupola. Culpeper County was created in 1748 from the great territory of Orange. Culpeper is at the southern junction with US 29 (*see Tour 4b*).

Left from Culpeper on State 3, an asphalt road, to Germanna Bridge over the Rapidan, 14.4 *m.*; L. 0.7 *m.* on a dirt road to the site of GERMANNA, where a crumbling stone chimney and half-buried foundations are reminders of Virginia's first industrial village. Here lived the miners brought from the German Palatinate by Governor Alexander Spotswood in 1714. When the governor's efforts to have iron deposits developed as a public enterprise failed, he lent a willing ear to the private schemes of adventurers, one of whom was the Swiss Baron von Graffenreid. But by the time the Germans arrived in the spring of 1714, von Graffenreid had returned to Switzerland, and the governor was beset by difficulties. Fearful of the hostile council's learning of his 'risque of Censure . . . for transporting Forreigners into these parts,' he proposed having them settled at this point as a barrier against Indian attacks. The council ordered a road cleared and two cannon dragged through 'the wild woods,' and set up on a 'stockade of stakes stuck in the ground . . . and of a substance to bear out a musket shot.' That summer the thrifty Germans had 'nine houses, built all in a row, and before every house, about twenty feet distant from it, . . . small sheds built for their hogs and hens, so that the hogsties and houses make a street.' In 1720 this frontier village became the seat of the newly-created Spotsylvania County. By 1722, when the governor retired, he had, through shrewd grants to subordinates to be held in trust for his own use, accumulated more than 85,000 acres of 'excellent Land among ye Little Mountains.' Here he lived in style suited to his lordly tastes. When the Germans moved farther north, slaves worked the iron enterprises, supervised by a 'master.' Here was his 'enchanted castle,' described by William Byrd II, with its terraced gardens, marble fountain, spacious drawing rooms 'elegantly set off with pier glasses' and where 'a brace of tame deer ran familiarly through the house.'

In 1732 the little county seat was abandoned for the growing town of Fredericksburg. Discouraged by a Parliament fearful that Colonial manufactures would interfere with British exports, the industrial activities dwindled after Spotswood's death in 1740.

At 19.4 *m.* on State 3 is junction with State 20 (*see Tour* 10).

Section c. CULPEPER to SPROUSE'S CORNER; 80.8 *m.* *US* 15

Orange is another center for sporting country life, but below Gordonsville the forest closes about the route; farms are to be seen only occasionally; and peaks of the distant mountains are frequently visible against the western horizon.

South of CULPEPER, 0 *m.*, is GREENWOOD (L), 1.3 *m.*, an attractive, rambling, story-and-a-half frame house with low wings, painted white. It stands far back from the highway among tall trees.

CEDAR MOUNTAIN, two miles away (L) at 5.1 *m.*, gave its name to the battle of August 9, 1862, between General T. J. Jackson and his old antagonist of the Valley, General Nathaniel P. Banks. Jackson, having left Richmond in advance of Lee's army, with the intention of watching Pope until Lee could join him, found Banks advancing with 9,000 men. Attacking Jackson's 23,000, Banks was defeated. Other Federal divisions arrived late in the evening and Jackson withdrew southward to await Lee (*see Tour* 10).

At 14.9 *m.* is a junction with County 622.

Left here to WOODBERRY FOREST, 1 *m.*, a boys' preparatory school, established in 1888. The school occupies a group of modern, white-pillared, red brick buildings at the head of a terraced slope above the Rapidan River. The campus was the Woodberry Forest plantation of General William Madison, brother of President James Madison. Madison's home, The Residence, is a one-story white frame structure built about 1783 among magnificent oaks.

At 17.9 *m.* on US 15 is a junction with County 633.

Left here to County 632, 0.4 *m.*; R. 0.2 *m.* to MONTEBELLO (L), a dignified mansion of dark red brick behind the great Tuscan columns of a white, two-story portico. The beauty of the old house, which overlooks rolling country, is enhanced by masses of boxwood, magnolia, and other evergreens, and by a formal garden.

In 1750 Benjamin Cave built the house that has had numerous additions and alterations.

ORANGE, 19.3 *m.* (524 alt., 1,381 pop.), seat of Orange County and trade center of a fertile agricultural area, lies on steep hillsides. Narrow, irregular Main Street, thickly-built near the courthouse green, rises at each end on hills where are attractive homes. On Saturday evenings, when the country 'comes to town,' there is barely room to breathe on Main Street.

The long-established farm trade and the business of the county have been increased by the establishment of a silk mill, a wood-flooring mill, and an assembly plant for metal office equipment.

The brick COURTHOUSE, built in 1858 and now painted gray, with deep overhanging eaves and a square central tower, is a Victorian departure from the red brick, white-columned type of courthouse traditional in rural Virginia. Orange County, created in 1734, was named for the Prince of Orange, who became England's William III. As originally constituted, the county boundaries were loosely defined and court was held in various places until 1748, when Orange was divided to create Culpeper County, and the courthouse, then 'absurdly near the very edge of the county,' was ordered moved to a more central site.

ST.THOMAS'S CHURCH, on a box-bordered lawn, has a recessed portico with white columns and is surmounted by a white cupola. It was built in 1833.

Orange is at a junction with State 20 (*see Tour* 10).

Left from Orange on County 615 to GREENFIELD (L), 0.8 *m.*, well back from the highway in a grove of trees. The house is of red brick with the usual white-columned portico, and has some good interior trim. It was erected about 1825.

The JAMES WADDELL MONUMENT (R), 27.4 *m.*, a granite block, is near the probable site of the 'ruinous old wooden house' in which Waddell, a blind Presbyterian evangelist, preached between 1785 and his death 20 years later. In 1803 Waddell was described as a tall, thin patriarch of supernatural appearance. His oratory could produce wailing and gnashing of teeth and had the power to quiet the storm it had created. William Wirt made Waddell's eloquence the subject of an incident in his book, *Letters of the British Spy*.

GORDONSVILLE, 28.4 *m.* (442 alt., 462 pop.) (*see Tour* 9), is at a junction with US 33, which coincides with US 15 for a few miles (*see Tour* 9); at 33.3 *m.* is the southern junction with US 33.

ZION CROSS ROADS, 40.9 *m.*, is at the junction with US 250 (*see Tour* 17*a*).

PALMYRA, 48.9 *m.* (145 pop.), is the seat of Fluvanna County. The COURTHOUSE (1838), an attractive small red brick building with four white Doric columns beneath a pediment, shares the village green with lawyers' tiny brick offices. The ancient two-story COUNTY JAIL, of field stone, faces the courthouse across a rambling lane; flat wrought-iron strips bar its heavy windows. Fluvanna County was created in 1777 from part of Albemarle County, and its name, Anne River, is a tribute to the popular queen.

DIXIE, 55.9 *m.*, is at a junction with State 6 (*see Tour* 23).

Near FORK UNION, 57.7 *m.* (200 pop.), is overrun during the school term with boys in uniform from FORK UNION MILITARY ACADEMY, a preparatory school founded in 1898. The brick and concrete buildings in pseudo-Gothic style are at the edge of town. 'The Academy is remote,' its catalogue avers, 'from the evil influence of the small towns and the dangers of the large city.'

At 61.6 *m.* is a junction with the private Bremo Plantation Road.

Right on this road through a large tract of field and woodland extending to the banks of the James. These acres were organized into a plantation about 1803 by General John Hartwell Cocke (1780–1866), who built the three large houses on the estate. Warm advocate of popular education, he helped Jefferson and Cabell found the University of Virginia and served as chairman of the building committee. Intemperate in youth, he became a teetotaler and was elected first president of the American Temperance Union, organized in 1836. He thoroughly denounced slavery as 'the great cause of all the great evils of our lands,' educated his own Negroes to useful trades, and then emancipated those who seemed fit for citizenship, sending them off to the Liberian colony.

BREMO RECESS (*open daily, adm.* 50¢), 0.2 *m.*, is a brick house (R) of moderate size almost hidden by trees. It is painted yellow and has tall lancet openings and cusped gables characteristic of the Jacobean style. Between house and road sprawl former stables, now falling into decay. Recess was the Cocke family home until the mansion nearer the river was completed.

LOWER BREMO (*private*), 1.9 *m.*, is (L) a cream-colored brick house with clustered chimneys and pseudo-Jacobean gables. It was built about 1843 by General Cocke for his son, Dr. Cary Cocke. A stone outbuilding near by was probably a 'hunting lodge' built soon after 1725 by Richard Cocke, who held the grant.

BREMO, 2.3 *m.* (*open* 9–5 *daily, April* 15 *to Nov.* 1*; adm.* $1*; to grounds only,* 50¢), is the main mansion, and one of Thomas Jefferson's most successful creations. The well-proportioned building with its massive Roman Doric portico in striking relief against rose-colored brick walls stands among great oaks and beeches behind a shallow ha-ha wall that sweeps in a semicircle between two pavilions. Crowning the one-story walls is a full entablature beneath an open roof balustrade. Small side porticoes face terraces beyond which are the pavilions. These dependencies, like the central block, have porticoes on the garden façade and a full basement story on the south and are connected by a passageway on the lower level. The garden façade is broken by a recess holding a veranda, with pilasters and two columns in antis above a basement arcade. The wide lawn drops away to fields where the outlines of a formal garden are traceable.

The classical interior is designed in Jeffersonian style. The entrance hall and two large chambers are cubical, with 20-foot ceilings and cornices four feet deep. Two bedrooms have bed alcoves. In the drawing room is a fine Adam mantel of Carrara marble. A pair of staircases in the lateral passageways are narrow, like those of Monticello. From the marble-floored dining room on the lower garden level, a revolving door carries shelves to simplify the change of courses.

Construction of Bremo was begun in 1815 and continued for four years. Here General Lee's family stayed during part of the War between the States.

Among the many outbuildings is the main barn, a palatial structure of stone on the plan of a Greek cross, with a portico forming one arm; at the intersection of the gable ridges is a belfry, in which still hangs a convent bell presented by La Fayette. Near the entrance gate stands a cast-iron TEA POT that formerly stood in a Doric temple at Temperance Spring close to the old canal. General Cocke erected the temple as an inspiration to canal boat travelers, who were reputed to have used its crystal waters to mix with stronger liquids.

On the north bank of the James River is BREMO BLUFF, 62.8 *m.* (82 pop.), a handful of houses and a railroad station near a hydroelectric plant.

At 65.9 *m.* is a junction with County 675.

Right here to ARVONIA, 0.8 *m.*, a village where huddled frame houses are overshadowed by huge piles of waste slate. Seven quarries are in operation by the state in this area.

Around DILLWYN, 78.3 *m.* (645 alt., 442 pop.), are acres of lumber-drying yards, piled high with railroad ties and pulpwood logs.

SPROUSE'S CORNER, 80.8 *m.*, is a cluster of dwellings, store, and filling station at a junction with US 60 (*see Tour 8b*).

Section d. SPROUSE'S CORNER to JUNCTION WITH US 360; 39.5 *m.* US 15.

This section of US 15 passes through long stretches of hilly woodland and open tobacco fields.

South of SPROUSE'S CORNER, 0 *m.*, at 4.6 *m.* is a junction with a dirt road.

Left on this road, which winds through woods to the top of WILLIS MOUNTAIN, 1 *m.* (1,200 alt.), a lone peak.

SHEPPARDS, 11.2 *m.*, is a store and a few houses at a crossroads. On the night of April 7, 1865, Lee's army passed here in retreat westward. While two corps of Grant's army closely pursued, two other corps forged west from Farmville to block Lee's advance toward Appomattox. Near Sheppards on the evening of April 7 Lee received Grant's note suggesting surrender.

Right from Sheppards on County 636 to NEW STORE, 4.6 *m.*, where Peter Francisco kept a tavern after the Revolution. Francisco's life history is richly embellished with legend. His origin was obscure, but historians believe he was kidnapped in Spain. Left near City Point in 1765, he was later adopted by Judge Anthony Winston. When the Revolution broke out, Francisco, then only about 16 years old but more than 6 feet tall and of great muscular strength, joined the Continental army. He distinguished himself by his courage in numerous battles. Stories of how he pulled a 1,100-pound cannon up a hill and of a special sword made to fit his great hands cling to his army record. His most notable feat was at West's Ordinary (*see Tour 20b*). His reputation grew as he disposed of all comers rash enough to dispute his prowess. In records of his life it is told that he once threw a man from the ground onto the roof of a house. A stranger, who announced to Francisco that he had come from Kentucky to decide which was the better man, was tossed over a fence. A moment later Francisco threw the intruder's horse after his master.

At 15.7 *m.* on US 15 is a junction with US 460.

Right here to APPOMATTOX, 24.2 *m.* (704 pop.), a scattered community typical of Virginia county seats established late in the nineteenth century. Frame and brick dwellings circle a main street closely packed with nondescript store fronts. The town is the local tobacco market and ships lumber.

Near the center in a fieldlike green is the COURTHOUSE, a one-story brick building on a high stone basement. Appomattox County was formed in 1845 but the courthouse was not erected here until 1892.

Right from Appomattox 0.4 *m.* on State 131 to State 24; R. here 2.4 *m.* to OLD APPOMATTOX COURTHOUSE, now consisting of a few modern residences, several dilapidated buildings, two monuments, and a small cemetery. Near the old courthouse is the SITE OF WILMER MCLEAN'S HOUSE, where the Confederate surrender took place.

On the evening of April 8, 1865, Lee's weary army encamped here—two corps, under Longstreet and Gordon, starved and ill-equipped, flanked by four times its number at the beginning of its retreat and surrounded by many times its number here, depleted by desertions, and convinced that further resistance was futile since two more Federal corps were in their rear.

At 8:30 on the morning of April 9, while sporadic fighting continued in front, General Lee accompanied only by his aide, Colonel Charles Marshall, rode to the rear to meet General Grant. Expecting the conference he had requested and intending to surrender, Lee received a letter from Grant, declining the interview. Lee replied with an offer to surrender. Grant, however, having changed his headquarters to a point some 15 miles away, did not receive Lee's offer until almost noon. Meanwhile, Lee was warned that a Federal attack had been ordered and that he must return to his own lines. General G.A.Custer, riding over the field demanding a surrender in the name of Sheridan, suffered rebukes from both Longstreet and Gordon; several hotheaded clashes threatened trucemaking efforts; and at a critical moment, General G.G.Meade, ill in an ambulance, was forced to assume the responsibility of declaring a truce. At about one o'clock Colonel Orville E. Babcock, of Grant's staff, arrived with word that Grant was hurrying to the field.

Soon the two generals met in McLean's parlor—Lee in a new uniform and dress trappings and Grant dusty, in fatigue dress, and without side arms. They had known each other slightly in years past. Once in Mexico years before, Lee had reprimanded Grant for his unkempt appearance. Now the tension was relieved by the casual conversation of old friends. It was General Lee who introduced a businesslike note into the conference by requesting General Grant to tell him the terms of surrender. After further conversation Grant wrote out the terms, and handed the paper to Lee. The officers and men were to be paroled and disqualified from taking up arms again until properly exchanged. Only public property was to be surrendered, and officers were to retain their side arms and horses. Lee was pleased. The cavalry and artillery horses, he said, were owned by the rank and file in the Confederate service, and would be of great help to the men when they got home. Grant gave orders to exempt these animals when they were claimed by their riders. Generously he ordered Sheridan to supply Lee's commissary with 25,000 rations. Then Grant apologized for the condition of his dress and lack of side arms, saying that he had been some distance from his headquarters and believed that Lee would rather receive him as he was than to be detained. After more conversation, the meeting ended. When firing of salutes and the playing of bands began in the Federal camps, Grant gave orders that all such demonstrations cease.

Another meeting took place, at Grant's request, the following day. Of this little is known except that Grant wished Lee to meet President Lincoln, in the belief that Lee's, Lincoln's, and his own influence would restore a condition of rest to the country. As the Confederate Government still existed, Lee declined the assumption of political prerogatives.

Grant set out for Washington on the evening of the 10th, and two days later Lee left for Richmond.

About 10,000 muskets were surrendered at Appomattox. About 28,000 men, including noncombatants, were paroled. The tragic, unnecessary war had come to an end; and another era, more tragic and equally unnecessary, was about to begin.

FARMVILLE, 19.9 *m.* (337 alt., 3,133 pop.), seat of Prince Edward County, is a progressive-looking town, with a long and busy Main Street, bulky tobacco warehouses, and red brick factories along the river. The town's retail trade is stimulated for several months of the year by the influx of students. Dark tobacco marketing and various small industries add to the local income.

On the afternoon of April 6, 1865, Lee's retreating army was attacked by Sheridan's cavalry and two corps of infantry at Sailor's Creek, 10 miles to the east. The Confederate rear was cut off, and 6,000 men and six generals were taken prisoners. The following morning the retreating army pushed westward.

PRINCE EDWARD COURTHOUSE, a small, brick structure built about 1873, stands back from the street, almost invisible among the business places. Prince Edward County was created in 1753 and named for Edward, Prince of Wales, younger brother of George III. The seat was moved from Worsham to Farmville in 1871.

The STATE TEACHERS' COLLEGE, in the center of the town, is housed in five modern three-story buildings of red brick with Ionic porticoes; they are connected by colonnaded passages. Before 1835 *Martin's Gazeteer* recorded '1 female school' here. By 1839 this school had become the Farmville Female Seminary, and in 1860 the Farmville Female College. The property passed to town authorities in 1884 and was turned over to the State for a 'female normal school.' The enrollment (1937–38) was 2,193.

In KINGSVILLE, 25.6 *m.*, now a few modern dwellings, was born in 1787 Dr. John Peter Mettauer, internationally known surgeon and teacher. He was the son of François Joseph Mettauer, a physician attached to French troops billeted in this neighborhood after the battle of Yorktown. After graduating at Hampden-Sydney College and attending medical school in Philadelphia, the younger Mettauer taught medicine in his home. With this group as the nucleus, he established in 1848 the first medical department at Randolph-Macon College.

Right from Kingsville on State 133 to State 134, 0.8 *m.;* L. here 0.2 *m.* to HAMPDEN-SYDNEY COLLEGE. Vine-clad buildings of mellowed brick are scattered over a 250-acre campus, much of it a natural woodland. Hampden-Sydney Academy was established here by Presbyterian elders in 1776 and incorporated as a college in 1783. It is the second oldest college in Virginia. In 1937–38 the college had an enrollment of 238.

WORSHAM, 26.7 *m.*, a cluster of small buildings, was formerly Prince Edward Courthouse. The old jail (R), its massive stone walls crumbling, was built in 1789; and the former County Clerk's Office (L), now a dwelling, dates from 1820.

At 39.5 *m.* is a junction with US 360 (*see Tour 20b*), which coincides with US 15 for 19.6 miles.

Section e. JUNCTION WITH US 360 to NORTH CAROLINA LINE; 43.6 *m.* *US* 15–360

Tobacco is seen increasingly as the route progresses south. As the money crop, tobacco leaves room for small attention to balancing crops of food and forage. At intervals are wide sections of pine and hardwoods.

South of the junction with US 360, 0 *m.*, is KEYSVILLE, 1.6 *m.* (589 pop.), largest town of Charlotte County and a tobacco market.

WYLLIESBURG, 17.1 *m.*, is a crossroads hamlet.

Right from Wylliesburg on County 607 to County 631, 1.8 *m.*; R. here to ROANOKE PLANTATION (R), 12.7 *m.*, home of John Randolph of Roanoke (*see Tour* 19), representative in Congress 1799–1813, 1815–17, 1819–25; senator 1825–27; member of the Virginia Constitutional Convention 1829–30; and minister to Russia 1830. Though brilliant and forceful, John Randolph was definitely unbalanced all his life. He suffered from insomnia, stomach disorders, rheumatism, and probably died from tuberculosis. Apparently not clearly demented until after 1818, he was for years dangerously near the border of insanity. In Congress he shone as a caustic orator, terrifying his opponents and, for hours on end, flinging shafts of bitter eloquence upon his fascinated audience.

After 1810, unmarried and more and more given to eccentricity, he lived here in solitude, building two small houses, one of logs. About this time he added 'of Roanoke' to his name to distinguish himself from a kinsman, who was known as 'Possum John.' Although he frequently lacked cash, at his death he owned 8,000 acres of land, 400 slaves, and a stud of blooded horses.

He died in Philadelphia May 24, 1833, while waiting to take a ship for England, and was buried at Roanoke with his face to the west in accordance with his request that he might keep an eye on Henry Clay. In 1879 his remains were removed to Richmond.

At 19.6 *m.* is BARNES JUNCTION, southern junction with US 360 (*see Tour 20b*).

PRESTWOULD (R), 34 *m.*, is a mansion on a wooded plateau overlooking the Staunton Valley. Built about 1765 of native limestone cut into smooth blocks by plantation slaves, the house has the stout, rugged appearance of a frontier home. Its thick walls, two stories above a basement, rise to a hip roof covered with heavy copper shingles and pierced along the ridge by 10-foot chimneys. Small porches are river front and land front. Great, high-ceilinged rooms with carved marble mantels and deep window seats open from a central hall holding a broad staircase.

Prestwould plantation was part of the 10-mile tract along the Roanoke River patented in 1730 by William Byrd II and called by him Blue Stone Castle. From his son, William Byrd III, the land passed as stakes in a three-day card game to Sir William Skipwith, grandson of Sir Gray Skipwith, who fled to Virginia during the Protectorate. Sir William's son, Sir Peyton Skipwith, built the house.

At 35.8 *m.* is a junction with US 58 (*see Tour 7b*), which coincides westward with US 15 to CLARKSVILLE, 36.7 *m.* (800 pop.) (*see Tour 7b*), at the western junction with US 58.

At 43.6 *m.* US 15 crosses the North Carolina Line, 17 miles north of Oxford (see *North Carolina Guide*).

Tour 4

(Washington,D.C.)—Fairfax—Warrenton—Culpeper—Charlottesville—Lovingston—Amherst—Lynchburg—Danville—(Greensboro,N.C.). US 29.

District of Columbia Line to North Carolina Line, 254.2 *m.*

Paved roadbed throughout—chiefly asphalt with long stretches of concrete.
Southern Ry. parallels route roughly throughout.
All types of accommodations.

West of the Virginia suburbs of Washington for about 50 miles US 29 follows an almost straight line through rolling farm country where the inhabitants are engaged principally in dairying, the breeding and training of horses, and in fox hunting. Then curving almost directly south, it wanders among Blue Ridge foothills—a country of fertile farms, apple orchards, and pastures for beef cattle. Plantation homes and villages, established here as settlement flowed westward from the Tidewater in the early part of the eighteenth century, have a seasoned flavor. The southern third of the route passes through tobacco country.

Section a. POTOMAC RIVER to WARRENTON; 42.5 *m. US* 29–*US* 211

Beyond a thickly populated suburban section US 29 traverses an extensive battlefield area.

US 29 crosses the District of Columbia Line at the south end of Key Bridge in ROSSLYN, 0 *m.* (1,500 pop.), a business and residential town.

At 0.4 *m.* is a junction with State 237.

Left on this road is AURORA HEIGHTS, 0.8 *m.*, one of the many residential communities along the south side of the Potomac. On North Uhle Street is ARLINGTON COURTHOUSE, a porticoed brick building on a green.

Arlington County, ceded to the Federal Government in 1789 as part of the District of Columbia and returned to Virginia in 1846, is small but densely populated. First called Alexandria for its biggest city, it in 1920 took the name of the Custis-Lee estate (*see Tour* 12).

CHERRYDALE, 1.9 *m.* (6,000 pop.), closely built up, with homes of Government workers, whose bungalows rise among a hodgepodge of business places.

Right from Cherrydale on a military road to a junction with State 9, 2.3 *m.*, by the remains of FORT ETHAN ALLEN (L), erected during the War between the States to guard the approaches to Chain Bridge.

Right on State 9, 0.8 *m.*, to the SITE OF THE CLAY-RANDOLPH DUEL (L), the outcome of John Randolph's tirade on the floor of the Senate against Henry Clay's acceptance of the post as Secretary of State under John Quincy Adams. The duel took place April 8, 1826. When the duelists appeared, the tall thin Randolph was dressed in a large flowing coat, the kind often used by duelists to throw off an opponent's aim. When Randolph's pistol was discharged prematurely, he was given another. At the command both men fired and missed. With fresh weapons they again faced each other. Clay fired and missed. Randolph, who had deliberately waited, raised his pistol in the air, fired, and advanced with hand outstretched. Clay met him halfway.

At 3.1 *m.* on US 29 is a junction with State 9.

Right on this road to the WASHINGTON GOLF AND COUNTRY CLUB (R), 0.8 *m.*, an 18-hole course.

FALLS CHURCH, 5.7 *m.* (364 alt., 3,800 pop.), is a pleasant suburban community with comfortable-looking homes and well-kept grounds.

The FALLS CHURCH is an austere, rectangular block with an unbroken hip roof. Surrounded by a large grassy yard, the walls in Flemish bond with blackened headers rise from a wide water table to a bold cornice with widely-spaced dentils. The windows of the upper tier have round arches of rubbed brick, those below, similar flat arches. Especially notable is the classical wood enframement of the door at the center of the long side, and the molded brick pilasters and pediment framing the door. This church, of Fairfax Parish, was erected in 1767–69 on the site of a structure built in 1734 by Colonel Richard Blackburn of Rippon Lodge, 'a builder of skill.' During the Revolution it was a military recruiting station. After the disestablishment of the Church of England, it was abandoned until 1830. During the War between the States it was used as a hospital and later a stable for cavalry horses. After the war, Congress appropriated $1,300 for its rehabilitation.

In Falls Church is a junction with State 7 (*see Tour* 13).

Left from Falls Church on County 649 to OSSIAN HALL (R), 6 *m.* This white frame house, flanked by boxwood and oak trees, was built on the Ravensworth estate before the Revolution as an overseer's house. After 1804 it was the home of Dr.David Stuart, who in 1783 married Eleanor Calvert, widow of John Parke Custis—Washington's stepson.

At 6.4 *m.* is a junction with County 620; R. here 0.3 *m.* to RAVENSWORTH (L), once an estate covering 35 square miles. A white stuccoed brick barn formally designed and one other building are all that remain of the old plantation buildings. The Ravensworth estate was acquired in 1695 by William Fitzhugh (1651–1701). In 1830, the estate passed to Mrs.Robert E. Lee. General Lee's mother died here, his wife came here after leaving Arlington in 1861, and W.H.F.Lee died here in 1891.

At 12 *m.* are junctions with US 50, with which US 29 unites for 2.9 *m.* (*see Tour* 12), and with State 237.

Left 2 *m.* on State 237 to State 236; R. here to FAIRFAX, 2.2. *m.* (640 pop.), seat of Fairfax County, a compact village.

The COURTHOUSE, a red brick rectangle with gabled roof, arcaded loggia, and a cupola, is within a stone-walled green. It was built in 1800 when the county seat was moved from Alexandria. The wills of George and Martha Washington are displayed in a wing added in 1929. Fairfax County was formed from Prince William in 1742 and named for Thomas, Lord Fairfax. On the court green is CAPTAIN JOHN Q. MARR MONUMENT, honoring a soldier thought to have been the first Confederate to die in battle.

The SITE OF FAIRFAX TAVERN is occupied by a bank building. On October 1, 1861, President Jefferson Davis with General Joseph E. Johnston, General P.G.T.Beauregard, and General Gustavus W. Smith conferred here and decided that the Confederates were in no condition to take advantage of the success of the First Battle of Manassas and begin an offensive against Washington.

The MOSBY–STOUGHTON HOUSE, now the Episcopal rectory, was the quarters of General Edwin H.Stoughton in 1863. March 8, in the dead of the night, the general was awakened by a spanking. Colonel John S. Mosby and 29 of his partisans had stolen through Federal lines, captured pickets and horses, and ended their episode by playing havoc with the commanding officer's dignity. The escapade ended with the officer's capture.

The ANTONIA FORD HOUSE, a remodeled brick building that dates from about 1800, was the home of a charming Confederate who entertained Federal officers to spy on them. Major Joseph C. Willard arrested her for supplying information to Mosby. He delivered the lady to a Federal prison, but later worked for her release and eventually married her.

The FAIRFAX FEDERAL ART GALLERY, sponsored by the Fairfax County Art Guild, was opened in the Fairfax Elementary School on December 12, 1938.

At 3.1 *m.* State 237–State 236 rejoins US 29 (*see below*).

On US 29, at 14.9 *m.*, are junctions with US 50 and State 236 (*see above*).

CENTERVILLE, 20.3 *m.* (24 alt., 100 pop.), was the center of war activities in 1861 and 1862. General Irvin McDowell concentrated his Union army here prior to and during the First Battle of Manassas, and here General Joseph E. Johnston and his Confederates spent the following winter.

Between Centerville and US 15–29, State 28–233–295 provides an alternate and shorter route, by-passing Warrenton (*see Tour Key Map*).

Left from Centerville on State 28 to MANASSAS, 7 *m.* (312 alt., 1,215 pop.), one long business street, several blocks of closely built houses and stores, and a wide outer fringe of well-spaced dwellings on landscaped lawns that lend a suburban atmosphere. The seat of Prince William since 1893, Manassas has grown from a railroad junction, which gave its name to two battles, into a trading center for a populous farming area.

The PRINCE WILLIAM COURTHOUSE, a red brick structure in a park, is surrounded by numerous monuments, cannon, and pyramids of shells. This courthouse, completed in 1893, was the fifth for the county. Prince William County, formed in 1730 from Stafford and King George, embraced all the backwoods of the Northern Neck proprietary.

1. Left from Manassas 0.5 *m.* on County 612 to County 614; L. here to County 615, 1.8 *m.*; L. again to a farm lane, 2 *m.*; L. here to SIGNAL HILL (L), 2.1 *m.*, on which was erected the signal tower used during the First Battle of Manassas. On the hill are the remains of earthworks and emplacements for 16 cannon.

2. Left from Manassas on State 234 to County 649, 2.4 *m.*; R. here 3 *m.* to BRENTSVILLE (75 pop.), seat of Prince William County from 1822 to 1893. The old brick courthouse is now a community center. Brentsville is at the apex of the Brent Town Tract, a grant of 30,000 acres made to George Brent, Richard Foote, Robert Bristow, and Nicholas Hayward in 1686 by James II, last Roman Catholic King of England (*see Tour 1a*). Brent Town was a sanctuary for people of all creeds, and a real-estate venture.

On State 234 at 3.6 *m.* is LAKE JACKSON (*fishing, cabins, picnicking facilities*), formed by a hydroelectric dam on Occoquan Run. The lake, though privately owned, has been stocked by the State with bass and trout. On the bluff overlooking the dam is a small but exact reproduction of Arlington Mansion.

3. Right from Manassas on State 234 to a shale road, 5.9 *m.*, leading to HENRY HILL (*see below*).

At 11.6 *m.* on State 28 is a junction with County 619.

1. Right here 1.9 *m.* to LINTON HALL MILITARY ACADEMY (R), a Roman Catholic school for boys, established in 1894 and housed in several large brick buildings on a 1,700-acre campus.

2. Left 0.8 *m.* on County 619 to BRISTOW (203 alt., 40 pop.), where Jackson cut Pope's communications on August 26, 1862.

At 13.2 *m.* from Centerville on State 28 is a junction with County 645; L. here 1.9 *m.* to County 653; L. again 1.7 *m.* to PARK GATE (L), a small frame house believed to have been built before 1750. The rear one-story wing is a later addition. The house was once the home of Thomas Lee, eldest son of Richard Henry Lee.

On County 645, at 4.8 *m.* from State 233, is a junction with County 607; here (R) is PILGRIM'S REST, a square, two-story frame house with gabled roof. Heavy beaded pine clapboards cover the house. The dining room is paneled in pine, and the other interior woodwork is simple. Pilgrim's Rest was built about 1750 by Richard Foote.

At 19.4 *m.* from Centerville on State 28 is CATLETT (200 pop.), a small railroad community where, on August 22, 1862, General J.E.B.Stuart raided General John Pope's headquarters, seizing Pope's personal effects and capturing a number of staff officers.

At 25.2 *m.* from Centerville on State 28 is a junction with County 649.

1. Right on County 649 to County 602, 0.4 *m.*; R. here to the SITE OF GERMANTOWN (R), 0.9 *m.*, settled in 1720 by the Siegenian contingent of the Germanna Colony (*see Tour 3b*). The ruins of several houses and a long neglected graveyard filled with undecipherable tombstones are all that remain.

At odds with Governor Spotswood and perhaps with the Alsatian Lutherans, who had joined them in 1717, the Germanna miners, all members of the Evangelical Reformed Church, decided to move elsewhere. In 1718 they received a warrant for 1,805 acres of land lying on both sides of Licking Run. Agreeing to share equally the purchase price of the tract, the group of 12 Siegenians divided the land into 12 parts of 150 acres each and two years later, with their wives and children, 'packed all their provisions on their heads' and trekked over the Iroquois Trail to their new home. Their first crops flourished; 'in a few years they had large stocks of tame and very large cattle.' Concentration on tobacco followed; the profitable leaves started on their way to the Falmouth market over the German Rolling Road, which the settlers had constructed.

The village of the ex-miners grew apace, its spiritual needs cared for by Henry Haeger (1644–1738), 'minister of the Germans in Virginia.' In the spring of 1748, Matthew G. Gottschalk, the Moravian minister who visited Germantown, wrote: 'It is like a village in Germany where the houses are far apart.' But already the settlers had begun to disperse. In 1746 part of the land was sold and by the time the Revolution arrived, Germantown as a settlement had ceased to exist.

2. Left from State 295 on County 649 to a lane, 0.6 *m.*; L. here through two gates and to a tall, conical stone marker, 1.2 *m.*, indicating the SITE OF THE MARSHALL HOUSE, birthplace of John Marshall (1755–1835), Chief Justice of the U.S.Supreme Court (1801–35). His father, Thomas Marshall, a surveyor who became in time one of Fauquier's leading citizens, acquired this land on Licking Run about 1754. The first of nine children, John Marshall, lived here in a pioneer environment until 1775, when his family moved west to Goose Creek.

At 29.4 *m.* from Centerville on State 28 is a junction with State 17 (*see Tour 1a*), and at 31.4 *m.* is a junction with US 15–US 29 (*see Tour 36*).

The NATIONAL BATTLEFIELD MUSEUM (*adm.* 50¢), 24.4 *m.*, a long, one-story white painted brick building (R), has a collection of war relics, including bullets, shells, uniforms, arms, and various bits of equipment.

At the STONE BRIDGE (R), 24.5 *m.*, the First Battle of Manassas began on July 21, 1861. Along the stream here—Bull Run—and the hills to the west, the first major battle of the War between the States was fought.

Commanded by Generals Joseph E. Johnston and P.G.T.Beauregard, the Confederate army was south of the bridge when General Irvin McDowell attacked here with one division and sent two other divisions three miles north to sweep down Bull Run in a flank attack. A Confederate observer six miles south signalled by wigwag and the Confederates were able to hold McDowell on Matthews Hill until late in the morning, when they fell back to the turnpike. There, reinforced, they held McDowell for two hours until forced to withdraw to Henry Hill. It was here that General Barnard E. Bee exclaimed, 'There stands Jackson like a stone wall.' The Confederates rallied, held their position while reinforcements were hurried forward, and two hours later drove the Federals from the hill. Again on the turnpike, McDowell's lines were broken and, in his own words, 'The retreat soon became a rout, and this degenerated into a panic.'

The STONE HOUSE (R), 25.5 *m.*, a well-preserved two-story building of brown sandstone, served as a hospital for both Union and Confederate soldiers. It was used by John Esten Cooke for a ghostly episode in his novel, *Surry of Eagle's Nest.*

1. Right from the Stone House on State 234 to MATTHEWS HILL (R), 1 *m.*, where a small force from the Stone Bridge was posted to delay McDowell's flank movement.

2. Left from the Stone House on State 234 to a shale road, 0.3 *m.*; L. here 0.4 *m.* to HENRY HILL, on which there are numerous markers that indicate battle maneuvers. The possession of Henry Hill gave victory to the Confederate army in the First Battle of Manassas and largely determined the fate of a retreating Federal army August 30, 1862, in the Second Battle of Manassas.

The fighting of August 30, 1862, is sometimes designated the Second Battle of Manassas, but the designation is more generally applied to the fighting from August 28 to 30, 1862.

The rebuilt HENRY HOUSE (*adm. free*), a small two-story frame building here on the hill, is now a museum, containing many battlefield relics. Badly damaged during both battles, the house was later demolished. Mrs.Henry, an 85-year-old invalid and widow of Dr.Isaac Henry, was killed by a shell during the first battle.

On State 234 is MANASSAS, 6.2 *m.* (*see above*).

At 26.8 *m.* is the GROVETON CONFEDERATE CEMETERY (R), with monuments to regiments that fought in this vicinity. Near by are other war memorials.

The DOGAN HOUSE (R), 27 *m.*, a small barnlike frame structure, was in the center of fighting during the Second Battle of Manassas, August 29–30, 1862. This battle brought to a close a series of events that gave victory to a co-ordinated Confederate army and defeat to a confused and misdirected Federal army.

General John Pope, confused by Confederate tactics to relieve Richmond, scattered his army and exhausted his cavalry. He ordered it successively to Warrenton, Gainesville, Manassas, and Centerville, and finally concentrated it at Groveton. Orders were delayed and lost. He refused for days to believe that Jackson was in his rear or to acknowledge the presence of Lee and Longstreet, despite Porter's protest, until he was finally defeated and routed, with Longstreet in pursuit. He ordered a pursuit of Jackson while Jackson lay in wait for him to attack. He lost his communications at Bristow, a vast store of supplies at Manassas, and his personal papers at Catlett's Station. And, as a climax, he centered blame on Fitz-John Porter. With an initial force equal to Lee's—about 50,000 men—he was thwarted in his attempts to derive material aid from McClellan's 100,000 men, who were hurried to him by way of the Potomac River. General George H. Gordon, under Pope, stated that the army fought gloriously, but that 'Whipped in detail should be Pope's epitaph.'

During the two days of battle Jackson's corps, in an abandoned railroad cut to the north, withstood repeated Federal assaults by Pope, now commanding 75,000 men, while Longstreet, to the south, was ignored until his artillery, with an enfilading fire, broke the final charge. Routed and pursued by Longstreet, the defeated troops streamed down the same road followed one year before by McDowell's defeated army.

In GAINESVILLE, 30.4 *m.* (357 alt., 100 pop.), on August 28, 1862, a battle was brought on by Jackson to prevent the Federal army from concentrating east of Bull Run.

In Gainesville is a junction with State 55 (*see Tour 4A*).

BUCKLAND, 34.1 *m.* (50 pop.), founded in 1798, manages to preserve a bustling air, though it has now only a small mill. To the MOSS HOUSE, a small century-old building, Mrs.Moss, wife of the clerk of Fairfax County, brought the county records, including the volume that contained George Washington's will, during the War between the States.

'Buckland Races' is the common name of an engagement of October 19, 1863, between the cavalry forces of General J.E.B.Stuart and General H.J.Kilpatrick. The Federals abandoned all equipment and fled to their lines at Gainesville.

At NEW BALTIMORE, 36.8 *m.* (100 pop.), is the BROAD RUN BAPTIST CHURCH (L), a frame building erected in 1870. Prior to 1782 this congregation, organized in 1762, included in its membership Nancy Hanks and Luke Hanks, believed to have been the parents of Lincoln's mother, Nancy Hanks.

At 40.2 *m.* is a junction with County 605, once a section of the Dumfries-Winchester Road. Over this road George Washington, in 1748, accompanied George William Fairfax, to begin surveys of Fairfax lands.

Left here to County 670, 5 *m.*; R. 1.1 *m.* to AUBURN (26 pop.), at a junction with County 602, the old Caroline Road. AUBURN MILL, a stone mill on Cedar Run, is said to date from 1712, though a partly obliterated date on a stone in the wall may be 1742. Auburn was the home of the McCormick family, of harvester fame.

At 41.3 *m.* US 29 forks to a by-pass around Warrenton.

WARRENTON, 42.5 *m.* (635 alt., 1,450 pop.) (*see Tour 22*), is at junctions with US 211 (*see Tour 22*) and with US 15 (*see Tour 3a*), with which US 29 coincides for 24.9 miles (*see Tour 3b*).

Section b. CULPEPER to CHARLOTTESVILLE; 44.8 *m.* *US* 29

South of Culpeper the highway traverses the middle Piedmont, through apple orchards, farms, and fields of dark tobacco.

CULPEPER, 0 *m.* (423 alt., 2,379 pop.) (*see Tour 3b*), is at the southern junction with US 15 (*see Tour 3b*).

BRIGHTWOOD, 12.3 *m.* (55 pop.), specializes in the manufacture of hickory-rod shipping containers for chickens. A local manufacturer of grain cradles originated this type of coop in 1885, but failed to patent his device.

At 16.6 *m.* is a junction with State 16.

Right on this road to a junction with County 603, 1 *m.*; R. here 1 *m.* to HEBRON CHURCH (L), a frame T-shaped building with gabled roofs and simple ornamentation. The main part was built in 1740 by the Lutheran congregation; the transept was added in 1802. The communion silver service bears the dates 1727 and 1729. The pipe organ, encased in soft and hard wood, was made at Lititz, Pennsylvania, in 1802. The church was founded by Germans, who migrated from Germanna (*see Tour 3b*) and settled in this community in 1724.

At 5 *m.* on State 16 is a junction with State 231; L. here 2 *m.* to County 649, and L. to the HOOVER CAMP, 9.6 *m.* This vacation retreat of President Herbert Hoover is now in Shenandoah National Park.

MADISON, 17.1 *m.* (430 pop.), the seat and principal commercial center of Madison County, is strung out along one street. The community was established when a log courthouse was built here in 1793, the year in which William Wirt (1772–1834) began his practice of law here. He became attorney general under Monroe and John Quincy Adams and a prosecutor of Aaron Burr (1807). Wirt was the author of several books, of which *The Letters of the British Spy* (1803) is the best known.

The COURTHOUSE, of red brick, has an arcaded front, and an octagonal cupola above the gabled roof. Built in 1829, this courthouse shows architectural forms much used in the previous century. Thinly settled Madison County, formed in 1792, was taken from Culpeper and named for James Madison.

Three Madison buildings bear the mark of some enterprising workmen, who added novelty to the conventional brick work of a century ago. Laying alternate courses of brick slightly off center, the experimenter changed the usual Flemish bond pattern. These buildings are the OLD MASONIC HALL AND CAVE HOME, erected in 1834 as the Washington Hotel; the HARRISON HOME, built about 1823; and the PIEDMONT EPISCOPAL CHURCH, built in 1834.

Left from Madison on State 230 to the MADISON COUNTY HOMESTEADS (L), 1 *m.*, a Resettlement Administration Project. The 16 frame farm houses built on 15- to 40-acre tracts by the Federal Government are in sharp contrast to the dwellings from which their occupants have been removed. These mountain folk from the Shenandoah National Park area have left log-bodied, mud-daubed cabins in remote coves for attractive four- to six-room houses, well-built and wired for electricity.

RUCKERSVILLE, 29 *m.* (108 pop.) (*see Tour 9*), is at the junction with US 33 (*see Tour 9*).

At 39.6 *m.* is a junction with County 643.

Left here to BENTIVAR (R), 1.9 *m.*, a square brick house, one story above an English basement. Bentivar was erected about 1795 by Garland Carr. Double floors enclose a layer of sand as a means of fire prevention.

On the lowlands below the house was the Indian village Monasukapanough, which, though never visited by white men, was indicated on early maps. Here was the Indian burial mound that Thomas Jefferson investigated and described in his *Notes on Virginia.*

CARRSBROOK (L), 40.4 *m.*, is a two-story house with one-story wings; it was built about 1794 by Peter Carr, whose father, Dabney Carr, had married Thomas Jefferson's sister, Martha. In 1773 Dabney Carr introduced the resolution to put into effect Richard Henry Lee's idea for establishing the Committee of Correspondence that co-ordinated Colonial resistance. After his death, his son Peter became the ward of Thomas Jefferson, served as Jefferson's secretary, and was prominent in the founding of the University of Virginia.

At 43.8 *m.* is a junction with County 654.

Right on this road to County 601, 2.4 *m.*; R. here to a junction with County 658, 4.1 *m.*; R. here to THE BARRACKS (R), 5.4 *m.*, a large square brick house with double end chimneys, built in 1819 on the site of the prison camp to which British and Hessian prisoners were brought following the Battle of Saratoga. Colonel John Harvie, a member of the Continental Congress, was able to have the prison camp established on his lands. The prisoners arrived in midwinter of 1779. Many complaints were made of the hardships to which they were subjected. Before the camp was abolished in October 1780, many prisoners had escaped to the mountains—400 at one time—where they remained and intermarried with the inhabitants.

CHARLOTTESVILLE, 44.8 *m.* (480 alt., 15,245 pop.) (*see Charlottesville*).

In Charlottesville are junctions with US 250 (*see Tour 17a*), State 239 (*see Tour 23*), and County 613 (*see Tour 10*).

Section c. CHARLOTTESVILLE to NORTH CAROLINA LINE; 142 *m. US* 29

South of Charlottesville, the highway passes through the foothills just east of the Blue Ridge, and then descends to the flattened south Piedmont. Apple and peach orchards along the route mingle with farms and vineyards, then give way to lands producing bright leaf tobacco.

South of the junction with US 250 in CHARLOTTESVILLE, 0 *m.*, is a junction with Frye's Spring Road, 1.1 *m.*

Left here to County 1014, 0.4 *m.*; R. to County 631, 1.6 *m.* and R. again to BALLY-LES-BRADEN (R), 2.5 *m.*, a three-story brick house with a lower rear wing. As Tudor Grove, this was the childhood home of Colonel John S. Mosby, the Confederate partisan leader. His force, with which he harassed large bodies of troops, did not average more than 200 men.

At 11.7 *m.* on US 29 is a junction with County 712.

Left here to EDGEMONT (R), 6 *m.* (*see Tour 23*).

At 21.1 *m.* on US 29 is a junction with State 6.

Left here to State 6-Y, 6 *m.*; R. here 2 *m.* to SCHUYLER (700 pop.), where quarrying and processing of soapstone is the chief occupation. The stratum of soapstone extends about 30 miles. Soapstone is highly refractory, a good insulator, impervious to water, and unaffected by acids and alkalis.

LOVINGSTON, 32 *m.* (330 pop.), seat of Nelson County, is a one-street community in the center of a large apple-raising area.

The brick COURTHOUSE with arcaded front entrance, cupola, and a gabled roof, was erected in 1809.

At 32.5 *m.* is a junction with State 56.

Left here to County 626, 11.8 *m.*; L. here 2.9 *m.* to County 604.

1. Right on County 604 to WARMINSTER (36 pop.), 0.2 *m.*, where in the middle of the eighteenth century Dr. William Cabell, first of the Virginia Cabells, established a terminal for batteaux carrying inland produce down the river.

2. Left on County 604 to EDGEWOOD, 0.1 *m.*, once the home of Joseph Carrington Cabell (1776–1856). The frame house, enlarged soon after Cabell bought it from Robert Rives in 1807, has an unusual charm rather than architectural distinction. Facing a neat grove of trees, the oldest part—altered considerably—is the bar of a double H. It opens onto small verandas at front and back and is linked to side wings by one-story passages. 'Jeffersonian' staircases are tucked out of view in the wings. Near by rises the top of an old circular icehouse of brick with a conical roof. A member of the Board of Visitors of the University of Virginia from the beginning in 1819, Cabell was twice rector, the second time from 1845 until his death in 1856.

On State 56 is WINGINA, 13.9 *m.*, a railroad station and store at a bridge across the James River.

Right from Wingina 0.4 *m.* on County 647 to SOLDIER'S JOY, constructed by Colonel Samuel J. Cabell shortly after the Revolution. The house was more than 140 feet in length but is now reduced to half its original size. Colonel Cabell (1756–1818) was congressman from 1795 to 1803.

On County 647 is UNION HILL (R), 1.9 *m.*, a large square frame house built in 1775 by Colonel William Cabell as the seat of a 25,000-acre estate. Here the Hanover Presbytery met November 1774 and prepared a petition to the house of burgesses asking that the 1772 Act of Toleration be amended to allow dissenters 'free exercise of our religion, without molestation or danger of incurring any penalty whatever.' June 5, 1781, the Virginia assembly and Governor Thomas Jefferson, in flight from British raiders under Tarleton, stopped here.

At 41.1 *m.* on US 29 is a junction with County 674.

Left here to County 665, 1.4 *m.*; L. to ROSE MILL (R), 1.5 *m.*, a stone and timber structure that was designated as a landmark at the division of Amherst Parish, 1778. It was owned by descendants of the Reverend Mr. Robert Rose, who came to Virginia about 1725 and took up great tracts of land.

At 42.1 *m.* on US 29 is a junction with State 151.

Right here to State 56, 2.6 *m.*; L. here 2 *m.* to MASSIES MILL (200 pop.), a shopping center.

Left from Massies Mill 1.7 *m.* on County 666 to County 679; R. to LEVEL GREEN (L), 1.8 *m.*, erected in 1801 by Major Thomas Massie, who delivered Washington's oral orders to his second in command, General Charles Lee, for the attack on General Clinton with full force at Monmouth Courthouse, New Jersey.

On State 56 at 4.3 *m.* is a junction with County 680; L. here 1.6 *m.* to PHARSALIA (R), on a hill among a heavy growth of foliage. The weatherboarded house has a small pedimented portico and a large addition that forms the stem of a T. Pharsalia, built in 1814, was Major Massie's wedding gift to his son, William.

State 56 continues to TYRO MILL (L), 5.1 *m.*, a log structure, now metal-covered, built by William Massie in 1820. Many parts of the old wooden machinery are still used.

Straight ahead from the mill on County 655 to CRABTREE FALLS, 12 *m.*, where the South Fork of the Tye River tumbles 2,000 feet in a series of cascades.

The VIRGINIA CHEMICAL COMPANY PLANT and the SOUTHERN MINERAL PRODUCTS CORPORATION PLANT, both at 43.6 *m.*, extract ilmenite and apatite from nelsonite, rock having a high content of titanium-phosphorus.

CLIFFORD, 48.7 *m.* (105 pop.), incorporated as Cabellsburg in 1785 and later known as New Glasgow, was for a short time the seat of Amherst County.

ST.MARK'S EPISCOPAL CHURCH, a simple rectangular brick building, was built about 1808.

The GRAVE OF SARAH WINSTON HENRY, mother of Patrick Henry, is on the grounds of WINTON, a large, white, well-preserved building on landscaped grounds. Mrs.Henry died here in 1784 at the home of her son-in-law, Colonel Samuel Meredith. So great was Colonel Meredith's esteem for his mother-in-law that he asked to be buried at her feet.

Left from Clifford on County 610 to TUSCULUM (R), 1.1 *m.*, a frame house erected in 1735 by David Crawford. Tusculum was the birthplace of William Harris Crawford (1772–1834), senator from Georgia, Secretary of the Treasury, Secretary of War, minister to France, and presidential candidate in 1824 on the Republican ticket.

AMHERST, 53.8 *m.* (628 alt., 576 pop.), seat of Amherst County, is surrounded by farms where life is placid and leisurely.

The COURTHOUSE, of stone and brick, was built in 1871. Amherst County, formed in 1761 from Albemarle's vast territory, was named for Sir Jeffrey Amherst, who was acclaimed in England as 'Conqueror of Canada.' Although named Governor of Virginia, he never came to the colony.

CENTRAL HOTEL, a long low building, was a pre-Revolutionary stagecoach tavern.

In Amherst is a junction with US 60 (*see Tour 8b*).

SWEET BRIAR COLLEGE (R), 56.2 *m.*, is housed in some 30 buildings on a large tract of meadow, orchard, and woodland. Lawns and gardens surround a central group of larger buildings, which are of red brick, white-trimmed adaptations of the Colonial Georgian styles.

SWEET BRIAR HOUSE, now the president's home, is an old yellow-painted structure with Victorian additions. It is surrounded and partly hidden by nearly 400 immense boxwood trees. The old part of the house, with 600 acres of land, was bought by Elijah Fletcher, a Vermont scholar who came to Virginia in 1810, married Marie Antoinette Crawford of Tusculum, and made a fortune from tobacco and real estate. In 1841 he made this house his home. Mrs.Fletcher named the estate 'Sweet Briar' because of the profusion of wild roses. The eldest Fletcher child, Indiana, inherited the land in 1858, and married James Henry Williams of New York City. Their only child, Maria, called Daisy, died at the age of 16. As a memorial to her, Mrs.Williams in 1900 left her entire estate for the founding of an institution 'to impart to students such an education in sound learning, and such physical, moral, and religious training as shall in the judgment of the Directors best fit them to be useful members of society.'

The college, opened in 1906, has an enrollment of about 450 young women.

MONROE, 61.6 *m.* (1,135 alt., 1,000 pop.), a division terminal of the Southern Railway, has a cluster of small houses on the hillside that slopes sharply down to the roundhouse from which locomotives, being prepared for service, belch forth an almost continuous column of heavy black smoke. Here, 'Pete' on a fateful day in 1903 got his orders to take 'Old 97' into Spencer, North Carolina on time. The tragedy that ensued inspired the ballad and song, 'The Wreck of the Old 97.' The hero of the song 'was found in the wreck . . . scalded to death by the steam.'

MADISON HEIGHTS, 66.9 *m.* (4,000 pop.), laid out in 1791, clings to a hill sloping to the James River. In 1757 young John Lynch, founder of Lynchburg (*see Lynchburg*), built a tobacco warehouse on these heights.

Left here on State 130 to the STATE COLONY FOR EPILEPTICS AND FEEBLEMINDED (R), 1.1 *m.*, with a group of 13 buildings. Opened in 1911, the colony cares for about 1,200 patients.

LYNCHBURG, 68.3 *m.* (721 alt., 40,661 pop.) (*see Lynchburg*).

In Lynchburg is a junction with US 501 (*see Tour 11a*).

At 72 *m.* is a junction with State 128.

Right on this road to County 676, 0.4 *m.*; R. here 0.1 *m.* to SANDUSKY (R), a two-story L-shaped brick house surrounded by magnolias, boxwood, and other shrubbery. Charles Johnston, who had been captured by Indians as a boy, built the house in 1797 and named it for an Indian village that figured in his boyhood experiences. In 1794, he told the story to the Duc de la Rochefoucauld-Liancourt, who incorporated it in *Travels through the United States*. Incensed because of errors in the retelling of the story, Johnston published his own version in 1827.

Among the soldiers quartered here in 1864 were three who became Presidents—James A. Garfield, Rutherford B. Hayes, and William McKinley.

On State 128 is the QUAKER MEMORIAL PRESBYTERIAN CHURCH (L), 0.5 *m.*, a small ivy-covered, steep-gabled stone building formerly the South River Quaker Meeting House, built between 1792 and 1798 and restored in 1901. The first meeting house on this site was built of logs in 1757 by a group organized by Mrs.Sarah Clark Lynch, mother of Colonel Charles Lynch and of John Lynch, the founder of Lynchburg. The meeting flourished until the nineteenth century, when many of the Friends yielded to pressure and, joining in the wars of the period, were 'turned out of meeting.'

The sentiments of Sarah Lynch-Terrell, a leader in the antislavery movement, forcibly set down just before her death in 1773, were read at meetings as 'the Last Sayings of Sarah Terrell,' and led to the passing of strong abolition resolutions.

It was from Quakers of the old South River Meeting that Mark Twain, Francis Scott Key, and Jefferson Davis were descended. Near by is the grave of John Lynch.

At 1.4 *m.* on State 128 is a junction with County 624, part of the old turnpike between Lynchburg and Salem.

Left on County 624, 6.7 *m.* to NEW LONDON (50 pop.), which in 1754 was made the first permanent seat of the vast frontier county of Bedford and later, as Bedford Alum Springs, became a popular spring resort and social center.

It was in court here that Patrick Henry pled the 'Beef Case.' His client, John Venable, a commissary for the American forces in the Revolution, was being sued by John Hook, a New London merchant, for two steers seized to feed the soldiers. He painted a word picture of hungry soldiers and carried his audience into patriotic frenzy with his description of the American triumph at Yorktown. At the climax of his speech he turned on Hook, 'But hark! What notes of discord are these which disturb the general joy, and silence the acclamations of victory? They are notes of John Hook, hoarsely bawling through the American camp, Beef! Beef! Beef!'

Right from New London on County 623, 0.9 *m.* to FEDERAL HILL (L), a frame house with a two-story central section and one-story wings that was the home of James Steptoe, for 54 years clerk of Bedford County Court. This house was built in 1805 and replaced another burned that year. The CLERK'S OFFICE is on the lawn. Born in 1750, James Steptoe was educated at the College of William and Mary and there began his lifelong friendship with Thomas Jefferson.

AVOCA (R), 93.3 *m.*, a modern frame house, is on the site of the home of Charles Lynch, for whom one tradition says the Lynch Law was named. The harsh measures that Lynch used to check the activities of Tories and criminals during the Revolution were condoned in 1782 by the Virginia legislature. Charles Lynch (1736–96) was a brother of John Lynch, founder of Lynchburg.

ALTA VISTA, 95.2 *m.* (2,367 pop.), is a thriving industrial town on a hill overlooking the Staunton River. A crowded business section spreads for several blocks. The town has a rayon plant and a large cedar chest factory.

In HURT, 96.5 *m.* (500 pop.), live workers from the Alta Vista industrial plants.

Right from Hurt on County 668 to CLEMENT HILL (R), 0.2 *m.*, the home of Captain Benjamin Clement (1700–80), who with Colonel Lynch made gunpowder here during the Revolution. Colonel Lynch advertised in *The Virginia Gazette* for saltpetre and explained how this important gunpowder ingredient could be extracted from the dirt floors of smokehouses on which it had dripped from meat.

CHATHAM, 117.8 *m.* (828 alt., 1,143 pop.), seat of Pittsylvania County since 1777, is a quiet town enlivened by students.

When a permanent courthouse was to be built, a long dispute over where it should be rent the community. When in 1807 the legislature settled the matter, the town was designated Competition and so remained until 1874, when it was renamed in honor of William Pitt, Earl of Chatham, for whom the county had been named in 1767. Henry St.George Tucker, clerk of the House of Delegates, wrote on the blotter:

Immortal Pitt! How great thy fame,
When Competition yields to Chatham's name!

The COURTHOUSE, a nondescript red brick building, was erected in 1885 after an earlier building was destroyed by fire. This county was formed from Halifax in 1767.

CHATHAM HALL, an Episcopal school for girls, stands amid gardens, athletic fields, and woodland. Founded in 1894 by the Reverend Mr.C.Orlando Pruden, who was president of its board of trustees for 30 years, the school has about 150 students.

The HARGRAVE MILITARY ACADEMY, a boys' preparatory school, was opened as the Chatham Training School in 1909. It has a cadet corps of more than 200.

1. Left from Chatham on County 685 to ELDON (L), 1.1 *m.*, an early eighteenth-century frame house with a columned portico. This was the home of Claude A. Swanson (1862–1939), who after practicing law in Chatham served successively as congressman, governor, senator, and Secretary of the Navy.

2. Left from Chatham on State 57 to County 702, 8.5 *m.*; L. here 4.3 *m.* to County 665; L. to Banister River, 6.7 *m.*; just beyond in a field to the SITE OF MARKHAM (L), 7.1 *m.*, home of Colonel John Donelson. Here was born in 1767 Rachel Donelson, who became the wife of Andrew Jackson. When Rachel, the youngest of 11 children, was 17, the Donelsons moved to the Tennessee-Kentucky frontier. A belle of the border, Rachel in 1785 married Lewis Robards. Misapprehension as to the legal technicalities of Robards' suit for divorce led to her marriage to Jackson two years before the decree was granted and provided the scandal that pursued the Jacksons' public and private life to the end of their days.

Over a period of 35 years John Donelson (1725–85) served as county militia officer, surveyor, justice, vestryman, burgess, and emissary to Indian tribes along the border. In 1779 he disposed of his Virginia holdings and led 120 women and children and 40 men into Tennessee.

BEAVER'S TAVERN (L), 128.2 *m.*, once a famous stopping place, has been remodeled into a modern dwelling. During the early 1800's the land near by was used as a muster ground for the militia of the county. The troopers, with sticks and cornstalks, were paraded over the field by officers, mounted and in full regalia, many of whom had as little military knowledge as the men whom they were trying to drill. One officer carried a digest of his manual in his plumed hat and was put to it to find some pretext for scanning it at convenient moments.

At 134.8 *m.* is a junction with US 360 (*see Tour 20b*), which coincides with US 29 to DANVILLE, 136.1 *m.* (408 alt., 22,247 pop.) (*see Tour 20b*).

At 142 *m.* US 29 crosses the North Carolina Line, 43 miles north of Greensboro, N.C. (*see North Carolina Guide*).

Tour 4A

Gainesville—Haymarket—The Plains—Marshall—Front Royal; 39.4 *m.* State 55 (also Skyline Drive).

Asphalt roadbed throughout.
Southern Ry. parallels route.
Accommodations include tourist camps, tourist homes, and hotels in Front Royal.

State 55 links US 29 with the northern entrance of the Skyline Drive. It crosses the small Bull Run Mountains, travels along a rolling plateau, climbs the Blue Ridge Mountains, and drops into the Shenandoah Valley, following Colonial roads that later were parts of the Manassas Gap Turnpike, constructed in 1811, and the Thorofare Gap Turnpike, opened in 1812. The raising of hunting horses and beef cattle, dairying, apple culture, and general farming are the profitable pursuits of the landowners.

State 55 branches west from US 29–211 (*see Tour 4a*) in GAINESVILLE, 0 *m.* (357 alt., 100 pop.) (*see Tour 4a*).

HAYMARKET, 2 *m.* (337 alt., 167 pop.), a score of neat houses and several general stores, was called in Colonial days Red House, for a tavern here. Federal troops burned all the buildings of the village except a church and two houses.

St. Paul's Church, a rectangular brick building with a sheet metal and wood addition and a belfry, was erected in 1799 as a county district courthouse. In 1807 it became a school; in 1830 it was remodeled and made a church; during the War between the States it served as hospital, barracks, and stable; after 1867 it became a church again.

Right from Haymarket on County 625 to Waverly (L), 2.1 *m.*, a large gabled roof house of brick built about 1840 by Frederick Foote. The carved interior trim is well preserved.

Chapman's Mill (R), 6.5 *m.*, a six-story stone building erected in 1742 by one Jonathan Chapman, is still in use.

THOROUGHFARE GAP, 6.8 *m.* (399 alt.), in the Bull Run Mountains, was a gateway to the west. Through this opening in August 1862 the troops of 'Stonewall' Jackson came in their march around General John Pope's army in the Second Battle of Manassas (*see Tour 4a*).

THE PLAINS, 11.5 *m.* (414 pop.) (*see Tour 3a*), is at a junction with US 15 (*see Tour 3a*).

MARSHALL, 16.3 *m.* (630 alt., 550 pop.), stretching along the highway for nearly a mile, is an important shopping center. On Saturdays the highway here is lined with automobiles. Sunday mornings even larger crowds assemble when services are held at the four churches. Marshall has a grain elevator, a stock sales ring, a cannery, fair grounds, and a polo field. The town was established in 1796 as Salem.

The railroad through Marshall, chartered as the Manassas Gap Railroad in 1850, was organized by local farmers to carry produce east. Federals controlled the line after 1863, but its tracks were repeatedly torn up by the Confederates.

Colonel Henry Dixon was the only man in Fauquier County who voted for Abraham Lincoln in 1860. He carried, it is said, a pistol in one hand and ballot in the other. After the war, sadly enough, Colonel Dixon was killed in a gun fight in the streets of Alexandria.

At 16.7 *m.* is a junction with County 721.

Left here to County 719, 0.5 *m.*; L. to Valley Mills, 1.8 *m.*, a stone gristmill erected about 1770 and still used. Huge hand-hewn oak beams, studding, and joists, fastened with wood pins, are well preserved. The top floor has been reconstructed, and the wooden wheel has been replaced. The mill is on the northeastern edge of the vast country once part of the great Fairfax proprietorship (*see Tour 5A*) and known as the Free State. Litigation over these acres culminated in the U.S. Supreme Court decision handed down in the case of Hunter *v.* Fairfax's devisees, that the U.S. Supreme Court had the right to set aside decisions of the state supreme courts.

Oak Hill (R), 20.1 *m.*, is a little house of brick stuccoed creamy white. A flat-roofed portico with six Doric columns extends across the lower half of the two story façade. This house was built in 1818 by John Marshall (*see Tour 1a, and Richmond*). Near by stands the small brick house erected by Thomas Marshall, father of John, in 1773.

At 21.4 *m.* is a junction with County 671.

Right here to YEW HILL (L), 0.1 *m.*, a small frame structure, with a steep-pitched gabled roof, and dormers, erected about 1743 by Robert Ashby (1710–92), great-grandfather of General Turner Ashby, Confederate cavalry leader. As a tavern called the Kitty Shacklett House the place enjoyed a wide reputation.

At 21.9 *m.* on State 55 is a junction with County 731.

Left here to COOL SPRING CHURCH, 0.2 *m.*, a rectangular red brick, gabled-roof building, now housing a Methodist congregation. It was erected in 1858 on the site of an Episcopal church, built about 1780. The first minister here was the Reverend James Thompson, who tutored Thomas Marshall's children.

MARKHAM, 25.7 *m.* (552 alt., 150 pop.), a shipping point for apples, lies at the eastern end of Manassas Gap and is flanked (R) by NAKED MOUNTAIN (1,400 alt.) and (L) by RED OAK MOUNTAIN (1,200 alt.).

ROSEBANK (R), birthplace of Confederate General Turner Ashby (1828–62), is a frame building on a knoll. Here were born Captain James Green Ashby and Captain Richard Ashby, brothers of Turner Ashby.

THE HOLLOW (R), a four-room brick and frame dwelling just behind Rosebank, was erected in 1764 by Thomas Marshall.

WOLF'S CRAG (L), a square brick-and-stucco house with a frame addition is on a steep hill. It was purchased by Turner Ashby in 1853. Here Ashby organized a troop of horsemen, known as the 'Mountain Rangers,' to control men working on the Manassas Gap railroad and troubling farmers near by. In 1859 he and his troops were assigned to picket duty during the John Brown insurrection at Harpers Ferry.

MANASSAS GAP, 30 *m.* (950 alt.), the lowest pass in the Blue Ridge was early an important gateway through the range. John Lederer is believed to have used it in 1670. George Washington and John Wood surveyed it in 1761. It is flanked (L) by HIGH KNOB (2,385 alt.).

At 38.6 *m.* is a junction with State 3.

Left on this road to the U.S. ARMY REMOUNT STATION, 2.2 *m.*, one of three breeding and training stations maintained by the army and the headquarters of a purchasing board that supplies mounts to the entire eastern area. In retirement here are Jeff and Kidron, mounts used by General John J. Pershing. Here also is the trick horse Solomon Levi. Other horses on the reservation include the 'royal family'—Lady Lou, her two sons, and three daughters—animals with one of the best blood strains in the army. An average of 50 colts are foaled here annually.

At 38.9 *m.* is the entrance to SKYLINE DRIVE (*adm.* 25¢).

Left on this route (*speed limit 35 miles an hour; picknicking facilities, campsites, restaurants*) through the SHENANDOAH NATIONAL PARK, established in 1935, an irregular strip, one to 13 miles wide along the crest of the Blue Ridge Mountains. Its acres—the very heart of the mountains—are precipitous and almost entirely forest-covered. The wide, paved road follows the older Appalachian Trail most of the way along the crest of the ridge, with an average elevation of more than 3,000 feet, and often higher. The trail has been rerouted but is accessible from the highway. The route affords a continuous series of magnificent views over steep, wooded ravines and occasional rocky crags to the rolling Piedmont Plateau on the east and across the fertile farmland of the Shenandoah Valley to the Alleghenies on the west.

In PANORAMA (Thornton Gap), 32.1 *m.* (2,304 alt.) (*restaurant, lodgings*), is a junction with US 211 (*see Tour 22*). Each season brings its own beauty to this wild, elevated world. The winter-dark forest is brightened in spring by dogwood breaking into bloom everywhere, like thin puffs of steam. Later rhododendron and mountain laurel flood the sheltered hillsides with pink and white. Summer pours warm sunlight from clear skies onto the peaks and into the valleys, where streams splash down over rocky beds and falls, and often, especially in the early morning, onto clouds covering the lowlands far below. Autumn tints the leaves of every tree but the evergreen and intensifies the blue haze ever-present along the ridge. The clear air of Indian summer becomes even clearer with winter, and then snow blankets the upper slopes intermittently until another late spring.

The entrance (R) to SKYLAND (*cabins and cottages, restaurant, horses for hire*), 42.1 *m.*, is near the crest of STONY MAN MOUNTAIN (4,010 alt.), from which many miles of bridle paths and hiking trails wind in many directions.

From HAWKSBILL GAP (3,361 alt.), 45.8 *m.*, a three-mile trail leads to the summit of HAWKSBILL MOUNTAIN (4,049 alt.), the highest peak in the Shenandoah Park.

At BIG MEADOWS, 51.1 *m.* (*restaurant, cabins, lodgings*), high on the ridge, President Roosevelt dedicated the Skyline Drive, July 3, 1936.

SWIFT RUN GAP, 66.1 *m.* (2,349 alt.) (*restaurant, tavern, and cottages*), is at a junction with US 33 (*see Tour 9*).

From JARMAN GAP, 97 *m.*, the road continues south to a junction at 105.5 *m.* with US 250 (*see Tour 17b*), and in the future will continue as the Blue Ridge Parkway (*see Tour 7c*).

FRONT ROYAL, 39.4 *m.* (508 alt., 2,424 pop.) (*see Tour 5A*), on State 55 is at the junction with State 12 and State 3 (*see Tour 5A*).

Tour 5

(Martinsburg, W.Va.)—Winchester—Woodstock—Harrisonburg—Staunton—Lexington—Roanoke—Pulaski—Wytheville—Marion—Abingdon—(Bristol, Tenn.). US 11.
West Virginia Line to Tennessee Line, 343.4 *m.*

Asphalt roadbed throughout.
Pennsylvania R.R. parallels route between West Virginia Line and Winchester, Baltimore and Ohio R.R. between Winchester and Lexington, Norfolk and Western Ry., roughly between Greenville and Bristol.
All types of accommodations.

US 11 passes southward between the Blue Ridge and main Allegheny Range, traversing the full length of Virginia's 'Great Valley,' an undulating plain drained by five rivers—the Shenandoah, James, Roanoke, New, and Holston. The region is divided into the Shenandoah Valley and Southwest Virginia. Mineral wealth, fertile lands, and natural beauty make the Valley the State's richest section. Isolated by mountains, it was not settled until the third decade of the eighteenth century.

During the entire period of the War between the States, the Shenandoah Valley was the scene of conflict, for the Valley was not only the granary of the Confederacy, but a perfect point from which to turn the flank of forces operating out of the District of Columbia. It was, moreover, the path twice taken by Lee for invasion of the North.

In 1862, General Stonewall Jackson, who had been ordered to threaten Washington and keep reinforcements from McClellan, fought the Valley Campaign, a model of military strategy. In four battles, Kernstown, Winchester, Cross Keys, and Port Republic, he crushed three Federal armies, and so frightened the Government in Washington that needed reinforcements were not sent to the Union army near Richmond.

During 1863, the Valley again echoed to the gun fire of contending armies when Ewell cleared the Valley of Milroy's troops and Lee swept across the Potomac to Gettysburg.

The next year, after General Jubal A. Early had marched up the Shenandoah, crossed into Maryland, and appeared before Washington, the available Union troops in northern Virginia were concentrated under General P.H.Sheridan, with orders to make the valley untenable to Confederate troops and completely useless as a source of supplies. Sheridan defeated Early at Winchester and Fisher's Hill, and was able to snatch victory from the hands of the Confederates at Cedar Creek. After this last battle had sent Early's forces whirling down the Valley, Sheridan systematically devastated the area, so successfully that, as he phrased it, 'a crow would have to carry his rations if he flew over it.'

Section a. WEST VIRGINIA LINE to STAUNTON; 101.6 *m.* *US* 11.

South of the West Virginia Line, US 11 follows the Shenandoah River between the gently rounded peaks of the Blue Ridge and the more rugged Allegheny mountains. Apple orchards, grain fields, bluegrass pastures, and poultry farms flourish on rich limestone land. Stone, brick, clapboarded log, and frame farm houses stand in the lee of commodious barns. The towns are brisk centers of shipping. Under the slopes are limestone caves, fairylands in water-worked stone.

In the first years of the eighteenth century Virginia offered trade monopolies to settlers west of the mountains; in 1716 the expedition of Governor Spotswood and his Knights of the Golden Horseshoe publicized the region; and in the late 1720's Pennsylvanians obtained large grants of land and began bringing settlers south.

US 11 crosses the West Virginia Line, 0 *m.*, 13 miles south of Martinsburg, W.Va. (*see West Virginia Guide*).

On both sides of the highway are large commercial orchards. The early settlers converted much of their prolific apple crops into brandy, but with the advent of good highways and the railroads they began to send apples to distant markets. Today, the 10,000,000 apple trees in the valley of Virginia produce annually 7,000,000 to 10,000,000 bushels.

At 2.9 *m.* is a junction with County 672.

Right here to HOPEWELL MEETING HOUSE (L), 1.3 *m.*, a large rectangular building of gray limestone erected in 1788–89; incorporated in it is a meeting house built by Thomas McClun in 1759. In the stone-walled graveyard is buried Alexander Ross, a Quaker who in 1732 received a large grant of land with the proviso that at least one family settle on each 1,000 acres.

Left from the meeting house on County 665 0.1 *m.* to the HOME OF ALEXANDER ROSS (R), a large stone house. After Ross and other Friends settled in the region Ross's lands proved to be within the Fairfax Proprietary of the Northern Neck. The arrival of Lord Fairfax in 1738 caused the grantees no little anxiety, for his lordship immediately declared that their purchases were defective. Since the western boundary of the Proprietary had never been established, Fairfax agreed to confirm many of the grants if the long disputed point was settled. Accordingly, the Fairfax Line was surveyed and the grantees' titles were secured, though quit rents were henceforth extracted—an annual tax of two shillings for each 100 acres.

KENILWORTH (R), 3.9 *m.*, a gray stone house behind a hedge, was during the War between the States the home of the Quaker, William Stephenson. Jackson's troops camped on Kenilworth lands after the Battle of Winchester, May 25, 1862, and here occurred the Battle of Stephenson's Depot, June 15, 1863, when General R.S.Ewell, commanding a corps of Lee's army, captured wagons, cannon, and 4,000 of General R.H.Milroy's force, which was retreating from Winchester. The Confederate victory cleared the Valley of Union troops and allowed Lee to formulate his plan for invading Union territory, and thus, if successful, induce England's aid. Gettysburg followed 15 days later.

At 4.8 *m.* is a junction with State 274.

Left on this road to a junction with County 664, 1.5 *m.*; R. here 0.8 *m.* to JORDAN'S WHITE SULPHUR SPRINGS (R), now largely a group of dismal old whitewashed buildings standing to the east of a more recent red brick structure. First used by the Indians during their ceremonials, the springs early became popular with the whites.

At 6.6 *m.* on US 11 is a junction with County 661.

Left on this road to HACKWOOD PARK (R), 0.9 *m.*, a massive gray stone house approached through a vast apple orchard. The house was built during the latter part of the Revolution by Major General John Smith, member of the Virginia legislature and later congressman. General Smith was made custodian of 300 Hessian prisoners interned at Winchester and 14 Philadelphia Quakers suspected of pro-British sympathies. When release for the survivors came, many of the Hessians settled in the valley, where their ability as masons was soon recognized, as it still is today.

At 7.4 *m.* is a view of STAR FORT, on a wooded hill (R). The fort, built by Federals in 1862, was abandoned a few months later. On the night of June 14, 1863, Union troops under General R.H.Milroy, withdrew from the fort after an attack by Ewell's corps had driven the Federals out of their outworks; several thousand Federals were captured the following morning. On September 19, 1864, when the Third Battle of Winchester took place between the armies of General Sheridan and General Early, Federal cavalry captured these works, turned the Confederate left flank, and forced evacuation of the town.

A red brick house (L), 8.1 *m.*, among many trees stands on the SITE OF FORT COLLIER, thrown up around the home of Isaac Stine in 1861 by General Joseph E. Johnston, then Confederate commander in the Valley. From Fort Collier, fortifications formed a semicircle around Winchester. On the afternoon of September 19, 1864, Early's hard-pressed Confederates were forced to this old line and later withdrew southward.

WINCHESTER, 9.7 *m.* (725 alt., 10,855 pop.) (*see Winchester*).

In Winchester are junctions with State 3 (*see Tour 5A*), US 50 (*see Tour 12*), and State 7 (*see Tour 13*).

The HOME OF ISAAC PARKINS (R), 10.5 *m.*, a stone house standing upon a hillside, was built before 1746. Parkins (or Perkins), a close friend of Lord Fairfax, opened what were probably the first mills in this region.

At 11.1 *m.* is a junction with County 628. Once barring the road at this point was the Hillman toll gate. According to local tradition, Charlotte Hillman, keeping the gate, delayed General Sheridan and his troops in their pursuit of General Early after the Third Battle of Winchester. She stood her ground, with the long bar held defiantly across the road until Sheridan agreed to pay for himself and staff. He could not, he said, answer for his soldiers; whereupon all marched through, unaware that Charlotte was counting the men. After the war, a bill was sent to Washington and was eventually paid.

From a vantage point at 11.9 *m.*, General Jackson on the morning of May 25, 1862 observed Union forces spread out in an arc and began the First Battle of Winchester, which ended with a Confederate victory.

KERNSTOWN, 12.6 *m.* (350 pop.), was first called Opequon, later Hogue's Ordinary for William Hogue's 'house of entertainment.'

The Battle of Kernstown, fought west of the village on March 23, 1862, was the first in Jackson's valley campaign. Although lost to the Confederates, the battle caused General Nathaniel P. Banks to return to the valley with his entire force and abandon his plans to join McClellan on the Peninsula. A small engagement took place on the same field, July 24, 1864, between part of General Jubal A. Early's troops and a detachment of Federals.

SPRINGDALE, 14.5 *m.*, a dignified small mansion of stone, stands close by the road, its two-and-a-half-story central section flanked by one-story wings. In the yard are the broken gray stone walls of JOIST HITE'S HOUSE, erected about 1734. John Hite, son of the pioneer, built Springdale in 1753. The dormers and portico were added in 1827. In 1730 Joist Hite, a native of Strasburg, Alsace, received a large grant upon condition that he bring 40 families here.

STEPHENS CITY, 16.9 *m.* (606 pop.), known previously both as Stephensburg and Newtown, was chartered in 1758.

The HOUSE OF JACOB CRISMAN (L), 19.1 *m.*, son-in-law of Joist Hite, is of gray stone, built in 1751. An underground passage gave safe access to a spring in case of need. A log building, still on the lawn, served as a powder magazine.

At 19.2 *m.* is a junction with County 638.

Right here to VAUCLUSE (L), 0.7 *m.*, a large brick house, painted yellow, in a grove above fertile acres. Here lived William Jones (b.1756), son of the explosive lawyer, Gabriel Jones of Bogota (*see Tour 5A*). Gabriel Jones disinherited his grandson, William Strother Jones, Jr., writing, 'The best I can say of him is (and God knows its bad enough) that he is an idol disapated young man, and is now left to live upon the reck of a miserable fortune left him by his father (which I gave him) now almost spent by his extravigance . . .'

MIDDLETOWN, 21.7 *m.* (416 pop.), spread out on a low plateau and first known as Senseny Town, was chartered in 1796 by Dr.Peter Senseny. As early as 1766 this village was recognized as a clockmaking center, and its reputation increased as wooden-wheeled timepieces gave way to those with brass, which bowed in turn to elaborately patterned eight-day clocks. The same artisans fashioned watches and surveyors' implements. One of them, Jacob Danner, constructed compasses of such mathematical precision that their reputation endures today. Here in 1817 a threshing machine demonstrated its superiority over flail and threshing-floor.

Right from Middletown on County 627 to County 622, 4.4 *m.*; R. here, with hills always in view, to MARLBORO, 5 *m.*, named for marl deposits near by. General Isaac Zane of Philadelphia in1771 built a mill here, an iron foundry, and a distillery—now a barn. In his day Zane was second only to Lord Fairfax in wealth.

Left 0.1 *m.* from Marlboro on County 628 to STEPHENS' FORT (R), a small whitewashed hexagonal building of stone erected before the Revolution.

At 23.3 *m.* on US 11 is a junction with County 625.

Left on this road to County 611, 0.7 *m.*; R. here to LONG MEADOWS (L), 2.4 *m.*, a substantial red brick house built in 1845 by Colonel George Bowman, grandson of Joist Hite, upon part of a tract Joist chose for his son Isaac. The house is on the site of Isaac's home. In the graveyard near by are buried Isaac Hite,Sr., Isaac Hite,Jr., and Samuel Kercheval (1767–1845), author of the *History of the Valley of Virginia.*

At 23.4 *m.* on US 11 is another junction with County 625.

Right here to BELLE GROVE (R), 0.5 *m.*, a dressed limestone house of one full story on a very high basement. The walls are quoined with rough-hewn stone, and keyed flat arches of stone emphasize each window opening. Four widely spaced chimneys, also of stone, rise symmetrically from the broad hip roof. Belle Grove, designed in the Classical Revival style, has been altered by removal of the north wing and three of four porticoes. Planned and constructed by Major Isaac Hite,Jr. (1758–1830), grandson of Joist Hite, it was completed in 1794. At the College of William and Mary in 1777, Isaac Hite became the first man to be elected by the charter members of the Phi Beta Kappa Society. Major Hite's first wife, Nelly Conway Madison, was sister of James Madison (*see Tour 16a*). Here James and Dolly spent two weeks of their honeymoon.

For a time General Sheridan had headquarters here. On October 19, 1864, his army was routed from these grounds in the Battle of Cedar Creek (or Battle of Belle Grove). A surprise attack at daybreak demoralized two corps of Sheridan's army, which retreated some miles northward. Returning from Washington and learning the news in Winchester, Sheridan rejoined his army and in turn routed Early.

HARMONY HALL (L), 25.4 *m.*, first called Fort Bowman, is a small stone house built about 1753 by George Bowman, son-in-law of Joist Hite, and enclosed by a stockade during the French and Indian War. George Bowman, who had married successively Anna Maria and Mary Hite, had four distinguished sons: John Jacob, later prominent in Kentucky; Abraham, a colonel during the Revolution; and Joseph and Isaac, members of the Lewis and Clark expedition.

CRYSTAL CAVERNS (*adm. 75¢, illuminated*), 26.4 *m.*, were formerly called Hupp's Cave.

HUPP'S FORT (R), 26.9 *m.*, is a barnlike stone structure built about 1755 and fortified against Indian attacks.

STRASBURG, 27.4 *m.* (1,901 pop.), a neat town with an atmosphere of thrift and efficiency, ships lumber, dairy products, flour, apples, and limestone and manufactures silk. Pottery making, begun during the nineteenth century, rose to such prominence here that at one time there were six potteries running full tilt. By 1908 the industry that had caused the place to be called 'Pot Town' had vanished.

Strasburg was German-born. Called in succession Shenandoah River, Funk's Mill, Funkstown, and Staufferstadt (Stovertown), the village received its name Strasburg and legal status in 1761. In 1799 Peter Stover left to the community land and $10,000 for schools.

The white-painted COLONIAL INN, SW. corner King and Massanutten Sts., was built of brick about 1807 and first called Hotel Spengler. It contains much fine woodwork.

Left from Strasburg on State 55 to WATERLICK, 4.9 *m.*, once a stagecoach stop on the Powell's Fort Valley Turnpike. The MENNONITE BAPTIST CHURCH here was founded by the Reverend Mr. James Ireland, who was born in Edinburgh, Scotland, in 1748.

Right 1.2 *m.* from Waterlick on an improved road, formerly Powell's Turnpike, to the state-maintained FRONT ROYAL FISH HATCHERY (L). Fish bred here include several varieties of sunfish, largemouthed bass, and smallmouthed bass.

The unpaved road continues (R) through PASSAGE CREEK GAP, 2.9 *m.*, into the Massanutten Section of the GEORGE WASHINGTON NATIONAL FOREST. This gap is one of the openings to Powell's Fort Valley, named for a counterfeiter, who made coins with a silver content greater than that of legal money. A rich deposit of silver, known only to him, is said to have been the source of his metal. John Esten Cooke used the valley as the locale for his novel *Lord Fairfax; or, The Master of Greenway Court.*

At 4.3 *m.* is a foot trail (R) to SIGNAL KNOB, used during the War between the States as a wigwag signal station by both armies.

At the Forest Service ELIZABETH FURNACE CAMP (*picnicking facilities; shelters*), 4.8 *m.*, are the ruins of one of several early furnaces operated in this area.

At 29.3 *m.* on US 11 is a junction with County 601.

Right here to the crest of FISHER'S HILL, 0.8 *m.* Following his defeat at Winchester, September 19, 1864, Early fell back to this position and was here again defeated by Sheridan on the 22nd. Sheridan's three victories over Early—and Read's poem 'Sheridan's Ride'—restored confidence in the Federal Administration and helped bring about Lincoln's re-election.

MAURERTOWN (pronounced Morrytown), 34.8 *m.* (125 pop.), laid out by Charles Maurer, was called for many years 'Jug Town' because the houses, of heavy logs and weatherboarding, were designed on a plan that simulated a jug.

WOODSTOCK, 38.9 *m.* (1,552 pop.), seat of Shenandoah County, assumes a metropolitan air. Its industrial plants include creameries, apple-grading plants, and farm-supply stores. First called Müllerstadt for Jacob Miller, it was legally established in 1761. Miller, with his wife and six children, came from Pennsylvania in 1752. In 1761 he laid off a tract of 96 acres for a town. In 1766 John Peter Gabriel Mühlenburg (1746–1807), a Lutheran minister, arrived to take charge of the church here. Son of the Reverend Henry Melchior Mühlenburg, organizer of the first Lutheran synod in America, John Mühlenburg was educated at the universities of Pennsylvania and Halle. Mühlenburg went to London in 1772, and was ordained a priest in the Established Church, but he and his parishioners met June 16, 1774, and drafted a resolution declaring they would 'pay due submission to such acts of government as His Majesty has a right to exercise over his subjects and to such only.' The smoldering rebellion reached its climax on a Sunday in January 1776. Mühlenburg mounted the pulpit of the log church and announced as his text Eccl.3.1–8: 'There is a time to every purpose . . . a time to war, and a time to peace.' The sermon rose to a dramatic finale: 'The time to fight has come!' he cried and, flinging aside the black folds of his cassock, he stood forth in the blue and buff of a Continental colonel and began to enroll his parishioners in the Eighth Virginia Regiment.

A weekly newspaper, the *Shenandoah Herald*, established in 1817 by Major Benjamin Hogan, a cousin of Washington's, is still published here.

In 1859 the artist Benjamin West Clinedinst was born in Woodstock. Educated at the Virginia Military Institute and the École des Beaux-Arts, this *genre* painter is best known in Virginia for his panorama of the Battle of New Market.

The stone SHENANDOAH COUNTY COURTHOUSE, but for modernizations, looks as it did when erected in 1791–92. In 1772 the county was cut from Frederick and named Dunmore, but it soon dropped the name because of the unpopularity of Governor Dunmore.

The MASSANUTTEN MILITARY ACADEMY, a boys' preparatory school on the southern outskirts of town, occupies red brick buildings, in front of which is a cannon. It was established in 1899 by the Reformed Church in America. The academy has about 125 cadets.

Right from Woodstock on State 261, through MT.CALVARY, 2 *m.*, to the SITE OF COLUMBIA FURNACE, 6.4 *m.*, built about 1803 by George Mayberry and Benjamin Pennybacker—George Mayberry & Co.—and operated until 1886.

Brick stacks and a boiler at 12.4 *m.* are the RUINS OF LIBERTY FURNACE, built about 1822 by William Newman, son-in-law of Benjamin Pennybacker. General Isaac Zane once made Liberty Furnace stoves embellished with Scriptural verses in German.

EDINBURG, 44.4 *m.* (498 pop.), between a graveyard and a gulley, is a line of frame houses flush with the street. Edinburg was founded on land owned by Philip Bishop. Captured by Indians, he had escaped and changed his name to Grandstaff. The town rose to prominence because of its rifle factory, which supplied many guns for the War of 1812.

For a month during 1862 the town was a basis of operations for General Turner Ashby, who involved the enemy in 28 skirmishes during that period. General Sheridan set the mills of the town on fire, but, persuaded by two young women that the people of the community depended on the mills for food, he had the flames extinguished.

Edinburg has mills that have steadily ground flour since Major George Grandstaff built them in 1848.

MOUNT JACKSON, 51.5 *m.* (575 pop.), which appears to have gathered accidentally around a group of shops, altered its homespun name of Mount Pleasant to honor the hero of New Orleans. Mount Jackson was for long the terminus of the valley division of the stage route and, until Reconstruction days, was the southern terminal of the valley's railroad.

The UNION CHURCH (L), a little brick building surrounded by trees and tombstones, was built about 1825 on land left by Reuben Moore, who wrote: 'It is my will that the . . . land . . . remain for the free use of a meetinghouse and burying-ground for ever to be free for all Christian ministers of any society to preach in.'

The CONFEDERATE CEMETERY (L) contains graves of 500 soldiers, 112 of them unknown.

Right from Mount Jackson on State 263, locally called the Orkney Grade, to the FUNKHOUSER HOUSE (R), 1.3 *m.*, a white plastered log building erected in 1775 by Jacob Funkhouser. Here was born George Funkhouser, one of the founders of Bonebrake Theological Seminary, Dayton, Ohio. A much older log cabin, close to the road, is typical of early homes.

At 11.7 *m.* is a junction with State 265; R. here 1 *m.* to a point where State 265 becomes County 717; straight ahead to a lane (R), 1.5 *m.*, that leads 0.7 *m.* through woods to BIRD HAVEN. The Shenandoah Community Workers were organized here 'to develop and demonstrate practical methods of applied forestry . . . to give its members education in craftsmanship . . . all income of which shall be used for Community purposes.' Here local craftsmen fashion furniture, toys, fireplace equipment, hooked rugs, and quilts, from patterns evolved by their ancestors.

On County 717 to SHENANDOAH ALUM SPRINGS (L), 1.7 *m.* The hotel, built in 1852 and extensively remodeled since, has grounds of 100 acres in the GEORGE WASHINGTON FOREST area.

State 263 continues to ORKNEY SPRINGS, 13.2 *m.* (1,750 alt., 75 pop.), greatly augmented in summer. It grew up around 11 chalybeate springs. Before the Revolution Dr. John McDonald acquired 360 acres including the 'Yellow Springs.' By 1785 traffic had increased to such an extent that an Indian trail to this place had been made a public road. The village, with its public square, was laid out in 1803.

Over the ORKNEY SPRINGS HOTEL hovers the spirit of the '60s, as epitomized by the name of one of the formal rooms: *Ladies' Parlor*. Chartered in 1838, the hotel entertained some 8,000 guests a season in the 1880's, and continues popular today. On its many acres are the usual facilities for strenuous relaxation.

On a wooded hillside near the public square, is an ecclesiastical retreat belonging to the Episcopal Diocese of Virginia. Scattered about the SHRINE OF THE TRANSFIGURATION, erected in 1924–25, are cottages, a community dining room, meeting halls, and a swimming pool.

At 54.1 *m.* on US 11 is a junction with County 730.

Right here to the SHENANDOAH CAVERNS, 1.5 *m.* (*adm.* $1.50, *children* 75¢; *special rates to parties*). Beyond lengthy passageways, subterranean rooms become, with the aid of a guide's suggestion, a cathedral, a theatre, a hunter's lodge, and a crystal lake.

Around the BUSHONG HOUSE (R), 57.2 *m.*, a two-story clapboarded structure, the Battle of New Market took place on Sunday afternoon,

May 15, 1864. While Grant and Lee battled in Spotsylvania and the Valley was almost bare of Confederate troops, General Franz Sigel marched from Winchester to destroy the Virginia Central Railroad at Staunton. General John C. Breckinridge, with several brigades, was rushed from Southwest Virginia and joined by 257 cadets from the Virginia Military Institute. The Confederates attacked Sigel here and drove him north of Mount Jackson. The cadets followed the veteran troops and filled gaps as they appeared, capturing many prisoners and guns. Ten lads were killed and 47 wounded. Grant, hearing of this battle, exclaimed, 'The South is robbing the cradle and the grave.'

The HINES MEMORIAL PYTHIAN HOME (R), 58 *m.*, housed in a red brick building on treeless land, is an orphanage named for Samuel Holder Hines, who died in an effort to save a fellow member of the order during a fire in a Richmond hotel in 1879. The tall house, first called Stanley Hall, was built in 1834 by Dr. John W. Rice, organizer and president of the company that built the Valley turnpike. Successfully preventing the extension of the railroad to New Market, he argued that cattle should not be frightened.

NEW MARKET, 58.4 *m.* (640 pop.), proud that there is not a smoke-stack in the town, has a few new houses around a group of old buildings that have not lost their German flavor. The town derives its sustenance from visitors to the commercialized caves and from produce of the surrounding farms.

In 1761 John Sevier, later governor of the short-lived State of Franklin, and six times governor of Tennessee, married and moved to this cross-roads, where he established an inn and a store. In 1774 Sevier sold his land. In 1785 Peter Palsel laid off a town.

Lewis Summers wrote in 1808: 'Proceeded to New Market, a very hand-some little town . . . The houses well built of brick, a good many stores & full of goods; containing 500 or 600 people.' In 1817 the New Market Academy was established, and in 1821, the Lutheran Seminary. Almost a century later, in 1908, another school joined these—the Shenandoah Valley Academy, a coeducational institution of the Seventh Day Adventists.

The HENKEL BUILDING, SW. corner Congress St., was occupied until 1925 by the Henkel Press, established by Ambrose Henkel in 1806, when he was only 20 years old. Henkel, both editor and printer, published a German newspaper and a series of books, many of them for children. In 1817 he sold the business to his brother Solomon.

OLD POLYTECHNIC HALL, Water St., a dilapidated brick building, housed a classical school opened September 5, 1870. Polytechnic Institute was operated until 1890. During the summers between 1874 and 1882 the building held Virginia's first Normal School of Music.

In New Market is a junction with US 211 (*see Tour 22*).

US 11 at 59.7 *m.* crosses the southwestern boundary of the Fairfax Grant. This disputed boundary was established in 1736. Fairfax's Proprietary had natural boundaries on all sides except the southwestern—an omission that permitted his lordship to lay claim to an unlimited amount of land until a line was established between points in the Blue Ridge and the Alleghenies.

At 61.7 *m.* is a junction with a paved road.

Left here 1.9 *m.* to the ENDLESS CAVERNS (*adm.* $1.50, *children* 75¢; *free camp grounds, rest rooms, shower baths, benches, tables*). The caverns were discovered in 1879 when Reuben Zirkle's dog ran a rabbit behind a large boulder.

COURT MANOR (L), 62.4 *m.*, is a brick house with Doric portico. The grounds are ornate, with trees, shrubs, gardens, and pools. As Moreland Hall, the house was built sometime after 1820. The enlarged house is now center of a stud farm belonging to Willis Sharp Kilmer, owner of such winners as *Sun Beau* and *Exterminator*.

At 69.4 *m.* is a junction with County 721.

Right here to EDOM, 4.8 *m.* (150 pop.), a compact village in a valley. Here lived Dr. Jesse Bennett, who in 1794 courageously performed a Caesarian operation on his wife and saved the lives of both the mother and child—for that time an amazing feat, which he failed to report. When conditions developed that made delivery of the child impossible and the mother's death seemed imminent, Dr. Bennett consulted Dr. Alexander Humphreys, teacher of medicine in Staunton (*see Staunton*), who refused to undertake the operation. Whereupon Dr. Bennett proceeded unassisted. It was not until 1809, 15 years later, that Dr. Ephraim McDowell, in the wilds of Kentucky, performed the oöphorectomy that has given him recognition as the father of abdominal surgery.

Right from Edom 2.7 *m.* on State 260 to the entrance (R) to the LINCOLN HOMESTEAD (*adm.* 50¢ *for party*), a substantial brick house painted buff. Its rear wing was built by Abraham Lincoln I, whose father, having come to Virginia from Pennsylvania in 1750, lived near by. Here was born Thomas Lincoln, the son of this Abraham and the husband of Nancy Hanks, mother of another Abraham Lincoln. When Thomas was six years old, his parents moved to Kentucky. The main portion of the house was built about 1800 by a Captain Jacob Lincoln. The graveyard on the hill above the house contains the graves of the immigrant and several members of his family.

On County 721 is SINGER'S GLEN, 9.3 *m.* (99 pop.), first called Mountain Valley. About 1798 Joseph Funk, a Mennonite and self-taught musician, brought his bride to this spot in the wilderness, cleared land, and built a log house. Here he raised a large family, which he himself taught, with emphasis on music. As the school grew, augmented by neighbors' children, so did Funk's collection of hymns and folk songs. In 1816, he had published a volume entitled *Choral Music*, which passed through many editions and furnished hymns for rural congregations throughout the country. In 1847, after publishing a Mennonite history, Funk opened a Mennonite printing house. Besides his hymnals, he published *The Musical Advocate*, a magazine devoted to music. Timothy Funk, a son, became one of the best known itinerant teachers of singing in the Valley. Joseph Funk's grandson, Aldine Kieffer, composer of 'Twilight Is Falling,' continued the publishing business and revived *The Musical Advocate* under the title *The Musical Million.*

The CAVERNS OF MELROSE (R), 69.7 *m.* (*adm.* $1), known first as Harrison's Cave, then as Virginia Caverns, were discovered about 1818 by David Harrison. Hundreds of names of both Union and Confederate soldiers decorate their walls.

SMITHLAND (L), 74.1 *m.*, a large white-painted brick house with a two-columned portico, was built about 1845 on the lands owned in Colonial times by Daniel Smith. The first session of the court of Rockingham County met here in an earlier house on April 27, 1778. Soon afterward, it was ordered that 'a square Log Jayle or prison 12 feet square' be erected 'on the most convenient spott of the sd. Daniel Smith's plantation.'

HARRISONBURG, 76.3 *m.* (1,937 alt., 7,232 pop.), called the 'Hub of the Valley,' is the efficient seat of Rockingham County. It is a city wherein the old and new are pleasantly merged. Manufacturing more than 50 products, this busy community ships poultry, dairy products, livestock, processed fruits, rayon, and air conditioning equipment in considerable quantity.

Harrisonburg was founded by Thomas Harrison, who, with his wife Sarah, had settled about 1739 at this point where the Indian Road crossed the Spotswood Trail. In 1779 the couple conveyed land to the county for the erection of a courthouse, and the following year Harrison procured the passage of an act establishing the town. Popularly known in its infancy as Rocktown, the settlement grew rapidly, fostered by Harrison's sons Reuben and Robert, who supplied lands in 1797 for municipal expansion. In 1794 Bishop Asbury started a Methodist school here, in which not only were gaming and 'instruments of music' outlawed, but no scholar was 'permitted on any account whatever to wear Ruffles or powder his hair.'

At the turn of the century hogs were excluded from the streets; in 1805 a new jail became part of the municipal equipment; in 1822 Lawrence Wartmen started the *Rockingham Register*, a vigorous weekly that lasted until 1912.

Charles Triplett O'Ferrall (1840–1905), member of Congress (1882–93) and governor of Virginia (1894–98), was a citizen of Harrisonburg from 1869 to 1893.

ROCKINGHAM COURTHOUSE, Court Square, is a towered granite building, erected in 1897 and fifth court building since 1781. Named for Charles Watson Wentworth, Marquis of Rockingham, Rockingham County was formed from Augusta in 1778. During the War between the States the Rockingham records were loaded in a wagon to be carried to a place of safety. Though General Hunter overtook the vehicles and set fire to the papers, the flames were smothered with green hay and some of the records were saved.

WARREN HOTEL, 28 N.Court Square, a three-story brick building painted white and fronted by verandas, was erected in the late 1700's by John Warren, a son-in-law of Thomas Harrison, and remodeled in 1858.

The STONE HOUSE, NW. corner Main and Bruce Sts., a story-and-a-half cottage with a single dormer in its slate roof, is now the rear wing of a brick house. It was built in 1753 by Thomas Harrison and his wife.

MADISON COLLEGE, 840–60 S.Main St., occupies 17 buildings, constructed of local blue limestone and arranged in a horseshoe on the campus. Established in 1908 as a state normal and industrial school, the name was changed in 1916 to the State Normal School for Women, in 1924 to the State Teachers' College at Harrisonburg, and in 1938 to Madison College. The college has an enrollment (1937–38) of 1360 students, confers bachelor degrees in education and the liberal arts, and offers a two-year teacher-training course.

The CITY PRODUCE EXCHANGE, 56 W.Gay St., in a four-story building with two acres of floor space, is equipped with a poultry-killing and dressing machine, and cold storage and packing rooms.

The highway at 79 *m.* passes a mile and a half west of the spot where Brigadier General Turner Ashby was killed, June 6, 1862, as he led a bayonet charge against the 13th Pennsylvania 'Bucktails' Infantry. After his horse—the one Jackson had ridden at Manassas—had been shot beneath him, he leaped to his feet and called, 'Virginians, charge!' A second later, as the shouts of his men announced the repulse of the enemy, Ashby himself was shot. Jackson wrote, 'As a partisan officer, I never knew his superior. His daring proverbial, his powers of endurance almost incredible . . .'

MT.CRAWFORD, 84 *m.* (272 pop.), is no larger today than it was in 1835 when *Martin's Gazetteer* credited it with '25 dwelling houses, 1 house of public worship free for all denominations, 2 common schools, 2 taverns,' and sundry stores and shops.

Right from Mt.Crawford on State 257 to BRIDGEWATER, 2.8 *m.* (900 pop.), with the North River twisting through its center. The one business street from which narrow lanes go winding is lined with stores that serve prosperous farm folk and college students. Beginning as a port for flatboats, the community was first called Dinkletown for John and S.J.Dinkle, who had a carding machine, a sawmill, and a gristmill here in 1810.

BRIDGEWATER COLLEGE, with five major buildings, is on a 25-acre campus that adjoins the college farm of 100 acres. The college is operated by the Church of the Brethren, or Dunkards. It confers bachelor degrees and has a student body of 235 (1937–38). Bridgewater College had its beginning in 1880 as the Spring Creek Normal and Collegiate Institute. In 1882, as Virginia Normal School, it was moved to this town, and in 1889 it became a college. In 1923 Daleville College (*see Tour 21a*) was combined with Bridgewater, and in 1929 Blue Ridge College of New Windsor, Maryland, became affiliated with Bridgewater.

FORT DEFIANCE, 93 *m.* (50 pop.), is a scattering of houses around a church and a school. On a tree-dotted knoll above outcroppings of rock stands AUGUSTA CHURCH (R), a dressed stone structure with gabled roof above cottage windows. A wing and portico have been added. Traces of an embankment, foundation for palisades erected in 1753 during Indian raids, remain around the church, which was built in 1748 by the Scotch-Irish Presbyterians.

The settlers' numerous 'supplications' for a pastor were finally appeased in 1740, when the Reverend John Craig 'was set apart for the work of the Gospel ministry in the south part of Beverley's Manor.' He had landed at New Castle, Delaware, three years before, after a voyage in which he had been washed overboard and then thrown back onto the ship.

In 1760 he here baptized a converted Mohammedan named Selim, an Algerian found starving in the forest sometime before. When Selim had acquired sufficient knowledge of English he said that a wealthy farmer had sent him to school in Constantinople; that on his way home the boat on which he was traveling had been captured by a Spanish man-of-war and he had been made prisoner. Transferred to a French vessel that landed in New Orleans, he had been given to the authorities and sent to the Shawnee towns on the Ohio River. Having learned of the settlements to the east, he had escaped and attempted to find them and seek passage home. Selim was given a letter to Robert Carter, who provided his return passage to

Algiers. But he reappeared in Virginia after his father had turned him away because of his new religion. His mind then became deranged and he was sent for a time to the Insane Asylum at Williamsburg. Free again, he made a round of protracted visits. Later he went to South Carolina where all record of him has disappeared.

Adjoining the church is AUGUSTA MILITARY ACADEMY (R), a preparatory school known as the Augusta Male Academy when founded in 1865 by Charles S. Roller. On the large campus are barracks, a parade ground, a gymnasium, and a library.

STAUNTON, 101.6 *m.* (1,385 alt., 11,990 pop.) (*see Staunton*).

In Staunton is a junction with US 250 (*see Tour 17b*).

Left from Staunton on State 254 to BELLEFONT (L), 2.2 *m.*, an unusually large two-story log house, now covered with brick veneer and enlarged. John Lewis (1678–1762), founder of Staunton, built the house. Charged with the murder of an oppressive landlord in Ireland, Lewis, accompanied by his family and a group of followers, had come to America in 1732. The GRAVE OF JOHN LEWIS, marked by a simple slab, is near the house.

Section b. STAUNTON to JUNCTION US 52; 164.2 *m. US* 11.

Within constant view of both the Blue Ridge and the Allegheny Mountains, US 11 passes through the valleys of the James, Roanoke, and New Rivers, where rounded hills, pastures, orchards, and grain fields vary the quiet scene. Wedge-shaped Southwest Virginia, settled after 1745, was developed through land companies.

US 11 continues south from the corner of Augusta and Beverley Streets, 0 *m.*, in STAUNTON.

FOLLY (R), 5.2 *m.*, is a red brick house, Jeffersonian in style and proportion. The single floor on a high basement is crowned by a decked hip roof. The two principal façades have classic porticoes and Palladian entrances. From the sides extensions ramble out beneath great oaks and elms in the picket-fenced yard. The Jeffersonian influence is also apparent in a serpentine brick wall around three sides of the garden. The house was built in 1818 by Joseph Smith, a friend of Jefferson.

At 10.8 *m.* is a junction with State 12 (*see Tour 5A*).

GREENVILLE, 12.3 *m.* (350 pop.), is the village which Kate Smith, the radio singer, recalls as her birthplace.

SMITH'S TAVERN (L), a brick structure with frame extension in front and large stone chimneys, served many nineteenth-century travelers. The Marquis de Chastellux wrote in 1782, before the building had become an inn, 'Mr.Smith, a poor planter . . . had neither forage for our horses nor anything for ourselves.'

At the hamlet of MIDWAY, 18.4 *m.*, is a junction with County 606.

Right here to WALNUT GROVE (L), 0.9 *m.*, the restored McCormick homestead. Working here Cyrus Hall McCormick (1809–84) perfected the mechanical grain reaper in 1831. By 1847, when his sale of reapers totaled 778, McCormick moved west to the grain country. The house and many outbuildings have been restored. In the workshop stands one of the original binders.

RAPHINE (needle; Gr. *raphis*), 2 *m*., so named to honor James Ethan Allen Gibbs, who in 1857 invented the 'twisted loop rotary hook sewing machine.' Gibbs was born in 1829 at RAPHINE HALL (L), a red brick house. In 1858 he and James Willcox of Philadelphia put on the market the Willcox & Gibbs Sewing Machine.

FAIRFIELD, 24.4 *m*. (175 pop.), small though it is, boasts several eighteenth-century houses. Once when George Washington was a guest at the ALBRIGHT TAVERN (L), a 14-room building, rain poured through the roof and ruined a painting he had just purchased.

CHERRY GROVE (R), 25 *m*., is a weatherboarded log structure in which was born James McDowell (1795–1851), governor of Virginia from 1843 to 1846, a Progressive Liberal who favored emancipation of slaves and wider educational facilities in Virginia.

In the brick-walled MCDOWELL BURYING GROUND (R), 25.7 *m*., is a shaft, thick, square, and Moorishly embellished, erected to the memory of Ephraim McDowell (1673–1777), first settler in this part of the valley, who died at the age of 104. Near by is the grave of his son, Captain John McDowell (*see Tour 11a*).

TIMBER RIDGE PRESBYTERIAN CHURCH (L), 29 *m*., is a low T-shaped limestone building incorporating one built in 1756. On the interior is a tablet to the 'Noble Women who Helped with their own Hands.'

On Timber Ridge Plantation, south of the cemetery, is the SITE OF THE BIRTHPLACE OF SAM HOUSTON (1793–1863), who became commander-in-chief of the Texans at the Battle of San Jacinto (1836), President of the Republic of Texas (1836–38 and 1841–44), and finally State governor (1859–61).

In LEXINGTON, 35.4 *m*. (1,000 alt., 3,752 pop.), seat of Rockbridge County, meander tree-shaded streets, some walled with houses, others lined with sloping, boxwood-filled lawns. The business district and spreading suburbs belong very much to the present. During scholastic sessions student voices break the pastoral symphony created by the agricultural affairs of a county seat. In summer, Lexington settles down to sociability and tourists.

A part of the Borden Grant, acquired in 1739 by Gilbert Campbell, who left his 'hoose and personality' to his son Isaac in 1750, this land became the town of Lexington in 1777. Wiped out by fire in 1796, it was rebuilt from the proceeds of a lottery. *The Rockbridge Repository*, now the *Lexington Gazette*, first appeared in 1801.

Lexington's peaceful seclusion was disturbed on June 10, 1864, by General David Hunter, who bombarded the town and later allowed his troops to burn many buildings.

Standing on a terraced square, the ROCKBRIDGE COURTHOUSE, SW. corner of Main and Washington Sts., erected in 1896, is a two-story red brick building, behind which is LAWYERS' ROW, a group of one-story brick offices that terminate in the JAIL, the stone part of which dates from 1779, the year the first courthouse was built. Formed from parts of Augusta and Botetourt Counties in 1777, Rockbridge County by 1835 was dotted with stores, grist mills, furnaces, and forges.

The OLD BLUE TAVERN, NW. corner of Main and Jefferson Sts., a three-story brick building with pillared porches, was built in part by Matthew Hanna in 1785.

In the LEXINGTON PRESBYTERIAN CEMETERY, E. side of Main St., are buried Stonewall Jackson, his grave marked by a bronze statue by E.V.Valentine; approximately 400 Confederate soldiers; and two governors of Virginia, James McDowell and John Letcher.

WASHINGTON AND LEE UNIVERSITY, W. end of Henry St., spread out along the crest of a sloping greensward at the northwest edge of town. The long WASHINGTON COLLEGE group (*center unit open 9–5 weekdays for information*), red brick with three tall white porticoes in line, was completed soon after 1824.

In 1749 the institution was founded by Presbyterians as Augusta Academy some 20 miles northeast, but in 1776 it was patriotically renamed Liberty Hall. In 1780 it was moved to the vicinity of Lexington, where it functioned until the rock building burned in 1802. Chartered in 1782 as Liberty Hall Academy, in 1796 it received 200 shares of James River Canal Company stock from George Washington, a strong reason for changing the name to Washington Academy two years later. In 1813 it became Washington College. Closed during the War between the States, it reopened in 1865 on borrowed funds with General R.E.Lee as president. In 1871, soon after Lee's death, it received its present name.

Washington and Lee University, which bestows both bachelor and master degrees, in 1869 became the first college to conduct courses in journalism. Its enrollment in 1937 was nearly 1,000.

Facing the long colonnade is the LEE MEMORIAL CHAPEL (*open 3–5 daily, adm. 25¢*), a brownish-red structure of Victorian-Gothic character, built in 1867. In the galleried interior, behind the altar, is the white marble recumbent FIGURE OF LEE by E.V.Valentine. Among a large number of portraits are Washington's first, in the uniform of a British colonel, by Charles Willson Peale, and one of La Fayette, also by Peale. In the crypt below lie the remains of Lee and members of his immediate family.

Adjacent to the University is the VIRGINIA MILITARY INSTITUTE, long known as the 'West Point of the South,' but more recently as the home of 'Brother Rat.' The institute occupies nearly 40 buildings, of which the 7 largest, in gray stone and stucco-covered brick, are buttressed and crenellated. East of the large parade ground are quadrangular BARRACKS. The Institute opened in 1839 with 23 Virginia cadets and Colonel Claude Crozet (*see Tour 17b*) as president of the board of visitors. During the period of the Confederacy the Institute temporarily closed. Reopening in January 1862 as an emergency training school, it was burned by General David Hunter. This was the pioneer normal school in the State. Before its first class had been graduated, the legislature decreed that its mission should be the training of teachers. Civil engineering, however, was a part of the first curricula. In 1846 courses in industrial chemistry were introduced; and in 1860 it became a general scientific college, with agriculture (since discontinued), engineering, and fine arts its three schools of application.

The present enrollment (1939) is about 700.

In the NICHOLS ENGINEERING HALL, S. side of parade grounds, a stuccoed building in Tudor style, are the GENERAL FRANCIS H. SMITH MEMORIAL ROOMS (*open* 9–5; *Sat.* 9–1), containing a large collection of interesting military relics. In front of the building stands a fine bronze seated figure of *Virginia Mourning Her Dead*, the NEW MARKET MONUMENT by Sir Moses Ezekiel, who, as a cadet, was present at the battle.

The castellated, gray stone residence (*private*), N. side of parade ground, was occupied by Matthew Fontaine Maury (*see Tour* 10), a member of the faculty from 1868 until his death five years later.

Over the rostrum of the STONEWALL JACKSON MEMORIAL HALL, S. side of parade ground, is a very large canvas by Benjamin Clinedinst, depicting the charge of the corps of cadets at the Battle of New Market.

In Lexington are junctions with US 60 (*see Tour 8b*) and US 501 (*see Tour 11a*).

NATURAL BRIDGE (*open 7 a.m.–9:30 p.m. daily; adm.* $1), 49.2 *m.* (736 alt.), is a 90-foot bridge of stone spanning a 215-foot gorge cut by Cedar Creek. This serviceable wonder, over which the highway passes, has long been the drawing-card for an adjacent summer hotel, a rambling old structure with gossipy verandas. Surrounding cottages and trailer and recreational facilities inject a modern note. On July 5, 1775, for the paltry sum of 20 shillings, Thomas Jefferson was granted '157 acres . . . including Natural Bridge on Cedar Creek,' on which he had long cast an appreciative eye. He built a log cabin of two rooms here, one of which was reserved for visitors, installed slaves as caretakers, and then thoughtfully introduced a large book 'for sentiments,' a tome time-crammed with illustrious names.

At Natural Bridge is a junction with State 249 (*see Tour 11a*).

FOREST TAVERN (L), 51.2 *m.*, of mellow rose brick and formerly called 'Forest Oak,' has been restored and is now an inn. Part of the slave quarters stand near by. The builder of Forest Oak was the Reverend Samuel Houston (1758–1839), who fostered the State of Franklin and helped draft its constitution. He returned to Virginia, however, and in 1791 became pastor of High Bridge Presbyterian Church near by.

At 58.7 *m.* is a junction with County 611.

Right here along Purgatory Creek past the ruins (R), 0.5 *m.*, of a stone furnace, operated in 1800 and abandoned in 1862; past the stone ruins (R), 0.7 *m.*, of a mill built in 1805 and washed out by a seven-day freshet in 1870, to (R) GREY LEDGE, 1.1 *m.*, a vast stuccoed brick bulk that clings like a medieval stronghold to an eminence. Part of the house was built in 1845.

Reversing the traditional directions, the road winds through a woodland paradise to reach PURGATORY SPRINGS (R), 3.7 *m.*, bubbling up in the lee of Purgatory Mountain. Creek, springs, and mountain got their names from the reply of General Andrew Lewis when asked about his journey after return from an Indian-harassed expedition up the valley in 1750.

BUCHANAN, 60.8 *m.* (834 alt., 625 pop.), rent in two by the rushing waters of the James, is in the shade of mountains. The combination of apples, wheat, bone-buttons, the Norfolk & Western Railway, and Scotch-Irish dispositions has produced an atmosphere of industry and complacency.

To prevent the eastward trend of French settlements, the Virginia government offered huge grants in this area on condition that homesteads be established. Colonel James Patton received a grant of 120,000 acres. His company—the Wood's River Land Company—and the Loyal Land Company, with Dr. Thomas Walker of Castle Hill (*see Tour 17a*) as its agent, were the principal operators.

In 1811 this town was established and it eventually became the terminus of the James River and Kanawha Canal and of the Buchanan & Clifton Forge Railroad.

The brick and frame house diagonally opposite the Botetourt Hotel is the BIRTHPLACE OF MARY JOHNSTON (*see Literature, Richmond, and Tour 21a*), writer of historical novels. In this mountain village Miss Johnston spent the first 15 years of her life, gaining from her father's large library the foundation for her literary career.

Left from Buchanan on State 43 to the PEAKS OF OTTER 12 *m.* (*see Tour 11a*).

Across the James from the former landing place of Looney's Ferry, 62 *m.*, is the SITE OF CHERRY TREE BOTTOM, selected by Colonel James Patton for a plantation, but not settled until 1756 when John Buchanan, husband of Margaret Patton and executor of his father-in-law's estate, moved to these lands.

At 74.3 *m.* is a junction with State 294.

Right here to County 676, 0.9 *m.*; R. again to BRICK UNION CHURCH (R), 1 *m.*, a Lutheran church built about 1835 by a congregation the Reverend John George Butler of Pennsylvania had organized in 1796. The congregation clings to its German Bible and its early records.

At 77.6 *m.* is a junction with US 220 (*see Tour 21a*), which unites with US 11 for 11 *m.*

CLOVERDALE, 78.7 *m.* (500 pop.), among rounded mountains, derives its name from the estate of James Breckenridge.

MEADOW VIEW INN (R) evolved from a fortlike log dwelling with 'peepholes' to the present rambling, modern-looking structure.

Across the creek is the SITE OF CLOVERDALE FURNACE, an iron works started about 1787 by Robert Harvey, operated in 1800 by Samuel G. Adams, in 1808 by Carter Beverley, and in 1810 by John Tayloe.

HOLLINS COLLEGE (R), 80 *m.*, occupies 11 structures which stand among faculty residences on a large campus. Behind them are mountains that vary in color with each change of season. The white-trimmed, rose-red brick buildings form an open quadrangle.

The Valley Union Educational Society opened here in 1842 a coeducational institution, the Valley Union Seminary. The society had purchased the Roanoke Female Seminary, founded in 1839 at Botetourt Springs. The history of Hollins began, however, in 1846, when Charles L. Cocke took charge. The seminary, encumbered by debt, could offer no salary and even borrowed the $1,500 that Mr. Cocke and his wife had saved. In his report to the trustees in 1857 Mr. Cocke said that 'in the present state of society in our country young ladies require the same thorough and rigid mental training that is afforded to young men . . .' In 1852 boys were excluded.

In 1855 Mr. and Mrs. John Hollins of Lynchburg gave $5,000 toward a new building, and the name of the school was changed to Hollins Institute. By 1900, when the dormitories accommodated 225 girls, the accumulated debt to the Cocke family was $101,253 and the trustees prevailed upon Mr. Cocke to accept the institution in settlement. He died the following year, and the family carried on, Miss Matty L. Cocke assuming the presidency. The name of the institute was changed to Hollins College in 1911. In 1932 the college was transferred to a self-perpetuating board of trustees. It confers bachelor of arts degrees and has more than 300 students. Among the students each year are daughters, granddaughters, and frequently great-granddaughters of former Hollins 'girls.'

ROANOKE, 87.7 *m.* (904 alt., 69,206 pop.) (*see Roanoke*).

In Roanoke is a junction with US 220 (*see Tour 21a*).

ZION LUTHERAN CHURCH (L), 92.2 *m.*, is a weatherboarded log building erected in 1828 by a congregation organized soon after 1796.

At 93.6 *m.* is a junction with County 700.

Right here to the VETERANS FACILITY HOSPITAL, 1 *m.*, established in 1933 for the care of soldiers injured in the World War.

SALEM, 96.1 *m.* (1,006 alt., 4,833 pop.), quiet, lengthy, and encircled by mountains, is the seat of Roanoke County. Though actively resisting the tentacles of aggressive Roanoke, the town appears leisurely and conservative after the Victorian manner. Ancestors of all people worth knowing are remembered; afternoon tea is still in good standing; and ladies lead lives not too hurried for formal calling. Yet coal trains rattle through the industrial section, where bricks, elevators, and cigarette machines are made, and on Main Street churches vie in number with shops that cater to college students and a rural clientele.

After purchasing 31 acres of the 625-acre grant made to Andrew Lewis in 1768, James Simpson laid out Salem on 16 acres in 1802. On the main line of travel down the Valley, Salem became a stopping-place with numerous inns: The Old Time Tavern, the Bull's Eye, the Indian Queen, the Globe, and the Mermaid Tavern—the last a 'tippling place' run by James Simpson's son-in-law, Griffin Lumpkin, whose interests ran to profitable horse-races and cock-fights.

The buff brick ROANOKE COUNTY COURTHOUSE (R), standing in the center of the town, was completed in 1910 and supplanted the building erected in 1841. Roanoke County was formed from Botetourt in 1838 and later received a part of Montgomery County. The 18 original justices held their first meeting in the convivial atmosphere of Farris Tavern; and the court convened for three years in the home of the jailor.

The LUTHERAN ORPHAN HOME OF THE SOUTH, end of Virginia Ave., cares for some 100 children, and the BAPTIST ORPHANAGE OF VIRGINIA, end of Broad St., for about 200 children.

The GRAVE OF GENERAL ANDREW LEWIS, East Hill Cemetery, is marked by an obelisk erected after the body of the general was reinterred here in 1897. Settling in the vicinity before 1769, Andrew Lewis (1716–81), son of the founder of Staunton, was soon a leader. During Dunmore's War, an uprising led by the Shawnee chieftain Cornstalk in 1774, General Lewis defeated the Indians at Point Pleasant, an event that freed Virginia from hostile Indians and brought Lord Dunmore, conveniently elsewhere during the fight, into political disrepute.

The red brick buildings of ROANOKE COLLEGE, a coeducational institution formally related to the Lutheran Church, are spread out on a campus below Fort Lewis Mountain and McAfee's Knob. Established in 1842 near Staunton as the Virginia Institute, the school was incorporated in 1845 as the Virginia Collegiate Institute, and two years later moved here. Today, Roanoke College, accommodating annually some 455 students majoring, for the most part, in pre-professional courses, offers the degrees of bachelor of arts and bachelor of science.

Right from Salem on State 311 to State 114, 10.2 *m.*; R. here 0.4 *m.*, to State 123, and L. to CATAWBA SANATORIUM, 1.1 *m.*, a State institution for the treatment of tuberculosis, established in 1909. Below thickly treed Catawba Mountain, the long, open-air wooden pavilions—with 300 beds—cluster around the administration building and dining hall.

On State 311 is NEW CASTLE, 23 *m.* (1,800 alt., 259 pop.), seat of Craig County. Overshadowed by three tall peaks, this isolated little mountain town, so long satisfied with a flour mill, a weekly newspaper, and two banks, has recently acquired public utility plants and a desire for more industry.

Established as one of the series of forts Governor Dinwiddie ordered built in 1756 along the western frontier, the town in time became New Fincastle. Subsequently, when its mail was confused with that of Fincastle, the town shed its 'Fin.'

The CRAIG COUNTY COURTHOUSE, a columned brick structure with belfry and wings, replaced in 1921 one erected soon after the county was formed in 1850 from parts of Botetourt, Roanoke, Monroe (now in West Virginia), and Giles Counties. The name doubtless honors Robert Craig, instrumental in the formation of the county.

FORT LEWIS MOUNTAIN and the village of the same name, 99.9 *m.*, derive their name from a stockade fort built by Major Andrew Lewis as a place of rendezvous for the troops intended for Lewis's expedition against the Cherokees (1758–62).

Brick, two-storied FOTHERINGAY (L), 110.4 *m.*, its rectangular length and tall end chimneys silhouetted against hazy-blue Poor Mountain, was probably built by George Hancock (1754–1820) on land first owned by William Robinson, who sold the property to Joseph Kent (*see Tour* 5*c*) about 1796. Eventually acquired by Colonel Henry Edmondson, Fotheringay became the Edmondson Place.

A marble vault, glistening on the the mountain side, contains the bodies of George Hancock and his daughter Julia, who was the first wife of William Clark, the explorer. Accustomed, from this vantage point, to watch his slaves labor in the valley below, George Hancock continued the supervision even after death, according to the Negroes, who insisted that 'de Gennul, he still set up dah in a stone chair so's he can see his slaves at deh work.'

In SHAWSVILLE, 112.4 *m.* (1,650 alt., 100 pop.), once stood Fort Vause. Built in 1754 by Captain Ephraim Vause at his own expense, this stockaded house was attacked when the Indians swept through, killed or took prisoner Captain Vause's 'Wife & two Daughters, two Servants, and one Negro,' 'burned to ashes' the stockade, the 'Barn & other Buildings,' and made off with 'above eighty head of Cattle & Horses.' The Council of War held in Augusta Courthouse (Staunton) the same year, ordered the stockade rebuilt.

CHRISTIANSBURG, 123 *m.* (1,970 alt., 2,100 pop.), seat of Montgomery County, is high up on the northern rim of the Blue Ridge Plateau and clings tenaciously to the expression, 'Down to the top of the mountain.' From the town's shaded public square flows justice; from its stock yards, beef; and from its factories, overalls, lumber, and canned vegetables.

Founded in 1792 on land donated by Colonel James Craig, the town was first called Hans Meadows—the result of an early Teutonic migration—and then Christiansburg for Colonel William Christian, brother-in-law of Patrick Henry.

The MONTGOMERY COUNTY COURTHOUSE, a gray limestone building topped with a gilded eagle, preserves the records of two counties: Montgomery, which it now serves, and extinct Fincastle. Montgomery County was named for General Richard Montgomery, who was killed at the Siege of Quebec in 1775.

The CHRISTIANSBURG INDUSTRIAL INSTITUTE, at the northern edge of the town, is a Negro high school supported jointly by Montgomery County and the Friends' Freeman's Association of Philadelphia. The institute is an outgrowth of a primary school established in 1866 by Charles S. Schaeffer, who settled in Christiansburg after the war and organized the first Negro Baptist church.

1. Right from Christiansburg on State 8 (*see Tour 5B*).

2. Left from Christiansburg on State 8 across Pilot Mountain and Little River to FLOYD, 21.6 *m.* (2,431 alt., 500 pop.), first called Jacksonville, the seat of mountainous Floyd County. A thin fringe of residences surrounds two business blocks that have captured none of the aggressive hum of the one town industry, a shirt factory.

In Floyd was born Robley Dunglison Evans (1846–1912), commander of the *USS Iowa* at the Battle of Santiago Harbor, 1898, who, after his appointment as rear admiral in 1901, commanded both the Asiatic (1902) and Atlantic Fleets (1905–08).

The brick FLOYD COUNTY COURTHOUSE was erected in 1845, replacing a log cabin that housed the first meeting of the court soon after the formation of Floyd from Montgomery County in 1831. Named for John Floyd, governor of Virginia from 1830 to 1834, the county was later increased in size by an addition from Franklin County.

In the HILL CEMETERY, at the western edge of the village, are the GRAVES OF DANIEL HENRY, a brother of Patrick Henry, and of ANNIE MARIA SMITH (1817–33), a New England school teacher who lived for a while in Richmond, and then taught in western Virginia. Her friendship with Edgar Allan Poe found permanent expression in his poem *For Annie*.

On the crest of a sloping lawn east of the courthouse is the PHLEGAR HOUSE, built of logs in 1822 by Abram Phlegar but now covered with clapboards.

RADFORD, 132.7 *m.* (1,800 alt., 6,227 pop.), flung out on the brink of New River's deep gorge, hides behind its corporate mask two separate units, Radford and East Radford, each with its own business center. Lumber yards, iron foundries, railroad repair shops, and education are the town's principal industries.

Successor to the village of Lovely Mount, Central Depot, equidistant from Lynchburg and Bristol, grew up after the Virginia & Tennessee Railroad established machine shops here in 1856. In the wake of the New Division of the Norfolk & Western Railway, opened in 1883, came a stove foundry, brick kilns, and iron furnace. Two years later the little town was incorporated and named for the man who had formerly owned the property, Dr. John Bane Radford.

On RADFORD STATE TEACHERS COLLEGE campus, a natural terrace overlooking the New River, are 10 large brick buildings that face each other across a walk-threaded sward. Exhibits in the museum, a log house built about 1776 on Meadow Creek and moved here, tell the story of southwestern Virginia's domestic past.

Since its opening in 1913, the college has increased steadily in size. Since 1935 it has offered the degrees of bachelor of arts and bachelor of science, and a two-year normal course. The winter and summer quarter enrollment for the 1937–38 session was 895 students.

ARNHEIM, a brick house on the high, school grounds, was the home of Dr. John Bane Radford, whose widow, née Harriet Kinnerly, became the second wife of William Clark, the explorer.

Left along the river on the main street of Radford, which becomes County 605, to a junction with County 611, 3.8 *m.*; R. here to INGLES FERRY, 4.1 *m.* (*toll* 25¢), where a flat boat attached to a cable is carried across the New River by the eddying current. On the east side, where William and Mary Draper Ingles settled after the Draper's Meadow Massacre (*see Tour* 5*B*), a threepence ferry was established in 1762.

From DUBLIN, 140.8 *m.* (500 pop.), large numbers of cattle are shipped.

Left from Dublin on State 100 through rich grasslands to County 611, 2.1 *m.*; L. here 2.4 *m.* to DUNKARD'S BOTTOM MONUMENT (R), a chimney-shaped memorial constructed from the chimney rock of a house built in 1771 by Colonel William Christian on the site of a settlement established about 1745 by a group of dissatisfied Dunkards that strayed south from Ephrata in Pennsylvania.

'The Duncards are an odd set of people,' explained Dr. Thomas Walker in 1750, 'who make it a matter of religion not to shave their Beards, ly on beds, or eat Flesh, though at present, in the last they transgress, being constrained to it, as they say, by want of sufficiency of Grain and Roots, they having not long been seated here. I doubt the plenty & deliciousness of the Venison & Turkeys has contributed not a little to this.'

On State 100 is NEWBERN, 2.9 *m.* (217 pop.), seat of Pulaski County from 1839 to 1893.

PULASKI, 148.9 *m.* (1,900 alt., 7,168 pop.), the present seat of Pulaski County, bustles with industry when farmers come in from the valleys. Into this town, spread out in a fertile pocket of the Alleghenies, pour grain, produce, iron, zinc, lumber, and coal.

Coal discovered to the northwest in 1877 suddenly rocketed this railroad flag stop, Martin's Tank, into industrial importance and a more dignified name, Martin's Station. Cheap fuel soon lured zinc and iron furnaces, nuclei for the town's subsequent growth. Railroad repair shops, textile factories, and lumber mills are the mainstays of its present commercial vigor.

The PULASKI COUNTY COURTHOUSE, of Peak Creek sandstone, was built after the county seat was brought here in 1893 from Newbern. The county was formed in 1839 from parts of Montgomery and Wythe Counties and named for Count Casimir Pulaski (*c.*1748–79), the Pole who fought for the American cause.

On the side of Draper's Mountain and overlooking a vast expanse of shimmering valley is PULASKI WAYSIDE PARK (*picnicking facilities*), 151.6 *m.*

At 154.1 *m.* is a junction with State 101.

Left on this road to State 100, 4.3 *m.*; R. here to RED HORSE TAVERN (L), 5.9 *m.*, a frame house that incorporates several rooms of an inn built about 1790 and sold in 1813 to Thomas Galbreth, husband of Katherine Kissecher, who feasted Washington and his cabinet in York, Pa., and prepared the wedding banquet for Jerome Bonaparte and Elizabeth Patterson in 1804. In 1813, armed with an early copy of the Declaration of Independence presented to her by Washington, a teapot whose contents had warmed the cockles of many a distinguished heart, an enviable culinary reputation, and a husband, she came to Southwest Virginia where her talents mellowed at the Sign of the Red Horse.

The SITE OF FORT CHISWELL (L), 163.4 *m.*, in the lee of Mays Mountain, is marked by a pyramid of boulders. Built in the fall of 1760 under the direction of William Byrd III, the fort was named for John Chiswell, owner of the lead mines near by (*see Tour 7c*). From 1778 until 1789 this was the seat of Montgomery County.

At 164.2 *m.* is a junction with US 52 (*see Tour 7c*) and State 121.

Right on State 121 to the SITE OF ANCHOR AND HOPE ACADEMY (L), 1.1 *m.*, where the Reverend Thomas E. Birch conducted a school of oratory and preached to congregations assembled from homes near by.

MAX MEADOWS, 2 *m.*, in rich lowlands, was once called the 'Valley of Contention and Strife' because of petty feuds among settlers. The MANSION HOUSE (R) is a two-storied log building with stone end chimneys. Built by Hugh McGavock, it was a mansion only in comparison with the cabins round about.

Left from Max Meadows on County 610, 0.5 *m.* to the HUGH MCGAVOCK HOUSE (L), a clapboarded structure that incorporates a late eighteenth-century log house that James McGavock willed in 1800 'unto my Sun Hugh and his heirs.'

Section c. JUNCTION US 52 to TENNESSEE LINE; 77.6 m. US 11.

This undulating southern section of US 11 pierces the valley between blue mountain walls. In the distance stand rounded knobs, with grass cropped close by cattle and sheep that are eventually shipped, along with farm produce, grain, and ores, through the valley towns.

US 11 continues south from the junction with US 52, 0 *m.* to a junction at 2.9 *m.* with a dirt road.

Right here through a gate to KENTON, 2.1 *m.*, a two-story, brick house overlooking wide lowlands. At the foot of a hill remains one of the many buildings that once surrounded the house built by Joseph Kent, who married Margaret McGavock in 1787 and seven years later, after the sale of Fotheringay, moved here. The Kenton land had been the frontier homestead of an uncle of John C. Calhoun, Ezekiel Calhoun, who was killed in an Indian raid.

WYTHEVILLE, 8.1 *m.* (2,350 alt., 3,327 pop.), seat of Wythe County, lies on a high plateau. Wide Main Street, a dressed-up section of the Wilderness Road, has pushed sidewalks back under the high porches of century-old houses. Jurisprudence, the sale of livestock, and flour, lumber, and textile mills give a commercial solidity to the town.

First called Abbeville, honoring the South Carolina birthplace of Jesse Evans, the settlement was legally established in 1792 as Evansham, a name that clung until its incorporation in 1839.

Being near the lead mines and the only salt works in the South, Wytheville was in a constant state of turmoil as the contending forces intermittently poured through. In July 1863 a Union cavalry detachment descended on the town intending to tear up the railroad, but was routed by the home guards forewarned by Mary Tynes (*see Tour* 15).

Two Virginia governors were born here: Henry Carter Stuart (1855–1933), governor from 1914 to 1918, and Elbert Lee Trinkle (1876–1939), governor from 1922 to 1926. Henry Carter Stuart's administration was characterized by efforts to promote agriculture and to raise the living standards in rural Virginia. Deeply interested in education and social problems, E.Lee Trinkle emphasized human welfare and did much to eradicate for a time sectionalism in Virginia.

In the WYTHE COUNTY COURTHOUSE, a porticoed structure of gray brick built in 1900, meet not only the county court but, once a year, the state court of appeals. In this courthouse is on display a bell cast in Germany, seized at the Battle of Lake Erie (1813), and presented to the county for use in an earlier courthouse. Wythe County was formed in 1789 from Montgomery County and named for George Wythe (*see Williamsburg*).

VILLA MARIA ACADEMY, a preparatory school for girls supervised by the Sisters of the Visitation, has a campus overlooking the town. This school, founded at Abingdon in 1867 and chartered a decade later, was moved here in 1902.

SAINT MARY'S ROMAN CATHOLIC CHURCH, a long, rectangular building with a wide white-columned portico, was built in 1842–43.

Right from Wytheville on US 21 (US 52) to ST.JOHN'S EVANGELICAL LUTHERAN CHURCH, 1 *m.*, a rectangular, frame building erected in 1851 by the oldest congregation in this region.

BLAND, 22.2 *m.* (250 pop.), is the seat of Bland County. Called Seddon when incorporated in 1872, this isolated town is the legal and business center of a remote agricultural district.

The BLAND COUNTY COURTHOUSE is a two-story, red brick building with a disproportionate white belfry.

In 1861 Bland County was formed from parts of Wythe, Tazewell, and Giles Counties and was named for Richard Bland (1710–76), called by Jefferson 'the wisest man south of the James River.' He was a delegate to the General Congress in Philadelphia (1774) and a political pamphleteer.

US 21 (US 52) crosses the West Virginia Line (*see West Virginia Guide*) at the crest of East River Mountain, 42.3 *m.*, three miles east of Bluefield (*see Tour* 15).

MARION, 34.2 *m.* (2,124 alt., 4,156 pop.), seat of Smyth County, has a Main Street liberally sprinkled with new façades and makes furniture, flour, leather, and brick. This aggressive county mart which has a private school, an asylum, and two newspapers, supposedly at political loggerheads but both edited by Robert Anderson, son of Sherwood Anderson, was founded in 1831 and named for the 'Swamp Fox' of South Carolina.

The Smyth County Courthouse, a massive stone building heavily embellished, is a twentieth-century creation. Smyth County, formed from parts of Wythe and Washington Counties in 1832, was named for Alexander Smyth (1765–1830), lawyer, soldier, and congressman.

Marion College (Junior), founded in 1873 by the Lutheran Synod of Southwestern Virginia and chartered the following year as the Marion Female College, has a student body of about 200.

Southwestern State Hospital, established in 1887, cares for the mentally ill from this section, and the criminal-insane from the entire State. With a farm, garden, and dairy, this institution has a capacity of about 1,350 patients.

In Marion are junctions with State 88 (*see Tour 7c*).

Right from Marion on State 88 to HUNGRY MOTHER STATE PARK, 3 *m.* (*open May 15 to Nov. 1, adm.* 10¢, *for overnight campsites* 25¢, *children under* 10 *free; rowboats* 25¢ *an hr.*, $1.25 *a day; overnight accommodations* $2.50 *a person; cabins equipped with electric lights, stoves, and water heaters, payment by coin meters;* $15 *a week for* 2 *persons*, $20 *for* 3 *or* 4 *persons*, $5 *for each additional person; reservations made at Virginia Conservation Commission, Richmond*), a large recreational area lying at the foot of Walker Mountain. Bathing from the sand beach of the lake, which twists among high, forested mountains, is no less popular than fishing in the water well-stocked with perch and bass. Bridle and foot paths lace through the knobs.

Tradition is that a woman and her baby, captured by raiding Shawnees and held prisoner, escaped and wandered into this region. Reaching the peak now known as Molly's Knob, she collapsed, while the child waded down the shallow creek to a group of houses, crying, 'Hungry–Mother, Hungry–Mother.'

On the small hill (R), 42.1 *m.*, is the Site of Aspenvale, home of General William Campbell (1745–81), who while on military duty in Williamsburg in 1776–77 married the sister of Governor Patrick Henry, whom he brought here. Together with Walter Crockett, he took the law in his own hands during the Revolution and ordered a number of British agents hanged—the unorthodox method of meting out justice later adopted by Colonel Charles Lynch (*see Tour 7c*).

CHILHOWIE, 44.5 *m.* (712 pop.), ships quantities of apples and cabbages. This was Central Settlement on Holston, established by Colonel James Patton.

Atop the steep hill (R) stands the Town House, a dilapidated weatherboarded building, which includes a log house believed to have been built by Colonel James Patton about 1748. The house became a tavern and popular meeting place.

Left from Chilhowie on State 79 to US 58, 3.7 *m.*; R. here to County 600, 3.8 *m.*; L. on County 600 to Konnarock Training School, 12.8 *m.*, a lengthy shingle-covered building, erected in 1925, among rounded hills overshadowed by White Top Mountain. Started by the United Lutheran Church in 1923, this school for mountain children gives elementary and grammar school work with emphasis on cooking, sewing, child care, and home making. For a week during the summer a doctor's helpers institute is conducted here to train local women in practical nursing and midwifery.

Right 2 *m.* from Konnarock Training School on County 603 to Iron Mountain Lutheran School, founded in 1931 by the Brotherhood of the United Lutheran Church for training mountain boys in agriculture. In addition to practical work on the 425-acre farm, the boys are trained in manual arts and crafts.

Above the Konnarock School, County 600 climbs wooded slopes to the summit of WHITE TOP MOUNTAIN, 17.8 *m.* (5,520 alt.), which affords a view of lofty and inaccessible MOUNT ROGERS (5,719 alt.), the highest peak in Virginia. A 500-acre prairie slithers across the crest of the mountain, giving the appearance, from a distance, of a glacier. Surrounding this white swathe are flora not found at lower altitudes and an evergreen locally called lashorn.

For two days in August every year the White Top Music Festival (*see Music*) is held on the plateau where several rustic cabins have been built.

A stone pyramid marks the entrance (L), 47.4 *m.*, to modernized FORT KILMACKRONAN, a stuccoed stone house with a white portico. Construction of the first unit was begun in 1776.

At 50.4 *m.* is a junction with State 81.

Right here to PLASTERCO, 8 *m.*, a community around the lime-dusted plant of the United States Gypsum Company.

The mineral, lying here at the base of Pine and Little Brushy Mountains, occurs in irregularly shaped masses.

The town of SALTVILLE, 9 *m.* (1,739 alt., 2,975 pop.), gazing up at the tall, black chimneys of the salt works that belch smoke and fumes, has been created through the commercial development of salt deposits that lie below large, marshy flats.

The MATHIESON ALKALI WORKS has several shafts, equipped with pumps, to varying depths, a few to 2,000 feet. Some 600 tons of limestone are used daily to change the sodium chloride into commercial products.

The development of the property, called Buffalo Lick, was begun by General William Russell, who left Aspenvale and settled here in 1788. More than 200,000 bushels of salt were being produced here annually in the early part of the nineteenth century. During the War between the States, the salt works, the main source of supply for the entire Confederacy, were heavily guarded. It was not until December 1864 that Saltville was captured and the salt works were destroyed.

ELIZABETH CEMETERY was the graveyard of Elizabeth Church established by Elizabeth Henry Campbell Russell, whose character resembled that of her brother, Patrick Henry. 'Madam Russell' was one of the first converts to Methodism in the Holston Valley and an opponent of slavery. Freeing the Negroes that had been left to her, she wrote: 'Whereas by the wrong of man it hath been the unfortunate lot of the following Negroes to be slaves for life . . ., and whereas, believing the same to have come into my possession by the direction of Providence, and conceiving from the clearest conviction of my conscience . . . that it is both sinful and unjust, as they are by nature equally free as myself, to continue them in slavery, I do, therefore, by these presents . . ., make free the said Negroes.'

At 53.6 *m.* is a junction with County 737.

Right here to EMORY AND HENRY COLLEGE (R), 1.2 *m.*, founded by the Methodist Church. The red brick buildings are on a sloping campus covered with trees and bluegrass.

Named for Bishop John Emory (1789–1836) and for either Patrick Henry or his sister, Elizabeth, the college opened in April 1838 as a manual labor school. During the war its buildings were used as a Confederate hospital. In 1922 the institution was made coeducational. It grants art and science degrees and has about 470 students.

ABINGDON, 62.6 *m.* (2,057 alt., 2,677 pop.), seat of Washington County, radiates from shady Courthouse Square. Old houses, chiefly of brick, wall in undulating Main Street, which is crowded on Saturday with townspeople, 'Knobites' in for the day, Negroes from the King's Mountain quarter, and, in summer, with slack-clad actors, set designers, and other people attached to the experimental theater. Chemical factories, wagon works, lumber mills, a milk condensory, and a cigar factory are the chief support of the town, though burley tobacco is also shipped in quantities.

Wolf Hills was the name given to the settlement made between 1765 and 1770 on land granted to Dr. Thomas Walker in 1752. The small fort built here was enlarged in 1776 to afford refuge for settlers terrified by the Cherokee uprising. Black's Fort was attacked several times during the year but survived and became the center of 120 acres of land donated for a county seat. In 1778 the village was established as Abingdon, and by 1793 it had become distributing center for all the mail sent to southwest Virginia.

On December 14, 1864, some 10,000 Federal troops, under General George Stoneman, burned the depot, jail, barracks, and wagon-shops—all storehouses for Confederate supplies. The following day, a straggler from the Federal army—a former resident of Abingdon—set fire to the remaining buildings on Main Street.

Abingdon was the home of John Campbell, Secretary of the Treasury (1829–39); the Confederate general, Joseph E. Johnston; George W. Hopkins (1804–61), congressman and chargé d'affaires to Portugal; and three Virginia governors, Wyndham Robertson (1836–37), David Campbell (1837–41), and John Buchanan Floyd (1849–52).

The columned, brick WASHINGTON COUNTY COURTHOUSE is the sixth to serve the county, which was formed in 1776 from vast Fincastle County.

SINKING SPRINGS CEMETERY, strewn with tombstones dating from 1776, is adjacent to the site of Sinking Springs Church, 'the mother church of the Appalachies,' built by a Presbyterian congregation organized in 1772.

MARTHA WASHINGTON INN is a large, two-story, brick building erected in 1830–32 by Brigadier General Francis Preston and his wife, Sarah Campbell Preston. Of the ten Preston children, William C. became a senator from South Carolina and minister to Italy; John S., a Confederate general; and three daughters, the wives of governors—John B. Floyd and James McDowell of Virginia, and Wade Hampton of South Carolina. Enlarged and remodeled, the house was occupied from 1858 to 1932 by Martha Washington College, a Methodist school for girls.

THE BARTER COLONY occupies the three brick buildings formerly used by the Stonewall Jackson Institute, a Presbyterian girls' school founded in 1869 and closed in 1932. Around an inn, theater, work-shop, and dormitory revolves the life of the Barter Theater, established in 1933 by Robert and Helen Fritch Porterfield. Edible commodities, from calves to huckleberries, are accepted on payment for tickets.

BRISTOL, 77.6 *m.* (1,695 alt., 8,845 pop.), with crowded, narrow streets, is separated from Bristol, Tennessee (12,000 pop.), only by the invisible State line that bisects State Street. Although welded physically, the two cities, studded with 35 churches, are separate municipal units, each with its city government, post office, school system, and water supply. Though a mart for produce from fertile lands near by, Bristol, Virginia, derives its brisk tempo from the production of iron, lumber, textiles, paper, and leather.

Surveyed in 1749 by John Buchanan, the Sapling Grove tract, part of James Patton's 120,000-acre grant, became after the French and Indian War the property of Colonel Evan Shelby and Isaac Baker,Sr. of Maryland. In 1771 they built their homes—Colonel Shelby on the present Tennessee section and Isaac Baker,Sr., on that which now lies in Virginia. When news was bruited about in 1850 that the State line would be the terminus of the Virginia and Tennessee Railroad, Colonel Samuel Goodson, who then owned the Baker area, envisioned the town of Goodsonville on his property, had it surveyed, and sold all the lots. When the railroad was completed in 1856, the flourishing town was incorporated as Goodson, a name that was changed to Bristol when it received a city charter in 1890.

The question of the long-disputed Virginia-North Carolina (and later Tennessee) boundary line—first run by Colonel William Byrd in 1728, continued in 1749 by Joshua Fry and Peter Jefferson, and momentarily settled by a compromise in 1803—flared up afresh in 1897 and again in 1900 when commissioners were appointed to re-establish the boundary between White Top Mountain and Cumberland Gap. Because of this long dispute, finally settled in 1903 by the U.S. Supreme Court's decision sustaining the boundary established in 1803, the site has been under the jurisdiction of North Carolina (1779), the State of Franklin (1785–89), the Federal Government (1789) in the territory south of the Ohio River, Tennessee (1796), and Virginia.

The porticoed brick buildings of SULLINS COLLEGE, a nonsectarian girls' preparatory school and junior college, overlook Bristol from Virginia Park, which contains Lake Sycamore. During July and August the school maintains Camp Sequoya for girls. The school was founded in 1870 by the Reverend David Sullins. After a fire in 1915, the college erected the present buildings, which accommodate 390 students and a faculty of 37 (1937–38).

VIRGINIA INTERMONT COLLEGE, a Baptist preparatory school and junior college for girls, is housed in a long series of connected buildings of varying architectural design shaded by a grove of oaks through which the wall of blue mountains looms in the distance. Founded at Glade Spring in 1884 as the Southwest Virginia Institute, the school was moved to Bristol in 1910. Two years later the name was changed. The student body numbers about 400.

In Bristol are junctions with US 11E, US 11W, and US 421 (*see Tennessee Guide*).

Tour 5A

Winchester—Front Royal—Luray—Waynesboro—Junction with US 11; 119.6 *m.* State 3–State 12.

Asphalt-paved roadbed throughout.
Between Front Royal and Waynesboro route paralleled by Norfolk & Western Ry.
All types of accommodations.

State 3–12, an alternate to US 11, passes through the eastern Shenandoah Valley. Winding beside rivers and streams, always in view of the Blue Ridge Mountains, it offers scenery far more beautiful than that of the arterial highways. Because the limestone soil creates rich pastures and produces wheat and corn, this section is thickly settled. Apple trees in serried ranks alternate with the open fields. There are many caverns which attract visitors in all seasons.

State 3 branches south from US 11 at Millwood Ave. and Loudoun St. in WINCHESTER, 0 *m.*, in union with US 50 (*see Tour* 12) to a point at 1.1 *m.*

A low earthworks on a hilltop (L), 4.8 *m.*, was constructed as part of the defenses of Winchester in the War between the States.

The highway crosses Opequon Creek (pronounced o-peck-on) at PARKINS' MILL, 5 *m.*, an important facility of frontier days.

Double Toll Gate, 8.7 *m.*, at a junction with State 277, was on an earlier turnpike.

Left on State 277 to WHITEPOST, 1.9 *m.*, a hamlet. Its outstanding feature is a tall white post surmounted by an old-fashioned lantern that duplicates one erected by Lord Fairfax to mark the route to his estate.

Right from Whitepost 1.2 *m.* on State 12 to Greenway Court (R), formerly the wilderness manor of Thomas Lord Fairfax, master of the 5,000,000-acre proprietary of the Northern Neck. Only the Land Office remains of the structures erected by Fairfax in 1748. This little house, two low stories of gray stone, stands close to the highway at the edge of stony fields. Here quit rents were collected and here George Washington, the youthful surveyor for Fairfax, is said to have kept his instruments. Lord Fairfax inherited the Northern Neck grant from his mother, a daughter of Thomas, Lord Culpeper. In 1669, Charles II had granted to several loyal friends all the land between the Rappahannock and the Potomac Rivers. In 1673 Lord Culpeper bought out the grantees and became sole proprietor.

Fairfax's life here was not happy. He had come to Virginia thoroughly embittered because his fiancée had married another man; he would invite no women to his lavish parties. Quit rents were not always willingly paid, and he was forever occupied with lawsuits over boundaries. Like many other landed Virginians he was a Tory. When the news of Cornwallis's surrender came, the old man turned in his bed to remark that it was time for him to die.

CEDARVILLE, 15 *m.*, a hamlet, stretches its gray houses and gray stone fences along a gray highway. A log-and-stone building on the top of a slight rise (R) was the HOME OF ROBERT MCKAY, a Quaker who received a large grant here on condition that he settle 100 families on the land in two years. He complied with the provision in 1737.

RIVERTON, 17.7 *m.* (500 pop.), against rocky hills, is on a high triangle formed by the north and south forks of the Shenandoah River. Important in the days of river transportation, it waned after 1854 when the railroad down the Valley was built.

At 18.6 *m.* the highway passes near the spot where two of Mosby's guerillas were hanged Sept. 22, 1864, by order of General George A. Custer. Five others were shot in Front Royal the same day. Later Mosby retaliated by capturing and executing an equal number of Custer's men.

FRONT ROYAL, 19.7 *m.* (508 alt., 2,424 pop.), seat of Warren County, with many houses of rough-hewn stone, has retained much of its nineteenth-century flavor despite a textile-mill boom and the flood of automobiles bound for the Skyline Drive. The town also does wood-working, canning and preserving, and distilling.

Front Royal, chartered in 1788, was at first a frontier village, called 'Hell Town,' on the packhorse road to the north. Two legends account for the name Front Royal. According to one, British officers during the Revolution, when drilling their men near a large oak tree, gave the command, 'Front the Royal Oak' and the sentence was shortened to 'Front Royal.' According to another story, the sentry's command 'Front' and the pass word 'Royal' were linked by common usage.

Front Royal was one of the bases from which the pretty Confederate spy Belle Boyd worked most effectively. In 1862 when a Federal regiment occupied Front Royal, she invited General Nathaniel P. Banks and his officers to a ball. While the weary officers slept after the festivities, according to the story, she made a daring horseback ride to give Jackson valuable information she had garnered. The next morning, May 23, 1862, the Confederates attacked the Union force here and captured 750 of the 1,000 men. In the afternoon General Jackson arrived.

The WARREN COUNTY COURTHOUSE, a large gray stone building erected in 1936, is on the site of the first one built in 1837, a year after Warren County was formed from parts of Shenandoah and Frederick counties and named for General Joseph Warren, a Revolutionary officer killed at Bunker Hill.

The AMERICAN VISCOSE CORPORATION PLANT (*visited by arrangement*), several large brick factory structures opened in 1939 at the western outskirts, is one of the chief artificial silk mills operated by Courtaulds, Ltd. (*see Roanoke*).

RANDOLPH-MACON ACADEMY, a unit of the Randolph-Macon System (*see Tour 1b*), is a military preparatory school for boys, housed principally in one large brick building on a wooded hill. The school, established here in 1892 by the Methodist trustees of Randolph-Macon College, has more than 200 students.

In Front Royal are junctions with State 55 (*see Tour 4A*), the Skyline Drive (*see Tour 4A*), and State 12.

South of Front Royal, State 12 winds close beside the Shenandoah River.

RILEYVILLE, 35.8 *m.* (350 pop.), on the high banks of the twisting stream, is a gathering place for gregarious countryfolk.

LURAY, 43.9 *m.* (835 alt., 1,459 pop.) (*see Tour* 22), is at a junction with US 211 (*see Tour* 22).

At 44.7 *m.* is a junction with County 642.

Left here to State 266, 1.6 *m.*, which runs straight ahead to IDA VALLEY HOMESTEADS, 6.6 *m.*, a resettlement project for mountaineers evacuated after the creation of Shenandoah National Park. About 20 small frame houses have been erected on farms of from 8 to 12 acres.

At 54.5 *m.* is a junction with County 616.

Right here to RIVERDALE FARM (L), 1.8 *m.*, called Fort Long. This land, which Philip Long settled before 1729, was a part of the Massanutten Grant.

Two small stone houses behind a mid-nineteenth-century brick farmhouse were homes of pioneers. From one of these an underground passage, now partly caved in, leads to a fort beneath a corn crib. This cellar fort is ingeniously built of rough limestone blocks. The arched ceiling is an interesting example of pioneer engineering. Loop holes extend upward at an angle of 45 degrees. From the cellar of the lower cottage a passage, restored and lighted, leads to a well.

NEWPORT, 57.4 *m.*, now a group of houses among craggy foothills, was once a bristling port.

SHENANDOAH, 64.5 *m.* (1,980 pop.), a railroad town on steep slopes of Massanutten foothills, grew up around the Shenandoah Iron Works, which shipped ore down the river on flat boats.

In BEAR LITHIA SPRINGS (R), 67.3 *m.*, once a popular resort around waters that were bottled and sold widely, are several old buildings, shabby reminders of another day. The springs are on land once owned by Jacob Bear.

The MILLER HOMESTEAD (R), 68.3 *m.*, is a large, sprawling frame farmhouse that incorporates a log house built about 1768 by Adam Miller, father-in-law of Jacob Bear.

ELKTON, 69.9 *m.* (971 alt., 965 pop.) (*see Tour* 9), is at a junction with US 33 (*see Tour* 9), with which State 12 unites for 8.5 miles (*see Tour* 9).

At 81.7 *m.* is a junction with County 659.

Left here to BOGOTA (L), 2.8 *m.*, built about 1847 by Jacob Strayer. Brick walls, rising above stone foundations, have three gabled ends with chimneys. Near by had been the home of Gabriel Jones, king's attorney, 'the man with the celestial name and the very uncelestial temper.' There is a story that a judge reprimanded another attorney for 'making Mr. Jones swear so.'

LYNNWOOD (R), 3.6 *m.*, a brick house built in 1813, incorporates a log house of 1751 that was the home of Thomas Lewis, a son of the pioneer John Lewis (*see Tour 5a*).

Around LEWISTON CHURCH, 4.2 *m.*, a narrow frame building with a belfry, was fought the Battle of Port Republic in which General Jackson on June 9, 1862, defeated the forces of General James Shields. This enabled Jackson to proceed eastward to help check McClellan before Richmond.

PORT REPUBLIC, 85 *m.* (200 pop.), at the head of the south fork of the Shenandoah River, flourished in the days of water transportation, and was notorious for the frequent fights among its river men, who used fists, thumbs, feet, and skulls as weapons.

GROTTOES, 87.4 *m.* (534 pop.), took its name from limestone caverns near by.

At 88.1 *m.* is a junction with County 664.

Left on County 664 to GRAND CAVERNS, 0.5 *m.* (*open 7 a.m. to 9 p.m., adm.* $1). Bernard Weyer discovered the passages in 1804 while looking for a groundhog trap.

WAYNESBORO, 104.3 *m.* (1,311 alt., 6,226 pop.) (*see Tour 17b*), is at a junction with US 250 (*see Tour 17b*).

STUART'S DRAFT, 112.9 *m.*, spreads over rolling lands to the northwest of acres that Colonel James Patton, monarch of Southwest Virginia, bought from William Beverley (*see Staunton*) in 1736 and 1740. Patton's house, Spring Hill, stood about two miles from the hamlet. Patton, a sea captain, transported colonists to Virginia and carried products from the New World to England. His sister Elizabeth, with her husband, John Preston, and several children, settled near Stuart's Draft in 1740.

At 119.6 *m.* is a junction with US 11 (*see Tour 5b*), at a point 10.8 miles south of Staunton.

Tour 5B

Christiansburg—Blacksburg—Pearisburg—Narrows—Rich Creek; 42 *m.* State 8.

Asphalt-paved roadbed throughout.
Virginian Ry. and Norfolk & Western Ry. parallel route.
Accommodations in Blacksburg and wayside tourist homes and camps.

After passing along a plateau, then through the rugged beauty of several mountain ridges, this route follows the valley of the rapid New River northwest to West Virginia.

State 8 branches north from a junction with US 11 (*see Tour 5b*) in CHRISTIANSBURG, 0 *m.* (1,970 alt., 2,100 pop.) (*see Tour 5b*).

BLACKSBURG, 6.9 *m.* (2,135 alt., 1,406 pop.), is dominated by Virginia Polytechnic Institute. Faculty houses stand between hotels and boarding houses along shaded streets, and robust youths in mufti and uniform crowd the movie houses and shops. The college and town are on lands once owned by Colonel James Patton. Homesteads were surveyed and sold to a handful of pioneers who formed a settlement here—Draper's Meadows—in 1745. On Sunday July 8, 1755, a band of Shawnee, in an attempt to repossess their lands, swooped down on the whites, killed four, took six prisoners, and destroyed the homes. Colonel James Patton, visiting here, cut down two Indians with his broadsword but was shot by a savage. William Ingles and John Draper escaped, but their wives and children were captured and taken to the Shawnee town on the Scioto River. After several months of captivity Mrs. Ingles, née Mary Draper, escaped at Big Bone Lick (now in Kentucky). Armed with a tomahawk and accompanied by an old Dutch woman, she followed streams east, finally reaching the home of Adam Harmon just west of Draper's Meadow. Mrs. John Draper, adopted by the family of an Indian chief, remained in captivity until 1761, when she was ransomed.

The VIRGINIA POLYTECHNIC INSTITUTE, an agricultural and mechanical college supported mainly by public funds, operates nine experiment stations and has a broad extension program. Part of the 32 buildings on a large campus are around an oval drill field. These structures, designed in neo-Gothic style and built of limestone, contrast sharply with the brick buildings, chiefly barracks and recreational centers, on the northeastern part of the campus. On the opposite side of the drill field is the stadium, beyond which lie the riding ring, the numerous barns and silos, green houses, and an amphitheater. During the winter session about 1,200 students become cadets and are instructed in military science and tactics by officers of the regular army. Some 800 other students, among whom are about 100 women, are in residence. Undergraduate and graduate courses are given, leading to both bachelor and master degrees in science, in agriculture, engineering, applied sciences, and business administration. A summer quarter, popular with Virginia public school teachers who pay no tuition, combines courses in academic subjects with a large number of technical courses. Informational bulletins on agriculture, industry, and rural sociology, prepared by the college, are widely disseminated throughout the State. The engineering experiment station conducts industrial investigations. Four branch schools in State industrial centers offer the first two years of the engineering curricula. The Virginia Agricultural Extension Service, with 500 acres of land here, carries on experimental work in horticulture, animal husbandry, dairying, plant pathology and bacteriology, agricultural chemistry and economics, wildlife conservation, and farm and household engineering. Through bulletins, correspondence, and farm and home demonstration agents the institution assists the rural population of the State.

Virginia Polytechnic Institute is a land-grant college established in 1872 under the provisions of the Morrill Act. Preston and Olin Institute, a Methodist school founded in 1854, became the nucleus of what was at first called the Virginia Agriculture and Mechanical College. In 1888 the agricultural experiment station became a department of the institution.

SMITHFIELD, on the west side of the campus, is an L-shaped, story-and-a-half frame house built between 1772 and 1774 by Colonel William Preston (1729–83). A small transom tops the double-doored entrance of the façade that is further relieved by dormers. In the basement is a huge fireplace flanked by generously proportioned ovens. The hall contains a stairway in Chinese Chippendale design. Three walls of the adjacent living room have a dado; the fourth—the chimney end—is paneled to the ceiling. At Smithfield was born James Patton Preston (1774–1843), governor of Virginia (1816–19), who inherited the estate from his father and left it to his three sons, two of whom built SOLITUDE and WHITEHORN, now on the campus. Their sister Letitia became the wife of John Floyd, governor of Virginia (1830–34), and mother of John Buchanan Floyd, governor of Virginia (1849–52), who was born at Smithfield.

Southeast of Smithfield is the Preston burial ground.

West of Blacksburg, State 8 crosses Brush and Gap Mountains affording views of the beautiful Alleghenies.

At 17.9 *m.* is a junction with State 112.

Right here up the steep side of Salt Pond Mountain to MOUNTAIN LAKE (*hotel accommodations*), 7 *m.* (3,500 alt.), a deep body of water (*bass, rainbow trout*) so clear that trunks of trees are visible far beneath the surface, an oval mirror reflecting rounded hills covered with hemlock, laurel, and azaleas.

PEARISBURG, 33 *m.* (688 pop.), seat of Giles County, is shadowed by a tall peak, Angel's Rest. A tannery, a lumber mill, and a chick hatchery are the town's industrial establishments.

In 1782, Captain George Pearis established a ferry here across New River. Later Captain Pearis provided land, together with timber and stone necessary to erect public buildings, as a seat for the court, and the town of Pearisburg was legally brought into existence.

The GILES COUNTY COURTHOUSE, a red brick building erected in 1836 and since enlarged by wings, is shaded by the huge oaks of the court green. An octagonal cupola on the hip roof dwarfs the two-story portico. Giles County, formed in 1806 from Montgomery, Tazewell, and Monroe (now in West Virginia) Counties, was named for William B. Giles, congressman for four terms and governor of Virginia (1827–30).

The very large CELANESE CORPORATION OF AMERICA PLANT (opened 1939), by New River on land acquired from the Giles County Chamber of Commerce, has capacity for more than 10,000 employees.

NARROWS, 37.9 *m.* (1,547 alt., 1,345 pop.), close by a deep gorge through which pass two railroads, the state highway, and the swirling waters of the New River, has a tannery, a hosiery mill, and a public utilities plant.

In the winter of 1863 about 1,000 Confederate soldiers, commanded by General John McCausland, were quartered here. A fort, built on an eminence, had its guns ranged on the gorge, which was further defended by the vigilant signal corps station on East River Mountain.

At RICH CREEK, 42 *m.*, close to the West Virginia Line, is a junction with US 219 (*see West Virginia Guide*).

Tour 6

Fredericksburg—Tappahannock—Saluda—Gloucester—Gloucester Point—Yorktown—Portsmouth—(Elizabeth City,N.C.). US 17. Fredericksburg to North Carolina Line, 170.7 *m.*

Hard-surfaced roadbed throughout, chiefly asphalt with stretches of concrete.
Norfolk Southern R.R. parallels route between Portsmouth and the North Carolina Line.
Ferry over York River and toll bridge over James River; for costs see below.
Accommodations only in towns.

US 17 parallels the south bank of the Rappahannock River, crosses the lower parts of the Middle Peninsula and the Peninsula, and passes through the Dismal Swamp of the Southside, traversing the areas of early settlement.

Section a. FREDERICKSBURG to GLOUCESTER POINT; 107.5 *m. US* 17.

The upper part of this section of US 17 crosses a plain between the Rappahannock and a low plateau. Along the way are plantations, old villages, small farms and patches of forest. Occupations vary from farming in the upper region, with lumbering and fishing minor pursuits, to oystering, fishing, and truck-farming in the lower.

US 17 branches southeast from US 1 (*see Tour 1b*) in FREDERICKSBURG, 0 *m.*, at the junction of Princess Anne St. and Lafayette Blvd., in union with State 2 (*see Tour 1A*).

Southeast of the city the highway traverses the area of HAMILTON'S CROSSING, scene of stirring activities during the Battle of Fredericksburg in December 1862 (*see Tour 1b*).

All that is left of MANNSFIELD (L), 2.6 *m.*, are the foundations and a vaulted cellar of cut stone. It was the home of Mann Page (1749–1803). When the militia assembled in this vicinity in 1775 after Governor Dunmore's removal of the gunpowder in Williamsburg, Mann Page rode to the capital without stopping, and returned at once with a letter advising against any violent action. After an animated discussion, a committee voted by a majority of one that the troops should not go to Williamsburg.

The MANNSFIELD HALL COUNTRY CLUB 3.3 *m.*, is (L) beyond a golf course. The main part of the large two-story brick house with Ionic portico was built by William Pratt in 1805. The grounds are part of an estate of Major Lawrence Smith, who in 1676 built and commanded the fort the general assembly had authorized near the falls of the Rappahannock. The family seat here, then called Smithfield, was built by Smith's son, Major Augustine Smith, who in 1716 entertained the Knights of the Golden

Horseshoe. Upon the marriage of Richard Brooke to Ann Hay Taliaferro, who inherited it, Smithfield became a home of the Brooke family. Here was born Dr.Lawrence Brooke (*c.*1752–1803), surgeon on John Paul Jones's ship, the *Bonhomme Richard*, and his brothers, Robert Brooke (1751–99), Governor of Virginia (1794–96), and General Francis Taliaferro Brooke (1763–1851), soldier and jurist. After Mannsfield, near by, was destroyed, its name was given to Smithfield.

At 5.7 *m.* is a junction with a dirt road.

Left here to the approximate SITE OF NEW POST, 1 *m.*, where Governor Alexander Spotswood (1676–1740) maintained a furnace for the manufacture of utensils from the pig iron produced at Germanna (*see Tour 3b*) and had headquarters for the postal service while he was deputy postmaster general of the Colonies. The large brick house later built here was the home of Spotswood's grandson, General Alexander Spotswood (1751–1818).

Colonel William Byrd, in *A Progress to the Mines*, tells of visiting here in 1732: 'The colonel . . . carried us directly to his air furnace . . . The use of it is to melt his sow iron in order to cast it into sundry utensils . . . which . . . can be afforded at twenty shilling a ton, and delivered at people's own homes. And, being cast from the sow iron, are much better than those which come from England.' Colonel Byrd had found Spotswood, at Germanna, 'very frank in communicating all his dear-bought experience . . . For his part, he wished there were many more iron works in the country, provided the parties concerned would preserve a constant harmony among themselves' in order to be 'better able to manage the workmen and reduce their wages to what was just and reasonable.'

At 5.8 *m.* State 2 (*see Tour 1A*) branches R. and US 17 proceeds L.

At 13.3 *m.* is a junction with a narrow lane.

Right here into the WINDSOR ESTATE, the seat of which has long since disappeared. This was the birthplace of General William Woodford (1734–80), who commanded the Virginians at the Battle of Great Bridge (*see Tour 6b*). The house was built in 1731–32 by his father, Major William Woodford. William Byrd, stopping here in 1732, wrote: 'We took our way . . . to major Woodford's . . . who lives upon a high hill that affords an extended prospect. On which account it is dignified with the name of Windsor. There we found Rachel Cocke, who stayed with her sister some time that she might not lose the use of her tongue in this lonely place.'

GAY MONT (R), 18.4 *m.* (*open April* 15 *to Nov.* 15; *adm.* 50¢), is approached through a tunnel of trees. The house among extensive gardens overlooks broad terraces descending toward the Rappahannock. The frame gabled roof house (1725) with a long recessed, colonnaded porch, is lengthened by one-story octagonal rooms of stuccoed brick (1798). At the rear an octagonal music room (1830) projects into the garden. Busts of several distinguished men ornament the porch. The frame part of the house, first called Rose Hill, was built by the Catlett family. The French wallpaper was hung in 1815.

At 18.9 *m.* is a dirt road.

Left here to the SITE OF HAZELWOOD, 0.5 *m.*, the home of John Taylor (1754–1824), who was born at Mill Hill. Taylor here conducted experiments that led to soil improvement and crop rotation on soil impoverished by two centuries of tobacco culture. In 1817 he organized the Agricultural Society of Virginia. The county societies he encouraged resulted in 1820 in the United Agricultural Societies of Virginia. Taylor wrote prolifically on both agricultural and political subjects and served in the United States Senate.

At 20.8 *m.* on US 17 is a junction with State 207.

1. Left here to PORT ROYAL, 0.5 *m.* (250 pop.), now merely a residential village with a few commercial establishments along unpaved shaded streets. It is connected with Port Conway on the opposite side of the river, by the JAMES MADISON MEMORIAL BRIDGE. Many of the residences, with large yards containing huge clumps of boxwood, have dormers. In a cemetery are several eighteenth-century tombstones. On one is chiseled:

'Beneath this humble stone a youth doth lie,
Most too good to live too young to dye;
Count his few years, how short the scanty span,
But count his virtues and he dyed a Man.'

Port Royal was constituted a town in 1744. It traded directly with Old World ports until the building of railroads rerouted the flow of commerce. Such was its importance that it was able to make a strong bid for selection as the seat of the Federal Government.

2. Right from US 17 on State 207 to the GARRETT HOUSE (R), 2.2 *m.*, now in ruins. Lincoln's assassin, John Wilkes Booth, and his accomplice, Herold, after crossing the Potomac River, the Northern Neck, and the Rappahannock River, took refuge in a barn here and were discovered by cavalrymen on April 26, 1865. Herold surrendered. When Booth refused to do so, the soldiers fired the barn and sent several shots into it. Taken out fatally wounded, Booth died on the porch of the residence.

VAUTER'S CHURCH (L), 30.6 *m.* (*open* 10–11 *and* 3–4), partly covered by English ivy amid old oaks and walnuts, is a simple T-shaped building. The rectangle was built in 1719 and the south transept in 1731. The brick walls above a high water table are laid in Flemish bond, with the patterns emphasized by unusual black glazed headers. The two small windows above each door light a gallery.

The chancel in the east end, raised one step above stone-paved aisles, has modern equipment, but against the north wall stands the Colonial reading desk and high pulpit, reached by a stairway. The tops of the original box pews, with benches of uncompromising rigidity and clanging doors that announced the arrival or retirement of the occupants, have been cut down. A communion service that was presented to the parish by Queen Anne is preserved here.

Vauter's was the Upper Church of St.Anne's Parish, formed in 1704. The Reverend Robert Rose, rector from 1725 to 1746, was 'a kind of universal genius.' 'His journal mentions all his visits,' said Bishop Meade, '. . . sometimes preaching, sometimes marrying, at other times baptizing . . . He once visited Western Virginia . . . sleeping out at nights in cold weather and drinking, as he records, wretched whiskey for want of something better . . . We find him repeatedly at Williamsburg . . . dining or suppering with the Governor and Council . . . Now he is in the house reading Cicero's Orations, now on the farm engaged in all kinds of employment, now at his neighbours' instructing them in various operations. Now he writes . . . a recipe for the best mode of curing tobacco

. . . He speaks of turning away an overseer for getting drunk . . . and yet . . . he brings home with him . . . "rum and wine and other necessaries."'

At 38.3 *m.* is a junction with County 631.

Right here to FONTHILL (R), 1.9 *m.*, built about 1835. This was the home of Robert Mercer Taliaferro Hunter (1809–87), who served in both houses of Congress, was Speaker of the House for one term, declined the post of U.S. Secretary of State but served as Secretary of State for the Confederacy and then as a member and president *pro tempore* of the Confederate Senate.

CARET, 41.2 *m.*, is near an early seat of the Old Rappahannock County, which was cut from Lancaster County in 1656 and, extending westward indefinitely, had two seats, the one here for the 'South Side.' It ceased to exist in 1692. Here Thomas and Benjamin Goodrich were ordered to appear in 1676 with halters around their necks to express penitence for participating in Bacon's Rebellion. The men, wearing strings around their necks, obeyed the order symbolically rather than literally.

Left from Caret on County 624 to a private road, 0.6 *m.*; L. here to BLANDFIELD, 2.1 *m.*, which stands on the ridge among a tangle of old trees. The front of the building, a central rectangle connected by shed-roofed passages to the smaller wings set forward, faces a rose garden in a wide forecourt. Beneath a hip-on-hip roof with four tall chimneys at the corners, the river front, like the garden front which it closely resembles, is broken by a slightly projecting pavilion with a pediment. On both fronts are neo-classic porches added in 1854. The most striking feature is the design of the flat arches over the openings, very deep brick arches with a splay of 45°.

Before 1750 William Beverley (1698–1756), son of Robert Beverley, the historian, and grandson of Robert Beverley, the immigrant (*see below*), built Blandfield, which he named for his wife, Elizabeth Bland. He acquired this large plantation about 1730.

Blandfield was stripped of its fine paneling when the porches were added seven years before the War between the States. During the war much of the furniture and all the portraits were taken away by Union soldiers.

In TAPPAHANNOCK, 48 *m.* (427 pop.), seat of Essex County, old and new houses look across the broad waters of the Rappahannock River from the dense foliage of large and beautiful trees. Since the Downing Bridge was built in 1927 the town has become one of two gateways to the once isolated Northern Neck; its old hotel among weeping willows by the river is notable for its soft shell crabs and shad.

Tappahannock (Ind., On the Rising Water) was constituted a town in 1680 when the general assembly, considering 'the greate necessity, usefullnesse, and advantage of cohabitation,' directed that 19 towns be established, one for each county. Everything went well until Charles II in 1681 vetoed the act 'for cohabitation and . . . trade and manufacture,' because planters objected violently to the provision that they should ship their tobacco only from the towns and only during stipulated periods. But in 1691, after William and Mary had ascended the throne, the towns were again made ports of entry—one 'ffor Rappahannock County at Hobs his hole . . . where the Court house, severall dwelling houses, and ware houses (are) already built.' But in 1693 the general assembly, grown bolder, itself suspended the ports act. In 1705, after Anne had become

Queen, ports were again constituted, this time only 16 but among them Hobbs' Hole, then renamed Tappahannock.

Tappahannock prospered. When created in 1680, it had been made the seat of Rappahannock County, and in 1692 after the old county was divided to form Essex and Richmond Counties it became the seat of Essex. Though the town was formally named, Washington, stopping here in 1752, referred to it as 'Hobs Hole.' A century and a half ago ships went hence to the remotest parts of the world and the town was something of a social center. But its importance declined after the construction of railroads. It was shelled in December 1814 by the British navy, under orders of Admiral Cockburn.

The ESSEX COUNTY COURTHOUSE, a large rectangle of brick with white columned-portico and a cupola, was erected in 1848. In the Clerk's Office are the records of Old Rappahannock County, as well as those of Essex County. They show that in 1688, when the birth of a Prince of Wales was celebrated, the court ordered 'as much Rum and other strong liquor with Sugar proportionable' as should amount to 10,000 pounds of tobacco distributed 'amongst the Troops of horse, company of foot' and other persons 'at the solemnitie.' Other records tell of a woman indicted for swearing 'seventy-five oaths,' and of another whipped for wearing Governor Spotswood's clothes.

The OLD COURTHOUSE, on the green and now part of a church, was built in 1728.

The OLD CLERK'S OFFICE, a small brick house built before 1750 and used after 1848 as a jail, is now a club.

The small brick DEBTORS' PRISON, now an office, was once the clerk's office. It became the last debtors' prison, succeeding one the court pronounced 'too foul for human beings.'

The story-and-a-half brick RITCHIE HOUSE, with dormers and outside chimneys—the remaining unit of three—was the birthplace of Thomas Ritchie (1778–1854), founder and for 40 years editor of the *Richmond Enquirer*. It was built about 1750 by Ritchie's father, Archibald Ritchie, a Scot who became a wealthy Virginia merchant. Though Thomas Ritchie was accused of being the 'son of a Scotch Tory,' records show that Archibald furnished gunpowder free to the patriots during the Revolution and later two sons for the American army.

ST.MARGARET'S SCHOOL, on a shaded campus by the river, is a preparatory school for girls, conducted by the Protestant Episcopal Diocese of Virginia. One of the buildings, the large frame BROCKENBROUGH HOUSE, was erected before the Revolution. A distinctive feature is the large projecting vestibule with a door flanked by narrow windows and surmounted by a fanlight. A triglyphed frieze beneath the cornice follows the roof line and is repeated in the heading above the windows to form an incomplete pediment. The house was built by Dr.John Brockenbrough.

Tappahannock is at a junction with US 360 (*see Tour 20a*), which is united with US 17 to a junction at 50.4 *m.*

GLEBE LANDING CHURCH (R), 65 *m.*, is of brick, built in 1839 with gabled roof and a loggia gracefully arched. A former building stood by a landing on a parish glebe. The Baptist congregation here was constituted in 1772 as the result of the preaching of the Reverend John Waller (*see Tour 1b*).

SALUDA, 77.5 *m.* (150 pop.), spreads along three roads and has changed little since 1852 when it became the seat of Middlesex County. The COURTHOUSE, a nondescript red brick building, has had several additions since the first part was erected to replace a courthouse burned during the War between the States. The Clerk's Office contains records that date from 1673. When the courthouse was burned, the early records were saved by the clerk, who hid them in a barn on an island in Dragon Run. Middlesex County was erected in 1668 out of part of Lancaster. The early history of the county is interwoven with the record of Robert Beverley, who settled here in 1663. Beverley was a supporter of Governor Berkeley in the rebellion of 1676, but later resisted unjust rule by royal authority and, as champion of the people, figured prominently in the Tobacco Rebellion of 1682.

The second Robert Beverley (1673–1722), in 1705 published his *History and Present State of Virginia*, which included an unbiased account of his father's career. The work has survived for two centuries, because of its originality, shrewd observations, and humorous comments.

Andrew Jackson Montague (1862–1937), governor of Virginia (1902–06) and a congressman (1913–37), was at one time a resident of Saluda. He did much to advance the public schools of Virginia, was a student of foreign affairs, and represented America at two international conferences.

Left from Saluda on State 33 to State 227, 2.1 *m.*; L. here 1.6 *m.* to ROSEGILL (R), on a 30-acre lawn. The long, many-windowed building has one brick and one frame story beneath a gabled roof. The white walls are accented by numerous green shutters. Several dependencies are survivors of 'at least 20 houses scattered along a charming plateau above the Rappahannock River,' as wrote a M.Durand, a Huguenot refugee visiting Virginia after a shipwreck in 1686.

Ralph Wormeley patented this estate in 1649 and began to build that year. Rosegill contained a chapel, picture gallery, large library, and 30 guest-chambers. One immense attic-room provided 14 beds for bachelor guests. The present main house contains part of the first. Two governors—Sir Henry Chicheley and Lord Francis Howard—lived here, and Rosegill was once temporary seat of the colony. In 1667 Sir Henry married Wormeley's widow and he resided here until his death in 1682. Telling of a visit in the time of the second Ralph Wormeley (1650–1703), councillor and later secretary of the colony, Durand wrote: 'The Council met during this time,' and he expressed surprise that the councillors were not robed, but 'sit officially in their boots and swords.'

'What persuaded me,' he said, 'that there is plenty of money among the people of quality in this country is that after supper they sat down to cards; and it was near midnight when Milor Parker, seeing that I was nodding, urged me to retire, "for," as he said, "it is possible we may be here all night;" and, in fact, I found them next morning still at play, and saw that Milor Parker had gained a hundred pieces of eight.' Bacon's Rebellion, only ten years before, had been caused by the intense poverty of the small land holders near by.

State 227 continues to URBANNA, 2.6 *m.* (432 pop.), on high ground above the Rappahannock. The town, created port for Middlesex County by the Act of 1680, was named in 1705 'City of Anne' to honor the Queen. Soon after its establishment it was made the county seat.

EPIPHANY CHAPEL, a low-pitched brick building with flanking wings, was built in the early eighteenth century as the courthouse of Middlesex County. In 1852 it was converted into a chapel. It was in this building that several itinerant Baptist ministers were tried and sentenced for preaching without license.

The old brick CUSTOM HOUSE is now a residence.

State 227 runs northwest and becomes County 602; at 3.3 *m.* from State 33 is HEWICK (R), T-shaped with brick walls laid in Flemish bond. The stem was built about 1678 by Christopher Robinson (1645–93), who arrived in Virginia about 1666, became a member of the Council in 1691, and was one of the first 'visitors and governors' of the College of William and Mary. His grandson, Speaker John Robinson, was born here in 1704.

REMLIK (R), 5.2 *m.*, is a training station for race horses, maintained by Willis Sharpe Kilmer, owner of Sun Beau and Exterminator.

On State 33 is CHRIST CHURCH (L), 3.3 *m.*, the 'mother Church' of Christ Church Parish, in a shaded and tomb-studded churchyard. Built in 1712–14, restored in the 1800's after it had been long neglected, it is low-pitched and has compass windows. Above the west entrance is a round window. The vestibule is a later addition. Part of an early communion set is still used here. The first church was erected in 1665–66 in accordance with an agreement to build a 'Mother Church . . . according to ye Modell of ye Middle-plantation Church' (at present Williamsburg). Governor Henry Chicheley, who died in 1682, is buried under the chancel.

In 1711 William Churchill left money from which the interest should pay the rector 'for preaching four quarterly sermons yearly against the four reigning vices, . . . atheism and irreligion, swearing and cursing, fornication and adultery, and drunkenness.' This he would have 'done forever.'

CHRIST CHURCH SCHOOL, adjoining the churchyard, is a preparatory school for about 50 boys, conducted by the Protestant Episcopal Diocese.

HARMONY VILLAGE, 7.3 *m.*, is at a junction with County 621; L. here 3.1 *m.* to County 640; L. to GREY'S POINT, 4.1 *m.*, terminus of IRVINGTON-GREY'S POINT FERRIES (*about every two hrs., car and driver* $1, *each passenger* 25¢).

On State 33 is the METHODIST LOWER CHAPEL (R), 9.8 *m.*, a small building with thick walls. Its gabled roof has hipped ends and a 'kick-out.' Within is the table-tomb of Mary, first wife of Robert Beverley. The little building, erected in 1717, was a chapel of ease in Christ Church Parish. After the Revolution it was used by other denominations.

On State 33 at 10.9 *m.* is a junction with State 225; R. here 2 *m.* to WILTON (R), a chunky T-shaped brick house with a gambrel roof and dormers. Wilton was built by William Churchill in 1762.

GLENNS, 80.7 *m.*, is at a junction with State 33 (*see Tour 6A*).

MT. PRODIGAL (L), 85.2 *m.*, is a story-and-a-half brick house with thick walls, tall chimneys, and dormers on a steep roof. Charles Roane built the house in the latter half of the seventeenth century.

At 88.9 *m.* is (L) the SITE OF POPLAR SPRING CHURCH, a once richly decorated church of Petsworth Parish, begun in 1723, completed after 1751, and destroyed about 1850. When Nathaniel Bacon died in this vicinity in 1676, his men, after secretly burying the body, interred a casket filled with stones in the yard of a former church on this site.

At 89.4 *m.* is a junction with County 615.

Right here to County 613, 0.3 *m.*, and R. 0.7 *m.* to County 612; R. here 0.4 *m.* to MARLFIELD (L), a T-shaped brick house built about 1732 and now falling into ruins. Here was the home of John Buckner, who brought the first printing press into Virginia. In 1682 he was reproved by Governor Culpeper for printing the laws of 1680 without a license and, with his partner, William Nuthead, was required to give bond not to do any further printing 'until his Majestys pleasure should be known.'

On County 613 at 3.1 *m.* is a junction with County 614 and County 669; straight ahead on County 669 to PURTON, 5 *m.*, a large, square brick house, erected before the Revolution, with two chimneys at one of its gabled ends.

The estate, patented in 1661 by Anne Corderoy Bernard, widow of Richard Bernard, was one of several managed by this astute business woman. The crisp courtesy of a letter she wrote in 1653 to Colonel Walter Brodhurst, who represented her in Westmoreland County, reveals her characteristics: 'I give you many thanks for your care of my business. I cannot resolve of my comeing to Potomac myselfe till ye return of ye shipps . . . In what charge you are at in my businesses these lines shall oblige me to pay & your love & care I shall ever study ye best way of returning.'

In 1663 an indentured servant at Purton, one Berkenhead, exposed a conspiracy of servants and prevented an insurrection. The general assembly 'resolved that Berkenhead—the discoverer of the horrid plot—have his freedom and 5,000 pounds of tobacco . . . that his master be satisfied . . . for his time,' and that September 13, the date fixed for the uprising, 'be annually kept holy.' The incident was the basis of Mary Johnston's novel, *Prisoners of Hope*.

GLOUCESTER, 94.2 *m.* (300 pop.), elm-shaded and leisurely, is the seat of Gloucester County. Its main street divides into one-way thoroughfares around the walled court-square. The number of business establishments in the small town indicates that Gloucester is the financial and commercial center of the county.

In 1769, the general assembly, having been assured that a town 'on the lands of John Fox, gentleman, adjoining the lands whereon the Court house . . . is erected . . . will be advantageous,' directed the laying off of 'sixty acres . . . into lots and streets' and constituted 'Gloucester Court House' a town 'by the name of Botetourt town'—a name that was never popular.

The GLOUCESTER COUNTY COURTHOUSE, a brick building with a hip roof and columned portico, was erected in 1766, the portico at a later date. In the court room are the usual portraits of prominent native sons and a tablet characterizing Nathaniel Bacon, leader in the rebellion of 1676, as 'soldier, statesman, and saint.' Gloucester County was formed in 1651 from York.

The small, brick DEBTORS' PRISON, adjoining the courthouse, was built before 1750 and equipped as prescribed, 'with iron-barred windows' and door 'secured with good locks and bars of iron.'

The CLERK'S OFFICE, erected about 1890, contains records dating chiefly from the 1860's. The early records were destroyed during a fire in 1820 and those covering the period from 1820 to 1860, taken to Richmond during the War between the States, were burned when the capital was evacuated. The OLD CLERK'S OFFICE, a small brick house, was built in 1821. Dr. John Clayton (*c.* 1685–1773) long served the county as a clerk. He accompanied his father, John Clayton, attorney-general of the colony, to Virginia in 1705. He corresponded with Karl von Linne, the noted Swedish botanist, and traveled all over Virginia in search of plants, which he described with laborious detail. From Clayton's name and work is derived *Claytonia*, a genus of low herbs. In 1748 and in 1762 editions of *Flora Virginica*, Clayton's scholarly work in Latin, classifying Virginia plants, were published at Leyden University.

The MASONIC HALL, a two-story frame building with a hip roof and tower, is the home of Botetourt Lodge, No.7, formed in 1757 and chartered in 1773.

HOTEL BOTETOURT, a long building, part frame and part brick, incorporates an inn built about the time Gloucester became the county seat.

LONG BRIDGE ORDINARY, a frame building, now a club, was built prior to 1730 and was a post station.

1. Right from Gloucester on County 616 to WALTER REED'S BIRTHPLACE (R), 3.9 *m.*, a one-room house restored as a memorial. Walter Reed (1851–1902), the physician who discovered the cause of yellow fever, was born here not long after a fire had forced his parents from the Methodist parsonage, their home.

2. Left from Gloucester on State 14, which circles eastward across the headwaters of North River, then turns southward through the low-lying peninsula almost surrounded by Chesapeake Bay and its tidal estuaries.

WARE CHURCH (R), 1 *m.*, within a brick-walled enclosure, is a large rectangular structure with steep gabled roof and walls three feet thick. Two large round arched windows light the chancel and five others are in the side walls. The church, built about 1700, has a door in both north and south walls. Before the chancel, but now covered by flooring, are table-tombs. The communion service is part of a set presented to Poplar Spring Church (*see above*) by Augustine Warner before 1681.

Ware Parish was constituted between 1652 and 1654. The Reverend Alexander Murray, who was with Charles II at the Battle of Worcester in 1652 and was the king's companion during his subsequent wandering, arrived in Virginia in 1653 and served here as rector until 1672.

ELMINGTON (R), 2.8 *m.*, is a brick house with a high-columned portico. Thomas Dixon was living here when he wrote *The Clansman* and *The Leopard's Spots* (*see Literature*). The fields of the estate are now used for the culture of narcissus bulbs.

TODDSBURY (R), 3.3 *m.*, is a brick house among broadnut, elm, and willow oak trees on a great lawn extending to the North River. To the T-shaped structure with steeply curbed roofs and nearly flush dormers has been added a porch with an enclosed second floor. The house is notable for its beautifully paneled rooms, for the cornice and staircase in the wide hall, and deep window recesses with round arches flanking the chimney in the dining room.

The estate was patented by Thomas Todd in 1665 and at least part of the house was probably built soon afterwards. The interior woodwork, however, could not have been done until sometime after 1700.

At 14 *m.* is a junction with State 198; L. here 1 *m.* to State 223, and R. 2.3 *m.* to CRICKET HILL, a landing place on Milford Haven, an arm of the bay. A free ferry plies between the mainland and GWYNN'S ISLAND, which was named for Hugh Gwynn, one of the first two representatives from Gloucester County in the house of burgesses. Its people are engaged principally in the sea food industries.

On Gwynn's Island Lord Dunmore made his last stand against the Virginia patriots. After having been driven from Portsmouth, he came here with his fleet, boasting that he would drive 'the crickets' away. But the Virginia forces erected a battery on Cricket Hill and opened fire upon the British fleet—and Dunmore sailed away.

State 198 continues to County 631, 5.4 *m.*; R. here 0.9 *m.* to HESSE (R), a brick house with a frame wing. The fine interior paneling has been removed. Judith, the daughter of Colonel John Armistead, who settled here before 1676 and built the house, was the first wife of Robert (King) Carter (*see Tour* 16 *b*).

MATHEWS, 16.2 *m.* (450 pop.), seat of Mathews County, is scattered along State 14. It began as a landing at the head of East River and became the county seat with the formation of the county in 1790.

The COURTHOUSE, a T-shaped building of brick, with dormers, was erected during the nineteenth century. Near by is the old square jail, now used as the sheriff's office. Mathews County was formed from Gloucester and named for General Thomas Mathews. The cultivation of narcissus bulbs on a commercial scale makes the county in early spring a veritable flower garden.

At 17.9 *m.* is a junction with County 614; R. here 0.5 *m.* to (R) CHRIST CHURCH of Kingston Parish, a simple brick rectangle built in 1840–43, gutted by fire about 1900, but later restored. The GRAVE OF CAPTAIN SALLY TOMPKINS (*see below*) is in the churchyard. The parish was formed about 1655.

On State 14 is POPLAR GROVE (R), 18.5 *m.*, a large rambling frame house with a tall portico and many other additions. It was the home of John Patterson, whose granddaughter, Captain Sally Tompkins, was born here in 1833. At her own expense and with help from friends, she conducted Robinson Hospital in Richmond during the War between the States. President Jefferson Davis commissioned her a captain in the Confederate Cavalry.

The TIDE MILL on the estate has a huge wheel that turns one way when the tide rushes into the cove and the other way when it goes out.

BAYSIDE, 25.2 *m.*, has a mile-long pier on Mobjack Bay, where fishermen land their catches.

Offshore here is NEW POINT COMFORT, an island where live oak and pine trees grow among sand dunes along a three-mile beach. Hunting and fishing grounds are excellent.

The GLEBE HOUSE (R), 97.7 *m.*, a T-shaped brick building with dormers and wings, was built before 1724. Here ministers lived until the glebe was confiscated in 1802.

At 100.2 *m.* is a junction with County 614.

Right here to County 632, 2.8 *m.*; L. to a lane, 4 *m.*, and L. again to ROSEWELL, 4.8 *m.*, thrusting upward vast, empty walls among the trees on a wide lawn by the York River. In spite of the fire that gutted them, the gigantic walls laid in Flemish bond present a fine specimen of brickwork of the Colonial period.

The land was left in 1692 by John Page to his son Matthew (1659–1703), whose tomb stands here beside that of Mann Page (1691–1730), only son of Matthew and Mary Mann Page. Construction was begun in 1725 by Mann Page, but when he died in 1730 the house was unfinished, though a great part of the combined Page and Mann fortunes had been spent on the work. Bishop Meade in his *Old Churches, Ministers and Families of Virginia* commented that the building of Rosewell caused the Pages to sink deep into debt. The central part of the house contained 23 rooms, 3 wide halls, and 9 minor passageways and the wings contained 6 rooms each. The wainscoting was carved mahogany, and the staircase was wide enough to accommodate eight persons walking abreast. In 1916 the mansion was destroyed by fire.

John Page (1744–1808), son of Mann Page II, was the only member of the Council who refused in 1775 to censure Patrick Henry for his warlike attitude toward Governor Dunmore. He was a member of Congress from 1789 to 1797 and governor of Virginia, 1802–05.

At 100.5 *m.* on US 17 is a junction with County 614.

Left here to County 658, 2.5 *m.* and R. to WARNER HALL (R), 3.8 *m.*, approached between rows of elms. The frame house, two-and-a-half stories with a portico, is the third on this site. The other two were destroyed by fire, the first about 1740, the second in 1849. Only the original brick dependencies remain.

Part of the estate was patented in 1642 by Augustine Warner (1610–74), who left it to his son Augustine (1642–81), speaker of the house of burgesses at the time of Bacon's Rebellion.

Warner's daughter Mildred, married here in 1690 to Lawrence Washington, became a grandmother of George Washington. After Lawrence Washington's death in 1698, she married George Gale, went to England on a business trip, died there in 1701, and was buried at the Church of St.Nicholas, Whitehaven, England. Her sister Elizabeth, who inherited Warner Hall, married John Lewis. Another John Lewis, father of Colonel Fielding Lewis (*see Fredericksburg*), became step-father of Councillor Robert Carter (*see Tour 16A*), who passed his childhood here.

In the cemetery are tombs of the Lewises, also those of the two Warners.

ABINGDON CHURCH (L), 101 *m.*, in a walnut grove and surrounded by a brick wall, was built in 1754–55. Cruciform in plan, with walls two feet thick laid in Flemish bond, the building has oval-topped windows and above each of three doors a graceful segmentally-arched pediment in molded brick.

Though the interior has been modernized in some respects, the galleries retain their high-backed pews. Back of the chancel is a pentagonal reredos 20 feet high, depicting the façade of a Greek temple. A handsome communion set presented to the parish in 1703 by Major Lewis Burwell is still used. During the War between the States Federal troops used the boxed pews as stalls for their horses.

At 103.9 *m.* is a junction with County 639.

Right here to County 638, 0.6 *m.*; straight ahead on an unmarked road to a junction; L. here to another junction and R. to POWHATAN'S CHIMNEY, 1.3 *m.*, marking what is believed to have been Werowocomoco, chief village of the Chief Powhatan. The chimney, constructed of marl, belonged, according to tradition, to a house the colonists built for the chief. It tumbled down about 1915 but was later painstakingly restored.

When Captain John Smith was captured by Indians in 1607 (*see Tour 8a*), he was led from village to village and finally to Werowocomoco, where he was rescued by Pocahontas. Later, Captain Smith and Captain Newport visited Powhatan and with a few glass beads procured supplies for the starving colonists at Jamestown. In 1608 James I directed that Powhatan be crowned. When Smith came here with a party to invite Powhatan to Jamestown for the coronation, the chief was away; so the women of his court entertained the visitors. Said Smith: 'In a fayre plaine field they made a fire . . . suddainly amongst the woods was heard . . . a hydeous noise and shreeking . . . thirtie young women came naked out of the woods, onely covered behind and before with a few greene leaves, their bodies all painted . . . These fiends with most hellish shouts and cryes, rushing from among the trees, cast themselves in a ring about the fire, singing and dauncing with most excellent ill varietie . . .'

Powhatan refused to go to Jamestown; so the coronation was held here. The English came again for supplies, but this time King Powhatan refused to exchange corn for glass beads and copper kettles. He demanded a white man's house.

HAYES' STORE, 105 *m.*, formerly called the 'Hook,' is the scene of Colonel Banastre Tarleton's last engagement during the Revolution. On October 3, 1781, he was attacked here by Virginia militia and French cavalry and forced to Gloucester Point, where he was trapped until after Cornwallis's surrender.

Left from the hamlet State 216 traverses low-lying Guinea Peninsula, between the York and Severn Rivers. The people of this section, descendants of early settlers, have retained many old customs and ancient English words. Since only a dozen or more surnames are borne by the residents, it is necessary often, even in court records, to designate them by such terms as 'Fred's Tom' or 'Kate's Mary.' A majority engage in sea food industries.

At 2.8 *m.* on State 216 is a junction with County 643; R. here to County 642, 3.5 *m.*, and R. again to LITTLE ENGLAND, 4.5 *m.*, a tall well-preserved brick house commanding an extensive view of the York River. Built about 1714 by John Perrin, the rectangular house has small dormers and formal rooms paneled full-length at their ends. In the central hall is a 'swinging stair.'

GLOUCESTER POINT, 107.5 *m.*, on the York River, once a Colonial port, is now chiefly a ferry terminal (*see Tour 6b*).

First named Tindall's Point, then Gloucester Town, it was one of the towns authorized in 1680. The site was patented by Argall Yeardley in 1640 and was named for Robert Tindall, who made a map of the area in 1608. When, in 1667, the general assembly directed that a fort 'bee built in each river,' one was erected here 'within command of which . . . all ships trading .... may conveniently and in all probability securely ride and load.' Just after Nathaniel Bacon's followers burned Jamestown in 1676, Governor Berkeley conducted courts-martial aboard a ship off Tindall's Point.

The place figured in the Siege of Yorktown in 1781, in the War of 1812, the War between the States, and the World War—in the last, when the Atlantic Fleet of the U.S. Navy used the adjacent waters as an anchorage.

Section b. GLOUCESTER POINT to NORTH CAROLINA LINE; 63.2 m. US 17

This section of US 17 crosses the Peninsula and the James River and traverses the edge of the Dismal Swamp. North of the James are small truck farms, dairies, and nurseries; southward grow peanuts, hogs, and cotton. The highway touches areas where Virginia's earliest history was made, where the Revolution was brought to its close, and where troops struggled in the Peninsular Campaign of 1862.

Ferries from Gloucester Point cross the York River (*every half-hour on the quarter-hour and three-quarter-hour; car and driver 50¢, each passenger 15¢*).

YORKTOWN, 0 *m.* (300 pop.), spread along a 50-foot bluff on the south of the river, is the seat of York County and is in the Colonial National Historical Park. Main Street, bisected by streets only two or three blocks long, parallels the river. Frame houses and brick houses mingle, some Colonial, some more modern. The older, with trees and boxwood hedges softening the contours, look fresh since their restoration.

Before 1630, though the settlers had gone nearly to the falls of the James to found Henricopolis and across the Chesapeake Bay to occupy 'ye kingdom of Accomacke,' none had yet settled the shores of the York. In that year land was offered to all persons who 'should adventure or be adventured to seate and inhabit on the southern side' of the river 'formerly known by ye Indyan name of Chiskiacke, as a reward and encouragement for this their undertakeing.' Whereupon, houses were built at Chiskiacke, west of present Yorktown, and at 'York,' at the mouth of Wormeley's Creek, three miles east of the present village. Meanwhile, Captain Nicholas Martiau, a French engineer employed by the colony, had patented land embracing the site of Yorktown. When, in 1680, the general assembly authorized the establishment of 19 ports, it directed that one be here, between the two settlements. The town at once assumed importance.

During May and June 1781 Lord Cornwallis led campaigns north and west of Richmond, opposed by La Fayette. When Wayne and his Pennsylvania troops joined La Fayette's Continentals northwest of Richmond,

Cornwallis turned eastward, pursued by La Fayette and Wayne. After several skirmishes in the Peninsula, he crossed to Portsmouth but decided to fortify Yorktown as a base for contact with the British fleet and brought his army here by water.

Washington and Rochambeau combined forces and joined La Fayette at Williamsburg. Meanwhile, Comte de Grasse, sailing his French fleet from the West Indies, met the British fleet outside the capes and forced it to retire. By September 29 the American and French forces had surrounded Yorktown, making the British surrender inevitable.

The land forces had dug trenches and fortified themselves. The shelling began on October 9. On October 16, Cornwallis attempted to cross the York River, but was prevented by a storm. The next day the British commander asked for a parley and on October 19, the English marched out between the American and French forces, laying down their arms while the band played 'The World Turned Upside Down.' Though a great many troops were involved in the siege, casualties were few.

In 1814 Yorktown, garrisoned by the militia, was threatened by a British fleet. In April 1862 the Confederates under General John B. Magruder fortified the town. After they were forced out, Federal forces under command of General George B. McClellan moved in. The U.S. Navy established a base here in 1917.

The YORK COUNTY COURTHOUSE, a two-story brick structure, was built in 1875 to replace the building destroyed in 1862 by the explosion of Federal munitions stored in it. The county was formed in 1634 when a wide area on both sides of the river was made into Charles River County. In 1642 the name of both river and county was changed to York to honor James, Duke of York and son of Charles I. Other counties were subsequently formed from it.

The CLERK'S OFFICE (1875), a long, low, plastered brick building beside the courthouse, contains records that date from 1633, before the county was formed, and constitute one of the most nearly complete sets in Virginia. Archaic script shows that court was held from place to place until 1691, when it was held 'upon Mr.Benjamin Reade's.' Apparently, the superior station of the gentry was maintained with the help of the court, for, when James Bullock, a tailor, ran his mare with a horse belonging to Dr.Matthew Slader for a high wager, he was fined and horseracing was declared 'a sport for gentlemen only.'

The LIGHTFOOT HOUSE (*headquarters of Colonial National Historical Park; free guide service for area*), a small brick building with a porch, was built in 1710. Philip Lightfoot (*see Tour* 24) purchased and made it his home in 1716.

The SWAN TAVERN, with kitchen, smokehouse, and stable in the yard, is a frame building with dormers on the gabled roof, which has hipped ends. The first tavern on the site, built in 1719–20, was destroyed in 1862 by the explosion of a powder magazine. A tavern built about 1880 was burned in 1915. The present one, a reconstruction, was erected in 1934. The kitchen and stable contain relics.

Rectangular GRACE CHURCH, with a cupola and carved doorway—late additions—was built in 1697. The walls, of local marl, have been hardened by the fires that have gutted the building. Though the furniture was acquired in 1928, the communion set was presented by Nathaniel Bacon,Sr., in 1649 to 'Hampton Parish in Yorke County, Virginia,' and was used in Hampton Church (*see below*) until this church was built. The bell, inscribed 'Yorktown, Virginia, 1725,' was broken when the church was burned during the War of 1812. It was taken away by Federal soldiers in 1865, found in Philadelphia, recast, and returned in 1889.

In the churchyard are the tombs of Thomas Nelson (1677–1745), a baroque saracophagus with the Nelson arms; of William Nelson (1711–72); and of General Thomas Nelson (1738–89)—father, son, and grandson.

Grace Church—the Colonial York-Hampton Church—was originally T-shaped. The interior has been burned twice, once during the Revolution when the church was used by the British as a magazine, and again in 1814. When it was used for military purposes during the 1860's, a signal tower was erected on its roof.

The CUSTOM HOUSE (*adm.* 25¢), a two-story building of brick with hipped roof, turns a plain end to Main Street and faces a brick-walled enclosure. It was built in 1706 and restored in 1929. Edward Ambler, collector of revenues, was among those who participated in Virginia's 'tea party' on November 3, 1774, when residents of the town boarded the *Virginia* and dumped overboard two half-chests of tea.

The NELSON HOUSE or York Hall (*open April* 1 *to Nov.* 1; *adm. to house* 75¢, *to garden* 50¢, *to both* $1), in a brick-walled garden, lifts a bulky rectangle of brick two stories to a deep cornice and a broad gabled roof. It has large dormers along the front, and two massive chimneys with heavily molded tops. The light stone corner quoins and unusually tall keystones in the deep segmental arches of brick over the windows add interest. There is considerable variety in the size and arrangement of the fully paneled rooms. The drawing room, off the paved transverse hall, has engaged columns to frame the openings.

The mansion was built in 1740–41 by William Nelson (1711–72), president of the Council, who was the father of Thomas Nelson (1738–89), later a signer of the Declaration of Independence, and Governor of Virginia. While Cornwallis occupied the house during the siege of 1781, General Nelson directed a cannonade against his own home; a ball is still embedded in one wall.

The one-story SHEILD HOUSE (*adm.* 25¢), on a high basement, lifts walls of large brick to a gabled roof with clipped ends. Outside chimneys and five dormers give character to the structure, which was built by Thomas Sessions about 1699.

The YORKTOWN MONUMENT, rising 95 feet above a green, is an elaborate and symbolically ornamented column of white marble bearing a figure of Liberty with arms outstretched. Though in 1781 Congress resolved to erect a marble column here, 'adorned with emblems of the alliance between the United States and His Most Christian Majesty (France) . . .' a century elapsed before another Congress provided the necessary money for it.

YORKTOWN BEACH (*bath houses* 25¢, *suits* 25¢), east of the ferry-landing, is of hard-packed sand and shelves rather quickly to deep water.

YORKTOWN GOLF COURSE (*greens fee* $1), administered by the National Park Service, is an 18-hole course.

1. Left from Yorktown on State 170 to the MOORE HOUSE (*adm.* 25¢), 1.3 *m.*, a compact frame building with steeply curbed hip roof and outside chimneys. Here representatives of General Washington and Lord Cornwallis met October 18, 1781, and arranged the terms of the British capitulation. The restored house is believed to have been built before 1750; during the Revolution, it was the home of Anne Moore, widow of Daniel Moore.

2. Right from Yorktown on the landscaped Colonial National Parkway to WILLIAMSBURG, 13 *m.* (*see Williamsburg*).

South of Yorktown white-painted signs along US 17 mark points of interest.

At 8.9 *m.* is a junction with State 27.

Left here to County 600, 2 *m.*, and R. 0.7 *m.* to an artificial lake, approximately the center of the BATTLEFIELD OF BIG BETHEL. On June 10, 1861, a force of 5,000 men, sent to seize two Confederate outposts, fought here for two hours to dislodge the 1,400 defenders, then withdrew to Hampton. Losses were slight on each side.

On State 27 at 4.1 *m.* is a junction with State 172; L. here 0.6 *m.* to the SITE OF CHESTERVILLE (R), heaps of bricks in a grove. This was the birthplace of George Wythe (1726–1806), first American professor of law (*see Williamsburg*). His father, Thomas Wythe, belonged to the landed gentry. His mother, Margaret Walker, was the daughter of George Walker, of merchant stock, and of Ann Keith, a woman with stamina not only to hold to the faith that was in her but also to resist, with frequent recourse to the council, her husband's interference with the religious training of her children. Margaret Walker Wythe was her son's first teacher.

MORRISON, 15.2 *m.*, is at a junction with US 60 (*see Tour 8a*), with which US 17 unites for 2.5 miles.

US 17 crosses the JAMES RIVER BRIDGE, 20.5 *m.*, one of three bridges in this section (*toll for this bridge alone or for all* 3: *car and driver* 80¢, *round trip* $1; *extra passenger* 20¢, *round trip* 30¢). The bridge, 4.5 miles long and completed in 1928, is of the lift-span type. The span rises 147 feet above the river, the towers 200 feet.

At 25.3 *m.* is a junction with an extension of US 17.

Right on the cross link to State 10 (*see Tour* 19), 3 *m.*

At 28 *m.* is CHUCKATUCK CREEK BRIDGE (*car and driver* 20¢, *round trip* 30¢; *each passenger* 10¢, *round trip* 15¢).

The NANSEMOND RIVER BRIDGE is crossed at 30.4 *m.* (*toll same as for Chuckatuck Bridge*).

PORTSMOUTH, 42.6 *m.* (11–12 alt., 45,704 pop.) (*see Portsmouth*).

DEEP CREEK, 49.7 *m.*, at the edge of the Dismal Swamp, was long a stagecoach stop and a shipping point for lumber.

The Dismal Swamp is a wilderness in which, through the centuries, trees have fallen and, with other plants, formed a mass of organic material. Much valuable timber had been cut in the swamp. The mass-material, reaching the peat stage, has raised the surface of the swamp at its center. Forest fires, burning to the depth of several feet, frequently continue for weeks. The swamp was described by Colonel William Byrd, one of the commissioners who in 1728 surveyed the boundary between Virginia and North Carolina. In his *History of the Dividing Line* he wrote: 'Since the surveyors had enter'd the Dismal, they had laid eyes on no living creature . . . Not so much as a Zealand frog cou'd endure so aguish a situation. It had one beauty . . . the moisture of the soil preserves a continual verdure . . . but at the same time the foul damps ascend without ceasing, corrupt the air, and render it unfit for respiration.'

If the swamp was ever as Colonel Byrd saw it, a remarkable change has taken place. The usual fauna of eastern Virginia are now found in the area. Black bear and wildcats are here, and copperhead snakes and rattlesnakes occur in large numbers.

In the village the Dismal Swamp Canal is crossed. This waterway, connecting the southern branch of the Elizabeth River with the sounds of North Carolina, was built largely to afford transportation for lumber from the swamp. The Dismal Swamp Canal Company was organized to cut the canal in 1787, but the canal was not completed until 1828.

Between the canal and Deep Creek, a tidal branch of the Elizabeth River, are locks. The canal water is amber colored because of the juniper logs that have been buried in the swamp for centuries. In the years before the development of refrigeration, the water of the swamp was highly valued for drinking purposes on ships, because it remained fresh for a long time.

Left from Deep Creek on State 166 to County 640, 3.8 *m.*, and R. to GREAT BRIDGE, 8.7 *m.* (100 pop.), at the western terminus of the Albemarle and Chesapeake Canal, a seven-mile canal connecting the North Landing River with the southern branch of the Elizabeth and forming part of the Intercoastal Waterway.

Here, on December 9, 1775, British troops suffered defeat in their first clash with Colonial regulars on Virginia soil. Governor Dunmore, having occupied Norfolk, fortified the northern end of the bridge and causeways then spanning this area, and blocked the only approach to Norfolk by land. About December 1 a force of 700 Colonials took position south of the bridge, began desultory firing that continued until December 9 when 200 British regulars, supported by 300 loyalists and Negroes, advanced over the causeway. The British abandoned their position during the night and evacuated Norfolk shortly thereafter.

South of Deep Creek the highway parallels the canal.

The OLD STONE HOUSE (*tea room*), 58.4 *m.*, built when the canal was opened, was the home of the superintendent of the canal locks.

At ARBUCKLE'S LANDING, 60.2 *m.*, a junction of the canal with the Feeder Ditch (*boats, with outboard motors, and guides to Lake Drummond available here and in vicinity;* $1 *a person, minimum* $3), is a U.S. Engineers' Station.

Right (by boat) on the ditch, which is 15 feet wide, to the locks of LAKE DRUMMOND, 3 *m.*, in the heart of the swamp. William Drummond, the first governor of North Carolina, who was hanged in 1677 by Governor William Berkeley for his share in Bacon's Rebellion, discovered the lake while hunting. The growth of juniper, cypress, gum, maple, poplar, ash, and oak is dense and continuous along the ditch; the undergrowth is filled with flowering water plants. The lake, with an altitude of 22, is upon an elevation much like an inverted saucer. It is five miles long and is rimmed with stumps of giant trees.

The swamp has inspired many legends. Thomas Moore, the Irish poet, visited it in 1803 and wrote *The Lake of the Dismal Swamp*, based on the local legend of a young man who became mentally deranged when his sweetheart died, and who imagined she was not dead but in the swamp. The poem describes his wanderings in search of the girl who had

> . . . gone to the Lake of the Dismal Swamp,
> Where all night long, by firefly lamp,
> She paddles her white canoe.

Fresh-water fish in fair quantities are in the lake and other waters of the swamp. (*Hunting and fishing subject to regulations of Federal Government in some parts of the swamp, of State in others.*)

At 63.2 *m.* US 17 crosses the North Carolina Line, 22 miles north of Elizabeth City,N.C. (*see North Carolina Guide*).

Tour 6A

Glenns—West Point—New Kent—Bottom's Bridge; 37.6 *m.* State 33.

Asphalt-surfaced roadbed throughout.
Accommodations at a few tourists camps and in West Point.

This highway crosses the Mattaponi and the Pamunkey and traverses wooded lowlands and elevations. The countryside has a charm derived from old homesteads, old churches, and neat farmhouses.

State 33 branches from US 17 (*see Tour 6a*) at GLENNS, 0 *m.*

CENTERVILLE, 8 *m.* (50 pop.), is at a junction with State 14 (*see Tour 1B*).

State 33 spans the Mattaponi River, 11.8 *m.*, cleared and improved after 1788 by order of the Virginia Assembly as far as the 'Mattaponi Trustees' believed necessary to give it 'a sufficient depth and width of water to navigate boats, batteaus, or canoes, capable of carrying four hogsheads of tobacco.'

WEST POINT, 12.7 *m.* (1,800 pop.), on the peninsula made where the Mattaponi and the Pamunkey unite to form the York, has developed since the completion of the railroad between West Point and Richmond in 1861. The town, which has a few industrial plants, is characterized by neat, shaded streets, bright residences, and steepled churches. Baltimore boats of the Chesapeake Steamship Company stop regularly at the West Point wharf.

West Point was named for the West brothers, Thomas, Francis, Nathaniel, and John—three of them governors of Virginia—but especially for John, who patented the land embracing the town's site. In 1607 West

Point was called Pamunkee or Pamunkey and was the chief village of the Pamunkey of the Powhatan Confederacy. From Pamunkey, Powhatan's brother and successor, Opechancanough carried out the massacres of 1622 and 1644. In 1646 Governor Berkeley led a company of soldiers against the chief, captured him, and bore him wounded on a stretcher to Jamestown, where he was shot by a sentry appointed to guard him. Opechancanough was succeeded by Necotowance, son of Powhatan's eldest sister, then by the Queen of Pamunkey, who was reigning in 1676. In that year, when trouble with northern Indians was threatening, she was invited to Jamestown to confer with the governor and council. The chairman asked her how many men she could furnish the colony in the war that seemed impending. At first she declined to speak, but finally uttered vehement reproaches against the English for their injustice and ingratitude. Her husband, Totopotomoi, had been slain with many of his men while assisting the settlers against the Ricahecreans, and she had never had 'any compensation for her loss.' After further parley, she 'abruptly quitted the room.'

In 1691 the general assembly directed that West Point be created a port of entry and in 1705 the burgesses authorized the town to qualify as a 'free borough' and named it Delaware, for Governor Thomas West, third Lord Delaware. The old name was resumed when the railroad was constructed.

The pulp and paper plant, western edge of town, odoriferously changes native pine wood into sulphate pulp and paper board. The olfactory nerves of local residents seem immune to the odor that other York River people, who have suffered because polluted water has brought about decline of the once profitable oyster business, find objectionable.

West Point is at a junction with State 30 (*see Tour 20A*).

State 33 crosses the PAMUNKEY RIVER, 13.1 *m.*, which was also an early transportation route. The traffic on the river was disturbed in June 1862, when boats conveying McClellan's supplies hurried upstream in the drive on Richmond, and later hurried down. A correspondent of the *New York Times* wrote: 'The river was crowded with descending crafts of all sizes and shapes laden with provisions and stores, barges lashed together and crowded, jibbering contrabands [Negroes] looking like flies upon a pancake . . .'

At 14.7 *m.* is a junction with a dirt road.

Right here 1.0 *m.* to the SITE OF ELTHAM, on the bank of the Pamunkey. The house, destroyed by fire in 1876, was built about 1730 by Colonel William Bassett, who married Martha Washington's sister, Anna Maria.

Washington often stopped here on his journeys between Mount Vernon and Williamsburg. In the spring of 1771 he was escorting his wife and her daughter, Martha Custis, whom he called 'Patcy,' to Williamsburg to obtain medical treatment for Patsy. On the journey Washington paid 'for 4 bottles of Fit Drops' for the invalid, who died two years later at the age of 16.

To Eltham General Washington galloped from Yorktown on November 5, 1781, to the bedside of his stepson, John Parke Custis, who had contracted camp fever during the Yorktown Campaign and lay here dying.

John Smith's map indicates that Matchot, an Indian village and scene of peace negotiations between the Indians and the settlers in 1613, had been on land that was later part of Eltham.

At 23.3 *m.* on State 33 is a junction with County 623.

Right here to a private road, 2.3 *m.*; L. to the SITE OF CHESTNUT GROVE, 3.4 *m.*, birthplace of Martha Dandridge, who became the wife of George Washington. The house burned in 1927.

Martha Dandridge was born on June 2, 1731, the first child of Colonel John Dandridge and Frances Jones. Her father came here from Hampton, following his brother William (*see Tour 20A*), and built his house about 1722.

NEW KENT, 24.1 *m.* (50 pop.), seat of New Kent County, is no larger now than it was in 1691, when it became the county seat.

The tiny COURTHOUSE (1906), upon a neat green, with the Confederate Monument before it, houses portraits of Martha and George Washington, executed by David Silvette, after Stuart. New Kent County, formed in 1654 from York County, was reduced in size in 1691 when its territory north of the Pamunkey River became King and Queen County.

The TAVERN, once a low brick building with dormers, has been given two full stories by a frame addition. When General George B. McClellan established communication headquarters here during the Peninsular Campaign of 1862, the town, for the only time in its history, heard the click of telegraph keys. It is told that a tavern keeper of *ante-bellum* days, a Mr.Howle, was so unwilling to cater to guests that the Reverend Mr.Jones was moved to reprove him with the grace: 'God bless the 'Owl that ate the fowl and left the bones for Servant Jones.'

At 26.1 *m.* is a junction with County 608.

Right here to County 609, 4.3 *m.*, and R. 0.3 *m.* to a private road; R. here to the SITE OF THE WHITE HOUSE, 0.8 *m.*, home of Martha Dandridge Custis at the time of her marriage to George Washington. The house was burned by Federal soldiers in 1862.

The estate was acquired by the eccentric John Custis IV (*see Tour 2*), who gave it to his son, Daniel Parke Custis, as a home for Martha Dandridge, his bride of 1749. Eight years later he died, leaving her with two children, John Parke Custis and Martha Parke Custis. Thus, when Martha Dandridge Custis met George Washington in May 1758, she was mistress of a large plantation.

The bride's home was probably the scene of her wedding with Washington, celebrated on January 6, 1759, 'at candle light.' Home weddings had become the custom because no church was ever lighted at night—a law of the colony prohibiting meetings of any kind at churches after sundown—and no church had any means of heating in winter.

White House passed to John Parke Custis, then to his son George Washington Parke Custis, George Washington's adopted son, who left it in 1857 to his grandson, William Henry Fitzhugh Lee, second son of General Robert E. Lee.

Not long after General Lee's family left Arlington (*see Tour 12*) in 1861, Mrs.Lee came here to stay with her daughter-in-law, Charlotte Wickham Lee, and she was here when McClellan's army began the march up the Peninsula. On May 11 the women left the White House, pinning on the front door a note: 'Northern soldiers who profess to reverence Washington, forbear to desecrate the home of his first married life, the property of his wife, now owned by her descendants.' A few days later there was penned under the note: 'Lady, a Northern officer has protected your property in sight of the enemy, and at the request of your overseer.' Though the Federal army stored supplies on the estate, General McClellan gave specific protection to the White House. None the less, in the confusion after McClellan's defeat at Gaines' Mill June 27, the White House was set afire and burned.

At 4.4 *m.* on County 608 is the entrance to a private dirt road; R. here 1.2 *m.* to Poplar Grove, a two-story brick house formerly L-shaped but now square with a hip roof. The house was built about 1725 by Colonel William Chamberlayne, whose son, Colonel Richard Chamberlayne, was owner in May 1758 when Colonel George Washington, attended by his body servant, Bishop, crossed the Pamunkey River by the ferry on his way to Williamsburg with dispatches. Colonel Chamberlayne, who happened to be at the landing, invited Washington to dine at his home. Acceptance of the invitation was impossible, Washington explained; the mission in Williamsburg was urgent. But when Colonel Chamberlayne promised an introduction to the 'prettiest and richest widow in Virginia,' George Washington yielded. He 'would dine—only dine'—and by 'borrowing of the night' could be in Williamsburg the following morning. While the faithful Bishop waited, holding by the bridle the handsome charger presented by General Braddock, Washington lingered on. At sunset Colonel Chamberlayne declared that no man left his house at such an hour. So Washington stayed the night. Though he went to Williamsburg the next day, he returned to visit Martha Dandridge Custis at White House before he set forth on the expedition against the French. And by July he was able to write to her that he embraced the opportunity 'to send a few words to one whose life is now inseperable from mine. Since that happy hour when we made our pledges to each other, my thoughts have been continually going to you as to another self.'

At 30 *m.* on State 33 is a junction with State 155.

Right on this road to County 614, 0.9 *m.*; L. here 0.6 *m.* to a junction with County 606 and L. again 6.2 *m.* to Hampstead (L), a large brick house among old trees and shrubbery. It has a hip roof with a platform and a parapet balustrade. There are tall-columned porticos on both fronts and pilasters adorn the walls. Ornamentation is even more elaborate in the interior. From the great central hall, a stairway winds to an observatory.

Hampstead was built in 1820 by Conrad Webb. Among the Webbs prominent in Colonial Virginia was George Webb, author of *The Office and Authority of a Justice of the Peace*, published in Williamsburg in 1736 and called 'Webb's Justice.'

On State 155 is St.Peter's Church (R), 1.6 *m.*, with its graveyard in a grove on a knoll. Though not built until 1701–03, its style is that of the low-pitched early-Colonial rectangular church, with arched windows. The arches of the huge tower rise to the level of the eaves. This tower, with porch and pyramidal steeple, was added in 1740. In 1719 a brick wall, since removed, was ordered built around the churchyard, 's'd wall . . . in all respects as well done as the Capitol wall in Williamsburg.' Except for mellowness of age, St.Peter's looks much as it did in the eighteenth century. Though St.Peter's survived the Revolution, its furnishings were destroyed during the War between the States. On the walls of the chancel remain two mural tablets, the only objects approaching ornamentation. One commemorates the Reverend David Mossom, who officiated at the marriage of George Washington; the other Colonel William Chamberlayne of Poplar Grove. Both are buried beneath the chancel. St.Peter's was the first brick church to be built in the parish and was called the 'Brick Church.' Only once in records of the Colonial era—in 1752—was it referred to as St.Peter's Church.

St.Peter's Parish, formed in 1679 from Blissland Parish, had four churches in 1704 when St.Paul's Parish was cut from it.

Here as elsewhere the colonial vestry concerned itself with matters material as well as those spiritual—one reason for the unpopularity of the Established Church at the time of the Revolution. But the Reverend Nicholas Moreau, rector from 1696 to 1697, wrote the Lord Bishop of Lichfield and Coventry: 'I don't like this Country at all, my Lord . . . Your clergy in these parts are of a very ill example . . . I have got in the very worst parish of Virginia and most troublesome . . . An eminent Bishop . . . sent over here . . . will make Hell tremble and settle the Church of England in these parts forever.'

Of the 17 rectors that served the parish from 1680 to 1789, the Reverend Mr.Mossom is the most noted—for longevity of service and irascibility of temper. He came to the Colonies in 1718, was minister at Marblehead, Mass., from 1718–26, and rector of St.Peter's Parish from 1727–67. Having a quarrel with the clerk, he threatened from the pulpit to thrash him. Undaunted, the clerk announced the hymn.

With restless and ungovern'd rage,
  Why do the heathen storm?
  Why in such rash attempts engage,
  As they can ne'er perform?

Bishop Meade wrote with masculine generosity: 'He was married four times and much harassed by his last wife . . . which may account for and somewhat excuse a little peevishness.'

BOTTOM'S BRIDGE, 37.6 *m.*, is at a junction with US 60 (*see Tour 8a*).

Tour 7

Virginia Beach—Norfolk—Suffolk—Emporia—South Hill—Boydton—Danville—Martinsville—Marion—Bristol—Gate City (Cumberland Gap, Tenn.). US 58, State 88, US 58.
Virginia Beach to Tennessee Line; 536.7 *m.*

Hard-surfaced roadbed throughout, chiefly asphalt, with three-lane concrete east of Suffolk.
Southern Ry. roughly parallels route between Norfolk and Danville; Danville & Western R.R. between Danville and Stuart; Southern Ry. between Bristol and Clinchport; Louisville & Nashville R.R. between Jonesville and Tennessee Line.
All types of accommodations throughout, chiefly in towns.

US 58, called the J.E.B.Stuart Memorial Highway to honor the Confederate cavalry leader killed during the War between the States, roughly parallels the southern State boundary, passing from the broad Tidewater region through the Southside tobacco country and across the Blue Ridge into the valleys and mountains of Southwest Virginia.

Section a. VIRGINIA BEACH to EMPORIA; 97.3 *m. US* 58

This section of US 58 crosses fertile lowlands where truck gardening prospers. Weathered frame buildings, including the inevitable garish filling station, mark the crossroads, but in byways are old houses that have survived the centuries. Here and there, as the highway pushes toward the tobacco belt, are occasional cotton fields.

US 58 runs west from a junction with US 60 (*see Tour 8a*) in VIRGINIA BEACH, 0 *m.* (12 alt., 1,719 pop.) (*see Tour 8a*).

Cities and Towns

LOWER PRINCE STREET, ALEXANDRIA

Photograph by courtesy of the Norfolk Advertising Bo

***U. S. S. OKLAHOMA* AGAINST NORFOLK'S SKYLINE**

FIVE O'CLOCK, NEWPORT NEWS SHIPYARD, NEWPORT NEWS

Photograph by courtesy of the Farm Security Administrat

otograph by courtesy of the Virginia Conservation Commission

AIRVIEW OF RICHMOND, SHOWING MONUMENT AVENUE

Photograph by W. Lincoln Hightc

SMITHFIELD

A TIDEWATER MAIN STREET, WITH COURTHOUSE AND CONFEDERATE SOLDIER'S MEMORIAL—TAPPAHANNOCK

Photograph by W. Lincoln Hightc

otograph by W. Lincoln Highton

VILLAGE STORE, YORKTOWN

Photograph by W. Lincoln Highto

AUTUMN RAIN, LEESBURG

RESIDENTIAL STREET, TANGIER ISLAND

graph by W. Lincoln Highton

SALUDA

Photograph by courtesy of the Norfolk Advertising Boc

THE BIG GUNS, FORT STORY

ARTIFICIAL WHIRLWIND—WORLD'S LARGEST WIND TUNNEL, LANGLEY FIELD

Photograph by courtesy of the National Advisory Committee for Aeronaut

SEA TACK, 1.1 *m.*, a handful of frame houses, has a name that is an abbreviated form of 'sea attack'—reminder of the time during the War of 1812 when cannon balls from guns of the British fleet fell here in an attack on the coast.

At 2.7 *m.* is a junction with County 615.

1. Right here to the HORATIO CORNICK HOUSE (R), 3.7 *m.*, a weathered frame building built about 1773. Originally a rectangle with a gambrel roof pierced by three shallow dormers, it was early enlarged. Outside end chimneys were then paired by smaller ones that serve the additions.

BROAD BAY MANOR (R), 4.4 *m.*, is a group of brick houses on a close-cropped lawn descending to Broad Bay. It is approached through a vast trucking field hemmed in by pine trees, against which the oxblood red of evenly-spaced tenant houses stands out in bold relief.

The nucleus and oldest of this series of houses is a diminutive building that has become a mere hyphen linking a new brick unit on the right with a Georgian dwelling. The thick brick walls form only one room. The two-and-a-half-story Georgian unit has recessed windows, high ceilings, and a fine stairway. The modern part of this multiple house is comparable to the Georgian structure in size but not in style.

Behind this group is a rectangular building with a gambrel roof, end chimneys, and two doors, side by side, overlooking the water. On the west end an open stairway glistens white against pink brick speckled with weathered blue headers.

In 1636, when this section was a part of New Norfolk County, Governor John West granted 550 acres to an enterprising bachelor, Thomas Allen, who spent most of his time transporting tobacco to England and had small need for a spacious domicile. It was he, perhaps, who built the small house and also the later gambrel-roof building, which were on the land when James Kempe conveyed the plantation in 1770 to Lemuel Cornick I.

Brick columns at 4.8 *m.* mark the entrance-lane (R) to GREEN HILL, a two-story house of brick laid in Flemish bond with blue headers. The date '1791' is cut in one of the bricks. The front of this rectangular house looks out past huge live oaks, while the rear faces a former kitchen at the head of a greensward that descends to sand-circled Broad Bay.

At 5.6 *m.* is the sandy entrance-lane (L) to the KEELING HOUSE, overlooking shimmering Lynnhaven River. Built late in the seventeenth century, the walls of this story-and-a-half house are notable for their fine Colonial brick work. In the gable ends, pierced by small windows that were apparently casement openings, the Flemish bonding gives way above the eave level to a striped pattern picked out in blue-glazed headers. End chimneys give height, and dormers relieve the severity of the steep-pitched roof. Enlarged by a modern brick kitchen wing, this substantial old house surveys flat truck fields that stretch to distant walls of pine.

When Adam Keeling I made his will in 1683, he left to his son Thomas this parcel of land 'commonly known by ye name of Dudlies . . . beinge near four hundred acres.' Thomas Keeling evidently built the house.

2. Left from US 58 on County 615 to SALISBURY PLAINS (L), 0.5 *m.*, a weathered house that looms against pine trees, across a field green with vegetables. It has one solid brick end-wall containing a chimney, while the rest is frame. The 60-foot façade is relieved by a porch and five dormers in the gambrel roof. The walls of the spacious hall are broken by wide doors and a graceful stairway. There is full paneling in the parlor.

William Cornick, son of 'Simond Cornix' of Salisbury, England, gave his sandy acres, patented in 1659, the name of his father's birthplace. The will of his son Joel, dated 1727, left part of the plantation to a son of the same name, with the responsibility of '. . . finishing the house I am now building.'

EASTERN SHORE CHAPEL (L), 0.9 *m.*, built in 1754 as a chapel of Lynnhaven parish, is a story-and-a-half rectangle of mellow red brick, its steep-pitched roof forming deep Victorian gables with slight returns. The openings are round-arched with brick. The original silver communion service, dated 1759, is still in use.

LONDON BRIDGE, 4.2 *m.*, is a scattered collection of bungalows, tourist cabins, and filling stations.

1. Right from London Bridge on County 632 to the lengthy entrance-lane (R), 0.4 *m.*, that runs arrowlike through a wide field of vegetables to the JACOB HUNTER HOUSE. This steep-pitched gambrel-roofed structure, covered with pinkish whitewash through which the Flemish bond of the old brick walls is visible, sits on a high foundation. The shallow dormers piercing the lower roof-surface have counterparts flanking the two slender outside chimneys that not only balance but give height to the rectangular building. In 1714 Adam Keeling sold to John Pallet I this plantation, called Wolf's Snare. Five years later, John Pallet II came into possession of the estate. It was doubtless he who built the house, for, in 1777, when he divided the plantation, he specified that he was giving his son Matthew the part containing a dwelling subject to his mother's use during her widowhood.

2. Left from London Bridge on County 632 to the BUTTS HOUSE (L), 6.2 *m.*—the Jonathan Woodhouse Plantation Home—a compact, gambrel-roofed building so pleasingly designed that not even the dilapidated frame kitchen wing at right angles detracts from its proportions. The old delicately pink brick walls taper at the ends beneath a roof so gently pitched as to seem curving. The entry door is between narrow windows topped with flat brick arches, and three dormers cast their shadows on the lower roof. Several Jonathan Woodhouses have lived in this house, all descended from Captain William Woodhouse, Sr., and his wife Pembroke, who are doubtless the people referred to by the initials 'W.W.P. 1760' cut on each side of the façade.

In a garden sheltered by huge oaks is the FRANCIS THOROWGOOD LAND HOUSE (L), 5.9 *m.*, a large brick gambrel-roofed building with five gabled dormers piercing the green shingles of the lower roof. The cellar is divided into two rooms, each with a fireplace. Much of the structure has been altered, including the roof, windows, and doors.

In 1753, sometime after Francis Thorowgood Land (born in 1736) had come into possession of this land, he added to the tract, and then, doubtless, built the house.

At 10.4 *m.* is a junction with County 647.

Right on this road to DONATION CHURCH (R), 2.4 *m.*, in a grass plot among pine and oak trees. The restored building is rectangular, of red brick with high-pitched roof. It was built in 1736 and succeeded a predecessor, erected in 1692, and Lynnhaven Parish's first church, completed by 1640 on another site. The Reverend Thomas Dickson in 1776 left his farm in trust to the vestry, the income to be used to employ 'an able and discreet teacher in the Latin and Greek languages and mixed mathematics' for the instruction of male orphans of the parish. This, according to tradition, led to the church's being called 'Dickson's Donation Church' and later 'Donation Church.' The old building was gutted by a forest fire in 1882, and only the walls were standing when restoration was begun in 1916. The old silver communion service, pewter collection plate, and marble font, recovered from the river, have survived.

Beside Donation Church is a private road (R) leading across flat fields to FERRY FARM in a wood. The house, its whitewashed brick walls rising in three sections to gabled roofs, overlooks an arm of Lynnhaven River. Anthony Walke II directed that if he 'should depart this life' before erecting 'a decent Dwelling House,' then '1000£ current money' should be 'laid out . . . in building on the Land . . . called "Ferry" Plantation at the old Court House.' The duty doubtless fell to his son William Walke (1762–95). This was the site of Princess Anne's second courthouse (*c.*1735–*c.*1751).

Close by Donation Church stood Princess Anne County's first courthouse. Soon after the county was formed in 1691 a courthouse was ordered built 'in Jno. Keelings old field by London Bridge,' but the courthouse was not erected until about 1696 and then here on 'land belonging to the Brick Church.' In this building one of Virginia's two witch trials was held. Early in 1706 Mrs. Grace Sherwood, a widow and mother of a family, having plagued the community with petty lawsuits, was haled before the county court on the charge of having bewitched the wife of Luke Hill. A jury of women examined Grace's body and declared they found physical signs by which witches were identified. The court stopped the proceedings. Whereupon Hill took the case before the Council of State, which evaded a decision and sent the case back to the county court. A second jury of women refused to act and was promptly fined for contempt of court. On July 7, Grace Sherwood agreed to be 'tried in the water by ducking,' but the 'weather being very rainy and bad so that it might possible endanger her health,' the trial was postponed until July 10. On the afternoon of that day, near 'William Harper's Plantation,' she was subjected to the test. Her hands were bound, and she was thrown into water 'above a man's depth.' To swim was proof of occult powers; to sink, a sign of innocence. Grace Sherwood swam—disregarding the boat provided to rescue her. Afterwards, she was searched by 'five ancient and knowing women' who 'all declared on oath' that 'she was not like them, or no other woman that they knew of . . .' Thus convicted, she was committed to the 'common gaol.' A land grant issued in Grace Sherwood's name in 1714 indicated that the jail term ended her legal punishment.

At 12.6 *m.* on US 58 is a junction with State 165.

Left on this road to the JAMES BARRY ROBINSON HOME FOR BOYS (R), 0.5 *m.*, a Roman Catholic institution, housed in a group of modern three-story brick buildings on a farm.

At 1 *m.* is a junction with County 654; R. here 1.5 *m.* on a poor road to the SITE OF NEW TOWN, in Colonial days a lively little port, established in 1697 and made the county seat in 1751. Near by lived Colonel Edward Hack Moseley, who, when Lord Dunmore was entertained in Norfolk in 1774, was summoned by an express 'to come to town with his famous wig and shining buckles, he being the finest gentleman we had, to dance the minuet with Lady Dunmore, the Mayor of Norfolk, Captain Abyvon, not being equal to the occasion.' In 1778 the county court was moved to Kempsville.

On State 165 is KEMPSVILLE, 3.2 *m.* (100 pop.), a village of old houses under arching trees. A severe moral note is frequently injected by the presence of traditionally garbed Dunkards from farms near by. With tobacco warehouses by the canal and a deep water landing, flourishing Kemp's Landing, as the place was called before its incorporation as Kempsville in 1783, reached the pinnacle of its importance during the Revolution.

In 1775 Lord Dunmore, persisting in his hunt for rebel 'Shirtmen,' came on foot to Kemp's Landing, where, on the night of November 14, a skirmish took place between his troops and the Colonial militia. 'They fire one Gun at our flanking partee & two at our advance Guard . . .' wrote John Brown, one of the British soldiers. 'This was returned with a heavee fire from the Grandeers, which instantly put the Villians to flight. We killed a few of them on the spott, drove them into a river where two of them drowned, took ninetten prisoners.' The victorious Dunmore immediately set up his standard at the home of George Logan, a Scotch Tory, where, says a local historian, 'those who could not conveniently run away came at once, took the oath of allegiance and had the red badge pinned on their breasts.'

EMMANUAL EPISCOPAL CHURCH, an ivy-covered brick building, with pillared façade, a square, white belfry, and pointed arches above the windows, was consecrated by Bishop William Meade in 1843. Beside it is LYNNHAVEN PARISH HOUSE, a frame building with four dormers in its gambrel roof. Its oldest part was built before 1762, probably by John Michael Kenline.

PLEASANT HALL, opposite the church, a two-story brick house, stands on a shaded lawn. Of the elaborate woodwork on the interior, the most notable is in the parlor, where white-painted paneling extends from wainscoting to rich cornice. Cut in a brick above a basement window is the date 'April 19, 1779,' which seems to indicate that the house was built by wealthy Peter Singleton, as extravagant in dress as he was reckless at cards.

Behind Pleasant Hall is the former COURTHOUSE, now abandoned. When the court was moved to Kemp's Landing in 1778, a levy was laid 'for fixing up and making convenient [George] Logan's dry good store for use as a court house, and a part of the wet goods store for the jail to be used until such places should be built.' The courthouse was built prior to 1789. The brick JAIL adjacent, erected in 1787, has been used as a school, and finally as a private residence.

PRINCESS ANNE, 11.2 *m.* (150 pop.), in flat, truck-farming country, has been since 1824 seat of Princess Anne County, created in 1691 from lower Norfolk County; its name is that of the princess who later became queen. The first county seat was at Lynnhaven; second (1751) at New Town; third (1778) at Kemp's Landing; and since 1824 at Princess Anne.

NORFOLK, 18.8 *m.* (11 alt., 129,710 pop.) (*see Norfolk*).

US 58 westward leaves Norfolk by way of the Norfolk-Portsmouth Ferry from the foot of Commerce St.

PORTSMOUTH, 19.1 *m.* (33 alt., 45,704 pop.) (*see Portsmouth*).

In Portsmouth is a junction with US 17 (*see Tour 6b*).

At 28 *m.* the highway, bordered by a deep ditch, begins to skirt the gray upper reaches of Dismal Swamp (*see Tour 6b*).

SUFFOLK, 38.6 *m.* (33 alt., 10,271 pop.) (*see Tour* 18), is at a junction with US 460 (*see Tour* 18) and State 10 (*see Tour* 19).

West of Suffolk the fields along US 58 have a rather pleasant monotony with their long rows of growing vegetables. Gray farm buildings and patches of swampland break the pattern.

At HOLLAND, 50.6 *m.* (371 pop.), in 1928, under the leadership of J.J. Gwaltney and T.V.Downing, the Ruritan National was organized as a service club for civic improvement in rural communities. Chartered as a National organization in 1929, it now has a membership of 2,500 farmers and business men in Virginia and the Carolinas.

FRANKLIN, 61.1 *m.* (20 alt., 2,930 pop.), is a flourishing town by the Blackwater River. Business places and pleasant residence streets are along the south side of the river; while on the north bank rise the tall chimneys of the mills, drying sheds, and yards of a large lumber company.

Left from Franklin on US 258 to the North Carolina line, 11 *m.* (*see North Carolina Guide*).

COURTLAND, 70.4 *m.* (355 pop.), a scattered village with a courthouse, stores, and homes deep on shady lawns along the highway, is the seat of Southampton County. Until 1888 the town was called Jerusalem.

The SOUTHAMPTON COUNTY COURTHOUSE, of brick, painted gray, with tall front portico, is on a narrow strip lying between the highway and the Nottoway River. The one-story CLERK'S OFFICE at the rear section of the building was built as the second county courthouse in 1749. Alterations made in 1825 included removal of a fence put up in 1751 to keep horse traders from using the courthouse steps as an auction block. Southampton County, created in 1748 from Isle of Wight, was named for the Earl of Southampton, treasurer of the London Company.

Right from Courtland on State 35 to CHARLIE'S HOPE PLANTATION (L), 7.7 *m.*, approached between broken rows of aged cedars. The L-shaped house was built in 1825 by Charles Fox Urquhart. The neglected interior has elaborately carved high mantels, wainscoting, and paneled doors. Behind the house are the former workshops and slave cabins.

The highway crosses the Nottoway River, 70.7 *m.*, bordered on both sides by swampland covered with gum, juniper, and high-kneed cypress trees.

At 72.5 *m.* is a junction with State 35. Plantations bordering this road (L) from Boykins to Courtland (at that time called Jerusalem) were in August 1831 the scene of the greatest slave uprising in the history of the United States. Leader of the uprising was one Nat Turner, who had taught himself to read the Bible and had impressed upon his followers that he had Divine guidance to free the slaves of the neighborhood and 'go into Jerusalem.' The county seat was the only Jerusalem known to Turner. Negroes at a Sunday camp meeting, exhorted to frenzy by Turner, armed themselves with corn knives, axes, and scythes and followed him in an orgy of butchery. They went first to the Travis plantation, home of Nat's master, near Cross Keys, where they killed the entire family. The slaves continued across the country, plundering and gathering recruits as they went. Fifty-five whites, including 12 pupils of a girls' school, were killed before troops summoned from Richmond and Norfolk arrived. Many slaves were killed by the soldiers, and of those captured 19 were later hanged. Turner escaped and for two months eluded hundreds of searchers. He was captured on October 30, 1831, in a cave under a fence near his old home, tried, and hanged.

Left on State 35 to State 194, 4.4 *m.*, and L. to County 671, 7.2 *m.*; L. again to the BIRTHPLACE OF MAJOR GENERAL GEORGE H. THOMAS (L), 9.6 *m.*, a plain white frame farmhouse, shaded by a magnificent oak tree. Here Thomas, one of the few Virginians to serve in the Union army during the War between the States, was born July 31, 1816. When General Thomas, a West Point graduate and veteran of the Mexican War, made his choice in 1861, it is said that his family turned his portrait to the wall. After the Battle of Chickamauga, September 1863, when his division held the Union line at a vital point, Thomas was called 'the Rock of Chickamauga.'

At 88.6 *m.* is a junction with County 615.

Right on County 615 to County 612, 2.6 *m.*, and L. to the MASON HOUSE (L), 4.2 *m.*, white frame, on a hill. Here, on April 18, 1799, was born John Y. Mason, member of Congress 1831–37, Secretary of the Navy 1844–45, Attorney-General 1845–46, Secretary of the Navy 1846–49, and minister to France until his death in 1859. Mason was one of the three diplomats who in 1854 met unofficially at Ostend, Belgium, and wrote the Ostend Manifesto, which called on the United States to take possession of Cuba. In 1846 Spain, refusing President Polk's offer of purchase, had said that she would rather sink the island than let the United States have it. The Ostend document, therefore, caused a diplomatic sensation.

At EMPORIA, 97.3 *m.* (2,144 pop.), is a junction with US 301 (*see Tour 14*).

Section b. EMPORIA to DANVILLE; 117.3 *m. US* 58

West of Emporia the highway cuts its way through vast tobacco fields chiefly cultivated by sharecroppers and other tenant farmers. Soil and climate combine here for the production of 'bright' tobacco, mainstay of the world's cigarette business. On farms where log curing-barns, chinked with red clay, dominate the fields, farmers grow, cure, and sell tobacco. The all-important event of the farm year is the late summer tobacco market, when high-piled trucks and farm wagons roll into town night and day, carrying the crop and the farmer's fortunes for the year. In this one-crop country, the singsong jargon of the warehouse auctioneer determines whether the grower will get a new automobile or an extension on the mortgage. In this world given over to tobacco, even the county fair of more diversified agricultural sections has been supplanted by an all-tobacco festival, a dressed-up, carnival-like affair of ceremonies, balls, and a big parade with bands and ornate floats dripping tobacco leaves, all presided over by a tobacco 'queen' and her court.

US 58 continues westward from the junction with US 301 in EMPORIA, 0 *m.*

LAWRENCEVILLE, 20 *m.* (1,629 pop.), on hills sloping gently to the Meherrin River, is the business center and seat of Brunswick County. The town's name honors Lawrence, a favorite horse of Colonel James Rice, who in 1814 gave land for the townsite and was granted the privilege of naming the settlement.

South of the business district is ST.PAUL'S NORMAL AND INDUSTRIAL SCHOOL FOR NEGROES, which was founded in 1888 by the Reverend James Solomon Russell. It now cares for 1,000 pupils in a group of modern red brick buildings, on a landscaped campus, and on a 1,600-acre farm. James Russell, born a slave, was educated at Hampton Institute and, through the efforts of Mrs.Pattie Buford, was enabled to study for the Protestant Episcopal priesthood. At Lawrenceville, in the heart of Virginia's five-county belt containing 60,000 Negroes, Dr.Russell opened St.Paul's Protestant Episcopal Chapel and acquired three acres of land and a dilapidated cabin for a school. Incorporated in 1890, the school three years later came under the supervision of the Protestant Episcopal Church Institute for Negroes.

The BRUNSWICK COUNTY COURTHOUSE, of red brick with tall white Ionic portico, was built about 1854. As Union troops approached Lawrenceville during the War between the States, the county clerk, realizing the hopelessness of trying to hide huge books, spread his Masonic apron on his desk and left the office door open. The records were not molested. Brunswick County was formed in 1720 from Prince George and named for the ducal lands of the House of Hanover. In 1733 Surry and Isle of Wight contributed territory, and in 1745 Lunenburg was cut from Brunswick.

Native to this county is Brunswick Stew, a flavorous brew first concocted by a group of hunters. One of the party, who had been detailed to stay in camp as cook, lazily threw all the supplies into a pot, it is said, and cooked the mixture over a slow fire. When his companions returned, cold and exhausted, they found the concoction a most appetizing dish. The time-honored directions for making this luscious meal are: boil about 9 pounds of game—squirrels are preferred—in 2 gallons of water until tender; add to the rich stock 6 pounds of tomatoes, 1 pound of butter-beans, 6 slices of bacon, 1 red pepper; salt to taste; cook 6 hours and add 6 ears of corn cut from the cob; boil for 8 minutes.

At 20.8 *m.* is a junction with State 34.

Left here to County 686, 0.9 *m.*, and R. to the SITE OF FORT CHRISTANNA (R), 3.1 *m.*, a stockade built by Governor Spotswood in 1714. An ancient unmounted cannon, one of five that guarded the palisades, marks the place. Spotswood persuaded the peaceful Saponi to move their village 'within musket shot' of Fort Christanna—the name combining the Savior's and the British queen's—and to patrol the country between the Appomattox and the Roanoke, favorite hunting ground of savage Tuscarora. He also set up a school for Indian children, regarding these youths as valuable hostages against Indian attacks. The Virginia Indian Company built the school, and the governor paid the salary of 'the worthy Mr. Charles Griffin,' the teacher.

In 1722, the Fort Christanna school was merged with the one at Williamsburg.

At 22.1 *m.* on US 58 is a junction with County 647.

Right here to a group of white-painted frame buildings (R), 0.2 *m.*, the CHURCH HOME FOR DISABLED AND INFIRM NEGROES, known as 'Mrs. Buford's Hospital.' In 1875 Mrs.Pattie Buford used a building on the family plantation as a refuge for homeless and bewildered Negroes. After Mrs.Buford's personal funds were exhausted, the Protestant Episcopal Church Institute for Negroes financed the home until the last inmate died in 1912.

LA CROSSE, 35.6 *m.* (427 pop.), rambles away from a railroad junction.

SOUTH HILL, 38.4 *m.* (1,405 pop.) (*see Tour 1c*), is at a junction with US 1 (*see Tour 1c*), which unites with US 58 to a junction at 44.6 *m.* (*see Tour 1c*).

BOYDTON, 55 *m.* (500 alt., 493 pop.), a pleasant town built around the shady courthouse square, was named for Alexander Boyd, a county judge who died in 1801 while holding court. BOYD'S GRAVE, on the lawn of a private home in the village, is marked by a curiously-worded epitaph giving in detail the circumstances of his death. Noteworthy among buildings in the town is ST. JAMES EPISCOPAL CHURCH, built about 1840, a simple red brick rectangle with graceful white cupola, and the METHODIST EPISCOPAL CHURCH, with modillioned cornice, cupola, and slender spire. The MECKLENBURG COUNTY COURTHOUSE, a handsome, well-proportioned red brick structure with tall white Ionic columns in its pedimented portico, was built about 1842. The county was created in 1764 from Lunenburg County and its name honors Princess Charlotte of Mecklenburg-Strelitz, queen of George III.

The FIRST HOME OF RANDOLPH-MACON COLLEGE (R), 56.1 *m.*, two red brick buildings, was given up in 1868 when the institution was moved to Ashland (*see Tour 1b*). This first Methodist Episcopal college in the United States was chartered in 1830, sponsored by the Virginia and North Carolina conferences, and named for John Randolph of Roanoke and Nathaniel Macon of North Carolina. From 1879 until 1916 the buildings here were occupied by the Boydton Academic and Bible Institute for Negroes.

At 64 *m.* is a junction with US 15 (*see Tour 3e*), which unites with US 58 for 1 mile.

OCCANEECHEE ISLAND (*private*) lies (R) as US 58 crosses the Roanoke River, 64.7 *m.*, formed above the island by the union of the Dan and Staunton Rivers. Now a stock farm, the island was once a village of the peaceful and industrious Occaneechee, who traded with other Indians of a broad area. These shrewd Indians, having established a fur monopoly, saw the white man not as a new enemy but as a new customer. On the trail of the marauding Susquehannock, who had fled here, Nathaniel Bacon brought his militia to the island in 1676 and persuaded the Occaneechee to join in expelling the visitors. This accomplished, trouble flared up between the whites and their Indian allies, ending in a two-day battle in which Occaneechee village was destroyed.

In CLARKSVILLE, 64.9 *m.* (800 pop.), on a hill above the river, a bustling little main street stretches toward a group of comfortable homes. The town is a market for flue-cured tobacco.

At 71.9 *m.* is a junction with County 732.

Right here to BUFFALO MINERAL SPRINGS, 0.3 *m.*, where frame boarding houses and cottages are reminders that the Springs have been popular since horse and buggy days. William Byrd II, in 1727 the Springs' first white visitor, is said to have so named the place because of the buffalo grazing near by.

At 86 *m.* is a junction with US 501 (*see Tour 11b*).

DANVILLE, 117.3 *m.* (413 alt., 22,247 pop.) (*see Tour 20b*), is at junction with US 360 (*see Tour 20b*) and US 29 (*see Tour 4c*).

Section c. DANVILLE to MARION; 170.3 *m.* *US* 58, *State* 88

West of Danville US 58 follows the north bank of the Dan River through a fringe of steel-fenced cotton mills, neighborhood stores, and workers' homes, and then swings across open farm country. The terrain gradually becomes more rugged as the highway rises to wind through foothills, and soon the Blue Ridge appears, first as a misty blue line against the horizon westward, then as blue-veiled peaks and sloping wilderness.

US 58 continues westward from Main St., 0 *m.*, in DANVILLE.

At 8.8 *m.* is a junction with County 863.

Left here to OAK HILL (L), 6.1 *m.*, a handsome brick house built in 1823 by Samuel Hairston. A wide flagstone path between English box leads to the pillared front entrance, and at the rear is a formal garden flanked by slave cabins. In large rooms with high ceilings are paneled wainscoting and elaborately carved mantels.

MARTINSVILLE, 29.2 *m.* (1,025 alt., 7,705 pop.) (*see Tour 21b*), is at a junction with US 220 (*see Tour 21b*).

SMITH RIVER DAM (R), 31.3 *m.*, furnishes electric power for Martinsville.

PATRICK SPRINGS, 55.4 *m.*, is a cluster of frame dwellings, a garage, and a railroad station below No Business Mountain (R).

STUART, 60.4 *m.* (1,450 alt., 588 pop.), in the foothills of the Blue Ridge, is a trading center and seat of Patrick County. Its one industrial venture, a silk mill, is no more. First called Taylorsville, the town in 1884 changed its name to honor the Confederate general, J.E.B.Stuart, born in the county February 6, 1833.

The PATRICK COUNTY COURTHOUSE, a red brick structure on a fenced-in green, was built in 1852 and remodeled in 1928. A weathered STATUE OF GENERAL STUART is near it. Patrick County was sliced from Henry County in 1790 and took the first name of the Revolutionary orator.

Westward US 58 runs through the shadowed, mountain gorge formed by the Mayo River in its swift descent from the mountains and then sweeps upward in long curves. All around are views of clouded peaks towering above valleys checkered with red plowed fields and green patches of pine woods.

From LOVERS' LEAP (R), 70.2 *m.* (3,300 alt.), a beautiful setting for the well-worn tale of lovers who chose death rather than separation, is a far reaching view across miles of mountains to sunny valleys.

At 76.1 *m.* is a junction with County 602.

Left here to County 607, 3.1 *m.*, and L. to County 614, 3.5 *m.*; R. here to the PINNACLES OF THE DAN (L), 5.1 *m.*, a deep gorge through which the Dan drops in a series of cascades. In the canyon is the PINNACLES HYDROELECTRIC DEVELOPMENT, a system of dams and reservoirs creating power for Danville. This P.W.A. project cost $3,400,000 and was completed in 1938.

At 76.2 *m.* is a junction with the Blue Ridge Parkway, an isolated section of a proposed 480-mile parked highway system that will follow the summit of the Appalachian Mountain ranges and connect the Shenandoah and the Great Smokies National Parks. Another completed section is the Skyline Drive (*see Tours 4A and 21B*).

In HILLSVILLE, 97.3 *m.* (2,570 alt., 485 pop.), seat of Carroll County, the highway widens to become the main street, bordered by spic-and-span cottages with flowery front yards, general stores, the neon-signed drugstore, the new buff brick school, and the county courthouse.

In the CARROLL COUNTY COURTHOUSE, a red brick building with white columned entrance, the mountain clan of Allen ran amok on March 12, 1912, during the trial of Floyd Allen, arraigned for freeing two youthful members of the clan who had been arrested for disturbing a church meeting. Trouble was expected when the mountaineers rode into town and the courtroom was crowded. After the jury's verdict of guilty and the refusal of a new trial, Judge Thornton L. Massie imposed sentence of a year in jail. As the prisoner stood up and shouted, 'I ain't a-goin'!' a volley blazed 'like the crackle of mountain laurel,' a witness said. The judge, the commonwealth attorney, the sheriff, the jury foreman, and a witness for the prosecution were killed, and the clerk of court was wounded. Then the Allens rode off into the hills. Subsequently caught, two were sentenced to death and four to prison. Of these, two were pardoned by Governor E.Lee Trinkle in 1924 and two by Governor Harry F. Byrd in 1926. In the mountains the shooting is remembered in the doleful ballad 'Claude Allen.'

Carroll County was cut from Grayson County in 1842 and named for Charles Carroll of Carrollton, who died in that year.

Right from Hillsville on US 52, which by-passes an old COVERED BRIDGE, 2.1 *m.*, that once carried it across Reed Island Creek.

At 11 *m.* is a junction with State 91; L. here 3.5 *m.* to County 636 and R. to AUSTINVILLE, 4.2 *m.*, successor to The Lead Mines, on the western side of the river, seat of old Fincastle County. The lead mines along New River were first developed by Colonel John Chiswell, who discovered deposits here in 1756. By the end of the eighteenth century numerous small industrial developments, including lead and zinc mines, furnaces and forges, had sprung up in the area, which became particularly important during the Revolution. In July 1775 the assembly directed the Fincastle Committee of Safety to contract with the mines for 'such quantities of lead as may be judged necessary,' and, should the owners be unco-operative, to operate the mines 'at the charge of the colony.' Both the Lead Mines and Fort Chiswell near by were later garrisoned for the protection of the mines. Production seems to have lagged, for, in October 1776, the assembly empowered the governor to engage 'slaves, servants or others' to work the mines 'to greater advantage.' When more serious difficulties threatened in 1780 Colonel Charles Lynch, superintendent of the mines, resorted to extra-legal methods to suppress Tory activities seeking to stop production. For his harsh actions he was later exonerated by the legislature (*see Tour 4c*).

Fincastle County was created in 1772 from part of Botetourt County as government kept pace with the tide of settlement pushing the frontier toward the southwest. Its boundaries embraced all Southwest Virginia, eastern Kentucky, and part of Tennessee. But Fincastle County disappeared from the map of Virginia in December 1776, when its territory was divided into the 'County of Kentucky' and the counties of Montgomery and Washington.

The farmhouse on the lead mine's land was the birthplace on November 3, 1793, of Stephen Fuller Austin (1793–1836), son of Moses Austin, a Connecticut Yankee who came to Virginia in 1784 and, with his brother Stephen, developed the village of Austinville as headquarters of their mining operations in this vicinity. In 1797 Moses Austin journeyed to southwestern Missouri, then a Spanish province, where he bought mining properties and established a home for his family. Later Stephen Fuller Austin planted the first Yankee settlement in Texas and played a leading part in Texas history.

OLD SHOT TOWER (L), 12.6 *m.*, on US 52, rising like a lighthouse on the south bank of New River, was built by Thomas Jackson about 1820. The grim fortresslike stone shaft is 75 feet above ground and 20 feet square, and its walls are 3 feet thick. Below ground it sinks 75 feet to a water tank at the bottom. Shot was made by pouring molten lead through sheetiron colanders at the top of the tower. During the 150-foot fall to the water at the bottom the drops of lead would assume a globular form. These pellets were then rolled down an inclined plane, as a sorting process: good shot rolled straight to waiting boxes; poor ones zigzagged off to another melting.

The highway crosses New River, first called Wood's River for Abraham Wood, a trader, whose couriers discovered the stream in 1671, and continues to FORT CHISWELL, 20.4 *m.*, at a junction with US 11 (*see Tour 5b*).

On US 58 is GALAX, 110.4 *m.* (2,341 alt., 2,544 pop.), with four furniture factories, two weekly newspapers, a hosiery mill, and a mirror factory. An unusual enterprise is the shipping of galax—a decorative mountain evergreen for which the town is named. This plant, with round, cordate leaves and tiny white blossoms, covers the surrounding mountain slopes, is gathered in the blooming season, and is held in cold storage for the higher-priced winter market. The town, which sits astride the Grayson-Carroll County line, sprang up in 1904, when a spur of the Norfolk and Western Railway opened up the timber regions. For a year it was called Bonaparte.

INDEPENDENCE, 127.8 *m.* (2,432 alt., 400 pop.), high on the slopes of the Blue Ridge, is busy only with county administration and farm-trade. In 1842 the county seat was moved here from Old Town, where it has been since Grayson County was created in 1792. Its name honored William Grayson, one of Virginia's first United States senators.

The GRAYSON COUNTY COURTHOUSE, of massive red brick with cusped gables and peaked turrets, was built in 1907–08.

US 58 continues to wind westward, passing MOUTH OF WILSON, 140.8 *m.* (125 pop.), a small settlement close to the North Carolina line where Wilson Creek joins New River, then swings northward.

At 144.8 *m.* is a junction with State 16; L. here on State 16.

TROUTDALE, 151.9 *m.* (357 pop.), shadowed (L) by MOUNT ROGERS (5,719 alt.) (*see Tour 5c*), is a small boom town that never grew up though its corporate limits have not been contracted.

After climbing Brushy Mountain, the highway zigzags down to MARION, 170.3 *m.* (*see Tour 5c*), at a junction with US 11 (*see Tour 5c*), with which US 58 unites below Abingdon.

Section d. BRISTOL to TENNESSEE-KENTUCKY LINE, 108.5 m. US 58

This section of US 58 sweeps in great curves, roughly paralleling the Southern Railway line. Through hilly farmland and broken foothills it crosses outlying ridges of the Alleghenies and passes through broad Powell's Valley toward Cumberland Gap. For the greater part of its way the road follows the easy levels of watercourses, skirting the mountains through shadowy gorges with glimpses of open gaps, tumbling waterfalls, and hilly corn patches beside gray, weathered cabins. West of Moccasin Gap the road traces the Indian path taken by Daniel Boone in 1769.

Westward on State St. from Piedmont St., 0 *m.*, in BRISTOL.

The highway climbs out of the valley to WALKER MOUNTAIN, 5.7 *m.*, named for Dr. Thomas Walker, who in 1750 explored this area while leading a party to survey the 800,000-acre Loyal Land Company grant.

HILTON (R), 23.1 *m.*, is a random gathering of houses along a railroad track.

At 27.2 *m.* is the line surveyed in 1772 under the treaty made at Lochaber, South Carolina, between representatives of the colony and Cherokee Nation chiefs. This line, defining the boundary between Colonial lands and those of the Cherokee, did not prevent whites from usurping native lands.

MOCCASIN GAP, 27.8 *m.*, is a pass in Clinch Mountain, used by Boone in 1769.

GATE CITY, 29.3 *m.* (1,342 alt., 1,216 pop.), rambling along the highway, is the seat of Scott County. An early tavern kept here by Elisha Faris was frequented by most travelers on the Boone trail. The Faris family was slain in 1791 by the notorious half-breed Benge, who led his red brothers in an attempt to drive out the intruding whites.

The SCOTT COUNTY COURTHOUSE is a substantial two-story red brick building in which are incorporated parts of an earlier structure. The county was created in 1814 from Lee, Washington, and Russell and named for General Winfield Scott, then being hailed for his exploits in the War of 1812. Court sessions were held in private homes throughout the county until 1817.

The highway follows Clinch River through a narrow, two-mile-long gorge, 40 *m.*, between Moccasin Ridge and Big Ridge. The tracks of two railroads pass through the mountain by means of tunnels, one about 100 feet above the other.

At 45.1 *m.* is an unobstructed view of the western end of NATURAL TUNNEL, a giant hole in Purchase Ridge, through which railway tracks and the waters of Stock Creek run. The tunnel is about 100 feet in diameter and nearly 900 in length.

PATTONSVILLE, 53.2 *m.*, a handful of frame houses and a crossroads store, was an old stagecoach service station.

Westward the highway begins long, swirling loops up the side of Powell Mountain and reveals inspiring views of primitive mountain country.

STICKLEYVILLE, 58.8 *m.*, a cluster of houses at the foot of the ridge, is near the spot where in 1795 Archibald Scott and four children were killed and Mrs.Scott and another child were taken captive by Indians led by 'Chief' Benge.

The highway traverses a narrow valley, where hilly rock-strewn pastures are netted with cowpaths, and ascends WALLEN'S RIDGE (2,100 alt.), 60.3 *m.*, which affords broad views of rolling country towards the Cumberlands.

JONESVILLE, 72.8 *m.* (1,300 alt., 384 pop.), with courthouse, hotel, bank, and general stores, is the seat of Lee County. In November 1781 Jonesville, a collection of log cabins, witnessed the arrival of a body of dissenters from upper Spotsylvania County on their way to Kentucky. These Separate Baptists had long defied the Colonial law requiring that ministers be licensed. Led by the Reverend Lewis Craig, about 200 church members left Spotsylvania County with their children, slaves, and earthly possessions. Along the pioneer trail they were joined by other westbound pioneers anxious for company on the journey through the Indian country. By the time it left Jonesville the caravan of staid religious folk, shepherded by a dozen preachers who held daily prayer services, had been augmented by soldiers, adventurers, land grabbers, Indian traders, backwoodsmen, and homeseekers (600 in all) and was trailed by droves of domestic animals.

The LEE COUNTY COURTHOUSE, of buff brick, was built in 1933. The county was organized in 1792 from Russell County and named for General Henry ('Lighthorse Harry') Lee, then governor.

At 74 *m.* is a junction with County 662.

Left here to a footpath, 2 *m.*, that leads (L) down a steep incline to NATURAL BRIDGE, an immense arch of limestone spanning Beatty Creek.

The highway at 89.2 *m.* passes near the SITE OF MARTIN'S FORT, built in 1768 by settlers whose leader was Joseph Martin, born in Albemarle County in 1740. Martin had run away at 16 and become a trader at Fort Pitt on the Ohio. By 1763, with a wild reputation as a gambler, he was again in Virginia. As an officer of militia he fought up and down the frontier from Virginia to Georgia.

In ROSE HILL, 89.6 *m.* (1,445 alt.), small homes and stores hug the road.

Two INDIAN BURIAL MOUNDS (R), 92.1 *m.*, in a field beyond the railroad tracks have never been explored. Lack of digging enthusiasm is attributed to a legend concerning a prying early settler who was killed by a cave-in while attempting to uncover their secrets.

EWING, 94.3 *m.* (1,388 alt., 500 pop.), is a farm trading center.

The highway at 98.5 *m.* passes near the spot where on October 10, 1773, Daniel Boone's oldest son, James, Henry Russell, and a son of Captain Drake were killed by Indians. In September 1773 the Boones—Daniel, his wife, and eight children—with five other families had left North Carolina. Along the way they were joined by 40 more homeseekers. Near this spot camp was made for the night. The boys left the party, lost their way, and spent the night in the woods, where they were surprised by Indians. The Boones abandoned the journey and spent the winter in a cabin near Russell's Fort (*see Tour* 15).

US 58 runs through a valley that narrows and is darkened by mountains to a junction at 108.5 *m.* with US 25, close to the Kentucky-Tennessee line and 0.8 miles north of Cumberland Gap, Tennessee (*see Tennessee and Kentucky Guides*).

Tour 8

Virginia Beach—Cape Henry—Willoughby—Old Point Comfort—Newport News—Williamsburg—Richmond—Buckingham—Amherst—Lexington—Clifton Forge—Covington—(White Sulphur Springs, W.Va.). US 60.
Virginia Beach to West Virginia Line, 315.6 *m.*

Hard-surfaced roadbed throughout, concrete east of Williamsburg, asphalt west of Williamsburg.
Chesapeake & Ohio Ry. parallels route between Old Point Comfort and Richmond, and Clifton Forge and W.Va. Line.
Ferry between Willoughby and Old Point Comfort; for cost see below.
All types of accommodations in towns.

US 60 crosses the center of the State, climbing to the Piedmont and then over the Blue Ridge Mountains; west of the Shenandoah Valley it crosses the crest of the Alleghenies.

Section a. VIRGINIA BEACH to RICHMOND; 114.6 *m. US* 60

The eastern end of this section of US 60 is in the country where the founders of Virginia first set foot upon American soil; north of Hampton Roads is the area of the first settlement.

VIRGINIA BEACH, 0 *m.* (13 alt., 1,719 pop., 12,000 summer pop.) is a seaside playground where from May to October holiday throngs line the six miles of white beach and jostle each other on the concrete walk above it in front of cottages, hotels, and amusement halls.

At the southern end of Virginia Beach is the STATE MILITARY RESERVATION, where units of the Virginia National Guard Infantry encamp each summer.

In Virginia Beach is a junction with US 58 (*see Tour 7a*).

US 60 runs northward on Virginia Beach's main street, passing large homes among dunes and the towering Cavalier Hotel, to FORT STORY (R), 5.7 *m.*, a unit of the defense system that guards the important naval base, shipyards, and ports of Hampton Roads and the water approach to the Nation's capital. Its long-range coast defense and antiaircraft batteries are manned by detachments from the Coast Artillery base at Fort Monroe.

CAPE HENRY, 6.2 *m.*, a sandy point, forms, with Cape Charles on the north, the entrance to the Chesapeake Bay. A cluster of buildings is dominated by the towering CAPE HENRY LIGHTHOUSE, which was erected in 1879 and supplanted the OLD LIGHTHOUSE, near by, built in 1791. Before there was any lighthouse, ships were guided by bonfires. A GRANITE CROSS marks the spot where on April 26, 1607, the passengers of three storm-driven little ships—the *Sarah Constant*, the *Goodspeed*, and the *Discovery*—came ashore. Here the adventurers opened the box that contained the sealed instructions of the London Company and here first encountered the Indians, who had not forgotten the vengeance of the Spanish after the killing of the Jesuits along the Potomac.

The entrance to SEASHORE STATE PARK is (L) at 9.4 *m.* (*open May 15 to Nov. 1; adm. 10¢, children under 10, free; space for overnight camping, 25¢; cabins for 4, $20 a week, $5 each additional person; cabins equipped with electric lights, stoves, water heaters—payment by coin meter; reservations for cabins made at Virginia Conservation Commission, Richmond*). The 3,400-acre park lies between Chesapeake Bay and inland waters of Lynnhaven Inlet, Broad Bay, Linkhorn Bay, and Crystal Lake. Its terrain, ranging from huge, creeping sand dunes along a five-mile beach to fresh-water lakes and inland swamps, gives natural sanctuary to landbirds and waterfowl.

At 10.1 *m.* is a junction with County 615 (*see Tour 7a*).

The highway crosses LYNNHAVEN BAY, 11.2 *m.*, an arm of the Chesapeake. Captain John Smith called the inlet Morton's Bay, for Matthew Morton, who, with Captain Gabriel Archer, was wounded here by the Indians. The present name was given by Adam Thoroughgood for Lynn, England.

At 13.7 *m.* is a junction with US 460.

Left here to a private road, 0.6 *m.*, and L., between brick gateposts, 1.4 *m.* on a road bordered by dense thickets and through a grove of pecans to the ADAM THOROUGHGOOD HOUSE (*open 10–6 weekdays, adm. 50¢*). The diminutive, brick plantation house, half-covered by vines, is a Jacobean remnant of early Virginia. Its one full story, capped by a steep gable roof with prim dormers, is between two massive T-shaped chimneys, one outside. The bonding of the walls is English except on the east front, which is Flemish. The openings are topped by low arches of brick with alternating glazed headers; but the sashes, like the dormers, must date from a much later period than that of the building. The interior, refurnished appropriately, is covered with simple pine paneling. Adam Thoroughgood (Thorowgood) came to Virginia in 1621 and settled at Kecoughtan (Hampton). In 1634 he patented much land here and built a home, possibly this one, for when he died in 1640, his will mentioned a brick dwelling on his land.

At 15.9 *m.* on US 60 is a junction with State 13 and a drive.

Right here to LITTLE CREEK-CAPE CHARLES FERRY TERMINAL (*see Tour* 2) (*cars* $2.50–$3.00, *each passenger* 75¢).

OCEAN VIEW, 22.1 *m.*, is the bay front section of Norfolk (*see Norfolk*).

West of Ocean View the highway traverses WILLOUGHBY SPIT, a narrow sand peninsula, jutting into Hampton Roads and lined with cottages. This sand spit is said to have been thrown up during a severe 'gust' about 1680. Madam Thomas Willoughby, surveying her domain after the storm and seeing land where before only the waters of the Chesapeake rolled, hastened to claim the 217 acres. Captain Newport's flagship, *Sarah Constant*, anchored near by April 28, 1607. Thence the voyagers 'rowed to a point where they found a channel which put them in good comfort.' This they named Cape Comfort, now Old Point Comfort.

At 24.5 *m.* is the OLD POINT-WILLOUGHBY FERRY TERMINAL (*intervals from* 15 *min. to* 1 *hr., depending upon the time of day; car and driver* $1.00; *each passenger* 20¢). (*See Hampton Roads Port.*)

OLD POINT COMFORT, 24.5 *m.*, is dominated by a towering hotel, which perpetuates the area's century-old reputation as a fashionable resort. In the background are the brick buildings of FORT MONROE, U.S. Army Coast Artillery Post and Coast Artillery School. US 60 passes officers' quarters and other post buildings. The septagonal-bastioned fortification, screened by trees, with quarters and administration buildings, covers about 80 acres and is 1.6 miles in circumference. It is surrounded by a moat.

In 1609 the Jamestown settlers built a defense they called Algernourne Fort against a possible attack by the Spaniards. It was described as a stockade 'without stone or brick,' with 50 men, women, and boys, and equipped with seven cannon. The defense was later called Point Comfort and in 1630–32 was rebuilt by Colonel Samuel Mathews. A new fortification, erected in 1727–30 and named Fort George, though constructed with double walls of brick, was destroyed by the 'great gust' of 1749. During the Siege of Yorktown, Count de Grasse strengthened his defenses of the area by placing batteries on the point. The construction of the present fort was begun in 1819 and completed about 1847. Among privates here in 1828–29 was Edgar Allan Poe, who enlisted in Boston as E.A.Perry. Chief Black Hawk of Illinois was held a prisoner here in 1832 after the Black Hawk War.

On the night of February 2, 1865, a steamer from Washington anchored in Hampton Roads, bringing President Lincoln for an informal peace conference with Confederate commissioners, headed by his old friend and fellow congressman, Alexander Stephens, then vice-president of the Confederacy. The conference came to nothing. Jefferson Davis was a prisoner here for two years (1865–67).

Old Point Comfort's career as a fashionable resort began at the time

Chief Black Hawk and his warriors were imprisoned at Fort Monroe. Curious crowds that flocked to stare at the proud old warrior soon overflowed the little Hygeia Hotel, housing civilian employees at the fort. The proprietor, Harrison Phoebus, built additions to his hotel, chartered boats to bring visitors, and soon Old Point was on its way to becoming a place where diplomats and Government officials mingled with the élite of Baltimore, Philadelphia, Richmond, and the Deep South.

PHOEBUS, 26.1 *m.* (3,500 pop.), is a fishing mart and residential town. During the fishing seasons, crowded lines of boats tie up along Mill Creek Wharf to dump their shimmering cargoes of shad, bluefish, croakers, spots, flounders, trout, oysters, and crabs. The town, built on land once owned by Harrison Phoebus, began about 1870 as a handful of catch-penny stores around the gates of the National Soldiers Home. Here during the War between the States was Camp Hamilton, concentration point for Union troops.

1. Right from Phoebus on State 169 to BUCKROE BEACH, 2.3 *m.*, a scattered collection of bungalows, frame hotels, shacks, and lunch rooms, most of them open only in summer. Raucous with shoot-the-chutes, venders' stands, a dance pavilion, fortune tellers' booths, and like contraptions, the place in summer is the mecca of one-day excursionists. The resort occupies part of Buck Roe Plantation, one of several estates set aside in 1619 for public use. In 1620 the London Company sent Frenchmen here to teach the colonists grape and silkworm culture. By 1637, however, the plantation had joined the rest of the colony as a tobacco field.

2. Left from Phoebus on Mallory St. to KECOUGHTAN, 0.8 *m.*, which has assumed the name of the Indian village here when the first whites arrived.

Here is the entrance (R) to the VETERANS' FACILITY (*open* 6:30 *a.m. to* 9:00 *p.m.; hospital* 2 *to* 4; *guide service*) on a peninsula. Commodious frame and brick buildings are on tree-shaded grounds. The facility, established in 1930 to care for disabled veterans of all wars, supplanted the National Soldiers Home. It provides quarters, recreational facilities, and medical treatment for 2,000 to 2,500 men.

HAMPTON, 27.8 *m.* (3 alt., 6,382 pop.) (*see Hampton*).

Right from Hampton on King St. to LANGLEY FIELD, 3 *m.*, military air base, named for Dr.Samuel P. Langley, aviation pioneer. The field, a scene of aeronautical activities during the World War and for years headquarters of the Second Wing, U.S. Army Air Corps, is now headquarters for the First Air Base Squadron, three pursuit squadrons, two bombardment squadrons, and an observation and reconnaissance squadron. Twenty-two hundred men are stationed here (1940). The field is also the most important research and experimental station of the National Advisory Council for Aeronautics, a non-military organization. On the 5,000 acres between the Back River and Chesapeake Bay are hangars, warehouses, wind tunnels, as well as the usual post facilities.

NEWPORT NEWS, 34.3 *m.* (25 alt., 34,417 pop.) (*see Newport News*).

At 37.3 *m.* is a junction with US 17 (*see Tour 6b*), which unites with US 60 for 2.6 miles.

HILTON VILLAGE, 38.5 *m.* (1,600 pop.), consisting of closely built rows of houses of the English villa style, grew up around 500 houses built by the Federal Government during the World War as homes for workers at the Newport News Shipyard.

The MARINERS' MUSEUM (L), 39.6 *m.* (*open weekdays* 9–5, *Sundays* 2–5; *park closes at sunset*), a simple one-story stuccoed building, was built in 1930 by Archer M. Huntington to house his collection of more than 45,000 marine antiquities. It is in a large park along the James River and is protected as a wildlife sanctuary, with an artificial lake for migratory waterfowl. At the museum entrance are sculptured animal figures and groups, the work of Anna Hyatt Huntington. On display are collections of ship models, figureheads, anchors, marine engines, deck and steering gear, and navigation instruments, volumes of sea lore, maps, charts, and globes.

At 39.9 *m.* is the western junction with US 17 (*see Tour 6b*).

At the JAMES RIVER COUNTRY CLUB (L), 41.4 *m.* (*golf, tennis, and swimming*), is a GOLF MUSEUM (*open to visitors*) housing the Archer M. Huntington collection of early golf paraphernalia.

DENBIGH PLANTATION (L), 45.3 *m.*, was patented by Colonel Samuel Mathews, who came to Virginia before 1618, filled several important posts, and became the father of Samuel Mathews, governor of the colony (1657–60). Said a writer in 1649: 'He . . . sowes yearly a store of Hemp and Flax, and causes it to be spun; he keeps Weavers and hath a Tan-house, causes Leather to be dressed, hath eight Shoemakers employed in their trade, hath forty Negro Servants, bringing them up in Trades in his house; . . . hath abundance of Kine, a brave Dairy, Swine great store, and Poltry; he married the daughter of Sir Thomas Hinton.' This daughter of Sir Thomas—Frances—had been the wife of Nathaniel West, brother of Lord Delaware, then of Colonel Abraham Peirsey.

Denbigh Plantation in 1630 had three representatives in the House of Burgesses. In 1631–32 monthly courts were authorized to be held at 'Warwick River.' Two years later Warwick County was constituted. In 1680 the general assembly directed that a town for Warwick County be laid out 'att the mouth of Deep Creek on Mr.Mathews land.' When, in 1691, towns were made 'ports of entry,' the village was referred to as Warwick Town and a brick courthouse and prison were built. But Warwick Town never materialized and in 1809, because 'the inhabitants of Warwick County' labored under 'great inconvenience by being compelled to attend their court at the place it is now holden,' the county seat was moved to 'two acres' belonging to Richard Gary, deceased, at Stony Run, which is now DENBIGH, 47.4 *m.* (50 pop.), a scattering of houses and stores.

The WARWICK COUNTY COURTHOUSE of red brick was built in 1884. The CLERK'S OFFICE, a pleasing one-story red brick structure with a Doric portico, was built in 1810, when the seat was moved here from Denbigh Plantation. All the early records of Warwick County were destroyed during the 1860's.

At 51.2 *m.* is a junction with a paved road.

Left here to FORT EUSTIS (L), 1.1 *m.*, a large reservation with many frame buildings—during the World War a cantonment, later an artillery post, in 1934–37 a Government rehabilitation camp for transients, and in 1938 a training school conducted by the N.Y.A. Within the reservation is the JONES HOUSE, built in the late seventeenth century and remodeled in 1757.

Beyond Fort Eustis on an old road 5 *m.* is MULBERRY ISLAND, a little peninsula where in June 1610 the starving colonists, who had abandoned Jamestown to return to England, stopped for the night. The following morning, when news came that Lord Delaware had arrived at Point Comfort with new colonists and supplies, all turned back.

LEE HALL, 52.3 *m.* (75 pop.), has sprung up on the grounds of a Colonial estate of the same name. The first frame house, called Oak Hill, was on the site of the present LEE HALL (R), a brick *ante-bellum* residence. Here General John B. Magruder had headquarters in April and May 1862.

West of Lee Hall, along the highway, was Martin's Hundred, the estate of a society of 'lords, knights, and gentlemen,' granted by the London Company in 1618 and named for Richard Martin, attorney for the London Company and member of the society. In March 1619 the *Gift of God* hove to with 250 persons, some of them indentured servants, sent to settle the plantation. The servants, however, fared none too well, and one Richard Frethorne wrote his father in England begging his redemption. He referred to his 'daily and hourly sighs, groans and tears.' This Hundred was one of the few that remained intact until counties were formed in 1634.

The entrance-lane (L) to CARTER'S GROVE, 56 *m.* (*open* 9–6, *March* 15 *to June* 15; *adm.* $1.10), lies between ancient cedars and locusts. Set behind a row of giant tulip-poplars, the two-and-a-half-story main unit and its wings, all with brick walls now rose-red, stretch out on an eminence 80 feet above the river. A fine cornice and classical enframements in rubbed brick over the two centered entrances, topped with pediments, are the chief adornments of this Georgian Colonial house, which relies for exterior beauty chiefly on the texture of the Flemish bonding and the nearly perfect proportions of every element, from windowpanes to the arrangement of the mass. From the ridge ends of the steep hipped roof rise a pair of large square chimneys with molded tops. The chimneys at the gable ends of the wings, which are linked to the main section by passages forming a single structure 200 feet long, have arches protecting their flues. Dormers punctuate each roof surface.

The interior woodwork is beautifully executed. The main hall is notable for the great arch rising across the middle from fluted pilasters of poplar wood and for the carved balusters of the stairway.

The estate was originally within Martin's Hundred. 'King' Carter (*see Tour* 16*b*) acquired it and gave it to his daughter Elizabeth, who married Nathaniel Burwell. It descended to Elizabeth's second son, Carter Burwell, who brought over David Minitree, a master craftsman, under whose direction the house was built between June and September of 1751. Carving of the woodwork was probably done by craftsmen from England, but the unskilled labor was done by the owner's slaves. The total cost was £500, of which £150 was Minitree's fee. To this the delighted Burwell added a bonus of £25. Restoration, begun in 1927, included raising the pitch of the roof, and the addition of dormers on the main unit and of the galleries between the central structure and the wings. Old furnishings have been installed and among the many portraits are one of William Henry Harrison by Charles Willson Peale and one of Charles Mordaunt, Earl of Peterborough.

KINGSMILL (L), 58.7 *m.*, which was patented before 1637 by Richard Kingsmill, passed in time by marriage to Lewis Burwell.

One of Burwell's nine daughters 'completely upset what little reason there was in Governor Francis Nicholson,' who was most 'passionately attached to her and demanded her of her parents in royal style.' When her parents refused his suit he became furious, and threatened to kill three persons if the young lady married any other but himself—the bridegroom, the officiating minister, and the justice that issued the license. The affair ended only when Nicholson was recalled by the queen.

At 59.8 *m.* is a junction with County 642.

Right here to the SITE OF FORT MAGRUDER, 0.6 *m.*, around which was fought the Battle of Williamsburg on May 5, 1862.

General Joseph E. Johnston, withdrawing from Yorktown, passed through Williamsburg pursued by three corps of McClellan's army. Finding his cavalry forced back on the Yorktown road, Johnston stationed a division of infantry here. General Joseph Hooker attacked the Confederate right on May 5. Longstreet ordered additional troops to the field and at noon ordered a counterattack. The Confederates, victorious over Hooker on the right, were in turn severely repulsed by General W.S.Hancock on the left. Longstreet withdrew during the night.

WILLIAMSBURG, 62.3 *m.* (78 to 84 alt., 3,778 pop.) (*see Williamsburg*).

In Williamsburg is a junction with State 31 (*see Tour 8A*).

TOANO, 73 *m.* (500 pop.), began in Colonial days with a tavern and, after the tavern's destruction by fire, became Burnt Ordinary.

HICKORY NECK CHURCH (R), 73.9 *m.*, of red brick with a steep gabled roof and modillioned cornice, is only part of the large T-shaped Lower Church of Blissland Parish. The main part was built in 1734–38 and the south transept, the present structure, in 1774–76. When militia camped here during the Revolution, the church was partly destroyed. Repaired in 1825, it was used for many years by Hickory Neck Academy. During the War between the States, the building was a barracks for both Confederates and Federals. After the war it was again a school, but in 1907 was ceded back to the parish, which restored and refurnished it.

At 74.5 *m.* is a junction with State 30.

Right here is BARHAMSVILLE, 4.5 *m.*, called in Colonial times Doncastle. Here was Doncastle Ordinary, stopping place on the way to Williamsburg. Patrick Henry halted at Doncastle with militia in May 1775 on his way to the capital to demand restoration of powder taken from the 'Powder Horn' by Lord Dunmore. Henry was persuaded to wait here while Carter Braxton sent to his father-in-law, Richard Corbin, receiver-general of the king's revenues, for payment for the powder (*see Tour 20a, and Tour 1B*).

The CHICKAHOMINY INDIAN COMMUNITY (L), 85.8 *m.*, is the home of descendants of the powerful tribe that participated in the capture of Captain John Smith in December 1607.

The STATE GAME FARM, 86.2 *m.*, is a 1,400-acre preserve for breeding partridge to restock game sanctuaries.

PROVIDENCE FORGE, 89.1 *m.* (159 pop.), a scattered community, took its name from a foundry set up here about 1770 to make farm implements. William Holt and the Reverend Charles Jeffrey Smith, a Presbyterian minister, built the forge. In 1771 they were joined by Francis Jordone.

In the village is the CHRISTIAN HOUSE (R), weatherboarded story-and-a-half, with high pitched roof, dormers, and double outside chimneys.

Since Colonel Burgess Ball, who visited here and also Pope's Creek, the house in which George Washington was born, left the statement that the two buildings were alike in design, the Christian House was used as a model in the reconstruction of Washington's birthplace (*see Tour* 16*a*).

BOTTOM'S BRIDGE, 100.3 *m.*, is at the crossing of Chickahominy River and a junction with State 33 (*see Tour 6A*), the old road to Williamsburg. General Joseph E. Johnston, retreating before McClellan, halted here for five days before withdrawing to the vicinity of Richmond on May 17, 1862. McClellan occupied this position two days later.

At 102.4 *m.* is a junction with State 156.

Left on this road is WHITE OAK SWAMP, 3.9 *m.* (*see Tour* 24).

SAVAGE STATION (R), 102.7 *m.*, was formerly a railroad stop that gave its name to the third battle in the Seven Days' Campaign. Following the Battle of Gaines' Mill (*see Tour* 20*a*), both armies spent June 28 seeking new positions. On this day McClellan abandoned his supply base at White House Landing (*see Tour 6A*) and began his retreat toward Harrison's Landing on the James. On the morning of June 29 half of McClellan's army was beyond White Oak Swamp, several miles south, and the remainder grouped around this station, awaited withdrawal. Lee's scattered army moved rapidly to intercept McClellan. In mid-morning, General John B. Magruder's division encountered General E.V.Sumner's Federal corps about a mile to the southwest. Sumner easily repulsed Magruder, then withdrew to this place. In the afternoon Sumner repelled a second attack by Magruder and withdrew southward during the night.

At SEVEN PINES, 106.1 *m.*, is the SEVEN PINES NATIONAL CEMETERY (R), with surrounding stone wall, 'row on row' of gravestones, and along the front wall in a straight line seven pines similar to those that gave the place its name.

Seven Pines was the field of action in indecisive fighting on May 31 and June 1, 1862, when McClellan's army, quiescent on the Chickahominy, was attacked by the Confederate army under Johnston. General Johnston, wounded at Fair Oaks one mile north, was succeeded by General G.W. Smith. During the afternoon of June 1, General Robert E. Lee was assigned to command the Confederate army in Virginia.

SANDSTON, 106.8 *m.* (800 pop.), a pleasant village of small residences with neat front yards, had its birth during the World War, when cottages were built here for employees at a munitions plant near by. Later, real estate promoters developed the town as a suburb of moderately priced homes.

RICHMOND, 114.6 *m.* (15 to 206 alt., 182,929 pop.) (*see Richmond*).

In Richmond are junctions with US 1 (*see Tour* 1), US 33 (*see Tour* 9), US 250 (*see Tour* 17), State 10 (*see Tour* 19), US 360 (*see Tour* 20), State 6 (*see Tour* 23), and State 5 (*see Tour* 24).

Section b. RICHMOND to LEXINGTON; 135 *m. US* 60.

West of Richmond US 60 straightens out to traverse the Piedmont on a modern course that touches older highways only here and there. In the rolling country west of the falls line tobacco and general farm crops are grown, but there is a vast acreage of unused eroded red land. The highway crosses the Blue Ridge near the crest of wooded peaks before dropping into the Valley of Virginia.

In RICHMOND US 60 runs south on 9th St. from Broad St., 0 *m.*

At 12.5 *m.* is a junction with State 147.

Right here to the SITE OF BLACK HEATH (L), 0.5 *m.*, in dense undergrowth.

This was the home of John Heth, who was an officer on the *Decatur*, United States gunboat captured during the War of 1812. Heth and two companions escaped from the British in Bermuda.

Here in 1825 was born John Heth's son Henry, who precipitated the Battle of Gettysburg. Sent forward by General A.P.Hill to obtain a supply of shoes and cautioned not to engage in hostilities, General Heth met a body of Union cavalry and brought on an engagement that grew rapidly into one of the decisive battles of history. Of 7,500 men in his command 2,850 were on the casualty list.

On this estate is the BLACK HEATH COAL MINE, one of many in the Richmond bituminous basin. Operations started here in 1785. An explosion in 1839 killed all but three of 54 miners. After a second such disaster in 1844 the mine was closed until 1938.

On State 147 is a junction with State 44, 1.5 *m.*; L. here 0.9 *m.* to County 673; R. here 1.8 *m.*, to the former BELLONA ARSENAL (L). Three brick buildings in a stone-walled enclosure, an unroofed powder magazine, and a position for testing cannon are the remains of the arsenal that was established by Major John Clarke of Keswick, in 1810, as a cannon foundry. Major Clarke supplied guns used in the War of 1812. In 1816–17 the Federal Government constructed an arsenal, barracks, workshop, officers' homes, and a hospital here. The arsenal, abandoned after 11 years, was reconditioned by the Confederates in 1861 and it supplied the Southern armies until the fall of Richmond in 1865.

On State 44 is MANAKIN CHURCH (L), 7 *m.*, a rectangular frame building, fourth of the name and built in 1894. It bears the name of a French settlement of the vicinity, derived from Monacan, the name of Indians, who once lived here and whom King Powhatan tried in vain to subdue.

Following the revocation of the Edict of Nantes in 1685, many French refugees came to Virginia. In 1690 the general assembly passed an act giving them a large tract of land on the south side of the James and exempting them from taxation for seven years. Governor Nicholson said in 1700 that this settlement 'would be a strengthening to the frontiers.'

In 1701 the land 'held by French refugees at Manakin town & adjacent' had been constituted 'King William Parish in the County of Henrico.' Four years later its people were exempted from the 'laws for ministers' maintenance' and were to be at liberty to 'pay their ministers as their circumstance will permit.' The service of the Church of England was used, and sermons were preached in both French and English. An old register, written in French and covering the period from 1721 to 1753, shows that more Negro than white children were baptized.

The Huguenots did not 'remain together as near as may be to the said Manakin Town,' but spread through Virginia, and some were before long among the most prominent families in the colony.

MIDLOTHIAN, 14.7 *m.* (400 pop.), is a widely scattered settlement that dates from the early mining days of this area. In 1831 the Chesterfield Railroad was completed from the mines to the head of tidewater at Richmond. This 13-mile line, with horse-drawn cars holding 56 bushels each, was Virginia's first railroad and continued in operation until 1851.

Right in Midlothian to the railroad station, 0.4 *m.*; R. here to a fork 0.7 *m.*, and L. to the SITE OF SALISBURY, 2.1 *m.*, one of the many homes of Patrick Henry. A fire left only the tall chimneys of the frame story-and-a-half house to which Henry moved his family after his election in November 1784 for his fourth term as governor. He remained here until 1786.

At 31.6 *m.* on US 60 is a junction with State 13.

Left here to POWHATAN, 1 *m.* (150 pop.), seat of Powhatan County and shopping center for a large rural area. The village came into being when the courthouse was built shortly after the formation of the county in 1777 from vast Cumberland County and was first called Scottsville for General Charles Scott, who was a native of the neighborhood. Because the county was created during the Revolution, its name has no English flavor but honors Emperor Powhatan of the Tidewater Indian confederacy.

The small POWHATAN COUNTY COURTHOUSE (R), with stuccoed brick walls, has a Roman Doric recessed portico between walls in antis and closely spaced pilasters. The front part of the CLERK'S OFFICE, a small brick T-shaped building, was built with the courthouse about 1817. The CONFEDERATE MONUMENT is an ornately carved piece of stone hidden by a circle of tall privet.

An old tavern, now an apartment house adjacent to the courtgreen, is a tall brick structure dating from the Revolutionary period.

CUMBERLAND, 50.3 *m.* (474 alt., 130 pop.), seat of Cumberland County, is a small town of dwellings and stores, strung out along the highway.

The CUMBERLAND COUNTY COURTHOUSE (R), erected in 1818, a small building with portico, is pleasant in appearance, its brick walls laid in an unusual bonding—one course of headers to three of stretchers. It has large chimneys and its windows contain old rippled panes of glass. The small square CLERK'S OFFICE was also built about 1818. Cumberland County, cut from Goochland County in 1749, was named for Prince William, the Duke of Cumberland.

The SITE OF THE EFFINGHAM TAVERN is opposite the courthouse. This old inn, burned in 1933, served many travelers on the early road to western Virginia and was in 1766 the scene of the murder of Robert Routledge by Colonel John Chiswell, a prospector, miner, and promoter. One late summer evening Chiswell was entertaining his fellow guests here with glowing accounts of his lead mines by the New River (*see Tour 7c*), when Routledge questioned his statements and a quarrel ensued. Chiswell sent a servant upstairs for his sword, called Routledge 'a fugitive rebel and a Presbyterian fellow,' and ran him through. Chiswell's good friends—John Blair, William Byrd, and Presley Thornton, members of Council—were able to have him released on bail. After the prosecutor, who proved to be John Blair, was selected by lot, Chiswell was found dead in his Williamsburg home. Although his physician testified under oath that his death was the result of 'nervous fits, caused by constant uneasiness of mind,' it is generally believed that he committed suicide.

Late in the eighteenth century Cumberland was the scene of the trial of Richard Randolph of Bizarre for the murder of a newly-born infant. Alexander Campbell, John Marshall, and Patrick Henry were counsels for the defense. Under Henry's cross-examining, the principal witness, a daughter of Archibald Cary, testified that, her suspicions having been aroused, she had peeped through a keyhole and had watched the woman in the case undress. Henry, with scornful tones, asked, 'Which eye did you peep with?' Without waiting for an answer he exclaimed, 'Great God, deliver us from eavesdroppers.'

At 51.3 *m.* is a junction with County 629, passable only in dry years.

Left here to TAR WALLET CHURCH (R), 1 *m.*, built about 1750 as a church of Southam Parish, later of Littleton Parish. A hog-drover of the frontier, camping here one night, had his wallet destroyed by hogs. 'Tear Wallet,' the name the incident gave to the creek,—spelled as pronounced in the vernacular 'Tar Wallet'—was later passed on to the church. Since 1835 the building has been used by the Methodists.

At 55.3 *m.* on US 60 is a junction with County 652.

Left here to County 632, 0.1 *m.*, and R. to CA IRA (Fr. It will go on) CHURCH (R), 0.3 *m.*, a small building with tall, flat-arched windows. The paneled doors, of heart pine, were fashioned by a slave locally famed for his craftsmanship. Known also as Grace Episcopal Church of Littleton Parish, it was built about 1840 to replace a former building. Its name, that of a once-flourishing community, may have been bestowed by French refugees, or it may have been adopted as a compliment to Benjamin Franklin, who, during the American Revolution, often used the expression that later became the slogan of the French revolutionists.

SPROUSES, 65.2 *m.*, is at a junction with US 15 (*see Tour 3c*).

BUCKINGHAM, 69.1 *m.* (92 pop.), seat of Buckingham County, has kept with unusual success the patina of a more tranquil day, in spite of the acid of modern highway traffic. No shop or filling station obtrudes to spoil the placid effect of vine-covered brick and ancient weatherboarding.

The BUCKINGHAM COUNTY COURTHOUSE (R), is of brick, with white-columned portico. The first courthouse, a wooden structure, stood west of the village, then called Maysville. The next, designed by Thomas Jefferson, was burned in 1869, when many of the county records were destroyed. Buckingham County, formed in 1761 from Albemarle, was from 1727 until 1745 part of the vaguely designated territory of Goochland. White men traveled through this region early, for in Woodson's Cave on Willis Mountain is painfully inscribed in the hard stone 'B.Bolling. I.Bell 1700,' and in another place 'W.Smith, P.Turpin 1709.'

The BUCKINGHAM HOTEL (L) is a large frame and weatherboarded log structure opposite the courthouse. According to local tradition, Lee and his staff attempted to find accommodations here on their return from the surrender. Because there was not room for the entire staff, General Lee refused quarters for himself. Tradition adds that he and his staff were served coffee on the inn porch. If the story is fact, the defeated general and his men probably drank one of the substitutes of the time, for coffee was a luxury not available in war-torn Virginia.

MAYSVILLE HOTEL (R), an H-shaped brick structure next to the courthouse, is a century-old inn now called Pearson's Hotel.

At 73.1 *m.* is a junction with State 24.

Left here to the SURRENDER GROUNDS at Old Appomattox Courthouse, 17.1 *m.* (*see Tour 3d*).

US 60 crosses the JAMES RIVER, 86.5 *m.*, broad and sluggish as it meanders in a bed cut below the Piedmont peneplain. The James River Division of the Chesapeake & Ohio Railway, a freight route following the bank of the river, is the transportation successor to the James River and Kanawha Canal (*see Richmond and Transportation*). West of the river the highway cuts through a section of second-growth woodland that borders the highway almost without a break.

AMHERST, 101.8 *m.* (628 alt., 876 pop.) (*see Tour 4c*), is at a junction with US 29 (*see Tour 4c*).

The highway crosses the eastern boundary of the GEORGE WASHINGTON NATIONAL FOREST (*see Tour 9*) at 116.5 *m.* and follows the Buffalo River between sharply rising slopes of the Blue Ridge foothills.

LONG MOUNTAIN WAYSIDE PARK, 118.6 *m.*, is a picnic and camp ground.

Left here on a dirt road (*impassable in wet weather*), winding steeply through forest and banked with thickets of mountain laurel, to PEDLAR LAKE, 4.4. *m.*, stocked with game fish. Fishing rights are restricted because this is a reservoir.

After crossing BROWN'S MOUNTAIN, 119.6 *m.*, the highway dips through a secluded valley, where life moves slowly, and climbs to cross BLUE RIDGE MOUNTAIN (2,290 alt.) at 124 *m.* On the western slope the route has been engineered with dramatic economy and curves along monstrously graded shoulders of the steep, pine-wooded mountainside toward the lowland, constantly in view. The beauty attending this descent is greatly enhanced in spring by various mountain bloom: dogwood, laurel, rhododendron, and Judas tree.

BUENA VISTA, 128.5 *m.* (1,000 alt., 4,002 pop.) (*see Tour 11a*), is at a junction with US 501 (*see Tour 11a*), which unites with US 60 to LEXINGTON, 135 *m.* (1,000 alt., 3,752 pop.) (*see Tour 5b*), at junctions with US 11 (*see Tour 5b*), and US 501 (*see Tour 11a*).

Section c. LEXINGTON to WEST VIRGINIA LINE; 66 *m. US* 60.

West of LEXINGTON, 0 *m.*, the highway, following older routes only intermittently, crosses the eastern ridge of the Allegheny Mountains, to the valleys of the Cowpasture and Jackson Rivers, and ascends the western ridge, after winding through stretches of beautiful mountain country.

MONMOUTH MILL (L), 2.6 *m.*, a tall weather-beaten frame building with a high over-shot wheel, is typical of mills that since Colonial times have met the Virginian demand for corn bread made of water-ground meal. Monmouth Mill has been in existence since 1750.

The KERR'S CREEK MONUMENT (pronounced 'Carr'), 6.2 *m.*, a small stone pillar, commemorates two Indian raids on the Kerr's Creek settlement. That at Big Springs was the more severe. The date of the lesser raid was July 17, 1763, according to the inscription on the monument; at the other, in 1764, 50 to 60 persons were killed.

The Pontiac War, a concerted Indian drive to clear the Allegheny country of white settlers, broke out in June 1763. It appears that a group of Shawnees was assigned to clean up this territory. Raiding the Greenbrier, Jackson River, and Cowpasture River sections, the band came down out of the mountains to Kerr's Creek on July 17, 1763. Four homes were visited, 12 persons killed, and others were taken away as captives. Three companies of militia quickly followed the raiders. The Indians, pursued and attacked at first unsuccessfully, were again overtaken and all killed except one. Loot recovered by the militiamen was sold for $1,200.

The Big Springs raid was probably better planned. The Indians were seen in the neighborhood for several days and frightened settlers congregated in a home near the Big Spring. Stories of the massacre seem to agree that the people, though expecting the attack, were surprised while saddling their horses for a trip to church. Witnesses said that men, women, and children scattered 'like chickens,' while the Indians gave chase. One woman stood over the body of her husband and fought until overwhelmed; another raced away on horseback with a baby in her arms, dropped it in a rye field, and was able later to recover it unhurt; still another, having hid her baby in the underbrush, was taken captive. Its bones were there when she returned from captivity. The treaty that ended the Pontiac War stipulated that the prisoners be returned.

The highway follows the Kerr Valley westward, passing many comfortable century-old homesteads as it climbs the Allegheny Range over North Mountain.

The RUINS OF LONGDALE FURNACE (R), 22 *m.*, operated from 1827 to 1911, face empty frame buildings across the highway, which is bordered for a mile or more by giant heaps of slag. The furnace was established by Colonel John Jordan and first called Lucy-Selina for two relatives. The Confederate Government took over the plant during the first year of the war for the production of ordnance material. Later it was operated by the Longdale Company as a hot blast furnace.

At 30.3 *m.* is a junction with a park road.

Right here to DOUTHAT STATE PARK, 5 *m.* (*open May* 15 *to Nov.* 1; *adm.* 10¢, *overnight camping,* 25¢, *children under* 10, *free; fishing, swimming; rowboats,* 25¢ *an hr., maximum* $1.25 *a day; overnight accommodations,* $2.50 *a person; cabins equipped with electric lights, payment by coin meter;* $15 *a week for* 2 *persons,* $20 *for* 4 *persons,* $5 *for each additional person; store and restaurant; reservation for cabins made at Virginia Conservation Commission, Richmond*). The 5,000-acre recreational area includes a large lake.

CLIFTON FORGE, 32.3 *m.* (1,047 alt., 6,850 pop.), is a city that a railroad built, for here are shops and a terminal of the Chesapeake & Ohio Railway. The Clifton Forge business district is along a narrow strip of bottom land by the Jackson River, while bungalow homes on brick pillars stand on the steep hillsides.

In 1861 the Virginia Central Railroad, extending from the east through Charlottesville, Waynesboro, and Staunton, had reached the Jackson River at the edge of the present town, and a roadbed had been graded westward to connect it with the Ohio River. But the War between the States intervened and tracks were not laid westward until 1867. The James River and Kanawha Canal Company was authorized in 1876 to build the Buchanan and Clifton Forge Railway to connect the westernmost point of the canal with the railroad. Two years later the Richmond and Alleghany Company was authorized to build a road along the James from Richmond to Buchanan. Thus Clifton Forge became the division point of the large east-to-west system that resulted when the pioneer roads were combined under the Chesapeake and Ohio Railway Company.

In Clifton Forge is a junction with US 220 (*see Tour* 21*a*), which coincides with US 60 to COVINGTON, 43.7 *m.* (1,245 alt., 6,550 pop.), seat of Alleghany County, a manufacturing city, and a compact block at the confluence of three tributaries of the Jackson River and hemmed in on three sides by the Warm Springs, Sweet Springs, and Lick Mountains. Covington is on land owned as early as 1746 by Peter Wright. Later, Fort Young was built here, and a settlement called Merry's Store grew around it. In 1819 town lots were laid out, and the settlement was named for its oldest inhabitant, Peter Covington. Though a village on the Midland Trail, which crossed the mountains, and later a station on the railroad to the west, Covington did not develop until the 1890's.

The large stone ALLEGHANY COUNTY COURTHOUSE was built in 1911. The first crude structure was erected in 1823, a year after Alleghany County was formed from parts of Bath, Botetourt, and Monroe (W.Va.) Counties.

In Covington is the western junction with US 220 (*see Tour 21a*). The highway follows Dunlop Creek up a pass.

CROW TAVERN (R), 60.1 *m.*, with stone chimneys and a double veranda across the entire front, is an eccentrically gabled frame structure. During the first half of the nineteenth century it overflowed with travelers on their way between White Sulphur and Old Sweet Springs. It was a rule of the house that no more than five persons should sleep in a bed. A good bed with clean sheets was advertised for 8⅓¢, but should the guest have to share his bed, the price was 5½¢. Persons so fortunate as to have blankets were charged nothing for the privilege of sleeping on the floor. A 'warm diet' meal cost 12⅔¢, while a 'cold diet' meal was 10½¢.

According to tradition, Colonel John Crow, the landlord, was a notable liar but a very entertaining host. To amuse his guests he often rode a huge tame bear about the inn grounds.

At 66 *m.* US 60 crosses the West Virginia Line 4 miles east of White Sulphur Springs, W.Va. (*see West Virginia Guide*).

Tour 8A

Williamsburg—Jamestown Island; 6.4 *m.* State 31.

Asphalt-paved roadbed throughout.
No accommodations.

This route connects the sites of the first and second capitals of Virginia. It slopes through woodland to the spot on the James River where Englishmen established their first successful settlement in America.

State 5 branches south from US 60 in WILLIAMSBURG, 0 *m.*

At 1.5 *m.* is a junction with State 5 (*see Tour 24*).

On JAMESTOWN ISLAND (*open 9–5 weekdays, 1–5 Sun.; adm. 25¢*),

6.4. *m.*, a flat, wooded oval nearly three miles long separated from the mainland by a marshy inlet, is the site of James Towne, where permanent settlement in British America began in 1607 and where in 1619 was set up the first representative government in the New World. Besides the ruins of the church tower and graveyard, all that remains of the capital of the Virginia Colony from 1607 to 1699, are the foundations of several dwellings and of the third and fourth statehouses. Much of the western end of the island, on which the first buildings stood, where a neck of land joined the island to the mainland, had been washed away by tides before a sea wall was constructed in 1901. Scattered about in clumps are gnarled descendants of the mulberry trees planted by order of the assembly of 1621 to feed silkworms that would provide one of the colony's first industries. Facing the river, near the spot at which the first landing is thought to have been made, are several memorials set up in recent years, including the JAMESTOWN NATIONAL MONUMENT, a 100-foot granite shaft dedicated in 1907; the ROBERT HUNT MEMORIAL SHRINE, a mounting of ancient brick with a bronze tablet, recalling the chaplain who on May 25, 1607, celebrated the first communion service in America of the Church of England; a STATUE OF POCAHONTAS, an appealing bronze figure of the Indian girl; and a bronze STATUE OF CAPTAIN JOHN SMITH, forceful leader and Virginia's first hero.

On May 13 (o.s.), 1607, the *Sarah Constant*, the *Goodspeed*, and the *Discovery* were 'moored to the Trees in six fathom of water' off the island. The next day the English adventurers—the first 105 Virginians—landed and 'set to worke about the fortification.' 'The Counsel was sworn, and the President elected . . . Maister Edm. Maria Wingfield.' Construction of a little fort, a chapel, a storehouse, and thatched huts within a stockade was begun.

Here the settlement persisted in spite of high mortality caused by the unhealthy situation, summer heat, recurring famine, Indian attacks, internal dissension, and the 'Starving Time' of the winter of 1609–10 that ended in June with a three-day abandonment of the site. From Jamestown Captain John Smith, who governed the colony sternly for a year ending in September 1609, sallied forth with followers on his many expeditions to explore the country and to seek Indian corn for the inexperienced colonists. More than once, by the force of his character, Smith kept the settlement from disintegrating, but his policy of browbeating and terrifying the natives, while immediately useful and bold, sowed seeds of perpetual war between the Indian and the white man.

Thirteen-year-old Pocahontas, daughter of the Indian leader, Powhatan, came often to the island to turn cartwheels about the stockade and to warn the English against attacks from her people, but particularly to see fascinating Captain Smith, whose life she had saved at Werowocomoco. Smith called her 'the only *Nonpariel*' of the country, but failed to realize the real love she bore him. Here in 1614, soon after she had been brought to Jamestown as a hostage, her first visit since Smith's departure in 1609, John Rolfe married her, not for any 'carnall affection; but for the good of this plantation, for the honour of our countrie . . .' When she met Smith again three years later in England, where she died, she was overcome with emotion—lost on the unsentimental captain. Smith reported: 'After a modest salutation, without any word, she turned about, obscured her face, as not seeming well contented; and in that humour . . . we all left her two or three houres, repenting my selfe to have writ she could speake *English*. But not long after, she began to talke, and remembered mee well what courtesies shee had done . . .' Finally she blurted out with tragic brevity: ' . . . They did tell us alwaies you were dead, and I knew no other till I came to Plimoth . . . because your Countriemen will lie much.'

It was to Jamestown that the 22 burgesses came in 1619 to sit in the first legislative body in America; that 20 Negroes, forerunners of Virginia's future slaves, were brought and sold the same year; and that the first considerable number of Virginia 'maides' were consigned a year later. By 1623, a year after the first massacre, there were only 183 inhabitants and 22 dwellings in Jamestown itself, which had not extended beyond the four original acres.

With the growth of the tobacco trade and the extension of the cultivated area, Jamestown became important as the seat of government, but it never achieved any considerable size. In 1676, the year of Bacon's Rebellion, when the town was burned on September 19 to prevent its reoccupation by Governor Berkeley, it was described by Mrs.An Cotton in *Bacon's Proseedings* as having '16 or 18 houses, most as is the church, built of brick, faire and large; *and in them about a dozen familees (for all of the howses are not inhabited) getting their liveings by keeping of ordnaries, at extreordnary rates.*' Rebuilt, the town was burned by accident almost entirely in 1698, and the next year the capital was moved to Williamsburg. Jamestown remained a place of ruins, described in 1772 as 'an abundance of bricks and rubbish with three or four inhabited houses.'

In July 1781 Cornwallis, retreating with his British army before La Fayette, crossed the James here on his way to Portsmouth. In 1861 the Confederates built a Jamestown fort on the site of the first one; a year later the island was occupied by Union troops. It had become a briar-choked wilderness in 1893, when twenty-three and a half acres were acquired by the Association for the Preservation of Virginia Antiquities. In 1933 the State and the Federal Governments jointly purchased the island as a part of the Colonial National Historical Park.

The JAMESTOWN CHURCH TOWER, standing by the site of the earlier churches, is a bulky, ivy-draped brick ruin—part of the fifth church at Jamestown, whose construction was begun in 1639 and completed about 1654. This church has been reconstructed—buttresses and all—behind the tower. The first church, 'a homely thing like a barne and set upon cratchetts,' was built inside the stockade in May 1607. It was burned the next winter in the colony's first fire. The second church, a similar crude structure within the stockade, was the scene in 1608 of the first wedding in Virginia, when John Laydon married Anne Burras. After Lord Delaware's arrival in 1610, another church—the largest erected on the island—was built on a site west of the present tower. Here Pocahontas was baptized in 1614. This third church, also a frail structure, hastily erected, had become a ruin by 1617. Then Governor Samuel Argall directed the building of a smaller church. It was in this fourth wooden church that America's first representative lawmaking body, following a prayer by the Reverend Richard Buck, held its initial session on July 30, 1619. The fifth church, built around the fourth while that was still in use, was a buttressed rectangular structure of brick with a huge tower. This brick church, its interior and roof restored after the rebellion of 1676, survived the fire of 1698 and served James City Parish until the Revolution.

Relics in the church include an ironstone tablet, believed to be part of the tomb of Sir George Yeardley, royal governor, who died in 1627. In the tomb were found silver epaulettes and spurs. A 100-year-old sycamore separates the tombs of the Reverend James Blair and his wife Sarah; legend connects this tree with the curse of her father, Colonel Benjamin Harrison, who opposed their marriage and vowed to separate the couple. Other old stones include that of William Sherwood, 'a greate sinner.' A timeworn fragment identifies the grave of proud Lady Frances Berkeley, wife of Sir William and later of Colonel Philip Ludwell. 'Lady Berkeley' she remained, even on her tombstone.

The RELIC HOUSE, a small new building by the sea wall, contains a collection of small articles found during excavations and provides a souvenir stand and rest rooms.

The brick RUINS OF THE JACQUELIN-AMBLER HOUSE stand gauntly at the eastern end of the island. The first house, its construction begun about 1710 by Edward Jacquelin, was later acquired by Richard Ambler. Burned during both the Revolution and the War between the States and twice rebuilt, it was destroyed finally by fire in 1895.

JAMESTOWN-SCOTLAND FERRY (*see Tour* 19) (*hourly service* 7 *a.m.–*9 *p.m.; from April* 15 *to Nov.* 1, *extra half-hour service between* 9 *a.m. and* 7 *p.m.; Sun. and holidays extra service at* 10 *p.m. and* 11 *p.m.; car and driver* 80¢, *round trip* $1, *additional passengers* 20¢, *round trip* 30¢, *pedestrians* 25¢).

Tour 9

Richmond—Louisa—Gordonsville—Stanardsville—Harrisonburg—(Franklin, W.Va.). US 33.
Richmond to West Virginia Line, 144 *m.*

Asphalt-paved roadbed throughout.
The Chesapeake & Ohio Ry. parallels route between Richmond and Gordonsville.
Accommodations in towns; few tourist homes and camps.

The eastern half of US 33 passes through country that produces food and forage crops and dark tobacco; westward are apple orchards, pastures, and grain fields. Yet farther westward the highway climbs the mountains, drops into the valley, and climbs again into the mountains.

US 33 runs west from Capitol Square in RICHMOND, 0 *m.*, on Broad Street, in union with US 250 (*see Tour 17a*) to a junction at 4.8 *m.*, where US 33 turns R. from US 250.

STAPLES MILL (L), 6.2 *m.*, a plain clapboarded structure beside a stone dam, is typical of early Virginia grist mills.

LAUREL GOLF COURSE (L), 9.6 *m.*, is a public links (*see Richmond*).

At 18.9 *m.* is a junction with County 670.

Left here to County 675, 1.8 *m.*, and R. to the RUINS OF AUBURN MILL (L), 2.9 *m.*, a large structure built before 1750 of local rock, 'laid dry'—that is, without mortar. After the walls were finished the outside cracks were 'pointed' or filled with plaster. Auburn shipped its product to a wide market. The loss of a cargo of flour that went down with a sailing ship bound for the Argentine led indirectly to the failure of its owner, Michiah Crew. During the War between the States the mill manufactured bayonets, sabers, and cutlasses.

At 24.9 *m.* on US 33 is a junction with County 657.

Right here to CEDAR CREEK, 1 *m.*, near the SITE OF CEDAR CREEK MEETING HOUSE, from which the Friends' influence spread westward as early as 1746.

MONTPELIER, 26.7 *m.*, a few houses, stores, and a post office, is in an area where are found rutile crystals, often called 'venus-hair stones' or 'love's-arrows' and ranging in size from small grains to masses weighing 20 pounds. One of the three crystal forms of the element titanium, rutile is, curiously, black by reflected light and deep red by transmitted light.

In the forks of the road at 43.3 *m.* is the SITE OF CUCKOO TAVERN, from which Jack Jouette, the son of the proprietor, began his ride on the night of June 3, 1781, to warn Thomas Jefferson at Monticello and the Virginia assembly in Charlottesville of the approaching British dragoons under Colonel Tarleton. Jouette had learned of their mission while the British rested here. In gratitude for his warning, the assembly voted ' . . . to present Captain John Jouette an elegant sword and a pair of pistols as a memorial of the high sense which the General Assembly entertains for his activity and enterprise . . . whereby the designs of the enemy were frustrated and many valuable stores preserved.'

Later, after Jouette moved to Kentucky, then a Virginia county, he served in the general assembly, where he sponsored a petition for the divorce of his brother-in-law, Lewis Robards, from Rachel Donelson (*see Tour 4c*), who was later Mrs.Andrew Jackson.

PENDLETON, 46.1 *m.* (69 pop.), is little more than a station on the Chesapeake & Ohio Railway. The Louisa Railroad, begun in 1836, was the first in this section. It reached Louisa in 1838 and Gordonsville in 1840 and caused diversion of trade from Fredericksburg to Richmond. During the War between the States the line transported supplies to Richmond and iron to Confederate armament factories.

MINERAL, 47.4 *m.* (463 alt., 416 pop.), with scattered stores, houses, and sawmills, was once a shipping point for iron, mica, sulphur, and some gold. In 1848 Robert and Colonel James Hart, brothers, operated a furnace here that they called 'Rough and Ready' to honor Zachary Taylor. After the War between the States the demand for sulphur increased; and iron pyrites, found near by, was mined and smelted for that product. After 1900, operations in Louisiana caused a decline in profits here.

LOUISA, 53.6 *m.* (437 alt., 300 pop.), seat of Louisa County, has remained a placid 'courthouse' in spite of the modern stores that line the highway. The town's beginning was in 1742 when it became the seat of Louisa County, taken from Hanover in 1742 and named for Queen Louisa of Denmark, daughter of George II of England.

The LOUISA COUNTY COURTHOUSE, a white-pillared brick building on a green, was built in 1905.

It was as a member from Louisa that the 29-year-old Patrick Henry in May 1765 began his fight for the common man when he spoke against the 'loan office,' an instrument intended to cloak certain questionable loans made from the public treasury by John Robinson, Speaker of the House and Treasurer of the Colony (*see Tour 1B*). Toward the end of this session when the House was in committee to consider the Greenville Stamp Act, Henry introduced his resolutions proposing 'That the General Assembly . . . have the only and sole exclusive right and power to lay taxes and impositions upon the inhabitants of this colony.' The startled members were brought to their feet when Henry cried, 'Caesar had his Brutus, Charles the First his Cromwell, and George the Third—' 'Treason, treason!' cried members of the assembly. Henry continued, ' . . . and George the Third may profit by their example. If this be treason, make the most of it!'

Though cautioned against sleeping at Louisa Courthouse—with 'the worst lodging . . . in all America'—the Marquis de Chastellux, when traveling in Virginia after the Revolution, had 'a curiosity to judge of it by my own experience' and went in. 'This man, called Johnson, is become so monstrously fat, that he cannot move out of his armchair . . . A stool supported his enormous legs, in which were large fissures on each side, a prelude to what must soon happen to his belly . . .'

During the Revolution and again during the War between the States Louisa lay in the path of hostile forces. Tarleton passed through in 1781; and on May 2, 1863, General George Stoneman's Union forces destroyed the railroad here. From the friendly side, however, came General Fitzhugh Lee, who camped near by on June 10, 1864, before the Battle of Trevilian.

A STONE MEMORIAL (R) at 60.4 *m.* commemorates the Battle of Trevilian Station, fought near here on June 11–12, 1864. As the Union army lay at Cold Harbor in June (*see Tour 20a*), Grant sent General Philip H. Sheridan with two cavalry divisions to cut Lee's communications and join General David Hunter, then advancing eastward from the Valley. General Wade Hampton overtook Sheridan here, and after a two-day battle turned him eastward.

At 64.4 *m.* is a junction with US 15 (*see Tour 3c*), which unites northward with US 33 for 5 miles. BOSWELL'S TAVERN (R), a story-and-a-half frame building with large end chimneys, was praised by the Marquis de

Chastellux, though he said that the innkeeper, Colonel Boswell, 'a tall, stout Scotsman . . . appeared but little prepared to receive strangers.'

GORDONSVILLE, 69.3 *m.* (442 alt., 462 pop.), in an area of prosperous estates, is concentrated along a main street lined with comfortable homes on shaded lawns, and places of business that close at sunset, except on Saturday. Until a few years ago, Gordonsville to travelers meant fried chicken. When the train stopped, vendors of pullet done to a turn circulated among passengers, who purchased almost to a man. The village had its first growth as the western terminus of the Louisa Railroad. In 1855 the Orange & Alexandria established its terminus here. To reach these, two toll roads were constructed in the 1850's across the Blue Ridge.

Interest in blooded horses began early here. Before the middle of the nineteenth century, local breeders set up a training stable under the care of an English trainer and dubbed it 'Horse College.' Here was kept Voltaire, a renowned sire.

GORDON INN, a tan-colored frame building in two sections built by Nathaniel Gordon about 1787, became a stage stop.

In Gordonsville is the northern junction with US 15 (*see Tour 3c*).

MONTE BELLO (L), 73.2 *m.*, is a frame house with a long porch. From the boxwood-covered lawn is a sweeping view of the Blue Ridge. According to one story (*see Tour 10*), Zachary Taylor, who became twelfth President of the United States, was born here on September 24, 1784.

BARBOURSVILLE, 75.2 *m.* (200 pop.), took its name from the home of Governor James Barbour (1775–1842) that once stood near by. Barbour, a conservative, was governor of Virginia (1812–14) and later United States senator.

BARBOURSVILLE RUINS stand at the end of a long oval 'green,' bordered half-around by tall box that halts opposite the entrance. Behind four Roman Doric columns, approached by steps of turf, rise ivy-covered brick walls, roofed only by the spreading branches of a large walnut tree that has grown up in the center. One of the old dependencies is the present house. Designs for the mansion were drawn by Jefferson about 1817, and construction began soon afterwards. Hospitality was dispensed here on a general scale until the mansion burned in 1884.

In Barboursville is a junction with State 20 (*see Tour 10*).

At RUCKERSVILLE, 82.3 *m.* (108 pop.), an old village, is a junction with US 29 (*see Tour 4b*).

At 83.4 *m.* is a junction with County 644.

Left here to RHEA HOUSE (L), 1.4 *m.*, a small frame building below the highway, once the home of William Thurman, the founder of a religious sect called Thurmanites, who believed they knew the day the world would end. The date passed unchaotically, and the sect died out.

STANARDSVILLE, 88.7 *m.* (350 pop.), seat of Greene County, is the largest settlement in a wide area of foothills. Along the western horizon flows the undulating line of the Blue Ridge.

The COURTHOUSE, a red brick building with a Doric portico and a cupola, was erected shortly after Greene County was cut from Orange

County in 1838 and named for General Nathanael Greene. The COUNTY OFFICE BUILDING was completed in 1938.

West of Stanardsville the highway follows small Swift Run to the summit of SWIFT RUN GAP, 97.2 *m.* Here is a junction with the Skyline Drive (*see Tour 4A*). Through this gap Indians in 1716 guided Governor Alexander Spotswood and his merry gentlemen. Hoping to find a new pass westward, they started from Germanna (*see Tour 3b*), on August 29, 1716, well provisioned, especially with liquors of several kinds. At the slightest provocation, they drank the health of the king and the governor. They traveled westward, by easy stages, amusing themselves shooting deer, bear, turkeys, and snakes and making the expedition a pleasure trip. The party reached the top of the Blue Ridge September 5, drank the special toasts to the king and to Governor Spotswood, and named a peak for each. Riding into the Shenandoah Valley, they ceremoniously claimed the land west of the mountains for the king, then returned east. A short time after their return Governor Spotswood presented each member of the party with a jeweled miniature horseshoe of gold. The owners of these elaborate mementoes became the Knights of the Golden Horseshoe.

From the crest (2,400 alt.), US 33 drops into the Shenandoah Valley, following the course of Elk Run, to ELKTON, 104.2 *m.* (965 pop.), which hugs the slope at the edge of fertile river bottom lands. Prior to 1908 it was called Conrad's Store—a name that appears in war records. The Confederates burned the bridge across Elk Creek June 3, 1862, to keep Union forces under Shields from crossing to join Fremont against Jackson.

In Elkton is a junction with State 12 (*see Tour 5A*), which unites westward with US 33 for 8.6 miles.

The highway crosses the SHENANDOAH RIVER, 104.9 *m.* When Governor Spotswood's party camped by this river, they named it Euphrates. According to the diary of one of the members of the party, 'The Governor buried a bottle with a paper inclosed, on which he writ that he took possession of this place in the name and for King George the First of England . . . and we drank the king's health in champagne and fired a volley, the Princess's health in Burgundy, and fired a volley, and all the rest of the Royal Family in Claret, and fired a volley. We drank the Governor's health and fired a volley. We had several sorts of liquiors, viz; Virginia red wine, Irish usquebaugh, brandy shrub, two sorts of rum, champagne, canary, cherry punch, water cider, etc.'

McGAHEYSVILLE, 110.9 *m.* (400 pop.), is an old village lying under the Peaks of the Massanutten Mountain. Like other villages in the Blue Ridge country, at the beginning of the nineteenth century McGaheysville was a manufacturing center supplying local needs for clothes, shoes, hats, furniture, and wagons.

About 1809, George Rockingham Gilmer, a native of this region who was later Governor of Georgia, wrote of numerous excavations on the side of 'Peaked Mountain,' 'made by the neighboring Dutch people in search of hidden treasure.' Gilmer told of a young man who 'had a club foot and was made a tailor of, as fit for nothing else,' and who told the treasure seekers that 'in his travels through Ohio, he had seen a factory of spyglasses, which so added to the power of sight, that he could see several feet into the earth with one of them.' On his suggestion, the Dutch made up a purse to send him to Ohio for a glass. On his return, without the glass, he told sorrowfully that he had bought the glass, but had lost it; he added that the glasses had been so much improved that without doubt it would be possible to see entirely through Peaked Mountain. The eager fortune hunters made up another purse and the tailor left again. This time he did not return.

At 112.9 *m.* is the western junction with State 12 (*see Tour 5A*).

PEALE'S CROSSROADS, 115.9 *m.*, also called Massanutten Crossroads, is at a junction with County 620. At the crossroads is MASSANUTTEN CROSSROADS CHURCH (R), a white frame successor to a church closely identified with the organizing of the Presbyterian denomination in this area. The Reverend John Hindman was sent here as a missionary from the Presbytery of Donegal Synod of Philadelphia in 1742.

Right on County 620 to KEEZLETOWN, 1.6 *m.* (116 pop.), which retains the charms of an earlier day. It was established about 1790 by George Keisell, who laid out his town shortly after Thomas Harrison established Harrisonburg farther west. Rivalry for the honor of being the county seat resulted in a horse race in which Harrison outdistanced Keisell.

Signs lead from the town to MASSANUTTEN CAVERNS, 2.8 *m.* (*adm.* $1.50), discovered in 1892 in a secondary ridge of the Massanutten.

At 117.5 *m.* on US 33 is a junction with County 687.

Left here 0.7 *m.* to MASSANETTA SPRINGS, a former resort now owned by the Presbyterian Synod of Virginia. Annual summer conferences, schools of music, and music festivals are held here.

HARRISONBURG, 121.6 *m.* (1,338 alt., 7,232 pop.) (*see Tour 5a*), is at a junction with US 11 (*see Tour 5a*).

At 127.7 *m.* is a junction with County 752.

Right here to MT. CLINTON, 1.5 *m.*, a small community. Its former name, Muddy Creek, was changed by election in 1833. Poultry raising is the leading commercial activity on farms near by.

WAR BRANCH, 128.8 *m.*, is a mountain stream named for an Indian battle along its banks. The low ridge in front and slightly to the left of the highway at 129.2 *m.* is a local landmark called Giant's Grave.

RAWLEY SPRINGS (L), 133 *m.*, is a spa that started its career when Joseph Hicks advertised in 1825 the benefits to be derived from its waters. Numerous fires have reduced its accommodations to cabins and campsites.

Just west of Rawley Springs the highway passes into the GEORGE WASHINGTON NATIONAL FOREST (*camp and picnicking facilities*), an area of many thousand acres of mountain land in Virginia and West Virginia set aside for the protection of watersheds and timber reserves. Since 1933 the recreational facilities of the forest have been greatly increased by the C.C.C.

The highway passes upward across the Allegheny Range, following the bed of Dry River through a parklike area.

US 33 crosses the crest of the Allegheny Range and the West Virginia line, 144 *m.*, at a point 21 miles east of Franklin, W.Va. (*see West Virginia Guide*).

Tour 10

Fredericksburg—Wilderness—Orange—Barboursville—Charlottesville; 66.8 *m.* State 3, State 20, County 613.

Asphalt-paved roadbed throughout.
Southern Ry. parallels route between Orange and Charlottesville.
Accommodations between termini only in a few tourist homes.

The eastern section of this route traverses an area of small farms, second-growth woodland, and parks that memorialize battles of the 1860's; westward are rolling hills with productive farms and large estates.

State 3 branches west from US 1 (*see Tour 1a*), 0 *m.*, on William St. in FREDERICKSBURG.

The SUNKEN ROAD (L), 0.6 *m.*, was a Confederate line of defense during the Battle of Fredericksburg (*see Tour 1b*).

MARY WASHINGTON COLLEGE (R), is at 0.8 *m.* (*see Fredericksburg*).

SALEM BAPTIST CHURCH (L), 4.2 *m.*, a red brick building erected shortly after the organization of its congregation in 1844, was within the Confederate lines during the Battle of Salem Church, May 3–4, 1863. Its walls show many battle scars. Moving toward Chancellorsville and reaching Fredericksburg at daybreak on May 3, the Union General John Sedgwick drove back General Jubal A. Early, and advanced westward against the brigade of General C.M.Wilcox, which was forced to retreat slowly toward Salem Church. There Wilcox was reinforced by General Lafayette McLaws' division. Repeated Federal attacks were repulsed before darkness ended the fighting. On May 4, Early began an offensive to connect with McLaws at the church; Anderson's division arrived to reinforce McLaws. As night fell before the attack could be made, Sedgwick withdrew across the river.

A junction with County 612 at 5.3 *m.* is locally called FIVE MILE FORK. County 612—the old Orange Plank Road—was paved in 1854 with planking.

At 6.6 *m.* is a junction with County 620.

Right here to the SITE OF SPOTSWOOD'S IRON FURNACE (L), 3.7 *m.*, where slag piles remain to mark the first air furnace in America operated by Alexander Spotswood early in the eighteenth century (*see Tour 3b*). Production of charcoal for iron furnaces early depleted the forests of this vicinity and produced the area of tangled second-growth woodland called The Wilderness.

At 8.7 *m.* is a junction with the Catherine Furnace Road. Before the Battle of Chancellorsville, the evening of May 1, 1863, the Confederates extended their lines along this road.

Left here to the MAURY MONUMENT (R), 1.6 *m.*, near the site of the birthplace of Matthew Fontaine Maury (1806–73). Maury has been called the father of the Naval Observatory and of the U.S. Hydrographic Office. His work in meteorology resulted in the establishment of what later became the U.S. Weather Bureau. He plotted the present North Atlantic ocean lanes, conceived the idea of an Atlantic cable, and furnished much data and advice for laying the first cable; he also wrote on naval education and reform.

CHANCELLORSVILLE, 10 *m.*, is a crossroads named for the CHANCELLOR HOUSE (R), used by General Joseph Hooker as headquarters during the Battle of Chancellorsville. The structure, burned during the battle and restored in 1908, was later destroyed again.

The Battle of Chancellorsville was the last of a series of Federal failures in Virginia, after each of which Lincoln changed Union commanders. General Hooker, who had supplanted General Ambrose E. Burnside, was placed in command of 130,000 men north of the Rappahannock. General Robert E. Lee had 57,000 Confederates on the south bank. Beginning an offensive on April 29, 1863, Hooker sent his cavalry raiding toward Richmond and placed a corps near Fredericksburg. Then hurriedly moving the greater part of his army up the river, he crossed to the south side and intrenched here.

General Lee, opposed by two forces, either of which, with a common reserve, outnumbered his entire army, left a division at Fredericksburg and moved the remainder to oppose Hooker. Here he retained 14,000 men to oppose the Federal front and sent Jackson with the main body to attack Hooker from the west. On May 2, Jackson's corps struck the Union rear and drove the corps of General O.O.Howard in rout over the main body.

While riding across the front of his lines at dusk to reform his tired and scattered troops, Jackson was shot down by Confederate bullets. Eight days later he died (*see Tour 1A*).

At dawn the next morning General J.E.B.Stuart attacked from the west and Lee from the east. The Union army, caught between these forces, fell back across the Rappahannock River. The Federals lost 17,000 men, and the Confederates about 13,000. The Union forces did not again cross the river until Gettysburg had been fought.

At 10.5 *m.* is a junction with a park road.

Left here to FAIRVIEW HEIGHTS (L), 0.1 *m.*, a small hill, where Federal gun pits have been restored. Between this point and HAZEL GROVE (R), 0.5 *m.*, held by the Confederates during the battle, some of the hottest fighting of the battle took place.

The JACKSON MONUMENT (R), 10.9 *m.*, marks the approximate spot where 'Stonewall' Jackson was shot. Wounded in the left shoulder, forearm, and right hand, he was removed to the Wilderness Tavern, where on the following day his left arm was amputated. On Monday evening, May 4, General Lee directed that he be sent to Guinea Station (*see Tour 1A*).

Adjoining the monument is a NATIONAL PARK CONTACT STATION (*information*).

At 14.4 *m.* is a junction with State 210 (L), the Brock Road. General Jackson, completing his flank march around Hooker, came into the turnpike at this point and moved eastward; on May 5–6, 1864 this was the central point of the Battle of the Wilderness, the first meeting of Grant and Lee, and the beginning of a struggle that lasted 11 months and ended with Appomattox. Grant, newly in command of the Union armies, planned that four major forces should converge on Richmond. With 102,000 men, he crossed the Rapidan and on May 5 started west from this point to attack Lee in Orange County. Lee, learning of the Federal activities from lookouts stationed on Clark Mountain (*see below*), met Grant with 64,000 men. The two armies, scattered along two roads, faced each other three miles west of this point and fought in the tangled underbrush.

The Federals, having fortified the Brock Road, concentrated the next day against General A.P.Hill's corps on the Plank Road. Thrown back and routed, the Confederates were rallied by the arrival of General James Longstreet's corps, which pushed the Federals back to their former position. Longstreet, leading an attack similar to Jackson's at Chancellorsville, was, like Jackson, wounded by his own men. His loss at this critical moment caused confusion that kept the Confederates from converting their advantage into a decisive victory. Federal losses were 14,000, Confederate 7,500.

Left on State 210 to the ALEXANDER HAYS MONUMENT (R), 1.4 *m.*, a mounted cannon. General Hays, killed here on May 5, 1864, commanded a brigade of Hancock's corps. Hays had commanded the Third Division of the Second Corps at Gettysburg, which, with Gibbon's Second Division, bore the brunt of Pickett's charge on the third day of that battle.

At 1.6 *m.*, is a junction with County 621, the Plank Road; R. here 0.3 *m.* to the spot (L) where General James Longstreet was wounded.

On County 621 is the WADSWORTH MONUMENT (R), 0.6 *m.*, a large block-stone pillar, to General James S. Wadsworth, who was mortally wounded near this spot on May 6, 1864. Commander of the Fourth Division of General G.K.Warren's Fifth Corps, he was attacking the Confederate left flank when Longstreet's reinforcements broke through.

County 621 continues westward to the place, 1.1 *m.*, where General Lee attempted to lead the Texas Brigade. Longstreet's assurance that his line would be recovered within an hour caused Lee to comply with the soldiers' plea, 'Lee to the rear.' In the clearing (R) is the SITE OF THE WIDOW TAPP'S HOUSE, near which General Lee had his headquarters.

On State 210, at 4.2 *m.*, is BROCK STATION of the Orange and Fredericksburg Railroad, the point from which Longstreet's flank movement began.

On State 210 are the SEDGWICK MONUMENT (L), 10.1 *m.*, and a PARK CONTACT STATION. General John Sedgwick, killed near by on May 9, 1864, was put in command of the Federal Sixth Corps shortly before the Battle of Chancellorsville.

At 10.4 *m.* on State 210 is a junction with County 648, near which, on May 8, began the 12-day Battle of Spotsylvania Courthouse. With Confederate cavalry opposing the Union advance along the Brock Road throughout the night of May 7–8, both armies had moved southward simultaneously along parallel roads. In the morning when the Federal force charged an improvised breastwork near this point, they found two brigades of infantry had replaced the cavalry. During the day the line was extended by other Confederate forces while the Federal line was being formed. In the meantime cavalry under General Stuart and General Sheridan were carrying their fight toward Richmond.

May 9 was given over chiefly to artillery fire, sharpshooting, and the formation of lines. On May 10 the Union forces made three unsuccessful attacks. May 12 brought the bloodiest fighting of the entire war. The Federals attacked at 4:30 in the morning, capturing General Edward Johnson's division of 4,000 men and 18 guns and pushing well into the Confederate lines. As the Southern reserve counterattacked, General Lee again tried to lead his men into battle. Terrific fighting followed in the 'Bloody Angle.' Federal guns, brought within 300 yards, threw shells into the Confederate masses; opponents struggled in hand-to-hand combat; blood ran in streams; fallen men were trampled and—sometimes four deep—had to be removed to provide standing room; and lines of men passed loaded muskets forward to those in position to fire. Between 50,000 and 60,000 men struggled viciously until past midnight.

For five days both armies maneuvered. A Federal offensive of May 18 was ineffective, and the next day a Federal movement began to the east and south. When fighting ended on the following day 17,000 of 110,000 Federals and about 14,000 of the 50,000 Confederates were dead, wounded, or captured.

Right 1.1 *m.* on County 648 to County 608 and R. 0.4 *m.* to MILLBROOK (L), an imposing house of red brick, two full stories above a high basement. The house, remodeled in 1836, was the last home of Mrs.Fielding Lewis, George Washington's sister, Betty (*see Fredericksburg*). Spotsylvania records show that Mrs.Lewis bought Millbrook in 1795. Two death notices that appeared in Fredericksburg newspapers, April 11 and April 12, 1797, both saying that 'Mrs. Betty Lewis, relict of the late Fielding Lewis,' died 'at her seat in this county,' would seem to fix Mrs.Lewis's death at Millbrook and not elsewhere as frequently asserted.

At 10.7 *m.* on State 210 is a junction with an improved road; L. here along the road that follows generally the Confederate line of defense during the Battle of Spotsylvania Courthouse. The central NATIONAL PARK CONTACT STATION, 0.8 *m.* is at the apex of 'Bloody Angle.'

SPOTSYLVANIA, 12 *m.*, on State 210, is at a junction with State 51 (*see Tour 1b*). This seat of Spotsylvania County is little but a green with a courthouse, jail, and tavern.

The two-story yellow brick COURTHOUSE, with its high pillared portico, was built in 1870, replacing one ruined during the fighting of 1864.

An act of the assembly of 1720, setting forth that 'the frontiers toward the high mountains are exposed to danger from the Indians and the late settlement of the French to the westward,' created the county as part of a defense for the Tidewater. A fund of £1,500 was provided for a church, a courthouse, and ammunition to equip each Christian tithable. The county extended to the Shenandoah River beyond the Blue Ridge Mountains. In 1732 the seat, first established at Germanna (*see Tour 3b*), was moved to Fredericksburg, in 1779 or thereabouts to a place two miles south of Spotsylvania, and in 1839 to its present site.

The SPOTSYLVANIA TAVERN, opposite the courthouse green, is a long rambling brick building with a roof that slopes forward to shelter a veranda with heavy columns. The southern half, built shortly after the Revolution, was added to in 1830. Though the building has been used continuously as an inn under various names, it has at times sheltered a school, a post office, and Confederate military leaders.

The SITE OF WILDERNESS TAVERN is (R) at 14.9 *m.* In a hospital tent behind this tavern Stonewall Jackson's left arm was amputated (*see above*). The tavern was the headquarters of General Grant and General George G. Meade during the Battle of the Wilderness.

At 15.3 *m.* is a junction with State 20 (L), from this point westward, the main route.

Right on State 3 to GERMANNA BRIDGE, 5 *m.*; R. here 0.7 *m.* to the SITE OF GERMANNA (*see Tour 3b*).

Near a NATIONAL PARK CONTACT STATION at 17.2 *m.* are restored Confederate trenches of the Battle of the Wilderness.

LOCUST GROVE, 20.1 *m.*, is a crossroads known in 1785 as Old Trap and subsequently as Robinson's, or Robertson's Tavern, for a tavern that stood here. Around this tavern, in November 1863, General Meade gathered his troops for a campaign in which he planned to surprise Lee, in winter quarters some distance west. The campaign came to nothing because confusion in assembling the Federal army gave Lee time to intrench on Mine Run, three miles west.

At 23.5 *m.* is a junction with County 614, the Gold Mine Road.

Left here to the GRASTY TRACT (L), 0.5 *m.* The Virginia Mining Company bought this five-acre gold field in 1831 for $30,000 and began operations that have continued sporadically ever since. In early years the yield of gold was worth from $6 to $32 a ton.

At VERDIERSVILLE, 25.5 *m.*, on the morning of August 18, 1862, General Stuart and several aides barely escaped capture by a Federal scouting party. Stuart lost his ostrich-plumed hat, but a week later turned the tables by capturing General Pope's tent and personal effects. When, on the night of the 17th, General Fitzhugh Lee failed to meet Stuart as ordered, Major Norman R. Fitzhugh was sent to find him. When Fitzhugh was captured during the night he was carrying a copy of the Confederate plan of campaign. Because of the information then obtained, Pope withdrew across the Rappahannock River and thereby postponed his defeat by a week (*see Tour 4a*).

RHODESVILLE, 27.2 *m.*, a hamlet formerly known as Lafayette, was on the Marquis Road, used by La Fayette in June 1781 when he marched southward to check Cornwallis. Returning on November 19, 1824, La Fayette found a triumphal arch erected here.

CHESTNUT HILL TAVERN (R), 32.9 *m.*, a 10-room frame structure built in 1822 and now a residence, is said to have been one of Henry Clay's favorite stopping places.

At 33 *m.* is a junction with County 628.

Right here to County 615, 3.2 *m.*

1. Left on this road 0.7 *m.*, to another junction with County 628 and R. to HARE FOREST (L), 2.6 *m.*, a long, white-painted, brick, two-story house. This is one of three places in Virginia that may have been the birthplace of Zachary Taylor (*see Tour 9*).

2. Right on County 615, 1.2 *m.*, to a junction with County 627; R. here 3.7 *m.* to a junction with a private trail that leads (L), 2 *m.*, to the top of CLARK MOUNTAIN (1,100 alt.), which was the site of a Confederate Signal Station built by Jackson in order to watch the movements of General Pope. Later it was used at intervals. Around the base of this mountain Lee gathered his troops in August 1862, preparing to attack Pope's army between the Rapidan and the Rappahannock Rivers. Moving rapidly from Richmond, where he had defeated McClellan, he wished to defeat Pope before McClellan arrived with reinforcements. Confederate movements did not progress as planned, and Pope retreated northward without attacking. On May 2, 1864, from this tower Lee saw the beginning of Grant's movement that preceded the Battle of the Wilderness.

On County 615 is the WADDELL MEMORIAL CHURCH (L), 2.3 *m.*, a frame structure honoring James Waddell (1739–1805), the blind preacher, who was buried here in 1880 (*see Tour 3c*).

BLOOMSBURY (R), 34.4 *m.*, a small weatherboarded house with dormers, a steep gabled roof, two large end chimneys, and a small four-columned portico, was built about 1722 by James Taylor (1674–1729), who was a member of Spotswood's expedition of 1716 and became a pioneer settler of the western country (*see Tour 3c*). He was a great-grandfather of James Madison and Zachary Taylor, and his sister was the mother of Edmund Pendleton.

At 37.3 *m.* is a junction with County 612.

Left here to MEADOW FARM (L), 1.6 *m.*, a white-painted brick mansion, now surrounded by boxwood and old shade trees, that was built in 1855 on the site of the home of Zachary Taylor (1707–68), whose grandson and namesake became President of the United States. In 1769 his sons, Hancock and Richard, made a trading trip by water from Pittsburgh to New Orleans. Hancock returned to Kentucky in 1773 and was killed by the Indians the following year. Richard, the father of the second Zachary, was an officer in the Revolution, married Sarah Strother in 1779, and moved to Kentucky in 1784 or 1785. General Longstreet, after being wounded at the Battle of the Wilderness, was brought to Meadow Farm for several days before he was taken farther south. Colonel Erasmus Taylor, then the owner, was Longstreet's quartermaster.

ORANGE, 37.9 *m.* (524 alt., 1,381 pop.) (*see Tour 3c*), is at a junction with US 15 (*see Tour 3c*).

At 41.8 *m.* is the pillared entrance (L) to MONTPELIER (*private*), once the home of James Madison, 'Father of the Constitution' and fourth President of the United States.

From among ancient trees the long, two-story house faces a wide view of the Blue Ridge Mountains. The brick walls are stuccoed and the roof, built in several hipped sections, extends over a finely denticulated cornice. The four widely spaced Roman Doric columns of the great portico rise directly from the ground, quite independent of an iron-railed porch terrace. The exterior, with simple window frames, is ornamented only by well-proportioned fanlights in the pediments of the portico and front door. The numerous and very spacious reception rooms have simple white woodwork.

The central part of the house—two rooms on each side of the transverse hall on both floors—was built by Colonel James Madison, about 1760. His son and namesake added the portico in 1793 at the suggestion of Thomas Jefferson. A few years later he built one-story wings and made other minor changes after plans drawn by William Thornton, amateur architect of the capitol in Washington. In 1907 new owners raised the wings to the level of the main part and extended the house toward the east, without destroying its fine proportions. The house was suited to the entertainment that President and Dolly Madison dispensed here, as in Washington, on a large and generous scale. On one occasion 90 persons were served dinner at Montpelier. Madison dealt graciously and successfully with a mother-in-law-in-the-house problem by giving his mother an apartment, with her own kitchen and servants.

Behind the house is a natural amphitheatre that has been made into a large formal garden on plans drawn by General La Fayette while visiting the Madisons in 1824. Until Madison's last years, the descending terraces, box-bordered paths, and geometrical flower beds were kept neatly groomed by a French gardener. The present owners have restored the garden. A charming little classical summer house, which concealed an icehouse and slave quarters, stands near by.

Born at Port Conway, Virginia (*see Tour 16a*), James Madison was graduated from Princeton College in 1771 but remained for a year studying theology. As a member of the Virginia Constitutional Convention of 1776, he proposed unsuccessfully an article providing for religious freedom. In 1785, however, he pushed through the general assembly Jefferson's Statute of Religious Liberty. As a delegate in the Continental Congress in 1780 he drafted instructions to John Jay, then representing the United States in Spain, to insist on free navigation of the Mississippi River, but it was not until 1803, when he was Secretary of State under Jefferson, that he saw this objective attained through the purchase of the vast Louisiana Territory.

In 1781 he favored an amendment to the Articles of Confederation that would give the Congress power to enforce its requisitions. At the expiration of his term in 1783, he took up the study of law and in 1784 was elected to the Virginia general assembly, where he paved the way for the National Constitutional Convention. On his proposal the Virginia and Maryland commissioners met to discuss navigation and commerce. When the Alexandria and Mount Vernon conference led to the Annapolis Convention, Madison and Alexander Hamilton worked together on the proposal that all States be invited to send representatives to consider commercial questions, and the Constitutional Convention resulted. The Virginia Plan, which served as the basis of deliberation in Philadelphia, was Madison's handiwork. As delegate he took a leading part in the debates and convinced of the historical importance of the occasion, kept full and careful notes that are the chief source of information on what happened during the secret sessions.

Though the Constitution did not wholly satisfy him, he was able to swing the Virginia delegates for its adoption; later he worked for ratification by his State and wrote 20 of the 85 Federalist papers, which had circulation through the Union. After being elected to Congress in 1789, he fulfilled a promise made first to George Mason by introducing the first nine amendments, which, along with the tenth, became the Bill of Rights. He was an opponent of slavery and deplored the compromise that permitted the slave trade to continue until 1808 and failed to provide for ultimate emancipation. Pressure, especially from New England, forced him to abandon the policy of commercial sanctions against Great Britain and brought on the War of 1812, declared during his presidency.

In 1789, in opposing the Alien and Sedition Laws, Madison wrote the Virginia Resolutions, reiterating the limitations of Federal powers, which, together with Jefferson's Kentucky Resolutions, served as the foundation for Calhoun's nullification policy in 1832 and furnished the basic argument for the rights of secession in 1861.

When his term as President expired in 1817, he retired to Montpelier, where he died June 28, 1836. Here Dolly Payne Madison, the beautiful widow whom he had married in 1793, the year he began to make plans for a mansion that would be a fitting background for her social graces, won her laurels as America's most accomplished hostess.

At 42.7 *m.* is a junction with County 639.

Left here to a dirt road, 0.8 *m.*, and L. to the MADISON CEMETERY, 1 *m.*, where a monolith, erected in 1856, marks the grave of James Madison and a smaller stone the grave of his wife. Mrs. Madison died in Washington July 12, 1849—not July 8 as is inscribed on the stone—and her body was moved to this place about 1858.

At 44.4 *m.* on State 20 is a junction with State 231.

Left here to (L) FRASCATI (*private*), 2.2 *m.*, screened by trees, undergrowth, and box hedges. A tall portico with four Greek Doric columns obscures more than half the two-story façade. The rectangular brick mansion has a deep cornice below the eaves of a hip roof, to which dormers have been added on the sides. The gracefully traced fanlight above the entrance door extends over the side-lights and is unusually large. The semicircular motif is repeated in a heavy round arch of carved wood with keystone motif spanning the transverse hall midway. That the house was built after the death of a man who inspired its design is evident in the stairs at the back of the hall—in open, un-Jeffersonian view. Only one drawing room is elaborately decorated. Here a deep gray wall is narrowed and framed by a low dado and a fine cornice, with a frieze carrying a design all around, in delicate plaster work. In the gardens, once enclosed by a serpentine brick wall, a double row of huge box trees has formed a vast arcade.

Frascati was built shortly before 1830 by Judge Philip Pendleton Barbour (1783–1841), brother of James Barbour (*see Tour 9*). William Thornton is said to have been the architect, but he can only have supervised the execution of what was clearly a typical Jeffersonian design. The work was done by 'workmen who had been engaged on the University.'

Judge Barbour was a member of the Virginia legislature, a speaker of the National House of Representatives, and presiding officer of the Virginia Constitutional Convention of 1829. Andrew Jackson appointed him to the U.S. Supreme Court. This democratic President liked Judge Barbour's liberal views as much as he disliked the Whiggishness of his brother, James Barbour.

BARBOURSVILLE, 50.2 *m.* (200 pop.) (*see Tour 9*), is at a junction with US 33 (*see Tour 9*). From this point the route continues on County 613.

At 57.1 *m.* on County 613 is a junction with County 600.

Left here 0.8 *m.* to (R) a small FRAME BUILDING, at the rear of a Negro church. Here shortly after the War between the States James Ferguson, a white man, gathered together 11 Negro children to be taught the three R's. He first gave his services but later was paid a nominal salary by the county.

The pillared entrance to BUENA VISTA (R) is at 64.1 *m.* This brick house, built in 1862, is near the site of the birthplace of George Rogers Clark (1752–1818), whose parents, John Clark and Ann Rogers Clark, moved here in 1750 from King and Queen County two years before he was born. The family later moved to Spotsylvania County. George spent several years exploring the Ohio River country and in 1774 was a captain of militia in Dunmore's War. In the early years of the Revolution, in response to Clark's challenge that 'if a country was not worth protecting, it was not worth claiming,' the Virginia assembly appropriated money for the defense of Kentucky. Commissioned lieutenant colonel and at the head of 175 men, Clark, on July 4, 1778, captured Kaskaskia, and in August Cahokia and Vincennes. This territory was ceded to the United States by the Treaty of Paris in 1783.

FRANKLIN (L), 64.6 *m.*, a story-and-a-half clapboarded house among trees, was in 1799 the home of Dr. William Bache, a grandson of Benjamin Franklin. It is said that Meriwether Lewis (*see Tour* 17*b*) once lived here and that he rode horseback every day to Monticello where he was secretary to Thomas Jefferson.

CHARLOTTESVILLE, 66.8 *m.* (480 alt., 15,245 pop.) (*see Charlottesville*).

In Charlottesville are junctions with US 250 (*see Tour* 17*a*), US 29 (*see Tour* 4*b*), and State 239 (*see Tour* 23).

Tour 11

(Marlinton, W. Va.)—Lexington—Buena Vista—Lynchburg—Brookneal—South Boston—(Roxboro, N.C.). State 501, US 501.
West Virginia Line to North Carolina Line, 183.2 *m.*

Asphalt-paved except for a long graveled stretch west of Warm Springs.
Chesapeake & Ohio Ry. parallels route between Glasgow and Lynchburg, Norfolk & Western Ry. between Lynchburg and North Carolina Line.
Limited accommodations and few filling stations west of Lexington. All types of accommodations elsewhere.

The western end of this route crosses the Allegheny and Blue Ridge Mountains—an area of great scenic beauty. The central and southern sections pass diagonally over the rolling Piedmont. With respect to both terrain and character of the people, the route presents a cross section of Virginia.

Section a. WEST VIRGINIA LINE to LYNCHBURG; 109.9 *m.* *State* 501, *US* 501

Southeast of the West Virginia line, at the crest of the Allegheny Range, the highway crosses the Jackson and Cowpasture River valleys and follows the North River. Settlers reaching these fertile valleys toward the middle of the eighteenth century clung to their holdings in spite of relentless Indian raids. This is a region of mineral springs, in the nineteenth century promoted as therapeutical aids to sufferers from fashionable ailments. Transformed into recreational centers, the resorts of the Warm Springs Valley have prospered, while other once popular spas have been abandoned.

State 501, a continuation of W.Va. 43, crosses the Virginia Line, 0 *m.*, 9 miles east of Marlinton, W.Va. (*see West Virginia Guide*).

The SITE OF FORT DINWIDDIE (L), 13.1 *m.*, is in the lowlands of the Jackson River. The stockaded structure was one of a chain, 15 to 30 miles apart, established in the mid-eighteenth century to guard the Virginia frontier against the Indians of the Ohio River Valley. George Washington, then a colonel, was in command of the project. He ordered Captain Peter Hog, commander of Fort Dinwiddie and good friend of Governor Dinwiddie, to raise a body of men, obtain tools, and work southward from Fort Dinwiddie. Because tools and men were scarce, progress was slow. Late in 1756 Washington wrote to the governor after inspecting the forts, 'I found them very weak for the want of men; but more so by indolence and irregularity.' Fort Dinwiddie was garrisoned from 1755 until 1789.

The entrance (R) to FASSIFERN FARM, a resort, is at 13.3 *m.* The small stone building down the hill (L) from the farmhouse was used as the clerk's office when Bath County was formed in 1791. Later the county seat was established at Warm Springs.

WARM SPRINGS, 18.4 *m.* (2,350 alt., 300 pop.) (*see Tour 21a*), is at a junction with US 220 (*see Tour 21a*).

At 20.3 *m.* is a junction with a dirt road.

Right here for a steep climb to FLAG ROCK, 0.7 *m.* (3,500 alt.), a high lookout point.

At BATH ALUM SPRINGS, 24 *m.*, a few decaying brick buildings remain to mark a once popular resort. Opposite the entrance to the grounds (R), at the base of a wall 100 yards from the highway, are springs of alum, iron, freestone, and lime water.

BLOWING CAVE (L), 31 *m.*, entered through a three-foot hole in the cliff beside the highway, was listed as 'a natural curiosity' in Thomas Jefferson's *Notes on Virginia.*

WINDY COVE CHURCH (R), 31.3 *m.*, a red brick structure built in 1838, is the third successor to a log church built by Presbyterians in the mid-eighteenth century.

At 31.4 *m.* is a junction with State 269.

Left here to GREEN VALLEY (L), 7.3 *m.*, a long two-story frame house with a porch across the front. The clapboarding hides the logs of the oldest part of the structure, which served at one time as a stagecoach tavern. It had been built as an addition to a frontier cabin.

At 11.6 *m.* is a junction with County 625; L. here 0.2 *m.*, to the SITE OF FORT LEWIS (L), once the home of Charles Lewis, youngest son of the founder of Staunton. It was protected about 1759 by a stockade, probably a crude affair, for it was called 'Lewis' Hog Pen.' Charles Lewis, like his brothers, was prominent in the affairs of the frontier. His lands included both Hot and Warm Springs. Lewis was killed in the Battle of Point Pleasant.

MILLBORO SPRINGS, 32.1 *m.*, was once a resort.

Right from Millboro Springs on State 42 to a monument, 1.2 *m.*, (L) in the woods, on the SITE OF THE FIRST WINDY COVE CHURCH—established by Presbyterians. Built about 1749, it was burned by Indians sometime after 1755, the year in which its first minister, uncertain of Presbyterian status in Virginia, emigrated to North Carolina.

At 2 *m.* is a junction with a dirt road; R. here 0.4 *m.* to SITLINGTON GRAVEYARD (R), a burying yard with many ancient unlettered slabs. About a third of a mile below (L) is the SITE OF FORT DICKENSON, garrisoned in 1756, with 40 men. Washington, reporting to Governor Dinwiddie on the condition of the frontier forts, wrote: 'None I saw in a posture of defence, and few that might not be surprised with the greatest of ease.' One Arthur Campbell, a young militiaman in no 'posture of defence,' was captured here while picking wild plums in the neighboring thicket.

The highway crosses a boundary of GEORGE WASHINGTON NATIONAL FOREST at 35.6 *m.*

GOSHEN, 40.1 *m.* (1,410 alt., 400 pop.), for sometime after 1890 a popular mountain resort, now produces textiles and refined glass sand, and quarries marble.

GOSHEN PASS, 45 *m.*, is a gap four miles long cut through the mountains by the Maury River, flanked on both sides by towering walls of green—brilliantly splashed with rhododendron in spring and early summer. The gap was first called Dunlap Pass, for Alexander Dunlap, who early established a homestead near by.

John Lederer is believed to have used this pass in 1669 or 1670 on one of his 'marches' westward. Later it was used by other adventurers and by General Andrew Lewis on his way to Point Pleasant. The stream in the gap was named for Matthew Fontaine Maury (*see Tour* 10), who became so fond of the magnificent scenery here while teaching in Lexington that on his deathbed he requested his body to be taken through the gap before burial in Richmond. The MAURY MEMORIAL, 46.9 *m.*, encircled with chains, is a granite shaft with a large iron anchor leaning against it.

ROCKBRIDGE BATHS, 50.8 *m.* (100 pop.), is merely a few stores and houses around the ruins of a resort, established in 1834 and so popular that it was sold for $150,000 in 1853. At that time as many as 400 guests registered in a single day.

Left from Rockbridge Baths on County 602 to the HAYES CREEK INDIAN MOUND (L), 2.5 *m.*, which, when opened in 1901 by representatives of the Valentine Museum (*see Richmond*), was found to contain well-preserved skeletons buried in four levels. Though single burials were frequent, many bodies were found in groups. Several had been weighted down with large stones.

Left from the mound 0.5 *m.* by a foot trail to the foot of JUMP MOUNTAIN, where is the GRAVE OF MAJOR JOHN HAYES, of Daniel Morgan's riflemen. According to local tradition, Major Hayes requested to be buried near the Indian mound in order that he might see the Indians arise on Judgment Day. The extent to which the Valentine Museum has interfered with Hayes's plans is a matter of conjecture.

LEXINGTON, 62.6 *m.* (946 alt., 3,750 pop.) (*see Tour 5b*), is at junctions with US 11 (*see Tour 5b*) and US 60 (*see Tour 8b*). In Lexington, State 501 becomes US 501, which coincides eastward for a few miles with US 60.

Stretching between towering mountains and the North River is BUENA VISTA, 69.9 *m.* (1,000 alt., 4,002 pop.), with silk mills, paper manufacturing plants, a tannery, brick kilns, and a saddlery. Buena Vista was one of the boom towns brought forth by a promotion company in the last decades of the nineteenth century, when paper towns were being created throughout western Virginia. A report of 1889 reads, 'The landed estate of the Buena Vista Company has been made by the consolidation of the historic iron and agricultural lands of Sam'l F. Jordan, known as the Buena Vista property, the Green Forest farm and the Hart's Bottom farm; all together making about 13,000 acres . . . Most of the lands of Green Forest and Hart's Bottom, amounting to over 1,000 acres, have been laid off into streets and building lots.'

GREEN FOREST (R), in a wooded area at the northern edge of town, with a large brick house having a two-storied porch, was established in the late eighteenth century by Arthur Glasgow, the immigrant who became a great-grandfather of Ellen Glasgow (*see Richmond*).

The SOUTHERN SEMINARY AND JUNIOR COLLEGE, on an elevation, is a girls' school whose main building is a towered brick structure.

In Buena Vista is a junction with US 501; R. here on US 501.

At 78.8 *m.* is a junction with State 249.

Right here to GLASGOW, 0.2 *m.* (500 pop.), the remnant of a town established in 1890. General Fitzhugh Lee was president of the promotion company. Neither the large hotel nor the power plant, hopefully built, was ever operated, and industries failed to materialize.

In December 1742, Captain John McDowell (*see Tour 5b*) and seven militiamen were killed near by in the first fight with the Indians in this vicinity. Captain McDowell had entertained the natives for a day on apparently friendly terms. But after the warriors left they hunted for a week or more along the South River and pillaged in the neighborhood. Captain McDowell raised a body of 34 men to expel the Indians from the area; in the fight that followed, there were casualties on both sides.

GLASGOW MANOR, with brick walls laid in Flemish bond, was built in 1810 by Joseph Glasgow, a son of Arthur Glasgow. The house was extensively remodeled at the time the town was established.

On State 249 is NATURAL BRIDGE STATION (L), 3.4 *m.*, of the Norfolk and Western Ry. Left here 0.5 *m.* on County 685 to County 1004 and R. to ARNOLD'S VALLEY, (*picnicking, boating, fishing, facilities and campsites*), 4.8 *m.*, a recreational area in the Jefferson National Forest. Close to the lake is a cascade that tumbles 80 feet, and a lookout point that commands a view of distant mountain ranges.

State 249 continues to US 11 at NATURAL BRIDGE, 6.3 *m.* (*see Tour 5b*).

BALCONY FALLS, 80.8 *m.*, is a series of rapids in the beautiful gap, four miles long, cut by the James through the Blue Ridge. Because the James and the Potomac are the only streams offering possibilities of water transportation between Chesapeake Bay and the valleys beyond the range, plans were made for their utilization as early as 1772.

Although the first section of the James River Canal was opened in 1789, more than 50 years had passed and $8,000,000 had been spent before the canal was carried beyond Balcony Falls. However, sluice navigation was being used by 1816. Long narrow batteaux loaded with produce were guided through the tortuous channel by boatmen whose services drew high pay. The railroad through this pass was completed in 1881.

SNOWDEN, 84.1 *m.*, consists of a half dozen houses around a plant generating electricity from the fall of the river.

BIG ISLAND, 90 *m.* (500 pop.), scattered between the highway and river centers around a plant manufacturing paper from pine pulp.

The highway climbs to EAGLE'S EYRIE (L), 97.6 *m.*, on the crest of the mountains, a large house built during the World War by Baron Quarles von Offert, a German refugee.

Right from Eagle's Eyrie on a dirt road several hundred yards to SUNSET LEDGE, which affords a wide view.

LYNCHBURG, 109.9 *m.* (731 alt., 40,661 pop.) (*see Lynchburg*), is at a junction with US 29 (*see Tour 4c*).

Right from Lynchburg on US 460 to County 661, 7.4 *m.*, and L. 0.6 *m.* to POPLAR FOREST (*private*), one of the most interesting of the houses designed by Thomas Jefferson. The octagonal brick 'country house' stands among poplars within a white-fenced octagon of ground. A formal portico with four slender Roman Doric columns and a perfectly proportioned fanlight in the pediment faces the box-bordered drive. From inconspicuous projections at the sides—accommodating the stairs and pantry—low terraces run out to turf-covered mounds, which screen various outbuildings that include octagonal privies, standing like sentry boxes and imitating the house. The sloping ground on the southern side gives the house two stories in the rear, where a second portico above a basement arcade faces a broad lawn.

The interior, finished simply, is divided into four rooms around a central hall 20 feet square. This hall, lighted only from above, is the dining room, from which one of Jefferson's renowned dumb-waiters descends to the kitchen below. Opposite the entrance passage is the drawing room, which opens through French windows onto the portico that overlooks the garden. In the bedrooms Jefferson as usual placed the beds in alcoves.

This property of more than 4,000 acres came into Jefferson's hands through Martha Wayles Skelton, whom he married in 1772. In order to superintend the management of the plantations, he came here often and stayed in the two-room cottage, then the only dwelling. It was while on such a visit in 1781 that he was thrown from his horse and suffered the enforced confinement that enabled him to write his *Notes on Virginia*. That same year Colonel Tarleton raided Poplar Forest, hoping—but failing—to find his important and long-sought quarry.

In 1806 Jefferson began to build the present house according to plans he had drawn for Pantops, one of his farms near Monticello. Although the building was finished within three years he continued to add details from time to time. The plantation, called Bedford at first, was his favorite retreat from the persistent admirers of his later years. In 1821 he praised its 'tranquility and retirement much adapted to my age and indolence.' The house was later gutted by fire. As restored, it lacks the original balustrade along the parapet, the pediment over the garden portico, depth of entablature, and the purity of style in which Jefferson executed the interior woodwork.

BEDFORD, 23.8 *m.* (900 alt., 3,719 pop.), is both the financial and geographical center of Bedford County and the seat of its government. Wide and shaded residential streets spread out from a business section crowded against the narrow thoroughfare by hills. To the west the land rises toward the Peaks of Otter (4,000 alt.), which form three massive blue humps on the skyline.

In the town are tobacco warehouses, the oldest automobile tire factory in Virginia, a mill that weaves cloth for military uniforms, a plant that manufactures asbestos products, and a label printing establishment.

After Campbell County was taken from the large Bedford area in 1781, the county seat was moved from New London (*see Tour 4c*) to a tract donated by William Downey and Joseph Fuqua. The new settlement was officially named Liberty, but local people called it Bedford Court House. In 1890 it was incorporated as Bedford City, shortened in 1912 to the present form.

The COURTHOUSE, a red brick building facing a small square, was constructed in 1930. The CONFEDERATE MONUMENT, an attractive monolithic obelisk in the court square, is a pleasing departure from the conventional soldier statue. The large stone in the courthouse square was chipped from the block used in cutting the stone that caps the Washington Monument in the Nation's capital.

Bedford County was formed in 1753 from Lunenburg County and Albemarle County and named for John Russell, Duke of Bedford.

The ELKS NATIONAL HOME for the aged, established in 1902, is housed in several pink stuccoed buildings.

Right from Bedford on State 43 to a junction with County 614, 12.9 *m.*, where, after passing between the PEAKS OF OTTER—(R) FLAT TOP (4,001 alt.) and (L) SHARP TOP (3,875 alt.)—the highway will join the proposed Blue Ridge Parkway (*see Tours 4A and 7c*). State 43 will be diverted south of a lake (2,505 alt.) to be formed north of this junction. Recreational areas (*camping, boating, swimming, picnicking*) will be provided.

Left on County 614 a short distance to (L) a toll road (*adm.* 50¢) leading 2 *m.* to SHARP TOP, a popular point for sunrise parties.

At 52.4 *m.* on US 460 is a junction with US 11 (*see Tour 5b*) in ROANOKE (950 alt., 69,206 pop.) (*see Roanoke*).

Section b. LYNCHBURG to NORTH CAROLINA LINE; 73.3 *m.* *US* 501

This section of highway traverses the rolling country of the south-central Piedmont. It passes through forests, farms producing diversified crops, and the tobacco belt. Towns are small and infrequent in the northern part of the route, but there are a few charming villages and one city in the lower section.

South of LYNCHBURG, 0 *m.*, at 2.3 *m.* is a junction with US 460.

Left on US 460 to State 24, 18.5 *m.*, and L. to the SURRENDER GROUNDS AT OLD APPOMATTOX COURTHOUSE, 21.3 *m.* (*see Tour 3d*).

RUSTBURG, 10.4 *m.* (350 pop.), is a leisurely village, established on land donated in 1783 by Jeremiah Rust for the seat of the newly formed Campbell County. *The Comprehensive Gazetteer* of 1835 said that Rustburg then had a population of 100, twelve houses, two taverns, one classical and one common school, two stores, a tanyard, 'several mechanics,' two physicians, and three attorneys. 'The mails,' it said, 'arrive and depart three times a week. The public buildings are large, neat and commodious.'

The CAMPBELL COUNTY COURTHOUSE, in a generous square, is a red brick structure built in 1848 to replace one that burned. Campbell County, formed in 1781 from the eastern part of the vast Bedford area, was named for General William Campbell, who the year before had won fame in the Battle of King's Mountain.

Facing each other are two old taverns. The FOUNTAIN HOTEL, a low rambling frame building with long low porch, has been in service since April 1786 when Bernard Finch was granted leave to keep an ordinary in his home. The RUSTBURG INN, established sometime after the Fountain Hotel, is a plain frame building.

GLADYS, 19.6 *m.* (200 pop.), was called Connelly's Tavern in the days when it was a relay station for mail brought overland by a carrier on horseback. Later it became Pigeon Run because of the extensive roosts of wild pigeons in the neighborhood.

1. Left from Gladys on County 652 to County 650, 1.7 *m.*, and L. to SHADY GROVE (L), 2.1 *m.*, home of Captain Alexander Spotswood Henry, son of Patrick Henry. The story-and-a-half brick house, with dormer windows, is set above a high basement. Window and door framing, the porch, and cornices are ornamented with beading, honeycombing, and dentils. This house, erected on one of the many pieces of land

bought by Patrick Henry for his children, was built by Dr. George Cabell as a wedding present for his daughter, Paulina, who married Captain Henry in 1814.

2. Right from Gladys on State 126 to LONG ISLAND, 7.3 *m.* (100 pop.), on the Staunton River, named for a large island opposite, on which Patrick Henry was living as early as 1793, when he wrote to his daughter, Betsey Aylett, 'We shall go to Red Hill, 18 miles below this, in a few days, to spend eight months, but spend the sickly months here.' In the autumn of 1794 he complained of the 'solitude' of Long Island, told of being 'very sickly with the ague,' and remarked on deaths from 'the flux' in the neighborhood. In this letter Henry announced without enthusiasm, 'We have another son, named Winston,' and added that he had decided to 'give out the law, and plague myself no more with business, sitting down with what I have.'

BROOKNEAL, 31.3 *m.* (692 pop.), is in rolling country near the confluence of the Falling and Staunton Rivers and clouded with dust from a plant that crushes feldspar for making pottery. New brick buildings mark the trail of three fires that destroyed parts of the town during recent decades. The town has a small tobacco market, a peanut processing plant, grist mills and stores that cater to the farmers of the neighborhood. This little settlement, named for the Brooke and Neal families, is on land where was established a tobacco inspection depot about 1790. Soon, a ferry was bringing tobacco from plantations and a settlement had appeared that in 1802 was established as a town.

Left from Brookneal on State 40 to County 605, 2.8 *m.*; L. here 1.2 *m.* to County 601; R. to HAT CREEK PRESBYTERIAN CHURCH (R), 4.6 *m.*, a small white frame structure on the site of a log church built about 1742 by Scotch-Irish Presbyterians from Pennsylvania. For more than 40 years Hat Creek was the only church in the scattered Hat Creek community; after a second building had been erected here, members of other churchless denominations were invited to join in services. There was a tempest in a teapot when an itinerant evangelist, one William Dodson, lured a prominent elder and his family from the Presbyterian to the Baptist fold and with a torchlight ceremony immersed his new converts at midnight in Little Falling River.

On State 40 is a junction with County 600, 3.9 *m.*; R. here 1.9 *m.* to County 619 and L. to a junction at 2.8 *m.* with County 677; R. on this road, 1.6 *m.*, to RED HILL, a modern frame house, on the site of one of Patrick Henry's many homes. For two years after Henry bought Red Hill, he divided his time between it and Long Island, then, in 1796, 'fixed his home' here. A family tradition is that Henry, standing in the house yard, would give orders to slaves working half a mile away, his voice carrying distinctly. In failing health, he refused high official appointment and a sixth term as Virginia's governor to lead the life of a country squire. The two youngest of his fifteen children by two marriages were born here. Only once—on the personal appeal of George Washington in January 1799—did the old warrior buckle on his armor and do battle in a political campaign. At Charlotte Courthouse he made his last speech—a fiery appeal for the support of the Federal Administration. In June of that year he died.

HENRY'S GRAVE, in the boxwood-bordered family burying ground, is marked, 'His fame his best epitaph.'

On County 619, at 6.4 *m.*, is the entrance (R) to STAUNTON HILL. The Gothic revival mansion, on a low hill in a large landscaped and wooded park, is an austere battlemented mass of gray stucco with turrets and pointed windows. A long porch has slender marble columns separated by shallow broad arches.

The house has 14 rooms of baronial proportions, in addition to kitchens and servants' quarters that face a long granite-flagged colonnade at the rear. The interior is richly ornamented in English Gothic style. The five-room lodge and plantation office is also modified Gothic in design, with deep gables and traceried eaves.

In 1848, when Charles Bruce began to build this house, marble for pillars, mantels, and floor sections was brought from Italy to Philadelphia, where it was fashioned. It was shipped from Philadelphia by way of Albemarle Sound and up the Staunton in batteaux to the plantation landing.

On State 40 is PHENIX, 12.9 *m.*, (100 pop.), a small shopping center.

Right from Phenix 2.7 *m.* on State 26 to County 649; and R. to County 619, 5.2 *m.*; R. here to the SITE OF CUB CREEK PRESBYTERIAN MEETING HOUSE (R), 6 *m.* A few rough gravestones and the foundations of the second church, built about 1800 and burned in 1937, mark the site of the little log church built here about 1742, one of the six churches of the first Presbytery of Virginia. A tall poplar is traditionally the shelter for the first crude pulpit around which the congregation gathered while outposts, armed with rifles, watched for lurking Indians. Founders of Cub Creek Church, as at Hat Creek, were Ulster Scotch-Irish.

On State 40 is CHARLOTTE COURTHOUSE, 19.6 *m.* (366 pop.), seat of Charlotte County, trading center, and gathering place for county residents on Saturdays and court days.

The COURTHOUSE, built in 1823, is the third. A court record of 1788 says that 'some evil disposed person' had burned the first. Charlotte County, formed from Lunenburg in 1764, was named for Princess Charlotte of Mecklenburg, young queen of George III. At Charlotte Courthouse during the political campaign of 1799 Patrick Henry and John Randolph of Roanoke matched oratory. It was the aged Henry's last appearance in public life, and Randolph's first.

Scotch-Irish Presbyterians and Huguenots, following the English into Charlotte County, fell easily under the influence of Methodist and Baptist evangelists.

Church customs of the late eighteenth century still prevail in Charlotte County. Women are found sitting together on one side of the middle aisle, and men on the other. It is a happy day indeed when a little boy graduates to the pews that no skirt ever touches. A timid bridegroom sometimes sheepishly sits beside his bride for a Sunday or two but it is a sign that the honeymoon is over when he returns to his brethren. During Sunday School and the first hymn and the long prayer the men remain outside the church. Someone gives the signal for entrance as the preaching begins.

In the summer the 'protracted meeting' dots the monotony of the year like a fiery exclamation point. When crops are 'laid by' a preacher arrives for one or two weeks to minister to the souls of saints and to call sinners to repentance. Young and old flock to the all-day meetings, while perspiration melts 'biled' collars and mingles with the permanent mustiness of the church. Dinner, spread on long tables in the grove near by, is an important feature. There is a rivalry among housewives as the board is loaded with fried chicken, piled high on paper plates, home-cured hams, legs of lamb, roast beef, and sometimes whole shoats. Chess pies—made by mysterious processes—and meringues and potato custards and cakes, variously colored and curiously ornamented, are drawn from beneath the covers of hampers. Every woman brings her best pickles and all the preserves and jellies by which her housewifery can be judged. At the end of the protracted meeting there is time for the people to recover before they need 'get in' the crops.

At 24 *m.* is a junction with County 656; R. here 0.6 *m.* to GREENFIELD (R), built by Isaac Read in 1730.

On County 656 at 2.6 *m.* is a junction with County 655; R. here 0.9 *m.* to County 651, and R. to ROANOKE BRIDGE (R), 1.1 *m.*, a house built by Colonel Joseph Morton on land granted by George II. When Colonel Morton settled here, his nearest neighbor was 30 miles away.

On State 40 is a junction with US 15, 30.4 *m.* (*see Tour 3e*).

VOLENS, 40.8 *m.*, is a crossroads village with a haphazard line of frame dwellings along the highway, several stores, and a county consolidated school.

Left from Volens on County 644 to County 646, 1.5 *m.*; L. here to County 641, 3.8 *m.*, and L. to CATAWBA BAPTIST CHURCH (L), 5 *m.*, a small frame building, painted white. On the opposite side of the road stood the church built in 1773. In 1785 the persuasive William Dodson arrived at Catawba, ousted the minister, and remained as pastor for two years.

At 45.8 *m.* on US 501 is a junction with County 754.

Left here to MILLSTONE CHURCH (R), 0.1 *m.* The Baptist congregation here was planted by the ubiquitous William Dodson in 1787, after he had left the Catawba.

The highway crosses the BANISTER RIVER, 53.7 *m.*, spread out to a great lake by the dam of the Halifax hydroelectric plant.

At 54.7 *m.* is a junction with US 360 (*see Tour 20b*), which is united with US 501 to HALIFAX, 55.4 *m.*, (753 pop.) (*see Tour 20b*), the southern junction with US 360 (*see Tour 20b*).

At 56.9 *m.* is a junction with County 654.

Right here to GREEN'S FOLLY (L), 0.5 *m.*, built about 1775 by Berryman Green, captain of the Light Dragoons and quartermaster on Washington's staff during the Revolution. The house, a tall white landmark, is of frame, two-and-a-half stories high and built in three sections. The two-story recessed portico has been enclosed and a free-standing portico, with square columns and a balustrade above the eaves, has been added. Dormers and a side porch also are new. When Green built his house before going away to war, he was clerk of Halifax County. He made the hall of his home large enough for use as a courtroom. Here county business was transacted until about 1800. The great hall and the size of the house in this, then remote, section gave the place its name.

SOUTH BOSTON, 60.7 *m.* (318 alt., 4,841 pop.), on the Dan River in the middle of the bright tobacco belt of the border counties, is the business center of Halifax County and one of the country's leading tobacco markets. Since its growth dates from the late decades of the nineteenth century, it has many red brick Victorian mansions among its more modern stuccoed and frame houses and bungalows. Although there are a cotton mill and a few other small industrial plants, the tobacco market dominates the town. Annually in September business and civic organizations sponsor a tobacco festival. A queen with attendants, chosen with much publicity, rules over a pageant, parade, and ball.

The town was chartered in 1796, nearly a century before it was incorporated in 1884. The settlement was made on land bought from George Carrington for £2,000 and disposed of in half-acre plots by lottery. Buyers were given five years to build dwellings with brick or stone chimneys.

Right from South Boston on State 152 to County 682, 0.7 *m.*; R. here to County 659, 3 *m.*, and L. to BERRY HILL (L), 4.1 *m.*, an imposing *ante-bellum* house at the head of a wide circular driveway. The mansion was modeled after the Parthenon, with eight Doric columns of fluted white marble supporting pediments on both front and rear. In adapting the Greek temple to the requirements of a plantation home, the architect departed from the classical design and made the house far broader than deep.

In the great hall, 25 by 40 feet, twin flights of stairs rise along the side walls to a landing at the second floor level and curve together again high above the center of the hall to reach the third floor.

At the rear of the house a colonnaded avenue leads to broad terraced and landscape gardens with flowering trees, shrubs, and evergreens, including cape jasmine, mimosa, and borders of towering boxwood, cedars, and lilacs.

James Coles Bruce, who built Berry Hill in the 1830's, was the oldest son of James Bruce, of Woodburn, Halifax County. The older Bruce, beginning with a chain of small general stores, amassed before his death in 1837 one of the largest fortunes of his day. In the decade before the War between the States the fortune of James Bruce, estimated at $4,000,000, including 3,000 slaves, was the largest in the South.

At 61.3 *m.* is a junction with US 58 (*see Tour 7b*).
At 66.3 *m.* is a junction with County 658.

Right here to CLUSTER SPRINGS, 0.7 *m.*, a shaded hamlet named for small lithia springs near by, well known in the days when it was fashionable to 'take the waters.'

At 73.3 *m.* US 501 crosses the North Carolina Line, 13 miles north of Roxboro (*see North Carolina Guide*).

Tour 12

(Washington,D.C.)—Fort Myer—Upperville—Ashby's Gap—Boyce—Winchester—(Romney, W.Va.). US 50.
District of Columbia Line to West Virginia Line, 87.8 *m.*

Paved roadbed throughout, chiefly asphalt.
All types of accommodations, chiefly in larger towns.

US 50, the Lee-Jackson Memorial Highway traverses the rolling fields of northern Virginia, the foremost dairying section of the State, and rises gradually through a country of fine horses and hunting, scales two mountain ranges, and crosses the Shenandoah Valley between them.

US 50 crosses the District of Columbia Line 0 *m.* at the western end of the Arlington Memorial Bridge at a point 1.4 miles from the zero milestone below the White House.

Left here on Memorial Avenue through a U.S. AGRICULTURAL EXPERIMENT FARM where rows of hothouses and other buildings stand among cultivated plots on what was once a part of Arlington, the Custis-Lee estate. Here George Washington Parke Custis kept the first flock of imported Merino sheep, brought to America in 1803 to stimulate the wool industry.

The highway comes to a dead end at Ridge Road and the Arlington Court of Honor, 0.5 *m.*

Left here into ARLINGTON NATIONAL CEMETERY (*open daily, sunrise to sunset*), entered between white pylons and iron gates. This largest of the National burial grounds contains the graves of more than 44,000 men and women of the service. Its 400 landscaped acres overlook the Potomac.

ARLINGTON HOUSE (*open* 9–5 *daily, March to Oct.;* 9–4:30, *Oct. to March;* 9–6, *April only*), built by the step-grandson of George Washington, became the home of Robert E. Lee. The mansion, high above the Potomac on the crest of a wooded hill, has a massive Doric portico with six heavy columns, effective at a distance but somewhat heavy when seen close at hand. Set between magnolias that screen flanking wings, the portico is reminiscent of the Greek temple at Paestum. The lines of the stuccoed brick house, painted buff with white trim, are simple. The present furnishings are largely copies of those first used here.

The estate of 1,100 acres was bought in 1778 by John Parke Custis, Martha Washington's son, and named for an older Custis estate (*see Tour 2*). Construction of the great house was begun about 1802 by George Washington Parke Custis but not entirely completed until after the War of 1812. In 1820 it was remodeled under direction of George Hadfield, an architect, who added the present portico. The large rooms were well designed for entertaining on a lavish scale.

Here in 1831 Mary Ann Randolph Custis, only child of George Custis, married Lieutenant Robert Edward Lee (1807–70). As a military man Lee was often absent, but Mrs.Lee and her seven children lived here until the three boys left for West Point or college. Driven out in 1861, the family never returned.

The estate was used as a training camp, and the title passed to the Federal Government in 1864, when the land was seized for unpaid taxes illegally imposed. Nearly 20 years later, the Government paid Custis Lee $150,000 for the property. Restoration of the house as a museum began in 1925.

Robert E. Lee was reared by his invalid mother. His father, the dashing, improvident, lovable 'Light Horse Harry' Lee, brilliant officer in the Revolutionary War, governor of Virginia, inmate of a debtors' prison, last saw Robert when the boy was six years old and the Revolutionary veteran was leaving for the south to regain his health. Five years later the older Lee died on Cumberland Island, Georgia. Graduating at West Point, second in the class of 1829, Robert E. Lee distinguished himself in the War against Mexico and was superintendent of West Point from 1852 to 1855. His last conspicuous service in the U.S. Army was the capture of John Brown at Harpers Ferry. In 1856 he wrote to his wife: '. . . slavery as an institution is a moral and political evil in any country . . . a greater evil to the white than to the black race . . .' But when the lines were drawn five years later, he resigned his commission in the U.S. Army, refusing to lead it against Virginia. He wrote, 'I shall return to my native state and share the miseries of my people and, save in defence, will draw my sword no more.' Eventually, however, he led the Confederate forces and proved himself one of the great military commanders of all time. Within six months of the surrender at Appomattox, he became president of Washington College in Lexington, where he died in 1870.

The MEMORIAL AMPHITHEATRE is a large open auditorium of white marble, designed by Carrère and Hastings after the theater of Dionysus at Athens and the Roman theater at Orange, France. It accommodates several thousand persons. At the east end is a pavilion (*open* 9–4:30 *daily*), containing a reception room, trophy room, stage, museum, and chapel. The TOMB OF THE UNKNOWN SOLDIER, dedicated in 1931 as a memorial to the unidentified dead in the World War and designed by Thomas Jones and Lorimer Rich, is on a terrace near the amphitheatre.

The U.S.S. MAINE MEMORIAL is an eagle-topped column, bearing the mast and conning tower of the sunken battleship. The CONFEDERATE MEMORIAL is a bronze monument in baroque style, the work of the Virginia sculptor and soldier, Moses Ezekiel, who is buried near by.

US 50 turns R. on Ridge Road and swings L. to the entrance (L) to FORT MYER, 2.4 *m.* (*exhibitions and polo matches, information at post headquarters*), home of the crack Third U.S. Cavalry, the first battalion of the Sixteenth Field Artillery, and the Machine Gun Troop, Tenth Cavalry. The administration building, officers' and enlisted men's quarters, and rows of brick stables bordering the parade ground are on land that was once part of Arlington. During the War between the States Fort Whipple, one of the chain of 127 forts defending Washington, was on the present reservation. It was renamed in 1881 to honor Brigadier General A.J.Myer, creator of the Army Signal Corps. U.S. Army Radio Station WAR is here.

At 2.8 *m.* is a junction with an unmarked road.

Left here 0.8 *m.* to (L) the U.S. NAVY RADIO STATION NAA (*visited only on pass from Director of Naval Communications*). Three tall towers, one 600 feet and two 450 feet, are visible for miles. Communication is maintained through a powerful short-wave system with U.S. warships in every part of the world.

At 6.9 *m.* is a junction with State 7 (*see Tour* 13).

At 13.4 *m.* is a junction with US 29–211 (*see Tour 4a*), which unites with US 50 for 2.8 miles (*see Tour 4a*).

At 16.2 *m.* is the western junction with US 29–211 (*see Tour 4a*).

CHANTILLY, 22.7 *m.*, is a crossroads, sometimes called Ox Hill, which Stonewall Jackson reached on Sept. 1, 1862, in a movement to prevent the Federal troops under General Pope from retreating to Alexandria. During spirited action here General Philip Kearny was killed.

Right from Chantilly on County 657 to FLORIS, 3.3 *m.*, a hamlet in which is FRYING PAN CHURCH (R), a small frame building with circular pulpit, a gallery, long benches, and an old floor of wide boards. The Reverend Mr. Jeremiah Moore, who became a Baptist dissenter in 1772, was one of the pastors here.

Near the SITE OF MOUNT ZION CHURCH (L), 33.4 *m.*, in July 1864, Colonel John S. Mosby attempted to cut off a Union cavalry force under Major W.H.Forbes. Mosby reached the road near the church, set his cannon, and charged. Forbes, pinned under his horse, was captured. This, oddly enough, was the beginning of a lifelong friendship between the families of the two leaders.

At 34.1 *m.* is a junction with US 15 (*see Tour 3a*), with which US 50 unites for 6.6 miles (*see Tour 3a*).

MIDDLEBURG, 40.5 *m.* (300 pop.) (*see Tour 3a*), is at the western junction with US 15 (*see Tour 3a*).

WELBOURNE (R), 41.8 *m.*, is an old house set back in a beautiful garden. Several skirmishes took place near by during the War between the States, when this was the home of Colonel R.H.Dulaney, organizer of horse shows and hunts. Harry Payne Whitney later established stables here.

At ATOKA, 44.7 *m.*, a hamlet, on June 10, 1863, Colonel John S. Mosby organized Company 'A' of his guerillas.

The UPPERVILLE HORSE SHOW GROUNDS (L), 47.5 *m.*, attract large numbers of sportsmen to annual shows—the oldest organized horse show in the United States, started by Colonel Dulaney in 1853.

UPPERVILLE, 49.5 *m.* (550 pop.), is a leisurely town lying in rolling country. Heavy trees arch over the long main street, where dignified homes make room here and there for general stores, an antique shop, a bank, and the post office. Upperville, once a post village on the Ashby Gap Turnpike, is the headquarters of the Piedmont Foxhounds, a pack established in 1840.

A small old stone TOLLGATE (R), 51.6 *m.*, is a relic of turnpike days.

PARIS, 53.1 *m.* (100 pop.), is a general store and a group of frame dwellings.

ASHBY GAP (1,150 alt.) 53.8 *m.*, through the Blue Ridge Mountains, was named for Captain Thomas Ashby, who settled near here about 1710. A hill here (L) was used as a signal station, first by the Confederates and later by the Federals.

ASHBY'S TAVERN (R), 55.1 *m.*, is a small, dilapidated wooden building at which British prisoners from Yorktown rested on their way to Winchester in 1781. Thomas Ashby's son John, who kept an ordinary here, was sent by Washington to convey to Governor Dinwiddie news of Braddock's defeat.

BURWELL'S MILL (R), 59 *m.*, a two-story field-stone structure with a steep pitched roof and heavy wooden door, was built in 1760 by Daniel Morgan (*see below*).

MILLWOOD, 59.6 *m.* (225 pop.), with a few stores, garages, churches, and a school, is a local service center for several large estates near by.

1. Right from Millwood on State 255 to CARTER HALL (R), 0.2 *m.*, a vast mansion with stuccoed brick walls, facing acres of rolling lawn and a wide view of the mountains.

The principal structure is behind a great flat-roofed portico 72 feet long with six Roman Ionic columns. In the hall a fine stairway rises in a circular sweep. Two dependencies—of stuccoed brick, like the main house they flank—are almost mansion-size.

Nathaniel Burwell built the house in 1790–92 and named it for his great-grandfather, 'King' Carter (*see Tour 16b*). The house was altered in 1830 and in 1855; the portico probably dates from one of these years. Edmund Randolph, governor of Virginia and first attorney general of the United States, died here in 1813, and here Stonewall Jackson had his headquarters in October 1862.

OLD CHAPEL (L), 3.1 *m.*, an ivy-covered stone building, was erected about 1790. Its high peaked roof, stone chimneys, heavy shutters, and whitewashed interior attract antiquarians. Bishop William Meade, the church historian, was rector here for many years. In the sycamore-shaded graveyard are buried Nathaniel Burwell, who donated two acres on which the first chapel stood; Edmund Randolph; members of the Page, Nelson, and Pendleton families; some Negro servants; John Esten Cooke, novelist; Philip Pendleton Cooke, poet; and 18 other Confederate soldiers.

2. Left from Millwood on County 624, 1.2 *m.*, to County 626 and R. to LONG BRANCH (L), 2.2 *m.*, a large brick dwelling, with an Ionic portico on one façade and a Doric portico on the other. From a deck roof rises an airy cupola. A large transverse hall, adorned with columns midway, has a gracefully curving staircase. There is fine scenic wallpaper in two rooms. Legend has it that secret rooms and a concealed staircase exist. Long Branch was built in 1805–6 by Captain Robert Carter Burwell.

The brick-arched entrance (L) to TULEYRIES is at 60.9 *m.* The large block of a mansion with portico and cupola was erected in 1833 by Colonel Joseph Tuly. It is said that Sheridan spared the house in 1865 because of the carved eagle over the door. After the war much of the furniture from the White House of the Confederacy in Richmond was kept here. Part of the estate is now an experimental farm operated by the University of Virginia.

SARATOGA (L), 61.1 *m.*, a gaunt but massive stone house, was the home of Daniel Morgan, hero of Saratoga and Cowpens. It is said that when Morgan erected the house in 1781–82, he used Hessian prisoners as workmen.

BOYCE, 61.6 *m.* (572 alt., 325 pop.), is a busy little town on the Norfolk and Western Ry.

At 64 *m.* is a junction with County 655.

Right here to County 620, 1.2 *m.*, and R. to THE BRIARS (R), 1.7 *m.*, a barnlike stuccoed stone house built about 1830 by Dr.R.P.Page. After 1869 it was the home of Dr.Page's son-in-law, John Esten Cooke, novelist, historian, and Confederate soldier, who died here in 1886. Born at Ambler's Hill in Winchester, Cooke was one of the 13 children of John R. Cooke.

At 69.3 *m.* is a junction with State 3 (*see Tour 5a*), with which US 50 unites to WINCHESTER, 70.5 *m.* (717 alt., 10,855 pop.) (*see Winchester*).

In Winchester are junctions with US 11 (*see Tour 5a*) and State 7 (*see Tour 13*).

GORE, 83.5 *m.* (125 pop.), is a trading post for mountaineers.

US 50 crosses the West Virginia line at 87.8 *m.* 26 miles east of Romney, W.Va. (*see West Virginia Guide*).

Tour 13

Alexandria—Falls Church—Tyson's Corner—Leesburg—Purcellville—Berryville—Winchester; 71.3 *m.* State 7.

Asphalt-paved roadbed throughout.
Washington & Old Dominion Ry. parallels route between Falls Church and Bluemont.
All types of accommodations.

Most northerly east-west route in Virginia, State 7 follows in general the eighteenth-century wagon road that became a turnpike in the 1820's and 1830's between Alexandria and Winchester. A hilly, suburban section changes west of Tyson's Corner into rolling pastureland, where prosperous dairy farms and cornfields alternate with wooded stretches. Many large estates, with white fenced meadows for fancy horses, give an air of rural fashion to the area around Leesburg. West of Leesburg the road winds and dips as it rises to a rolling plateau between low Clark's Gap and the Blue Ridge. Stone houses are scattered through this section, and near the Ridge stone fences predominate around fields used for orchards, general farming, and stock raising. West of Snicker's Gap the route drops abruptly to the Shenandoah before rising and falling gently through the horse-raising area around Berryville and stone-walled orchards nearer Winchester.

State 7 branches northwest from US 1 (*see Tour 1a*) at King and Washington Sts. in ALEXANDRIA, 0 *m.*

At 2.8 *m.* is a junction with Braddock Road.

Left here about 100 yards to a junction with Quaker Lane; L. here to EPISCOPAL HIGH SCHOOL (R), 0.2 *m.*, occupying a group of brick buildings on a hill from which there is a wide view of distant Washington. The school was founded in 1839 and prepares about 225 boys for college. The central structure, stuccoed like several others near it, is a former residence, built about 1785 by one of the Alexander families. The flat-roofed Doric portico in Greek Revival style must have been a later addition. The drawing room contains excellent woodwork in Adamesque style.

On Quaker Lane is the PROTESTANT EPISCOPAL THEOLOGICAL SEMINARY (R), 0.4 *m.*, second in the United States only to the seminary in New York City in age and size. Its large group of buildings in stone or brick, ponderously Gothic and Romanesque and dominated by a pagoda-like tower, stands in a grove of oaks. The seminary was founded in 1823 in Alexandria, largely through efforts of a society organized five years earlier under the influence of Dr. William H. Wilmer, the Reverend William Meade, and Francis Scott Key. In 1827 the seminary was moved to the present site. About 70 students are enrolled. At the seminary is kept the alms basin from the church that served Jamestown in the seventeenth century.

BAILEY'S CROSSROADS, 5.6 *m.*, a store-girt intersection, was named for a family one of whose members was the partner of P.T. Barnum, the circus impresario.

At 7.8 *m.* is a junction with US 50 (*see Tour* 12).

FALLS CHURCH, 8.8 *m.* (364 alt., 3,800 pop.) (*see Tour* 4*a*), is at a junction with US 29–211 (*see Tour* 4*a*).

At 12.9 *m.* is a junction with State 9.

Right here to SALONA (R), 3.9 *m.*, known locally as 'the Smoot House,' a large red brick structure, with a gabled roof. Built in 1801 for the Reverend William Maffit, the house sheltered President and Mrs. Madison when Washington was occupied by the British in 1814. Fleeing from the White House on the afternoon of August 24, and lugging with her among other things the Declaration of Independence and Stuart's portrait of George Washington, Dolly crossed the Potomac by the Chain Bridge, followed back roads, and stopped at the first large house. Mrs. Maffit took her in, loaded a musket, and ordered slaves to bar the doors. Later the President himself turned up with Mr. Maffit and several cabinet members. The company interrupted supper to watch the fire that gutted the White House and other public buildings in the Capital. President Madison soon left Salona, but Dolly stayed on. From October 1861 until the following April, the house was headquarters for General McClellan.

RIDGELAWN (R), 4.2 *m.*, an ivy-draped stone house in Hollywood style within a walled garden, is the home of Percy Crosby, cartoonist and creator of 'Skippy.'

At 4.7 *m.* is a junction with County 604, the old Georgetown Turnpike, in LANGLEY (114 pop.), a scattered rural community. L. here to SCOTT'S RUN, 2.7 *m.*, cascading toward the Potomac. A dirt road (R), 3.1 *m.*, leads down to a GOLD MINE (*closed to visitors*) on Bull Neck Run near the river. Gold was discovered in Maryland opposite this point in 1864, when a regiment of soldiers washing their skillets in the creek found traces of 'color.' Developed soon after the war, it continued in operation until 1896. It still yields a small amount of 'flour gold.'

The DOWER HOUSE (R), 3.2 *m.*, is a simple, two-story structure by the ruins of an older stone building. During the early days of the War between the States this structure was set afire by Confederates who mistook it for the home of James W. Jackson, who had killed the Union Colonel Elmer Ellsworth while defending a Confederate flag flying over his Alexandria hotel. Jackson in turn was shot down by Ellsworth's men.

MISS MADEIRA'S SCHOOL (R), 4.3 *m.*, occupying 11 neo-Georgian buildings, in the midst of white-fenced woods and meadow, is a finishing school for girls.

The entrance (R) to GREAT FALLS PARK (*fee for parking car* 25¢, *adm. for hikers* 10¢) is at 5.6 *m.* At the end of a dirt road through laurel-dotted woodland are the GREAT FALLS OF THE POTOMAC, a surprising volume of water lashing its way down a great cascade over wild heaps of rock before rushing on through a granite gorge. Near by are the stone RUINS OF GEORGE WASHINGTON'S IRON FOUNDRY AND MILL. Water continues to flow down the millrace from a section of the old Potomac Canal. Fostered by Washington and opened in 1800, the canal bore more than $10,000,000 worth of goods before being superseded by the more ambitious Chesapeake and Ohio Canal in 1825. Four of the five locks, lying three quarters of a mile to the south, are easily reached by trail.

County 604 continues to a junction with State 7 at DRANESVILLE, 11.3 *m.* (*see below*).

On State 9, 7.3 *m.* from State 7, is CHAIN BRIDGE (L), built in 1938 on the site of a series of bridges, the first of which was constructed in 1797. It was from the method of construction used for the third that successors have been named.

The entrance (L) to ASH GROVE is at 14 *m*. Among the remains of a grove of ash trees, stands the cream-painted frame house, with dormers along its gabled roof. A low rear wing is the hunting lodge built about 1790 by Thomas, Lord Fairfax. H-and-L hinges, brass locks, hand-hewn beams, and the ripple glass of the windowpanes attest its age. The rest of the structure was built a little later. On the lawn, among holly and boxwood dating from the Fairfax regime, is the well-preserved brick kitchen.

DRANESVILLE, 21.6 *m*. (100 pop.), a vague community of houses in rolling country, wooded and white-fenced, is the area around a junction with the old Georgetown Turnpike (*see above*). There was a skirmish here on December 20, 1861, called the Battle of Dranesville, in which General E.O.C.Ord forced General J.E.B.Stuart to retire. On June 27, 1863, after an engagement at Upperville, General Stuart led three brigades through Dranesville on their way to cross the Potomac and join General Early in Pennsylvania.

DRANESVILLE TAVERN (L), 22.5 *m*., close to the highway, is a gray weatherboarded building dating back in part perhaps to 1720. It was a popular stop in stagecoach days.

BROAD RUN BRIDGE, 27.3 *m*., carrying the highway on its humped back across the stream here, was built in 1820, according to a date on one of the massive stone buttresses. Wooden bridges, frequently repaired or rebuilt, spanned the water at this point before 1759, when the earliest of many similar records tells of repairs. There was an order in 1771 'to build a bridge at the usual place' over Broad Run for £150. From the garden (*open, adm. summer* 10¢) of the little whitewashed stone TOLL HOUSE (L) there is a full view of the sturdy bridgeside.

BELMONT (L), 30.7 *m*., a red brick mansion half overgrown with ivy, stands on a tree-shaded hill surrounded by rolling white-fenced fields. With a formal porch centered on the façade below a small Palladian window and flat stone arches heading the other window openings, the gabled main section is linked gracefully by long passages to a pair of low dependencies. This house was built about 1800 by Ludwell Lee (1760–1836). During a reception for La Fayette here in 1825, when Coton, the home of Thomas Ludwell Lee, stood near by, slaves in a double line with flaming torches lighted the way between the two houses. A marble mantel at Belmont attests the gratitude felt by the Marquis after his return to France. Sold soon after 1836 and turned into a girls' school, the mansion became a residence again about 1905.

GOOSE CREEK BRIDGE, 32.3 *m*., is another of the few stone spans in Virginia more than 100 years old.

LEESBURG, 35.8 *m*. (330 alt., 1,640 pop.) (*see Tour 3a*), is at a junction with US 15 (*see Tour 3a*).

CLARK'S GAP, 39.1 *m*., affording a view of the Blue Ridge Mountains northwestward beyond wide, rich lowlands, is at a junction with State 238.

Right here to County 662, 0.7 *m*., and R. to WATERFORD, 3.6 *m*. (256 pop.), the oldest settlement in Loudoun County, dozing between low hills that roll down to meadows along a lazy creek. Old houses—white frame or red brick—are set along lanelike streets. A stone MILL that has produced waterground meal for more than 100 years stands at the edge of the village, which was named for Waterford in Ireland, the native town of Asa Moore, who built his house here in 1733.

Right from Waterford 0.3 *m.* on County 698 to the abandoned FAIRFAX MEETING HOUSE, in fork with County 665 (L), a barnlike structure of roughhewn stone. The building was erected about 1868 and replaced a meeting house built here in 1740.

HAMILTON, 42.6 *m.* (500 pop.), is a settlement of trim white dwellings in broad yards—shallow barriers that hold back the fields. The village was named for James Hamilton (1720–75), one of the first local landholders.

A TOLL GATE LODGE (R), 43.8 *m.*, a little stone hut at the road's edge, is one of a few surviving stations at which tolls were once collected.

At 44.3 *m.* is a junction with County 722.

Left here is LINCOLN, 1.7 *m.* (101 pop.), a few frame houses and a store that form a hamlet begun in the 1730's by Friends from Pennsylvania. Here is Goose Creek Meeting, the only Quaker meeting to survive in Loudoun County, which grew out of the prayers Jacob Janney's wife, Hannah, offered up twice weekly under the trees in the forest. The first meeting house, built shortly after 1736, was replaced in 1765 by the SECOND GOOSE CREEK MEETING HOUSE (R), a stone building, now a dwelling, beside a stone-walled cemetery. The THIRD MEETING HOUSE (L), a large red brick structure in use today, was erected in 1817.

PURCELLVILLE, 45 *m.* (700 pop.), with rather standoffish houses behind hedge-bound lawns, is a marketing center with a crowded little block of stores. Here every October is held the Loudoun County Fair. At the town's western edge (L) is the LOUDOUN GOLF AND COUNTRY CLUB (*9-hole course; greens fee* $1, *Sun.* $1.50).

Right from Purcellville on County 690 is HILLSBORO, 5.2 *m.*, its one street curving among scattered houses, white frame alternating with gray stone. Here in 1831 was born Susan Koerner, mother of Wilbur and Orville Wright, whose experiments with heavier-than-air craft made aviation practicable.

Left from Hillsboro 5.3 *m.* on State 238, through pleasantly remote farm lands, to KEY'S GAP (987 alt.), where the highway crosses the West Virginia line 8 miles east of Charles Town (*see West Virginia Guide*). This was called Vestal's Gap in Colonial times for John Vestal, who ran a ferry across the Shenandoah below the ridge. Near by lived 'Edw. Thomson, ye Quaker,' whose home was a welcome stopping place for weary travelers jouncing over the rough road. On April 6, 1754, Major George Washington with his troops passed here, setting down 'expences of the Regt. at Edw. Thomson's marching up' and 'Bacon for do. of John Vestal & Ferriages.' In 1755 Sir Peter Halket, leading a detachment of Braddock's troops on the ill-fated expedition against the French at Fort Duquesne, stopped here, and noted, 'Mr.Thomson's, the Quaker, wh. is 3,000 wt. corn.' The present name honors Francis Scott Key of Georgetown.

ROUND HILL, 47.9 *m.* (557 alt., 359 pop.), overlooks the prosperous scene of trim farming country. The village, with a few stores in its middle, is strewn about the highway beneath the shade of plentiful trees.

At 51.5 *m.* is a junction with State 245.

Left here steeply to BLUEMONT, 0.4 *m.*, a handful of houses and a store or two at the foot of the mountain whose slopes are covered with hepatica in the spring. Until 1900 the hamlet was called Snickersville. Glimpsed through the trees on the mountainside are many summer homes of Washington's official and diplomatic set.

SNICKER'S GAP, 52.5 *m.* (1,150 alt.), is on the crest of the Blue Ridge. A trail (L) leads into BEAR DEN PARK (*open 9–5, May to Oct.; caretaker's fee 15¢*), a rocky ledge, from which there is a wide view westward of mountains and the Shenandoah Valley and River.

Snicker's was first known as Williams' Gap, and a grant made in 1731 notes 'the road that leads to Williams Cabbin in the Blew Ridge.' Williams, who was a squatter on the Fairfax lands, had a ferry here, which by 1760 had passed to Edward Snickers.

At 53.1 *m.* is a lookout (R) with a good view northwestward across the valley.

AUDLEY FARM (R), 59.3 *m.*, centers around a rambling old house, stuccoed white, and a vast collection of outbuildings. In the house, built by Warner Washington in 1774 and later enlarged, lived Nellie Parke Custis after the death of her husband, Major Lawrence Lewis, until her death in 1852. Today the estate is a large horse- and stock-farm.

BERRYVILLE, 60.5 *m.* (568 alt., 1,200 pop.), has a peaceful, antique charm. Nondescript commercial buildings huddle along the little main street, but round about cluster attractive houses amply interspersed with old trees and lawns. This center of a prosperous farming and apple country is a contrast to Battletown, as the tavern community at the crossroads here was known in the days when the foregathering of lusty frontiersmen led frequently to brawls. In 1798 a town was properly laid out on land belonging to a Benjamin Berry. Between 1835 and 1860 the community prospered greatly. Several skirmishes took place near by in 1862–64, but no important engagement. Part of Lee's army camped here on the way to Gettysburg.

The CLARKE COUNTY COURTHOUSE (R), built about 1840, is a red brick rectangle with a portico in Roman Doric style, and an arcaded wing, added in 1933. The county, an area of country estates, producing wheat, horses, and cattle, was carved in 1836 from Frederick County and named for George Rogers Clark, conqueror of the Northwest Territory. The extra letter, a slip in the incorporation papers, has persisted. The Clarke County Horse Show is held in Berryville every August.

THE NOOK (R), near the courthouse, a little frame house with low wings, was built sometime before 1800 by a Major John Smith.

1. Left from Berryville on State 12 to a junction with County 633, 2.7 *m.*; R. here through patches of woodland to ANNEFIELD (R), 4.1 *m.*, a bluish-gray mansion of stone, solitary and severe on a low hill. The graceful bulk is topped by a broad deck roof. Openings are treated simply, but a double-decked portico has slender Ionic columns, and the cornice is deep. The interior woodwork is rich and well proportioned. Among the few mansions constructed of stone in formal style, Annefield has a beauty and distinction that has been undeservedly neglected by connoisseurs. The house, on land settled by Robert Carter, son of the 'King,' and later a Carter home, was built in 1790 by Matthew Page and named for his wife, Anne Meade, Bishop William Meade's sister.

2. Right from Berryville 0.3 *m.* on a lane to the entrance (L) of SOLDIER'S REST, a long frame T, painted white, on stone foundations. About 1762 Daniel Morgan, the spectacular Revolutionary figure, married lovely Abigail Bailey and began construction of his house here. After 1781 he lived for a time at Saratoga near by but returned to Soldier's Rest, where he remained until 1800.

On this farm is so-called WASHINGTON SPRING (R), gushing from rocks at the foot of an old elm. According to a tradition, Washington used a log cabin that once stood near by as an office while surveying adjacent lands.

3. Right from Berryville 3.8 *m.* on US 340 to FAIRFIELD (R), a gray stone mansion among trees on a knoll. The mid-section, two stories beneath a hip roof with dormers and stone chimneys, is extended by lower wings. The house was apparently built about 1770 by Warner Washington, who had settled here with his second wife, Hannah Fairfax, about 1765. The vast barn of brick and stone and other outbuildings date from Warner Washington's time.

ROSEMONT (L), 61.4 *m.*, a modern, rambling, stuccoed frame structure with an eight-columned veranda across the front, is the home of Harry Flood Byrd, Governor of Virginia (1926–30), United States Senator since 1933. In his career Senator Byrd has emphasized efficiency and economy in government.

From this point west to Winchester the highway has an excellent macadam surface and passes through orchards, crossing a patch of rocky land and, between Opequon Creek and the city, a strip of shale that extends down the valley from the Potomac to Staunton.

At 71.3 *m.* is WINCHESTER (725 alt., 10,855 pop.) (*see Winchester*), at a junction with US 11 (*see Tour 5a*).

Tour 14

Petersburg—Emporia—(Weldon,N.C.); US 301.
Petersburg to North Carolina Line, 52.4 *m.*

Paved roadbed throughout, largely with asphalt.
Atlantic Coast Line R.R. parallels route.
Accommodations chiefly in towns.

US 301 passes through slightly rolling Southside where cotton, peanuts, and tobacco are grown. Much of the area was a battleground during the Revolution and the War between the States. The route runs through the center of the Petersburg National Military Park (*see also Tours 1c and 18*).

US 301 branches south from Washington St., 0 *m.*, on Sycamore St. in PETERSBURG.

The SITE OF FORT MAHONE (R), is at 2.2 *m.* This Confederate fortification was named for General William Mahone, whose division occupied it in 1864. On the remnants of the fort is a tall stone monument to the memory of the Third Division of the Federal Ninth Corps. Fort Mahone was lost during Grant's drive on the morning of April 2, 1865.

The PENNSYLVANIA MONUMENT (L), 2.3 *m.*, honors the dead of the 48th Regiment, Pennsylvania Volunteers, composed of coal miners who excavated the mine that was later exploded and formed the Crater (*see Tour* 18).

Here (L) is a junction with County 634, a part of the Jerusalem Plank Road over which farmers rolled tobacco to Petersburg.

Left on County 634 to the DEFENDERS' MONUMENT (R), 0.2 *m.*, erected in memory of the old men and boys of Petersburg who, on June 9, 1864, held off a cavalry force of 1,300 men under General A.V.Kautz until reinforced by Confederate cavalry.

The FEDERAL TUNNELS (L), 2.5 *m.* (*adm.* 40¢), are a reconstruction of Fort Sedgwick, named for General John Sedgwick, who was killed at the Battle of Spotsylvania Courthouse (*see Tour* 10). This Federal fortification was built as the Union lines were extended to the left in the early summer of 1864. The amount of ammunition used here when the fort was earning its nickname Fort Hell is said to have been enormous. Likewise owned privately is a museum containing many battlefield relics.

At 3.1 *m.* is a junction with a park road.

Right on this road, which circles westward along the line of Federal entrenchments and returns eastward along the Confederate line to the vicinity of Fort Mahone.

FORT DAVIS (L), 0.1 *m.*, formed another unit for the left flank of the Union army. When Grant had extended his lines to this vicinity, he began construction of Fort Davis, and on June 21, 1864, he sent two corps and a large force of cavalry to attempt to cut the railroads leading into Petersburg. The cavalry advanced to Reams' Station and turned westward on a raid. While the Sixth Corps swung southward and accomplished nothing, the Second Corps advanced against the railroad, three miles west, and was defeated by Mahone's Confederate division on June 22.

FORT WADSWORTH, 3.5 *m.*, was named for Federal General James S. Wadsworth, killed May 6, 1864, in the Battle of the Wilderness (*see Tour* 10). Just beyond the fort are the tracks of the former Petersburg and Weldon R.R., now part of the Atlantic Coast Line. Because it was one of the railroads that supplied Lee's army, Grant repeatedly sought its destruction, but Lee managed to protect it with only occasional breaks.

On August 18, 1864, the Federals cut the railroad at this point, began construction of Fort Wadsworth, and for four days defeated every effort on the part of the Confederates to dislodge them. Failing in a contemporaneous movement to break through to Richmond north of the James River (*see Tour* 24), Grant made an unsuccessful attempt to destroy this road at Reams Station (*see below*).

At 4.6 *m.* on US 301 is a junction with County 629.

Left here to the BELSCHES HOUSE (L), 1 *m.*, formerly called Bell Hill. The old remodeled house, a two-story frame structure, was at one time the home of Alexander Belsches, who distinguished himself during the War of 1812 in a battle between the *Constitution* and the British frigate *Guerrière*. For his bravery the State of Virginia bestowed upon him a sword.

Adjoining the Belsches House is FORT PATRICK KELLY, well-preserved breastworks now thickly covered by trees and underbrush. This Federal outpost was used by Grant during the Siege of Petersburg.

SECOND SWAMP, 5.7 *m.*, is the headwater of streams that once supplied power for several Colonial grist mills.

At 8 *m.* is a junction with County 608.

Right here to OLD GARY'S CHURCH (L), 0.5 *m.* The congregation was organized after a Methodist revival meeting held in 1787 by Jesse Lee at Jones's Hole near by. Built in 1880 the frame building was a successor to the barn given James Cary for the first meetings.

At 10.3 *m.* on US 301 is a junction with County 621.

Left here to County 638, 1.8 *m.*, and L. to LEE'S MILL (R), 2.3 *m.*, said to have been in use since the Revolution. Here, on July 12, 1864, part of General Fitzhugh Lee's command engaged in a lively skirmish with Federal cavalry, routing the enemy and capturing 33 prisoners and 30 horses.

At 11 *m.* on US 301 is a junction with County 622.

Right here to County 606, 2.2 *m.*, and L. to REAMS STATION, 3.3 *m.*, a depot on the former Petersburg and Weldon R.R.

On June 22, 1864, Generals James H. Wilson and A.V.Kautz, with 6,000 cavalry, tore up track, burned the station, and started on a raid westward. Upon returning, on June 29, they were surprised here by Confederate infantry and cavalry. Abandoning their wagons and guns, the Union cavalrymen fled southward with General Fitzhugh Lee's cavalry in pursuit. On August 25, General W.S.Hancock's Second Corps was badly beaten here by General A.P.Hill's corps and General Wade Hampton's cavalry.

At 13.8 *m.* on US 301 is a junction with County 604.

Right here to SHILOH BAPTIST CHURCH (R), 0.6 *m.*, with a congregation organized in 1836. When admitted to the Portsmouth Baptist Association, Shiloh had a membership of 24.

STONY CREEK, 21.4 *m.* (74 alt., 465 pop.), with freshly painted houses and well-kept yards, thrives with the support of lumber mills, a peanut plant, and the trade of a well-to-do farming area. There was much activity here during the last year of the War between the States. On May 7, 1864, General A.V.Kautz burned the railroad bridge over Stony Creek, just west of which, on June 28, the cavalry of General Wade Hampton defeated the cavalry of Wilson and Kautz, causing them to abandon silks, furniture, horses, silverware, and about 1,000 Negroes, the result of pillaging that later provoked a Federal headquarters investigation. Later, on December 1, Federal cavalry raided the depot and captured the station guard of 170 men. At Stony Creek during this winter was maintained a Confederate forage station, a source of supply for Lee's army that was cut off March 31, 1865, when Dinwiddie Courthouse was occupied by Federal troops.

At 22.1 *m.* is a junction with State 40.

Left here to SUSSEX, 7 *m.* (50 pop.), seat of Sussex County, a close-knit settlement with a general store and the usual buildings that surround a Virginia courthouse.

The SUSSEX COUNTY COURTHOUSE, built of brick in 1828 is on a large tree-shaded green. The central section projects over an arcaded loggia and at the center of the roof is a small bell tower. Sussex County was formed in 1754 from Surry and named for Sussex County, England.

The small TREASURER'S OFFICE was built simultaneously with the courthouse.

The CLERK'S OFFICE, erected in 1924, contains county records dating from the formation of the county, among them a deed signed by Thomas Rolfe, son of Pocahontas.

The large DILLARD HOUSE, built in 1802 by C.H.Bailey, was the repository of the clerk's records until the courthouse was built.

For about 10 miles south of a junction with County 640, at 26.1 *m.*, US 301 follows the old Halifax Road, which led to Halifax, in the North Carolina tobacco belt. Cornwallis marched over this road in his invasion of Virginia in May 1781. Because Lieutenant Colonel Banastre Tarleton had cleared the path for his general, Cornwallis met little opposition. On this march the British are said to have committed 'enormities that were a disgrace to the name of man.'

JARRATT (154 alt., 200 pop.), 31.5 *m.*, at a crossing of two railroads, began to grow in 1938 when the Johns-Manville Company established an insulating-board plant here.

On May 8, 1864, the village was burned by General Kautz to delay Beauregard. On December 8, track was torn up here by a large Federal force operating under Warren on retreat from Belfield. Warren withdrew to his lines near Petersburg in time to avoid conflict with General A.P. Hill's 16,000 Confederates, concentrating here on the morning of December 11.

EMPORIA, 42 *m.* (2,144 pop.), seat of Greensville County, is composed of North Emporia and South Emporia, two old towns formerly Belfield and Hicksford, separated by the Meherrin River. The town, of well-kept, attractive homes, has a lively air created by the presence of machine shops, lumber, cotton, and tapestry mills, veneer and candy factories, and peanut plants. It ships cotton and peanuts.

The old town of Hicksford, or Hicksville, grew up near the site of a ford, named for Captain Robert Hix, an Indian trader who was captain of the garrison at Fort Christanna (*see Tour 7b*) in 1717. He accompanied Governor Alexander Spotswood to Albany, N.Y., in 1722, to negotiate a treaty with the Five Nations, and in 1728 was a member of Colonel William Byrd's surveying expeditions.

On December 10, 1864, when Warren reached Belfield, he found Hampton protecting the railroad bridge from a well-fortified position. Repulsed, Warren returned to his lines at Petersburg. Hampton's cavalry remained here for a month while repairs were being made on the railroad.

The GREENSVILLE COUNTY COURTHOUSE, a two-story brick building with large, columned portico, was built in 1787. The county was formed in 1781 from Brunswick.

The REESE HOUSE, in North Emporia, was Butts Tavern for many years.

Emporia is at a junction with US 58 (*see Tour 7a*).

At 47.7 *m.* is a junction with County 621.

Right here to large GRANITE QUARRIES, 2 *m.*, which ships quantities of fine stone.

At 52.5 *m.* US 301 crosses the North Carolina Line at a point 12 miles north of Weldon, N.C. (*see North Carolina Guide*).

Tour 15

Bluefield—Tazewell—Lebanon—Appalachia—Big Stone Gap—Jonesville; 149.2 *m.* US 19, State 64.

Asphalt-paved roadbed.
Norfolk and Western Ry. parallels route between Bluefield and Norton; Louisville and Nashville R.R. between Norton and Jonesville.
Accommodations only in larger towns.

This route winds through the mountains of southwest Virginia, a rugged country with vast coalfields, bluegrass pastures, and fertile farmlands. Mining communities huddle in the valleys; coal dust smears the hillsides; handsome big-breasted cattle graze in the clearings.

This area, Virginia's last frontier, was not settled till the end of the eighteenth century. Before good roads and industrial developments brought the east and west together, the mountain folk held tenaciously to individualism, feuds, moonshining, old customs and forms of speech. Now, however, Southwest Virginia has transferred its attention from family to political feuds and has enough Republicans to make elections lively and to assure its citizens a good share of State offices.

US 19 crosses the Virginia Line at Bluefield, W.Va. (*see West Virginia Guide*), into BLUEFIELD, 0 *m.* (2,600 alt., 3,906 pop.), its twin, with which it unites to form a city of 23,245 persons. Physically inseparable despite civic independence, the towns share the advantages accruing from the presence of fertile land near by and from coal operations in the Pocahontas field. Bluefield is at the junction with US 21–52 (*see Tour 5c*).

1. Left from Bluefield on State 85 to BLUEFIELD COLLEGE, 2 *m.*, a coeducational junior college housed in several red brick buildings on a large campus. The school was established in 1920 by the Baptist General Association of Virginia.

2. Right from Bluefield on State 85 to FALLS MILLS, 3.9 *m.* (300 pop.), straddling the Bluestone River. Here General John Toland's troops camped in 1863 on their flight from Wytheville (*see Tour 5c*).

POCAHONTAS, 9.8 *m.* (2,500 alt., 2,800 pop.), with nondescript frame houses beside huge black shafts, is the focal point of the great Pocahontas semibituminous coal fields. The town sprang into existence around the first mine in the field, with the coming of the Norfolk & Western Railroad in 1882. A blacksmith discovered this field, used the coal for his forge, and allowed neighbors to dig enough for their homes. His frugal wife, fearing the supply would be exhausted, advised against such wanton generosity. Today there are 17 large areas of operation in this field.

These operations have an unusual feature. An 18-mile tunnel, supported by huge beams, has been driven along a coal seam to Dry Fork, West Virginia, and drains an area of approximately 12,000 acres. This outlet for water in mines saves a pumping cost of thousands of dollars annually.

At 10.1 *m.* on US 19 is a junction with County 655.

Right here to County 644, 7.4 *m.*, and R. to pass into fertile Abb's Valley, named for Absolom Looney, who discovered it in 1763.

On County 644 at 12.2 *m.* is the MOORE HOMESTEAD (L), a rambling frame farmhouse near the site of a cabin built by Captain James Moore in 1772. The Moore family's troubles with Indians began in 1784, when their 18-year-old son James was captured. In the summer of 1786, a party of 47 Indians swept down on the cabin and killed Captain Moore, a son, a daughter, and a sick man whose name history failed to record. Mrs.Moore, four children, and a girl visiting the family, Martha Evans, were taken captive. Mrs.Moore and two of the children were killed; while Martha Evans and Mary Moore were sold to a French Canadian family living near the place where James was held captive. The three were finally released, and James Moore returned to Abb's Valley and built a house on the site of his father's cabin.

At 16.9 *m.* on US 19 is a junction with County 645.

Left here to the SITE OF A BOONE CABIN-FORT (L), 0.5 *m.*, built by Daniel Boone and several companions on a hunting expedition in 1767–68. A brick farmhouse now occupies the spot. Here later Henry Harman,Jr., built the log house in which Tazewell County was organized and where the first court was held.

DIAL ROCK, a prominent crag beyond the house, was so named because its shadow is supposed to tell the time of day. Beyond it (R) is BUCKHORN, a grotesque summit resembling the horns of goats.

By a junction with State 61 at 17.7 *m.* is the PEERY HOUSE (L), a large frame building, in which Thomas Dunn English was a guest in 1843 when he wrote, 'Do You Remember Sweet Alice, Ben Bolt.' Captain W.E.Peery, a Confederate veteran, introduced purebred cattle to Clinch Valley.

Also at this intersection is (R) the SITE OF WYNNE'S FORT, now replaced by a frame house. William Wynne, a Friend, settled here in 1772. The Indians never attacked the fort, perhaps because the peace loving Quaker placed no garrison here.

Near this junction was Rocky Dell, the home of Samuel Tynes, whose daughter Molly, pretty and blond, made a daring 40-mile ride over the mountains in July 1863 to warn the countryside that General Toland was marching toward Wytheville. Having called her news at every farmhouse along the way, she reached Wytheville in time for a company of old men and boys to gather and resist the raiders (*see Tour 5c*). Molly—Mary Elizabeth formally—later married her soldier-sweetheart, William D. Davidson, who became a member of the West Virginia Legislature.

Left on State 61 to State 78, 4.4 *m.*, and R. 5.6 *m.* to the gap giving entrance to BURKE'S GARDEN, a broad oval basin (3,200 alt.), walled in by ridges that rise about 1,000 feet above it. Beside Garden Creek in the gap is a primitive grist mill operated for the benefit of the farmers on the fertile lands round about. Substantial homes stand amid bluegrass pastures where cattle graze.

At 7.1 *m.*, toward the center of the plateau where the road crosses the Creek, is a tumble-down springhouse (R), near the site of the house built by James Burke, who discovered these lands in 1749 and settled here. In 1756, when Indian fighters led by Andrew Lewis (*see Tour 5b*) camped near this spot, potatoes were growing in profusion near Burke's abandoned home. Thereafter the plateau was known as Burke's Garden.

In 1774 there was a frontier fortification here called Burke's Fort. In 1781 the wife and children of Thomas Ingles of Burke's Garden were captured by Indians. Ingles and a party of friends rescued Mrs.Ingles, but the children were killed (*see Tour 5B*).

TAZEWELL, 19.5 *m.* (2,373 alt., 1,211 pop.), is the seat of Tazewell County and financial capital of this agricultural and coal mining region. The substantial homes on the several hills offer convincing evidence of prosperity. After the formation of Tazewell County in 1799, two communities had champions in the contest for the seat of government. Those favoring Tazewell argued that here were the prime essentials of a frontier town —a grist mill and a blacksmith shop. A skull and fist fight settled the controversy. First called Tazewell Courthouse, then Jeffersonville, the town of Tazewell was incorporated in 1866.

The TAZEWELL COURTHOUSE, a severely plain stuccoed building with a large square central unit, a high columned portico, and flanking wings, replaced one destroyed by fire in the 1830's. Tazewell County was formed from parts of Russell and Wythe Counties and named for Henry Tazewell, United States senator from 1794 until 1799.

Stone foundations mark the SITE OF WITTEN'S MILL, built about 1800 by Thomas Witten, Jr. This 'tub mill' was a nucleus around which Tazewell grew.

A flat-roofed, two-story office building, 20 Main Street, stands on the site of a log house that was first an inn, then the home of John Warfield Johnston, United States Senator (1870–83), and father of George Ben Johnston (1853–1916), physician and pioneer in Virginia medical education, who was born in a second Johnston home in Tazewell. Dr. Johnston was an early disciple of Lister. He is credited with the first antiseptic operation performed in Virginia. Tazewell County is the birthplace and home of George C. Peery, governor of Virginia from 1934 to 1938.

Right from Tazewell on State 81, crossing the railroad tracks, to NORTH TAZEWELL, 1 *m.* (600 pop.), first called 'Kelly,' and now a small commercial center around a railroad station.

At 22.2 *m.* on US 19 is a junction with State 88.

Left from US 19 on this hard-surfaced road and up a slight grade through PLUM CREEK GAP. When the road was opened here over rough and inaccessible terrain, a judge told the road builders, 'You have put a road where God Almighty never intended one to be placed.'

At 22.5 *m.* on US 19 is a junction with State 81.

Left here at 0.3 *m.* a rounded peak is seen rising in the wide gap on top of the mountain (L), about a mile from the highway. This peak, BATTLE KNOB, was named for a bloody fight between the Cherokee and the Shawnee, who carried on perpetual strife for these hunting lands. The Cherokee fortified themselves on Battle Knob and were able to withstand the attacks of a much larger force of Shawnee. When their ammunition was exhausted during the battle, a runner obtained a fresh supply at Witten's Fort (*see below*) and thus was made possible victory for the smaller force.

At 6 *m.* on State 81 is the village of LIBERTY; L. here on County 608, 0.4 *m.*, to a lane (L), leading to the SITE OF LOST MILL. In a depression 80 feet deep are a bulging dam, the water wheel foundation, old timbers, and various pieces of machinery. Power was transmitted to the mill by some mechanical arrangement.

At MAIDEN SPRING (L), 8.7 *m.* on State 81, a remarkable flow of water gushes from the base of a cliff.

Above the spring, at 8.9 *m.* on State 81, is a junction with County 609; in the field (R) at this junction is the SITE OF MAIDEN SPRING FORT, built by Reese Bowen, who moved his family here about 1772.

In 1776, when the Indians of the Ohio River Valley came east along the Big Sandy River and terrorized the settlements west of Maiden Spring, Bowen and the other men of the neighborhood went to meet them, leaving their families here. Late one afternoon, Mrs. Bowen, rounding up the cows for the night milking, at the foot of Short Mountain came on imprints of mocassins. Believing that she was being watched, Mrs. Bowen walked calmly home and told the women to dress in men's clothing and take turns at sentry duty outside. Only she, however, and a Negro slave woman dared to carry out the proposal. One carrying a musket and the other a stick shaped like a gun, they guarded the fort all night and apparently succeeded in giving the impression that the fort was well manned; at least there was no attack.

The present BOWEN HOUSE was built in 1838 on the hill above the old site. It incorporates two rooms of Reese Bowen's cabins.

Reconstructed FORT WITTEN (L), 24 *m.*, marks the site of the first settlement in this part of the Clinch Valley. About 1767 Thomas Witten settled here on a tract called Big Crab Apple Orchard and built such a garrisoned house as was customary on the frontier.

At 35.4 *m.* is a junction with State 84.

Right here to CEDAR BLUFF, 3.5 *m.* (590 pop.), home of the Cedar Bluff Woolen Mills. Except after fires in 1898 and 1922, the mill has operated continuously since 1832. Beautifully patterned coverlets are woven here.

Just north of RICHLANDS, 5.8 *m.* (1,926 alt., 1,355 pop.), a coal miners' town, is a large brickmaking plant. Kentuckians, driving their cattle to the Lynchburg market, gave the place its name because of the excellent pastures they found here.

At RAVEN, 9.9 *m.*, State 84 turns north from Clinch Valley to GRUNDY, 39 *m.* (1,065 alt., 815 pop.), seat and principal settlement of Buchanan County. The buildings of the mountain town stand close together at the fork of the Levisa and Slate Rivers, hemmed in by steep slopes that rise almost from the rivers' edge.

The BUCHANAN COUNTY COURTHOUSE, a three-story building of stone, has a tall square clock tower at one corner. Buchanan County, wholly within the Cumberland Mountains, was formed in 1858 from parts of Tazewell and Russell counties and named for President James Buchanan.

At 43.8 *m.* the highway passes near the SITE OF FORT CHRISTIAN, erected in 1774 by Daniel Smith, surveyor and captain of a military company, stationed in the upper Clinch Valley.

At 52.1 *m.* is a junction with State 80.

Left here to the SITE OF ELK GARDEN FORT (R), 0.9 *m.* The large brick house just beyond was the home of Henry Carter Stuart, governor of Virginia from 1914 to 1918.

LEBANON, 59.1 *m.* (2,131 alt., 560 pop.), seat of Russell County, caps a rounded hill beside Cedar Creek. Lebanon, so named because of the cedars in the neighborhood, grew up after the county seat was moved here from Dickensonville in 1816.

The RUSSELL COUNTY COURTHOUSE, is a two-story brick building with a high Ionic portico, salvaged from the first courthouse which was completed in 1818 and burned in 1872. A clock tower rises from the center of its roof. Russell County was formed from Washington in 1786 and named for General William Russell, member of the House of Delegates from Washington County who introduced the bill providing for the creation of the new county. The original Russell County was a vast territory, from which six other Virginia counties and a part of West Virginia were eventually taken.

At 60.1 *m.* is a junction with State 64; straight ahead on State 64 from this point.

DICKENSONVILLE, 69.6 *m.*, a crossroads settlement of several houses, was the first seat of Russell County. When Henry Dickenson, hoping to have an important town bearing his name, offered to build a courthouse for the county, his offer was accepted; his courthouse, built of hewed logs, was 20 feet square, 'furnished with proper seats and a bar.'

At 70.8 *m.* is a junction with State 64; R. here on State 64.

On the hill (R) at 75.7 *m.*, above a junction with County 615, is the SITE OF RUSSELL'S FORT, built in 1774 by William Russell, Indian fighter and officer in the Revolution, who was actively engaged in the protection of the frontier in the 1770's. In the latter part of his life Russell married Elizabeth Henry Campbell, sister of Patrick Henry and widow of General William Campbell (*see Tour 5c*).

ST.PAUL, 81 *m.* (1,486 alt., 716 pop.), is a railroad junction and a lively shopping center that grew up near the old Wheeler's Ford on the Clinch River. Here, in the 1770's, was Moore's Fort. In the 1890's a promotion company, anticipating the construction of a railroad, acquired land on both sides of the river and proposed to establish twin cities, to be named St.Paul and Minneapolis. The company paid $100 to the postmaster of another St.Paul, in Carroll County, for the exclusive use of the name, and laid out streets; but the project was abandoned when the financing of the railroad failed. It was not until the Carolina, Clinchfield & Ohio Railway was built in 1904 that St.Paul began to grow.

In 1790, Baron François Pierre de Tubeuf, a French political exile, traded houses in London to one Richard Smith for 55,000 acres of land in this neighborhood. The next year Tubeuf arrived with his wife, a son, and servants, and among other supplies, a pair of specially made boots designed as a protection against snakes. In 1794 two visitors killed Tubeuf, his wife, and all the servants except one maid, who escaped but was drowned during her flight. Alexandre de Tubeuf, the son, was left for dead but recovered. The house was stripped of its valuables and burned by the brigands. Later the men were captured and placed in the Abingdon jail, from which they freed themselves.

In St.Paul is a junction with State 70; L. here on State 70.

At VIRGINIA CITY, 83.5 *m.*, local coal was first made into coke.

COEBURN, 94.4 *m.* (1,983 alt., 785 pop.), is a railroad junction and mining center by the Guest River. The settlement, first called Guest's Station, was incorporated in 1894 and supposedly named for an engineer named Coe and a judge named Burn.

NORTON, 105.4 *m.* (2,138 alt., 3,077 pop.), trade and shipping center in a region of large coal mining operations, is hemmed in by steep slopes. It spreads out along one principal street, which parallels the railroad tracks. First called Prince's Flats for William Prince, who settled here in 1787, the town changed its name in the 1890's. Norton is so close to a coal seam that it is possible for families to dig their winter's supply of fuel from the cellars of their homes.

In June, when rhododendron covers the neighboring hills with its beauty, Norton sponsors a Rhododendron festival. Scenes of Indian and festival pioneer days are reenacted; 'King Coal' reigns; and the usual 'princesses' are in evidence.

1. Right from Norton on US 23 to WISE, 4.5 *m.* (2,474 alt., 1,112 pop.), seat of Wise County, and shopping center for mountain folk and miners. The early settlement here was called Big Glades, then Gladeville.

The WISE COUNTY COURTHOUSE, a large winged brick building, built in 1865 and added to in 1897 and 1915, supplanted a log structure built in 1858 and burned by Federal troops in 1864. Behind the courthouse was the whipping post used during the first years of the county. In 1892 a scaffold was erected here on which seven men were hanged for murder, one of whom was Talt Hall, notorious bad man of the Cumberlands.

Wise County was formed in 1856 from Lee, Scott, and Russell Counties and named for Henry A. Wise, then governor of Virginia. Before the 1890's, when railroads began to steam their way through the narrow valleys, the mountain folk of Wise County were governed largely by the code of the hills. Rugged individualists, they settled their difficulties without recourse to the law, made and sold their 'mountain dew,' and viewed all 'furriners' with suspicion.

POUND, 15.9 *m.* (218 pop.), is a scattered village named for a pounding mill built here in 1815 by James Mullins. Here in 1935 Edith Maxwell, a young school teacher, was charged with killing her father when she struck him as he sought to punish her for staying out late at night. The code of the hills, as interpreted in the newsrooms, furnished a basis for many sensational stories. Edith Maxwell was convicted, retried, and sentenced to serve 20 years.

Right from Pound 11.5 *m.* on State 59 to CLINTWOOD (800 pop.), seat of Dickenson County. This was the settlement of Holly Creek before the establishment of the county government here in 1882.

The DICKENSON COUNTY COURTHOUSE, a tall two-story brick building with wings, a clock cupola, and a two-story portico, was erected soon after 1880. Dickenson was formed from parts of Wise, Buchanan, and Russell Counties and named for W.J.Dickenson, a member of the Virginia general assembly at the time.

The present Dickenson County area, in the Sandy River Valley and called the 'Basin of the Sandy,' was not settled until after 1816 when 'Fighting Dick' Colley built a cabin at Sand Lick. Before the settlements were made, however, the Sandy Valley had long been hunting grounds for the white men, as was evidenced by two trees that bore the legends 'D.Boone 176-,' the other 'D.Boone 1771.'

On State 59, at 35 *m.*, by the mouth of the McClure River, is HAYSI (500 pop.), serving as a trading point for a large territory in both Dickenson and Buchanan Counties. It was named for Charles M. Hayter and a Mr.Sypher, partners in a small store here.

Left from Haysi, 8 *m.* on State 80, to the BREAKS OF SANDY (L), a series of rapids in the gap cut through the Cumberland Mountains by the Big Sandy River on its way to join the Ohio River at Ashland,Ky.

West of Pound US 23 climbs through Pound Gap in the Cumberland Mountains, the country of *The Trail of the Lonesome Pine*. In the hollows of this slope John Fox, Jr., found the characters for his book, which portrayed the life of the Cumberland Mountain people. The Wright and Mullens families were among the prototypes of Fox's characters. 'Devil' John Wright, a patriarch who was married three times and was the father of 37 children, was 'Jud Tolliver' of the story. 'Devil John' spent his last years in a cabin that stood about half way up the slope. Just left of the place where the highway crosses the crest of the mountain, stood, until a few years ago, the huge evergreen known to mountain folk as the Lonesome Pine.

Until the end of the nineteenth century the long mountain rifle took its toll here. In 1892 Ira Mullens, his wife, a daughter, and a friend, riding in a wagon, were shot from ambush in this pass. Mullens' small son rolled off the wagon and escaped. The women's breasts were slashed away and the Mullens' possessions were looted. Marshall Taylor, physician, minister, and Federal marshal, and Calvin and Henon Fleming were accused of the crime. Calvin Fleming was killed and Henon wounded in a gun battle with officers; Henon Fleming was brought to trial and acquitted. Dr.Taylor had himself crated and secretly shipped by freight to Bluefield, W.Va., but he was captured, convicted of murder, and hanged. On the scaffold he preached a sermon and predicted his resurrection in three days. His family waited five days before burying the body.

At the CREST, 20.5 *m.*, US 23 crosses the Kentucky Line, 1 mile east of Jenkins, Ky. (*see Kentucky Guide*).

2. Left from Norton, State 73 passes through BENGE'S GAP, named for a half-breed Indian leader who used it for raids into the neighboring valleys.

At BENGE'S ROCK, 1 *m.*, a large boulder (R), Benge was ambushed and killed in 1794 as he and his party returned from a raid along the Clinch and Holston Rivers. The highway climbs the mountain to an unmarked dirt road, 4.1 *m.*; R. here 1.1 *m.* HIGH KNOB, from which many square miles of territory are visible.

APPALACHIA, 116.6 *m.* (1,900 alt., 3,595 pop.), is a mining town at a junction with three railroads.

Right from Appalachia on State 67, which follows Looney Creek and winds up Black Mountain, to the crest, 8.8 *m.*, providing an extensive view of the Cumberlands. State 67 crosses the Kentucky Line 9 miles east of Cumberland, Ky. (*see Kentucky Guide*).

BIG STONE GAP, 120 *m.* (1,455 alt., 3,908 pop.), built compactly about a business district on two crossing streets, is at the southern end of the pass cut through Stone Mountain by the Powell River. The town's substantial activity is dependent on mining in the neighborhood. Because the town site was at the gap and the junction of three forks of the river, it was a strategic spot when three railroads came into the coal fields in the 1890's. The settlement here, first called Three Forks, then Imboden, was chartered as Mineral City in 1882 and assumed its present name in 1888.

The HOME OF JOHN FOX, JR., 746 Shawnee St., is a low shingled cottage, still occupied by members of the Fox family. Here lived the author who gave the world its first, though somewhat idealized, story of life in these mountains. From 1894 until 1913 a dozen romances of the hills followed each other in quick succession. The first two were only mildly successful, but *Hell-for-Sartin* (1896) received National attention. The whole country then wept over the plight of *The Little Shepherd of Kingdom Come* (1903), read breathlessly *Christmas Eve on Lonesome* (1904), fell in love with 'June' and fought with the Tollivers in *The Trail of the Lonesome Pine*, then sang the geographically inaccurate song, 'In the Blue Ridge Mountains of Virginia, on the Trail of the Lonesome Pine . . .'

In 1908 Fox married Fritzi Scheff, a winsome light opera star in her heyday. As Mademoiselle Modiste, she had set young and old to singing 'Kiss Me Again' and had dazzled the world with jewels, gowns, pompadour, wasp waist, and sprightly charm. She had divorced her Baron von Bardeleben and married Fox after a courtship of less than 24 hours. When she followed the new husband to Big Stone Gap, she arrived with servants and with trunks that aging natives now declare to have been 80 in number. Perhaps Fritzi Scheff was disappointed to find the hills not as romantic as they had been portrayed; at any rate, she soon departed.

The FEDERAL ART GALLERY, the first of its kind in the State, opened in the Big Stone Gap Elementary School on March 4, 1936.

PENNINGTON GAP, 141.2 *m.* (1,460 alt., 1,553 pop.), is the trade center of a prosperous trucking country.

Right from Pennington Gap on State 66 to NIGGER HEAD ROCK, 3 *m.*, an immense rock jutting out from the mountain, which has the profile of a head, neck, and shoulders.

JONESVILLE, 149.2 *m.* (384 pop.) (*see Tour 7d*), is at a junction with US 58 (*see Tour 7d*).

Tour 16

Fredericksburg—King George—Montross—Warsaw—Lancaster—Kilmarnock—Westland; 104.5 *m.* State 3.

Asphalt-paved roadbed throughout.
All types of accommodations.

State 3 traverses the Northern Neck, the peninsula between the Rappahannock and the Potomac. Occupations here vary from dairying and forestry in the upper section to truck farming, fishing, canning, and shipping in the lower. Along the waters are small summer resorts.

The route through farm lands and pine forests was first called the King's Highway for Robert 'King' Carter, who 'opened' it between the 'Lease Land' (Fredericksburg) and his seat, Corotoman. Along the way are old seats of distinguished Virginia families, modern houses, old villages, and a few small modern towns.

Section a. FREDERICKSBURG to WARSAW; 56.9 *m. State* 3.

East of Fredericksburg, the highway runs across the Rappahannock flats, where farms are large, houses few, and dairy products are the principal source of income. Corn, wheat, and tomatoes are chief crops farther south.

State 3 branches east from US 1 (*see Tour 1a*) in FREDERICKSBURG (*see Fredericksburg*), 0 *m.*, and crosses the Rappahannock River on the FREE BRIDGE.

At the eastern end of the bridge, 0.3 *m.*, is a junction with County 607.

Left here to CHATHAM (R) (*open April Garden Week*), 0.2 *m.*, amid wide-spreading trees and boxwood, on a hill top. The long, brick house has one-story wings flanking the taller, central mass, with modillioned cornices beneath hipped roofs. A large, pedimented two-deck porch shelters an entrance classically enframed.

Chatham was built about 1765 by Colonel William Fitzhugh (1741–1808), grandson of King Carter and great-grandson of William Fitzhugh. In Colonial days, the place was famed for its private race track, its horses, and its hospitality. Washington wrote Colonel Fitzhugh: 'I have put my legs oftener under your mahogany at Chatham . . . and have enjoyed your good dinners, good wines, and good company more than any other.' Late in life, Colonel Fitzhugh was forced to move to Ravensworth because, he said, he could not feed the horses of his guests here, having at times as many as 50 in his stables. The builder was the father of Mary Lee Fitzhugh, who married George Washington Parke Custis.

On FERRY FARM (R), 1.6 *m.*, nothing remains of the house in which George Washington lived between the ages of 6 and 11 and again during the second half of his sixteenth year. To be near his mines Augustine Washington moved here in November 1738 from Hunting Creek, now Mount Vernon, with his five children, George, Elizabeth, Samuel, John Augustine, and Charles. There were also two half-brothers, Lawrence, who was in the British Navy, and Augustine II, who was managing the Pope's Creek estate. If George Washington ever threw a Spanish silver dollar across a river or ever cut down a cherry tree, Ferry Farm was the scene of his skill and cunning.

After the death of her husband in 1743, Mary Washington sent George to Pope's Creek to live with Augustine. She remained here until 1772. 'My wants are few in this life,' she told her children, 'and I feel perfectly competent to take care of myself.' When Lawrence and his brother secretly planned to put George in the British navy and obtained a commission for him, the strong-minded woman got wind of the plan and abruptly brought George back to Ferry Farm and sent him to school in Fredericksburg.

After 1772 Mary Washington continued to manage Ferry Farm from Fredericksburg, riding out each day in a chaise. When her son-in-law, Colonel Fielding Lewis, offered to take the responsibility off her shoulders, she replied: 'Keep my books, for your eyesight is better than mine, but leave the management to me.'

Paralleling the highway for a few miles is STAFFORD HEIGHTS (L), from which, during the Battle of Fredericksburg in December 1862, General Henry J. Hunt kept up a continuous fire to hold off the Confederates while the Federal forces crossed the Rappahannock under a barrage of their own guns.

At 12.7 *m.* is a junction with County 607.

Left here to LAMB'S CREEK CHURCH (R), 0.5 *m.* (*open on application at residence near by*), of Brunswick Parish, built in 1769 to succeed Muddy Creek Church. The building, two-thirds as wide as long, with a high-pitched hip roof, has walls laid in Flemish bond. Above both main doors and a side door at the center of the south wall are rubbed brick pediments. The interior was wrecked when the building was used as a stable during the War between the States. A copy of the 'Vinegar' Bible (1716) and a Prayer Book (1739) are preserved here. Brunswick Parish was formed in 1732.

At 13.6 *m.* on State 3 is a junction with County 607.

Right here to the entrance to POWHATAN (L), 1.9 *m.*, a square two-story brick house with one-story wings and connecting pavilions. Powhatan was built in 1830 by Edward Thornton Tayloe, grandson of John Tayloe (*see below*).

At 3.2 *m.* on County 607 is a junction with County 610; R. here 1.5 *m.* to a private road and straight ahead 0.6 *m.* to CLEVE, in a wide lawn by the river. The modern frame house is on the foundation of the mansion erected in 1729 for Charles Carter, a son of 'King' Carter.

SHELBURNE (L), 14.4 *m.*, a small two-story house (*c.* 1860), part brick and part frame, was a home of Paul Kester (1870–1933), novelist and dramatist (*see Literature*).

COMORN, 15.5 *m.* (20 pop.), is at a junction with County 609.

Left here to (R) MARMION (*adm.* 50¢), 1.9 *m.*, built about 1750 by Colonel William Fitzhugh (1725–91), a cousin of the builder of Chatham. The external simplicity of the frame structure, which is approached by brick-paved walks, belies the elegance of its interior. Massive chimneys lift molded tops above a gabled roof. A piazza is a fairly recent addition.

The parlor has been stripped of its woodwork, which was used in a reconstruction of the room in the Metropolitan Museum of Art in New York. Flanking each door and window in the house are fluted pilasters with Ionic capitals, and the paneled walls are decorated with deep cornices. Most of the handsome, carved woodwork is marbleized, and panels are decorated in rococo style. The execution of this work was the grateful expression of a Hessian soldier whom the Fitzhugh family found wounded and nursed back to health.

William Fitzhugh, the immigrant, gave the estate to his youngest son, John (1693–1734), whose son William built the house.

At 2.4 *m.* on County 609 is a junction with State 218.

1. Left on State 218 1 *m.* to County 609 and R. to FAIRVIEW BEACH, 1.9 *m.*, a small resort by the Potomac River. On a hill (L) is the SITE OF THE SMITH HOUSE in which was born, September 6, 1797, William Smith, Governor of Virginia from 1846 to 1849 and again from 1864 to the fall of the Confederacy. In 1827 Smith made a contract with the Federal Government to carry mails once a week from Fairfax to Culpeper. In 1835 he established a daily four-horse post coach route between Washington and Milledgeville, Georgia. Because of his repeated demands for more compensation, he acquired the sobriquet 'Extra Billy.' The excessive drunkenness he saw at the taverns along his routes caused him to become a lecturer on prohibition.

2. Right on State 218 to EAGLE'S NEST (L), 1.9 *m.*, an immense barnlike frame house among ancient myrtle, lilac, locusts, and mulberries. The present *ante-bellum* house succeeded one built about 1730 by Henry Fitzhugh, whose wife was Lucy, a daughter of 'King' Carter, and whose son, William, builder of Chatham, was born here August 24, 1741.

At 5.7 *m.* on State 218 is CALEDON (L), a small story-and-a-half brick house, all that remains of the home of John Alexander, for whom Alexandria was named (*see Alexandria*).

At 6.9 *m.* on State 218 is a junction with State 206 (*see below*).

At 16.6 *m.* on State 3 is a junction with State 206.

Left here to DIXON'S CABIN (L), 4.6 *m.*, the log house of Junius and Patsy Dixon, house servants who served John Wilkes Booth when he fled across this peninsula after his assassination of President Lincoln.

CLEYDALE (R), 4.7 *m.*, was built in 1859 as the summer home of Dr.Richard H. Stuart. It was here that Booth and his accomplice Herold came at dusk on April 22, 1865, to beg food and medical aid. The doctor, becoming suspicious, declined to admit them to the house but gave them permission to rest at the barn. The following morning Booth sent the doctor a note, contemptuously thanking him for 'what we did get' and enclosing $5. Dr.Stuart threw the note into the fire, but his son-in-law recovered it. Later, when the doctor was imprisoned for complicity in the assassination, the note exonerated him.

At 6.4 *m.* on State 206 are junctions with County 632 and State 218 (*see above*).

Right here 0.2 *m.* on County 632 to (R) ST.PAUL'S CHURCH (*open upon request at house near by*), designed on a cruciform plan. Its brick walls, broken by two tiers of windows—those above topped by round arches—rise to a cornice with closely spaced dentils and support a hipped roof. Little of the original furniture remains, but a silver communion service presented by Henry Fitzhugh and a large Bible given by the Reverend William Stuart, rector in 1762, have been preserved.

The church, built in 1766, belonged to St.Paul's Parish, which was formed before 1680 from Potomac Parish.

In ruins when visited by Bishop Meade in 1813, the church was subsequently repaired and used as an academy. In 1830 it was restored by the parish.

State 206 continues northward to OWENS, 8.5 *m.*, a crossroads.

Left here 0.4 *m.* on County 624 to BEDFORD (L), established in 1674 by William Fitzhugh (1651–1701). The present oddly designed brick house was built during a later generation. Here by the Potomac Fitzhugh built homes for each of his five sons.

William Fitzhugh came to Virginia in 1670 with John Newton (*see Tour 16A*), with whom he lived at first. Together they patented large estates in the upper Northern Neck, and in 1674 Fitzhugh married Newton's step-daughter, Sarah Tucker, and sent the eleven-year-old girl to England to be educated. Fitzhugh's diversions were those of lawyer, planter, merchant, burgess, and member of the council. 'As to your wonder that I have never been troubled therewith,' he replied in 1698 to a friend who had just recovered from a severe attack of gout, 'I'll tell you Sr. I never much frequented Bacchus' Orgyes & always avoided Ceres' shrine, & never was one of Venus' votarys.'

At 10.6 *m.* on State 206 is a junction with County 614; R. here 0.9 *m.* to the frame QUESENBURY HOUSE, on Upper Machodoc Creek. After crossing the Potomac, John Wilkes Booth avoided the public landing near by and rowed to the wharf of the Quesenbury House, where he passed the night.

On State 206 is DAHLGREN, 11.1 *m.* (600 pop.). Its residents are chiefly military and civilian, serving at the U.S. NAVAL PROVING GROUND (*visitors admitted to operating area only by permit*), where high-powered naval rifles are tested. The guns have a possible range of 50 miles down the Potomac. The lower part of the river is used also as a torpedo speed trial course.

The houses of KING GEORGE, 18 *m.* (75 pop.), seat of King George County, are almost entirely modern, though the village maintains an eighteenth-century atmosphere. The farmers of the surrounding territory come in each day, about the time the U.S. mail truck arrives, to receive their mail or merely to gossip on such important topics as hunting and fishing.

The COURTHOUSE (L), on a neat green, was built in 1915. The CONFEDERATE MONUMENT on the square is a simple shaft lacking the usual figure of a Southern soldier. The original King George County was formed in 1720 from Richmond.

PERKINS' CORNER, 19.1 *m.*, is at a junction with State 205.

Left here to Rozier's Creek, 7.7 *m.*, named for the Reverend John Rozier, who patented lands upon it about 1651. On the west bank is the SITE OF WASHINGTON'S MILL (L), built about 1665 by the immigrant John Washington (1632–77).

POTOMAC BEACH, 11 *m.* (40 pop.), is a resort and a terminus of the POTOMAC BEACH-MORGANTOWN (Md.) FERRIES (*hourly service in summer, hour-and-a-half in winter;* $1 *for car and driver,* 25¢ *extra passenger,* $1.50 *maximum*).

COLONIAL BEACH, 12.8 *m.* (928 pop., 5,000 to 10,000 summer pop.), is a river resort (*canoes, motor boats, sailboats; fishing for trout, rock, perch, and croakers*). Many of the cottage owners work in Washington but spend summer vacations here and come down on election days to vote. Two of the cottages were built by Alexander Graham Bell, inventor of the telephone. In the Colonial Beach Hotel is incorporated a house once owned by 'Light Horse Harry' Lee. The little Ionic portico has echoed diminishing elegance during a century and a half, from powdered wigs and epaulettes, through crinoline to slacks and shorts, and from minuet and waltz to big apple and jitter-bug.

The SITE OF MONROVIA (L), 14 *m.*, is marked by a clump of locust trees. James Monroe, born here April 28, 1758, was the son of Spence Monroe and Elizabeth Jones Monroe and the great-great-grandson of Andrew Monroe, who came to Virginia in 1647. The following year Andrew returned to Scotland and fought in the Battle of

Preston. Captured and banished, he came again to Virginia and in 1650 patented the first tract of the estate here.

At 17.1 *m.* State 205 crosses Mattox Creek, on the south bank of which is MATTOX (L), a wharf, a cannery, and one house. Barges and sailing vessels still come up the winding stream to receive cargoes, as they have since 1648 when Colonel Nathaniel Pope built a wharf and warehouse here. When young John Washington, engaged in transatlantic shipping, came to Virginia in 1656, he anchored at Mattox, and when he had subsequent litigation, Colonel Pope offered to go security for him in beaver skins. Washington decided to remain in Virginia and stayed at Pope's house. Two years later he married his friend's daughter Anne, his first wife. Her father gave the couple 700 acres of land including Mattox. They lived here until December 1664, when they purchased land along Bridges' Creek (*see below*).

OAK GROVE, 18.4 *m.* (40 pop.), is at a junction with State 3 (*see below*).

In OFFICE HALL, 20.7 *m.*, is the ROLLINS HOUSE (L), where John Wilkes Booth passed the night of April 23, 1865.

Right from Office Hall on State 207 to a private road, 5.1 *m.*; R. here 0.1 *m.* to EMANUEL CHURCH (R), a small brick rectangle erected about 1840 as a church of Hanover Parish.

At 0.3 *m.* on the private road is (L) BELLE GROVE (*open April Garden Week*), a large white clapboarded house with graceful wings. Near the main entrance door is a 35-foot holly tree. Belle Grove was built about 1830 by John Bernard.

On State 207 is PORT CONWAY, 5.3 *m.*, by the Rappahannock River, formerly an important shipping point but now a riverside hamlet with a few houses. In the wake of John Wilkes Booth, who used the ferry here on April 24, 1865, came a company of cavalry that had trailed him from Washington. The cavalry overtook Booth at the Garrett House (*see Tour 6a*). Washington crossed here on numerous occasions, ferried by one James Bowie, and later by his widow, Sarah, who, on November 4, 1779, petitioned the general assembly to repeal an act 'which required James Bowie or heirs of his public ferry to set foot-passengers across the Rappahannock free.' On December 24, 1801, she asked 'authority to increase ferriage rates from Port Royal to Port Conway.'

On the bluff (L) above the bridge is the unmarked SITE OF THE CONWAY HOUSE, once home of Francis Conway, whose grandson, James Madison (*see Tour 10*) was born here March 16, 1751, the son of James Madison and Eleanor Rose Conway Madison.

At Port Conway State 207 crosses the Rappahannock on the James Madison Memorial Bridge (*see Tour 6c*).

At 27.3 *m.* on State 3 is a junction with County 627.

Right here to WILMONT, 2.0 *m.*, a former steamboat-landing below high cliffs from which diatomaceous clay (fuller's earth) is taken at intervals.

OAK GROVE, 31.2 *m.* (40 pop.), is at junctions with County 638 and State 205 (*see above*).

Right here on County 638, which becomes County 637, to LEEDSTOWN, 6.7 *m.*, on a bank above a horseshoe bend in the Rappahannock River. In 1766, in this then lively port, 115 citizens called together by Thomas Ludwell Lee signed the Leedstown Resolutions. These were drafted by his brother Richard Henry Lee and enunciated principles embodied later in the Declaration of Independence. Among those present at the meeting of February 27, 1766, were two brothers of Thomas Ludwell and Richard Henry Lee and two of their cousins; three of George Washington's brothers; and Spence Monroe, the father of James Monroe. The presiding officer was Judge Richard Parker, whose great-grandson, Richard Parker, was presiding judge at the trial of John Brown.

Settlement began here in 1681 but the 'Town of Leeds' was not constituted until 1742.

At 32.4 *m.* on State 3 is a junction with a poor dirt road.

Left here to a private road, 0.5 *m.*, leading L. to the SITE OF HENRY WILLIAMS' SCHOOL (L), occupied now by a residence. From 1743 to 1747 George Washington attended this school.

At 34 *m.* on State 3 is a junction with State 204.

Left here to the GEORGE WASHINGTON BIRTHPLACE NATIONAL MONUMENT (*open* 8 *to* 6; *adm.* 10¢), 1.7 *m.* At the entrance is a 50-foot granite shaft, and beyond a gate is a reconstruction of the story-and-a-half brick house in which Washington was born on February 22, 1732. Dormers and double outside chimneys are distinguishing features. The rooms and central hall have paneled wainscoting; the floors, old-fashioned wide boards; and the doors, heavy hand-wrought locks with brass knobs. A 'boxed' stair leads from the hall to the upper floor. The house has old furnishings and some relics.

Rows of thick untrimmed dwarf boxwood border a brick walk that extends to the herb and flower gardens. A footbridge across Dancing Marsh and a road from the monument circle lead to the LOG HOUSE (*meals, lodging, souvenirs*) and a picnic ground. In a walled enclosure at the end of a lane is the WASHINGTON CEMETERY, 1.1 *m.*, containing the dust of 31 members of the family. Washington's father, grandfather, and great-grandfather are buried under table tombs. In 1923, Josephine Wheelwright Rust, a descendant of the immigrant Washington, organized the Wakefield National Memorial Association to rescue the estate from weeds and briars. That agency, with the co-operation of the Federal Government and John D. Rockefeller, Jr., brought the reservation to its present condition. Though research failed to produce an authentic picture of Pope's Creek, the foundations indicated its size. Of value was information passed down by Colonel Burgess Ball, Washington's kinsman, that the house resembled the Christian House at Providence Forge (*see Tour* 8*a*). The house was completed in 1931.

On December 3, 1664, the immigrant John Washington purchased 150 acres and built a house 50 yards east of the spot he later selected for a burial lot. He left the estate to his son John, who, in turn, passed it to his son John. The immigrant left the estate at Mattox (*see above*) to his older son, Lawrence, who willed it to his son Augustine. In 1717–18 Augustine Washington purchased three tracts of land here adjoining the lands of his cousin, and in 1720 built the brick house in which Jane Butler, his first wife, died in 1729. Two years later he married Mary Ball of Sandy Point (*see Tour* 16*A*). George was their first child.

On the headstream of Pope's Creek, at 34.7 *m.*, is WASHINGTON'S MILL (R), built in 1713 by Nathaniel Pope, purchased in 1728 by Augustine Washington, and owned by the Washington family through several generations. Repaired and remodeled at intervals, it is still in use.

At 38.9 *m.* is a junction with County 642.

Left here to WESTMORELAND STATE PARK, 1.5 *m.* (*open May* 15 *to Nov.* 1; *adm.* 10¢; *overnight camping,* 25¢, *children under* 10, *free; rowboats* 25¢ *an hr., maximum,* $1.25 *a day; dock privileges,* 25¢ *a day; cabins with electric lights, stoves, water heaters—payment by coin meters*—$15 *a week for* 2 *persons,* $20 *for* 3 *or* 4 *persons,* $5 *for each additional person; reservations made at Virginia Conservation Commission, Richmond*). This large park extends along the Potomac River, with a beach below high steep cliffs.

At 39.6 *m.* on State 3 is a junction with State 214.

Left here to STRATFORD HALL (L), 1.1 *m.* (*open* 9–6; *adm.* 50¢, *children* 25¢). The house stands near a grove of beeches on cliffs high above the Potomac River. It is a massive brick structure dominated by two arcaded groups of four chimneys with heavily molded tops rising solidly from the multiple hipped roof. Though simple and robust in architectural style, it has dignity. Its H-plan, a survival from Elizabethan and Jacobean times, occupies the center of a great square marked at the corners by four large dependent buildings. A 'ha-ha' wall has been restored across the front of this square. The main floor, reached from outside by long flights of steps, is above an exceedingly tall ground floor that held several other rooms. The bricks of the ground floor wall, of the face of the main floor, and of the chimneys, are laid in Flemish bond and form a strikingly checkered pattern. Over both entrance doorways are simple brick pediments broken at the lower corners.

The five rooms of the main floor are spacious and lofty. The hall forming the bar of the H is 30 feet square. Beneath a coved ceiling are pine panels divided at unequal intervals by Ionic pilasters. Passages lead to a pair of rooms in each wing. A single inside stairway, at the end of the east passage, descends to the ground floor.

The Robert E. Lee Memorial Foundation, organized in 1929, completed the purchase of Stratford in 1932 and is gradually restoring the estate as a memorial to the Confederate commander and to provide a model Colonial plantation with characteristic industries and plants. The house had had no great structural changes since Colonial times. But the wharf, mill, shop, and springhouse, and the formal gardens with box-bordered walks and box mazes had disappeared and are being replaced. The vista, long obscured by trees, again provides a view of the river.

The estate, called the 'Clifts Plantation,' was patented in 1651 by Nathaniel Pope, one of George Washington's great-great-grandfathers, and in 1716 was purchased by Thomas Lee (1690–1750). Colonel Lee was building the house and other buildings in 1729, when fire destroyed his birthplace and former home, Matholic (*see Tour 16A*). Thomas Lee was the only native Virginian to be appointed by the Crown as governor of Virginia. In 1722 he married Hannah Ludwell, who became the mother of 11 children, among them: Philip Ludwell, Thomas Ludwell, Richard Henry, Francis Lightfoot, William, and Arthur—all except Philip Ludwell born here. A daughter, Hannah, was one of America's first suffragists.

The eldest, Philip Ludwell Lee (1727–75), married Elizabeth Steptoe, inherited Stratford, and had two daughters, Matilda and Flora. In 1775 Matilda inherited Stratford and in 1782 married her cousin, General Henry (Light Horse Harry) Lee. She died in 1790, leaving three children, Philip Ludwell, Lucy Grymes, and Henry. In the next year General Henry Lee was elected governor of Virginia and in 1793 he married Ann Hill Carter. Among their children was Robert Edward Lee, born here January 19, 1807.

The estate descended to Henry Lee (1787–1837), son of 'Light Horse Harry' Lee and Matilda Lee, Philip Ludwell having died. When Robert Edward was four years of age, 'Light Horse Harry,' in order to permit Henry to have full possession of Stratford, moved to Alexandria.

Stratford exemplified the pinnacle of Colonial cultural, social, and plantation life. 'The owner [Philip Ludwell Lee] . . . lived here in great state,' said General Robert E. Lee, 'and kept a band of musicians to whose airs his daughters, Matilda and Flora, with their companions, danced in the saloon or promenaded on the housetop.' Philip Vickers Fithian, tutor at Nomini Hall (*see Tour 16A*) in 1773, wrote of a visit here in his *Journals & Letters*: 'When the candles were lighted, we all repaired, for the last time, into the dancing-room. First each danced a Minuet; then all joined as before in the country dances; these continued till half after Seven when Mr.Christian retired; and, at the proposal of several (with Mr.Carter's approbation), we played Button, to get Pauns for Redemption . . . Half after eight we were rung in to Supper. The room looked luminous and splendid; four very large candles burned on the table where we supped; three others in different parts of the Room; a gay sociable Assembly, and four well instructed waiters. So soon as we rose from supper, the Company formed into a semicircle round the fire, and played "break the Pope's neck." Here we had great Diversion in the respective Judgments upon the offenders, but we were all dismissed by ten and retired to our several Rooms.'

State 214 becomes County 645; at 3.5 *m.* is a private road; L. here to an unimproved road, 4.7 *m.*, and R. to the SITE OF CHANTILLY, 5.2 *m.*, marked by clumps of jonquils —once the home of Richard Henry Lee, who built it after his return from school in Europe and named it for a chateau near Paris.

Richard Henry Lee (1732–94) was one of the first to advocate separation of the colonies from Great Britain and the emancipation of American slaves. His first address as a member of the Virginia house of burgesses in 1757 was against the importation of slaves. Lee was the author of the resolution of the Continental Congress for a declaration of independence and was to have been chairman of the committee appointed to draw up a declaration, but was called home by illness in his family. He helped draft the Articles of Confederation and was president of the Congress in 1784. He declined membership in the Constitutional Convention of 1787 on the grounds that the plan was to submit the new constitution to Congress for approval, that he was a member of that body, and that he did not think the men that wrote the constitution should review their own work. He opposed ratification of the Constitution by Virginia because it did not contain a bill of rights, and was the author of the Tenth Amendment, which, with the first nine amendments, constituted the Bill of Rights as it finally stood.

MONTROSS, 43.9 *m.* (200 pop.), seat of Westmoreland County, is largely a village of modern houses. The residents have inherited not only the property but also the hospitable and genial nature of their ancestors.

The WESTMORELAND COUNTY COURTHOUSE, on a green, is a tall oblong structure with a hip roof. An addition made in 1936 under the Williamsburg influence—including a Doric portico—converted it into a T-shaped building. The first courthouse here was built in 1673–74, when Montross became the county seat. Part of the third courthouse, erected in 1817, has been incorporated in this one. Westmoreland County was carved from the western part of Northumberland County in 1653 and, when constituted, stretched westward beyond the present District of Columbia. Territorial changes in 1664 and in 1778 brought about the final boundaries.

In the CLERK'S OFFICE in the courthouse are records that date from the formation of the county. Portraits on the walls of the courtroom include one of James Monroe, by Willis Pepoon, after Vanderlyn; of Richard Henry Lee, by Pepoon, after one by Charles Willson Peale; and of Francis Lightfoot Lee, a copy of one by Charles S. Forbes. The most valuable portrait is that of William Pitt (Lord Chatham), painted in 1768–69 by Charles Willson Peale and restored in 1935. Here also is a full-length portrait of General Robert E. Lee, by E.F.Andrews.

TEMPLEMANS, 47.5 *m.* (20 pop.), is at a junction with State 202 (*see Tour 16A*).

By a junction with an alternate of State 202, 48 *m.*, is NOMINI BAPTIST CHURCH (L), a simple rectangular brick building that belongs to the second oldest Baptist congregation in the Northern Neck, organized in 1786. There had been early dissenters from the Established Church in the area, among them nine persons who, in 1717, were committed to the 'County Gaol of Westmoreland' for convening 'under pretence of religious worship . . . in Concenticles, contrary and repugnant to Law.' The court had directed that the prisoners, 'severally, in the presence of the persons congregated at Yeocomico Church [*see Tour 16A*] . . . own their fault and acknowledge their error . . . and humbly ask God and this congregation forgiveness of the offense . . . promise never to commit the like again.'

Right on State 202-alternate to a private road, 5.1 *m.*; R. here 1 *m.* to MENOKIN (pronounced Mee-no-kin), on a high bluff. The square main building, two stories high with a hip-on-hip roof, is constructed of blocks of dark-colored stone, now covered with stucco and trimmed with light sandstone. The 12 rooms have hand-carved mantels. Only one dependency remains. Menokin, built about 1770 by the Tayloe family, became the home of Francis Lightfoot Lee, who was born at Stratford Hall October 14, 1734, and in 1769 married Rebecca, second daughter of Colonel John Tayloe of Mount Airy (*see below*). With his brother, Richard Henry Lee, he signed the Leedstown Resolutions and the Declaration of Independence.

At 9 *m.* on State 202 is a junction with State 3 (*see below*).

At 53.7 *m.* on State 3 is a junction with State 203.

Left here to a private road, 0.6 *m.*, and R. to BLADENSFIELD, 1.2 *m.* (*adm.* 50¢, *children* 25¢), a large frame house on a brick basement. The walls of nogging covered with clapboards rise two stories to a gabled roof with several dormers, the largest of which is over the entrance. There are hand-carved mantels and cornices, dial-pinned flooring, and H-L hinges. The rear door, with peep-hole, is fastened by the hard-timbered bar that held it secure against the Indians in the 1690's.

Behind the house is a flower garden containing rare old-fashioned plants.

The original estate of 1,000 acres was patented by John Jenkins May 14, 1653, and the present house was built for Jenkins by Nicholas Rochester, who came from England in 1689. At Jenkins's death in 1719, Bladensfield was added to the Nomini Hall estate (*see Tour 16A*). When, about 1775, John Peck, who had succeeded Philip Vickers Fithian as tutor to the Carter children, eloped with his pupil, Ann Tasker Carter, her father, Councillor Carter, was irate at first but relented and gave Bladensfield to them as a wedding gift.

In later years 'the Laying of the Ghosts,' was occasionally conducted here. 'Vast crowds' of Negroes arrived—'until the hills were covered.' A preacher backed through the rear door, wearing his coat inside out and upside down and reading a page of the Bible, from the bottom line upwards. After the ceremony the ghosts were 'never quite so bad.'

At 56.5 *m.* is a junction with State 202 (*see above*).

WARSAW, 56.9 *m.* (400 pop.), the tree-strewn seat of Richmond County, is redolent of the past, despite its modern stores and a predominance of new residences. On court days and Saturdays the county people gather here to gossip and to buy and barter, and the citizenry still clings to traditions of decanter and frosted julep cup. The village received its present name in 1845 because of local sympathy for the Poles, who were fighting for independence.

The brick RICHMOND COUNTY COURTHOUSE, on a green, has a low-pitched hip roof, round-arched and deeply recessed windows, and a front canopy. It was built in 1748–49. Richmond County, constituted in 1692, included all Old Rappahannock County that had lain north of the Rappahannock River. In 1720 it was reduced to its present small area.

The two-room CLERK'S OFFICE near by, also erected in 1748–49, had only one room until 1935. The walls of the old part are two feet thick and are of blocks of stone. The building is heated now, as formerly, by an open fireplace. Here are musty records, including deeds and wills, recorded by professional scribes, who spelled 'God' with a small *g* and 'Rum' with a capital *R*.

Warsaw was the home of William Atkinson Jones, who worked for the independence of the Philippine Islands. In the yard of St. John's Church here is the costly mausoleum erected over his grave by the people of the Islands.

Right from Warsaw on US 360, which unites briefly eastward with State 3, to a private road, 1.2 *m.*; L. here 0.9 *m.*, between hedges, to SABINE HALL (*adm. to house* 50¢, *to garden* 50¢), on high ground close to a gate lodge. The brick walls of the mansion, laid in Flemish bond and now covered with a light cement wash, are a softly mottled pink and gray. A tall portico with four slender hand-hewn Tuscan columns breaks the façade of the main unit, which is extended by low wings to a length of 180 feet. White stone trim includes flat arches over the windows and a heavy enframement of the entrance. On the south front, broad verandas overlook a large garden, laid out for the builder by an English gardener. In early spring old gardenia-narcissus blooms here in profusion. Five grassy terraces lead down toward the flat land along the river, a mile or two away.

The interior is paneled with heart pine, carved in the heavy style of the first half of the eighteenth century. The staircase, in a side hall, opening through a wide pilastered arch off an immense transverse hall, leads to a similar hall above. The finest woodwork is in the library and halls. Most of the furnishing belongs to the early days of the house. Among the many portraits of Carters is one of Robert 'King' Carter. The Colonial library is intact.

The estate was acquired by 'King' Carter, who gave it to his son Landon. The house was built about 1730. Young Carter named his new home for the hillside estate of the Roman, Horace. The portico was added shortly after the Revolution. The east wing is a reconstruction.

At 1.6 *m.* on US 360 is another private road; R. here 0.5 *m.* to MOUNT AIRY (*private*), most noted of the several houses built by the Tayloes. The lane leads through park, meadow, and lawn to the house that looks across terraced lawns toward the river. Dwarf boxwood of giant proportions still takes its undulating course among the remains of a formal garden.

Built of brown stone, with light stone trim, Mount Airy consists of a massive central block, curving passageways, and two large dependencies set forward. The broad hip roof of the main unit is pierced by four chimneys near the ridge. The walls, three feet thick, are broken by slightly projecting pavilions, the one in front on the first floor square-columned in antis and that at the rear arcaded. These pavilions, the framing of every opening, the wide string course, and the deeply emphasized water table are all constructed of light Aquia stone.

A fire in 1844 swept away the fine interior woodwork but left the walls undisturbed. The wide central hall opens into a lateral hall that leads to front and back parlors and into the dining room, to which food is still carried from the kitchen dependency, as in the days of myriad servants. Old furniture, rarest of which perhaps is a cylinder piano played by turning a handle, and valuable pieces of glass, china, and silver are cherished here. The walls are lined with a large collection of family portraits, including work of Gilbert Stuart, Thomas Sully, Thomas Hudson, and John Wollaston, and etchings by St.Mémin.

The estate, acquired by William Tayloe, who built the first house, descended first to his son, Colonel John Tayloe (1687–1747), and then to Colonel John Tayloe II (1721–79), who built the present house about 1758. The formal setting and character of this Georgian mansion and the monumental scale of the original garden suggest a European designer. On Colonel Tayloe's death in 1779, Mount Airy passed to his only son, Colonel John Tayloe III (1771–1824), builder of the Octagon House in Washington.

John Tayloe II had a deer park and maintained a band of musicians among his servants. He was an importer and breeder of fine race horses. Philip Vickers Fithian, a visitor here in 1774, wrote, 'Fish, Feasts, and Fillies! . . . Loud disputes concerning the Excellence of each others Colts—concerning their Fathers, Mothers (for so they call the Dams), Brothers, Sisters, Uncles, Aunts, Nephews, Neices, and Cousins to the fourth Degree! All the Evening Toddy constantly circulating. Supper came in, and at Supper I had a full, broad, satisfying view of Miss Sally Panton. I wanted to hear her converse, but, poor Girl, anything she attempted to say was drowned in the more polite and useful Jargon about Dogs and Horses . . . In the Dining-Room, beside many other fine Pieces, are twenty four of the most celebrated among the English Race-Horses, Drawn masterly, and set in elegant gilt Frames.'

On the grounds are the tombs of Francis Lightfoot Lee and Rebecca, his wife, who was second daughter of the builder of Mount Airy.

At 2.4 *m.* on US 360 is a junction with State 204; R. here 4.7 *m.* to County 636 and L. to NAYLOR'S HOLE, 6.8 *m.*, now a wharf and a few houses but once a shipping point for the ancestral seat of the Fauntleroy family. Colonel Moore Fauntleroy settled here in 1651. During a later period, Naylor's Hole was the home of Elizabeth Fauntleroy, George Washington's mysterious 'Lowland Beauty,' who turned Washington down on account of the smallpox scars on his face. In 1752, Washington wrote her father, Colonel William Fauntleroy: 'I purpose . . . to wait on Miss Betsy, in hopes of a revocation of the former cruel sentence and see if I can meet with any alteration in my favor.'

US 360 crosses the Rappahannock River on the Downing Bridge, erected in 1927, to TAPPAHANNOCK, 6.4 *m.* (427 pop.) (*see Tour 6a*), at a junction with US 17 (*see Tour 6a*), and US 360 westward (*see Tour 20a*).

Section b. WARSAW to WESTLAND; 47.6 *m.* *State* 3.

This section of State 3 traverses the lower Northern Neck, crossing many side roads that lead to old plantations near the Bay and the Rappahannock. The people engage in seafood industries, shipping, and agriculture.

East of WARSAW, 0 *m.*, State 3 is united with US 360 for 0.8 miles.

At 7.2 *m.* is a junction with State 228.

Right here to SHARPS, 6.1 *m.* (300 pop.), with old and new houses along its unpaved streets. A shipping point since Colonial days, and still sending out seafood, the village is now more important as a resort on the Rappahannock (*boats available for fishing*).

In FARNHAM, 9.9 *m.* (45 pop.), on a pleasant greensward, is (L) NORTH FARNHAM CHURCH, Greek-cruciform in plan, with a single tier of windows. Though the church was once almost demolished by fire, the present walls are those erected in 1737. Above the door is a fanlight; in the gable are two round lights; and in the side walls of the transepts are oval-topped windows.

North Farnham Parish was formed in 1692. After the Revolution the church was deserted for many years. Bishop Meade reported that the bricks of the wall around the plot had been used for hearths, chimneys, and other purposes and that the church itself was used 'as a granery, stable, a resort for hogs . . . For years it was also used as a distillery . . . while the marble font was circulated from house to house, on every occasion of mirth and folly . . . until at length it was found bruised, battered, and deeply sunk in the cellar of some deserted tavern.' The walls show bullet holes, scars of a skirmish during the War of 1812, when the Richmond County Militia repelled Admiral Cockburn's raiders.

The church was restored in 1835, but during the War between the States was again stripped of its furniture and occupied by both Federal and Confederate troops. Restored, it was burned in 1887 and restored again in 1920–24. The communion silver and the communion font have been returned.

EPPING FOREST (R) is at 19.9 *m.* The present oddly-designed two-story frame house on a wide shady lawn replaced one built by Colonel Joseph Ball (1649–1711), who inherited this 'forest estate' in 1680 from his father, Colonel William Ball. Joseph Ball married Elizabeth Romney and reared a son and four daughters. In February 1708, when a widower 59 years of age, he deeded his farm to his son Joseph and divided all his personal property among his five mature children, reserving the right to continue to reside here and also certain dower rights for a wife in the event he again married. He forthwith married a widow, Mary Montague Johnson, who in 1708 or 1709 became the mother of Mary Ball.

When Mary was a small child, her father died, and her mother married Captain Richard Hawes, who took her and her three children to his home in Cherry Point Neck, Northumberland County. At her mother's death in 1721, Mary Ball went to live with her guardian at Sandy Point (*see Tour 16A*). Mary Ball married Augustine Washington and became the mother of George.

LIVELY, 21.7 *m.* (75 pop.), warns motorists by a conspicuous sign that its speed limit is five miles an hour.

Right from Lively on State 201 to FARMVILLE (R), 2.4 *m.*, a brick *ante-bellum* house on the site of the home of David Fox, who settled here about 1650, and became a leader in church and civil affairs.

By a junction with County 622, at 3.2 *m.* is (R) ST.MARY'S WHITE CHAPEL (*keys at house near by*), quiet and lovely among trees and tombs. The chapel suggests not a church but a cottage. Its brick walls beneath a hip roof are covered with a cloak of ivy. Beneath a barrel ceiling are aisles paved with 'good Smooth well burnt tile.' Built in 1740–41, the church was originally cruciform in plan. When it was restored in 1830, after long abandonment, the transepts were removed. Here are the marble font, a silver chalice (1699), and a paten (1691), which were used in the first church. St.Mary's White Chapel is one of two churches of Christ Church Parish, formed in 1668 from Lancaster Parish.

Left from St.Mary's White Chapel 4.2 *m.* on County 622 to County 625; L. here to MILLENBECK, 6.8 *m.*, an old village by Corotoman River. It has grown up around the private wharf built in 1651 by William Ball (1615–80). In 1652 Millenbeck became the first seat of Lancaster County.

LANCASTER, 26.1 *m.* (150 pop.), seat of Lancaster County, maintains an atmosphere of eighteenth-century leisure except on court days.

The COURTHOUSE, a tall brick building erected about 1800, contains the usual portraits of native sons and daughters, among them one of Mary Ball Washington. The monument on the green, a simple marble shaft, is among the first erected to the soldiers of the Confederacy. Lancaster County, constituted in 1652, at first embraced territory on both sides of the Rappahannock River, extending westward indefinitely.

The CLERK'S OFFICE contains records that date from the county's formation.

At 26.7 *m.* is a junction with County 604.

Right here to a private road, 3.7 *m.*, and L. 0.2 *m.* to VERVILLE, a brick house, built between 1680 and 1690 on a mound above the flats of Corotoman River. The two-story central unit, beneath a steeply curbed roof with dormers almost flush, is flanked by low, gabled wings. A pair of chimneys pointing up the gambrel ends are unusually tall. Interior woodwork includes high wainscoting and carved mantels. Verville was built by Dr. James Madison, an eccentric Scottish immigrant.

WHITE MARSH CHURCH (R), 28.9 *m.*, a plain brick structure, was built in 1848 by a Methodist congregation that organized in 1792. The first

Methodist camp meeting in this section was held here. Bishops Enoch George and David S. Doggett were members of the congregation.

Despite its small population KILMARNOCK, 33.1 *m.* (900 pop.), has 82 licensed business establishments. Henrietta Hall (1817–44), the first American woman to go to China as missionary, was born here.

Left from Kilmarnock on State 200 to County 607, 2 *m.*, and R. 0.2 *m.* to County 669; L. here 1 *m.* to a private road (R) that leads 0.9 *m.* to COBB'S HALL, between the two branches of Dividing Creek. The present frame residence, fourth on this site, is a successor to that built by Richard Lee, forebear of the Lees of Virginia, who moved here in 1651, and became burgess, a member of the council, and Secretary of the Colony. He was loyal to the Crown during the Cromwell regime. John Gibbons, poet and great-granduncle of the historian, said that in 1659 he was 'most hospitably entertained by the Honourable Collonel Richard Lee, who after the King's martydom hired a Dutch vessel, freighted her himself, went to Brussels, surrendered up Sir William Barcklaie's old commission and received a new one from his present Majesty.'

On County 607 is the entrance, 1.5 *m.*, to DITCHLEY (L). The massive walls of the brick dwelling, in a shaded yard, rise two stories to a full cornice and hip roof. A one-story wing extends one end of the rectangle, and porches are centered on both façades. The house was built in 1752 by Kendall Lee on the site of a house built by his grandfather, Hancock Lee, who is buried near by.

The immigrant Richard Lee patented the estate in 1651. His fifth son, Hancock Lee (1651–1709), built the first Ditchley house in 1686 and named it for an estate near Oxford, England. He and his second wife Sarah were the great-grandparents of Zachary Taylor.

On State 200 is MORATTICO CHURCH (L), 2.7 *m.*, a large rectangular brick building erected in 1856 by a congregation formed in 1778.

WICOMICO CHURCH, 7.4 *m.* (75 pop.), an old village on County 200, took its name from a church that stood on a site beside the modern Episcopal Mission Church (R). Wicomico Church (pronounced Y-kom-eye-ko), built in 1771, was reduced to ruins after the Revolution. Its communion sets are preserved in the present church. A silver cup bears the inscription: 'Ex Dono Hancock Lee to ye Parish of Lee 1711.' Other pieces have inscriptions with the dates 1726, 1728, and 1736.

Right from Wicomico Church 1.4 *m.* on County 609 to County 665 and L. to a private road (R), 3.3 *m.*, that leads 0.1 *m.* to WICOMICO VIEW, a brick, two-and-a-half-story house with gabled roof, dormers, and thick walls. A circular stairway winds, without any newel, from the first to the top floor. This has been a home of the Hudnall family since 1656, when John Hudnall acquired his first tract of 100 acres.

State 200 continues northward and crosses the Great Wicomico River to BURGESS STORE, 12.7 *m.* (20 pop.), at a junction with US 360 (*see Tour 16A*).

State 3 turns R. in Kilmarnock and passes small farms and numerous crossroad-communities.

At 36.5 *m.*, where State 3 turns L. at a junction with State 222, is the tomb-strewn yard (R) of CHRIST CHURCH (*open* 8–6, *contributions*), probably the finest Greek-cruciform Colonial church in Virginia. Its heavy brick walls laid in Flemish bond support a steep, swag roof with four hips. The three wide entrance doors have classical frames of rubbed brick and are under small oval windows. The tall windows have round arches of brick with stone keys. The ceiling within, 30 feet above the floor, has groined arches. The aisles are paved with large slabs of sandstone. Except for a new roof-covering in 1896 and a recent treatment of the furniture to preserve it, the church remains almost as it was when completed in 1732. The wine-glass pulpit and sounding-board are intact. The tables with inscriptions of the Ten Commandments and the Creed are above the chancel. Near the chancel is the vault in which were buried 'King' Carter's father, John Carter, who died in 1669, his three wives, a son, and also two daughters, Elinor and Sarah. An ambiguous inscription on the tomb has given rise to the story that John Carter had five wives.

This church sprang from the arrogance of 'King' Carter, autocratic viceroy of the Northern Neck Proprietor. 'King' Carter, insisting that the new church be on the site of the church erected in 1669–75, offered to build the church at his own expense, so that the church would continue to embrace the vault of his parents. Bishop Meade said that, though it was the custom for the rector to sign the vestry minute book first and then the members in the order of their rank, in Christ Church Parish the Carters always signed first. In the churchyard are the ornate sarcophagi of 'King' Carter and his two wives.

Right on State 222 to a junction with a private road, 3 *m.*; R. here 0.8 *m.* to WHARTON GROVE, formerly a camp-meeting ground but now a summer resort.

At 3.2 *m.* on State 222 is a private road leading (R) 0.3 *m.* to the SITE OF COROTOMAN, on the bank of the Rappahannock. Of this ancestral seat of the Carter family, only ruins of one out-building remain.

The immigrant John Carter settled here about 1650. At his death in 1669 his son Robert (1663–1732) inherited the place, later built an elaborate home-plant, acquired vast estates for his services as agent for the proprietors of the Northern Neck, and developed the wide sphere of influence that won his sobriquet. Speaker of the house of burgesses, treasurer of the colony, and acting governor, 'King' Carter was also a pioneer road builder. Greatness, however, came to him from his descendents, largely through the female line, among whom were eight governors of Virginia, three signers of the Declaration of Independence, two Presidents (the two Harrisons), Bishop William Randolph Meade, General Robert E. Lee, Chief Justice Edward Douglas White, Carter Harrison, and Lila Meade Valentine.

Ann Hill Carter, the mother of Robert E. Lee, was born here in 1773. Corotoman passed to 'King' Carter's eldest son, John Carter (1690–1743), then to his son Charles (1732–1806). By his marriage to Elizabeth Hill, John acquired Shirley (*see Tour* 24), which Charles inherited and to which he moved in 1776.

IRVINGTON, 38.1 *m.* (700 pop.), by Carter's Creek, is noted for its seafood and fishing grounds. The winter occupation of those who live in the small frame houses, spread along the tree-lined streets in the newer section, is primarily oyster and herring packing. Plants here extract oil from menhaden and manufacture fertilizer from fish. But in summer the town becomes festive. Urban people open their cottages, motor launches arrive, and boats are made ready for fishing parties.

On Rappahannock Day, usually the Fourth of July, people from the entire Northern Neck come for the motorboat racing, athletic contests, and the crowning of 'Miss Rappahannock.'

The IRVINGTON-GRAY'S POINT FERRY (*see Tour 6a*) connects the neck with the mainland (*about every 2 hrs.; $1 for car and driver, 25¢ each passenger*).

WHITE STONE, 40 *m.* (300 pop.), is a modernized commercial community.

At 40.3 *m.* is a junction with County 639.

Right here to WHITE STONE BEACH, 1.1 *m.*, a resort on the Rappahannock (*fishing and salt-water swimming*).

State 3 traverses a tiny odd-shaped peninsula formed by the Rappahannock and Oyster Creek, passing residences of fishermen.

WESTLAND, 47.6 *m.* (35 pop.), is at the southeastern tip of the Northern Neck. Here a steamboat unloads supplies used in the seafood industries and receives oysters or packed-herring for Northern points. It carries both passengers and freight.

Tour 16A

Templemans—Hague—Callao—Heathsville—Burgess Store—Reedville; 39 *m.* State 202–US 360.

Asphalt-surfaced throughout.

This route traverses the northern part of the lower Northern Neck, roughly paralleling the Potomac and crossing the upper reaches of its estuaries. At its lower end the road traverses the neck between the Little Wicomico and the Great Wicomico. The section comprises fertile farms and also an area of the menhaden industry. Along the way are old homesteads, modern houses, old grist mills on quietly flowing creeks, and villages that dream of other days.

State 202 crosses State 3 (*see Tour 16a*) at TEMPLEMANS (*see Tour 16a*), 0 *m.*, and proceeds northeastward.

On the east bank of the Nomini River is NOMINY CHURCH (L), 3.4 *m.*, a simple brick rectangle with gabled roof, built in 1704, burned by the British in 1813 and rebuilt. Though the church of Cople Parish, which was constituted in 1664, has lost most of its old furnishings, it has preserved its silver intact.

In 1773 Philip Vickers Fithian, tutor in the Carter family at Nomini Hall (*see below*), wrote: 'Between my window and the Potowmack is Nominy Church, in a pleasant agreeable place . . . We were rowed [there] by slaves . . . The river was alive with boats, some fishing, some going to church.'

At 4.3 *m.* is a junction with County 621.

Left here to a private road, 1.7 *m.*, and L. 1.2 *m.* to BUSHFIELD, a large, vine-covered brick house approached through a flower garden. Built about the middle of the nineteenth century, the bulky structure has a long portico and a dormer-dotted roof topped by a cupola with weather vane.

Richard Bushrod, who acquired the estate in 1659, left it to his son John, whose widow, Hannah Keene, though twice remarried, was buried here, at her request, between her first and third husbands. Her eldest son, John Bushrod II, whose wife was Mildred Corbin of Pecatone, willed Bushfield to his daughter Hannah, who married

John Augustine Washington and was mistress at Mount Vernon during George Washington's bachelorhood. Her son, Bushrod Washington, who became a justice of the U.S. Supreme Court, was born here June 5, 1762.

Events at Bushfield in 1782, just after the marriage of Justice Washington's brother Corbin to Hannah Lee, are recorded in the *Journal of a Young Lady of Virginia*: 'When we got here we found the House pretty full . . . Milly Washington is a thousand times prettyer than I thought her at first . . . About sunset, Nancy, Milly, and myself took a walk in the Garden . . . We were mighty busy cutting thistles to try our sweethearts when Mr.Washington [Corbin] caught us; and you can't conceive how he plagued us—chased us all over the Garden, and was quite impertinent. I must tell you of our frolic after we went in our room. We took it into our heads to want to eat . . . While we were eating the apple pye in bed . . . in came Mr.Washington, dressed in Hannah's short gown and peticoat, and seazed me and kissed me twenty times, in spite of all the resistance I could make; and then Cousin Molly. Hannah soon followed, dress'd in his Coat. They joined us in eating the apple pye, and then went out. After this we took it in our heads to want to eat oysters. We got up, put on our rappers, and went down in the Seller to get them. Do you think Mr.Washington did not follow us and scear us just to death!'

At 3.2 *m.* on County 621 is a junction with County 626; L. here 0.4 *m.* to a private road, on which R. 1.2 *m.* to the GLEBE OF COPLE PARISH, on a broad lawn by Glebe Creek. The old two-story part of this brick house, built in 1680, has been altered and enlarged considerably. The Reverend John Waugh, the first rector to occupy the Glebe, was fined 10,000 pounds of tobacco in 1674 for marrying Restitute Whitson, an orphan, to Matthew Steel, after having been forbidden to do so by the girl's guardian. Restitute was of 'good lineage and estate,' while Steel was of 'no estate.' In this house was born John Augustine Smith (1782–1865), who was the son of the Reverend Thomas Smith, and became the ninth president of the College of William and Mary and later president of King's College (now Columbia University).

On December 27, 1773, Fithian wrote: 'Mrs.Carter gave me an invitation to wait on her to Parson Smith's . . . Mrs.Carter, Miss Prissy, Miss Fanny, and Miss Betsy in the chariot; Bob and I on horseback . . . When we had dined the ladies retired, leaving us a bottle of wine and a bowl of toddy for companions.'

Among the Colonial clergymen buried near by was the Reverend Walter Jones, who officiated at the marriage of Washington's parents.

At 6.5 *m.* on State 202 is a junction with County 626.

Right here to County 612, 1 *m.*, and R. to NOMINI HALL (R), 1.6 *m.* The large brick house, built by Robert 'King' Carter about 1725 for his son Robert, and home of Robert's son, Councillor Robert Carter, was destroyed by fire in 1850. Near its site is a frame *ante-bellum* house. Two rows of large old poplar trees border the driveway.

Councillor Robert Carter (1728–1804), perhaps the most accomplished and distinguished of the sons or grandsons of 'King' Carter, became a Baptist, and opened Nomini Hall as a forum for the dissemination of new doctrines. In 1761 he had moved his family to Williamsburg, but in 1770 he came back to Nomini Hall. The Princetonian, Philip Vickers Fithian, served here as tutor for the Carter children, from October 1773 to October 1774, and here wrote the *Journal & Letters* that give one of the best descriptions of Virginia plantation life. Nothing escaped Fithian's notice—church, wines and liquors, bedbugs, parsons, and cock-fighting; epidemics of 'flux, ague, and putrid quinsy,' prevalent illiteracy, pronunciations and locutions—'sho-er' for shower, 'sale' for vendue; fox hunting and social events—'blow high, blow low, Virginians . . . will dance or die.'

Councillor Carter emancipated all his slaves except those he had given with the marriage portion of one of his daughters, but later 'wrote a serious letter to Mr.Ball [his son-in-law], exhorting him to free his Negroes or he would assuredly go to hell. Mr.Ball . . . returned answer to the old gentleman's letter, "Sir, I will run the chance."'

HAGUE, 8.1 *m.* (50 pop.), colloquially 'The Hague,' is a gay community, cultured, and ancestor conscious. Its people cling to leisurely living and class distinctions; but, like other descendants of Northern Neck settlers, they are liberals, awake to new social trends that threaten the security of their snug little world.

Left from the western limit of Hague, through a field behind a house to the SITE OF LEE HALL, 0.5 *m.*, marked by foundations and a cemetery. The large brick house, abandoned after 1839, was built about 1720 by Thomas Lee (*see Tour 16a*) for his brother Henry (1691–1747). Lee Hall is best known as the home of Henry Lee's second son, Richard (1726–95), called 'Squire Lee.' This Richard remained a bachelor until he was about 60 years of age, then married his cousin, Sally Poythress, and had three daughters—Mary, Lettice, and Richarda. After his death, Sally Poythress married Willoughby Newton. But she rests here beside her first husband, 'Squire Lee of Lee Hall.'

On May 18, 1774, Fithian wrote of a ball here 'attended by over seventy persons, of whom forty-one were ladies.' With occasional intermissions for sleep, the party continued for three days. The music 'was from a French horn and two violins. The Ladies were Dressed Gay and splendid, and when dancing their Skirts and Brocades rustled and trailed behind them . . . There were parties in Rooms made up, some at Cards; some drinking for Pleasure; some toasting the Sons of America; some singing "Liberty Songs," as they call them, in which six, eight, ten or more would put their heads near together and roar.'

The entrance to LINDEN (R) is at 8.4 *m.* The present white frame house, amid shrubbery and old trees, was built in 1929, replacing a house erected a century earlier by Willoughby Newton (1802–74). The old brick outbuildings remain. Willoughby Newton, a congressman, was an associate of Edmund Ruffin in 1845 in the founding of the Virginia State Agricultural Society. Mrs.Willoughby Newton, as a refugee in Hanover County, officiated in 1862 at 'the burial of Latané' (*see Tour 20a*). At Linden was born her granddaughter, Mary Newton Stanard (1865–1929), whose book *The Story of Bacon's Rebellion* (1907), constitutes the most authentic account of the rebellion of 1676. Among Mrs.Stanard's works are several social histories.

At 8.5 *m.* is a junction with County 612.

Left here to MOUNT PLEASANT (L), 0.3 *m.*, with a large frame house on what was once part of the Lees' Matholic estate. The house, built in 1886 by John Emerson Randolph Crabbe, became the last home of Paul Kester (*see Tour 16a*), the dramatist and novelist.

West of the lawn is the site of the first Mount Pleasant, built in 1729 by Thomas Lee for his brother Richard, who had been sent to school in England, married there, and never returned. His only son, George (1714–61), who occupied the house that had been built for his father, married Anne Fairfax, widow of Lawrence Washington. Soon after this marriage and George Washington's purchase of the widow's dowry, a quarrel arose between George Lee and George Washington over the division of the Mount Vernon slaves, causing Washington to ask for a leave of absence from his military duties. However, the 'very important dispute,' as Washington called it, was settled amicably. Here, beside her second husband, is buried Mount Vernon's first mistress.

At 0.7 *m.* is a junction with a dirt road; L. here 0.2 *m.* and R. to another turn, 1.1 *m.*; L. again to the SITE OF MATHOLIC, 1.3 *m.*, in an area now called 'Burnt House Field.' The house on Machodoc Creek, destroyed in 1729, had been built in 1666. Here is the Lee family's ancient cemetery, enclosed by a brick wall. Within are the tombs of Richard Lee II, Thomas Lee, and Richard Henry Lee—father, son, and grandson.

The immigrant Richard Lee I founded this seat of the Lees when in 1650 he patented 1,000 acres here. He added more acreage and gave the estate to his eldest son, John Lee (1645–73), who built the house. John died unmarried, and Matholic passed to his brother Richard, then to Richard's eldest son, Richard III, who, being in England, leased the place to his brothers, Thomas and Henry—for 'the yearly rent of one pepper corn only on the feast day of the birth of our Lord God.'

The second Richard Lee (1647–1714) sided with Berkeley in Bacon's Rebellion and was captured by Bacon's men. Thomas Lee (1690–1750) lived here while he was engaged in building Stratford Hall and was here when, in 1729, Matholic was set on fire and destroyed by persons who had been convicted while he sat as a justice.

At 9.8 *m.* on State 202 is a junction with County 611.

Left here to County 606, 1.6 *m.*

1. Left on County 606 to WILMINGTON (L), 0.3 *m.*, a story-and-a-half frame structure with dormers, on a knoll and surrounded by old trees. John Newton, who came to Virginia with several sons, settled here in 1670. Soon after his arrival he married his third wife, Rose Tucker.

On County 606 at 1.2 *m.* is the junction with a private lane; R. 0.1 *m.* to the SITE OF THE BANQUETING HOUSE (L), in Peckatown's (Peckatoan's) Field. This was a country club, built in 1670 by the four planters whose estates met at this point—John Lee, Henry Corbin, Isaac Allerton, and Thomas Gerard—'for the continuance of good Neighborhood' and as a meeting-place for 'processioning the bounds . . . to make an Honourable treatment, fit to entertain the undertakers thereof, their wives, mistress & friends, yearly & every year, to begin upon the 29th of May (1671).'

On the private road is WILTON, 0.9 *m.*, on a lawn bounded by a stream. Its thick brick walls, beautifully laid about 1685, rise two stories, with the glazed headers forming an attractive pattern. The large house is set between two outside chimneys that break the widely overhung eaves of the hipped roof. The small porches are later additions.

The estate was acquired in 1662 by Dr.Thomas Gerard, whose grandson, John Gerard, built this house. Wilton passed to the Eskridge family, then in 1737 to Richard Jackson.

Dr.Thomas Gerard was in 1639 'Lord of St.Clement's Manor' in Maryland. Though a member of the Governor's Council, this upright Catholic, for some strange reason, stole books and a key from a Protestant church and was forthwith fined. Later he became dissatisfied with conditions in Lord Baltimore's Proprietary and crossed the Potomac. After the death of his wife, Susannah Snow, Gerard married Rose, the widow of John Tucker, and she, after Gerard's death, married John Newton. Anne, one of Dr.Gerard's daughters, became the second wife of the immigrant, John Washington; and her sister Frances, his third wife.

2. Right on County 606 to another junction with County 611, 0.1 *m.*; L. here 1.1 *m.* to County 661 and L. again to a private road, 1.7 *m.*; R. here to PECATONE, 2.2 *m.*, by the Potomac. Ruins and one brick outbuilding remain of the house that was built in 1670 and destroyed by fire in 1888.

The estate was purchased in 1662 by Henry Corbin, who built the house. Corbin's grandson, Gawin, who inherited the estate from his father, married his cousin Hannah Lee, daughter of Colonel Thomas Lee. When Gawin died in 1759, Hannah Lee Corbin was the mistress of the estate. Heavily taxed, yet denied the right to vote, she protested bitterly against the injustice. 'I have wrote to my brother' (Richard Henry Lee), she wrote in 1778, '& I beg you will use your interest with him to do something for the poor desolate widows.' Her vigorous letter to Lee produced a long and understanding reply: 'The doctrines of representation is a large subject, and it is certain that it ought to be extended as far as wisdom and policy can allow; nor do I see that either of these forbid widows having property from voting, notwithstanding it has never been the practice either here or in England . . . I . . . would at any time give my consent to establish their right of voting.'

County 606 continues eastward, paralleling State 202; at 1.3 *m.* is YEOCOMICO CHURCH (*see below*); at 2.5 *m.* is a junction with County 604 (*see below*).

State 202 traverses a prosperous farm area and passes occasional patches of forest. At 11 *m.* is a junction with County 604.

Left here to County 606, 2.1 *m.*, and L. again 1.2 *m.* (L) to YEOCOMICO CHURCH (*keys at post office near by*), in a shady, brick-walled yard in the woods. T-shaped and low, the church and its vestibule are covered by steep swagged roofs. Yeocomico (pronounced Yo-kom′-i-ko) was built in 1706 on the site of a frame church erected in 1655.

A small porch with floor of flagstone provides approach to the great door. Here the communicants have always paused, before and after services, to exchange greetings and to indulge in a bit of gossip. The main door is of heavy timbers and swings on clumsy wrought-iron hinges. Within are the original exposed beams of the roof's framework. The high-backed pews were destroyed by British soldiers during the War of 1812, when the building was used as a barracks. The lectern is part of the original furniture, as is the walnut communion table.

Yeocomico, still a church of Cople Parish, was used for a time after the Revolution as a courthouse and later by a Methodist congregation. An all-day 'home-coming,' usually on the third Sunday in July, is an annual event.

On County 604 is SANDY POINT (L), 5.5 *m.*, by the Potomac. The present nondescript frame house, near a row of summer cottages, was erected about the middle of the nineteenth century on the site of the first house. About 1700 Colonel George Eskridge, a lawyer, acquired the estate. Formerly he had been a neighbor of Mary Ball's mother and, when Mary's mother died in 1721, her will appointed her 'truly and well-beloved friend,' Colonel Eskridge, one of her executors and her daughter's guardian. Here Mary Ball was living when she met her guardian's client, Augustine Washington, and here the parents of George Washington were married in 1731. In more recent years this estate was the home of the author, John Dos Passos.

At 13 *m.* on State 202 is a junction with State 203.

Left here to KINSALE, 1.6 *m.* (350 pop.), by a prong of the Yeocomico River. This shipping point and trade center, though constituted in 1705, is not much larger now than it was during the late eighteenth century. The Yeocomico here is lovely at all seasons and at all hours, but especially so at twilight, when an old fishing boat, long anchored here, is starkly outlined against the horizon. Old homes and new are on the slopes above the river. On their lawns in the late evening, sociable folk often gather for oyster roasts. The oysters are tossed upon metal sheets that roof great outdoor fireplaces, then retrieved—rare, medium, or well-done—and served by the tough hands of professional oyster openers. Long tables are loaded with the pickles and sauces, the pride of local housewives.

On a bluff is the BAILEY GREAT HOUSE, with grounds terraced to the water's edge. The story-and-a-half frame structure, with walls of nogging, dormers, and end chimneys, is not the large house its name suggests. It serves as a lighthouse; in one of its windows a light has been placed every evening since about 1750. In its burial lot is the tomb of Midshipman James B. Sigourney, a native of Boston, who commanded the *Asp* during a battle fought in the cove before the house on July 14, 1813. After five barges of the British navy entered the river four of them retreated; the fifth, however, came alongside the *Asp*, giving the British the opportunity to rush onto the deck of the American ship. Finding her commander propped against a mast, fatally wounded but still directing his men, one of the enemy leveled a gun and ended the heroic defense.

CALLAO, 17.6 *m.* (100 pop.), with its filling stations, bank, and high school, spreads at the confluence of three roads.

Left from Callao on County 616 to LODGE, 2.2 *m.*, a hamlet by a small stream. Here is the CHAMBERS ENGRAVING PLANT, which until 1928 made dies for postmarking the U.S. mail. The enterprise, begun in Washington in 1844 by Benjamin Chambers, was moved here in 1877.

At Callao the main route becomes US 360, on which at 19.5 *m.* is a junction with County 624.

Left here to MOUNT ZION (L), 0.2 *m.*, a Victorian house on the site of one built about 1750 by Colonel Thomas Jones (1726–86). With Colonel Jones lived his much younger brother, Walter, who became 'Physician-General of Hospitals' during the Revolution.

At Mount Zion was born Thomas Catesby Jones (1789–1858), who served as a naval officer in the War of 1812 and in the Mexican War. In 1842, when he commanded the Pacific Squadron, he took possession of Monterey on receiving erroneous information that war existed between the United States and Mexico. His twin brother, Roger (1789–1852), served in the War of 1812 and was adjutant-general of the army from 1825 to 1852. It was his son, Catesby Roger Jones, who commanded the *Virginia* (*Merrimac*) during her engagement with the *Monitor*.

LEWISETTA, 7.0 *m.* (200 pop.), on a half-moon-shaped peninsula, at the mouth of the Coan River, is a shipping point, packing center, and a resort with summer cottages along the beach on the Potomac side. Across the river, on another peninsula, is Walnut Point. Sail vessels and motorboats ply the salty waters here.

At 24.2 *m.* is the entrance (L) to SPRINGFIELD, a large brick house with unusual, low wings. It was built by William Harding in 1828 on the site of a house called Black Point, which had been a home of John Heath (1761–1810), who organized the Phi Beta Kappa Society in 1776 while he was a student at the College of William and Mary. His son, James Ewell Heath (1792–1862), was one of the founders of the *Southern Literary Messenger*, and kept the publication alive during its first eight years. After anonymously publishing *Edge Hill, or The Family of the Fitzroyals* (1825), a two-volume romance of plantation life, he wrote a comedy, *Whigs and Democrats, or Love of No Politics* (1839), to demonstrate that 'our own country furnishes ample material for the drama' as well as to ridicule 'the despicable arts of demagoguism.' Heath married his cousin Fannie, daughter of 'Parson' Mason Locke Weems.

HEATHSVILLE, 24.7 *m.* (200 pop.), seat of Northumberland County, is a shaded village of new and old houses. Named for the family of John Heath, the village was first called Hughlet's Tavern, then Heath's Store. Before the coming of bridges, its people, remote as they were from the centers of population, became fixed in habits of unhurried living. They have time for much reading, and they have not lost the art of conversation. Even recently, a judge adjourned court to chat with friends passing by. But there is little insular conservatism in Heathsville.

The NORTHUMBERLAND COUNTY COURTHOUSE, erected in 1851 and enlarged in 1934, is a two-story brick structure with a hip roof and a veranda. When the first courthouse was being erected, Joseph Humphries and Captain Richard Haynie did 'oblige themselves joyntly in penal sum 140,000 pounds tobacco that said Humphries shall compleate the new court house according to contract by May 1706.' In the courthouse are the Clerk's Office, with ample county records and among many portraits of native sons and daughters those of General Walter Jones, General Roger Jones, Juliana Gordon Hayes, and Edward Bates, Attorney General of the United States under Lincoln.

Northumberland, originally an Indian district called Chickacoan (or Chickawane) and embracing all northern Virginia, was constituted a county in 1645. In 1648 it was formally named Northumberland for a county in England.

The TAVERN, a long two-story frame building, has served court-day crowds for nearly two centuries.

At 26.3 *m.* is a junction with County 630.

Left here to County 629, 1.5 *m.*, and L. 0.9 *m.* to a private road; R. here to MANTUA, 1.7 *m.*, on a hill overlooking both the Coan River and the Potomac. The large brick house has huge end chimneys, slightly lower wings, and a two-story Doric entrance portico. There are six different floor levels. Mantua was built about 1795 by James Smith, who came from County Derry, Ireland, accumulated great wealth in Baltimore, and then settled here.

On County 630 at 1.9 *m.* is another junction with County 629; R. here 1.1 *m.* to FONT HILL (L), a dilapidated L-shaped frame house, birthplace of Juliana Gordon Hayes (1813–95), missionary and first president of the Women's Missionary Society of the Methodist Episcopal Church, South, elected in 1878.

On County 630 is COAN HALL (L), 3.5 *m.*, by the Coan River, the seat of a large estate with an *ante-bellum* residence and *ante-bellum* outbuildings. Here and along the bank of the river to the southward were the first settlements in northern Virginia.

The seat that John Mottrom established in 1640 soon became the headquarters of Protestants—and some Catholics—who had become disaffected with conditions at the 'Cittie of St.Marys' (Maryland).

Colonel Mottrom presented himself at Jamestown on November 20, 1645—the first representative in the house of burgesses from northern Virginia. When Northumberland County was constituted, his home became the county seat. Mottrom's daughter Frances, born here in 1645, became the wife of Governor Nicholas Spencer.

At 32.1 *m.* on US 360 is a junction with County 640.

Left here to County 604, 1.1 *m.*, and R. to POTOMAC VIEW BEACH, 3.6 *m.*, a small resort.

SHILOH BAPTIST CHURCH (R), at 34 *m.*, a large frame building, has a congregation (Negro) formed in 1867 when another church granted its 38 Negro members permission to withdraw and organize as a separate body. On February 18, 1898, Shiloh Baptist Church organized 'The Moral Association' and adopted resolutions that declared: 'Matrimony was instituted of God in the time of man's innocency and should be highly commended, but licentiousness should be abhored as degrading in its tendency and ruinous in its consequences . . . that we consider the man who will, by his attention to a woman, lead her to believe that it is his desire to make her his companion for life, then rob her of her virtue and abandon her to fate, should be looked upon with scorn and contempt . . . that from this date any man who ruins the character of a woman . . . shall not be a welcome visitor to our house, but shall be considered as a vile libertine . . . and should be shunned as unworthy of the recognition of a gentleman.'

LILLIAN, 36.3 *m.* (75 pop.), where US 360 turns L., is at a junction with County 646.

Right (straight ahead) on County 646 to FAIRPORT, 2.7 *m.*, a community spread along Cockrell's Creek.

Here are FACTORIES OF THE MENHADEN INDUSTRY, large brick and frame buildings with towering smokestacks. Here oil is extracted from menhaden, and fertilizer is manufactured from the residue. The fish—called also 'ale-wives'—of a variety not commonly used as food, are related to both shad and herring and resemble shad in form and color. They are caught in the Atlantic off the coast of Virginia and Maryland, from steamers equipped with 'purse nets' from 1,080 to 1,200 feet long. These nets are hauled between two row (purse) boats. When a school of fish is sighted by the lookout, the small boats are rowed parallel to each other until they reach 'striking distance.' Then the boats describe a circle in their course, each paying out its part of the net. When the boats meet, completing the circle, the ends of the net are fastened together, and a 'tom' (a ball of lead) is thrown overboard to form a fulcrum by which to 'purse' the net at the bottom. This is accomplished by means of a line attached to a ring in the tom and by other ropes passed through rings attached to the net at bottom and sides. The bottom of the net thus is brought together, forming a bag and enclosing the fish.

The steamer conveys its catch to the factory where the fish are boiled in large vats to extract the oil. Some steamers are equipped to 'cook' aboard during the fishing. The average catch is about 350,000 fish. The yield of oil is from five to six gallons per 1,000 fish. The product is marketed as whale oil, olive oil, and cod-liver oil, in diminutive bottles, the labels of which proclaim it as cure for many ills.

The JULIUS ROSENWALD TRAINING SCHOOL (R), at 37.7 *m.*, is one of several schools for Negro youths instituted with the co-operation of State school departments and the philanthropy of Julius Rosenwald (1862–1932). In the frame two-story houses agriculture, shop-mechanics, home economics, and many other subjects are taught. This school, established in 1918, has an average enrollment of 400.

At 38.5 *m.* is a junction with County 657.

Left here to County 656, 1 *m.*, and R. to CHESAPEAKE BEACH, 1.8 *m.*, a resort on Chesapeake Bay (*facilities for fishing and swimming*).

REEDVILLE, 39 *m.* (700 pop.), on a narrow peninsula, is spread along a single street. It is the center of the menhaden industry and at the time of the World War was the richest town per capita in the United States. Reedville has sprung up since 1875 and was founded by Northerners. The upper part has all the ear-marks of a prosperous Northern suburb. At the lower end are wharves, where all manner of fishing craft tie up—often beside a dapper yacht or an immaculate Government launch.

Tour 17

Richmond—Charlottesville—Waynesboro—Staunton—Monterey—(Bartow, W.Va.). US 250.
Richmond to West Virginia Line, 170.2 *m.*

Asphalt-paved except for shale-surfacing west of Monterey.
Chesapeake & Ohio Ry. parallels route between Charlottesville and Staunton.
Hotels, tourist homes, and cabins plentiful in the towns only; summer hotels in mountains.

US 250 runs across the Piedmont Plateau between the fall line and the foothills, scales the Blue Ridge, crosses the Shenandoah Valley, and rises again to the mountain wilderness of the high Alleghenies.

Section a. RICHMOND to CHARLOTTESVILLE; 70.5 *m.*

Between Richmond and Shadwell the highway has been regraded and straightened across fairly level country, largely worn-out tobacco land covered with brush and second growth woodland; not a single town breaks the monotony. In general the road follows old Three Chopt Road, so named for the three 'chops' or notches blazed on trees to mark it in early days. West of Shadwell it is bordered almost continuously by elegant estates, with houses usually far back from the road.

West of Capitol Square, 0 *m.* in RICHMOND, US 250 runs on Broad St. At 4.8 *m.* is a junction with US 33 *(see Tour 9)*.

A FOREST FIRE LOOKOUT TOWER (R), 13 *m.*, is the usual tall lean skeleton of steel holding a boxlike hut aloft. Guards are on watch during 'fire seasons,' and are connected by telephone with the homes of district fire wardens.

SHORT PUMP, 13.3 *m.*, is a crossroads hamlet named for Short Pump Tavern, where long ago 'the pump being under the porch gave the why for its naming . . .'

WOODLAWN (R), 21.1 *m.*, is a well-preserved brick house of two stories with double end chimneys, white marble lintels, and small white-painted porches. Its paneled doors, carved mantels, and hewn timbers are good examples of eighteenth-century workmanship. Restored in 1938, it is denied its full measure of charm by proximity to the highway, which has been cut through the grounds. Woodlawn, for many years a tavern, is believed to have been built about 1770 by Elisha Leake.

At 43 *m.* is a junction with State 162.

Left here to County 603, 2 *m.*, and L. on a dirt road leading to the WALLER GOLD MINE (L), 2.5 *m.*, one of several operated in the late eighteenth and early nineteenth centuries along the gold-bearing stratum through the central Piedmont. These mines, which had been worked by slave labor, were abandoned after the War between the States. A sheet metal building caps the main shaft of a recent development.

At 54.6 *m.* on US 250 is a junction with US 15 *(see Tour 3c)*.

At 61.4 *m.* is a junction with County 616.

Left here to BOYD'S TAVERN (R), 0.4 *m.*, a tall frame building with outside chimneys. Largely rebuilt after a fire in 1868 and now a residence, it was constructed not long after 1780, when the first tavern on this site burned. This was a well-known stopping place on the Three Chopt and River Roads, which joined at this point.

At 65 *m.* is a junction with State 22. Lands near by were once part of Colle, the plantation of Filippo Mazzei, a liberal, who was born in Tuscany in 1730, studied medicine in Florence and practiced in Smyrna before becoming a wine merchant in London. There, about 1770, he made the acquaintance of Benjamin Franklin and Thomas Adams, a Virginian, and formed an association with Thomas Adams and others to introduce grape-growing, wine-making, and silk worm culture into Virginia. When, in 1773, Mazzei arrived with Tuscan vineyard workers on a ship he had chartered, he was welcomed at Williamsburg by notables including Washington. He also brought 10,000 vine cuttings from famous wine districts of

Along the Highway I

graph by courtesy of the Virginia State Chamber of Commerce

IN THE HILLS, NEAR LEXINGTON

Photograph by courtesy of the Farm Security Administra

A BLUE RIDGE MATRON

MOUNTAINEER POSTMASTER

Photograph by courtesy of the Farm Security Administra

hotograph by courtesy of the Farm Security Administration

APPLE PEELER, SHENANDOAH NATIONAL PARK

'THE BEST MEAL IS WATER-GROUND'

hotograph by courtesy of the Farm Security Administration

Photograph by W. Lincoln Hight

WAITING FOR TRADE, URBANNA

ograph by W. Lincoln Highton

TIME OFF

Photograph by W. Lincoln Hight

BOXWOOD, SWEET BRIAR

GRAVEYARD, JAMESTOWN

Photograph by courtesy of the Virginia Conservation Commissi

hotograph by W. Lincoln Highton

FALLS CHURCH (1767–69), FAIRFAX COUNTY

Photograph by W. Lincoln Highton

CITY MARKET, RICHMOND

SOHPIE'S ALLEY, RICHMOND

Photograph by Robert McNeil

France, Italy, Portugal, and Spain; 4,000 olive trees; lemon trees; silk worms; and 'a sufficient number of Seeds, Stones, Grafts and small plants . . . which may . . . render the living more agreeable and comfortable.' The ship returned to Italy loaded with tobacco, grain, flour, and 'some presents' for Mazzei's patron, the Grand Duke of Tuscany; these included a brace of deer and a live rattlesnake.

To the small acreage Mazzei bought, Thomas Jefferson added a considerable tract of Monticello land. By the time his vineyards were planted, Mazzei was up to his ears in political intrigue, making fiery speeches and writing pamphlets, which Jefferson translated. In 1779, when on his way to Europe as financial agent for Virginia, he was captured by a privateer and spent three months in New York as a British prisoner. Having thrown overboard his official papers, he was without credentials when he finally arrived in Europe and had no success in raising loans. He served zealously, however, sending letters of advice and information to Jefferson, Adams, Madison, and other Virginians. To refute foreign criticism of the Revolution, he wrote a history of the colonies, signing his two-volume work merely 'A Citizen of Virginia.' Returning to America in 1783, he sought a foreign consulship but failed, and left the next year for France.

When Mazzei went abroad in 1779, Colle was rented to the Baron de Riedesel, taken prisoner at Saratoga. Jefferson afterwards wrote that the baron's horses 'destroyed in one week the whole labor of three or four years.' After 1784, Colle was the home of the Comte de Rieux, who had married Mazzei's stepdaughter. Scenes in *Janice Meredith*, by Paul Leicester Ford, were laid here.

Right on State 22 to State 231, 5.5 *m.*; L. here to GRACE CHURCH (R), 6.2 *m.*, a stone building in Gothic Revival style with a little tower. It was erected between 1848 and 1855 on the site of the 'mountain chapel' of Fredericksville Parish.

CASTLE HILL (L), 7.7 *m.*, is surrounded by gardens and heavy shrubbery on a hill at the end of a long drive and is approached through two double rows of towering tree-box. A garden is separated from the deep lawn by another box hedge that in some places is nearly 40 feet high. The mansion consists of two parts, connected by a short passage. In front is the main house, built about 1840, two stories of brick. Behind it is Dr. Thomas Walker's home, a diminutive story-and-a-half frame structure built about 1764.

Dr. Walker was one of several agents whose vast speculations in frontier land helped to settle Southwest Virginia. As a young physician from King and Queen County (*see Tour 1B*), Walker came into control of about 17,000 acres here in 1741 by his marriage to the widow of Nicholas Meriwether. Dr. Walker practiced medicine in the neighborhood and became so close a friend of Colonel Peter Jefferson that he was made guardian of Peter's young son, Thomas, after the colonel's death.

In 1748 Walker accompanied Colonel James Patton (*see Tour 5b*) on an expedition into what is now Southwest Virginia and, with Colonel Jefferson and Thomas and David Meriwether, filed claim to a large tract of those promising lands. Dr. Walker immediately gave up medical practice for a more exciting and remunerative career as explorer and speculator. Two years later, as agent of the Loyal Land Company, he headed his own expedition westward—the first that penetrated into what later became Kentucky. He was guided by a hunter called Stalnaker to the gap that he named in honor of the then Duke of Cumberland. The land company, composed of Walker and 45 others, was granted 800,000 acres of wilderness on condition that they be settled within four years. Walker was occupied during the rest of his active life surveying and selling these lands and others to which claims were so questionable that the disputes over them had to be settled by the passage of an act by the assembly.

Captain Anbury, sent to Albemarle with other British prisoners (*see Tour 4b*), wrote, 'In this neighborhood I visited Colonel Walker . . . and found his home a hospitable house but unpleasant, because the family chiefly conversed on politics, though with moderation. His father (Dr. Walker) is a man of strong understanding, though considerably above eighty years of age. He freely declared his opinions of what America would be a hundred years hence, and said the people would reverence the resolution of their fathers, and impress the same feeling on their children, so that they would adopt the same measures to secure their freedom, which had been used by their brave ancestors.'

Jack Jouett (*see Tour 9*), on his ride to Charlottesville to warn Governor Jefferson and the Virginia Legislature of Tarleton's approach, was given a fresh mount at Castle Hill. When Tarleton arrived by another road, he was pressed to accept a sumptuous breakfast at Castle Hill that Jouett might have more time.

Through marriage to a granddaughter of Dr. Walker, William Cabell Rives became owner of Castle Hill. He was a member of the U.S. Senate and minister to France under President Andrew Jackson. Amelie Rives (Princess Troubetzkoy), his granddaughter, to whom the estate descended, has written novels, short stories, poems, essays, and successful dramas. Her first husband, whom she divorced, was the eccentric John Armstrong Chaloner, who contributed a phrase to American speech when, from an insane asylum, he telegraphed, 'Who's looney now?' to his brother on the occasion of his brother's marriage to beauteous Lina Cavalieri.

EDGEHILL (R), 65.1 *m.*, a two-story brick house above the highway, has a wide view though a grove conceals it from the road. The square, central section, in Classical Revival style, is unexpectedly simple. On the front is a one-story flat-roofed portico surmounted by a Chippendale balustrade. Four chimneys are grouped close to the short ridge of the low hipped roof. A rear wing is a later addition.

Although William Randolph of Tuckahoe patented land here on the north side of the Rivanna in 1735, none of the family lived here until his grandson, Colonel Thomas Mann Randolph, married Martha Jefferson. Colonel Randolph, who managed Thomas Jefferson's estates during his long absences and was governor of Virginia 1819–22, died in 1828. Colonel Thomas Jefferson Randolph, his son, found the old brick house too small and had it moved back in the yard, where it stands now, covered with clapboarding. That same year he erected the front part of the present structure, according to drawings prepared long before by Jefferson.

Here in 1836 Mrs. Jane Nicholas Randolph, wife of Jefferson's grandson, opened a boarding school for girls. Closed during the War between the States, it was reopened and functioned until 1896. Before the end of the nineteenth century, the interior had been burned and then restored.

At 66.1 *m.* is SHADWELL (L), the birthplace of Thomas Jefferson. On this site was Colonel Peter Jefferson's house, in which his son Thomas was born April 13, 1743, and lived until it burned in 1770, when he moved to Monticello (*see Tour 23A*). Shadwell stood upon a small farm acquired by Peter Jefferson in 1736 from William Randolph of Tuckahoe. The deed of transfer shows that the consideration for the land was: 'Henry Weatherburn's biggest bowl of Arrack punch to him delivered' (*see Williamsburg*).

At 69.1 *m.* is a junction with County 613 (*see Tour 10*).

CHARLOTTESVILLE, 70.5 *m.* (480 alt., 15,245 pop.) (*see Charlottesville*).

In Charlottesville is the junction with State 239 (*see Tour 23*).

Section b. CHARLOTTESVILLE to WEST VIRGINIA LINE; 99.7 m. US 250.

West of Charlottesville, where Main Street coincides with the ghost of Three Notched Road, the highway closely follows the course of the road through rolling foothills and passes elaborate estates. Pastures and occasional orchards border the highway. After a steep climb to Rockfish Gap in the Blue Ridge, with a vast stretch of wooded peaks and of cultivated fields far below, US 250 drops swiftly to peach and apple country of the broad valley floor. West of Staunton the route follows in general the older Staunton-Parkersburg Turnpike. Parallel ridges and valleys, including Calf Pasture, Cow Pasture, Bull Pasture, and Jackson Rivers, are curiously uniform in contour and size. Where limestone predominates, lush bluegrass fattens beef cattle. Near the West Virginia Line the highway climbs among the lofty Alleghenies, which rise more than 4,000 feet.

West of Courthouse Square in CHARLOTTESVILLE, 0 *m.*, US 250 follows High St., then Main St. to a junction with US 29 (*see Tour 4b*) at 2 *m.*

The FARMINGTON COUNTRY CLUB (R), 4.1 *m.*, occupies a large tract with views of the mountains. Part of the property is a residential development, and another part is a golf course (*see Charlottesville*). The clubhouse, a large rose-brick *ante-bellum* structure, has a portico with four tall modified-Doric columns. Part of the rooms of the former mansion have been united to form a single room two stories high.

A wing of the structure was the pre-Revolutionary home of Francis Jerdone, an alleged Tory, whose estate was confiscated and then returned to him. About 1785 the estate passed to George Divers. With plans drawn by Thomas Jefferson, Divers began to enlarge and remodel the house in 1802–03, but displeasure on the part of Jefferson over the way his plans were being executed and then the death of Divers stopped the work. Construction was completed in the 1850's, under Bernard Peyton, and the central section was added. Opened in 1929 as a country club and hotel, the building has been enlarged and modernized.

IVY, 7.4 *m.* (200 pop.), is a scattered village of retired, middle-income folk.

On the northern fringe of this community is the SITE OF LOCUST HILL (R), birthplace in 1774 of Meriwether Lewis, who, accompanied by William Clark, younger brother of George Rogers Clark, commanded the expedition that started westward in the summer of 1803, wintered in the vicinity of St.Louis, set out again on May 14, 1804, and reached the mouth of the Columbia River in Oregon on November 15, 1805—a journey of 4,000 miles through unknown wilds, including passage across the Rocky Mountains. The expedition began its return in March 1806 and reached St.Louis on September 23, 1806, in possession of copious notebooks bursting with information. In recognition of his services, Jefferson made Lewis governor of Louisiana Territory. Lewis died under mysterious circumstances in 1809, while stopping at a tavern in Tennessee, on a journey to Washington. Jefferson inclined to the idea that he had committed suicide but there is some evidence that he was a victim of one of the many bandits on the Natchez Trace.

CROZET, 13.4 *m.* (718 alt., 300 pop.), is an attenuated community, including large storage warehouses, strung out along highway and railroad. The crop grown in neighboring orchards and packed in Crozet reaches a yearly value of half a million dollars. The town was named for Colonel Benoît Claude Crozet (1789–1864), a distinguished engineer who came to America from France. Educated at the École Polytechnique, he served in Napoleon's army until taken prisoner in Russia. After his exchange he rejoined Napoleon before Waterloo. In America, he was an instructor at West Point, then State engineer of Virginia; he supervised the early growth of the Virginia Military Institute, and finally headed Richmond Academy. Besides supervising the construction of canals, highways, tunnels, railroads, and aqueducts, Crozet was a cartographer and author of textbooks on mathematics.

SEVEN OAKS (R), 17.7 *m.*, a gleaming white frame house in Greek Revival style with large Ionic portico, stands on a hill above the road on the site of Black Tavern, kept by James Black. Part of the tavern, a small log building, is behind the present house. It was moved back when Seven Oaks was built in 1847–48 by Dr. John Bolling Garrett, long associated with educational enterprises in the county, especially with the University of Virginia.

EMMANUEL CHURCH (L), 18.7 *m.*, a red brick structure with cloister and tower, was erected in 1914 as a memorial to Mrs. Chiswell Dabney Langhorne, mother of Lady Nancy Astor and of Mrs. Charles Dana Gibson, who was her husband's model for the 'Gibson Girl.'

At 21 *m.* is a clear view of ELK MOUNTAIN (R), a castellated eyrie simulating a feudal stronghold, in which a greater and a lesser capitalist have nested. Perched high on the Blue Ridge, the gray mass thrusts tower and crenellations against the sky in a pseudo-baronial style. The house was erected in 1925–26 by Thomas Fortune Ryan.

AFTON, 23 *m.* (1,374 alt., 50 pop.), perched on the mountainside, is a station on the Chesapeake & Ohio, which passes here over the route of the Virginia Central Railroad, extended west from Charlottesville in 1854. Beneath the mountains westward, Colonel Crozet cut a railroad tunnel that was the longest in the world when opened in 1856.

The highway crosses the Blue Ridge through ROCKFISH GAP (1,900 alt.), at 25 *m.*, which in clear weather commands magnificent views of farm-filled valleys on both sides of the ridge. The gap played an important part in the early settlement of western Virginia especially after a buffalo path through the gap had become a well-known travel route. In the gap is a junction with Skyline Drive (*see Tour 4A*).

By the Drive junction is the entrance (L) to huge SWANNANOA, built of white marble in Italian Renaissance style. Once the home of Major James H. Dooley, Richmond philanthropist, and then used as a country club, the estate is about to be converted (1939) into a center for the promotion of world-wide peace. On the grounds is the SITE OF LEAKE TAVERN, where a commission met in 1818 to decide upon a location for the nascent University of Virginia.

Westward the highway uncoils itself precipitously down the mountain to WAYNESBORO, 29 *m.* (1,295 alt., 6,226 pop.), sprawling before a hillside stripped by extensive gravel operations. The town retains some of an earlier pleasantness despite current industrial developments. A small hamlet had gathered here before the Revolution on this early road to the West. Chastellux found a tavern here, 'the worst in all America . . . Mrs.Teaze, the mistress of the house, was sometime since left a widow; she appears also to be in fact the widow of her furniture, for surely never was a house so badly furnished.'

On March 2, 1865, General Philip H. Sheridan, with a force of Union cavalry, drove General Jubal A. Early and 1,000 Confederates from their strategic position near by. Early's force was captured almost to a man, but the general and his staff escaped to the woods. This was one of the last contests of the war in western Virginia.

About 1895, citizens of Waynesboro were victims of an oil hoax. A group proclaiming it had found oil in the vicinity began to sell stock and made a show of drilling. As the work progressed with no signs of oil, the sale of stock began to lag. One night several barrels of oil were poured into the drilled hole. The next day this hopeful evidence stimulated sales, and several business men retired to enjoy their oil royalties. The only product of the well was good drinking water.

FISHBURNE MILITARY SCHOOL, occupying a large red brick building and several smaller structures, is a boys' preparatory school established in 1879. At present (1939) the enrollment is 176.

FAIRFAX HALL, a girls' preparatory school and junior college housed in a large towered building on a shaded campus, was named, with unintentional irony, for Thomas, Lord Fairfax, the staunchest misogynist of Virginia history (*see Tour 5A*).

In Waynesboro is a junction with State 12 (*see Tour 5A*).

West of Waynesboro the highway passes extensive apple orchards in the warm valley, rimmed by mountains.

FISHERVILLE, 34.1 *m.* (150 pop.), a rural shopping center that grew up as a stagecoach station, has a plant for the manufacture of fruit containers.

Left from the village on State 273 to TINKLING SPRING CHURCH (R), 1.2 *m.*, a log-bodied, weatherboarded structure built about 1790 and since remodeled. The first church, built here in 1740, was the place of worship for settlers from a wide area that included the settlement at Staunton. John Craig, first Presbyterian minister to settle in Virginia, preached here on alternate Sundays (*see Tour 5a*). The spring at the edge of the churchyard gave the church its name. Craig favored another site for the church and refused to drink water from the spring, bringing a bottle of water, which he placed beside him in the pulpit.

STAUNTON, 41 *m.* (1,385 alt., 11,990 pop.) (*see Staunton*).

In Staunton is a junction with US 11 (*see Tour 5a*).

At 45.7 *m.* is a junction with County 732.

Right here to MT.PLEASANT, 0.3 *m.*, a brick house with end chimneys and octagonal bay windows. The house was built by Colonel George Moffett, soldier in the French and Indian War and commander of a company of militia at the Battle of Guilford

Courthouse during the Revolution. Some of the Virginia legislators, fleeing from Charlottesville at the approach of Tarleton in 1781, found refuge here.

US 250 crosses Middle River, at 47.3 *m.*, near which in 1764 was the home of John Trimble. Indians, led by a white man or half breed, killed Trimble and carried off his son, his sister-in-law, and a Negro boy. Neighbors, led by Colonel Moffett of Mt.Pleasant, surprised the Indians in camp and rescued young Trimble and the sister-in-law. The Negro was killed in the fray.

CHURCHVILLE, 49.5 *m.* (303 pop.), is appropriately named for the number of churches on its short main street—LOCK WILLOW PRESBYTERIAN (1781), ST.JAMES METHODIST CHURCH (1826), ST.PETER'S LUTHERAN (1850), and UNITED BRETHREN CHURCH (1878).

In the middle of the nineteenth century two brothers, Jed and Nelson Hotchkiss, came to Churchville from New York. Jed Hotchkiss established a school for boys, while the wife of Nelson Hotchkiss opened a school for girls. Jed Hotchkiss, a captain and topographical engineer on Stonewall Jackson's staff in the War between the States, made maps of the State for the Confederate army.

Through JENNINGS GAP, 53.6 *m.*, ran the old Staunton-Warm Springs road.

The highway crosses the eastern boundary of the GEORGE WASHINGTON NATIONAL FOREST at 53.9 *m.* This mountain area of timber reserves and watersheds is under the protection of U.S. Forestry Service.

BUCKHORN TAVERN, 56.5 *m.*, a two-story frame building with a long double veranda, is the remnant of a much larger building that was once a popular shopping place for travelers.

The crest of the Shenandoah Mountains, 66.9 *m.*, is a vantage-point (2,950 alt.).

Right along the ridge 100 yards from the crest parking space to FORT EDWARD JOHNSON, occupied by General Edward Johnson's Confederate command of 3,000 men in February 1862. This unit, a remnant of the Army of the Northwest, had been left at Camp Allegheny, 25 miles west, to guard against invasion of the Shenandoah Valley by means of the Staunton-Parkersburg turnpike. Upon withdrawal of other Confederate forces west of the Alleghenies, Johnson retired to this position. He was followed by General R.H.Milroy, whom he had defeated at Camp Allegheny on December 13, 1861. When General T.J.Jackson retired from Harrisonburg on April 19, Johnson withdrew toward Staunton, and Milroy, acting now as General John C. Frémont's advance force, occupied this position. Jackson, before attempting his larger plan in the valley, combined half of his army with that of Johnson and, on May 7, advanced against Milroy, who, retreating, was reinforced. On the following afternoon the combined force, under Schenck, attacked Jackson.

On the west side of the BULL PASTURE MOUNTAIN, 75 *m.*, the Battle of McDowell was fought between the forces of Jackson and Schenck. The two small forces met on May 8. Because field pieces could not be brought into action over the rough ground, the fight was almost entirely with small arms. During the night the Union forces, followed by Jackson, withdrew northward toward Franklin.

McDOWELL, at 76 *m.*, is a mountain hamlet.

Left from McDowell, 6.5 *m.* on State 269, to the SITE OF FORT GEORGE (L), an early refuge in Indian attacks. Its outlines are remarkably well preserved in the meadow between the river and a brick house (R). Clearly outlined also are two bastions, a hole for the powder magazine, and a tunnel or trench by which water could be brought from the river in case of a siege.

Settlements were established in this valley prior to 1743. The brick house, on land near the old fort, was built about 1844. The mill, on the opposite side of the river, was built about 1840.

MONTEREY, 85.4 *m.* (3,100 alt., 290 pop.) (*see Tour 21a*).

From Monterey the highway crosses the Allegheny Mountains. The CREST, 99.7 *m.*, was fortified in 1861 by forces under General Johnson to guard the Staunton-Parkersburg turnpike.

Here US 250 crosses the West Virginia Line (*see West Virginia Guide*) at a point 7 miles east of Bartow, W.Va.

Tour 18

Suffolk—Wakefield—Waverly—Petersburg; 61.4 *m.* US 460.

Asphalt-paved roadbed, chiefly four-lane.
Norfolk & Western Ry. parallels route.
All types of accommodations in towns.

US 460 runs northwest, traversing flat or slightly rolling country, partly wooded but largely used for the raising of peanuts, and some vegetables, cotton, and tobacco. The combination of sandy fields and proximity to markets make peanut growing and hog raising, allied activities, the backbone of small-farm income. In the villages along the railroad are sawmills that cut the yellow pine and hardwood.

US 460 branches northwest from US 58 (*see Tour 7a*) in SUFFOLK, 0 *m.* (58 alt., 10,271 pop.), the peanut capital of the world and the birthplace of 'Mr.Peanut.' The city is at the head of the Nansemond River, close to the Dismal Swamp, and surrounded by flat country. In the crowded little commercial district, where two buildings tower seven stories high, chain grocery stores, installment clothing stores, hardware and produce stores hobnob with the few father-to-son businesses that have survived modern trends. Along tree-vaulted residential streets old houses stand sedately beside those of later vintage. Fringing the town are jumbled Negro districts—Boston, Philadelphia, Pleasant Hill, and Jericho.

The people of Suffolk, friendly though ancestor-conscious, live in century-old houses or in new houses built on old designs. They faithfully support all socially accepted organizations, patriotic, civic, and philanthropic, and deal courteously with both their fellow townsmen and accredited strangers within their gates. Here mint juleps, pickled artichokes, pickled oysters, and Christmas 'tipsy-cakes'—a spongy confection soaked in brandy—are at their best.

Suffolk has reason to be peanut conscious. Though 22 concerns, producing a variety of other products, employ about 2,500 workers here, the peanut easily dominates the commercial picture. Peanut farms of lower Tidewater Virginia and North Carolina send more than 50,000 tons of nuts yearly to Suffolk processing plants and the town's 9 large warehouses. All day long during the harvesting season trucks, piled high with nut-filled sacks, rumble through the streets; and in any season, when the wind blows from the factory quarter, the air is heavy with the oily-sweet odor that means local prosperity.

Of several varieties of *arachis hypogaea*—the peanut or 'ground pea' that flourishes in the sandy soil of the region—three are favorites: Virginia Bunch, Virginia Runner, and Jumbo. The crop, planted in April, blooms in July and is harvested in October. After pollination, the blossom fades, the stem lengthens and thrusts its head into the earth, where the pod matures. Most crop operations—planting, cultivating, and harvesting—are done by machines, some of which work as many as four field rows at one time. Digging of the nuts is done with a complicated machine, which also strips off loose dirt; it is followed by a hand job of shocking the vines in the field, pods innermost, and by three weeks of curing. Next comes the whirring thresher, which, amid clouds of dust, strips the pods from the vines and feeds them into burlap bags. The nuts are then whisked away to storage warehouses, where a constant temperature of 40° F. prevents the growth of the saw-toothed weevil larvae. The vines make stock forage.

Processing plants are the principal peanut buyers. In the plants high-powered fans blow out stems and trash. Then the nuts to be sold raw for roasting are culled and graded; those to be used for confections, salting, and oil go first to shelling machines, where lightly-crushed shells are blown away and nuts drop through grading slots in a jiggling, inclined table. These operations separate large, plump nuts from the inferior grades that will be crushed, to extract oil for cooking and butter substitutes. The residue from this process is sold as stock feed. Candy- and salting-nuts are lightly roasted to loosen the red skins and then blanched in rotary suction machines that also carry off the skins. After this, they pass an electric eye, sensitized to color, which selects the whitest nuts, and then are further culled by hand. Nuts for salting are conveyed to a huge machine, where they are cooked in oil, salted, and subjected to a final check by fluoroscope. Those for candy go straight to dipping machines for chocolate coating, or to mixing machines for a syrup bath before being pressed and scored into bars.

Captain John Smith explored the Nansemond River in 1608, and Edward Waters settled here in 1618. The first group of Puritans to reach Virginia settled in this section but were driven out of the colony by orthodox Governor Berkeley just as the Puritan revolt triumphed in England;

the 300 of them who migrated from Nansemond to tolerant Maryland and established Providence on the Severn River took their turn at carrying on religious persecution in that State.

Suffolk itself did not come into being until 1742 when the general assembly authorized a town at Constance's Warehouse, to care for the then dominant tobacco business. It was not until 1808 that the town was incorporated. The town early began to look out for its poor. It took seriously a law passed in 1755 by the general assembly that every person receiving aid must wear a badge with the name of his parish, under penalty of loss of allowance or lashes not to exceed five. And a vestry book of this period reveals that 500 pounds of tobacco were paid to a doctor for 'salevating Mary Brinkley and keeping her salevated.'

The little town suffered during the Revolution and the War between the States. On May 13, 1779, General Matthews burned it, and on May 12, 1862, Federal troops took possession.

In SUFFOLK CEMETERY, E. end of Mahan St., where tombstones stand row on row, is CONSTANTIA HOUSE, a story-and-a-half structure covered with beaded weatherboards and having buttressed outside end chimneys and two dormers in each slope of its gabled roof. The house is a faithful restoration of the Widow Constance's home, which was at Constance's Warehouse on Sleepy Hole Point in the river.

WITHERS HOUSE (*private*), 510 N.Main St., is a dignified two-and-a-half-story brick structure on a high basement and fronted by a Doric porch. Built in 1837, the house encountered its first exciting adventure in the 1860's when its upper stories were Federal headquarters and its basement stabled the horses of Union officers.

NANSEMOND COUNTY COURTHOUSE, SE. corner Milner and N.Main Sts., a building with brick walls laid in Flemish bond, has an unusually tall entrance portico with four Tuscan columns. Built in 1840, it serves the county of which Suffolk is a geographical but, as a city, not a political part.

In 1634 Nansemond County lay within Elizabeth City County; in 1636 that part of Elizabeth City lying south of the James became the county of New Norfolk; in 1637 New Norfolk was divided into Upper Norfolk and Lower Norfolk; and in 1642 Upper Norfolk was designated as Nansemond County, the name commemorating the Indians of the Powhatan Confederacy whom Captain John Smith found here in 1608. In 1750 the county seat was moved to Suffolk from Jarnigan's or Cohoon's Bridge.

WINDSOR, 12.2 *m.* (371 pop.), is a farmers' marketing and school center.

Right from Windsor on State 158 to ISLE OF WIGHT, 7.8 *m.* (50 pop.), seat of Isle of Wight County. A few houses, stores, and gasoline stations are comfortably settled near the Confederate Soldier, who stands at the center of a circular grass plot just outside the wall that encloses the county buildings. The red brick COURTHOUSE has a look of adequate solidity. The CLERK'S OFFICE, originally a one-story rectangle of brick with built-in chimneys and wooden lintels, has a matching addition, which, by means of a connecting passageway, forms an H. The older part of the building was begun in the first years of the nineteenth century. The records are in a fair state of preservation in spite of the vicissitudes through which they have passed. During the Revolution

Mrs. Francis Young, wife of a deputy clerk, buried them to prevent their destruction by the raiding Tarleton; and during the War between the States they were first hidden in the woods and then carted into other counties for safekeeping.

One of the eight shires constituted in 1634 was Warrosquoyacke, an unpronounceable name that was soon changed to Isle of Wight. The boundaries, at first so indefinite as to cause considerable dispute, were fixed in 1705 and redefined in 1733, when a southwestern slice of the county was added to Brunswick, and again in 1748, when Southampton was carved from Isle of Wight. The county seat was moved here from Smithfield (*see Tour* 19) in 1800.

Enterprising WAKEFIELD, 30 *m.* (881 pop.), is centered around the railroad station. The part touched by the highway is marked by two 'diner' lunchrooms and several filling stations. The little town owns its electric light and water systems and a modern high school building. It has a weekly newspaper, a bank, general stores, a peanut factory, and a stave mill.

Right from Wakefield on State 31 to DENDRON, 5.9 *m.* (671 pop.), which enjoyed ephemeral prosperity while lumbering despoiled the wooded area around it.

WAVERLY, 37.8 *m.* (1,355 pop.), Sussex County's largest town, has the usual main street with general stores, a bank, weekly newspaper office, and small business places that cater to farm trade. The town's industrial activity, once centered in peanut factories and sweet potato shipping, is now dependent on lumber mills and a ham curing plant.

Legend has it that DISPUTANTA, 46.6 *m.* (120 pop.), a crossroads village, was so named because of lack of agreement on a suitable title for the place when the railroad came through in the late 1850's.

NEW BOHEMIA, 54.3 *m.*, a hamlet with one church, a general store, and handful of frame dwellings, is the social and trade center of a Slav farming community, which, at its beginning in the early decades of the present century, was something of a sensation in this rural section with its English tradition and distrust of aliens. First to invade this country, where farming had long been carried on by sharecroppers, was a group of Bohemians and Slovaks from the industrial and mining sections of western Pennsylvania and eastern Ohio. Their success in rehabilitating worn-out farms, where production had almost vanished under one-crop planting year after year, led to the immigration of other Bohemians and Slovaks, with a sprinkling of Poles and Lithuanians, many of whom came directly from their homelands.

At 54.4 *m.* is a junction with County 630.

Right here to State 37, 3.4 *m.*, and R. to PRINCE GEORGE, 4.7 *m.* (75 pop.), seat of Prince George County, with its few houses and stores that are supported by court days and court business. Compactly set within the courthouse square are the county buildings, facing an obelisk of roughhewn stone, the monument to the Confederate dead.

The COURTHOUSE, a two-story red brick building with gabled roof and arcaded porch, is flanked by two single-story buildings, one separate and the other connected by a continuation of the arcade. Prince George County was created from Charles City County in 1702 and named in honor of Queen Anne's consort, Prince George of Denmark. Court sessions were held successively at City Point, Jordan's Point, Merchant's Hope, and Fitzgerald's, until 1785, when the seat of government was moved here.

At 58.1 *m.* is an entrance (R) to the PETERSBURG NATIONAL MILITARY PARK (*see also Tours* 1c *and* 14).

Right on the park road, along a line of Federal forts and entrenchments, to FORT STEDMAN (R), 1.2 *m.*, a well-fortified position taken by the Confederates on March 25, 1865, and lost again within a few hours. In a last desperate attempt to cut Grant's line, Lee placed half of his army of about 35,000 under command of General John B. Gordon and ordered an assault here. Fort Stedman was taken at 4:30 a.m., but misinformation as to other Federal works, failure of a large part of Lee's troops to arrive from Richmond, and heavy artillery cross fire from flanking forts caused a collapse of the offensive, with a loss of 3,000 to the Confederates and 1,000 to the Federals. Within a week Grant broke Lee's lines and forced the evacuation of Petersburg and Richmond.

1. Left from Fort Stedman 200 yards to COLQUITT'S SALIENT, from which the Confederate offensive began on March 25, 1865. On a line from this vicinity to the Appomattox River, a distance of two miles, and eastward one mile, a Confederate defense under General P.G.T.Beauregard held off an advancing Federal force on June 15–18, 1864, until Lee could be convinced that Grant had crossed the James River. Federal losses for the period were about 10,000; Confederate about 5,000.

2. Right from Fort Stedman to a junction with two park roads, 1.3 *m.*; R. here to a park road, 2.2 *m.*, and L. to State 36, 3 *m.*; R. here to a park road, 3.3 *m.*, and L. to a NATIONAL PARK CONTACT STATION, 3.5 *m.* (*maps, free guide service*).

This part of the Battlefield Park was in Camp Lee, one of the large cantonments of the World War period. Camp Lee was established June 21, 1917, and cost more than $21,000,000. Ninety thousand troops—among them the Eightieth, or Blue Ridge Division, composed of men from the mountain regions of Virginia, West Virginia, Maryland, and Pennsylvania—were trained here.

At 58.9 *m.* is a junction with County 634 (L), which follows the Battlefield Park Route to US 301 (*see Tour* 14).

The MASSACHUSETTS MONUMENT (R), 59 *m.*, in a fortlike enclosure, commemorates soldiers and sailors killed in Virginia between 1861 and 1865. This monument has been the means of bringing together veterans of the North and the South. After the Massachusetts Legislature had appropriated in 1909 funds for its erection, a commission was sent to Virginia to arrange necessary details, and established friendly relations with the A.P.Hill Camp of Confederate Veterans in Petersburg. The next year Massachusetts veterans entertained the Petersburg veterans and later returned the visit. On a gala night in the Petersburg armory, when veterans were swapping stories above buried hatchets, Colonel James Anderson, chairman of the Massachusetts Commission, told of the many commendatory letters that had come to him after the visit of the Southern soldiers. But, he added, a lady from Paterson, New Jersey, had written chiding him for permitting a 'vile band of Rebels' to walk through the streets of a fair Northern city to the tune of that 'rebel song, Dixie.' Colonel Anderson returned the letter to its sender with these words appended: 'There will be Confederates in Heaven. If you don't want to associate with Confederates, go to Hell.'

Right at the monument on a park road to THE CRATER, 0.2 *m.*, a large elliptical pit surrounded by a high embankment and behind several monuments and a NATIONAL PARK CONTACT STATION AND MUSEUM (*free guide service*). A regiment of Pennsylvania miners had dug a 500-foot tunnel under this sector of the Confederate line while a Federal offensive had drawn the larger part of Lee's army north of the James (*see Tour* 24), weakening the lines around Petersburg. Early on the morning of July 30,

1864, a charge of 8,000 pounds of gunpowder was fired in the subterranean cavity while General A.E.Burnside's four divisions waited to rush through the breach and occupy the city. The explosion blew 278 men of Confederate General Stephen Elliott's brigade into the air, and also two guns of a four-gun battery, momentarily demoralizing the Confederates and stunning the Federal divisions. The blast left a pit 135 feet long and 30 feet deep. Three charging Federal divisions, crowding the crater, spilled into the Confederate lines, while a terrific cannonade began on both sides. The Union troops, fearing to advance, were further crowded by the Negro division, thrown in later.

On the Confederate side strenuous efforts were made to hold the enemy to the breach until reinforcements could reach the field. After three charges by the reinforced Confederates, all Federal troops who had not retreated were driven into the pit, and there began a virtual massacre as the Confederates gathered around the cavity, throwing in, points first, armfuls of bayonetted rifles, while mortars, brought close, dropped shells into the struggling mass. The Confederates then jumped into the pit and struggled hand-to-hand until the remaining Federals surrendered. The Federal loss was about 4,400, of which 1,100 were prisoners; the Confederate loss was about 1,500.

PETERSBURG, 61.4 *m.* (28,564 pop.) (*see Petersburg*).

Petersburg is at junctions with US 1 (*see Tour 1c*) and US 301 (*see Tour 14*).

Tour 19

Richmond—Chesterfield—Hopewell—Surry—Smithfield—Suffolk—(Sunbury,N.C.); State 10.
Richmond to N.C. Line, 107.7 *m.*

Hard-surfaced roadbed throughout, chiefly asphalt.
Norfolk Southern R.R. parallels route between Suffolk and North Carolina Line.
Hotel accommodations only in cities, tourist homes in smaller communities.

This highway follows the southern bank of the James River through land that lay within the earliest grants to English colonists in America. Much of the soil, once highly productive and later impoverished through unscientific farming, is being reclaimed by means of diversified plantings and modern agricultural methods. Northward the small farm prevails, producing grain, poultry, and milk. Southward is a fertile peanut and tobacco area, with here and there acres given over to cotton. Near the North Carolina line the route skirts the vast Dismal Swamp.

On the bank of the river, remote from the highway, are mansions that were once the seats of many of Virginia's most distinguished families. Some of these have passed into the hands of newcomers; others are occupied by descendants of the first owners; a few of the oldest and most beautiful are occupied by tenants.

State 10 branches south from US 360 (*see Tour 20b*) from Hull St.,

0 *m.*, on Broad Rock Road in RICHMOND and traverses a suburban district where among bungalows and nondescript cottages are older houses that conform to the dignity of an earlier architectural era.

BRANCH'S BAPTIST CHURCH (R), 3 *m.*, is a T-shaped brick building, with Doric columns and Gothic windows. The congregation, organized May 10, 1828, was served until 1839 by neighboring ministers. Branch's Church was an arm of Chesterfield Church, organized in 1773.

The highway passes FALLING CREEK, 4.1 *m.*, by which in 1619 John Berkeley established the first iron furnace in America. The revenue from the furnace was to be used by the proposed College at Henricopolis (*see Tour 1c*). Projected by Sir Edwyn Sandys, the enterprise cost the London Company £4,000. In the early spring of 1622 it was described as being 'in a very great forwardness.' Shortly afterwards Berkeley and all his workers were slain, and the furnace was not revived.

Later, on these ruins, rose another iron foundry that passed into the hands of Archibald Cary (*see Tour 1c*). The enterprise lasted until 1781 when it was destroyed by British guns.

CHESTERFIELD, 10.4 *m.* (150 pop.), seat of Chesterfield County, has maintained its atmosphere of eighteenth-century leisure. The brick COURTHOUSE, with a Tuscan portico, in an enclosure thickly shaded by old trees, was erected in 1917. The well-kept records date back to 1748, the year that Chesterfield County was carved from Henrico. The British destroyed the first courthouse in 1780–81. The OLD CLERK'S OFFICE, built in 1828, is a one-storied cottage-like rectangle of mellowed brick, now used by the superintendent of schools and the county auditor. The present CLERK'S OFFICE, built in 1889, was enlarged in 1930. On the site of the old jail is a granite shaft bearing the inscription: 'On this spot were imprisoned 1770–1774 John Tanner, David Tinsley, Joseph Anthony, Augustine Eastin, Jeremiah Walker, John Weatherford, Apostles of Religious Liberty.' Probably the most famous prisoner of the old jail was Colonel Henry Hamilton, former Governor General of Canada, known as the 'scalptaker' or 'hair buyer,' captured in 1779 by George Rogers Clark at Vincennes and brought first to Williamsburg and then to Chesterfield. 'While at Chesterfield,' wrote Hamilton, 'our confinement was rendered very tolerable . . . We had liberty to walk about in the neighborhood.' In Williamsburg he had had far less courteous treatment, for there 'the people were much incensed against him, on account of his dealing with the savages, and he was put in irons and kept in jail for some time.'

During the Revolution, Virginia militia were trained here by the great drillmaster, Baron von Steuben. The local barracks were one of the principal objectives of General William Phillips, who, with the aid of General Benedict Arnold, succeeded toward the end of the war in destroying them and large stores of tobacco.

The left section of CASTLEWOOD was built about 1776 by Charles Poindexter. Pavilions connect three small units on a high foundation.

Right from Chesterfield on County 655 to SWIFT CREEK RECREATION PARK (R), 3 *m.* (*picnicking, bathing, boating, and fishing facilities*), a large public recreational area including two lakes.

CHESTER, 15.4 *m.* (1,000 pop.), a sprawling residential village, was laid out in 20 lots of equal size. It was once an important shipping point and market center on the Petersburg Railroad. On May 10, 1864, the Union army destroyed the railroad tracks near Chester in their efforts to cut off supplies from Richmond.

SALEM BAPTIST CHURCH, a simple frame building, houses a congregation constituted in 1802. In his *History of the Middle District Association*, Semple says that Salem started with 117 members and adds, 'It is worthy of remark that generally the Baptist cause prospered most extensively where it met with the most severe opposition.' In recounting the tribulations of Baptist ministers in Chesterfield County, he said, 'Some were whipped by individuals, several fined. They kept up their persecutions after other counties had laid it aside.'

At 17.4 *m.* is a junction with US 1 (*see Tour 1c*).

At 22.7 *m.* is a junction with County 619.

1. Left here to County 618, 0.9 *m.*, and R. to BERMUDA HUNDRED, 4.2 *m.*, now a group of fisher-folks' shacks lining dusty roads. When the English settled at Jamestown, Opussoquionuske, the Indian woman who reigned over a village here, received her white visitors in regal state. In retaliation for an attack on the colonists, Captain George Percy drove the Indians from the town in 1611. Two years later the Bermuda Hundred settlement was effected, the name having been derived 'by reason of the strength of the situation' and a fancied similarity to Bermuda. Governor Dale assigned about 300 indentured men the task of building 'a commodious habitation and seat for the English.' Bermuda Hundred was long an important shipping point.

2. Right on County 619 to County 617, 1 *m.* Just south of this junction is the SITE OF POINT OF ROCKS, once the seat of the plantation granted in 1642 to Peter Batte. Henry Stratton, who acquired it from the Batte heirs, was the owner of ships that traded with the West Indies. In 1864 General B.F.Butler built a pontoon bridge here across the James and over it sent General A.V.Kautz's cavalry and other troops to attack Petersburg June 9, 1864.

Adjoining Point of Rocks to the west are the lands of COBBS, early home of the Bolling family. John Bolling, who settled here toward the end of the seventeenth century, was the son of Colonel Robert Bolling and Jane Rolfe, daughter of Thomas Rolfe and granddaughter of Pocahontas. This Colonel Bolling prospered mightily through trade with the whites and with the Indians, and 'partook freely at the same time of all the pleasures of society, for which his gay and lively spirit eminently fitted him.'

Congenital deafness manifested itself in the Bolling line. Thomas Bolling had three deaf children whom he sent to a school in Scotland conducted by Thomas Braidwood. William Bolling, another son of Thomas and heir of Cobbs, had a son, William Albert, who was born deaf. Hearing that John Braidwood, a grandson of the distinguished Scotch teacher, had come to America, he sent for him and started a school for his own son and other afflicted children. Soon, however, Mr. Braidwood 'fell into bad habits, contracted large debts with merchants of Petersburg, and suddenly fled to the North.' Returning to Richmond in 1818, 'friendless, penniless, and almost naked,' he applied to William Bolling for aid. When six or seven pupils, including William Albert, were turned over to him, he managed to conduct himself in exemplary manner for some months before his old habits gripped him again. 'Braidwood finally fell to be a barkeeper in a tavern, where he died a victim to the bottle, in 1819 or 1820.' The State took over the work in 1838 with the establishment of its school for the deaf (*see Staunton*).

On December 22, 1935, a bus plunged through the open draw of the APPOMATTOX RIVER DRAWBRIDGE, 25 *m.*, and carried to death 14 occupants, only one surviving.

HOPEWELL, 25.8 *m.* (41 alt., 11,327 pop.), the youngest of Virginia cities but one of the oldest Virginia communities, has broad streets but many of its houses show that they were built in haste during the boom days. At the outskirts, lanes wind to old houses that stand aloof to the inroads of progress. Hopewell owes its origin and its recent development to its position at the confluence of the two rivers, for ocean-going vessels can reach its harbor on the James and smaller vessels can run up the Appomattox to Petersburg.

City Point, now part of Hopewell, first lay within Bermuda City (renamed Charles Hundred), a plantation laid out by Sir Thomas Dale in 1613. In 1619, when the four 'corporacouns' were formed, City Point was one of the hundreds in the Charles City Corporation. Its first designation, Bermuda City, was changed to Charles City, lengthened to Charles City Point, and later abbreviated to City Point. But on March 22, 1622 (N.S.), its population was almost entirely wiped out during the Indian attack and the city did not materialize for many years. However, the deep waters off shore served the cities of Petersburg and Richmond as a harbor and in both the Revolution and the War between the States it witnessed naval and military maneuvers.

Hopewell is a city that munitions built. After the E.I. du Pont de Nemours Company erected its munitions plant on Hopewell Farm in 1913, the city was born. Incorporated July 1, 1916, it had during America's participation in the World War a population of approximately 40,000, augmented from time to time by soldiers from Camp Lee, five miles away, who came to Hopewell on their days of leave. Houses for workers went up overnight; large and small businesses prospered. After the lull that followed the signing of the Armistice, steady growth began with the coming of peacetime industries.

Now factories stretch far and wide within and beyond its corporate limits, and the air is filled with both profitable odors and sulphuric smoke. Several huge mills produce kraft and synthetic textiles, and an enormous plant lives off air, using the synthetic ammonia process for the fixation of the inactive nitrogen in the atmosphere. Other products of Hopewell are pottery, car liners and doors, insect sprays, sheet metal, machine equipment, and building supplies.

Probably the most illustrious son of Hopewell was John Randolph of Roanoke (1773–1833), the site of whose birthplace, Cawsons, is within the limits of the new city. William Randolph of 'Turkey Island' was his great-grandfather; John Randolph (1742–75), his father; and Frances, daughter of Theodoric Bland,Sr. (whose home Cawsons was) and sister of Theodoric Bland,Jr. (1742–90), was his mother. Soon after his father's death Mrs.Randolph married St.George Tucker (*see Williamsburg*), amiable and brilliant scholar of law, whose influence was of first importance in molding his stepson's mind. After attending private school and the College of William and Mary, Princeton, and Columbia intermittently, he studied law. In 1810 he moved permanently to Charlotte County (*see Tour 3e*).

APPOMATTOX MANOR, end of Cedar Lane, on the curved shore of the Appomattox River, is a rambling T-shaped frame house representative of several architectural eras. Surrounded by spreading trees and ancient garden, it has successfully maintained its air of detachment from the city at its gates. The section that is the stem of the T, a story-and-a-half in height, with peaked roof and small dormers, antedates the larger section, which is now the front of the house and across which extends a veranda embellished with iron fretwork. Shell holes in the chimneys and grass-covered breastworks beyond the garden are reminders that the manor, on an exposed river front, was in a perilous situation during two wars.

The older part of the house, though built in the middle of the eighteenth century, is believed to incorporate timbers of a house built not long after 1635, when Captain Francis Eppes received the plantation for transporting himself, three sons, and 30 servants to the colony. During the Revolution British soldiers set fire to the house and trampled the lovely garden. Slaves put out the flames, however, and the garden was restored. The house was shelled by Federal gunboats and later General Grant had his headquarters here during the siege of Petersburg. The garden, much more beautiful than ever because of the seeds and cuttings that had been brought from abroad, was again destroyed. The house was later restored, the garden replanted and replanned with a Confederate rampart as one of its enclosures.

CITY POINT HOUSE, E. side Prince Henry St., facing Maplewood Ave., a gray, two-story weatherboarded building, with outside chimneys and a low wing, was built before the middle of the eighteenth century as a stage stop.

The SITE OF THE PROPOSED EAST INDIA SCHOOL, Pierce St., overlooking the James, is in the old part of Hopewell. In 1621, while the *Royal James*, of the fleet captained by Martin Pring, lay at anchor off the Cape of Good Hope, the Reverend Patrick Copeland chaplain of the *Royal James*, whom Dale had interested in the Virginia Colony, gathered from the 'gentlemen and marriners' aboard the sum of £70. 8*s*. 6*d*. to be used for the benefit of the English Colony in North America. The committee appointed to handle the money later decided that the sum should be used for the building of a school at Charles City. An unknown benefactor brought the contribution to an even £100. The Virginia Company ratified the action of the committee and set aside 1,000 acres for the school. At the next Quarter Court, February 9, 1622, a 'person, not willing as yet to be knowne' sent £25 in gold 'to helpe forward the East Indie Schoole'; and 'the gentlemen and mariners that lately came from the East Indies in two ships called the Hart and the Roe-Bucke . . . gave toward the building of the aforesaid free-schoole in Virginia the summe of £66, 13*s*, 4*d*.' In March 1622, the court appointed a Mr.Dike as usher and agreed to furnish free text books to the students. But the massacre of 1622 put an end to the plans. Consequently, the proposed school, designed for 'the education of children and grounding them in the principles of religion, civility of life and humane learning,' suffered the same fate that overtook the proposed university at Henricopolis (*see Tour 1c*), upon which 'it should have dependence.'

1. Right from Randolph St. (State 10) on Broadway in Hopewell to Crescent Ave. and L. to County 648, 2.3 *m.*; R. here to County 645, 2.6 *m.*, and R. to (R) a U.S. REFORMATORY, 4.7 *m.*

Within the grounds is the story-and-a-half JOHN BUREN HOUSE, built on part of the Bolling estate. Wainscoting and other details place its construction at the beginning of the eighteenth century. Here also is the SITE OF FORT CONVERSE, used by the Union forces during the War between the States. Besieging Petersburg, General Butler stationed Negro troops here to protect his pontoon bridges.

2. Right from Randolph St. on Broadway to Main St.; L. on Main St. to State 36, 1.7 *m.*; R. here to County 648, 3.4 *m.*, and R. 0.2 *m.* to CEDAR LEVEL (L), a neglected weatherboarded, story-and-a-half house, with dormers on a roof that extends over porches, front and rear. At each end are two massive chimneys. Heavy oak timbers, paneled doors, and wainscoting are other features. Cedar Level was the home of Robert Bolling (1682–1749), a surveyor and a son of the builder of Kippax (*see below*).

It was once Halfway House, a tavern on the City Point—Petersburg stage route.

On County 648 at 0.6 *m.* is the entrance to KIPPAX (R), a two-story frame house, with massive chimneys, and an ell. It stands on the site of the home of Jane Rolfe, wife of Robert Bolling, daughter of Thomas Rolfe and Jane Poythress, and granddaughter of John Rolfe and Pocahontas. Robert Bolling (1646–1709) came to Virginia at the age of 15. Jane Rolfe died the year after her marriage, leaving one son, Major John Bolling (1676–1729). Both she and her father are buried here. Mrs.Edith Bolling Galt Wilson, second wife of Woodrow Wilson, is a descendant of Jane Rolfe's son, John.

At 29.7 *m.* on State 10 is a junction with State 36.

Left here to HOPEWELL AIRPORT (R), 1.6 *m.*, on land settled in 1619 by Samuel Jordan, who built his house on this point jutting into the James River and still bearing his name. When Jordan died in 1623 he left a charming widow, Cecily, the first Virginia woman whose coquetry is a matter of record. Upon two of her suitors, the Reverend Greville Pooley and William Farrar, owner of Farrar's Island near by, she practiced her wiles so effectively as to cause the governor and council to issue a proclamation against women who engage themselves 'to two several men at the same time.' The Reverend Mr.Pooley, moreover, sued pretty Cecily for breach of promise, the first such suit in English America. The council, hearing the case, was divided. Then Cecily married Mr.Farrar and put an end to the matter. Pooley soon married another woman, and lived happily or unhappily till both he and his wife were killed by Indians.

At 2 *m.* is the HOPEWELL-CHARLES CITY FERRY (*see Tour* 24) (***hourly service between 7 a.m. and 7 p.m.; car and driver 65¢, round trip $1, extra passenger 20¢, round trip 30¢***).

At 32 *m.* on State 10 is a junction with County 641.

1. Right here to MERCHANT'S HOPE CHURCH (R), 0.5 *m.*, a gaunt rectangular brick structure, its floor still paved with the original flagstones. Because a crown was found engraved on one of these, it is believed that the stones were brought from England. Though the interior has been greatly altered, an old Bible remains, declared by experts to be a New Testament of 1639 appended to the Old Testament of 1640. The year 1657, cut in one of the huge rafters of the barrel vaulted roof, has been considered the date of construction, though the design does not belong to such an early period. Merchant's Hope, a church of Martin's Brandon Parish, was named for a grant made in 1635 to the owners of a barque, *The Merchant's Hope*, in the transatlantic trade. Richard Quiney, brother of Thomas Quiney, who married Shakespeare's daughter Judith, later owned the land. The Reverend Mr.Peter Fontaine, who came to Virginia in 1716, was a rector of Martin's Brandon Parish, Weyanoke Parish, and Wallingford Parish, and, in order to discharge his pastoral duties, must have spent most of his time crossing the river.

2. Left from State 10 on County 641 to a dirt road, 0.3 *m.*; L. here 0.6 *m.* to TAR BAY HOUSE (R), on a tree-shaded lawn with gardens terraced toward a bend in the

river. Daniel Colley built the two-story brick house in the first half of the eighteenth century and named it for his home in England.

The dirt road continues to BEECHWOOD (L), 0.9 *m.*, almost demolished during the War between the States and subsequently restored. Situated on an eminence, it is surrounded by a sweeping lawn. This plantation was the home of Edmund Ruffin, whose writings on agriculture and experiments in scientific farming were the means of reclaiming impoverished lands in Virginia and who fired the first gun at Fort Sumter. Federal gunboats, cannonading along the river, took pot shots at the home of the man who was connected with the beginning of hostilities. On the hillsides are remnants of the marl beds that played a major role in Edmund Ruffin's efforts to redeem the Tidewater soil. Here Ruffin wrote many of the articles that might have revolutionized farming throughout the South. His later years were spent at Marlbourne (*see Tour 20a*).

On County 641, at 1.5 *m.*, is the junction with another dirt road; L. here 2 *m.* to COGGIN'S POINT, where piles of bricks, a burying ground, and flowers and shrubbery mark the site of a house in which lived George Ruffin, the father of Edmund Ruffin. The Ruffin estate once covered more than 1,300 acres. From this point on January 10, 1781, Baron von Steuben observed Benedict Arnold retreating down the James after his raid on Richmond. On July 31, 1862, from the same place, General D.H.Hill bombarded the camp of General McClellan on the north bank of the river.

At GARYSVILLE (25 pop.), 34.5 *m.*, the RUINS OF GARY'S MILL and two old houses beyond the creek constitute the only evidence of the community's antiquity. The mill was built in the middle of the seventeenth century. Powell's Creek, at the edge of the scattered settlement, gives nominal honor to Nathaniel Powell, acting governor of the colony in 1619.

At 34.9 *m.* is a junction with County 639.

Left here to County 640, 2.1 *m.* and L. 1.3 *m.* to MAYCOCK PLANTATION. Near the river are breastworks thrown up during the War between the States. Samuel Maycock (or Maycox), one of the settlers slain in the Indian uprising of 1622, patented the land in 1618. It was bought in 1774 by David Meade, of whose garden a commentator reported, 'Forest and fruit trees are here arranged as if nature and art had conspired together to strike the eye most agreeably.' From the jutting point of the plantation Cornwallis crossed the James, on May 24, 1781, advancing northward in pursuit of La Fayette.

On County 639 is FLOWER DE HUNDRED, 4.1 *m.*, on an elevation above vestiges of terraced lawns and gardens. This frame plantation house, despite many years of neglect, has not lost its quiet charm. A two-storied central section with end chimneys is flanked by matching wings. In 1618 Sir George Yeardley patented and named the plantation and on it in 1621 built the first American windmill.

In 1862 to prevent the landing of Northern troops on the south side of the James, the Confederate Government ordered the burning of the new wharf here. In 1864, when General Grant crossed the river here, soldiers trampled standing corn, camped in fields and on the lawns, and destroyed woodwork and old furniture in the house; one of them gaily marched off wearing the bridal veil of a newly married daughter of the house.

BURROWSVILLE, 40 *m.*, has allowed filling stations and general stores to obscure its few old homes.

Left from Burrowsville on County 616 to the SITE OF FORT POWHATAN and HOOD'S FORT, 4.9 *m.*, on a high bluff above the James. Still visible are the piles of an early wharf and earthworks of the fortifications. This place at which tobacco was received, inspected, and shipped began its military career on September 13, 1776, when the Council of Virginia ordered the 'whole amount of cargoes of salt, medicines, clothing for the Army . . . also 90 hogshead of tobacco and 900 barrels of flour to be stored at Hood's' and had fortifications thrown up for their protection. With the outbreak of the War of 1812 the fortifications were strengthened. Toward the end of the War between the States the point was occupied by a regiment of Negro troops under command of General E.A.Wilde.

At 40.6 *m.* on State 10 is a junction with County 611.

Left here to BRANDON CHURCH (L), 0.2 *m.*; a nineteenth-century successor to the church in the part of Weyanoke Parish that in 1720 was added to Martin's Brandon Parish.

On County 611 is a junction with County 600, 1.2 *m.*: L. here 5.6 *m.* to UPPER BRANDON (L), on a slope above the James River. Boxwood in untutored growth surrounds the house, and the lawn is shaded by enormous willow oaks, ashes, and magnolias. Like its older neighbor, Brandon (*see below*), the red brick house differs in design from other plantation homes in Virginia, and resembles those of early Maryland. A two-story central unit, with one-story wings and square portico, is linked with separate two-story buildings on high basements.

Here are portraits of Maria Byrd by Charles Bridges, and of Martha Blount, reputedly the sweetheart of the misogynistic Alexander Pope.

The estate is part of the original Brandon grant. William Byrd Harrison, the son of Benjamin Harrison of Brandon and Evelyn Taylor Byrd—niece of the beautiful Evelyn whose ghost still lingers at Westover (*see Tour* 24)—built the house early in the nineteenth century. Along with Ruffin, Harrison was a pioneer in the use of lime to counteract the acidity of impoverished lands.

On County 611 is BRANDON, 5.7 *m.*, among old trees, high above a broad expanse of the river. The house looks toward the river through a vista bordered by a formal garden, outlined by dwarf boxwood that has grown to gigantic proportions. In one garden, faithfully preserved, are ancient cucumber trees, yews, and a pecan more than 300 years old and 30 feet in girth.

The house, measuring 210 feet from end to end, consists of a central unit two stories high and flanked by one story wings, connected with separate two-story rectangular buildings by hyphens. On the one-story porch are four fluted Corinthian columns. A large pineapple, symbolizing hospitality, caps the peak of the hip roof. A hall, from which rises a graceful stairway, separates the living room and the dining room. The mahogany balustrade is decorated with shell carvings, and the rooms of this unit are trimmed with carved paneling. Exquisite simplicity is the dominant characteristic of Brandon.

This land was patented in 1616 by John Martin and subsequently, with Merchant's Hope, came under the joint ownership of Quiney and Sadler, brothers-in-law. Quiney's moiety passed to his son Thomas, and then to Thomas's great-nephew, Robert Richardson. By 1720 the property was in the hands of Nathaniel Harrison. The oldest part of the house, the east wing, was built in the first half of the eighteenth century. The main section shows the influence of Thomas Jefferson. British ships fired on the house in 1776, and Federal forces in the 1860's burned outbuildings and tore away wainscoting.

CABIN POINT, 44 *m.*, a cluster of houses and filling stations, is the 'Cabin Poynt' of commercial importance as early as 1639. In 1753 a town called Guilford was laid out here by John Cocke. In time it became a crossroads stage stop.

SPRING GROVE at 47.9 *m.* is a few stores and scattered houses.

Left here on State 40 to County 610, 0.3 *m.*, and R. 4 *m.* to FLOOD HOUSE (L), a tiny frame structure in poor condition, on land that John Flood patented before 1639. In October 1646 it was enacted 'that Captain John ffloud be interpreter for the collony and that for his service therein and transporting such Indians as shall be employed from tyme to tyme to the Gov'r in message or otherwise, he be allowed from the publique the salary of four thousand pounds of tobacco yearly.'

On County 610, at 4.6 *m.*, is the entrance to EASTOVER (L), a weatherboarded house with one unit built in the late seventeenth century by George Jordan on a part of the Pipsico Plantation.

FOUR MILE TREE (L), 7.6 *m.*, on land by the river, is a story-and-a-half house with hipped gambrel roof. In an ancient graveyard here is a blackened granite slab inscribed: 'Here lyeth buried Alyce Myles, daughter of John Myles of Branton near Herreford Gent: and late wife of Mr.George Jordan in Virginia, who departed this life the 7th of January 1650. She touched the soil of Virginia with her little foot and the wilderness became a home.'

The plantation received its name from a tree that in 1619 marked the western limit of the Jamestown corporation.

At 8.6 *m.* is the entrance to MOUNT PLEASANT (L), a two-story brick house above a garden with massive boxwood. The house, once burned, was rebuilt within its original walls. The land here and much more was included in a grant made in 1620 to Richard Pace and known as Pace's Paines. With Pace lived a converted Indian by the name of Chanco, who, in 1622, learning of Opechancanough's plan to murder all white settlers, revealed the plot to his patron. Pace provided for the safety of his family and 'before day rowed to Jamestowne, and told the Governor of it.' According to Captain John Smith, thousands were saved 'by this one converted Infidel.'

The entrance to SWANN'S POINT is at 9.5 *m.* Here an isosceles triangle commands a near view of Jamestown across the water and a far view of the James. A new house has been built here. A lane (L) leads to the GRAVE OF COLONEL THOMAS SWANN, 'who departed this Life Ye 16th Day of September in Ye Yeare of our Lord God 1680.'

During the War between the States the Federals established a telegraph line at the Point.

On State 40 CLAREMONT, 5 *m.* (434 pop.), is a leisurely village by the James, with modern homes in striking contrast to exquisite Claremont Manor. A granite marker in a circle near the water front commemorates the landing here on May 5, 1607, of English settlers. Prior to white settlement, the Quioughconock had a village here.

At the edge of the village is CLAREMONT MANOR, amid gardens that slope toward the curving James. Old trees, among which are giant magnolias, frame a garden outlined by dwarf boxwood whose size belies its name. Between the river and the house stretches a lane bordered by linden trees. The story-and-a-half main section of the house has five dormers in its gabled roof. The square central hall, from which the stairway rises, opens into large rooms. An ell stretching rearward also has dormers and a central chimney. Mantels, elegantly simple, carved woodwork and paneling, and a double-landing stairway are important architectural features. Close by are the bake house, loom house and other buildings essential to old plantation economy.

In 1632 Arthur Allen, who is said to have come to America because of a turbulent love affair, patented vast tracts of land in the present county of Surry and in 1649 the Claremont estate. In 1655 he built in lower Surry County a house that is now called Bacon's Castle (*see below*). It is believed that construction of Claremont Manor was started in the middle of the seventeenth century and that additions were made during the following decades. Claremont Manor, like its neighbors along the river, suffered at the hands of pillaging Federal forces.

From Claremont is a FERRY TO SANDY POINT (*see Tour* 24). (*Hourly service from* 6:45 *a.m. to* 7:45 *p.m.; from April* 15 *to Nov.* 1, *half-hourly service between* 9 *a.m. and* 7 *p.m.; car and driver* 80¢, *round trip* $1.00, *each additional passenger* 20¢, *round trip* 30¢, *other passengers* 25¢).

THE GLEBE (L), 52.1 *m.*, is a brick story-and-a-half house, on a high basement. Almost flat against the gambrel roof are three small dormers. In 1724 John Cargill reported to the Bishop of London that his house, an earlier one, was in such poor condition that it would be necessary for him to 'look for a house elsewhere.' Doubtless remedial measures caused the building of this house, which served a parish constituted in 1642 as Chippoakes and in 1647 renamed Southwark.

SURRY, 56.8 *m.* (243 pop.), seat of Surry County, an agreeable village that, holding to its past, has reluctantly accepted such modern innovations as electricity, filling stations, and water works. Along shaded streets old houses of diversified design merge in the modern pattern. The village was called the Cross Roads, McIntosh's Cross Roads, Scuffletown, and Smithville before it settled down to its courthouse town designation.

The SITE OF THE SURRY INN, at the crossroads, is occupied by a filling station. Here in early days stagecoaches changed horses and travelers stopped for the night. In 1782 Robert McIntosh, the tavern keeper, was hauled to court for failing to keep his liquor prices posted. Revolutionary officers and soldiers slept beneath this roof, and officers in the War of 1812 stopped here on their way to Norfolk.

The SURRY COUNTY COURTHOUSE, a modern brick building with a shallow, Ionic portico, was completed in 1923. In 1797 the county seat was moved here from Troopers, where it had been established in 1754, following its removal from Ware Neck, and the courthouse was built on land presented the county by Robert McIntosh and wife, March 23, 1796, 'in consideration for the friendly respect and attachment which they have for the said county.' In 1652 Surry had been cut off from James City County. The oldest building in the square is the CLERK'S OFFICE, a simple oblong brick structure, erected in 1825–26; the chimneys at its gable ends are ivy-covered. The CONFEDERATE MONUMENT differs somewhat from its fellows in that the soldier atop the granite shaft rests peacefully against his bent saber. THE MONUMENT TO CHANCO is a block of rough granite in which is embedded a bronze plaque commemorating the services of the Indian who saved many colonists in 1622.

Left from Surry on State 31 to the ROLFE [WARREN] HOUSE (L), 1.8 *m.* (*open* 9–5 *daily; adm.* 25¢), a charming story-and-a-half brick house, with a central hall opening, upstairs and down, into a room on each side. In the basement, an end chimney serves a huge fireplace. The mantels, wainscoting, and balustrades are exquisitely carved, and the walls are painted the true Colonial blue, which much scraping revealed beneath coats of many colors. Though long neglected, the house had suffered so little that in the restoration nothing of importance had to be replaced.

The house stands on property that was a gift from Powhatan or Opechancanough, either to John Rolfe or to Thomas Rolfe. By deed dated June 10, 1654, Thomas Rolfe conveyed to William Corker 'one hundred & fivety Acres of land in Surry County lyeing betweene Smith's fort old feild & the Divill's Woodyard Swampe . . . being due unto the said Rolfe by Guift from the Indyan King.' A suit recorded in 1677 fixes the construction date for the house as 1651 or 1652. Deponents stated that Thomas Rolfe was commonly on the place 'before & after & whilst ye said house was building.'

This only son of Pocahontas and John Rolfe had remained in England after the death of his mother in 1617 and was reared in London. He returned to America in early manhood and married Jane Poythress. Through an only daughter, Jane, the prolific line was established.

Near the house is a remnant of Smith's Fort, erected in 1609 and called on John Smith's map 'The New Fort.' In Early Colonial days a public landing here accommodated the usual warehouses.

On State 31 is a junction with County 637, 4.1 *m.*; R. here 1 *m.* to PLEASANT POINT (L), a frame house with brick ends, much like the Rolfe House. From its terraced slope it commands a far view of Hog Island and the shores of the James. The house was undoubtedly built before the end of the seventeenth century. Here the Confederates established one of their many signal stations on the James River.

On State 31 is old SCOTLAND WHARF, terminus of the JAMESTOWN (*see Tour 8A*) and SCOTLAND FERRY, 4.2 *m.* (*hourly service from* 6:45 *a.m. to* 8:45 *p.m.*; *from April* 15 *to Nov.* 1 *half-hourly service between* 9 *a.m. and* 7 *p.m.*; *Sun. and holidays extra service at* 10 *p.m. and* 11 *p.m.; car and driver* 80¢, *round trip* $1.00, *each additional passenger* 20¢, *round trip* 30¢, *other passengers* 25¢).

At 61.3 *m.* on State 10 is County 633.

Left here to RICH NECK (L), 1 *m.*, with a story-and-a-half above a high basement. Set almost flush with its steep gambrel roof are five dormers. The walls are sandy pink against the dark green of encircling boxwood, on a lawn sloping riverward. The house was built by Robert Ruffin, son of William Ruffin, the immigrant who settled in Isle of Wight County, and great-great-great-grandfather of Edmund Ruffin (*see above*). The house was the seat of the tract in Lawne's Creek Parish acquired by Robert Ruffin in 1685.

Construction of CHIPPOKES, 3.5 *m.*, a commodious house named for an Indian Chief, was started before the War between the States and completed immediately thereafter. Close to the river stands the first Chippokes, simpler and much lovelier than its imposing descendant. It was built to conform with the early pattern that involved a river view, beaded weatherboarding, end chimneys, and dormers. On the plantation are slave houses that bear testimony, in their comfortable and well-designed simplicity, to the *ante-bellum* prosperity of the plantation.

The RUINS OF LAWNE'S CREEK CHURCH (L), 63.2 *m.*, are roofless, vine-covered walls pierced by arched windows. Within, trees are growing above a carpet of ivy and periwinkle. Lawne's Creek Parish, created in 1639, became extinct in 1738. During Reconstruction days the church was set on fire by Negroes, who had used its cemetery and were loath to relinquish their occupancy when white people attempted to regain possession.

At 63.5 *m.* is a junction with County 630.

Left here 0.4 *m.* to (L) BACON'S CASTLE (*open daily, adm.* 25¢) at the end of a wide avenue of ancient maples. The west end, marred only by a small frame extension by the chimney, is now the most distinguished part. On the warm red brick front façade is a two-story gabled vestibule, a projection matched in the rear by a gable stairtower, giving the structure a cruciform floor plan. The steep, medieval gable end with the stepped and curved parapet, typical of Tudor and Jacobean architecture, is centered by three tall, slender, clustered stacks with molded tops. The thick walls of the first story are cut by doors and windows with segmentally arched brick heads. Although half obliterated, the brick enframements of the second story windows still suggest architraves, and in spite of neglect, the interior, with deep window seats, low ceilings, and oaken beams, still suggests the period of construction. The plain paneling is of later era.

Bacon's Castle, built by Arthur Allen about 1655, was first called Allen's Brick House. Nathaniel Bacon, the rebel leader, never lived at the house that now bears his name; the 'castle' was seized in 1676 by William Rookings, Robert Burgess, and Arthur Long, his followers, and became a rebel stronghold. Depositions filed in 1677 record that 'Arthur Allen was by the late wicked Rebels forbid from his house.'

On County 630 at 5 *m.* is HOG ISLAND, so named because for many years after 1608 the colonists kept their hogs here. A garrison warned the settlers of approaching enemies. It is said that the keepers of the hogs did wood carving in their spare time and that the delicate tracery in wainscoting, balustrades, and mantels of many early houses was their handiwork. In 1610, when the colonists were abandoning Jamestown (*see Tour 8A*), they stopped here. During the War between the States the island was a Confederate signal station.

At 68.7 *m.* on State 10 is a junction with County 621.

Left here to BURWELL'S BAY, 0.4 *m.*, frequented by swimming parties, picnickers, and amateur fishermen. The river, wide and deep, has a sandy beach. In the curve, popularly called a bay, was the Warrascoyack village where in 1608 Captain John Smith got corn for the starving colonists across the river.

At SHOAL BAY (L), 70 *m.*, a modern house surrounded by boxwood and crepe myrtle, is a smokehouse and a two-story brick kitchen belonging to the early seat of the estate granted to Edward Bennet in 1621 and later owned by Dr.Richard Cocke, who scandalized the neighborhood by his lack of piety. He went so far as to tear down a church and use the bricks from its walls to build this kitchen and the wood from its chancel and pulpit for partitions in a barn—which on the very day it was finished was struck by lightning. In spite of Federal bombardment, the house survived, only to be destroyed by fire much later.

At 70.3 *m.* is a junction with County 677.

Right here to WRENN'S MILL (R), 1 *m.*, still grinding meal after the manner it adopted 300 years ago. One of the original stones continues in use; the brick foundations are unchanged; and the miller does his work on shares and not for money.

Waterground meal from mills such as this—and many remain to fill the demand—is the stuff from which Virginia cornbread is made. Along State 10, spoon bread is found at its best. The delectable concoction is made by scalding white meal with boiling water, cooking it into a smooth mush, and then adding generous quantities of eggs and milk and shortening, salt, and baking powder. The mixture is baked slowly in a deep dish for about 45 minutes. The bread, encased by its crispy crust, is so soft that it must be eaten with a spoon.

George Hardy built the mill, first called Hardy's Mill and known to have been standing in 1646. The name of the mill was changed when the Wrenns came into possession of Hardy's land.

At 71.4 *m.* on State 10 is a junction with County 673.

Left here to FORT BOYKIN (L), 2.5 *m.*, on a bluff commanding two bends in the James River. Beyond swinging gates are an undulating lawn, old oak and black walnut trees, mulberries and tulip poplars, and a garden, fragrant and varicolored. Within a 16-acre enclosure are earthworks, now grass-covered, that form the seven points of a star; a gun emplacement, almost hidden; and an ivy-covered earthen bank that was once a bomb-proof magazine. A small fort was built here during the War of 1812, probably on the site of fortifications thrown up during the Revolution. During the War between the States the fort was enlarged. The poet, Sidney Lanier, while stationed here in 1863, played his flute on the ramparts by the moonlight, wrote home of glorious nights and beautiful Virginia girls, composed one of his first poems, and started his war novel *Tiger Lilies*.

MORGART'S BEACH, 3.4 *m.*, is a resort on the James. Roundabout are groves of Japanese persimmon trees.

SMITHFIELD, 74.9 *m.* (1,179 pop.), on Pagan's Creek, is the home of the Smithfield ham. Colonial houses stand beside those of the most ornate Victorian era and others of the early twentieth century yet, withal, the town has maintained its air of ancient tranquility.

A tobacco warehouse was here in 1633 and in the eighteenth century the place was the seat of Isle of Wight County. First known commercially as a point from which tobacco was shipped to foreign ports, Smithfield is now famed principally for its hams, though it also cleans and ships peanuts. From the Indians here the first settlers learned the process of curing the meat of razorback hogs. In the eighteenth century Mallory Todd perfected the primitive technique. According to an invoice, Mallory Todd, founder of E.M.Todd & Co., was shipping hams to the West Indies in 1779. The best of the hams come from the hog that is allowed to roam through the woods and fields in the spring and summer and thus grow strong and lean. In the fall he is turned into fields from which the major part of the peanut crop has been taken but where enough has been left to fatten him. After the killing, hams are packed in salt, then subjected to a slow smoking above smoldering hickory fires. Afterward they are stored for at least a year, though the thicker the mold the more the connoisseur is pleased. In and around Smithfield real 'Virginia hams' are procurable. Local cooks advise that hams be boiled 20 minutes to the pound, allowed to cool, be skinned, baked, and, for serving, sliced to paper thinness. The experts disdain coatings of brown sugar, cloves, and dressings of wine. Well-cured and cooked, Smithfield ham is deep red, with the fat translucent amber. In Smithfield are preserved orders from Windsor Castle for hams that were sent to Queen Victoria.

The OLD COURTHOUSE OF ISLE OF WIGHT COUNTY, NE. corner Main and Mason Sts., is a two-story brick building, now covered with plaster. This building was used from 1750 to 1800 for the legal business of the county. The OLD CLERK'S OFFICE, adjoining the former courthouse, is an ivy-covered cottage, now a beauty salon. The OLD COUNTY JAIL, the corner of Mason St., is a red brick building that has been converted into a residence.

MASONIC HALL, East Mason St., a two-story gabled building painted gray, houses Union Lodge No. 18 of the Ancient, Free, and Accepted Order of Masons, chartered in October 1787. The following year meetings were held in a building that had housed a school for which Elizabeth Smith, wife of Arthur Smith II, had donated £125, but which had fallen into disuse because hatred of all things British caused resentment against Mrs. Smith's stipulation that the principal of the school be a clergyman of the Church of England.

WINDSOR CASTLE, off Church St., in a section of Smithfield known as Jericho, is a story-and-a-half stuccoed brick house with dormers. Its tree-shaded enclosure was once terraced to the water's edge. The wide center hall opens into four square rooms on each floor. Here lived Arthur Smith upon whose land Smithfield was built.

Right from Smithfield on State 158 to ISLE OF WIGHT, 13.9 *m.* (*see Tour* 18).

At 79.2 *m.* on State 10 is a junction with County 659.

Left here to ST. LUKE'S CHURCH (L), 0.1 *m.*, the Old Brick Church, as it was first known, in a quiet yard screened from the highway by a grove of large trees. The mellow red brick building is typical of early rural churches in England.

The massive square tower, which forms almost the whole front of the gabled nave, has a Norman character, especially in its broad, low, central portal beneath a round arch of brick. The quoined corners of brick and a rudimentary pediment just above the door are the only architectural suggestions of the classical influence. String courses of raised brick divide the tower into three stages, the second of which is pierced on each side by a round-arched window composed of two lancet openings divided by brick tracery. The highest stage is pierced by plain round-arched openings. The thick walls of the body of the church, laid in Flemish bond like the tower, are cut by round-arched, double-lancet windows, four to a side, between heavily graceful buttresses that break back thrice above the high water table. The steep roof is terminated at the back by a many-stepped gable in brick that helps to frame a 'great' window. The design of this opening is late Gothic, and the lights of its upper tier are lancet, but the two lower tiers, of four lights each, have round arches in pre-Gothic style. The furnishings of the restored interior, including pulpit and boxpews, have been copied from the simplest style common in England in the mid-seventeenth century.

Warrascoyack Parish was created in 1632 and a church was built almost at once, under the supervision of Joseph Bridger. Evidence from the oldest vestry book, Volume Two, that the cypress shingles, generally serviceable for a century, were replaced in 1737 and the discovery of a brick apparently marked 1632, buttress the strong local tradition that the present church is the first building. Yet a brick church comparable in size was not completed at Jamestown, the capital, until the 1650's. The present St.Luke's was probably built about the same time or shortly afterwards, as the style of the two churches was similar.

Neglected from 1777 to 1821 and abandoned again after 1830, the church lost its roof in a storm in 1887, when part of the east wall also fell. This damage awakened interest in the venerable edifice, and its restoration was begun the same year.

SUFFOLK, 94.5 *m.* (58 alt., 10,271 pop.) (*see Tour* 18), is at junctions with US 460 (*see Tour* 18) and US 58 (*see Tour 7a*), and State 32.

South of Suffolk State 10 passes through a trucking district of small fertile farms that stretch westward from the Dismal Swamp (*see Tour 6b*).

At 107.7 *m.* State 10 crosses the North Carolina Line, 9 miles north of Sunbury, N.C. (*see North Carolina Guide*).

Tour 20

Tappahannock—Richmond—Amelia—Burkeville—Halifax—Danville; 201.8 *m.* US 360.

Asphalt-paved throughout.
Southern Ry. parallels route between Richmond and Danville.
All types of accommodations in towns.

Southwest of the Rappahannock River US 360 traverses Tidewater lowlands and woodlands. West of Richmond it passes through the tobacco lands of the southside.

Section a. TAPPAHANNOCK to RICHMOND; 46.5 *m. US* 360.

This section of the highway, paralleling the early zigzag post road, is the main thoroughfare between the once-isolated Northern Neck and the State capital.

East of the Rappahannock US 360 belongs to the Northern Neck (*see Tour 16a*). In TAPPAHANNOCK, 0 *m.* (427 pop.) (*see Tour 6a*), on the western bank, US 360 meets US 17 (*see Tour 6a*), with which it unites to BRAY'S FORK, 2.4 *m.*, where US 360 swings R.

MILLER'S TAVERN, 9 *m.*, a hamlet named for an early stage station, is at a junction with County 620.

Right here to the SITE OF THE MATTAPONI VILLAGE, 3.9 *m.*, on Piscataway Creek. After the massacre of 1644, the Indians, driven from Pamunkey Neck, moved northward, settling here, where they lived peacefully until 1668.

MT.ZION CHURCH (L), 5.2 *m.*, built in 1854, a small brick rectangle, belonging to a congregation organized secretly March 13, 1774. Ministers at the first meeting—John Waller, John Shackleford, Robert Ware, and Ivison Lewis—were arrested and all except Lewis, who had not spoken, were thrown into jail. Near by at Piscataway, now called Dunbrooke, followers of Nathaniel Bacon clashed with supporters of Governor Berkeley in July 1676. After the fight Bacon's forces marched to the Pamunkey River, where their leader joined them.

ST.PAUL'S CHURCH (R), 10.1 *m.*, a small brick building, has a graceful, diamond-paned window above two doors with lintels. St.Paul's of South Farnham Parish was built in 1838 to replace a church destroyed about 1820.

At 14.3 *m.* is a junction with County 631.

Left here to SHEPHERD'S CHURCH (L), 0.3 *m.*, a simple brick structure built in 1859 by a Methodist congregation organized about 1790 at the home of William Shepherd.

ST.STEPHEN'S CHURCH, 16.3 *m.*, a crossroads community that has taken the name of a former church of St.Stephen's Parish, is at a junction with State 14 (*see Tour 1B*).

HOLLY HILL (L), 17.6 *m.*, is a tall brick L-shaped house built about 1810 by the Fauntleroys. Samuel Fauntleroy was the last person in this section to abandon his 'coach and four'; his arrival in high style at church was always an event.

AYLETTS, 18.9 *m.* (250 pop.), by the formerly navigable Mattaponi, was named for the Aylett family on whose land it was founded. Before the War between the States the town bristled with activity each Tuesday and Friday, when people of the countryside drove in to meet the stage, which brought the 'United States mail'—including newspapers. The lumbering stage, drawn by four horses, ran between Tappahannock and Richmond; on its 'boot' were trunks, and on its top packages and mail bags. 'Mail days' were shopping days and people brought their lunches with them. In 1856 Ayletts had a carriage factory, an iron foundry, tailoring and millinery shops, a tavern, harness and saddle-making plants, and a variety of stores.

MONTVILLE (L), 20 *m.*, an Aylett estate, was a home of Patrick Henry's daughter Elizabeth, who married Philip Aylett. William Aylett built twin frame houses here, one of them for Patrick Henry Aylett. That young man, supplied with two horses, a Negro, $500, and a gold watch that belonged to his grandfather Patrick Henry, went to practice law in Tennessee but returned to Virginia and became a prominent attorney.

At 21.4 *m.* is a junction with State 30.

Right here to County 639, 0.8 *m.*, and L. 0.2 *m.* to CAT-TAIL CHURCH (L), a simple low-pitched brick structure erected in 1751. Twin frame towers and outside flues designed as Gothic buttresses have been added and the walls have been covered with stucco. The church was first in St.Margaret's Parish, constituted in 1721, but subsequent changes placed it in St.David's. After the disestablishment, the building was used by other denominations. About 1850 Cat-Tail was given to Negro Baptists.

At 10.1 *m.* on State 30 is a junction with County 638; L. here 0.2 *m.* to MANGOHICK CHURCH (L), built in 1732 and starkly unornamented. Its walls rise to a steeply gabled roof. 'The new Brick church' that Colonel William Byrd passed in 1732 on his way to the mines was later given the name of an Indian tribe that had lived in the vicinity. Mangohick, first a church of St.Margaret's Parish, then of St.David's, was deserted by its communicants after the Revolution. In 1825 the Union Baptist Church was organized here, with both white and Negro members. In 1854 the white members moved to a new building.

At 15.5 *m.* on State 30 is a junction with State 2 (*see Tour 1A*).

CENTRAL GARAGE, 22.4 *m.*, is at a junction with State 30 (*see Tour 20A*).

At 24.6 *m.* is a junction with County 618.

Left here to FONTAINEBLEAU (L), 1.4 *m.*, where the foundations of the former 'great house,' destroyed in 1932, now form the enclosure of a garden. In the garden and about the grounds are figures of animals, fauns, and wood nymphs, the handiwork of a resident of the small brick house that remains. Her studio is an abandoned streetcar, gaily decorated.

Fontainebleau was the home of Colonel William Spotswood Fontaine (1810–82). He was a great-grandson and his wife was a granddaughter of Patrick Henry, a fact that helped save the *ante-bellum* house when Federal soldiers came here. The family had fled to a neighboring plantation. The furniture had been piled in the hall and saturated with kerosene, when a subordinate officer noticed a portrait of Patrick Henry and questioned the servants about it. Discovering that the house belonged to descendants of the Revolutionary hero, the officer ordered the soldiers away.

US 360 crosses the PAMUNKEY RIVER, 27.4 *m.*, a narrow winding stream fringed by dense woodlands and giant sycamores.

At 29 *m.* is a junction with County 605.

1. Left here to the SITE OF NEW CASTLE, 0.8 *m.*, on the bank of the Pamunkey. When seen by the Marquis de Chastellux the 'little capital' contained 'twenty-five or thirty houses, some of which are pretty enough.' The New Castle fairs were gala occasions, with 'Horse-Races and several other Diversions.' In 1737 subscribers proposed: 'that 20 Horses or Mares do run round a three-mile Course for a Prize of Five Pounds . . . that a Violin be played for by 20 Fiddlers; no person to have the liberty of playing unless he bring a fiddle with him; after the prize is won, they are all to play together and each a different tune, and to be treated by the company . . . that a Flag be flying on said Day 30 feet high; that a handsome Entertainment be provided for the subscribers and their wives; and such of them as are not so happy as to have wives may treat any other Lady; . . . that a Quire of Ballads be sung for by a number of Songsters, all of them to have liquor sufficient to clear their Wind-Pipes.'

At New Castle in May 1775 Patrick Henry assembled the Hanover County Militia to force Governor Dunmore to return the colony's powder taken from the Powder Horn.

2. Right from US 360 on County 605 to the SITE OF HANOVERTOWN (R), 3.9 *m.*, a few scattered houses. In 1751 this place, then called Page's Warehouse, missed by a few votes being made the State capital. John Blair, incensed because the prestige of Williamsburg was threatened, accused Speaker John Robinson of having been 'at the bottom of this hellish plot.' Page's Warehouse became a town, however, when, in 1762, the general assembly directed that 100 acres be laid off with streets and lots and be called Hanover.

Here the Virginia Militia assembled to await orders May 29, 1776. There was a hospital here during the Revolution, and at the wharves army ordnance was loaded and unloaded. After the Revolution British prisoners were kept here for several weeks, and did 'as they please—burnt three empty houses, all fences within half a mile of town, and most piling around their gardens.' Here, on May 27–28, 1864, Grant's army crossed the Pamunkey in his attempt to advance on Richmond.

SUMMER HILL (R), 4.9 *m.*, a frame house, was the home of Colonel William B. Newton of the Confederate army. Here General Grant stopped a few days in 1864 after crossing the river at Hanovertown. Finding the family ill and with little food, he sent them a wagonload of provisions from his headquarters at Cold Harbor. Two years before, Captain William Latané, killed at Linney's Corner, June 13, had been buried in the Summer Hill burial lot near the house. The funeral service was read by Mrs. Willoughby Newton of Westmoreland County, who was a refugee in Hanover. The incident inspired 'The Burial of Latané'—a painting by William D. Washington and a poem by John R. Thompson.

MARLBOURNE (L), at 30.7 *m.*, is the burial place and one time home of Edmund Ruffin (*see Tour* 19). The frame, two-story house, overlooking broad lowlands, has a two-story porch and one-story wings.

Moving to Marlbourne in 1843, Ruffin here developed fully his agricultural practices and received ample reward, monetary and honorary, for his incessant labors. He forsook experimental farming in 1855 to promote secession, and traveled through the South making fiery speeches. At Charleston he was allowed to fire the first shot on Sumter. Too old for military service, Ruffin retired to Marlbourne where he stayed until the approach of Union troops.

At 31.9 *m.* is a junction with County 606.

1. Left here to OLD CHURCH, 1.5 *m.*, an almost deserted village that was once a trading center. The tavern, no longer accommodating guests, is part brick and part frame with a two-story full length porch. Near by is the SITE OF THE OLD CHURCH, built in 1718 and rebuilt in 1753. The Reverend Patrick Henry, uncle of the orator, was rector for 40 years.

2. Right from US 360 on County 606 to LINNEY'S CORNER, 0.3 *m.* (*see Tour 1A*).

Southward, US 360 traverses battle grounds of the Seven Days' Campaign of 1862 and of the Cold Harbor Campaign of 1864. McClellan, advancing up the Peninsula in 1862, fought a drawn battle at Seven Pines (*see Tour 8a*) and one month later was defeated in a series of battles and forced to abandon his drive on Richmond.

After the fighting at the Wilderness and at Spotsylvania in May 1864, Grant moved toward Richmond. Finding the Confederates in a strategic position on the North Anna River, he swung eastward, then southward. Lee continued to parallel Grant, keeping always between Richmond and the Federal army. After lingering in this vicinity for three days, the armies moved to Cold Harbor.

The SITE OF BETHESDA CHURCH (L) is at 35.1 *m.* Among Brady's photographs of war scenes is one showing Grant and his staff seated on benches before the church.

REMNANTS OF BREASTWORKS (L), 35.7 *m.*, mark the advanced position of Ewell's Confederate Corps, preceding the Battle of Cold Harbor in 1864.

MECHANICSVILLE, 40 *m.* (100 pop.), is now a gathering of filling stations and brick barbecue stands but in *ante-bellum* days it had taverns, livery stables, and blacksmith shops, with hucksters' carts, farm wagons, and carriages about them—'the last stop' on the stage-route to Richmond. On the hill (R) is the wooden antenna tower of Radio Station WRVA.

Left here on State 156 to BEAVER DAM CREEK, 1.1 *m.*, along which on June 26, 1862, was fought the Battle of Mechanicsville, or Beaver Dam Creek. Following three weeks of Federal inactivity, during which Jackson had marched from the Valley to Richmond, Lee ordered an attack here on McClellan's right wing, under General Fitz-John Porter. Jackson and A.P.Hill, coming from the west, were to drive Porter from the town, thus opening the river bridge to Longstreet and D.H.Hill. Jackson delayed; A.P.Hill attacked prematurely; Porter fell back to his fortifications on this creek; and Longstreet and D.H.Hill, crossing, followed A.P.Hill. The battle lasted six hours, with no advantage to the Confederates. The following morning Porter abandoned his position and fell back to New Cold Harbor. Confederate losses were 1,350, Federal 361.

At 6.1 *m.* is a junction with a battlefield park road; R. here 0.5 *m.* to BOATSWAIN CREEK, across which, on June 27, 1862, was fought the Battle of Gaines' Mills, or New Cold Harbor. Porter had drawn up his corps on a hill to resist the advance of Lee's army. The Confederate attack, begun about 2 p.m., lacked co-ordination and until 7 had made little progress. About sundown Lee ordered a general advance without regard to connecting troops. Porter pushed back at dusk, crossed the river during the night and joined the main army. Federal losses were 6,837; Confederate 8,358.

Along State 156 is the BATTLEFIELD OF OLD COLD HARBOR with a contact station (*information; riding horses rented*) at 6.4 *m.* The field is within the Richmond National Battlefield Park; miles of trenches have been restored, and foot and bridle paths cross fields and earthworks. Farmlands here were the bloody ground of the 1862 campaign and of the Battle of Cold Harbor, June 3, 1864, when, outnumbering Lee's army two to one, the Federals made a concerted attempt to dislodge the Confederates from entrenchments. Though the assault lasted only 22 minutes, the Federal losses were more than 7,000 compared with a Confederate loss of less than 2,000. Sporadic firing continued for some days, but no further assault was made.

From this battlefield Lee sent Early's corps to the Valley and Grant sent Sheridan westward to tear up the Virginia Central Railroad (*see Tour* 9) and to join General David Hunter, approaching Lynchburg. On June 12 Grant moved eastward to Wilcox's Landing (*see Tour* 24).

At 14.8 *m.* on State 156 is a junction with US 60—at SEVEN PINES (*see Tour* 8*a*).

At 42.4 *m.* are REMAINS OF THE INTERMEDIATE LINE, breastworks built in the 1860's. Richmond's defense included 25 inner forts and batteries, this encircling earthwork, and a third or outer line.

RICHMOND, 46.5 *m.* (15 to 206 alt., 182,929 pop.) (*see Richmond*).

In Richmond are junctions with US 1 (*see Tour* 1*b*), State 2 (*see Tour* 1*A*), US 33 (*see Tour* 9), US 250 (*see Tour* 17*a*), State 6 (*see Tour* 23), US 60 (*see Tour* 8), State 10 (*see Tour* 19), and State 5 (*see Tour* 24).

Section b. RICHMOND to DANVILLE; 155.3 *m.* *US* 360.

Southwest of Richmond US 360 traverses a country of small farms and scattered villages with here and there a plantation established prior to the Revolution. In the middle section are scenes of the stirring events of the last tragic days of the Confederate army, as Lee's troops retreated westward from Petersburg. Near Danville bright leaf tobacco dominates country and village life; tobacco fields and curing barns are constantly in sight.

In RICHMOND, 0 *m.*, US 360 runs south on 14th St. to Hull St. and straight ahead on Hull St.

At 22.7 *m.* is a junction with County 605.

Left here to State 153, 4.9 *m.*, and R. to abandoned water-filled pits of the CLOVER HILL MINES, 5.7 *m.*, opened about 1840. These workings were in the Richmond coal basin, a low grade bituminous seam developed in 1770. As early as 1789 Richmond coal was shipped to Philadelphia.

State 153 becomes County 602, which continues to County 664, 6.4 *m.*; L. here to the mile-long entrance lane (L), 8.1 *m.*, of EPPINGTON, built in the 1730's. The two-and-a-half story central block of the house is flanked by one-story wings, designed with beautiful proportions. The walls of beaded weatherboard rise to a denticulated cornice under the eaves of a steep hip roof. Richard Eppes built the house on the plantation inherited from his father, Colonel Francis Eppes.

The crossroads settlement, SKINQUARTER, at 23.6 *m.*, was so named, according to the story, because Indians gathered at a spring close by after hunts to skin and quarter their game.

The highway dips to cross the Appomattox River at GOODE'S BRIDGE, 29.2 *m.* Near by in July 1781 General 'Mad Anthony' Wayne's Continentals took position to halt British troops, moving southward. On April 3, 1865, Hill's, Longstreet's, and Gordon's Corps of Lee's army crossed here in retreat from Petersburg.

At 36.7 *m.* is a junction with County 609.

Right here to ST. JOHN'S CHURCH (L), 3 *m.*, first called Grubhill Church. The little brick building among old trees is simple, with high pitched roof, tall chimneys, and arched windows holding small, diamond-shaped panes. Erected in 1855, it replaced a church built before 1768. One Sunday, at the outbreak of the Revolution the Reverend John Brunskill, rector of the parish, arose and, 'seeing men dressed in regimentals, called them rebels and expressed himself indignantly to see such indications of a general rebellion . . . Whereupon nearly everyone . . . got up and left the house, not before warning him, however, never to repeat such language or he would receive harsh treatment added to disrespect.' The Tory parson was not allowed to hold further services but retained the title of rector and lived at the glebe until his death in 1803, 'after a solitary and uncomfortable life.'

The SITE OF THE FOREST (R) is at 6.4 *m.* This was the birthplace of John Banister Tabb (1845–1909), who was 17 when war broke out in 1861. Barred from army service by poor eyesight, he enlisted as captain's clerk on the blockade-runner, *Robert E. Lee.* In 1884 he entered the Roman Catholic priesthood and was later a member of the faculty of St. Charles College in Maryland. His poems had much popularity in the South.

At 9.9 *m.*, by a junction with County 637, is a water-powered GRIST MILL (R) that has ground grain since about 1830. Left here 2 *m.* to THE WIGWAM (R), built by William B. Giles, congressman and governor of Virginia (1827–30). The frame house, now much dilapidated and marred by a late two-story porch, is T-shaped with deep, sloping roof pierced by dormers. The interior woodwork is richly carved.

AMELIA, 37.8 *m.* (333 alt., 887 pop.), seat and trading center of Amelia County, spreads small stores, filling stations, and warehouses along the highway. The green and shady Courthouse Square is bordered by a bank building, lawyers' offices, and small homes in flowery yards.

By the narrow margin of a few hours Amelia Courthouse escaped both a final battle in the War between the States, and the surrender. On April 4, 1865, Lee's harassed army arrived here on its retreat from Petersburg, failed to find expected provisions, and remained a day while foraging parties had frequent clashes with Federal cavalry and lost about 200 wagons. On the evening of the 5th, with Grant at Nottoway Courthouse blocking the route to Danville, Lee circled north then west. From Nottoway Courthouse on April 6 Grant sent the greater part of his army against Lee here, only to find the town evacuated. At Sailor's Creek that afternoon three Federal columns struck Lee's moving lines, captured 8,000 men, but failed to stop the retreat (*see Tour 3d*).

The AMELIA COUNTY COURTHOUSE, a red brick and white columned building, was built in 1924. Amelia County was created in 1734 from Prince George and Brunswick Counties and named for Princess Amelia, daughter of George II. Under the trees in the square is the CONFEDERATE MEMORIAL, a stalwart bronze soldier. In the CLERK'S OFFICE is a letter Patrick Henry wrote in 1797; in it he said that, 'having got some money,' he was in the market for a tract of land—his perpetual state of mind.

Left from Amelia on State 38 to County 614, 1 *m.*, and R. to DENNISVILLE, 8 *m.*, a hamlet that was the birthplace of Virginia Hawes Terhune (1831–1922), better known as Marion Harland, pioneer newspaper woman and versatile writer. Beginning before she was 16 with an article, 'Marrying through Prudential Motives,' which was published in *Godey's Magazine*, she wrote fiction, travel books, and lectured on various subjects, but her greatest reputation was as the author of cook books and syndicated newspaper articles on household topics.

JETERSVILLE, 46.5 *m.* (428 alt., 100 pop.), is a post office, store, and a few frame houses. While Lee's army was at Amelia, a partial Federal concentration took place here.

Right from Jetersville on County 642 to County 616, 7.8 *m.*, and R. to PAINESVILLE, 8.4 *m.*, a handful of houses so named because a Tom Paine Infidel Club was organized here in 1800. In this vicinity on the afternoon of April 5, 1865, Sheridan's cavalry destroyed more than 200 Confederate supply wagons.

At 50.6 *m.* on US 360 is a junction with County 631.

Left here to County 619, 2.3 *m.*, and L. to a dirt road, 4.6 *m.*; L. again to the SITE OF WEST CREEK, 4.9 *m.*, home of Colonel Benjamin Ward. Here in July 1781 Peter Francisco, Virginia's Hercules of the Revolutionary War (*see Tour 3d*), met in hand-to-hand combat some of Tarleton's raiding dragoons, killed one, and seized their horses. Francisco fought off the dragoons with his broadsword and, pretending that Colonial troops were near, called lustily for help. The raiders made off, abandoning their dead comrade and nine horses. A popular steel engraving depicting the episode shows the dragoons falling back in terror, while the hero, his hair a bit ruffled, suffers only the loss of a garter.

JENNINGS' ORDINARY, at 52.9 *m.*, is a scattered group of white frame dwellings named for an old stage station that has been so much remodeled as to have lost all semblance of antiquity.

Left here on County 615 to County 630, 3.6 *m.*, and R. to MOUNTAIN HALL (L), 4.1 *m.*, with high pitched hip roof and front and side porticos. The house was built about 1800 by Dr. James Jones, who served in Congress and was a surgeon in the War of 1812.

At 56.3 *m.* on US 360 is a junction with US 460.

Left here to PIEDMONT SANATORIUM (L), 0.7 *m.*, a 150-bed State institution for the treatment of Negro tuberculosis patients.

In CREWE, 4.2 *m.* (2,152 pop.), business and residential areas flank the huge Norfolk & Western Ry. roundhouse, Y.M.C.A. building, and yards. At the southeastern edge of town stands a new hosiery mill that migrated hither when Crewe citizens offered special inducements.

NOTTOWAY, 8.5 *m.* (50 pop.), seat of Nottoway County, is a handful of county buildings, dwellings, and a general store that may well be those described in *Martin's Gazetteer* of 1835: 'a courthouse, clerk's office and criminal and debtor's jail, besides 15 dwelling houses, one mercantile house, one hotel, one saddler, one tailor and one blacksmith shop . . . population seventy persons.' On April 5, 1865, General Grant spent the night here.

The NOTTOWAY COUNTY COURTHOUSE, built in the 1830's, is a red brick structure with low wings and a white pedimented portico. Guarding its front entrance is the CONFEDERATE MONUMENT, a little soldier leaning wearily on his gun. Federal troopers ransacked the county clerk's office, hacked record books, and threw them into the courtyard horse trough. In one is scrawled 'Abraham Lincoln, President of Virginia 1865.'

The SITE OF ROSE HILL (R) is at 10.7 *m.* This was the birthplace of Roger A. Pryor (1828–1919), newspaper man, minister to Greece (1855), and congressman (1857–59). In 1861, having failed in efforts to influence secession in Virginia, he went to South Carolina where he made speeches urging that 'a first blow be struck.' 'The very moment,' he declared, 'that blood is shed Old Virginia will make common cause with her sisters of the South.' He was one of the four aides of General P.G.T.Beauregard. After the war he practiced law in New York, where he was a justice of the State supreme court.

BLACKSTONE, 15.3 *m.* (423 alt., 1772 pop.), is a tobacco market and trading center known before 1885 as Black's and White's for two taverns that faced each other across the route of the Petersburg-North Carolina stage.

Bishop James Cannon, Jr. (1864–) was president of the college here from 1894 to 1918. As superintendent of the Anti-Saloon League of Virginia, he gained both limelight and political influence. In 1928 under his leadership Virginia voted against Alfred E. Smith, momentarily joining the Republican ranks.

BLACKSTONE COLLEGE, a Methodist Episcopal junior college for young women, is housed in buildings of modern design on a 34-acre campus at the edge of the town. Its student body numbers about 200.

BURKEVILLE, 57.3 *m.* (515 alt., 775 pop.), straddles the tracks of the railroads that cross here. As the railroad stop for the community near Burke's Tavern, the place was first called Burke's Junction. Tarleton's British dragoons came here pillaging in July 1781, and in June 1864 Union cavalry, in order to cut off Confederate supplies to Richmond and Petersburg, tore up railroad tracks in the vicinity. On April 3, 1865, Jefferson Davis and cabinet passed through as they fled from Richmond to Danville; and three days later Union troops, pursuing the retreating Confederates, camped here.

In July 1910 Miss Ella G. Agnew was appointed State Home Demonstration Agent with Burkeville as her base and a program began in Nottoway and Halifax Counties that has provided an example for similar work among rural women all over the country.

Left from Burkeville on State 49 to the SITE OF NOTTOWAY MEETING HOUSE (R), 3.3. *m.* Granite blocks mark the four corners of a church built in 1769.

A handful of houses called HUNGRYTOWN, 10.7 *m.*, was really named Hungarytown, for Hungarian settlers.

In VICTORIA, 16 *m.* (1,568 pop.), primarily an industrial town, haphazard rows of two-story red brick and frame buildings house drug stores, the variety store, the groceries, the 'cafe,' and dry goods emporia. The town has grown up around the shops of the Virginian Railway, a line carrying coal from West Virginia to Virginia seaports. The town ships lumber, some furniture, and silk. To bring the silk mill here, local citizens provided the plant and gave a period of tax-exemption.

1. Left (straight ahead) from Victoria 6.5 *m.* on State 40 to KENBRIDGE (753 pop.), which vies with Petersburg and South Hill as a leading market for bright tobacco. Among the usual rows of small stores are four tobacco warehouses, a tobacco redrying plant, a fertilizer plant, a cotton gin, and a flour mill. During the tobacco season the streets are as lively as those of much larger towns.

Right from Kenbridge 2.4 *m.* on County 637 to the SITE OF CRAIG'S MILL (L), operated in early days by James Craig, a Baptist minister. In July 1781 Tarleton's British raiders came here to carry off flour and meal, only to find that Craig, warned of their approach, had dumped his stock into the mill stream. The disappointed redcoats burned the mill, put the parson to work butchering his hogs for their use, and carried off his slaves.

2. Right from Victoria on State 49, here united with State 40, is LUNENBURG, 19.1 *m.* (35 pop.), seat of Lunenburg County, with a pleasant cluster of county buildings, an unusually attractive country inn that dates from 1803, half a dozen substantial white frame dwellings and a general store. The little crossroads settlement was incorporated in 1816 as Lewiston.

The red brick COURTHOUSE, with an Ionic portico, was erected in 1826. Lunenburg County was cut from Brunswick County in 1746; its area has since been broken up into ten counties. Lunenburg was called The Old Free State in 1861, when its fiery citizens, irked at the delay of the Virginia Convention called to consider secession, threatened, in case Virginia should remain in the Union, to secede from the State and Nation.

At 58.1 *m.* on US 360 is a junction with County 621.

Right here to BURKE'S TAVERN (R), 1.3 *m.*, built in 1731. Now a dwelling, the two-and-a-half-story structure, with red brick first story and weatherboarded upper section, deep pitched roof and tall outside end chimneys, was a famous stage tavern stop.

GREEN BAY, 65.2 *m.* (588 alt., 100 pop.), with a consolidated school and general stores, is a shipping point for pulpwood and railroad ties.

MEHERRIN, 68.7 *m.* (585 alt., 200 pop.), spreads along the highway with stores and small frame dwellings.

At 75.7 *m.* is a junction with US 15 (*see Tour 3e*), which unites with US 360 for 19.7 miles.

At BARNES JUNCTION, 95.3 *m.*, is the southern junction with US 15 (*see Tour 3e*).

Left here on State 47 to CHASE CITY, 8.6 *m.* (1,590 pop.), a tobacco market and trading center for farmers. Among the stores, tobacco warehouses, comfortable homes, and churches, a motion picture house with ultra-modern decorations is conspicuous.

CLOVER, 104.8 *m.* (486 alt., 251 pop.), its main street a mixture of business places and white frame homes, shade trees, and flowery yards, is a rural trading and social center. From this place, on the night of April 5, 1865, John S. Wise, 19-year-old son of the former governor, Henry A. Wise, secretly carried a telegram from President Davis, then at Danville, to General Lee, at Farmville. Leaving Farmville on April 7 with Lee's reply, young Wise recrossed the Federal lines and made his way back to Danville.

At 111.5 *m.* is a junction with County 725 and State 304.

1. Left on County 725 through SCOTTSBURG, 2.3 *m.* (100 pop.), to County 716, 7.3 *m.*; R. here 2.2 *m.* to FALKLAND FARM (L), a 7,000-acre hunting preserve with a rambling, white frame house on a hill. Here Henry Sydnor Harrison (1880–1930) began to write the novels that were popular in the early part of the twentieth century—*Queed*, *V.V.'s Eyes*, and *Angela's Business*.

On County 725, at 10.8 *m.*, is STAUNTON RIVER STATE PARK (*open May 15 to Nov. 1; adm. 10¢, children under 10 free, overnight camping, 25¢; cabins $15 a week for 2 persons, $20 a week for 4, $5 for each additional person; reservations made at Virginia Conservation Commission, Richmond*). This large recreational area contains a swimming pool and a wading pool.

2. Left from US 360 on State 304 to BANISTER LODGE (L), 2.1 *m.*, a gaunt two-and-a-half-story brick dwelling incorporating parts of the 20-room house built here about 1820 by William H. Clark, whose wife was a granddaughter of Patrick Henry.

At 118.4 *m.* is a junction with US 501 (*see Tour 11b*), which unites with US 360 to HALIFAX, 119.2 *m.* (753 pop.), seat of Halifax County. This charming town typifies the rural centers of romantic fiction, with a green and shady courthouse square, quiet-looking stores, and white-pillared homes set far back from the street among old oaks, magnolias, and evergreens. The only business is trade and county legal affairs, though in 1890 new railroad facilities caused it to change its name from Banister to Houston for a railroad executive, who was to be asked to send factories into the town. Unfortunately, the committee sent to New York to acquaint the gentleman with his new honor made the disastrous mistake of mispronouncing his name. Whereupon he denied his interest in the town and thereafter influenced no industries to come. In 1920 the little community went back to its historic designation as the county town of Halifax County.

GRAND OAKS, Main Street, in grounds beautiful with shrubbery, boxwood, and giant oaks, is a spacious red brick mansion with a white-columned two-story portico.

REST-A-WHILE, adjacent, a brick and white columned structure in traditional style, was called Elm Hill by its builder, Captain Henry Edmunds.

ST. JOHN'S CHURCH, diagonally across Main Street, is a nineteenth-century brick structure painted white, without ornament except fluted pilasters set into the walls and an octagonal cupola from which rises a slender spire. The Reverend Charles Dresser, rector here from 1823 to 1831, migrated to Illinois, where he performed the marriage ceremony of Abraham Lincoln and Mary Todd in 1842.

The METHODIST CHURCH, in the same block, built in 1827 as the first Episcopal church, was bought by the Methodists when St. John's was built. Its brick bulk is relieved by a cupola.

OLD MASONIC TEMPLE, a simple red brick structure, was built about 1830.

HALIFAX COURTHOUSE, of red brick with white columned portico, stands among tall trees in a green square surrounded by a stone wall. At one side is a row of tiny red brick lawyers' offices and in front is the CONFEDERATE MONUMENT, the usual soldier on a pedestal. The county, organized in 1752 and then including what is now Halifax, Pittsylvania, Henry, Franklin, and Patrick Counties, was named for the Earl of Halifax. The first seat was at Peytonsburg now in Pittsylvania County. In 1800 it was established here.

In Halifax is a junction with US 501 (*see Tour 11b*).

West of Halifax the highway runs between small farms, where tobacco is the chief crop and the fields are dotted with clay-chinked log barns in which the leaf is cured. Not even crossroads hamlets break the rural scene for many miles.

At 154.2 *m.* is a junction with US 29 (*see Tour 4c*), which unites with US 360 into DANVILLE, 155.3 *m.* (408 alt., 22,247 pop.), spread over hills that slope gradually toward a wide bend in the Dan River.

This aggressive city, typical of the New South, is one of Virginia's purely industrial cities. While tobacco is the backbone of income in its shipping and trading activities, cotton manufacturing dominates the city. On both sides of the river sprawl huge textile mills and at the western edge of the city are more acres of red brick mills, fenced in and surrounded by a company town with rows of houses and the usual facilities of an independent community. Yet Danville is a Main Street town. An artery, on which seven main highways converge, climbs from the river on North Main Street through a cramped area of cotton mills and pungent, cavernous tobacco warehouses, redrying, and storage plants; reaches a business section where neon signs imitate the rainbow at night, and a 12-story Masonic Temple, an opulent-looking Municipal building of conventional classic design, and a new Federal building give a metropolitan touch; and as West Main Street climbs again to the residential area where impressive homes, two junior colleges, and Ballou Park with miles of road through natural woodland show the profits of industrial activity. In this prosperous upper area is Lady Astor Street, named for a local daughter, one of the Langhorne beauties, who became a member of the British Parliament.

As Virginia cities go, Danville is young. It boasts of no tavern where Washington spent a night, no home where La Fayette was feted, and among its many stores is not one 'antique shoppe' to lure tourists with spinning wheels and old glass. But the city slogan 'Danville Does Things' rests on solid achievements. The large mills annually turn an average of 60,000,000 pounds of cotton into textiles, and smaller ones convert some of the textiles into garments. At the heart of the 'old belt' of bright tobacco growing, it gathers for a world market the flue-cured leaf known in the tobacco world as U.S. Type 11, basis of various cigarette blends and mainstay of the world's cigarette industry. In the late summer its auction warehouses, with floor space for selling 2,250,000 pounds of leaf daily, resound with the singsong jargon of auctioneers, and buyers, led by bidders for the 'big four' of American cigarette corporations and for the two that dominate European markets, make the signs that bring prosperity or ruin to the tobacco farmer.

In 1876 Danville adopted the principle of municipal ownership of public utilities. The municipally owned water, electric power, and gas plants return nearly a $500,000 yearly into city coffers. Results are municipal solvency, low service charges—which attracts industries—and one of the lowest real estate tax rates in the State. The city has turned down fat bids for its utilities by private interests and has provided a backlog of future cheap power by establishing, with Federal aid, a gigantic development at the headwaters of the Dan, 82 miles away (*see Tour 7c*).

Like other tobacco-market towns, Danville began as an inspection warehouse. In 1793, Piedmont planters, irked by the hardship of rolling hogsheads over red clay roads to Richmond or Petersburg for the required inspection, petitioned the legislature for inspection facilities at this central point by the river. The petition was granted and trustees were appointed to take over 25 acres of land, which were to be divided and sold in half-acre lots. Inspection began at once, but it was two years before the first tier of lots, hugging the old Salisbury road, now Main Street, was offered for sale.

Early tobacco marketing was a haphazard business. Many inland growers sold their tobacco by the acre or barnful, letting the buyer worry about getting it out. First impetus to Danville's growth was improvement of river transportation, which began about 1820 when the Roanoke Navigation Company built a canal around the falls and opened the way for bateaux carrying tobacco to ships in Albemarle Sound. Real expansion began when the organized auction warehouse system was introduced in 1852—though the first was a small, poorly-lighted structure and a Negro advertised the sales by blowing a horn along the streets.

Though Danville escaped material damage during the War between the States, its position at the junction with the railroad bringing food and military supplies to Richmond and the fighting zone from Atlanta and gulf ports made it a valuable base. Idle tobacco warehouses were turned into hospitals, and one became a prison for captured Yankees. For seven days—April 3–10, 1865—Danville was the capital of the fast dying Confederacy. When the Richmond-Petersburg area was evacuated, President Davis and his Cabinet came to Danville, and here the President called the last full cabinet meeting and issued his last official proclamation, going to a newspaper office to see it set up and printed. When news of Lee's surrender came on April 10, Davis set out immediately for Greensboro,N.C. The same day Governor William (Extra-Billy) Smith arrived on horseback from Richmond, having stopped first at Lynchburg. For five days thereafter the town was the seat of the State administration.

Danville's industrial era began in 1881 with the opening of a small yarn mill. The Riverside Mill, parent of the present Riverside and Dan River Cotton Mills, was organized in 1882 and by 1890 had taken over a small rival, Morotock Mills. With the harnessing of the Falls of the Dan to create cheap electric power, and the influx of cheap labor from farms and mountain settlements, the business has grown fairly steadily. In 1931, 4,000 textile workers struck, demanding union recognition in a wage dispute. The strike, which loomed large in National importance as an early attempt by organized labor to capture textile strongholds in the South, began in September with a huge parade led by blaring bands, mass meetings with National organizers exhorting the strikers, meetings of those with sympathy for the mill owners, and charges and counter-charges. By midwinter the strike had dwindled to a bitter endurance test, with bread lines, soup kitchens, evictions from mill houses, and the guns of the National Guard policing the mill districts. The affair ended in early spring, neither side conceding defeat.

The CONFEDERATE MEMORIAL MANSION, Main St. between Sutherlin and Holbrook Aves., is occupied by the Danville Public Library. It was here that Jefferson Davis and his cabinet staged their last meeting. The mansion at that time was the home of Major W.T.Sutherlin. The central unit of the public library, with periodical, reference, lending, and reading rooms, occupies the first floor of this house. A Negro branch circulates more than 2,000 volumes monthly from quarters in the Langston Negro High School on Gay Street.

AVERETT COLLEGE, West Main St., in well-shaded grounds, has a handsome four-story main building with high white columned portico. Behind this are the dormitory, gymnasium, the science and music halls, an open air theater, and athletic fields. This junior college for young women is operated under the Baptist General Association of Virginia. Founded in 1859, before 1910 it had been called Union Female College, Roanoke Female College, Roanoke College for Women, and Roanoke Institute, when after the construction of new buildings it assumed its present name.

DANVILLE MILITARY INSTITUTE, S.Main St., a preparatory school, occupies a group of turreted, vine-covered, gray stone buildings on a heavily-wooded campus. Founded in 1920 as a private school, in 1921 it passed to the control of the Presbyterian Synod of Virginia. In 1933 military training was dropped and it became the Virginia Presbyterian School; but in 1937 it again became the Danville Military Institute.

STRATFORD COLLEGE, 1119 Main Street, another junior college for young women, with STRATFORD HALL, a preparatory school, occupies an ivy-clad red brick and white porticoed building. During the century of its history the institution has been the Danville Female College, Danville College for Young Ladies, Randolph-Macon College, and Stratford.

In Danville are junctions with US 58 (*see Tour 7b*) and US 29 (*see Tour 4c*).

Tour 20A

Central Garage—King William—West Point; 25.2 *m.* State 30.

Asphalt-paved roadbed throughout.

This highway traverses a peninsula lying between the Mattaponi and the Pamunkey and formerly called Pamunkey Neck. It prospered in Colonial days when tobacco was king, and in the *ante-bellum* era, when, with slave labor, its plantations yielded bumper crops of corn, wheat, and black-eyed peas. The large plantations have been divided into small farms.

State 30 branches east from US 360 (*see Tour 20a*) at CENTRAL GARAGE, 0 *m.*

RUMFORD, 2.7 *m.* (20 pop.), is at a junction with County 600.

Left here to RUMFORD ACADEMY (R), 0.3 *m.*, a dilapidated brick building that held one of the many private schools for boys operated before the inauguration of a State high school system. It was established in 1804.

The entrance to MOUNT PISGAH (R), is at 1.4 *m.* The large brick house is in a grove, and its lawn sweeps toward the river. Thick walls, recessed windows, wide floor boards, the trim, and a basement containing kitchen, dining room, and storage pantries attest its age, as does a brick in a fireplace bearing the date 1760. The house has been beautifully restored. Its builder was Henry Robinson, a brother of Speaker John Robinson (*see Tour 1B*).

In 1870 Miss Fannie Page Robinson opened a seminary here for young ladies and had the roof of the house lifted to provide more bedrooms for her students. Just what 'Miss Page' taught is not a matter of record; yet from Mount Pisgah and other such seminaries students were prepared for the early women's colleges of Virginia, which patterned their curricula after 'The University' and Richmond College.

At 3.9 *m.* on State 30 is a junction with County 616.

Right here to CHERRY GROVE (R), 1.1 *m.*, a remodeled frame house on a slight eminence. Ambrose Edwards, who came to Virginia in 1745, built the house and lived here until his death in 1810. Wealthean Butler was his first wife. Late in life, he married a rich widow, Barbara Finch, who, like many another woman of her day, managed to evade the rigors of the Common Law through a prenuptial contract stipulating that her husband should not interfere with the management of her property and in turn agreeing to make no claim upon his.

Close by the house is the family burying ground, now a tangle of vines and mulberry shoots. Because seven Negroes died soon after working among the graves, it is now well nigh impossible to employ men to clear away the underbrush.

At 6.6 *m.* on State 30 is a junction with County 629.

Left here to ENFIELD (R), 1.8 *m.* (*see Tour 1B*).

At 6.7 *m.* on State 30 is a junction with County 629.

Right here to ACQUINTON CHURCH (R), 1.8 *m.*, gaunt ghost of another day. Its flagstone flooring is gone; its brick walls are now covered with stucco; its pews and pulpit have been taken away. Yet Acquinton, built in 1732, was one of the four Colonial churches in the rich Pamunkey Neck area, embraced originally by St.John's Parish. Of the Reverend Henry Skyron, rector from 1773 to 1787, Bishop Meade wrote, 'He was an elegant scholar . . . alike remarkable for his eloquence and piety, never participating in any of the worldly amusements so common with the clergy . . . When Mr.Skyron preached Acquinton Church was always so crowded that the people used to bring their seats and fill up the aisle after the pews were full.' The Bishop added, 'His widow, who was too amiable to refuse a favor . . . allowed the ministers of the neighboring parishes to pick over and take away his sermons, which were never returned.'

For a time after the Revolution Acquinton Church was abandoned; later it was used by Methodist and Baptist congregations.

At 3.5 *m.* is a junction with County 623; L. here 3.9 *m.* to a private road and R. to ELSING GREEN, 5.1 *m.*, a large brick house in a wide lawn near the Pamunkey River. This large, solid Georgian Colonial building, built in part about 1719, has a pair of gable-roofed dependencies. Large halls form a cross. At each end of the side hall is a fine stairway with such an easy rise that a daughter of William Browne, one of the owners, once rode her pony up one flight and down the other.

Captain William Dandridge, captain in His Majesty's Navy and uncle of Martha

Washington, built part of the structure, which was the home of Carter Braxton (*see below*) from 1758 to 1767.

At 5.3 *m.* on County 629 is a junction with County 600; L. here 1 *m.* to a private road, and R. 1 *m.* to CHERICOKE, a square hip roofed brick house shaded by old locust trees and surrounded by hedges of mockorange. The house was built in 1767 by Carter Braxton, gutted by fire during the Revolution, restored, burned, and again restored.

Carter Braxton (*see Tour 1B*) lived here until 1786. He was educated at the College of William and Mary; served in the house of burgesses almost continuously from 1761 until 1775; was a member (1774–76) of the Virginia Conventions and of the Continental Congress in 1776; and signed the Declaration of Independence.

KING WILLIAM, 7.8 *m.* (50 pop.), seat of King William County, with its few scattered stores and homes, bustles mildly on court days. It is no larger than it was in Colonial days and only slightly changed in appearance and way of life. The automobiles parked outside the court green seem an anachronism. Most prominent in the enclosure formed by the Colonial brick wall, one of the few still standing in Virginia, is the COURTHOUSE, a T-shaped building, with hip roof, end chimneys, and an arched loggia across its façade. On the court green are also the CLERK'S OFFICE and JAIL, both built since 1885, and the usual CONFEDERATE MONUMENT.

King William County was formed in 1701 from King and Queen County and named for William III. King and Queen had been cut from New Kent in 1691.

At 8.5 *m.* is a junction with State 293.

Right on this road, which becomes County 633, to a junction with County 623, 7.8 *m.*; R. here to the PAMUNKEY INDIAN RESERVATION, 8.8 *m.*, home of the Indians whose tribe has lived on this neck since the land was assigned to it by the colony in 1677. The treaty announced that 'The Respective Indian Kings and Queens doe henceforth acknowledge their immediate dependency on, and Own all Subjection to, the great King of England, Our now dread Soveraigne.' The Queen of the Pamunkey (*see Tour 6A*), then ruler of the Tidewater Confederacy, signed the treaty by a symbol that resembles a script capital *U*. Charles II sent a gift to each of the signers; and the English Queen 'decorated' the Queen of the Pamunkey with a velvet hat adorned by a silver chain. This 'crown' is now preserved by the Virginia Historical Society.

On the reservation the wards, supervised by the State and exempted from taxation and continuing a semblance of their tribal customs, are governed by a chief and council of their own choosing. They live in small frame houses along dirt roads, worship in a church affiliated with the Baptist General Association, send their children to a school provided by the State, and gain their livelihood through farming, hunting, and fishing. The women make and sell pottery, shape beads, and fashion pocketbooks, watch fobs, and other articles. Following custom, the chief and his men make a pilgrimage to Richmond each Thanksgiving and on the steps of the capitol present freshly killed game—quail, rabbits, turkeys, and occasionally a deer—to the governor of Virginia, whom they address as 'Great White Father.' For the occasion the Indians wear beaded doeskin suits and feathered headgear. They are frequently seen about the legislative halls, particularly when they fear that the passage of bills aimed to stop miscegenation will result in classifying them as negroid.

At 13.1 *m.* is a junction with County 640.

Left here to County 625, 1.1 *m.*, and L. to the MATTAPONI INDIAN RESERVATION, 2.3 *m.*, home of another small remnant of the former Tidewater Indian Confederacy. After the massacre of 1644, the Mattaponi were driven from Pamunkey Neck by William Claiborne to a site near the Rappahannock, but returned here in 1668.

ST. JOHN'S CHURCH (*open upon application at house near by*), at 15.4 *m.*, was erected in 1732 as one of the four brick churches that replaced former frame churches of old St. John's Parish. The building is T-shaped, and each unit of its roof is gabled. The aisles are paved with flagstones, and above both the north door and the main entrance are galleries. First a single rectangle, it was later enlarged. Abandoned after the Revolution, St. John's suffered at the hands of vandals. Though no longer used regularly, the church has been restored.

At 17.7 *m.* is a junction with County 634.

Right here to SWEET HALL (L), 1.7 *m.*, a sturdy story-and-a-half brick house on a bluff above the Pamunkey River. The house is distinguished by clusters of built-in chimneys at each end and by its fortlike brick walls. It was built about 1720 by Thomas Claiborne, grandson of William Claiborne.

The estate is part of a tract patented in 1653 by William Claiborne, who had contended with Lord Baltimore over the ownership of Kent Island.

RUFFIN'S FERRY, 1.9 *m.*, is a river landing and terminal of a ferry from Colonial times until the river was bridged in 1926. At this 'poynt,' states the patent to his estate, William Claiborne 'landed the Army under his command in 1644,' when he led an attack against the Pamunkey after the uprising of that year.

Here La Fayette placed in camp the 'light infantry' August 13, 1781, while observing Cornwallis.

At 21.1 *m.* on State 30 is a junction with County 635.

1. Right here to a private road, 0.4 *m.*, and straight ahead 0.5 *m.* to ROMANCOKE, seat of the estate that belonged from 1653 to 1925 successively to Clairbornes, Custises, and Lees. The present frame house by the Pamunkey succeeds the *ante-bellum* house burned in 1925. On part of this estate William Claiborne spent his last years. George Washington purchased Romancoke about 1770 and in his diary often referred to it as 'my Quarter.' He gave it to his stepson, John Parke Custis, through whom it descended to Captain Robert E. Lee, youngest son of General Lee.

2. Left from State 30 on County 635 to (L) CHELSEA, 0.9 *m.*, a brick house built in two sections, by the Mattaponi. The first section forms the stem of a T and has a steep gambrel roof with dormers. Boxwood, fine trees, and flowers adorn the wide lawn.

The older part of the house was built about 1710 by Colonel Augustine Moore (1685–1743), who patented the estate; the hip roofed front section was added about 1740.

At Chelsea Governor Alexander Spotswood assembled the Knights of the Golden Horseshoe for the expedition beyond the Blue Ridge in 1716. Colonel Moore was one of the 'Knights.'

PORT RICHMOND, 23.5 *m.* (800 pop.), was incorporated in 1924 as a town, separate from West Point, which it adjoins. At this farm town, which has developed since 1920, intensive experimental truck-farming on 10-acre farms is conducted.

WEST POINT, 25.2 *m.* (1,800 pop.) (*see Tour 6A*) is at a junction with State 33 (*see Tour 6A*).

Tour 21

(Franklin, W.Va.)—Warm Springs—Hot Springs—Covington—Clifton Forge—Roanoke—Rocky Mount—Martinsville—(Winston-Salem, N.C.). US 220.
West Virginia Line to North Carolina Line, 187.4 *m.*

Paved throughout, chiefly with asphalt.
Chesapeake & Ohio Ry. parallels route between Hot Springs and Eagle Rock; Norfolk & Western Ry. roughly between Roanoke and North Carolina Line.
Accommodations, resort hotels, tourist homes in villages, and commercial hotels in towns.

This route takes a north-south course across Virginia and affords a diversified view of the 'back country,' settled in the middle of the eighteenth century during the desperate last stand of the Indians against encroachment by the whites. It is now punctuated by textile mills.

Section a. WEST VIRGINIA LINE to ROANOKE; 119.4 *m. US* 220.

This section of the highway follows the Jackson River between lofty peaks of the Alleghenies, passes through an area of thermal and mineral springs, and enters the Roanoke Valley.

US 220 crosses the West Virginia Line, 0 *m.*, at a point 15 miles south of Franklin, W.Va. (*see West Virginia Guide*) and runs to a junction with State 284 at 1.1 *m.*

Right on this road, which affords beautiful views along the South Fork of the Potomac River, to CRABBOTTOM, 2.7 *m.* (3,000 alt., 100 pop.), in the fertile limestone soil of Crabbottom Valley. East of the village is a curious limestone formation that arches up from the river like the vertebrae of some monstrous prehistoric animal and gives the place the name of Devil's Backbone.

Left from Crabbottom 1.3 *m.* on County 640 to NEW HAMPDEN (50 pop.), a mountain hamlet between two long ridges. An old water-powered mill in the settlement grinds the grain of the neighborhood.

Right from New Hampden 0.5 *m.* on a foot trail crossing a ridge to INDIAN FLINT QUARRIES, where unfinished and broken implements mark the site of extensive primitive manufacturing operations. A local legend is that through treaty the quarries were considered neutral ground by the Indians, even during wars.

At 3.7 *m.* on US 220 is a junction with County 629.

Left here to SEYBERT HILLS (L), 2 *m.*, a two-story clapboarded structure built in 1872 on the site of former Seybert homes. Stones in the present double end chimneys are relics, having been used in the chimney of the first house, a log cabin, built before the Revolution probably by Henry Seybert. He had been captured by Indians in 1758 during the raid on Fort Seybert, in what is now West Virginia. At the stockaded frontier post, Shawnee, led by Chief Killbuck, killed about 40 settlers, after having agreed to spare their lives in return for money and guns. The whites were lined up against a wall and tomahawked, the fort was burned, and four children—the oldest, Henry, 16—were taken captive; Henry later escaped and settled in this area.

MONTEREY, 7.4 *m.* (3,100 alt., 290 pop.), seat of Highland County, rests on an elevation between the valley and the mountains. Though as early as 1774 Samuel Black had a cabin here, in 1848 the site was still only a small clearing on the Staunton and Parkersburg turnpike across the Allegheny Range.

The HIGHLAND COUNTY COURTHOUSE, a red brick structure with a large white columned portico, was built in 1848. It was the first courthouse of Highland County, which was formed the year before from parts of Bath County and Pendleton County (W.Va.).

The CONFEDERATE MONUMENT, on the court square, differs from its comrades in other Virginia counties in that the soldier shades his eyes with one hand and grips his gun with the other.

In Monterey is a junction with US 250 (*see Tour 17b*).

Below the highway is MACKEY SPRING (L), 11.8 *m.*, which swirls up in tremendous volume.

At 27.8 *m.* the highway begins the climb up the southern tip of Jack Mountain, which separates Jackson and Warm Springs valleys.

The brick BARNER HOUSE (L), 36.7 *m.*, of two-and-a-half stories, dates from the early nineteenth century. Its thick walls, laid in Flemish bond, rise to an ornate cornice of brick set flush with the roof line.

WARM SPRINGS, 38.7 *m.* (2,350 alt., 300 pop.), seat of Bath County, is a pleasant little town cupped in a valley. Besides county administration, the business of the town is chiefly catering to tourists.

WARM SPRINGS INN, at the northern end of town, is composed of three red brick buildings on a spacious lawn close to the western base of Warm Springs Mountain. Two of the buildings, built about 1842, served the county until 1907 as courthouse and jail. The third, a small building, was built in 1820 for a law office.

Opposite the inn are two large bath houses and a pavilion. The springs supply sulphur water at a temperature of 96.5° and at a rate of 1,200 gallons per minute.

In 1750 Dr.Thomas Walker wrote of this valley: 'We visited the hot springs and found six invalids there. The spring is very clear and warmer than new milk . . . The settlers would be better able to support travelers was it not for the great number of Indian warriors that frequently take what they want from them, greatly to their prejudice.'

After the Indians had been driven back by the tide of settlement following the Revolution, the wealth and fashion of the Tidewater journeyed to the mountains to escape the miasma of lowland summers, and resorts flourished. According to Peregrine Prolix—pseudonym of a young Philadelphia lawyer who toured the country in the 1830's in a search for health—the costume suitable for resort use was 'a large cotton gown of a cashmere shawl pattern lined with crimson, a fancy Greek cap, Turkish slippers and a pair of loose pantaloons—a garb that will not consume much time in doffing and donning.' According to a writer of 1845, the springs were so popular that the bath house was run on schedule,' . . . two hours for ladies . . . and the same period for gentlemen' and 'a white flag hoisted as a signal that it is occupied by the former.'

The COURTHOUSE, a red brick structure built in 1908, serves Bath County which was created in 1790 from Augusta, Greenbrier (now in West Virginia), and Botetourt Counties, and so named because of the many springs within its boundaries.

In Warm Springs is a junction with State 501 (*see Tour 11a*).

Left 0.5 *m.* from Warm Springs to THREE HILLS, which was the home of Mary Johnston, the novelist (*see Literature; Tour 5b; and Richmond*), from 1913 until her death in 1936. In these years she wrote *Silver Cross*, *Croatan*, *The Slave Ship*, *The Great Valley*, *Michael Forth*, and *The Exile*, books influenced by the philosophy of the mystics.

The HOMESTEAD HOTEL, at 43.1 *m.*, an expansive four-story winged, red brick structure built around a 12-story tower, is surrounded by many acres of landscaped grounds, and many miles of territory used for amusement by its opulent clientele. Although its advertising pamphlets remind the public that Hot Springs 'is a place where hydrotherapy is administered,' emphasis is placed on golf, tennis (hard-surfaced courts are called 'En-Tout-Cas' here), riding, driving, skeet, swimming, badminton, dancing, and honeymooning.

Thomas Bullitt, a frontier militiaman, about 1765 acquired 300 acres of land here and built a hotel. Overshadowed in the early days by the fashionable Warm Springs, to the extent of once having been called 'Little Warm Springs,' this hotel had little expansion until it was acquired in 1832 by Dr.Thomas Goode. Peregrine Prolix spoke of 'The old frame hotel' and of its proprietor, 'Dr.Goode, an intelligent physician, who is using great exertion and investing much money to render the establishment pleasant to travelers, and comfortable and useful to valetudinarians.' Prolix described the baths as 'the Spout and the Boiler; the former is said to be preferred by Orators, the latter by Poets and Warriors.' The Spout, Prolix explained, was made by the direction of the spring water through a 'perforated log . . . affording the bather an opportunity of receiving the stream upon any part of his body or limbs, into which rheumatism has thrust his uncomfortable claws.' The Boiler was a hot pool, into which the patient submerged his body. The water, 'a little scalding at first, becomes pleasant as soon as the bather is chin deep in the health-restoring fluid.' Adjoining both baths were rooms into which each bather retired, wrapped in blankets. 'Perspiration soon starts from every pore . . . Sometimes it penetrates the blankets, mattress and sackonbottom, and streams on the floor.'

During the War between the States, the hotel buildings were used as hospitals. In the 10 years that followed the war, Hot Springs forged ahead as a resort of fashion. In 1890, the property was purchased by the Southern Improvement Company, headed by M.E.Ingalls, president of the Chesapeake and Ohio Railway. A fire of 1901 destroyed most of the buildings, thereby furnishing an opportunity for the construction of the first part of the present hotel.

HOT SPRINGS (2,250 alt., 1,004 pop.), adjoining the hotel grounds, owes its existence to the trade and employment the resort provides.

1. Right from the hotel entrance on an unmarked road to the HOMESTEAD SKEET FIELD, 1 *m.*, which affords an excellent view of Warm Springs Valley.

2. Left through the hotel grounds on a roadway that rises 1,200 feet to a road, 2.7 *m.*, running along the ridge; R. here to a fork at 5.8 *m.* and straight ahead to the Airport Road, 6.1 *m.*; L. on this road 0.5 *m.* to the HOT SPRINGS AIRPORT, a private landing field on top of Warm Springs Mountain (3,850 alt.).

South of the junction with the Airport Road, the fork road continues to BALD KNOB FIRE TOWER (4,200 alt.), 9 *m.*, from which several hundred miles of mountain country are visible.

HEALING SPRINGS, 46 *m.* (700 pop.), a well-kept village, contains year-round homes. Water from its mineral springs is bottled and sold.

The CASCADE INN, at the southern end of town, is a sprawling two-story building, operated as an annex to the Homestead Hotel. The inn, built before 1850, was named for cascades that tumble westward into the Jackson River. Wounded Confederate soldiers were treated here during the War between the States. The hotel golf ground is rated a championship course.

The MEMORIAL TO 'MAD ANN' BAILEY, a boulder at 54.7 *m.*, commemorates a frontier woman whose shooting, riding, and profanity out-masculined the fiercest masculine proficiency of her day (*see Staunton*). The boulder marks the site of Mad Ann's hut, on what is now known as Mad Ann Ridge.

By the boulder is a parking space that overlooks small FALLING SPRINGS (R). Thomas Jefferson in his *Notes on the State of Virginia* said, 'The only remarkable cascade in this country, is that of Falling Spring in Augusta . . . it falls over a rock 200 feet into the valley. This cataract will bear no comparison with that of Niagara, as to the quantity of water . . . but it is half as high again.'

COVINGTON, 62.1 *m.* (1,245 alt., 6,550 pop.) (*see Tour 8c*), is at a junction with US 60 (*see Tour 8c*), which unites eastward with US 220 to CLIFTON FORGE, 74 *m.* (1,047 alt., 6,850 pop.) (*see Tour 8c*).

Just south of Clifton Forge the highway parallels Jackson River through a gap in RAINBOW RIDGE, passing under a towering arc of stratified rock cut by the river.

The confluence of the Jackson and Cow Pasture Rivers is at 78.7 *m.*

The hills surrounding EAGLE ROCK, 89 *m.* (600 pop.), which is on bottom lands of the James, are scarred by quarries that feed raw stone to the lime-making plants of the town. Lime is produced from limestone by the application of heat. Lime-burning, for domestic purposes, has been carried on since the first homesteads were established in this area. For local consumption, portable and make-shift stone-grinding and -burning contraptions still work small outcroppings throughout the valleys.

FINCASTLE, 100.6 *m.* (1,250 alt., 517 pop.), seat of Botetourt County, overlooks valley lands from the top of a small rounded hill. Fincastle was established in 1772 on land donated by Israel Christian for a county seat in 1770, one year after the original Botetourt County was formed and two years before much of its territory was separated to form Fincastle County.

In 1828 it was incorporated. Botetourt County was named for Norborne Berkeley, Baron de Botetourt, then governor of Virginia, when it was formed during the first of a series of divisions of Augusta County, necessitated by the rapid increase in the number of western Virginia settlements. Botetourt first covered an area now included in 19 Virginia counties, 32 West Virginia counties, and the State of Kentucky.

The BOTETOURT COUNTY COURTHOUSE (L), a brick building with a portico, was erected about 1850.

The FINCASTLE PRESBYTERIAN CHURCH, built about 1832 and remodeled in 1850, is a charming structure—red brick with white columns in a recessed entrance porch, and a slender spire rising from a square, white pilastered belfry. When Israel Christian gave the land for the townsite, an 'eligible lot' was set aside for a church. The building, erected soon thereafter and abandoned when the Revolution separated church and state, was taken over by the Presbyterians, then in majority. A remembered occasion in the old church was the sermon preached for six Negro slaves, convicted of murdering their master, an itinerant slave trader. Afterwards they were hanged from a walnut tree in the presence of most of the inhabitants of the county.

At 105.5 *m.* is a junction with County 665.

Right here to GREENFIELD (L), 0.8 *m.*, a large double-winged weatherboarded house on an estate established in 1761 by William Preston (1729–83), colonel of the Augusta militia and one of the first trustees of Staunton. The first house, incorporated in the present structure, was a garrison with portholed walls built about 1762. In 1763, Preston came here from Staunton, bringing his family, and two others. Although neighboring plantations were deserted when Indian raids threatened, Colonel Preston wrote to a friend: 'I have built a little fort in which are 87 persons, twenty of whom bear arms. We are in a pretty good posture of defence, and with the aid of God are determined to make a stand . . . No enemy have appeared here as yet. Their guns are frequently heard and their footing observed, which make us believe they will pay us a visit.'

After the Indian menace was past, the house was remodeled and added to; there has been little change since the Revolution. Without gardens and on an elevation where the view of hills and distant mountain peaks is unobstructed, Greenfield is typical of the later frontier home.

Colonel William Preston, born in north Ireland, was brought to the colonies in 1740 by his father, John Preston. When he died in 1783, his holdings approximated 15,000 acres. James Patton Preston, Colonel Preston's son, born at Greenfield, was governor of Virginia from 1816 to 1819.

AMSTERDAM, 106.9 *m.*, a small collection of houses, was once center of a Dunkard community. The town, laid out in 1796, became a stage stop on the road to Old Sweet Springs, a popular resort now in West Virginia. In the late nineteenth century carriages and chairs were manufactured here; and until the establishment of Roanoke, the village had hopes of industrial development. The split-bottom chairs manufactured here by the Keeling factory are now prized by collectors.

DALEVILLE, 107.6 *m.* (100 pop.), several stores and a scattered group of houses, is now the shopping center of the Dunkards.

This was the seat of Daleville College, founded in 1891 as the Botetourt Normal School, established by the Dunkards or Church of the Brethren.

The school was operated as the Daleville Junior College from 1914 until 1924, when its college department was transferred to Bridgewater College (*see Tour 5a*). The secondary school here was discontinued in 1932.

At 109.6 *m.* is a junction with US 11 (*see Tour 5b*) with which US 220 unites for 10 miles (*see Tour 5b*).

ROANOKE, 119.4 *m.* (950 alt., 69,206 pop.) (*see Roanoke*).

In Roanoke is the western junction with US 11 (*see Tour 5b*).

Section b. ROANOKE to NORTH CAROLINA LINE; 68 *m. US* 220.

Between Roanoke and the newly industrialized towns near the North Carolina border the highway winds among the Blue Ridge Mountains and drops gradually through rounded foothills and fertile valleys.

US 220 runs south from Salem Ave. 0 *m.* on Jefferson St. in ROANOKE.

Left from Roanoke 0.4 *m.*, on US 221 to BENT MOUNTAIN POST OFFICE, 18.5 *m.*; L. here 0.8 *m.* to ADNEY GAP, in which is a junction with a completed section of the Blue Ridge Parkway. Left here 43 miles along the Blue Ridge to a junction with US 58 (*see Tours 4A and 7c*).

BOONE MILL, 14.1 *m.* (1,128 alt., 388 pop.), at the head of a beautiful valley, has a wood working plant, a barrel factory, a vegetable cannery, a grist mill, and general stores. In 1782 Jacob Boone, cousin of Daniel Boone, arrived here from North Carolina and built his little mill and cabin on the banks of Maggodee Creek. Because the Carolina Road was near by, a community soon grew around the mill. A house built in 1820 by John Boone, son of Jacob, stands on the mill site at the northern end of the hamlet.

ROCKY MOUNT, 26.2 *m.* (1,100 alt., 2,000 pop.), with its pretentious section of new buildings on top of a hill, is the seat of Franklin County. The once quiet village now has an overlay of industrial activity, producing furniture, mirrors, and overalls, in addition to selling tobacco. For nearly 100 years the community was two rival villages, Rocky Mount and Mount Pleasant. Though in 1873 Rocky Mount swallowed its smaller rival, the town buildings of the two villages still glare at each other across a narrow street.

Sharing honors with the CONFEDERATE MONUMENT in the courthouse square is a rough granite GENERAL JUBAL A. EARLY MEMORIAL, a boulder commemorating the Confederate leader who was born in the county on November 3, 1816. After being graduated from West Point, Early resigned from the army to practice law, was elected to the general assembly, and was a member of the Virginia Secession Convention of 1861.

The FRANKLIN COUNTY COURTHOUSE, dignified in red brick with white-columned portico, was built in 1909. Franklin County was organized and named in 1785 when Benjamin Franklin was a popular hero because of the aid he had gained for the Revolutionists in France.

County records are rich in human interest stories. Here is the inventory of November 23, 1861, of the estate of James Burroughs, a planter, including 'One Negro boy, "Booker," value $400.00.' This little Negro boy, listed with other slaves among household goods and farm implements, grew up to be Booker T. Washington, leader and educator of his race. His birthplace was on the Burroughs plantation in the Hale's Ford area. When slaves were freed, the boy went with his mother to Malden, West Virginia, and at night, after having worked long hours in the salt mines, studied Webster's *Blue Back Speller*. As a child in Virginia, he had acquired the name Booker because of his passion for books. He added the Washington on his first day in school when roll call caused him to realize that other children had two names. In 1872 he set out on foot from West Virginia for Hampton Institute. In Richmond, after spending a night beneath the planks of a sidewalk, he earned enough for transportation to Hampton. In his autobiography, *Up from Slavery*, Booker T. Washington told the story of the hard but pleasant work that followed—of his graduation in 1875; of his return to Malden as teacher in a Negro school; of his years at Hampton as a member of the faculty; and then of the big chance that came to develop Tuskegee Institute in Alabama.

A marriage bond dated January 7, 1811, recalls a story still fondly remembered in the countryside. The bond gave notice that Joseph Hix, a plantation overseer, intended to marry his employer, Polly Early, a widow. Mrs.Early's relatives were outraged by her choice of a social inferior. When the couple entered the bridal chamber on the night of their marriage, they were confronted by the coffin of the first husband, dug up and placed there by the bride's brothers. Before the bridal pair had recovered from their shock the brothers appeared, carried the bridegroom off to a steep hilltop, thrust him into a spike-studded hogshead, and rolled him down the hill. The overseer lived to institute a damage suit against his assailants.

Another record dated February 19, 1830, shows that William B. Williams, the groom of a May-December romance, applied for divorce on the grounds that on his wedding night his young bride first drugged his liquor and, when he fell asleep, tried to murder him by pouring molten lead into his ear from a fire-shovel.

In 1888, on Snow Creek near by, a farmer's plow uncovered an egg-shaped stone weighing nearly 100 pounds. Cut into the stone was: 'Here may be found my tools and E-15-P-A- God mine. Z.K. 1611.' Iron pyrites —'fool's gold'—is found in the vicinity, and the word 'God mine' is interpreted as 'gold mine.' The modern phrasing of the message is in marked contrast with the date, and is generally considered a hoax.

Right from Rocky Mount on State 40 to County 640, 2.2 *m.*; L. here 0.6 *m.* to the old stone HILL HOUSE (R), built in the early eighteenth century by Robert Hill, an Irish immigrant, whose grant of several thousand acres extended along Pigg River from Chestnut Creek to Story Creek. The house was a stout refuge and is still called 'the Indian fort.' Two of Robert Hill's sons were killed by Indians and another by a panther.

On State 40, at 10.3 *m.*, is a junction with State 120; R. here 0.1 *m.* to FERRUM TRAINING SCHOOL, a high school and junior college under the auspices of the Methodist Church. The pine-covered foothills of the Blue Ridge make an effective background for the early Federal-style red brick buildings.

The SITE OF WASHINGTON IRON WORKS (R), 26.7 *m.*, is marked by crumbled stone walls and a chimney overgrown with vines and saplings. The furnace, then called 'the bloomery,' was operated between 1774 and

1779 by Colonel John Donelson (*see Tour 4c*) father of Rachel, afterwards the wife of Andrew Jackson. When Donelson left Virginia to settle in Tennessee, he sold the furnace to Colonel Jeremiah Early and the latter's son-in-law, Colonel James Callaway, who renamed it the Washington Iron Works. Its first business of making farm implements and 10-gallon 'potts' and ovens was put aside during the Revolution for the job of manufacturing arms.

At 47.5 *m.* is a junction with State 57.

Right here to STANLEYTOWN, 1.5 *m.* (600 pop.), which has a furniture factory surrounded by rows of company houses and small stores.

BASSETT, 2.5 *m.* (3,000 pop.), sprawling along the bends of Smith River, was named for its leading family, whose chair factory was the nucleus of the village. The retail section of the town, close to the river's edge, thins out to a border of factories, where furniture, wood veneer, mirrors, and knit goods are produced by hundreds of workers, who live near by in frame bungalows. Streets of small dwellings reach to the outlying hills, where the more showy homes of the industrial executives stand.

At 12.5 *m.* is the entrance (R) to FAIRY STONE STATE PARK (*open May* 15 *to Nov.* 1; *adm.* 10¢, *overnight camping,* 25¢, *children under* 10, *free; rowboats* 25¢ *an hr., maximum* $1.25 *a day;* 2-*person cabins,* $15 *a week,* 4-*person cabins,* $20 *a week—each additional person* $5; *store and restaurant; reservations for cabins made at Virginia Conservation Commission, Richmond*). This 5,000-acre park contains a lake and facilities for swimming and fishing. It was so named because of the small staurolite crystals, locally called fairystones, found in profusion in the area.

At 47.8 *m.* the highway passes near the SITE OF FORT TRIAL, one of the frontier forts ordered built by the assembly in 1756 and inspected in that year by George Washington, then colonel of State militia. A later visitor, who recorded lively impressions of the wilderness stockade, was the English traveler, J.F.D.Smythe; he stopped here in 1774 and 10 years later published *A Tour of the United States of America.* Though traveling alone on horseback and warned that 'the Indians had taken up the hatchet' against the whites, he determined to continue. On his way to Fort Trial he was lost in the dense thickets bordering Smith River, when he came upon an Indian war party so suddenly that his only chance was to appear friendly. The Indian leader, friendly as Indians usually were with courteous folk, was attracted at once by the gold braid on the white man's hat and pleased greatly when Smythe gave it to him as a headband. The Englishman spent the night in the woods with the natives—which proved no recommendation for him when he got to the fort the next day. The settlers, convinced that the stranger was conniving with the Indians, refused to let him enter the stockade. After a day of arguing, he was admitted, though only after he had threatened to fire the fort. In his book Smythe evens the score with very unflattering comments on the settlers and their living conditions.

At 49.9 *m.* is a junction with County 609.

Right here to FIELDALE, 0.5 *m.*, in a beautiful valley where Marshall Field & Company of Chicago in 1919 built a textile plant and homes for employees. The houses of varied architectural designs with well-kept lawns and streets make a far more attractive appearance than that of the usual industrial town.

MARTINSVILLE, 54.3 *m.* (1,128 alt., 7,705 pop.), seat of Henry County, rises to heights from the banks of the Smith River and is encircled by foothills of the Blue Ridge. Although its beginning was as a county seat village in 1793, the city now bears little suggestion of its age, having become a lively industrial town. The principal business is the manufacture of furniture and allied products—mirrors, paint, varnish, and wood veneer. Other factories produce textiles and knitted goods and various other articles, employing thousands of workers from neighboring farms and mountain settlements. The new retail business section, a long main street overhung with neon signs, has modern shops, banks, office buildings, 'modernistic' motion picture theaters, and chain stores. Martinsville was named for General Joseph Martin, and its site was given by George Hairston, who reputedly bought his 30,000-acre tract in 1770 for 10¢ an acre. Martin was a robust figure in the history of the early frontier. He was born in Albemarle County in 1740, ran away to fight Indians at 17, became an Indian agent, land agent, and officer of militia, fighting Indians all up and down the frontier. In 1774 he came to Henry County, established himself at Belle Monte on Leatherwood Creek, for nine years sat for his district in the general assembly, and in 1793 was made a brigadier general of State militia. He was a brawny, picturesque man, more than six feet tall and the father of 18 children; wore buckled knee breeches and a great beard, braided and thrust inside his shirt.

The HENRY COUNTY COURTHOUSE faces the old court square which is now eclipsed by the new business section, but a century ago was the center of county life, enlivened on court days by arguing politicians, lawyers, and planters and their muddy horses hitched to its rail. The building is a rectangle of red brick, its proportions marred at the white-pillared front entrance by a misbegotten outside stairway. Henry County, originally including the territory now in Franklin and Patrick Counties, was organized in 1776 and named for Patrick Henry.

In Martinsville is a junction with US 58 (*see Tour 7c*), with which US 220 unites to a junction at 56.5 *m.*

At 59.4 *m.* is a junction with County 641 (*slippery when wet*).

Right here to BELLEVIEW (L), 3.7 *m.*, the home of Major John Redd, Indian fighter, and officer in the Continental forces at Yorktown. The house commands a view of miles of rolling farmlands. It is well-preserved, clapboarded, L-shaped, with two-storied front porch. Family tradition is that Major Redd, master of hundreds of slaves, kept a watchful eye on plantation work through a field glass from the front porch of his home.

For a brief period in the middle 1800's, RIDGEWAY (400 pop.), 63.8 *m.*, was a busy little tobacco market. It is now the home of Danville workers.

The highway passes near Matrimony Creek, at 67.8 *m.* The Virginia Commission to establish the Virginia-North Carolina line camped on its banks in 1728. William Byrd II, who headed the party of Virginians, wrote that the creek was 'called so by an unfortunate marry'd man because it was exceedingly noisy and impetuous. However, tho the stream was clamorous, like those women who make themselves plainest heard, it was perfectly clear and unsully'd.'

At 68 *m.* US 220 crosses the North Carolina Line, 45 miles north of Winston-Salem, N.C. (*see North Carolina Guide*).

Tour 22

Warrenton—Washington—Sperryville—Luray—New Market; 58.9 *m.* US 211.

Asphalt-paved throughout.
All types of accommodations, chiefly in towns.

US 211 bisects northern Virginia, rises through the Piedmont to the Blue Ridge and Massanutten Mountains, and descends into the Shenandoah Valley, traversing rolling pastures, vast forest preserves, ruggedly beautiful mountains, and many fertile valleys. General farming, stock raising, and fruit culture are the pursuits of the region.

US 211 branches west from US 29 (*see Tour 4a*) in WARRENTON, 0 *m.* (635 alt., 1,450 pop.), seat of Fauquier County and the social and trading center for a prosperous area. Here in the foothills of the Blue Ridge Mountains, old and new Virginia meet. 'Horsey' folk in breeches share the crowded little business street with farmers in jeans. Old buildings stand beside newer ones in the few steep streets that are liberally shaded by trees. The Warrenton Junior Hunt Pony Show is the oldest in this country and the Warrenton Garden Club, the first organized in the South, is a charter member of the Garden Club of America. Named in honor of General William Warren, hero of Bunker Hill, the town was incorporated in 1810. But Fauquier Courthouse already had a history coupled with that of the county. As early as 1712 there were settlers in this vicinity and Thomas Lee received a large grant of land here in 1718. By direction of his son, Richard Henry Lee, a survey was made in 1790 and 12 half-acre lots were staked.

The FAUQUIER COUNTY COURTHOUSE is an undistinguished, mid-nineteenth-century building of brick, painted cream. There is a four-columned Ionic portico above a high flight of steps across its narrow front. Among the portraits in the courthouse are the only one in existence of Governor Francis Fauquier, painted by Lesley Bush Brown from a miniature, and a portrait of Chief Justice John Marshall by William D. Washington. Both Marshall and William Washington were natives of Fauquier County. Fauquier was formed in 1759 from Old Prince William and named in honor of the lieutenant governor.

A MONUMENT TO MOSBY, N. side of courthouse, celebrates, by a modest roughhewn obelisk of red stone, the partisan ranger, Colonel John Singleton Mosby, who came to Warrenton after the War between the States. He was arrested, however, by the Federal Government. After his release he practiced law here.

The WARREN GREEN HOTEL, erected shortly after 1875 on the site of the Norris Tavern, is a rambling three-story building of red brick with a double-decked veranda. When in 1819 Thaddeus Norris conceived the idea of erecting a brick tavern, 'he right worthily carried out his conception, and mason and joiner, and even Mr.Baker, the old silversmith at the corner of Main and Culpeper streets, who has a penchant for taming mice, heartily seconded and encouraged it.' The old gentleman's contribution was a thin plate of silver with the date the work began—found beneath the cornerstone in 1875 when the tavern was destroyed by fire. After the death of Norris, the building housed a private school but later, under the name of the Warren Green, was again an inn.

The MARR HOUSE, 342 Culpeper St., a small frame dwelling on a brick basement hidden by bushes, was the home of Captain John Quincy Marr, a Confederate who was shot June 1, 1861, at Fairfax Courthouse.

The SMITH HOUSE, 521 Culpeper St., courthouse-like with its portico and cupola, is constructed of brick, stuccoed yellow. On the grounds are long old brick stables. Most of the house was built in 1845 by Governor William ('Extra Billy') Smith (*see Tour 16a*).

Left of Warrenton on State 29 to County 744, 1.1 *m.*; L. here 0.9 *m.* to LEETON FOREST (L) a low, red brick house with a gabled roof and a small Ionic portico. This was the home of Charles Lee, attorney general of the United States from 1795 to 1801. Lee was a naval officer during the Revolution and one of the counsel for the defense in Aaron Burr's trial for treason. Leeton Forest was part of the tract of 4,200 acres granted in 1718 to Thomas Lee. The ridge on which the house stands commands a far view of the Piedmont and the Blue Ridge.

ST.LEONARDS (R), 3.1 *m.* on State 29, is a long, two-story mansion constructed of fieldstone, at the end of a lane that winds through a grove of old trees. This was the residence of John Barton Payne (1855–1935), Secretary of the Interior under President Wilson, chairman of the U.S. Shipping Board and chairman of the Red Cross under four Presidents. Judge Payne's philanthropy made possible the Virginia Museum of Fine Arts (*see Richmond*).

CLOVELLY (L), 3.2 *m.*, first called Cedar Grove, has a stone house with two long rambling additions and a columned porch. It is on a small hill landscaped with trees, hedges, stone walks, and lawns. The oldest part was built in 1746 by Peter Kemper.

The entrance (L) to NORTH WALES (L), 3.5 *m.*, is marked by a stone lodge. This structure, now a country club, has foundation walls six feet thick. The central section and its irregular wings, almost entirely covered with ivy, open onto porches with slim columns. Paneling and old iron locks are features of the interior. An old grandfather clock here, once the property of Governor Spotswood, is reputed to have been the first in Fauquier County. There is a stable for 40 hunters, a three-quarter-mile track, and a tanbark ring. The oldest part of the house was built in 1773 by William Allison.

At 4.3 *m.* is a junction with County 681; R. here 0.8 *m.* to WOODBOURNE (L), a T-shaped stone house of two stories on a high basement. It has a small entrance portico, and the wings are buttressed by two massive stone chimneys. Woodbourne was the home of Isham Keith, soldier in the Revolution and son of the Reverend James Keith, first of that name in Virginia. Isham's sister Mary became the mother of Chief Justice John Marshall.

FAUQUIER WHITE SULPHUR SPRINGS (R), 7.1 *m.* on State 29, is chiefly a pavilion and a group of red brick buildings in various stages of dissolution. For more than half a century before the War between the States, this was one of the fashionable watering places of the East. As many as 600 guests were entertained at one time. Two great hotels, 90 double cabins, as well as servants' quarters and stables, were here. In a huge ballroom assembled belles and elegant young men from many States. Many people of national importance came here, and the Virginia assembly sat here from June 11 to August 17, 1849.

A Tanxnitania Village Site is at the northern edge of the grounds, spread along the Rappahannock for half a mile. It was noted by Captain John Smith in 1608, and a land grant in this section, made in 1717, mentions 'a poison field where an Indian town formerly stood.'

On August 22, 1862, during Lee's campaign against Pope (*see Tour 4a*), General T.J. Jackson's corps, moving westward along the south bank of the Rappahannock River, arrived opposite this point. General John Pope ordered a force of 25,000 men to operate against the Confederates here but accomplished nothing. During the evening of the 24th Jackson, replaced by Longstreet, withdrew to Jeffersonton.

In JEFFERSONTON, 10.3 *m.* (82 pop.), a crossroads hamlet, is the McDermott House, a three-story stone building erected early in the nineteenth century; it has been a home, store, barroom, and post office. In early days the postmaster would dump the mail on the floor and allow customers to find their own letters. From this village, on August 24, 1862, General Jackson, after conferring with General Lee, started at midnight with 22,000 men on the great march that covered 56 miles in two days and circled the Federal army.

US 211 runs westward from Warrenton across the rolling Piedmont country.

At 17.1 *m.* is a junction with State 49.

Right on State 49 to the entrance of Ben Venue (R), 0.2 *m.*, a 5,000-acre estate with a very large, brick house, painted yellow. Built in mid-nineteenth century, it now stands deserted in a tangle of vines and weeds. Among many outbuildings are an overseer's house and, across the road, four slave cabins of red brick. Twenty miles of old stone fences divide the vast property into fields of workable size.

Little WASHINGTON, 22.7 *m.* (693 alt., 550 pop.), is the seat of Rappahannock County. An apple grading plant here ships 30,000 barrels a year. A stone monument, setting forth the town's principal claim to fame, recites: 'The First Washington of All, surveyed and platted by George Washington, with the assistance of John Lonem and Edward Corder as chainmen, August 4, 1749 . . . Town organized Dec. 14, 1796—Incorporated Feb. 12, 1894.'

The Rappahannock County Courthouse, a plain, rectangular structure of red brick with four white stuccoed pilasters, was erected in 1871. The clerk's office, smaller but of similar construction, adjoins it. The Confederate Monument near by is a stone shaft inscribed with the names of soldiers and their organizations and surmounted by four stacked muskets. Rappahannock County was formed in 1833 from Culpeper and named for the river forming its eastern boundary.

SPERRYVILLE, 28.4 *m.* (350 pop.), has an apple grading plant and a score of houses by the Thornton River. General John Pope's Army of Virginia, ordered June 26, 1862, was organized from troops under Generals Banks, Frémont, and McDowell. The troops began to arrive in this vicinity early in July and took up positions extending east and west about 30 miles. On August 7 Pope arrived to review the corps of General Franz Sigel who succeeded General Frémont in command of his corps.

Left from Sperryville on State 16 to Montpelier (L), 5.9 *m.*, a huge, stuccoed block of a house, 112 feet long. Across its three-story façade stretches a great veranda with eight massive columns and Victorian scrollwork trim. The older, middle section of stone was erected before 1760 by Colonel Francis Thornton for his son William. In the nineteenth century the house was lengthened in brick, and the portico was added. Thornton's Gap and Thornton River were named for this family.

At 31.3 *m.*, the highway crosses the eastern boundary of SHENANDOAH NATIONAL PARK (*see Tour 4A*).

BRYAN BAPTIST MEETING HOUSE (R), 33 *m.*, a small, one-story frame structure with a stone chimney, was built in 1797. Chiefly responsible for its erection was an ancestor of William Jennings Bryan. In his *Memoirs* Mr.Bryan says: 'William Bryan is the most remote forefather of whom I have knowledge. He lived in what was then a part of Culpeper (now Rappahannock) County and near the town of Sperryville, Virginia . . . He belonged to the Baptist Church in that neighborhood, which was known as the Bryan Meeting House.' William's cabin, now part of a larger house and about half a mile north of Sperryville, became the birthplace of Silas Lillard Bryan, father of William Jennings Bryan. When Silas was a child, the family moved to Mount Pleasant on the Ohio River in what is now West Virginia. In the little meeting house are two pulpit chairs, presented by Mr.Bryan about 1908.

THORNTON GAP or PANORAMA, 35.6 *m.* (2,300 alt.), is the summit of the Blue Ridge Mountains. Here is a junction with the Skyline Drive (*see Tour 4A*). The highway climbs steadily from Sperryville to the gap in a series of curves and hairpin turns, from which open views, more impressive at each higher level, of mountains, deep valleys with sparkling runs, and the twisting ribbon of road far below. Just south of the gap are two of the highest peaks in the Blue Ridge: Stony Man, 4,010 feet; and Hawks Bill, 4,049 feet. To the north are other peaks—many more than 3,000 feet high. The Massanutten Mountain rears a jagged crest beyond, and on the far western horizon lie the hazy peaks of the Alleghenies. Confederate and Union troops used Thornton Gap constantly throughout the war.

LURAY, 44.6 *m.* (835 alt., 1,450 pop.), seat of Page County, is shopping headquarters for the central Shenandoah Valley, and a tourist center. Its principal streets are lined with stores, agencies for farm implements and automobiles, restaurants, small hotels, and tourist homes. Luray produces flour, corn meal, and stock feed and ships thousands of baby chicks and turkey poults from hatcheries near by.

The town was laid out in 1812 by William Staige Marye, son of Peter Marye, who built the first turnpike—a toll road—to cross the Blue Ridge from Culpeper into the Shenandoah Valley. The site of Luray was part of a tract that belonged to the family of William Marye's wife.

The PAGE COUNTY COURTHOUSE, a two-and-one-half-story brick structure surmounted by a cupola, is entered through a loggia that extends also along the front of low wings.

Page County was formed in 1831 from Rockingham and Shenandoah and named for Governor John Page. Although Luray is the county seat, it is not within the section that was settled first. In 1729 Jacob Stover received a grant of 5,000 acres along the South Fork of the Shenandoah River at the base of Massanutten Mountain, which forms the western boundary of the county. A group of German-Swiss settlers, chiefly from Pennsylvania, founded along the river a colony known as Massanutten Town.

The SALTPETER CAVE is at the southern edge of the town. Here the Confederate forces established a nitrate plant and used the product in the manufacture of ammunition.

Luray is at the junction with State 12 (*see Tour 5A*).

The BELLE BROWN NORTHCOTT MEMORIAL TOWER (R), 45.7 *m.*, is a carillon, a square stone tower with a vaulted entrance in the base, which is slightly larger than the shaft. Under the peaked roof are 47 bells behind three Gothic arches. Programs are given at frequent intervals.

Here is the entrance (R) to the grounds of LURAY CAVERNS (*open daily; adm.* $1.50, *children* 75¢), the largest cave in Virginia. Among the subterranean rooms are the 'Cathedral,' in which there is a remarkable organ-like formation of stone, 'Giants' Hall,' 'Throne Room,' and the 'Ball, Room.' Two small bodies of water, 'Dream Lake' and the 'Silver Sea,' help to vary the underground wonders. The Smithsonian Institution long ago reported: 'It is safe to say that there is probably no cave in the world more completely and profusely decorated with stalactitic and stalagmitic formations than Luray.'

OLD MEETING HOUSE (R), 47.8 *m.*, built in 1770 and known as Mill Creek Church, is a rectangular structure of weatherboarded logs. Inside, a small gallery looks down on the old pulpit and upon austere benches to which comfort-loving modern worshipers have added backs. A stove bears the inscription: 'D.Pennybacker, 1799.' Records show that the Reverend John Koontz, a Baptist, came in 1770 to Mill Creek and organized a church. Under his persuasive influence almost every one in the vicinity—including Mennonites—became Baptists.

At 49.1 *m.* is a junction with County 646.

Right here to WHITE HOUSE (R), 0.5 *m.* a two-story structure built of stone and wood. A cellar with vaulted stone roof is similar to others in the neighborhood. The cellar and first-story walls are pierced for loopholes. A large paneled room occupying the entire first floor was used by Mennonites for meetings. White House is believed to have been built about 1750 by sons of Martin Kauffman, whose stone house survives not far away. He was a Mennonite convert of the Reverend Mr.Koontz.

At 50 *m.* on US 22 is a junction with County 615.

Left here to LOCUST GROVE (R), 0.8 *m.*, a two-story house constructed partly of brick and partly of stone, with stone chimneys at each end. The cellar, built about 1760, was fortified against Indian raids. Window sills are fastened with wooden pins. This was once the home of Isaac Strickler and in its day the most pretentious on the Massanutten grant. A chimney bears the date: 1791. A veranda that ran the length of one side was swept away in the flood of 1870.

On County 615 is the WILLIAM BRUBAKER HOUSE (R), 1.6 *m.*, built of brick on the site of the Brewecker (Brubaker) ancestral home, which was plundered and burned by the Indians in 1758. Tradition is that the Brubaker family was saved by a premonition of Mrs.Brubaker's. One evening she told her husband she could see a party of Indians on the mountains—could even count them as they sat around a camp fire. She insisted that the Indians would attack the next morning and persuaded her husband to take the family to a safe place. The neighboring Stone family ridiculed Mrs.Brubaker's premonition and were victims of the attack she had accurately prophesied. John Stone was killed in his house. His wife, baby, a son about seven, and a young George Grandstaff were carried off as prisoners. It was found that the Indians, tallying even in number with Mrs.Brubaker's count, had camped at the very spot she had pointed out, two miles away. Mrs.Stone and her baby were killed later by their captors, but Grandstaff returned to the settlement after three years. The Stone boy grew up with the Indians. Years later he returned, claimed his father's property, sold it, went back to his Indian friends and was never heard of again.

The highway crosses the eastern boundary of the GEORGE WASHINGTON NATIONAL FOREST, 52.2 *m.* (*see Tour 8b*), and climbs Massanutten Mountain, following a road laid out in 1746 along an older Indian trail.

A FOREST SERVICE CAMP is at 54.1 *m.*

NEW MARKET GAP, 55 *m.* (1,850 alt.), was formerly known as Massanutten Pass.

At 55.1 *m.* (R) is a road maintained by the Forest Service and leading northward along the mountain crest.

NEW MARKET, 58.9 *m.* (540 pop.) (*see Tour 5a*), is at the junction with US 11 (*see Tour 5a*).

Tour 23

Richmond—Goochland—Columbia—Scottsville—Charlottesville; 89.6 *m.* State 6, County 613, State 239.

Asphalt-paved throughout.
Chesapeake & Ohio Ry. parallels route between Richmond and Columbia.
Hotels in Richmond and Charlottesville, few tourist homes between termini.

Between Richmond and Scottsville this route parallels the James River through fertile bottom lands, then winds north into the hills. For a short distance at the eastern end it has a trim modern appearance but it quickly settles down to the leisurely course of its ancestor, the primitive Indian trail that became the first westbound route of white men on the James. This route has great charm, looping gracefully through alternating stretches of woodland and open fields. It once joined Three Notched Road near Boyd's Tavern after turning north at Point of Fork along the Rivanna River. The Huguenots about Manakin were among the first to use it frequently.

In RICHMOND State 6 runs west from Capitol Square, 0 *m.*, on Broad St. to the Boulevard, then west on Kensington Ave.

At 13.6 *m.* is a junction with County 649.

Left here to County 650, 1.1 *m.*, and R. to TUCKAHOE (L), 1.3 *m.*, a large white frame house approached through an avenue of elms and designed in the severe style of the early period. It rises two stories from foundations of brick in Flemish bond and consists of two gabled structures connected by a thick hyphen, which completes an H-shaped plan reminiscent of a similar Elizabethan survival at Stratford Hall. Entrance is through formal little porches on front and river façades. The interior is paneled and decorated throughout with carved woodwork of great beauty. Most of the wood is pine, but black walnut gives a fine somber effect in the central hall or 'saloon,' in the stairway of the north wing, and in the 'Burnt Room,' once slightly damaged by fire—17 coats of paint were scraped from it during the restoration. The floral carving on the riser-ends and slender balusters of the stairway are notable. Doors, swinging on H-and-L hinges, have heavy, heraldically-decorated locks, and on certain of the small iridescent windowpanes are names cut with diamonds by eighteenth-century visitors.

Just south of the house, across the lawn that sweeps toward the river, stands the little brick school house in which Thomas Jefferson received part of his early education; his childish autograph is still on its plastered wall. Beyond lies an old-fashioned garden with one of the most elaborate box-labyrinths in America. Slave quarters and the detached old brick kitchen also stand near by.

The Tuckahoe lands were patented in 1695 by William Randolph of Turkey Island (*see Tour* 24). This plantation he left to his son Thomas (1689–1730), who built the house perhaps as early as 1712.

Colonel Peter Jefferson, father of Thomas, was a friend of Thomas Randolph's son, William, who inherited the estate and married Jane, daughter of William's uncle, Isham Randolph. Thus it happened that Thomas Jefferson went to school here with the Randolph children.

William Byrd, visiting here in 1732 during a rain lasting several days, wrote: 'I learned all the tragical story of her [Mrs.Thomas Randolph's] daughter's humble marriage with her uncle's overseer'—a man without 'one visible qualification, except impudence.' The wine gave out, and Byrd could not fortify himself against 'vapors . . . laden with blight, coughs, and pleurisies,' except with endless doses of 'bark' and 'Indian physic.'

During the Revolution the Randolphs entertained officers of both armies. Captain Thomas Anbury, a British officer, on parole from the prison camp near Charlottesville, wrote in his diary, 'We found many gentlemen of this province very liberal and hospitable to British officers, among whom I may mention Messers, Randolph, of Tuckahoe, Goode, of Chesterfield, and Cary, of Warwick. In conversing with prisoners, they carefully refrain from politics. So warm and bigotted was the prevailing spirit, that those who exercised such courtesy incurred much criticism and censure. Some went so far on this account as to threaten to burn Colonel Randolph's mills.'

The estate was named for Tuckahoe Creek, which Captain John Smith called 'Tochawhoughe' (an edible water plant).

On County 650 is POWELL'S TAVERN (R), 1.7 *m.*, a relic of the days when taverns such as this were placed along the River Road at intervals of about 12 miles. It consists of two buildings, one brick and one frame, close but unconnected.

At 15.4 *m.*, by a junction with County 650, State 6 begins to follow the old River Road westward.

MANAKIN, 16.4 *m.* (150 pop.), stretching new and old houses about a single street, is the successor to Mannakin Towne (*see Tour 8b*), a Huguenot settlement south of the James River that was named for Monacan settlements near this point.

'Monsieur Marij, the minister of the Parish,' whom Byrd met here in 1732, had been 'a Romish priest, but found reason, either spiritual or temporal, to quit that gay religion.' Observing more closely, the colonel wrote, 'He looks for as much respect from his protestant flock, as is paid to the popish clergy, which our ill-bred Hugonots do not understand.'

The DOVER BAPTIST CHURCH (R), a rectangular frame building with a broad gabled roof and many windows, houses a congregation organized in 1773. The first minister was William Waller, who was locked in Chesterfield and Middlesex jails 'for preaching without authority except from above.'

This village was at the center of the Dover coal operations, the first successful commercial production of coal in America. After rich outcroppings had been discovered by a Huguenot hunter, Colonel William Byrd quickly patented the lands and in 1740–50 operations began. Bituminous coal was marketed as far north as Philadelphia until railroads brought cheaper coal from Pennsylvania.

At 19.1 *m.* is a junction with County 644.

Left here to SABOT, 0.1 *m.*, named for a small island near by that seemed to Huguenot settlers to resemble the outline of a shoe. Sabot, now only a railroad station and a few paintless shacks, was for a time the prosperous village of Dover Mills. A large mill, operated by water from the James River and Kanawha Canal, was an important source of supply for the Confederates.

The entrance (R) to SABOT HILL is at 19.9 *m.* A modern brick house is on the site of one built in 1855 by James A. Seddon, United States congressman for many years and later Secretary of War for the Confederacy. When Colonel Ulric Dahlgren, ordered to make a surprise attack on Richmond for the purpose of releasing war prisoners, advanced through this region in 1864 with 500 Federal cavalrymen, his soldiers burned the Seddon barns and sacked the house. He then attempted to follow the north bank of the James River into Richmond. Though the city was virtually unprotected at the time, a small hastily assembled home guard turned back the Union cavalry. The expedition ended in Dahlgren's death in King and Queen County (*see Tour 1B*).

CROZIER, 22.5 *m.*, a few buildings and a post office gathered loosely along the highway, is near the SITE OF COXE'S TAVERN, a stage stop.

The STATE FARM at 24.6 *m.* has accommodations in various nondescript brick and frame buildings for 750 male short-term and well-behaved long-term convicts from the State penitentiary and misdemeanants from the several sections of Virginia. Annually from 1,500 to 2,000 prisoners, convicted of minor offenses, serve sentences here. Penal reforms point to the replacement of county jails entirely by regional prisons such as this. The farm lands produce food for the use of the institution. There is also a 40-patient tuberculosis hospital here.

At 28 *m.* is a junction with State 49.

Left here to a bridge, 0.9 *m.*, that is near the SITE OF MASSINACACK, an Indian village found by Captain Christopher Newport, who in 1608 set forth 'with 120 chosen men . . . for the discovery of Monacan.' Said one account of the trip, 'the people neither used us well nor ill, yet for our securitie we tooke one of their petty Kings, and led him bound to conduct us the way.' John Lederer visited the village in 1670 and showed it on the map that accompanied the account of his exploration west of the Blue Ridge.

South of the river is the VIRGINIA INDUSTRIAL SCHOOL FOR BOYS (R), 1.2 *m.*, a reform school for delinquent youths committed by the juvenile and domestic relations courts. The number of boys in the school generally approximates the capacity of 280.

The STATE INDUSTRIAL FARM FOR WOMEN (L), 28.6 *m.*, is housed in several attractive dormitories of pink brick behind white fences on a 174-acre prison farm. The institution, where vocational training has been successfully employed, has accommodations for 100. The farm lies close to the riverside hamlet, Maidens, which used to be called Maidens Adventure and celebrates the legendary exploit of a young girl who is supposed to have crossed the river here to rescue her lover from Indian marauders.

GOOCHLAND, 29.1 *m.* (105 pop.), seat of Goochland County, is on open, rolling hills. The small group of structures sheltering rural commerce and county law practice and residences, old or new, surround GOOCHLAND COURTHOUSE (R), which is among trees within a brick-walled yard. The roof of this red brick building extends forward to form the pediment of a full-width portico with four Tuscan columns. Built in 1826, its design was undoubtedly copied from that of the pavilions at the University of Virginia, then under construction. The jail, constructed of uncut stone, was built in 1848. Goochland County, formed from Henrico in 1727, was the first Virginia county entirely in the Piedmont.

The most publicized of Goochland records are the marriage bond of the parents of Thomas Jefferson and a deed for Peter Jefferson's part of the Shadwell estate, which was transferred 'for and in consideration of Henry Weatherburn's biggest bowl of Arrack punch' (*see Tour 17a*).

When Colonel Byrd visited Goochland in 1732 he wrote of a home just west of the county seat as 'a new settlement' in a 'retired part of the country.' 'A Goochland store,' he averred, was a place where 'the way of dealing . . . is for some small merchant or pedler to buy a Scots pennyworth of goods, and clap one hundred and fifty per cent upon that.'

BELMONT (R), at 30.5 *m.*, is the farm on which was born Edward Bates (1793–1869), United States Attorney General during the War between the States. The house has been destroyed. Taken by his father, Thomas Fleming Bates, to Missouri when he was 10 years old, Bates in time reached the National legislature, where he became a passionate antislavery candidate for Republican nomination to the presidency.

At 33.4 *m.* is a junction with County 625.

Left here to BOLLING HALL (L), 1.9 *m.*, a large two-story frame house, built early in the nineteenth century by Colonel William Bolling (*see Tour 19*). A conservatory at one end of the house was a notable feature when it was erected.

At 3.9 *m.* is a junction with County 627; L. here to County 600, 2.6 *m.*, and R. to ROCK CASTLE (R), 3.6 *m.*, where a modern brick house with a neo-Tudor air takes precedence over the old white frame house, probably built before 1732 by Tarleton Fleming. Tiny dormer windows in the old gabled roof with hipped ends light a half story. In 1732 Colonel Byrd said that Mrs.Fleming, formerly a Miss Mary Randolph of Tuckahoe, was 'packing up her baggage with design to follow her husband . . . who was gone to a new settlement in Goochland.' He added that Mr. and Mrs.Fleming had 'been about seven years persuading themselves to remove to that retired part of the country.' When Colonel Tarleton, raiding during the Revolution, found the Tarleton coat-of-arms hanging here, he angrily cut down the plaque and carried it away.

GEORGES TAVERN, 39.7 *m.*, a crossroads settlement of half a dozen houses, carries on the name of a vanished stage inn on the River Road.

Left from Georges Tavern on State 45 to HOWARDS NECK (R), 4.1 *m.*, a plantation that has been the home of Randolphs, Cunninghams, and Hobsons. The red brick house, built about 1825 after plans of Robert Mills, is nearly square, with a broad hip roof. Well-spaced windows with shutters break the wall surfaces, which are set off by the white stone of lintels and of ornamental plaques set midway between each pair of window openings. A formal porch is half hidden by tree-box. Edward Cunningham built his house in front of a much older frame one constructed early in the eighteenth century by the first settler here, a Randolph.

At 7.7 *m.* is a junction with County 602; R. here 3 *m.* to AMPTHILL, a one-story red brick house facing the fertile lowlands along the James. Its fine portico has four Tuscan columns. Large windows with shutters and white marble lintels take up much of the wall space between a high basement and a severe cornice.

To Randolph Harrison, who married Thomas Jefferson's granddaughter, Jefferson wrote in 1815: 'I have had leisure to think of your house. You seemed to require six rooms, neither more nor less, and a good entrance or passage of communication. The enclosed is drawn on that plan. The ground plat is in detail, and exact, the elevation is merely a sketch to give a general idea. The workman, if he is anything of an architect, will be able to draw the particulars. Affectionately yours . . .' This house appears to have been constructed, however, sometime between the death of Mrs.Harrison in 1835 and her husband's death, four years later. And then only part of Jefferson's plan was used.

Joined to the rear of the house by a wide passage chamber is the much older frame dwelling constructed about 1732, soon after these frontier lands were first taken up. Similar in outline and parallel to the newer part, it has two stories beneath its hip roof and low wings. The central staircase has carved paneling. Near by stand several of the old brick outbuildings.

At 40.7 *m.* on State 6 is a junction with County 608.

Left here to a lane (L), 1.6 *m.*, the entrance to ELK HILL, a gray-stuccoed brick house high on a hill among box bushes and a grove of elms. Thomas Jefferson inherited this estate from his father-in-law. At the approach of the British in May 1781, Mrs. Jefferson and her little family fled to her husband at Monticello and left Elk Hill to Cornwallis, who made it his headquarters from June 7 to 15, 1781, while waiting for Colonel Tarleton to return from Charlottesville with Governor Jefferson and the Virginia legislature in tow. When Tarleton turned up empty-handed, Cornwallis marched eastward, leaving the house ransacked, supplies destroyed, livestock killed, and with Jefferson's slaves as booty.

Elk Hill was again sacked in 1865, this time by Sheridan's raiders.

COLUMBIA, 46.3 *m.* (154 pop.), at the confluence of the James and Rivanna Rivers, is a collection of frame houses and country stores, filling stations, and a saw mill with attendant lumber yards. Rising on the site of Rassawek, capital of the Monacans, this was called Point of Fork until an act of the general assembly in 1788 directed that land here 'shall be laid off with convenient streets, and shall be established as a town by the name of Columbia.' Later the town became important as the meeting place of two canals. Produce from the north was floated down the Rivanna and its tributaries as early as 1756, for in that year the Reverend James Fontaine Maury of Albemarle wrote, 'Nothing is more common than to see two of these tottering vehicles [flatboats], when lashed together side by side, carrying down our upland streams eight or nine heavy hogsheads of tobacco.'

In the latter part of the Revolution, Baron von Steuben, then in charge of Virginia militia, commanded a training post and supply depot here. When he thought that the forces of Simcoe and Tarleton were about to converge here, von Steuben moved the stores and most of his force across the Rivanna. On Simcoe's arrival he retreated, abandoning most of the supplies.

In 1783 an ammunition and ordnance depot was established here, and in 1792 a contract was given for the movement of military supplies from Richmond. In March 1865 Columbia was raided by General Sheridan.

At 50.9 *m.*, by the rural post office DIXIE, is a junction with US 15 (*see Tour 3c*) which unites with State 6 to FORK UNION, 53.1 *m.* (*see Tour 3c*).

SCOTTSVILLE, 69.5 *m.* (341 pop.), serves the neighborhood as shopping center and awakes to mild hilarity on Saturday nights. It was the seat of Albemarle County until Charlottesville was established in 1762. Later it became the terminal of the James River-Staunton Turnpike.

At the outskirts of the village on Warren St. is CHESTER, a two-story frame house built in 1747 by Joseph Wright, a retired English gardener who designed the formal gardens.

At 70.1 *m.*, R. on County 613, a narrow, somewhat rough hard-surfaced road, now the main route, that dips and winds among the foothills of the Blue Ridge. Between Scottsville and Charlottesville are many small 'gentlemen's estates.'

GLENDOWER (L), 73.6 *m.*, a large brick house with a wide, two-tiered portico, was built about 1808 by Samuel Dyer.

At KEENE, 75.8 *m.*, an almost invisible hamlet, county roads branch in five directions.

1. Right from Keene on County 712 to County 713, 1.6 *m.*

a. Right on County 713, 0.3 *m.*, to CHRIST CHURCH (R), a rectangular brick structure with gabled roof and full entablature. It was built in 1831–32 and dedicated by Bishop Meade. The chancel rail and gallery are as they originally were. St.Anne's Church is the successor to the Forge Church of St.Anne's Parish, which was formed from St.James's Parish in 1745.

b. Left from County 712 0.1 *m.* on County 713 to PLAIN DEALING (L), an informal two-story frame house with brick ends. Samuel Dyer, who bought the place in 1787, incorporated the small house he found here as a wing of the present structure.

2. Left from Keene on County 712 to ESTOUTEVILLE (R), 1.5 *m.*, a large red brick house behind a formal Doric portico. The large central part is flanked by one-story wings. Construction of the house was begun by John Coles III in 1828 according to plans drawn by James Dinsmore, a Philadelphian who for 10 years assisted Jefferson with architectural work. The 50 ox skulls in bas-relief, in the hall frieze, were carved in Charlottesville at a cost of $5 each.

The first house here, built in 1800, was named Calycanthus Hill. A Coles marriage with a member of the Skipwith family of Mecklenburg County caused the place to be renamed for the Norman baron d'Estouteville, an ancestor of the Skipwiths.

At 1.6 *m.* is a junction with County 627; L. here 0.7 *m.* to ENNISCORTHY (R), a large, comfortable-looking brick house, with a square two-story unit having a hip roof and flanked by lower wings. It was built in the 1850's to replace a house burned in 1840. About 1769 John Coles II, of Hanover, settled here on land named for the family seat in Leinster, Ireland.

'The Cabin,' a little brick cottage overlooking wide gardens, was probably the first house Coles built on his lands.

At 2 *m.* on County 627 is the entrance (R), through handsome Italian wrought-iron gates, to TALLWOOD, a two-story brick house, its main section woodsheathed. Additions to the one-story wings have given rise to a local jest that the house has both wings and pinions. Each of the four chimneys has four arches protecting the flue. The detail of the carved mantel in the living room is exceptionally fine. Tucker Coles built Tallwood between 1810 and 1827 on his share of the Enniscorthy estate.

At 4.4 *m.* on County 712 is EDGEMONT (L), a small frame structure of fine proportions. Rising one generous story from a stone basement to a sweeping hip roof pierced by slender chimneys, the square structure displays Roman Doric porticoes on three sides. Centered on the fourth side, opposite the main entrance, is the projecting bay of an octagonal salon. Every element of the design is characteristic of Jefferson's best plans. The walls were originally painted to simulate stone block construction.

Colonel James Powell Cocke, suffering from malaria, traded his James River home, Malvern Hills, for Robert Nelson's estate here in the more salubrious mountain air. Plans for the house, dated 1806, have been identified in the Coolidge Collection of Jeffersoniana.

RUINS OF VIEWMONT (R), 78.2 *m.*, hulks of two great buttressed chimneys, are all that remain of a fine frame dwelling burned in 1939. Colonel Joshua Fry, who was already living here in 1744, entertained Dr. Thomas Walker during his explorations in 1749–50. In 1786 the estate was purchased by Governor Edmund Randolph.

CARTER'S BRIDGE, 79.1 *m.*, is at a junction with County 627 (*see Tour 23A*), an alternate route into Charlottesville.

BLUE RIDGE SANATORIUM (R), 88.1 *m.*, is a State institution for the treatment of tubercular patients. Its gray stuccoed buildings, on elevated land, accommodate 270 patients.

At 88.3 *m.* this route is rejoined by Tour 23A (*see Tour 23A*); L. here on State 239, the main route into CHARLOTTESVILLE, 89.6 *m.* (480 alt., 15,245 pop.) (*see Charlottesville*).

Tour 23A

Junction with County 613—Monticello—Ash Lawn—Carter's Bridge; 11.2 *m.* State 239 and County 627.

Asphalt-paved roadbed between Junction with County 613 and Ashlawn; gravel Ashlawn to Carter's Bridge.
No accommodations.

This route winds through the foot hills, passing the homes of James Monroe and Thomas Jefferson, and several less noteworthy estates.

State 239 branches southeast from a junction with County 613, 0 *m.*, at a point 1.3 miles south of Charlottesville (*see Tour 23*).

MICHIE TAVERN (R), 0.7 *m.* (*open 9–5 daily, adm. 50¢*), is a small rectangular frame building painted white that was moved in 1927 from its original site northwest of Charlottesville. The oldest part of the inn, built before 1740, has fine interior woodwork. It was enlarged about 1763, not long after Major John Henry, father of Patrick Henry, had sold it to John Michie. It contains Colonial tavern furnishings.

MONTICELLO (*open* 8–5 *daily; adm.* 50¢), 1.2 *m.*, is approached by a private road that winds up through woods from a brick lodge. The notable mansion, on the leveled top of a 'little mountain,' looks across a wide lawn shaded by scattered trees to far horizons, embracing the crest of the Blue Ridge and many miles of the Piedmont.

The red brick house with snow-white trim, roughly oval in plan and in a green frame of trees, is an example of Classical Revival design. To the southwest it presents a fine Roman Doric portico before the projecting end of a salon designed in the French manner. The room is topped by a large white-domed octagonal clerestory with circular windows. Behind a similar portico, the eastern and newer side has a low second story with half windows immediately above the lintels of the first floor windows, and a half story set back inconspicuously. The whole, tied together by a balustraded parapet and by a continuous Doric entablature, seems much smaller than it is. The house is at the center of a formal plan that embraces sunken and terrace-covered passages leading away from it on both sides to small templelike pavilions at the far ends of service quarters set in the hillside.

The interior is distinguished by beauty of woodwork and many evidences of Jefferson's ingenuity. The large entrance hall opens, beneath a balcony, into the salon. Lateral halls lead to four chambers, to the dining room with monumentally proportioned arches over alcove, and to Jefferson's study. Two steep staircases, hidden in closetlike alcoves because the builder regarded stairs as unattractive architectural features, lead to low bedrooms above the high first floor and to a 'ballroom' in the cupola.

Jefferson loved a gadget and invented many clever devices still in use. At Monticello are dumb-waiters, disappearing beds, unusual lighting and ventilating arrangements, one of his duplicate-writing machines, the forerunner of the one-arm lunch chair, folding doors of the type now used in streetcars—all devised by the builder of Monticello, who attached a contrivance to a wheel of his carriage to record the revolutions. Over the entrance is an extraordinary clock with a series of weights and pulleys that are incongruous in the formal room.

Assimilating the Graeco-Roman designs of Palladio and using materials —even nails—made by his slaves on the spot, Jefferson began building with painstaking care from his own design in 1770 and by 1775 had completed the western part, including a two-tiered portico. In 1771 after Shadwell (*see Tour 17a*) burned, he moved into the first completed pavilion and a year later he brought his bride to it on horseback through a blizzard. Stimulated by what he saw on his European travels, he enlarged the house between 1796 and 1809 in a style even more Roman, making it an example of classical design adapted to its environment and uses. Jefferson was the leader in as purifying a movement in architecture as in government. His careful symmetrical arrangement, the drawing room with an octagonal bay and the emphasized white portico, had a far-reaching influence in developing the style of architecture now called Early Republican or Federal. The Marquis de Chastellux, visiting here as early as 1782, wrote later: 'We may safely aver that Mr. Jefferson is the first American who has consulted the fine arts to know how he should shelter himself from

Along the Highway II

otograph by courtesy of the Virginia Conservation Commission

NATURAL BRIDGE, ROCKBRIDGE COUNTY

Photograph by Virginia Skyline Company, Incorporated

A SKYLINE DRIVE VISTA, SHENANDOAH NATIONAL PARK

IN THE BLUE RIDGE

Photograph by courtesy of the Virginia Conservation Commission

otograph by courtesy of the United States Forest Service

SHARP TOP, PEAKS OF OTTER, BEDFORD COUNTY

Photograph by courtesy of the Norfolk Advertising Board

LAKE DRUMMOND, DISMAL SWAMP, NORFOLK COUNTY

TYE RIVER, NELSON COUNTY

Photograph by courtesy of the United States Forest Service

otograph by courtesy of American Airlines, Incorporated

ABRAMS FALLS, NEAR BRISTOL

Photograph by courtesy of the Norfolk Advertising Boar

ALONG THE ATLANTIC

BEFORE THE GOLD CUP STEEPLECHASE, NEAR WARRENTON

Photograph by W. Lincoln Highto

Photograph by courtesy of the Virginia Conservation Commission

VALLEY OF VIRGINIA FROM SKYLINE DRIVE, SHENANDOAH NATIONAL PARK

FOX HUNT

Photograph by courtesy of the Virginia Conservation Commission

Photograph by courtesy of the Virginia Conservation Commission

BOATING, HUNGRY MOTHER PARK

SHENANDOAH RIVER, WARREN COUNTY

Photograph by W. Lincoln Highton

the weather.' Though the house has great interest it is less satisfactory from an architectural point of view than others Jefferson designed.

During Jefferson's last years Monticello was a mecca for all distinguished travelers, European and American. He often received 40 or 50 guests a day in spite of his love of quiet for study and contemplation, which he rarely achieved except at Poplar Forest (*see Tour 11a*).

Soon after Jefferson's death in 1826 the house and estate were sold for his only surviving child, Mrs.Martha Jefferson Randolph. Much hospitality and generosity had helped to impoverish a 'founding father' who never indulged in speculation. Generally valued at more than $70,000, the house and remaining 552 acres were bought in 1831 in a depressed market for a tenth of that amount by a Mr.Barkley, who had newly come to the neighborhood, disliked Jefferson, and largely destroyed his gardens. When Barkley's silk worm project failed after three years, there was an abortive movement by the Federal Government to buy the place as a National monument. Two hundred and eighteen acres and the house were bought for $2,500 and partly restored by Uriah Levy, who admired Jefferson. But after 1839 he turned it over to tenants and gradual ruin. The house was confiscated in 1861 and the furnishings were sold. After the war, however, Monticello was restored to Commodore Uriah Levy, who recovered some of the furniture and attempted to leave Jefferson's house to the Nation or to the people of Virginia. His will having been broken, a nephew, Jefferson Levy, acquired full possession, restored the house, and enlarged the estate to about 2,000 acres. In 1923 he sold Monticello and 650 acres for $500,000, to the Thomas Jefferson Memorial Foundation, successor to another association organized for the same purpose in 1912.

Thomas Jefferson was born near by at Shadwell (*see Tour 17a*), the farm of his father, Peter Jefferson, on April 13, 1743. His mother was Jane Randolph, daughter of Isham Randolph. In 1760, after attending school in several places, Jefferson entered an advanced class at the College of William and Mary. He was admitted to the bar in 1767. Entering the house of burgesses in 1769, he became almost at once the author of the first American antislavery bill, which failed, however, of passage. His marriage in 1772 to Mrs.Martha Wayles Skelton doubled his fortune. The next year he helped devise the intercolonial activities of the Committees of Correspondence and was a member of the Virginia Committee. He was only 32 when sent to the Continental Congress in 1775 and only 33 when he phrased the Declaration of Independence.

In 1779 Jefferson succeeded Patrick Henry as governor of Virginia and while in office wrote the Statute of Virginia for Religious Freedom. He served his country as minister to France during the years 1785–89 and was thus abroad at the time of the Constitutional Convention. His known aversion to strengthening the Federal Government caused considerable concern to Washington and Madison, who kept him apprised of what was going on and endeavored to disarm the objection they knew he would raise. On his return he reluctantly agreed to argue out his objections privately provided the sponsors would move immediately after adoption for inclusion of a bill of rights. Washington appointed him the first Secretary of State. It was as antagonist of Alexander Hamilton, Secretary of the Treasury, that he drew to his side the agrarian, democratic, antifederal elements throughout the States, enabling him to found the Democratic (then Republican) party, to become Vice President in 1797, and third President in 1801. The most important acts during his two terms in office were the purchase of Louisiana in 1803, the promotion of the Lewis and Clark expedition, and his advocacy of the Embargo Act of 1807. After his retirement from public life in 1809, Jefferson devoted much of his time to promoting education. In 1819 he founded the University of Virginia. America's 'great commoner' died on July 4, 1826, the fiftieth anniversary of the Declaration of Independence.

His self-composed epitaph on a simple shaft in the graveyard reads:

Here was buried
Thomas Jefferson
Author of the Declaration of American Independence
of the Statute of Virginia for Religious Freedom
and Father of the University of Virginia.

At Monticello, State 239 becomes County 627.

At 2.5 *m.* is a junction with County 732.

Left here to TUFTON (L), 0.6 *m.*, an unobtrusive country house on part of the first estate patented in Albemarle by Colonel Peter Jefferson. The middle section of the house—of logs covered with weatherboarding—was built about 1790 by Thomas Jefferson. The rear wing—of stone—was built by Thomas Jefferson's grandson, Thomas J. Randolph, and the brick part, in front, about 1833 by a later owner.

At 3.6 *m.* on County 627 is the entrance (R) to ASH LAWN (*adm.* 50¢), a plain frame structure of two stories with a low one-story L at the rear. It stands on a hill at the head of a long lawn studded with great ash trees, lofty Norway pines, dwarf and tree boxwoods, magnolias, rhododendron, and English ivy. James Monroe built this house to be near his friend and mentor, Thomas Jefferson. During his hard years as minister to France he wrote yearningly to Jefferson 'of the house to be built in two sections, a part to be finished first and the whole to cost not more than three or four thousand dollars.' But Monroe completed only the small rear part of Ash Lawn, and this between 1796–98. From that time until 1820, he constantly returned to Ash Lawn as a refuge from troublous experiences. After 1820 he lived at Oak Hill (*see Tour 3a*).

James Monroe (1758–1831) was born in Westmoreland County (*see Tour 16a*). The early part of his career, including his attendance at the College of William and Mary, soldiering during the Revolution, practice of law, and election to the Virginia Constitutional Convention, the Virginia general assembly, and the United States Senate, was not unlike that of several other ambitious young Virginians of the time. First the disciple, then the trusted friend of Thomas Jefferson, he was finally the man who completed the work the aging Jefferson was unwilling to continue. In 1794 he served as envoy to France, from 1799 to 1802 as Governor of Virginia; in 1803 he was sent abroad by Thomas Jefferson to assist in the negotiations over a port of deposit on the Mississippi that resulted in the Louisiana

Purchase, and remained abroad as minister to England and later to Spain; he became Secretary of State and later Secretary of War under Madison and President of the United States from 1817 to 1825. As President he brought to a close boundary disputes between the United States and Great Britain, eliminated fortifications from the Canadian border, effected the purchase of Spanish Florida, and enunciated the doctrine that bears his name. Like Jefferson and Madison, Monroe opposed slavery. As early as 1801, he corresponded with Jefferson concerning the possibility of settling Negroes in Africa. Monrovia, the capital of Liberia, is his namesake.

The 16-foot marble STATUE OF MONROE on the lawn is by Attilio Piccirilli. Commissioned by the Venezuela government, Piccirilli finished the figure after a revolutionary movement in Venezuela had placed in power officials who did not appreciate the Monroe Doctrine as much as did their predecessors. The statue stood in a New York studio from the 1880's until 1931.

MORVEN (R), 5 *m.*, is a tall stone house built about 1820 by David Higginbotham. Prior to the construction of the present house, this spot was the home of William Short, minister to the Netherlands during Washington's administration. The estate was first called Indian Camp because of the ruins of an Indian village in the neighborhood. The extensive old-fashioned garden has recently been formalized.

ELLERSLIE (R), 7.2 *m.*, is a square, red brick house among white-fenced fields. The Ellerslie Stud, operated for the past half century here and in Kentucky, was established by Captain Richard Hancock, a Louisiana Confederate veteran who recovered from wounds in this section and married. Gallant Fox and Omaha, both outstanding winners on American turf, and the renowned sire Wrack were from Ellerslie stables.

At 7.6 *m.* is a junction with County 727.

Left here to BLENHEIM (L), 0.5 *m.*, a long, low frame house with a pair of formal entrance porches on the front. The gable roof is punctuated by small dormers and three chimneys. In this house, one of two John Carter maintained on this plantation, lived his son, Edward.

In 1836 Blenheim became the home of Andrew Stevenson. During the period (1836–41) when he was American minister to England, Mrs.Stevenson—Sarah Coles of Enniscorthy—received a barrel of Albemarle pippins from friends. In her note of thanks she wrote, 'They were eated and praised by royal lips . . . Mr.Stevenson proposed sending two dozen to the Queen . . . and dining with Lord Durham soon after, he told me my apples had created a sensation at the palace . . .' Queen Victoria, so the story goes, became a steady customer of the pippin growers of Albemarle and regularly served this crisp, juicy apple.

At 11.1 *m.* on County 627 is a junction with County 708.

Left here to REDLANDS (L), 0.2 *m.*, a tall brick house soberly designed. It was built in 1798 by Robert Carter, on part of the large tract patented here by his grandfather, John Carter, Secretary of the Colony and eldest son of Robert 'King' Carter.

At 11.2 *m.* County 627 rejoins County 613 (*see Tour 23*) at Carter's Bridge, a point 10.5 miles south of Charlottesville.

Tour 24

Richmond—Charles City—Barrett's Ferry—Junction State 31; 53.6 *m.* State 5.

Roadbed asphalt-paved.
Accommodations at scattered tourist homes.

State 5 parallels the north bank of the James River through woodland and crosses the Chickahominy. The route is exceptionally beautiful, particularly in seasons when heavy foliage frames its ever-changing vistas. It traverses some of the oldest plantations of Anglo-America.

State 5 branches southeast from US 60 (*see Tour 8a*) in RICHMOND, at the east end of Broad St., 0 *m.*, and for a short distance is a winding cobble-paved road, downhill.

At 3.2 *m.* is a junction with the Osborne Road.

Right here 5.4 *m.* to State 156, which traverses the Richmond National Battlefield Park and parallels the line of fortifications that formed the Confederates' outer defenses during the War between the States. FORT HOKE (L), at the junction, has been restored with sandbags and gabions.

Paralleling the Osborne Road is CHAFFIN'S BLUFF (R), which, like Drewry's Bluff (*see Tour 1c*) on the south side of the river, was strongly fortified and formed part of Richmond's defenses.

At 6.4 *m.* on State 5 is a junction with State 156.

Right here to FORT HARRISON (L), 2.5 *m.*, now a PARK HEADQUARTERS AND MUSEUM (*open* 9 *to* 6), where relics and a plaster model of the James River area in relief are on display. Fort Harrison, a strong position in the outer defense line, was captured by the Federals September 29, 1864, when General B.F.Butler attacked in Grant's third major attempt to break through to Richmond while two corps diverted Lee's attention south of the James. The next day a division of Longstreet's corps failed in an attempt to retake Fort Harrison. The Confederates at this point fell back to a second line, which they held to the end.

At 3.8 *m.* is FORT HOKE (*see above*).

At 6.6 *m.* on State 5 is a junction with the Varina Road.

Right here to the FORT HARRISON NATIONAL CEMETERY, 1.8 *m.* The soldiers buried here were killed when the fort was taken.

The Varina Road becomes a private road leading to VARINA (pronounced Va-rye-na), 6.2 *m.*, a large brick residence, seat of a plantation by the James. It was on this land in 1612 that John Rolfe introduced the cultivation of tobacco for export to England and began an enterprise that salvaged the struggling colony and formed the basis of early Virginia prosperity. The estate was the home of John Rolfe and Pocahontas for two years following their marriage in 1614 and the birthplace of their son Thomas (*see Tour 19*). When the counties were formed in 1634, Varina became the seat of Henrico County and so remained until 1752. When in 1680 the general assembly directed that each county should have a town or port, one was laid out here for Henrico County. Here in the Henrico Glebe-House the Reverend James Blair (1653–1743) conceived the plan for a college in Virginia (*see Williamsburg*). And here, in the Glebe-House, the Reverend William Stith (1707–55) wrote his *History of the First Discovery and Settlement of Virginia*, printed in 1747 (*see Williamsburg*).

The present brick house was built in 1857 by Albert M. Aiken and was the headquarters of General B.F.Butler while he was digging the Dutch Gap Canal. Called Aiken's Landing, Varina was a place for the exchange of prisoners; the brick barn was used as a detention station.

At 10.7 *m.* on State 5 is a junction with the Kingsland Road.

Right here to the Deep Bottom Road, 0.7 *m.*, and L. to DEEP BOTTOM, 2.2 *m.*, a landing on the James. Here General Grant disembarked heavy forces several times in attempts to take Richmond. On July 27, 1864, the 2nd Corps and Sheridan's cavalry were landed here to distract attention from Burnside's Mine (*see Tour* 18). A second unsuccessful attempt, paired with a heavy movement against the Weldon R.R. (*see Tour* 14), was made by two corps that landed here August 12. In a third attempt on September 29—paired with movements against railroads south of Petersburg—the Federals were successful in capturing Fort Harrison (*see above*).

Stone gateposts (R) at 11.6 *m.* mark the entrance to CURLES NECK, a modern dairy farm that was the seat of the leader of Bacon's Rebellion. The Colonial house has been supplanted by the large brick mansion. On a steeplechase course here the owner holds horse shows each spring.

Curles Neck was patented in 1617 by Edward Gurgany. Later it was acquired by Nathaniel Bacon, who, campaigning without authority against the Indians in June 1676, offended Governor Berkeley, was arrested, brought to trial, acquitted and 'forgiven.' When the governor attempted his arrest for a second trial, 500 Virginia farmers, who had resented the governor's failure to give them protection from the aborigines, gathered here and began a civil war.

In 1698 'Curles, formerly Longfield,' and 'Slashes,' 'late in the seizen and inheritance of Nathaniel Bacon . . . and found to escheat to his most sacred Majesty by the attainder of . . . Nathaniel Bacon, Junr., of high treason,' were purchased for £150 by the immigrant, William Randolph, who gave the land to his son Richard.

Brick gateposts (R), 13.7 *m.*, are at the entrance to TURKEY ISLAND, ancestral seat of the Randolph family. The present house, near the James, is relatively modern. Within a walled enclosure are ironstone table tombs, that of the immigrant bearing the Randolph arms. The plantation, so named for an island near by where the first explorers of the river found many wild turkeys, was owned in 1676 by Colonel James Crews, who was hanged for participating with his neighbor, Bacon, in the rebellion. In 1684 the land was sold to William Randolph (1657–1711).

At 13.9 *m.* is a junction with State 156, the Battlefield Route.

Left here to the BATTLEFIELD OF MALVERN HILL, 1.2 *m.*, scene of the final engagement on July 1, 1862, of the Seven Days' Campaign. Here Lee and McClellan had their armies concentrated for the first time. McClellan's five corps occupied this hill, with flanks by the river; Lee's army stretched in a semicircle to the northward across this road, the only feasible means of approach. The Confederates, retarded more by the fire of artillery than by small arms, were repeatedly repulsed. The assaults, however, were such a threat that General Fitz-John Porter, virtually in command of the field and fearing capture at one period, tore up his diary and campaign book. During the night the Federal army withdrew to their base at Harrison's Landing (*see below*).

In the GLENDALE NATIONAL CEMETERY (R), 3.1 *m.*, are a vertically mounted cannon and symmetrically circular rows of headstones. Of the 1,192 buried here 958 are unknown.

GLENDALE, 3.9 *m.*, a hamlet where several roads converge, was the central point during the Battle of Glendale, or Frayser's Farm. On June 30, following the Battle of Savage Station, Lee's divisions encountered the Federals at Malvern Hill, at White Oak Swamp, and at this crossroads. Though several Federal divisions maintained their ground throughout the afternoon, fighting stopped as darkness came on, and the Federal forces withdrew to Malvern Hill.

At WHITE OAK SWAMP, 6.5 *m.*, General W.B.Franklin held Jackson. Reaching the north side of the stream about noon and finding the bridge destroyed, Jackson remained here until Franklin withdrew after nightfall.

At 10.4 *m.* is a junction with US 60 (*see Tour 8a*).

At 14.7 *m.* on State 5 is a junction with a dirt trail.

Right here through woods to another trail, 0.3 *m.*, and R. to the RANDOLPH MONUMENT, 0.5 *m.* This area—Park Woods—was part of the Turkey Island estate and maintained by the Randolph family as a park. The obelisk, 18 feet high, relates that, 'The Foundation of this Pillar was laid in the calamitous year 1771 when all the Great Rivers of this Country were swept by inundations never before experienced which changed the face of Nature and left traces of their violence that will remain for ages. In the year of 1772 this monument was raised to the memory of the first Richard and Jane Randolph of Curles.'

At 17.5 *m.* on State 5 is a junction with County 607.

Left here to County 605, 1.3 *m.*, and R. to the SITE OF THE FOREST (R), 1.5 *m.*, where Thomas Jefferson and Martha Wayles Skelton, widow of Bathurst Skelton, were married New Year's Day 1772.

At 19.6 *m.* on State 5 is a junction with County 608.

Right here 1.5 *m.* to (R) SHIRLEY (*gardens open week days, adm.* 50¢; *house open April Garden Week*), one of the largest Tidewater mansions, built between 1720 and 1740; it is on a lawn sloping to the river. Large outbuildings are behind it. The square three-story brick structure is unusually high and has a deep denticulated cornice. The double-hipped roof has no ridge; there is a single fineal at the peak, and plain gabled dormers are packed closely about its four sides. Glazed headers, now almost black, laid in Flemish bond, make a checkered pattern against the dull pink of the stretchers. The entrance and river fronts are half hidden by large two-story porches with plain columns and low pediments, added in 1800.

The asymmetrical interior is notable for its woodwork especially for the number of completely paneled rooms. In the very large hall, occupying more than a quarter of the main floor, is a 'hanging stair,' which seems to have no support as it swings out over the center of the chamber on its way up a square well three stories high. Deep cornices, mantels, overmantels, and broken pediments—each different—over doors that connect the hall and three large reception rooms have carved details. Besides old furniture, the house contains a large collection of portraits. In the great hall hangs an oil of 'King' Carter, elegant in bright red coat and other eighteenth-century finery; and in the parlor are crayons of a later Robert Carter and his wife, and of William Carter, by Saint-Mémin.

The estate was settled in 1613 as a hundred called 'West-and-Sherley,' owned by Thomas West, third Lord Delaware, and his brothers, Francis, Nathaniel, and John—all, except Nathaniel, in turn, governors of Virginia. It was early patented by Colonel Edward Hill. Commemorating in its name Sir Thomas Sherley, the father of Cecilly, Lady Delaware, Shirley passed to Colonel Edward Hill II (1637–1700), treasurer of the colony, attorney-general, and also councillor and speaker of the house of burgesses. In 1720 the estate was inherited by Elizabeth Hill, who in 1723 married

John Carter (1690–1743), eldest son of 'King' Carter (*see Tour 16b*). Their granddaughter, Ann Hill Carter, was married here to 'Light Horse Harry' Lee in 1793 (*see Tour 16b*).

At 20.8 *m.* on State 5 is a junction with State 36.

Right here to HARRISON'S POINT, 1.1 *m.*, terminus of the HOPEWELL-CHARLES CITY FERRY (*see Tour 19*) (*hourly service 7:30 a.m. to 7:30 p.m.; car and driver 65¢, round trip $1, each passenger 20¢, round trip 30¢*).

The highway crosses Kimage's Creek, 21.5 *m.*, which flows by CAWSEY'S CARE, patented by Nathaniel Causey in 1620. The estate was owned during the time of Bacon's Rebellion by Colonel Thomas Grendon, whose wife Sarah took so prominent a part in the uprising against autocratic rule that she had the honor of being the only woman excepted under the act of 1677 for 'indemnitie and free pardon.'

At 23 *m.* on State 5 is a junction with a dirt road.

Right here to BERKELEY (R), 0.2 *m.*, the birthplace of a signer of the Declaration of Independence—Benjamin Harrison—of a president of the United States—William Henry Harrison—and ancestral home of another president—Benjamin Harrison. Berkeley stands between detached dependencies at the head of low terraced gardens above the James. Its warm red brick walls rise two stories to a deep cornice beneath a massive gabled roof. Two tall chimneys pierce the ridge near the ends above widely spaced dormers.

The chalk white of an unusual quantity of interior hand-tooled woodwork is accentuated by plaster-tinted walls. The spacious, deeply corniced, transverse hall is broken midway by a broad elliptical arch springing from fluted pilasters. A pair of drawing rooms are attractively joined by double-arched openings that flank their common chimney. A glass panel in the wall now reveals 'B.Harrison,' traced undoubtedly by the builder in the temptingly wet base plaster.

The estate was a part of Berkeley Hundred, a grant made to Sir George Yeardley, Richard Berkeley, and others in 1619. The proprietors instructed the settlers of the 'Town and Hundred' that 'the day of our ships arrival . . . shall be yearly and perpetually kept as a day of Thanksgiving.' The *Margaret* landed her passengers at Berkeley, December 4, 1619—a year and 17 days before the Pilgrims arrived to establish their Thanksgiving Day.

Abandoned after the massacre of 1622, the Hundred was later acquired by John Bland, whose son Giles lived here until executed for his part in Bacon's Rebellion. Confiscated by Governor Berkeley, the land was purchased by Benjamin Harrison (1673–1710), attorney-general of the colony, treasurer and speaker of the house of burgesses. Benjamin Harrison, his son, began to build this mansion in 1726. With two daughters, he was killed by lightning during a 'violent Thunder Gust' in July 1745. His son, Benjamin Harrison (1726–91), who installed the handsome interior woodwork, was the signer, a governor of Virginia, and father of William Henry Harrison (1773–1841), who emigrated to the Ohio Territory. William Henry Harrison achieved his distinction in the Northwest Territory, of which he was the first secretary, and which he represented in Congress. The victory of Tippecanoe in 1811 gave him a lasting epithet and 19 years later the campaign slogan that won for the Harrison-Tyler Whig ticket success at the polls. He died, however, one month after his inauguration. His grandson, Benjamin Harrison visited his ancestral home as President of the United States.

Benedict Arnold plundered Berkeley in 1781, and the estate, called Harrison's Landing, served as a base and camping-ground for the Federal army after McClellan's withdrawal from Malvern Hill. Near his transports and under protection of gunboats, McClellan was safe from attack by pursuing Confederate infantry, who stopped short of the river. Though McClellan remained in this position until mid-August, Lee began to withdraw his army on July 13, to oppose General John Pope in northern Virginia.

On the same road WESTOVER, at 2.3 *m.* (*grounds open daily, adm. $1; house open*

April Garden Week), once home of the Byrd family and one of the earliest houses built on the grand scale in Virginia, stands at the end of a road that winds between woods and fields. Gates of wrought-iron, made in England long ago, swing between simple posts on which are perched two leaden eagles with half-spread wings. The over-throw is probably the finest piece of old English ironwork in America. The dark red brick mansion looks upon the James across a semi-elliptical lawn framed by great tulip poplar trees. Flanked by a pair of story-and-a-half wings connected by passages, the central rectangular mass rises two stories to a steep hipped roof, with dormers. Windows with shutters and low-arched headings of brick are evenly spaced in two tiers, separated by a string course of brick painted white. The extremely tall chimneys, in pairs at both ends, are important features of the composition. But the exterior chiefly depends for accent on the centered entrances, which are framed by pilasters that support a frieze, cornice, and elaborate pediment. The pediment over the north portal is segmental, while the cornice of the pediment over the garden door is of the broken scroll type with the scrolls framing a pineapple. Within, four large rooms are divided by a transverse hall. The walls are paneled between high dadoes and deep cornices. At the back of the wide hall, an open-string stairway with scroll step-ends ascends behind delicate spiral balusters in sets of three. On the east side, next to the library, where once reposed Colonel Byrd's outstanding collection of almost 4,000 volumes, is the drawing room. Tall pilasters frame the doors and the mantel, which is faced with black marble having a white marble trim—imported from Italy.

Westover Plantation was selected by Captain Francis West in 1619 for his nephew Henry, son and heir of Thomas, third Lord Delaware. At the time of the massacre of 1622 Francis, John, and Nathaniel West had separate plantations here; the Indians killed two men at each. In 1633 Thomas Pawlett represented the plantations in the house of burgesses and in 1637 purchased the Westover tract. The Bland family in 1688 conveyed 1,200 of these acres to 'Will Bird' for £300 and 10,000 pounds of tobacco. This first William Byrd, son of a London goldsmith, had settled at 'The Falls,' where he founded a business fortune. His son, William Byrd II (1674–1744), built the present mansion and a tradition of abundant living. Construction, begun about 1730, was completed before 1735. Westover suffered early from two fires, the last in 1749. Most of the fine interior trim was probably installed during the second renovation. The 'Black Swan,' as Colonel William Byrd II was called, wrote amusing records of his travels about Virginia and spent a good deal of his life in London, where, as a grandee from the 'new wilderness,' he astonished society with his elegance. He thwarted the romance of his eldest daughter with the Catholic son of the dissolute Earl of Peterborough and the beautiful Evelyn Byrd returned to Westover, where she died at the age of 28, a disconsolate spinster. The other five cygnets, four daughters and a son, offspring of two marriages, married well into the 'closed corporation' of Tidewater society. Byrd's tomb in the garden bears his long, self-composed epitaph, which leaves a reader equally impressed by the record of his remarkable accomplishments and his serene egotism in thus advertising them. The son, William Byrd III, was a prodigious gambler and dissipated the family fortune.

During the Revolution Benedict Arnold landed here more than once and corresponded regularly with the Byrd family, whose Tory sympathies are clearly shown in letters written later by Cornwallis. He said in part to the Lords of the Treasury in 1789, 'She [Mrs.Byrd] had, to my knowledge, reason to expect that she should receive reimbursement at New York for the supplies which were furnished from her plantation to the various corps of British troops which passed by Westover, but she was utterly disappointed [in her claim for £6,600].' Cornwallis refers also to the Byrds as 'sufferers of a certain description.' But Arthur Lee guessed correctly when he wrote to Colonel Bland in 1781: 'I have reason to think she [Mrs.Byrd] will not be tried at all, because care having been taken to keep the witnesses out of the way.' Sales and good marriage alliances dispersed a large collection of portraits belonging to a family that has been an outstanding contributor to Virginia's tradition of expansive social life.

During the War between the States, the fields and lawns were frequented by Federal troops, who destroyed the east wing and damaged the main building. The house has, however, been restored, fairly well, on the whole, though the symmetry of one dependency has been altered.

At the site of the church are horizontal slabs—one of them covering the dust of the first Benjamin Harrison of Berkeley—and Evelyn's elaborate tomb. Here also is the tombstone of Captain William Perry, who died the '6th day of August Anno Domini 1637.'

At 24.4 *m.* on State 5 is a junction with County 609.

Left on this road, which at 3.3 *m.* becomes County 607 and leads to SALEM CHURCH (L), 3.8 *m.*, a small frame building in a woods. Sheridan, returning from Trevilian Station (*see Tour* 9), picked up a supply train of 800 wagons at White House Landing (*see Tour 6A*), and set out for the James. At Nance's Shop, north of this church, Hampton attacked the train but was held at bay by General D.McM.Gregg's division of the Federal cavalary while the wagons escaped to the river. Hampton pursued them. The wounded soldiers were brought to this church for care and some of the dead were buried in the churchyard.

At 24.8 *m.* on State 5 is a junction with a narrow flower-and-shrub-bordered lane.

Right here 0.2 *m.* to WESTOVER CHURCH (*open* 9 *to* 6), on the bank of Herring Creek in a wide yard dotted with tombstones and shaded by old trees. Built in 1737, the church was before restorations a notable example of Georgian Colonial design—low-pitched, with gabled roof, wide overhanging eaves, arched windows at the sides, a main door in the west end, and a door in the south wall. The walls, laid in Flemish bond, are specked with glazed headers to display the quincunx patterns. Modern interior arrangements have caused the south door to be replaced by another arched window, and one of the narrow windows in the east end has been made a door. The modern-oval-topped window in the front gable lights the gallery. Modern furniture has replaced the high-backed pews, but in the gallery old 'stalls' remain. After the Revolution, Westover Church was used as a barn and during the War of the 1860's it was used by Federals as a stable.

The first Westover Church was at Westover. The Byrd family gave this site that the congregation might be remote from the house, because—tradition says—all would remain after services for dinner.

GREENWAY (L), 29.8 *m.*, on a wide lawn among old trees and old outbuildings, was built before 1790. The story-and-a-half frame structure on a brick basement, has dormers and outside chimneys. John Tyler (1747–1813), governor of Virginia from 1808 to 1811, described it as 'a genteel well-furnished dwelling-house, containing six rooms all wainscoted chair-board high.' His son John, who became President of the United States, was born here March 29, 1790.

CHARLES CITY, 30.3 *m.* (25 pop.), a hamlet with a few houses and stores clustered about the grassy court square, is the seat of Charles City County. Named for a proposed city (*see Tour* 19), the county is part of one of the oldest political units in America—the four 'incorporations' into which settlements in Virginia were divided in 1619. This 'Incorporation' in 1634 made it one of the eight original counties.

The COURTHOUSE, facing the Confederate Monument and away from the highway, was built in 1730. It is a T-shaped brick building with a gabled roof, low-pitched, and with the bar forming the façade.

The CLERK'S OFFICE, erected in 1902, contains—except for some volumes taken away by Federal soldiers in the 1860's—early records of the county as well as subsequent documents.

At 31.1 *m.* is a junction with County 615.

Left here to the GLEBE (L), 1.6 *m.*, the Colonial rectory of Westover Parish, approached by an avenue bordered by old trees. A box garden is enclosed by a picket fence. The brick house, built before 1750, is story-and-a-half high with dormers, thick walls, and outside chimneys.

At 31.9 *m.* on State 5 is a junction with County 619.

Right here to a private road, 2 *m.*, and R. to WEYANOKE, 3 *m.*, on a neck at a bend of the river above a jut called Weyanoke Point. The present hip-roofed frame residence replaced a colonial house.

Weyanoke—'place where the river goes around land'—was called by the Indians 'Tanks Weyanoke' (Little Weyanoke) to distinguish it from 'Great Weyanoke,' on the opposite side of the river. In May 1607, when Captain Newport and 23 'Gentlemen,' 'Maryners,' and 'Saylours' made a voyage up the river to its falls, they stopped on their return at Weyanoke Point, after visiting, in the vicinity of present Hopewell, 'Queene Opussoquionuske, a fatt lusty manly woman.' In 1617 Opechancanough gave this land to Sir George Yeardley, and in 1619 the gift was confirmed by the London Company. In June 1864 part of Grant's army crossed the river from Weyanoke Point on a pontoon bridge nearly one-half mile long.

The entrance (R) to SHERWOOD FOREST (R) is at 34 *m.* This was the home of John Tyler, who became President of the United States, and birthplace of his son, Lyon Gardiner Tyler, long president of the College of William and Mary and eminent Virginia historian.

Though the estate has the James as one of its boundaries, the house is a mile or more from the river. The frame structure rambles from a two-and-a-half-story central unit through lower wings and dependencies, all connected by passageways, to a total length of about 300 feet.

In 1842 President Tyler purchased the estate, called Walnut Grove, from Collier Minge and remodeled a Colonial house on it. Lateral additions from time to time finally produced the present structure, completed during ownership of David Gardiner Tyler (1846–1927). Among mementos preserved here is the silver pitcher that was presented to President Tyler by the ladies of Brazoria County, Texas, upon the admission of the 'Lone Star State' in 1845. Though it was burned black in the Richmond fire of 1865, its inscription is still legible.

John Tyler (1790–1862), born at Greenway (*see above*), a stone's throw from the birthplace of the Whig President whom he succeeded in the White House, was graduated from the College of William and Mary, served as Virginia assemblyman, congressional representative and senator, and as governor of his State. Though he cast his lot with the Whigs in 1833 and with the Democrats in 1844, neither party could claim his wholehearted allegiance or ever gave him its support. In 1840 the Whigs nominated William H. Harrison for the presidency, and Tyler for the vice-presidency, because they thought he could hold the southern Whigs who were being deflected from the party by antislavery agitation. When President Harrison died one month after his inauguration and was succeeded by Tyler, storms, long gathering, broke immediately. Tyler had become the nominal leader of a party whose policies he actually disapproved; Henry Clay remained the real Whig leader. Congressional debates were focused upon the occupation of the Oregon country and the annexation of

Texas. Slavery and the extension or limitation of slaveholding territory were the real issues. The Whig President, who was a Calhoun Democrat, favored annexing Texas, a vast slaveholding country, and defied the Whigs who had elected him. Though neither party renominated him in 1844, the election of James K. Polk, Democrat and annexationist, was in a sense a vindication of Tyler's policy and enabled him to sign the annexation bill shortly before the inauguration of his successor.

In 1845 Tyler retired to Sherwood Forest. In 1861 the Virginia legislature commissioned him to confer with President Buchanan concerning Federal occupation of Fort Sumter. On February 4, 1861, he presided over the ineffectual peace conference in Washington, from which he returned to urge secession. After his State had seceded, Tyler was made chairman of the committee that conferred with Alexander H. Stephens, Vice President of the Confederate States, who had been sent to Richmond to form a treaty of alliance between Virginia and the Confederate Government. He was a member of the provisional Confederate Congress and was elected to the permanent congress January 18, 1862, but died before that body met.

At 34.5 *m.* is a junction with County 618.

Right here to the gates of LION'S DEN (L), 1 *m.* The frame house, a story-and-a-half with dormers, on a wide lawn by the James, was Dr.Lyon Gardiner Tyler's place of retirement after 1919 when he relinquished the presidency of the College of William and Mary, a post he had held for 31 years. Born to John Tyler and Julia Gardiner Tyler in 1853, he was the son of his father's later years. In 1883 he was instrumental in the re-founding of the Richmond Mechanics Night School. As a member of the general assembly he was patron of a bill in 1888 for the re-opening of the College of William and Mary, then a poorly endowed deserted institution. The appropriation of $10,000 he obtained was the first State contribution to that college. Elected president of the college, he cleared the campus of weeds and the building of debris. During his administration the endowment was increased from practically nothing to $154,000 and an expansion in buildings and equipment inaugurated. Against great odds he made the college a State institution in 1906 and against equally great odds coeducational in 1918. He was one of the first men in Virginia to make public his belief in woman suffrage. In 1910 he shocked his conservative friends by presenting Dr.Anna Howard Shaw to a Richmond audience.

Dr.Tyler was also an eminent historian. In 1892 he founded the *William and Mary College Quarterly Historical Magazine*, which he edited until 1919, when he founded and edited *Tyler's Quarterly Historical and Genealogical Magazine.* His works include many scholarly histories and biographies.

At 38 *m.* on State 5 is a junction with County 617.

Right here to SANDY POINT, 5.8 *m.*, terminal of the CLAREMONT-SANDY POINT FERRY (*see Tour* 19) (*hourly* 7 *a.m. to* 8 *p.m., Sundays and holidays to* 9 *p.m.; half-hourly service* 9–7, *April* 15 *to Nov.* 1; *car and driver* 80¢, *round trip* $1, *each passenger* 20¢, *round trip* 30¢; *others* 25¢).

The CHICKAHOMINY RIVER, 44.3 *m.*, is crossed by BARRETT'S FERRY (*free*).

At 48.8 *m.* is a junction with County 614.

Right here to GREEN SPRING, 0.2 *m.* Nothing remains of the home of Sir William Berkeley, governor of the colony (1642–52 and 1660–77), except foundations and the grim little prison where Berkeley wreaked vengeance on the followers of Nathaniel Bacon. But the 'very green spring' that gave the estate its name is still flowing.

Here in 1608, under the supervision of Captain John Smith, a house was erected for the manufacture of glass, and when Captain Newport went to England that year he took specimens of the product. The manufacture of glass was continued here at intervals with success during the seventeenth century. In 1619, 3,000 acres were laid out here as the Governor's Land and tilled for the support of the governor's office. After 1624 this public land was leased for terms of 99 years, a system that continued until after the Revolution.

Berkeley's house of which construction was begun before 1650, had a main section nearly 100 feet long and two full stories, with a high roof pierced by two tiers of dormers. During Cromwell's regime, Berkeley retired to Green Spring where he entertained royalist refugees and developed the place after the fashion of an English estate. He set out 1,500 fruit trees, also mulberry trees to feed silk worms, grew orange trees in a hothouse and had extensive rose gardens on the terraced lawn. He presented Charles II with 300 pounds of silk for a robe. Later he experimented with a windmill and dug an ice house. Berkeley also dabbled in glassmaking. This was revealed in 1931 when ruins of a small glass furnace and bits of Colonial-type bottles were unearthed. A brick of the furnace was inscribed 'H.A.L. 1666.' Bacon and his 'rebels' visited Green Spring after the burning of Jamestown in September 1676; and, his lordship being absent, they regaled themselves from the well-filled storehouses.

The solid old house was taken down in 1796 by William Ludwell Lee to make way for a new one designed by Benjamin Latrobe. Recent excavation has yielded a fragment of leaded glass in lozenge lights.

At 53.6 *m.* on State 5 is a junction with State 31 (*see Tour 8A*).

1. Left here to WILLIAMSBURG, 1.5 *m.* (74 to 84 alt., 3,778 pop.) (*see Williamsburg*).

2. Right here to JAMESTOWN, 4.9 *m.* (*see Tour 8A*).

PART IV
Appendices

Chronology

Dates used are old style. Prior to 1752, when the calendar was changed, the year began on March 25 and ended March 24.

1585 August 17. Sir Walter Raleigh's first settlers reach Roanoke Island in 'Virginia.'

1591 Roanoke Island settlers having disappeared, the colony is abandoned.

1606 April 10. James I grants joint charter to two companies to colonize 'Virginia.'

1607 May 14. First permanent English settlement in the New World established at Jamestown.

1607 August. Colonists of Plymouth Company land at Kennebec (Maine) but make only temporary settlement.
December. Captain John Smith saved by Pocahontas.

1608 January 12. Arrival of 'First Supply.'

1609 May 23. London Company granted second charter.

1609–10 'Starving Time'; between September and June population drops from about 500 to 60.

1610 May 23. Sir Thomas Gates, first governor, arrives at Jamestown.
June 8. Colonists having abandoned Jamestown, return upon arrival of Thomas West, Lord Delaware, at Point Comfort.

1611 March 12. London Company granted third charter. (March 22, 1612, n.s.)

1612 John Rolfe introduces the cultivation of tobacco for export.

1614 April 5. John Rolfe marries Pocahontas at Jamestown.

1619 July 30. First representative legislature in America—House of Burgesses—meets in Jamestown.
August 30. First Negroes arrive at Jamestown.
First iron foundry in America established on Falling Creek.

1620 First shipload of 'maids' arrives to become wives of settlers.
December 11. Pilgrims, authorized to settle in southern Virginia, land at Plymouth, having been thrown off course.

1622 March 22. Indian Massacre wipes out about one third of colonists.

1624 June 16. London Company's charter revoked by King's Bench; Virginia becomes royal colony.
Doctrine of no taxation without representation is first asserted in Virginia by burgesses.

1628–29 Population about 3,000.

1629 October 30. Province of Carolina carved from Virginia by royal grant to Sir Robert Heath.

1632 Province of Maryland carved from Virginia by royal grant to Lord Baltimore.

1634 First eight counties formed.
February 12. Syms Free School endowed—first educational institution endowed and oldest free school in the United States.

1635 Population about 5,000.
Sir John Harvey 'thrust out' by council and burgesses, who make first assertion of colonists' right to order own government.

1644 April 18. Second Indian massacre kills about 300 colonists.

1649 Virginians assert their allegiance to Charles II.

1650 Population about 20,000, including 5,000 indentured whites, 300 Negroes.
Southwest Virginia explored by Abraham Wood and Edmund Bland.
October. First navigation act passed by Parliament, banishing Dutch vessels from Virginia.

1651 March 12. Virginia capitulates to the Commonwealth. (March 22, 1652, n.s.).

1652–60 Only period of almost complete self-government in Colonial Virginia.

1652 May 5. Burgesses declare that 'the right of election of all officers of the Colony appertain to the Burgesses.'

1659 March 13. Burgesses declare the 'Supreme power of the government' in Virginia rests in them; Berkeley elected governor.

1660 July 31. Charles II reappoints Berkeley as royal governor.

1670 Population about 40,000, including 6,000 indentured whites, 2,000 Negro slaves.

1673 Northern Neck of Virginia, granted to Lord Hopton and associates in 1649 by Charles II, actually becomes a proprietary when Lord Culpeper assumes control. Proprietary rights to all Virginia are bestowed upon Lord Arlington and Lord Culpeper.

1675 Susquehannock Indian War.

1676 Bacon's Rebellion.

1680 An act for the establishment of one town for each county passed by general assembly; Charles II suspends its operation.

1682 Tobacco Riots.

1691 General assembly re-enacts law providing for towns, but suspends operation of the act in 1693.

1693 February 8. The College of William and Mary, second institution of higher learning in America, founded at Middle Plantation (Williamsburg).

1699 Seat of government moved to Middle Plantation.
Act for religious tolerance passed.
First group of Huguenots reach Virginia.

1700 Population about 70,000, including 5,000 to 6,000 Negroes.

1705 Basis of independence from counties of Virginia's future cities laid by general assembly.

1716 First theater in United States built in Williamsburg.

1722 Williamsburg, capital of the colony, becomes first incorporated municipality in Virginia.

1730 Population 114,000, including 30,000 Negroes.

1736 August 6. First newspaper in Virginia founded at Williamsburg.

1749 In transmontane Virginia 500,000 acres granted to Ohio Company and

800,000 to Loyal Company; Christopher Gist explores Ohio tract to falls of Ohio River (present Louisville).

1754 George Washington with Virginia troops advances against the French in the Ohio Valley, precipitating French and Indian War.

1755 July 9. Upon fatal wounding of General Edward Braddock, Washington rallies British regulars and Colonials near Fort Duquesne.

1755–56 Population 294,000, including 120,000 Negroes.

1758 November 25. Fort Duquesne occupied.

1759 General assembly creates standing committee of correspondence to exchange information with colony's agent in London.

1763 December 1. Patrick Henry flouts British rule in the Parsons' Cause.
French and Indian War ends; transmontane region ceded to British.
Royal proclamation forbids further grants west of Alleghenies.

1765 May 29. Patrick Henry, protesting the Stamp Act, delivers in house of burgesses 'Caesar-Brutus' speech.

1766 February 27. One hundred and fifteen patriots sign Leedstown Resolutions embodying principles later incorporated in Declaration of Independence.

1769 First 'lunatic asylum' in America established at Williamsburg.

1773 March 14. Burgesses develop intercolonial committee of correspondence, which includes four members of old committee.

1774 May 27. Burgesses meet in Raleigh Tavern, call convention, and propose congress of the Colonies.
June 1. Virginia observes Fast Day in protest of Boston Port Bill.
August 1. First Virginia Convention meets, chooses delegates to Continental Congress.
September 5. Peyton Randolph of Virginia elected president of First Continental Congress.
October 10. General Andrew Lewis defeats Shawnee at Point Pleasant (now West Virginia).

1775 March 23. Patrick Henry delivers 'liberty or death' speech in Second Virginia Convention in Richmond.
June 15. Washington chosen commander in chief of Continental Army.
October 24. First bloodshed of Revolution in Virginia at Hampton.

1776 May 6–June 29. Fifth Virginia Convention meets in Williamsburg, declares Virginia independent State, instructs Virginia's delegates to Continental Congress to propose independence; adopts George Mason's declaration of rights and first constitution of a free and independent state, and elects Patrick Henry first governor of Commonwealth.
June 7. Richard Henry Lee offers in Continental Congress resolutions for independence, foreign alliances, and a form of confederacy.
July 2. Lee's resolutions adopted by Congress.
July 4. Declaration of Independence, phrased by Thomas Jefferson, adopted by Congress.
December 5. Phi Beta Kappa Society, first intercollegiate fraternity in United States, founded at Williamsburg.
Kentucky established as a county of Virginia.

1778 July 9. Virginia ratifies Articles of Confederation.

1779 February 25. George Rogers Clark with Virginia troops takes Vincennes.
May 9. First formal invasion of Virginia by British who came by sea.
June 15. Act passed authorizing removal of capital to Richmond.
First law school in America established at College of William and Mary, which that year became first American university.

1780 April 30. Governor Jefferson moves executive office to Richmond.
December 30. Benedict Arnold with 27 ships arrives in James River.

1781 April 29. La Fayette reaches Richmond.
May 20. Cornwallis reaches Petersburg, taking command of combined British forces.
May 24. La Fayette begins retreat before Cornwallis.
June 4. Warned by Jack Jouette, Jefferson and Virginia Legislature escape Colonel Tarleton, who arrives in Charlottesville.
October 19. Cornwallis surrenders at Yorktown.

1782 Population 567,114, including 270, 262 Negro slaves.

1784 March 1. Virginia cedes Northwest Territory to United States.
February 5. *Alexandria Gazette*, State's first daily newspaper, founded.

1785 Virginia Statute for Religious Liberty passes legislature.
March 28. Mt.Vernon Conference, called by Virginia Legislature, results in movement toward Constitutional Convention.

1786 September 11. Annapolis Convention meets at invitation of Virginia Legislature—second step toward Constitutional Convention.

1787 May 25. George Washington elected president of Constitutional Convention, meeting at Philadelphia.
May 29. Governor Edmund Randolph submits to Convention Madison's Virginia Plan—basis of deliberations.

1788 June 26. Virginia ratifies Federal Constitution, 89 to 79.

1789 April 30. George Washington inaugurated first President of United States.
December 3. Virginia cedes to United States part of area for seat of government.

1790 Population 747,610, including 305,493 Negroes of whom about 12,000 are free.
Virginia Legislature remonstrates against Assumption Bill—first remonstrance of a state against a Federal act.

1791 December 15. America's Bill of Rights added to the Constitution when nine amendments offered by James Madison and tenth by Richard Henry Lee are ratified.

1798 December 21. Legislature adopts 'Virginia Resolutions,' protesting Alien and Sedition laws.

1799 First ship constructed by the Federal Government—the Chesapeake—is built at the Gosport Navy Yard.

1800 Population 880,200, including 345,896 slaves and 20,124 free Negroes.

1801 March 4. Thomas Jefferson inaugurated President.

1803 February 23. Chief Justice John Marshall of Virginia hands down opinion asserting U.S. Supreme Court's right of Judicial review.
April 30. James Monroe, Jefferson's emissary, concludes treaty with France for Purchase of Louisiana Territory.

1804 May 14. Lewis and Clark, commissioned by Jefferson, begin exploration of Louisiana Territory.

1807 May 22. Trial of Aaron Burr begins in Richmond.
June 22. British frigate *Leopard* attacks *Chesapeake* off Virginia capes.
December 22. Congress passes Jefferson's Embargo Act.

1809 March 4. James Madison inaugurated President.

1810 Population 974,600, including 392,510 slaves and 30,573 free Negroes.

1812 June 18. President Madison signs Congressional act declaring war upon England.

1813 British fleet ravages areas contiguous to Virginia waters.

1814 August 24. President and Mrs.Madison flee to Virginia before British entering Washington.

1816 August 19–23. Western Virginians, meeting at Staunton, demand new State constitution equalizing representation.

1817 March 4. James Monroe inaugurated President.

1819 January 25. University of Virginia established.
February 22. President Monroe's envoys conclude treaty with Spain for acquisition of Floridas.

1820 Population 1,065,366, including 425,153 slaves and 36,889 free Negroes.

1823 April 24. Stephen F. Austin of Virginia obtains grant of land in Texas from Mexico for colonization.
December 2. President Monroe promulgates the 'Monroe Doctrine.'

1825 January 11. President Monroe's signature concludes treaty with Russia establishing Northwest boundary.
March 4. End of 'Virginia Dynasty.'

1829 February 21. Legislature condemns 'Tariff of Abominations' as unconstitutional.

1830 Population 1,211,405, including 469,757 slaves and 47,348 free Negroes.

1831 August 21. Nat Turner's slave insurrection.

1832 Bill to abolish slavery in Virginia lost in house of delegates by vote of 67 to 60.

1835 Edgar Allan Poe becomes editor of *Southern Literary Messenger*, in which his first short stories have already appeared.

1836 October 22. Sam Houston of Virginia elected first President of Republic of Texas.

1840 Population 1,239,797, including 449,087 slaves and 49,852 free Negroes.

1841 March 4. William Henry Harrison of Virginia inaugurated President.
April 4. John Tyler of Virginia inaugurated President.

1842 January 24. Thomas Walker Gilmer of Virginia moves that Congress censure John Quincy Adams for presenting petition from abolitionists for peaceful dissolution of Union.

1845 March 1. President Tyler signs bill annexing Texas.

1846 May 1. Southern Methodists, meeting in Petersburg, organize Methodist Episcopal Church, South.

1847 September 13. General Winfield Scott of Virginia takes Mexico City.

1849 March 4. Zachary Taylor of Virginia inaugurated President.

1850 Population 1,421,661, including 472,528 slaves and 54,333 free Negroes.

1851 October 23–25. New constitution, providing liberal white male franchise, ratified by big majority.

1859 October 16. John Brown and band seize U.S. Arsenal at Harpers Ferry, are later suppressed by troops under Colonel R.E.Lee.
December 2. John Brown hanged.

1860 Population 1,596,318, including 490,865 slaves and 58,042 free Negroes.

1861 February 4. 'Peace Conference,' called by Virginia Legislature, meets in Washington, attended by representatives of 21 states.
February 13. State Convention (Secession Convention) meets, but refuses to consider secession until peace overtures are exhausted.
April 17. State Convention votes for secession 88 to 55.
April 25. Virginia joins the Confederate States.
May 21. Richmond chosen capital of Confederacy.
July 21. First Battle of Manassas.

1862 March 9. Battle between *Monitor* and *Merrimac* in Hampton Roads.
March 23. Battle of Kernstown (beginning of Jackson's Valley Campaign).
June 26. Seven Days' Battles around Richmond begin.
August 29–30. Second Battle of Manassas.
December 13. Battle of Fredericksburg.

1863 May 2–3. Battle of Chancellorsville; Jackson mortally wounded.
June 20. Virginia divided; West Virginia admitted as a State.

1864 May 5–6. Battle of Wilderness.
May 8–18. Battle of Spotsylvania Courthouse.
June 3. Second Battle of Cold Harbor.
June 15–18. Battle of Petersburg; siege begins.

1865 April 2–3. Richmond and Petersburg evacuated by Confederates.
April 9. Lee surrenders at Appomattox.
May 22. Jefferson Davis imprisoned at Fort Monroe.

1867 March 2. Virginia designated as Military District No.1 under Reconstruction Act.
May 13. Jefferson Davis, arraigned in Richmond and indicted for treason, is admitted to bail.

1869 July 6. New State constitution ratified.
October 8. Fourteenth and Fifteenth Amendments to Constitution ratified.

1870 Population 1,225,163, including 512,841 Negroes.
January 26. Virginia readmitted to Union.

1880 Population 1,512,565, including 631,616 Negroes.

1889 April 24. Simpson dry dock, largest in world, opened at Newport News.

1890 Population 1,655,980, including 635,438 Negroes.

1894 March. Legislative Act provides for secret balloting.

1900 Population 1,854,184, including 660,722 Negroes.
May 12. Legislature passes 'Jim Crow' law.

1902 July 10. New State constitution, effective by proclamation, improving public education and governmental efficiency and virtually eliminating Negro vote through poll tax and 'understanding clause.'

1907 April 26. Jamestown Exposition opens to commemorate 300th anniversary of first landing of English settlers at Cape Henry.

December 16. Atlantic Fleet, commanded by Rear Admiral Robley D. Evans of Virginia, leaves Hampton Roads for World Cruise.

1908 Staunton, Virginia, is first city to adopt city manager form of government.

1910 Population 2,061,612, including 671,096 Negroes.

1913 March 4. Woodrow Wilson of Virginia inaugurated President.

1914 November 18. Wilson signs Federal Reserve Bank Act, fathered by Congressman Carter Glass of Virginia.

1915 June 14. U.S. Supreme Court decision places upon West Virginia obligation to share Virginia's *ante-bellum* State debt.

1917 April 6. President Wilson signs Congressional Act declaring war upon Germany.

Hampton Roads becomes great naval and military base.

1918 The College of William and Mary admits women.

The budget system, sponsored by Governor Westmoreland Davis, is adopted.

1920 Population 2,309,187, including 690,017 Negroes.

Women admitted to graduate and professional schools of University of Virginia.

November 2. Virginia women vote, though Virginia had voted against ratification of Nineteenth Amendment.

1922 February 27. State Board of Public Welfare evolves from State Board of Charities and Corrections.

March 24. State Highway Commission created.

March 27. Juvenile and Domestic Relations Court established.

1924 March 20. Act provides for sterilization of persons committed to State institutions.

1927 April 27. Act for reorganization of State government, sponsored by Governor Harry Flood Byrd, passes general assembly.

1930 Population 2,421,851, including 650,165 Negroes.

March 17. Legislative act exempts new manufactories from taxation for five years under specified conditions.

1936 December 18. Act approved, in conformity with Federal Social Security Act, creating Unemployment Compensation Commission.

1938 March 31. Public assistance Act revised and approved, in conformity with Federal Social Security Act, to render old age assistance, aid to dependent children, aid to the blind, and for general relief.

Bibliography

Current information is readily available in the tourist guides issued by the Virginia Conservation Commission; commercial, industrial, and tourist publications, issued by the State Chamber of Commerce and chambers of commerce of cities; booklets of the Department of Agriculture and Immigration of Virginia; and information and maps issued by the Virginia Department of Highways. The industrial and agricultural surveys, issued by the Engineering Extension Division and Agricultural Extension Division of Virginia Polytechnic Institute, and the economic and social surveys in the University of Virginia Record Extension Series are published separately for each county, with about half of the counties covered.

GENERAL INFORMATION

American Automobile Association. *Southeastern Tour Book.* Washington,D.C., 1939. 408p.,illus.,maps. See pp.181–224. Issued annually.

Latimer, James C.,ed. *Virginia newspaper directory and market information.* Bristol,Va., by the author, 4th annual ed.,1939. 60p. Begun as an annual in 1936.

DESCRIPTION AND TRAVEL

Alvord, Clarence Walworth, and Lee Bidgood. *Travels in Virginia.* The first explorations of the trans-Allegheny region by the Virginians, 1650–74. Cleveland, Arthur H. Clark Co.,1912. 275p.,maps.

Anburey, Thomas. *Travels through the Interior Parts of America*; in a series of letters, by an officer. London, W.Lane,1791. 2 vols.,maps. First pub.1789. The letters begin at Cork in 1776 and end at Falmouth in 1781.

Burnaby, Rev.Andrew. *Travels through the Middle Settlements in North America, in the Years 1759 and 1760, with Observations upon the State of the Colonies.* 2nd ed. London, T.Payne,1775. 198p.

Chastellux, (Francois-Jean) Marquis de. *Travels in North America, in the Years 1780–81–82.* Tr. from the French by an English gentleman, who resided in America at that period. Copied from Grieve's 1787 translation, with notes and corrections by the American editor. New York, White,Gallaher,& White,1827. 416p. Reprinted in New York, no publisher given, in 1828. Pub. Paris 1786, Dublin and London 1787.

Davis, John. *Travels of Four Years and a Half in the United States of America during 1798,1799,1800,1801,and 1802.* New York, H.Holt & Co.,1909. 429p. First ed. London, 1803. 2 vols., edited by John Vance Cheney for the Bibliographical Society, Boston,1910.

Hale, Mrs.Louise C. *We Discover the Old Dominion.* New York, Dodd,Mead,& Co.,1916. 374p.,sketches. An account of travel; personal incidents and bits of history.

Jefferson, Thomas. *Notes on the State of Virginia.* A new edition, printed from Jefferson's own copy of the London edition, with his last additions and corrections in manuscript and four maps of caves, mounds, fortifications, etc. Translations of all Jefferson's notes in foreign languages by Prof.Schele de Vere. Richmond,1853. 275p. First pub. in Paris in 1784, in London,1787; Philadelphia,1788; and subsequently in many editions.

Kern, M.Ethel Kelley. *The Trail of the Three Notched Road.* Rev.ed. Richmond, The William Byrd Press,Inc.,1929. 334p.,illus.,maps,bibl. An account of the old road from Richmond to Staunton.

La Rochefoucauld-Liancourt, Francois Alexandre Frederic, duc de. *Travels through the United States of North America . . . in the years 1795–1796, and 1797.* Trans. by H.Neuman . . . London, R.Phillips, 2nd ed.,1800. 4 vol., maps.

Lederer, John. *The Discoveries of John Lederer, in Three Several Marches from Virginia, to the West of Carolina, and Other Parts of the Continent; begun in March 1669, and ended in September 1670.* Collected and translated out of Latin from his discourse and writings by Sir William Talbot, London,1672. Reprinted for G.P.Humphrey, Rochester,N.Y.,1902. 30p.

Moorman, John J. *The Virginia Springs: Comprising an Account of All the Principal Mineral Springs of Virginia . . .* 2d ed.,enl. Richmond, J.W. Randolph,1857. 319p.,maps,plates. With appendix describing the natural curiosities of Virginia.

Morrison, Alfred J.,ed. *Travels in Virginia in Revolutionary Times.* Lynchburg, J.P.Bell Co.,Inc.,1922. 138p.

Rothery, Agnes E. *New Roads in Old Virginia.* Rev.ed. Boston and New York, Houghton Mifflin Co.,1937. 186p.,illus. First pub.1929.

Smyth, J.F.D. *Tour in the United States of America; Containing an Account of the Present Situation of That Country . . . with a Description of the Indian Nations . . .* London, G.Robinson,1784. 2 vols. Smyth, traveling in Virginia during latter part of the Revolution, is at times bitterly critical.

Speed, Thomas. *The Wilderness Road.* Louisville,Ky., Jno.P.Morton & Co.,1886. 75p.,map. A description of the routes to Kentucky used by pioneers.

Verrill, A.Hyatt. *Romantic and Historic Virginia.* New York, Dodd,Mead & Co., 1935. 242p.,illus.,map.

PLANT AND ANIMAL LIFE

Bailey, Harold H. *The Birds of Virginia.* Lynchburg, J.P.Bell Co.,1913. 362p., colored plates, half-tones. Treats of 185 species and subspecies that breed within the State, but lacks descriptive identifications and all half-tones are of nests and the young.

Bushnell, David I.,Jr. *The Five Manocan Towns in Virginia, 1607.* Washington, Govt.Print.Off.,1930. 38p.,illus.,maps. (Smithsonian Miscellaneous Collections, vol.82, no.12.)

——— *Native Villages and Village Sites East of the Mississippi.* Washington,

Govt.Print.Off.,1919. 111p. (Smithsonian Inst.Bureau of Am.Ethnology. Bulletin 69.)

——— *The Manahoac Tribes in Virginia, 1608.* Washington, Govt.Print.Off., 1935. 56p.,plates. (Smithsonian Miscellaneous Collections, vol.94, no.8.)

——— *Research in Virginia from Tidewater to the Alleghanies.* Lancaster,Pa., New Era Printing Co.,1908, pp.531–48. (Repr. from *American Anthropologist.*) Historical sketch of Indians from 1716 to 1763.

——— *Tribal Migrations East of the Mississippi.* Washington, Govt.Print.Off., 1934. 9p.,4 maps. (Smithsonian Miscellaneous Collections, vol.89, no.12.)

Fowke, Gerard. *Archeologic Investigations in James and Potomac Valleys.* Washington, Govt.Print.Off.,1894. 80p. (Smithsonian Inst.Bureau of Am.Ethnology. Bulletin 23.)

Holmes, William Henry. 'Stone Implements of the Potomac-Chesapeake Tidewater Province.' (In *Fifteenth Annual Report of the Bureau of American Ethnology . . . 1893–94.* Washington, Govt.Print.Off.,1897. pp.3–152.)

——— 'Aboriginal Pottery of the Eastern United States.' (In *Twentieth Annual Report of the Bureau of American Ethnology . . . 1898–99.* Washington, Govt.Print.Off.,1903. pp.1–237,plates.)

——— 'Aboriginal Shell-Heaps of the Middle Atlantic Tidewater Region.' *American Anthropologist.*1907. vol.9, pp.113–28.

Mooney, James. *The Siouan Tribes of the East.* Washington, Govt.Print.Off., 1894. 101p. (Smithsonian Inst.Bureau of Am.Ethnology. Bulletin 22.)

Speck, Frank G. *Chapters on the Ethnology of the Powhatan Tribes of Virginia.* New York, Museum of the American Indian, Heye Foundation,1928. 455p.

Tooker, William Wallace. *The Algonquian Names of the Siouan Tribes of Virginia.* New York, F.P.Harper,1901. 83p. (Repr. from *American Anthropologist.*)

Virginia Conservation Commission. *Common Forest Trees of Virginia.* Charlottesville,1936. 64p. (Virginia Forest Service Publication No.26, in cooperation with Forest Service of U.S. Dept.of Agriculture.)

HISTORY

Cappon, Lester Jesse. *Bibliography of Virginia History since 1865.* University, Virginia, Institute for Research in the Social Sciences,1930. 900p. A classified list, with critical notes, of all published matter touching on the period since 1865, including locations of known copies.

General

Adams, James Truslow. *America's Tragedy.* New York, London, Charles Scribner's Sons,1934. 415p.,illus.,maps.

——— *The Epic of America.* Boston, Little,Brown & Co.,1932. 433p.,illus.

Andrews, Matthew Page. *Virginia, the Old Dominion.* Garden City,N.Y., Doubleday,Doran & Co.,1937. 664p.,illus.,maps,bibl.

Bruce, Philip Alexander,*et al. History of Virginia.* I. Colonial Period, by Philip Alexander Bruce; II. Federal Period, by Lyon Gardiner Tyler; III. Virginia since 1861, by Richard L. Morton; IV–VI, Biography, by special staff. Chicago and New York, American Historical Society,1924. 6 vols.

Fiske, John. *Old Virginia and Her Neighbors*. Boston and New York, Houghton Mifflin Co.,1900. 2 vols.,illus. First pub.1897.

Robinson, Morgan Poitiaux. *Virginia counties; those resulting from Virginia legislation*. Richmond, Virginia State Library bulletin, Davis Bottom, Supt. of Public Printing,1916. 283p. A study on the derivation of counties.

Squires, W.H.T. *Through Centuries Three; a Short History of the People of Virginia*. Portsmouth,Va., Printcraft Press,Inc.,1929. 605p.,illus.,map.

Tyler's Quarterly Historical and Genealogical Magazine, 1919 to date. Ed. by L.G.Tyler and later by Mrs.L.G.Tyler. Richmond, Whittet & Shepperson, 1919–39. Vols.1–20.

Virginia Historical Index, compiled by E.G.Swem. Roanoke,Va., sponsored by a group of 16 . . . 1934–36, 2 vols. A complete index of the *Calendar of State Papers*, vols.1–11; *Henings Statutes*, vols.1–13; *Lower Norfolk County Antiquary*, vols.1–5; *Virginia Historical Register*, vols.1–6; *Tyler's Quarterly*, vols.1–10; *Virginia Magazine of History and Biography*, vols.1–38; *William and Mary Quarterly*, 1st series vols.1–27, 2nd series vols.1–10.

Virginia Historical Register (a quarterly). Ed. by William Maxwell. Richmond, for the Proprietor, 1848–53. Vols.1–6.

Virginia Magazine of History and Biography, 1893 to date. Ed. successively by P.A.Bruce, W.G.Stanard, and R.A.Lancaster,Jr. Richmond, pub.quarterly by the Virginia Historical Society, 1893–1939. Vols.1–47.

William and Mary College Quarterly Historical Magazine. Ed. by L.G.Tyler, 1892–1919; J.A.C.Chandler, E.G.Swem,1921 to date. Pub. by William and Mary College at Williamsburg,Va.
First Series, July 1892–April 1919. Vols.1–27. (Vols.4–27 Richmond.)
Second Series, January 1921–38. Vols.1–18.

Early Period

Abernathy, Thomas Perkins. *Western Lands and the American Revolution*. New York, D.Appleton-Century Co.,1937. 413p.,maps. (University of Virginia for Research in the Social Sciences.)

Ambler, Charles Henry. *Sectionalism in Virginia from 1776 to 1861*. Chicago, Univ.of Chicago Press,1910. 366p.,maps.

Andrews, Charles M.,ed. *Narratives of the Insurrections, 1675–1690*. New York, Charles Scribner's Sons,1915. 414p.

Andrews, Charles M. *The Colonial Period of American History*. New Haven and London, Yale Univ.Press, Oxford Univ.Press,1934. 256p. (Pub. on the Louis Stern Memorial Fund.)

Ballagh, James Curtis. *White Servitude in the Colony of Virginia*. Baltimore, Johns Hopkins Press,1895. 99p.,refer. (Johns Hopkins University Studies.) A study of the system of indentured labor in the American colonies.

Bayne, Howard R. *A Rebellion in the Colony of Virginia*. New York,1904. 16p. Bacon's rebellion—1676. (From the Historical papers of the Society of Colonial Wars in the State of New York, No.7,1904.)

Beverley, Robert. *History of Virginia, in Four Parts*. Reprinted from the author's 2nd rev. ed., London,1722, with an intro. by Charles Campbell. Richmond, J.W.Randolph,1855. 264p. First printed in London in 1705; translated and printed in Paris and in Amsterdam in 1707; 2nd London ed.,1722, revised and brought up to 1720. Beverley affords a vivid, comprehensive, instructive, and entertaining picture of Virginia at his time.

Bouldin, Powhatan. *The Old Trunk, or Sketches of Colonial Days.* Richmond, Andrews, Baptist, and Clemmitt,1888. 53p.

Brown, Alexander. *The First Republic in America.* Boston and New York, Houghton Mifflin Co.,1898. 688p. An account of the origin of the nation, written from the records then (1624) concealed.

Brown, Alexander,ed. *The Genesis of the United States.* Boston and New York, Houghton Mifflin Co.,1890, reprinted 1897. 2 vols. A series of historical manuscripts now first printed, together with a reissue of rare tracts, bibliographical memoranda, notes, brief biographies, and maps.

Bruce, Philip Alexander. *Economic History of Virginia in the Seventeenth Century.* New York and London, The Macmillan Co.,1896. 2 vols.,refer. Repr. 1907. A standard work.

——— *Institutional History of Virginia in the Seventeenth Century.* New York and London, G.P.Putnam's Sons,1910. 2 vols.,refer. A companion work to the Economic History.

——— *Social Life of Virginia in the Seventeenth Century.* 2d. ed., rev. and enl. Lynchburg, J.P.Bell,Inc.,1927. 275p. First pub. in Richmond in 1907.

Burk, John Daly. *The History of Virginia from Its First Settlement to the Present Day.* Petersburg, Dickson & Pescud,1804–16. 4 vols. Vol.4, begun by Burk, added to by Skelton Jones, and completed by Louis Hue Girardin, brings the history to 1781.

Byrd, William. *Writings of 'Col. William Byrd of Westover in Virginia Esqr.'* Ed. by John Spencer Bassett. New York, Doubleday,Page & Co.,1901. 461p. Contains 'The History of the Dividing Line between Virginia and North Carolina, 1728–29'; 'A Progress to the Mines, 1732'; 'A Journey to the Land of Eden, 1733'; and other papers. These papers have been published in other editions, at Petersburg in 1841; at Richmond in 1866; and at New York in 1928.

Calendar of Virginia State Papers and Other Manuscripts Preserved in the Capital in Richmond; Covering the Period from 1652 to 1869. Ed.by H.W.Flournoy, Wm.P.Palmer, S.McRae, and R.Colston. Richmond, by authority of the Legislature,1875–93. 11 vols.

Campbell, Charles. *History of the Colony and Ancient Dominion of Virginia.* Philadelphia, J.B.Lippincott Co.,1860. 765p.

Cooke, John Esten. *Virginia; a History of the People.* Boston and New York, Houghton Mifflin Co.,1897. 523p. (American Commonwealth Series.) First pub. in 1883 and reprinted in numerous editions. Authoritative, but brief treatment of period since 1865.

Dunaway, Wayland Fuller. *History of the James River and Kanawha Company.* New York, Longmans,Green & Co.,1923. 251p. (Columbia University Studies.) A scholarly study of the canal company.

Eckenrode, H.J. *The Revolution in Virginia.* Boston and New York, Houghton Mifflin Co.,1916. 311p. Repr. in 1926.

English, William Hayden. *Conquest of the Country Northwest of the River Ohio, 1778–1783, and Life of Gen. George Rogers Clark.* Indianapolis and Kansas City, Bowen-Merrill,1896. 2 vols.,illus.,maps.

Foote, Rev. William Henry. *Sketches of Virginia—Historical and Biographical.* First Series: Philadelphia, William S. Martien, 1850. 568p. Second Series, Philadelphia, J.B. Lippincott Co., 2nd ed., 1856. 596p. Vast collection of material on Presbyterian Church in Virginia, stories of Indian wars, etc.

Force, Peter (Collector). *Tracts and Other Papers, Relating Principally to the Origin, Settlement, and Progress of the Colonies in North America, from the Discovery of the Country to the Year 1776.* Washington, P. Force, 1836–46. 4 vols. A valuable collection that includes much on Virginia.

Hale, John P. *Trans-Allegheny Pioneers.* 2nd ed. Charleston, W.Va., Kanawha Valley Pub.Co., 1931. 340p., illus., maps. First pub. in Cincinnati in 1886.

Hariot, Thomas. *Narrative of the First English Plantation of Virginia.* First printed in London in 1588, now reproduced after De Bry's illustrated edition, Frankfort, 1590, the illustrations having been designed in Virginia in 1585 by John White. London, B. Quaritch, 1893. 111p. Thomas Hariot was one of the voyagers to Roanoke Island.

Howe, Henry. *Historical Collections of Virginia.* Charleston, S.C., W.R. Babcock, 1849. 544p. Traditions, biographical sketches, anecdotes, and geographical and statistical descriptions.

Johnston, Henry P. *The Yorktown Campaign and the Surrender of Cornwallis, 1781.* New York, Harper & Bros., 1881. 206p., maps.

Jones, Hugh. *The Present State of Virginia.* New York, J. Sabin, 1865. 151p. (Sabin's Reprint, No. 5, of the London ed. of 1724.) Jones was rector at Jamestown and professor at the college at Williamsburg.

Kingsbury, Susan Myra, ed. *Virginia Company of London.* Washington, pub. by Library of Congress. Vols. 1 and 2, 1906; Vols. 3 and 4, 1933–35. Minutes and documents of the Company, 1619–24.

Lee, Henry. *Memoirs of the War in the Southern Department of the United States.* New ed. with revisions and a biography of the author by Robert E. Lee. New York, University Pub.Co., 1869. 620p. Describes the Revolution in Virginia and the Carolinas in 1781.

Lewis, Virgil A. *History of the Battle of Point Pleasant, Monday, October 10th, 1774.* Charleston, W.Va., 1909. 131p., illus. Authoritative. Describes the chief event of Lord Dunmore's War.

McDonald, James J. *Life in Old Virginia.* Ed. by J.A.C. Chandler. Norfolk, Old Virginia Pub.Co., 1907. 374p.

Neill, Edward D. *The English Colonization of America during the Seventeenth Century.* London, Strahan & Co., 1871. 352p.

——— *Virginia Carolorum: the Colony under the Rule of Charles the First and Second . . . 1625–1685, based upon manuscripts and documents of the period.* Albany, N.Y., Joel Munsell's Sons, 1886. 446p.

Sams, Conway Whittle. *The Conquest of Virginia: the Forest Primeval.* An account . . . of the Indians in that portion of the continent in which was established the first English colony in America. New York, J.P. Putnam's Sons, 1916. 432p., illus., maps.

——— *The Conquest of Virginia: the First Attempt.* An account of Sir Walter Raleigh's colony on Roanoke Island . . . Norfolk, Keyser-Doherty Printing Corp., 1924. 547p., illus., maps.

——— *The Conquest of Virginia: the Second Attempt.* An account . . . of the attempt . . . to found Virginia at Jamestown, 1606–10. Norfolk, Keyser-Doherty Printing Corp.,1929. 916p.,illus.,maps.

Smith, Captain John. *Travels and Works of Captain John Smith, President of Virginia, and Admiral of New England, 1580–1631*, Ed. by Edward Arber. A new edition, with a biographical and critical introduction by A.G.Bradley. Edinburgh, John Grant,1910. 2 vols.,illus.,maps. Contemporary documents are included, pp.i–cxxxvi, and a bibliography includes the various editions of Smith's works and of works on Smith.

Squires, W.H.T. *The Days of Yester-year in Colony and Commonwealth.* Portsmouth,Va., Printcraft Press,Inc.,1928. 301p.,illus. A sketch book of Virginia.

Stanard, Mary Newton. *Colonial Virginia: Its People and Customs.* Philadelphia and London, J.B.Lippincott Co.,1917. 376p.,illus.

——— *The Story of Virginia's First Century.* Philadelphia and London, J.B. Lippincott Co., 1928. 322p.,illus.

Stewart, Robert Armistead. *The History of Virginia's Navy of the Revolution.* Richmond, Mitchell and Hotchkiss,1934. 279p.

Stith, William. *The History of the First Discovery and Settlement of Virginia.* New York, J.Sabin,1865. 331p. The history ends with 1624. (Sabin's reprint of Williamsburg ed. of 1747.)

Thwaites, Reuben Gold,ed. *Original Journals of the Lewis and Clark Expedition, 1804–1806.* New York, Dodd,Mead & Co.,1904–05. 7 vols. text and 1 vol. maps. The only complete edition of Lewis and Clark.

Tyler, Lyon Gardiner. *The Cradle of the Republic; Jamestown and James River.* 2d ed.,rev.and enl. Richmond, Hermitage Press,1906. 286p.,maps,plates. First pub.1900.

——— *England in America.* New York and London, Harper & Bros.,1904. 355p (American Nation Series.)

Tyler, Lyon Gardiner,ed. *Narratives of Early Virginia, 1606–1625.* New York, Charles Scribner's Sons,1907. 478p.,map.

Wertenbaker, Thomas J. *Virginia under the Stuarts, 1607–1688.* Princeton, Princeton Univ.Press,1914. 271 p.,illus.,maps.

Williams, Lloyd Haynes. *Pirates of Colonial Virginia.* Richmond, The Dietz Press,1937. 139p.,illus.,maps,bibl.

Withers, Alexander S. *Chronicles of Border Warfare; or a History of the Settlement by the Whites, of North-western Virginia, etc.* A new edition, edited and annotated by R.G.Thwaites . . . Cincinnati, R.Clarke Company,1895. 477p. First pub.1831.

Civil War Period

Alexander, E.P. *Military Memoirs of a Confederate.* New York, Charles Scribner's Sons,1907. 634p.,sketch-maps,statistical charts. A critical and authoritative narrative of operations in Virginia.

Allan, William. *History of the Campaigns of Gen.T.J.(Stonewall) Jackson in the Shenandoah Valley of Virginia from November 4, 1861, to June 17, 1862.* Maps by Jed Hotchkiss. Philadelphia, J.B.Lippincott Co.,1880. 175p. A standard reference work.

——— *The Army of Northern Virginia in 1862.* With intro. by John C. Ropes. Boston and New York, Houghton Mifflin Co.,1892. 537p.,folded tinted maps.

Allan, William, and Hotchkiss, Jed. *Chancellorsville.* New York, D.Van Nostrand,1867. 152p.,fold.maps. Authoritative.

American Annual Cyclopaedia and Register of Important Events of the Year 1861. New York, Appleton & Co.,1862. 780p. Contains a good account of the Secession Convention in Richmond and a list of all engagements in Virginia during the year.

Blanton, Wyndham Bolling. *Medicine in Virginia in the Nineteenth Century.* Richmond, Garrett and Massie,Inc.,1933. 466p.,bibl. Includes surgeons during the War between the States. The author has published similar books on the seventeenth and eighteenth centuries, respectively 1930 and 1931.

Butler, B.F. *Butler's Book.* Boston, A.M.Thayer & Co.,1892. 1154p.,illus.,maps. Autobiography and personal reminiscences of Major General Benj.F.Butler.

Craven, Avery. *Edmund Ruffin, Southerner. A Study in Secession.* New York, Appleton & Co.,1932. 283p. A well-documented study of agricultural conditions from 1820 to 1850; of secession in which Ruffin was a leader; and of the period during the war.

Davis, Jefferson. *The Rise and Fall of the Confederate Government.* New York, Appleton & Co.,1881. 2 vols.,portraits,maps.

Dodd, William E. *Jefferson Davis.* Philadelphia, George W. Jacobs (1907). 396p. (American Crisis Series.) A well-documented biography of the president of the Confederacy.

Freeman, Douglas Southall. *R.E.Lee, a Biography.* New York, London, Charles Scribner's Sons,1934–35. 4 vols.,illus.,maps,foot-notes,bibl. A history of the War between the States.

Gordon, George H. *Brook Farm to Cedar Mountain, in the War of the Great Rebelion, 1861–62.* (Cambridge,1883.) 376p.,maps. A narrative, by a commander under General Banks, of operations in the Valley, of political commanders, of people of the Valley, and of the formation of Pope's army.

——— *History of the Campaign of the Army of Virginia under John Pope, . . , from Cedar Mountain to Alexandria, 1862.* Boston, Houghton,Osgood & Co., 1880. 498p.,maps. A critical treatment, by a subordinate commander, of Pope's campaign which ended with the second battle of Manassas.

Henderson, Col.G.F.R. *Stonewall Jackson and the American Civil War.* With an introduction by Field Marshall the late Right Hon. Viscount Wolseley. New York and London, Longmans,Green & Co.,1927. 2 vols.,maps. First ed.1898.

Henry, Robert Selph. *The Story of the Confederacy.* New and rev.ed. with foreword by Douglas S. Freeman. Indianapolis, The Bobbs-Merrill Co. (1936). 514p.,maps and chronological table of engagements on land and along the coast.

Hotchkiss, Maj.Jed. *Virginia.* Atlanta, Confederate Publishing Co.,1899. 571p. of text, remainder biographical; 1295p. for distribution in Virginia, 692p. for distribution in other states. (Evans, C.A.,ed. *Confederate Military History.* vol.3.)

Johnson, Robert Underwood, and Clarence Clough Buel, editors. *Battles and Leaders of the Civil War.* New York, Century (1887–88). 4 vols. First pub. in *Century Magazine,* being for the most part contributions by Union and Confederate officers.

McClellan, H.B. *The Life and Campaigns of Major-General J.E.B.Stuart, Commander of the Cavalry of the Army of Northern Virginia.* Boston and New York, Houghton Mifflin Co.; Richmond, J.W.Randolph & English,1885. 468p.,maps. The history of the corps, from its records, to the death of Stuart in 1864.

McGregor, James C. *The Disruption of Virginia.* New York, The Macmillan Co., 1922. 328p. A documented account of the formation of West Virginia.

Official Records of Union and Confederate Navies in the War of the Rebellion. Series 1 and 2. Washington, Govt.Print.Off.,1894–1914,1927. 31 vols.

Official Records of Union and Confederate Armies in the War of the Rebellion. Series 1,2,3, and 4 of army orders, reports, and correspondence, and civil correspondence. Washington, Govt.Print.Off.,1881–1901. 128 vols.

Pearson, Charles Chilton. *The Readjuster Movement in Virginia.* New Haven, Yale Univ. Press,1917. 191p. Covers period of Mahoneism in Virginia.

Rhodes, James Ford. *History of the Civil War, 1861–1865.* New York, The Macmillan Co.,1919. 454p.,maps. A comprehensive abridgment of the author's three-volume work.

Richardson, James D. *A Compilation of the Messages and Papers of the Confederacy, including the Diplomatic Correspondence, 1861–1865.* Nashville, United States Publishing Co.,1906. 2 vols.

Schaff, Morris. *The Sunset of the Confederacy.* Boston, J.W.Luce and Co. (1912). 302p.,maps.

Scharf, J.Thomas. *History of the Confederate States Navy from its origin to the surrender of its last vessel.* New York, Rogers and Sherwood,1887. 824p.,illus., tables.

Scott, Major John. *Partisan Life with Col. John S. Mosby.* New York, Harper & Bros.,1867. 492p.,illus. and sketches. A history of Mosby's command.

Southern Historical Society Papers, 1876—ed. by R.A.Brock, *et al.* First Series, 1876–1910; vols.1–6 published two a year; vols.7–38 annually; 38 vols. Second Series, 1910—; vols.1–9 published occasionally; 9 vols. Richmond, Va., by the Society, whole number 47 vols. Latest vol. published 1930. This series of papers contain a comprehensive collection of original narratives, anecdotes, reports, and miscellaneous documentary material concerning the Southern Cause in the War between the States.

Southern Historical Society Papers Index; 1876–1910. First series of 38 vols.; compiled by Mrs.Kate Pleasants Minor. Richmond, D.Bottom, Supt.of Public Printing,1913. 139p.

Tremain, Henry Edwin. *Last Hours of Sheridan's Cavalry.* A reprint of war memoranda. New York, Bonnell,Silver and Bowers,1904. 563p.,maps. A valuable contribution on the ten days preceding Lee's surrender.

Walker, Francis A. *History of the Second Army Corps in the Army of the Potomac.* New York, Charles Scribner's Sons,1886. 737p.,maps,ports. A history of the activities of this, probably the most outstanding, corps of the Federal army in Virginia.

BIOGRAPHIES, MEMOIRS, REMINISCENCES, ETC.

Adams, James Truslow. *The Living Jefferson.* New York and London, Charles Scribner's Sons,1936. 403p.

Alderman, Edwin Anderson, and Gordon, Armistead Churchill. *J.L.M.Curry, A Biography.* New York, The Macmillan Co.,1911. 468p.,bibl. A prominent figure during the War between the States and most active in education after the war.

Andrews, Matthew Page, compiler. *Women of the South in War Times.* Baltimore, The Norman Remington Co., new ed., rev.,1927. 466p.,illus. First pub.1920 and reprinted several times.

Asbury, Herbert. *A Methodist Saint; the Life of Bishop Asbury.* New York, A.Knopf,1927. 355p.,bibl.

Avary, Myrta Lockett. *Dixie after the War.* Introduction by Gen.Clement A. Evans. New York, Doubleday,Page & Co.,1906. 435p.,illus. Reissued in Boston in 1937 with minor changes. An exposition of social conditions in the South.

Beveridge, Albert J. *The Life of John Marshall.* Boston and New York, Houghton Mifflin Co.,1916. 4 vols.

Bruce, William Cabell. *John Randolph of Roanoke, 1773–1833.* New York and London, G.P.Putnam's Sons,1922. 2 vols. plates,ports.

Chestnut, Mary Boykin. *A Diary from Dixie.* Ed. by Isabella D. Martin and Myrta Lockett Avary. New York, D.Appleton and Co.,1905. 424p.,illus. A diary of events in Charleston, Montgomery, and Richmond during the War between the States.

Chinard, Gilbert. *Thomas Jefferson, the Apostle of Americanism.* Boston, Little, Brown and Co.,1929. 548p.,plates,ports.

Claiborne, John H. *Seventy-Five Years in old Virginia.* New York and Washington, Neale Pub.Co.,1904. 360p. The author was surgeon in the Confederate army and in charge of all military hospitals at Petersburg,Va.

Conway, Moncure Daniel. *Barons of the Potomac and the Rappahannock.* New York, The Grolier Club,1892. 290p.

Custis, George Washington Parke. *Recollections and Private Memoirs of Washington.* By his adopted son . . . with a memoir of the author by his daughter. New York, Derby and Jackson,1860. 644p.

Davis, Arthur Kyle,ed. *Virginians of Distinguished Service of the World War.* State Capitol, Richmond, Va. Published by Order of the Executive Committee,1923. 243p.

Dodson, Leonidas. *Alexander Spotswood, governor of colonial Virginia, 1710–1722.* Philadelphia, University of Pennsylvania Press, London, Oxford Univ. Press,1932. 323p.

du Bellet, Louise Pecquet. *Some Prominent Virginia Families.* Lynchburg, J.P. Bell (1907). 4 vols.

Durand, of Dauphiné. *A Huguenot Exile in Virginia.* From the Hague ed. of 1687, with an intro. and notes by Gilbert Chinard. New York, Press of the Pioneers,Inc.,1934. 189p.

Fithian, Philip Vickers. *Journal and Letters, 1767–1774.* Ed. for the Princeton Historical Association by John Rogers Williams. Princeton,N.J., The University Press, 1900–34. 2 vols. Fithian was a student at Princeton and a traveler and tutor in Virginia.

Garland, Hugh A. *The Life of John Randolph of Roanoke.* New York, D.Appleton and Co., 1850. 2 vols. Reissued in 1853 in 1 vol.

Goode, John. *Recollections of a Lifetime.* New York and Washington, Neale Pub. Co.,1906. 266p. Goode was a member of the Secession Convention, of the Confederate Congress, and president of the 1901–02 constitutional convention.

Gwathmey, John H. *Legends of Virginia Courthouses.* Richmond, Press of the Dietz Printing Co.,1933. 141p.,plates.

Harrison, Mrs.Burton. *Recollections Grave and Gay.* New York, Charles Scribner's Sons,1911. 386p. *Ante-bellum* Virginia, Richmond and Virginia during the war, and cosmopolitan life after the war.

Henry, William Wirt. *Patrick Henry: Life, Correspondence and Speeches.* New York, Charles Scribner's Sons,1891. 3 vols.

Hocker, Edward W. *The Fighting Parson of the American Revolution*; a biography of General Peter Muhlenberg. Philadelphia, by the author, 1936. 191p.

Irving, Washington. *Life of George Washington.* New York, G.P.Putnam and Sons,1856. 5 vols. Reissued in 1860.

Jefferson, Thomas. *The Writings of Thomas Jefferson.* Ed. by Paul Leicester Ford. New York and London, G.P.Putnam's Sons,1894. 10 vols.

——— *Writings of Thomas Jefferson.* Ed. by Andrew A. Lipscomb and Albert E. Bergh. Washington, issued under auspices of the Thomas Jefferson Memorial Association,1903. 20 vols.

Jones, J.B. *A Rebel War Clerk's Diary at the Confederate States Capital.* Philadelphia, J.B.Lippincott and Co.,1866. 2 vols.

Jones, John Paul. *Life and Correspondence of John Paul Jones, including his narrative of the campaign of the Liman.* From original letters and manuscripts in possession of Miss Janette Taylor. New York, stereotyped by A.Chandler, 1830. 555p.

Lee, Edmund Jennings, ed. *Lee of Virginia.* Biographical and genealogical sketches of the descendants of Colonel Richard Lee. Philadelphia, by the author,1895. 586p.

Lee, Richard Henry. *The Letters of Richard Henry Lee, 1762–1794.* Collected and ed. by James Curtis Ballagh. New York, The Macmillan Co.,1911–14. 2 vols. Pub. under the auspices of the National Society of the Colonial Dames of America.

Lee, Richard Henry. *Life of Arthur Lee*; with his political and literary correspondence. Boston, Wells and Lilly,1829. 2 vols. Arthur Lee was the colony's agent in London prior to the Revolution.

Lewis, Charles Lee. *Matthew Fontaine Maury, the Pathfinder of the Seas.* Annapolis, The U.S. Naval Institute,1927. 264p.

Madison, James. *The Writings of James Madison.* Ed. by Gaillard Hunt. New York, London, G.P.Putnam's Sons,1900–10. 9 vols.

Maury, Ann. *Memoirs of a Huguenot Family.* Trans. and comp. from the original autobiography of the Rev.James Fontaine, and other family manuscripts; comprising an original journal of travels in Virginia,etc., in 1715 and 1716. New York, G.P.Putnam's Sons, new ed.,1872. 512p. First pub. 1838 as 'A tale of the Huguenots.'

Monroe, James. *The Writings of James Monroe.* Ed. by Stanislaus Murray Hamilton. New York and London, G.P.Putnam's Sons,1898–1903. 7 vols.

Morgan, George. *The Life of James Monroe.* Boston, Small,Maynard and Company (1921). 484p. Authoritative.

——— *The True Patrick Henry.* Philadelphia, London, J.B.Lippincott Co.,1907. 492p.,maps,plates.

Mosby, Colonel John S. *The Memoirs of Colonel John S. Mosby.* Ed. by Charles Wells Russell. Boston, Little,Brown and Co.,1917. 414p.

Nock, Albert Jay. *Jefferson.* New York, Harcourt,Brace and Company (1926). 340p.

Owen, Wm.Miller. *In Camp and Battle with the Washington Artillery of New Orleans.* Boston, Ticknor and Company,1885. 467p.,illus.,maps. An interesting narrative of events from Bull Run to Appomattox, including portions of a diary; social events, Drewry's Bluff, defense of Fort Gregg, etc.

Parton, James. *The Life and Times of Aaron Burr.* Boston and New York, Houghton Mifflin Co., enl. ed. (1892). 2 vols. First pub. 1857 and reissued many times.

Pollard, Jno.Garland, comp. *Virginia Born Presidents.* Addresses delivered by various persons on the occasions of unveiling the busts . . . at old hall of the House of Delegates. New York, Boston, American Book Company,1932. 232p.,ports.

Randall, Henry S. *The Life of Thomas Jefferson.* Philadelphia, J.B.Lippincott Co.,1871. 3 vols. First pub.1857.

Randolph, Sarah N. *The Domestic Life of Thomas Jefferson*; compiled from family letters and reminiscences, by his great-granddaughter. New York, Harper & Bros.,1871. 432p.,illus. Reissued in 1872.

Richardson, E.Ramsay. *Little Aleck; a life of Alexander Stephens, the fighting vice-president of the Confederacy.* Indianapolis, The Bobbs-Merrill Company (1932). 359p.,illus.

Rowland, Kate Mason. *The Life of George Mason, 1725–1792.* With an introduction by Gen.Fitzhugh Lee. New York, G.P.Putnam's Sons,1892. 2 vols. A standard.

Sale, Edith Tunis. *Old time belles and cavaliers.* Philadelphia, London, J.B.Lippincott Co.,1912. 285p.,illus. plates,ports.

Simms, Henry H. *Life of John Taylor.* Richmond, The William Byrd Press,Inc., 1932. 234p. The story of a brilliant leader in the early Virginia state rights school.

Smith, George G. *Life and Labors of Francis Asbury, Bishop of the Methodist Episcopal Church in America.* Nashville, Publishing house M.E. Church, South, 1898. 311p.

Wandell, Samuel H. and Minnegerode, Meade. *Aaron Burr.* New York and London. G.P.Putnam's Sons,1925. 2 vols. plates,ports.

Washington, George. *The Diaries of George Washington, 1748–1799.* Ed. by John C. Fitzpatrick. Boston and New York, Houghton Mifflin Co.,1925. 4 vols.

——— *Writings of George Washington.* Collected and edited by Worthington Chauncey Ford. New York and London, G.P.Putnam's Sons,1889. 14 vols.

Weems, Mason Locke. *A History of the Life and Death, Virtues and Exploits of General George Washington.* Philadelphia and London, J.B.Lippincott Co., 1918. 288p. First pub. 1800 as a pamphlet, later enlarged and reprinted many times.

Welles, Gideon. *Diary of Gideon Welles*. Introduction by John T. Morse,Jr. Boston and New York, Houghton Mifflin Co.,1911. 3 vols. The diary of the Secretary of the Navy under Lincoln and Johnson.

Wirt, William. *Sketches of the Life and Character of Patrick Henry*. Philadelphia, James Webster,1817. 427p. Reissued several times.

Wise, John S. *The End of An Era*. Boston and New York, Houghton Mifflin Co., 12th impression (1899). 474p. A readable narrative of events prior to and during the War between the States, by the youngest son of Governor Henry A. Wise.

Wilstach, Paul. *Patriots off their Pedestals*. Indianapolis, The Bobbs-Merrill Co. (1927). 240p. Washington, Henry, Jefferson, Marshall, Madison, etc.

POLITICS AND GOVERNMENT

Acts of the Assembly. Published separately for each session of the Legislature, beginning with the session 1807–1808 and continuing to the present time. Printed by the public printer, Richmond,Va.

Ambler, Charles Henry. *Thomas Ritchie; A Study in Virginia Politics*. Richmond, Bell Book and Stationery Co.,1913. 303p. Political parties of the post-Revolutionary period.

Brenaman, J.N. *A History of Virginia Conventions*. Richmond, J.L.Hill Printing Co.,1902. 122 + 87p. Brief treatment of the Revolutionary conventions; in greater detail for subsequent conventions; constitutions of 1868 and 1902 given in full.

Colonial Records of Virginia. Richmond, by authority of Sub-Committee in Charge of Library, R.F.Walker, Supt.of Public Printing,1874. 106p. Contains the proceedings of the First Assembly,1619; list of living and dead in 1623; a list of the inhabitants . . . in 1634; a list of the parishes in 1680; etc.

Cooper, Hon.Thomas V. and Fenton, Hector T. *American Politics*. Philadelphia, Fireside Publishing Co.,1882. 1058p. Contains history of political parties and their platforms; great speeches; texts of all political laws; tables—elections, financial, etc.

Eckenrode, Hamilton James. *Political History of Virginia during the Reconstruction*. Baltimore, Johns Hopkins Press,1904. 128p. (Johns Hopkins University Studies.)

——— *Separation of Church and State in Virginia*. Richmond, D.Bottom, Supt. Public Printing,1910. 164p. (Special report of the Department of Archives and History.)

Executive Journals of the Councils of Colonial Virginia. Ed. by Henry Read McIlwaine. Richmond, pub. by the Virginia State Library,1925–30. 4 vols. Contains proceedings of the council from 1680 to 1739.

Hening's and Shepherd's Statutes at Large; being a collection of all the laws of Virginia from the first session of the legislature in 1619 to the session of 1807–08. (First series), vols. 1–13, by William Waller Hening; Second series, vols. 1–3, by Samuel Shepherd. Various imprints—Richmond, New York, Philadelphia. Pub. by Act of the General Assembly, February 1808, 1823–36. 16 vols. (Continued as *Acts of the Assembly*.)

Journals of the Council of the State of Virginia. Ed. by H.R.McIlwaine. Richmond, pub. by the Virginia State Library, 1931–32. 2 vols. Contains proceedings July 1776 to November 1781.

Journals of the House of Burgesses of Virginia, 1619–1776. Ed. by John P. Kennedy and H.R.McIlwaine. Richmond, by authority of the Library Board of the Virginia State Library, 1905–15. 13 vols.

Journals of the House of Delegates, 1776– . Published separately for each session of the Legislature, beginning with the session of 1776 and continuing to the present time. Printed by the public printer at the capital, Richmond (Williamsburg until 1780).

Journals of the Senate, 1776– . Published separately for each session of the Legislature, beginning with the session of 1776 and continuing to the present time. Printed by the public printer at the capital, Richmond (Williamsburg until 1780).

(*Journals of Virginia's Revolutionary Conventions.*) The proceedings of the conventions of delegates for the counties and corporations in the Colony of Virginia, held at Richmond and Williamsburg, 1775–76. Richmond, Ritchie, Truehart & Du-Val, reprinted by a Resolution of the House of Delegates, 1816. 229p.

Legislative Journals of the Council of Colonial Virginia. Ed. by H.R.McIlwaine. Richmond, Library Board, Virginia State Library, 1918–19. 3 vols.

McBain, Howard L. *Government and Politics in Virginia.* Richmond, The Bell Book and Stationery Co., Rev. ed.,1922. 332p.,illus. A well-written text book.

McPherson, Edward. *The Political History of the United States of America during the Great Rebellion.* Washington, Philp and Solomons, 2nd ed.,1865. 653p. A standard work. The author was clerk of the House of Representatives; he published a political history of Reconstruction and a number of political year-books.

Stanard, William G. and Mary Newton, compilers. *The Colonial Virginia Register.* Albany,N.Y., Joel Munsell's Sons,1902. 249p. A list of governors, councillors, members of the house of burgesses and of the Revolutionary conventions, and other high officials.

RACIAL ELEMENTS AND FOLKLORE

Ballagh, James Curtis. *A History of Slavery in Virginia.* Baltimore, Johns Hopkins Press,1902. 160p.,bibl. (Johns Hopkins University Studies in Historical and Political Science. Extra vol. 24.)

Caperton, Helena Lefroy. *Legends of Virginia.* Richmond, Garrett and Massie, 1931. 74p.

Dew, Thomas Roderick. *An Essay on Slavery.* Richmond, J.W.Randolph,1849. 115p. Published in 1832 as a 'review of the debate in the Virginia legislature of 1831 and 1832.'

Davis, Arthur Kyle,Jr.,ed. *Traditional Ballads of Virginia.* Cambridge, Harvard Univ.Press,1929. 634p. Collected under the auspices of the Virginia Folklore Society. A priceless volume of folk literature.

Ezekiel, Herbert T., and Lichtenstein, Gaston. *History of the Jews of Richmond, 1769–1917.* Richmond, H.T.Ezekiel,1917. 374p.

McConnell, John Preston. *Negroes and Their Treatment in Virginia from 1865 to 1867*. Pulaski, Va., B.D. Smith (1910). 126p. refer.

Maury, Richard L., comp. *The Huguenots in Virginia*. n.p. (Huguenot Society of America) (*c.*1900). 116p. (Carries no title page.)

Morton, Richard L. *The Negro in Virginia Politics, 1865–1902*. Charlottesville, University Press, 1919. 199p. (Publications of the University of Virginia. Phelps-Stokes Fellowship Papers, No. 4.)

Russell, John H. *The Free Negro in Virginia, 1619–1865*. Baltimore, Johns Hopkins Press, 1913. 194p., refer. (Johns Hopkins University Studies.)

Scarborough, Dorothy, assisted by Ola Lee Gulledge. *On the Trail of Negro Folk-Songs*. Cambridge, Harvard Univ. Press, 1925. 289p. illus., music.

AGRICULTURE, INDUSTRY, LABOR

Arnold, Benjamin William. *History of the Tobacco Industry in Virginia from 1860 to 1894*. Baltimore, Johns Hopkins Press, 1897. 86p. (Johns Hopkins University Studies.)

Bruce, Kathleen. *Virginia Iron Manufacture in the Slave Era*. New York, London, The Century Co. (1930). 482p. A doctorial dissertation.

Department of Agriculture of Virginia. *Virginia*. Compiled and edited by Charlotte Allen under direction of George W. Koiner, Commissioner. Richmond, by the department, 1937. 264p., illus. An excellent general work on the resources of the State.

Handy, R.B. *Peanuts: Culture and Uses*. Washington, Govt. Print. Off., 1896. 24p. (U.S. Department of Agriculture, Farmers' Bulletin, No. 25.)

McCormick, Cyrus. *The Century of the Reaper*. Boston and New York, Houghton Mifflin Co., 1931. 307p., plates, ports. An account of Cyrus Hall McCormick, the McCormick harvester, and the business he created.

Newman, Clarence W., ed. *Virginia, Economic and Civic*. Prepared in the Virginia Polytechnic Institute in collaboration with the Virginia State Chamber of Commerce by R. Lee Humbert, Willard H. Humbert, and Melville L. Jeffries; foreword by the Hon. John Garland Pollard. Edited for the Virginia State Chamber of Commerce by Clarence W. Newman. Richmond, Whittet and Shepperson, 1933. 427p., bibl.

Starnes, George Talmage, and Hamm, John Edwin. *Some Phases of Labor Relations in Virginia*. New York, London, D. Appleton-Century Co., 1934, 151p. (University of Virginia Institute for Research in the Social Sciences. Monograph No. 20.)

Watson, Thomas Leonard. *Mineral Resources of Virginia*. Lynchburg, J.P. Bell Co., 1907. 618p., illus., maps, tables, bibl. A valuable survey of the State's mineral wealth and its development.

EDUCATION AND RELIGION

Bruce, Philip A. *History of the University of Virginia, 1819–1919; the lengthened shadow of one man . . .* New York, The Macmillan Co., Centennial ed. (1920–22). 5 vols. bibl. The standard history of the university.

Goodwin, Edward Lewis. *The Colonial Church in Virginia*. Milwaukee, Morehouse Pub.Co.; London, A.R.Mawbray and Co.,1927. 344p.

Heatwole, Cornelius J. *A History of Education in Virginia*. New York, The Macmillan Co.,1916. 382p.

Meade, William. *Old Churches, Ministers and Families of Virginia*. Philadelphia, J.B.Lippincott Co.,new ed. (including Wise's index), 1931. 2 vols. A standard work, first printed in 1857 and reprinted in 1861 and 1872. J.M. Toner's index to Meade was issued in 1872, and Jennings Cropper Wise's index was issued in 1910.

Morrison, A.J. *The Beginnings of Public Education in Virginia, 1776–1860*. Richmond, D.Bottom, Supt.of Public Printing,1917. 195p. Issued by the State Board of Education.

Neill, Edward D. *History of Education in Virginia during the Seventeenth Century*. Washington, Govt.Print.Off.,1867. 27p. Prepared for the U.S. Commissioner of Education.

Semple, Robert B. *A History of the Rise and Progress of the Baptists in Virginia*. Revised and extended by Rev.G.W.Beale. Richmond, Pitt and Dickinson, 1894. 536p. Revision of a work published in 1810.

Trent, William P. *English Culture in Virginia*. A Study of the Gilmer letters and an account of the English professors obtained by Thomas Jefferson for the University of Virginia. Baltimore, Johns Hopkins University,1889. 141p. (Johns Hopkins University Studies.)

SPORTS AND RECREATION

Harrison, Fairfax. *The Equine F.F.Vs*. Richmond, privately printed, the Old Dominion Press,1928. 184p.,plates, ports.

Potomac Appalachian Trail Club. *Guide to Paths in the Blue Ridge*. 2nd ed. Washington,D.C.,1934. 452p.,illus.,maps. A handbook that plots distances of the Virginia-Maryland section of the Maine-to-Georgia hiker's trail and gives data on geology, wild-flowers, trees, first aid, and a selected bibliography.

LITERATURE AND JOURNALISM

Bagby, George William. *The Old Virginia Gentleman and Other Sketches*. Ed., with an introduction, by Thomas Nelson Page. New York, Charles Scribner's Sons,1910. 312p. Repr.1911.

Cappon, Lester J. *Virginia Newspapers, 1821–1935*. A bibliography, with historical introduction and notes. New York, London, D.Appleton-Century Company, for the Institute of Research in the Social Sciences, University of Virginia,1936. 299p.

Cooke, John Esten. *Stories of the Old Dominion, from the settlement to the end of the Revolution*. New York, Harper & Bros.,1879. 337p.

Gordon, Armistead C.,Jr., ed. *Virginia Writers of Fugitive Verse*. New York, J.T.White & Co.(1923). 404p.,bibl.

Minor, Mrs.Kate Pleasants, and Harrison, Miss Susie B. 'A List of Newspapers in the Virginia State Library, Confederate Museum, and Valentine Museum.' Compiled under direction of Earl G. Swem. *Virginia State Library Bulletin* (Issued quarterly), Oct.1912, vol.5, no.4:285–425.

Page, Thomas Nelson. *The Old South; essays social and political.* New York, Charles Scribner's Sons,1892. 344 p.

Painter, F.V.N. *Poets of Virginia.* Richmond, Atlanta, B.F.Johnson Publishing Co. (1907).,336p.

Thomas, Ella Marshall. *Virginia Women in Literature, a partial list.* Richmond, B.F.Johnson Publishing Co.,1902. 61p.

Woodberry, George E. *Edgar Allan Poe.* Boston and New York, Houghton Mifflin Co.,1892. 354p. (American Men of Letters series). The standard biography.

ART AND ARCHITECTURE

Architectural Record. *The Restoration of Colonial Williamsburg in Virginia.* New York, F.W.Dodge Corp.,1935. 458p. Reprinted from the Architectural Record, December 1935. The whole issue is devoted to the restoration.

Chandler, Joseph Everett, ed. *The Colonial Architecture of Maryland, Pennsylvania, and Virginia.* Boston, Bates,Kimball and Guild,1892. 3p.,50 plates.

Coffin, L.A., and Holden, A.C. *Brick Architecture of the Colonial Period in Maryland and Virginia.* New York, Architectural Book Pub.Co.,1919. 29p.,illus.

Dunlap, William. *History of the rise and progress of the arts of design in the United States.* New edition, edited with additions, by Frank W. Bayley and Charles E. Goodspeed. Boston, C.E.Goodspeed and Co.,1918. 3 vols.,illus.,bibl.

Kimball, Fiske. *American Architecture.* Indianapolis and New York, The Bobbs-Merrill Co. (1928). 262p.,plates,notes.

——— *Domestic Architecture of the American Colonies and of the Early Republic.* New York, Charles Scribner's Sons,1922. 314p.,illus., biographical footnotes. Published under auspices of the Metropolitan Museum of Art committee on educational work.

——— *Thomas Jefferson, Architect.* Original designs in the collection of Thomas Jefferson Coolidge,Jr., with an essay and notes by Fiske Kimball. Cambridge and Boston, Riverside Press,1916. 205p.,223 facsimiles.

——— *Thomas Jefferson and the First Monument of the Classical Revival in America . . .* Harrisburg,Pa., and Washington,1915. 48p. Reprinted from the Journal of the American Institute of Architects, vol.III.

——— *Thomas Jefferson and the Origins of the Classical Revival in America.* n.p. (1915). pp.219–27,illus. (Reprinted from Art and Archaeology.)

Quesnay de Beaurepaire, Alexandre Marie. *Memoir concerning the Academy of the Arts and Sciences of the United States of America at Richmond, Virginia.* Translated by Rosewell Page and published as part of the Report of the Virginia State Library for 1920–21. Richmond, D.Bottom,1922, 50p.

Sale, Edith Tunis. *Colonial Interiors, second series.* With an introduction by J. Frederick Kelly. New York, W.Helburn Inc.,1930. 159p.,plans,illus.

———*Interiors of Virginia houses of colonial times, from the beginnings of Virginia to the Revolution.* Richmond,The William Byrd Press,Inc.,1927. 503p., 371 plates,etc.

Waterman, Thomas Tileston, and Barrows, John A. *Domestic colonial architec-*

ture of tidewater Virginia. New York, London, Charles Scribner's Sons,1932. 191p.,illus.

Weddell, Alexander Wilbourne, ed. *Memorial Volume of Virginia Historical Portraiture, 1585–1830*. With an introduction by Ellen Glasgow and a review of early American portraiture by Thomas B. Clarke. Richmond, The William Byrd Press, Inc.,1930. 556p.,plates, ports.,map,bibl. Commemorates an exhibit . . . under the auspices of the Virginia Historical Society . . . 1929.

HISTORIC HOMES, GARDENS, ETC.

Alexander, Frederick Warren, comp. *Stratford Hall and the Lees Connected with Its History*. Oak Grove,Va., The Author,1912. 332p.,illus.

Armes, Ethel. *Stratford Hall, the Great House of the Lees*. With intro. by Franklin D. Roosevelt. Richmond, Garrett & Massie,Inc.,1936. 575p.,illus.

Chase, Enoch Aquilla. *The History of Arlington*. Washington, National Art Service Co.,1929. 22p.,pencil sketches.

Lancaster, Robert A.,Jr. *Historic Virginia Homes and Churches* . . . with 316 illustrations. Philadelphia and London, J.B.Lippincott Co.,1915. 527p.

Lowther, Minnie Kendall. *Mount Vernon; Its Children, Its Romances, Its Allied Families and Mansions*. Rev. and enl. ed. Philadelphia, John C. Winston, 1932. 302p. First pub.1930.

Massie, Susanne Williams, and Frances Archer Christian, eds. *Homes and Gardens in Old Virginia*. With intro. by Douglas S. Freeman. 4th ed. Richmond, Garrett & Massie,Inc.,1932. 367p. First pub.1930.

Sale, Edith Tunis,ed. *Historic Gardens of Virginia*. Rev.ed. Richmond, The William Byrd Press, Inc.,1930. 376p.,illus. Compiled by James River Garden Club.

——— *Manors of Virginia in Colonial Times*. Philadelphia and London, J.B. Lippincott Co.,1909. 309p.,illus.

U.S. Quartermaster Corps. *Arlington House and Its Associations*. Washington, Custis, Lee. (Fort Humphreys),1932. 45p.,illus. Lists furnishings and explains their acquisitions.

Wayland, John W. *Historic Homes of Northern Virginia and the Eastern Panhandle of West Virginia*. Staunton,Va., McClure Co.,Inc.,1937. 625p.,illus., maps.

Wilstach, Paul. *Mount Vernon, Washington's Home and the Nation's Shrine*. 4th ed. Indianapolis, The Bobbs-Merrill Co. (1930). 301p.,illus. First pub.1916.

CITIES, TOWNS, COUNTIES, SECTIONS

Bagby, Alfred. *King and Queen County, Virginia*. New York and Washington, Neale Publishing Co.,1908. 402p.,maps.,plates,ports.

Boley, Henry. *Lexington in old Virginia*. Richmond, Garrett and Massie,1936. 235p.illus.

Brydon, G.MacLaren. 'The Huguenots of Manakin Town and Their Times.' *The Virginia Magazine of History and Biography*, Richmond, Oct.1934, vol.42, no.4:325–35.

Burrell, Charles Edward. *A History of Prince Edward County, Virginia, from its formation in 1753, to the present.* Richmond, Williams Printing Co.,1922. 408p.

Carrington, J.Cullen, comp. *Charlotte County, Virginia.* Richmond, The Hermitage Press,Inc.,1907. 142p.,illus. Briefly historical; agricultural.

Carrington, (Mrs.) Wirt Johnson. *A History of Halifax County (Virginia).* Richmond, Appeals Press,1924. 525p.

Cartmell, T.K. *Shenandoah Valley Pioneers and Their Descendants.* (Winchester, Va. Eddy Press Corp.,1909). 587p.,plates. A history of Frederick County.

Christian, W.Asbury. *Lynchburg and Its People.* Lynchburg, J.P.Bell Co.,1900. 463p.,plates, ports. Chronological history, with biographical sketches.

——— *Richmond, Her Past and Present.* Richmond, L.H.Jenkins,1912. 618p., plates,map.

Clarke, Peyton Neale. *Old King William Homes and Families.* Louisville, J.P. Morton and Company,1897. 211p.,plates.

Clement, Maud Carter. *The History of Pittsylvania County, Virginia.* Lynchburg J.P.Bell Company,Inc.,1929. 340p.,ports.,maps. A documented history of the area from first settlement; brief treatment after 1865.

Davis, Arthur Kyle. *Three Centuries of an old Virginia town (Petersburg).* Richmond, W.C.Hill Printing Co., 8th printing,1923. 30p. Reprinted from the Magazine of History, New York,1914.

Early, R.H. *Campbell chronicles and family sketches, embracing the history of Campbell County, Virginia, 1782–1926.* Lynchburg, J.P.Bell Company,1927. 554p.,illus.

Embrey, Alvin T. *History of Fredericksburg.* Richmond, Old Dominion Press, 1937. 202p.,illus.

Eubank, H.Ragland. *Historic Northern Neck of Virginia.* Richmond, Northern Neck Association (Colonial Beach) (1934). 109p.,illus.,road map. History treated through families and homes.

Fauquier Historical Society, Warrenton,Va. *Bulletins*; First Series, 1921–24. Richmond, Old Dominion Press,Inc.,n.d. 520p.,ports.,maps. Four annual bulletins treating of aboriginal inhabitants, surveys, marriage bonds, letters, biographical sketches, statistics, etc.

Gold, Thos.D.,*et al. History of Clarke County, Virginia, and its connection with the War between the States. . . .* (Berryville,Va., C.R.Hughes,1914.) 337p., plates,ports.

Goodwin, Rutherford. *A Brief and True Report for the Traveller concerning Williamsburg in Virginia.* Richmond, printed for Colonial Williamsburg, Inc., 2nd ed., rev. and improved,1936. 192p.,plates,maps. First printed in 1935.

Gordon, Armistead C. *In the Picturesque Shenandoah Valley.* Richmond, Garrett and Massie,Inc.,1930. 201p.,plates,maps.

Groome, H.C. *Fauquier during the Proprietorship.* A chronicle of the colonization and organization of a Northern Neck county. Richmond, Old Dominion Press,1927. 255p.,map showing old roads.

Harris, Malcolm H. *History of Louisa County.* Richmond, Dietz Press,1936. 525p. Includes biographical sketches, genealogies, marriage bonds 1767–1800.

[Harrison, Fairfax.] *Landmarks of Old Prince William; a Study of Origins in North-*

ern Virginia. Richmond, privately printed by the Old Dominion Press, 1924. 2 vols. A well-documented history.

Head, James W. *History and Comprehensive Description of Loudoun County, Virginia.* (Washington), Park View Press (1909). 186p. Descriptive, historical, statistical.

Jack, George S., *et al. History of Roanoke County*, by George S. Jack; *History of Roanoke City and History of the Norfolk and Western Railway Company*, by E.B. Jacobs. (Roanoke, Stone, 1912). 255p., illus.

James, Edward Wilson, ed. *Lower Norfolk County Virginia Antiquary.* Vol.1–5; 1895–1906. (n.p. 1895–1906). 5 vols.

Kegley, F.B. *Virginia Frontier; the beginning of the Southwest; the Roanoke of colonial days, 1740–83.* Roanoke, Southwest Virginia Historical Society, 1938. 786p.

Kellam, Sadie Scott, and U. Hope. *Old Houses in Princess Anne, Virginia.* Portsmouth, Printcraft Press, Inc., 1931. 235p., illus.

Kercheval, Samuel. *A History of the Valley of Virginia.* Strasburg, Va., Shenandoah Publishing House, 4th ed., rev. and ext., 1925. 405p. First pub. 1833.

Kibler, J. Luther. *Colonial Virginia Shrines.* A complete guide book to Jamestown, Williamsburg, and Yorktown. Richmond, Garrett and Massie, Inc. (1936). 98p., illus.

Mordecai, Samuel. *Virginia, Especially Richmond, in By-gone Days; with a glance at the present.* 2nd ed., with many corrections and additions. Richmond, West and Johnston, 1860. 359p. First pub. in 1856 as 'Richmond in by-gone days.' A valuable contemporary account of the city during the life of the author.

Morton, Oren F. *A Centennial History of Alleghany County, Virginia.* Dayton, Va. J.K. Ruebush Co., 1923. 226p. Based, generally, upon reliable sources.

——— *A History of Highland County.* Monterey, Va. by the author (1911). 419p., plates, maps. Based largely upon county and State records.

——— *A History of Rockbridge County, Virginia.* Staunton, The McClure Co., 1920. 574p.

——— *Annals of Bath County, Virginia.* Staunton, The McClure Co., 1917. 208p.

Morton, Frederic. *The Story of Winchester in Virginia, the oldest town in the Shenandoah Valley.* Strasburg, Va., Shenandoah Publishing House, 1925. 336p.

Page, Rosewell. *Hanover County; its history and legends.* (Richmond 1926.) 153p.

Pedigo, Lewis G. and Virginia G. *History of Patrick and Henry counties.* Roanoke, Stone Printing and Mfg. Co., 1933. 400p., plates, ports.

Pendleton, Wm.C. *History of Tazewell County and Southwest Virginia, 1748–1920.* Richmond, W.C. Hill Printing Co., 1920. 700p. Based, generally, upon reliable sources.

Powell, Mary G. *The History of Old Alexandria, Virginia, from July 13, 1749 to May 24, 1861.* Richmond, The William Byrd Press, Inc. (1928). 366p.

Quinn, S.J. *The history of the city of Fredericksburg, Virginia.* Prepared and printed by authority of the common council. Richmond, Hermitage Press, 1908. 349p., plates, ports.

Scott, W.W. *A History of Orange County, Virginia, from its formation in 1734* (o.s.) to the end of Reconstruction in 1870 . . . Richmond, Everett Waddey Co., 1907. 292p., plates, map. Generally from the records.

Squires, W.H.T. *Through the years in Norfolk.* Norfolk, by the Norfolk Advertising Board,*et al.*,1936. 359p.,illus.

Stanard, Mary Newton. *Richmond, its people and its story.* Philadelphia and London, J.B.Lippincott Co.,1923. 238p.,illus.,ports.,map.

Stansbury, Charles Frederick. *The Lake of the Great Dismal.* With a preface by Don Marquis. New York, A. & C. Boni,1925. 238p.,plates,port.,map. Description of the region and reference to economic conditions.

Starkey, Marion L. *The First Plantation: a history of Hampton and Elizabeth City county, Virginia, 1607–1887.* (Hampton) by the author,1936. 95p.

Summers, Lewis Preston. *History of Southwest Virginia, 1746–1786, Washington County, 1777–1870.* Richmond, J.L.Hill Printing Co.,1903. 921p.,illus.,map.

Trudell, Clyde F. *Colonial Yorktown. Being a brief Historie of the Place; together with Something of its Houses and Publick Buildings.* Richmond, The Dietz Press,1938. 206p.,illus.,maps.,bibl.

Tyler, Lyon Gardiner. *Williamsburg, the Old Colonial Capitol.* Richmond, Whittet and Shepperson,1907. 285p.,illus.,maps.

Waddell, Joseph A. *Annals of Augusta County, Virginia, from 1726 to 1871.* Staunton, C.R.Caldwell, 2nd ed.rev.,1902. 545p. First pub. in 1888.

Wayland, John W. *A history of Shenandoah County, Virginia.* Strasburg,Va., Shenandoah Publishing House,1927. 874p.,illus.,maps.

——— *A history of Rockingham County, Virginia.* Dayton,Va., Ruebush-Elkins Company,1912. 466p.,illus.,maps.

———*The German Element of the Shenandoah Valley of Virginia.* Charlottesville, by the author, 1907. 272p.

Wertenbaker, Thomas J. *Norfolk; historic southern port.* Durham,N.C., Duke Univ.Press,1931. 378p.,plates,ports.,maps,bibliographical footnotes.

Williams, Harrison. *Legends of Loudoun.* Richmond, Garrett and Massie,1938. 248p. An account of the history and homes of the county.

Wilson, Goodridge. *Smyth County History and Traditions.* (Kingsport,Tenn.) published in connection with the Centennial Celebration of Smyth County, 1932. 397p.

Wilstach, Paul. *Potomac Landings.* Indianapolis, The Bobbs-Merrill Co. (1932). 378p.,plates,ports.,map. First pub. in 1921.

——— *Tidewater Virginia.* Indianapolis, The Bobbs-Merrill Co. (1929). 326p., illus.

Wingfield, Marshall. *A history of Caroline County, Virginia, from its formation in 1727 to 1924.* Richmond, Press of Trevvet Christian & Co.,Inc.,1924. 528p.

Wise, Jennings Cropper. *Ye Kingdome of Accawmacke; or the Eastern Shore of Virginia in the Seventeenth Century.* Richmond, The Bell Book and Stationery Co.,1911. 406p.

Woods, Edgar. *Albemarle County in Virginia.* (Charlottesville,Va., The Michie Co.,1901.) 412p. Reprinted at Bridgewater,Va., in 1932. Much material from the records.

1940 Census Figures

STATE TOTAL	2,677,773	RURAL TOTAL	1,733,098
URBAN TOTAL	944,675		

Independent Cities

Alexandria	33,523	Newport News	37,067
Bristol	9,768	Norfolk	144,332
Buena Vista	4,335	Petersburg	30,631
Charlottesville	19,400	Portsmouth	50,745
Clifton Forge	6,461	Radford	6,990
Danville	32,749	Richmond	193,042
Fredericksburg	10,066	Roanoke	69,287
Hampton	5,898	South Norfolk	8,038
Harrisonburg	8,768	Staunton	13,337
Hopewell	8,679	Suffolk	11,343
Lynchburg	44,541	Williamsburg	3,942
Martinsville	10,080	Winchester	12,095

Incorporated Towns

Abingdon	3,158	Branchville	153
Alberta	416	Bridgewater	993
Altavista	2,919	Broadway	506
Amherst	930	Broadnax	536
Appalachia	3,010	Brookneal	736
Appomattox	922	Buchanan	868
Arlington County	57,040	Buckingham	190
Ashland	1,718	Burkeville	658
Bedford	3,973	Cambria	810
Belle Haven	277	Cape Charles	2,299
Berryville	1,262	Capron	291
Big Stone Gap	4,331	Cedar Bluff	823
Blacksburg	2,133	Charlotte Courthouse	399
Blackstone	2,699	Chase City	1,896
Bluefield	3,921	Chatham	1,230
Bond Town	288	Chilhowie	889
Boone Mill	377	Chincoteague	2,142
Bowling Green	541	Christiansburg	2,299
Boyce	342	Claremont	380
Boydton	424	Clarksville	826
Boykins	699	Clifton	194

Clinchport	346	Hillsboro	115
Clintwood	1,106	Hillsville	656
Clover	252	Holland	378
Coeburn	764	Honaker	851
Colonial Beach	1,105	Independence	429
Colonial Heights	3,194	Iron Gate	719
Columbia	144	Ivor	339
Courtland	459	Jarratt	458
Covington	6,300	Jonesville	588
Crewe	2,048	Kenbridge	847
Culpeper	2,316	Keysville	607
Damascus	1,441	Kilmarnock	614
Dayton	632	La Crosse	524
Dendron	465	Lawrenceville	1,703
Dillwyn	436	Lebanon	622
Drakes Branch	438	Leesburg	1,698
Draper	241	Lexington	3,914
Dublin	576	Louisa	365
Duffield	83	Lovettsville	248
Dumfries	480	Luray	1,511
Dungannon	333	McDowell	110
Eastville	316	McKenney	453
Edinburg	565	Madison	281
Elkton	1,050	Manassas	1,302
Emporia	2,735	Marion	5,177
Fairfax	979	Meadow View	596
Falls Church	2,576	Mendota	173
Farmville	3,475	Middleburg	629
Fincastle	442	Middletown	361
Floyd	479	Mineral	427
Franklin	3,466	Monterey	309
Fries	1,677	Mount Crawford	290
Front Royal	3,831	Mount Jackson	562
Galax	3,195	Narrows	1,489
Gate City	1,565	Newcastle	253
Glade Spring	686	New Market	629
Glasgow	938	Nickelsville	256
Glen Lyn	259	North Tazewell	688
Gordonsville	508	Norton	4,006
Goshen	187	Occoquan	213
Gretna	619	Onancock	1,283
Grottoes	759	Orange	1,980
Grundy	1,476	Pamplin City	273
Halifax	536	Parksley	701
Hamilton	409	Pearisburg	987
Haymarket	156	Pennington Gap	1,990
Haysi	623	Phoebus	3,503
Herndon	1,046	Phoenix	340

Pocahontas	2,623	Surry	254
Port Royal	123	Tangier	1,020
Pulaski	8,792	Tappahannock	783
Purcellville	787	Tazewell	1,374
Quantico	1,139	The Plains	372
Remington	226	Timberville	252
Richlands	2,203	Toms Brook	219
Ridgeway	422	Troutdale	334
Rocky Mount	1,366	Urbanna	482
Round Hill	337	Victoria	1,555
Rural Retreat	440	Vienna	1,237
St. Charles	482	Vinton	3,455
St. Paul	746	Virgilina	358
Salem	5,737	Virginia Beach	2,600
Saltville	2,650	Wachapreague	548
Scottsburg	239	Wakefield	687
Scottsville	368	Warrenton	1,651
Shenandoah	1,829	Washington	245
Singers Glen	120	Waterford	247
Smithfield	1,178	Waverly	1,288
South Boston	5,252	Waynesboro	7,373
South Hill	1,739	West Point	1,947
Stanardsville	212	Wiehle	91
Stanley	317	Windsor	411
Stephens City	600	Wise	1,226
Stony Creek	493	Woodstock	1,546
Strasburg	1,968	Wytheville	4,653
Stuart	720	Yorktown	521

Radio Stations

Location	*Station*	*Kilocycles*
Charlottesville	WCHV	1450
Danville	WBTM	1400
Fredericksburg	WFVA	1290
Harrisonburg	WSVA	550
Lynchburg	WLVA	1230
Martinsville	WMVA	1450
Newport News	WGH	1340
Norfolk	WTAR	790
Petersburg	WPID	1240
Richmond	WMBG	1380
"	WRNL	910
"	WBBL	1240
"	WRVA	1140
Roanoke	WDBJ	960
"	WSLS	1490
Suffolk	WLPM	1450
Winchester	WINC	1400

Recent Changes In Highway Numbering

(Before using the Guide, the traveler may find it best to pencil in the following corrections on the pages indicated.)

On pages	*Change*	*To*
xii,414,418,442,524	State 3	State 522
340,407	6Y	335
344,525	9	123
400,401	9	120
587	10	32
406,614	16	27
33,234–5,246–7,462	27	170
475	34	46
572	37	106
614	49	242
619	49	522

On pages	*Change*	*To*
538	59	83
537	64	71
539	67	160
535 (line 26)	81	16
439,535	81	91
536	84	4
xiii,438,468,476,535	88	16
477	91	81
609	120	245
433	123	320
234–5,571,586	158	258
33,462	170	238
450,544	207	301
403	233	28
400	237	Wilson Blvd.
526–7	238	9
527	245	234
421	261	59
350,392,403	295	28
234–5	299	13
xiii,511–12,605	501	39
430,492	US 501	39
438	58	81

Index